The Sociology
of
Mental Illness
BASIC STUDIES

The Sociology
of
Mental Illness

BASIC STUDIES

Edited by

OSCAR GRUSKY *The University of California, Los Angeles*

MELVIN POLLNER *The University of California, Los Angeles*

HOLT, RINEHART AND WINSTON

NEW YORK   CHICAGO   SAN FRANCISCO   DALLAS
MONTREAL   TORONTO   LONDON   SYDNEY

Library of Congress Cataloging in Publication Data
Main entry under title:

The Sociology of mental illness.

   Bibliography: p.
   Includes index.
   1. Social psychiatry. I. Grusky, Oscar, 1930–
II. Pollner, Melvin. [DNLM: 1. Community mental health services.
2. Mental disorders. 3. Community psychiatry. WM30.6 S678]
RC455.S644   362.2'042   80-22616

ISBN 0-03-053211-6
© 1981 by Holt, Rinehart and Winston
Printed in the United States of America
1 2 3   144   9 8 7 6 5 4 3 2 1

Publisher: RAY ASHTON
Acquiring Editor: PATRICK POWERS
Managing Editor: JEANETTE NINAS JOHNSON
Senior Project Editor: ARLENE KATZ
Production Manager: ANNETTE MAYESKI
Art Director: ROBERT KOPELMAN

Preface

The last two decades have witnessed many changes in ways of thinking about mental illness. Numerous developments have radically altered the nature and distribution of mental health services. Whereas the mental hospital dominated the horizon of the 1950s, the community mental health center and the sheltered care facility are the edifices of the 1970s and probably the 1980s as well. On the academic side, theorizing and research about mental illness moved in an unusual and promising direction with the advent of labeling or societal reaction theory. While the traditional medical model conceptualized mental illness as a disease entity within the individual, societal reaction theory, augmented by the antipsychiatry movement, argued that mental illness was best understood as a role that powerless individuals were encouraged or required to accept and enact.

While the consequences of these changes are diverse and tangled, several facts are clear enough. The deinstitutionalization movement has succeeded in drastically reducing the population of hospitalized mental patients. While more people than ever are in contact with some form of psychiatric service, long-term hospitalization is no longer the norm. Services intended to care, cure, or otherwise respond to individuals whose problems of living are defined as psychological have rapidly proliferated and dispersed. On the academic side, there is sufficient evidence to demonstrate that as useful as the epidemiological and societal reaction perspectives assuredly are, they cannot account for all the multileveled, multiprocessed textures of events, interactions, and institutions subsumed under the term mental illness. Thus, labeling theory has difficulty assimilating recent persuasive studies which indicate that a proportion of individuals designated as schizophrenic have a genetically transmitted disposition toward the disorder. Difficulty with the theory also arises when one considers the political and economic factors that shape the mental illness enterprise.

The dispersion of mental health services and the limitations of current theory have implications for the disciplines that strive to understand mental illness. First, the dispersion suggests that patienthood and the processes involved in becoming a patient are no longer of as great interest as they were in a system where the hospital was, if not the hub, then a major node or collecting point. Indeed, the diffusion of services requires a more subtle conception of the phenomena than the one needed when patienthood provided the main characterization of the field. At the very least, a new sociology of mental illness must attend to the new agencies that deal with the mentally ill, most notably those comprising the community mental health movement. Second, the limitations of current theory demand a more comprehensive, subtle, and differentiated view of all aspects of the mental illness enterprise. For example, an adequate sociological treatment cannot focus on mental illness *per se* but must recognize the vastly different syndromes ranging from depressive and mood disorders to schizophrenia. Similarly, an adequate sociology of mental illness must attend to both the sociohistorical processes that shape the idiom and agencies of the mental health enterprise *and* the microorganization of the episodes that the enterprise makes possible.

The recognition of the fairly recent developments and their implications for the sociology of mental illness provided the initial impetus for this collection. While several fine readers are available, they suffer from two major deficiencies. Either they are dated because they were unable to anticipate how new concepts and agencies would reshape the mental illness enterprise or they are so committed to a single perspective that they fail to encourage the more comprehensive, multileveled thinking we believe is essential.

This reader seeks to reground and update the sociology of mental illness. These intentions are reflected in the collection's distinctive features. We emphasize articles that provide a comprehensive, theoretically grounded understanding of the mental illness enterprise. Without ignoring the empirical we selected articles that offer a deeper, theoretical interpretation or a firmer outline of the "frontier of the possible." The most concrete expression of our concern with theory is found in the book's early sections, which are devoted to the important fountainheads of ideas—the work of Freud, Durkheim, Lemert, and Parsons. The concern with thoughtful and provocative theory is further reflected in the organization and selection of papers that represent current theoretical and empirical work styles in sociology. We emphasized the debatable, criticizable, and incomplete character of various models not out of an abstract commitment to presenting both sides of an issue, but because current models are debatable, criticizable, and incomplete.

Our concern with updating is reflected in the recency of many of the articles and in the final section devoted to community organization. Developments in this area have occurred so quickly that there are few significant efforts to understand their origin, nature, and consequences. We have included the most important representatives of the extant literature.

Another expression of the update is the small number of articles devoted to hospitalization. At an earlier time the mental hospital deserved more attention. The diminished import of the hospital has made an extensive section out of place.

The collection lacks an epilogue and its absence marks our inability to complete the task that the collection inaugurates. In the absence of a grand synthesis we adopted an eclectic stance; we advocate this stance simply because a single perspective is unable to encompass the multileveled, multipathed processes comprising the sociology of mental illness. It is unlikely that there will ever be such an overall perspective. Eclecticism is advocated as the most fruitful and realistic stance because the mental illness enterprise is diverse, amorphous, and loose. To use Jules Henry's (1965) phrase, there are many pathways to madness: some are dominated by organic components, others by structural and sociopsychological factors, and others by interactions of these.

Not only is the mental illness enterprise multipathed, it is multileveled, and this too makes the eclectic stance a reasonable one. One level of reality of the mental illness enterprise is the concrete interactions between the agents and agencies of the enterprise and individuals. But social structure and process move both "behind" and "above" these situated episodes and contribute to their shape and flow. Structure and process move "behind" the episodes in the sense that they affect the social class distribution of people's problems in everyday living and availability of resources for coping with those problems. The consequence here is that members of the lower class will be more apt to encounter the mental illness enterprise. Social structure and process move "above" the concrete interactions by shaping the organizational and ideological contexts within which encounters occur. For example, the possibility of mental illness rests upon the existence of a mental illness idiom as well as on the existence of concrete agencies for institutionalizing and enforcing that idiom. The idioms and agencies that make possible interactions between psychiatric personnel and the mentally ill are sociohistorical emergents. Appreciation of their development requires consideration of their cultural, structural, and historical context.

This volume is a direct product of our deep involvement in the UCLA Sociology Department's NIMH-sponsored postdoctoral mental health evaluation research training program (USPHS NIMH-14583). We are very grateful to NIMH and to Dr. Kenneth Lutterman, in particular, for support. (The National Institute of Mental Health is, of course, not responsible for the views presented.) Grusky directs this program and Pollner serves on the Steering Committee. Participation in this program has affected us in several respects. First, and most importantly, it has brought us into close contact with outstanding postdoctoral scholars whose ideas have been most stimulating: John Weiler, Mark Baldassare, Wayne Alves, Robert Broadhead, Gina Miller, Dean Gerstein, Paul Freddolino, and John Fleishman. Second, it has led us to make contact with UCLA's Neuropsychiatric Institute and over a dozen community mental health agencies in the Los Angeles area where our trainees work regularly as consultants. Third, it has encouraged us to develop new mental health research projects and new courses as well.

Due to the variety of sources and diversity of authors, the studies collected here show a variety of writing and editorial styles. Other than basic typographics, no attempt has been made to impose a uniform style on this collection. Unless otherwise noted, methods of documentation, numbering systems, spelling, punctuation, and other stylistic features are reproduced here as in the original sources.

The value of any collection of readings rests primarily on the contributions of the authors. We are indebted to them. We also wish to acknowledge the typing assistance of Andrea Anzalone, the editorial assistance of Patrick Powers and Arlene Katz, and a helpful overall review by our colleague, Robert Emerson. The decisions and work involved in developing, assembling, and preparing this collection were shared equally in every respect. The same responsibility, of course, applies to any errors. The editors' names are listed alphabetically.

O.G.
M.P.

Los Angeles
May, 1980

Contents

Preface *v*

────────── PART ONE ──────────

Influential Paradigms *1*

INTRODUCTION *2*

────────── PART TWO ──────────

Major Sociological Orientations *23*

A

Bio-Medical Perspective and Issues *24*

INTRODUCTION *24*

ix

B
Societal Reaction Perspectives and Issues 40

C
Epidemiological Perspectives and Issues 90

————————————PART THREE————————————

Family and Community 162

—————————————PART FOUR—————————————

Entering the Psychiatric Enterprise   *240*

INTRODUCTION *241*

—————————————PART FIVE—————————————

Structures and Ideologies of Institutional Treatment Settings   *279*

INTRODUCTION *280*

———————————PART SIX———————————

Structures of Community-Based
Treatment *354*

The Sociology
of
Mental Illness
BASIC STUDIES

PART ONE

Influential Paradigms

INTRODUCTION   A major concern of the sociology of mental illness is the social etiology of mental disorder. The search for causes is guided by the researcher's assumptions regarding the nature of society and of individuals and the relations between the two. Contemporary formulations of mental illness, although numerous and disparate, often prove to be variations from a relatively small number of basic conceptions regarding the way in which society and psyche are related. It is useful to return to primary expressions of basic themes in order to gain one's bearings. Accordingly, we sample some classic and consequential statements on the implications of collective life for mental well-being. As seminal as these works are, they reflect ideas that have a long heritage.

For Freud society and psyche are in deep conflict and the ultimate consequence of the battle are the neuroses. Civilization requires the sublimation, suppression, or repression of fundamental human drives: "In all that follows I adopt the standpoint . . . that the inclination to aggression is an original, self-subsisting intellectual disposition in man, and I return to the view that it constitutes the greatest impediment to civilization" (*Civilization and Its Discontents,* 1961). If there is to be civilization, the instinctive drives of the organism must be constrained. Through internalization man's ego seeks to reconcile the powerful instinctual demands of the id (the forces of sex and aggression) with the requirements of society and its norms, depicted in Freud's model by the superego. Man's feelings of guilt reflect the tension aroused by the primordial struggle between biological and social needs. Psychopathologies therefore represent the "working out" or expression of these internalized conflicts. Neurosis by this view is assured by virtue of the tension between the dispositions inherent in the human organism and the requirements of collective life.

If the constraints imposed by collective life are for Freud the source of malaise, guilt, and anxiety, it is the absence of those constraints that Durkheim argued accounted for other forms of psychological suffering and ultimately suicide. The dark forms of agitation and despair described by Durkheim do not rise from a stifling yoke of collective life but from the absence of direction, control, and structure furnished by integrated, stable socionormative structures. When these structures are weakened or disrupted, there is a corresponding weakening or disruption of the individual's psychic economy. Where Freud argued that the demands of collective life were inimical to the pleasure of the psyche, Durkheim argued that they were precisely what staved off an order of suffering that often ended in self-dissolution. The imagery sketched in both the Freudian and Durkheimian excerpts is of the collectivity exerting its force for better or worse upon the psyches of members. Other influential models suggest a more dynamic interplay of the relations between collectivity and the individual.

In the important statement on *Social Pathology* by Edwin Lemert, the individual is more than a passive recipient of societal forces. Lemert invites us to recognize that just as the collectivity or community responds to and affects the individual, the individual adjusts and responds to the action of the collectivity. It is in the course of this dynamic interchange that aspects of the individual's self and psyche are created or transformed.

Lemert makes an important distinction between primary and secondary deviation. Primary deviation refers to the person's original deviant act, such as the first criminal violation, the first stutter, or a child's first classroom prank. Secondary deviation, the main interest of the theory, involves the actual assumption of the deviant role. This occurs when the person's deviancy serves ". . . as a means of defense, attack, or adjustment to the overt and covert problems created by the consequent societal reaction to him. . . " For example, Lemert cites the case of the child who performs a prank and is punished by the teacher. Later, because of simple clumsiness he makes a disturbance in the classroom and is punished once again by the teacher. Next, he is punished for something he did not do, and eventually he is tagged with the label "mischief-maker" or "bad boy." At the same time the child finds that this role foisted upon him by the teacher actually elevates his status among his cohorts and provides him with new attention and rewards, just as his position declines in the eyes of the teacher. The combined stigmatization and reward created by the societal reaction strengthens the child's behavior pattern and encourages acceptance of his deviant position in the classroom. The adjustment of the child to this situation, and more generally, the adjustment of any deviant to his or her situation, is a dynamic one and is determined by the person's choices, which are, in turn, constrained by both external and internal limits. External limits include social participation barriers (mental patients encounter difficulties in finding jobs), physical characteristics (attractive female mental patients are responded to differently than unattractive ones), and other constraints. Internal limits are set by structural components of one's personality, and by the knowledge and acquaintance one has with the skills and values of the deviant role. The two types of limits, external and internal, cluster together and reinforce one another.

While it is highly arguable whether the work of Parsons provides the grand synthesis to which we recurrently allude, it is exemplary in its efforts to conceptualize the concrete acts with which a sociology of mental illness must deal in terms of motivational, cultural, and social systems. Parsons' contributions to sociological theory are massive (as Freud's to psychology, Durkheim's to sociology, and so forth) and we can represent only a small portion of his work here. In particular, we focus on his approach to social deviance. In the section of *The Social System* selected, Parsons emphasizes the interaction of the motivational and social system-created aspects of deviance, but "it is clearly the conception of deviance as a disturbance of the equilibrium of the interactive system, which is the more important perspective for the analysis of social systems." If a deviant act is committed in the family—a teenage son assaults his father, for example—the family system acts quickly to restore the equilibrium disrupted by this act. In this instance, the son deviates by violating the norm "Honor thy father and mother." A complete understanding of this deviant act requires knowledge of the son's and the father's motivational systems, the family as a social system including each member and his or her relationship to the other members including the son, the family's normative structure, each individual member's adaptation to his or her role, and the impact of the larger society and cultural values on both the family as a whole and each member. Suppose the immigrant father criticized his son for studying and accused him of being too passive, a "namby-pamby." These taunts aroused the son's anger and led to counterattacks, eventually culminating in the deviant act. The father's traditional values, carried from the "old country," demean soft, intellectual activity and conflict with American achievement values and their attainment through educational channels, values internalized by the son. In part, then, the son's hostile response toward his father can be understood as a response to role strain created by value conflict. The son is ambivalent; the father is likewise ambivalent. The son wishes to conform to the norm of honoring his father, but finds it frustrating to do so. Unstructuredness in their mutual expectation systems and a gradual build-up in the conflict level by means of the vicious cycle process exacerbates strain in the family system. Most of the time the son's commitment to his family and all it represents is powerful enough to overcome the motivation to deviate. In general, as Parsons notes, social systems are organized so as to limit deviance, since deviant behavior creates stronger role and system strains than conformity. These limitations operate through the combination of socialization and social control mechanisms. Since both devices are incapable of eliminating deviant behavior, system disequilibrium is a continual occurrence. The excerpt from Parsons concludes with an analysis of three features of social control: support, permissiveness, and reciprocation restriction. As is pointed out, psychotherapy is a prototype of these three social control processes, although one with a number of special features.

Although it is possible to cast these models in competition with one another, it is more fruitful to view each as offering a special insight into the relation between the individual and society. A fundamental task for a social etiology of mental illness is to provide an understanding of how social relations induce or preclude the tensions or strains that are the raw material of mental illness, and an understanding of how these strains are amplified, channeled, or curtailed as the individual interacts with others. The cry for a grand synthesis is easily made but not easily followed. While it is clear he has not completely succeeded, Parsons' work offers an ambitious attempt to synthesize Freudian, Durkheimian, and Lemertian models while maintaining a respect for the ways in which socially induced strains are socially patterned and controlled.

SIGMUND FREUD

Civilization and Its Discontents

In the first place, I suspect that the reader has the impression that our discussions on the sense of guilt disrupt the framework of this essay: that they take up too much space, so that the rest of its subject-matter, with which they are not always closely connected, is pushed to one side. This may have spoilt the structure of my paper; but it corresponds faithfully to my intention to represent the sense of guilt as the most important problem in the development of civilization and to show that the price we pay for our advance in civilization is a loss of happiness through the heightening of the sense of guilt.[1] Anything that still sounds strange about this statement, which is the final conclusion of our investigation, can probably be traced to the quite peculiar relationship—as yet completely unexplained—which the sense of guilt has to our consciousness. In the common case of remorse, which we regard as normal, this feeling makes itself clearly enough perceptible to consciousness. Indeed, we are accustomed to speak of a 'consciousness of guilt' instead of a 'sense of guilt'.[2] Our study of the neuroses, to which, after all, we owe the most valuable pointers to an understanding of normal conditions, brings us up against some contradictions. In

Reprinted from Sigmund Freud, *Civilization and Its Discontents*, translated by James Strachey, pages 81−84, with permission of the publishers (Copyright 1961, W. W. Norton and Co., Inc. in the USA, and Sigmund Freud Copyrights, Ltd., The Institute of Psycho-Analysis, and the Hogarth Press Ltd., elsewhere.)

1. 'Thus conscience does make cowards of us all . . .'
That the education of young people at the present day conceals from them the part which sexuality will play in their lives is not the only reproach which we are obliged to make against it. Its other sin is that it does not prepare them for the aggressiveness of which they are destined to become the objects. In sending the young out into life with such a false psychological orientation, education is behaving as though one were to equip people starting on a Polar expedition with summer clothing and maps of the Italian Lakes. In this it becomes evident that a certain misuse is being made of ethical demands. The strictness of those demands would not do so much harm if education were to say: 'This is how men ought to be, in order to be happy and to make others happy; but you have to reckon on their not being like that.' Instead of this the young are made to believe that everyone else fulfils those ethical demands—that is, that everyone else is virtuous. It is on this that the demand is based that the young, too, shall become virtuous.

2. ['*Schuldbewusstsein*' instead of '*Schuldgefühl*'. The second of these terms is the one which Freud has been using for the most part. They are synonyms apart from their literal meaning, and both are translated by the usual English 'sense of guilt' except on such special occasions as this.]

one of those affections, obsessional neurosis, the sense of guilt makes itself noisily heard in consciousness; it dominates the clinical picture and the patient's life as well, and it hardly allows anything else to appear alongside of it. But in most other cases and forms of neurosis it remains completely unconscious, without on that account producing any less important effects. Our patients do not believe us when we attribute an 'unconscious sense of guilt' to them. In order to make ourselves at all intelligible to them, we tell them of an unconscious need for punishment, in which the sense of guilt finds expression. But its connection with a particular form of neurosis must not be over-estimated. Even in obsessional neurosis there are types of patients who are not aware of their sense of guilt, or who only feel it as a tormenting uneasiness, a kind of anxiety, if they are prevented from carrying out certain actions. It ought to be possible eventually to understand these things; but as yet we cannot. Here perhaps we may be glad to have it pointed out that the sense of guilt is at bottom nothing else but a topographical variety of anxiety; in its later phases it coincides completely with *fear of the super-ego*. And the relations of anxiety to consciousness exhibit the same extraordinary variations. Anxiety is always present somewhere or other behind every symptom; but at one time it takes noisy possession of the whole of consciousness, while at another it conceals itself so completely that we are obliged to speak of unconscious anxiety or, if we want to have a clearer psychological conscience, since anxiety is in the first instance simply a feeling,[3] of possibilities of anxiety. Consequently it is very conceivable that the sense of guilt produced by civilization is not perceived as such either, and remains to a large extent unconscious, or appears as a sort of *malaise*,[4] a dissatisfaction, for which people seek other motivations. Religions, at any rate, have never overlooked the part played in civilization by a sense of guilt. Furthermore—a point which I failed to appreciate elsewhere[5]—they claim to redeem mankind from this sense of guilt, which they call sin. From the manner in which, in Christianity, this redemption is achieved—by the sacrificial death of a single person, who in this manner takes upon himself a guilt that is common to

everyone—we have been able to infer what the first occasion may have been on which this primal guilt, which was also the beginning of civilization, was acquired.[6]

Though it cannot be of great importance, it may not be superfluous to elucidate the meaning of a few words such as 'super-ego', 'conscience', 'sense of guilt', 'need for punishment', and 'remorse', which we have often, perhaps, used too loosely and interchangeably. They all relate to the same state of affairs, but denote different aspects of it. The super-ego is an agency which has been inferred by us, and conscience is a function which we ascribe, among other functions, to that agency. This function consists in keeping a watch over the actions and intentions of the ego and judging them, in exercising a censorship. The sense of guilt, the harshness of the super-ego, is thus the same thing as the severity of the conscience. It is the perception which the ego has of being watched over in this way, the assessment of the tension between its own strivings and the demands of the super-ego. The fear of this critical agency (a fear which is at the bottom of the whole relationship), the need for punishment, is an instinctual manifestation on the part of the ego, which has become masochistic under the influence of a sadistic super-ego; it is a portion, that is to say, of the instinct towards internal destruction present in the ego, employed for forming an erotic attachment to the super-ego. We ought not to speak of a conscience until a super-ego is demonstrably present. As to a sense of guilt, we must admit that it is in existence before the super-ego, and therefore before conscience, too. At that time it is the immediate expression of fear of the external authority, a recognition of the tension between the ego and that authority. It is the direct derivative of the conflict between the need for the authority's love and the urge towards instinctual satisfaction, whose inhibition produces the inclination to aggression. The superimposition of these two strata of the sense of guilt—one coming from fear of the *external* authority, the other from fear of the *internal* authority—has hampered our insight into the position of conscience in a number of ways. Remorse is a general term for the ego's reaction in a case of sense of guilt. It contains, in little altered form, the sensory material of the anxiety which is operating behind the sense of guilt; it is itself a punishment and can include the need for punishment. Thus remorse, too, can be older than conscience.

3. [See Chapter VIII of *Inhibitions, Symptoms and Anxiety* (1926*d*), *Standard Ed.*, **20**, 132.—Feelings cannot properly be described as 'unconscious' (cf. *The Ego and the Id, Standard Ed.*, **19**, 22–3.]

4. ['*Unbehagen*': the word which appears in the title of this work.]

5. In *The Future of an Illusion* (1927*c*).

6. *Totem and Taboo* (1912–13) [*Standard Ed.*, **13**, 153–5].

EMILE DURKHEIM

SUICIDE

Egoistic Suicide

We have thus successively set up the three following propositions:

- *Suicide varies inversely with the degree of integration of religious society.*
- *Suicide varies inversely with the degree of integration of domestic society.*
- *Suicide varies inversely with the degree of integration of political society.*

This grouping shows that whereas these different societies have a moderating influence upon suicide, this is due not to special characteristics of each but to a characteristic common to all. Religion does not owe its efficacy to the special nature of religious sentiments, since domestic and political societies both produce the same effects when strongly integrated. This, moreover, we have already proved when studying directly the manner of action of different religions upon suicide.[1] Inversely, it is not the specific nature of the domestic or political tie which can explain the immunity they confer, since religious society has the same advantage. The cause can only be found in a single quality possessed by all these social groups, though perhaps to varying degrees. The only quality satisfying this condition is that they are all strongly integrated social groups. So we reach the general conclusion: suicide varies inversely with the degree of integration of the social groups of which the individual forms a part.

But society cannot disintegrate without the individual simultaneously detaching himself from social life, without his own goals becoming preponderant over those of the community, in a word without his personality tending to surmount the collective personality. The more weakened the groups to which he belongs, the less he depends on them, the more he consequently depends

Reprinted from Emile Durkheim, *Suicide* (translated by John Spaulding and George Simpson; edited by George Simpson), Glencoe, Ill.: The Free Press, 1951, pages 208–212, 219–221, 241, and 252–254, by permission of the publisher.

1. See above, Book II. Ch. 2.

only on himself and recognizes no other rules of conduct than what are founded on his private interests. If we agree to call this state egoism, in which the individual ego asserts itself to excess in the face of the social ego and at its expense, we may call egoistic the special type of suicide springing from excessive individualism.

But how can suicide have such an origin?

First of all, it can be said that, as collective force is one of the obstacles best calculated to restrain suicide, its weakening involves a development of suicide. When society is strongly integrated, it holds individuals under its control, considers them at its service and thus forbids them to dispose wilfully of themselves. Accordingly it opposes their evading their duties to it through death. But how could society impose its supremacy upon them when they refuse to accept this subordination as legitimate? It no longer then possesses the requisite authority to retain them in their duty if they wish to desert; and conscious of its own weakness, it even recognizes their right to do freely what it can no longer prevent. So far as they are the admitted masters of their destinies, it is their privilege to end their lives. They, on their part, have no reason to endure life's suffering patiently. For they cling to life more resolutely when belonging to a group they love, so as not to betray interests they put before their own. The bond that unites them with the common cause attaches them to life and the lofty goal they envisage prevents their feeling personal troubles so deeply. There is, in short, in a cohesive and animated society a constant interchange of ideas and feelings from all to each and each to all, something like a mutual moral support, which instead of throwing the individual on his own resources, leads him to share in the collective energy and supports his own when exhausted.

But these reasons are purely secondary. Excessive individualism not only results in favoring the action of suicidogenic causes, but it is itself such a cause. It not only frees man's inclination to do away with himself from a protective obstacle, but creates this inclination out of whole cloth and thus gives birth to a special suicide which bears its mark. This must be clearly understood for this is what constitutes the special character of the type of suicide just distinguished and justifies the

7

name we have given it. What is there then in individualism that explains this result?

It has been sometimes said that because of his psychological constitution, man cannot live without attachment to some object which transcends and survives him, and that the reason for this necessity is a need we must have not to perish entirely. Life is said to be intolerable unless some reason for existing is involved, some purpose justifying life's trials. The individual alone is not a sufficient end for his activity. He is too little. He is not only hemmed in spatially; he is also strictly limited temporally. When, therefore, we have no other object than ourselves we cannot avoid the thought that our efforts will finally end in nothingness, since we ourselves disappear. But annihilation terrifies us. Under these conditions one would lose courage to live, that is, to act and struggle, since nothing will remain of our exertions. The state of egoism, in other words, is supposed to be contradictory to human nature and, consequently, too uncertain to have chances of permanence.

In this absolute formulation the proposition is vulnerable. If the thought of the end of our personality were really so hateful, we could consent to live only by blinding ourselves voluntarily as to life's value. For if we may in a measure avoid the prospect of annihilation we cannot extirpate it; it is inevitable, whatever we do. We may push back the frontier for some generations, force our name to endure for some years or centuries longer than our body; a moment, too soon for most men, always comes when it will be nothing. For the groups we join in order to prolong our existence by their means are themselves mortal; they too must dissolve, carrying with them all our deposit of ourselves. Those are few whose memories are closely enough bound to the very history of humanity to be assured of living until its death. So, if we really thus thirsted after immortality, no such brief perspectives could ever appease us. Besides, what of us is it that lives? A word, a sound, an imperceptible trace, most often anonymous,[2] therefore nothing comparable to the violence of our efforts or able to justify them to us. In actuality, though a child is naturally an egoist who feels not the slightest craving to survive himself, and the old man is very often a child in this and so many other respects, neither ceases to cling to life as much or more than the adult; indeed we have seen that suicide is very rare for the first fifteen years and tends to decrease at the other extreme of life. Such too is the case with animals, whose psychological constitution differs from that of men only in degree. It is therefore untrue that life is only possible by its possessing its rationale outside of itself.

Indeed, a whole range of functions concern only the individual; these are the ones indispensable for physical life. Since they are made for this purpose only, they are perfected by its attainment. In everything concerning them, therefore, man can act reasonably without thought of transcendental purposes. These functions serve by merely serving him. In so far as he has no other needs, he is therefore self-sufficient and can live happily with no other objective than living. This is not the case, however, with the civilized adult. He has many ideas, feelings and practices unrelated to organic needs. The roles of art, morality, religion, political faith, science itself are not to repair organic exhaustion nor to provide sound functioning of the organs. All this supra-physical life is built and expanded not because of the demands of the cosmic environment but because of the demands of the social environment. The influence of society is what has aroused in us the sentiments of sympathy and solidarity drawing us toward others; it is society which, fashioning us in its image, fills us with religious, political and moral beliefs that control our actions. To play our social role we have striven to extend our intelligence and it is still society that has supplied us with tools for this development by transmitting to us its trust fund of knowledge.

Altruistic Suicide

Besides the old men, women are often required among the same peoples to kill themselves on their husbands' death. This barbarous practice is so ingrained in Hindu customs that the efforts of the English are futile against it. In 1817, 706 widows killed themselves in the one province of Bengal and in 1821, 2,366 were found in all India. Moreover, when a prince or chief dies, his followers are forced not to survive him. Such was the case in Gaul. The funerals of chiefs, Henri Martin declares, were bloody hecatombs where their garments, weapons, horses and favorite slaves were solemnly burned, together with the personal followers who had not died in the chief's last battle.[3] Such a follower was never to survive his chief. Among the Ashantis, on the king's death his officers must die.[4] Observers have found the same custom in Hawaii.[5]

Suicide, accordingly, is surely very common among primitive peoples. But it displays peculiar characteristics. All the facts above reported fall into one of the following three categories:

---

2. We say nothing of the ideal protraction of life involved in the belief in immortality of the soul, for (1) this cannot explain why the family or attachment to political society preserves us from suicide; and (2) it is not even this belief which forms religion's prophylactic influence, as we have shown above.

3. *Histoire de France,* I, 81, cf. Caesar, *de Bello Gallico,* VI, 19.
4. See Spencer, *Sociology,* Vol. II, p. 146.
5. See Jarves, *History of the Sandwich Islands,* 1843, p. 108.

1. Suicides of men on the threshold of old age or stricken with sickness.
2. Suicides of women on their husbands' death.
3. Suicides of followers or servants on the death of their chiefs.

Now, when a person kills himself, in all these cases, it is not because he assumes the right to do so but, on the contrary, *because it is his duty*. If he fails in this obligation, he is dishonored and also punished, usually by religious sanctions. Of course, when we hear of aged men killing themselves we are tempted at first to believe that the cause is weariness or the sufferings common to age. But if these suicides really had no other source, if the individual made away with himself merely to be rid of an unendurable existence, he would not be required to do so; one is never obliged to take advantage of a privilege. Now, we have seen that if such a person insists on living he loses public respect; in one case the usual funeral honors are denied, in another a life of horror is supposed to await him beyond the grave. The weight of society is thus brought to bear on him to lead him to destroy himself. To be sure, society intervenes in egoistic suicide, as well; but its intervention differs in the two cases. In one case, it speaks the sentence of death; in the other it forbids the choice of death. In the case of egoistic suicide it suggests or counsels at most; in the other case it compels and is the author of conditions and circumstances making this obligation coercive.

This sacrifice then is imposed by society for social ends. If the follower must not survive his chief or the servant his prince, this is because so strict an interdependence between followers and chiefs, officers and king, is involved in the constitution of the society that any thought of separation is out of the question. The destiny of one must be that of the others. Subjects as well as clothing and armor must follow their master wherever he goes, even beyond the tomb; if another possibility were to be admitted social subordination would be inadequate.[6] Such is the relation of the woman to her husband. As for the aged, if they are not allowed to await death, it is probably, at least in many instances, for religious reasons. The protecting spirit of a family is supposed to reside in its chief. It is further thought that a god inhabiting the body of another shares in his life, enduring the same phases of health and sickness and aging with him. Age cannot therefore reduce the strength of one without the other being similarly weakened and consequently without the group existence being threatened, since a strengthless divinity would be its only remaining protector. For this reason, in the common interest, a father is required not to await the furthest limit of life before transferring to his successors the precious trust that is in his keeping.[7]

This description sufficiently defines the cause of these suicides. For society to be able thus to compel some of its members to kill themselves, the individual personality can have little value. For as soon as the latter begins to form, the right to existence is the first conceded it; or is at least suspended only in such unusual circumstances as war. But there can be only one cause for this feeble individuation itself. For the individual to occupy so little place in collective life he must be almost completely absorbed in the group and the latter, accordingly, very highly integrated. For the parts to have so little life of their own, the whole must indeed be a compact, continuous mass. And we have shown elsewhere that such massive cohesion is indeed that of societies where the above practices obtain.[8] As they consist of few elements, everyone leads the same life; everything is common to all, ideas, feelings, occupations. Also, because of the small size of the group it is close to everyone and loses no one from sight; consequently collective supervision is constant, extending to everything, and thus more readily prevents divergences. The individual thus has no way to set up an environment of his own in the shelter of which he may develop his own nature and form a physiognomy that is his exclusively. To all intents and purposes indistinct from his companions, he is only an inseparable part of the whole without personal value. His person has so little value that attacks upon it by individuals receive only relatively weak restraint. It is thus natural for him to be yet less protected against collective necessities and that society should not hesitate, for the very slightest reason, to bid him end a life it values so little.

Anomic Suicide

But society is not only something attracting the sentiments and activities of individuals with unequal force. It is also a power controlling them. There is a relation between the way this regulative action is performed and the social suicide-rate.

It is a well-known fact that economic crises have an aggravating effect on the suicidal tendency.

6. At the foundation of these practices there is probably also the desire to prevent the spirit of the dead man from returning to earth to revisit the objects and persons closely associated with him. But this very desire implies that servants and followers are strictly subordinated to their master, inseparable from him, and, furthermore, that to avoid the disaster of the spirit's remaining on earth they must sacrifice themselves in the common interest.

7. See Frazer, *Golden Bough, loc. cit.,* and *passim.*
8. See *Division du travail social, passim.*

In Vienna, in 1873 a financial crisis occurred which reached its height in 1874; the number of suicides immediately rose. From 141 in 1872, they rose to 153 in 1873 and 216 in 1874. The increase in 1874 is 53 percent[9] above 1872 and 41 percent above 1873. What proves this catastrophe to have been the sole cause of the increase is the special prominence of the increase when the crisis was acute, or during the first four months of 1874. From January 1 to April 30 there had been 48 suicides in 1871, 44 in 1872, 43 in 1873; there were 73 in 1874. The increase is 70 percent.[10] The same crisis occurring at the same time in Frankfurt-on-Main produced the same effects there. In the years before 1874, 22 suicides were committed annually on the average; in 1874 there were 32, or 45 percent more.

It is not true, then, that human activity can be released from all restraint. Nothing in the world can enjoy such a privilege. All existence being a part of the universe is relative to the remainder; its nature and method of manifestation accordingly depend not only on itself but on other beings, who consequently restrain and regulate it. Here there are only differences of degree and form between the mineral realm and the thinking person. Man's characteristic privilege is that the bond he accepts is not physical but moral; that is, social. He is governed not by a material environment brutally imposed on him, but by a conscience superior to his own, the superiority of which he feels. Because the greater, better part of his existence transcends the body, he escapes the body's yoke, but is subject to that of society.

But when society is disturbed by some painful crisis or by beneficent but abrupt transitions, it is momentarily incapable of exercising this influence; thence come the sudden rises in the curve of suicides which we have pointed out above.

In the case of economic disasters, indeed, something like a declassification occurs which suddenly casts certain individuals into a lower state than their previous one. Then they must reduce their requirements, restrain their needs, learn greater self-control. All the advantages of social influence are lost so far as they are concerned; their moral education has to be recommenced. But society cannot adjust them instantaneously to this new life and teach them to practice the increased self-repression to which they are unaccustomed. So they are not adjusted to the condition forced on them, and its very prospect is intolerable; hence the suffering which detaches them from a reduced existence even before they have made trial of it.

It is the same if the source of the crisis is an abrupt

growth of power and wealth. Then, truly, as the conditions of life are changed, the standard according to which needs were regulated can no longer remain the same; for it varies with social resources, since it largely determines the share of each class of producers. The scale is upset; but a new scale cannot be immediately improvised. Time is required for the public conscience to reclassify men and things. So long as the social forces thus freed have not regained equilibrium, their respective values are unknown and so all regulation is lacking for a time. The limits are unknown between the possible and the impossible, what is just and what is unjust, legitimate claims and hopes and those which are immoderate. Consequently, there is no restraint upon aspirations. If the disturbance is profound, it affects even the principles controlling the distribution of men among various occupations. Since the relations between various parts of society are necessarily modified, the ideas expressing these relations must change. Some particular class especially favored by the crisis is no longer resigned to its former lot, and, on the other hand, the example of its greater good fortune arouses all sorts of jealousy below and about it. Appetites, not being controlled by a public opinion become disoriented, no longer recognize the limits proper to them. Besides, they are at the same time seized by a sort of natural erethism simply by the greater intensity of public life. With increased prosperity desires increase. At the very moment when traditional rules have lost their authority, the richer prize offered these appetites stimulates them and makes them more exigent and impatient of control. The state of de-regulation or anomy is thus further heightened by passions being less disciplined, precisely when they need more disciplining.

But then their very demands make fulfillment impossible. Overweening ambition always exceeds the results obtained, great as they may be, since there is no warning to pause here. Nothing gives satisfaction and all this agitation is uninterruptedly maintained without appeasement. Above all, since this race for an unattainable goal can give no other pleasure but that of the race itself, if it is one, once it is interrupted the participants are left empty-handed. At the same time the struggle grows more violent and painful, both from being less controlled and because competition is greater. All classes contend among themselves because no established classification any longer exists. Effort grows, just when it becomes less productive. How could the desire to live not be weakened under such conditions?

This explanation is confirmed by the remarkable immunity of poor countries. Poverty protects against suicide because it is a restraint in itself. No matter how one

9. Durkheim incorrectly gives this figure as 51 percent.—Ed.
10. In 1874 over 1873.—Ed.

acts, desires have to depend upon resources to some extent; actual possessions are partly the criterion of those aspired to. So the less one has the less he is tempted to extend the range of his needs indefinitely. Lack of power, compelling moderation, accustoms men to it, while nothing excites envy if no one has superfluity. Wealth, on the other hand, by the power it bestows, deceives us into believing that we depend on ourselves only. Reducing the resistance we encounter from objects, it suggests the possibility of unlimited success against them. The less limited one feels, the more intoler-

able all limitation appears. Not without reason, therefore, have so many religions dwelt on the advantages and moral value of poverty. It is actually the best school for teaching self-restraint. Forcing us to constant self-discipline, it prepares us to accept collective discipline with equanimity, while wealth, exalting the individual, may always arouse the spirit of rebellion which is the very source of immorality. This, of course, is no reason why humanity should not improve its material condition. But though the moral danger involved in every growth of prosperity is not irremediable, it should not be forgotten.

EDWIN LEMERT

Social Pathology

The deviant person is a product of differentiating and isolating processes. Some persons are individually differentiated from others from the time of birth onward, as in the case of a child born with a congenital physical defect or repulsive appearance, and as in the case of a child born into a minority racial or cultural group. Other persons grow to maturity in a family or in a social class where pauperism, begging, or crime are more or less institutionalized ways of life for the entire group. In these latter instances the person's sociopsychological growth may be normal in every way, his status as a deviant being entirely caused by his maturation within the framework of social organization and culture designated as "pathological" by the larger society. This is true of many delinquent children in our society.

The same sort of gradual, unconscious process which operates in the socialization of the deviant child may also be recognized in the acquisition of socially unacceptable behavior by persons after having reached adulthood. However, with more verbal and sophisticated adults, step-by-step violations of societal norms tend to be progressively rationalized in the light of what is socially acceptable. Changes of this nature can take place at the level of either overt or covert behavior, but with a greater likelihood that adults will preface overt behavior

changes with projective symbolic departures from society's norms. When the latter occur, the subsequent overt changes may appear to be "sudden" personality modifications. However, whether these changes are completely radical ones is to some extent a moot point. One writer holds strongly to the opinion that sudden and dramatic shifts in behavior from normal to abnormal are seldom the case, that a sequence of small preparatory transformations must be the prelude to such apparently sudden behavior changes. This writer is impressed by the day-by-day growth of "reserve potentialities" within personalities of all individuals, and he contends that many normal persons carry potentialities for abnormal behavior, which, given proper conditions, can easily be called into play.[1]

Personality Changes Not Always Gradual

The importance of the person's conscious symbolic reactions to his or her own behavior cannot be overstressed in explaining the shift from normal to abnormal behavior or from one type of pathological behavior to another, particularly where behavior variations become systematized or structured into pathological roles. This is not to say that conscious choice is a determining factor in the differentiating process. Nor does it mean that the

Reprinted from Edwin Lemert, *Social Pathology*, New York: McGraw-Hill Publishing Co., Inc., 1951, pages 73–79, 81–87, by permission of the author and publisher.

1. Brown, L. Guy, *Social Pathology*, 1942, pp. 44–45.

awareness of the self is a purely conscious perception. Much of the process of self-perception is doubtless marginal from the point of view of consciousness.[2] But however it may be perceived, the individual's self-definition is closely connected with such things as self-acceptance, the subordination of minor to major roles, and with the motivation involved in learning the skills, techniques, and values of a new role. *Self-definitions or self-realizations are likely to be the result of sudden perceptions and they are especially significant when they are followed immediately by overt demonstrations of the new role they symbolize.* The self-defining junctures are critical points of personality genesis and in the special case of the atypical person they mark a division between two different types of deviation.

Primary and Secondary Deviation

There has been an embarrassingly large number of theories, often without any relationship to a general theory, advanced to account for various specific pathologies in human behavior. For certain types of pathology, such as alcoholism, crime, or stuttering, there are almost as many theories as there are writers on these subjects. This has been occasioned in no small way by the preoccupation with the origins of pathological behavior and by the fallacy of confusing *original* causes with *effective* causes. All such theories have elements of truth, and the divergent viewpoints they contain can be reconciled with the general theory here if it is granted that original causes or antecedents of deviant behaviors are many and diversified. This holds especially for the psychological processes leading to similar pathological behavior, but it also holds for the situational concomitants of the initial aberrant conduct. A person may come to use excessive alcohol not only for a wide variety of subjective reasons but also because of diversified situational influences, such as the death of a loved one, business failure, or participating in some sort of organized group activity calling for heavy drinking of liquor. Whatever the original reasons for violating the norms of the community, they are important only for certain research purposes, such as assessing the extent of the "social problem" at a given time or determining the requirements for a rational program of social control. From a narrower sociological viewpoint the deviations are not significant until they are organized subjectively and transformed into active roles and become the social criteria for assigning status. The deviant individuals must react symbolically to their own behavior aberrations and fix them in their sociopsychological patterns.

2. Murphy, G., *Personality*, 1947, p. 482.

The deviations remain primary deviations or symptomatic and situational as long as they are rationalized or otherwise dealt with as functions of a socially acceptable role. Under such conditions normal and pathological behaviors remain strange and somewhat tensional bedfellows in the same person. Undeniably a vast amount of such segmental and partially integrated pathological behavior exists in our society and has impressed many writers in the field of social pathology.

Just how far and for how long a person may go in dissociating his sociopathic tendencies so that they are merely troublesome adjuncts of normally conceived roles is not known. Perhaps it depends upon the number of alternative definitions of the same overt behavior that he can develop; perhaps certain physiological factors (limits) are also involved. However, if the deviant acts are repetitive and have a high visibility, and if there is a severe societal reaction, which, through a process of identification is incorporated as part of the "me" of the individual, the probability is greatly increased that the integration of existing roles will be disrupted and that reorganization based upon a new role or roles will occur. (The "me" in this context is simply the subjective aspect of the societal reaction.) Reorganization may be the adoption of another normal role in which the tendencies previously defined as "pathological" are given a more acceptable social expression. The other general possibility is the assumption of a deviant role, if such exists; or, more rarely, the person may organize an aberrant sect or group in which he creates a special role of his own. *When a person begins to employ his deviant behavior or a role based upon it as a means of defense, attack, or adjustment to the overt and covert problems created by the consequent societal reaction to him, his deviation is secondary.* Objective evidences of this change will be found in the symbolic appurtenances of the new role, in clothes, speech, posture, and mannerisms, which in some cases heighten social visibility, and which in some cases serve as symbolic cues to professionalization.

Role Conceptions of the Individual Must Be Reinforced by Reactions of Others

It is seldom that one deviant act will provoke a sufficiently strong societal reaction to bring about secondary deviation, unless in the process of introjection the individual imputes or projects meanings into the social situation which are not present. In this case anticipatory fears are involved. For example, in a culture where a child is taught sharp distinctions between "good" women and "bad" women, a single act of questionable morality might conceivably have a profound meaning for the girl so indulging. However, in the absence of reactions by the person's family, neighbors, or the larger community, reinforcing the tentative "bad-girl" self-definition, it is questionable whether a transition to secondary deviation would take place. It is also doubtful whether a temporary exposure to a severe punitive reaction by the community will lead a person to identify himself with a pathological role, unless, as we have said, the experience is highly traumatic. Most frequently there is a progressive reciprocal relationship between the deviation of the individual and the societal reaction, with a compounding of the societal reaction out of the minute accretions in the deviant behavior, until a point is reached where ingrouping and outgrouping between society and the deviant is manifest.[3] At this point a stigmatizing of the deviant occurs in the form of name calling, labeling, or stereotyping.

The sequence of interaction leading to secondary deviation is roughly as follows: (1) primary deviation; (2) social penalties; (3) further primary deviation; (4) stronger penalties and rejections; (5) further deviation, perhaps with hostilities and resentment beginning to focus upon those doing the penalizing; (6) crisis reached in the tolerance quotient, expressed in formal action by the community stigmatizing of the deviant; (7) strengthening of the deviant conduct as a reaction to the stigmatizing and penalties; (8) ultimate acceptance of deviant social status and efforts at adjustment on the basis of the associated role.

As an illustration of this sequence the behavior of an errant schoolboy can be cited. For one reason or another, let us say excessive energy, the schoolboy engages in a classroom prank. He is penalized for it by the teacher. Later, due to clumsiness, he creates another disturbance and again he is reprimanded. Then, as sometimes happens, the boy is blamed for something he did not do. When the teacher uses the tag "bad boy" or "mischief maker" or other invidious terms, hostility and resentment are excited in the boy, and he may feel that he is blocked in playing the role expected of him. Thereafter, there may be a strong temptation to assume his role in the class as defined by the teacher, particularly when he discovers that there are rewards as well as penalties deriving from such a role. There is, of course, no implication here that such boys go on to become delinquents or criminals, for the mischief-maker role may later become integrated with or retrospectively rationalized as part of a role more acceptable to school authorities.[4] If such a boy continues this unacceptable role and becomes delinquent, the process must be accounted for in the light of the general theory of this volume. There must be a spreading corroboration of a sociopathic self-conception and societal reinforcement at each step in the process.

The most significant personality changes are manifest when societal definitions and their subjective counterpart become generalized. When this happens, the range of major role choices becomes narrowed to one general class.[5] This was very obvious in the case of a young girl who was the daughter of a paroled convict and who was attending a small Middle Western college. She continually argued with herself and with the author, in whom she had confided, that in reality she belonged on the "other side of the railroad tracks" and that her life could be enormously simplified by acquiescing in this verdict and living accordingly. While in her case there was a tendency to dramatize her conflicts, nevertheless there was enough societal reinforcement of her self-conception by the treatment she received in her relationship with her father and on dates with college boys to lend it a painful reality. Once these boys took her home to the shoddy dwelling in a slum area where she lived with her father, who was often in a drunken condition, they abruptly stopped seeing her again or else became sexually presumptive.

Social Participation—Alternatives and Choices

Given a person who has identified with a general class of people held undesirable by society at large, what explains his or her selection of a specific role within the broader range of pathological behavior patterns? Again, what factors operate in the selection of approved or disapproved roles subsidiary to the major role? In dealing with these rhetorical questions it is well to dispense with the deterministic logic explicit and implicit in much statistical analysis, or at least restate it in another form. The human personality, whether it is normal or abnormal, has to be understood as a dynamic, creative, choice-making organism. Human behavior is always in the form of urgent thrusting and seeking in terms of positive satisfactions as well as avoidances, powered by animal energies and rhythms. Recognition of this dynamic cast of human behavior has led some theorists to search for direct relationships between physiological processes and the strictly human aspects of behavior. The sociologist's position is distinctive in that these physiological mainsprings of action are looked upon as always or "90 percent of the time" asserting themselves as social and cultural transmutations. In other words, the goals of human action are inevitably social and cultural

3. Mead, G. "The Psychology of Punitive Justice," *American Journal of Sociology,* 23, March, 1918, pp. 577–602.

4. Evidence for fixed or inevitable sequences from predelinquency to crime is absent. Sutherland, E. H., *Principles of Criminology,* 1939, 4th ed., p. 202.

5. Sutherland seems to say something of this sort in connection with the development of criminal behavior. *Ibid.,* p. 86.

goals. Man does not desire glucose or carbohydrates, he desires French pastry or certain varieties of candies. He does not want to release gonadal secretions but rather wants a date with a "cute blonde girl" or whatever his particular socially derived tastes in femininity happen to dictate. For these reasons the satisfaction sought by the person cannot be defined by any narrow physiological, implicit, pain-pleasure calculus, or by any principle of "least effort." Furthermore, it is the specific differentiation of the goals from one person to another rather than the fact that there are generalized goals, wishes, desires, and drives which becomes the factor of transcending importance in human motivation. Finally, it must be noted that means tend to become ends and that their separation is a methodological convenience. Many of the aspects of social roles are originally means of reaching goals, but in time these techniques become satisfactions or ends in themselves. Hence, factoring a role into ends and means is not always necessary; in the analysis here the social role will be taken as embracing the goals as well as the means of behavior.

The search for reasons why the individual settles upon one form of pathological behavior in place of another is made difficult by some of the same methodological problems which are met in accounting for the growth of sociocultural systems. The part played by fortuitous and accidental factors is a very great one. The operation of hereditary processes which give one person a brown or yellow skin cannot be explained directly in sociological terms. Disfigurement, maiming, or blindness, deafness, and invalidism ensuing from accident or disease arbitrarily impose role definitions and status upon the persons so differentiated. The geographic presence of persons in social situations conducive to deviation is often a happenstance. Explaining why a particular individual chances to be in a situation where a given set of role choices confront him lies beyond the scope of this volume. Certain facts must be taken as "given" with analysis proceeding from that point.

The External Limits

The most immediate external limits imposed upon the person identified and stigmatized as pathological or as socially disadvantaged are those erected by the community or society in the form of barriers to social participation. These barriers not only exclude the deviant from many general and special social and economic roles in the socially respectable community but also isolate the deviant from opportunities to participate in sociopathic roles. The ex-convict finds most occupations closed to him in the normal segment of society, except the low-paying, low-status, menial positions, with only the odd

chance at better jobs in dubious tension-generating roles, such as that of a strikebreaker or a marginal criminal role. The criteria for membership in organized sociopathic groups may be just as rigid and exclusive. If the ex-convict is a Negro, he may be denied entrance into certain criminal gangs in the same way that he is barred from other groups, simply because he has a black skin. A person who has been a beggar may have difficulty in entering the more "aristocratic" criminal trades. A college boy running away from a scandal in his home community may aspire to the fellowship of a group of fast-traveling hobos, only to be ignored because of his faulty skills or because of his obvious class affiliations. Patriotic considerations may lead prostitutes to shun the girl who has willingly submitted to the sexual advances of enemy troops or civilians.

All these illustrations make it plain that any person aspiring to a given role, whether it is organized around approved or disapproved behavior, will be restricted by the social definition of his preexisting social status. This status will be indicated by such things as age, sex, physical characteristics, nativity, kinship, religious affiliation, economic position, and social class. Not all of these dimensions of one's social status are of equal importance, hence we shall consider here only those which seem to have a more direct effect upon the life choices of the deviant.

Limits Based upon Age, Sex, and Physical Characteristics

Rules, regulations, prejudices, and stereotypes associated with age, sex, size, degree of beauty, physical stigmas, and physical defects all have the effect of facilitating or ruling out a person's potential enactment of various social roles, abnormal as well as normal. We know considerably more about the effects of such limits upon the choices of nondeviant persons than upon those of sociopathic individuals. A little-known and little-explored area is the effect of sociological aging upon the status of deviants. Much knowledge is needed about the occupational life spans of such deviants as prostitutes, criminals, homosexuals, hobos, and radicals. We need to know how much cultural discontinuity and crisis is created by the aging of persons of this class and what alternatives and choices remain open to them as they move into their older years. In the case of prostitutes the general consequences of aging are fairly obvious, but not so for the others we have mentioned. In the case of homosexuals there is reason to believe that the crisis of middle age may be as great as it is for women in general in our society. With the loss of his physical attractiveness, other homosexuals apparently come to reject the older sex pervert in a heartless fashion, referring to him as an "old aunty." Yet while these things come out in occasional case histories, we still do not know in much detail what necessary modifications are made in the role of the homosexual as a result of such rejections.

Limits of Strength, Agility, and Endurance Are Socially Ascribed to Age, Sex, and Physical Handicaps

At first thought such things as strength, agility, and energy seem to be largely internal limits growing out of age, sex differences, and damage to the organism. However, closer inspection reveals that they are originally external limits in the sense that the real debilities are overlaid or obscured by the putative limitations which the culture ascribes to age, sex, and physical defect. This is most easily seen in the isolating reactions toward physically handicapped persons—the deaf, epileptic, crippled, physically ill, and speech defectives. The spastic child, for example, is commonly thought to be feeble-minded—sometimes even by its parents. Consequently it is often treated on such an assumption, and little effort is made to teach it to talk or to educate it up to the physical limits of its handicap. Many of the blind are surprised and irritated to find others reacting to them as if they were deaf as well as visually disabled.

The sociocultural limits which tend to exclude the physically handicapped from full economic participation in our society have been rationalized largely in terms of biological incapacities. Thus many employers have the idea that handicapped workers are more likely to have accidents in the plant and to have higher absenteeism rates than other workers and that consequently they will be less productive. The fallacy of such employer attitudes was brought out during the Second World War when personnel managers, following empirical procedures in hiring and firing, were surprised to discover that many of the physically handicapped persons could effectively perform jobs of which they were previously thought incapable.

Economic Limits

The economic status of the deviant does much to determine what groups he may enter and those which are closed to him. This works in two ways: (1) The possession of adequate money permits deviants to move more freely in their environments and is means for formal entree into many groups. (2) The conspicuous expenditure of money becomes a prestige or "success" symbol for the deviant, which has a "halo" or whitewashing effect upon the less enviable aspects of his role. Thus we see how wealthy criminals or gamblers are able to stay at the best hotels and live in upper class residential areas in our larger communities. They have been known to consort informally with socially elite persons at fashionable summer and winter resorts. The part played by the possession of adequate income in differentiating the role and status of criminals can also be observed very clearly within prisons.

A deviant whose role and status varies quite closely with his financial resources is the drug addict. If he is poor he is practically forced into criminal pursuits, but if he has a substantial income he avoids this necessity. The status of any of the physically handicapped deviants who are unable to find gainful employment can be greatly modified and improved by the possession of an ample income. We recall here the case of a blind woman who inherited considerable money from her husband. With this the whole problem of movement in her environment was solved, for she simply hired taxicab drivers who took her through city traffic and escorted her on shopping tours.

Limits Based upon Geographic and Demographic Factors

The location, size, technological specialization, and demographic composition of the community in which the deviant happens to be located are other sources of externally imposed limits upon his life choices. In a small, geographically isolated town the deviant person may have no opportunity to engage in homosexual behavior or to make habitual use of narcotic drugs. On the other hand, in a rural community a feeble-minded person may be tolerated in certain roles by the conforming members of the community and also by nonconforming groups. We know of one such community in which a feeble-minded man enjoys a virtual monopoly of cesspool digging. Interestingly enough, this same man prior to settling down to these labors had run with a gang of rowdies in the township, who put up with him largely in order to use him as a scapegoat for their petty crimes. In contrast to this, it is very unlikely that there will be any place for a person of defective intelligence in more highly organized crime found in urban areas. However, the large, complex urban community is ordinarily thought of as being more congenial to the deviant person. The diversity of social roles and the range of sociopathic behavior systems in existence there maximizes the opportunities the deviant has to gravitate into a role or roles most compatible with his particular deviant tendencies.

Mobility as a Limit

Mobility of the deviant person or deviant group member is another important external limit upon social participation. Persons with low spatial and vertical mobility must live within a closely circumscribed participational area determined by their immediate locality or social class. On the other hand, if persons who are culturally disenfranchised in one area are in a position to migrate, they may gain status in a different social organization or they may move back and forth between different communities and by this means widen their range of choices.

The Internal Limits

In addition to the external limits precluding the choice of roles and blocking avenues of social participation, the reacting individual is bound and hedged by the internal structuring of his personality. It is pretty well agreed that there is a selective economy in personality which sorts and picks among the social stimuli coming to it from the external world. At any given point in the personality development of the individual there is a definable set of alternative roles which are subjectively congenial to him, in terms of his covert symbolic processes and perhaps in terms of his unverbalized responses. This subjectively delimited area of choice may lie within the range of the external limits or it may fall outside, and while the external limits may be comparable for different persons, these internal limits tend to be much more variable. Aspirations to status and roles arise within the scope of the internal limits; likewise, social pressures upon the individual to accept certain roles and status which fall beyond the internal limits will be resisted, circumvented, selected out, and rejected.

Internal Limits Are the Structural Aspect of Personality

The subjective component which has here been called "internal limits" and which reacts upon social stimuli has been described in various ways and from different points of view. Some writers have spoken of the "apperceptive mass"; others choose to think in terms of "sets in human nature," personality traits, or personality patterns, or "regions" and "barriers" with differing communicability between the regions, or, finally "status personality." It matters little what we call these factors so long as we admit that there is a structural and delimiting aspect of personality.

The case of a delinquent boy who had organized his life around the role of a "jack-roller" (one who makes a living by robbing drunken men) reveals how internal limits function to demarcate congeries of congenial roles. The boy in the case was characterized as being egocentric, aggressive, and rebellious toward authority, which characteristics became the basis for his selection of delinquent roles and later nondelinquent roles. In the boy's ultimate "reformation" he attempted a number of different occupational roles, all involving direct supervision by his employers, before he fell into a job compatible with his personality structure; as a high-pressure salesman he found a role in which his "traits" were put to a definite advantage.[6] Although the case history does not dwell upon the point, it can be inferred from the data that certain forms of crime were as unattractive as certain legitimate jobs. A criminal role making imperative close cooperation with others and providing no outlets for aggressiveness presumably would have little appeal for such a person. Not only because of the compulsives of the criminal code to which he adheres but also because of his hostilities toward the police, the role of a stool pigeon would be unthinkable to such a person. Similarly, a man disposed to painful stomach disorders and who is penurious may find the role of the alcoholic beyond his tolerance simply because of the inroads excessive drinking would make upon his health and his pocketbook. A girl with a strong fear of venereal disease or hatred of bodily contacts will be fortified to that extent against situational pressures to enter prostitution. Some few people apparently are incapable of securing any sensations at all from morphine injections, which means that addiction to the drug in their cases becomes an impossibility.

Attitudinal Limits

Many persons whose status is well secured within the community have a fairly wide knowledge of deviant roles, including the language, mannerisms, and skills involved. Social caseworkers become adept at imitating the mannerisms of their pauperized and sexually casual clients; professors of criminology occasionally can delectate their students with exhibitions of pocket picking and the reproduction of criminal argot. The internal limits which presumably make such roles undesirable to the persons concerned consist in the verbalized and unverbalized fears and antipathies to playing them in any other than specious social contexts. In some cases such as these, normal persons go as far as to make a subjective identification with a sociopathic role, but some strongly encysted deterrent facts prevent them from making the transition to overt participation in the role.

6. Shaw, *op cit*.

Knowledge and Skill as Limits

In other instances the internal limits are simply the lack of acquaintance with the skills and values of the role and an inability to conceptualize it. Children and mentally deficient adults are internally limited in this respect more than others. It can be supposed that limits of this sort, unless they are reacted to symbolically and become an emotional blocking or a sense of inferiority, more easily give way in the face of situational pressures to play a given sociopathic role than is true of the outer limits we have classed as internal.

TALCOTT PARSONS

The Social System

It has been evident from the beginning of this work that the dimension of conformity-deviance was inherent in and central to the whole conception of social action and hence of social systems. One aspect, that is, of the common cultural patterns which are part of every system of social interaction, is always normative. There is an expectation of conformity with the requirements of the pattern, if it be only in observing the conventions of a communication pattern, for example, by speaking intelligibly. The complementarity of expectations, on which such great stress has been laid, implies the existence of common standards of what is "acceptable," or in some sense approved behavior. . . . We have dealt with the processes by which motivational structures required for behavior in conformity with such normative social expectations are built up. We must now turn to the other side of the coin, the processes by which resistances to conformity with social expectations develop, and the mechanisms by which these tendencies are or tend to be counteracted in social systems.

It is a cardinal principle of the present analysis that all motivational processes are processes in the personalities of individual actors. The processes by which the motivational structure of an individual personality gets to be what it is are, however, mainly social processes, involving the interaction of ego with a plurality of alters. Thus the sectors of the motivation of the individual which are concerned with his motivation to deviant behavior, are the outcome of his processes of social interaction in the past and the whole problem must therefore be approached in social interaction terms. In the analysis of deviance as well as of socialization we must focus on the

interactive processes as it influences the orientation of the individual actor in his situation and in orientation to the situation itself, including above all the significant social objects, and to the normative patterns which define the expectations of his roles.

Deviance and the mechanisms of social control may be defined in two ways, according to whether the individual actor or the interactive system is taken as the point of reference. In the first context deviance is a motivated tendency for an actor to behave in contravention of one or more institutionalized normative patterns, while the mechanisms of social control are the motivated processes in the behavior of this actor, and of the others with whom he is in interaction, by which these tendencies to deviance tend in turn to be counteracted. In the second context, that of the interactive system, deviance is the tendency on the part of one or more of the component actors to behave in such a way as to disturb the equilibrium of the interactive process (whether a static or a moving equilibrium). Deviance therefore is defined by its tendency to result either in change in the state of the interactive system, or in re-equilibration by counteracting forces, the latter being the mechanisms of social control. It is presumed here that such an equilibrium always implies integration of action with a system of normative patterns which are more or less institutionalized.

It is clearly the conception of deviance as a disturbance of the equilibrium of the interactive system, which is the more important perspective for the analysis of social systems. But we must still be quite clear that it is essential to be able to follow this analysis from the level of ascertaining uniformities in the processes of change in the structure of the social system, to that of analyzing the relevant motivational processes in the personalities of

Reprinted from Talcott Parsons, *The Social System*, Glencoe, Ill.: The Free Press, 1951, pages 249–256; 267–268; 297–301, by permission of the publisher.

the individual actors. Hence there is always *also* a reference to the first context implied.

It should also be made clear that there is a certain relativity in the conceptions of conformity and deviance. These are concepts which refer to problems of the integration and malintegration of social systems and sub-systems. It is therefore not possible to make a judgment of deviance or lack of it without specific reference to the system or sub-system to which it applies. The structure of normative patterns in any but the simplest sub-system is always intricate and usually far from fully integrated; hence singling out one such pattern without reference to its interconnections in a system of patterns can be very misleading, e.g., the judgment that a person who tells a "white lie" as a way out of a conflict situation is a "dishonest person." Similarly the concrete individual actor never acts in one role only, but in a plurality of roles and situations, with complex possibilities of variation in the expectations and tensions to which they subject the actor. Furthermore, there is the problem of the time sector which is taken as relevant to the analysis of a system. Actions are mortised together in time sequence as well as in other respects, and conflicts can focus on time-allocation as well as on the conflicting claims of different interaction-partners.

Interaction and the Genesis of Deviant Motivation

Let us go back then to the fundamental paradigm of social interaction including the assumption . . . that a stably established interactive process, that is, one in equilibrium, tends to continue unchanged. We will further assume that ego and alter have, in their interaction, developed mutual cathectic attachments to each other, so that they are sensitive to each other's attitudes, i.e., attitudes are fundamental as sanctions, and that the interaction is integrated with a normative pattern of value-orientation, both ego and alter, that is, have internalized the value-pattern. We have stated many times that such an interaction system is characterized by the complementarity of expectations, the behavior and above all the attitudes of alter conform with the expectations of ego and vice versa.

This paradigm provides the setting for the analysis of the genesis of motivation to deviance. Let us assume that, from whatever source, a disturbance is introduced into the system, of such a character that what alter does leads to a frustration, in some important respects, of ego's expectation-system vis-à-vis alter. This failure of the fulfillment of ego's expectations places a "strain" upon him, that is, presents him with a problem of "adjustment" in the terms which we have used. There are

always, we may presume, three terms to this problem. First ego's expectations in the interaction system are part of his own system of need-dispositions which in some sense press for gratification. Second, these expectations are organized to include an attachment to alter as a cathected object, and third the value-pattern governing the relationship has been internalized and violation of its prescriptions is directly a frustration of some of ego's need-dispositions. In so far as the adjustment problem is "serious," in that alter's disturbing behavior is more than momentary and in that it touches some strategic area of ego's orientation system, ego will be forced to restructure his orientation in one or more of these three respects. He can first restructure his own need-dispositions, by inhibition and by one or more of the mechanisms of defense, such as simply repressing the needs which are no longer gratified. He can, secondly, seek to transfer his cathexis to a new object and relieve the strain that way and, finally, he can renounce or seek to redefine the value-orientation pattern with which alter is no longer conforming.

In any one or more of these three directions there may be resolution of the strain by a successful learning process; ego may learn to inhibit his need-disposition, he may cathect a new object which will fulfill his expectations, or he may extinguish or alter the value-pattern. This would be the obverse of alter abandoning his changed behavior. In either case equilibrium would be re-established, in one case with a changed state of the system, in the other with a restoration of the old state.

But another outcome is possible, and in many cases very likely. That is that, in one or more of the above three respects, a "compromise" solution should be reached. Our primary interest is not in the internal integration of the personality but in ego's adjustment to social objects and to normative patterns. Hence first, ego may not abandon his cathexis of alter by substituting an alternative object, but may retain his cathexis, but this cathexis can no longer be "undisturbed." Ego must have some reaction to the frustration which alter has imposed upon him, some resentment or hostility.[1] In other words the cathectic orientation acquires an ambivalent character, there is still the need to love or admire alter, but there is also the product of his frustration in the form of negative and in some sense hostile attitudes toward alter. In so far as this happens of course ego is put in an emotional conflict in his relation to alter. Similarly, the integration of ego's expectations with the value-pattern has been disturbed by alter's failure to conform with it, the pattern may be too strongly internalized for ego to be able to abandon it and accept one in conformity with alter's

1. Another very important phenomenon of reaction to strain is the production of phantasies.

behavior. Here again ego may develop an ambivalent attitude structure, at the same time adhering to the normative pattern and resenting the "cost" of this adherence in that it involves him in conflict with alter and with aspects of his own personality.

There are many complications involved in the possibilities of handling the strains inherent in such an ambivalent motivational structure. For our purpose, however, they may be related to two fundamental alternatives. The first is repression of one side of the ambivalent structure so that only the other side receives overt expression. If it is the negative side which is repressed, ego will continue to be attached to alter and/or to be motivated to conform with the normative pattern in question. If the positive side is repressed, conversely ego will tend to abandon his attachment to alter, in the sense of giving it overt expression, and to refuse to conform with the normative pattern. The second fundamental possibility is for ego to try to find a way to gratify both sides of his ambivalent motivation. Presumably in the same concrete relationship this is impossible[2] since the two are in conflict. But in a more extensive and complex interaction system there may be such possibilities either because contexts and occasions can be segregated, or because it is possible to find alternative objects for one or both sides of the need-disposition structure. This latter possibility will become very important to the discussion of the social structuring of deviance later in this chapter. But for the present let us adhere to the simpler case.

The negative component of such an ambivalent motivational structure relative to a system of complementary expectations will be called an *alienative* need-disposition, the positive component, a *conformative* need-disposition. It should be noted that in these theoretical terms alienation is conceived *always* to be part of an ambivalent motivational structure, while conformity need not be. Where there is no longer *any* attachment to the object and/or internalization of the normative pattern, the attitude is not alienation but *indifference*. Both social object and pattern have become only neutral objects of the situation which are no longer a focus of ego's cathectic need-system. The conflict in such a case would have been solved by full resolution, through substitution of a new object, through inhibition or extinction of the need-disposition, and/or through internalization of a new normative pattern.

Where alienative motivation is present, but the conformative component is dominant over the alienative, we may speak of *compulsive conformity,* where on the other hand the alienative component is dominant over the con-

formative, we may speak of *compulsive alienation.* The psychological reasons for using these terms are not far to seek. The essential point is that ego is subject not only to a strain in his relations with alter, but to an internal conflict in his own need-disposition system. Precisely because he has a negative feeling toward alter, but at the same time a powerful need to retain his relation to alter and to the normative pattern, he must "defend himself" against his need to express his negative feelings, with the attendant risk of disturbing his relation to alter still further or provoking him to retaliatory action, in the more extreme case, of losing alter. This is, indeed, in relation to social interaction relationships, the basis of the defense mechanism of reaction formation. The pattern is to "accentuate the positive," to be compulsively careful to conform with what ego interprets as alter's expectations (which by institutionalization are also his own) so as to minimize the risk of disturbing the relationship still further.

Conversely, if the alienative component is dominant, the fact that the attachment to alter as a person and to the normative pattern is still a fundamental need, means that ego must defend himself against the tendency to express this need-disposition. He must therefore not only express his negative reaction, but be doubly sure that the conformative element does not gain the upper hand and risk his having to inhibit the negative again. Therefore his refusal to conform with alter's expectations becomes compulsive. This defense against the repressed component is in both cases the primary basis of resistance against the abandonment of "symptoms," even though they involve ego in serious negative sanctions in his social relationships.

It is here that we have the focus of the well-known vicious circle in the genesis of deviant behavior patterns, whether they be neurotic or psycho-somatic illness, criminality or others. It may be presumed that the reaction of ego to the change in alter's behavior, which resulted in resort to adjustive and defensive mechanisms involving ambivalence, will be in some way complementary to the change alter introduced. For example, alter, instead of recognizing the merit of a piece of work ego has done, may have shown marked disapproval, which ego felt to be in contravention of the value-pattern with respect to competent achievement shared by both. Ego reacted to this with resentment which, however, he repressed and became compulsively anxious to secure alter's approval. This compulsive element in ego's motivation makes him excessively "demanding" in his relation to alter. He both wants to be approved, to conform, and his need for approval is more difficult to satisfy because of his anxiety that alter may not give it. This in turn has its effect on alter. Whatever his original motivation to

---

2. It is of course possible within limits through time allocation. At certain times ego's resentment may break through into hostile acts (including verbal) and the positive attitude then regains ascendancy.

withhold the approval ego expected, ego has now put him in a position where it is more difficult than it was before for him to fulfill ego's expectations; the same level of approval which would have sufficed before is no longer sufficient. Unless a mechanism of social control is operating, then, the tendency will be to drive alter to approve even less, rather than more as ego hopes. This will still further increase the strain on ego and intensify his resentment, hence, if the alienative component does not break through, it will add to the compulsiveness of his motivation to seek approval through conformity with alter's expectations. The pressure of ego's conflict may also of course lead to cognitive distortion so that he thinks that alter's expectations are more extreme than they really are, and that therefore he is being held to intolerable standards.

This is the essential structure of the generation of cumulative motivation to deviance through the interaction of complementary ambivalences in the motivational systems of ego and alter. Of course this is a highly simplified and abstract paradigm. The "direct line" of development of the vicious circle could not empirically proceed far without some modification for two sets of reasons. First the need-dispositions of ego and alter which are the focus of the developing conflict are only parts of a complicated system of need-dispositions in the personalities of each. The alterations in these parts growing out of the interaction process would lead to repercussions in the rest of the personality systems which would modify the development of the interaction itself. Secondly, the interaction of ego and alter on which we have focused is only a sector of a larger system of social interaction which involves other actors than ego and alter, and perhaps their interaction in other roles. These complications must duly be taken into account, and are of course extremely important for the mechanisms of social control. But the vicious circle in the interaction of two actors is the fundamental paradigm of the genesis of the motivation for deviant behavior.

Some Further Situational Aspects of the Genesis and Structuring of Deviance

We must now supplement the above considerations about the roots of alienative need-dispositions in the personality, and the processes of mutual stimulation of these alienative tendencies in the interaction process with an analysis of certain crucial features of normative patterns themselves and their variability. The problem of conformity cannot be dissociated from a consideration of that with which conformity is expected.

The most fundamental classification of the compo-

nents of normative patterns which is derived from the pattern variable scheme need not be further discussed just now. Here only a few observations on points of relevance to the present context are necessary. The first point to emphasize is that the ways in which "pressure" is exerted on the motivational system of the actor will vary as a function of the kind of pattern with which he is expected to conform.

This is in the nature of the case a very complicated field. Yet considerations such as those advanced earlier relative to the process of socialization would make it seem likely that in spite of socio-cultural variations some types of value-pattern impose inherently greater strains on most human beings than others; some such factor is for example essential to the meaning of the concept of regression. For present purposes we need not consider whether the principal sources of these strains are to be found in constitutional features of the human organism or in certain constants of the process of socialization. A good example is the degree of stress on affective neutrality.

There is a sense in which as we have seen, all normative patterning involves an element of affective neutrality, in that as was noted, conformity with a normative pattern cannot in itself be a source of direct and immediate gratification. However, some types of normative pattern impose the disciplines of affective neutrality far more stringently and over far wider segments of the action system than do others. Some on the other hand seem more concerned with the organization of and selection among direct gratifications, rather than their postponement or diversion from particular contexts. These are above all the patterns which organize social relationships to a high degree about diffuse love attachments, and further stabilize expressive activities in terms of relatively definite and rigorous systematization of expressive symbol and action systems, as for example in a large amount of ritual and etiquette. On the other hand our own society, with its very strong instrumental emphases and very long-range planning, puts a strong accent on affective neutrality and requires exceptionally high levels of discipline in certain respects.

Somewhat similar considerations, as we have seen, apply to achievement patterns and to universalism. Indeed in this respect the latter is probably the more fundamental. This seems to derive above all from the fact that universalistic requirements cut across the particularism of attachments to persons. The fundamental importance of the latter in all human socialization seems to be established beyond question. Hence where patterns involve a prominent universalistic emphasis, it is necessary not merely to inhibit certain "natural" cathectic tendencies, but to transcend them, in the sense of developing a capacity of cathexis of all members of a universalistically defined class of social objects and correspondingly to internalize the valuation of abstract principles. This latter step is thus, in the universalistic case, possible only through a special elaboration of the development of "secondary" motivational structures.

The upshot of all this is that one focus of strains consists in the difficulty of conformity with the expectations involved in the particular type of pattern in question. In general this difficulty can be analyzed in the same fundamental terms which were used above. It will, that is, involve elements of ambivalence and conflict.

The Mechanisms of Social Control

The theory of social control is the obverse of the theory of the genesis of deviant behavior tendencies. It is the analysis of those processes in the social system which tend to counteract the deviant tendencies, and of the conditions under which such processes will operate. Like the theory of deviance, it must always be stated relative to a given state of equilibrium of the system or sub-system which include specification of the normative patterns institutionalized in that sub-system, and the balance of motivational forces relative to conformity with and deviance from these patterns.

Hence the stable equilibrium of the interactive process is the fundamental point of reference for the analysis of social control just as it is for the theory of deviance. But our attention will be focused on one aspect of the interactive process, the forestalling of the kinds of deviant tendencies we have analyzed earlier, and the processes by which, once under way, these processes can be counteracted and the system brought back, in the relevant respects, to the old equilibrium state. This latter is, of course a theoretical point of reference. In empirical fact no social system is perfectly equilibrated and integrated. Deviant motivational factors are always operating, and become established so that they are not eliminated from the motivational systems of the relevant actors. In that case the mechanisms of social control account not for their elimination but for the limitation of their consequences, and for preventing their spread to others beyond certain limits.

There are such close relations between the processes of socialization and of social control that we may take certain features of the processes of socialization as a point of reference for developing a framework for the analysis of the processes of control. The preventive or forestalling aspects of social control consist in a sense of processes which teach the actor not to embark on processes of deviance. They consist in his learning how not to rather than how to in the positive sense of socialization. The re-equilibrating aspects on the other hand are a special case of the learning process in that they involve the unlearning of the alienative elements of the motivational structure.

Perhaps the key to the relationship of the two sets of processes is to be found in the fact that both socialization and social control consist from one point of view in processes of adjustment to strains. The strains either may eventuate in deviant motivation or, previous strains already having done so, a secondary strain may be introduced into the system by the pressure on it of the established deviant motivations.

Strain, we may assume without going into all the psychological complexities, provokes four main types or components of reaction namely anxiety, fantasy, hostile or aggressive hitting-back or hitting-out reactions, and defensive measures in the sense of attempts to limit the deviation from ego's expectations and/or restore the status quo ante. Indeed all the reactions may on one level be interpreted in the latter light, but at a more differentiated level it is useful to distinguish these elements. Effective measures of control must in some sense operate on all these elements of the motivational structure.

One whole important class of such measures operates only on the level of dealing with overt behavior. These are the measures which by compulsion, and by appeal to rational decision through coercion or inducement, prevent certain actions or deter from them or from carrying them beyond narrow limits. The empirical significance of these aspects of the social control system is not to be doubted, but our concern is with the subtler underlying motivational aspects.

The first element of any social control mechanism in the latter sense may be called "support." Its primary direct significance is in relation to the anxiety component of the reaction to strain, to give a basis of reassurance such that the need to resort to aggressive-destructive and/or defensive reactions is lessened. Support may be of various kinds, but the common element is that somewhere there is the incorporation or retention of ego in a solidary relationship so that he has a basis of security in the sense of the above discussions. The stability of the love attitudes of the mother in critical phases of socialization is one fundamental type of case. The collectivity-orientation of the therapist, his readiness to "help" and his "understanding" of the patient is another. These types differ fundamentally as role-pattern types and yet they have this common element. In one sense the consequence of support is to localize the focus of strain, by making it possible for ego to feel that his insecurity is not "total" but can be focused on a limited problem area for adjustment.

Quite clearly, however, the element of support cannot be unconditional in the sense that *whatever* ego does is met with a favorable response from alter; in that case there could be no control exerted over ego's motivation; he would be directly rewarded for continuing and possibly extending his deviance.

Support could not be effective as reassurance if there were no element of permissiveness relative to the pattern system from which ego deviates. We may say that people under strain are, whether alter is fully aware of it or not, expected to deviate in some ways and to some extent, to do and say things which would not be tolerated if the circumstances, or their own states were wholly normal. (The child is understood to be under strain in "having to learn.") In general this permissiveness is to be interpreted as toleration of "natural" reactions to the frustration of expectations. These will of course be of one order if alienative motivation has not become established, and of another order if it has. This is the basis for a fundamental differentiation of types of mechanisms of social control, namely, whether it is necessary to cope with the vicious circle phenomena or not.

Permissiveness, must, however, be strictly limited if it is not to lead to the encouragement instead of the forestalling of the vicious circle. Hence there is a balance between areas of permissiveness and of restriction on it. The most fundamental form of the latter may, in the light of our analysis, be seen to be the refusal of alter to reciprocate certain of the expectations which ego develops under the pressure of his anxiety, his fantasies, his hostility and his defensiveness. Indeed support itself is in one sense a refusal on alter's part to "justify" ego's anxieties by reacting as ego fears that he might. Similarly, alter will refuse normally to reciprocate ego's hostility by being hostile in return, or will for example not accept either dominance or submission from ego. The most fundamental difference between a vicious circle-building reaction on alter's part and a social control reaction seems thus to be the combination of permissiveness with the discipline of refusal to reciprocate. Exactly in what areas this combination will operate and how the balance will be held will vary with the nature of the strains to which ego is exposed and with the role structure of the interaction system. There is, however, the common element that the refusal to reciprocate, like the support, is legitimized in terms of the institutionalized value patterns which in this case we may assume ego has previously internalized.

With respect to all three basic aspects, support, permissiveness and restriction of reciprocation, there is a further important distinction between the extents to which alter's action is consciously manipulative or is not. Many of the most fundamental elements of social control are built into the role structure of the social system in such a way that neither ego nor alter is conscious of what goes on. Their functions are wholly latent functions. On occasion, however, one or more of them may be manipulated with greater or less awareness of what the actor is doing. These are deliberately imposed sanctions, and may touch any one of the three aspects of the control problem we have distinguished. Again in line with our previous analysis we may hold that the most fundamental elements of this manipulation concern the "relational rewards," that is, alter's attitudes of love, approval and esteem. There are of course other extremely important aspects of the control relationship, notably the control of communication, but the attitude elements must, it is clear, have a critically important place.

The process of psychotherapy is the case in our own society where these fundamental elements of the processes of social control have been most explicitly brought to light. For certain purposes, as we shall point out a number of times, it can serve as a prototype of the mechanisms of social control. It should not, however, be forgotten that psychotherapy has a number of special features not shared by many other mechanisms involving the same fundamental elements. First, it is carried out in a professional role of a specialized type, and qualifications must be made for the differences of this role structure from those involved in many other types of social control. Secondly, in its classic form, it is carried out in a one-to-one relationship of two persons, not a group interaction process, whereas many mechanisms operate through more complex group situations. Third, the cultural patterns of scientific knowledge of psychological processes and, hence, the value-standards of scientific objectivity play a prominent role not to be found in many other cases, and, finally, the therapist extends his conscious manipulation of the situation and of the reward system in the light of his own theory, much farther than the case for many other types of mechanism.

PART TWO

Major Sociological Orientations

A

Bio-Medical Perspective and Issues

Medicine, psychiatry, and mental illness are deeply intertwined. The persons who direct and staff major agencies dealing with the mentally ill are typically medically trained professionals. Major conceptions of the causes, courses, and cures of mental illness fundamentally derive from medical idioms. Indeed, the vocabulary of the mental illness enterprise is replete with terms originally used to describe physical illness. As Maher (1966) suggests, "Society currently uses the model of physical illness as a basis for the terms and concepts to be applied to deviant behavior. Such behavior is termed *pathological* and is classified on the basis of *symptoms,* classification being called *diagnosis.* Processes designed to change behavior are called *therapies* and are applied to *patients* in mental *hospitals.* If the deviant behavior ceases, the patient is described as *cured".*

What has come to be termed the medical model argues that aberrant patterns of affect, thought, and behavior are best viewed as "symptoms" produced by an underlying pathological condition. The medical model asserts that disease is caused by physiobiological factors that may involve genetic, metabolic, biochemical, or other organic pathology. Mental illness is like any other illness and is unique only in that the symptoms are not fevers and aches, but unusual patterns of behavior. At times the medical model is employed in a metaphorical way. Even when there is no discernible organic basis psychiatrists hold that it is useful to treat deviant behaviors *as if* they resulted from an illness not of the body, but of the mind. The cause of the illness may be any of a number of psychosocial factors ranging from unusual patterns of upbringing and socialization to intense and stressful life experiences.

As later readings will suggest, sociological models often have a dramatically different point of view and conflict with the medical model. But the medical model in either literal or metaphorical form so deeply permeates the idiom and organization of the mental illness enterprise that it demands attention prior to turning to the major sociological orientations.

David Mechanic, in "What Are Mental Health and Mental Illness?", a selection from his book on *Mental Health and Social Policy* (1969), provides an overview of the perspectives, problems, and controversies of psychiatric medical models. Focusing upon schizophrenia—the disorder most studied by research-oriented psychiatrists—Mechanic reviews the spectrum of explanations currently existing regarding its causes. He reviews as well some of the arguments delivered against the notion of mental illness itself. Mechanic considers the costs associated with adoption of the medical model by psychiatrists. He notes that the medical model stigmatizes the patient and places responsibility for the problem on the individual. Mechanic compares the disease model with psychodynamic models (although it should be noted that the latter is a metaphorical application of the medical model). While the psychodynamic view is more attuned to sociological considerations, the emphasis is on personality-based explanations: "This approach is characterized by a very strong bias—that most problems stem from defects in people and their personality development rather than from external difficulties".

The medical model is a potent way of accounting for certain types of eccentric behavior. There are several historical episodes in which investigators succeeded in discovering organic bases for crazy behavior despite support for the conflicting opinion that the causes lay in the individuals' social environments. For example, in the nineteenth century leading authorities argued that "general paralysis" or "paresis" was due to socio-psychological as well as physical factors. The fact that former members of Napoleonic armies had a higher incidence of the disorder was explained by "the privations experienced by these men, the terrors of war, their excessive drinking, and the disappointment resulting from the defeat of Napoleon" (Rosen, 1969). By 1906 Wasserman had perfected the blood test for identifying syphilitic antibodies and soon thereafter it was conclusively demonstrated that paresis was caused by syphilitic infection. Numerous cures were developed in the ensuing years and in the 1940s penicillin was found to act directly upon and destroy the syphilitic organism. The steadily declining rate of first admissions to mental hospitals for general paresis is impressive testimony to the power of the biomedical model. The promise of this episode in medical history is quite seductive: "All ye students of irrational behavior, wait long enough and all will be explained as this disease was!" (Torrey, 1975).

In "The Biological Roots of Schizophrenia," Seymour S. Kety, one of the world's foremost psychobiologists, reviews recent evidence in support of biochemical and genetic components in the etiology of schizophrenia. Kety notes that the 1950s and 1960s were characterized by many simplistic and premature explanations of biochemical processes. Many of these studies suffered from the fact that only hospitalized patients were studied. Thus, while there may have been significant biochemical differences between hospitalized and normal persons, it was not clear that the differences were due to schizophrenia or to the fact that hospitalized patients often received unusual or deficient diets, little exercise, and extraordinary quantities of drugs and medication. Relatedly, it was often difficult to determine whether the madness was caused by a biochemical imbalance, or if the imbalance produced the madness.

Early studies that sought to assess the presence and extent of a genetic contribution to schizophrenia were equivocal. The finding that "schizophrenia runs in families" is as congenial to a genetic interpretation as it is to a psychosocial one. By studying the biological and adopting families of persons who were adopted at an early age and later hospitalized as schizophrenic, Kety was able to separate environmental and genetic effects. Kety and his colleagues found that the biological relatives of schizophrenics were more likely to be schizophrenic than were members of the adopting family. Even though the genetically linked family members had scarcely lived with their schizophrenic offspring, they were significantly more likely (than the adoptive parents who raised the children) to have schizophrenia.

He points out that although these studies demonstrate the presence of a genetic component, one cannot rule out environmental factors. If schizophrenia were purely hereditary, for example, we would expect *all* fraternal twins of schizophrenics to be schizophrenic. The fact that the percentage is considerably less than 100 percent suggests that psychosocial or other environmental influences interact with genetic dispositions to produce schizophrenia.

While Kety's studies provide impressive evidence of the presence of a genetic component for a proportion of schizophrenics, it would be misleading to assume that they demonstrate that all schizophrenia is the outcome of the interaction between genetic and environmental factors. Although Kety's studies show a significant concentration of schizophrenia in the biological families of schizophrenics, the actual proportion of schizophrenic family members is quite modest. Thus, the concentration of schizophrenia in the biological families of schizophrenics examined in one study amount to 13 of 153, less than 10 percent. This suggests that a substantial proportion of schizophrenics come from families without any indication of manifest schizophrenia. While complex genetic patterns might be invoked to preserve a genetic explanation despite the absence of schizophrenia in a very large proportion of family members, it is also possible that only a small proportion of schizophrenics are genetically predisposed to the disorder.

Other aspects of Kety's research suggest that two major types of schizophrenia—acute (or reactive) as opposed to chronic (or process)—may have very different etiologies. Chronic schizophrenics have long histories of disorder, and families often recall that since earliest childhood these individuals did not relate well to other children. The chronic schizophrenic grows progressively more withdrawn and disintegrated regardless of therapeutic countermeasures. Chronic schizophrenics have the poorest prospects for recovery. By contrast, the early histories of reactive schizophrenics are relatively free of major difficulties, symptoms arise suddenly, and prospects of recovery are comparatively favorable (Snyder, 1974).

In comparing both types of schizophrenics with normal persons, Kety found that *none* of the biological relatives of acute schizophrenics were diagnosed as schizophrenics of any type. Indeed, Kety *et al.* (1971) suggest this finding calls into question whether acute schizophrenia is truly a schizophrenic disorder. While such issues are best left to psychiatric nosologists, the possibility exists that there are at least two paths to schizophrenia—one carved by bioorganic factors and the other heavily shaped by factors of a psychosocial nature.

The sociological implications of research like Kety's remain unassessed. In the first place, it is important to note that schizophrenia represents a very small portion of mental illness. Second, the research does not conclusively indicate that a genetic factor is necessarily involved in diagnosed schizophrenia. Nevertheless, these studies do establish a parameter that future sociological research must consider: A proportion of individuals diagnosed and hospitalized as schizophrenic have a distinctive genetic and biochemical makeup.

References

Seymour S. Kety, David Rosenthal, Paul H. Wender, and Fini Schulsinger, "Mental Illness in the Biological and Adoptive Families of Adopted Schizophrenics," *American Journal of Psychiatry*, **128**:3, September, 1971, 82−86.

B. A. Maher, *Principles of Psychopathology*, New York: McGraw-Hill Book Co., Inc., 1966.

David Mechanic, *Mental Health and Social Policy*, Englewood Cliffs, N.J.: Prentice-Hall, Inc., 1969.

George Rosen, *Madness In Society*, New York: Harper and Row, Inc., 1969.

Solomon H. Snyder, *Madness and the Brain*, New York: McGraw-Hill Book Co., Inc., 1974.

E. Fuller Torrey, *The Death of Psychiatry*, New York: Penguin Books, Inc., 1975.

DAVID MECHANIC

What Are Mental Health and Mental Illness?

If we are to discuss mental health policy, we must be aware of the scope and limits of our topic. If our goal is to develop policies to deal with the prevention and treatment of mental illness and the facilitation of mental health, then we must clearly outline the dimensions of each of those concepts. Are mental health programs to be limited to persons who come under the care of mental health workers, or are they to extend to those who see no need for psychiatric services and who have not been defined as problems by their communities? Are such programs to be restricted only to persons suffering from clear psychiatric syndromes, or should they include those with ordinary problems such as nervousness, unhappiness, and social and family conflict? Are deviations such as delinquency and criminal behavior part of the mental health problem, or are they more fruitfully dealt with outside the sphere of psychiatry? Are such situations as poverty, discrimination, and unemployment central aspects of the mental health problem, or do they relate more significantly to other fields? Is failure in performance resulting from a low level of education a mental health problem, or is it primarily a problem of education? Each of these questions and many others must be answered before it is possible to consider alternative mental health policies.

Psychiatrists, mental health workers, and the public in general disagree considerably about the appropriate criteria for ascertaining the presence of mental illness. Much of this disagreement stems from a lack of consensus as to how broad or narrow the conception of mental illness should be. While some psychiatrists restrict the definition of mental illness to a limited set of disorders, others include a great variety of problem situations within the psychiatric sphere.

Reprinted from David Mechanic, *Mental Health and Social Policy*, Englewood Cliffs, N.J.: Prentice-Hall, Inc., 1969, pages 12−22, by permission of the author and publisher.

Psychiatric Diagnostic Models

Traditionally, psychiatrists have developed descriptive diagnostic labels which they use in categorizing and dealing with patients. Although most psychiatrists use these designations, they do not agree on their nature, significance, or utility. Some psychiatrists maintain that the labels denote different disease conditions; others maintain that they apply to reaction patterns having manifest similarities and in no way describe disease conditions. The opinions of most psychiatrists probably fall somewhere between these two; they accept some of the diagnostic categories as disease categories, and they view others as convenient ways of grouping reaction patterns.

The American Psychiatric Association divides psychiatric conditions into three major groups: (1) those conditions caused by or associated with impairment of brain tissue (i.e., disorders caused by infection, intoxication, trauma, metabolic disturbances, etc.); (2) mental deficiency; and (3) disorders without clearly defined clinical cause, those not caused by structural change in the brain, and those attributed to psychogenic causes. We will focus our discussion on this third category.

The American Psychiatric Association further divides this category into five subcategories: (1) psychotic disorders; (2) psychophysiologic, autonomic, and visceral disorders; (3) psychoneurotic disorders; (4) personality disorders; and (5) transient situational personality disorders. Although each of these subcategories is quite ambiguous and has limited diagnostic reliability (that is, psychiatrists frequently disagree as to what the condition is), they descriptively depict the gross reaction patterns recognizable among patients.

From the point of view of psychiatric inpatient care, the psychotic conditions and mental disorders of old age are the central problems. Old persons now constitute approximately one-quarter of all first admissions for long-term care in mental hospitals. Although classified by the American Psychiatric Association as suffering from chronic brain disorders, many of these patients are only moderately senile and could live quite adequately in sheltered environments other than mental hospitals. They often require some nursing attention and are very difficult to care for within a small household. Because of the lack of other suitable facilities, such aged persons are often sent to mental hospitals. The assumption that most of the problems of old age are the result of brain disorders is unproved, and apart from the diagnosis of arteriosclerosis these assumptions are based totally on observations of behavior (Clausen, 1966). Even the influence of arteriosclerosis is unclear since senility and evidence of arteriosclerosis are not always correlated. Although problems of old age are important and require careful attention, we shall emphasize here psychotic conditions that develop earlier in life.

The psychotic disorders to which we shall give main emphasis are the affective, the paranoid, and the schizophrenic reactions. The affective disorders involve extreme states of depression or mania, although the former is more common. Depression and other psychoses occurring in late adulthood are given a special designation— involutional psychotic reactions—since they are believed to have some relationship to metabolic and endocrine functions. The paranoid reactions are usually characterized by persecutory or grandiose delusions, without the occurrence of hallucinations. The suspiciousness characteristic of the paranoid occurs commonly in the general population and does not ordinarily lead to treatment. Some persons with paranoid inclinations become sufficiently disordered and disruptive that they require hospitalization. The schizophrenic reactions—the most important in terms of public policy and the need for continuing care—account for approximately one-quarter of all first admissions to mental hospitals and one-half of all patients residing in them. Although psychiatrists generally agree that schizophrenic reactions encompass many different conditions, there is little evidence that subtypes can be reliably differentiated, and under ordinary conditions of practice even the gross diagnosis is less than fully adequate in its reliability. Since schizophrenia is one of the most important psychiatric conditions—and the most studied and written about—we shall illustrate some of the general problems of psychiatric conceptualization using schizophrenia as an example.

Schizophrenia: An Example in Psychiatric Conceptualization

Psychiatrists usually diagnose schizophrenia on the basis of bizarre behavior characterized by inappropriate verbalizations and distortions of interpersonal perception as evidenced by the presence of delusions and hallucinations. Schizophrenics often withdraw from interpersonal contacts and engage in a rich and unusual fantasy life. In its more extreme manifestations, schizophrenia is associated with disregard for conventional expectations and with habit deterioration. According to this description schizophrenia is a set of reactions involving disturbances in reality relationships and concept formation, accompanied by a variety of intellectual, affective, and behavioral disturbances varying in kind and degree. A. McGhie and J. Chapman (1961) note that early schizophrenia often involves disturbances in the processes of attention and perception (including changes in sensory quality and in the perception of speech and movement), changes in motility and bodily awareness, and changes in thinking and affective processes. Patients classified as schizophrenics often give the impression that they are retreating from reality and appear to be suffering from unpredictable disturbances in their streams of thought. Depending on the stage of the condition and the level of personal deterioration, schizophrenia may be easy or difficult to identify, as F. C. Redlich and D. X. Freedman (1966) note:

> The diagnosis of schizophrenia is either very easy or very difficult. The typical cases, and there are very many such, can be recognized by the layman and the beginner; but some cases offer such difficulties that the most qualified experts in the field cannot come to any agreement. Such difficulties can hardly be surprising; there is no clear fundamental definition of schizophrenia and there are marked differences in international psychiatry as to what is meant by the term. In the United States, the concept of schizophrenia is broader than in the rest of the world and includes marginal types. In general, the diagnosis of schizophrenia is made too frequently; we are inclined to believe that the less skilled the psychiatrist, the more often the diagnosis of schizophrenia. As the diagnosis still has a connotation of malignancy and grave implications for patients and their families, it encourages drastic therapies and should be made with great circumspection. It is based entirely upon psychological and rather subjective criteria. All too often the diagnosis is made without specification of state and severity. (pp. 507–8)

Investigators disagree considerably about the causes of schizophrenia, and theories of conditions so labeled range from biologically oriented models to those which posit the roots of schizophrenia in social interaction, particularly in family life. Implicated in such differences of perspective is the question of whether it is valuable to view schizophrenia as a group of diseases or as a group of problems in living. Those who view schizophrenia as a disease are more careful in specifying precise diagnostic criteria, are more restrictive in the use of the diagnostic label, and are more concerned about diagnostic reliability (Wing, 1967). In contrast, those who view schizophrenia as a convenient term for characterizing a particular reaction pattern which has no generic base use the label more loosely and are less concerned with the reliability of the concept since the diagnosis is not seen as the primary factor in decisions concerning the care and treatment of the patients. This difference in point of view is apparent from the statements below:

Constitutional resistance to the main genotype of schizophrenia is determined by a genetic mechanism which is probably non-specific and certainly multifactorial. . . . For various reasons it does not seem likely, however, that the genetic mechanisms controlling susceptibility and lack of resistance to schizophrenia—that is, the ability to develop a schizophrenic psychosis and the inability to counteract the progression of the disease—are entirely identical with each other. (Kallman, 1956, pp. 96−97)

Social withdrawal, for example, is a characteristic of most forms of chronic schizophrenia, irrespective of social setting, and a biological component (seen at its most extreme in catatonic stupor) must be accepted. (Wing, 1963, p. 635)

Confusion may arise if one does not keep in mind the nature of the concept of schizophrenia. It is not, and should not be treated as, a disease entity of a biochemical or genetic nature, but merely a reaction type which has been selected more or less arbitrarily because of its operational usefulness. (Ødegaard, 1965, p. 296)

In psychoanalytic terms, the schizophrenics represent those who have failed, due to either somatic or psychogenic forces, to evolve the ego integrative processes or strengths necessary to resolve flexibly conflicts between their (id) drives and overdemanding superego attitudes and aspirations. They are thus defective in their capacity to adapt to the social demands confronting them and to their own drives and they thereby lack a harmonious self-concept and ego ideal with clear goals and motivations. Much of their adaptation is made, instead, through partially satisfying regressive or fixated infantile behavior. (Noyes and Kolb, 1963, p. 325)

We suggest that the double bind nature of the family situation of a schizophrenic results in placing the child in a position where if he responds to his mother's simulated affection her anxiety will be aroused and she will punish him . . . to defend herself from closeness with him. Thus the child is blocked off from intimate and secure associations with his mother. However, if he does not make overtures of affection, she will feel that this means that she is not

a loving mother and her anxiety will be aroused. Therefore, she will either punish him for withdrawing or make overtures to the child to insist that he demonstrate that he loves her. . . . In either case in a relationship, the most important in his life and the model for all others, he is punished if he indicates love and affection and punished if he does not. . . . This is the basic nature of the double bind relationship between mother and child. (Bateson *et al.,* 1956, p. 258)

When gross rule-breaking is publicly recognized and made an issue, the rule-breaker may be profoundly confused, anxious, and ashamed. In this crisis it seems reasonable to assume that the rule-breaker will be suggestible to the cues that he gets from the reactions of others toward him. . . . The rule-breaker is sensitive to the cures provided by these others and begins to think of himself in terms of the stereotyped role of insanity, which is part of his own role vocabulary also, since he, like those reacting to him, learned it early in childhood. In this situation his behavior may begin to follow the pattern suggested by his own stereotypes and the reactions of others. That is, when a residual rule-breaker organizes his behavior within the framework of mental disorder, and when his organization is validated by others, particularly prestigeful others such as physicians, he is "hooked" and will proceed on a career of chronic deviance. (Scheff, 1966a, p. 88)

Varying Conceptions of Mental Illness

The descriptions above indicate the many conceptions of the nature and cause of schizophrenia; this situation equally applies to most other mental disorders, and it has led to a vigorous discussion of the concept of mental illness. At one extreme stands Thomas Szasz (1960), a professor of psychiatry and a psychoanalyst, who vociferously maintains that mental illness is a myth and that the standards by which patients are defined as sick are psychosocial, ethical, and legal but not medical. Although Szasz's use of myth metaphor does little to stimulate reasonable and rational debate, he does present a point of view that requires serious scrutiny.

Szasz argues that the concept of mental illness results from conditions such as syphilis of the brain in which it is demonstrable that peculiarities in behavior and thought are linked with a brain condition. He argues that, in contrast, most symptoms designated as mental illness are not brain lesions or similar physical indications, but rather deviations in behavior or thinking. Thus Szasz contends that the metaphor of illness is used to characterize problems having no biological basis and that such judgments are based primarily on ethical or psychosocial criteria. He concedes that specific disorders in thinking and behavior result from brain dysfunctions, but he argues that it is more correct to say that some people labeled as mentally ill suffer from disease of the brain rather than to assert that all of those called mentally ill are sick in a medical sense. In Szasz's opinion, the use of the concept of mental illness to characterize both disorders of the brain and deviations in behavior, thinking, and affect due to other causes results in confusion, abuses of psychiatry, and the use of medical terminology to deprive patients of their civil liberties through involuntary hospitalization and other coercive techniques.

Psychiatrists who oppose Szasz's viewpoint—and they appear to be the majority—contend, in contrast, that they diagnose mental illness not only through the recognition of maladaptive and nonconforming behavior but also through the recognition of manifest disturbances of psychological functioning—delusions, confused perceptions, hallucinations, and such disturbed emotional states as extreme anxiety or depression (Lewis, 1953). Further, they believe that these psychopathological criteria are as valid as the pathological criteria used in the diagnosis of physical conditions. The problem which leads to such great controversy is that in the psychiatric area assessments of pathology depend almost exclusively on the clinician's judgment, while in physical medicine more objective investigatory procedures are frequently available in making such assessments.

One of the typical problems in such debates is that the adversaries are really not addressing themselves to the same point. Szasz bases his argument on the observations that frequently psychiatrists define mental illness solely on the basis of social and psychosocial criteria, that psychiatrists often become involved in questions of ethics and in conflicts of interest rather than being concerned with illness per se, and that the psychiatric role is used to deal with social problems and to achieve social goals which are only remotely related to clinical assessments of pathology; he is correct in all these observations. However, he never really adequately addresses himself to the possibility of assessing mental illness on the basis of disturbances in psychological processes, and it is to this question that his critics usually respond.

Szasz assumes that the disease concept should be reserved for observations demonstrable on a physical basis and therefore that psychological phenomena do not appropriately belong within a disease model. In an essay entitled ''Personality Disorder Is Disease,'' David Ausubel (1961) presents four opposing arguments to the Szasz viewpoint. First, symptoms need not necessarily be a physical lesion to be regarded as a manifestation of disease. Consider, for example, the importance of subjective pain in medicine. Second, it is appropriate to regard psychological symptoms as manifestations of dis-

ease if they impair the personality and distort behavior. Third, there is no contradiction in regarding psychological symptoms both as manifestations of illness and as problems. Like physical indications, psychological symptoms may or may not threaten the social adjustment of the person. Finally, immoral behavior and mental illness are clearly distinguishable conditions; the issue of culpability is irrelevant in handling behavior disorders.

Disease concepts are pragmatic instruments, and the reasonableness of applying the diagnostic disease concept to psychiatry depends on its potential use. Medical diagnoses are hypotheses based on some underlying theory or set of assumptions. These underlying theories may be of a scientific or a nonscientific nature, and scientific disease theories may vary widely in their degree of confirmation. The usefulness of a diagnostic disease model depends on its level of confirmation, which depends in turn on the reliability of the diagnosis (the amount of agreement among practitioners in assigning the diagnostic label) and its utility in predicting the course of the condition, its etiology, and how it can be treated successfully (Mechanic, 1968).

The disease models that doctors use in ordinary medical practice vary from those (such as pernicious anemia) based on underlying theories that are well confirmed, to those (such as heart disease, diabetes) based on partially confirmed theories, to those (such as multiple sclerosis) based on unconfirmed theories. Most diseases fall somewhere within the partially confirmed designation. In other words, we know a considerable amount about these conditions, but many important questions are still unanswered. With confirmed disease theories, all the necessary information concerning the cause of the condition, what is likely to occur if it is untreated, and what regimen to apply to retard it is available. A correct diagnostic assessment thus leads to correct action. It should be obvious why diagnostic reliability is so important; if the patient has pernicious anemia and the physician diagnoses his condition as tuberculosis, he will be proceeding on incorrect inferences concerning the cause of the problem and the appropriate actions which will remedy it. (For more complete discussion of this issue, see Mechanic (1968), pp. 90–114.)

From a theoretical standpoint, we do not have to consider psychiatric conditions as being qualitatively different from nonpsychiatric ones, but, on the whole, the underlying theories concerning psychiatric disorders have a lower level of confirmation than do ordinary medical theories. When a physician assigns the label of pernicious anemia to his patient's condition, his understanding of the patient's problem and his treatment procedure follow directly from the diagnosis. In contrast if, as Ø. Ødegaard (1965) maintains, assignment of the label of schizophrenia to a patient's condition does not affect the choice of therapy or his chance of recovery, we can seriously question the advantage of using the disease model.

In psychiatry, the diagnoses made are not entirely unassociated with the treatment process. Although psychiatrists with a psychodynamic perspective tend to apply a similar approach to most conditions which they regard as treatable, a growing tendency is to use very specific treatments for particular disorders. For example, electroshock therapy appears to be more useful for depressive psychoses than for schizophrenia; behavior therapy, a technique based on learning theory, is used more frequently for phobic reactions than for involutional depression; and the psychiatric drugs used in treating a schizophrenic patient are different from those used in treating a depressed or anxious patient. Obviously, the great deal of overlap in treatment techniques for these various conditions reflects the ambiguous and uncertain state of the field, but the overall level of ignorance is not so large as some would imply.

In deciding whether a disease orientation is useful, it is necessary to balance the gains achieved from using such a perspective against its various disadvantages. The adoption of a disease perspective involves certain risks. For example, characterizing a particular problem as a mental disease may lead to greater stigmatization than would some other way of describing the difficulty. Moreover, the implications that the condition is within the individual rather than in his social situation and that is it not subject to his control or that of others may under some circumstances lead to attitudes on his part and on the part of others in the community that are a serious deterrent to rehabilitation. The most serious result of using disease models when they yield little information is the possible encouragement such a model may provide for failing to explore alternatives for rehabilitation outside the disease perspective. Gerald Grob (1966), an intellectual historian who has studied the history of mental hospital care, notes the following problems.

> The continued insistence by psychiatrists that their profession was truly scientific, however, exerted a profound, though negative, influence over the character of the mental hospital. As we have seen, the assumption that mental disease was somatic in nature invariably led to therapeutic nihilism. Moreover, somaticism often precluded alternative approaches, particularly along psychological and other nonsomatic lines. Lacking any visible means of therapy, psychiatrists tended to engage in a vast holding operation by confining mentally ill patients until that distant day when specific cures for specific disease entities would become available. (pp. 356–57)

The major competing view to the disease perspective is one which conceptualizes problems in terms of their psychodynamics. Instead of concerning himself with establishing a disease diagnosis, the psychodynamic psychiatrist attempts to reconstruct a developmental picture of the patient's personality; he believes that such an exploration will provide an understanding of how the disturbed state of the patient has developed and what functions the disturbed behavior has in his adaptation to the environment. A. P. Noyes and L. C. Kolb (1963), in instructing the psychiatrist on the examination of the patient, make the following observation.

> It will be seen that the mental examination should be a clinical study of personality and aims at a comprehensive appraisal of the patient. Such a study must be made by a genetic and dynamic rather than by a cross sectional method. Only by a genetic-dynamic investigation, with its emphasis on developmental sequence, can one ascertain how the individual came to express himself in his particular form of behavior—that of the neurosis, psychosis, or behavior disorder. The examiner does not seek to make a "diagnosis" in terms of some disease entity. (p. 111)

A basic assumption of the psychodynamic psychiatrist is that disturbed behavior is part of the same continuum as normal behavior and is explained by the same theories that govern our understanding of normal personality development and social functioning. If disturbed behavior is a form of adaptation of the personality in response to particular situations and social stresses, then it is logical to study such behavior from the same perspectives and orientations as those from which we study any other kind of behavior.

The psychodynamic psychiatrist does not make a serious attempt to ascertain whether the patient is mentally ill for this is not a meaningful perspective within his frame of reference. He tends to assume the existence of mental illness or personality disturbance by the fact that the patient is suffering and has come for help or by the fact that the patient's social behavior is sufficiently inappropriate to lead others to bring him to the attention of psychiatric facilities. Using a developmental approach, the psychiatrist attempts to ascertain what aspects of the person's past experience have led him to develop the patterns of functioning that have created the present difficulty. Strong inferences in this approach are that the source of the difficulty is within the person himself and his personality development and that the problem can be alleviated or remedied by changing some aspect of his personality.

Since the psychodynamic perspective does not differentiate mental illness from ordinary problems of mental discomfort or social adjustment, psychiatrists of this persuasion tend to accept for treatment people with a wide variety of problems such as marital dissatisfaction, poor adjustment to school, homosexuality, alcoholism, neurosis, and feelings of lack of fulfillment. Although the psychiatrist may be attuned to some extent to the social aspects of some of these problems, he basically proceeds as though they largely result from the personality of the patient rather than his social situation, deprivation and injustice, or other environmental contingencies. Thus this approach is characterized by a very strong bias—that most problems stem from defects in people and their personality development rather than from external difficulties.

As traditional psychodynamic views have become modified, psychiatrists tend to see difficulties and mental discomfort as the complicated outcomes of the interaction between an individual's personality and the nature of his social environment. Thus, they increasingly recognize that persons with similar personality strengths and weaknesses may make successful or unsuccessful adjustments depending on the social circumstances. For example, a person with strong aggressive needs may or may not have problems depending on whether he is in a position of authority or in a subordinate job. Although this perspective takes the social environment into account, psychiatrists still feel that a well-integrated personality can cope with most circumstances and that persons who get into difficulty usually have significant personality weaknesses. The problem with this assumption is that few people are perfect, and so it is easy to blame any difficulties a person may have on weaknesses or deficiencies in his personality. Negro mothers of illegitimate children may very well have a wide variety of personality problems; but the high rate of illegitimacy among Negroes results largely from the structure of Negro family life, which is the consequence of slavery, impoverishment, discrimination, lack of knowledge about and access to the means of birth control, and a welfare system structured to punish members of intact families. To treat this problem and many others as if responsibility resides in the victim rather than in the social structure is to impose a particular set of values which may have little relationship to reality. The psychodynamic theorist argues that a person raised in an impoverished and deprived environment develops a different personality structure from that of a person raised in privileged and affluent circumstances. Since the psychodynamic theorist does not differentiate the processes underlying normal and abnormal behavior, he might view the personalities of individuals raised under some circumstances as being inimical to adequate social adjustment. Although different social conditions lead to

the development of different personality traits, the basis for viewing some traits as adaptive and others as maladaptive is not clear. In the end what is viewed as maladaptive may depend on who the judge is and from what perspective he sees the problem. In short, the psychodynamic view depends very heavily on the value judgments of the therapist.

In contrast, those who view failures in adjustment as being purely the result of environmental circumstances approach the field of mental health with a very different bias. A strict environmental perspective fails to explain why, in the same circumstances, most persons manage to adapt while others have great difficulty. Persons vary widely in their skills, training, and personal characteristics, and a simple situation for some to handle may introduce insuperable barriers and difficulties for others. In the long run, the question of whether it is most appropriate to view the field of mental disorder primarily from the perspective of disease, of psychodynamic development, or environmental causation depends on future research. No argument, regardless of its sophistication and refinement can, at this point, settle the matter. While it is important to keep an open mind about the ultimate value of using disease models in relation to mental disorders, we must also make sure that the assumption that mental disorders are diseases does not undermine the use of other approaches in helping afflicted persons. Whatever the disease character of mental disorders, such conditions tend to be characterized by various aspects that make them socially different from most nonpsychiatric conditions and which present unique problems in their recognition and care.

REFERENCES

Ausubel, D. P. 1961. "Personality disorder is disease." *American Psychologist* **16** (February):69–74.

Bateson, G., *et al.* 1956. "Toward a theory of schizophrenia." *Behavioral Science* **1** (October):251–264.

Clausen, J. 1966. "Mental disorders," in R. Merton and R. Nisbet (eds.), *Contemporary Social Problems* (rev. ed.), pp. 26–83. New York: Harcourt, Brace & World, Inc.

Grob, G. 1966. *The State and the Mentally Ill.* Chapel Hill: University of North Carolina Press.

Kallman, F. 1956. "The genetic theory of schizophrenia," in C. Kluckhohn and H. A. Murray (eds.), *Personality in Nature, Society and Culture,* pp. 80–99. New York: Alfred A. Knopf, Inc.

Lewis, A. 1953. "Health as a social concept." *British Journal of Sociology.* **4** (June): 109–124.

McGhie, A., and J. Chapman. 1961. "Disorders of attention

and perception in early schizophrenia." *British Journal of Medical Psychology* **34** (June): 103–116.

Mechanic, D. 1968. *Medical Sociology: A Selective View*. New York: The Free Press.

Noyes, A. P., and L. C. Kolb. 1963. *Modern Clinical Psychiatry* (6th ed.). Philadelphia: W. B. Saunders Company.

Ødegaard, Ø. 1965. "Discussion of 'sociocultural factors in the epidemiology of schizophrenia.' " *International Journal of Psychiatry* **1** (April):296–305.

Redlich, F. C., and D. X. Freedman. 1966. *The Theory and Practice of Psychiatry*. New York: Basic Books.

Scheff, T. 1966. *Being Mentally Ill: A Sociological Theory*. Chicago: Aldine Publishing Co.

Szasz, T. 1960. "The myth of mental illness." *American Psychologist* **15** (February):113–118.

Wing, J. 1963. "Rehabilitation of psychiatric patients." *British Journal of Psychiatry* **109** (September):635–641.

———. 1967. "The modern management of schizophrenia," in H. Freeman and J. Farndale (eds.), *New Aspects of the Mental Health Services*, pp. 3–28. New York: Pergamon Press, Inc.

SEYMOUR S. KETY

The Biological Roots of Schizophrenia

What is madness?

Philosophers, physicians, and psychologists have debated this question for centuries. Hippocrates was among the first to believe that insanity was a form of illness, originating in imbalances in the brain; but a view more widely held by his contemporaries was that the insane owed their unfortunate condition to supernatural influences. In the Middle Ages, people who thought and acted strangely were persecuted as witches. At least one physician, Johann Weyer, believed that the insane were sick and could be healed, but he was villified by the public and the church. Even when the insane began to be seen clearly as "sick" rather than possessed, their lot was not tremendously improved. Since no one understood their disorder at either the biological or psychological level, the mentally ill were placed primarily under custodial care that at best was woefully inadequate. (The very word "bedlam" first evolved as a corruption of Bethlehem, the name of an early English mental hospital, and accurately described the condition of that place.) Today, in apparent reaction against the slow progress in understanding madness, there are those who claim that the insane are not really ill at all, but are simply making a "creative adaptation" to an impossible social situation. Unfortunately, this view of mental illness is not generally shared by the sufferers themselves.

Paradoxically, the development of antiscience and antipsychiatry attitudes over the past decade has coincided

Reprinted from *Harvard Magazine*, Vol. **78**, No. 9 (May, 1976), pages 20–26, by permission of the author and publisher.

with the discovery of strong new evidence that mental illness is truly a medical and psychobiological problem. Some promising advances have even been made in our understanding of the most serious and the most puzzling of the psychoses: schizophrenia.

The term "schizophrenia," coined by the Swiss psychiatrist Eugen Bleuler in 1911, means "split mind" in Greek. Bleuler felt that the basis of the disorder was a split between the emotions and the intellect that made it impossible for the schizophrenic to function as a fully integrated person able to relate to the world in an appropriate way.

While schizophrenia may take many different forms the dissociation between thought and feeling remains one of its hallmarks. Schizophrenics suffer from severe thought disorder, which manifests itself in bizarre speech and behavior. They have difficulty establishing close relationships, tend to withdraw from the outside world, may be unable to experience pleasure, and may have hallucinations and delusions. Schizophrenia primarily affects adolescents and young adults, and severely interferes with educational, occupational, sexual, amd marital adjustments. And schizophrenia is a widespread problem; everywhere in the world that its incidence has been estimated, it is found that approximately 1 percent of the people will manifest schizophrenia in their lifetime.

Although schizophrenia has been recognized as such (or by its earlier designation, dementia praecox) for nearly a hundred years, our understanding of its causes or even where to look for its causes has barely begun. In the past thirty years, knowledge of the brain and its relationship to behavior has burgeoned, and we have probably learned more in that period than we had in centuries before. Today, for the first time, we are beginning to develop plausible hypotheses that specifically link schizophrenia to abnormal—but, we hope, correctable—processes in the brain.

One of the first triumphs of biochemistry was the delineation of the metabolic pathways by which energy was made available from the oxidation of foodstuffs. Not surprisingly, an early biochemical hypothesis viewed schizophrenia as a disorder in the utilization of oxygen by the brain. My first research in schizophrenia thirty years ago examined that hypothesis.

One can measure the oxygen consumed by an organ if one can measure the rate of blood flowing through it. But how could one measure the rate of blood flow through the conscious human brain? The answer came from the physical principles involved in the exchange of inert gases between blood and body tissues.

Anesthesiologists had known for a long time that anesthesia was induced more rapidly in patients with faster circulation. Apparently the uptake of anesthetics by the brain was related to cerebral blood flow. Many anesthetics are inert gases; they are not used by the brain as fuel, and are not metabolized by the brain. The uptake of these inert gases by the brain is unaffected by the metabolic processes that regulate the rate at which the brain takes up and uses oxygen. Instead, their uptake is governed by physical factors, and, of these, blood flow is the most important variable. Equations were derived relating blood flow in the brain to the rate of uptake of an inert gas, its solubility characteristics, and concentration in the blood, all of which could be directly measured.

Using low concentrations of inhaled nitrous oxide and these equations, researchers found that the brain of a normal conscious man receives about three-quarters of a liter of blood per minute, and utilizes, in that time, 46 milliliters of oxygen and 76 milligrams of glucose (the sugar that is the brain's main fuel). From this, the rate of energy utilization could be calculated and was found to be twenty watts for the thinking human brain—a remarkably small power requirement compared with the kilowatts used by most electronic computers.

Next, biochemists measured the rate of cerebral oxygen metabolism in different mental states. They soon found that when the energy supply to the brain was disturbed by disorders of the cerebral circulation or metabolism, consciousness was seriously affected. In comas of various types, cerebral oxygen consumption and the energy it provided was reduced by 50 percent. But no such results were found for schizophrenia.

In fact, both the rate of blood flow to the brain and its oxygen metabolism in schizophrenia are perfectly normal; one uses just as much oxygen to think an irrational thought as a rational one.

This observation, as well as the finding that the sleeping brain is using energy at a normal rate, clearly demonstrated that the brain is not like the heart or most machines, which use more energy when they do more work. The energy consumed by the brain has relatively little to do with its output. The brain of a statesman making a speech that will change the history of the world uses no more oxygen than that of a comedian telling a silly joke. The brain is like a radio, whose power supply keeps it running but doesn't determine its output. A severe disturbance in the power supply of a radio will interfere with its working; on the other hand, one cannot improve its fidelity or the quality of the program by supplying more energy.

If there was a biochemical disturbance in schizophrenia, scientists realized, it would have to be found in much more subtle and complex processes than the plumbing and heating system of the brain. But 25 years ago no one had any idea what those processes might be. A wide gap of ignorance lay between what was known about the brain and what was known about disorders of the mind, although there was no dearth of attempts to bridge that gap, with hypotheses of varying plausibility.

One of these, the adrenochrome hypothesis, had an interesting origin. Every physician knows that if one keeps adrenaline (used as a heart stimulant; to constrict the blood vessels; and to relax the bronchi in asthma) in solution for a long time, it turns pink as the adrenaline changes to a new substance, adrenochrome. During the blitz in England, some physicians had used pink adrenaline because they didn't have any fresh adrenaline. A patient thus treated reported some strange subjective sensations, and the idea developed that adrenochrome might be a hallucinogenic agent. Two investigators in Canada prepared some adrenochrome, gave it to each other in a rather uncontrolled experiment, and convinced themselves that it did produce hallucinations. This led them to the hypothesis that schizophrenia was caused by the abnormal metabolism of circulating adrenaline; the schizophrenic was making his own adrenochrome, they suggested, and becoming psychotic as a result.

In 1955 we didn't know very much about the normal metabolism of adrenaline, let alone its metabolism in schizophrenia. Two years later, Julius Axelrod solved that problem by describing a new enzyme and the several pathways of adrenaline metabolism. This enabled us to compare the metabolism of adrenaline in schizophrenics with that in normal individuals, and to learn that they were the same. There was thus no evidence that schizophrenics were manufacturing adrenochrome from the adrenaline circulating in their blood.

The late Fifties and early Sixties was a discouraging time for investigators interested in the problem of schizophrenia. The adrenochrome hypothesis was only one of many simplistic and premature explanations that sober research was unable to support.

From one week to the next, great claims would appear, usually in the Sunday supplements, that some chemical substance or some chemical process was defective in schizophrenics. All of these claims turned out to be fruitless. In retrospect, this is hardly surprising; our store of basic information about the brain and the nervous system was so inadequate even ten or twenty years ago that these hypotheses were like bridges thrown across a great chasm, but bridges that had no supports. They were heroic and premature hypotheses that tried to solve the problem of mental illness all at once, even though most important scientific discoveries must actually come through the slow accretion of facts, whose relevance to an ultimate problem may not be appreciated until the problem is actually solved. Not only did these early theories not solve the problem, but their failure also led some to become completely disillusioned with biology and to develop doctrines that psychosis was not at all biological in nature but something that certain parents taught to their children, or even that schizophrenia was a myth, that it was not an illness at all, but a creative adaptation to an evil society.

At the time, there was little to support a belief that biology had much to offer to psychiatry. The brain contains more than 10 billion neurons, each of which receives signals from many close and distant neighbors and sends signals to many others. For a long time, the connections between one neuron and the next (a link called the synapse) in the chain of communication were thought to be electrical junctions. The brain was thus considered closely analogous to a modern computer with billions of electrical switches; biochemical processes provided the energy for the circuits but the computer itself was largely physical. To unravel these billions of circuits in search of a hypothetical short circuit or defective component that caused schizophrenia seemed beyond the realm of possibility.

Yet there was one area that seemed to imply that biochemistry really was relevant to the understanding of mental illness. That was the possibility that schizophrenia and serious emotional disorders (such as manic depression) had important genetic components.

Many psychiatrists had thought for years that genetic factors were important in schizophrenia; but the evidence was inconclusive. Schizophrenia runs in families: 5 percent of the parents of schizophrenics and 10 percent

of the children and siblings of schizophrenics will suffer from the disorder. That doesn't prove the illness is genetic, however, for many characteristics run in families—wealth, poverty, nutritional disorders like pellagra. Families share their life experiences as well as their genetic endowment.

Studies of the twins of schizophrenics were somewhat more compelling. Identical twins had been shown to have a greater chance of sharing schizophrenia than fraternal twins: the identical twin of a schizophrenic has approximately a 50-percent chance of developing the illness, while a fraternal twin (like any sibling) has only a 10-percent risk. This is compatible with the view that genetic factors are important; identical twins are genetically identical, and are thus much more likely than fraternal twins to "share" a genetic disease. But identical twins also share much more of their environment than do fraternal twins—their parents usually dress them alike and parade them in a double perambulator, they are rarely separated, their friends can't tell the difference between them; in short, they identify with each other for many nongenetic reasons. (The identical twins of physicians are, interestingly, often also doctors, but this would hardly be evidence that becoming a physician was genetically determined.)

There were loopholes, then, in the genetic evidence available before the 1960s. And these loopholes must have been large, because whole schools of psychiatry marched through them, ignoring the evidence on either side.

But there was another approach yet to be tried; it seemed to offer investigators the capability of disentangling the genetic from the environmental variables in schizophrenia. This was the study of adopted individuals. An adopted person derives his genes from one family but shares his life experience and environment with another family. By tracing the biological relatives and the adoptive relatives of adopted individuals who eventually become schizophrenic, one could hope to determine to what extent the tendency of schizophrenia to run in families was due to genetic or to environmental influences.

Over the past fourteen years, David Rosenthal (chief of the Laboratory of Psychology at the National Institute of Mental Health), Paul Wender (professor of psychiatry at the University of Utah), Fini Schulsinger (chief of psychiatry at Copenhagen's Kommunehospitalet), and I have compiled a total sample of all of the legally adopted people in Denmark who are now between 25 and 50 years of age. Out of the 14,500 who had not been adopted by biological relatives, there were 74 that all four of us agreed were schizophrenic. We selected 74 adoptees with no history of mental disorder who matched the schizophrenics in age, sex, length of time spent with the biological family, and socioeconomic status of the rearing family; these made up our control group. Through Denmark's remarkable population registers, it was possible to find the biological and adoptive relatives of the schizophrenic and control adoptees. The total sample of about 1,100 close relatives—parents, siblings, or half-siblings on the biological or adoptive side—was then examined for evidence of schizophrenia. These relatives were diagnosed on the basis of hospital, clinic, military, and court records: each analysis was made without knowing whether the individual was related to a member of the schizophrenic or the control group of adoptees.

Our findings strongly supported the hypothesis that genetic factors operate in schizophrenia. We found a significant concentration of definite schizophrenia and "uncertain" schizophrenia in only the biological relatives of adopted schizophrenics—people who were genetically related to schizophrenics, even though they hadn't lived with them. The adoptive relatives who had reared the 74 schizophrenics did not show any more schizophrenia than did adoptive relatives of the control—nonschizophrenic—group; and neither the adoptive nor the biological relatives of the control adoptees showed any greater prevalence of schizophrenia than exists in the general population. Our results were corroborated when roughly half of the biological and adoptive relatives were rediagnosed on the basis of extensive interviews carried out by the Danish psychiatrist Bjørn Jacobsen.

This study, however, had a possible flaw—it had still not totally separated genetic from environmental factors. Even an adopted child experiences a certain amount of environmental influence from his mother, in utero and in the few days or weeks he spends with her before he is transferred away. Possibly, some environmental influence from the biological mother—viral, nutritional, or psychological—could have affected the child, determining the development of schizophrenia fifteen or more years later. (Clearly, the study should have been carried out on individuals adopted at the time of conception!)

We did have another approach available that made it possible to rule out the influence of even these environmental factors. The biological parents of the adoptees tended to have other children, often with other partners. These adoptees had an especially large number of biological paternal half-siblings, who had the same father but different mothers; the paternal half-siblings obviously didn't share the same uterus or the same early mothering experience as the adoptees under study. And since they were reared apart after that as well, they didn't share any environmental influences at all. In having the same father, they had only a genetic background—albeit only 50-percent—in common.

This genetic relationship, once again, carried with it a strong predisposition to schizophrenia. Thirteen percent of the biological paternal half-siblings of adopted schizophrenics were schizophrenic themselves, in comparison with 2 percent of the control group's half-siblings. This is probably the best evidence we have that genetic factors operate significantly in the transmission of schizophrenia.

Schizophrenia may not be a single disorder; in fact, there are differences among the various subgroups of schizophrenia that suggest we may be dealing with a heterogeneous syndrome like enteric fever or mental retardation. Nevertheless, we can now say that among the various forms of schizophrenia, there is certainly a large percentage (more than half) in which genetic factors seem to play a major role. And, in the face of these observations, it is also difficult to maintain that schizophrenia is a myth. How could independent judges diagnose a mythical illness in the same people, and then find this mythical illness at high prevalence only among those people who turned out to be their biological relatives? If schizophrenia is a myth, it is a myth with a strong genetic component.

The evidence for the heritability of schizophrenia raises some intriguing questions. Since schizophrenia is clearly a maladaptive condition, why haven't the genes that predispose the individual to schizophrenia been eliminated from the population by natural selection? Schizophrenics have a low fertility rate—they tend not to get married, and not to have as many children as nonschizophrenics—and so one would expect to find a smaller proportion of schizophrenics in each succeeding generation, if the disorder were related to genetic factors. And yet, as far as we know, this has not been the case. One fascinating hypothesis that has been proposed to explain this paradox is that schizophrenia may be genetically related to creativity, a characteristic that may help the individual adapt to his environment. Schizophrenics are known for their ability to generate novel and undreamed-of associations. This ability is also the basis of creativity: the creative person is one who can come up with an idea that no one else has had. The difference, however, is that the productively creative person is also very critical, evaluates his ideas as they arise, and rejects most of them. It may be that the schizophrenic lacks that critical ability. Some evidence indicates that among the relatives of schizophrenics there may be more creative individuals than one sees in the rest of the population; however, this has not yet been established, though it remains a provocative hypothesis.

If genetic factors are involved in the transmission of

schizophrenia, are environmental factors irrelevant in the causation of this disease? Emphatically not. Some of the same studies that have revealed the significance of genetic factors in schizophrenia have simultaneously shown that the disorder cannot be entirely hereditary. If schizophrenia were a purely genetic illness, for example, 100 percent rather than 50 percent of the identical twins of schizophrenics would be schizophrenic themselves. But even though the environment is clearly important, no specific environmental factor has been unequivocally implicated. Our study of adopted schizophrenics has demonstrated that schizophrenia in the rearing family is not a necessary prerequisite for the development of schizophrenia; however, the study has not ruled out other parental personality traits or methods of child-rearing that may favor the development of the disorder—or, for that matter, a wide variety of environmental influences: physical, chemical, dietary, infectious, as well as psychological.

Apart from these other considerations, the important implication of our studies at the present time is that if genetic factors are significantly involved in the disorder, then schizophrenia must have biochemical components, since genes can only operate through biochemical processes.

While these genetic studies were going on, neurobiologists did not remain idle. Great advances have been made in the neurosciences and none had a more revolutionary impact on the study of the brain than the discovery of the chemical nature of the synapse.

It is now clear that the brain is not a complex *electronic* computer, but one in which chemical and electrical processes interact at every level. Through the microscopically narrow space between neurons pass chemical substances (called neurotransmitters) that are synthesized in one neuron and affect specific receptors in the next. The hundreds of billions of synapses in the brain that mediate mental processes are not electrical connections but chemical junctions. The fact that they are chemical means that metabolic processes as well as chemical substances like hormones and drugs can all affect them. If there are biochemical disturbances in mental illness, one would expect them to operate there, and it is the synapses upon which the drugs ameliorating these illnesses should exert their influence.

Demonstration of the chemical nature of synapses required the development of fundamental knowledge and new techniques to demonstrate the existence of specific chemical substances in certain neurons and at their junctions. One of these was a technique for chemically altering certain neurotransmitters so that they would fluoresce with specific colors under ultraviolet light. When this method was applied to the brain, scientists

discovered neurons that were loaded with particular chemical substances, like noradrenaline, serotonin, and dopamine, which, like acetylcholine, certain amino acids, and polypeptides, appear to serve as neurotransmitters.

As a result of this kind of basic research as well as advances in electron microscopy, neurobiology, and neuropharmacology, it is now possible to make theoretical models of the synapse. These models change as new discoveries are made, but the basic features of the model appear to be well established.

Chemical transmission can go in only one direction at any given synapse; signals are always transmitted from the "presynaptic" to the "postsynaptic" neuron. Synaptic transmission involves some very complicated biochemical processes. The presynaptic neuron carries out the synthesis of the neurotransmitter and stores it in small packets called vesicles. When the presnyaptic neuron is stimulated, an electrical signal passes down the nerve fiber to its ending, where the vesicles release the neurotransmitter into the microscopically small "synaptic cleft" that separates the two neurons. The chemical transmitter diffuses rapidly across the synaptic cleft to interact with special receptors on the post-synaptic neuron; these receptors react to the presence of the neurotransmitter by initiating a series of biochemical events in the postsynaptic neuron, and the neuronal signal is then transmitted. Finally, the presynaptic neuron contains mechanisms for enzymatically inactivating or reabsorbing the neurotransmitter from the synaptic cleft, thus terminating its action.

We know now that a number of drugs act directly on the synapse. In 1950, a revolutionary new drug, chlorpromazine, was first used in the treatment of schizophrenia. This drug had much greater specificity for the symptoms of schizophrenia than any drug available before. Previously, a psychiatrist could control a very disturbed schizophrenic patient by giving him a large enough dose of a barbiturate to sedate him. But chlorpromazine, not just a powerful tranquilizer, acted very specifically upon the psychotic manifestations of schizophrenia. In fact, the same dose of chlorpromazine that will control the bizarre behavior, delusions, and hallucinations of a schizophrenic patient will have little effect on a normal person. The use of chlorpromazine and related drugs has considerably revamped and improved the treatment of the major psychoses, although we will have much to learn about these agents and many improvements to make on them.

There was one major problem with chlorpromazine, however. As soon as it was introduced, it was observed to produce a side effect that closely resembled the neurological disorder called Parkinson's disease. The pharmaceutical companies synthesized many related drugs and some that were entirely different, but, somehow, virtually every drug that was effective in the treatment of schizophrenia was also capable of producing symptoms of Parkinson's disease.

No one understood this strange coincidence. More than ten years passed before the basic research on neurotransmitters and their pathways in different parts of the brain produced the answer. One neurological pathway emanating from a group of neurons called the substantia nigra was found to use dopamine as a neurotransmitter. Neuropathologists had already shown that Parkinson's disease is associated with lesions in the substantia nigra, and the Viennese physician Oleh Hornykiewicz speculated that these lesions might involve damage to the dopamine-containing cells of the area. This hypothesis was correct: the brains of patients who had died of Parkinson's disease were found on chemical analysis to be very low in dopamine. Once this was understood, it became possible to treat the disease with l-dopa, the precursor of dopamine, which partially restores the levels of that transmitter. The introduction of l-dopa in the treatment of Parkinson's disease was one of the most important advances in neurology in the past decade.

The understanding of Parkinson's disease also had great implications for psychiatry. Arvid Carlsson in Sweden immediately recognized the possibility that the drugs used in the treatment of schizophrenia might also cause Parkinsonian symptoms by acting on dopamine pathways in the brain. Soon Carlsson produced the first experimental evidence that chlorpromazine and related drugs do in fact block dopamine synapses in the brain. During the past decade, Carlsson's work has been confirmed and expanded. Two groups at Yale, through neurophysiological studies on individual neurons and biochemical studies on dopamine receptors, produced compelling evidence that the drugs effective in the treatment of schizophrenia have an important pharmacologic action in common: their ability to block dopamine synapses.

One cannot conclude from that, however, that overactive dopamine synapses are the cause of schizophrenia. The interrelationship of the many different types of neurons in the brain, the various neurotransmitters they use, and the different effects of psychoactive drugs are much too complex—and too little understood—to permit simple conclusions. But it is obvious that further study of the functions of dopamine and other transmitters in the brain and their relationship to behavior can only improve our understanding of schizophrenia, and possibly of other mental disorders, as well.

Biochemistry does not hold all the answers to mental illness. But, for the first time, this discipline has meaningful questions to ask, plausible hypotheses to pose, and powerful techniques with which to test them. The gap between our knowledge of the brain and our understanding of the biological substrates of mental illness has narrowed considerably.

B

Societal Reaction
Perspectives and Issues

INTRODUCTION

Many of the leading histories of psychiatry celebrate the emergence of the medical metaphor. The metaphor is often regarded as an important humanitarian and scientific advance over earlier ideas regarding the nature and cause of madness and deviant behavior. Social scientific thinking in the last two decades, by contrast, has been dominated by an attitude skeptical of such claims. Proponents of the societal reaction perspective contend that mental illness is not a disease entity lodged within an individual's psyche, but a pattern of conduct that the individual is induced to enact by the responses of significant others. While there is considerable variation in the specification of how the response of the community brings about bizarre behavior, societal reaction theorists agree that extended displays of such behavior are best understood as emerging through interaction and not as expressions of a disposition to madness. Further, there is agreement that community response is critical in shaping and organizing the nature and extent of what will come to be seen as pathology. The image of the actor implied by the theory is not the psychically impaired person portrayed by clinicians, but an observant, sensitive, and powerless individual whose symptoms are created in an attempt to accommodate the oppressive interactional overtures of significant others.

Scheff's "The Role of the Mentally Ill and the Dynamics of Mental Disorder: A Research Framework" provides a consequential statement of this theory. The formulation is indebted to Lemert's distinction between primary and secondary deviance. Many, perhaps all, individuals perform deviant acts at one point or another in their lives for diverse situational reasons and without lasting consequence for self-identity or character. While primary deviance may be ubiquitous, secondary deviance arises insofar as the individual's primary deviance is noticed and responded to by significant others. In the course of reacting to the community response, the individual may be propelled into ever more extensive and identity-altering deviant acts. Scheff proposes that most psychiatric symptoms, like primary deviance generally, are of diverse origin and apt to terminate if they are ignored or denied by significant others. If they are responded to and regarded as instances of mental illness, a self-fulfilling process is initiated that culminates with the individual capitulating to pressures and rewards to accept the role of a mentally ill individual. Indeed, the process goes beyond mere role enactment for the new self-identity and may actually impair the ability to organize and control one's activities. Mental illness is a myth, but a myth that because it is believed and used by members of the society is transformed into reality.

The ascendancy of the labeling approach in the 1960s channeled a good deal of sociological thinking and research. Given the understanding that the mentally ill were virtually no different from normal persons, save for the fact that the former had been detected in the violation of rules that everyone violates at one time or another, the mentally ill were regarded as suffering not so much from illness as from contingencies. Since anyone was ripe for a career as a mentally ill person, the prime focus of interest was not the person (or as some would call him or her, the victim) but factors that determine whether and how segments of the community interpret and respond to transgressions of residual rules. Thus, labeling theory promoted studies that emphasized the confrontation between the individual and social control agents. Many of these studies implied that the label "mentally ill" had little to do with the behavior of the individual so labeled and much to do with the context of confrontation and the social properties of the individual.

Societal reaction theory in its unqualified form is almost the antithesis of the medical model. It argues that the mental health enterprise is not a solution to the problem of mental illness. On the contrary, the mental health enterprise (the agencies and idioms that are predicated upon, promote, and use the medical model) comprise the major institutional vehicle for the production and perpetuation of mental illness! Accordingly, the model yields unusual and startling hypotheses regarding the effects of the mental health enterprise. It is a truism of common sense and medical thinking that the more effective the facilities and personnel for treating mental illness, the more rapid the recovery. In contrast, the societal reaction model predicts a *negative* relation between the sophistication, extensiveness, and efficiency of care and speed and quality of recovery. Perhaps more surprising than this dismal hypothesis is the supportive empirical evidence it has stimulated. For example, clinical and social outcomes of patients treated at the relatively simple mental health facility in the island society of Mauritius have been compared with outcomes of those treated at facilities in England.

> If we compare the findings from patients who are discharged from the three British hospitals with those from the Mauritius hospital, we discover that across the four treatment facilities, that is, the three hospitals in Great Britain and one on Mauritius, as the psychiatric treatment given becomes better or more modern the outcome for the patients who are treated becomes worse. The Mauritius hospital, with its limited facilities for following patients and its narrow range of medications, leads to the best outcome; the next best outcome

comes, generally, from the two more limited British hospitals; tendencies for the poorest outcome come from the model community mental health center at Mapperly. (Waxler, 1974)

The theory emphasizes the role of cognitive definitions and labels in the creation of secondary deviance. But in focusing on the reaction of the community, the theory is sensitive to complex, subtle interactional processes, of which the formal act of labeling is but a component. Lemert (1962), for example, suggests that paranoia develops through a process in which groups feel jeopardized by initially impolite (and hence impolitic) colleagues and undertake covert and collaborative efforts to contain and ultimately exclude them. The individuals, in turn, become increasingly belligerent as they try to determine the nature and meaning of what appear to be organized conspiratorial efforts against them.

> While the paranoid person reacts differentially to his social environment, it is also true that "others" react differentially to him and this reaction commonly if not typically involves covertly organized action and conspiratorial behavior in a very real sense. A further extension of our thesis is that these differential reactions are reciprocals of one another being interwoven and concatenated at each and all phases of a process of exclusion which arises in a special kind of relationship. Delusions and associated behavior must be understood in a context of exclusion which attenuates this relationship and disrupts communication. (Lemert, 1962)

Laing and Esterson's (1970) analysis of the interaction between schizophrenic daughters and their families suggests that parents induce and reinforce "symptomatic behavior" in their daughters by creating double-binding or otherwise untenable interactional contexts. Further, family members are unaware of or even deny their unusual interactional maneuvers. Even though the daughters' behavior may be an intelligible adaptation to a mystifying and confusing family context, the daughters' behavior appears bizarre and schizophrenic to uninformed outsiders, other family members, and on some occasions even to the daughters themselves.

Szasz is not a societal reaction theorist. Nevertheless, his vivid analysis is congenial to the societal reaction thesis and draws from similar conceptual wellsprings, such as G. H. Mead. Moreover, his work has been a fertile source of ideas for societal reaction theorists and, together with their writings, comprises part of what has come to be called the "antipsychiatry movement." Szasz's writings are controversial and the debate is exacerbated by his aphoristic, contentious style. The aphorisms, however, are but an aspect of an extensive analysis of the historical, structural, and situational genesis and maintenance of the mental illness enterprise. In *The Myth of Mental Illness* (1961), Szasz explores the sociohistorical origins of the idioms (mental illness) and practices (psychiatry) that comprise the contemporary context for describing, explaining, and responding to persons who have difficulty dealing with "problems in living." For example, Szasz describes how Charcot and Freud were instrumental in having hysteria (physical disability in the absence of a discernible organic cause) conceptualized and responded to as an illness rather than as malingering. Charcot and Freud succeeded in changing the rules of what Szasz calls the "Original Medical Game." The old rules held that only physiochemically based disabilities were illnesses, while the new rules asserted that "persons disabled by phenomena which only look like illnesses of the body (i.e., hysteria) should also be classified as ill." The treatment of hysteria as an illness despite the lack of an organic basis paved the way for the metaphor of mental illness and "formed the nucleus around which the vast structure of psychopathology gradually crystallized."

Szasz proposed that particular diagnoses as well as entire systems of classification are conditioned by the sociohistorical context of the physician-patient relation. Thus, for example, the use of the mental illness idiom is most apt to occur in a context in which the diagnoser is sympathetic to and is an agent of the patient. The diagnosis of malingering, on the other hand, occurs in a context where the physician owes his primary loyalties to the state and identifies with prevalent social values, particularly the value of industrial productivity. The nature of the relation between physician and patient, conditioned by social structural features, significantly affects the ways in which an individual's apparent inability to function will be explained.

While Szasz regards the mental illness metaphor as a dubious and debasing myth, he acknowledges that a person may behave in an ostensibly bizarre and inexplicable fashion. The appropriate metaphor, argues Szasz, is not illness but language. "The problem of hysteria," Szasz writes, "is more akin to the problem of a person speaking a foreign tongue than it is to that of a person having a bodily disease." Hysteria is the "language of illness" and is "employed either because another language has not been learned well enough, or because this language happens to be especially useful." Hysterical language performs a number of functions, such as allowing a person to be granted what he or she desires (for instance, relief from everyday routines) without having to ask for it explicitly. Further, the efficacy of the language of illness in achieving certain effects, such as help, stems from a variety of implicit and explicit values derived primarily from the Judeo-Christian tradition that emphasize dependency and that assert that the sick must be helped. We are surrounded by "an unseen ocean of human commands to be incompetent, impoverished and sick."

Societal reaction theory is not without empirical support. (For example, see Rosenhan's "On Being Sane in Insane Places" in Part V.) We have briefly indicated some cross-societal comparisons that conform to the theory's expectation of an inverse relation between the extensiveness of mental health care facilities and prognosis. The theory also comports well with some qualitative and quantitative observations regarding the effects of hospitalization, the lack of diagnostic consensus among mental health practitioners, cross-cultural differences in symptomatology, and the stigmatizing consequences of hospitalization. At the same time, however, it has become evident that societal reaction theory, particularly in its narrowest sense, is oblivious to or at odds with some key empirical phenomena. While Scheff's formulation postulates that most residual deviance is denied and subsequently terminates, in "Societal Reaction as an Explanation of Mental Illness: An Evaluation" Gove shows that while residual deviance is often denied, it nevertheless persists and may, in fact, grow in severity. Gove also demonstrates that psychiatric screening and evaluation agencies do not simply endorse the labels or diagnoses applied at some earlier point but, in fact, screen out a large portion of persons who come before them. Further, Gove's review displays evidence that hospitalization does not invariably have stigmatizing and disabling consequences. Gove concludes that "the societal reaction formulation of how a person becomes mentally ill is substantially incorrect." He is particularly critical of the theory's emphasis on secondary deviance.

> Contrary to the position taken by the societal reaction theorists, the primary deviance may reflect a serious disturbance, one that in some cases may be considerably more important than the problems associated with secondary deviance. Most of the hospitalized cases of mental illness appear to reflect a psychiatric disorder that requires societal intervention (treatment). If the treatment is rapid, intensive, and effective, the psychiatric crisis can be handled without any significant development of secondary deviance.

In "Psychiatric Labeling in Cross-Cultural Perspective" Jane M. Murphy, an anthropologist, challenges the validity of the cultural relativism that informs much of societal reaction theory. Drawing upon her experience with Eskimos and with the Yoruba people of the eastern Guinea coast, Murphy investigates the extent and consequences of cross-cultural variations in the conceptualization and formulation of and response to unusual behavior. Her review suggests that many cultures have explicit concepts of insanity and that they are applied to patterns of actions similar to those labeled mentally ill in Western European societies. Some differences do exist, but they do not have the effect postulated by societal reaction theory. For example, neither the Yoruba nor Eskimos have a single term for neuroses. This does not mean that neurotic behavior patterns do not occur or that they are not recognized. Indeed, "they form a major part of what the shamans and healers are called upon to treat." These and similar observations, particularly the similarity in rates of schizophrenia between complex and traditional societies, prompt Murphy's conclusion that the symptoms of mental illness are not products of sociocultural processes, but the "manifestations of a type of affliction shared by virtually all mankind." These are important criticisms, but they are by no means the concluding phase of the dialogue between societal reaction theory and other perspectives. Even if societal reaction theory must concede aspects of its position on etiology and recognize the role of primary deviance, it nevertheless remains an important sociological heuristic. In emphasizing the socially constructed character of mental illness, the contingencies that condition its application, and the dynamics of the relation between individuals, significant others, and social control agents, the theory furnishes the sociology of mental illness with ways of moving beyond medical models of madness.

References

Erving Goffman, *Asylums: Essays on the Social Situation of Mental Patients and Other Inmates,* Garden City, N.Y.: Anchor Books, 1961.

R. D. Laing and A. Esterson, *Sanity, Madness and the Family,* Harmondsworth, England: Penguin Books, Ltd., 1970.

Edwin M. Lemert, "Paranoia and the Dynamics of Exclusion," *Sociometry,* Vol. **25**, No. 1 (March 1962), 2–20.

Nancy E. Waxler, "Culture and Mental Illness," *Journal of Nervous and Mental Disease,* Vol. **159**, No. 6 (December 1974), 379–95.

THOMAS SZASZ

The Myth of Mental Illness

Hysteria as a typical example of mental illness was chosen as the starting point for our inquiry into the nature of self-experience and personal conduct. Charcot, Breuer, Freud, and many of their contemporaries observed that certain patterns of human behavior—or, more precisely, certain modes of nonverbal communication—resembled neurological illnesses, yet differed from them in crucial ways. For historical and social reasons, the phenomena in question were *defined* and *classified as* members of the class "disease." Thus, hysteria as a quasi-neurological illness formed the nucleus around which the vast structure of "psychopathology" gradually crystallized.

Reprinted from Thomas Szasz, *The Myth of Mental Illness,* New York: Hoeber-Harper, 1961, pages 294–310, by permission of the author and publisher.

Origin of the Modern Concept of Mental Illness

Hysteria and the Concept of Illness

The error of classifying hysteria as an illness, with emphasis on its similarities to known neurological diseases, is attributable mainly to the nineteenth-century reductionist conception of personal conduct. According to this view, all behavior was regarded as a problem in muscle and nerve physiology. As a tabetic ataxia was explained by certain nerve lesions, it was assumed that normal behavior too could be adequately explained by describing its neuroanatomical and neurophysiological correlates. This approach rested on the erroneous belief that there were no significant differences between complex items of learned behavior on the one hand, and the behavioral manifestations of *defects of the body* on the other hand. It followed that whenever defective functioning of the body was encountered it was regarded as *prima facie* evidence of illness. In view of the practical task of the neurologist, it is easy to see why he should have been especially prone to make this mistake. It often happens that diseases of the nervous system (for example, multiple sclerosis, brain tumor) first manifest themselves by peculiarities in personal conduct. It was tempting to conclude from such occurrences that brain and behavior stand in a simple type of cause-and-effect relationship to each other.

This approach was consistent with the prevalent philosophical preconceptions of medical workers concerning the principles of their science. It allowed them to treat as medical problems all manner of complicated human situations that found overt expression in the patient's belief that he was ill. If known methods of physiochemical examination failed to reveal the presence of bodily disease, this was of no great concern. The late nineteenth-century physician's model of disease was derived from his experiences with tuberculosis, syphilis, and typhoid fever. As the causes of these illnesses had been discovered by medical science, so it would be with hysteria and mental illnesses.

Charcot succeeded in making hysteria acceptable to the medical profession. This achievement, however, was in the nature of a social reform, not a scientific discovery. Although some members of suffering humanity were promoted, as it were, to higher social rank, this was attained at the cost of obscuring the logical character of the observed phenomena.

Because of the conceptual make-up of late nineteenth-century psychiatry, hysteria was compared and contrasted with malingering on the one hand, and with "real illness" on the other. The persistent medical and psychiatric opinion that behavior which imitated illness was an effort to cheat or fool doctors made it necessary to condemn it. Hence, physicians who wished to prevent the condemnation of people exhibiting this type of behavior had to insist that such patients *were* "ill." In this way their behavior could still be described as essentially illness-imitating—and could be studied scientifically—while at the same time the pejorative diagnosis of malingering could be avoided. This strategy contained a hidden danger. The notion of illness, at first used mainly with a socially promotive aim in mind, rapidly became accepted as the correct description of "facts." The expression "mental illness" was not understood in a metaphorical sense as it should have been, but attained a high degree of concretization and began to lead a life of its own. Now it is a *panchreston* (Hardin, 1956), a word that is supposed to explain everything,

whereas it explains nothing and serves only to hinder our critical understanding. In modern psychiatry this thesis is exemplified by the persistent denial that a person may *wish* to imitate sickness and *play the role* of a disabled person without necessarily being sick. The nosological categorization of every possible feature of malingering as a manifestation of mental illness is a result of this tendency.

Sociology of the Physician-Patient Relationship

In late nineteenth-century Europe and America, medical care could be obtained by purchase and owned, much as private property. Private medical practice became an integral part of capitalistic, individualistic society. Those who could not afford to buy this commodity were forced to obtain it—as they did many other things in life—through the charity of others. The private practice type of relationship between physician and patient was a crucial antecedent of the psychoanalytic situation. In both, the therapist was the patient's agent, in contrast to being the agent of some other person or group.

Nineteenth-century medical practice may be profitably compared to contemporary Western practices. Today, medical practice is characterized by a mixture of *private* and *insured* situations. The insurance scheme introduces third (and fourth, etc.) parties into the transaction between sufferer and healer. Finally, in the Soviet system of medical practice the physician is an agent of the state. Depending on the type of disability the patient has, the Soviet medical system readily leads to various conflicts between physician, patient, and state. The concept of malingering is very much in vogue in Russia, whereas in Western countries it has largely been displaced by the concepts of hysteria, neurosis, and mental illness. None of these terms denotes or describes a "disease entity." Actually, they arise from and reflect characteristic features of the social matrix of the therapeutic situation. They point to covert preferences of individualistic or collectivistic ethics and their attendant notions concerning the duties and privileges of citizen and state in regard to each other.

What is Psychiatry?

It is customary to define psychiatry as a medical specialty concerned with the study, diagnosis, and treatment of mental illnesses. This is a worthless and misleading definition. Mental illness is a myth. Psychiatrists are not concerned with mental illnesses and their treatments. In actual practice they deal with personal, social, and ethical problems in living.

I have argued that, today, the notion of a person "having mental illness" is scientifically crippling. It provides professional assent to a popular rationalization, namely, that problems in human living experienced and expressed in terms of bodily feelings or signs (or in terms of other "psychiatric symptoms") are significantly similar to *diseases of the body*. It also undermines the principle of personal responsibility, upon which a democratic political system is necessarily based, by assigning to an external source (i.e., the "illness") the blame for antisocial behavior. We know that for the individual patient this attitude precludes an inquiring, psychoanalytic approach to problems which "symptoms" at once hide and express. Codifying every type of occurrence that takes place in a medical setting as, *ipso facto,* a medical problem makes about as much sense as suggesting that when physicists quarrel their argument constitutes a problem in physics.

Although powerful institutional pressures lend massive weight to the tradition of keeping psychiatric problems within the conceptual fold of medicine, the scientific challenge seems clear. The task is to redefine the problem of mental illness so that it may be encompassed under the general category of the science of man. Medicine itself contributes to this enterprise, as do numerous other disciplines. The psychiatric and psychoanalytic approaches to this task, however, must be defined more clearly. It is inevitable that these disciplines must stand or fall with whatever value their special methods possess. Since their methods pertain to the analysis of communications, and since their concepts involve those of psychosocial structure and sign-using behavior, we should delay no longer in describing our work in terms appropriate to these methods and concepts. This, of course, would necessitate a thoroughgoing revision—and indeed, a scuttling—of many of our notions concerning both psychopathology and psychotherapy. The former should be conceived in terms of object relationships, sign-using, rule-following, social roles, and game-playing. As to psychotherapy, it should be systematized as a theory of human relationships, involving special social arrangements and fostering certain values and types of learning.

Semiotical Analysis of Behavior

The bodily signs of conversion hysteria—for example, an hysterical seizure or paralysis—were chosen as typical examples of at least one type of so-called psychiatric symptom. Our inquiry was focused on the following questions: (1) What type of language, or communication system, is employed by persons exhibiting this kind of behavior? (2) What type of object rela-tionship is secured and maintained by means of hysterical communications? (3) What are the specific interpersonal functions of indirect communications in general, and of dreams and certain "psychiatric symptoms" in particular?

The "Psychiatric Symptom" as a Form of Picture Language

It was found that a sign relation of iconicity was the chief characteristic of signs typically encountered in hysterical symptom-communications. An iconic sign is defined as an object, X, which because of its similarity to another object, Y, is used to denote the latter. The relation of similarity (iconicity) is usually based on appearance, as for example in a photograph. It may also be based on function. Thus, animals may symbolize (represent) people, as in cartoons, because both exhibit manifestations of life.

The observation that hysterical symptoms depict certain occurrences was originally made by Freud. He asserted that hysteria was like a pantomime, or dumbshow, in which the patient expressed a message by means of nonverbal signs. Pseudocyesis is a good example. It is a pictorial representation of the idea "I am pregnant." Hysterical body language therefore consists essentially of pictures. As such, it is similar to other picture languages, such as *picture puzzles* or *charades*. In each of these, communication is achieved by means of pictures (iconic signs) instead of words (conventional signs). In a picture puzzle, the name "Forrestal" may be depicted by showing a picture of several trees to the right of which is placed a tall man. Given such a puzzle, the task is to translate from picture language to word language. Similarly, in the game of charades, a proverb, quotation, or almost anything "spelled out" in words must be so "acted out" by one of the players that his teammates shall recognize the message. In both of the examples cited, there is a two-way process of translation or sign-transformation. In charades, the person who acts out the message must translate from English (or some other ordinary language) to pantomime, while his teammates must reverse the process by transforming pantomime back into English. In hysteria, and in many other behavioral phenomena as well, the task of the psychiatrist is similar to that confronting a person who tries to unravel a picture puzzle. The meaning of hysteria—stated in the form of a picture language, or, more precisely, in the form of a language composed of iconic signs—must be rendered into everyday verbal language.

The logical character of communications composed of iconic body signs was then compared to other types of communications. Since hysterical body language constitutes a mode of communication logically inferior to that of object and metalanguages, it was designated a protolanguage. Ordinary object language stands in a meta relation to protolanguage.

The Functions of Protolanguage

Protolanguage may serve all the cognitive and instrumental uses of ordinary language. The differences in usefulness between an iconic sign language and a conventional symbol language lie in the degree to which the various language functions may be exercised by means of each. Thus, for purely cognitive purposes, protolanguage is greatly inferior to object and metalanguages. It is superior, however, for purposes of affective and promotive communication. Thus, the facial expression of grave suffering, perhaps accompanied by tears and groans, usually is more effective in imparting a mood and in inducing a wished-for action, than the simple statement "I am in pain."

Protolanguage is relatively nondiscursive. This is inherent in its being composed of iconic rather than conventional signs. The former mode of symbolization embodies a more idiosyncratic or private sign relationship than does the latter. The most public or impersonal language systems (for example, mathematics, the Morse code) are the most discursive, while the typically private or personal idioms (for example, an "hysterical" or "schizophrenic" symptom) are relatively nondiscursive. Because of the iconicity and nondiscursiveness of hysterical body language, it affords vast possibilities for mistakes and misunderstandings in cognitive communication. Exploration of the cognitive or informative use of iconic body signs made it possible to ask whether such communication might be similar to mistakes and lies in everyday language. An analysis of this problem disclosed that there is a compelling parallelism between the concepts of malingering, hysteria, and (ordinary "organic") illness on the one hand and the concepts of lying, making a mistake, and telling the truth on the other.

Considerations of the uses of iconic body signs in a psychiatric context led, finally, to highlighting an hitherto unrecognized function of this mode of communicative behavior. The object-seeking and relationship-maintaining function of any type of communication was arrived at by a combined semiotical and object relations approach to problems of communication in psychiatry. This point of view lends special force to the interpretation of such things as the dance, religious ritual, and the representative arts. In each of these, the participant or the viewer is enabled *to enter into a significant human relationship by means of a particular*

system of communication. The same is true, of course, for logically higher levels of language, such as mathematics. Scientists achieve and maintain object contact with their colleagues by means of special languages, just as members of primitive tribes may gratify similar needs by means of a ritual dance. It is significant, however, that the language of science has, in addition to its object-relations aspect, a cognitive facet as well, and that this is largely, although not entirely, absent in the more primitive communicative modes. Still, considerations of object contact are at least potentially relevant in connection with all sign-using functions.

The Uses of Indirect Communications

Hysteria or any mental illness may also be considered an indirect communication or language that is used ambiguously, usually in order to give the recipient of the message a choice between several alternative replies. Hints, allusions, and metaphorical expressions of all kinds are everyday examples of indirect communications. The need for this mode of communication arises typically in the family. The social conditions of this unit make it necessary that family members curb their wishes and hence also the explicit symbolic representations of them. This leads to the inhibition ("repression") of direct forms of communication and provides the stimulus for the development of relatively more devious, or indirect, forms of need-communicative behavior. The function of hinting was illustrated by an analysis of dream communication. The "hysterical symptom" may also be regarded as a hint addressed to the patient's significant objects or to physicians.

The chief advantages of hinting—and hence of hysteria—are the following: (1) It provides a mode of sending a message whose effect is feared, either because the communication pertains to the expression of an ego-alien wish or because it is an aggressive reproach against a loved but needed person. (2) It permits the expression of a communication without full commitment to it. In other words, it provides an escape route should the message misfire or backfire. (3) It makes it possible for a person to be granted what he desires without having to ask for it explicitly. It thus protects the help-seeking person from being humiliated should his request be denied. This is an exceedingly important mechanism, commonly used by children. It is also employed by adults, either because they have retained certain childish ideals (for example, "I should not need anything or anybody"), or because they find themselves in a situation in which they feel more strongly committed to a person than the "objective conditions" would warrant (for example, "love at first sight"). In these situations, hinting—whether by means of socially acceptable metaphors or ''mental symptoms''—provides an exploratory mode of communication.

Situations of close personal interdependence favor indirect communications, whereas certain more impersonal, functional types of social relations foster direct communications. In the psychoanalytic situation, the hinting functions of hysteria, dreams, and other ''mental symptoms'' are subjected to persistent scrutiny. Indeed, it may be said that one of the aims of the analytic process is to induce the patient to relinquish his indirect (''symptomatic,'' ''transference'') communications and to substitute for them direct messages framed in the straightforward idiom of ordinary English. This is accomplished by placing him in a situation in which hinting is not rewarded, as it might be in ordinary life, but direct communication is. This is inherent in the conditions of the analytic situation, in which an explicit positive value is placed on direct communication (absolute truthfulness, privacy of the two-person situation, etc.). Thus, the interpersonal conditions of analysis are such as to favor a process of change in regard to the patient's (habitual) sign-using behavior.

In this regard, being in analysis could be compared to going to a foreign country for purposes of study. By means of this analogy, the double impact of psychoanalysis on the patient's sign-using behavior may be illustrated. First, it induces him to give up his habitual mode of communicating (mother tongue, symptom language) and to substitute for it a *new language* (foreign language, direct communication in ordinary language). To accomplish this alone, however, might be merely a ''transference cure.'' Ideally, psychoanalysis accomplishes more than this, just as going abroad to study physics enables the student to learn a foreign language *and* physics. Similarly, in the psychoanalytic situation the analysand is not only induced to shift from symptom-language to ordinary verbal communication but is *also taught to examine and understand the particular patterns of object relationships which he has had and the communicative patterns to which these gave rise*. Thus, the basic aim of psychoanalytic treatment is to enable the patient to learn about his object relationships and communicative behavior. A shift from protolanguage to object and metalanguage must be successfully achieved before mastery of the more far-reaching task of self-knowledge can be attempted.

The chief purpose of iconic body language may be merely to make contact with objects. For some people, sometimes, no verbal language may be available with which legitimately to address their fellow man. If all else fails, there still remains the language of illness—a language that virtually everyone the world over knows how to speak and understand. This is the idiom which the lonely, the downcast, the poor, and the uneducated can still use and thereby hope to ''get something'' which they had failed to obtain in other ways. Thus, the language of illness—and of social deviance, too—constitutes the last, and perhaps the firmest, bastion on the grounds of which unsatisfied and ''regressed'' man can make a last stand and claim his share of human ''love'' (Szasz, 1957a). For the average layman, or for the therapeutically dedicated physician or psychiatrist, this message of nonspecific help-seeking may, of course, be difficult to hear, since all labor under the assumption that what they see and hear are manifestations of ''illness.'' This leaves them no choice but to endeavor to ''cure'' or at least ''ameliorate'' the ''disease.'' Yet, it seems that this whole imagery is false. The spectacle that faces us is simply an aspect of the *human condition*—call it fate, destiny, life style, character, existence, or what you will—and what we hear and see are *the cries for help* and their *pictorial representations*.

The Rule-following Model of Behavior

''Social life,'' as Peters (1958) reminded us, ''is never like the jungle life popularized by evolutionary theories, a matter of mere survival; it is a matter of surviving in a certain sort of way'' (p. 127). To ask, then, ''In what sort of way?'' and to provide answers to this question, is the task of the sciences concerned with man as a social being. Since survival by means of exhibiting ''hysteria'' (or ''mental illness'') is one distinctively human form of survival, it is necessary to study the factors that contribute to this pattern of human existence.

Classification of Rules

Three broad categories of rules may be distinguished. In the first group, designated as natural laws or biological rules, belong the regularities that must be obeyed lest sheer physical survival be jeopardized. Examples are the need to satisfy hunger or thirst and the prevention of injuries from falling, drowning, burning, and the like. Prescriptive laws constitute the next group. These are the rules—whether social, religious, or moral—that govern social life among particular groups of men. The Bible or the American Constitution and Bill of Rights are typical examples. They define the rules of the game by which social living in a given community shall be played. The third group, named ''imitative or interpersonal rules,'' is composed of those patterns of action which must be copied by children, more or less accurately, from the behavior of the adults about them, if they are to partake of the social life of the group: for example, the learning of one's mother tongue, the use of household items, patterns of eating, and the like. Biological rules are of the utmost importance for the survival of the human (and animal) body and species. The exploration, the elucidation, and sometimes the alteration of these rules are the aims of the basic medical sciences (physiology, biochemistry, genetics, etc.) and of clinical medicine. Social and interpersonal rules, on the other hand, constitute the core-subject of the sciences of man (anthropology, psychiatry, psychoanalysis, psychology, sociology, etc.).

The Family Situation, Religion, and the Rules for Getting and Giving Help

Childhood patterns of help-seeking and help-getting form the core of a system of rules that in later life may foster the seeking or imitating of illness or disability in order to induce others to care for one. This communicative, coercive feature of disabilities of all sorts is often enhanced by Jewish and Christian religious teachings. In this connection, an examination of the Bible as a rule-book was undertaken. It was shown that the Judaeo-Christian religions contain numerous incentives to being ill or disabled. States of distress and failure—whether because of stupidity, poverty, sickness, or what not—may be interpreted as potentially desirable goals for as the hungry infant is given the mother's breast, so the disabled human being is promised God's all-embracing helpfulness and benevolence. This pattern of human interaction and communication is regarded as the main source of a vast number of rules, all of which conspire, as it were, to foster man's infantilism and dependence. These may be contrasted with rules emphasizing the need for man's striving for mastery, responsibility, self-reliance, and mutually cooperative interdependence.

Witchcraft and Hysteria

The specific effects of certain Biblical rules on human conduct were illustrated by means of the social phenomenon of medieval witchcraft. The psychiatric and the rule-following theories of witchcraft were compared. According to the former, witches were misdiagnosed hysterics. According to the latter, they were persons sacrificed as scapegoats in a real-life game in which the activities of God and devil were taken too literally and too seriously.

Witchcraft existed as an integral part of the medieval Christian game of life. This game was theologically de-

fined, and demanded that the players conduct themselves according to rules which were impossible to follow. Violation of the game-rules—that is, cheating—was thus unavoidable. Hence, virtually everyone was a cheat. In general, persons of high social status could cheat much more easily and safely than persons of low status. Poor old women were especially expendable and most of the witches were recruited from among their ranks. High officials of the Roman Catholic Church—who themselves disobeyed the rules of the game most flagrantly and whose activities sparked the Protestant Reformation—fostered the persecution of those who were alleged to cheat.

In the language of chess, the persecution of witches meant that poor, unimportant people (pawns) were sacrificed to insure the safety and well-being of the ruling classes (king and queen). By this maneuver, victory for God (the master player) was assured. In addition to insuring God's continued glory, this operation also served to preserve the social *status quo*. Witch-hunts and witch-trials were, accordingly, a safety valve of society. Some aspects of contemporary psychiatric practices—especially psychiatric operations involving involuntary patients and legal actions—appear to serve a function analogous to that served by the medieval witch-trials.

The contest between theological persecutor and witch is closely paralleled by the contest between institutional psychiatrist and involuntary mental patient. The former is always the victor, the latter forever the vanquished. The concept of mental illness and the social actions taken in its name serve the self-seeking interests of the medical and psychiatric professions, just as the notion of witchcraft served the interests of the theologians, acting in the name of God. As the theological game was the "opiate of the people" in past ages, so the medical-psychiatric game is the opiate of contemporary peoples. By draining interpersonal and group tensions, each game fulfills the function of social tranquilization.

The Game-playing Model of Behavior

Developmental and Logical Aspects of Games

The model of games was selected as offering the most comprehensive map by which to chart the social behavior of human beings. The models of sign-using and rule-following, used earlier, may be subsumed under this more general scheme.

Initially, games were considered as they are encountered in everyday experience, in familiar card and board games (bridge, checkers, chess, etc.). Children's attitudes toward game-rules show an interesting and exceedingly significant progression. Briefly summarized, preschool children are virtually unable to adhere to rules; they play games idiosyncratically, in the presence of other children but not with them. Subsequently, children learn to adhere to the rules of the game, but regard the rules—and the game as a whole—as "sacred." At this stage, rules are rather poorly understood and slavishly followed. Usually not before their early teens do children gain an appreciation of game-rules as conventional and cooperatively constructed. Relatively mature, autonomous game-playing behavior may thus be contrasted with immature, heteronomous game-playing behavior. In addition to the important developmental distinctions among different types of game-playing behaviors, a logical hierarchy of games similar to the logical hierarchy of languages may be constructed. The concept of game-hierarchies has important applications both in everyday life and in psychiatry. The familiar moral conflict that sometimes exists between ends and means is a conflict involving game-hierarchies. End-goals occupy a logically higher level than strategies used in pursuing them.

Ethics, Games, and Psychiatry

As long as the socioethical values of psychiatric theories and therapies remain obscure and inexplicit, their scientific worth is bound to be rather limited. This is simply because human social behavior is fundamentally ethical behavior. It is difficult to see, therefore, how such behavior could be described, or how modifications of it could be advocated, without at the same time coming to grips with the issue of ethical values. Psychoanalytic descriptions of behavior and of therapy, for example, have emphasized instinctual forces, pathogenic occurrences, and mental mechanisms at the expense of explicitly specifying norms and values. The concept of genital primacy (Fenichel, 1945, p. 61) as a norm or value is a typical example of the psychiatric-psychoanalytic dilemma that must be resolved. In this concept, a norm of adult human functioning is described and covertly advocated without, however, specifying the socioethical context in which a person's "genital primacy" is supposed to occur. It is left open whether genital primacy in the social context of king and concubine, master and servant, soldier and prostitute, or husband and wife is considered the ideal goal. Thus, we have no provisions either for describing or for judging the variations in, say, marital relations in societies that are autocratic and democratic, or those that are patriarchal, matriarchal, and pediarchal (child-dominated).

In the theory of personal conduct which I have put forward—and implicitly, in the theory of psychotherapy

that may be based upon it—I have endeavored to correct this deficiency, emphasizing the urgent need to clearly specify norms and values first and techniques of behavior second. This approach was illustrated by emphasizing the end-goals of the hysterical game which were identified as domination of interpersonal control. It follows from this goal that coercing strategies may be employed in pursuit of it. In contrast, one might espouse the goals of self-reliant competence and dignified human interdependence. It is evident that these goals could not be secured by coercive techniques, for pursuing them in this fashion would conflict with the very ends that are sought. Since the ends determine, within a certain range, the means that may be used to attain them, failure to specify clearly and to bear in mind end-goals cannot be corrected by concentration on, or training in, specific techniques of living.

Impersonation and Cheating

"Impersonation" refers to taking someone else's role under false pretenses; or, what is essentially the same, to claiming to play game A while, in fact, playing game B. The word "cheating" refers to a similar concept, but one that is more limited in scope. It is applied to the behavior of persons whose game-playing activity is judged to deviate from the correct or agreed-upon rules. For example, malingering, the Ganser syndrome, and hysteria all include elements of cheating, meaning thereby violation of the rules in order to maximize one's advantages.

The significance of impersonation as a theoretical-explanatory conception for psychiatry is considerable. This notion touches on the familiar psychoanalytic concepts of identification, ego-formation, ego-identity, self-system, etc., but expands on them by introducing considerations of social role and interpersonal strategy. In this light, the modern concept of "mental illness" and its "psychiatric treatment" presents us with a double impersonation. On the one hand so-called psychiatric patients impersonate the sick role: the hysteric acts as though he were bodily ill, and invites "treatment" in accordance with the rules of the medical game. Concomitantly, psychiatrists and psychoanalysts, by accepting the problems of their patients as manifestations of "illness," commit a complementary act of impersonation: they impersonate physicians and play the role of the medical therapist. This act of impersonation, however, also goes on independently of the machinations of patients. It is actively fostered by the present-day professional organizations of psychotherapeutic practitioners, as well as by the members as individuals.

I refer here to the *credo* of most contemporary psychiatrists, that psychiatry—including psychotherapy—is significantly similar to other branches of medicine, and belongs to it. It seems to me, however, that medical psychotherapists, having had a medical training, only look like other doctors—just as hysterics only look like organically sick persons. The difference between the purely communicational interventions of the psychotherapist and the physiochemical actions of the physician represents an instrumental gulf between the two groups that no institutional resemblance can convincingly close. It is common knowledge that when clinical psychologists press their claims to practice independent psychotherapy, they tend to be regarded (especially by physicians) as impersonators of the medical role of "taking care of sick people." But the same could be said for medically trained psychotherapists whose work also differs in crucial ways from that of the surgeon or internist.

Until now, this impersonation has served the apparent interests of both mental patients and psychiatrists. Thus, no one has really protested against this variation on the theme of the myth of the emperor's clothes. I think the time is now ripe to consider seriously the possibility that the medical aspects of psychotherapy are about as substantial as the legendary emperor's cloak which was so finely woven that only the wisest and most perspicacious men could perceive it. To claim that he was naked was, therefore, tantamount to self-confessed stupidity, as well as an affront against a powerful personage.

Analyses and arguments attempting to clarify the differences between medicine and psychiatry (or psychoanalysis) have been hampered by similar factors. It is almost as though medicine and psychiatry (psychotherapy) were husband and wife united in an unstable marriage. Those who emphasize what the couple have in common, hoping thereby to stabilize the relationship, are honored and rewarded as the doers of meritorious deeds. On the other hand, those who notice and comment on the differences between them are treated as though it were *they* who were breaking up an otherwise perfect union. As could be expected, marriage counseling to save the union—expressed partly as a propagandizing "psychosomatic medicine" and partly as a redefining of psychoanalysis as "psychoanalytic medicine"—has tended to flourish, whereas work clarifying the differences between medicine and psychiatry (irrespective of where this might lead) has been virtually nonexistent.

Games, Objects, and Values

In conclusion, some connections between the theories of object relationships and game-playing were pre-

sented. For adults (and probably also for children after the age of ten to twelve years), games and their constituent rules often function as objects. In other words, loss of game—that is, the inability to play a game, either because of the unavailability of other players or because of changes in one's own game-playing propensities—no less than loss of object, leads to serious disequilibrium within the personality, requiring adaptive, reparative measures. Indeed, objects and games are interdependent, since the players are of necessity *people*. Hence, psychology and sociology are interlocking and interdependent.

The game model of human behavior appears well suited for unifying psychology, sociology, and ethics. For example, the sociological concept of anomie—a state of social unrest resulting from the dissolution of established rules—could readily be integrated with the psychoanalytic concepts of object loss, anxiety-depression, and ego identity. Loss of a sense of satisfying personal identity is linked to *modern man's inevitable loss of the "games" learned early in life*. In other words, modern man, if he is at all educated, cannot play the same sorts of games which he played as a youngster, or which his parents played, and remain satisfied with them. Cultural conditions are changing so rapidly that everyone tends to share the problem of the immigrant who *must* change games because he has moved from one country to another. Even those who stay put geographically find themselves in a world other than that of their parents. Indeed, as they grow older they usually find themselves in a world other than that of their youth. In this dilemma, man is confronted by the imperative need to relinquish old games and to learn to play new ones. Failing this, he is forced to play new games by old rules, the old games being the only ones he knows how to play. *This fundamental game-conflict leads to various problems in living. It is these that the modern psychotherapist is usually called on to "treat."*

Three general types of game-conflict may be distinguished. One is characterized by the person's inability to forget the old rules, or by his outright unwillingness to relinquish playing the old game. This may result in a refusal to play any of the games that others play: It is a kind of "strike" against living. Various so-called disability states—malingering, hysteria, and "dependency reactions"—illustrate such a "strike" or revolt against the challenge to learn. A second type of game-conflict consists of the superimposition of old goals and rules upon new games. Illustrative is the "transference neurosis" or reaction, the "neurotic character structure," the foreign accent, and so on; in each of these, we are confronted by a pattern of behavior that is the result of mixing different, to some extent mutually incompatible games. Finally, a third type of game-conflict, manifested in a general disappointment-reaction, develops from the realization that man can play no transcendentally valid (God-given) game. Many react to this insight with the feeling that, in this case, *no game is worth playing!* The significance of this condition—namely, *that no game is really worth playing*—appears to be especially great for contemporary Western man.

Epilogue

In Pirandello's play, *The Rules of the Game* (1919, p. 25), the following conversation takes place:

> LEONE: Ah, Venanzi, it's a sad thing, when one has learnt every move in the game.
> GUIDO: What game?
> LEONE: Why . . . this one. The whole game—of life.
> GUIDO: Have you learnt it?
> LEONE: Yes, a long time ago.

Leone's despair and resignation come from believing that there is such a thing as *the* game of life. Indeed, if mastery of *the* game of life were the problem of human existence, having achieved this task, what would there be left to do? But there is no game of life, in the singular. The games are infinite.

Modern man seems to be faced with a choice between two basic alternatives. On the one hand, he may elect to despair over the lost usefulness or the rapid deterioration of games painfully learned. Skills acquired by diligent effort may prove to be inadequate for the task at hand almost as soon as one is ready to apply them. Many people cannot tolerate repeated disappointments of this kind. In desperation, they long for the security of stability—even if stability can be purchased only at the cost of personal enslavement. The other alternative is to rise to the challenge of the unceasing need to learn and relearn, and to try to meet this challenge successfully.

The momentous changes in contemporary social conditions clearly forewarn that—if man survives—his social relations, like his genetic constitution, will undergo increasingly rapid mutations. If this is true, it will be imperative that all people, rather than just a few, *learn how to learn*. I use the term "to learn" rather broadly. It refers, first, to the adaptations that man must make to his environment. More specifically, man must learn the rules that govern life in the family, the group, and the society in which he lives. Further, there is the learning of technical skills, science, and learning to learn. Clearly, there is no "objective" limit to learning. The limiting

factor is *in man*—not in the challenge to learn. Leone's dilemma is the dilemma of a man so far withdrawn from life that he fails to appreciate, and hence to participate in, the ever-changing game of life. The result is a shallow and constant life which may be encompassed and mastered with relative ease.

The common and pressing problem today is that, as social conditions undergo rapid change, men are called upon to alter their modes of living. Old games are constantly scrapped and new ones started. Most people are totally unprepared to shift from one type of game-playing to another. They learn one game or, at most, a few, and desire mainly the opportunity to live out life by playing the same game over and over again. But since human life is largely a social enterprise, social conditions may make it impossible to survive without greater flexibility in regard to patterns of personal conduct.

Perhaps the relationship between the modern psychotherapist and his patient is a beacon that ever-increasing numbers of men will find themselves forced to follow, lest they become spiritually enslaved or physically destroyed. By this I do not mean anything so naive as to suggest that "everyone needs to be psychoanalyzed." On the contrary, "being psychoanalyzed"—like *any* human experience—can itself constitute a form of enslavement and affords, especially in its contemporary institutionalized forms, no guarantee of enhanced self-knowledge and responsibility for either patient or therapist. By speaking of the modern psychotherapeutic relationship as a beacon, I refer to a simpler but more fundamental notion than that implied in "being psychoanalyzed." This is the notion of being a *student of human living*. Some require a personal instructor for this; others do not. Given the necessary wherewithal and ability to learn, success in this enterprise requires, above all else, the sincere desire to learn and to change. This incentive, in turn, is stimulated by hope of success. This is one of the main reasons why it is the scientist's and educator's solemn responsibility to clarify—never to obscure—problems and tasks.

I hope that I have been successful in avoiding the pitfalls of mysticism and obscurantism which, by beclouding the problems to be tackled and solved, foster feelings of discouragement and despair. We are all students in the school of life. In this metaphorical school, none of us can afford to become discouraged or despairing. And yet, in this school, religious cosmologies, nationalistic myths, and lately psychiatric theories have more often functioned as obscurantist teachers misleading the student, than as genuine clarifiers helping him to help himself. Bad teachers are, of course, worse than no teachers at all. Against them, skepticism is our sole weapon.

REFERENCES

O. Fenichel, *The Psychoanalytic Theory of Neurosis,* New York: W. W. Norton, 1945.

G. Hardin, "The meaninglessness of the word protoplasm," *Scientific Monthly,* Vol. **82** (1956), 112.

R. S. Peters, *The Concept of Motivation,* London: Routledge & Kegan Paul, 1958.

L. Pirandello, "The Rules of the Game," (translated by Robert Rietty), in L. Pirandello, *Three Plays,* E. Martin Browne (editor), Harmondsworth, England: Penguin Books, 1959.

K. R. Popper, *The Open Society and Its Enemies,* Princeton, N.J.: Princeton University Press, 1950.

T. S. Szasz, *Pain and Pleasure. A Study of Bodily Feelings,* New York: Basic Books, 1957.

THOMAS J. SCHEFF

The Role of the Mentally Ill and the Dynamics of Mental Disorder: A Research Framework*

Although the last two decades have seen a vast increase in the number of studies of functional mental disorder, there is as yet no substantial, verified body of knowledge in this area. A quotation from a recent symposium on schizophrenia summarizes the present situation: "During the past decade, the problems of chronic schizophrenia have claimed the energy of workers in many fields. Despite significant contributions which reflect continuing progress, *we have yet to learn to ask ourselves the right questions.*"[1] Many investigators apparently agree; systematic studies have not only failed to provide answers to the problem of causation, but there is considerable feeling that the problem itself has not been formulated correctly.

One frequently noted deficiency in psychiatric formulations of the problem is the failure to incorporate social processes into the dynamics of mental disorder. Although the importance of these processes is increasingly recognized by psychiatrists, the conceptual models used in formulating research questions are basically concerned with individual rather than social systems. Genetic, biochemical, and psychological investigations seek different causal agents, but utilize similar models: dynamic systems which are located within the individual. In these investigations, social processes tend to be relegated to a subsidiary role, because the model focuses attention on individual differences, rather than on the social system in which the individuals are involved.

Recently a number of writers have sought to develop an approach which would give more emphasis to social processes. Lemert, Erikson, Goffman, and Szasz have notably contributed to this approach.[2] Lemert, particularly, by rejecting the more conventional concern with the origins of mental deviance, and stressing instead the potential importance of the societal reaction in stabilizing deviance, focuses primarily on mechanisms of social control. The work of all of these authors suggests research avenues which are analytically separable from questions of individual systems and point, therefore, to a theory which would incorporate social processes.

The purpose of the present paper is to contribute to the

Reprinted from Thomas J. Scheff, "The Role of the Mentally Ill and the Dynamics of Mental Disorder: A Research Framework," *Sociometry,* **26,** 1963, pages 436–453, by permission of the author and publisher.

*This project was supported in part by the Graduate Research Committee of the University of Wisconsin. The help of many persons, too numerous to list here, who criticized earlier drafts is gratefully acknowledged.

1. Nathanial S. Apter, "Our Growing Restlessness with Problems of Chronic Schizophrenia," in Lawrence Appleby, *et al., Chronic Schizophrenia,* Glencoe, Ill.: Free Press, 1958.

2. Edwin M. Lemert, *Social Pathology,* New York: McGraw-Hill, 1951; Kai T. Erikson, "Patient Role and Social Uncertainty—A Dilemma of the Mentally Ill," *Psychiatry,* **20** (August, 1957), pp. 263–274; Erving Goffman, *Asylums,* New York: Doubleday-Anchor, 1961; Thomas S. Szasz, *The Myth of Mental Illness,* New York: Hoeber-Harper, 1961.

formulation of such a theory by stating a set of nine propositions which make up basic assumptions for a social system model of mental disorder. This set is largely derived from the work of the authors listed above, all but two of the propositions (#4 and #5) being suggested, with varying degrees of explicitness, in the cited references. By stating these propositions explicitly, this paper attempts to facilitate testing of basic assumptions, all of which are empirically unverified, or only partly verified. By stating these assumptions in terms of standard sociological concepts, this paper attempts to show the relevance to studies of mental disorder of findings from diverse areas of social science, such as race relations and prestige suggestion. This paper also delineates three problems which are crucial for a sociological theory of mental disorder: what are the conditions in a culture under which diverse kinds of deviance become stable and uniform; to what extent, in different phases of careers of mental patients, are symptoms of mental illness the result of conforming behavior; is there a general set of contingencies which lead to the definition of deviant behavior as a manifestation of mental illness? Finally, this paper attempts to formulate special conceptual tools to deal with these problems, which are directly linked to sociological theory. The social institution of insanity, residual deviance, the social role of the mentally ill, and the bifurcation of the societal reaction into the alternative reactions of denial and labeling, are examples of such conceptual tools.

These conceptual tools are utilized to construct a theory of mental disorder in which psychiatric symptoms are considered to be violations of social norms, and stable "mental illness" to be a social role. The validity of this theory depends upon verification of the nine propositions listed below in future studies, and should, therefore, be applied with caution, and with appreciation for its limitations. One such limitation is that the theory attempts to account for a much narrower class of phenomena than is usually found under the rubric of mental disorder; the discussion that follows will be focused exclusively on stable or recurring mental disorder, and does not explain the causes of single deviant episodes. A second major limitation is that the theory probably distorts the phenomena under discussion. Just as the individual system models under-stress social processes, the model presented here probably exaggerates their importance. The social system model "holds constant" individual differences, in order to articulate the relationship between society and mental disorder. Ultimately, a framework which encompassed both individual and social systems would be desirable. Given the present state of knowledge, however, this framework may prove useful by providing an explicit contrast to the more conventional medical and psychological approaches, and thus assisting in the formulation of sociological studies of mental disorder.

The Symptoms of "Mental Illness" as Residually Deviant Behavior

One source of immediate embarrassment to any social theory of "mental illness" is that the terms used in referring to these phenomena in our society prejudge the issue. The medical metaphor "mental illness" suggests a determinate process which occurs within the individual: the unfolding and development of disease. It is convenient, therefore, to drop terms derived from the disease metaphor in favor of a standard sociological concept, deviant behavior, which signifies behavior that violates a social norm in a given society.

If the symptoms of mental illness are to be construed as violations of social norms, it is necessary to specify the type of norms involved. Most norm violations do not cause the violator to be labeled as mentally ill, but as ill-mannered, ignorant, sinful, criminal, or perhaps just harried, depending on the type of norm involved. There are innumerable norms, however, over which consensus is so complete that the members of a group appear to take them for granted. A host of such norms surround even the simplest conversation: a person engaged in conversation is expected to face toward his partner, rather than directly away from him; if his gaze is toward the partner, he is expected to look toward his eyes, rather than, say, toward his forehead; to stand at a proper conversational distance, neither one inch away nor across the room, and so on. A person who regularly violated these expectations probably would not be thought to be merely ill-bred, but as strange, biazarre, and frightening, because his behavior violates the assumptive world of the group, the world that is construed to be the only one that is natural, decent, and possible.

The culture of the group provides a vocabulary of terms for categorizing many norm violations: crime, perversion, drunkenness, and bad manners are familiar examples. Each of these terms is derived from the type of norm broken, and ultimately, from the type of behavior involved. After exhausting these categories, however, there is always a residue of the most diverse kinds of violations, for which the culture provides no explicit label. For example, although there is great cultural variation in what is defined as decent or real, each culture tends to reify its definition of decency and reality, and so provide no way of handling violations of its expectations in these areas. The typical norm governing decency or reality, therefore, literally "goes without saying" and its violation is unthinkable for most of its members. For the convenience of the society in construing those instances of unnamable deviance which are called to its attention, these violations may be lumped together into a residual category: witchcraft, spirit possession, or, in our own society, mental illness. In this paper, the diverse kinds of deviation for which our society provides no explicit label, and which, therefore, sometimes lead to the labeling of the violator as mentally ill, will be considered to be technically *residual deviance*.

The Origins, Prevalence and Course of Residual Deviance

The first proposition concerns the origins of residual deviance. *1. Residual deviance arises from fundamentally diverse sources.* It has been demonstrated that some types of mental disorder are the result of organic causes. It appears likely, therefore, that there are genetic, biochemical or physiological origins for residual deviance. It also appears that residual deviance can arise from individual psychological peculiarities and from differences in upbringing and training. Residual deviance can also probably be produced by various kinds fo external stress: the sustained fear and hardship of combat, and deprivation of food, sleep, and even sensory experience.[3] Residual deviance, finally, can be a volitional act of innovation or defiance. The kinds of behavior deemed typical of mental illness, such as hallucinations, delusions, depression, and mania, can all arise from these diverse sources.

The second proposition concerns the prevalence of residual deviance which is analogous to the "total" or "true" prevalence of mental disorder (in contrast to the "treated" prevalence). *2. Relative to the rate of treated mental illness, the rate of unrecorded residual deviance is extremely high.* There is evidence that grossly deviant behavior is often not noticed or, if it is noticed, it is rationalized as eccentricity. Apparently, many persons who are extremely withdrawn, or who "fly off the handle" for extended periods of time, who imagine fantastic events, or who hear voices or see visions, are not labeled as insane either by themselves or others.[4] Their deviance, rather, is unrecognized, ignored, or

rationalized. This pattern of inattention and rationalization will be called "denial."[5]

In addition to the kind of evidence cited above there are a number of epidemiological studies of total prevalence. There are numerous problems in interpreting the results of these studies; the major difficulty is that the definition of mental disorder is different in each study, as are the methods used to screen cases. These studies represent, however, the best available information and can be used to estimate total prevalence.

A convenient summary of findings is presented in Plunkett and Gordon.[6] This source compares the methods and populations used in eleven field studies, and lists rates of total prevalence (in percentages) as 1.7, 3.6, 4.5, 4.7, 5.3, 6.1, 10.9, 13.8, 23.2, 23.3, and 33.3.

How do these total rates compare with the rates of treated mental disorder? One of the studies cited by Plunkett and Gordon, the Baltimore study reported by Pasamanick, is useful in this regard since it includes both treated and untreated rates.[7] As compared with the untreated rate of 10.9 per cent, the rate of treatment in state, VA, and private hospitals of Baltimore residents was .5 per cent.[8] That is, for every mental patient there were approximately 20 untreated cases located by the survey. It is possible that the treated rate is too low, however, since patients treated by private physicians were not included. Judging from another study, the New Haven study of treated prevalence, the number of patients treated in private practice is small compared to those hospitalized: over 70 per cent of the patients located in that study were hospitalized even though extensive case-finding techniques were employed. The overall treated prevalence in the New Haven study was reported as .8 per cent, which is in good agreement with my estimate of .7 per cent for the Baltimore study.[9] If we accept .8 per cent as an estimate of the upper limit of treated prevalence for the Pasamanick study, the ratio of treated to untreated cases is 1/14. That is, for every treated patient we should expect to find 14 untreated cases in the community.

One interpretation of this finding is that the untreated patients in the community represent those cases with less severe disorders, while those patients with severe im-

3. Philip Solomon, *et al.* (eds.), *Sensory Deprivation*, Cambridge: Harvard, 1961: E. L. Bliss, *et al.*, "Studies of Sleep Deprivation—Relationship to Schizophrenia," *A.M.A. Archives of Neurology and Psychiatry*, **81** (March, 1959), pp. 348–359.

4. See, for example, John A. Clausen and Marian R. Yarrow, "Paths to the Mental Hospital," *Journal of Social Issues*, **11** (December, 1955), pp. 25–32; August B. Hollingshead and Frederick C. Redlich, *Social Class and Mental Illness*, New York: Wiley, 1958, pp. 172–176; and Elaine Cumming and John Cumming, *Closed Ranks*, Cambridge: Harvard, 1957, pp. 92–103.

5. The term "denial" is used in the same sense as in Cumming and Cumming, *ibid.*, Chap. VII.

6. Richard J. Plunkett and John E. Gordon, *Epidemiology and Mental Illness*, New York: Basic Books, 1960.

7. Benjamin Pasamanick, "A Survey of Mental Disease in an Urban Population, IV, An Approach to Total Prevalence Rates," *Archives of General Psychiatry*, **5** (August, 1961), pp. 151–155.

8. *Ibid.*, p. 153.

9. Hollingshead and Redlich, *op. cit.*, p. 199.

pairments all fall into the treated group. Some of the findings in the Pasamanick study point in this direction. Of the untreated patients, about half are classified as psychoneurotic. Of the psychoneurotics, in turn, about half again are classified as suffering from minimal impairment. At least a fourth of the untreated group, then, involved very mild disorders.[10]

The evidence from the group diagnosed as psychotic does not support this interpretation, however. Almost all of the cases diagnosed as psychotic were judged to involve severe impairment, yet half of the diagnoses of psychosis occurred in the untreated group. In other words, according to this study there were as many untreated as treated cases of psychoses.[11]

On the basis of the high total prevalence rates cited above and other evidence, it seems plausible that residual deviant behavior is usually transitory, which is the substance of the third proposition. *3. Most residual deviance is "denied" and is transitory.* The high rates of total prevalence suggest that most residual deviancy is unrecognized or rationalized away. For this type of deviance, which is amorphous and uncrystallized, Lemert uses the term "primary deviation."[12] Balint describes similar behavior as "the unorganized phase of illness."[13] Although Balint assumes that patients in this phase ultimately "settle down" to an "organized illness," other outcomes are possible. A person in this stage may "organize" his deviance in other than illness terms, e.g., as eccentricity or genius, or the deviant acts may terminate when situational stress is removed.

The experience of battlefield psychiatrists can be interpreted to support the hypothesis that residual deviance is usually transitory. Glass reports that combat neurosis is often self-terminating if the soldier is kept with his unit and given only the most superficial medical attention.[14] Descriptions of child behavior can be interpreted in the same way. According to these reports, most children go through periods in which at least several of the following kinds of deviance may occur: temper tantrums, head banging, scratching, pinching, biting, fantasy playmates or pets, illusory physical complaints, and fears of sounds, shapes, colors, persons, animals, darkness, weather, ghosts, and so on.[15] In the vast majority

10. Pasamanick, *op. cit.,* pp. 153–154.

11. *Ibid.*

12. Lemert, *op. cit.,* Chap. 4.

13. Michael Balint, *The Doctor, His Patient, and the Illness,* New York: International Universities Press, 1957, p. 18.

14. Albert J. Glass, "Psychotherapy in the Combat Zone," in *Symposium on Stress,* Washington, D. C.: Army Medical Service Graduate School, 1953. Cf. Abraham Kardiner and H. Spiegel, *War Stress and Neurotic Illness,* New York: Hoeber, 1947, Chaps. III–IV.

15. Frances L. Ilg and Lousie B. Ames, *Child Behavior,* New York: Dell, 1960, pp. 138–188.

of instances, however, these behavior patterns do not become stable.

If residual deviance is highly prevalent among ostensibly "normal" persons and is usually transitory, as suggested by the last two propositions, what accounts for the small percentage of residual deviants who go on to deviant careers? To put the question another way, under what conditions is residual deviance stabilized? The conventional hypothesis is that the answer lies in the deviant himself. The hypothesis suggested here is that the most important single factor (but not the only factor) in the stabilization of residual deviance is the societal reaction. Residual deviance may be stabilized if it is defined to be evidence of mental illness, and/or the deviant is placed in a deviant status, and begins to play the role of the mentally ill. In order to avoid the implication that mental disorder is merely role-playing and pretense, it is first necessary to discuss the social institution of insanity.

Social Control: Individual and Social Systems of Behavior

In *The Myth of Mental Illness,* Szasz proposes that mental disorder be viewed within the framework of "the game-playing model of human behavior." He then describes hysteria, schizophrenia, and other mental disorders as the "impersonation" of sick persons by those whose "real" problem concerns "problems of living." Although Szasz states that role-playing by mental patients may not be completely or even mostly voluntary, the implication is that mental disorder be viewed as a strategy chosen by the individual as a way of obtaining help from others. Thus, the term "impersonation" suggests calculated and deliberate shamming by the patient. In his comparisons of hysteria, malingering, and cheating, although he notes differences between these behavior patterns, he suggests that these differences may be mostly a matter of whose point of view is taken in describing the behavior.

The present paper also uses the role-playing model to analyze mental disorder, but places more emphasis on the involuntary aspects of role-playing than Szasz, who tends to treat role-playing as an individual system of behavior. In many social psychological discussions, however, role-playing is considered as a part of a social system. The individual plays his role by articulating his behavior with the cues and actions of other persons involved in the transaction. The proper performance of a role is dependent on having a cooperative audience. This proposition may also be reversed: having an audience which acts toward the individual in a uniform way may lead the actor to play the expected role even if he is not particularly interested in doing so. The "baby of the family" may come to find this role obnoxious, but the uniform pattern of cues and actions which confronts him in the family may lock in with his own vocabulary of responses so that it is inconvenient and difficult for him not to play the part expected of him. To the degree that alternative roles are closed off, the proffered role may come to be the only way the individual can cope with the situation.

One of Szasz's very apt formulations touches upon the social systemic aspects of role-playing. He draws an analogy between the role of the mentally ill and the "type-casting" of actors.[16] Some actors get a reputation for playing one type of role, and find it difficult to obtain other roles. Although they may be displeased, they may also come to incorporate aspects of the type-cast role into their self-conceptions, and ultimately their behavior. Findings in several social psychological studies suggest that an individual's role behavior may be shaped by the kinds of "deference" that he regularly receives from others.[17]

One aspect of the voluntariness of role-playing is the extent to which the actor believes in the part he is playing. Although a role may be played cynically, with no belief, or completely sincerely, with whole-hearted belief, many roles are played on the basis of an intricate mixture of belief and disbelief. During the course of a study of a large public mental hospital, several patients told the author in confidence about their cynical use of their symptoms—to frighten new personnel, to escape from unpleasant work details, and so on. Yet these *same* patients, at other times, appear to have been sincere in their symptomatic behavior. Apparently it was sometimes difficult for them to tell whether they were playing the role or the role was playing them. Certain types of symptomatology are quite interesting in this connection. In simulation of previous psychotic states, and in the behavior pattern known to psychiatrists as the Ganser

syndrome, it is apparently almost impossible for the observer to separate feigning of symptoms from involuntary acts with any degree of certainty.[18] In accordance with what has been said so far, the difficulty is probably that the patient is just as confused by his own behavior as is the observer.

This discussion suggests that a stable role performance may arise when the actor's role imagery locks in with the type of "deference" which he regularly receives. An extreme example of this process may be taken from anthropological and medical reports concerning the "dead role," as in deaths attributed to "bone-pointing." Death from bone-pointing appears to arise from the conjunction of two fundamental processes which characterize all social behavior. First, all individuals continually orient themselves by means of responses which are perceived in social interaction: the individual's identity and continuity of experience are dependent on these cues.[19] Secondly, the individual has his own vocabulary of expectations, which may in a particular situation either agree with or be in conflict with the sanctions to which he is exposed. Entry into a role may be complete when this role is part of the individual's expectations, and when these expectations are reaffirmed in social interaction. In the following pages this principle will be applied to the problem of the causation of mental disorder.

What are the beliefs and practices that constitute the social institution of insanity?[20] And how do they figure

16. Szasz, *op. cit.*, p. 252. For discussion of type-casting see Orrin E. Klapp, *Heroes, Villains and Fools,* Englewood Cliffs, New Jersey: Prentice-Hall, 1962, pp. 5–8 and *passim.*

17. Cf. Zena S. Blau, "Changes in Status and Age Identification," *American Sociological Review,* **21** (April, 1956), pp. 198–203; James Benjamins, "Changes in Performance in Relation to Influences upon Self-Conceptualization," *Journal of Abnormal and Social Psychology,* **45** (July, 1950), pp. 473–480; Albert Ellis, "The Sexual Psychology of Human Hermaphrodites," *Psychosomatic Medicine,* **7** (March, 1945), pp. 108–125; S. Liberman, "The Effect of Changes in Roles on the Attitudes of Role Occupants," *Human Relations,* **9** (1956), pp. 385–402. For a review of experimental evidence, see John H. Mann, "Experimental Evaluations of Role Playing," *Psychological Bulletin,* **53** (May, 1956), pp. 227–234. For an interesting demonstration of the inter-relations between the symptoms of patients on the same ward, see Sheppard G. Kellam and J. B. Chassan, "Social Context and Symptom Fluctuation." *Psychiatry,* **25** (November, 1962), pp. 370–381.

18. Leo Sadow and Alvin Suslick, "Simulation of a Previous Psychotic State," *A.M.A. Archives of General Psychiatry,* **4** (May, 1961), pp. 452–458.

19. Generalizing from experimental findings, Blake and Mouton make this statement about the processes of conformity, resistance to influence, and conversion to a new role:

. . . an individual requires a stable framework, including salient and firm reference points, in order to orient himself and to regulate his interactions with others. This framework consists of external and internal anchorages available to the individual whether he is aware of them or not. With an acceptable framework he can resist giving or accepting information that is inconsistent with that framework or that requires him to relinquish it. In the absence of a stable framework he actively seeks to establish one through his own strivings by making use of significant and relevant information provided within the context of interaction. *By controlling the amount and kind of information available for orientation, he can be led to embrace conforming attitudes which are entirely foreign to his earlier ways of thinking.*

Robert R. Blake and Jane S. Mouton, "Conformity, Resistance and Conversion," in *Conformity and Deviation,* Irwin A. Berg and Bernard M. Bass (eds.), New York: Harper, 1961, pp. 1–2. For a recent and striking demonstration of the effect on social communication in defining internal stimuli, see Stanley Schachter and Jerome E. Singer, "Cognitive, Social, and Physiological Determinants of Emotional State," *Psychological Review,* **69** (September, 1962), pp, 379–399.

20. The Cummings describe the social institution of insanity (the "patterned response" to deviance) in terms of denial, isolation, and insulation. Cumming and Cumming, *loc. cit.*

in the development of mental disorder? Two propositions concerning beliefs about mental disorder in the general public will now be considered.

4. Stereotyped imagery of mental disorder is learned in early childhood. Although there are no substantiating studies in this area, scattered observations lead the author to conclude that children learn a considerable amount of imagery concerning deviance very early, and that much of the imagery comes from their peers rather than from adults. The literal meaning of "crazy," a term now used in a wide variety of contexts, is probably grasped by children during the first years of elementary school. Since adults are often vague and evasive in their responses to questions in this area, an aura of mystery surrounds it. In this socialization the grossest stereotypes which are heir to childhood fears, e.g., of the "boogie man," survive. These conclusions are quite speculative, of course, and need to be investigated systematically, possibly with techniques similar to those used in studies of the early learning of racial stereotypes.

Assuming, however, that this hypothesis is sound, what effect does early learning have on the shared conceptions of insanity held in the community? There is much fallacious material learned in early childhood which is later discarded when more adequate information replaces it. This question leads to hypothesis No. 5.

5. The stereotypes of insanity are continually reaffirmed, inadvertently, in ordinary social interaction.

Although many adults become acquainted with medical concepts of mental illness, the traditional stereotypes are not discarded, but continue to exist alongside the medical conceptions, because the stereotypes receive almost continual support from the mass media and in ordinary social discourse. In newspapers, it is a common practice to mention that a rapist or a murderer was once a mental patient. This negative information, however, is seldom offset by positive reports. An item like the following is almost inconceivable:

> Mrs. Ralph Jones, an ex-mental patient, was elected president of the Fairview Home and Garden Society in their meeting last Thursday.

Because of highly biased reporting, the reader is free to make the unwarranted inference that murder and rape occur more frequently among ex-mental patients than among the population at large. Actually, it has been demonstrated that the incidence of crimes of violence, or of any crime, is much lower among ex-mental patients than among the general population.[21] Yet, this is not the picture presented to the public.

21. Henry Brill and Benjamin Malzberg, "Statistical Report Based on the Arrest Record of 5354 Male Ex-patients. Released from New York State Mental Hospitals During the Period 1946–48," mimeographed

Reaffirmation of the stereotype of insanity occurs not only in the mass media, but also in ordinary conversation, in jokes, anecdotes, and even in conventional phrases. Such phrases as "Are you crazy?", or "It would be a madhouse," "It's driving me out of my mind," or "It's driving me distracted," and hundreds of others occur frequently in informal conversations. In this usage insanity itself is seldom the topic of conversation; the phrases are so much a part of ordinary language that only the person who considers each word carefully can eliminate them from his speech. Through verbal usages the stereotypes of insanity are a relatively permanent part of the social structure.

In a recent study Nunnally demonstrated that reaffirmation of stereotypes occurs in the mass media. In a systematic and extensive content analysis of television, radio, newspapers and magazines, including "confession" magazines, they found an image of mental disorder presented which was overwhelmingly stereotyped.

> . . . media presentations emphasized the bizarre symptoms of the mentally ill. For example, information relating to Factor 1 (the conception that mentally ill persons look and act different from "normal" people) was recorded 89 times. Of these, 88 affirmed the factor, that is, indicated or suggested that people with mental-health problems "look and act different": only one item denied Factor 1. In television dramas, for example, the afflicted person often enters the scene staring glassy-eyed, with his mouth widely ajar, mumbling incoherent phrases or laughing uncontrollably. Even in what would be considered the milder disorders, neurotic phobias and obsessions, the afflicted person is presented as having bizarre facial expressions and actions.[22]

Denial and Labeling

According to the analysis presented here, the traditional stereotype of insanity becomes the guiding imagery for action, both for those reacting to the deviant and, in childhood and are continuously reaffirmed in the mass media and in everyday conversation. How do these beliefs function in the processes leading to mental disorder? This question will be considered by first referring to the earlier discussion of the societal reaction to residual deviance.

It was stated that the usual reaction to residual deviance is denial, and that in these cases most residual deviance is transitory. The societal reaction to deviance

document available from the authors; L. H. Cohen and H. Freeman, "How Dangerous to the Community are State Hospital Patients?", *Connecticut State Medical Journal,* **9** (September, 1945), pp. 697–701.

22. Jum C. Nunnally, Jr., *Popular Conceptions of Mental Health,* New York: Holt, Rinehart and Winston, 1961, p. 74.

is not always denial, however. In a small proportion of cases the reaction goes the other way, exaggerating and at times distorting the extent and degree of deviation. This pattern of exaggeration, which we will call "labeling," has been noted by Garfinkel in his discussion of the "degradation" of officially recognized criminals.[23] Goffman makes a similar point in his description of the "discrediting" of mental patients.[24] Apparently under some conditions the societal reaction to deviance is to seek out signs of abnormality in the deviant's history to show that he was always essentially a deviant.

The contrasting social reactions of denial and labeling provide a means of answering two fundamental questions. If deviance arises from diverse sources—physical, psychological, and situational—how does the uniformity of behavior that is associated with insanity develop? Secondly, if deviance is usually transitory, how does it become stabilized in those patients who became chronically deviant? To summarize, what are the sources of uniformity and stability of deviant behavior?

In the approach taken here the answer to this question is based on hypotheses Nos. 4 and 5, that the role imagery of insanity is learned early in childhood, and is reaffirmed in social interaction. In a crisis, when the deviance of an individual becomes a public issue, the traditional stereotype of insanity becomes the guiding imagery for action, both for those reacting to the deviant and at times, for the deviant himself. When societal agents and persons around the deviant react to him uniformly in terms of the traditional stereotypes of insanity, his amorphous and unstructured deviant behavior tends to crystallize in conformity to these expectations, thus becoming similar to the behavior of other deviants classified as mentally ill, and stable over time. The process of becoming uniform and stable is completed when the traditional imagery becomes a part of the deviant's orientation for guiding his own behavior.

The idea that cultural stereotypes may stabilize primary deviance, and tend to produce uniformity in symptoms, is supported by cross-cultural studies of mental disorder. Although some observers insist there are underlying similarities, most agree that there are enormous differences in the manifest symptoms of stable mental disorder *between* societies, and great similarity *within* societies.[25]

These considerations suggest that the labeling process is a crucial contingency in most careers of residual deviance. Thus Glass, who observed that neuropsychiatric casualties may not become mentally ill if they are kept with their unit, goes on to say that military experience with psychotherapy has been disappointing. Soldiers who are removed from their unit to a hospital, he states, often go on to become chronically impaired.[26] That is, their deviance is stabilized by the labeling process, which is implicit in their removal and hospitalization. A similar interpretation can be made by comparing the observations of childhood disorders among Mexican-Americans with those of "Anglo" children. Childhood disorders such as *susto* (an illness believed to result from fright) sometimes have damaging outcomes in Mexican-American children.[27] Yet the deviant behavior involved is very similar to that which seems to have high incidence among Anglo children, with permanent impairment virtually never occurring. Apparently through cues from his elders the Mexican-American child, behaving initially much like his Anglo counterpart, learns to enter the sick role, at times with serious consequences.[28]

Acceptance of the Deviant Role

From this point of view, then, most mental disorder can be considered to be a social role. This social role complements and reflects the status of the insane in the social structure. It is through the social processes which maintain the status of the insane that the varied deviancies from which mental disorder arises are made uniform and stable. The stabilization and uniformization of residual deviance are completed when the deviant accepts the role of the insane as the framework within which he organizes his own behavior. Three hypotheses are stated below which suggest some of the processes which cause the deviant to accept such a stigmatized role.

6. Labeled deviants may be rewarded for playing the stereotyped deviant role. Ordinarily patients who display "insight" are rewarded by psychiatrists and other personnel. That is, patients who manage to find evidence of "their illness" in their past and present behavior, confirming the medical and societal diagnosis, receive benefits. This pattern of behavior is a special case of a more general pattern that has been called the "apostolic func-

23. Harold Garfinkel, "Conditions of Successful Degradation Ceremonies," *American Journal of Sociology,* **61** (March, 1956), pp. 420–424.

24. Goffman, "The Moral Career of the Mental Patient," in *Asylums, op. cit.,* pp. 125–171.

25. P. M. Yap, "Mental Diseases Peculiar to Certain Cultures: A Survey of Comparative Psychiatry," *Journal of Mental Science,* **97** (April, 1951), pp. 313–327; Paul E. Benedict and Irving Jacks, "Mental Illness in Primitive Societies," *Psychiatry,* **17** (November, 1954), pp. 377–389.

26. Glass, *op. cit.*

27. Lyle Saunders, *Cultural Differences and Medical Care,* New York: Russell Sage, 1954, p. 142.

28. For discussion, with many illustrative cases, of the process in which persons play the "dead role" and subsequently die, see Charles C. Herbert, "Life-influencing Interactions," in *The Physiology of Emotions,* Alexander Simon, *et al.,* eds. New York: Charles C. Thomas, 1961.

tion'' by Balint, in which the physician and others inadvertently cause the patient to display symptoms of the illness the physician thinks the patient has.[29] Not only physicians but other hospital personnel and even other patients, reward the deviant for conforming to the stereotypes.[30]

7. *Labeled deviants are punished when they attempt to return to conventional roles*. The second process operative is the systematic blockage of entry to nondeviant roles once the label has been publicly applied. Thus the ex-mental patient, although he is urged to rehabilitate himself in the community, usually finds himself discriminated against in seeking to return to his old status, and on trying to find a new one in the occupational, marital, social, and other spheres.[31] Thus, to a degree, the labeled deviant is rewarded for deviating, and punished for attempting to conform.

8. *In the crisis occurring when a primary deviant is publicly labeled, the deviant is highly suggestible, and may accept the proferred role of the insane as the only alternative*. When gross deviancy is publicly recognized and made an issue, the primary deviant may be profoundly confused, anxious, and ashamed. In this crisis it seems reasonable to assume that the deviant will be suggestible to the cues that he gets from the reactions of others toward him.[32] But those around him are also in a crisis; the incomprehensible nature of the deviance, and the seeming need for immediate action lead them to take collective action against the deviant on the basis of the attitude which all share—the traditional stereotypes of insanity. The deviant is sensitive to the cues provided by these others and begins to think of himself in terms of the stereotyped role of insanity, which is part of his own role vocabulary also, since he, like those reacting to him, learned it early in childhood. In this situation, his behavior may begin to follow the pattern suggested by his own stereotypes and the reactions of others. That is, when a primary deviant organizes his behavior within the framework of mental disorder, and when his organization is validated by others, particularly prestigeful others such as physicians, he is ''hooked'' and will proceed on a career of chronic deviance.

The role of suggestion is noted by Warner in his description of bone-pointing magic:

The effect of (the suggestion of the entire community on the victim) is obviously drastic. An analogous situation in our society is hard to imagine. If all a man's near kin, his father, mother, brothers and sisters, wife, children, business associates, friends and all the other members of the society, should suddenly withdraw themselves because of some dramatic circumstance, refusing to take any attitude but one of taboo . . . and then perform over him a sacred ceremony . . . the enormous suggestive power of this movement . . . of the community after it has had its attitudes (toward the victim) crystallized can be somewhat understood by ourselves.[33]

If we substitute for black magic the taboo that usually accompanies mental disorder, and consider a commitment proceeding or even mental hospital admission as a sacred ceremony, the similarity between Warner's description and the typical events in the development of mental disorder is considerable.

The last three propositions suggest that once a person has been placed in a deviant status there are rewards for conforming to the deviant role, and punishments for not conforming to the deviant role. This is not to imply, however, that the symptomatic behavior of persons occupying a deviant status is always a manifestation of conforming behavior. To explain this point, some discussion of the process of self-control in ''normals'' is necessary.

In a recent discussion of the process of self-control, Shibutani notes that self-control is not automatic, but is an intricate and delicately balanced process, sustainable only under propitious circumstances.[34] He points out that fatigue, the reaction to narcotics, excessive excitement or tension (such as is generated in mobs), or a number of other conditions interfere with self-control; conversely, conditions which produce normal bodily states, and deliberative processes such as symbolization and imaginative rehearsal before action, facilitate it.

One might argue that a crucially important aspect of imaginative rehearsal is the image of himself that the actor projects into his future action. Certainly in American society, the cultural image of the ''normal'' adult is that of a person endowed with self-control (''willpower,'' ''back-bone,'' ''strength of character,'' etc.). For the person who sees himself as endowed with the trait of self-control, self-control is facilitated, since he can imagine himself enduring stress during his imaginative rehearsal, and also while under actual stress.

29. Balint, *op cit.*, pp. 215–239. Cf. Thomas J. Scheff, ''Decision Rules, Types of Error and Their Consequences in Medical Diagnosis,'' *Behavioral Science,* **8,** (April, 1963), pp. 97–107.

30. William Caudill, F. C. Redlich, H. R. Gilmore, and E. B. Brody, ''Social Structure and the Interaction Processes on a Psychiatric Ward,'' *American Journal of Orthopsychiatry,* **22,** (April, 1952), pp. 314–334.

31. Lemert, *op. cit.*, provides an extensive discussion of this process under the heading of ''Limitation of Participation,'' pp. 434–440.

32. This proposition receives support from Erikson's observations: Kai T. Erikson, *loc. cit.*

33. W. Lloyd Warner, *A Black Civilization,* rev. ed., New York: Harper, 1958, p. 242.

34. T. Shibutani, *Society and Personality,* Englewood Cliffs, N. J.: Prentice-Hall, 1961, Chapter 6, ''Consciousness and Voluntary Conduct.''

For a person who has acquired an image of himself as lacking the ability to control his own actions, the process of self-control is likely to break down under stress. Such a person may feel that he has reached his "breaking-point" under circumstances which would be endured by a person with a "normal" self-conception. This is to say, a greater lack of self-control that can be explained by stress tends to appear in those roles for which the culture transmits imagery which emphasizes lack of self-control. In American society such imagery is transmitted for the roles of the very young and very old, drunkards and drug addicts, gamblers, and the mentally ill.

Thus, the social role of the mentally ill has a different significance at different phases of residual deviance. When labeling first occurs, it merely gives a name to primary deviation which has other roots. When (and if) the primary deviance becomes an issue, and is not ignored or rationalized away, labeling may create a social type, a pattern of "symptomatic" behavior in conformity with the stereotyped expectations of others. Finally, to the extent that the deviant role becomes a part of the deviant's self-conception, his ability to control his own behavior may be impaired under stress, resulting in episodes of compulsive behavior.

The preceding eight hypotheses form the basis for the final causal hypothesis.

9. *Among residual deviants, labeling is the single most important cause of careers of residual deviance.* This hypothesis assumes that most residual deviance, if it does not become the basis for entry into the sick role, will not lead to a deviant career. Most deviant careers, according to this point of view, arise out of career contingencies, and are therefore not directly connected with the origins of the initial deviance.[35] Although there are a wide variety of contingencies which lead to labeling rather than denial, these contingencies can be usefully classified in terms of the nature of the deviant behavior, the person who commits the deviant acts, and the community in which the deviance occurs. Other things being equal, the severity of the societal reaction to deviance is a function of, first, the degree, amount, and visibility of the deviant behavior; second, the power of the deviant, and the social distance between the deviant and the agents of social control; and finally, the tolerance level of the community, and the availability in the culture of the community of alternative nondeviant roles.[36] Particularly crucial for future research is the importance of the first two contingencies (the amount and degree of deviance), which are characteristics of the deviant, relative to the remaining five contingencies, which are characteristics of the social system.[37] To the extent that these five factors are found empirically to be independent determinants of labeling and denial, the status of the mental patient can be considered a partly ascribed rather than a completely achieved status. The dynamics of treated mental illness could then be profitably studied quite apart from the individual dynamics of mental disorder.

Conclusion

This paper has presented a sociological theory of the causation of stable mental disorder. Since the evidence advanced in support of the theory was scattered and fragmentary, it can only be suggested as a stimulus to further discussion and research. Among the areas pointed out for further investigation are field studies of the prevalence and duration of residual deviance; investigations of stereotypes of mental disorder in children, the mass media, and adult conversations; studies of the rewarding of stereotyped deviation, blockage of return to conventional roles, and of the suggestibility of primary deviants in crises. The final causal hypothesis suggests studies of the conditions under which denial and labeling of residual deviation occur. The variables which might affect the societal reaction concern the nature of the deviance, the deviant himself, and the community in which the deviation occurs. Although many of the hypotheses suggested are largely unverified, they suggest avenues for investigating mental disorder different than those that are usually followed, and the rudiments of a general theory of deviant behavior.

35. It should be noted, however, that these contingencies are causal only because they become part of a dynamic system: the reciprocal and cumulative inter-relation between the deviant's behavior and the societal reaction. For example, the more the deviant enters the role of the mentally ill, the more he is defined by others as mentally ill; but the more he is defined as mentally ill, the more fully he enters the role, and so on. By representing this theory in the form of a flow chart, Walter Buckley pointed out that there are numerous such feedback loops implied here. For an explicit treatment of feedback, see Edwin M. Lemert, "Paranoia and the Dynamics of Exclusion," *Sociometry,* **25,** (March, 1962), pp. 2–20.

36. *Cf.* Lemert, *op cit.,* pp. 51–53, 55–68: Goffman, "The Moral Career of the Mental Patient," in *Asylums, op cit.,* pp. 134–135; David Mechanic, "Some Factors in Identifying and Defining Mental Illness," *Mental Hygiene,* **46** (January, 1962), pp. 66–74; for a list of similar factors in the reaction to physical illness, see Earl L. Koos, *The Health of Regionville,* New York: Columbia University Press, 1954, pp. 30–38.

37. *Cf.* Thomas J. Scheff, "Psychiatric and Social Contingencies in the Release of Mental Patients in a Midwestern State," forthcoming; Simon Dinitz, Mark Lefton, Shirley Angrist, and Benjamin Pasamanick, "Psychiatric and Social Attributes as Predictors of Case Outcome in Mental Hospitalization," *Social Problems,* **8** (Spring, 1961), pp. 322–328.

WALTER R. GOVE

Societal Reaction As An Explanation of Mental Illness: An Evaluation

During the 1960s the societal reaction perspective, sometimes referred to as "labeling theory," has been one of the most pervasive and influential sociological approaches to deviance.[1] However, this perspective has received little systematic evaluation. In this paper I will attempt to assess the empirical validity of the explanation of mental illness provided by the societal reaction theorists.

The Societal Reaction Perspective

One of the most fundamental distinctions made by the societal reaction theorists is between primary deviance, which may cause someone to be labeled as a deviant, and secondary deviance, which is the behavior produced by being placed in a deviant role. Regarding primary and secondary deviance, Lemert (1967:17) says: "Primary deviation is assumed to arise in a wide variety of social, cultural, and psychological contexts, and at best has only marginal implication for the psychic structure of the individual; it does not lead to symbolic reorganization at the level of self-regarding attitudes and social roles. Secondary deviation is deviant behavior, or social roles based upon it, which becomes a means of defense, attack or adaptation to the overt and covert problems created by the societal reaction to primary deviation."

The societal reaction theorists do not appear to attach significance to an act of primary deviance except insofar as others react towards the commission of the act. To them deviance is not a quality of an act, but instead deviance is produced in the interaction between a person

Reprinted from Walter Gove, "Societal Reaction as an Explanation of Mental Illness: An Evaluation," *The American Sociological Review,* **35,** 1970, 873–884, by permission of the author and publisher.

*The research for this paper was conducted under a grant from the Vanderbilt University Research Council. I would like to thank James Thompson, John McCarthy, and particularly Mayer Zald for comments on an earlier draft of this paper.

1. Some of the most important statements of this approach are Lemert, 1951, 1967; Becker, 1963; Scheff, 1966; Erikson, 1957, 1964; Kitsuse, 1964; Goffman, 1961; Schur, 1969.

who commits an act and those who respond to it (Becker, 1963:14). As Erikson (1964:11) says: "Deviance is not a property *inherent in* certain forms of behavior; it is a property *conferred upon* these forms by the audiences which directly or indirectly witness them. The critical variable in the study of deviance, then, is the social audience rather than the individual actor, since it is the audience which eventually determines whether or not any episode of behavior or any class of episodes is labeled deviant." Similarly Becker (1963:9) states: "*Social groups create deviance by making rules whose infractions constitute deviance,* and by applying those rules to particular people and labeling them as outsiders. From this point of view, deviance is not a quality of the act a person commits, but rather a consequence of the application by others of rules and sanctions to an 'offender.' The deviant is one to whom the label has successfully been applied; deviant behavior is behavior that people so label." Becker goes on to emphasize the distinction between rule breaking and deviance, noting that many persons who commit rule-breaking acts do not receive a deviant label while others, who have committed no rule-breaking act may, by mistake, be labeled deviant.

Persons do not usually commit acts that would place them in a deviant status without some reason. Although the societal reaction theorists have not been particularly concerned with explaining acts of primary deviance, they have provided a number of explanations of why a person might commit such acts. (1) A person may belong to a minority group or subculture whose values and ways of behaving may lead to violations of the rules of the dominant group. (2) He may have conflicting responsibilities, and the adequate performance of one role may produce violations in a second role. (3) He may violate rules for personal gain, usually with the expectation that he won't be caught. (4) He may be simply unaware of the rules and violate them unintentionally. Primary deviance is thus attributed to inconsistencies in the social structure, to hedonistic variables or to ignorance, while psychological characteristics such as personality or psychiatric disorders are ignored.[2] What concern the societal reaction theorists have with an individual's personal and social attributes is focused on how these attributes affect the way others respond to an act of primary deviance. Their argument is that the more powerful a person, the less likely the deviant label will be imposed upon him.

According to this approach, usually the most crucial step in the development of a stable pattern of deviant behavior is the experience of being caught and publicly labeled deviant. Whether or not this happens to a person "depends not so much on what he does as on what other people do"[3] (Becker, 1963:31). Erikson (1964:16), writing about the public labeling process, states: "The community's decision to bring deviant sanctions against the individual . . . is a sharp rite of transition at once moving him out of his normal position in society and transferring him into a distinctive deviant role. The ceremonies which accomplish this change of status, ordinarily, have three related phases. They provide a formal confrontation between the deviant suspect and representatives of his community (as in the criminal trial or psychiatric case conference); they announce some judgment about the nature of his deviancy (a verdict or diagnosis for example), and they perform an act of social placement, assigning him to a special role (like that of a prisoner or patient) which redefines his position in society."

Erikson (1964:16) goes on to state: "An important feature of these ceremonies in our own culture is that they are almost irreversible."[4] Why might this be the case? According to the societal reaction theorists, the status of deviant is a master status which overrides all other statuses in determining how others will act towards one (Becker, 1963:33). Once a person is stigmatized by being labeled a deviant, a self-fulfilling prophecy is initiated with others perceiving and responding to the person as a deviant (Becker, 1963:34; Erikson, 1964:16). Furthermore, once persons are publicly processed as de-

2. For the exception to this otherwise apparently uniform trend, see Lemert (1967:55–59).

3. Becker does note the possibility that the person might brand himself as "deviant" and "punish himself."

4. Becker (1963:37) notes that in the situation where a person is apprehended for the first time, the act of apprehension does not necessarily lead to secondary deviance if the person is still in a position to choose alternative lines of action. Similarly, Lemert (1967:42) indicates that the importance of degradation rituals is not in their drama but in their consequences and that "for stigmatization to establish a total deviant identity it must be disseminated throughout the society." In any case, it would appear that when a person's mental disorder leads to a public hearing which results in hospitalization, that person has no alternative lines of action and that his "deviance" is well established.

viants, they are typically forced into a deviant group (usually by being placed in an institution). As Becker notes (1963:38), such groups have one thing in common, their deviance. They have a common fate, they face the same problems and because of this they develop a deviant subculture. This subculture combines a perspective on the world with a set of routine activities. According to Becker (1963:38), "membership in such a group solidifies a deviant identity" and leads to rationalization of their position.

In the view of the societal reaction theorists, once this has occurred it is extremely difficult for the person to break out of his deviant status. As Lemert (1967:55) states, "Once deviance becomes a way of life the personal issue often becomes the cost of making a change rather than the higher status to be gained through rehabilitation or reform. Such costs are calculated in terms of the time, energy and distress seen as necessary for change." The deviant has learned to carry on his deviant activities with a minimum of trouble (Becker, 1963:39). He has already failed in the normal world, suggesting to himself and others an inability to make it even when things are relatively normal; now he faces the world as a stigmatized person. If he is in an institution, such as a mental hospital, to become a candidate for reinstatement in society he must, as Lemert (1967:45) notes, give allegiance to an often anomalous conception of himself and the world. Denial of the organizational ideology may lead to the judgment that the deviant is "unreformed" or still "sick." Even if he is returned to the community, he presumably will face an audience which anticipates the worst and which will take steps to protect itself, steps which make it difficult for the person to succeed. Furthermore, in the community he may be on a form of probation which forces him to live by extremely rigorous rules, the violations of which are grounds for reinstitutionalization.

In summary, the argument of the societal reaction theorists is that persons who have passed through a degradation ceremony and have been forced to become members of a deviant group have experienced a profound and frequently irreversible socialization process. They have acquired an inferiority status and have developed a deviant world view and the knowledge and skill that go with it. And perhaps equally important, they have developed a deviant self-image based upon the image of themselves they receive through the actions of others. Although the societal reaction perspective of deviance has been very much in vogue during the 1960s, most of the work based on this perspective has been intuitive and/or theoretical, and there has been very little systematic evaluation and testing of the perspective.

What follows in this paper is an attempt to meet this lack of critical evaluation by examining the evidence in a particular area of deviance—that of mental illness.

Entrance into the Mentally Ill Role

The Theoretical Explanation

A fairly explicit statement of how the societal reaction perspective may be used to explain how a person becomes mentally ill has been provided by Scheff.[5] Following Becker, he makes a distinction between rule-breaking and deviance. He then goes on to note that: "the culture of the group provides a vocabulary of terms for categorizing many norm violations: crime, perversion, drunkenness, and bad manners are familiar examples. Each of the terms is derived from the type of norm broken, and ultimately, from the type of behavior involved. After exhausting these categories, however, there is always *a residue of the most diverse kinds of violations* for which the culture provides no explicit label" (italics added), (Scheff, 1966:34).

Scheff terms these types of violations residual rule-breaking and then indicates that it is the violation of these diverse kinds of rules that lead to labeling someone mentally ill. He notes that "we can categorize most psychiatric symptoms as instances of residual rule-breaking or residual deviance" (Scheff, 1966:33). Throughout the remainder of his work he equates the diverse behaviors of residual deviance with the symptoms of the mentally ill. According to him (Scheff, 1966:40) there "should be an unlimited number of sources" of residual rule-breaking. In giving an example of residual rule-breaking, he discusses Goffman's (1964) position that there is a rule that the adult be "involved" when in public view. According to Scheff (1966:34−39), if a person is uninvolved or "away" without giving the appropriate signals, he is a residual rule-breaker. Other examples of residual rule-breaking presented by Scheff are the Dada movement and the reactions to LSD-25, to monotony, and to sleep and sensory deprivation. Scheff holds that: (1) acts of residual rule-breaking are frequent and they are committed by a very wide segment of the "normal" population; (2) they are caused by very diverse (and frequently benign) factors; and (3) they should not be taken to indicate personal abnormality or disorder. Scheff's point appears to be that we do not need to be concerned with the act of

residual deviance or its cause, but that instead we need to focus on the reactions of others to acts of residual deviance. Scheff (1966:54) explicitly states that the societal reaction is the single most important factor in the stabilization of mental illness.

To explain the public's reaction to an act of residual rule-breaking, Scheff turns to the public stereotype of mental illness. He notes that "stereotyped imagery of mental disorder is learned in early childhood" (1966:64) and that these "stereotypes of insanity are continually reaffirmed, inadvertently in ordinary social interaction"[6] (p. 67). According to Scheff (1966:67) an important component of the public stereotype of insanity is an unreasoned fear of the mentally ill which makes the public unwilling to take risks that would routinely be accepted in ordinary living. He holds that sometimes this stereotype is applied to a person who commits an act of residual rule-breaking and at other times it is not. He notes a general tendency to deny that an act of residual rule-breaking is an indication of mental illness. When denial occurs, residual rule-breaking is presumed to be transitory. However, if for some reason "the deviance of the individual becomes a public issue, the traditional stereotype of insanity becomes the guiding imagery for action" (Scheff, 1966:82). When this happens it is assumed that procedures to initiate hospitalization will be quickly taken.

Once a person enters the domain of officials responsible for the hospitalization of the mentally ill, it is argued that he will be almost invariably hospitalized. Scheff (1966:105−155) presents a number of reasons for this position based upon his research. (1) Psychiatrists are more sensitive to signs of mental illness than the general public; they tend to see a broad array of persons as disturbed and in need of care. (2) Once the question of whether or not a person is ill has been raised, officials, following the medical ideology, feel that it is safer to treat someone who may not be ill than it is to release someone who may be ill. And (3) there are a number of features built into the commitment process, such as established routines, lack of facilities, the payment schedule for examiners, etc., that make it difficult to reverse the commitment process. Scheff's investigation of commitment procedures thus leads him to conclude that "the official societal reaction . . . exaggerates both the amount and degree of deviance," and once the offi-

---

5. It should be clear by now that mental illness, as Scheff and other societal reaction theorists use the term, refers to the occupancy of a social role and not to a state of personal distress or disorganization.

6. At this point, Scheff's argument appears to me somewhat inconsistent. I find it difficult to associate a stereotype that is well-established and continually reinforced with a set of diverse behaviors (acts of residual deviance) whose primary similarity is that no explicit label can be attached to them. For a more detailed discussion of this problem see Fletcher and Reynolds (1968).

cial process is initiated the person is almost invariably routed to a mental hospital (Scheff, 1966:154).

In summary, Scheff views mental illness as an ascribed status, entry into which is primarily dependent upon conditions external to the individual. His formulation is (1) that virtually everyone at some time commits acts that correspond to the public stereotype of mental illness; (2) if, by some happenstance, these acts become public knowledge, the individual may, depending upon various (unspecified) contingencies, be referred to the appropriate officials; and (3) once this happens the person will be routinely processed as mentally ill and placed in a mental institution. This is an original formulation which very neatly gets around a potentially troublesome aspect of the societal reaction perspective, namely, why does the person commit an act of primary deviance? In most cases it would be very difficult to argue that the person publicly presents psychiatric symptoms for personal gain or because he belongs to a subculture with values in conflict with the dominant group. Instead, Scheff argues that psychiatric symptoms are a common phenomenon, that their presentation is unintended, and only rarely and fortuitously do they cause someone to be labeled mentally ill. The question we must now confront is whether or not this formulation is consistent with available evidence.

The Empirical Evidence

A number of investigations (Star, 1961; Nunnally, 1961; Cumming and Cumming, 1957) have been made of the public's image of mental illness. These studies indicate that the public lacks accurate knowledge about mental disorder, distorting and exaggerating the amount and type of disturbance. In addition, "the mentally ill are regarded with fear, distrust and dislike" (Nunnally, 1961:46). In the public conception, mental illness appears to involve unpredictable and potentially dangerous behavior. Furthermore, there is a halo effect: once a person is perceived as mentally ill, he is not only thought to be unpredictable and dangerous but also "dirty, unintelligent, insincere and worthless" (Nunnally, 1961:233). These investigations clearly indicate that the public has a negative, highly stereotyped image of mental illness and suggest that the public generally views mental illness as a master status that overrides other characteristics of the individual. The question, however, is whether people are treated as mentally ill because they inadvertently perform an act that activates the stereotype of mental illness. The evidence from field surveys and from studies of the path to the mental hospital indicates that this is not the case.

In a pioneering study, Yarrow et al. (1955) investi-

gated how wives came to define their husbands as mentally ill. The research demonstrated that the wives utilized strong defenses to avoid seeing their husbands' behavior as deviant. The wives would make every effort to interpret their husbands' behavior as normal. If that failed, they would minimize the importance of the behavior and balance it off against more normal behavior. Only when the husband's behavior became impossible to deal with[7] would the wife take action to have her husband hospitalized. Even at this time the husband was not always viewed as mentally ill.[8] This pattern appears to be consistent with the findings of other investigators (Schwartz, 1957:290; Sampson et al., 1964; Hollingshead and Redlich, 1958; also see Jaco, 1960:18). Furthermore, investigations have indicated that rehospitalization does not typically occur because of the expectations of others but because of the manifestation of severe psychiatric symptoms which have become impossible to handle in the community (Freeman and Simmons, 1963; Angrist et al., 1968).

The results of field surveys also bear upon how people identify the mentally ill. When people are presented with descriptions of persons with various types of mental disorder, the disturbed behavior is not regarded as an indication of mental illness except when the person is presented as dangerous (Star, 1961; Cumming and Cumming, 1957). Phillips (1963), using the same case materials, has shown that rejection of the mentally ill is not related to their behavior[9] but to their being labeled as mentally ill by being in treatment. In sum, the evidence strongly suggests that persons, typically, are hospitalized because they have an active psychiatric disorder which is extremely difficult for themselves[10] and/or

7. In the example provided by Yarrow et al. (1955), the husband, in a two-day period, thought a TV program was about him and the set was after him, threatened to kill his wife, got the shakes, kept his wife up and talked to her all night in a bizarre fashion (for example, he asked her if she were his mother or God), created a serious disturbance where his wife worked, said his male organs were blown up and little seeds covered him, and finally chased his wife around the apartment growling like a lion.

8. After a person is hospitalized, he is not necessarily perceived by himself or others as mentally ill. Yarrow, et al. (1955) found that even after the husband's hospitalization one fifth of the wives did not view their husbands as mentally ill and another fifth did so only sporadically. The wives Schwartz (1957) studied also tended to deny their husbands were mentally ill. Scheff (1966:86) himself notes many hospitalized patients deny they are mentally ill, and a group of ex-mental patients which I studied (Gove and Lubach, 1969) generally acknowledged they had needed and benefited from hospitalization but denied they had been mentally ill. Also see Cumming and Cumming (1965).

9. The exception again is the paranoid schizophrenic who appears dangerous.

10. As state hospitals improve, an increasing proportion of patients seek voluntary admission. For example, Northern State Hospital, located in the State of Washington, has shown a marked improvement over the years, and the admission rate rose from 3% in 1955 to 57% in 1967. A

others to handle. It would appear that the public's stereotype of mental illness does not lead to persons being inappropriately labeled mentally ill through an inadvertent act of residual rule-breaking. Instead, the evidence suggests that the gross exaggeration of the degree and type of disorder in the stereotype fosters the denial of mental illness, since the disturbed person's behavior does not usually correspond to the stereotype.

Once a person is brought to the attention of public officials as mentally ill, do the officials, as Scheff suggests, act on the assumption of illness and routinely route him to a mental hospital? We might first look at persons who voluntarily seek hospitalization. Mechanic (1962) and Brown (1961:60) feel that public mental hospitals accept virtually all such patients, but they present no data. To my knowledge there are only two studies that have systematically evaluated hospital acceptance of voluntary mental patients. Mishler and Waxler (1963) found that the public mental hospital they studied accepted for admission only 39% (n = 246) of the applicants and the private mental hospital accepted 58% (n = 137) of the applicants. Similarly, Mandel and Rapport (1969) found that the public mental hospital they studied accepted for admission 41% (n = 269) of the applicants. Both studies thus found that the public mental hospitals only admitted approximately 40% of the voluntary applicants. Although there probably are hospitals that routinely assume illness and admit virtually all voluntary mental patients, it is clearly inappropriate to assume this is always or even usually the case.

Let us turn to involuntary patients. Such persons may be thought of as going through three stages in their contact with public officials: (1) a screening stage where the police or some other screening agency makes the decision to hold or not to hold the person for examination and possible commitment, (2) an examination by a court psychiatrist or other duly qualified board and (3) the court hearing where the official decision is made to release the person or to commit him to a mental hospital.

First, let us examine the limited data available on the screening stage. A recent study of police discretion in the apprehension of the mentally ill by Bittner (1967:280) found that the police "like everyone else avail themselves of various forms of denial when it comes to doing something about it (mental illness)." Furthermore, it is Bittner's impression that "except for cases of suicide attempts, the decision to take someone to the hospital is based upon overwhelmingly conclusive evidence of illness" (Bittner, 1967:285). He goes on to

note that the police regularly assist persons in the community whom they and others recognize as having a serious mental disturbance while making no effort to have them hospitalized. There is, to my knowledge, only one study (Wilde, 1968) of a psychiatric screening agency that presents the agency's response to requests to initiate commitment proceedings. In this study when a nonpsychiatrist made a request to initiate commitment proceedings, the screening agency approved the request in only 33% of the cases[11] (n = 6000). In contrast, when a psychiatrist made a request, the request was apparently routinely approved—the approval rate for hospital psychiatrists being 98% (n = 2000), and for court psychiatrists 100% (n = 250)—presumably on the assumption that the psychiatrist had carefully and expertly evaluated the need for hospitalization. Support for this assumption is provided by the fact that the court psychiatrists examined approximately 1000 suspected mental cases sent by the jails but only requested commitment proceedings on 250 (Wilde, 1968:216). These studies clearly suggest that during the initial screening stage officials do not assume illness but in fact proceed rather cautiously, screening out a substantial number of persons.

Let us shift to the outcomes of the psychiatric examination of persons held for commitment. Scheff in his study of these examinations found them to be unsystematic, arbitrary, and prejudicial. He felt that "except in very unusual cases, the psychiatric examiner's recommendation to retain the patient is virtually automatic" (Scheff, 1968:287). Nonetheless, in each of the studies reviewed release was recommended for at least some persons (see Chart 1). Generally, such recommendations were relatively rare; however, in the largest study (Haney and Michielutte, 1968) only 50% of the persons under 65 were found to be incompetent.

When we look at the outcome to the court hearing, we find a similar pattern with most, but usually not all, persons being committed (see Chart 2). The description of commitment proceedings (Miller and Schwartz, 1966; Wenger and Fletcher, 1969; Scheff, 1967) indicate that they are very rapid, that there is rarely any real exploration of the facts surrounding the case, and that proper legal procedures are not closely observed. From their experience Miller and Schwartz (1966:34) guess that "the judgment about mental illness had already been made earlier in the commitment process and that the hearing was a rubber stamp to an earlier decision." From the rates presented by Wilde (1968), it would ap-

---

study (Gove, 1968) of a sample of these patients found that most of the voluntary patients initiated their own hospitalization due to their acute distress (and occasionally disorientation), a reason for hospitalization not readily explained by the societal reaction perspective.

11. Wilde (1968), from a study of a sample of persons processed by the screening agency, came to the conclusion that there was no relationship between degree of disturbance and the initiation of procedures. His study, however, suffers from methodological problems, and it can be shown that his conclusion is probably erroneous (see Gove, 1970).

CHART 1.

Outcome of the Psychiatric Examination

Wilde (1968:216−17)

		Recommendation of Examiners		
		Release [a]	Commit	N
		4.8% (200)	95.2% (4000)	4200

Haney and Michielutte (1968) [b]

		Examiners' Evaluation of Prospective Patients		
		Temporarily		
Age	Competent	Incompetent [c]	Incompetent	N
up to 64	35.7% (158)	13.6% (61)	50.0% (221)	442
65−over	8.5% (11)	3.1% (4)	88.4% (129)	129
Total	29.6% (169)	11.4% (65)	59.0% (337)	571

Kutner (1962)

	Recommendation for Examiners		
	Release	Commit	N
	33%	77%	not given

Scheff (1968:284) [d]

		Recommendation of Examiners		
	Release	30 Day Observation	Commit	N
	7.7% (2)	23.1% (6)	69.2% (18)	26

[a] Over half of the requests for commitment came from psychiatrists. If we assume that the court psychiatrists in such cases agreed with their colleagues, then in those cases where the proceedings were initiated by a layman, the proportion of persons for whom commitment is recommended drops to about 90%.

[b] Although the authors do not explicitly say so, the examining board apparently had the power not only to examine but also to commit.

[c] The authors do not indicate whether or not persons judged to be temporarily incompetent were to be committed to a mental hospital.

[d] Elsewhere Scheff (1968:281) notes that in the examination of 196 court records there was not a single recommendation for release (he does not indicate the outcomes of these hearings). This may be taken as an indication of an almost uniform presumption of illness, but it may be the case that when the psychiatrists recommend the person be released, the officials try to settle out of court by getting the participants to agree to the release of the subject.

CHART 2.

Outcome of Court Hearings

Wilde (1968:216−17)

Proportion of Cases		
Released		Committed
4.8% (200)		95.2% (4000)

Miller and Schwartz (1966)

Proportion of Cases [a]		
Released	Held Over	Committed
22% (13)	10% (6)	68% (39)

Wenger and Fletcher (1969)

Proportion of Cases		
Released		Committed
19.7% (16)		80.3% (65)

Scheff (1967:113)

Proportion of Cases		
Released		Committed
0% (0)		100% (43)

[a] Of the 58 prospective patients, 13 were voluntarily seeking admission.

pear that those persons who are released are exclusively those for whom the psychiatrists had recommended such action. Wenger and Fletcher (1969:68) explicitly state this to be the case in their study. Miller and Schwartz (1966:34), however, found that "the judge reversed the medical recommendation for commitment . . . in nearly one-fourth of the cases."

In summary, the available evidence on how people enter the mentally ill role indicates that the societal reaction formulation, at least as stated by Scheff, is false. The evidence is that the vast majority of persons who become patients have a serious disturbance, and it is only when the situation becomes untenable that action is taken. The public officials who perform the major screening role do not simply process all of the persons who come before them as mentally ill but instead screen out a large portion. If the person passes this initial screening, he will probably be committed, and there is reason to assume the process at this point frequently becomes somewhat ritualized. But even here a number of persons are released either through the psychiatric examination or the court hearing.

Consequences of Hospitalization

Let us now turn to what happens to a person who enters a mental hospital. As noted in the introductory section, the societal reaction theorists feel that once a person has gone through a public hearing, and has been certified as a deviant and placed in an institution, it is extremely difficult for the person to break out of his deviant status. For a number of reasons, the impact of this process is held to be especially pronounced for the mental patient (see Goffman, 1961). First, the mental patient may have been misled, lied to, jailed and testified against by those he trusted; and by the time he arrives at the hospital, he is presumed to feel deserted, betrayed and estranged from his family and friends, a condition that should promote the acceptance of the mentally ill role. Second, in the hospital the patient is surrounded by severe restrictions and deprivations which are presented as "intended parts of his treatment, part of his need at the time, and therefore an expression of the state his self has fallen to," (Goffman, 1961:149). Third, the events recorded in the patient's case history are selected in such a manner that they are almost uniformly defamatory and discrediting. These events tend to be public knowledge, and they may be used to keep the patient in his place and to validate his mental illness.

Unfortunately, the research in the societal reaction tradition dealing with the effects of hospitalization has focused almost exclusively on what goes on in the hospital. Such studies have probably focused primarily on long-term patients who make up the bulk of the resident population; they tend to ignore the majority of psychiatric patients whose hospitalization is relatively brief. For this reason much of this research may present an unrepresentative picture. Let us agree, however, that mental hospitals may, in many ways, be debilitating places where patients *may* come to accept the preferred role of the insane and *may*, over time, develop skills and a world view adapted to the institutional setting and gradually lose their roles and even interest in the community.[12]

Restitutive Processes

The fact that debilitating processes may be present does not mean that restitutive processes are not also in operation. One such process may of course be treatment, but that is not the only one. An important study by Sampson *et al.* (1961, 1964), which looked at the patient before, during, and after hospitalization, found that hospitalization initiated major restitutive processes, most of which were not consciously guided by hospital personnel. Let us outline these processes. It was found that hospitalization interrupted a situation which was experienced as untenable and, by doing so, it blocked actions

---

12. A study by Wing (1962) of the effects of prolonged institutionalization on the mentally ill found length of hospitalization was associated with a growing apathy towards events outside the hospital and with an increased contentment with institutional life. However, contrary to what one might expect, if one felt that psychiatric symptoms were primarily a response to cues in the immediate environment, prolonged hospitalization was not associated with changes in symptomatic behavior.

which threatened irremediable damage to family life. This interruption was "legitimated by the act of hospitalization which ratified the wife as ill and in need of special isolation and treatment" (Sampson *et al.*, 1961:144). This ratification of illness was decisive in blunting and redefining the negative implications of the interruption. The acts leading to the hospital were not viewed as alienative, "but as actions of an involuntary nature required by and serving the present and future interests of the patient and her family" (Sampson *et al.*, 1961:144). Furthermore, through moral and legal obstacles the husband was forced to defer a sometimes planned divorce allowing other solutions to marital difficulties to be considered and attempted.

As hospitalization occurred "at a relatively late stage in family and personal disorganization" (Sampson *et al.*, 1961:143), frequently a number of alienative acts had occurred which seriously jeopardized the resumption of the marriage. In such situations a certain "undoing" must be accomplished if the marital family is to be restored. Hospitalization was found to facilitate this "undoing" by a number of processes. (1) It enabled the patient and family to separate the deviant behavior and ideation from the real self of the patient. (2) Treatment was interpreted as an important and successful "undoing" process. According to Sampson *et al.* (1961:148), "patients and their spouses often assigned remarkable diagnostic acumen and therapeutic efficiency to the hospital, and they strained to view their eventual release as a carefully determined medical judgment of recovery." (3) During and following hospitalization there was a transition period of construction where the family evolved a new "working consensus." During this period, as is consonant with the concept of illness, relatives were advised not to upset the patient, and they in fact tended to avoid touchy subjects.

Hospitalization was also found to have initiated processes which served in a positive way to move the family toward reintegration. In some cases the removal of the patient and the conflict situation promoted a revival of positive ties and feelings. In many other cases the dislocation in family life produced by the wife's absence caused considerable problems and "at the first sign of improvement the husband often began to pleasurably anticipate his wife's return and resumption of responsibilities" (Sampson *et al.*, 1961:152). Furthermore, the hospital, by treating the husband as responsible for his wife and eager for her recovery, put him into a role which frequently reinstituted a relationship of concern and improved marital communication.

A major issue is whether the processes just presented generally have a major impact on the patient or if they are overshadowed by the processes pointed to by the societal reaction theorists. Before the era of the tranquilizers and the open door policy, the average patient was probably heavily influenced by the deadening institutional procedures of the traditional mental hospital. Now, however, the vast majority of mental patients receive fairly rapid and intensive treatment.[13] In such cases the restitutive factors of hospitalization may well dominate; and, in any case, with a brief hospitalization the impact of many of the processes outlined by the societal reaction theorists should be minimal.

Stigma

There is, of course, the possibility that the patient is so stigmatized by having been labeled mentally ill that when he returns to the community he is not *allowed* to resume his previous interpersonal and instrumental roles. In an attempt to evaluate the question of whether or not the stigma of having been a patient in a mental hospital necessarily leads to the chronic occupancy of the mentally ill role, let us turn to a detailed study of 287 women after treatment conducted by Angrist *et al.* (1968). Their sample of women tended to be severely disturbed but to have an acute rather than chronic illness (for example, only one third of their sample had been hospitalized previously). Their patients had received fairly intensive treatment and on the average had been in the hospital 52 days. The study was concerned with those patients who had been returned to the community and who were able to remain there for 15 days.

One of the first things to be noted is that the ex-patients were not like their neighbors, or like a random sample of females in the community, the ex-patients being atypical in their lack of education, their singleness, and their household living arrangements. These factors apparently predated their hospitalization and could not be considered a consequence of being publicly labeled mentally ill. Once the former mental patients and their neighbors were matched on these characteristics, the groups were extremely similar "in the areas of instrumental role performance, role expectations and tolerance of deviant behavior" (Angrist *et al.*, 1968:161). The ex-patients, however, manifested significantly more psychiatric handicaps. The authors also found that "as performance (or the ability to perform) degenerates, the expectations of family members are corroded, so that they become accustomed to expect less of their relative" (Angrist *et al.*, 1968:171). This suggests that expectations for poor performance may be determined more by ineffectual behavior than the reverse, a conclusion that

appears to be consistent with the work of Freeman and Simmons (1963).

For former patients, probably the most important indicator of continued occupancy of the mentally ill role is rehospitalization. Of the patients in this study 15% had been rehospitalized after six months; 24% after two years; and 32% after seven years (Angrist *et al.*, 1968: *passim*). Thus, over two-thirds of these patients had not been rehospitalized after seven years, and probably a significant proportion of these never will.

What caused rehospitalization? The evidence indicated that following the initial hospitalization, the readmitted patients had exhibited more deviant behavior and more psychiatric symptoms (particularly extreme and acutely disordered symptoms) than ex-patients who avoided rehospitalization. Furthermore, the data showed that in spite of the fact that ex-patients had previously been labeled as mentally ill, the relatives viewed "readmission as a last resort for behavior which cannot be handled without medical help" (Angrist *et al.*, 1968:100). In conclusion, the authors (Angrist *et al.*, 1968:176) state that "the fact that the returnees were decidedly sicker than community patients indicates that intrinsic features of the illness are of greater consequence in precipitating readmission than are the variations in the way significant others perceive, evaluate or tolerate such illness."

Although this study clearly suggests that the stigma attached to a former mental patient does not generally have serious consequences, it does not specifically deal with the question of stigma. Unfortunately, very little work has focused directly on this issue. A study of psychiatric patients by Jones *et al.* (1963) found that patients, typically, felt that the lay public would not view a person as undesirable because he had been in a mental hospital. Cumming and Cumming (1965) found, in a study of 22 former mental patients, that 41% felt stigmatized, four expressing shame and five having a generalized expectation of discrimination. They suggest that with the passage of time, or with the occupancy of normal roles, feelings of stigma will disappear. Freeman and Simmons (1961) in a study of feelings of stigma by relatives of ex-mental patients found that only 24% of the families (n = 394) felt stigmatized. Furthermore, their findings indicate that feelings of stigma are associated with the perception that the patient is acting in an abnormal fashion and with a fear that persons in the community will discriminate against the family because of the patient's current bizarre behavior. In general, the evidence on stigma, although far from conclusive, suggests that stigma is not a serious problem for most ex-mental patients and that, when stigma is a problem, it is more directly related to the person's current psychiat-

---

13. For example, in the State of Washington the median length of stay for the admissions to the state mental hospitals was only 2.0 months in 1966 (State of Washington, 1966).

ric status, or general ineffectiveness, than it is to having been in a mental hospital.

Discussion

The societal reaction perspective does not view the deviant as someone who is suffering from an intra-personal disorder but instead as someone who, through a set of circumstances, becomes publicly labeled a deviant and who is forced by the societal reaction into a deviant role. In essence, they view the deviant as someone who is victimized (see Gouldner, 1968). The available evidence, however, indicates that the societal reaction formulation of how a person becomes mentally ill is substantially incorrect. There is very little systematic evidence of victimization. The evidence shows that a substantial majority of the persons who are hospitalized have a serious psychiatric disturbance quite apart from any secondary deviance that may be associated with the mentally ill role. Furthermore, persons in the community do not view someone as mentally ill if he happens to act in a bizarre fashion. On the contrary, they persist in denying mental illness until the situation becomes intolerable. Once prospective patients come into contact with public officials, a substantial screening still occurs, presumably sorting out persons who are being railroaded or who are less disturbed. It is only in the last stages of the commitment process that some ritualization appears to occur, and even here a noticeable proportion of persons are sorted out.

The evidence also indicates that the societal reaction theorists have overstated the degree to which secondary deviance is associated with mental hospitalization. (1) There appear to be many restitutive processes associated with hospitalization even apart from the question of therapy. (2) Patients treated in a modern psychiatric hospital typically do not spend enough time in the hospital to become truly institutionalized. (3) In most cases the stigma of having been a former mental patient does not appear to affect greatly one's performance in the community following discharge. In summary, the studies reviewed, while in no way denying the existence of the processes outlined by the societal reaction theorists, suggest that mental hospitalization does not necessarily or even typically lead to a prolonged occupancy of the mentally ill role. Furthermore, the available evidence indicates that when former patients continue to have difficulty, these difficulties are generally due to the person's confronting a troubled situation or to some psychiatric disorder, and not to the social expectations of others.

It would appear, from what we know of mental illness, that it is useful to make a distinction between primary and secondary deviance. However, contrary to the position taken by the societal reaction theorists, the primary deviance may reflect a serious disturbance, one that in some cases may be considerably more important than the problems associated with secondary deviance. Most of the hospitalized cases of mental illness appear to reflect a psychiatric disorder that requires societal intervention (treatment). If the treatment is rapid, intensive, and effective, the psychiatric crisis can be handled without any significant development of secondary deviance (see for example Gove and Lubach, 1969). Clearly in the past a great deal of secondary deviance was produced by mental institutions. However, mental hospitals have moved a long way from the traditional insane asylum, and the amount of secondary deviance has been greatly reduced.[14]

The inability of the societal reaction theorist to explain the development of mental illness together with their exaggeration of the amount of secondary deviance produced by treating someone as mentally ill is probably indicative of a general bias in the perspective. The societal reaction perspective does not explain why people initially commit deviant acts; it deals mainly with secondary processes that may not always be of crucial importance. Just as focusing only on the processes involved in producing primary deviance may lead to an unrealistic image of a deviant behavior, so also will an exclusive focus on the societal reaction to an act of primary deviance.

The evidence reviewed suggests that a person's behavior determines the expectations of others to a much greater degree than the reverse. This relationship between behavior and expectations is probably generally true in the short run; it certainly appears that it is the person's disturbed behavior that generally leads to the mentally ill role. In the long run, however, the expectations of others may play an important role in determining the behavior of a person, and such expectations should be taken into account in a general theory of mental illness.[15] Unfortunately, the societal reaction theorists

14. Modern mental hospitals, however, still have demonstrable detrimental effects (see for example Pasamanick *et al.*, 1967).

15. As has been shown, a focus on the expectations of others does not in general lead to an explanation of why someone becomes mentally ill. However, whether or not a person who is mentally ill remains mentally ill may depend in part on the social expectations he confronts. Let me, as an illustration, indicate one way in which the expectations of others would appear to relate to mental illness. As a general rule, people normalize the behavior of others; i.e., they interpret it in light of the situation and the person's past behavior. If in the past a person has acted in a normal (appropriate) fashion and then, for a brief period, acts inappropriately, others will tend to normalize his behavior (see it as being within the bounds of normality). However, if the person has a long history of inappropriate behavior and then starts to act in an appropriate fashion, others will again normalize his behavior (still see him as inappropriate).

have generally treated their framework as a sufficient explanatory system. In doing so they have underemphasized the importance of acts of primary deviance and overemphasized the importance of the forces promoting secondary deviance.[16] Future attempts at explaining mental illness will have to redress the balance.

REFERENCES

Angrist, Shirley, Mark Lefton, Simon Dinitz and Benjamin Pasamanick. 1968. *Women After Treatment*. New York: Appleton-Century-Crofts.

Becker, Howard. 1963. *Outsiders: Studies in the Sociology of Deviance*. New York: The Free Press.

Bittner, Egon. 1967. "Police discretion in apprehending the mentally ill." *Social Problems* 14 (Winter):278–292.

Brown, E. L. 1961. *Newer Dimensions of Patient Care*. New York: Russell Sage Foundation.

Cumming, Elaine and John Cumming. 1957. *Closed Ranks*. Cambridge: Harvard University Press.

Cumming, John and Elaine Cumming. 1965. "On the stigma of mental illness." *Community Mental Health Journal* 1:135–143.

Erikson, Kai. 1957. "Patient role and social uncertainty: A dilemma of the mentally ill." *Psychiatry* 20:263–274.

——. 1964. "Notes on the sociology of deviance." Pp. 9–21 in Howard Becker (ed.), *The Other Side*. New York: The Free Press.

Fletcher, C. Richard and Larry Reynolds. 1968. "Residual deviance, labeling, and the mentally sick role: A critical review of concepts." *Sociological Focus* 1 (Spring): 9–27.

Freeman, Howard and Ozzie Simmons. 1961. "Feelings of stigma among relatives of former mental patients." *Social Problems* 8:32–321.

——. 1963. *The Mental Patient Comes Home*. New York: Wiley.

Goffman, Erving. 1961. *Asylums: Essays on the Social Situation of Mental Patients and Other Inmates*. Garden City, N.Y.: Anchor Books.

——. 1964. *Behavior in Public Places*. New York: The Free Press.

Gouldner, Alvin. 1968. "The sociologist as partisan: Sociology and the welfare state." *The American Sociologist* 3 (May):103–116.

Gove, Walter. 1968. A Theory of Mental Illness: An Analysis of the Relationship Between Symptoms, Personality Traits, and Social Situations. Unpublished Dissertation, University of Washington.

——. 1970. "Who is hospitalized: A critical review of some sociological studies of mental illness." *Journal of Health and Social Behavior*. Forthcoming.

——. 1970. A General Theory of Mental Illness. In Preparation.

Gove, Walter and John Lubach. 1969. "An intensive treatment program for psychiatric in-patients: A description and evaluation." *Journal of Health and Social Behavior* 10 (September):225–236.

Haney, C. Allen and Robert Michielutte. 1968. "Selective factors operating in the adjudication of incompetency." *Journal of Health and Social Behavior* 9 (September):233–242.

Hollingshead, August and Fredrick Redlich. 1958. *Social Class and Mental Illness*. New York: Wiley.

Jaco, E. Gartly. 1960. *The Social Epidemiology of Mental Disorders*. New York: Russell Sage Foundation.

Jones, Nelson, Marvin Kahn and John MacDonald. 1963. "Psychiatric patients' view of mental illness, hospitalization and treatment." *Journal of Nervous and Mental Disease* 136:82–87.

Kitsuse, John. 1964. "Societal reaction to deviant behavior: Problems of theory and method." Pp. 87–102 in Howard Becker (ed.), *The Other Side*. New York: The Free Press.

Kutner, L. 1962. "The illusion of due process in commitment proceedings." *Northwestern University Law Review* 57 (September):383–399.

Lemert, Edwin. 1951. *Social Pathology*. New York: McGraw-Hill.

——. 1967. *Human Deviance, Social Problems and Social Control*. Englewood Cliffs, N.J. Prentice-Hall.

Mechanic, David. 1962. "Some factors in identifying and defining mental illness." *Mental Hygiene* 46 (January): 66–74.

Mendel, Werner and Samuel Rapport. 1969. "Determinants of the decision for psychiatric hospitalization." *Archives of General Psychiatry* 20 (March):321–328.

Miller, Dorothy and Michael Schwartz. 1966. "County lunacy commission hearings: Some observations of commitments to a state mental hospital." *Social Problems* 14 (Summer):26–35.

Mishler, Elliott and Nancy Waxler. 1963. "Decision processes in psychiatric hospitalization." *American Sociological Review* 28:576–587.

Thus, although it is the psychiatric disturbance of the individual that generally places a person in the mentally ill role, once he becomes firmly entrenched in that role (the evidence would indicate that a single brief psychiatric hospitalization is generally not sufficient for this), the expectations of others may make it very difficult to leave it. Elsewhere I am presenting in considerable detail the relationship between social expectations and mental illness (Gove, 1970).

16. For example, I suspect that they have generally overstated the difficulties a stigmatized person will have when dealing with the public. Such findings are reported in the literature. Kitsuse (1964:100), for example, would on theoretical grounds posit "extreme negative sanctions against homosexuality" but found his subjects to have "generally mild reactions."

Nunnally, Jim. 1961. *Popular Conceptions of Mental Health*. New York: Holt, Rinehart and Winston.

Pasamanick, Benjamin, Frank Scarpitti and Simon Dinitz. 1967. *Schizophrenics in the Community*. New York: Appleton-Century-Crofts.

Phillips, Derek. 1963. "Rejection: A possible consequence of seeking help for mental disorders." *American Sociological Review* 28:963–972.

Sampson, Harold, Sheldon Messinger and Robert Towne. 1961. "The mental hospital and marital family ties." *Social Problems* 9 (Fall):141–155.

——. 1964. *Schizoprenic Women: Studies in Marital Crisis*. New York: Atherton.

Scheff, Thomas. 1966. *Being Mentally Ill*. Chicago: Aldine.

——. 1967. "Social conditions for rationality: How urban and rural courts deal with the mentally ill." Pp. 109–118 in Thomas Scheff (ed.), *Mental Illness and Social Progress*. New York: Harper & Row.

——. 1968. "The societal reaction to deviance: Ascriptive elements in the psychiatric screening of mental patients in a Midwestern state." Pp. 276–290 in Stephen Spitzer and Norman Denzin (eds.), *The Mental Patient*. New York: McGraw-Hill.

Schur, Edwin. 1969. "Reactions to deviance: A critical assessment." *American Journal of Sociology* 75 (November):309–322.

Schwartz, Charlotte. 1957. "Perspectiv Wives' definitions of their husband *Psychiatry* 20:275–291.

Star, Shirley. 1961. The Dilemmas of Mental Illness Cited in the Joint Commission on Mental Illness and Health. *Action for Mental Health*. Pp. 74–76. New York: Science Editions.

State of Washington. 1966. "Reference report." Department of Institutions.

Wenger, Denis and C. Richard Fletcher. 1969. "The effect of legal counsel on admissions to a state mental hospital: A confrontation of professions." *Journal of Health and Social Behavior* 10 (March):66–72.

Wilde, William. 1968. "Decision-making in a psychiatric screening agency." *Journal of Health and Social Behavior* 9 (September):215–221.

Wing, J. K. 1962. "Institutionalism in mental hospitals." *British Journal of Social and Clinical Psychology* 1:38–51.

Yarrow, Marion, Charlotte Schwartz, Harriet Murphy and Leila Deasy. 1955. "The Psychological meaning of mental-illness in the family." *The Journal of Social Issues* XI, (No. 4):12–24.

JANE M. MURPHY

Psychiatric Labeling in Cross-Cultural Perspective

In recent years labeling (or societal reaction) theory has aroused strong interest among people concerned with mental illness. From the perspective of labeling theory, the salient features of the behavior patterns called mental illness in countries where Western psychiatry is practiced appear to be as follows: (i) these behaviors repre-

Reprinted from *Science*, Vol. **191**, 1976, pages 1019–1028, by permission of the author and publisher.

The author is associate professor of anthropology in the Harvard School of Public Health, Boston, Massachusetts 02115. A portion of this article was presented at the 1973 meeting of the Atlantic Provinces Psychiatric Association in Halifax, Nova Scotia.

sent deviations from what is believed to be normal in particular sociocultural groups, (ii) the norms against which the deviations are identified are different in different groups, (iii) like other forms of deviation they elicit societal reactions which convey disapproval and stigmatization, (iv) a label of mental illness applied to a person whose behavior is deviant tends to become fixed, (v) the person labeled as mentally ill is thereby encouraged to learn and accept a role identity which perpetuates the stigmatizing behavior pattern, (vi) individuals who are powerless in a social group are more vulnerable to this process than others are, and (vii) because social agencies in modern industrial society contribute to the labeling process they have the effect of creating problems for those they treat rather than easing problems.

This school of thought emerged mainly within sociology, as an extension of studies of social deviance in which crime and delinquency were originally the major focus (*1*). It is also associated with psychiatry through, for example, Thomas Szasz and R. D. Laing (*2*). These ideas have come to be called a "sociological model" of mental illness, for they center on learning and the social construction of norms. They began to be formulated about 25 years ago (*3*), commanded growing attention in the late 1960's, and have been influential in recent major changes in public programs for psychiatric care, especially the deinstitutionalization which is occurring in a number of states (*4, 5*).

Several aspects of the theory receive support from a study reported in *Science* by David Rosenhan (*6*), based on the experiences of eight sane subjects who gained admission to psychiatric hospitals, were diagnosed as schizophrenic, and remained as patients an average of 19 days until discharged as "in remission." Rosenhan argues that "we cannot distinguish insanity from sanity" (*6*, p. 257). He associates his work with "anthropological considerations" and cites Ruth Benedict (*7*) as an early contributor to a theme he pursues, which is that "what is viewed as normal in one culture may be seen as quite aberrant in another" (*6*, p. 250). He indicates that the perception of behavior as being schizophrenic is relative to context, for "psychiatric diagnosis betrays little about the patient but much about the environment in which an observer finds him." He argues that, despite the effort to humanize treatment of disturbed people by calling them patients and labeling them mentally ill, the attitudes of professionals and the public at large are characterized by "fear, hostility, aloofness, suspicion, and dread." Once the label of schizophrenia has been applied, the "diagnosis acts on all of them"—patient, family, and relatives—"as a self-fulfilling prophecy. Eventually, the patient himself accepts the diagnosis, with all of its surplus meanings and expectations, and behaves accordingly" (*6*, p. 254).

The research to be described here presents an alternative perspective derived from cross-cultural comparisons, mainly of two widely separated and distinctly contrasting non-Western groups, Eskimos of northwest Alaska and Yorubas of rural, tropical Nigeria. It is concerned with the meanings attached to behaviors which would be labeled mental illness in our society. I interpret these data as raising important questions about certain assumptions in the labeling thesis and therefore as casting doubt on its validity as a major explanation of mental illness, especially with respect to schizophrenia. These cross-cultural investigations suggest that relativism has been exaggerated by labeling theorists and that in widely different cultural and environmental situations sanity appears to be distinguishable from insanity by cues that are very similar to those used in the Western world.

The Labeling Orientation

As Edwin Schur (*8*) points out, if labeling theory is conceived broadly it is the application of George Herbert Mead's theories about self-other interactions to a definition of social deviance extended to include human problems ranging from crime to blindness. Labeling theory emphasizes the social meanings imputed to deviant behavior and focuses on the unfolding processes of interaction whereby self-definition is influenced by others. Further, "it is a central tenet of the labeling perspective that neither acts nor individuals are 'deviant' in the sense of immutable, 'objective' reality without reference to processes of social definition." Schur states that "this relativism may be viewed as a major strength" of labeling theory (*8*, p. 14).

Edwin Lemert's concept of secondary deviance (*9*) is of critical importance in linking self-other considerations to deviations. Secondary deviation occurs when a person learns the role and accepts the identity of a deviant as the basis of his life-style. It is a response to a response, negative feedback from significant others reinforces and stabilizes the behavior that initially produced it. Applied to criminality, this idea has created general awareness of a process whereby a young person on being labeled a juvenile delinquent may enter a network of contingencies that lead ultimately to his learning criminal activities and "hardening" as a criminal rather than to the correction of behavior.

In *The Making of Blind Men*, Robert Scott points to a similar process regarding a very different type of deviance (*10*). If a person is labeled blind by certain administrative criteria he is likely to become enmeshed in care-giving agencies that encourage him to accept a definition of himself as helpless and to learn to play the role of the blind man. These experiences may even inhibit the use of residual vision. Scott shows that institutions for the blind vary in the degree to which they encourage acceptance or rejection of the deviant role and that these differences are related to differences in the life-style of blind men. Insofar as the labeling concept has been employed in this way I believe it is sound and has disclosed new and valuable information.

The application of labeling ideas to mental illness has tended to take a different course (*11*) and has aroused considerable controversy, as indicated, for example, in the continuing exchange between Thomas Scheff and

Walter Gove *et al.* *(12 – 15)*. One question in this controversy is whether mental illness should be considered a "pure case" of secondary deviation or a more complex case. Lemert's formulation of the concept of secondary deviation was influenced by his investigation of stuttering, and he suggests that stuttering represents the pure case: "Stuttering thus far has defied efforts at causative explanation. . . . It appears to be exclusively a process-product in which, to pursue the metaphor, normal speech variations, or at most, minor abnormalities of speech (primary stuttering) can be fed into an interactional or evaluation process and come out as secondary stuttering" *(9,* p. 56).

The important point here is that primary deviance is considered to be normal variation or only "minor abnormalities," and the influence of societal reactions is considered genuinely causative. Societal reactions "work on" and "mold" normal variations of speech to "create" stuttering. For mental illness, the labeling theorists have tended to use the "pure case" model rather than the more complex model represented by blindness, where lack or loss of sight is primary deviance and the role of blind man is secondary deviance.

Scheff has provided the most systematic theoretical statement regarding labeling and mental illness, and in his formulation the primary deviations that are fed into interactional processing to come out as mental illness are described as "amorphous," "unstructured," and "residual" violations of a society's norms *(11,* p. 33, 82). Rosenhan suggests that the behaviors labeled schizophrenic might be " 'sane' outside the psychiatric hospital but seem insane in it . . . [because patients] are responding to a bizarre setting" *(6,* p. 257). Lemert says that social exclusion can "create a paranoid disposition in the absence of any special character structure" *(9,* p. 198). Further, many have posited that behavior we call mental illness might be considered normal in a different culture or in a minority social class. Thus, the primary deviations of mental illness are held to be for the most part insignificant, and societal reactions become the main etiological factor.

This view is reminiscent of ideas about human plasticity, cultural determinism, and cultural relativism which were prominent in what used to be called the culture-personality studies of anthropology. In fact the influence of culture-personality on labeling theory is explicitly stated by Lemert, who was trained jointly in sociology and anthropology and who has drawn on non-Western studies throughout his career. The influence is equally acknowledged by Rosenhan *(6)*. It seems to me that numbers of proponents of labeling theory assume that the expanding body of data from non-Western areas has supported the relativist propositions put forth by Bene-

dict and others in the 1930's and '40's *(16)*. Indeed, it was my own assumption when I began anthropological work with Eskimos. I thought I would find their conception of normality and abnormality to be very different, if not opposite, from that held in Western culture. This did not prove to be the case, and my experience is not unique. Anthropologists who have been conducting field research in recent years using more systematic methods but continuing to work on the relations between individual behavior and cultural context tend to hold a greatly modified view of the extent of individual plasticity and the molding force of culture *(17, 18)*.

It would be misleading on my part to imply that all theory building and investigation regarding the relation of labeling and mental illness have followed the pure-case model. In their studies on mental retardation Robert Edgerton and Jane Mercer use moderate labeling ideas and show that social reactions are related to differences in the ways subnormal individuals are able to function both in and outside of institutions *(19)*. A growing number of studies of alcoholism, many of them influenced by labeling views, have demonstrated that social attitudes and the variable meanings attached to drinking are correlated with marked differences in alcoholism rates in various cultural groups *(20)*. There are, in addition, numbers of studies of the social pathways leading to hospitalization, the impact of hospitalization, attitudes toward discharged mental patients, and so on which reveal important outcomes for the mentally ill without imputing to societal reactions the degree of significance given them in the more deterministic formulations.

Most labeling studies of mental illness have been carried out in the United States and the United Kingdom. Variations in the definition and tolerance of mental illness have mainly been studied in groups at different social class levels in industrialized society *(21)*. Since cultural relativism is one of the main elements of the orientation, it seems useful to put some of the basic labeling questions to non-Western data. As background for this, I quote from four contributors to labeling theory: Scheff, Erving Goffman, Theodore Sarbin, and David Mechanic. These references do not encompass the breadth and elaboration of each contributor's own approach to the problem of mental illness, but they do reflect the view of cultural relativity which runs throughout the labeling orientation.

Scheff says that "the culture of the group provides a vocabulary of terms for categorizing many norm violations" *(11,* pp. 33, 82). These designate deviations such as crime and drunkenness. There is a residual category of diverse kinds of deviations which constitute an affront to the unconscious definition of decency and reality uniquely characteristic of each culture. Scheff posits that the "culture provides no explicit label" for these deviations but they nevertheless take form in the minds of societal agents as "stereotypes of insanity." When people around a deviant respond to him in terms of these stereotypes, "his amorphous and unstructured rule-breaking tends to crystallize in conformity to these expectations." Scheff further suggests that these cultural stereotypes tend to produce uniformity of symptoms within a cultural group and "enormous differences in the manifest symptoms of stable mental disorder between societies."

It has been pointed out that there appears to be a contradiction in one aspect of Scheff's theory (*12*, p. 876:22). It is difficult to accept that a socially shared image of behavior that can influence action and has the concreteness of a stereotype should lack a name. It is possible Scheff meant that in the evolution of language a label for insanity was the last to emerge because it refers to a residue of norm violations. The dating of words is beyond the scope of the data to be presented here, but it will be possible to see whether an explicit label currently exists in the two cultures studied, a hunting-gathering culture (Eskimo) and an agricultural society (Yoruba), neither of which developed a written language. If a word for insanity occurs we can then investigate the kinds of behaviors therein denoted.

Regarding our own society, Goffman stresses that the "perception of losing one's mind is based on culturally derived and socially engrained stereotypes as to the significance of symptoms such as hearing voices, losing temporal and spatial orientation, and sensing that one is being followed" (*23*). He further indicates that there is cultural variation in this kind of imagery and differential encouragement for such a view of oneself. This makes it appropriate to ask whether hallucinations, delusions, and disorientations are present or absent from the conception of losing one's mind in Yoruba and Eskimo cultures, assuming they have a stereotype of insanity at all.

Labeling theorists express considerable dissatisfaction with the concept of mental illness, pointing out that it is a vague and euphemistic metaphor and ties together phenomena that are neither "mental" nor "illness." They argue that mental illness is a myth developed in Western societies, that the term represents an abortive effort to improve the treatment of people previously called lunatics, that in the name of this myth we continue to incarcerate, punish, and degrade people for deviating from norms. Sarbin suggests that defining behavioral aberrations as illness occurred in medieval Europe as a way to relabel people who might otherwise have been burned at the stake as witches (*24*). He further suggests that it was during this phase of Western history that the concept of mind came into being. It was used as a way to

explain perplexing behavior that could not be related to occurrences external to the person. It is "*as if* there are states of mind" that cause these patterns of conduct. The "as if" was transmuted into the myth that the mind exists as a real entity and can therefore be sick or healthy.

In the data to be given, it will be possible to ask whether the idea of an inner state that influences conduct is found in these non-Western groups and, since both groups believe in witchcraft, whether a stereotype of insanity is associated with the conduct of witches. Everywhere that witchcraft has been systematically studied the role of the witch involves deviances that are heavily censured. The witch carries out practices that are believed to harm people through supernatural means. If the insane person and the witch are equated in the beliefs of non-Western groups, it would appear to follow that in those groups, mental illness is thought of as social deviance; and this would be a telling point for labeling theory.

Mechanic makes the point that "although seemingly obvious, it is important to state that what may be viewed as deviant in one social group may be tolerated in another, and rewarded in still other groups" (*25*). He emphasizes that the social response may influence the frequency with which the deviant behavior occurs. It has been hypothesized by a number of researchers that holy men, shamans, or witch doctors are psychotics who have been rewarded for their psychotic behavior by being made incumbents of highly regarded and useful roles (*26*). This is the obverse of the possibility that the insane are thought of as witches. The role of the healer carries great power and approval. The idea of social rewards for mental illness underscores the lengths to which relativity can be carried, for it suggests that the social definition of one kind of behavior can turn it into such opposing roles as the defamed witch or the renowned shaman. Mechanic's points make it appropriate, therefore, to ask whether the shamans in Eskimo culture and the healers in Yoruba culture are thought by the people to be mentally ill and whether the rates of such mental illness in these groups are similar to or different from those in the West.

Scheff, Goffman, Sarbin, and Mechanic share the view that in our society the appellation "mentally ill" is a "stigmatizing" and "brutalizing" assessment. It robs the individual of identity through profound "mortification" and suggests that he is a "non-person." It forces him into an ascribed role, exit from which is extremely difficult. Thus another question is posed: If Eskimos and Yorubas have a stereotype of insanity, are they less harsh than we with those defined as insane?

To illustrate the model I have in mind for exploring

these questions I will first describe a non-Western event which suggests that certain aspects of labeling theory are valid. It does not concern mental illness but it demonstrates the use of labels as arbitrary social definitions in the labeling theory sense. The case is reported by W. H. R. Rivers in connection with his analysis of the concept of death among the Melanesians (*27*).

Some persons who are seriously ill and likely to die or who are so old that from the Melanesian point of view they are ready to die are labeled by the word *mate*, which means "dead person." They become thereby subjects of a ceremonial live burial. It can be argued that the Melanesians have a concept of death which is a social fiction. It embodies what they arbitrarily agree to define as death and is a distortion of reality as seen by most cultural groups. The label *mate* involves a degradation ceremony in which an elderly person is deprived of his rights and is literally "mortified." He is perceived "*as if* dead" and then buried. The linguistic relativist might even say that this use of the word *mate* shows that the Melanesians do not perceive death by means of the indicators of vital functioning applied in Western society (*28*).

Rivers's own conclusion is that the Melanesians view death the way we do and are cognizant of the difference between biological and social *mate*. Biological *mate* is by far the commoner phenomenon. In their practice of live burials the Melanesians in fact take close note of two typical precursors of death: old age and illness.

It seems clear, however, that socially sanctioned acts based on symbolic meanings, such as those involved in social *mate*, are powerful in influencing the course of human affairs. They can be treacherously abused and lead to what we think of as cruel outcomes. Rivers says that the practice is not conceived to be cruel or degrading by the Melanesians because in their meaning the burial relieves the person of a worn-out earth-life so that he can enter the higher status of the spiritual afterlife. By our standards the Melanesian interpretation would nevertheless be considered a collective rationalization of "geronticide." Whatever the intent, the socially defined death of elderly Melanesians is a myth and serves as a model of what I understand the labeling theorists to mean by the "myth of mental illness." Thus a final question: Do the Eskimos and Yorubas subscribe to such fictions about mental illness through which they perpetuate inhumanity and degradation?

Method of Study

The data to be presented derive mainly from a year of field work. In 1954–55, in a village of Yupik-speaking Eskimos on an island in the Bering Sea, and an investigation of similar length in 1961 and 1963, among Egba Yorubas. I also draw on shorter periods of field work in Gambia, Sudan, and South Vietnam.

Some of the Eskimo data came from a key informant, who systematically described the life experiences of the 499 Eskimos who constituted a total village census over the 15 years previous to and including the year of investigation. In addition, a dictionary of Eskimo words for illness and deviance was developed. Extended life histories of a small number of Eskimos were gathered. Also daily observations and comments from Eskimos about Eskimos (both in their own village and in other areas known to them) were recorded for the purpose of understanding their conceptions of behavior (*29*).

The approach among the Yorubas was different in that I worked with a group of three native healers and a member of an indigenous cult. Interviews were directed toward understanding Yoruba concepts of behavior in the abstract and centered on actual people only to the extent that acquaintances and patients were brought into the discussion as illustration (*30*).

The Eskimo data served as the base for an epidemiological study of the village in 1955, and the Yoruba data constituted one of the first phases of a larger epidemiological study carried out with a group of Nigernian and U.S. colleagues in which we studied 416 adults, of whom 245 constituted a representative sample from 14 villages (*31*).

In *The Social Meanings of Suicide,* a study affiliated with the labeling tradition, Jack Douglas has shown the weakness of official statistics as a basis for judging the social significance of behavioral phenomena in groups (*32*). The Eskimo and Yoruba studies reflect a similar orientation about the inadequacies of mental hospital statistics for the purposes at hand. As has been done in many labeling studies, I relied on participant observation and interviewing about microcultural events. The focus was on indigenous meanings. These meanings were then used as a basis for counting similar behavior patterns, so that they were defined from within a cultural group rather than by imposed criteria.

In these studies I have considered language to be the main repository of labels. Insofar as there is a counterpart to the official recognition of mental illness involved in hospital commitment in a Western society, it resides in what Eskimos and Yorubas say are the kinds of people treated by shamans and native healers.

Labeled Behavior Patterns

The first specific question is: Do Eskimos and Yorubas have labels for psychological and behavioral differences that bear any resemblance to what we mean by mental illness? These groups clearly recognize differences among themselves and describe these in terms of what people do and what they say they feel and believe. Some of the differences lead people to seek the aid of healers and some do not, some differences arouse sympathy and protection while others arouse disapproval, some are called sickness and others health, some are considered misconduct and others good conduct. Some are described by a single word or nominative phrase. Some that seem to have common features are described in varying circumlocutions and sentences. If a word exists for a complex pattern of behavior it seems acceptable to assume that the concept of that pattern has been crystallized out of a welter of specific attributes and that the word qualifies as an explicit label.

Of major importance is whether or not the Yorubas and Eskimos conceptualize a distinction between body and mind and attribute differences in functioning to one or the other. The first indication of such a distinction arose early in the Eskimo census review when a woman was described in these terms: "Her sickness is getting wild and out of mind . . . but she might have had sickness in her body too." The Eskimo word for her was *nuthkavihak*. It became clear from other descriptions that the word refers to a complex pattern of behavioral processes of which the hallmark is conceived to be that something inside the person: the soul, the spirit, the mind is out of order. Descriptions of how *nuthkavihak* is manifested include such phenomena as talking to oneself, screaming at someone who does not exist, believing that a child or husband was murdered by witchcraft when nobody else believes it, believing oneself to be an animal, refusing to eat for fear eating will kill one, refusing to talk, running away, getting lost, hiding in strange places, making strange grimaces, drinking urine, becoming strong and violent, killing dogs, and threatening people. Eskimos translate *nuthkavihak* as "being crazy."

There is a Yoruba word, *were*, which is also translated as insanity. The phenomena include hearing voices and trying to get other people to see their source though none can be seen, laughing when there is nothing to laugh at, talking all the time or not talking at all, asking oneself questions and answering them, picking up sticks and leaves for no purpose except to put them in a pile, throwing away food because it is thought to contain *juju*, tearing off one's clothes, setting fires, defecating in public and then mushing around in the feces, taking up a weapon and suddenly hitting someone with it, breaking things in a state of being stronger than normal, believing that an odor is continuously being emitted from one's body.

For both *nuthkavihak* and *were* indigenous healing practices are used. In fact, among the Yorubas some native healers specialize in the treatment of *were* (*33, 34*).

The profile of *were* behaviors is based not only on what the healers described in the abstract but also on data concerning two members of the sample identified as *were* by the village headman and a group of 28 *were* patients in the custody of native healers and in a Nigerian mental hospital. The profile of *nuthkavihak* is built from information about four individuals within the 15-year population of 499 persons and six Eskimos from earlier times and from a related Eskimo settlement in Siberia.

Of paramount significance is the fact that *were* and *nuthkavihak* were never used for a single phenomenon such as hearing voices, but rather were applied to a pattern in which three or four of the phenomena described above existed together. It is therefore possible to examine the situations in which a person exhibited one or another of the listed behaviors but was not labeled insane.

The ability to see things other people do not see and to look into the future and prophesy is a clearly recognized and highly valued trait. It is called "thinness" by Eskimos. This ability is used by numerous minor Eskimo diviners and is the outstanding characteristic of the shaman. The people called "thin" outnumber those called insane by at least eight to one. Moreover, there were no instances when a "thin" person was called *nuthkavihak*.

When a shaman undertakes a curing rite he becomes possessed by the spirit of an animal: he "deludes" himself, so to speak, into believing that he is an animal. Consider this description (*35*):

> The seance is opened by singing and drumming. After a time the shamaness falls down very hard on the floor. In a while, the tapping of her fingers and toes is heard on the walrus skin floor. Slowly she gets up, and already she is thought to "look awful, like a dog, very scary." She crawls back and forth across the floor making growling sounds. In this state she begins to carry out the various rites which Eskimos believe will cure sickness, such as sucking the illness out of the body and blowing it into the air. Following this the shamaness falls to the floor again and the seance is over.

Compare this to the case, reported by Morton Teicher, of a Baffin Island Eskimo who believed that a fox had entered her body (*36*). This was not associated with shamanizing but was a continuous belief. She barked herself hoarse, tried to claw her husband, thought her feet were turning into fox paws, believed that the fox was moving up in her body so that she could feel its hair in her mouth, lost control of her bowels at times, and finally became so excited that she was tied up and put into a coffin-like box with an opening at the head through which she could be fed. This woman was thought to be crazy but the shamaness not. One Eskimo summarized the distinction this way: "When the shaman is healing he is out of his mind, but *he is not crazy*." Figure 1 is a picture selected by an Eskimo to illustrate the shaman's appearance during a seance *(37)*.

This suggests that seeing, hearing, and believing things that are not seen, heard, and believed by all members of the group are sometimes linked to insanity and sometimes not. The distinction appears to be the degree to which they are controlled and utilized for a specific social function. The inability to control these processes is what is meant by a mind out of order; when a mind is out of order it will not only fail to control sensory perception but will also fail to control behavior. Another

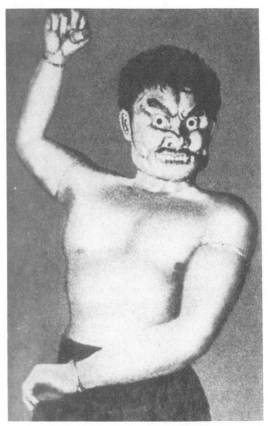

Figure 1 *The shaman during seance; "he is out of mind but not crazy."*

Eskimo who was asked to define *nuthkavihak* said that it means "the mind does not control the person, *he is crazy*." I take this to mean that volition is implicated, that hearing voices, for example, can be voluntary or involuntary, and that it is mainly the involuntary forms that are associated with *were* and *nuthkavihak*.

In cultures such as Eskimo and Yoruba, where clairvoyant kinds of mental phenomena are encouraged and preternatural experiences are valued, something similar to what we might call hallucinations and delusions can probably be learned or simulated. A favorable audience reaction is likely to stabilize the performance of the people who fill the roles of fortune-teller and faith healer. For example, the shamaness described above was unable to keep her patient alive but her performance was considered to have been well executed; she was said to have done "all her *part, acting* like a dog." The Eskimos believe that a person can learn to be a shaman. Their view of *nuthkavihak* is something that befalls the person, a pattern of behavioral processes that can appear and disappear, lasting a long time with some people and a short time with others.

A number of researchers in the field of cross-cultural psychiatry take the position that the underlying processes of insanity are the same everywhere but that their specific content varies between cultural groups *(38)*. A psychotic person, it is thought, could not make use of the imagery of Christ if he had not been exposed to the Christian tradition and he could not elaborate ideas about the *wittiko* cannibalistic monster if not exposed to Cree and Ojibwa Indian traditions *(39)*. It would seem that if a culture-specific stereotype of the content of psychosis exists in a group it might have the kind of influence suggested in labeling theory. If the content stereotype were applied to the unstructured delusions of a psychotic his thought productions might be shaped and stabilized around the theme of that stereotype.

There have been several attempts to study phenomena such as *wittiko* and *pibloktoq*, the former being thought of as the culturally defined content of a psychotic process in which the person believes himself to be a cannibalistic monster and the latter as a culture-specific form of hysteria found in the arctic *(40,* p. 218; *41)*. The evidence of their existence comes from early ethnographies. It has been difficult in the contemporary period to locate people who have these illnesses *(42)*. If the availability of a content stereotype has the effect one would expect from labeling theory, the stereotype should have sustained the pattern, but in fact these content patterns seem to have disappeared.

Prominent in the descriptions of the images and behavior of people labeled *were* and *nuthkavihak* were cultural beliefs and practices as well as features of the natural environment. Eskimo ideation concerned arctic animals and Eskimo people, objects, and spirits. The Yoruba ideation was based on tropical animals and Yoruba figures. The cultural variation was, in other words, general. There was no evidence that if a person were to become *were* or *nuthkavihak* he would reveal one specific delusion based on cultural mythology. In this regard I reach the same conclusion as Roger Brown did when he set out to see how far labeling ideas would aid his understanding of hospitalized schizophrenics: "Delusions are as idiosyncratic as individual schizo-phrenics or normals. . . . There seems to be nothing like a standard set of heresies, but only endless variety" (*15*, p. 397).

The answer to the first specific question, whether Es-kimos and Yorubas have labels for psychological and behavioral differences resembling what we call mental illness, is to my mind a definite yes. The expanding ethnographic literature on this topic indicates that most other non-Western groups also have such labels [in addi-tion to the papers already cited see (*43*)]. From this broad perspective it appears that (i) phenomenal proc-esses of disturbed thought and behavior similar to schizophrenia are found in most cultures; (ii) they are sufficiently distinctive and noticeable that almost everywhere a name has been created for them; (iii) over and above similarity in processes, there is variability in content which in a general way is colored by culture; and (iv) the role of social fictions in perceiving and defining the phenomena seems to have been very slight.

Unlabeled Behavior Patterns

The questions of this section are: Do phenomena labeled mental illness by us go unlabeled elsewhere, and if so what are the consequences? Are there natural exper-iments of culture which allow us to gain some un-derstanding of the effects of not labeling? From the lin-guistic relativist's viewpoint, if phenomena are not named they are screened out of the perception of the people who speak that language; thus not only would mental illness go unrecognized if unlabeled but also the negative effects of labeling could not pertain.

Although one cannot speak of mental illness without reference to insanity and psychoses, most people in our culture mean more by the term and include some or all of the phenomena described in a textbook of psychiatry. Elsewhere I have presented data about Eskimo and Yoruba terms, lack of terms, and levels of generalization for mental retardation, convulsions, and senility (*30, 44*). According to the healers with whom I worked, the Yorubas have no word for senility but they recognize that some old people become incapable of taking care of

themselves, talk to themselves, are agitated, wander away and get lost. In such cases they are watched, fed, and protected in much the same way as might be done in a nursing home. The lack of an explicit label seems to make little difference in how they are treated.

In contemporary Western society psychoneurotic pat-terns are thought of as one of the main types of mental illness, yet neurosis has a minor role in the labeling theory literature (*45*). Since labeling theory is addressed to the concept of mental illness per se, one feels it ought to apply to the neurotic as well as the psychotic.

In working with the Eskimos and Yorubas I was un-able to find a word that could be translated as a general reference to neurosis or words that directly parallel our meaning of anxiety and depression. On the other hand, their words for emotional responses that we might clas-sify as manifestations of anxiety or depression constitute a very large vocabulary. The Yoruba lexicon includes, for example, words for unrest of mind which prevents sleep, being terrified at night, extreme bashfulness which is like a sense of shame, fear of being among people, tenseness, and overeagerness. The Eskimo terms are translated as worrying too much until it makes the person sick, too easy to get afraid, crying with sadness, head down and rocking back and forth, shaking and trembling all over, afraid to stay indoors, and so on. The point is that neither group had a single word or explicit label that lumped these phenomena together as constitut-ing a general class of illness by virtue of their underlying similarities or as a pattern in which several components are usually found in association (*46*). In the terms of this article, these symptoms are unlabeled but they do exist. People recognize them and try to do something about them. Some of them are conceived as severely disabling and cause people to give up aspects of their work (such as being captain of a hunting boat); others appear to be less serious. Some of them are transient; others are life-long characteristics.

Of special significance to the problem at hand is the fact that most of these emotional phenomena are defi-nitely thought of as illnesses for which the shaman and witch doctor have effective cures. The number of people who exhibit these phenomena is considerably in excess of those labeled *were* and *nuthkavihak*. Among the Yorubas the ratio is approximately 12 to 1 and among the Eskimos 14 to 1. In the clientele of a typical shaman or healer a large proportion would be people who came with symptoms such as "unrest of mind that prevents sleep" or "shaking and trembling all the time."

The answer to the question whether phenomena we label mental illness go unlabeled elsewhere is thus also yes. These Eskimos and Yorubas point out a large number of psychological and behavioral phenomena which we would call neuroses but which they do not put together under such a rubric. The consequence is not, however, a reduction in the number of persons who display the phenomena or great difference in how they are treated. The fact that these peoples cannot categorically define someone as "a neurotic" or that the Yorubas do not talk about "a senile" appears mainly to be a classification difference, and I am led to conclude that the phenomena exist independently of labels.

Evaluation of Behavior Patterns

Do non-Western groups evaluate the labeled behaviors of mental illness negatively or positively? Are they more tolerant of deviance than we are? I shall consider first the related institutional values of the culture, its roles and ceremonies, and then the noninstitutionalized actions and attitudes toward the mentally ill.

As pointed out earlier, it has been proposed that the shaman role is a social niche in which psychopathology is socially useful and that therefore mental disorder is positively valued. Since the Eskimos do not believe the shaman is *nuthkavihak*, it cannot be insanity that invests the role with prestige in their eyes. It could be, however, that some other form of mental illness, possibly a neurotic disorder like hysteria, is considered essential to what a shaman does and therefore is accorded the same respect that the role as a whole commands.

Among the 499 Eskimos 18 had shamanized at some time in their lives. None was thought to be *nuthkavihak*. No other personality characteristic or emotional response was given as typical of all of them, and in these regards the shaman seemed to be a random sample of the whole. The only feature I was able to determine as common to the group was that they shamanized, and they did that with variable success.

The Yoruba healer has not been described in the literature as a mentally ill person, though some of the Yoruba healing cults consist of individuals who have been cured and thereafter participate in curing others. The healers known to me and my conversations with Yorubas about their healers gave no evidence that mental illness was a requisite. Thus as far as the groups reported here are concerned, mental illness does not appear to be venerated in these roles. If the shaman is to be considered either psychotic or hysterical it seems to require that a Western definition be given to the portion of behavior specific to shamanizing.

If not institutionalized in an esteemed role, is mental illness institutionalized in a contemptible role? Both the Yorubas and the Eskimos have a clearly defined role of witch as the human purveyor of magically evil influences. Though feared, the man or woman who is be-

lieved to use magic in this way is held in low esteem.

Is insanity or other mental illness prima facie evidence that a person is a witch? If one tries to answer this by identifying the people labeled *were* or *nuthkavihak* and then the people labeled witches and comparing the two groups to see how much they overlap in membership, as I did regarding the shamans, a serious problem arises. The difficulty is in identifying the witches. Unlike shamanizing, which is a public act, the use of evil magic is exceedingly secretive. I did note, however, that there was no correspondence between the group of Eskimos said to have been insane at some point in their lives and the six people named as *auvinak* (witch) by at least one Eskimo.

In the more generalized information from the Yoruba healers it was evident that insanity was often believed to result from the use of evil magic but an insane person was rarely believed to use it against others. Thus my interpretation of whether mental illness is built into the role of witch is similar to the view presented about the role of healer. Some insane people have probably been accused of being witches, but it has been by happenstance, not because witching and insanity are considered to be the same thing and equally stigmatized.

In these regards the Eskimos and Yorubas seem to have much in common with the Zapotecs studied by Henry Selby (*47,* pp. 41–42). His work focuses on witchcraft as a major form of social deviance, and he interprets his information as supporting labeling ideas (*48*), especially the vulnerability of outsiders to labeling. He found that accusations of witchcraft are more likely to be leveled at someone outside the immediate group of kin and neighbors than at a group member. However, after "talking about deviance for months" with his Zapotec informants, Selby realized that he had no information on mental illness. He explored this topic separately and "found out that there were people who were 'crazy' " and that the condition was defined as having "something to do with the soul and was symptomized by agitated motor behavior, ataraxia, violent purposeless movement, and the inability to talk in ways that people could readily understand." Clearly, the Zapotecs have a conception of insanity, and like Eskimos and Yorubas, they do not classify it in the same frame of reference with such norm transgressions as witching, envy, stinginess, and adultery.

Another way in which a culture might institutionalize a negative view of mental illness is through a degradation ceremony or ritual slaying, as in the case of the Melanesian social *mate*. Ceremony is a preservative of custom, and there is voluminous information on ceremonies for healing, ceremonies for effecting fertility of land, animals, and humans, and rites of passage, as well as ceremonies in which various forms of human sacrifice are carried out.

In view of the wide elaboration of customs whereby groups of people enact their negative and positive values, it is perhaps surprising that no groups seem to have developed the idea of ceremonially killing an insane person in the prime of life just because he is insane. Infanticide has sometimes been conducted when a child was born grossly abnormal in a way which might later have emerged as brain damage, and senility may have been a contributing factor in live burials. Also there is no doubt that insane people have sometimes been done away with, but that is different from ritual sacrifice. There is no evidence as far as I can determine that killing the insane has ever been standardized as a custom. There are, on the other hand, numerous indications from non-Western data that the cermony appropriate for people labeled mentally deranged is the ceremony of healing (*34, 36, 38, 43*). Even the word ''lunatic'' associates the phenomena with healing, since it was usually the healer who was believed to have power over such cosmic forces as the lunar changes which were thought to cause insanity.

Regarding informal behavior and attitudes toward the mentally ill it is difficult to draw conclusions, because there is evidence of a wide range of behaviors that can be conceptualized as audience reactions. Insane people have been the objects of certain restrictive measures among both the Eskimos and the Yorubas. The Eskimos physically restrain insane people in violent phases, follow them around, and force them to return home if they run away; and there is one report of an insane man's being killed in self-defense when, after killing several dogs, he turned on his family. In describing the Chukchee, a Siberian group known to these Bering Strait Eskimos, Waldemar Bogoras reports the case of an insane woman who was tied to a pole during periods of wildness (*49*). Teicher describes, in addition to the coffin-like box mentioned earlier, the use of an igloo with bars across the opening through which food could be passed (*36*). This is again similar to Selby's observations of Zapotecs who barred the door of a bamboo hut as a way of restraining a psychotic man (*47*).

The Yoruba healer of *were* often has 12 to 15 patients in custody at one time. Not infrequently he shackles those who are inclined to run off, and he may use various herbal concoctions for sedation. In Nigeria, where population is much denser than in the arctic, it was not uncommon to see *were* people wandering about the city streets, sometimes naked, more often dressed in odd assortments of tattered clothing, almost always with long, dirt-laden hair, talking to themselves, picking up objects to save. In studying a group of such vagrant psychotics, Tolani Asuni noted that they usually stayed in one locale, that people fed them generously, allowed them to sleep in the market stalls, teased them mildly or laughed at them for minor deviations, and took action to control them only if the psychotics became violent (*50*).

A case I encountered in Gambia illustrates the complexities of the situation and indicates that compassion and rejection are sometimes both engaged. The case is of a man, identified as insane, who lived some 500 yards outside a village. The villagers lived in thatched mud houses. The madman lived on an abandoned anthill. It was about 2.5 meters long and 1.5 meters high and the top had been worn away to match the contours of his body (Figure 2). Except for occasional visits to the village, he remained on this platform through day and night and changing weather. His behavior was said to have become odd when he was a young man, and when I saw him he had not spoken for years, although he sometimes made grunting sounds. In one sense he was as secluded and alienated from his society as patients in back wards are in ours. On the other hand, the villagers always put food out for him and gave him cigarettes. The latter act was accompanied by laughter, because the insane man had a characteristic way of bouncing several leaps into the air to get away from anyone who came close to him, and that was considered amusing. Once a year someone would forceably bathe him and put new clothes on him.

If one defines intolerance of mental illness as the use of confinement, restraint, or exclusion from the commuity (or allowing people to confine or exclude themselves), there does not appear to be a great deal of difference between Western and non-Western groups in intolerance of the mentally ill. Furthermore, there seems to be little that is distinctively cultural in the attitudes and actions directed toward the mentally ill, except in such matters as that an abandoned anthill could not be used as an asylum in the arctic or a barred igloo in the tropics. There is apparently a common range of possible responses to the mentally ill person, and the portion of the range brought to bear regarding a particular person is determined more by the nature of his behavior than by a preexisting cultural set to respond in a uniform way to whatever is labeled mental illness. If the behavior indicates helplessness, help tends to be given, especially in food and clothes. If the behavior appears foolish or incongruous (in the light of the distinctive Eskimo and Yoruba views of what is humorous), laughter is the response. If the behavior is noisy and agitated, the response may be to try to quiet, sometimes by herbs and sometimes by other means. If the behavior is violent or threatening, the response is to restrain or subdue.

The answer to the question posed at the beginning of

Figure 2. *A man living on an abandoned anthill; "he is out of mind and crazy."*

this section seems to be that the patterns these groups label mental illness (*were* or *nuthkavihak*) are not evaluated in either a starkly positive or starkly negative way. The flavor and variability of the audience reactions to mental illness suggest the word "ambivalence." Two recent studies in the United States also indicate that stigma is not automatically and universally applied to mental illness and that complex responses are typical in our society as well (*51*).

Norm Violations

If these Eskimos and Yorubas are ambivalent about mental illness, do they strongly condemn any behaviors at all? Both groups have words for theft, cheating, lying, stinginess, drunkenness, and a large number of other behaviors which they consider to be specific acts of bad conduct. These, like the practice of witchcraft, are thought of as transgressions against social standards and are negatively sanctioned.

In addition, the Eskimos have a word, *kunlangeta*, which means "his mind knows what to do but he does not do it." This is an abstract term for the breaking of many rules when awareness of the rules is not in question. It might be applied to a man who, for example, repeatedly lies and cheats and steals things and does not go hunting and, when other men are out of the village, takes sexual advantage of many women—someone who does not pay attention to reprimands and who is always being brought to the elders for punishment. One Eskimo among the 499 was called *kunlangeta*. When asked what would have happened to such a person traditionally, an Eskimo said that probably "somebody would have pushed him off the ice when nobody else was looking." This suggests that permissiveness has a limit even in a cultural group which in some respects, such as attitude toward heterosexual activity, is very lenient. The Yorubas have a similarly abstract word, *arankan*, which means a person who always goes his own way regardless of others, who is uncooperative, full of malice, and bullheaded.

There are parallels between *kunlangeta* and *arankan* and our concept "psychopath"—someone who consistently violates the norms of society in multiple ways. Also, some of the specific acts of wrongdoing which Eskimos and Yorubas recognize might in our society be called evidence of "personality disorders." In Western psychiatry, this term refers to sexual deviations, excessive use of drugs or alcohol, and a variety of behaviors that primarily cause trouble for other people rather than for the doer.

It is of considerable interest that *kunlangeta* and *arankan* are not behaviors that the shamans and healers are

believed to be able to cure or change. As a matter of fact, when I pressed this point with the Yoruba healers they specifically denied that these patterns are illness. Both groups, however, believe that specific acts of wrongdoing may make an individual vulnerable to illness or other misfortune. For example, Eskimos hold to a hunting ethic which prescribes ownership and sharing of animals; cheating in reference to the hunting code is thought of as a potential cause of physical or mental illness. The social codes among the Yorubas are somewhat different, but they also believe that breaking taboos can cause illness. It has been recognized by anthropologists for nearly half a century that among peoples who believe in magic there is remarkable similarity in the explanations of illness, and that transgression as well as witchcraft ranks high in the accepted etiology of many non-Western groups (*52*). Believing that transgression causes illness is nevertheless quite different from believing that transgression *is* illness.

Thus the answer to the question of this section appears to be that these groups do have strong negative sanction for a number of behaviors. A difference between their opinions and those embodied in Western psychiatry is that the Eskimos and Yorubas do not consider these transgressions symptomatic of illness or responsive to the techniques used for healing.

Prevalence

Is the net effect of a non-Western way of life such that fewer people suffer from something they label mental illness than is the case in the West? In view of the focus on *were* and *nuthkavihak*, attention will mainly be directed to this pattern of behavior and it will be compared with schizophrenia.

There are available now a number of epidemiological studies of mental illness in different countries and cultures. Warren Dunham has compared prevalence rates for schizophrenia from 19 surveys in Europe, Asia, and North America; Table 1 is adapted from tables he presents (*53*). Like several others who have studied these figures, Dunham concludes that the prevalence rates "are quite comparable" despite the fact that some are based on hospital data and some on population surveys, despite differences in definitions and methods, and despite the cultural variation involved.

The rates of *were* and *nuthkavihak* can be compared to rates of schizophrenia in two Western surveys, one in Sweden and one in Canada. The Swedish study was carried out by Erik Essen-Möller and colleagues in two rural parishes for which a population register existed. Each member of the population was interviewed by a psychiatrist. A prevalence rate of schizophrenia is re-

TABLE 1.

Compilation of prevalence rates for schizophrenia, from Dunham (53).

Investigator	Date	Place	Population	CASES No.	CASES Rate per 1000
Brugger	1929	Thuringia, Germany	37,546	71	1.9
Brugger	1930–31	Bavaria, Germany	8,628	22	2.5
Stromgren	1935	Bornholm, Denmark	45,930	150	3.3
Kaila	1936	Finland	418,472	1,798	4.2
Bremer	1939–44	Northern Norway	1,325	6	4.5
Sjogren	1944	Western Sweden	8,736	40	4.6
Böök	1946–49	Northern Sweden	8,931	85	9.6
Fremming	1947	Denmark	5,500	50	9.0
Essen-Möller	1947	Rural Sweden	2,550	17	6.6
Mayer-Gross	1948	Rural Scotland	56,000	235	4.2
Uchimura	1940	Hachizo, Japan	8,330	32	3.8
Tsugawa	1941	Tokyo, Japan	2,712	6	2.2
Akimoto	1941	Komoro, Japan	5,207	11	2.1
Lin	1946–48	Formosa, China	19,931	43*	2.1
Cohen and Fairbank	1933	Baltimore, U.S.	56,044	127	2.3
Lemkau	1936	Baltimore, U.S.	57,002	158	2.9
Roth and Luton	1938–40	Rural Tennessee, U.S.	24,804	47	1.9
Hollingshead and Redlich	1950	New Haven, U.S.	236,940	845†	3.6
Eaton and Weil	1951	Hutterites, U.S.	8,542	9*	1.0

*Inactive as well as active cases.
†Cases treated six months or more.

ported, with figures for cases in the community and cases in a hospital during a specific year (54). This design is similar to the one I used among the Eskimos, where a census register provided the base for determining the population, and each person was systematically described by at least one other Eskimo. Focusing on the people living in the specified year reduces the Eskimo population studied from 499 to 348.

The Canadian study, in which I was one of the investigators, was based on a probability sample of adults in a rural county (55). We designed the Yoruba study to explore the possibilities of comparing mental illness rates, and so used similar sampling procedures. The rates in these two surveys are based on compilations of interview data with selected respondents as well as systematic interviews about those respondents with local physicians in Canada and local village headmen in Nigeria.

The results of comparing these studies is that the proportion of people who exhibited or had at some time exhibited the pattern of behavior called schizophrenia, *were* or *nuthkavihak* appears to be much the same from

group to group (Table 2). At the time these studies were carried out, mental hospitals existed all over the world. The Canadian and Swedish populations are similar to the United States in having a sizable number of large mental hospitals. The Eskimo population was considered to be in the catchment area served by a mental hospital in the United States, and the Yoruba villages were in the vicinity of two mental hospitals (56). For the Canadian and Yoruba studies we do not know the number of people who might otherwise have been in the communities but were hospitalized during the period when prevalence was surveyed. The Swedish and Eskimo studies, by virtue of starting with census registers, provide information on this point. The age-adjusted prevalence rate in the Swedish survey is 8.1 per 1000 when hospitalized schizophrenics are included and the Eskimo rate of *nuthkavihak* is increased to 8.8 when the one hospitalized case is added.

The number of schizophrenics, *were* and *nuthkavihak* in a population is small, but this comparison suggests that the rates are similar. With a broader definition of mental illness which I have explained elsewhere (it in-

TABLE 2.

Rates of nonhospitalized schizophrenia in two Western samples and of indigenously defined insanity in two non-Western samples. Rates are per 1000 population after adjustment by the Weinberg method (58).

			CASES	
Group	Date	Size	No.	Rate per 1000
Swedish	1948	2550	12	5.7
Eskimo	1954	348	1	4.4
Canadian	1952	1071	7	5.6
Yoruba	1961	245	2	6.8

cludes the neurotic-appearing symptoms, the senile patterns, and so on) the total prevalence rates for the three groups I have studied are: Canadian, 18 percent; Eskimo, 19 percent; and Yoruba, 15 percent (57).

The answer to the last question above seems thus to be that the non-Western way of life does not offer protection against mental illness to the point of making a marked difference in frequency. The rates of mental illness patterns I have discussed are much more striking for similarity from culture to culture than for difference. This suggests that the causes of mental illness, whether genetic or experiential, are ubiquitous in human groups.

Summary and Conclusions

Labeling theory proposes that the concept of mental illness is a cultural stereotype referring to a residue of deviance which each society arbitrarily defines in a distinct way. It has been assumed that information from cultures that are markedly different from Western society supports the theory. This paper presents systematic data from Eskimo and Yoruba groups, and information from several other cultural areas, which instead call the theory into question.

Explicit labels for insanity exist in these cultures. The labels refer to beliefs, feelings, and actions that are thought to emanate from the mind or inner state of an individual and to be essentially beyond his control; the afflicted persons seek the aid of healers; the afflictions bear strong resemblance to what we call schizophrenia. Of signal importance is the fact that the labels of insanity refer not to single specific attributes but to a pattern of several interlinked phenomena. Almost everywhere a pattern composed of hallucinations, delusions, disorien-

tations, and behavioral aberrations, appears to identify the idea of "losing one's mind," even though the content of these manifestations is colored by cultural beliefs.

The absence of a single label among Eskimos and Yorubas for some of the phenomena we call mental illness, such as neuroses, does not mean that manifestations of such phenomena are absent. In fact they form a major part of what the shamans and healers are called upon to treat. Eskimos and Yorubas react to people they define as mentally ill with a complex of responses involving first of all the use of healing procedures but including an ambivalent-appearing mixture of care giving and social control. These reactions are not greatly dissimilar from those that occur in Western society. Nor does the amount of mental illness seem to vary greatly within or across the division of Western and non-Western areas. Patterns such as schizophrenia, *were*, and *nuthkavihak* appear to be relatively rare in any one human group but are broadly distributed among human groups. Rather than being simply violations of the social norms of particular groups, as labeling theory suggests, symptoms of mental illness are manifestations of a type of affliction shared by virtually all mankind.

REFERENCES AND NOTES

1. H. S. Becker, *Outsiders* (Free Press, New York, 1963), reprinted in 1973 with a new chapter, "Labeling theory reconsidered."
2. T. S. Szasz, *The Myth of Mental Illness: Foundations of a Theory of Personal Conduct* Hoeber-Harper, New York, 1961); R. Laing and A. Esterson, *Sanity, Madness, and the Family* (Basic Books, New York, 1964).
3. Notably in E. Lemert's distinction between primary and secondary deviance, which appeared initially in his book *Social Pathology* (McGraw-Hill, New York, 1951).
4. "In California, labeling theory itself contributed to the formulation of the Lanterman-Petris-Short act, a law which makes it difficult to commit patients to mental hospitals, and still more difficult to keep them there for long periods of time" (5, p. 256).
5. T. Scheff, *Am. Sociol Rev.* **40**, 252 (1975).
6. D. Rosenhan, *Science,* **179**, 250 (1973).
7. R. Benedict, *J. Gen. Psychol.*, **10**, 59 (1934).
8. I. Schur, *Labeling Deviant Behavior: Its Sociological Implications* (Harper & Row, New York, 1971).
9. E. Lemert, *Human Deviance, Social Problems and Social Control* (Prentice-Hall, Englewood Cliffs, N.J., 1967).
10. R. Scott, *The Making of Blind Men* (Russell Sage Foundation, New York, 1969).
11. T. Scheff, *Being Mentally Ill: A Sociological Theory* (Aldine, Chicago, 1966).
12. W. Gove, *Am. Sociol. Rev.* **35**, 873 (1970).

13. ———— and P. Howell, *ibid.* **39,** 86 (1974); W. Gove, *ibid.* **40,** 242 (1975); R. Chauncey, *ibid.* 248; T. Scheff (*5, 14*). In addition to the Rosenhan study (*6*), Scheff (*24*) evaluates the following six investigations as strongly supporting labeling: J. Greenley, *J. Health Soc. Behav.* **13,** 25 (1972); A. Linsky, *Soc. Psychiatr.* **5,** 166 (1970); W. Rushing, *Am. J. Sociol.* **77,** 511 (1971); M. Temerlin, *J. Nerv. Ment. Dis.* **147,** 349 (1968); W. Wilde, *J. Health Soc. Behav.* **9,** 215 (1968); D. Wenger and C. Fletcher, *ibid.* **10,** 66 (1969). For several articles unfavorable to labeling theory see W. Gove, Ed.. *The Labelling of Deviance, Evaluating a Perspective* (Wiley, New York, 1975). Also not favorable are R. Brown (15; N. Davis, *Sociol. Q.* **13,** 447 (1972); J. Gibbs, in *Theoretical Perspectives on Deviance,* R. Scott and J. Douglas, Eds. (Basic Books, New York, 1972), p. 39; S. Kety, *Am. J. Psychiatr.* **131,** 957 (1974); R. Spitzer, *J. Abnorm. Psychol.* **84,** 442 (1975); D. Ausubel, *Am. Psychol.* **16,** 69 (1961).

14. T. Scheff, *Am. Sociol. Rev.* **39,** 444 (1974).

15. R. Brown, *Am. Psychol.* **28,** 395 (1973).

16. R. Benedict, *Patterns of Culture* (Houghton Mifflin, Boston, 1934); M. Mead, *Sex and Temperament in Three Primitive Societies* (Morrow, New York, 1935); *Male and Female* (Morrow, New York, 1949).

17. W. Caudill, in *Transcultural Research in Mental Health,* W. Lebra, Ed. (Univ. Press of Hawaii, Honolulu, 1972), p. 25; R. Edgerton, in *Changing Perspectives in Mental Illness,* S. Plog and R. Edgerton, Eds. (Holt, Rinehart & Winston, New York, 1969), p. 49; R. Levine, *Culture, Personality and Behavior* (Aldine, Chicago, 1973); M. Field, *Search for Security: An Ethnopsychiatric Study of Rural Ghana* (Northwestern Univ. Press, Chicago, 1960); A. Wallace, *Culture and Personality* (Random House, New York, 1970); B. Whiting and J. Whiting, *Children of Six Cultures* (Harvard Univ. Press, Cambridge, Mass, 1975).

18. J. Honigmann, *Personality in Culture* (Harper & Row, New York, 1967).

19. R. Edgerton, *The Cloak of Competence* (Univ. of California Press, Berkeley, 1967); J. Mercer, *Labeling the Mentally Retarded* (Univ. of California Press, Berkeley, 1973).

20. R. Jessor, T. Graves, R. Hanson, S. Jessor, *Society, Personality and Deviant Behavior* (Holt, Rinehart & Winston, New York, 1968); J. Levy and S. Kunitz, *Indian Drinking* (Wiley, New York, 1974); H. Mulford, in *The Mental Patient: Studies in the Sociology of Deviance,* S. Spitzer and N. Denzin, Eds. (McGraw-Hill, New York, 1968), p. 155; D. Pittman and C. Snyder, *Society, Culture and Drinking Patterns* (Wiley, New York, 1962).

21. S. Spitzer and N. Denzin, Eds., *The Mental Patient: Studies in the Sociology of Deviance* (McGraw-Hill, New York, 1968).

22. C. Fletcher and I. Reynolds, *Sociol. Focus* **1,** 9 (1968).

23. E. Goffman, *Asylums: Essays on the Social Situation of Mental Patients and Other Inmates* (Aldine, Chicago, 1962), p. 132.

24. I. Sarbin, in *Changing Perspectives in Mental Illness,* S. Plog and R. Edgerton, Eds. (Holt, Rinehart & Winston, New York, 1969), pp. 11, 15, 19.

25. D. Mechanic, *Ment. Hyg.* **46,** 68 (1962).

26. G. Devereux, in *Some Uses of Anthropology: Theoretical and Applied,* J. Casagrande and T. Gladwin, Eds. (Anthropological Society of Washington, Washington, D.C., 1956), p. 23; A. Kroeber, *The Nature of Culture* (Univ. of Chicago Press, Chicago, 1952), pp. 310−319; R. Linton, *Culture and Mental Disorders* (Thomas, Springfield, Ill., 1956), pp. 98, 118−124; J. Silverman, *Am. Anthropol.* **69** (No. 1), 21 (1967).

27. W. Rivers, *Psychology and Ethnology* (Harcourt Brace, New York, 1926), pp. 38−50.

28. B. Whorf, *Language, Thought and Reality* (Technological Press of MIT, Cambridge, Mass., 1956).

29. J. Hughes [Murphy], thesis. Cornell University (1960). The recording of Eskimo words was conducted by Charles C. Hughes. The spelling given here follows the principles used in C. Hughes (with the collaboration of J. Murphy), *An Eskimo Village in the Modern World* (Cornell Univ. Press, Ithaca, N.Y., 1960). The census of 1940 which served as a baseline was prepared by Alexander Leighton and Dorthea Leighton. The extended statements by Eskimos and Yorubas which appear in quotation marks in the text are taken from my unpublished field notes, 1954−55, 1961, 1963. Most of the Eskimo and Yoruba phrases are also taken directly from these sources. In a few instances I have needed to paraphrase for intelligibility and therefore I have not used quotation marks for phrases.

30. A. Leighton and J. Murphy, in *Comparability in International Epidemiology.* R. Acheson, Ed. (Milbank Memorial Fund, New York, 1965), p. 189.

31. A. Leighton, T. Lambo, C. Hughes, D. Leighton, J. Murphy, D. Macklin, *Psychiatric Disorder among the Yoruba* (Cornell Univ. Press, Ithaca, N.Y., 1963).

32. J. Douglas, *The Social Meanings of Suicide* (Princeton Univ. Press, Princeton, N.J., 1967).

33. Prince found that *were* was defined for him in terms almost identical to those I present here; he studied 46 *were* specialists (*34,* p. 84).

34. R. Prince, in *Magic, Faith, and Healing.* A. Kiev, Ed. (Free Press of Glencoe, New York, 1964).

35. J. Murphy, in *Magic, Faith, and Healing.* A. Kiev, Ed. (Free Press of Glencoe, New York, 1964), p. 53.

36. M. Teicher, *J. Ment. Sci.* **100,** 527 (1954).

37. In looking through a magazine with me, an Eskimo pointed to a picture and said that it resembled the shaman in seance: Fig. 1 is a photograph of that picture retouched to eliminate garments which the Eskimo said were irrelevant to the similarity.

38. A. deReuck and R. Porter, Eds., *Ciba Foundation Symposium: Transcultural Psychiatry* (Churchill, London, 1965); A. Kiev, *Transcultural Psychiatry* (Free Press, New York, 1972).

39. S. Parker, *Am. Anthropol.* **62**, 603 (1960).

40. Z. Gussow, in *Psychoanalytic Study of Society*, W. Muensterberger, Ed. (International Univ. Press, New York, 1960), p. 218.

41. M. Teicher, *Windigo Psychosis* (American Ethnological Society, Seattle, 1960).

42. Gussow (*40*) provides a description of *pipbloktoq* based on 14 recorded cases, mainly from explorers and ethnographers in the area from Greenland to the west coast of Alaska during the first part of this century. Recently a serious attempt was made to study *pibloktoq* properly and measure its prevalence. Ten cases were located from a population of 11,000 Innuit Eskimos. These cases were found on further study to be exceedingly heterogeneous: "Several subjects had epilepsy; several were diagnosed as schizophrenic; most had low normal serum calcium levels; one had hypomagnesiumia and possible alcoholism" [F. Foulk's, *The Arctic Hysterias of the North Alaskan Eskimo* (American Anthropological Association, Washington, D.C., 1972), p. 117]. This information suggests that *pibloktoq* is and may always have been a rare and ill-defined phenomenon. Regarding *wittiko* my assessment of the evidence is similar to Honigmann's when he says, "I can't find one [case] that satisfactorily attests to someone being seriously obsessed by the idea of committing cannibalism" (*18*, p. 401).

43. M. Beiser, J. Ravel, H. Collomb, C. Egelhoff, *J. Nerv. Ment. Dis.* **155**, 77 (1972); M. Micklin, M. Durbin, C. Leon, *Am. Ethnol.* **1**, 143 (1974); H. Kitano, in *Changing Perspectives in Mental Illness*, S. Plog and R. Edgerton, Eds. (Holt, Rinehart & Winston, New York, 1969), p. 256; R. Edgerton, *Am. Anthropol*, **68**, 408 (1966); the following in *Magic, Faith, and Healing*, A. Kiev, Ed. (Free Press of Glencoe, New York, 1964); S. Fuchs, p. 121; K. Schmidt, p. 139; M. Gelfand, p. 156; B. Kaplan and D. Johnson, p. 203; M. Whisson, p. 283.

44. J. Murphy and A. Leighton, in *Approaches to Cross-Cultural Psychiatry*, J. Murphy and A. Leighton, Eds. (Cornell Univ. Press, Ithaca, N.Y., 1965), p. 64.

45. A. Rose, in *Human Behavior and Social Processes*, A. Rose, Ed. (Houghton Mifflin, Boston, 1962), p. 537.

46. Western society also lacked a comprehensive concept of neurosis prior to Freud's influence, but at the present time neurotic patterns hold a firm position in the official classifications of Western Psychiatry; see *Diagnostic and Statistical Manual of Mental Disorders* (American Psychiatric Association, Washington, D.C., 1968).

47. H. Selby, *Zapotec Deviance, The Convergence of Folk and Modern Sociology* (Univ. of Texas Press, Austin, 1974).

48. Much of the support for labeling theory which Selby finds in his evidence stems from the following statement: "To the villagers, witches have an objective reality 'out there.' To me, they do not. I, the sociologist-anthropologist, do not believe that there are people in the world who have the capacity to float foreign objects through the air, insert them into my body, and make me sick or kill me" (*47*, p. 13). He concludes, "*We* create the deviants; they are products of our minds and our social processes." It seems to me this is a mistaken conclusion. I agree that the people who use witchcraft do not actually kill their victims by their incantations, burning effigies, boiling nail parings, and so on. The question, however, is whether some people actually carry out these maliciously intended acts. My work with Eskimos and Yorubas suggests that the idea of witchcraft is widely available to these groups, just as the idea of lethal weapons is to us and that a few people in such groups really do conduct the rites that they believe will harm others (the artifacts of witchcraft attest to this), that they are genuinely deviant in these practices, and that they are the brunt of strong disapproval because of them. In this regard witchcraft involves real acts. It just happens that because these acts are by definition secret they give rise to distortions, false accusations, and misidentifications.

49. W. Bogoras, in *The Jesup North Pacific Expedition*, F. Boas, Ed. (Memoir of the American Museum of Natural History, New York, 1904−1909), p. 43.

50. T. Asuni, in *Deuxième Colloque Africain de Psychiatrie* (Association Universitaire pour le Développement de l'Enseignement et de la Culture en Afrique et à Madagascar, Paris, 1968), p. 115.

51. W. Bentz and J. Edgerton, *Soc. Psychiatr.* **6**, 29 (1971); H. Spiro, I. Siassi, G. Crocetti, *ibid.* **8**, 32 (1973).

52. F. Clements, *Primitive Concepts of Disease* (Univ. of California Publications in American Archeology and Ethnology, Berkeley, 1932).

53. W. Dunham, *Community and Schizophrenia, An Epidemiological Analysis* (Wayne State Univ. Press, Detroit, 1965), pp. 18, 19. Dunham indicates that 21 cases of schizophrenia were discovered in the Essen-Möller study. I use 17 of these (those for whom the author had high confidence that the pattern was schizophrenia). For comparability between Tables 1 and 2, I recalculated the rate for this one study. See also T. Lin, *Psychiatry* **16**, 313 (1953), for a similar use and interpretation of several of the studies cited here.

54. E. Essen-Möller, *Individual Traits and Morbidity in a Swedish Rural Population* (Ejnar Munksgaard, Copenhagen, 1956). The rates for schizophrenia in the community and in the hospital were calculated from information on pp. 85, 86.

55. A. Leighton, *My Name is Legion* (Basic Books, New York,

1959); D. Leighton, J. Harding, D. Macklin, A. Macmillan, A. Leighton, *The Character of Danger* (Basic Books, New York, 1963).

56. T. Lambo, in *Magic, Faith, and Healing,* A. Kiev, Ed. (Free Press of Glencoe, New York, 1964), p. 443; T. Asuni, *Am. J. Psychiatry* **124**, 763 (1967).

57. J. Murphy, in *Transcultural Research in Mental Health,* W. Lebra, Ed. (Univ. Press of Hawaii, Honolulu, 1972), p. 213.

58. W. Weinberg, *Arch. Rassen, Gesellschaftsbiol.* **11**, 434 (1915). The Weinberg method of adjusting the rate of mental illness for the probable age period of susceptibility is useful when the age distributions of the populations compared are different. Comparison of Western and non-Western populations particularly need such adjustment. The age of susceptibility for schizophrenia is assumed by Weinberg to be 16 to 40 years. I used 20 to 40 years because that age breakdown is available in the four studies compared.

59. The Eskimo and Yoruba studies which form the core of this paper, and the Canadian study used for comparison, have been carried on as part of the Harvard Program in Social Psychiatry directed by Alexander H. Leighton and supported by funds from the Social Science Research Center of Cornell (for the Eskimo studies), the National Institute of Mental Health, the Ministry of Health of Nigeria, and the Social Science Research Council (for the Yoruba studies), the Carnegie Corporation of New York, the Department of National Health and Welfare of Canada, the Department of Public Health of the Province of Nova Scotia, the Ford Foundation, and the Milbank Memorial Fund.

C

Epidemiological Perspectives and Issues

Social epidemiology is a methodology for exploring macrostructural aspects of mental illness and not an explicit theory of the social organization and production of madness. In recent years, epidemiologists have emphasized the importance of socially created stress as an explanatory mechanism. Thus, differences in rates of mental disorder among social groups are accounted for by the greater stress experienced by one or another group and the lack of resources available to cope with the stress. This is not a novel way of accounting for madness. It has a venerable place both in common sense and in early attempts to explain mental illness (Plog, 1969). Nevertheless, it is an advance over earlier theoretically uninformed studies and has had payoffs both in the design and interpretation of epidemiological research.

In this section we have gathered some of the more sophisticated explorations of the relation between social structure and mental illness. The studies consider a variety of sociologically relevant and timely factors, such as socioeconomic status and gender, and deal with conditions ranging from untreated depression to diagnosed schizophrenia. Several articles are highly reflective about basic assumptions and basic practice and therefore display the epidemiological approach at its best.

Social epidemiology is the study of the distribution of an illness or pathological condition within the social structure. Social epidemiologists are concerned with both the *incidence* and *prevalence* of particular conditions among social groups and categories. In asking questions regarding the incidence of mental disorder, the epidemiologist is concerned with the rate at which new cases appear within a given time period. In focusing on the prevalence of a disorder, the epidemiologist examines the proportion of cases that exist within a population at a particular point in time. Since incidence and prevalence rates are logically independent of one another, it is possible for groups to have high incidence rates and low prevalence rates, and vice versa.

For many years the epidemiological study of mental illness was the sociological approach *par excellence.* In some measure the preeminence of the epidemiological approach derived from its demonstrated usefulness in the study of physical disease (Arthur, 1971) and from the impact of Durkheim's *Suicide.* Despite Durkheim's arguments that suicide was distinct from and varied independently of rates of "mania," this first great work of twentieth-century sociology amounted to an epidemiological study in the sociology of mental illness.

The epidemiological approach has had considerable success in discovering important and interesting relations. For example, the aggregate of epidemiological studies convincingly demonstrates that the incidence of schizophrenic disorders is highest among the lower socioeconomic classes. But facts ultimately require interpretation, and it is here that the epidemiological approach falters. Indeed, in some of its cruder expressions, the approach has raised more questions than answers. Two types of recurrent problems are of interest.

Some earlier epidemiological studies were conducted without a clearly articulated understanding of the phenomenon considered. Consequent research designs were unable to demonstrate etiological or process factors because they were constructed with little consideration of what those factors might be. The result was an intriguing relationship (schizophrenics come from the central "disorganized" zones of the city), an *ad hoc* explanation ("social isolation"), and a frustrating inability to answer obvious questions, such as whether the relation between the incidence of schizophrenia and zones of the city was a function of poorer, disorganized zones spawning more schizophrenics or of schizophrenics drifting into poorer, less organized areas of the city.

Many studies used admission to a mental hospital as an index of mental disorder. The reliance upon admissions (typically first admissions), although economically and practically attractive, introduces special problems of interpretation. For example, a strong inverse correlation between social class and diagnosed or treated mental illness may mean a greater incidence of disorder among lower socioeconomic classes *or* that disordered lower class individuals are more apt (than their upper class but equally disordered counterparts) to be hospitalized.

Contemporary epidemiological researchers are aware of these and related problems, although weaknesses in interpretation endure. As vulnerable as such studies are, they represent an important attempt to examine mental illness within the context of the social system and, consequently, they comprise a powerful argument for the importance of sociological factors in the production and organization of mental illness. Moreover, the growing sophistication of epidemiological researchers has recently yielded several sensitive theoretical and empirical examinations of the processes that mediate between social category and mental disorder.

Hollingshead and Redlich's "Social Stratification and Psychiatric Disorders" is one of the discipline's most consequential and enduring studies. Using an ambitious case-finding procedure, the authors identified New Haven residents who were psychiatric patients in late 1950. Comparison of the psychiatric population with a sample of the general population of New Haven confirmed that the diagnosed prevalence of psychiatric disorder was related to individual position in the class structure. Although the lowest socioeconomic class included 17.8 percent of New Haven's population, it contributed 36.8 percent of the psychiatric patients. The findings also revealed that type of illness and type of treatment patients received were significantly related to social class. Members of lower socioeconomic classes were more apt to be diagnosed as psychotic and less likely to receive psychotherapy than their upper class counterparts.

Hollingshead and Redlich were well aware that they were examining the relation between social class and *treated* mental illness. They were likewise aware of the equivocalities in interpretation induced by that limitation. As noted earlier, an inverse relation between class position and treated illness does not necessarily mean that those lower in the socioeconomic hierarchy are more apt to be mentally ill. It could mean, alternatively, that persons of lower class standing are more apt to be hospitalized. Determination of the relation between class and all forms of mental illness, treated and untreated, requires sampling of the general population and a procedure for assessing mental health (since one cannot validly use patienthood as the index of mental illness).

One of the most intensive efforts to carry out such a study entailed sampling the population of a vibrant section of New York City. The Mid-Town Study, as it came to be called, questioned, tested, examined, and psychiatrically evaluated over fifteen hundred individuals. One of the study's more astounding findings was that only 18 percent of the sample was free from noticeable psychiatric symptoms! Srole et al. (1977) demonstrated that the mental health of respondents (measured by an arguable index of symptoms) correlated positively with the socioeconomic status of their parents and their own status. The authors also found that downwardly mobile individuals were more apt than upwardly mobile individuals to be psychiatrically impaired.

Srole et al. examined the relation of psychiatric symptoms to many other variables and the excerpt from Langner and Michael's *Life Stress and Mental Health* furnishes a concise catalogue of the major findings. The authors conclude that socioeconomic status and, to a lesser extent, age, exhibited the most substantial and consistent relation to psychiatric impairment.

Although the relation between social class and mental disorder is virtually incontestable, interpretation of the relation is not. In "Social Class and Schizophrenia: A Critical Review and a Reformulation," Kohn attempts to fathom the meaning of over forty years of epidemiological research. His effort critically evaluates the methodological vulnerabilities and alternative interpretations of the key studies of this problem. Kohn proposes that the relation between class and schizophrenia is not the linear outcome of genetics, stress, or internal resources for coping with stress, but a function of the interaction of all three factors.

The relation between social class and schizophrenia is but one expression of economic factors that figure importantly in the social organization of mental illness. Ever since Durkheim's suggestion that economic crises can contribute to anomie in persons or populations, with presumptive effects on suicide, sociologists have appreciated the possibility that emotional and mental stability are related to aspects of the economy. Until recently, the hypothesis has had little empirical substance. In "Economic Change and Mental Hospitalization: New York State, 1910–1960," Brenner demonstrated that employment rates were significantly related to mental hospital admissions. Even more interesting was the variation in the strength of the relation for different subgroups. For example, the relation between the rate of employment and rate of hospitalization was particularly strong among the poorly educated and so by implication weaker for the better educated. Although the paper does not provide very specific information on this point, there are indications that the relation between employment and hospitalization rates may actually be reversed for the better educated, that is, the rate of hospitalization for this group may actually increase as economic conditions improve. Other evidence (Brenner, 1973) led Brenner to suggest that no single factor was responsible for the relations between the economy and mental illness.

Recently, Brenner (1977) examined the relation of unemployment to a range of "pathological indices" for the United States, Sweden, England, and Wales and for several selected areas within the United States. The data indicated that the employment rate was related not only to rate of first admissions to mental hospitals but to rates of imprisonment, homicide, suicide, mortality from cardiovascular disease, cirrhosis of the liver, and general mortality.

Many noneconomic variables, such as ethnicity, religious orientation, ecological location, and age, are also of interest to epidemiologists. In recent years gender has occupied a prominent position in epidemiological research. Are there sex differences in mental illness? Gove and Tudor (1973) observed that for a wide range of indices, including first admissions to mental hospitals, private outpatient care, and community surveys, "more women than men are mentally ill" and that the disproportionate presence of women in the psychiatric population began some time around World War II. They reasoned that the increase was due to postwar changes in the role of housewife in industrial societies that made it a less meaningful and more stressful role. In "Sex Differences and Psychiatric Disorders," Bruce P. and Barbara Snell Dohrenwend take issue with Gove and Tudor's analysis. They argue that the increase in rates of mental illness for both men and women since 1950 is a function of expanded concepts of what constitutes psychiatric disorder. They note that many of the later epidemiological studies have used measures of mental health that are more sensitive to symptoms of anxiety, depression, and physiological disturbances and are more apt "to identify persons, disproportionately female, whose neurotic problems are more private" than men's. Such ailments were less apt to be identified by first admissions to hospitals, which was the measure of mental illness often employed in earlier epidemiological studies. They do not deny that there are important sex differences in mental illness as their own review of epidemiological studies suggests that women have higher rates than men of neurosis and manic-depressive psychosis. The Dohrenwends recommend abandoning the use of an undifferentiated concept of mental illness in favor of focusing on more specific problems, such as the high rates of manic-depressive disorders among females or the high rate of so-called personality disorders among men. "The important question then becomes," write the Dohrenwends, "what is there in the endowments and experiences of men and women that pushes them in these deviant directions?"

George W. Brown and his colleagues have been carrying out a number of sophisticated and complicated analyses that partially respond to the Dohrenwends' exhortation to develop a more differentiated conception of mental illness and to examine factors that organize and produce such gender-linked disorders. In "Social Class and Psychiatric Disturbance Among Women in an Urban Population," the researchers examine factors that render women particularly vulnerable to severe psychiatric and especially depressive disturbance. They demonstrate that in the absence of severe stress the likelihood of psychiatric disorder is low and unaffected by factors such as employment or the presence of young children at home. However, when there are indications of stress, the likelihood of psychiatric disturbance is strongly affected by factors such as whether or not the individual has a job. Brown et al. also find that the higher rate of working class women's disorder is not entirely explained by the greater amount of life stress to which they are exposed. Rather, the higher rate is a product of the interaction between stress and factors, such as lack of employment, that render women vulnerable, which are common among working class women.

The significance of Brown's findings turns on leaps of interpretation that one may be reluctant to make. For example, if the factors rendering individuals vulnerable to stress are interpreted as operationalizations of resources for coping with stress, then the data are congenial to Kohn's interactional model. To be sure, there are major differences between Kohn's proposal and Brown's study (not the least of which is Kohn's concern with schizophrenia and Brown's with depression), but Brown's study is complementary to a framework that proposes that disorder is the outcome of several interacting factors, at least two of which include stress and coping resources. Brown's findings on the role of employment in mediating the effects of stress also complements the relation between unemployment and mental illness rates described by Brenner. This evidence and that of the other epidemiological studies reported in this section provide useful links between mental illness, stress, and key social and economic processes.

References

Ransom J. Arthur, *An Introduction to Social Psychiatry*, Harmondsworth, England: Penguin Books, Ltd., 1971.

M. Harvey Brenner, "Health Costs and Benefits of Economic Policy," *International Journal of Health Services*, Vol. **7,** No. 4 (1977), 581–623.

M. Harvey Brenner, *Mental Illness and the Economy*, Cambridge, Mass.: Harvard University Press, 1973.

Walter R. Gove and Jeannette F. Tudor, "Adult Sex Roles and Mental Illness," *American Journal of Sociology*, Vol. **78,** No. 4 (1973), 812–25.

Stanley C. Plog, "Urbanization, Psychological Disorders, and the Heritage of Social Psychiatry," in Stanley C. Plog and Robert B. Edgerton (eds.), *Changing Perspectives in Mental Illness*, New York: Holt, Rinehart and Winston, Inc., 1969, 288–312.

Leo Srole, Thomas S. Langner, Stanley T. Michael, Price Kirkpatrick, Marvin K. Opler, and Thomas A. C. Rennie, *Mental Health in the Metropolis*, Book Two, Revised Edition, Leo Srole and Anita K. Fisher (eds.), New York: Harper and Row, 1977.

AUGUST B. HOLLINGSHEAD • FREDERICK C. REDLICH*

Social Stratification and Psychiatric Disorders

The research reported here grew out of the work of a number of men, who, during the last half century, have demonstrated that the social environment in which individuals live is connected in some way, as yet not fully explained, to the development of mental illness.[1] Medi-

cal men have approached this problem largely from the viewpoint of epidemiology.[2] Sociologists, on the other

Reprinted from *The American Sociological Review*, 1953, Vol. 18, No. 2, pages 163–169, by permission of the authors and publisher.

* Paper read at the annual meeting of the American Sociological Society, September 3–5, 1952. The research reported here is supported by a grant from the National Institute of Mental Health of the United States Public Health Service to Yale University under the direction of Dr. F. C. Redlich, Chairman, Department of Psychiatry, and Professor August B. Hollingshead, Department of Sociology.

1. For example, see, A. J. Rosanoff, *Report of a Survey of Mental Disorders in Nassau County, New York*, New York: National Committee for Mental Hygiene, 1916; Ludwig Stern, *Kulturkreis und Form der Geistigen Erkrankung*, (Sammlung Zwanglosen Abhandlungen aus dem Gebiete der Nerven-und-Geiteskrankheiten), X, No. 2, Halle a. S:C. Marhold, 1913, pp. 1–62; J. F. Sutherland, "Geographical Distribution of Lunacy in Scotland," *British Association for Advancement of Science*, Glasgow, Sept. 1901; William A. White, "Geographical Distribution of Insanity in the United States," *Journal of Nervous and Mental Disease*, XXX (1903), pp. 257–279.

2. For example, see: Trygve Braatoy, "Is it Probable that the Sociological Situation is a Factor in Schizophrenia?" *Psychiatrica et Neurologica*, XII (1937), pp. 109–138; Donald L. Gerard and Joseph Siegel, "The Family Background of Schizophrenia," *The Psychiatric Quarterly*, 24 (January, 1950), pp. 47–73; Robert W. Hyde and Lowell V. Kingsley, "Studies in Medical Sociology, I: The Relation of Mental Disorders to the Community Socio-economic Level," *The New England Journal of Medicine*, 231, No. 16 (October 19, 1944), pp. 543–548; Robert W. Hyde and Lowell V. Kingsley, "Studies in Medical Sociology, II: The Relation of Mental Disorders to Population Density," *The New England Journal of Medicine*, 231, No. 17 (October 26, 1944), pp.

hand, have analyzed the question in terms of ecology,[3] and of social disorganization.[4] Neither psychiatrists nor sociologists have carried on extensive research into the specific question we are concerned with, namely, inter-relations between the class structure and the development of mental illness. However, a few sociologists and psychiatrists have written speculative and research papers in this area.[5]

571–577; Robert M. Hyde and Roderick M. Chisholm, "Studies in Medical Sociology, III: The Relation of Mental Disorders to Race and Nationality," *The New England Journal of Medicine,* 231, No. 18 (November 2, 1944), pp. 612–618; William Malamud and Irene Malamud, "A Socio-Psychiatric Investigation of Schizophrenia Occurring in the Armed Forces," *Psychosomatic Medicine,* 5 (October, 1943), pp. 364–375; B. Malzberg, *Social and Biological Aspects of Mental Disease,* Utica, N.Y.: State Hospital Press, 1940; William F. Roth and Frank H. Luton, "The Mental Health Program in Tennessee: Statistical Report of a Psychiatric Survey in a Rural County," *American Journal of Psychiatry,* 99 (March, 1943), pp. 662–675; J. Ruesch and Others, *Chronic Disease and Psychological Invalidism,* New York: American Society for Research in Psychosomatic Problems, 1946; J. Ruesch and others, *Duodenal Ulcer: A Socio-psychological Study of Naval Enlisted Personnel and Civilians,* Berkeley and Los Angeles: University of California Press, 1948; Jurgen Ruesch, Annemarie Jacobson, and Martin B. Loeb, "Acculturation and Illness," *Psychological Monographs: General and Applied,* Vol. 62, No. 5, Whole No. 292, 1948 (American Psychological Association, 1515 Massachusetts Ave. N.W., Washington 5, D.C.); C. Tietze, Paul Lemkau and M. Cooper, "A Survey of Statistical Studies on the Prevalence and Incidence of Mental Disorders in Sample Populations," *Public Health Reports,* 1909–27, 58 (December 31, 1943); C. Tietze, P. Lemkau and Marcia Cooper, "Schizophrenia, Manic Depressive Psychosis and Social-Economic Status," *American Journal of Sociology,* XLVII (September, 1941), pp. 167–175.

3. Robert E. L. Faris and H. Warren Dunham, *Mental Disorders in Urban Areas,* Chicago: University of Chicago Press, 1939; H. Warren Dunham, "Current Status of Ecological Research in Mental Disorder," *Social Forces,* 25 (March, 1947), pp. 321–326; R. H. Felix and R. V. Bowers, "Mental Hygiene and Socio-Environmental Factors," *The Milbank Memorial Fund Quarterly,* XXVI (April, 1948), pp. 125–147; H. W. Green, *Persons Admitted to the Cleveland State Hospital,* 1928–1937, Cleveland Health Council, 1939.

4. R. E. L. Faris, "Cultural Isolation and the Schizophrenic Personality," *American Journal of Sociology,* XXXIX (September, 1934), pp. 155–169; R. E. L. Faris, "Reflections of Social Disorganization in the Behavior of a Schizophrenic Patient," *American Journal of Sociology,* L (September, 1944), pp. 134–141.

5. For example, see: Robert E. Clark, "Psychoses, Income, and Occupational Prestige," *American Journal of Sociology,* 44 (March, 1949), pp. 433–440; Robert E. Clark, "The Relationship of Schizophrenia to Occupational Income and Occupational Prestige," *American Sociological Review,* 13 (June, 1948), pp. 325–330; Kingsley Davis, "Mental Hygiene and the Class Structure," *Psychiatry,* I (February, 1938), pp. 55–56; Talcott Parsons, "Psychoanalysis and the Social Structure," *The Psychoanalytical Quarterly,* XIX, No. 3 (1950), pp. 371–384; John Dollard and Neal Miller, *Personality and Psychotherapy,* New York: McGraw-Hill, 1950; Jurgen Ruesch, "Social Technique, Social Status, and Social Change in Illness," Clyde Kluckhohn and Henry A. Murray (editors), in *Personality in Nature, Society, and Culture,* New York: Alfred A. Knopf, 1949, pp. 117–130; W. L. Warner, "The Society, the Individual and his Mental Disorders," *American Journal of Psychiatry,* 94, No. 2 (September, 1937), pp. 275–284.

The present research, therefore, was designed to discover whether a relationship does or does not exist between the class system of our society and mental illnesses. Five general hypotheses were formulated in our research plan to test some dimension of an assumed relationship between the two. These hypotheses were stated positively; they could just as easily have been expressed either negatively or conditionally. They were phrased as follows:

I. The *expectancy* of a psychiatric disorder is related significantly to an individual's position in the class structure of his society.

II. The *types* of psychiatric disorders are connected significantly to the class structure.

III. The type of *psychiatric treatment* administered is associated with patient's positions in the class structure.

IV. The *psycho-dynamics* of psychiatric disorders are correlative to an individual's position in the class structure.

V. *Mobility* in the class structure is neurotogenic.

Each hypothesis is linked to the others, and all are subsumed under the theoretical assumption of a functional relationship between stratification in society and the prevalence of particular types of mental disorders among given social classes or strata in a specified population. Although our research was planned around these hypotheses, we have been forced by the nature of the problem of mental illness to study *diagnosed* prevalence of psychiatric disorders, rather than *true* or *total* prevalence.

Methodological Procedure

The research is being done by a team of four psychiatrists,[6] two sociologists,[7] and a clinical psychologist.[8] The data are being assembled in the New Haven urban community, which consists of the city of New Haven and surrounding towns of East Haven, North Haven, West Haven, and Hamden. This community had a population of some 250,000 persons in 1950.[9] The New Haven community was selected because the community's structure has been studied intensively by sociologists over a long period. In addition, it is served by a private psychiatric hospital, three psychiatric clinics,

6. F. C. Redlich, B. H. Roberts, L. Z. Freedman, and Leslie Schaffer.

7. August B. Hollingshead and J. K. Myers.

8. Harvey A. Robinson.

9. The population of each component was as follows: New Haven, 164,443; East Haven, 12,212; North Haven, 9,444; West Haven, 32,010; Hamden, 29,715; and Woodbridge, 2,822.

and 27 practicing psychiatrists, as well as the state and Veterans Administration facilities.

Four basic technical operations had to be completed before the hypotheses could be tested. These were: the delineation of the class structure of the community, selection of a cross-sectional control of the community's population, the determination of who was receiving psychiatric care, and the stratification of both the control sample and the psychiatric patients.

August B. Hollingshead and Jerome K. Myers took over the task of delineating the class system. Fortunately, Maurice R. Davie and his students had studied the social structure of the New Haven community in great detail over a long time span.[10] Thus, we had a large body of data we could draw upon to aid us in blocking out the community's social structure.

The community's social structure is differentiated *vertically* along racial, ethnic, and religious lines; each of these vertical cleavages, in turn, is differentiated *horizontally* by a series of strata or classes. Around the socio-biological axis of race two social worlds have evolved: A Negro world and a white world. The white world is divided by ethnic origin and religion into Catholic, Protestant, and Jewish contingents. Within these divisions there are numerous ethnic groups. The Irish hold aloof from the Italians, and the Italians move in different circles from the Poles. The Jews maintain a religious and social life separate from the gentiles. The *horizontal* strata that transect each of these vertical divisions are based upon the social values that are attached to occupation, education, place of residence in the community, and associations.

The vertically differentiating factors of race, religion, and ethnic origin, when combined with the horizontally differentiating ones of occupation, education, place of residence and so on, produce a social structure that is highly compartmentalized. The integrating factors in this complex are twofold. First, each stratum of each vertical division is similar in its cultural characteristics to the corresponding stratum in the other divisions. Second, the cultural pattern for each stratum or class was set by the "Old Yankee" core group. This core group provided the master cultural mold that has shaped the status system of each sub-group in the community. In short, the social structure of the New Haven community is a parallel class structure within the limits of race, ethnic origin, and religion.

This fact enabled us to stratify the community, for our purposes, with an *Index of Social Position*.[11] This *Index* utilizes three scaled factors to determine an individual's class position within the community's stratificational system: ecological area of residence, occupation, and education. Ecological area of residence is measured by a six point scale; occupation and education are each measured by a seven point scale. To obtain a social class score on an individual we must therefore know his address, his occupation, and the number of years of school he has completed. Each of these factors is given a scale score, and the scale score is multiplied by a factor weight determined by a standard regression equation. The factor weights are as follows: Ecological area of residence, 5; occupation, 8; and education, 6. The three factor scores are summed, and the resultant score is taken as an index of this individual's position in the community's social class system.

This *Index* enabled us to delineate five main social class strata within the horizontal dimension of the social structure. These principal strata or classes may be characterized as follows:

Class I. This stratum is composed of wealthy families whose wealth is often inherited and whose heads are leaders in the community's business and professional pursuits. Its members live in those areas of the community generally regarded as "the best;" the adults are college graduates, usually from famous private institutions, and almost all gentile families are listed in the New Haven *Social Directory*, but few Jewish families are listed. In brief, these people occupy positions of high social prestige.

Class II. Adults in this stratum are almost all college graduates; the males occupy high managerial positions, many are engaged in the lesser ranking professions. These families are well-to-do, but there is no substantial inherited or acquired wealth. Its members live in the "better" residential areas; about one-half of these families

10. Maurice R. Davie, "The Pattern of Urban Growth," G. P. Murdock (editor), in *Studies in the Science of Society*, New Haven: 1937, pp. 133–162; Ruby J. R. Kennedy, "Single or Triple Melting-Pot: Intermarriage Trends in New Haven, 1870–1940," *American Journal of Sociology*, 39 (January, 1944), pp. 331–339; John W. McConnell, *The Influence of Occupation Upon Social Stratification*, Unpublished Ph.D. thesis, Sterling Memorial Library, Yale University, 1937; Jerome K. Myers, "Assimilation to the Ecological and Social Systems of a Community," *American Sociological Review*, 15 (June, 1950), pp. 367–372; Mhyra Minnis, "The Relationship of Women's Organizations to the Social Structure of a City," Unpublished Ph.D. Thesis, Sterling Memorial Library, Yale University, 1951.

11. A detailed statement of the procedures used to develop and validate this *Index* will be described in a forthcoming monograph on this research tentatively titled *Psychiatry and Social Class* by August B. Hollingshead and Fredrick C. Redlich.

belong to lesser ranking private clubs, but only 5 per cent of Class II families are listed in the New Haven *Social Directory*.

Class III. This stratum includes the vast majority of small proprietors, white-collar office and sales workers, and a considerable number of skilled manual workers. Adults are predominately high school graduates, but a considerable percentage have attended business schools and small colleges for a year or two. They live in "good" residential areas; less than 5 per cent belong to private clubs, but they are not included in the *Social Directory*. Their social life tends to be concentrated in the family, the church, and the lodge.

Class IV. This stratum consists predominantly of semi-skilled factory workers. Its adult members have finished the elementary grades, but the older people have not completed high school. However, adults under thirty-five have generally graduated from high school. Its members comprise almost one-half of the community; and their residences are scattered over wide areas. Social life is centered in the family, the neighborhood, the labor union, and public places.

Class V. Occupationally, class V adults are overwhelmingly semi-skilled factory hands and unskilled laborers. Educationally most adults have not completed the elementary grades. The families are concentrated in the "tenement" and "coldwater flat" areas of New Haven. Only a small minority belong to organized community institutions. Their social life takes place in the family flat, on the street, or in neighborhood social agencies.

The second major technical operation in this research was the enumeration of psychiatric patients. A Psychiatric Census was taken to discover the number and kinds of psychiatric patients in the community. Enumeration was limited to residents of the community who were patients of a psychiatrist or a psychiatric clinic, or were in a psychiatric institution on December 1, 1950. To make reasonably certain that all patients were included in the enumeration, the research team gathered data from all public and private psychiatric institutions and clinics in Connecticut and nearby states, and all private practitioners in Connecticut and the metropolitan New York area. It received the cooperation of all clinics and

institutions, and of all practitioners except a small number in New York City. It can be reasonably assumed that we have data comprising at least 98 per cent of all individuals who were receiving psychiatric care on December 1, 1950.

Forty-four pertinent items of information were gathered on each patient and placed on a schedule. The psychiatrists gathered material regarding symptomatology and diagnosis, onset of illness and duration, referral to the practitioner and the institution, and the nature and intensity of treatment. The sociologists obtained information on age, sex, occupation, education, religion, race and ethnicity, family history, marital experiences, and so on.

The third technical research operation was the selection of a control sample from the normal population of the community. The sociologists drew a 5 per cent random sample of households in the community from the 1951, New Haven *City Directory*. This directory covers the entire communal area. The names and addresses in it were compiled in October and November, 1950—a period very close to the date of the Psychiatric Census. Therefore there was comparability of residence and date of registry between the two population groups. Each household drawn in the sample was interviewed, and data on the age, sex, occupation, education, religion, and income of family members, as well as other items necessary for our purposes were placed on a schedule. This sample is our Control Population.

Our fourth basic operation was the stratification of the psychiatric patients and of the control population with the *Index of Social Position*. As soon as these tasks were completed, the schedules from the Psychiatric Census and the 5 per cent Control Sample were edited and coded, and their data were placed on Hollerith cards. The analysis of these data is in process.

Selected Findings

Before we discuss our findings relative to Hypothesis I, we want to reemphasize that our study is concerned with *diagnosed* or *treated* prevalence rather than *true* or *total* prevalence. Our Psychiatric Census included only psychiatric cases under treatment, diagnostic study, or care. It did not include individuals with psychiatric disorders who were not being treated on December 1, 1950, by a psychiatrist. There are undoubtedly many individuals in the community with psychiatric problems who escaped our net. If we had *true* prevalence figures, many findings from our present study would be more meaningful, perhaps some of our interpretations would be changed, but at present we must limit ourselves to the data we have.

Hypothesis I, as revised by the nature of the problem, stated: *The diagnosed prevalence of psychiatric disorders is related significantly to an individual's position* in the class structure. A test of this hypothesis involves a comparison of the normal population with the psychiatric population. If no significant difference between the distribution of the normal population and the psychiatric patient population by social class is found, Hypothesis I may be abandoned as unproved. However, if a significant difference is found between the two populations by class, Hypothesis I should be entertained until more conclusive data are assembled. Pertinent data for a limited test of Hypothesis I are presented in Table 1. The data included show the number of individuals in the normal population and the psychiatric population, by class level. What we are concerned with in this test is how these two populations are distributed by class.

When we tested the reliability of these population distributions by the use of the chi square method, we found a *very significant* relation between social class and treated prevalence of psychiatric disorders in the New Haven community. A comparison of the percentage distribution of each population by class readily indicates the direction of the class concentration of psychiatric cases. For example, Class I contains 3.1 per cent of the community's population but only 1.0 per cent of the psychiatric cases. Class V, on the other hand, includes 17.8 per cent of the community's population, but contributed 36.8 per cent of the psychiatric patients. On the

TABLE 1.

Distribution of Normal and Psychiatric Population by Social Class

Social Class	NORMAL POPULATION*		PSYCHIATRIC POPULATION	
	Number	Per cent	Number	Per cent
I	358	3.1	19	1.0
II	926	8.1	131	6.7
III	2500	22.0	260	13.2
IV	5256	46.0	758	38.6
V	2037	17.8	723	36.8
Unknown**	345	3.0	72	3.7
Total	11,422	100.0	1,963	100.0

Chi square=408.16, P less than .001.

*These figures are preliminary. They do not include Yale students, transients, institutionalized persons, and refusals.

**The unknown cases were not used in the calculation of chi square. They are individuals drawn in the sample, and psychiatric cases whose class level could not be determined because of paucity of data.

TABLE 2.

Distribution of Neuroses and Psychoses by Social Class

Social Class	NEUROSES		PSYCHOSES	
	Number	Per cent	Number	Per cent
I	10	52.6	9	47.4
II	88	67.2	43	32.8
III	115	44.2	145	55.8
IV	175	23.1	583	76.9
V	61	8.4	662	91.6
Total	449		1,442	

Chi square=296.45, P less than .001.

basis of our data Hypothesis I clearly should be accepted as tenable.

Hypothesis II postulated a significant connection between the *type* of psychiatric disorder and social class. This hypothesis involves a test of the idea that there may be a functional relationship between an individual's position in the class system and the type of psychiatric disorder that he may present. This hypothesis depends, in part, on the question of diagnosis. Our psychiatrists based their diagnoses on the classificatory system developed by the Veterans Administration.[12] For the purposes of this paper, all cases are grouped into two categories: the neuroses and the psychoses. The results of this grouping by social class are given in Table 2.

A study of Table 2 will show that the neuroses are concentrated at the higher levels and the psychoses at the lower end of the class structure. Our team advanced a number of theories to explain the sharp differences between the neuroses and psychoses by social class. One suggestion was that the low percentage of neurotics in the lower classes was a direct reaction to the cost of psychiatric treatment. But as we accumulated a series of case studies, for tests of Hypotheses IV and V, we became skeptical of this simple interpretation. Our detailed case records indicate that the social distance between psychiatrist and patient may be more potent than economic considerations in determining the character of psychiatric intervention. This question therefore requires further research.

The high concentration of psychotics in the lower strata is probably the product of a very unequal distribution of psychotics in the total population. To test this idea, Hollingshead selected schizophrenics for special

12. *Psychiatric Disorders and Reactions,* Washington: Veterans Administration, Technical Bulletin 10A–78, October, 1947.

study. Because of the severity of this disease it is probable that very few schizophrenics fail to receive some kind of psychiatric care. This diagnostic group comprises 44.2 per cent of all patients, and 58.7 per cent of the psychotics, in our study. Ninety-seven and six-tenths per cent of these schizophrenic patients had been hospitalized at one time or another, and 94 per cent were hospitalized at the time of our census. When we classify these patients by social class we find that there is a very significant inverse relationship between social class and schizophrenia.

Hollingshead decided to determine, on the basis of these data, what the probability of the prevalence of schizophrenia by social class might be in the general population. To do this he used a proportional index to learn whether or not there were differentials in the distribution of the general population, as represented in our control sample, and the distribution of schizophrenics by social class. If a social class exhibits the same proportion of schizophrenia as it comprises of the general population, the index for that class is 100. If schizophrenia is disproportionately prevalent in a social class the index is above 100; if schizophrenia is disproportionately low in a social class the index is below 100. The index for each social class appears in the last column of Table 3.

The fact that the Index of Prevalence in class I is only one-fifth as great as it would be if schizophrenia were proportionately distributed in this class, and that it is two and one-half times as high in class V as we might expect on the basis of proportional distribution, gives further support to Hypothesis II. The fact that the Index of Prevalence is 11.2 times as great in class V as in class I is particularly impressive.

Hypothesis III stipulated that the type of psychiatric treatment a patient receives is associated with his posi-

tion in the class structure. A test of this hypothesis involves a comparison of the different types of therapy being used by psychiatrists on patients in the different social classes. We encountered many forms of therapy but they may be grouped under three main types; psychotherapy, organic therapy, and custodial care. The patient population, from the viewpoint of the principal type of therapy received, was divided roughly into three categories: 32.0 per cent received some type of psychotherapy; 31.7 per cent received organic treatments of one kind or another; and 36.3 per cent received custodial care without treatment. The percentage of persons who received no treatment care was greatest in the lower classes. The same finding applies to organic treatment. Psychotherapy, on the other hand, was concentrated in the higher classes. Within the psychotherapy category there were sharp differences between the types of psychotherapy administered to the several classes. For example, psychoanalysis was limited to classes I and II. Patients in class V who received any psychotherapy were treated by group methods in the state hospitals. The number and percentage of patients who received each type of therapy is given in Table 4. The data clearly support Hypothesis III.

At the moment we do not have data available for a test of Hypotheses IV and V. These will be put to a test as soon as we complete work on a series of cases now under close study. Preliminary materials give us the impression that they too will be confirmed.

Conclusions and Interpretations

This study was designed to throw new light upon the question of how mental illness is related to social environment. It approached this problem from the

TABLE 3.

Comparison of the Distribution of the Normal Population with Schizophrenics by Class, with Index of Probable Prevalence

Social Class	NORMAL POPULATION		SCHIZOPHRENICS		*Index of Prevalence*
	No.	*Per cent*	*No.*	*Per cent*	
I	358	3.2	6	.7	22
II	926	8.4	23	2.7	33
III	2,500	22.6	83	9.8	43
IV	5,256	47.4	352	41.6	88
V	2,037	18.4	383	45.2	246
Total	11,077	100.0	847	100.0	

TABLE 4.

Distribution of the Principal Types of Therapy by Social Class

Social Class	PSYCHOTHERAPY		ORGANIC THERAPY		NO TREATMENT	
	Number	Per cent	Number	Per cent	Number	Per cent
I	14	73.7	2	10.5	3	15.8
II	107	81.7	15	11.4	9	6.9
III	136	52.7	74	28.7	48	18.6
IV	237	31.1	288	37.1	242	31.8
V	115	16.1	234	32.7	367	51.2

Chi square=336.58, P less than .001.

perspective of social class to determine if an individual's position in the social system was associated significantly with the development of psychiatric disorders. It proceeded on the theoretical assumption that if mental illnesses were distributed randomly in the population, the hypotheses designed to test the idea that psychiatric disorders are connected in some functional way to the class system would not be found to be statistically significant.

The data we have assembled demonstrate conclusively that mental illness, as measured by diagnosed prevalence, is not distributed randomly in the population of the New Haven community. On the contrary, psychiatric difficulties of so serious a nature that they reach the attention of a psychiatrist are unequally distributed among the five social classes. In addition, types of psychiatric disorders, and the ways patients are treated, are strongly associated with social class position.

The statistical tests of our hypotheses indicate that there are definite connections between particular types of social environments in which people live, as measured by the social class concept, and the emergence of particular kinds of psychiatric disorders, as measured by psychiatric diagnosis. They do not tell us what these connections are, nor how they are functionally related to a particular type of mental illness in a given individual. The next step, we believe, is to turn from the strictly statistical approach to an intensive study of the social environments associated with particular social classes, on the one hand, and of individuals in these environments who do or do not develop mental illnesses, on the other hand.

THOMAS S. LANGNER

Life Stress and Mental Health: The Midtown Manhattan Community Setting and Initial Demographic Findings

A separate sociographic operation[1] was undertaken early in the project's history, in order to gather materials that would describe the community and its people. Historical data, newspaper clippings, and comments about Manhattan in novels and autobiographies were collected. These data, together with some field interviews and observations and the demographic statistics derived from the U.S. Census and our own Home Interview Survey, comprise what we know of Midtown.

The Place

Midtown is one small part of the "New York-Northeastern New Jersey Area," the largest urban complex in the United States, consisting of 13 million people in 4000 square miles. New York City covers only 315 square miles of this land, but contains 8 million people. Midtown is a residential area adjoining the central business section of the island of Manhattan, which in turn is one borough of New York City. Midtown is virtually the residential heart of the entire urban complex.

In addition to being a place of residence, Midtown lies in the center of a vast communications network. Commuters and produce pour into it by rail, highway, air, and water. It is a cosmopolitan area, for it has contact with the whole world.

Midtown's 175,000 residents live in relatively crowded conditions. The United States averages 50

Reprinted from Thomas S. Langner and Stanley T. Michael, *Life Stress and Mental Health*, London: The Free Press of Glencoe, 1963, pages 66–84, by permission of the author and publisher (Copyright 1963 The Macmillan Co., Inc., Publishers). The first volume reporting the study results was Srole, L., T.S. Michael, and T.A.C. Rennie, *Mental Health in the Metropolis: The Midtown Manhattan Study*, New York: McGraw Hill, 1962.

people per square mile, the New York metropolitan area 3,300, New York City proper 25,000, and Manhattan about 90,000. Residential land is land occupied only by residential buildings. Manhattan has 380,000 people per square mile of *residential* land. This is over four times the population density figure that includes all land.

Midtowners tend to live in buildings with five or more dwellings. Most common are the four- or five-story "brownstones" that are "walk-ups," and the huge elevator apartment houses, from ten to thirty stories high. Many tenement or substandard dwellings (approximately 19 per cent of Midtown's 65,000 occupied dwellings) are still in existence. They lack running water, are run down, or were inadequately constructed. As of the 1950 Census, 26 per cent of all Midtown dwellings also lacked central heating. The greatest shortage is in middle-income housing, although there is an over-all shortage of dwellings. The continuation of rent control, a wartime emergency measure, has partially alleviated one of the problems of housing in Midtown.

Many changes have taken place since 1953, when the survey was conducted. The destruction of many of the substandard dwellings and the construction of new luxury apartments, with monthly rentals of $50 to $100 per room, has driven out some of the people interviewed in 1953.

The People

Midtown is a typical "Gold Coast and Slum" area with high population density and a heterogeneous population. It is 99 per cent white; Manhattan is 79 per cent white. In the age range studied (twenty to fifty-nine) about one-third are immigrants, one-third are in-migrants from other cities or towns in the United States, and one-third were born in New York City. The national backgrounds of the Midtowners (traced back to the country of birth of their grandparents) are varied, but principally European. In order of their contribution to total population (in per cent) were those of German or Austrian background 20.3, Irish 14.8, Italian 8.6, Russian, Polish, and Lithuanian 8.4, Czech and Slovak 7.5, English, Scotch, and Welsh 6.0, Hungarian 4.5, and Puerto Rican 1.7. Persons of other nationality backgrounds constituted 12.2; 13.6 were fourth-generation Americans (all four grandparents born in the United States) and were not traced to their families' countries of origin. Only 2.4 per cent of the national backgrounds could not be determined from the Home Interview Survey.[2] Of course, a considerable number of the second and third generation (about 33 per cent) had parents of different nationality backgrounds. These people were asked which national background they felt they "belonged" to, which languages they spoke, and which national holidays and customs they observed. Such considerations were the final determinants of their *ethnic identification*.

In round figures, 41 per cent of the Midtowners are foreign-born immigrants, 29 per cent the children of immigrants, 16 per cent the grandchildren of immigrants, and 14 per cent are the great-grandchildren of immigrants (fourth generation or more). The immigrants are older, poorer, and more predominantly female. As the number of generations in the United States increases, the average age decreases and the average socioeconomic level increases.

Midtown immigrants, in contrast to their predecessors, are not predominantly from rural areas of Europe. About one-fourth were from large cities of more than 500,000 people, two-fifths from smaller cities, and one-third from farms or villages. However, in-migrants to New York City were predominantly from towns and villages, particularly in the fourth generation. They comprise 30 per cent of the second, 47 per cent of the third, and 72 per cent of the fourth generation. In-migrants are therefore younger, wealthier, and more acculturated than immigrants.

The rapid assimilation of the third and even the second generation has reduced the evidences of cultural homogeneity within the several nationality or "ethnic" groups. Although the Irish, Germans, Czechs, and Italians are more concentrated in some clusters of blocks, in no area is any one group a numerical majority. Ethnic restaurants, bakeries, grocery stores, recreation and athletic halls, travel agencies, and newspapers reflect the "old" cultures, but these stores and restaurants also serve all members of the community.

In our interview sample we found that about half are of Catholic, one-third of Protestant, and one-sixth of Jewish parentage. The Catholics are predominantly of lower and middle economic status; the Protestants and Jews are of middle or upper economic status.

Children under fifteen years of age comprise 28 per cent of the American "urban" population (towns of 2500 or more), but only 15 per cent of the Midtown population. The proportion of people sixty-five and over is similar to that in the United States as a whole, about 10 per cent. The fact that there are 32 per cent unmarried over the age of fourteen in Midtown (compared with 22 per cent in the urban United States) may account in part for the lack of children, coupled with the relatively low birth rate in metropolitan areas. One-fourth of Midtowners live alone, more than twice the proportion in the urban United States. This is tied to in-migration and the low marriage rate.

Forty-three per cent of the resident-employed in Midtown are women, compared with 30 per cent nationally. Over half of Midtown wives are holding full- or part-time jobs, compared with 26 per cent of white married women in the urban United States. This may be associated with, if not causally related to, the low birth rate.

Women also outnumber men 125 to 100 in Midtown, and this imbalance holds true at all age levels above eighteen. The sex ratio is equal for children under fifteen, and for those born in New York City. For immigrants and in-migrants it is 160:100 and 175:100 respectively.

The socioeconomic diversity of Midtown can be clearly seen in the great range of income, rent, education, and occupation, the four factors on which the index of socioeconomic status was based. While 3 per cent paid less than $20 rent per month, about 5 per cent paid $300 or more per month, or 15 times as much. The modal rent category was from $30 to $39 a month. Over half the sample (51.4 per cent) had rents between $20 and $49 a month. Their dwellings are, of course, under New York City rent control, for $50 per month is not an unusual rental for a single room not under rent control.

The range of education is equally striking. Six respondents had no schooling whatsoever. Although 12.8 per cent did not complete grammar school, 17.4 per cent did; another 16.9 per cent had some high school, and 22.7 per cent completed high school. Again, 11.9 per cent did not complete college, whereas 18.3 per cent were graduated from college and in many cases had further professional training. There are rather similar proportions of persons at the college and grammar school level, but an over-all predominance of those with a high school education. The typical Midtowner would have completed one year of high school.

Family income clearly reflects the "Gold Coast and

Slum'' character of Midtown. Whereas 11.7 per cent have a family income under $50 a week, another 9.8 per cent have an income of over $300 a week (over $15,600 a year). Forty-nine per cent have incomes between $50 and $99 a week, making the modal income around $75 a week. There is a ''bi-modal'' income distribution indicated by a hump at $75 and a hump at $300 a week, due to a larger proportion of people with these incomes. This shows us that the middle income people earning between $100 and $300 per week are rather less populous in Midtown.[3]

By far the largest occupational category[4] in Midtown is the Middle White Collar—owners or managers of middle-sized businesses, semiprofessionals, highly paid sales personnel, and artists employed by others (26.9 per cent). The next largest group were High White Collar people, receiving income from investments as well as salary—owners, managers, and officials of large corporations, professionals and self-employed artists (18.4 per cent). The Low White Collar group—lesser sales and clerical personnel, and small owners, managers, and officials—comprised 14.9 per cent.

The Blue Collars usually change to work clothes on the job, and their work usually involves manual labor. The High Blue Collars, skilled labor, and upper status service workers, numbered 12.6 per cent. The Middle Blue Collars, or semiskilled, totaled 11.9 per cent. The Low Blue Collars, unskilled labor and low status service personnel, constituted 15.3 per cent of the sample. It is of interest that many of the Middle White Collar people with relatively high income and skills are living in low-rent apartments. Thus the modal rents are out of keeping with the modal occupational and income levels. Many families have been living in these same dwellings for twenty or thirty years, and they cannot move because of the dearth of true middle-income apartments. The middle and upper-middle occupational group is most likely to move voluntarily from New York City to the suburbs, for they feel the housing squeeze most directly. The poor cannot afford to move, and the wealthier do not need to. Moreover, the recent (1955–1963) increase in new buildings has made for involuntary moves of large numbers of low SES people from Midtown.

The wide range of these indices of social and economic status demonstrates the extreme heterogeneity of Midtown. Adding to this variegated picture is the fact that many Midtowners are in a state of *status disequilibration*; that is, some are educated and poor, some are rich but uneducated *arrivistes*. Many pay more rent or less rent than their incomes call for. ''Proper'' monthly rent is estimated by the Department of Welfare as one week's pay or 20 to 25 per cent of income. However, a substantial number of Midtowners are paying up to 50 per cent of their income for rent.

The SES, religious, and ethnic subdivisions of Midtown are too numerous and complex to recount in detail, but they all spell heterogeneity. Midtown is not really a ''community'' in the sociological sense; rather, it is a part of a ''society,'' with many sets of values, languages, institutions, and organizations.

The study area is probably representative of other metropolitan areas on the Eastern seaboard. It is somewhat different in composition from the other boroughs of New York, but it is very close to the characteristics of the 1.6 million white population of Manhattan (of which it represents 11 per cent). Its similarity to other immigration centers is striking. Its unmarried adults, low fertility, working wives, predominance of women, crowdedness, ethnic, religious, and socioeconomic heterogeneity attest to this.

Community Organization

Sociologists picture societies as composed of major areas of social organization. These major areas are called ''institutions,'' and include the family, the military, educational, economic, legal, and other institutions. These institutions are in turn made up of organizations, both formal and informal. A school is an organization within the institution of education; a court is an organization within the legal institution. Teachers and pupils, judges, lawyers, jury, plaintiffs, and defendants all act more or less in accordance with a prescribed set of rules for behavior in school or court. These rules define *roles* for the members of an organization, and thus an organization is viewed as a set of interrelated roles.

The social structure of Midtown can be briefly described in terms of some of its institutions. Such a description will consist mainly of enumerating the actual organizations, for the most part formal, that comprise the institutions. The economic structure of Midtown is essentially that of a residential area. Although it borders on the main shopping section of Manhattan, Midtowners shop largely in local stores. There are a few chain stores, and many small dress shops, pet shops, bookstores and the like, catering to the entire socioeconomic range.

Most Midtowners work in the downtown office section of Manhattan; this is not true of the medical and allied professions, who practice by and large within the area. Although Midtown and Manhattan have equal proportions of dentists, chiropractors, and morticians, Midtown has four times the proportion of practicing physicians. Offices for private practice number about 250 per 100,000 population, compared with 18 for the rest of Manhattan and 3 for the United States.

Midtown has more than twice as many hospital beds per person as Manhattan or the United States; it also constitutes a medical center serving the metropolitan region and even areas beyond.

There are many religious organizations in Midtown. More than thirty Protestant churches, nearly twenty Catholic parishes, a number of synagogues, and several Eastern Orthodox churches were counted. The congregations vary greatly in size, from under 100 to over 2000 persons. The results of the survey show, however, that only 45 per cent attend church more than three times a year. These churchgoers are predominantly of the Catholic faith. The churches and synagogues have auxiliary organizations, such as nurseries, orphanages, residence clubs, adult education programs, and centers for the handicapped, the aged, and the young. These more or less secular appendages reach into the lives of as many or perhaps more people than the strictly religious church functions.

Higher status persons seem to belong to secular clubs exclusively, while those of middle and lower status often belong to both church and lay groups. The middle-class associations are less numerous and less powerful than in most American cities; they include a Chamber of Commerce, Lion's Club, businessmen's associations, veterans' groups, political clubs, the PTA's, League of Women Voters, and a chapter of Alcoholics Anonymous.

The working class individual, if he has membership in any formal organization, is most likely to belong to a church group, a union, or an "ethnic" social club, such as the "Sokol" and "Turn Verein," where eating, drinking, singing, and athletics are the chief activities. However, only 18 per cent of the first generation and 6 per cent of the second generation report attending meetings of these ethnic organizations.

The educational structure is best viewed in terms of the public, private, and parochial systems, each of which is independent (again indicating Midtown's diversity). There are twelve public, twenty private, and ten Catholic parochial schools. The private schools are almost exclusively attended by the children of wealthy families.

The institution of government is composed of two organizations: first the municipal government, which provides police, fire, sanitation, public education, and other services; second, the voluntary Citizens' Council, which guides health, housing, and family welfare. The Midtown Welfare and Health Council, composed chiefly of resident professionals, has attempted to improve housing and health services, and often includes city officials at its meetings. The rapid construction of new middle and high income housing and the consequent decrease in the lower socioeconomic population during the last five years has posed some difficult problems in planning services.

It is impossible at this point to cover in any detail the most basic institution of all, the family. Midtown families run the gamut in size, but seldom exceed six to a household. The number of children is well below average, and the number of unmarried adults and childless couples is high. A casual visitor would be struck by the large proportion of people living alone, in rooming houses, enjoying little contact with other human beings. The Midtown family is rather typical of the American family in general, consisting of parents and children, but not usually including the grandparents. A three-generation household is, of course, more common among lower status children of immigrants, who live in the parents' home and often derive the benefit of "built-in baby sitters." Typically, however, the later generations move toward the isolated nonextended family unit of parents and children. Even the practice of having godparents, such as the Puerto-Rican *comadre* and *compadre,* loses its meaning rapidly in the metropolitan environment.

While reviewing aspects of community organization, it might be informative to look at statistics that are usually considered indices of social *dis*organization. Compared with the other boroughs of New York City, Midtown and the borough of Manhattan have an infant mortality rate one-fourth greater. This is in spite of the much greater "accessibility" of medical services in Midtown. Midtown has higher rates for deaths due to alcoholism and nonvehicular accidents. Midtown has twice the rate of active cases of tuberculosis. Its juvenile delinquency is half again as much as in most other comparable districts of the city. Taken together, these higher rates of death and disease in Midtown indicate a surprising degree of social pathology. In view of the better medical facilities in Midtown, the higher death and disease rates may indicate inadequate use of services, in itself another index of social disorganization.

The Emotional Climate

Midtown and its parent borough, Manhattan, have been described as a place for the ambitious, the social climbers, and not a proper place to raise children. It seems that many other commentators have viewed it as the home of the poor, a slum environment more suited to breeding delinquency and poverty than to making a new generation of Horatio Algers. *Mental Health in the Metropolis* reviewed in detail what the novelists, biographers, poets, and historians have had to say about New York City. Their views seem to run the gamut, and it can be concluded only that the city is "all things to all people." They bring to it their own hopes and fears, their own values, their own way of perceiving the world. Small wonder, then, that some found it a fearful, threatening town, while others thought it a heavenly haven from persecution, a city of opportunity welcoming the stranger.

Whether the immigrants and in-migrants were pre-selected in terms of personality or of mental health we do not know. It is only logical to think that not only the mentally disturbed, dissatisfied, and dyssocial people but also the more skilled, interpersonally gifted, and emotionally integrated people tend to migrate. If selective migration has operated to produce Midtown, it has brought both the mentally disordered and the well to our shores, and taken both the disturbed and the gifted from our farms and villages.

The tensions of city life, the physical crowdedness, the emotional isolation, the striving for financial improvement, the competition, the physical threat of automobiles, the lack of sunshine, to name but a few, have been cited in the literature on urbanism as factors that would make for worse mental health in the city. Although we tend to revere the farm and the village, as they are part of our historical development, similar objections can be raised to rural life. The physical crowdedness of many farmhouses and villages, the physical isolation from other families, the struggle for economic survival, the rigid conformity often associated with a homogeneous community (although homogeneity and absence of value conflicts are often cited as advantages of rural life), the low level of education and poor medical care are typical indictments.

Only longitudinal studies will tell us what influence selective migration has on the mental health of city populations. Assuming that some migrants come to New York because of poverty, others because of persecution, and still others because of ambition or other motives, such as leaving their families, avoiding emotional contact, seeking new social or marital ties, it is impossible to estimate what effect this combination of motives for migration will have on the total prevalence of mental disorder.

We know that younger people have better mental health, on the average. If younger people tend to migrate (particularly younger women, who are the chief in-migrants to Midtown), then the mental health of the area has been improved. On the other hand, we know that older, poorer women were the chief immigrants to Midtown, and their mental health was below average. The average mental health of the area has probably been improved by the in-migrants who come chiefly from villages and towns, and are predominantly younger women of middle socioeconomic status and of third and fourth generation "Yankee" stock.

Thus, although three out of four Midtowners are migrants in some sense of the word, we have no evidence implying that their mental health is better or worse. Nor, on the other hand, have we any evidence that "city life" has injured their psyches in any manner that would not have occurred had they been exposed only to "country life."

Regardless of where they spent their childhood, and regardless of migration, all these adults seem to have been affected by their parents' physical and mental health, the frequency with which their parents quarreled, the death or divorce of their parents before age six, and other factors to be enumerated below. The socioeconomic level of their parents (their father's occupation and education) also was predictive of their current mental health. The characteristics of the family unit probably have the greatest effect on the developing personality. A home can be quarrelsome in the country or the city. Farmers can be poor or rich, similar to city dwellers. Children may migrate because they have achieved independence and courage in a happy home or because they must flee family conflict in a last effort at self-preservation.

Our task will be to show what factors in the family and community during childhood and in adult life may be connected with mental disturbance. These *stress factors* associated with mental disturbance were isolated and analyzed after the relationship of the demographic factors to mental disturbance had been established. This initial phase, reported in Volume I, came up with one overriding finding among many; namely, *socioeconomic status is more closely associated with mental disturbance than any other demographic factor*. It was therefore necessary to demonstrate that the stress factors operated independently of socioeconomic status. Once this had been done, an attempt was made to explain the poorer mental health of the low status group in terms of what we know about their personality structure and their modes of adapting to life stress.

Before explaining the methods and findings of this second phase of the study, we will review the findings of the first phase.

The Demographic Variables and Mental Health: Initial Findings Reported in *Mental Health in the Metropolis*

It is not easy to compress a highly technical book of several hundred pages into a few choice paragraphs. The reader desiring more information on method and some interpretation of the data can only be referred to the first volume, where all is spelled out. Our purpose here is to fill in the gap between the first and second phase of the analysis and to provide a base upon which to build interpretations of the stress factor material.

A. The Mental Health Rating Distributions

Kirkpatrick and Michael made independent psychiatric evaluations of each of the 1660 respondents on a seven-point scale of impairment. Because each psychiatrist assigned a rating from 0 to 6, each respondent had two ratings. These were combined to form a composite thirteen-point scale (0–12). This scale in turn was "collapsed," yielding final distributions of Ratings I and II (see Table 1).

In terms of Mental Health Rating II, based upon the larger amount of data,[5] less than one-fifth of the population is well, about three-fifths exhibit subclinical forms of mental disorder, and one-fourth shows some impairment and constitutes the clinical or morbid range of the scale. We are fairly confident that at least 23.4 per cent exhibit some impairment in life functioning, for all the evidence indicates that our methods tended to *underestimate* the level of psychopathology. Dr. Rennie felt that the Impaired category of the Midtown sample corresponded roughly to the impairment range of patients he had seen in psychiatric clinics and hospitals.

Supporting evidence for the clinical validity of the study comes from the fact that the majority of the symptoms elicited by the questionnaire were validated on a hospitalized and screened well population. A large number of symptoms discriminated between the known sick and known well groups, thus indirectly validating the psychiatric judgments made on the basis of the questionnaires.

The Home Interview Survey, in addition to giving an estimate of psychiatric impairment in the community, also aimed at establishing relationships between major demographic variables or biosocial groups and mental disturbance. The findings are reported under the headings of the typical background or demographic categories.

B. Age

Mental disturbance increased with increasing age. In the twenties we found 15.3 per cent Impaired, in the thirties and forties 23.2 per cent, and in the fifties 30.8 per cent. There was a "plateau" between thirty and fifty, but the rate increased sharply after fifty to twice the rate of the twenties.

C. Sex

No sex differences in impairment were found at the four age levels. However, women reported a greater number of psychoneurotic and psychophysiological symptoms.

D. Marital Status

While age and sex are factors upon which mental health can have little influence, marital status can be directly affected by one's mental health. By this token it is a reciprocal variable, acting as *both* "cause and effect." Marital status groups were compared while holding both age and sex constant. No sex differences appeared among the married. Single men had much higher impairment rates than did single women when age was held constant. The divorced and separated of both sexes had even higher rates.

TABLE 1.

Distribution of 1660 Respondents According to Severity of Symptoms and Associated Impairment

CATEGORY	MENTAL HEALTH RATINGS		PER CENT RATING I		PER CENT RATING II	
Well	0–1		18.8		18.5	
Mild Symptoms	2–3		41.6		36.3	
Moderate Symptoms	4–5		21.3		21.8	
Impaired	6–12		18.3		23.4	
Marked Symptoms		6–7		10.7		13.2
Severe Symptoms		8–9		6.2		7.5
Incapacitated		10–12		1.4		2.7
Total Number of Cases (N = 100 per cent)			1660		1660	

E. Father's Socioeconomic Status

Since the SES of the respondent's father could not have been greatly influenced by the respondent's mental health, it was considered an independent variable. The father's SES was based upon his education and occupation during the respondent's childhood. Respondents were divided into six groups of approximately equal size according to their father's SES. From high to low status, the proportions of Impaired (in per cent) were: 17.5, 16.4, 20.9, 24.5, 29.4, and 32.7. There was a definite increase in impairment as status decreased. The lowest third of the sample contained about twice the proportion of Impaired persons as the highest third.

This same trend appeared with even greater strength when the respondent's mental health was examined according to his present (adult) SES. In the Impaired category were 12.5 per cent of the highest of the six status groups and 47.3 per cent of the lowest status. Some of this increment, however, is due to the effect of mental disorder on socioeconomic status, as well as vice versa. No sex differences were observed in the SES trends. However, the age differences in impairment rates were maintained within each SES category. Within each age bracket, the relationship between impairment and SES origin was also maintained. Thus SES and age were both found to be related to the Mental Health Rating *independently of each other*.

F. Occupational Mobility

Male respondents were classified as upward, downward, or nonmobile according to whether they were higher, lower, or at the same occupational level as their fathers. The upwardly mobile were healthiest, the nonmobile less healthy, and the downwardly mobile the most impaired.

G. Generation

Immigrants were designated generation I, their children generation II, their grandchildren generation III, and their great-grandchildren or even more distant descendants generation IV. Functional impairment varied inversely with advancing generation position. Starting with generation I, the proportions of Impaired were 26.7, 22.9, 22.0, and 17.2 per cent. This relatively minor trend disappeared almost completely when age and parental SES were standardized (25.3, 23.0, 22.7, and 23.0 per cent). Thus the generation differences we have come to believe were a product of the rigors of

acculturation in actual fact seem to be attributable to the more advanced age and lower socioeconomic status of immigrants. Had these immigrants been younger and wealthier when we interviewed them, it is doubtful that they would have been "worse off" than the rest of the population with respect to mental health.

H. Religious Origin

The parental religion was selected as the only proper antecedent variable, because mental health itself may effect a change in religious persuasion. When rates were standardized by age and SES origin, Protestants and Catholics appeared to be quite similar (24.7 per cent and 23.5 per cent). Jews had a somewhat lower rate (17.2 per cent), but they had a much higher proportion of Moderately disturbed. On any measure taking into account the entire range of pathology, no sharp religious differences would appear.

I. Parental Religiosity

No relationship between parental religiosity and impairment was found among Jews. This was also true of high SES Protestants. On the other hand, Catholics and lower-status Protestants whose parents felt religion was "Not Important at All" were more likely to be Impaired. In this same religious and SES category, those whose parents felt religion was "Somewhat Important" were healthiest. Those from homes where religion was "Very Important" showed an intermediate proportion of Impaired.

J. Religious Mobility

The present religious identification of the respondent was compared with his religious origins (parental religion). Interfaith changers showed less impairment than nonchangers no matter what their religious origins. On the other hand, those who changed from a childhood faith to "No religion" as adults had a higher Impaired rate.

K. Rural-Urban Origins

In general, when age and SES origins are controlled, no difference in impairment is found between persons who spent their childhood in the Farm or Village, Town or Small City, Medium or Big City, and New York City. In the middle and high SES parental strata, there is some increase in impairment with progressively more urban origins. It may well be that minor socioeconomic variations *within* the parental SES categories are being caught or reflected by the rural-urban variable.

L. National Origin

Some sharp differences in Impaired rates appeared between the various "ethnic" groups in Midtown, but these disappeared almost completely when parental socioeconomic status was standardized.

In the first generation 37.5 per cent of the Italians and 52.2 per cent of the Puerto Ricans were in the Impaired category. However, only 18.2 per cent of the first-generation Hungarians were Impaired. This seems due in part to the fact that both Puerto Rican and Italian immigrants were of low SES origins, whereas the Hungarians were predominantly from the middle stratum. Thus socioeconomic status again helps to account for the ethnic differences in mental health.

Within the second generation the socioeconomic background largely explains interethnic differences in mental health. The rural or urban background as well as the economic origins of an ethnic group will in part determine its average proportion of Impaired ratings.

Taken all together, the most sizable, consistent, and independent relationship to impairment rates was exhibited by the factor of socioeconomic status (both parental and that of the adult respondent). Second in importance was age, which consistently showed a positive relationship to impairment rates. These factors form a foundation for the further investigation of the influence of sociocultural background on mental health.

In this volume we are attempting to investigate the relationship to mental health of broken homes, parental quarrels, parental mental health, parental physical health, the physical health of the respondent in childhood, and many other factors. Whether these stressful experiences or factors occurred more frequently in low status homes is always considered. The relationship between these factors and mental health is established within each socioeconomic category and each age category. In other words, a stress factor had to have a relationship with mental health independent of these two major demographic factors, SES and age. This did not mean, however, that a factor could not be *correlated* with SES. On the contrary, somewhat more homes among the low SES were "broken" before the respondent was age seven. Although there was some variation in the *proportion* of "early" broken homes, there was still a relationship between mental health and broken homes within each SES category.

M. The Gross Typology and the Symptom Group Classification

Drs. Michael and Kirkpatrick classified each respondent according to a Gross Typology that included the major diagnostic types. They also indicated the major areas of symptomatology evidenced by each respondent. These tasks were performed in addition to assigning the two Mental Health Ratings. Although little of this material could be reported in Volume I, it became of cardinal importance in the attempt to unravel the reasons for the disproportionate mental disturbance found in the low SES group.

There was a general finding that character disorders and psychoses are more common among those of low SES origin, while neuroses are more common in the high SES. The greater prevalence of suspiciousness, passive-dependency, and depressive symptoms among the low SES was also discovered. Such facts as the obsessive-compulsive tendencies of the upwardly mobile, and the alcoholism of the downwardly mobile will also help us to understand how certain personality types tend to accumulate at the extreme ends of the social ladder. This might be called the circulation of "emotional elites and non-elites."

N. The Patient Census

Careful examination of the records of all psychiatric hospitals, clinics, and private therapists having patients from Midtown resulted in a huge mass of data. This was analyzed in a fashion parallel to the Home Interview Survey data: by age, sex, SES, religion, and other variables. The many lacunae in the records, the difficulty of constructing comparable demographic categories, and countless other problems make these data anything but dependable. Although the results are of interest to those dealing primarily with studies of treated mental disorder, we feel that the space of this volume should be devoted entirely to the analysis of data on untreated mental disorder; namely, the Home Interview Survey. Many detailed analyses of prevalence rates according to age, sex, and socioeconomic categories are available in Volume I. These are analyzed according to private and public patients and by in-patients and out-patients. Data on incidence (first admissions) are also available from the project files.

On the basis of these data one thing is certain: the treated ill are in many respects radically different from the untreated ill in Midtown. The treated ill are wealthier, of later generations, have more positive attitudes toward doctors and psychiatrists, are better educated, and are probably of very different diagnostic composition. The psychopaths, the dyssocial types, and the paranoid schizophrenics are less apt to get into treatment unless they come in conflict with the police. Some types of dissociation and withdrawal are socially acceptable in certain social strata. Thus different diagnostic types are drawn from different class levels in an elaborate selection process based in various parts upon the availability of therapy, attitudes toward such services, the subcultural definitions of what constitutes ''illness,'' what is abnormal or socially unacceptable behavior, and the very recognition of and attitude toward mental disturbance by the potential patient, his family, and family doctor (if any). It is clearly paradoxical when the day laborer gets arrested and is sent to the emergency ward of a city hospital because he acted out his problems by punching his foreman in the nose, while his wealthier but not necessarily healthier counterpart is encouraged during his psychoanalysis to conquer his neurosis and understand or even express his repressed feelings toward the vice-president in charge of sales. One man's ''character disorder'' may be another man's therapeutic goal!

Thus the attempt to draw etiological conclusions from data on hospitalized, clinic, or private patients is seriously questioned. While individual dynamics and the progress of therapy and theory are constantly being fed by patient data, the current patient group—at least in Midtown—is grossly unrepresentative of mentally disturbed persons as a whole. Etiological generalizations should not be drawn from study of such groups alone. For example, ''broken homes'' has always loomed large as a factor in mental disturbance; many patients report they came from broken homes. We will see, however, that only 20 per cent of patients in Midtown came from broken homes, as compared with 36 per cent of nonpatients. *The products of broken homes, then, are overwhelmingly healthy adults!* Only in the perspective of data on the *total population* is the broken-home factor assigned its proper etiological emphasis.

Summary

Midtown is an area of tremendous heterogeneity, in terms of socioeconomic status, ethnic background, religious affiliation, immigrant status, and rural-urban origin. It is a metropolis that has meant all things to all people, reflecting their predispositions as well as preselecting certain types for migration. Both ill and well are attracted to the metropolis, and mental health rates are probably unaffected as a whole, since the two tendencies may balance each other. Midtown has fewer children, fewer married, and more childless couples. It

also has more working women and working mothers.

It is not a community, but part of a metropolitan complex, being governed by state, municipal, and local bodies simultaneously. It has a disproportionate number of professionals, particularly doctors, and less of a middle class than other boroughs. There is only negligible participation in the ''ethnic'' organizations, and church attendance is moderate to infrequent except among Catholics. The family is typically the isolated unit of parents and children. Many people live alone.

The Mental Health Ratings assigned to each of the 1660 Home Interview Survey respondents were examined in relation to various demographic factors. Socioeconomic origin, present socioeconomic status, and age were highly related to the Mental Health Ratings, independently of all other factors examined, and of each other. These two factors, particularly socioeconomic status, constitute a demographic overlay, so to speak, through which we can view the interaction of environmental stresses and mental health more fruitfully.

An elaborate patient census covering all forms of treated mental disorder led us to the conclusion that records on patients, particularly those of private therapists, are never completely available, and many of the available records are woefully inadequate, particularly where detailed demographic data are concerned. The comparison of treated and untreated psychopathology leaves no doubt that the preselection of persons for treatment makes them totally unrepresentative of the mentally disturbed as a whole. Patient data, therefore, should not be used alone in testing etiological hypotheses.

NOTES

1. The sociographic operation was performed by a team composed of Alice M. Togo, Ann Jezer, Samuel Reber, and Maurice Bloch, working under the direction of Dr. Srole.
2. Since the sample was found to be accurate for all age and sex categories according to the 1950 U.S. Census, proportions of other population characteristics are reported from the sample on the assumption that they will be good estimates of the true proportion in the population of Midtown as a whole.
3. The complete income distribution of the Midtown sample (in per cent) was as follows: under $15 (0.6), $15−24 (1.3), $25−49 (9.8), $50−74 (26.4), $75−99 (22.5), $100−124 (9.5), $125−149 (5.2), $150−174 (3.4), $175−199 (3.1), $200−299 (4.3), $300 and over (9.8).

4. For persons such as housewives or unmarried women who are not working outside the home, the husband's or father's occupation was taken as an indication of the occupational level of the respondent.

5. Rating II was unsuitable for correlational analysis against sociocultural variables without the methodological "insurance" of Rating I.

BRUCE P. DOHRENWEND • BARBARA SNELL DOHRENWEND

Sex Differences and Psychiatric Disorders[1]

In their 1973 study of sex roles and mental illness, Gove and Tudor discovered much in the writings of contemporary social scientists to suggest that "women find their position in society to be more frustrating and less rewarding than do men and that this may be a relatively recent development" (p. 816). Accordingly, they "postulate that, because of the difficulties associated with the feminine role in modern Western societies, more women than men become mentally ill" (p. 816).

To investigate this hypothesis, Gove and Tudor focused on research conducted since World War II, on the grounds that the war marked a high point of change in the role of women, with significant portions of married women entering the work force for the first time. They also restricted their coverage to North America and Europe where, they assumed, economic and technological conditions related to industrialization have promoted the posited change in the role of women. They concluded that the epidemiological evidence demonstrates that women do in fact have higher rates of "mental illness" than do men and that this is, indeed, a relatively recent development.

However, most of the evidence on which they base their conclusion is inadequate for the problem: It does

not deal with trends over time; it omits data on the personality disorders; it includes treatment statistics that are limited and can often be misleading (e.g., Dohrenwend and Dohrenwend 1969); and, where it consists of a presentation of results from some community studies that are not restricted to treated rates (Gove and Tudor 1973, p. 819), the findings are refracted through Gove and Tudor's highly idiosyncratic definition of "mental illness" (p. 812). In this definition, such disparate types of diagnosed psychiatric disorder as psychoses and neuroses are lumped together and tallied along with objective measures of milder signs and symptoms of personal distress whose relation to clinical psychiatric disorder is far from evident, especially when, as in some of the studies considered by Gove and Tudor, the test items are not calibrated against psychiatric evaluations or patient criterion groups (e.g., Dohrenwend 1973).

The most important data that Gove and Tudor bring to bear on the issue, and the only data on trends over time, consist of overall rates of functional disorder (not excluding the personality disorders) that we summarized in our 1969 review of epidemiological studies of "true" prevalence conducted since the turn of the century (Dohrenwend and Dohrenwend 1969). All of these studies identify cases of psychiatric disorder in general populations by one of the following procedures or some combination of them: evaluations by psychiatrists of data from key informants and agency records; evaluations by psychiatrists of data from direct interviews with community residents; and, especially in more recent studies, scores on screening test questions that have been calibrated against psychiatric evaluations or against criterion groups of psychiatric patients (Dohrenwend and Dohrenwend 1969, 1974*b*).

Reprinted from *The American Journal of Sociology,* Vol. 81, No. 6 (May 1976), pages 1447–1454 by permission of the authors and publisher.

1. This is a revised and shortened version of a paper presented at the 8th World Congress of Sociology, Toronto, Ontario, August 19–24, 1974. The analysis was supported in part by research grant MH 10328 and by Research Scientist Award K5 MH 14663 from the National Institute of Mental Health, U.S. Public Health Service. We would like to express appreciation to Frederick S. Mendelsohn for his very useful criticism and to Catherine K. Riessman for her help with the results for manic-depressive psychosis.

Perceptively, Gove and Tudor divided the North American and European studies that we included in our 1969 review into, roughly, pre-World War II and post-World War II groups (because of the gap in publication between 1943 and 1950, the division is actually on the basis of whether they were published before 1950 or in 1950 or later). They found that overall rates were consistently higher for men in the earlier studies and for women in the later ones (Gove and Tudor 1973, p. 828). Other things being equal, it would seem that these results provide the strongest support that Gove and Tudor have for their hypothesis. Other things, however, are not equal.

Analysis of Epidemiological Studies of "True" Prevalence Conducted in the United States and Europe

Since our 1969 review, we have updated our coverage of the epidemiological literature. Altogether, we have found over 80 studies of the "true" prevalence of psychiatric disorder in community populations. The majority of them provide at least some relevant data on sex differences, and 33 of those that do were conducted in North America and Europe.[2]

Table 1 shows that, as Gove and Tudor found on the basis of data from our 1969 review, overall rates in the North American and European studies are consistently higher for men in the pre-1950 investigations and for women in those published in 1950 or later. Accepted at face value, this apparent change provides striking support for Gove and Tudor's hypothesis. Note, however, that by contrast with the overall rates trends on sex differences for the major subclassifications of functional psychiatric disorder do not show such reversals between the earlier and the later studies. Rates of personality disorder in particular are consistently higher for men in both the earlier and the later studies, and there is no consistent evidence of higher male rates of either neurosis or psychosis in the pre-1950 studies. These results for the various subtypes of disorder are difficult to explain in terms of Gove and Tudor's theory of changing sex roles.

2. However, some of these studies present findings based on ratings or screening scores that do not distinguish among diagnostic types and can be tallied with other studies only for total or overall rates of functional psychiatric disorder. Moreover, not all of the studies that give diagnostic breakdowns do so for the same subtypes of disorder; hence, the more detail we seek beyond overall rates, the more studies we are forced to omit from our analysis. Because of space limitations, we present summary tables only. Interested readers can obtain more detailed tables and bibliography by writing to us at the Social Psychiatry Research Unit, Columbia University, 100 Haven Avenue, New York, New York 10032.

TABLE 1

Number of European and North American Studies Reporting Higher Rates of Psychiatric Disorder for Men or for Women According to Publication Prior to 1950 or in 1950 or Later

DATE OF PUBLICATION AND TYPE OF PSYCHOPATHOLOGY	STUDIES IN WHICH RATE IS HIGHER FOR (N)	
	Males	*Females*
Before 1950:		
All types	7	2
Psychosis	3	3
Neurosis	1	2
Personality disorder	3	0
1950 or later:		
All types	2	22
Psychosis	5	10
Neurosis	0	15
Personality disorder	11	3

Table 2 shows that something else has happened to reported rates of psychiatric disorders since 1950. Overall rates and rates for the major subclassifications of psychosis, neurosis, and personality disorder have all increased dramatically from the earlier to the later studies—for men and for women. Accepted at face value, these results not only would be consistent with the hypothesis that the role of women has become more stressful, but also would imply more stress in the male role since World War II. Moreover, the increase in the median of the overall rates from under 2% to over 15% for both sexes appears to be of epidemic proportions.

Amidst a plethora of possible speculations about the reasons for such an extraordinary increase, there is one firm fact. One thing that we know has increased is the breadth of our definitions of what constitutes a psychiatric case. A great impetus to this expansion was provided by the experience of psychiatrists in screening and treatment during World War II. As Raines wrote in his foreword to the 1952 *Diagnostic and Statistical Manual* of the American Psychiatric Association, which reflected that experience: "Only about 10% of the total cases fell into any of the categories ordinarily seen in public mental hospitals. Military psychiatrists, induction station psychiatrists, and Veterans Administration psychiatrists, found themselves operating within the limits of a nomenclature specifically not designed for 90% of the cases handled" (p. vi).

The expansion has been a continuing process. One can

TABLE 2

Medians and Ranges of Percentages of Psychiatric Disorder Reported for European and North American Studies Before 1950 and in 1950 or Later

	BEFORE 1950		1950 OR LATER	
	Males	*Females*	*Males*	*Females*
Overall:				
Median.................	1.89	1.91	15.4	23.5
Range...................	1.1−9.0	1.0−6.0	2.0−51.8	2.7−75.2
Studies *(N)*		9	22*	
Psychosis:				
Median.................	0.445	0.43	1.20	1.69
Range...................	0.23−0.90	0.247−0.91	0.006−4.6	0.009−56.0
Studies *(N)*		6	14†	
Neurosis:				
Median.................	0.20	0.26	3.56	8.0
Range...................	0.14−0.22	0.11−0.42	0.30−44.0	0.31−64.0
Studies *(N)*		3	15	
Personality disorder:				
Median.................	0.63	0.12	5.85	2.94
Range...................	0.11−1.08	0.01−0.18	0.046−18.0	0.047−11.0
Studies *(N)*		3	13†	

*Two studies reported only the relative ranking of men and women.
†One study reported only the relative ranking of men and women.

see it in the development of such concepts as "pseudoneurotic schizophrenia" (Hoch and Polatin 1949) and, reflecting the efforts of the mental health education movement, in a dramatic increase between the 1950s and the 1960s in the willingness of the public to broaden its own definition of what it identifies, at least attitudinally, as "mental illness" (e.g., Dohrenwend and Chin-Shong 1967). Consistent with these changes in conceptions of what constitutes a case, there has been an increase, as Table 3 shows, in rates of psychiatric disorder reported in the true prevalence studies not only between the pre- and post-World War II periods but also during the latter period.

While the expanding concepts of what constitutes a case appear to provide an economical explanation of the general tendency for reported rates of all types of functional psychiatric disorders to increase over time for both men and women, they do not explain why the rate of increase should be so much greater for women than for men (Table 2) that sex differences in overall rates are actually reversed between the earlier and the later studies (Table 1). We think that the most plausible and parsimonious explanation is again methodological rather than substantive.

In the studies published prior to 1950, there was a far greater tendency than in later ones for the investigators

TABLE 3

Medians and Ranges of Overall Percentages of Psychiatric Disorder Reported for European and North American Studies, by Date of Publication

	BEFORE 1950		1950−59		1960 OR LATER	
	Males	*Females*	*Males*	*Females*	*Males*	*Females*
Median.........	1.89	1.91	12.1	13.6	18.43	26.75
Range..........	1.1−9.0	1.0−6.0	2.0−22.1	2.7−26.0	4.8−51.8	2.4−75.2
Studies *(N)*		9		6		16

to rely on key informants and official records to identify potential cases (Dohrenwend and Dohrenwend 1974*b*, p. 425). Such procedures are well suited to identifying the types of personality disorder characterized by chronic antisocial behavior and addiction to alcohol or drugs: persons, disproportionately male, who show such problems tend to leave records with police and other agents of social control or, at the least, to develop unfavorable reputations in their communities (cf. Cawte 1972; Mazer 1974).[3] Correspondingly, such procedures are less likely to identify persons, disproportionately female, whose neurotic problems are more private (cf. Cawte 1972).

By contrast with the earlier epidemiological studies of true prevalence, the investigations published in 1950 or later tended to rely for the most part on direct interviews with all respondents for data collection. Moreover, beginning in the 1960s when, as can be seen in table 3, the strong trend for women to show higher overall rates than men emerged, a growing number of the investigators have adopted screening inventories such as the ones developed by Langner (1962), Macmillan (1957), and several investigators who have used variations on the Cornell Medical Index (e.g., Rawnsley 1966) to identify cases. Typically, these inventories focus on symptoms of anxiety, depression, and physiological disturbances that are more indicative of neurosis and some aspects of manic-depressive psychosis than of personality disorders or schizophrenia. Given their content, it is not surprising that scores on such measures are generally higher for women than for men (cf. Cawte 1972; Mazer 1974).

These contrasts in method are confounded with date of publication in the studies whose results are summarized in table 2, so that a direct test of their impact is difficult to make. There are, however, four studies concerning the United States and Europe published after 1950 that relied on key informants and records instead of direct interviews with all subjects to identify potential cases. The median of the ratio of female to male overall rates for these studies is 1.18. By contrast, the corresponding median for the seven post-1950 studies in Western communities that relied on the Langner screening items or a similar measure is 1.92. Moreover, one study reports for the same subjects both sex differences based on key informant reports and sex differences based on

3. It can be argued, in fact, that none of the "true" prevalence studies, cross-sectional in nature, use the appropriate methods for identifying the mobile and hazard-prone individuals who show the antisocial types of personality disorder. Far better for this purpose would be prospective studies of cohorts identified from birth records or early childhood records and followed to their destinations, whether residence in the community of birth, another community, a jail or other institution, or an early grave (cf. Robins 1966). Such studies, unfortunately, are extremely rare in psychiatric epidemiology.

self reports to questions adapted from the Cornell Medical Index (CMI) (Cawte 1972). The men are found by the informants to be more disturbed (p. 59); the women report more symptoms on the CMI (pp. 74–75).

It is possible, then, to speculate that the results in tables 2 and 3 indicate that there have been increases in rates of the functional psychiatric disorders in modern Western societies since World War II and that, particularly since 1960, these increases have been greater for women than for men. It seems more plausible, however, to interpret these results as being a function of changes in concepts and methods for defining what constitutes a psychiatric case.

Where Truth Lies in the Epidemiological Studies of True Prevalence

For us, the truth of these epidemiological studies does not lie in the accuracy of their estimates of rates for this or that type of psychiatric disorder, much less for overall rates. Such estimates, as we have shown, vary with contrasts in the concepts and methods used at different times and in different places by the various investigators. Instead, their truth lies in the consistent relationships they report between various social variables and various types of disorder across—even in spite of—such methodological differences. We have found such relationships with social class (Dohrenwend and Dohrenwend 1969, 1974*b*) and with rural versus urban location (Dohrenwend and Dohrenwend 1974*a*).

More recently we have been able to reach certain conclusions about sex differences, which we summarize here. With time since the turn of the century specified as pre- and post-World War II, with place specified as rural and urban settings in selected United States and European communities in contrast with selected communities in the rest of the world, and with the functional psychiatric disorders defined as operationalized by the various epidemiological investigators who have worked in these communities: (1) There are no consistent sex differences in rates of functional psychoses in general (34 studies) or one of the two major subtypes, schizophrenia (26 studies), in particular; rates of the other subtype, manic-depressive psychosis, are generally higher among women (18 out of 24 studies). (2) Rates of neurosis are consistently higher for women regardless of time and place (28 out of 32 studies). (3) By contrast, rates of personality disorder are consistently higher for men regardless of time and place (22 out of 26 studies).

These results cannot easily be explained by role theories arguing that at some time and place one or the other sex is under greater stress and, hence, more prone to psychiatric disorder in general. Instead, the findings suggest that we should discard undifferentiated, unidimensional concepts of psychiatric disorder and with them false questions about whether women or men are more prone to "mental illness." In their place we would substitute an issue posed by the relatively high female rates of neurosis and manic-depressive psychosis, with their possible common denominator of depressive symptomatology, and the relatively high male rates of personality disorders with their possible common denominator of irresponsible and antisocial behavior. The important question then becomes, What is there in the endowments and experiences of men and women that pushes them in these different deviant directions?

REFERENCES

Cawte, J. 1972. *Cruel, Poor and Brutal Nations*. Honolulu: University of Hawaii Press.

Dohrenwend, B. P. 1973. "Some Issues in the Definition and Measurement of Psychiatric Disorders in General Populations." Pp. 480–89 in *Proceedings of the 14th National Meeting of the Public Health Conference on Records and Statistics*. DHEW Publication no. (HRA) 74–1214, National Center for Health Statistics. Washington, D.C.: Government Printing Office.

Dohrenwend, B. P., and E. Chin-Shong. 1967. "Social Status and Attitudes toward Psychological Disorder: The Problem of Tolerance of Deviance." *American Sociological Review* 32 (June): 417–33.

Dohrenwend, B. P., and B. S. Dohrenwend. 1969. *Social Status and Psychological Disorder*. New York: Wiley.

——. 1974a. "Psychiatric Disorders in Urban Settings." Pp. 424–47 in *American Handbook of Psychiatry*. 2d ed. Vol. 2. *Child and Adolescent Psychiatry, Sociocultural and Community Psychiatry*, edited by S. Arieti and G. Caplan. New York: Basic.

——. 1974b. "Social and Cultural Influences on Psychopathology." *Annual Review of Psychology* 25:417–52.

Gove, W. R., and J. F. Tudor. 1973. "Adult Sex Roles and Mental Illness." *American Journal of Sociology* 78 (January): 812–35.

Hoch, P., and P. Polatin. 1949. "Pseudoneurotic Forms of Schizophrenia." *Psychiatric Quarterly* 23 (April): 248–76.

Langner, T. S. 1962. "A Twenty-two Item Screening Score of Psychiatric Symptoms Indicating Impairment." *Journal of Health and Social Behavior* 3 (Winter): 269–76.

Macmillan, A. M. 1957. "The Health Opinion Survey: Technique for Estimating Prevalence of Psychoneurotic and Related Types of Disorder in Communities." *Psychological Reports* 3 (September): 325–39.

Mazer, M. 1974. "People in Predicament: A Study in Psychiatric and Psychosocial Epidemiology." *Social Psychiatry* 9 (July): 85–90.

Raines, G. N. 1952. "Foreword." Pp. v-xi in *Diagnostic and Statistical Manual: Mental Disorders*, Committee on Nomenclature and Statistics of the American Psychiatric Association. Washington, D.C.: American Psychiatric Association.

Rawnsley, K. 1966. "Congruence of Independent Measures of Psychiatric Morbidity." *Journal of Psychosomatic Research* 10 (July): 84–93.

Robins, L. N. 1966. *Deviant Children Grown Up*. Baltimore: Williams & Wilkins.

M. HARVEY BRENNER

Economic Change and Mental Hospitalization: New York State, 1910–1960

The Research Problem

This research is concerned with the role of economic situations as proximal precipitating factors in the occurrence of hospitalized mental illness. More specifically it is a study of relationships between changes, over time, in the structure of the economy and concomitant changes in the distribution of mental illness in the population. The hypothesis is tested by a systematic examination of the covariation of fluctuations in mental hospital admissions and fluctuations in the employment index in New York State over the period 1910–1960. The major research hypothesis is that during economically depressed periods mental hospital admissions increase and during economically prosperous periods they decrease.

The argument begins with the empirically established proposition that the distribution of mental illness in the population (prevalence) is not random but occurs in inverse proportion to the socioeconomic structure of society: the higher the socioeconomic stratum, the lower the probability of mental illness.

The question is raised whether this inverse relationship is constant or varies over time. If it does vary over time, then mental illness may substantially be a response to precipitating conditions in the social environment. If, in addition, its variation over time coincides with changes in the structure of the economy, then mental illness may be, in part, a reaction to changes in the social-economic situation.

This initial research problem sets the stage for a study of the relationship between economic changes and mental hospitalization. But another series of problems of interpretation is raised by our findings. We do indeed find that mental hospital admissions are related to economic downturns, and that decreases are related to

Reprinted from *Social Psychiatry*, Vol. 2, No. 4, 1967, pages 180–188, by permission of the publisher and author (copyright 1967 by Springer-Verlag New York, Inc.)

upturns. Our second major research question, then, asks to what extent these fluctuations in mental hospital admissions may actually reflect variations in the level of psychiatric symptomatology.

Prevalence and Economic Status

The prevalence of treated mental disorders was studied in great detail in the New Haven community at a single point in time. This study included all persons in treatment with a psychiatrist or under the care of a psychiatric clinic or mental hospital on December 1, 1950 (Hollingshead and Redlich, 1958). The study concluded that the prevalence of treated mental illness is inversely related to socioeconomic status: the lower the socioeconomic status, the greater the proportion of persons in psychiatric treatment.

The New Haven study was preceded by an attempt to examine the prevalence of mental illness in the Eastern Health District of Baltimore in 1936. The Baltimore study included information drawn from "all institutions and agencies in the community that deal with the various types of mental hygiene problems" (Lemkau et al., 1941; 1942). This study reported a strong inverse relationship between socioeconomic status (as measured by income-level) and the age- and sex-adjusted prevalence rate of psychosis.

The Baltimore study of prevalence was followed by a more comprehensive true prevalence survey of a sample of the non-hospitalized population in a New York City area. This study found that the rate of diagnosed "psychotic type" individuals was inversely related to socioeconomic status (Rennie et al., 1957; Srole et al., 1962). The same study later reported an inverse relationship between the number of diagnosed psychiatric symptoms per person examined and socioeconomic status (Langner and Michael, 1963).

A true prevalence survey of Stirling County, an area of small fishing, lumbering, and farming towns located at the Northeastern tip of Canada, similarly found mental disorder inversely correlated with socioeconomic status (Leighton et al., 1963).

The above studies of the prevalence of mental disorder are consistent in suggesting the inverse relationship between mental illness (treated and untreated) and the socioeconomic structure of society. The central question of this study is whether this relationship is constant or varies over time. *If it varies over time, then mental illness may respond to conditions in the social environment.*

Fluctuations Over Time

One way to test the idea that mental illness may substantially be a response to conditions in the social environment is to examine admissions to treatment facilities in a defined population over a specified period of time, and link the treatment data to known conditions existing in the *economic* structure of society during the same period.

The research hypothesis of this study therefore proposes that: *a significant relationship exists between economic conditions and admissions to mental hospitals.* Ideally, of course, we should use an indicator of mental status in the population which would include all mentally ill persons, regardless of whether or not they are in treatment. Practically, this is impossible since no such data are extant. Then too, it may be argued that the inability of the individual to remain within his community—i.e., not hospitalized—is in itself an indicator of the presence of mental disturbance. Proponents of this argument would point out that the criterion for "recovery" used in relation to many chronic, physically disabling illnesses is whether or not further hospitalization is required (Joint Comm., 1961, pp. 34–35). In any case, the paucity of data requires us to confine our indicator of mental status to admissions to licensed public and private mental hospitals.

In viewing mental hospital admission as an indicator of the emergence of mental illness in the general population, *over time,* we are dealing with the problem of precipitation; we are considering only the latest, or most immediate, in a series of developmental factors which may be significant in the appearance of mental illness.

We therefore wish to hold "predisposing" factors constant and ask simply, *when* does mental illness appear most frequently in the population. A predisposing factor is understood in this discussion as any event in the development of an individual which interferes with the most efficient adaptation to a given environmental stress

factor (or precipitating factor) which occurs *later* in the life of that individual. The precipitating factor is then an event—a stress-producing situation—to which the individual maladapts (relative to social norms) because of the earlier weakness or adaptive handicap engendered by the predisposing factor or set of factors.

Until recently (Brenner et al., 1967), studies of the possible relationship between economic change and mental hospitalization did not appear to support our major research hypothesis. Reviewers of the literature were consistent in stating that psychiatric hospitalization did not appear to have been influenced by the large-scale economic fluctuations which occurred during the present century (Reid, 1961; Fried, 1964).

Brenner et al. (1967), however, compared New York State first admissions rates for functional psychosis (during 1922–1941 for all state mental hospitals and 1947–1954 for all private hospitals) with that state's employment index and found substantial inverse correlations.

The present study seeks to determine (1) whether the inverse relationship found for New York public hospitals extends beyond, and earlier than, the period of the Great Depression, and (2) to what extent a detailed breakdown of admissions trends by subpopulation is necessary in order to observe this relationship.

Methodology

The general procedure involves correlating the variations, over time, in an employment index with variations in mental hospital admissions. A first important step in this procedure is to remove the long-term trends from the employment and admissions data. The detrending is done in order to eliminate at least some of the more disturbing effects of extraneous factors on the particular variables we wish to correlate. For example, we would like to be able to eliminate the influences of long-term increased capacity of mental hospitals to accommodate mental patients and of more favorable attitudes of families of the mentally ill toward psychiatric hospitalization. Similarly, we would like to eliminate from the employment index the long-term trends of increased female participation in the labor force and the additions of industries to the economy. It is not possible, however, to remove short-term confounding factors from our data (such as variations in the availability of hospital beds or dramatic variation in the presence of a particular population group within the labor force). The fact that we cannot remove such short-term extraneous factors from our analysis will, of course, tend to *decrease* our ability to account for short-term variation in the admissions data by *sole* reference to variation in the employment index.

For the purposes of presenting the data in this paper we have used what is perhaps the least complex detrending technique. The data essentially remain in almost their "raw" form. A straight-line trend is mathematically fitted to the two sets of data. These linear (trend) data are then algebraically subtracted from the original data. What remains are the deviations or residuals which represent the difference between the actual data and their linear trend (Thomas, 1927; Henry and Short, 1954).

A further reason for fitting the data with a linear trend, rather than a more complex curve (such as a parabolic or logistic curve), is to demonstrate that predictability of the relationship can be perceived graphically on a relatively ordinary level of observation.

This procedure was used in correlating[1] New York State mental hospital admissions over the period 1910–1960 with the New York State employment index (manufacturing industries) for the same period.

Initial Findings

We first used this methodology in analyzing total admissions for each sex, to New York State mental hospitals, but found the correlation to be relatively low (Table 1). This is true despite the fact that the graphic representation of these two sets of data does appear to show some degree of inverse matching with the employment index (especially for males). This finding leads us to suspect that, since earlier research (Brenner et al., 1967) has shown considerably higher inverse corre-

---

1. This correlation remains low even if we use the best estimate of the relationship, which would attempt to account for variability in the distance in time between the effect of changes in employment and mental hospitalization. It is possible, for example, that the population of hospital admissions that is particularly sensitive to employment changes may experience changes in employment status significantly earlier or later than the average as represented by the employment index for the state as a whole. One way to deal with this problem is to correlate the admissions data with the employment index at various temporal synchronizations (as in Thomas, 1927) and obtain the optimum correlation which best represents the temporal relationships between employment and admissions changes. Another commonly used technique attempts to summarize the effects of one variable upon another, where these effects may be distributed over a substantial period of time. For example, the stressful effects of employment- or income-changes on a population may be felt over a period of years. Also, different subpopulations of hospital admissions may be affected relatively early or late. The net effect may be that different proportions of the stressful effects of employment changes on mental hospitalization may occur during several years *after which* a particular group experiences a change. To account for a *distributed lag* relationship between a specific stress and its predicted response, the multiple correlation is frequently used (eg., Johnston, 1963).

The (1) *synchronous* or "raw" correlation coefficient is therefore supplemented by the (2) *optimum* (among those found for three years of lag and three of lead of employment to admissions) and (3) *multiple* (lags and leads as for the *optimum*) coefficients.

lations of first admissions with functional psychosis (1922–1941) to an employment index, only certain categories of the population of admissions may show sensitivity to variations in employment.

Expanding on the earlier study, we examined first admissions with functional psychosis (schizophrenia, manic-depressive psychosis, involutional psychosis) for both sexes for the period 1910–1960. We now find that for first admissions with functional psychosis the relationship extends substantially beyond the earlier study, which dealt with the period 1922–1941. In fact, the period for which we can accurately predict hospital admissions from the employment index has more than doubled. In the present study the initial correlations are only moderate, but the graphic representation shows a high level of predictability (Table 1 and Figure 1).

Since it is important to our hypothesis to identify the *largest* subpopulation of hospital admissions that is sensitive to economic changes, we further selected from first admissions with functional psychosis the largest identifiable population group obtainable from the New York State data. This is the grammar school educated group (category of educational status) which represents an average of slightly over 60 percent of first admissions with functional psychosis for the 50-year period under consideration.

The correlations for this large group, for both sexes, are substantially higher than for all first admissions with functional psychosis (Table 1). This can clearly be seen in the graphic representations (Figure 1).

Situations Intervening in the Relationship

Two models of the possible relationship between *economic* change and changes in the level of mental hospitalization may be distinguished. The first model treats the economic change as *the* (or at least one of the) most proximal precipitating factors in the emergence of mental illness.

In the second model the *economic* change may be far from the most proximal factor in the increase in mental hospitalization. In this model of economic change as precipitant, it may *initiate* a fairly lengthy sequence of (say) family, peer-relation, and physical health problems which, in turn, may snowball and either singly, or as a group, precipitate psychiatric hospitalization. In this model the economic change provides a sufficiently stressful climate so that any substantial additional stress is critical for the appearance of mental illness.

Thus, regardless of the temporal proximity of the economic change to the "last" factor in the developmental chain leading to hospitalization, the argument maintains that economic change is related to the appearance

TABLE 1.

Correlations[1] between First Admissions and First Admissions Rates, Civil State Mental Hospitals and the Employment Index, New York State, 1910−1960*
Linearly detrended data: (Least-squares technique)

	ADMISSIONS		RATES	
	"raw" Cor.	Optimum Cor.	"raw" Cor.	Optimum Cor.
Male				
Total Admissions	−.51	−.58	−.51	−.54
First Admissions	−.62	−.62	−.57	−.59
First Admissions, Total Functional	−.62	−.62	−.62	−.68
First Admissions, Total Functional, Grammar School Educated	−.82	−.83	**	**
Female				
Total Admissions				
First Admissions	.34	.44	.34	.45
First Admissions, Total Functional	−.14	−.16	−.13	−.14
First Admissions, Total Functional, Grammar School Educated	−.16	−.16	−.16	−.30
	−.80	−.80	**	**

*N=45
**Data on rates not available.
[1]See footnote 1, in text.

of mental illness. It is clear, however, that unless the most significant stressful effects of economic change occur within a "relatively" short period of the appearance of mental illness, it would be quite difficult to observe and chart the extent of changes in mental hospital admission-levels that were *related to* economic changes.

In concentrating on the concept of economic changes, we focus on change in the general state of the economy. We are thereby attempting to define a period of time within which the rate of socioeconomic status mobility is *either* decreasing or increasing for the population *as a whole*. In other words, it is a situation in which the majority of socioeconomically mobile persons in a population are mobile in the same direction at approximately the same time. The concept of economic change thus subsumes economic downturns and upturns. During economic downturns a greater proportion of the population loses than gains socioeconomic status. During upturns the opposite is true.

Theoretically and empirically, the closest approximation to *this* conception of economic change is the concept of the business-cycle. Similarly, our concepts of upturns and downturns are reasonably close to those of expan-

sion and concentration and prosperity and depression commonly found in the business-cycle literature (Mitchell, 1951, p. 6; von Haberler, 1958, p. 259).

Specification of the Population at Risk

It is apparent from the studies of economic change in the population as a whole that its constituent groups are often very differently affected by the same "general" economic event. This study has repeatedly shown the necessity to specify the population that one thinks might show an unusually high risk of being severely damaged by economic changes. This especially has come to light in our finding that only when first admissions are distinguished from total admissions does our predictive relationship appear in high relief. Similarly, first admissions with a grammar school education appear far more sensitive to economic change, in terms of their mental hospitalization, than the entire group of first admissions.

One possible reason for the outstanding sensitivity of some groups and the apparent lack of sensitivity in others may be related to the socioeconomic position of the group in question. Menderhausen (1946), for example, has shown that during the Great Depression dif-

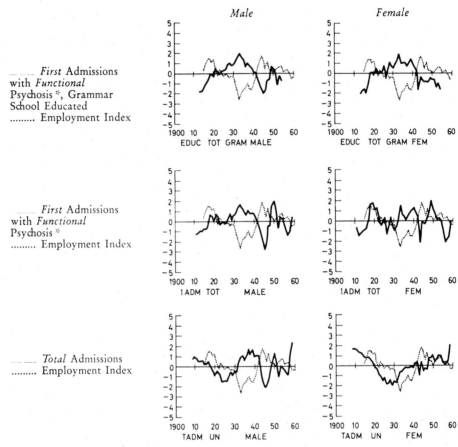

First Admissions with *Functional* Psychosis *, Grammar School Educated .... Employment Index

First Admissions with *Functional* Psychosis * .... Employment Index

Total Admissions .... Employment Index

FIGURE 1.   Admissions to Civil State Mental Hospitals Compared with the Employment Index *New York State, 1910–1960* Linearly Detrended Data (Least-Squares Technique), in Standard Deviations

ferent economic groups were very differently affected by the "general" economic downturn represented by "the depression." In fact, he found that whereas certain groups experienced great loss of income (high-income and lower-middle income persons), other groups experienced relatively slight income-loss, and some indeed showed moderate gains in income (the very lowest and certain upper-middle income groups). The fact that there is considerable variation in the effects of a general economic downturn on specific income groups has been confirmed by more recent studies (e.g., Sexton, 1961), and has been traced through much of the present century

(Creamer, 1956). This factor of variation in the degree to which economic loss occurs during a general downturn may in part account for the fact that the first admissions show particular economic sensitivity among total admissions; that admissions with functional disorders show unusually high sensitivity among total admissions; and that the grammar school educated show high economic sensitivity among first admissions with functional disorders.

It is possible that the sensitivities of the population categories showing high inverse correlations are related to their behavior in the economy. First admissions, for example, are known to be far more active in the labor force than readmissions (Freeman and Simmons, 1963). Again, among first admissions, those with functional

* Includes admissions with schizophrenia, manic-depressive psychosis and involutional psychosis.

psychosis are probably more heavily involved in the labor force because of their substantially lower average age. Finally, the grammar school educated, who possess a lower level of occupational skill than the better educated, might be more rapidly discharged during periods of economic emergency.

Economic Change and Specific Disorders

Remaining with our assumption that a detailed description of particularly sensitive populations is useful, we examined first admissions distinguished by classification of mental disorder. Here the pattern of differences is striking (Table 2). Among the major diagnostic groups (functional, alcoholic, senile, psychosis with cerebral arteriosclerosis, and paresis), it is clear that the patterns of relationship to economic changes are widely different.

Unfortunately, the great number of possible factors involved in this wide variation makes causal speculation difficult within the space of the present article. Among such possible factors are age, occupational status, labor force status, income rank, ethnic background, and marital status (Rose, 1956). In fact, it is possible that the multifactorial maze of causal factors, and their interrelationships, can scarcely even be guessed at without more

detailed epidemiological information than currently exists.

In any case, however, it appears that many different diagnostic categories do have a pattern of response to economic changes.

An important question now arises as to the mechanism whereby mental hospitalization for varying mental disorders might be precipitated. Under the stress of an economic downturn, it is possible that: (1) psychiatric symptomatology is generally increased (or is less well contained), (2) the degree to which persons are perceived and dealt with as mentally ill is increased, or (3) both of these sequences can occur.

The first hypothetical mechanism allows for the following possible sequences in the relationship of social stress to the development of psychiatric symptoms:

(a) an initial spell of mental illness in the life history.

(b) the flare-up of symptoms of a previously dormant mental illness.

(c) the remission of symptoms of an illness that appears in cycles.

(d) an increase or accentuation of symptoms of a continuous illness.

(e) the superimposition of a psychotic, neurotic, or behavioral reaction *upon* a previously established mental disorder. (Thus, for example, if psychosis is present in

TABLE 2.

Correlations[1] between First Admissions and First Admissions Rates, Civil State Mental Hospitals and the Employment Index, New York State, 1910–1960*
Linearly detrended data: (Least-squares technique)
Classification of First Admissions, and First Admissions Rates, by Diagnostic Category of Psychosis

	ADMISSIONS			RATES		
	"raw" Cor.	*Optimum Cor.*	*Multiple Cor.*	*"raw" Cor.*	*Optimum Cor.*	*Multiple Cor.*
Male						
Total Functional	−.62	−.62	−.72	−.62	−.68	−.73
Alcoholic	−.50	−.64	−.78	−.40	−.66	−.75
Senile	.60	.70	.80	.58	.69	.79
Cerebral Arteriosclerosis	−.26	−.72	−.82	−.19	−.69	−.79
Paretic	−.62	−.71	−.79	−.45	−.72	−.79
Female						
Total Functional	−.16	−.16	−.51	−.16	−.30	−.50
Alcoholic	.07	−.18	−.30	.10	−.29	−.33
Senile	.67	.69	.80	.67	.74	.82
Cerebral Arteriosclerosis	.11	−.46	−.81	−.02	−.61	−.76
Paretic	−.46	−.70	−.77	−.31	−.73	−.78

*N=41.
[1]See text footnote 1.

paresis, the *psychosis* may well be a reaction to additional social stresses.)

In the second mechanism the predisposed, or actually disturbed, individual's *family or other role-associates* experience the most direct effects of economic or other social stress. In this case, the *group under stress* might find itself unable to nurture the potentially or frankly symptomatic person.

Passive rejection may have a particularly devastating effect upon the severely neurotic or psychotic who, often alienated from much of his society, may require an unusual amount of tolerance from the few persons with whom he may still identify (Tyhurst, 1957, p. 164; Joint Commission, 1961, Ch. III). Overt rejection (e.g., Clausen, 1959; Freeman and Simmons, 1963), on the other hand, may often include the most repressive and punitive measures against the deviant or mentally ill person:

> . . . the mentally ill lack appeal. They eventually become a nuisance to other people and are generally treated as such. . . . People do seem to feel sorry for them; but in the balance, *they do not feel as sorry as they do relieved to have out of the way persons whose behavior disturbs and offends them.* (Joint Comm., 1961, p. 58)

But regardless of whether passive or overt rejection of the potentially or actually mentally ill occurs, the available evidence indicates that lack of tolerance has a profound effect on the containment of psychiatric symptoms among a large proportion of disturbed individuals. In an extensive review of the results of psychiatric treatment, the Joint Commission on Mental Illness and Health argued that the primary responsibility of the physician is to give the sick confidence and comfort and certainly do nothing to harm them. They went on to say:

> In treating the functional psychoses, we believe that this primary approach is scientifically sound; *the available evidence indicates it is possible to double or triple the spontaneous remission rate and achieve improvement or recovery in the majority of cases so approached.* Good results are discernible in how the patient thinks, feels and behaves—in the *subjective* conviction of the patient and of his doctor that he *is* better. These results then remain to be demonstrated to the patient's family and friends, *since his continued improvement depends not only on his own behavior but on how others accept him—on his reacceptance as a member of human society.* (Joint Comm., 1961, p. 55. The first and last emphases are supplied.)

The direct precipitation of symptomatology and intolerance of mental illness afford two explanations of why hospitalization for a variety of specific mental disorders should respond strongly to economic changes.

Specific Ethnic Group Reactions

The New York State Annual Reports classified first admissions to all state mental hospitals according to ethnic background.[2] This classification enables us to observe some of the effects of interaction between hospital admissions patterns by specific disorder and by economic-subcultural groupings. With these data we continue to examine the possibility that variations in hospitalization patterns may be due to differential response to economic changes. In the case of the ethnic groups, (1) differential economic *loss* and (2) differential *attitudes* toward economic loss seem particularly fruitful possibilities for study.

We may examine in detail the patterns of those groups whose admissions appear particularly sensitive and particularly insensitive to economic change (Table 3, and Figure 2). Of the 34 ethnic groups classified, the two most sensitive groups (who have average admissions of at least 10 persons per year) are the Jewish and German, and the two least sensitive are the Negro and Spanish-American.

It is interesting that the two most sensitive groups are among the highest in socioeconomic status of the 34 ethnic groups, and the two least sensitive are among the very lowest in socioeconomic status (Bogue, 1959, p. 74). The great differential in socioeconomic status alone suggests two interpretations of these ethnic admissions patterns. Taking, first, the approach of a somewhat mechanistic economic-loss model, it is possible that relatively high status persons suffer more during an economic downturn than those of relatively low socioeconomic status because they have more to lose. Even in "good times," low status persons experience relatively high unemployment and earn comparatively meager incomes (Henry and Short, 1954, p. 57). Then secondly, it is possible that higher status groups generally have a greater *concern* with socioeconomic status and, therefore, experience greater psychological loss during the downturn.

It has also been observed that strong economic achievement motivation is found more often in the subcultural role-definitions of higher than in lower socioeconomic status groups. Rosen (1959), for example, found that mean age of independence training, achievement values, educational aspirations, and vocational aspirations all increased linearly with Hol-

---

2. This classification is similar to that of the U.S. Bureau of Immigration (New York, 1934).

TABLE 3.

Correlations[1] between First Admissions to Civil State Mental Hospitals and the Employment Index, New York State, 1910–1960*

Linearly detrended data: (Least-squares technique)

Classification of First Admissions by Diagnostic Category of Psychosis

	RELATIVELY SENSITIVE GROUP						RELATIVELY INSENSITIVE GROUP					
	JEWISH			GERMAN			NEGRO			SPANISH-AMERICAN		
	Method of Correlation											
	Syn-chron.	Opti-mum	Mul-tiple	Syn-chron.	Opti-mum	Mul-tiple	Syn-chron.	Opti-mum	Mul-tiple	Syn-chron.	Opti-mum	Mul-tiple
Male												
Total	-.34	-.67	-.79	-.59	-.69	-.77	-.08	.25	-.37	.36	.58	.59
Total Functional	-.64	-.73	-.78	-.69	-.75	-.81	.15	.46	.55	.36	.55	.56
Alcoholic	-.45	-.59	-.71	-.27	-.50	-.60	-.35	-.39	-.60	.24	.49	.55
Senile	.75	.76	.83	.53	.69	.68	.12	.46	-.51	.28	.44	.47
Cerebral Arteriosclerosis	.10	.51	.78	-.58	-.74	-.82	.01	.34	-.58	.27	.47	.48
Paretic	-.36	-.37	-.48	-.33	-.41	-.50	-.34	-.50	-.64	.08	.33	.46
Female												
Total	-.14	-.61	-.75	.51	.51	.54	.32	.48	.49	.36	.52	.53
Total Functional	-.68	-.69	-.76	-.21	-.59	-.64	.24	.55	.62	.36	.51	.53
Alcoholic	-.04	-.08	-.11	.21	.31	.37	-.08	-.15	-.25	.20	.40	.48
Senile	.78	.78	.83	.72	.74	.88	.20	.44	-.51	.33	.37	.43
Cerebral Arteriosclerosis	.13	-.46	-.70	.05	-.28	-.39	.16	.47	.64	.27	.41	.43
Paretic	-.56	-.58	-.73	-.17	-.49	-.64	-.19	-.34	-.51	.10	.29	.42

*N = 41.

[1] See text footnote 1.

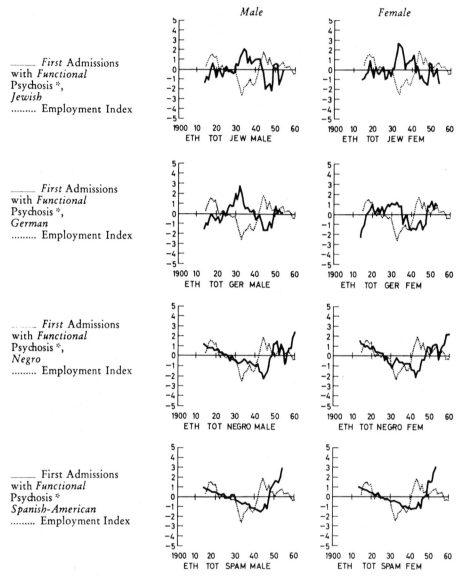

_____ First Admissions
with *Functional*
Psychosis *,
Jewish
.... Employment Index

_____ First Admissions
with *Functional*
Psychosis *,
German
.... Employment Index

_____ First Admissions
with *Functional*
Psychosis *,
Negro
.... Employment Index

_____ First Admissions
with *Functional*
Psychosis *
Spanish-American
.... Employment Index

FIGURE 2.   Admissions of Four Ethnic Groups to Civil State Mental Hospitals Compared
with the Employment Index *New York State, 1910–1960*

lingshead's scale of socioeconomic class. Hyman (1953) reported similar findings for high status educational and occupational "preferences" and "recommendations"

by socioeconomic class. Again, in an examination of class and family dynamics in the mental illness of Class III and V (Hollingshead's Index) mental patients, Myers and Roberts (1959) found the theme of frustrated achievement aspirations prevalent in Class III but not in Class V.

* Includes admissions with schizophrenia, manic-depressive psychosis and involutional psychosis

The graphic representation of the admissions pattern of the two relatively low status and insensitive groups tends to support the idea that a predominant factor in the response of a group to economic change is its relative economic position. Prior to World War II, it appears that the response of these low status groups to the economic changes was minimal (Figure 2). After World War II, however, the response of the low status groups to economic change appears at least as pronounced as that of the higher status groups. One possibility is that over the long-term trend, and particularly after World War II, significantly higher proportions of the populations in the low status groups increased their earnings. It may be, then, that the lower socioeconomic status groups increase their sensitivity to economic downturns as they approach the economic and attitudinal position of the higher groups.

In addition to the differential effects of the ethnic group categories, it appears that each illness category has an admission pattern of its own *across* the ethnic groupings (Table 3). It is clear that the populations represented by these illness categories (*within* the ethnic groups) behave differently in response to economic changes.

One of the more striking findings, finally, which runs through these data is that several groups respond with increased admissions—not during the downturn, but during the upturn. Certain classifications of illness (especially senile), ethnic groups (especially Spanish-Americans), and sex (females), at times, show strong *positive* correlations.

Interpretations of the General Relationship

We find that large numbers of mental hospital admissions in New York State show strong inverse correlations with the state's employment index during 1910–1960. In addition we find a wide range of variation in the patterns of response to economic change among different subgroups of the population of admissions.

The great variety in patterns of response to economic change would seem to exclude the possibility that any single causal factor might be responsible for the "general" inverse relationship. Perhaps several quite different causal mechanisms are involved. In the course of this paper, we have given particular attention to the two explanations of mental hospitalization which have greatest currency in the literature: increased psychopathology and increased intolerance of psychopathology.

An additional factor of possible importance in the response of mental hospitalization to economic stress may actually be the extent of economic resources of the mentally ill person. For certain groups of admissions, it may not even be absurd to ask whether the mental hospital is serving as an almshouse. Similarly, it is possible that the mental hospital acts as a shelter for those who are escaping other types of intolerable social circumstances.

The interpretive model given most attention in this paper, however, has been that the level of psychiatric symptomatology is frequently increased by precipitating sociocultural stresses, among which economic factors loom large in the sequence of causation.

There are several reasons why we feel this particular interpretation should be given prominent consideration. First, recent studies have shown that psychiatric symptom-formation is related to life stresses (Langner and Michael, 1963; Rogler and Hollingshead, 1965). Second, recent evidence appears to indicate that intolerance of deviance does not play the predominant role in the process of mental hospitalization (Freeman and Simmons, 1963). Third, the "precipitation of symptomatology" model is actually consistent with the intolerance of deviance model, but argues that intolerance of mental illness will at least exacerbate symptomatology in a disturbed or predisposed individual. This argument is well-supported by studies of the effectiveness of supportive treatment (Joint Commission, 1961).

REFERENCES

Bogue, D. J.: *The population of the United States.* Glencoe, Ill.: Free Press 1959.

Brenner, M. H., W. Mandell, S. Blackman, and R. M. Silberstein: Economic conditions and mental hospitalization for functional psychosis. *J. nerv. ment. dis.* **145,** No. 5, November (1967).

Clausen, J. A.: The sociology of mental illness. In *Sociology today* (R. K. Merton, L. Broom, and L. S. Cottrell, Jr. eds.). New York: Basic Books 1959.

Creamer, D.: *Personal income during business cycles.* National Bureau of Economic Research 1956.

Freeman, H. E., and O. G. Simmons: *The mental patient comes home.* New York: Wiley 1963.

Fried, M.: Effects of social changes on mental health. *Amer. J. Orthopsychiat.* **34,** 12 (1964).

Henry, A. F., and J. F. Short: *Suicide and homicide.* Glencoe, Ill.: Free Press 1954.

Hollingshead, A. B., and F. C. Redlich: *Social class and mental illness.* New York: Wiley 1958.

Hyman, H. H.: The value systems of different classes: a social psychological contribution to the analysis of stratification.

In *Class, status and power: a reader in social stratification* (R. Bendix and S. M. Lipset eds.). Glencoe, Ill.: Free Press 1953.

Johnston, J.: *Econometric methods.* New York: McGraw-Hill 1963.

Joint Commission on Mental Illness and Health: Action for mental health. New York: Basic Books 1961.

Kaplan, O. J.: *Mental disorders in later life* (2nd ed.). Stanford, Calif.: Stanford U.P. 1956.

Komarovsky, M.: *The unemployed man and his family.* New York: Institute of Social Research 1940.

Langner, T. S., and S. T. Michael: *Life stress and mental health: the Midtown Manhattan study.* Vol. II. New York: Free Press 1963.

Leighton, D. C., J. S. Harding, D. B. Macklin, J. S. Macmillan, and A. H. Leighton: *The character of danger, psychiatric symptoms in selected communities: the Stirling County study of psychiatric disorder and sociocultural environment.* Vol. III. New York: Basic Books 1963.

Lemkau, P., C. Tietze, and M. Cooper: Mental hygiene problems in an urban district. *Ment. Hyg.* **25**, 624−647 (1941); **26**, 100−119 (1942).

Menderhausen, H.: *Changes in income distribution during the great depression.* New York: National Bureau of Economic Research 1946.

Mitchell, W. C.: *Measuring business cycles.* New York: National Bureau of Economic Research 1951.

Myers, J. K., and B. H. Roberts: *Family and class dynamics in mental illness.* New York: Wiley 1959.

New York State: Annual report of the commissioner of mental hygiene (title varies) of the State of New York. Albany: 1910−1960.

New York State Department of Mental Hygiene: Statistical guide. Albany: New York State Dept. of Ment. Hyg. 1934.

Reid, D. D.: Precipitating proximal factors in the occurrence of mental disorders: epidemiological evidence. In *Causes of mental disorders: a review of epidemiological knowledge,* 1959. (Milbank Memorial Fund ed.) New York: Milbank 1961.

Rennie, T. A. C., L. Srole, M. K. Opler, and T. S. Langner: Urban life and mental health. *Amer. J. Psychiat.* **113**, 831−836 (1957).

Rogler, L. H., and A. B. Hollingshead: *Trapped: families and schizophrenia.* New York: Wiley 1965.

Rose, A. M. (ed.): *Mental health and mental disorder.* Section II. London: Routledge and Kegan Paul 1956.

Rosen, B. C.: Race, ethnicity and the achievement syndrome. *Amer. Sociol. Rev.* **24**, 47−60 (1959).

Sexton, P. C.: *Education and income.* New York: Viking 1961.

Srole, L., T. S. Langner, S. T. Michael, and T. A. C. Rennie: *Mental health in the metropolis: the Midtown Manhattan study.* New York: McGraw-Hill 1962.

State of New York, Department of Labor, Division of Research and Statistics. Adjusted indexes of manufacturing production worker employment and payrolls by principal industrial areas in New York State (monthly) 1914−1948. Handbook of labor statistics, 1948 (special Bulletin No. 226), p. 16. Nov., 1959. (The table referred to is adjusted by its compiler to join two separate tables which include several slightly different items of manufacture where 1936 = 100). The table was then readjusted by the present writer to include the years 1949−1960, as represented in a second table. The second monthly table was adapted from a series of Employment Tables (manufacturing industries) prepared by the Research and Statistics staff of the Division of Employment and Manpower Statistics of the Bureau of Labor Statistics, U.S. Department of Labor. Adjustment of the two tables was accomplished by computing the regression line (Y-97.61 + 12.23 x) of the correlated 10 years of (x) series in terms of the latter (Y) series. Finally, since monthly data were available, the yearly employment series was readjusted to conform to the fiscal year used in the first admissions accounting.

Stouffer, S. A., and P. F. Lazarsfeld: *Research memorandum on the family in the depression.* New York: Social Science Research Council (Bull. 29) 1937.

Thomas, D. S.: *Social aspects of the business cycle.* New York: Knopf 1927.

Tyhurst, J. S.: The role of transition states—including disasters—in mental illness. In *Symposium on preventive and social psychiatry* (Walter Reed Army Institute of Research and the National Research Council, sponsors). Washington, D.C.: Walter Reed Army Inst. of Res. 1957.

von Haberler, Gottfried: *Prosperity and depression.* Cambridge, Mass.: Harvard U.P. 1958.

MELVIN L. KOHN

Social Class and Schizophrenia: A Critical Review and a Reformulation

My intent in this essay is to review a rather large and all-too-inexact body of research on the relationship of social class to schizophrenia and to explore its implications for etiology.[1] Instead of reviewing the studies one by one, I shall address general issues and bring in whatever studies are most relevant.[2] It hardly need be stressed that my way of selecting these issues and evaluating the studies represents only one person's view of the field and would not necessarily be agreed to by others.

Before I get to the main issues, I should like to make four prefatory comments:

(1) When I speak of schizophrenia, I shall generally be using that term in the broad sense in which it is usually employed in the United States, rather than in the more limited sense used in much of Europe.[3] I follow American rather than European usage, not because I think it superior, but because it is the usage that has been employed in much of the relevant research. Any comparative discussion must necessarily employ the more inclusive, even if cruder, term.

(2) I shall generally not be able to distinguish among various types of schizophrenia, for the data rarely enable one to do so. This is most unfortunate; one should certainly want to consider "process" and "reactive" types of disturbance separately (Garmezy 1968), to distinguish between paranoid and nonparanoid types, and to take account of several other possibly critical distinctions. Worse yet, I shall at times have to rely on data about an even broader and vaguer category than schizophrenia—severe mental illness; in general, only the demonstrably organic disorders are excluded from this category. I shall, however, do this sparingly and emphasize studies that focus on schizophrenia.

(3) Social classes will be defined as aggregates of individuals who occupy broadly similar positions in the hierarchy of power, privilege, and prestige (Williams 1951, p. 89). In dealing with the research literature, I shall treat occupational position (or occupational position as weighted somewhat by education) as a serviceable index of social class for urban society. I shall not make any distinction, since the data hardly permit it, between the concepts "social class" and "socioeconomic status." And I shall not hesitate to rely on less than fully adequate indices of class when relevant investigations have employed them.

(4) Much of what I shall do in this essay will be to raise doubts and come to highly tentative conclusions from inadequate evidence. This is worth doing because we know so little and the problem is so pressing. Genetics does not seem to provide a complete explanation,[4] and, I take it from Kety's critical reviews (1960 and 1969), biochemical and physiological hypotheses have thus far failed to stand the test of replication. Of all the social variables that have been studied, those related to social class have yielded the most provocative results.[5] Thus, inadequate as the following data are, they must be taken seriously.

Reprinted from *Schizophrenia Bulletin*, No. 7, Winter, 1973, pages 60–79, by permission of the author.

1. This essay is an amalgam of two previously published papers (Kohn 1968 and 1972).

2. The rationale for doing such a review as this is to organize the evidence around certain central issues and to make use of all studies relevant to those issues. There are no definitive studies in this field, but most of them contribute something to our knowledge when placed in perspective of all the others. For an alternative approach, deliberately limited to those few studies that meet the reviewers' standards of adequacy, see Mishler and Scotch (1963). Dunham (1965) has recently argued for a more radical alternative; he disputes the legitimacy of using epidemiological data to make the types of social-psychological inferences I attempt here and insists that epidemiological studies are relevant only to the study of how social systems function.

Some other useful reviews and discussions of issues in this field are Clausen (1956, 1957, and 1959), Dohrenwend and Dohrenwend (1969), Dunham (1947, 1948, and 1953), Felix and Bowers (1948), Hollingshead (1961), Roman and Trice (1967), and Sanua (1963).

3. The classic definition of schizophrenia (Bleuler 1950) considers it to be a group of disorders whose "fundamental symptoms consist of disturbances of association and affectivity, the predilection for fantasy as against reality, and the inclination to divorce oneself from reality" (p. 14). In common with most American investigators, I use the term to refer to those severe functional disorders marked by disturbances in reality relationships and concept formation (Rosenbaum 1970, pp. 3–16).

4. I shall discuss the genetic evidence later in this essay.

5. For appraisals of the evidence about other social variables and about intersocietal differences in rates of schizophrenia, see Demerath (1955), Eaton and Weil (1955), Goldhamer and Marshall (1953), Leighton et al. (1963a), Lin (1953), and Mishler and Scotch (1963).

It must be emphasized, however, that there are exceedingly difficult problems in interpreting the data that I am about to review. The indices are suspect, the direction of causality is debatable, and the possibility that one or another alternative interpretation makes more sense than the one I draw is very real indeed. These problems will all be taken up shortly; first, though, I should like to lay out the positive evidence for a meaningful relationship between class and schizophrenia.

Evidence on the Possible Relationship of Social Class to Rates of Schizophrenia

Most of the important epidemiological studies of schizophrenia can be viewed as attempts to resolve problems of interpretation posed by the pioneer studies—Faris and Dunham's (1939) ecological study of rates of schizophrenia for the various areas of Chicago and Clark's (1948 and 1949) study of rates of schizophrenia at various occupational levels in that same city. Their findings were essentially as follows:

Faris and Dunham: Rates of first hospital admission for schizophrenia are highest in the central city areas of lowest socioeconomic status and diminish as one moves toward higher status peripheral areas.[6]

Clark: Rates for schizophrenia are highest for the lowest status occupations and diminish as one goes to higher status occupations.

The concentration of high rates of mental disorder, particularly schizophrenia, in the central city *areas* of lowest socioeconomic status has been confirmed in a number of American cities—Providence, R.I. (Faris and Dunham 1939, pp. 143–150); Peoria, Ill. (Schroeder 1942); Kansas City, Mo. (Schroeder 1942); St. Louis, Mo. (Dee 1939, Schroeder 1942, and Queen 1940); Milwaukee, Wis. (Schroeder 1942); Omaha, Neb. (Schroeder 1942); Worcester, Mass. (Gerard and Houston 1953); Rochester, N.Y. (Gardner and Babigian 1966); and Baltimore, Md. (Klee et al. 1967). The two ecological studies done in European cities—Sundby and Nyhus' study of Oslo, Norway (1963), and Hare's of Bristol, England (1956b)—are in substantial agreement, too.[7]

The concentration of high rates of mental disorder, particularly of schizophrenia, in the lowest status *occupations* has been confirmed again and again. The studies conducted by Hollingshead and Redlich in New Haven, Conn. (1958), and by Srole and his associates in midtown, New York City (1962), are well-known examples; a multitude of other investigations in the United States have come to the same conclusion.[8] Moreover, Svalastoga's (1965, pp. 100–101) reanalysis of Strömgren's data for northern Denmark is consistent, as are Leighton et al.'s data for ''Stirling County,'' Nova Scotia (1963b, pp. 279–294), Ødegaard's for Norway (1956, 1957, and 1962), Stein's for two sections of London (1957), Brooke's for England and Wales (see Morris 1959), Lin's for Taiwan (1969), and Stenbäck and Achté's for Helsinki (1966).

But there are some exceptions. Clausen and I happened across the first (Clausen and Kohn 1959), when we discovered that for Hagerstown, Md., there was no discernible relationship between either occupation or the social status of the area and rates of schizophrenia.[9] On a reexamination of past studies, we discovered a curious thing: the larger the city, the stronger the correlation between rates of schizophrenia and these indices of social class. In the metropolis of Chicago, the correlation is large, and the relationship is linear: the lower the social status, the higher the rates. In cities of 100,000 to 500,000 (or perhaps more), the correlation is smaller and not so linear: It is more a matter of a concentration of cases in the lowest socioeconomic strata, with not so much variation among higher strata. When you get down to a city as small as Hagerstown—36,000—the correlation disappears.

8. See, for example, Locke et al. (1958), Frumkin (1955), Dunham (1965), Lemkau, Tietze, and Cooper (1942), Fuson (1943), Turner and Wagenfeld (1967), and Rushing (1969). Relevant, too, are some early studies whose full significance was not appreciated until later: Nolan (1917), Ødegaard (1932), and Green (1939). One puzzling partial exception comes from Jaco's (1960) study of Texas. He finds the highest incidence of schizophrenia among the unemployed, but otherwise a strange, perhaps curvilinear relationship of occupational status to incidence. It may be that so many of his patients were classified as unemployed (rather than according to their pre-illness occupational status) that the overall picture is distorted.

9. In that paper, the data on occupational rates were incompletely reported. Although we divided the population into four occupational classes, based on U.S. Census categories, we presented the actual rates for only the highest and lowest classes, which led some readers to conclude, erroneously, that we had divided the population into only two occupational classes. In fact, the average annual rates of first hospital admission for schizophrenia per 100,000 population aged 15–64 were:

(a) professional, technical, and managerial personnel, and officials and proprietors:	21.3
(b) clerical and sales personnel:	23.8
(c) craftsmen, foremen, and kindred workers:	10.7
(d) operatives, service workers, and laborers:	21.7

Our measures of occupational mobility, to be discussed later, were based on movement among the same four categories.

6. The pattern is most marked for paranoid schizophrenia, least so for catatonic, which tends to concentrate in the foreign-born populations of slum communities (pp. 82–108). Unfortunately, subsequent studies in smaller cities dealt with too few cases to examine the distribution of separable types of schizophrenia as carefully as did Faris and Dunham.

7. There are some especially difficult problems in interpreting the ecological findings, which I shall not discuss here because most of the later and crucial evidence comes from other modes of research. The problems inherent in interpreting ecological studies are discussed in Robinson (1950) and Clausen and Kohn (1954).

Subsequent studies in a number of different places have confirmed our generalization. Sundby and Nyhus (1963), for example, showed that Oslo, Norway, manifests the typical pattern for cities of its half-million size: a high concentration in the lowest social stratum, little variation above. Hollingshead and Redlich's (1958, p. 236) data on new admissions for schizophrenia from New Haven, Conn., show that pattern, too. There is also substantial evidence for our conclusion that socioeconomic differentials disappear in areas of small population (Buck, Wanklin, and Hobbs 1955 and Hagnell 1966).

I think one must conclude that the relationship of socioeconomic status to schizophrenia has been demonstrated only for urban populations. Even for urban populations, a linear relationship of socioeconomic status to rates of schizophrenia has been demonstrated only for the largest metropolises. The evidence, though, that there is an unusually high rate of schizophrenia in the lowest socioeconomic strata of urban communities seems to me to be nothing less than overwhelming. The proper interpretation of why this is so, however, is not so unequivocal.

The Direction of Causality

One major issue in interpreting the reports of Faris and Dunham, Clark, and all subsequent investigators concerns the direction of causality. Rates of schizophrenia in the lowest socioeconomic strata could be disproportionately high either because conditions of life in those strata are somehow conducive to the development of schizophrenia or because people from higher social strata who become schizophrenic suffer a decline in status. Or, of course, it could be some of both. Discussions of this issue have conventionally gone under the rubric of the *drift hypothesis,* although far more is involved.

The drift hypothesis was first raised in an attempt to explain away the Faris and Dunham findings. The argument was that, in the course of their developing illness, schizophrenics tended to ''drift'' into lower status areas of the city. It is not that more cases of schizophrenia are ''produced'' in these areas, but that schizophrenics who are produced elsewhere end up at the bottom of the heap by the time they are hospitalized, and thus are counted as having come from the bottom of the heap.

When the Clark study appeared, the hypothesis was easily enlarged to include ''drift'' from higher to lower status occupations. In its broadest formulation, the drift hypothesis asserts that high rates of schizophrenia in the lowest social strata come about because people from

higher classes who become schizophrenic suffer a decline in social position as a consequence of their illness. In some versions of the hypothesis, it is further suggested that schizophrenics from smaller locales tend to migrate to the lowest status areas and occupations of large metropolises; this would result in an exaggeration of rates there and a corresponding underestimation of rates for the place and class from which they come.

One approach to this problem has been to study the histories of social mobility of schizophrenics. Unfortunately, the evidence is inconsistent. Three studies indicate that schizophrenics have been downwardly mobile in occupational status,[10] three others that they have not been.[11] Some of these studies do not compare the experiences of the schizophrenics to those of normal persons from comparable social backgrounds. Those that do are nevertheless inconclusive—either because the comparison group was not well chosen, or because the city in which the study was done was too small to have a concentration of schizophrenia in the lowest social class. Since no study is definitive, any assessment must be based on a subjective weighing of the strengths and weaknesses of them all. My assessment is that the weight of this evidence clearly indicates either that schizophrenics have been no more downwardly mobile (in fact, no less upwardly mobile) than other people from the same social backgrounds, or at minimum, that the degree of downward mobility is insufficient to explain the high concentration of schizophrenia in the lowest socioeconomic strata.

There is another and more direct way of looking at the question, however, and from this perspective the question is still unresolved. The reformulated question focuses on the social class origins of schizophrenics; it asks whether the occupations of fathers of schizophrenics are concentrated in the lowest social strata. If they are, that is clear evidence in favor of the hypothesis that lower class status is conducive to schizophrenia. Even if they are not, class still might be important in schizophrenia—it might, for example, be a matter of stress experienced by lower-class adults, rather than of the experience of being born and raised in the lower

10. Evidence that schizophrenics have been downwardly mobile in *occupational* status has been presented in Lystad (1957), Schwartz (1946), and Turner (1968). In addition, there has been some debatable evidence that the ecological concentration of schizophrenia has resulted from the migration of unattached men into the high-rate areas of the city. (See Dunham 1965, Gerard and Houston 1953, and Hare 1956a.)

11. Evidence that schizophrenics have not been downwardly mobile in occupational status is presented in Clausen and Kohn (1959), Dunham (1964), and Hollingshead and Redlich (1954 and 1958, pp. 244–248). Evidence that the ecological concentration of schizophrenia has not resulted from inmigration or downward drift is presented in Hollingshead and Redlich (1954), LaPouse, Monk, and Terris (1956), and, if I interpret his data correctly, in Dunham (1965).

class; but certainly the explanation that would require the fewest assumptions would be the drift hypothesis.

The first major study to evaluate the evidence from this perspective argued in favor of lower class origins being conducive to mental disorder, although not necessarily to schizophrenia. Srole and his associates (1962, pp. 212–222) found, in their study of midtown New York, that rates of mental disorder do correlate with parents' socioeconomic status, although not so strongly as with the subjects' own socioeconomic status. But then Goldberg and Morrison (1963) found that, although the occupations of male schizophrenic patients admitted to hospitals in England and Wales show the usual concentration of cases in the lowest social class, their fathers' occupations do not. Since this study was addressed specifically to schizophrenia, the new evidence seemed more directly in point. One might quarrel with some aspects of the study—the index of social class is debatable, for example, and data are lacking for 25 percent of the originally drawn sample—but this is much too good a study to be taken lightly. Nor can one conclude that the situation in England and Wales is different from that in the United States, for Dunham (1965)[12] reports that two segments of Detroit show a similar picture.

There is yet one more study to be considered, however, and this the most important of all, for it offers the most complete data about class origins, mobility, and eventual class position of male schizophrenics. Turner and Wagenfeld (1967), in a study of Monroe County (Rochester), N.Y., discovered a remarkable pattern: Rates of first treatment for schizophrenia are disproportionately high, both for patients of lowest occupational status and for patients whose fathers had lowest occupational status, but these are by and large not the same patients. Some of those whose fathers were in the lowest occupational category had themselves moved up and some of those ending in the lowest occupational category had come from higher class origins. Thus, there is evidence both for the proposition that lower class origins are conducive to schizophrenia and for the proposition that most lower class schizophrenics come from higher socioeconomic origins. Downward social mobility does not explain the class-schizophrenia relationship, but it does contribute to that relationship.

How much downward mobility is there, and how does it occur? Turner and Wagenfeld's data (p. 110) indicate that the absolute amount of downward mobility is almost nil: 36 percent of the schizophrenics in their sample have fallen and 35 percent have risen from their fathers' occupational levels, for a net decline of less than

one-tenth of a step on a 7-point occupational scale. In the general population, though, there has been a net rise of nearly one-half step on the same 7-point scale. Thus, one could say that, *relative to the general population*, schizophrenics have been downwardly mobile. More precisely, they have lagged behind the general population in not rising above their fathers' occupational levels. This has happened, not because the schizophrenics lost occupational positions they had once achieved, but because many of them failed ever to achieve as high an occupational level as do most men of their social class origins.

These findings argue strongly against a simple drift hypothesis; it is not, as some have argued, that we have erroneously rated men at lower than their usual socioeconomic levels by classifying them according to occupations at time of hospitalization, after they have suffered a decline in occupational position. It is likely, though, that a more sophisticated drift hypothesis applies—that some people genetically or constitutionally or otherwise predisposed to schizophrenia show debilitating effects at least as early as the time of their first jobs, for they are never able to achieve the occupational levels that might be expected of them. If so, the possibilities of some interaction between genetic predisposition and early social circumstances are very real indeed. It is also possible that downward social mobility has occurred in earlier generations—that because of genetic or other defects, schizophrenics' parents and grandparents failed to achieve as high a position as might have been expected of them. I defer consideration of this possibility until I have discussed the evidence for a genetic component in schizophrenia.

For the present, I think it can be tentatively concluded that, despite what Goldberg and Morrison found for England and Wales, the weight of evidence lies against the drift hypothesis' providing a sufficient explanation of the class-schizophrenia relationship. In all probability, lower class families produce a disproportionate number of schizophrenics, although not perhaps by so large a margin as one would conclude from studies that rely on schizophrenics' own occupational attainments.

The Adequacy of Indices

The adequacy of indices is another major issue in interpreting the Faris and Dunham, Clark, and all subsequent investigations. Most of these studies are based on hospital admission rates, which may not give a valid picture of the true incidence of schizophrenia. Studies that do not rely on hospital rates encounter other and perhaps even more serious difficulties, with which we shall presently deal.

---

12. See also Dunham, Phillips, and Srinivasan (1966), and Rinehart (1966).

The difficulty with using admission rates as the basis for computing rates of schizophrenia is that lower class psychotics may be more likely to be hospitalized and, if hospitalized, to be diagnosed as schizophrenic, especially in public hospitals. Faris and Dunham tried to solve this problem by including patients admitted to private as well as to public mental hospitals. This was insufficient because, as later studies have shown (Kaplan, Reed, and Richardson 1956), some people who suffer serious mental disorder never enter a mental hospital.

Subsequent studies have attempted to do better by including more and more social agencies in their search for cases; Hollingshead and Redlich (1958) in New Haven and Jaco (1960) in Texas, for example, have extended their coverage to include everyone who enters any sort of treatment facility; Jaco even went so far as to question all the physicians in Texas. This is better, but clearly the same objections hold in principle. Furthermore, Srole and his associates (1962, pp. 240–251) have demonstrated that there are considerable social differences between people who have been treated, somewhere, for mental illness, and severely impaired people, some large proportion of them schizophrenic, who have never been to any sort of treatment facility. So we must conclude that using treatment—any sort of treatment—as an index of mental disorder is suspect.

The alternative is to go out into the community and examine everyone—or a representative sample of everyone—yourself. This has been done by a number of investigators; for example, Essen-Möller (1956 and 1961) in Sweden, Srole (1962) in New York, and Leighton et al. (1963b) in Nova Scotia. They have solved one problem, but have run into three others.

The first is that most of these investigators have found it impossible to classify schizophrenia reliably, and have had to resort to larger and vaguer categories—severe mental illness, functional psychosis, and such. For some purposes, this may be justified. For our immediate purposes, it is exceedingly unfortunate.

Second, even if you settle for such a concept as "mental illness," it is difficult to establish criteria that can be applied reliably and validly in community studies (Dohrenwend and Dohrenwend 1965). For all its inadequacies, hospitalization is at least an unambiguous index, and you can be fairly certain that people who are hospitalized are disturbed. But how does one interpret Leighton et al.'s (1963c, p. 1026) estimate that about a third of their population suffer significant psychiatric impairment, or Srole's (1962, p. 138) that almost a quarter of his are impaired?

The third problem in community studies is that it is so difficult to secure data on the incidence of mental disturbance that most studies settle for prevalence data (Kramer 1957). That is, instead of ascertaining the number of new cases arising in various population groups during some period of time, they count the number of people currently ill at the time of the study. This latter measure—prevalence—is inadequate because it reflects not only incidence but also duration of illness. As Hollingshead and Redlich (1958) have shown, duration of illness—insofar as it incapacitates—is highly correlated with social class. Clearly, what is needed is repeated studies of the population, to pick up new cases as they arise and thus to establish true incidence figures. The crucial problem, of course, is to develop reliable measures of mental disorder, for without these our repeated surveys will measure nothing but the errors of our instruments. Meantime, we have to recognize that prevalence studies use an inappropriate measure that exaggerates the relationship of socioeconomic status to mental disorder.

So, taken all together, the results of the studies of class and schizophrenia are hardly definitive. They may even all wash out—one more example of inadequate methods leading to premature, false conclusions. I cannot prove otherwise. Yet I think the most reasonable interpretation of all these findings is that they point to something real. Granted that there isn't a single definitive study in the lot, the weaknesses of one are compensated for by the strengths of some other, and the total edifice is probably much stronger than you would conclude from knowing only how frail are its component parts. A large number of complementary studies all seem to point to the same conclusion: that rates of mental disorder, particularly of schizophrenia, are highest at the lowest socioeconomic levels, at least in moderately large cities, and this probably isn't just a matter of drift or inadequate indices or some other artifact of the methods we use. In all probability, more schizophrenia is actually produced at the lowest socioeconomic levels. At any rate, let us take that as a working hypothesis and explore the question further. Assuming that more schizophrenia occurs at lower socioeconomic levels—why?

Alternative Interpretations[13]

Many discussions of the class-schizophrenia relationship have focused on interpretations that, in effect, explain away its theoretical significance. This is obviously true of those interpretations that consider the relationship to be artifactual, the result of methodological error. It is equally true of interpretations, of which the drift

13. Although some of the interpretations discussed in this section have been addressed to mental illnes in general, they are equally applicable to schizophrenia.

hypothesis is prototypic, that assert that schizophrenics are found disproportionately in lower social classes because of the impairment they have suffered or because of some characterological defect of nonsocial origin. The social statuses of schizophrenics, from this point of view, may tell us something about how schizophrenics fare in society but little or nothing about what produces schizophrenia.

Others argue that class matters for schizophrenia, not because lower class conditions of life are conducive to the development of the disorder, but because a person's social class position affects other people's perceptions of and reactions to his behavior. One such interpretation asserts that psychiatric and other authorities are especially prone to stigmatize and hospitalize lower class people: They victimize the powerless.[14] Similar, though more subtle, explanations focus on the processes by which families, employers, police, and others come to label some deviant behaviors as mentally disordered, thereby setting in motion complex changes in social expectation and self-conception that sometimes eventuate in hospitalization.[15] From this point of view, the class-schizophrenia relationship documents the discriminatory readiness of many people to see signs of mental disorder in lower class behavior.

Even interpretations that accord a primary causal significance to social structural conditions have generally deemphasized the importance of social class, per se. Faris and Dunham, for example, did not take class very seriously in interpreting their data. From among the host of variables characteristic of the high-rate areas of Chicago, they focused on such things as high rates of population turnover and ethnic mixtures and hypothesized that the really critical thing about the high-rate areas was the degree of social isolation they engendered. Two subsequent studies, one by Jaco (1954) in Texas, the other by Hare (1956b) in Bristol, England, are consistent in that they, too, show a correlation between rates of schiz-

14. This interpretation is a logical outgrowth of Goffman's (1959) analysis of the "moral career of the mental patient," which sees hospitalization as the end-product of a "funnel of betrayal," with the psychiatrist as a major culprit. Goffman deals only in passing with the possibility of class differences in the likelihood of victimization, but some of his followers argue that psychiatrists are especially prone to hospitalize lower class people and to diagnose them as schizophrenic; middle class people are spared, if not hospitalization, at least the stigma of being called schizophrenic.

15. Scheff (1966) presents a cogent formulation of the labeling theory approach as applied to mental disorder. But Gove (1970) marshals evidence that this approach is based on assumptions that are inconsistent with what is known: principally, that people strongly resist seeing deviant behavior as mentally disordered; the pressures, instead, are to interpret even grotesque behavior as somehow normal and situationally explainable.

ophrenia and various ecological indices of social isolation. The only study that directly examines the role of social isolation in the lives of schizophrenics however, seems to demonstrate that, while social isolation may be symptomatic of developing illness, it does not play an important role in etiology (Kohn and Clausen 1955).

Several other possibilities have been suggested, some supported by intriguing, if inconclusive, evidence. One is that it is not socioeconomic status as such that is principally at issue, but social integration; Leighton et al. (1963b) have produced plausible evidence for this interpretation. Another is that the high rates of schizophrenia found in lower class populations are a consequence of especially high rates for lower class members of some "ethnic" groups who happen to be living in areas where other ethnic groups predominate. In their study in Boston, for example, Schwartz and Mintz (1963) showed that Italian Americans living in predominantly non-Italian neighborhoods have very high rates of schizophrenia, while those living in predominantly Italian neighborhoods do not; the former group contributes disproportionately to the rates for lower class neighborhoods. Wechsler and Pugh (1967) extended this interpretive model to suggest that rates should be higher for any persons living in a community where persons of their social attributes are in a minority. Their analysis of Massachusetts towns provides some surprisingly supportive data.

Other interpretations focus on the occupational component of socioeconomic status. Ødegaard (1956) showed that rates of schizophrenia are higher for some occupations that are losing members and lower for some that are expanding; in recent times, declining occupations have generally been of lower status. Alternatively, some investigators see the key in discrepancies between schizophrenics' occupational aspirations and achievements, arguing that the pivotal fact is not that they have achieved so little but that they had wanted so much more (Kleiner and Parker 1963, Parker and Kleiner 1966, and Myers and Roberts 1959).

These several interpretations are, for the most part, consistent with existing data and must be acknowledged to be plausible. But they largely neglect the most straightforward possibility of all—that social class is related to schizophrenia primarily because the conditions of life built into lower social class position are conducive to that disorder.

I think it is time to devote a larger portion of our efforts to devising and testing formulations about how and why lower class conditions of life might contribute to schizophrenia. The remainder of this essay is devoted to presenting one such formulation. It is necessarily ten-

TABLE 1

Some Principal U.S. Studies of Socioeconomic Differentials in Rates of Serious Mental Disorder, Particularly Schizophrenia.

INVESTIGATOR & LOCALE	CRITERION OF MENTAL DISORDER	CENTRAL FINDINGS
Faris & Dunham (1939, Map XI) Chicago, Ill.	First hospital admission, diagnosis of schizophrenia, 1922–1934, public & private hospitals combined.	The average annual rate per 100,000 population, aged 15–64, is 102.3 for the central city area of lowest socioeconomic status, with gradually diminishing rates to less than 25 in the highest status areas at the periphery of the city.
Clark (1948, table 3) Chicago, Ill.	First hospital admission, diagnosis of schizophrenia, 1922–1934, public & private hospitals combined.	Using the respondents' own educational 20–49 years old: The rank-order correlation between occupational status & hospitalization rate for schizophrenia is -0.81, the rates increasing from less than 100/100,000 population for large owners, professionals, & "major salesmen" to more than 600/100,000 for semi-skilled & unskilled workers.
Hollingshead & Redlich (1958, table 17) New Haven, Conn.	(a) Incidence: First treatment by any psychiatric agency, diagnosis of schizophrenia, between May 31 & Dec. 1, 1950. (b) Prevalence: Persons in treatment by any psychiatric agency at any time from May 31–Dec. 1, 1950, diagnosis of schizophrenia.	(a) Using the Hollingshead Index of Social Position, which combines the education & occupational status of head of household & social status of neighborhood as the basis for classifying social-class position: Age- & sex-adjusted rates per 100,000 population are 6 for two highest social classes (combined), 8 for class 3, 10 for class 4, & 20 for class 5. (b) Age- & sex-adjusted rates per 100,000 population are: 111 for social classes 1 & 2 (combined), 168 for class 3, 300 for class 4, and 895 for class 5.
Srole et al. (1962, tables 12-1 & 12-4 & figure 5) Midtown, New York City	Psychiatric ratings of degree of impairment, based on structured interviews with a representative sample of the population, aged 20–59. (Fieldwork conducted in 1954.)	Using age-adjusted rates for white males, & occupational levels as the basis for classifying socioeconomic status, respondents judged to be "impaired, with severe symptom formation" or "incapacitated," increase from 5.8% in the highest of 12 socioeconomic levels to 30.6% in the lowest; using respondents' fathers' educational & occupational levels, those severely impaired or incapacitated increase from 5.7% in the highest of 6 socioeconomic levels to 14.7% in the lowest.
Dunham (1965, tables 75 & 76) Two small areas of Detroit, Mich. (one a high-rate area, the other a low-rate area).	First contact with any psychiatric facility, diagnosis of schizophrenia, during 1958.	Using the patients' own educational & occupational levels as the basis for classifying social-class position, the incidence of schizophrenia for the two areas combined is 0.0 for class 1, 0.32 for class 2, 0.35 for class 3, 0.21 for class 4, & 1.45 for class 5. Using patients' fathers' occupational levels (not education) as the basis for a comparable classification, the corresponding rates are 0.87, 0.79, 0.44, 0.43, & 0.69.

TABLE 1 continued.
Some Principal U.S. Studies of Socioeconomic Differentials in Rates of Serious Mental Disorders Particularly Schizophrenia.

INVESTIGATOR & LOCALE	CRITERION OF MENTAL DISORDER	CENTRAL FINDINGS
Turner & Wagenfeld (1967, table 1) Monroe County (Rochester), N.Y.	First contact with any psychiatric agency, diagnosis of schizophrenia, Jan. 1, 1960 to June 30, 1963. (Limited to white males, aged 20–50.)	Using patients' own occupational levels, the ratio of observed/expected number of schizophrenic patients is 0.4 for professionals, 0.8 for minor professionals & managerial personnel, 1.4 for clerical & sales personnel, 0.9 for skilled manual workers, 0.9 for semiskilled workers, & 3.1 for unskilled workers. The corresponding ratios, based on patients' fathers' occupational levels, are 0.6, 0.9, 0.8, 1.5, 0.6, & 2.5.
Rushing (1969, table 1) Washington State	First hospital admission (State hospitals only), diagnosis of schizophrenia, between Dec. 31, 1954 & April 31, 1965.	Using patients' occupational levels as the basis for classification, the average annual rates of first hospitalization for schizophrenia per 100,000 employed males, for males aged 21–65, are 21 in the highest of five socioeconomic levels, 39 in level 2, 49 in level 3, 64 in level 4, & 270 in level 5.

tative, for it is based on seriously incomplete information; at critical places, there is no directly pertinent evidence, and I can only speculate.

Genetics and Stress

To try to explain the relationship of class to schizophrenia without bringing other variables into play would be extremely difficult. One would be hard-pressed to resolve the apparent contradiction that, although lower class conditions of life appear to be conducive to schizophrenia, the vast majority of lower class people never become schizophrenic (Roman and Trice 1967, p. 65). When, however, one brings genetics and stress into consideration, the task becomes more manageable. It is no longer necessary to find in class itself an explanation of schizophrenia. Instead, the interpretive task is to explain how social class fits into an equation that includes genetics, probably stress, and undoubtedly other, as yet unrecognized, factors.

Genetics

Recent studies of monozygotic twins and of adopted children demonstrate that, although genetics alone cannot provide a sufficient explanation of schizophrenia, some genetic mechanism is almost undoubtedly in-

volved.[16] Geneticists do not agree on what is inherited—whether it be a vulnerability specifically to schizophrenia, a vulnerability to mental disorder more generally, or even a type of personality structure. Nor is it certain whether the mode of genetic transmission is monogenic or polygenic. Important as these questions may be, they can for my immediate purposes be passed over; all that need be accepted is that genetics plays some substantial part in schizophrenia.

One could argue, in fact, that genetics explains why *class* is related to schizophrenia. If there is a heritable component in schizophrenia, there must have been higher than usual rates of the disorder among the parents and grandparents of schizophrenics. Moreover, since schizophrenia is debilitating, there would have been downward social mobility in earlier generations. Thus, schizophrenics could come disproportionately from lower class families, not because the conditions of life experienced by lower class people have pernicious effects, but because there is a concentration of genetically susceptible people in the lower social classes.

These processes of "multigenerational drift" may well contribute to the increased probability of schizo-

16. For a comprehensive assessment of the genetic evidence, see Rosenthal (1970). Other valuable discussions are to be found in Rosenthal (1962 and 1968); Kringlen (1966 and 1967); Slater (1968); and Shields (1968). For discussions of the mode of genetic transmission, see Gottesman and Shields (1967); Rosenthal (1970); and Heston (1970).

phrenia for people of lower class position. The question, though, is whether there could have been *enough* downward mobility attributable to the genetically induced disabilities of earlier generations to account for the heightened incidence of schizophrenia found today in the lower social classes.

Since there are no data about the mobility rates of parents and grandparents of schizophrenics, one can only come to a tentative appraisal based on data about schizophrenics themselves. As indicated earlier, male schizophrenics have not actually declined from their fathers' occupational levels, but they have lagged behind the general population in not rising above those levels. These data make it doubtful that there could have been enough of an increase in genetic susceptibility to schizophrenia in the lower social classes, even over several generations, to account for all or even the major part of the class-schizophrenia relationship. It would take a large amount of downward mobility, not just a moderate lag in upward mobility, to have a pronounced effect on the total amount of genetic susceptibility in the lower social classes. Moreover, data based on the occupational histories of schizophrenic patients probably exaggerate the amount of occupational lag that occurred in earlier generations; it can reasonably be assumed that the parents and grandparents were, on the average, less disturbed and therefore less likely to lag in mobility than were the schizophrenics themselves. Finally, we need not assume that all deficits in occupational attainment are genetically induced or have genetic consequences. In all probability, genetically induced, intergenerational social mobility has contributed to, but falls far short of explaining, the higher incidence of schizophrenia in the lower social classes.

Stress

Investigators of the role of stress in schizophrenia face a perplexing problem in defining and indexing stress (Lazarus 1966, Dohrenwend and Dohrenwend 1969, Scott and Howard 1970). A narrow conception would have that term apply only to externally induced events that can be assumed to be psychically painful to virtually everyone who experiences them. Such a conception achieves rigor at the price of excluding from its purview those traumas that may have been self-induced, as well as all those traumas that are painful for some people but not for everyone. It also excludes such real, if self-defined, misfortunes as failure to attain a longed-for goal. In fact, the only experiences that can be assumed to be externally induced and to be painful for everyone are such crises as serious illness, death of close relatives, hunger, and loss of one's job; and even these misfortunes

may not be equally painful to all who experience them. But broader conceptions of stress are also problematic. At the extreme, if any event that produces subjectively experienced pain in some individual is considered to be stressful, formulations that attribute to stress a causal role in schizophrenia become tautological.

Research workers have for the most part dealt with this dilemma by (explicitly or implicitly) defining as stressful those events that usually are externally induced and that can be expected to be painful to most people who experience them. Such events occur with greater frequency at lower social class levels: People at the bottom of the class hierarchy experience great economic insecurity and far more than their share of serious ill health, degradation, and the afflictions attendant on inadequate, overcrowded housing, often in overpopulated, underserviced areas.

Is stress conducive to schizophrenia? A definitive study would require direct, rather than inferential, measurement of stress; a research design that takes social class explicitly into account; and, of course, an adequate index of schizophrenia. Not surprisingly, no study meets all these criteria. Therefore, one can make only a tentative overall appraisal, recognizing that some pertinent studies do not index stress so well as we should like, others do not explicitly control social class, and some are addressed to mental disorder in general rather than specifically to schizophrenia.

My appraisal of the research evidence is based primarily on the studies by Birley and Brown (1970), Brown and Birley (1968), Eitinger (1964), Langner and Michael (1963), and Rogler and Hollingshead (1965). These studies do indicate that stress is associated with the occurrence of schizophrenia. Moreover, Rogler and Hollingshead (1965, pp. 409–411) show that the relationship between stress and schizophrenia does not simply reflect the high levels of stress prevalent in the lower social classes. From their investigation of schizophrenics and matched controls in the lowest social class of San Juan, Puerto Rico, they report that during the year before the onset of symptoms, the schizophrenics experienced notably greater stress than did the controls.[17] Even when judged by the harsh standards of life in the

---

17. A cautionary note: the Rogler-Hollingshead study is based on schizophrenics who are married or living in stable consensual unions. One would assume them to be predominantly "reactive" schizophrenics—precisely the group whom clinical studies describe as having had normal childhood social experiences, good social adjustment, and extreme precipitating circumstances. So these findings may apply only to reactive schizophrenia, not to process schizophrenia. It may also be that some of the stress experienced by the schizophrenics resulted from their already disordered behavior. Still, Rogler and Hollingshead present a strong case that externally induced stress is important for some types of schizophrenia.

San Juan slums, the stresses that preceded the onset of schizophrenia were unusually severe.

As with genetics, one must reverse the question and ask whether stress can explain the relationship of class to schizophrenia. The Rogler-Hollingshead study cannot help us here, for it is limited to one social class. Unfortunately for our purposes, the only study that does provide data for all levels of social class, that by Langner and Michael, is addressed to mental disorder in general rather than specifically to schizophrenia. This study is nevertheless germane, for it indicates that, at any given level of stress, people of lower social class position are more likely to become mentally disturbed than are people of higher social class position. In fact, the more sources of stress, the greater the class difference in the proportion of people who manifest psychotic symptoms. The implication is that the relationship of class to mental disorder (hence, if we may extrapolate, to schizophrenia) is not attributable to the amount of stress that people endure. There must also be important class differences in how effectively people deal with stress.

Part of the explanation for lower class people dealing less effectively with stress may be that the stress-producing situations they face are less alterable by individual action than are those encountered by people of higher social class position. Many of the stresses they encounter arise from economic circumstances over which few individuals have much control, lower class individuals least of all. Moreover, lower class people have little money or power to employ in coping with the consequences of stress. It also appears (Dohrenwend and Dohrenwend 1969, pp. 137–139) that fewer institutional resources, are available to them, either for escaping stressful situations or for mitigating the consequences of stress. Finally, there is reason to believe that lower class conditions of life limit people's *internal* resources for dealing with stress (Dohrenwend and Dohrenwend 1969, pp. 140–143).[18]

While recognizing that all these factors may make it difficult for lower class people to deal effectively with stress, my formulation emphasizes only one: that their conditions of life may impair lower class people's internal resources. I shall argue, more generally, that these life conditions may adversely affect people's ability to deal, not only with situations that by my limited definition are stressful, but also with many other dilemmas and uncertainties in a rapidly changing, complex society.

A critic might contend that an adequate explanation of the class-schizophrenia relationship can be formulated without taking internal resources into account—that one can explain the heightened incidence of schizophrenia in the lower social classes as resulting from a combination of greater genetic vulnerability, greater exposure to stress, and lesser external resources for dealing with stress. Present evidence is too scanty for a definitive judgment, but I think this formulation too narrow; it ignores much of what we know about the social psychology of class. And so I shall devote much of the remainder of this essay to laying out the reasons for believing that lower class conditions of life may adversely affect people's internal resources for dealing with stressful, problematic, or complex situations, and for believing that such impairment may be important in the schizophrenic process.

Class, Family, and Schizophrenia

If internal resources for dealing with complex and stressful situations are at issue, then that primary socializing institution, the family, is probably somehow involved. The many studies of the role of the family in the development of schizophrenia are pertinent here, even though most of them have been addressed to a question quite different from ours. The purpose of these investigations has generally been to find some pattern of interpersonal relationship unique to the families of schizophrenics. To the best of my knowledge, though, no well-controlled study has shown a substantial difference between the patterns of parent-child relationship characteristic of families that produce schizophrenic offspring and those characteristic of ordinary lower and working class families.[19] From a traditional, single factor perspective, two interpretations of this negative finding are possible.

One would be that the family plays no important part in the genesis of schizophrenia. This interpretation holds that the patterns of parent-child relationship typical of schizophrenia-producing families merely reflect those of the lower social classes from which schizophrenics disproportionately come,[20] without having been instrumental in the disorder.

---

18. Pertinent, too, are the discussions by Brewster Smith (1968) of "the competent self," by Foote and Cottrell (1955) of "interpersonal competence," and by Phillips (1968) of "social competence."

19. This sweeping conclusion is based on my inability, and that of others who have reviewed the research literature, to find a single study that finds important differences in patterns of parent-child relationship between schizophrenics and ordinary persons of lower social class background. Several well-controlled studies find an absence of difference; see, for example, Kohn and Clausen (1956), Rogler and Hollingshead (1965), and Mishler and Waxler (1968).

For a comprehensive, if now dated, review of research on family and schizophrenia, see Sanua (1961); see also the introduction to, and references included in, Kohn and Clausen (1956); the discussion and references in Mishler and Waxler (1965); and pp. 140–163 of Rosenbaum (1970).

20. For an incisive review of research on class and family, see Bronfenbrenner (1958). For references to studies completed since Bronfenbrenner's review, and to studies done outside the United States, see Kohn (1969, p. 4).

The alternative interpretation would assert that the family does play a critically differentiating role in schizophrenia, but that the statistical evidence is not yet in. From this point of view, most well-controlled studies have been too limited in focus. They have dealt with such relatively concrete aspects of family life as the overall pattern of role allocation, parental bestowal of warmth and affection, and disciplinary practices, but have missed more subtle interpersonal processes that recent clinical investigations have emphasized.[21] Future studies may show clear and convincing evidence of important differences between schizophrenia-producing families and ordinary families of lower social class position.

There is, however, a third possible interpretation. Instead of looking to the family for a total explanation of schizophrenia, this interpretation attempts only to explain how lower class families may contribute to the disorder in genetically vulnerable people who are subject to great stress. From this perspective, the family is important for schizophrenia, not because the family experiences of schizophrenics have differed in some presently undisclosed manner from those of other people of lower social class background, but precisely because they have been similar. If this be the case, there is no reason to restrict our interest to processes that are unique to the family, such as its particular patterns of role allocation. We should expand our focus to include, even to emphasize, processes that the family shares with other institutions—notably, those processes that affect people's ability to perceive, to assess, and to deal with complexity and stress.[22]

The family, I suggest, is important principally because of its strategic role in transmitting to its offspring conceptions of social reality that parents have learned from their own experience. In particular, many lower class families transmit to their offspring an orientational system[23] too limited and too rigid for dealing effectively with complex, changing, or stressful situations. This point of view is, I believe, consonant with recent psychiatric thinking about the family and schizophrenia, which emphasizes those communicational and cognitive processes in schizophrenia-producing families that con-

tribute to the schizophrenic's difficulties in interpreting social reality.[24] What is new is the assertion that these conceptions of reality, far from being unique to families whose offspring become schizophrenic, are widely held in the lower social classes, and in fact arise out of the very conditions of life experienced by people in these segments of society.

Social Class and Conceptions of Reality

The heart of my formulation is the hypothesis that the constricted conditions of life experienced by people of lower social class position foster conceptions of social reality so limited and so rigid as to impair people's ability to deal resourcefully with the problematic and the stressful. Although speculative, this hypothesis is a direct extrapolation from what is known about the relationship between social class and conceptions of reality (see, for example, the review by Rossi and Blum 1968). My own research (Kohn 1969, chapters 4 and 5) indicates that the lower a man's social class position, the more likely he is to value conformity to external authority and to believe that such conformity is all that his own capacities and the exigencies of the world allow; in particular, the lower a man's social class position, the more likely is his orientational system to be marked by a rigidly conservative view of man and his social institutions, fearfulness and distrust, and a fatalistic belief that one is at the mercy of forces and people beyond one's control, often, beyond one's understanding.

One need not argue that this orientational system is held by all lower class people, or that lower class people hold these beliefs and values to the exclusion of others more characteristic of higher social classes (Rodman 1963 and Miller 1964). It does seem to be well established, though, that these conceptions of social reality are most prevalent at the bottom of the social hierarchy.

The existence of class differences in beliefs and values is hardly accidental, nor even cultural in the sense employed by "culture of poverty" theorists who see lower class orientations as something handed down from generation to generation independently of current social conditions.[25] On the contrary, social class embodies

---

21. In support of this position are indications that lower class families with schizophrenic offspring, although no different from other lower class families in role patterning, may manifest disturbed, even pathological patterns of communication (Rosenthal, Behrens, and Chodoff 1968 and Behrens et al. 1968).

22. One implication is that it is not only the social class of one's parental family, but also one's adult social-class position, that matters for schizophrenia. This point is often overlooked, particularly in discussions of the drift hypothesis.

23. By orientation (or orientational system), I mean conceptions of the external world and of self that serve to define men's stance toward reality.

24. Especially relevant here is the work of Lyman Wynne and his associates (Wynne and Singer 1963, Singer and Wynne 1965, and Wynne 1967). See also Mishler and Waxler (1965), Bateson et al. (1956), and Schuham (1967).

25. For a systematic statement of the culture of poverty thesis, see Lewis (1965, pp. xlii–lii). For critiques of this and related concepts, see Valentine (1968), Roach and Gursslin (1967), and Rossi and Blum (1968). The principal issue, as I see it, is not whether there are class differences in values, orientation, and cognitive style—there certainly are—but whether the lower class orientational systems, once transmitted from parents to children, are amenable to change. My data show that, if there is a discrepancy between early family experience and later educa-

such basic differences in conditions of life that subjective reality is necessarily different for people differentially situated in the social hierarchy. Lower class conditions of life allow little freedom of action, give little reason to feel in control of fate. To be lower class is to be insufficiently educated, to work at a job of little substantive complexity, under conditions of close supervision, and with little leeway to vary a routine flow of work. These are precisely the conditions that narrow one's conception of social reality and reduce one's sense of personal efficacy (Kohn 1969, chapters 9 and 10).

There is, then, ample evidence that class differences in conditions of life are productive of differences in conceptions of social reality. But do these differences in orientation contribute to class differences in schizophrenia? There are three reasons for thinking that they might.

• The first is a consideration of theoretical strategy. Instead of searching aimlessly among the innumerable correlates of social class for one or another that might help explain its relationship to schizophrenia, I think it strategic to look to what underlies the social psychology of class: Members of different social classes, by virtue of enjoying (or suffering) different conditions of life, come to see the world differently—to develop different conceptions of social reality, different aspirations and hopes and fears, different conceptions of the desirable. Class differences in orientation are an important bridge between social conditions and psychological functioning.

• The second reason for thinking orientations pertinent is that our analysis of the interrelationship of class, genetics, and stress points to the desirability of taking into account any factor that might have an important bearing on class differences in how effectively people are able to deal with stressful or problematic situations. It seems to me that the conformist orientational system characteristic of the lower social classes is less adequate for dealing with such situations than is the self-directed orientational system more prevalent at higher social class levels.

Admittedly, the characteristically lower class orientational system, molded as it is by actual conditions, may often be useful. It is, for example, attuned to the occupational demands that lower class people must meet; a self-directed stance would probably bring few rewards and might easily lead to trouble. Moreover, participant-observation studies of lower class life (Whyte 1943 and Liebow 1966) make it vividly apparent

that, in an environment where one may be subject to diverse and often unpredictable risks of exploitation and victimization, this perspective may serve other protective functions as well. It is a way of keeping one's guard up. It provides a defensive strategy for people who really are vulnerable to forces they cannot control.

But there are times when a defensive posture invites attack, and there are times when the assumption that one is at the mercy of forces beyond one's control—even though justified—leaves one all the more at their mercy. An orientational system predicated on conforming to the dictates of authority sees social reality too simply and too fearfully to permit taking advantage of options that might otherwise be open. It is too inflexible for precisely those problematic and stressful circumstances that most require subtlety, flexibility, and a perceptive understanding of larger social complexities.

• The third reason for thinking class differences in orientations pertinent is that orientations—conceptions of reality—are fundamental to schizophrenia. Fearful, inflexible reactions to threat are integral to the schizophrenic experience. One reason for the disproportionately high incidence of schizophrenia at lower social class levels may be that schizophrenic disorders build on conceptions of reality firmly grounded on the experiences of these social classes.

Conclusion

My proposed formulation attempts to bring genetics, stress, and the conditions of life attendant on social class position into one coherent interpretation of schizophrenia. The thrust of the argument is that the conditions of life experienced by people of lower social class position tend to impair their ability to deal resourcefully with the problematic and the stressful. Such impairment would be unfortunate for all who suffer it, but would not in itself result in schizophrenia. In conjunction with a genetic vulnerability to schizophrenia and the experience of great stress, however, such impairment could well be disabling. Since both genetic vulnerability and stress appear to occur disproportionately at lower social class levels, people in these segments of society may be at triple jeopardy.[26]

How would one test such a formulation? Since the formulation posits that schizophrenia is produced by the

---

tional and occupational conditions, the latter are likely to prevail (Kohn 1969, pp. 135–137). The practical implications of this finding are as important as they are obvious: The most efficacious way to alleviate the burdens of lower social-class position is not by therapy, resocialization, or other efforts to teach middle class values and orientation, but by changing the social conditions to which lower class people are subject.

26. In trying to make my point forcefully, I may have exaggerated statistical tendencies, making it seem as if class differences in orientational systems were differences in kind rather than in degree. I hope it is clear from the general argument, though, that all the relevant variables—genetics, stress, conceptions of reality—must be seen as probabilistic; the formulation depends on the joint occurrence of these necessary conditions.

interaction of genetic vulnerability, stress, and the disabilities attendant on a conformist orientation, a rigorous test clearly requires that all three elements be considered together. I speak of interaction in its precise statistical sense: The relevance of any of the three factors depends on the strength of the other two. It may also be that the critical threshold for each of the factors depends on the strength of the other two. If, for example, the genetic predisposition is exceptionally strong, less stress may be required (Rosenthal 1963, pp. 507−509); if there is exceedingly great stress, perhaps only minimal genetic vulnerability will be sufficient (Eitinger 1964); if a person's orientation is strongly conformist, even moderately stressful situations may overwhelm him. These possibilities, and the numerous variations they imply, suggest that my model may be only a simple prototype of a family of models. Fortunately, research designed to test any one of them can assess the others as well, for they are all based on the interplay of the same three factors.

If the effects of genetics, stress, and orientation were assumed to be additive, we could test any of them by comparing schizophrenics to nonschizophrenics of the same social class on that factor alone. But with an interactive model of the type I have proposed, a single-factor comparison is inadequate. Since no one factor could produce schizophrenia except in combination with the others, it would be possible for *all* members of a given social class to surpass the threshold for any factor, provided they did not exceed the thresholds for the others. Thus, an absence of difference between schizophrenics and nonschizophrenics of the same class level on any of the factors in the model is no disproof of the pertinence of that factor. Correspondingly, finding a difference provides prima facie evidence that the factor is pertinent to schizophrenia, but no proof that its place in the model has been correctly established. An important corollary is that different factors may distinguish schizophrenics from nonschizophrenics in different social classes.

To be concrete: The correlations between class and the pertinent facets of orientation range from 0.13 to 0.38 (Kohn 1969, pp. 81, 83). If one took the moderate size of these correlations to imply that many lower class people do not hold a conformist orientation, he would predict substantial differences in orientation between those lower class people who do and those who do not become schizophrenic. But I interpret the moderate correlations between class and orientation to mean that a conformist orientation is widely held at lower social class levels and is far from absent, though less widely held, at higher social class levels. I should therefore predict little or no difference in orientation between

lower class schizophrenics and nonschizophrenics. From either perspective, we should expect lower class schizophrenics and nonschizophrenics to differ most decidedly in genetic vulnerability, perhaps also in exposure to stress, and least of all in orientation. Since present evidence suggests that the correlation between class and orientation is greater than that between class and genetics, or than that between class and stress, differences between schizophrenics and nonschizophrenics should center more and more on orientation at increasingly higher social class levels.

REFERENCES

Bateson, G.; Jackson, D. D.; Haley, J.; and Weakland, J. Toward a theory of schizophrenia. *Behavioral Science*, 1:251−264, 1956.

Behrens, M. I.; Rosenthal, A. J.; and Chodoff, P. Communication in lower class families of schizophrenics: II. Observations and findings. *Archives of General Psychiatry*, 18:689−696, 1968.

Birley, J. L. T., and Brown, G. W. Crises and life changes preceding the onset or relapse of acute schizophrenia: Clinical aspects. *British Journal of Psychiatry*, 116:327−333, 1970.

Bleuler, E. *Dementia Praecox or the Group of Schizophrenias.* New York: International Universities Press, 1950.

Bronfenbrenner, U. Socialization and social class through time and space. In: Maccoby, E. E.; Newcomb, T. M.; and Hartley, E. L., eds. *Readings in Social Psychology.* New York: Henry Holt and Company, 1958. pp. 400−425.

Brown, G. W.; and Birley, J. L. T. Crises and life changes and the onset of schizophrenia. *Journal of Health and Social Behavior*, 9:203−214, 1968.

Buck, C.; Wanklin, J. M.; and Hobbs, G. E. An analysis of regional differences in mental illness. *The Journal of Nervous and Mental Disease*, 122:73−79, 1955.

Clark, R. E. The relationship of schizophrenia to occupational income and occupational prestige. *American Sociological Review*, 13:325−330, 1948.

Clark, R. E. Psychoses, income, and occupational prestige. *American Journal of Sociology*, 54:433−440, 1949.

Clausen, J. A. *Sociology and the Field of Mental Health.* New York: Russell Sage Foundation, 1956.

Clausen, J. A. The ecology of mental illness. In: *Symposium on Social and Preventive Psychiatry.* Walter Reed Army Medical Center, Washington, D.C., 1957. pp. 97−108.

Clausen, J. A. The sociology of mental illness. In: Merton, R. K.; Broom, L.; and Cottrell, L. S., Jr., eds. *Sociology Today, Problems and Prospects.* New York: Basic Books, Inc., 1959. pp. 485−508.

Clausen, J. A., and Kohn, M. L. The ecological approach in social psychiatry. *American Journal of Sociology,* 60:140—151, 1954.

Clausen, J. A., and Kohn, M. L. Relation of schizophrenia to the social structure of a small city. In: Pasamanick, B., ed. *Epidemiology of Mental Disorder.* Washington, D.C.: American Association for the Advancement of Science, 1959. pp. 69—94.

Dee, W. L. J. "An Ecological Study of Mental Disorders in Metropolitan St. Louis." Unpublished M.A. thesis. Washington University, 1939.

Demerath, N. J. Schizophrenia among primitives. In: Rose, A. M., ed. *Mental Health and Mental Disorder.* New York: W. W. Norton & Company, Inc., 1955. pp. 215—222.

Dohrenwend, B. P., and Dohrenwend, B. S. The problem of validity in field studies of psychological disorder. *Journal of Abnormal Psychology,* 70:52—69, 1965.

Dohrenwend, B. P., and Dohrenwend, B. S. *Social Status and Psychological Disorder: A Causal Inquiry.* New York: John Wiley & Sons, Inc., 1969.

Dunham, H. W. Current status of ecological research in mental disorder. *Social Forces,* 25:321—326, 1947.

Dunham, H. W. Social psychiatry. *American Sociological Review,* 13:183—197, 1948.

Dunham, H. W. Some persistent problems in the epidemiology of mental disorders. *American Journal of Psychiatry,* 109:567—575, 1953.

Dunham, H. W. Social class and schizophrenia. *American Journal of Orthopsychiatry,* 34:634—642, 1964.

Dunham, H. W. *Community and Schizophrenia: An Epidemiological Analysis.* Detroit, Mich.: Wayne State University Press, 1965.

Dunham, H. W.; Phillips, P.; and Srinivasan, B. A research note on diagnosed mental illness and social class. *American Sociological Review,* 31:223—227, 1966.

Eaton, J. W., in collaboration with Weil, R. J. *Culture and Mental Disorders: A Comparative Study of the Hutterites and Other Populations.* Glencoe, Ill.: Free Press, 1955.

Eitinger, L. *Concentration Camp Survivors in Norway and Israel.* Oslo: Universitetsforlaget, 1964.

Essen-Möller, E. Individual traits and morbidity in a Swedish rural population. *Acta Psychiatrica et Neurologica Scandinavica, Supplement,* 100:1—160, 1956.

Essen-Möller, E. A current field study in the mental disorders in Sweden. In: Hoch, P. H., and Zubin, J., eds. *Comparative Epidemiology of the Mental Disorders.* New York: Grune and Stratton, Inc., 1961. pp. 1—12.

Faris, R. E. L., and Dunham, H. W. *Mental Disorders in Urban Areas: An Ecological Study of Schizophrenia and Other Psychoses.* Chicago: University of Chicago Press, 1939.

Felix, R. H., and Bowers, R. V. Mental hygiene and socioenvironmental factors. *The Milbank Memorial Fund Quarterly,* 26:125—147, 1948.

Foote, N. N., and Cottrell, L. S., Jr. *Identity and Interpersonal Competence: A New Direction in Family Research.* Chicago: University of Chicago Press, 1955.

Frumkin, R. M. Occupation and major mental disorders. In: Rose, A., ed. *Mental Health and Mental Disorders.* New York: W. W. Norton & Company, Inc., 1955. pp. 136—160.

Fuson, W. M. Research note: Occupations of functional psychotics. *American Journal of Sociology,* 48:612—613, 1943.

Gardner, E. A., and Babigian, H. M. A longitudinal comparison of psychiatric service to selected socioeconomic areas of Monroe County, New York. *American Journal of Orthopsychiatry,* 36:818—828, 1966.

Garmezy, N. Process and reactive schizophrenia: Some conceptions and issues. In: Katz, M. M.; Cole, J. O.; and Barton, W. E., eds. *The Role and Methodology of Classification in Psychiatry and Psychopathology.* (PHS Publication No. 1584) Washington, D.C.: U.S. Government Printing Office, 1968. pp. 419—466. Reprinted in *Schizophrenia Bulletin,* No. 2:30—74, Fall 1970.

Gerard, D. L., and Houston, L. G. Family setting and the social ecology of schizophrenia. *Psychiatric Quarterly,* 27:90—101, 1953.

Goffman, E. The moral career of the mental patient. *Psychiatry,* 22:123—142, 1959.

Goldberg, E. M., and Morrison, S. L. Schizophrenia and social class. *British Journal of Psychiatry,* 109:785—802, 1963.

Goldhamer, H., and Marshall, A. W. *Psychosis and Civilization: Two Studies in the Frequency of Mental Disease.* Glencoe, Ill.: The Free Press, 1953.

Gottesman, I. I., and Shields, J. A polygenic theory of schizophrenia. *Proceedings of the National Academy of Sciences,* 58:199—205, 1967.

Gove, W. R. Societal reaction as an explanation of mental illness: An evaluation. *American Sociological Review,* 35:873—884, 1970.

Green, H. W. *Persons Admitted to the Cleveland State Hospital, 1928—37.* Cleveland Health Council, 1939.

Hagnell, O. *A Prospective Study of the Incidence of Mental Disorder.* Stockholm: Svenska Bokförlaget, 1966.

Hare, E. H. Family setting and the urban distribution of schizophrenia. *Journal of Mental Science,* 102:753—760, 1956a.

Hare, E. H. Mental illness and social conditions in Bristol. *Journal of Mental Science,* 102:349—357, 1956b.

Heston, L. L. The genetics of schizophrenic and schizoid disease. *Science,* 167:249—256, 1970.

Hollingshead, A. B. Some issues in the epidemiology of schizophrenia. *American Sociological Review,* 26:5—13, 1961.

Hollingshead, A. B., and Redlich, F. C. Social stratification and schizophrenia. *American Sociological Review,* 19 (June): 302—306, 1954.

Hollingshead, A. B., and Redlich, F. C. *Social Class and Mental Illness: A Community Study.* New York: John Wiley & Sons, Inc., 1958.

Jaco, E. G. The social isolation hypothesis and schizophrenia. *American Sociological Review,* 19:567–577, 1954.

Jaco, E. G. *The Social Epidemiology of Mental Disorders: A Psychiatric Survey of Texas.* New York: Russell Sage Foundation, 1960.

Kaplan, B.; Reed, R. B.; and Richardson, W. A comparison of the incidence of hospitalized and nonhospitalized cases of psychosis in two communities. *American Sociological Review,* 21:472–479, 1956.

Kety, S. S. Recent biochemical theories of schizophrenia. In: Jackson, D. D. ed. *The Etiology of Schizophrenia.* New York: Basic Books, Inc., 1960. pp. 120–145.

Kety, S. S. Biochemical hypotheses and studies. In: Bellak, L., and Loeb, L., eds. *The Schizophrenic Syndrome.* New York: Grune and Stratton, Inc., 1969. pp. 155–171.

Klee, G. D.; Spiro, E.; Bahn, A. K.; and Gorwitz, K. An ecological analysis of diagnosed mental illness in Baltimore. In: Monroe, R. R.; Klee, G. D.; and Brody, E. B., eds. *Psychiatric Epidemiology and Mental Health Planning.* Psychiatric Research Report No. 22. Washington: The American Psychiatric Association, 1967. pp. 107–148.

Kleiner, R. J., and Parker, S. Goal-striving, social status, and mental disorder: A research review. *American Sociological Review,* 28:189–203, 1963.

Kohn, M. L. Social class and schizophrenia: A critical review. In: Rosenthal, D., and Kety, S. S., eds. *The Transmission of Schizophrenia.* Oxford: Pergamon Press, 1968. pp. 155–173.

Kohn, M. L. *Class and Conformity: A Study in Values.* Homewood, Ill.: The Dorsey Press, 1969.

Kohn, M. L. Class, family, and schizophrenia: A reformulation. *Social Forces,* 50:295–313, 1972.

Kohn, M. L., and Clausen, J. A. Social isolation and schizophrenia. *American Sociological Review,* 20:265–273, 1955.

Kohn, M. L., and Clausen, J. A. Parental authority behavior and schizophrenia. *American Journal of Orthopsychiatry,* 26:297–313, 1956.

Kramer, M. A discussion of the concepts of incidence and prevalence as related to epidemiologic studies of mental disorders. *American Journal of Public Health,* 47:826–840, 1957.

Kringlen, E. Schizophrenia in twins: An epidemiological-clinical study. *Psychiatry,* 29:172–184, 1966.

Kringlen, E. *Heredity and Environment in the Functional Psychoses: An Epidemiological-Clinical Twin Study.* Oslo: Universitetsforlaget, 1967.

Langner, T. S., and Michael, S. T. *Life Stress and Mental Health.* New York: The Free Press of Glencoe, 1963.

Lapouse, R.; Monk, M. A.; and Terris, M. The drift hypothesis and socioeconomic differentials in schizophrenia. *American Journal of Public Health,* 46:978–986, 1956.

Lazarus, R. S. *Psychological Stress and the Coping Process.* New York: McGraw-Hill, Inc., 1966.

Leighton, A. H.; Lambo, T. A.; Hughes, C. C.; Leighton, D. C.; Murphy, J. M.; and Macklin, D. B. *Psychiatric Disorder Among the Yoruba.* Ithaca, N.Y.: Cornell University Press, 1963a.

Leighton, D. C., with Harding, J. S.; Macklin, D. B.; MacMillan, A. M.; and Leighton, A. H. *The Character of Danger: Psychiatric Symptoms in Selected Communities.* New York: Basic Books, Inc., 1963b.

Leighton, D. C.; Harding, J. S.; Macklin, D. B.; Hughes, C. C.; and Leighton, A. H. Psychiatric findings of the Stirling County study. *American Journal of Psychiatry,* 119:1021–1026, 1963c.

Lemkau, P.; Tietze, C.; and Cooper, M. Mental-hygiene problems in an urban district: Second paper. *Mental Hygiene,* 26:100–119, 1942.

Lewis, O. *La Vida: A Puerto Rican Family in the Culture of Poverty—San Juan and New York.* New York: Random House, Inc., 1965.

Liebow, E. *Tally's Corner: A Study of Negro Streetcorner Men.* Boston: Little, Brown and Company, 1960.

Lin, T. A study of the incidence of mental disorder in Chinese and other cultures. *Psychiatry,* 16:313–336, 1953.

Lin, T.; Rin, H.; Yeh, E. K.; Hsu, C. C.; and Chu, H. M. Mental disorders in Taiwan, fifteen years later: A preliminary report. In: Caudill, W., and Lin, T., eds. *Mental Health Research in Asia and the Pacific.* Honolulu: East-West Center Press, 1969. pp. 66–91.

Locke, B. Z.; Kramer, M.; Timberlake, C. E.; Pasamanick, B.; and Smeltzer, D. Problems of interpretation of patterns of first admissions to Ohio State public mental hospitals for patients with schizophrenic reactions. In: Pasamanick, B., and Knapp, P. H., eds. *Social Aspects of Psychiatry.* The American Psychiatric Association (Psychiatric Research Reports No. 10), 1958. pp. 172–196.

Lystad, Mary H. Social mobility among selected groups of schizophrenic patients. *American Sociological Review,* 22:288–292, 1957.

Miller, S. M. The American lower classes: A typological approach. In: Riessman, F.; Cohen, J.; and Pearl, A., eds. *Mental Health of the Poor.* New York: The Free Press of Glencoe, 1964. pp. 139–154.

Mishler, E. G., and Scotch, N. A. Sociocultural factors in the epidemiology of schizophrenia: A review. *Psychiatry,* 26:315–351, 1963.

Mishler, E. G., and Waxler, N. E. Family interaction processes and schizophrenia: A review of current theories. *Merrill-Palmer Quarterly of Behavior and Development,* 11:269–315, 1965.

Mishler, E. G., and Waxler, N. E. *Interaction in Families: An Experimental Study of Family Processes and Schizophre-*

nia. New York: John Wiley & Sons, Inc., 1968.

Morris, J. N. Health and social class. *The Lancet* (February): 303–305, 1959.

Myers, J. K., and Roberts, B. H. *Family and Class Dynamics in Mental Illness.* New York: John Wiley & Sons, Inc., 1959.

Nolan, W. J. Occupation and dementia praecox. *State Hospitals Quarterly,* 3:127–154, 1917.

Ødegaard, Ø. The incidence of psychoses in various occupations. *International Journal of Social Psychiatry,* 2:85–104, 1956.

Ødegaard, Ø. Occupational incidence of mental disease in single women. *Living Conditions and Health,* 1:169–180, 1957.

Ødegaard, Ø. Psychiatric epidemiology. *Proceedings of the Royal Society of Medicine,* 55:831–837, 1962.

Parker, S., and Kleiner, R. J. *Mental Illness in the Urban Negro Community.* New York: Free Press, 1966.

Phillips, L. *Human Adaptation and Its Failures.* New York: Academic Press, Inc., 1968.

Queen, S. A. The ecological study of mental disorders. *American Sociological Review,* 5:201–209, 1940.

Rainwater, L. The problem of lower-class culture and poverty-war strategy. In: Moynihan, D. P., ed. *On Understanding Poverty: Perspectives from the Social Sciences.* New York: Basic Books, Inc., 1968. pp. 229–259.

Rinehart, J. W. On diagnosed mental illness and social class. *American Sociological Review,* 31:545–546, 1966.

Roach, J. L., and Gursslin, O. R. An evaluation of the concept "culture of poverty." *Social Forces,* 45:383–392, 1967.

Robinson, W. S. Ecological correlations and the behavior of individuals. *American Sociological Review,* 15:351–357, 1950.

Rodman, H. The lower-class value stretch. *Social Forces,* 42:205–215, 1963.

Rogler, L. H., and Hollingshead, A. B. *Trapped: Families and Schizophrenia.* New York: John Wiley & Sons, Inc., 1965.

Roman, P. M., and Trice, H. M. *Schizophrenia and the Poor.* Ithaca, N.Y.: New York State School of Industrial and Labor Relations, 1967.

Rosenbaum, C. P. *The Meaning of Madness: Symptomatology, Sociology, Biology and Therapy of the Schizophrenias.* New York: Science House, 1970.

Rosenthal, A. J.; Behrens, M. I.; and Chodoff, P. Communication in lower-class families of schizophrenics: I. Methodological problems. *Archives of General Psychiatry,* 18:464–470, 1968.

Rosenthal, D. Problems of sampling and diagnosis in the major twin studies of schizophrenia. *Journal of Psychiatric Research,* 1:116–134, 1962.

Rosenthal, D. *The Genain Quadruplets: A Case Study and Theoretical Analysis of Heredity and Environment in Schizophrenia.* New York: Basic Books, Inc., 1963.

Rosenthal, D. The heredity-environment issue in schizophrenia. In: Rosenthal, D., and Kety, S. S., eds. *The Transmission of Schizophrenia.* Oxford: Pergamon Press, Inc., 1968. pp. 413–427.

Rosenthal, D. *Genetic Theory and Abnormal Behavior.* New York: McGraw-Hill, Inc., 1970.

Rossi, P. H., and Blum, Z. D. Class, status, and poverty. In: Moynihan, D. P., ed. *On Understanding Poverty: Perspectives from the Social Sciences.* New York: Basic Books, Inc., 1968. pp. 36–63.

Rushing, W. A. Two patterns in the relationship between social class and mental hospitalization. *American Sociological Review,* 34:533–541, 1969.

Sanua, V. D. Sociocultural factors in families of schizophrenics: A review of the literature. *Psychiatry,* 24:246–265, 1961.

Sanua, V. D. The etiology and epidemiology of mental illness and problems of methodology: With special emphasis on schizophrenia. *Mental Hygiene,* 47:607–621, 1963.

Scheff, T. J. *Being Mentally Ill: A Sociological Theory.* Chicago, Ill.: Aldine Publishing Company, 1966.

Schroeder, C. W. Mental disorders in cities. *American Journal of Sociology,* 48:40–48, 1942.

Schuham, A. I. The double-bind hypothesis a decade later. *Psychological Bulletin,* 68:409–416, 1967.

Schwartz, D. T., and Mintz, N. L. Ecology and psychosis among Italians in 27 Boston communities. *Social Problems,* 10:371–374, 1963.

Schwartz, M. S. "The Economic and Spatial Mobility of Paranoid Schizophrenics and Manic Depressives." Unpublished M.A. thesis, University of Chicago, 1946.

Scott, R., and Howard, A. Models of stress. In: Levine, S., and Scotch, N. A., eds. *Social Stress.* Chicago: Aldine Publishing Company, 1970. pp. 259–278.

Shields, J. Summary of the genetic evidence. In: Rosenthal, D., and Kety, S. S., eds. *The Transmission of Schizophrenia.* Oxford: Pergamon Press, Inc., 1968. pp. 95–126.

Singer, M. T., and Wynne, L. C. Thought disorder and family relations of schizophrenics: Methodology using projective techniques; results and implications. *Archives of General Psychiatry,* 12:187–212, 1965.

Slater, E. A review of earlier evidence on genetic factors in schizophrenia. In: Rosenthal, D., and Kety, S. S., eds. *The Transmission of Schizophrenia.* Oxford: Pergamon Press, Inc., 1968. pp. 15–26.

Smith, M. B. Competence and socialization. In: Clausen, J. A., ed. *Socialization and Society.* Boston: Little, Brown and Company, 1968. pp. 270–320.

Srole, L.; Langner, T. S.; Michael, S. T.; Opler, M. K.; and Rennie, T. A. C. *Mental Health in the Metropolis: The Midtown Manhattan Study.* New York: McGraw-Hill, Inc., 1962.

Stein, L. "Social class" gradient in schizophrenia. *British Journal of Preventive and Social Medicine,* 11:181−195, 1957.

Stenbäck, A., and Achté, K. A. Hospital first admissions and social class. *Acta Psychiatrica Scandinavica,* 42:113−124, 1966.

Sundby, P., and Nyhus, P. Major and minor psychiatric disorders in males in Oslo: An epidemiological study. *Acta Psychiatrica Scandinavica,* 39:519−547, 1963.

Svalastoga, K. *Social Differentiation.* New York: David McKay, 1965.

Turner, R. J. Societal mobility and schizophrenia. *Journal of Health and Social Behavior,* 9:194−203, 1968.

Turner, R. J., and Wagenfeld, M. O. Occupational mobility and schizophrenia: An assessment of the social causation and social selection hypotheses. *American Sociological Review,* 32:104−113, 1967.

Valentine, C. A. *Culture and Poverty: Critique and Counter-Proposals.* Chicago: University of Chicago Press, 1968.

Wechsler, H., and Pugh, T. F. Fit of individual and community characteristics and rates of psychiatric hospitalization. *American Journal of Sociology,* 73:331−338, 1967.

Whyte, W. F. *Street Corner Society: The Social Structure of an Italian Slum.* Chicago: University of Chicago Press, 1943.

Williams, R. M., Jr. *American Society: A Sociological Interpretation.* New York: Alfred A. Knopf, Inc., 1951.

Wynne, L. C. Family transactions and schizophrenia: Conceptual considerations for a research strategy. In: Romano, J., ed. *The Origins of Schizophrenia.* Amsterdam: Excerpta Medica International Congress Series No. 151, 1967, pp. 165−178.

Wynne, L. C., and Singer, M. T. Thought disorder and family relations of schizophrenics: A classification of forms of thinking. *Archives of General Psychiatry,* 9:191−206, 1963.

GEORGE W. BROWN • MÁIRE NÍ BHROLCHÁIN • TIRRIL HARRIS

Social Class and Psychiatric Disturbance among Women in an Urban Population*

Introduction

The traditional sociological method of studying psychiatric phenomena has been to explain *rates* in terms of characteristics of the encompassing social system. There have now been many population surveys of treated and untreated psychiatric disturbance. A recent review

Reprinted from *Sociology,* Vol. **9**, No. 2, (May 1975), pages 225−254, by permission of the author and publisher. A fuller statement covering a larger number of women may be found in George W. Brown and Tirril Harris, *Social Origins of Depression,* London: Tavistock and New York: Free Press, 1978.

* The research was supported by the Foundations' Fund for Research in Psychiatry, the Medical Research Council and the Social Science Research Council. We would like to thank Dr. John Copeland of the Institute of Psychiatry for his help in interviewing patients and for his help, with Dr. Michael Kelleher, in interviewing in the general population.

of psychiatric epidemiological work lists sixteen studies which take some account of background social factors in urban communities, although only eleven examined social class (Dohrenwend and Dohrenwend, 1969). Of these eleven studies (which covered populations in the U.S.A., U.K., Canada, Formosa, and India) eight reported the highest rate of psychiatric disturbance in the lowest social class group. A study in Manhattan, New York, showed that this held when the occupations of parents were used to define social class of the respondents, thus ruling out the possibility that results were affected by a decline in occupational level as a result of the psychiatric disorder (Srole *et al.,* 1962).

While there is unanimity about the correlation between class and rates of psychiatric disturbance, nothing has been convincingly established about causality or the meaning of the social class differences. Statements about associations between demographic-type variables (and sometimes global community characteristics) and disturbance are simply used as a vehicle for speculation about causal processes. The Dohrenwends' review was, in part, an attempt to examine the rival hypothesis that social class differences are the result of the accumulation over a number of generations of genetically vulnerable individuals in the lower socioeconomic groups as opposed to the effect of environmental and social factors correlated with social status. The question however still remains an open one despite a considerable amount of research.

Reasons for failure are many, but not least among them is the tendency of investigators to rely on a combination of the perennial demographic-type measures and the meretricious fixed-choice questionnaire with its magical ability to measure almost anything with a few standard questions. In recent years a quite different approach has increased in popularity—the so-called labelling perspective on deviance: whatever its shortcomings, it conveys a greater willingness to struggle with the full complexities of the individual's life and circumstances and their meaning for him. Its emphasis is almost entirely on the ascribed status of deviance and the consequent handling in 'corrective' or 'treatment' institutions. 'Deviance is not a property *inherent* in certain forms of behaviour: it is a property *conferred upon* these forms by the audiences which directly or indirectly witness them' (Erikson, 1966). While there can be no dispute about the fact that most schizophrenic patients are considered deviant by society at large, we know of no studies suggesting similar processes in the case of depressive conditions—with which we are concerned in this paper. It is possible that sleeplessness, feelings of hopelessness and other features forming the cluster of symptoms called a 'depressive' condition are perceived as rule-breaking by both psychiatric personnel and lay people. If this is the case it remains to be demonstrated. Whether depressed women perceive themselves as rule-breakers or deviants is also an open question. On the other hand, we believe that the depressive conditions dealt with in this paper are, independent of such possible ascription, inherently unpleasant. They involve, among other bodily states, what Tomkins has termed the fundamental affect of *distress-anguish:* no one has to learn to consider it unpleasant in nature (Tomkins, 1963). When, as in depressive disorders, distress-anguish is associated with complaints such as early-morning wakening, lack of energy, feelings of worthlessness and so on, and they persist for months on end, the experience becomes scarcely endurable.

We will use the term psychiatric to refer to such conditions whether or not seen or treated by psychia-

trists; but we make no assumptions about their nature—whether or not they should be considered as illness or disease or a 'normal' response to certain kinds of adversity. We claim no more than that the conditions are similar in type and extent of symptoms to those seen by psychiatrists in their day-to-day practice and usually considered by them to require treatment.

Experiences such as these call for sociological attention for several reasons, irrespective of whether they are recognized or labelled as 'mental illness' by the individual himself, his immediate circle or members of the helping professions. First, depressive conditions are not only common, but in large part the result of experiences that are strongly related to social position. Psychiatric disturbance and in particular the depressive conditions we deal with are in a critical sense *social* phenomena, and their distribution in a population is therefore an important way of evaluating and understanding the workings of a society. In this paper we are particularly concerned with the aetiological role of certain kinds of adverse life-events. But we show that much more is involved than the random occurrence of such events; for instance, vulnerability to events is greatly increased by the presence of specific kinds of ongoing social circumstances. Second, they are sociologically important because in many cases depressive conditions and the suffering they imply are *ignored* by the institutions in our society whose function is to alleviate them. We will see that hardly any of the women whom we considered in the present study to be psychiatrically disturbed had seen a psychiatrist—scarcely half had seen any medical practitioner. Third, if our claim that many, if not most, depressive conditions are to a large extent the result of aetiological factors of a directly sociological nature is valid, it has important implications as to the kinds of intervention which might more profitably be directed toward prevention rather than 'cure.' Preventive measures, as we see them, would require the manipulation of social structural features. Labelling theory has tended understandably to place its emphasis on the subject-labeller interaction (and often its untoward consequences); but it is equally important to look at the situation where relatively little is labelled or 'processed' through societal institutions. We have therefore established the frequency of certain 'psychiatric' phenomena in a district in south London irrespective of whether they have been labelled by anyone as 'psychiatric' and have attempted to explain their occurrence in social terms. However, we have also been concerned to see how far these same conditions have been recognized and 'processed' by the medical and helping professions.

We would criticize attempts at investigating aetiology and 'processing' without reference to each other for failing to see that sociological understanding is gravely handicapped unless we take more account of both at the same time. We will show, for instance, that the same social factors that *increase* the risk of developing psychiatric disorder greatly *reduce* the chances of reaching psychiatric services. There are also different views of the conditions to be taken into account. A woman might not see her depressive symptoms as requiring medical attention as they are so obviously related to her daunting and intractable social problems; her husband may merely see her as typical of women in similar circumstances; her general practitioner may be content to recognize and deal only with her accompanying physical symptoms, and the psychiatrist who *would* see her as requiring his help *if* she should present herself at his clinic is never made aware of her existence. Phenomena of this kind of complexity cannot be studied by treating 'aetiology' and 'processing' as separate issues.

The main purpose of the study was to investigate the aetiology of depressive conditions in a way that would allow us to specify factors intervening between structural variables and psychiatric disorder and therefore develop a convincing link between theory and research findings. With this in mind, the two broad aims of the project can be outlined. (i) The first was to establish whether there is a causal link between life-events and the onset of depressive conditions: to concentrate on phenomena that had meaning for the individual in terms of his whole way of life, rather than on abstract demographic factors. We were concerned with events occurring to the respondent or to close relatives or friends. All involved some element of danger, significant changes in health, status or way of life, the promise of these or important fulfilments or disappointments. Much previous work on life-events had been open to serious criticism on methodological grounds, and for this reason particular care was taken in the design of this study and in the development of measures for selecting and characterizing life-events. Previous accounts of our work give details of the life-events approach (see Brown *et al.*, 1973a and Brown, 1974). (ii) The next stage was to investigate social class and other group differences in life-event rates and to establish (a) to what extent the group differences in event rates account for group differences in rates of psychiatric disturbance and (b) what factors affect vulnerability to onset of disturbance once events have occurred. In view of the recurrent finding that the lowest social status groups display relatively high rates of psychiatric disturbance, it was of particular interest to establish whether this could be accounted for by social class differences in the frequency of events.

Two samples of women aged between 18 and 65

living in one of the former Inner London boroughs were obtained:[1] (i) a group of 114 patients who were, at the time of interview, undergoing either in- or out-patient treatment whose diagnosis was one of primary depression and who had had an onset of depression in the year prior to interview and (ii) a random sample of 220 women.[2] Each respondent of the latter group was screened for psychiatric disturbance using an interview developed at the Institute of Psychiatry in London. It is based on a lengthy list of standard questions about symptoms, but allows for such further questioning as the interviewer considers necessary. The 35 women judged to have suffered from a definite psychiatric disorder (16 per cent) at any time in the three months up to interview were termed *cases*.[3] Of these 21 (10 per cent) had an onset in the year prior to interview and 14 (6 per cent) had been disturbed continuously for over a year: these are called *recent* and *chronic* cases respectively. The community cases although typical of many treated patients were, on the whole, less severely disturbed than the patients receiving in- and out-patient treatment; all were suffering from affective disorders of some kind.[4] Patients and cases were not defined simply by depressed mood, however severe. Both reported *clusters* of symptoms such as loss of weight, lack of energy, various forms of sleep disturbance, heightened anxiety and other basically unpleasant experiences which distinguish them from other women. We refer to them as psychiatric cases, but, as we have made clear, we place no particular weight on this term other than to convey that they appear to have specific characteristics in common with many, if not most, of the women actually treated by psychiatrists.

Forty-five other women who had definite symptoms but who were not considered severe enough to be rated cases were termed *borderlines*. (In general such women would be expected to be seen in an out-patient clinic only rarely.) There is evidently an arbitrary element in choosing a cut-off point between a case and a borderline. The important point is that a criterion despite its arbitrariness should be applied consistently, and this we believe we have done.[5] In general we will refer to non-cases as *normals*—that is, the term normal will usually include borderline conditions as well as those considered relatively symptom-free. This will be clear from the context.

Life-events and long term difficulties were asked about systematically and the circumstances surrounding them were covered in as free-flowing a way as possible. A description of the interviewing procedure and of the data collected on life-events appears in Brown *et al.*, 1973a and Brown, 1974. Briefly, we set out to establish what events had occurred irrespective of how the respondent felt about them. We then went on to obtain systematic and detailed information about anything in the respondent's past, present or future plans which had potential relevance for an understanding of the meaning of the event for her. Some of this material was used to rate each event on a four-point scale of severity (marked, moderate, some, none) according to the amount of threat implied, on common sense grounds, by the event about one week after it occurred. In this rating the respondent's account of her reaction to the event was ignored in order to avoid possible bias that would vitiate attempts to arrive at causal statements. However, everything else known about the woman, the event and her circumstances was taken into account. The rationale for this procedure is set out in some detail in Brown, 1974. Briefly, to establish causality it is necessary in a retrospective study to guard against post-onset reinterpretations on the respondent's part of events and reactions to them. This involves a blanket ignoring of all respondents' reports as to how threatening events were and their substitution by an observer assessment. The argument hinges on the point at which one is willing as an investigator to begin constructing, in Schutz's terms, 'typical patterns of motives and ends' (1954). We would argue that this should be done only when the investigator has taken account as much as possible of the 'biographically determined circumstances'—that is, that judgements about how threatening the typical individual in the same set of circumstances, would find a given event, should be based on a very detailed and full account of the circumstances surrounding the event in question: indeed on the whole available account ignoring only the respondent's reported feeling of threat.

Severe Events and Major Difficulties as Aetiological Factors

Using this rating of threat we found that 26 per cent of the community sample and 61 per cent of the patient group had a severely threatening event in an average

nine month period before interview (for the community) or onset (for patients). (Severe events include all marked events and certain moderate events.)[6] Applying the correction formula which allows for the chance juxtaposition of event and onset, the proportion ('x') of patients having a severe event of causal importance is 48 per cent (see Brown, 1973b). Using the same correction, 57 per cent of recent cases in the community had a severe event of causal significance in an average nine month period before onset. The distinctive feature of the majority of severe events is the *experience of a threatened or actual major loss*—a factor frequently cited in theoretical work as of major importance in the genesis of affective disorders.[7] Of those having a severe event, 77 per cent of patients, 86 per cent of recent cases and 68 per cent of normal women had at least one severe event involving a major loss.

In addition to life-events we considered 'long term difficulties' that had gone on for at least one month during the year prior to interview. Unpleasant and difficult circumstances were covered in all areas of the respondent's life such as housing, money, children, health of self and others, and marriage. Since we were unable, as with events, to develop an exhaustive list of specific questions that did not become impossibly cumbersome, there was a risk of over-reporting on the part of cases and patients. However only a small proportion of difficulties (11 per cent) was found to be of any causal importance. These were problems rated high on severity which had gone on for at least two years and which involved non-health problems only. These we will term *major difficulties*. If patients and cases were 'over-reporting' their difficulties it would be reasonable to assume they would also report more health difficulties and more difficulties of lesser severity. Since neither of these categories was more common among patients and cases than among normals, a general tendency to over-report difficulties because of the depression itself seems

TABLE 1A

Proportion with at Least One Severely Threatening Event or at Least One Major Difficulty in the Period before Onset for Patiens and Recent Cases or Interview for 'Normal' and 'Borderline' Women

	PATIENTS (N = 114)	RECENT CASES (N = 21)	'NORMAL' AND 'BORDERLINE' WOMEN (N = 185)
	%	%	%
1. Severe Event Alone	28 ⎤	38 ⎤	17 ⎤
2. Severe Event *and* Major Difficulty	32 ⎥ 75	29 ⎥ 86	4 ⎥ 31
3. Major Difficulty	15 ⎦	19 ⎦	9 ⎦
4. No Severe Event or Major Difficulty	25	14	69

(The period before onset was on average 38 weeks for patients and recent cases: and a comparison of 38 weeks before interview was therefore taken for 'normal' women. Chronic cases were excluded: 8 of the 14 were positive on 1, 2, or 3.)

TABLE 1B

Corrected Value (x) for the Proportion Involved in the Causal Effect

	PATIENTS	RECENT CASES
	%	%
Based on Marked Events Alone	34	23
Based on Severe Events Alone	48	57
Based on Severe Events and Major Difficulties	59	79

(See Brown *et al.*, 1973b, p. 162 for account of the '*x*' correction).

unlikely. These findings can now be added to the results for events. When we base our corrected figures on the proportion having *either* a severe event *or* a major difficulty, the '*x*' for patients increases to 59 per cent and for recent cases to 79 per cent (see tables 1a and 1b). Major difficulties therefore, although of lesser aetiological importance than events, do appear to play a causal role along with events in the aetiology of affective disturbance.

It is important to note there has been a close correspondence between the patient series and recent cases (in the results so far presented) on the aetiological importance of severe events and major difficulties.

Background Factors

The relation of such background social factors as social class to psychiatric disturbance rates can only be established unequivocally from a random sample of the general population. Results for a patient group are, when considered alone, of limited value as the operation of numerous and little understood selective factors—both personal and institutional—which intervene between the occurrence of disturbance and referral to psychiatric services means that they cannot be considered a representative sample of all disturbed persons in a particular population. For this reason we will now concentrate largely on the community sample.

The two most important background variables related to the rate of disturbance are social class and life-stage. Our measure of social status is largely based on the occupational level of the head of household and is described in the Appendix. The life-stage groups are based on the age of the respondent, her marital status and the age of her youngest child *living at home*.[8] We have divided the sample into five life-stage groups as follows: (a) a group of *younger* women (aged less than 35) who are either single or married, and have no children at home; (b) married women whose youngest child at home is aged less than 6; (c) married women whose youngest child at home is aged between 6 and 14; (d) married women whose youngest child is 15 or over; (e) a group of *older* women (aged 35 and over) who have no children at home, including the divorced, widowed, and separated who have never had children or whose children have left home, as well as single women.

Consistent with the findings of many other investigators we find that the lower status groups had a particularly high rate of disturbance. Combining the low and the intermediate status groups gives a disturbance rate of 25 per cent in the 'working class' group compared with 5 per cent of the high status or 'middle class' group[9] (*p* < .001).[10] The group of women whose youngest child is aged less than 6 has a particularly high rate of disturbance (see Table 2, top row). The breakdown by class, however, reveals that life-stage differences in disturbance rate are almost entirely restricted to the working class group.

Working class women who have a child aged less than 6 have a very high proportion of cases (42 per cent) as

TABLE 2

Percentage of Recent and Chronic Cases by Social Class and Life-Stage

	YOUNGER WITH NO CHILDREN	YOUNGEST CHILD AT HOME			OLDER WITH NO CHILDREN	TOTAL
		Less than 6	*6 to 14*	*15 and over*		
All	4 (1/28)	27 (13/49)	11 (5/45)	13 (5/39)	17 (11/59)	16 (35/220)
Middle Class	0 (0/21)	5 (1/22)	5 (1/21)	11 (2/18)	6 (1/17)	5 (5/99)
Working Class	14 (1/7)	42 (12/27)	17 (4/24)	14 (3/21)	24 (10/42)	25 (30/121)
MC vs WC	n.s.	*p*<.01	n.s.	n.s.	n.s.	*p*<.001

compared with women of similar status in other stages of life, and very much higher than their middle class counterparts. There is a suggestion, again only among working class women, that the rate of disturbance rises in the older group compared with women with adolescent and adult children at home. The only statistically significant differences, however, are the class comparison within the *child less than 6 group* and the *overall* class difference comparison. Similar results emerge when we consider only women with an onset of psychiatric disorder in the year of study (i.e. recent cases) and we will first examine these differences.

We deal first with the problem of whether the class and life-stage differences in the proportion of recent cases can be accounted for by differential rates of events and difficulties. Middle class women with children at home are much less at risk, having lower rates of severe events and major difficulties than the comparable working class women (see Table 3). When events alone are considered, the *younger* women of all classes have the highest rate of severe events of all life-stage groups, despite their relatively low rate of disturbance. These revolve largely around friendship and sexual matters—with boyfriends, unplanned pregnancies, a close friend going abroad and so on. The divergence in event rates between the classes occurs when women have children—and particularly when the children are young. Eighteen per cent of the middle class and 41 per cent of the working class women with a child at home had at least one severe event in the year.

Events concerning health, and friends and relatives not living in the respondent's household, show *no* social class difference. The differences are entirely due to crises (other than those related to health) involving husband, children, or housing. Working class women have, for example, more threats of eviction, more often have a husband sent to prison, a son arrested for

breaking and entering, a husband losing his job and so on.[11] But in the *older* group this class difference in rate of events again disappears.

Class differences in the experience of events and difficulties are therefore restricted to women with children at home. But the key question remains: can these differences in the rate of severe events and major difficulties explain the differential disturbance rates *between* classes? The answer to this question is no. Although the class groups are comparable in the absence of a severe event or major difficulty. Table 4 indicates that the working class women and in particular those who have children at home, are much more vulnerable to onset of psychiatric disturbance when they *do* have a severe event or major difficulty than are the middle class: 39 per cent of working class women with children who had a severe event or major difficulty developed psychiatric disorder in contrast to 6 per cent of the middle class group. Indeed, standardization for the proportions having a severe event or major difficulty reduces the working class/middle class ratio in disturbance rate by only one-fifth.

We could have stopped here and concluded that the results in Table 4 constitute an explanation of the class differences in disturbance. We might have argued that greater vulnerability to environmental stresses is a sufficient explanation of group differences; young working class women, it might be suggested, are simply not able to cope, have less 'toughness' and so on. This would however have prevented the emergence of perhaps the most interesting of all our results. Rather than stopping with a simple model which links severe events and difficulties directly with onset of disturbance, we assumed that further social factors intervene which modify or amplify the impact of events and difficulties and it is these factors that explain the vulnerability of working class women.

TABLE 3

Percentage with a Severe Event or Chronic Major Difficulty by Life-Stage and Social Class

	YOUNGER WITH NO CHILDREN	YOUNGEST CHILD AT HOME			OLDER WITH NO CHILDREN	TOTAL
		Less than 6	*6 to 14*	*15 and over*		
Middle Class	52	23	33	33	35	30
	(11/21)	(5/22)	(7/21)	(6/18)	(6/17)	(18/61)
Working Class	57	52	54	57	45	54
	(4/7)	(14/27)	(13/24)	(12/21)	(19/42)	(39/72)
MC vs WC	n.s.	*p*<.05	n.s.	n.s.	n.s.	*p*<.01

TABLE 4

Percentage of Recent Cases by Class, Life-Stage, Severe Events and Major Difficulties*

	SEVERE EVENT AND/OR MAJOR DIFFICULTY			NO SEVERE EVENT OR MAJOR DIFFICULTY		
	Younger and Older Women	*Women with Children at Home*	*Total*	*Younger and Older Women*	*Women with Children at Home*	*Total*
Middle Class	**6**	**6**	**6**	**0**	**2**	**2**
	(1/17)	(1/17)	(2/34)	(0/21)	(1/42)	(1/63)
Working Class	**15**	**39**	**30**	**5**	**0**	**2**
	(3/20)	(14/36)	(17/56)	(1/22)	(0/31)	(1/53)
	n.s.	$p<.05$	$p<.05$			

*Chronic cases are excluded from the totals: a women who is chronically disturbed cannot, of course, go on to develop an acute disorder. The figures are based on the numbers 'at risk'.

Intervening Factors

1. Support and Quality of Interpersonal Relationships

One of the ratings made for each event and difficulty was a scale of the practical and emotional support received from friends and relatives. Although women with most support were only a little less vulnerable to events and difficulties than those with lesser support, it seemed worthwhile to look at the more enduring characteristics of interpersonal relationships.[12] A new measure (which we call the 'intimacy' scale, possibly misleadingly) was therefore constructed, which rates the closeness to and intimacy with other adults but which also takes into account the frequency and quality of social contacts in general.[13] Each respondent was asked to name people to whom she could talk about things that were troubling her, and we call the persons, if any, mentioned *confidants*. The scale is a four-point one: the high point 'a' is used only for women considered to have a close, intimate, and confiding relationship with their husband or boyfriend, or in exceptional cases a woman with whom they live. A relationship with a husband or boyfriend was rated 'a' if the respondent mentioned him as a confidant, provided that there was nothing in the overall account based on evidence from the whole interview that contradicted this answer. We also occasionally placed in an 'a' relationship a husband who had not been named as a confidant in this way but where the overall account made it clear he was treated as such.[14] We found no relationship with a woman that merited the rating. There is, of course, the possibility that women who were psychiatrically disturbed might give a more jaundiced view of their close ties. In this respect we can only state that a 'non-a' rating was given to such women only when there was convincing evidence that the lack of closeness had clearly antedated the onset of the disorder. (In a third of the women rated 'non-a' the problem did not arise as they had no husband or boyfriend.) The second point 'b' was kept for women without such an intimate tie (in practice with a husband or boyfriend) but who nevertheless had a confiding relationship with someone else, such as mother, sister, or friend whom they saw at least weekly. The third point 'c' covered all other women who had a confidant who was seen less than once a week or more and the final point 'd' those women who mentioned no confidant at all.

The rationale for distinguishing women with a confiding relationship with a husband or boyfriend was influenced by Robert Weiss' stimulating discussion of the failure of various kinds of friendship and social relationships to substitute for each other (Weiss, 1970). We do not, however, wish to prejudge the issue of the necessity of a sexual relationship for reaching the highest point of intimacy and would certainly have rated as 'a' any relationship with another woman that had some of the qualities of a marital relationship—particularly where there was joint domicile. A sexual relationship is not an essential prerequisite for an 'a' rating.

Intimacy acts as a powerful mediator between a severe event or a major difficulty and onset of psychiatric disorder. In fact in the community severe events and major difficulties are effective causal agents only when they occur to women without an 'a' relationship.[15] Table 5 shows that high intimacy gives almost complete protection: only 4 per cent of those with an event or difficulty but who had an intimate tie with husband or boyfriend subsequently became disturbed.[16] But lack of such a tie does not itself provoke onset: considering only

TABLE 5

Percentage of Women Who Suffered on Onset in the Year of Study by Whether They Had a Severe Event or Major Difficulty, and Intimacy Context

	INTIMACY		
	High ('a')	*Low ('non-a')*	
Severe Event or Major Difficulty	**4** (2/45)	**38** (17/45)	$p < .001$
No Severe Event or Major Difficulty	**1** (1/82)	**3** (1/34)	n.s.

Intimacy scale dichotomized at the high point ('a') vs the rest ('b', 'c' and 'd'). Chronic cases excluded.

women without a severe event or major difficulty, of the 34 rated low on intimacy one woman (6 per cent) became a case in comparison with 1 per cent of those rated high on intimacy.

Other types of context (i.e. 'b' and 'c') failed to provide even relative protection: of those with a severe event or major difficulty, 35 per cent (9/26) broke down of the 'b's and 42 per cent (8/19) of the 'c's and 'd's. There is no suggestion that any kind of confidant, no matter how often seen, serves to modify the impact of a severe event or difficulty. Nor is there any suggestion that mere frequency of contact is protective: when the intimacy rating is controlled for, there is no relationship between frequency of social contacts and disturbance.

Since the intimacy scale is based on the situation existing *subsequent* to any severe event that occurred, it is important to test the results for possible circularity. It might be suggested that a low intimacy context could be the *result* of a particularly disruptive event which occurred during the year of study and that those women who have a low intimacy rating *and* a severe event have simply experienced an event of greater severity than those rated high on intimacy and with a severe event. Seven women were judged to have dropped from an initially high 'a' rating to a 'non-a' rating as the result of a severe event occurring during the year of study (e.g. death of husband). However, when these women are excluded, the results remain substantially the same.

The intimacy context also forms part of the explanation of the higher vulnerability of working class women relative to their middle class counterparts to severe events and major difficulties. Figure 1 shows the percentage of married women rated high on intimacy (i.e. 'a') by social class and life-stage. Married middle class women show a decline with successive life-stages: all have a high intimacy relationship with their husband when young, but only 73 per cent of the older women with no children at home do. Working class women also

start well: but there is a dramatic change as soon as they have children: only 37 per cent with a child under 6 at home are rated 'a', half the proportion of the corresponding middle class group. Thus working class women in the early stages of rearing their families are doubly at risk: firstly because, as we saw earlier, they experience more severe events and major difficulties than the comparable middle class group, and secondly because the quality of their marriages at this stage is, on the

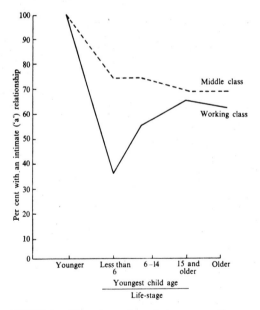

FIGURE 1. Percentage of married women with an intimate ('a') relationship with husband by life-stage and social class (N = 187: single, widowed, and divorced excluded)

whole, poor. However low intimacy does *not* appear to be a permanent feature of working class marriages. With successive life-stages their marriages steadily improve and by the last life-stage when their children have left home, the proportion with an intimate tie is much the same as in the middle class group.[17]

2. Further Factors Affecting Vulnerability

Three further factors mediate the effect of severe events and major difficulties: loss of mother by death or separation before the age of 11, having three or more children aged 14 or less at home and lack of full- or part-time employment.[18] As with low intimacy the presence of these factors does not raise the chances of onset in the absence of either a severe event or a major difficulty (see Table 6: these figures are restricted to married women with children only).

Of course, both number of children and employment relate to life-stage. Only a third of the women with a child aged less than six are employed, compared with three-quarters of the women with older children: there are no social class differences in this. There are, however, class differences in number of children: of those whose youngest child is less than 15, 43 per cent of the working class women have three or more children aged 14 or less, and 14 per cent of the middle class group. More of the working class women had suffered an early loss of mother—9 per cent (6/67) vs 3 per cent (2/59).

Among the *younger* and *older* women only a 'non-a' relationship emerged as a clear vulnerability factor.

With a sample of 220 women, of whom only 10 per cent are recent cases, it is evidently impossible to sort out in detail the complex inter-relationships between all these factors; it is possible that the four vulnerability factors we have isolated interact with each other in affecting the chances of developing psychiatric disturbance, but the demonstration of such effects is beyond the scope of our small sample. It is quite likely, however, that certain types of interaction, if convinc-

TABLE 6

Percentages of Women With a Child at Home Who Developed Psychiatric Disturbance in the Year of Study by Whether They Had a Severe Event or Major Difficulty and by (a) 3 Children Under 14 at Home (b) in Full or Part-Time Employment and (c) Loss of Mother Before the Age of 11 (Chronic Cases Excluded)

	SEVERE EVENT OR MAJOR DIFFICULTY		NO SEVERE EVENT OR MAJOR DIFFICULTY	
a)	*3 Children Less than 14*	*Others*	*3 Children Less than 14*	*Others*
	67 (8/12)	**17** (7/41)	**0** (0/12)	**2** (1/61)
		$p<.01$		n.s.
b)	*Not Employed*	*Employed*	*Not Employed*	*Employed*
	44 (11/25)	**14** (4/28)	**0** (0/28)	**2** (1/45)
		$p<.02$		n.s.
c)	*Loss of Mother*	*No Loss of Mother*	*Loss of Mother*	*No Loss of Mother*
	80 (4/5)	**23** (11/48)	**0** (0/3)	**1** (1/70)
		$p<.05$		
d)	*Positive on a or b or c*	*Not Positive on a, b or c*	*Positive on a or b or c*	*Not Positive on a, b or c*
	43 (13/30)	**9** (2/23)	**0** (0/34)	**3** (1/39)
		$p<.02$		n.s.

TABLE 7

Percentage of Women with a Child at Home who Developed Psychiatric Disturbance in the Year by Vulnerability Score and by Whether They Had a Severe Event or Major Difficulty (Chronic Cases Excluded)

	SEVERE EVENT OR MAJOR DIFFICULTY		NO SEVERE EVENT OR MAJOR DIFFICULTY		
0	1/11 }		1/30 }		
1	1/23 }	6	0/29 }	2	n.s.
2	5/11	**45**	0/13	**0**	
3+	8/8	**100**	0/1	**0**	*p*<.005

ingly documented, would have important implications for the prevention of affective disorders provoked by largely unpredictable and unavoidable life-events. For example, if having a job is protective, even in the presence of all the other three 'amplifiers,' a vulnerable woman would be well-advised to seek employment. There is a hint of such a possibility. Of women *with* a child at home with an event or difficulty but without an intimate tie with their husband, 79 per cent of those who were unemployed (11/14) as against 14 per cent (2/14) of those employed became disturbed—*p* < .005.

In the absence of large numbers we must be content with a relatively crude summary of the results we have outlined so far. It is reasonable to ask whether the sheer number of amplifying factors affects the chances of onset subsequent to a severe event or major difficulty, and, if so, whether the class differences can be accounted for in this way. Therefore for women with children a vulnerability score was obtained by assigning

to each woman one point for the presence of each of the four vulnerability factors. The score, which ranged from 0 to 4, is highly related to degree of vulnerability. The proportion with an onset among those with an event or difficulty ranges from 6 per cent for those with a score of 0 or 1, 45 per cent for 2 and 100 per cent for 3 or more (see Table 7).

Furthermore there is a large class difference in the distribution of vulnerability scores; when chronic cases are excluded, 14 per cent (8/59) of the middle class women scored 2 or more compared with 37 per cent (25/67) of the working class women (*p* < .05). When this is allowed for, the class differences in rate of disturbance are entirely accounted for.[19]

Patients and Vulnerability

On three of the four vulnerability factors results for patients are similar to those obtained for cases. Table 8 shows that for those with children at home over twice as many patients as normal women have had an early loss of mother, double the proportion lack an intimate tie with their husband and over a third more were not employed before onset (the latter is, however, not statistically significant). However, patients do *not* differ from normal women in the proportion having three or more children under 14 at home.[20] We do not think this last result inconsistent with the explanation we have so far developed. We would suggest that a young and relatively densely spaced family does increase the chances of onset of psychiatric disorder in the presence of an event or difficulty but once onset has occurred, makes contact with psychiatrists *less* likely. Twenty-two per cent of the chronic cases (4/14) and as many as 57 per cent (12/21) of recent cases were not currently seeking help for the psychiatric symptoms from a gen-

TABLE 8

Percentages of Patients, Recent Cases and Normal Women With Various Vulnerability Factors for Women with a Child at Home

	EARLY LOSS OF MOTHER	LOW INTIMACY WITH HUSBAND PRIOR TO ONSET	UNEMPLOYED PRIOR TO ONSET	3 OR MORE CHILDREN LESS THAN 14	SEVERE EVENT OR MAJOR DIFFICULTY
Patients (*N* = 62)	11	66	52	15	85
Recent Cases (*n* = 16)	25	81	75	50	94
Normal Women (*N* = 110)	4	27	38	15	34
Row 1 vs 3	*p*<.05	*p*<.01	n.s.	n.s.	*p*<.01
Row 1 vs 2	n.s.	n.s.	n.s.	*p*<.05	n.s.
Row 2 vs 3	*p*<.05	*p*<.01	*p*<.01	*p*<.01	*p*<.01

eral practitioner.[21] While women with a child under six at home sought help as often as other women when they had a *chronic* condition, many fewer did so among those who had an onset in the year (22 per cent of those with a child under six (2/9) vs 69 per cent of the remaining women (9/13)—$p < .05$). While these are obviously small numbers, and we do not rely on the statistical significance in blind faith, the figures do suggest that women with young children at home may have a much lower rate of contact with *any* doctor for psychiatric symptoms. We have not found any account of such an association. One related finding, that of Cartwright and Jefferys (1958), reports a lower than average rate of *all* contacts with general practitioners with an increasing number of children for all women under 45.

There is some suggestion that other such effects exist. For example, persons with a severe event or major difficulty who are high on intimacy seem to be selected *into* treatment. This may be due to encouragement by their husband to seek help. Among the married patients 67 per cent of those with an 'a' relationship came to treatment at the suggestion of their husband, compared with only 33 per cent of those without such a relationship ($p < .01$). Since middle class women much less often have 3 children aged less than 14 at home and more often have an 'a' relationship, they are probably much more likely to see a psychiatrist when suffering from a psychiatric disturbance. Of course there may well be other reasons for any greater chance they have of contacting psychiatrists.

Borderline Conditions

In addition to women who were cases, a further 21 per cent of the general population had definite psychiatric symptoms at some point in the three months prior to interview, which were considered sufficiently severe to be counted as a separate disturbed *borderline* group.[22] Somewhat more than half (26/45) had lasted more than a year, i.e. were *chronic*. There was little by way of class difference among those whose onset occurred in the year—indeed, if anything, there are proportionately more middle class recent borderlines. It is as though women from all social classes stand an equal chance of suffering a marked mood change, but that minor conditions of working class women are more likely to develop into severe disorders. This is however speculative: we do not know whether and if so, how often, such progressions take place.[23] No attempt was made to date the onset of the borderline conditions occurring in the year before interview. It is nevertheless of interest that there is a definite tendency for severe events and major difficulties to have the same relationship to borderline

conditions as they have to cases, and that the vulnerability score, dichotomized at 0 vs 1+ shows a similar though modified interaction with severe events and major difficulties and borderline disturbance.

Chronic Conditions

The class difference in chronic disturbance remains to be discussed. Five times more working class women were chronic cases and over twice as many were suffering from a chronic borderline condition. Overall a tenth of middle class women were suffering from some form of chronic condition and a quarter of working class women.[24]

Long term difficulties show the clearest relationship with such chronicity. But in order to examine their causal role we first had to apply a criterion of 'independence' developed originally for use with life-events.[25] Difficulties were rated as independent if it seemed likely *on logical grounds* that they could not have been *brought about* by the chronic disturbance. Many of these difficulties concerned poverty and housing which, at least on the information we have, were extremely difficult for the respondent herself to do anything about.

Table 9 shows that substantially more of those who had an 'independent' difficulty suffered from a chronic condition than women with no such difficulty—37 per cent and 13 per cent respectively: $p < .05$. It is notable that most of these difficulties are housing problems: 43 per cent (6/14) of the chronic cases have a major housing problem, 24 per cent (6/25) of chronic borderlines and 5 per cent (7/140) of the normal women. It suggests that it is housing difficulties more than any other which are the key to chronicity—both for cases and borderline conditions. Indeed, 55 per cent (12/22) of those with a major housing problem were suffering from a chronic condition, compared with only 13 per cent (2/16) of those with other kinds of major 'independent' difficulty—$p < .01$. The latter figure is in fact no different from the 14 per cent (25/182) who suffer from a chronic condition among those *without* a major 'independent' difficulty. Housing difficulties are of course about the 'hardest' set of difficulties that are available at present (i.e. most objective and least likely to be subject to reporting effects due to the disturbance since respondents were interviewed in their homes). All of them involved either severe overcrowding, extreme physical shortcomings or major problems to do with noise or security of tenure. It is likely that other difficulties, particularly marital problems, also contribute to chronicity but they cannot be used at present because of the possibility of lack of 'independence.'

There is a clear class difference in the frequency of

TABLE 9

Percentage of Those Having/Not Having a Major 'Independent' Difficulty by Various 'Disturbance' Groups

	MAJOR 'INDEPENDENT' DIFFICULTY		NO MAJOR 'INDEPENDENT' DIFFICULTY	
	%	(n)	%	(n)
Chronic Cases	16 ⎫	(6)	4 ⎫	(8)
	⎬ 37		⎬ 13	
Chronic Borderline	21 ⎭	(8)	9 ⎭	(17)
Recent Case or Borderline	34	(13)	15	(28)
Normal	29	(11)	71	(129)
	100	(38)	100	(182)

marked difficulties—78 per 100 in the middle class and 134 per 100 in the working class group. The occurrence of *new* difficulties within the year also shows a clear class difference (24 per 100 in the middle class and 36 per 100 in the working class group).[26] Furthermore the marked difficulties of the middle class women tend to be of shorter duration than those of the working class. Just over a quarter of those of middle class women that had started in the year had cleared up by the time of interview, which is four times the proportion found among working class women. In most instances the working class women seemed to have been drawn into difficulties not directly of their own doing and about which they were relatively helpless—a son on probation who says he is unable to get a job, a woman whose landlord wanted to split her rented house into flats, a home due for demolition where three offers of alternative housing had been much too expensive. It rarely seemed to us to reflect any personal inability to cope effectively with their problems. Many of the difficulties of the middle class women also seemed quite intractable, but there did seem to be more hope of ameliorative action than with those of the working class.

Major difficulties (i.e. marked non-health difficulties that have lasted over two years) show the greatest class differences.[27] For middle class women both health and non-health difficulties appear to clear up at about the same rate; while health difficulties of working class women conform to much the same pattern as those of middle class women, those concerned with housing, money, marriage, and children take much longer to be resolved. We have seen that it is just these difficulties that play a role in provoking the onset of depressive conditions; and it now seems likely that they are also the root cause of the greater prevalence of chronic disorder among working class women.

Summary and Conclusion

Events with severe, long term, threatening implications, most of which involve some major loss, play an important role in bringing about depressive and other affective disorders in women—at least until they reach the verge of old age. This is true for the whole range of severities of psychiatric disturbance.[28] Certain kinds of long term difficulties also appear to play a causal role, though a less important one than severe events. However, greater frequency of such life-events and difficulties in the working class does not account for the higher rate of disturbance among working class women. Class differences in the frequency of disturbance are restricted to those having a severe event or major difficulty. Working class women are about five times more likely to develop a psychiatric disturbance when only those with a severe event or major difficulty are considered—30 per cent of such working class women as against 6 per cent of such middle class women became cases (see Table 4). Can this greater vulnerability be explained?

So far we have identified four factors which increase the chances of developing a psychiatric disorder in the presence of an event or difficulty but which have no effect in their absence: loss of mother in childhood, three or more children aged under 14 living at home, lack of an intimate confiding relationship with a husband or boyfriend, and lack of full- or part-time employment. The first three are more common in the working class and between them they explain the class difference in vulnerability; a precise investigation of their relative contributions however, is not possible with our present sample size.

One crucial issue is the meaning of our measure of intimacy. At present it is very largely based on the availability of a confidant. But since confidants other than a husband or boyfriend appear to play no protective role at all, it may well be that the critical fact is not so much the availability of a confidant as such but, for example, the general level of satisfaction with the marriage or the amount of emotional support that a husband gives his wife in her role as a mother and housewife.

There are equal difficulties in interpreting the role of employment: does it have a protective function by improving economic circumstances, alleviating boredom, bringing greater variety in social contacts, or an enhanced sense of personal worth and so on? We have presented evidence suggesting that being employed can reduce the chances of developing psychiatric disorder after an event or difficulty even when women lack an intimate tie with a husband or boyfriend. We were particularly interested in a few of these women in our sample who took up employment a few weeks *after* the occurrence of a severe event, none of whom developed psychiatric disturbance. Their comments suggest that a sense of achievement might be crucial. One working class woman who had previously not worked for six years, commented that 'the money was not much' but that it gave her 'a great boost' and 'greater self-esteem.' Indeed, it may be that the relevance of the circumstances implied by at least three of the vulnerability factors is in generating a sense of failure and dissatisfaction in meeting internalized expectations of being a good mother and wife, and that this in turn leads to chronically low self-esteem, leaving the women particularly vulnerable to the effects of loss. Loss of self-esteem has long been recognized by psychoanalysts as a critical component of depression itself, but Bibring seems to have been the first to argue that it had a role in aetiology (Bibring, 1953). We would see the threat to self-esteem as being more severe subsequent to an acute loss if there has already been a slow erosion resulting from a sense of relative failure. We thus tie features of psychological importance with the characteristics of the social and familial situation.

The events with which we have been dealing are largely unavoidable, in the sense that the *individuals* to whom they occurred could not have prevented them. Social structural factors are certainly at the root of some of the events we have called severe (footnote 11) and partly explain their greater rate among working class women. Social change such as the reduction of economic and educational inequalities would reduce this difference, but on the whole it is doubtful whether measures aimed at the *prevention* of event occurrence can have more than a partial success. The majority of events involved the kind of loss which is more or less

inevitable (e.g. death of close relatives, migration of children, broken love affairs, miscarriages etc.).

Major difficulties and the various vulnerability factors present a different picture. Poor housing, size and spacing of family and employment are open to some control. While other factors such as marital difficulties and quality of supportive ties would be more difficult to influence, they are in the longer term probably a better bet for some kind of intervention than most kinds of life-events. One only needs to point out the likely effect on marriage of improved housing and increased economic security. Future research can be expected to throw up more subtle links: for example, the effect of increased provision of nursery schools on the life of mothers of young children obviously needs investigation.

There is also the possibility of other mediators. We have discussed low self-esteem as a mediating psychological factor; boredom is an equally interesting one, though it has received less attention in the psychological literature. One writer has pointed out the similarity of the state of boredom to that of being depressed: 'In boredom, goal directed activity is blocked and interfered with by repression of true goals; and in depression, the ego feels incapable of living up to its goals and narcissistic aspirations. Because of this similarity, depression may follow from boredom when a sense of helplessness and inescapability develop' (Izard, 1972, p. 203). This may well be a further feature of working class women's lives which puts them additionally at risk. Our preliminary attempts to test this, though crude, do however tend to discount it. We have taken as an indicator of the extent of vitality and excitement of women's lives, the number of life-events to which they report a positive emotional response combined with the number of incidents reported in response to a direct question about pleasant experiences. This measure shows little relationship to social status and even less to risk of onset.[29] Other measures will need to be developed before we can investigate the possible 'positive' effect of the degree of vitality in the day-to-day environment and the correlative 'negative' effect of an uneventful life. We hope to explore this further in future work.

The recurrent finding that depressed women have more often lost a parent in early childhood is one about which there has been much discussion (e.g. Bowlby, 1973, Chapter 15). However results have been curiously contradictory and Granville-Grossman's conclusion in 1968 that there had been no consistent evidence that early environment is of aetiological importance was a reasonable one. Indeed our results for the treated depressive group as a whole are also negative: 8 per cent of patients and 7 per cent of the *total* Camberwell sample had lost a mother before the age of 11. We have presented evidence that those in the general population who lost a mother before the age of 11 were more likely to develop affective disorders when they experience a severe event or major difficulty (this is reflected also in the patient series where all but one of those with an early loss had an event or difficulty). Conclusions at present must remain cautious: but the fact that a quarter of the 35 general population cases had experienced an early loss of mother and that 9 of the 16 women in the general population who had suffered such a loss were cases is certainly an impressive suggestion that such a loss is of aetiological importance. The correlation of early loss with the two vulnerability factors that not only increase the chance of psychiatric disturbance but also *lower* the chance of coming into contact with a psychiatrist may explain the inconsistency of previous research findings most of which are based on patient populations; and it is just one more example of the importance of taking *both* 'treatment seeking' and aetiological factors into account when dealing with a patient group.

While we have concentrated on explaining the onset of affective disorders, social factors also appear to be significant in determining whether these and less severe conditions (borderline) become chronic. There is again a class link. Major non-health difficulties, such as housing problems, probably play a crucial role in the greater prevalence of all forms of chronic condition among working class women. The explanation of this link may take a quite different form from that between class and vulnerability to onset itself, but it is possible that a greater sense of failure and low self-worth among working class women helps to explain both phenomena.

As a way of summarizing the results concerning onset, a schematic model is given in Figure 2. A full model will have to include 'treatment seeking' factors, such as the tendency for women with young children to seek treatment less often and for women who have an intimate tie with their husband to be encouraged more often to contact medical services. At present possible explanations for differential treatment seeking seem more obvious than those for the aetiological processes. For instance, women with children may just feel that they have less time to go to the doctor; or because of the greater salience of their difficulties they may be more likely to see medical help as irrelevant.

The relationship between social class and psychiatric disturbance has, as already mentioned, been repeatedly demonstrated in previous inquiries. The link between life-events and depression has also been reported in other work. Paykel (1973) using a different approach to the recording of life-events found higher rates of what he

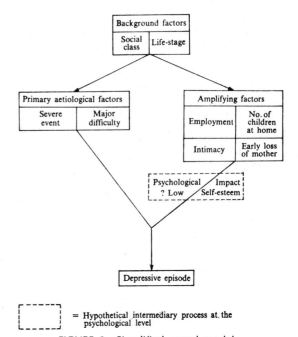

FIGURE 2   Simplified causal model.

classed as 'exit' events among a group of depressed patients than among a control group. Perhaps most important for the present paper is a check on the surprisingly high rate of disturbance among working class women with young children at home. We have found only one relevant study. In 1971 a psychiatrist, Naomi Richman, carried out a survey of the health of children under five years old living in a council housing estate in a district of north London. The children's mothers were screened, using a semi-structured interview, for psychiatric symptoms. Forty-two per cent of them were considered to be clearly psychiatrically disturbed and 16 per cent very seriously so (Richman, 1974).

The model outlined in this paper is a schematic one which leaves many questions unanswered and many others unasked. We have not, for example, kept touch with women we found to be psychiatrically disturbed in the community sample and thus have not been able to determine whether their low rates of contact with medical services was maintained, what factors promoted any subsequent help seeking and what effect such consultation had on the course of their conditions. Our approach has been to inquire into rate-producing factors of a sociological character. In this, it differs in intent and scope from that typical of the labelling perspective; we have focussed on the 'pre-history' of depressive conditions as opposed to the predominantly 'post-history' interests of the labelling approach. Two further factors limit the relevance of the latter for the present paper. Firstly, its theories of mental illness rely very heavily on the characteristic manifestations of schizophrenia, paranoia, and related conditions. Their applicability to depressive conditions is much less obvious. Indeed the approach can be faulted for its global concern with 'mental illness'—a term covering highly diverse phenomena that have radically different evaluations and images in social life. Depression is not 'madness,' the depressed woman is not 'crazy' in the public eye—apart perhaps from the manic phases of manic-depressive conditions with which we have not been concerned. Secondly, the perspective tends to be concerned with those who have been processed by helping agencies or agents of various kinds, or who have at least been labelled explicitly by members of their social circle. The psychiatrically disturbed women in our community sample, most of whom had not been processed or labelled in this way, presumably fall therefore into the category of 'secret deviants' (Becker, 1963, p. 20). We fail to see how this particular characterization is conducive to an understanding of the experiences of these women, or to the formulation of effective prevention or treatment programmes.

There remains the issue of normality. Are the conditions of cases and patients normal—in the sense that a burnt hand is a normal consequence of putting one's hand on a hot poker? We have made the point that to use psychiatric classifications does not imply that any position is taken on this issue. A recent study has been unable to demonstrate in a convincing way any clear differences between 'normal' bereavement reactions and so-called 'pathological' depressive conditions (Clayton, 1972). We believe psychiatrists label as a matter of course most depressive disorders they see in their everyday practice as 'pathological' or 'illness' and since they tend to see the more severe conditions, 'illness' is equated with the kind of condition commonly seen in their in-patients and in their out-patient clinics. This is probably not all that serious for psychiatry as it is currently practised, but it has left psychiatrists uncomfortably exposed to criticism about the nature and limits of some of the conditions they treat as mental illness. It could be considered simply a matter of words. Whether a woman who remained depressed for, say, three months after the loss of her husband or enforced rehousing is reacting 'normally' to a traumatic experience might be considered in relation to the reaction of *all* the women

who have similar experiences, their reactions ordered along a continuum of, say, severity or duration of the reaction and some arbitrary cut-off point chosen at each end of the continuum: those within the limits chosen might be labelled as having 'normal' and those outside as having 'abnormal' reactions. We suspect that this is *probably* the type of logic *implicit* in the judgements of psychiatrists (and indeed of society at large).

Sociological work on mental illness has recently been displaying such a lack of confidence in the medical model and the diagnostic procedures and categories that accompany it, that some comment on our use of psychiatric criteria may be necessary. We have identified our 'cases' and 'patients' by their reports of clusters of symptoms such as loss of weight, lack of energy, various forms of sleep disturbance and heightened anxiety. While we do not share this scepticism about the validity of categories based on such indicators, it is possible to view these women in a different way. Quite apart from this clustering of symptoms and regardless of whether they are homogeneous groups or of whether they should be called 'ill' or 'disturbed,' one extremely important feature of similarity unites them: these women *had been in much distress, did suffer* and were all certainly *most unhappy* women. In this their experiences in the year of study distinguish them from most of the women who were not considered 'psychiatrically disturbed' and this alone we believe justifies treating them as a group. Failure or refusal to recognize them in this way would mean that we are unable to document the social factors, some of which are undoubtedly the direct or indirect outcome of inequalities in the distribution of societal resources and rewards, contributing to their distress.

Before any firm conclusion can be drawn about the nature of depressive conditions, we will need more study of them as social as well as clinical phenomena. We must not only know about the clustering of symptoms, but also about the factors that bring people into care and that influence medical decisions about diagnosis and treatment, much more about the degree of handicap and distress, the effectiveness of traditional treatment and other forms of intervention as well as extending our knowledge of social factors involved in the onset and course of these conditions. For any of these tasks it is essential to have a reliable system of classification. The results and arguments outlined have, however, more farreaching implications. Certain groups of women in our society have a significantly greater than average risk of suffering from depressive conditions. To the extent that the unequal distribution of such risk is the result of more widely recognized inequalities within our society, and our findings certainly point in this direction, we believe that it constitutes a major social injustice.

Appendix

Social Status Index

Our original measure of social class was a simplified version of the General Register Office classification of occupations. The high group included professional, managerial positions and owners of small concerns/businesses. The intermediate group consisted of skilled manual and routine non-manual occupations such as clerk, tailor, typist and builder's foreman. The low group covered semi-skilled and unskilled manual workers. Women were rated by the level of occupation of their (i) husband, if living with him, or (ii) father if living in the parental household, or (iii) by their own occupation if living elsewhere. There were 42, 122 and 56 women in the high, intermediate and low groups respectively, in the community sample. Since the intermediate group formed more than half the sample and was quite heterogeneous, we wished to reduce its relative size in a way that would have some theoretical justification. We finally chose age of leaving full-time education and an index of 'prosperity' as criteria for dividing the group.* Women of the original intermediate group whose husband had finished full-time education to the age of 16 or later *or* who had themselves been in full-time education to the age of 16 or later *or* had both a car and a telephone, we reassigned into the high group. The remainder of the original intermediate group formed the new intermediate status group and the low group remained unchanged.

The small sample size and the relative rarity of cases in the general population meant that for purposes of analysis a dichotomy was preferable to this revised three-fold classification. We therefore combined the intermediate and low categories to form a 'working-class' group and left the high or 'middle-class' group as it was.

We believe this amended categorization makes more sense from our knowledge of the women and their lives than the occupational classification on its own: but it should be noted that all results in this paper hold when the original occupational classification is used.

NOTES

1. Camberwell, the area from which we selected our respondents, has a population of about 170,000. It is a working class district in the sense that in 1961, 69 per cent of the

---

* We did not have income data and so this obvious choice of discriminator could not be used.

---

economically active males were manual workers and 13 per cent were in unskilled manual employment. These figures compare with 54 per cent and 9 per cent for Greater London as a whole, and 33 per cent and 6 per cent for a 'middle class' borough such as Chelsea. In an analysis of the 1961 census material by the Centre for Urban Studies 45 per cent of enumeration districts in Camberwell were grouped as 'stable working class', 28 per cent as 'almost suburban', 23 per cent as 'local authority housing' and 5 per cent as 'poor' (Wing *et al.*, 1972, p. 53). In our own community sample 30 per cent were in local authority housing, 52 per cent in private tenancy and 18 per cent 'owner occupiers'. The small proportion of West Indian women in Camberwell were excluded.

2. For this second group, the sampling unit was the household and the final figure represents a response rate of 85 per cent. The occupational level of any male 'head of household' was 67 per cent manual workers and 12 per cent unskilled manual, percentages very close to those provided by the 1961 census.

3. Cases were those women judged by one of three psychiatrists from the Institute of Psychiatry to be similar to those women coming for in- or out-patient treatment.

4. The following is an extract from a description of a 'typical' case. 'Since this onset she had more difficulty in relaxing, was even more restless than usual and felt very anxious. She felt very depressed about half the time and "cried buckets" about once a week. The Librium helped her but did not alleviate her depression completely. She sometimes felt her life was not worth living, and has thought of harming herself, but not seriously. She was preoccupied with thoughts about an incident involving her husband (he apparently made advances to the daughter of a neighbour). She wanted to avoid people, though she was trying hard to overcome this, and felt nervous and shaky when she made herself go out. Similarly she did not want to do housework, but forced herself to keep it up. She was much more irritable in the month prior to interview and argued a lot more. Though she normally drank only at weekends, she had had a drink every evening in the month prior to interview. In general she had less energy than usual.'

5. Two psychiatrists from the Institute of Psychiatry visited most of the women whom we had considered as *cases* or *borderlines* and also a sample of the 'normal' women. The women were given the full standardized psychiatric interview. Of the persons rated by us as a case or borderline case there was 84 per cent agreement about the rating of 'case' or 'borderline'. There was complete agreement about the women who were 'normal'.

6. Twelve per cent of the community sample and 42 per cent of the patient group had a markedly threatening event in an average nine month period prior to interview (or onset of the disturbance in the case of patients). We showed in an

earlier paper how these events can bring about depression (Brown *et al.*, 1973b). Since then we have found that a subcategory of moderately threatening events—those focussed on the respondent herself or jointly on the respondent and some other person (which we call subject-focussed)—are also implicated in the onset of depression. It is these markedly threatening and moderately threatening subject-focussed events that we call *severe events*. An illustration may make the rating of 'focus' clear. Take the example of a car accident, the event would be rated as subject-focussed if the respondent was in the accident either alone or with another person; it would not be rated as subject-focussed if, say, the respondent's husband was involved but she herself was not.

7. We subsequently use the term major loss broadly to include: threat of or actual separation from a key figure, such as threatened or actual separation from husband; an unpleasant revelation about someone close forcing a major reassessment about the person and the relationship, such as finding out about a husband's unfaithfulness; a life-threatening illness to someone close; a major material loss or disappointment or threat of this, such as a couple living in poor housing learning that their chances of being rehoused by the local authority are minimal, and enforced change of residence or threat of it; and finally, miscellaneous crises involving such loss as redundancy after a period of steady employment.

8. There was only one instance of a married woman with a young child living away from home. The 'living at home' restriction largely applies therefore to older women whose children have left home.

9. The terms 'middle-class' and 'working-class', which do not coincide with the usual manual/non-manual split, are explained in the Appendix. Twenty-nine per cent (16/56) of the low status groups and 22 per cent (14/65) of the intermediate status groups were cases.

10. Fisher's exact test is used where the minimum expected cell frequency is less than five. In all other cases, the X^2 test of significance has been applied.

11. Proportions with at least one husband/house/child event are 5 per cent of the high (3/61), 22 per cent for the intermediate (8/37) and 31 per cent for the low (11/35) status groups; for other events the proportions are 16 per cent, 11 per cent and 17 per cent respectively. Some of these events are undoubtedly class-specific in the sense that certain types of events by the very nature of class occur only exceptionally in the middle class. A middle class woman has a close to zero risk of eviction, for example, or of having her husband sent to prison. The working class woman is not only subject to a higher frequency of the *same kind* of severe event that the middle class woman experiences, but also has an overlay of specifically 'working class' events.

12. Taking the most favourable report if there was more than one severe event, the proportions becoming cases who experienced a severe event were 11 per cent (2/19) of those reporting 'marked' support and 26 per cent (12/47) of those reporting 'some' or 'none' (n.s.).

13. This scale is the only one of our major measures to have been developed after the data had been collected. The information required for the rating was therefore not always entirely adequate. We had, however, as a routine procedure obtained information on (a) who the respondent confided in, (b) the frequency of contact and degree of satisfaction/dissatisfaction with other relatives and friends, (c) the frequency of contact with confidant(s), (d) the degree of satisfaction/dissatisfaction with the relationship with husband or boyfriends. The scale is of course in an exploratory stage.

14. We tended if anything to place women in 'a' on too little evidence. The reported level of general discussion between husband and wife often appeared sparse but, in the absence of a specific report that either held things back from the other, we rated the marriage as 'a' as long as the husband had been mentioned as a confidant. In some cases we felt that we were only able to do this because the relationship had not been tested by a recent crisis. However, this doubt was not really important. It is precisely for women with a severe event or major difficulty that we wished to know whether an intimate relationship was protective.

15. Age is not a confounding factor. It has *no* association with the rate of psychiatric disorder; and the association of intimacy, social class, and life-stage is not changed when age is controlled. Distribution of 'caseness' by age is:

18—25	26—35	36—45	46—55	56—65
13%	17%	17%	10%	21%
(4/32)	(8/47)	(8/46)	(4/42)	(11/53)

16. Results held independently for women in the *younger* and *older* life-stage groups: of those with a severe event or major difficulty none had an onset (0/20) in an 'a' context, and 22 per cent (4/18) in a 'non-a'. Results for those without an event or difficulty were none (0/24) and 6 per cent (1/18) respectively.

17. This is a stumbling block for any critic tempted to suggest that the results are due to cultural bias on the part of the middle class interviewers incapable of appreciating the quality of working class marriages.

18. To suggest that an event (loss of parent) occurring in early childhood 'mediates' between events occurring in adult life is possibly a misuse of language. We can at present only guess at the process by which early loss of mother operates: perhaps coping skills are affected by early loss?

Perhaps a recurrence of loss (which is what most severe events imply) in adulthood is amplified by memories of an early loss? It should also be noted that loss of father at any time or a mother when over 11 years did not increase vulnerability.

19. It might be argued that in controlling for vulnerability score, 'class' is being 'controlled out' of the class comparison. This may well be the case. If so, it simply means that we have identified the essential class-related factors relevant to our specific purpose.

20. This is corroborated by a further set of results, we have not presented, for 34 women attending general practitioners as recent cases. Since these were not a random series, merely consecutive cases of affective disorder presenting themselves at general practices, these results can only be considered suggestive rather than conclusive, but the results were almost identical with the patient series in every respect, including the result for the vulnerability factors.

21. Six of the 16 women not seeing a general practitioner for their *psychiatric* symptoms, were currently attending their G.P. for *physical* (usually chronic) symptoms such as high blood pressure and arthritis. They said they had never mentioned their 'nervous' symptoms.

22. The proportion of *borderline conditions* represents, as with cases, a three-month prevalence.

23. Grouping recent borderlines and cases together, the class difference in disturbance among women with children remains, but it is less than for cases alone—12 per cent (7/59) of the middle class and 40 per cent (27/67) of the working class women developed either a definite disorder or a borderline condition in the year. The results suggest that the inclusion of more minor conditions in defining disturbance in a psychiatric survey of a general population (as for instance in certain measures used by Taylor and Chave, 1964, in their survey of psychiatric disturbance in an English New Town) may well attenuate class differences.

24. Nine per cent (8/94) of middle class and 21 per cent (19/91) of working class ($p < .05$) women had a chronic borderline condition. Recent and chronic cases are excluded from the totals.

25. See Brown and Birley, 1968, for a discussion of the concept of 'independence'.

26. Marked difficulties refer to those difficulties rated at the top 3 points on a 6-point scale of severity. The greater class difference on prevalence than on incidence does not necessarily mean that working class difficulties take longer to terminate than those of the middle class. There may well be a ceiling effect involved—a group which already has a high prevalence of difficulties probably has fewer *potential new* difficulties. However it is not easy here to obtain the type of incidence figure usually used in the epidemiological field. Unlike the case of clearly defined illnesses, a person may have *multiple* difficulties. It is therefore not clear how to define the group 'at risk' on which a true incidence figure would be based.

27. Working class women have about 50 per cent more health *and* non-health difficulties of less than two years' duration than middle class women. For health difficulties lasting *over* two years, they have about a third as many again as middle class women, but for non-health difficulties the difference was four times as great as this, i.e. while 20 per cent and 27 per cent of middle class and working class had at least one marked health difficulty lasting more than two years, 18 per cent and 41 per cent respectively had a marked non-health difficulty of this duration.

28. We have argued elsewhere (Brown *et al.*, 1973b) that the effect of severe events is to 'bring forward' in time onsets of disturbance which would not, in the absence of the events, occur for a considerable time afterwards, if at all. Events are therefore of major aetiological importance.

29. The number of 'positive' events reported by middle class women is 1.89 and by working class women is 1.64 (standardizing for differences in life-stage); the average for recent cases, when standardized for life-stage is 2.01 compared with an average of 2.10 for the rest of the sample. The frequency of such events does, however, relate to life-stage, declining over the five life-stage groups: the averages are 3.42, 2.22, 1.96, 1.46, and 1.19. To give some idea of the types of events involved, we have divided them into three broad groups: 'Material' (purchases, winnings at bingo, etc.), 'achievements' (son passing examinations, learning to crochet, etc.) and 'social' (making a new friend, the birth of a grandchild, taking a holiday, etc.) Thirty-six per cent of 'positive' events involved material possessions, 26 per cent with achievements and 38 per cent were 'social'; there were no class differences in frequency of the first two categories. However middle class women mentioned social events more than twice as often—an average of 0.37 and 0.16 per person for middle class and working class women respectively ($p < .05$).

BIBLIOGRAPHY

Becker, H. S. 1963. *Outsiders: Studies in the Sociology of Deviance*. New York: Free Press.

Bibring, E. 1953. The Mechanism of Depression. In Greenacre, P. (ed.): *Affective Disorders*. New York: International University Press.

Bowlby, J. 1973. *Attachment and Loss: Volume 2*. London: Hogarth Press and the Institute of Psychoanalysis.

Brown, G. W. 1974. Meaning, Measurement and Stress of Life-Events. In: Dohrenwend, B. S. and B. P. (eds.): *Stressful Life-Events: Their Nature and Effects*. New York: John Wiley and Sons Inc.

Brown, G. W. and Birley, J. L. T. 1968. Crises and Life Changes and the Onset of Schizophrenia. *J. Health and Social Behav.*, 9: 203−214.

Brown, G. W., Sklair, F., Harris, T. O. and Birley, J. L. T. 1973a. Life Events and Psychiatric Disorder: 1. Some Methodological Issues. *Psychol. Med.*, 3: 74−87.

Brown, G. W., Harris, T. O. and Peto, J. 1973b. Life Events and Psychiatric Disorder: 2. Nature of Causal Link. *Psychol. Med.*, 3: 159−176.

Cartwright, A. and Jefferys, M. 1958. Married Women Who Work: Their Own and Their Children's Health. *Brit. J. of Prev. Soc. Med.*, 12: 159−172.

Clayton, P. J., Halikas, J. A. and Maurice, W. L. 1972. The Depression of Widowhood. *Brit. J. Psychiat.*, 120, 554: 71−78.

Dohrenwend, B. P. and B. S. 1969. *Social Status and Psychological Disorder: A Causal Inquiry*. New York: John Wiley.

Erikson, K. T. 1966. *Wayward Puritans*. New York: John Wiley.

Granville-Grossman, K. L. 1968. The Early Environment of Affective Disorder. In Coppen, A. and Walk, A. (eds.): *Recent Developments in Affective Disorders*. London: Headley Brothers.

Izard, C. E. 1972. *Patterns of Emotions: A New Analysis of Anxiety and Depression*. New York: Academic Press.

Paykel, E. S. 1973. Life Events and Acute Depression. In: *Separation and Anxiety*. American Association for the Advancement of Science.

Richman, N. 1974. The Effects of Housing on Pre-School Children and Their Mothers. *Devel. Med. Child Neurol.*, 16: 53−58.

Schutz, A. 1954. Concept and Theory Formation in the Social Sciences. *J. of Philosophy*, 51: 257−73. Reprinted in Thompson, K. and Tunstall, J. (eds.), 1971: *Sociological Perspectives*. Harmondsworth: Penguin Books.

Srole, L., Langner, T., Michael, S. T., Opler, M. K., and Rennie, T. A. C. 1962. *Mental Health in the Metropolis*. New York: McGraw-Hill.

Taylor, L. and Chave, S. 1964. *Mental Health and Environment*. London: Longman Green.

Tomkins, S. 1963. *Affect, Imagery and Consciousness. Volume 2: The Negative Affects*. London: Tavistock.

Weiss, R. 1970. The Fund of Sociability. *Transaction*, 7, 5: 36−43.

Wing, J. K., Birley, J. L. T., Cooper, J. E., Graham, P., and Isaacs, A. D. 1967. Reliability of a Procedure for Measuring and Classifying 'Present Psychiatric State'. *Brit. J. Psychiat.*, 113: 499−515.

Wing, J. K. and Hailey, A. M. 1972. *Evaluation of a Community Psychiatric Service*. Oxford: Oxford University Press.

PART THREE

Family and Community

INTRODUCTION   Regardless of how one chooses to define mental illness, it is useful to conceive of the transactions that are of concern to a sociology of mental illness as occurring within two domains of activity. On the one hand, there are the everyday relations between individuals and their families and proximate communities. It is in this domain that the stresses and strains, troubles and problems in living referred to by a number of the preceding theorists arise. While these problems may be engendered by any of a number of factors including the biological and the psychological, they manifest themselves initially in the relations between an individual and significant others. Lay members of the immediate community will be the first to be affected by problematic behaviors, to offer explanations and definitions of the trouble situation, and to attempt some sort of remedy or accommodation. In traditional societies, of course, lay interpretations and efforts would exhaust the repertoire of possible responses. In contemporary Western societies, there are a variety of options that derive from the second domain of activity or what we have referred to as the mental illness enterprise. The mental illness enterprise consists of all the agencies and institutions that manifestly treat and define problems in living as deriving from the deficiencies of an individual's psyche, self, or behavior. It is difficult to draw a firm boundary around this domain because it is diffuse and continually expanding. Indeed, its expansive propensities define this domain as an ongoing enterprise, encompassing many professions and occupations disposed to a psychological or individualistic idiom of interpretation, including psychiatry, clinical psychology, social work, and nursing, as well as a host of therapeutic settings and groups, such as mental hospitals, mental health clinics, board and care homes, est, and Alcoholics Anonymous.

   The following sections explore sociological aspects of these domains and of the flow between them. In this section, the processes through which the family and community define and respond to illness and the sociological factors, notably social class standing, that condition the response are considered.

Many efforts to study mental illness, particularly those informed by the medical model, begin by examining a population of individuals already identified and defined as mentally ill. For example, a researcher may compare a group of hospitalized schizophrenics with "normals" in an attempt to locate the psychobiological features that distinguish the former from the latter. From a sociological point of view, such studies take for granted an important aspect of the mental illness enterprise—the definitional process itself. While psychiatry has developed sophisticated definitions of mental illness, the identification of an individual as mentally ill is not first made by a psychiatrist but by a member of the family or local community. Often a psychological interpretation of a problem in living is not proffered immediately but is entertained as one of several alternative explanations. In "The Micro-Politics of Trouble," Emerson and Messinger identify some of the major contingencies that affect the definitional process and the likelihood that a psychological interpretation of a problem situation will prevail. They suggest that various forms of officially recognized deviance begin as vague, amorphous problems in living, or "trouble." In the absence of a clear-cut definition of the situation, the specification of trouble is open and provisional. The discovery of a successful remedy may retroactively establish the definition of the trouble. If the new job eases the husband's tension, then the anger is seen as the outcome of the pressures of the old job. If initial remedies fail, then outside parties may be brought in as troubleshooters. The appeal to outside intervention transforms the situation from a private argument to a public dispute and also politicizes the relation in that parties now have to argue on behalf of a particular definition of trouble and troublemaker. The role and stance of the troubleshooter, in turn, are affected by contingencies such as the extent to which his or her authority is dependent upon the support of both parties.

What is the nature of the trouble most apt to be interpreted as mental illness? According to Goffman, it is typically engendered by individuals who fail to honor and enact their place in social networks. Trouble is induced by individuals who show that they have assumptions about themselves—and therefore about others—that the family or work setting cannot allow as everyday, operative assumptions. If the individuals persist in such behaviors, they must "create organizational havoc and havoc in the minds of members." In "The Insanity of Place," Goffman provides a dramatic portrait of how middle-class family life is thoroughly disrupted by someone who fails to enact a definition of self that closely enmeshed others can orient to in everyday activity. It is not the bizarreness *per se* of the individual's behavior that upsets others, but the pragmatically disruptive aspects of his or her behavior.

> Bizarreness itself is not the issue. Even when the patient hallucinates or develops exotic beliefs, the concern of the family is not simply that a member has crazy notions, but that he is not keeping his place in relationships.

> Someone to whom we are closely related is someone who ought not to have beliefs which estrange him from us.

Goffman provides only a partial depiction of a complex array of interactional possibilities. For example, his description focuses on manic disorders and on families most apt to be disrupted by manic behaviors—those of the middle and upper class. Further, the family reaction is painted in broad strokes—they are upset, confused, watchful, and collusive. But manic syndromes comprise only one trouble configuration, middle-class families are only one socioeconomic station, and the reaction occurs along affective, cognitive, and interactional dimensions. A large literature addresses many of these issues and Kreisman and Joy's "Family Response to the Mental Illness of a Relative: A Review of the Literature" provides a comprehensive review and critique of this research.

There is a substantial literature that suggests that the family does not merely react to relatively well-defined symptomatic behavior but actually elicits or induces such behavior in the first place. Further, there are indications that symptomatic behavior is not simply a mechanical reaction to stressful circumstances, but action that is a functional adaptation to (or at least intelligible within) the family context. Over two decades ago Gregory Bateson and his colleagues (1956) hypothesized that the "word salad" character of certain forms of schizophrenic speech was analyzable as attempts to deal with difficult communicational patterns. The Palo Alto group proposed that schizophrenic individuals were subject to contradictory messages from one or both parents. These "double-binding" messages were constructed so that children would be punished regardless of their responses—the children were in a "damned if you do, damned if you don't" situation. A mother ambivalent in her feelings for her children might ask them in a distant way to kiss her good night. If the children sense the distance and refuse, they are admonished for lack of affection. If they approach, the mother withdraws. In a situation in which such communicational sequences are recurrent, the symptoms of schizophrenia may be strategies for dealing with impossible situations.

Quite complementary ideas about the familial creation of schizophrenia permeate the work of Laing and Esterson (1964), who have also argued that the behavior of schizophrenics is socially intelligible when viewed in the context of the family nexus. Their investigations of families led them to conclude that what appear to be the symptoms of schizophrenia when viewed out of context by psychiatrists are intelligible adaptations to extremely confused and confusing parental interaction. The parents often deny their confusion-inducing sequences and further confuse the child.

Although provocative, these and related perspectives are besieged with problems that inhibit acceptance of their central tenets. For example, some sequences that family researchers argue are distinctive of schizophrenogenic families occur in normal families, too. Recall the proverbial Jewish mother's response to her son who wears one of two gift shirts: "What's the matter? The other one you didn't like?" In the absence of control groups of normal families it is difficult to identify the extent to which double-binding is endemic to family life in general or is a process that occurs only in families producing schizophrenic children. The family interaction studies are also generally unable to establish a causal sequence. Even if it were demonstrated that families with schizophrenic individuals exhibit unique interactional patterns, it would not necessarily mean that the interactional pattern caused the symptomatic behavior. As several studies in this section suggest, while symptomatic behaviors may be a response to confusing interactional patterns, they induce confusion in interactional patterns as well. The presence of unusual interactional patterns is equally interpretable by a model that holds that family patterns induce mental illness and one that holds that mental illness elicits unusual family patterns.

Though methodologically questionable, the family interaction studies suggest the possibility of subtle interactional sequences in which the family both reacts to and induces symptomatic behaviors. More subtle interactional possibilities are suggested by researchers who have adopted a dialectical stance and examined not one or another side of the conflict comprising a trouble situation, but each side and its meaning as perceived by the other. Lemert (1962) recommends a "cubistic" perspective in the study of the relations between individuals ultimately labeled paranoid and their interpersonal network. Through retrospectively reconstructed case histories, he discovered that while the individuals reacted in a suspicious fashion to their workmates, the workmates reacted in an unusual and collusive fashion to them. The mild abrasiveness and suspicions of the individuals crystallized others into a covert effort to cope with, evade, or avoid them. This had the effect of minimizing the flow of information to the individuals about what was going on and prompted them to engage in blunt and aggressive confrontations. From the point of view of the group, the individuals were unwarrantably hostile and threatening, even paranoid. From the point of view of the individuals, the group was engaged in a coordinated, covert effort to exclude them—and, in fact, according to Lemert, they were!

Regardless of whether the family and community induces or merely responds to symptomatic behavior, a critical moment for the individual and significant others occurs when outside agencies are appealed to for assistance. In some situations, the individual may define the trouble in psychological terms, agree that the problem is his or hers, and willingly enter treatment or a hospital. In other situations, however, there may be furious differences as to the nature and remedy of the trouble situation, with the consequence that even the appeal for help becomes an extremely stressful event for everyone. Goffman's statement in "The Moral Career of the Mental Patient: The Prepatient Phase" reviews the mental patient's career sequences over time, emphasizing especially the person's view of him- or herself during the prepatient phase as various segments of the community coordinate their activity in order to hospitalize the individual.

The author differentiates between willing and unwilling prepatients. He is most interested in the unwilling, since at the time he wrote these were by far the most common. The preeminent distinguishing feature of hospitalized mental patients, as compared to the nonhospitalized mentally ill, is career contingencies. Contingencies such as one's social status, the availability of treatment facilities, and offense visibility interact with the specific activities of key agents in determining whether hospitalization ever takes place. Three agents act interdependently to propel the patients (or to avoid propelling them) into a situation leading to their incarceration. First and foremost are members of the persons' families or "next-of-kin," then the "complainants" (the persons who effectively take action against the patients that leads to their hospitalization), and finally the "mediators," those persons such as police, clergy, psychiatrists, teachers, lawyers, and social workers, who process the patients on their way to the hospital. Of course, one person may fill more than one role, for example, a parent may also be a complainant.

Not infrequently patients become embittered and feel betrayed once they discover that a family member whom they had previously trusted has formed a coalition against them with a mediator (often a psychiatrist). Goffman artfully describes what he calls the "betrayal funnel," a process whereby prepatients are led systematically through a series of situations that induce them to be considerate of others whom they have trusted and at the same time lead them tidily and quietly into the mental hospital ward.

In "Paths to the Psychiatrist," which is excerpted from the authors' powerful study of the New Haven, Connecticut, mentally ill population, Hollingshead and Redlich systematically explore the relationship between a patient's social status and social decision processes that eventuate in or fail to eventuate in that person's entering into psychiatric treatment. Hollingshead and Redlich propose that upper- and upper-middle-class people are much more apt to interpret problems in psychological terms than are members of the working class. Other studies support the Hollingshead and Redlich interpretation. Gurin, Veroff, and Feld (1960) in a national survey found a positive relationship between education and readiness for self-referral for help for psychological distress. In a recent study comparing the 1957 Gurin et al. data with comparable data collected in 1976, Kulka, Veroff, and Douvan (1979) found that the highly educated seek psychological help more often than the less educated. They are also more likely to seek such help in the future. It is upper- and upper-middle-class persons who are perceptive of the implication of failure, or personal frustration, and who are most likely to define these in terms of intrapsychic conflict. Since the upper classes are more inclined to psychological interpretations, more or at least different types of deviant behavior are presumably tolerated by members of the working class without pathological interpretations being applied. Hollingshead and Redlich conclude that while middle-class persons are more likely to interpret problems in psychogenic terms, working-class persons are more likely to interpret their problems in terms of criteria such as tough luck, meanness, physical illness, or laziness.

Not only do different classes offer different interpretations, but similar types of behavior by working-class or by middle- and upper-class persons will be interpreted differently by others and will lead to different social consequences. This theme is vividly illustrated by contrasting "promiscuous" behavior by an upper-class and by a working-class girl. Not only was there a difference in the way in which the authorities responded to the two girls, but there also were pronounced differences in the psychiatrist's orientation to them. In the case of the working-class patient, the psychiatrist recommended against treatment because "she was not able to profit from psychotherapy," whereas in the case of the upper-class girl, there was no difficulty in securing the services of the psychiatrist. Hollingshead and Redlich suggest that this type of professional judgment is not atypical, and that the underlying reason is that psychiatrists do not understand the cultural values of the working class. Since they themselves are of upper-class status, they find it easier to enter into a treatment relationship with patients of similar class position. (It is also more profitable.) This supports the proposition that whether or not troublesome behavior is judged to be indicative of mental illness or criminal or delinquent tendencies, or is simply idiosyncratic depends upon *who* appraises that behavior and *how* that person appraises it. The perspective and values of the appraisers are a critical aspect of the definition of the person as one in need of psychiatric care.

Hollingshead and Redlich find a strong relationship between the class position of the patients and the path through which they arrive at treatment. For example, lower social status individuals were more likely to be referred for psychiatric treatment by police officials and officials in social agencies, while upper- and middle-class persons were more likely to be referred for treatment by family, by friends, or by themselves. Thus, Hollingshead and Redlich demonstrate that the appraisal and implementation of decisions regarding treatment for mental illness was closely linked to the persons' class status and presumably their and their family's level of psychological knowledge. By this approach, mental illness is a state of mind not only of the sufferers, but also of the appraisers and of the therapists, and therefore is closely connected to the social status of all three.

These rich, textured articles describe significant aspects of the relations between the individual, the community, and trouble. There are, however, additional salient sociological dimensions that must be considered by a comprehensive sociology of mental illness. It is important to recognize that what counts as trouble depends upon its broader social relations context. The refusal or inability to work has one meaning in the extended family in an agrarian setting and quite another in the nuclear family in an industrialized, urban setting. The family and community form make certain troubles difficult to accommodate. It is even the case that different family configurations make certain problems in living possible while precluding others. As Goffman suggested, upper-middle-class families are particularly vulnerable to the financial extravagances of the manic individual. Insofar as family configurations condition different types of trouble and are themselves affected by economic and social factors, a full understanding of trouble situations that may mark the beginning of a mental illness career ultimately requires appreciation of the complete social, political, and economic context that shapes the form and function of family life.

References

Gregory Bateson et al., "Toward a Theory of Schizophrenia," *Behavioral Science,* Vol. **1** (October 1956), 251–264.

James C. Coyne, "Toward An Interactional Description of Depression," *Psychiatry,* Vol. **39** (February, 1976), 28–40.

James C. Coyne, "Depression and the Response of Others," *Journal of Abnormal Psychology,* Vol. **85,** No. 2 (1976), 186–193.

Gerald Gurin, Joseph Veroff, and Sheila Feld, *Americans View Their Mental Health,* New York: Basic Books, Inc., 1960.

Richard Kulka, Joseph Veroff, and Elizabeth Douvan, "Social Class and the Use of Professional Help for Personal Problems: 1957 and 1976," *Journal of Health and Social Behavior,* Vol. **20,** No. 1 (March, 1979), 2–17.

R. D. Laing and A. Esterson, *Sanity, Madness, and the Family,* city, state, country Pelican Books, 1970.

R. D. Laing and A. Esterson, *Sanity, Madness, and the Family,* Middlesex, England: Penguin Books, 1970.

Row, 1965.

Edwin Lemert, "Paranoia and the Dynamics of Exclusion," *Sociometry,* Vol. **25** (1962), 2–20.

ROBERT M. EMERSON • SHELDON L. MESSINGER

The Micro-Politics of Trouble

In his early evaluation and criticism, Gibbs (1966) argued that proponents of the labeling approach to deviance "might reasonably be expected to develop a theory of the reaction process." A number of recent

Reprinted from *Social Problems,* Vol. **25,** No. 2 (December 1977), pages 121–134, by permission of the authors and publisher.

statements from within the perspective have echoed this call (Kitsuse, 1972; Orcutt, 1973). Two issues demand particular attention. First, as Kitsuse has emphasized (1972:241), labeling proponents have provided few studies of *informal reaction.* Yet informal processes can establish deviant status independently of, but affecting "official labeling." Second, the labeling tradition has neglected relations between informal and official systems of reactions. Little existing research explores the conditions under which informal systems of control prove inadequate (but see Goffman, 1969), or the reciprocal effects of informal and formal control measures. In this paper we want to make a programmatic statement of a sociology of trouble, to provide a theoretical approach to these two types of societal reaction.

Our argument assumes that any social setting generates a number of evanescent, ambiguous difficulties that may ultimately be—but are not immediately—identified as "deviant." In many instances what is first recognized is a vague sense of "something wrong"—some "problem" or "trouble." Consideration of the natural history of such problems can provide a fruitful approach to processes of informal reaction and to their relation to the reactions of official agencies of social control. Specifically, this paper will explore the processes whereby troubles are identified, defined, responded to, and sometimes transformed into a recognized form of deviance.[1] Two points in this process hold particular significance for the movement toward deviance, and will receive major attention. The first arises when parties outside the trouble are mobilized around it, the second when those outsiders' involvement rests on formal authority rather than personal ties.

Preliminary Considerations of Troubles and Remedies

Problems originate with the recognition that something is wrong and must be remedied. Trouble, in these terms, involves both definitional and remedial components. Some state of affairs is experienced as difficult, unpleasant, irritating, or unendurable. The perception of "something wrong" is often vague at the onset: a woman notices that she is gaining weight, or that she is frequently depressed; a husband realizes that his wife is drinking more than usual, or is beginning to stay out later after work; parents see their daughter getting overly interested in boys, or their son starting to hang out with a tough gang of friends. Clearly, a person may come to recognize the existence of these or other problems, and yet never do anything in response. It may be that after mulling the problem over the person decides it is really no problem after all (everybody feels down at times, a

few pounds don't matter, or sexual mores have changed in today's world); or that while there is indeed something wrong, there is nothing that can be done or that the attempt to do something would be doomed from the start. A problem ignored may fester; or it may disappear. But often the recognition that something is wrong coincides with a weighing of remedies, perhaps resulting in an attempt to implement an appropriate one.

Sometimes an initial remedy will work; other times it will not. The latter case may lead to a search for other remedies, and as the search continues, troubles may assume a cyclical pattern (e.g., Goffman, 1969:361–69). A difficulty arises, a remedy is sought and applied; it works temporarily or not at all; then some new remedy is sought. The result tends to be a recurring cycle of trouble, remedy, failure, more trouble, and new remedy, until the trouble stops or the troubled person forsakes further efforts. As a consequence of these processes, the trouble is progressively elaborated, analyzed, and specified as to type and cause—"organized" to use the term Balint (1957) has applied to the early stages of illness.

Again, on first apprehension troubles often involve little more than a vague unease. This feeling may derive internally from the person affected, or externally, from the remark of an observant acquaintance. An understanding of the problem's dimensions may only begin to emerge as the troubled person thinks about them, discusses the matter with others, and begins to implement remedial strategies. The effort *to find and implement a remedy* is critical to the processes of organizing, identifying, and consolidating the trouble.

Consider the kind of remedial cycle that may evolve with certain physical ailments. As some bodily trouble comes to be recognized and some "tentative self-diagnosis" (Freidson, 1961) made, some remedial measures—perhaps absolutely minimal may be undertaken. In the case of a cold for example, this may involve taking it easy while waiting to see if the trouble disappears. If it does not, "more active measures like staying in bed for a day or so and taking aspirin" (Freidson, 1961:143) may be tried. Such remedies may end the trouble. If they do not, or if the "same trouble" recurs at some later time, the prior "cold" diagnosis may be questioned. An initially accepted interpretation of the trouble may then be recast, sometimes quite radically. For example:

> When the husband was in the Army he had a 'cold' that lasted several weeks. After observing the symptoms for a few days, the man's wife insisted that the ailment could not be a cold—it must be an allergy and he should see a doctor. The husband felt that his wife was wrong and he refused to

---

1. Our approach parallels, on the interactional level, that recently proposed by Spector and Kitsuse (1973) for analyzing the definition and crystallization of *social* problems on a collective level. They propose a natural history model to examine the "claim-making and responding activities" (146) that lead to the identification of an emergent social problem.

consult a doctor for treatment of a mere cold. The symptoms persisted for six or seven weeks and then vanished. The husband was discharged from the Army the following year and returned to civilian work. During that second year he again had a 'cold' which lasted several weeks. His wife again insisted that he must have hay fever. She reminded him that in a conversation about it his uncle—a physician—also said he must be suffering from an allergy, and she finally persuaded him to consult a physician who was a friend of theirs. The physician-friend diagnosed the ailment as a cold and joked about the wife's diagnostic qualifications. Eventually the 'cold' disappeared. During the third year the husband began sneezing again and his wife insisted that he consult another doctor. This time hay fever was diagnosed and the symptoms were henceforth controlled (Freidson, 1961:142–3).

This illustration suggests why "trouble" should not be conceptualized as simply the establishment of a particular definition of a problematic situation.[2] Such a view would imply that having defined or diagnosed a trouble in a certain way, the appropriate remedy is more or less specified: if overweight is the trouble, then dieting is the appropriate response; if illness, then visiting a doctor and getting the appropriate treatments seem required. In fact, the process of remedying troubles is much more open and emergent than this diagnose-then-respond formulation allows. As the foregoing incident dramatizes, any initial formulation of what the trouble "really is" is conditional upon the subsequent effects of the attempted remedy. The use of a remedy, while following from a particular definition of the trouble, simultaneously serves as a test of that definition. That the remedy works the first time is taken to confirm the initial diagnosis and the trouble's cause.[3] But this diagnosis only holds "until further notice" (Garfinkel, 1967), until, for example, a worsening of the trouble reopens the whole matter of just what is wrong and what can be done about it.

We do not deny that definition of what a trouble is affects what is done about it. But the effect is neither as linear nor as direct as is posited by the define-then-respond model. Naming something a problem has implications, prefiguring some solutions and removing others. To identify one's problem as "overweight," for example, is to preclude a formulation such as discrimina-

2. Hewitt and Hall (1973), for example, adopt this perspective: In looking at how "quasi-theories" may further the imputation of deviance in problematic situations, they conceptualize the process as essentially one whereby disorderly events are explained (defined) and made meaningful.
3. Note that in Freidson's illustration, it is just because the remedies based upon the hay fever diagnosis stopped the problem that all those involved—including the sociologist-analyst—accept the validity of that diagnosis to define the trouble.

tion and social exclusion based arbitrarily on bodily appearance (the position advanced by advocates of Fat Power; see Allon, 1973), a formulation with very different remedial implications. But even the definition "overweight" tends more to delimit a range of possible remedies than to prescribe a particular one necessary response. A man, deciding he is too fat, may diet or he may decide to exercise. Or he can look to causes rather than consequences, and enter psychotherapy.

In sum, many troubles, particularly when first noted, appear vague to those concerned. But as steps are taken to remedy or manage that trouble, the trouble itself becomes progressively clarified and specified. In this sense the natural history of a trouble is intimately tied to—and produces—the effort to do something about it. Thus, remedial actions of varying sorts—living with, ignoring, isolating, controlling, correcting the trouble—are highly significant events not only in determining the fate of the trouble, but also in shaping how it is first perceived. Conceptually, the definition of a trouble can be seen as the emergent product, as well as the initial precipitant, of remedial actions.

Relational Troubles and Intrinsic Remedies

We have largely drawn upon situations in which troubles begin and are remedied *intrapersonally*. Of particular sociological interest, however, are troubles that are inextricably *interpersonal* matters. Important variations arise with such *relational troubles*—that is, those in which remedial efforts are addressed to another in a recognized relationship with the troubled person. For, unlike efforts to remedy personal troubles, trying to resolve relational troubles raises issues concerning the distribution of rights and responsibilities in that relationship.

The difference between individual and relational troubles, and their radically variant remedial implications, is readily apparent in the advice and trouble formulations offered a woman interviewed about how she came to begin psychotherapy:

> She noticed her problems 'when I found myself crying on my job, while I worked. Bursting into tears in the face of a friend, while talking. And finally sobbing so continuously I could not leave the house without sobbing into the face of the first person I'd meet who greeted me with the words, 'Hello, how are you?' After several months of this a neighbor, who was a school teacher, 'told me to go to a mental hygiene clinic for aid.' This advice was judged helpful. Other unsolicited advice came from two physicians, one of whom 'told me I had no heart trouble but

mental aggravation that caused me pains in (my) chest,' and another who 'told me to get rid of my husband because he was no good,' and this was not helpful.

She solicited advice from several friends and from her husband. 'Friends all advised me to leave my husband. My husband will never listen to me when I talk without ridiculing me' (Kadushin, 1969:172).

This troubled person received advice both to seek help for her mental condition, a remedy assuming an intra-psychic core to her problem, and to leave her husband, a remedy positing an essentially relational character to her trouble.

This distinction should not be taken to imply that certain troubles are necessarily or mainly individual, others inherently relational. The difference derives less from the troubles themselves than from the perspective or framework from which they come to be viewed and treated. What begins as a personal trouble can be redefined and treated as a relational one, and vice versa. With bodily illness, for example, a psychosomatic diagnosis can transform any physical symptom, such as chest pains in the above case, into a product of some relational strain. Conversely, the relational dimensions of many forms of mental illness may disappear upon application of the medical model, or upon discovery of an organic cause for the troubled behavior.[4]

Moreover, movement of a trouble from an individual to a relational frame and vice versa is often propelled by the remedial cycle discussed previously. Thus, if a personal trouble persists despite intrapersonally directed remedies, the troubled person tends to become progressively uncertain as to just what the trouble is and what ought to be done about it. Here, as earlier, the troubled person may receive a variety of often conflicting interpretations about what is wrong, typically imparted in advice on managing the problem. As a result both intrapersonal and relational versions of the trouble may be entertained sequentially, or even simultaneously.

When troubles are addressed in relational terms, first remedial actions typically involve one party directly responding to and trying to influence the behavior of the other. Such corrective actions can be termed *intrinsic remedies,* since they can draw upon the interpersonal resources inherent in that relationship. Intrinsic remedies may first assume indirect and implicit forms. A wife disturbed by some behavior of her husband, may offer a variety of subtle cues that something is wrong: an

awkward silence, a raised eyebrow, a grimace (e.g., see Goffman on "remedial interchanges," 1971:95 – 187). Then a process of interactional negotiation is possible between participants to resolve the trouble without explicit recognition that it has arisen; the subtle sanction the offended person offers may work, moderating the behavior of the offender accordingly, sometimes by "stopping," sometimes by "stopping and apologizing." Alternatively, the offender may ignore the attempted sanction, and the sanctioner may let it pass.

But the issue may continue, initially in fairly muted, even covert ways. Joking references may be made of it, humor here as elsewhere allowing involved parties to avoid explicit acknowledgement of the trouble between them, while communicating its underlying seriousness (J. P. Emerson, 1969). Or the trouble may become an open issue in the relationship. Management strategies may vary from "we need to have a talk about it" to accusations that the other's behavior is wrong and must change.

A direct complaint made to the other alters the basic dynamics of the trouble. This move publicizes, explicates, and radically changes a purely individual trouble. With a direct complaint, buried differences in perceptions of the nature or source of the trouble may be brought to light. Implicit expectations about relational rights and responsibilities may be explicitly asserted and perhaps contested. The trouble may become the direct focus of the relationship, generating a continuing dialogue in which what is wrong and what should be done about it are explored, possibilities elaborated, and options specified. In this way, a complaint not only organizes and consolidates the trouble, but also constitutes that trouble as a fully interpersonal matter.

Initial complaints may only mark the beginning of an extended remedial cycle. Early interpersonal remedies may have little or only temporary effect, and further strategies may be used to influence the other's behavior, with varying degrees of success. Jackson (1954:572) has described a typical series of remedies unsuccessfully invoked by wives in trying to control a husband's emerging drinking problem:

> Threats of leaving, hiding his liquor away, emptying the bottle down the drain, curtailing his money, are tried in rapid succession, but none is effective. Less punitive methods, as discussing the situation when he is sober, babying him during hangovers, and trying to drink with him to keep him in the home, are attempted and fail.

Such remedial attempts reveal and highlight the nature and severity of the problem.

---

4. In these situations, troubles are moved back and forth between "social" and "natural" frames (Goffman, 1974:21ff). One attraction of the medical model is that it "de-relationizes" troubles, thus, in the case of psychiatric disorders, relieving those close to the disturbed person of any responsibility for the disordered state of affairs.

Understanding these matters is complicated by the partial and retrospective character of troubles and accounts of their development. Particular versions of what the trouble is, how it arose, and what was done in response, are likely to be highly partisan and hotly contested. Those involved in the trouble need never come to an agreement about what the trouble is or even that it exists. A husband may complain to his wife about her staying out nights, for example, but the wife need neither see nor acknowledge her behavior as a problem. When confronted by her spouse's rebuke or threat, she may identify his behavior as the trouble—an unreasonable insistence that she stay home. Claims about the existence or nature of a trouble, are embedded in and products of the troubled situation itself.

Second, many troubles will only be formulated retrospectively, often in furtherance of such partisan interests. Earlier relational incidents may be interpreted in light of subsequent diagnoses of the trouble. Thus, an aggrieved party may come to the realization: now I see what it is that has been bothering me about the way you treat me; or, now I appreciate how I have always hated it when you did that. Moreover, it is often only later that parties to a trouble explicitly formulate the distinctive stages and components of the remedial process. The beginning of the trouble, for example, may only be discovered in retrospect; pin-pointing the cause stands as part of the ongoing interpersonal struggle to determine what the trouble is and what can be done. Similarly, that relational rights and responsibilities, or which ones, are at issue, may be articulated only later. Finally, the meaning of actions as complaints or attempted remedies can often be grasped only in retrospect: at some later, intolerable point, for example, the complainant may point to his or her past toleration of the trouble as evidence of persistent attempts to handle the problem fairly and justly.

As with incipient intrapersonal troubles, relational troubles may not become more difficult. The complaint and attendant remedy may work sufficiently to satisfy the troubled party. The trouble may simply continue as neither party accepts the other's version of what is wrong. The complaint may be made and then dropped and ignored, as the initially offended individual learns to live with the problem. Or, as Goffman (1969:364–5) notes, the troubled party may accede to the demands of the other, redefining what was trouble as legitimate behavior and reallocating relational rights and responsibilities accordingly. In these circumstances, willingness to accept (or at least to endure) the problem behavior of the other—and alternatively, the inclination to keep pressing the trouble by looking for further remedies or responses—provide critical contingencies in the development of a trouble. But there is a limiting condition: that neither party to the trouble ends the relationship that surrounds it. While in fleeting public contacts with others, denial or withdrawal are readily available responses (Goffman, 1963), this strategem is not as available or acceptable in troubles arising in enduring relations (Goffman, 1969:365). Where exit is precluded, troubles and remedial strategies greatly increase in complexity. Under such circumstances, pressures to seek outside remedies often accelerate.

Complaints and Third-Party Intervention

As intrinsic remedies fail and accommodation is not forthcoming, outside parties are apt to be brought into the trouble in active and central ways. Outsiders may have been involved in a relational trouble from its inception; the husband of the philandering wife, for example, may talk to his mother, sister, or best friend about his wife's behavior, why it occurs, and how to respond. And his understanding of what the trouble is and how to cope may be critically shaped by the views and analyses provided by such third parties. Yet as long as these outside parties function only in advice and support roles, the trouble remains essentially private. In particular, efforts to do something still come only from those originally party to the problem. However, when an outside party moves from giving advice to active intervention the structure of the trouble undergoes significant change.

In many instances the line between advising and more active intervention may be blurred. There are strong pressures for converting advisors into direct participants. Friends, counsellors, and therapists of one party may decide to become directly involved in the trouble, as, for example, by taking a husband aside and pointing out how upset his wife is with his drinking. Critical involvement emerges when the third party directly intervenes and establishes a relationship with the troubled parties, who thus no longer deal exclusively with one another. With this event the remedies considered are no longer intrinsic, but *extrinsic*, to the troubled relationship.

With the request for third party intervention, the following roles (see Goffman on "agent roles," 1961:136) become differentiated in the remedial process: First, there is a *complainant* announcing the presence of trouble by seeking remedial action. The complainant role may be distinct from the role of *victim*, the person held injured, harmed, or wronged. Next, there is the remedy agent or *troubleshooter* to whom the trouble is taken for remedy. Finally, one party to the trouble may come to be designated the *troublemaker* responsible.[5]

In general terms, the decision to seek outside intervention and the kind desired seem intricately linked with prior attempts to deal with the trouble—to avoid, isolate, or remedy it. Such factors as the kinds of controls and remedies available in the particular social situation, the availability of and limitations upon their use, the presence and strength of ties with outside parties and possible troubleshooters, and the degree of legitimacy accorded each outsiders' potential involvement in the troubled situation, all shape not only the nature of initial efforts to respond to the trouble within the relationship, but also the occasion and nature of outside intervention.

Efforts to obtain outside intervention tend to move through several stages. First, those initially invited to troubleshoot are typically close friends or relatives of at least one of the involved parties. The involvement of such intimate troubleshooters rests exactly on their personal relationship with one or all of the parties to the trouble. While such personal troubleshooters may be able to remedy the trouble, their intimacy may also prove a hindrance. For example, the legacy of their prior dealings with the parties may preclude a mutually acceptable solution from the start, as when the troubleshooter is already identified as an ally of one of the parties.

Second, troubles may evolve with the increasing movement toward official, licensed troubleshooters. In some cases, such involvement may proceed on a highly unplanned and episodic basis. As Jackson (1954) has noted of the drinking husband, outside agents may be drawn into the situation on an emergency basis (for example, a call for police protection), and then through more regular contacts with social agencies, doctors, and perhaps sanitaria and Alcoholics Anonymous. In other situations, specific official troubleshooters may be sought out by the troubled parties or their allies because of their expertise or neutrality, as when a couple decides to take their problems to a marriage counsellor.

Usually, the first such official agents to become involved in troubles are "generalists," including the police (Cumming, Cumming and Edel, 1965; Parnas, 1967), family doctors (Freidson, 1961, 1970), and

ministers (Cumming and Harrington, 1963; Weiss, 1973). Initial preference for such troubleshooters reflects a variety of factors. Such agents are relatively available to lay complainants and their orientations are similar to what laypersons already know (Freidson, 1961): the generality and inclusiveness of their occupational mandates attract those-seeking remedies for relational troubles.

Even the initial choice of troubleshooter may prove highly consequential for the trouble. For the selection of a particular troubleshooter may preemptorially impose a definition on a trouble previously open or contested. Moreover, this selection may expose the differences between the troubled parties as irreconcilable. To suggest that one's spouse see a psychiatrist, for example, may bring previously latent discordances to a head. The proffered remedy thus exacerbates the prior trouble: "You want me to see a psychiatrist! You think I'm the crazy one?"

Furthermore, the effects of initial choice of troubleshooter may be consequential, if not necessarily irreversible, in determining whether, where, and how a trouble enters subsequent referral networks. When a trouble has resisted remedial efforts, or when it seems more appropriately handled elsewhere, initial troubleshooters tend to pass intractable problems on to new, often more specialized, troubleshooters. As in Goffman's notion of a "circuit of agents" (1961), troubles may be shifted from one agent to another, perhaps moving upward toward greater and greater specialization, perhaps toward increasingly coercive and punitive outcomes.

In moving through a circuit of troubleshooters, an initially ambiguous trouble tends to crystallize, as new ways and means of dealing with the problem are sought out and implemented and prior ways are determined to be ineffective and rejected. In this process, an individual may be definitely assigned the role of troublemaker and explicitly identified as deviant. As full-scale deviant remedies are tried and found to fail, the troublemaker may be referred to specialists in other areas of deviance, the nature of his or her trouble undergoing reinterpretation as new ways of eliminating, reducing, or confining the troublemaking are implemented.

It is important to understand how outside intervention radically transforms what were previously private troubles, for this transformation shows most clearly the negotiated (rather than intrinsic) nature of problems. Whereas disagreements about the nature of the trouble and how to remedy it were previously confined to (and under the control of) the initial parties, the involvement of a third party reconstitutes the trouble as a distinctly

---

5. Many remedial agents expect victim and complainant roles to be performed by the same person, and while this is not inevitably forthcoming, "disinterested" complainants may have to provide some sort of account for their involvement. The more general point is that victim and non-victim complainants may encounter different presentational problems in getting their complaints validated. Furthermore, complaints can be advanced, and interventions implemented, without definite allocation of victim and wrongdoer roles. Remedies involving mediation, to be considered below, either avoid these roles, or attribute part of each to both parties.

public phenomenon. As Gulliver (1969:14) has noted with regard to processes of dispute settlement, "the initial disagreement (is raised) from the level of dyadic argument into the public arena." With movement to a triadic situation, the original dyad can no longer orient exclusively to one another. Rather, each must attend to and seek to present his or her side to the third party. In the process relational assumptions, claims, and expectations previously taken for granted will have to be openly proclaimed and justified. Moreover, to the extent that the troubleshooter holds standards for weighing relational claims divergent from those of the original parties, new grounds for asserted rights and responsibilities may have to be provided. Tacit claims and conduct treated as idiosyncracies of the relationship, for example, may now have to be explained and justified in more universal terms; indeed the parties may learn to their surprise and dismay that some behaviors on which they founded their claim of being troubled are seen by others as "normal" or even "desirable."

Taking a problem to an outside party may provide the first occasion for seeing the trouble as a coherent whole and formulating an explicit history of the trouble. As troubled individuals try to have their claims validated by the newly involved third party, earlier behaviors, problems, and situations may be reinterpreted and organized into progressing incidents of the trouble, while still others may be framed as attempted remedies. Thus, the need to account for past actions and to justify desired remedial responses to the third party may generate more closely documented histories of the origin, causes, and persistence of the trouble, along with the new and extended accusations of wrongdoing.

Finally, outside intervention directly affects the remedial circumstances as well as the definitional dimension of the trouble. In proposing remedial actions the concerns and reactions of the third party now have to be anticipated and attended to, as these factors assume crucial roles in how the trouble will be defined and treated. If official troubleshooters are involved, the trouble may be treated as a "case" and accumulate a distinctive official history as it moves through the system of referrals. Different sets of remedial concerns may become salient, and solutions may be imposed that neither of the original disputants wanted.

In summary, the attempt to obtain and shape the course of intervention may lead to the progressive clarification and specification of the nature and seriousness of the trouble. More concretely, what is done about outside complaints—in particular, when and how the troubleshooter intervenes, if that happens—defines and organizes the trouble. The intervention, then, may fun-

damentally shape what the trouble will become. To highlight the theoretical significance of these processes, we will now consider the issues troubles pose to a troubleshooter at the point of initial intervention.

Dealing with Complaints: Contingencies in Intervening

To an outside troubleshooter, troubles pose issues of alignment: the troubleshooter must decide what stance to take toward the parties and issues. As Aubert (1965) has emphasized, troubleshooters may assume two general stances, responding to the trouble as conflict or as deviance.

In responding to trouble as conflict, the troubleshooter adopts a stance of nonalignment, either by refusing commitment to either side, or by equal commitment to both. In the former the troubleshooter refuses to intervene. In the latter the troubleshooter may try to become involved equally with the two parties by trying to mediate a settlement. For example the police routinely respond to calls concerning family violence by mediating between husband and wife to provide an immediate if temporary resolution (Parnas, 1967:932−3). In adopting the role of mediator, the troubleshooter treats the trouble as a dispute or conflict, in that intervention is symmetrical (Aubert, 1965:18) with regard to the positions and claims of the two parties.

In contrast, in responding to troubles as deviance a troubleshooter confronts the problem of alignment head on, orienting to the complaint and trouble in terms of whose side to take. In special circumstances, police will foresake mediating domestic disputes and respond openly on the side of one of the troubled parties, for example, by arresting and removing from the home an assaultive husband (Parnas, 1967). With one-sided intervention of this sort, the trouble is established not as conflict but deviance, as the disputelike, relational core of the trouble is dissolved with the asymmetrical allocation of all wrongdoing to one party (now the deviant) and of all right to the other (now the victim).

A variety of factors determine the likelihood of symmetrical or asymmetrical intervention. In the first place, on the structural level, the assertion of certain types of rights and claims may be legally proscribed, as when the criminal law denies workers a legitimate right to strike, or a disputant a legitimate right to kill or rob an enemy. Such denial of legitimacy to the assertion of particular claims, of course prescribes one-sided intervention against the illegitimized claimant.

Second, troubleshooters often operate with a distinctive theory of trouble and interventional ideologies which require symmetrical or asymmetrical responses. The assumptions of the criminal law, for example, encourage absolute judgments in the allocation of blame, and its agents typically dispense one-sided sanctions against the wrongdoer. The medicalization of troubles, locating the source of the trouble in some physiological disfunctioning within the individual, similarly promotes asymmetrical solutions. Finally, those who handle instances of child abuse are precommitted to the ideology of wrongdoing and proceed by determining whether or not there is a perpetrator. In contrast, some troubleshooters operate with distinctive remedial theories that facilitate or even require not taking sides. Marriage counsellors frequently employ a therapeutic ideology to eschew judgments of right and wrong, adopting a uniformly neutral, "no fault" stance toward troubles. Any and every problem must be treated as a relational matter, even though the counsellor may privately conclude that one party is more to blame.

Third, the form of intervention is affected by the power of the troubleshooter relative to that of the original parties to the trouble. Intervention by third parties whose authority is dependent upon the support or agreement of those in the entered trouble tends to assume symmetrical forms.[6] Personal troubleshooters (friends, relatives) may take sides, but usually cannot impose their solution against the resistance of the other. Thus, personal troubleshooting tends to be an act of mediation: the third party has to negotiate a mutually acceptable settlement relying upon personal resources and sanctions. In contrast, many official troubleshooters possess the power to impose one-sided solutions through adjudicated decisions (Eckhoff, 1966) even in the face of opposition from one or both parties. When mediating efforts have proved unsatisfactory, official intervention may be sought by one or another side, to obtain exactly this sort of forced ending to an intractable situation.

The nature of outside intervention is also fundamentally shaped by contingent, situational factors. Troubles will move toward asymmetrical outcomes to the extent that one or both parties are resistant to compromise and have reserves of power and resources to support that position. In addition, the conditions under which third party intervention is sought may prefigure symmetrical and asymmetrical response. Troubleshooters may be sought as mediators, as when a couple agrees to take their marital difficulties to a marriage counsellor. On

other occasions one or another party to a trouble may seek intervention directly on his or her side. The result is frequently sought by directing accusations of wrongdoing at the other, in this way formulating the trouble as onesidedly as possible in order to gain the desired intervention. When one party's accusation is made from a position of greater power, the likelihood of one-sided intervention on that persons's terms increases.

A complaint to a third party, whether in the form of an accusation or a request for mediation, marks only the starting point for ensuing intervention. Complaints are subject to scrutiny and to possible revision by troubleshooters, who proceed with some awareness that allegations may be distorted or false, that the proposed allocation of blame and responsibility may be misleading or invalid, that the remedial action sought may be exploitative, subversive, or illegitimate. In light of such understandings, the troubleshooter may implement remedial strategies unrelated to initial proposals. Thus, the troubleshooter may refuse to take any side where one or both parties seek partisan intervention. A juvenile court probation officer may respond to allegations that a teenager is actively misbehaving and "beyond control" by cooling out the parental accusers. A troubleshooter may come to take one side in a trouble brought in for neutral mediation. A troubleshooter may come to respond within the framework initially proposed for the trouble, but either redefine the problem (for example, parent-child differences reflect "a lack of communication"), or, with accusatory complaints, reverse the proposed allocation of victim and wrongdoer roles. Goffman's mental patient who "thought he was taking his wife to see the psychiatrist" (1961:138fn) provides a classic example of this last possibility.

These considerations highlight the importance of how direction and terms of the troubleshooter's intervention may determine what the trouble becomes. Even where the troubleshooter's intervention is shaped by the actions of one or both of the troubled parties, such that the remedy implemented merely ratifies what has already been proposed, in analytic terms it is the nature and direction of the outside intervention, particularly when authoritatively enforced, that determines what the trouble is. This is not to say that troubleshooters can intervene freely. Intervention may be tightly constrained by the need to take into account the prior history, positions, power, and concerns of the troubled parties, by the dictates of the troubleshooter's professional or institutional ideology, and by practical institutional and situational factors. Any troubleshooter's intervention may be radically overturned and revised by a subsequent intervention (although the ease with which this can be achieved declines as the trouble accumulates a documented history). Yet, it

---

6. Symmetrical intervention of a mediative character tends to be characteristic of legal processes in tribal and traditional societies as legal agents usually lack any such authority. Anthropological studies of disputing and dispute settlement (e.g., Nader, 1965: Gulliver, 1969) provide a rich source of materials on these processes.

is the nature and direction of outside intervention, particularly where carried out by officials, that produces the forms of alignment distinctive of deviance and conflict, and which ultimately constitutes the trouble as one or the other of these forms.

The processes of intervention that provide the key to the consolidation of troubles do not involve simply defining the situation as one meriting either a balanced or a one-sided treatment and responding accordingly. For third party aligning responses can proceed according to their own logic and dynamic, at times at odds with a trouble's definitions as deviance or as conflict. Professional ideologies may prescribe a pre-set response to all troubles without regard to the particulars of a given case, as when marriage counsellors respond relationally to any and all marital problems. But pragmatic, situational concerns may take intervention in a direction which could not be predicted on the basis of the troubleshooter's assessment of specific instances of wrongdoing. Those committed to relational treatments may find themselves stymied in efforts to work out a mutually acceptable solution, and may have to resort to onesided responses as a practical expedient. Thus, community mental health workers may encounter a situation where they clearly assess both parties as psychiatrically disturbed, yet may hospitalize only one, deciding that the situation is too volatile to remain unchanged (Emerson and Pollner, 1976). Conversely, troubleshooters may respond in an even-handed fashion, while recognizing unequal distribution of rightness and wrongness among the parties (for example, Bittner on police peacekeeping, 1967). Troubleshooters may even intervene on behalf of the party seen to be in the wrong, if such a response promises to provide a permanent end to the trouble (see, for example, Bittner's analysis of police handling of the case of "Big Jim," 1967:709–10). These instances highlight the way particular forms of trouble, including deviance and conflict, are produced *procedurally* by the responses of troubleshooters, and not simply by their definitions of the trouble.

Toward a Sociology of Trouble

In conclusion, we would like to explore some implications of the micro-politics of trouble proposed here for prevailing interactional approaches to deviance.

First, many such approaches cut into the production of deviants at late stages. Frequently, those who have suffered some major, perhaps irrevocable sanction, such as institutional placement, are identified as the subject population. Such sanctioning or placement provides an "end point" (which may later turn out to have been a "stage," of course), for treating an actor as a particular sort of deviant, and past activities and events are ordered as leading to this "end point." These sorts of deviant career notions, however, often organize events in ways foreign to perceptions prevailing earlier, when outcomes were in doubt and definitions ambiguous. In addition, these approaches focus on cases that have made it to an eventual deviant designation, neglecting those that have failed to do so. If not neglected outright, such cases are addressed in terms of this failure; why did they not make it? In this sense, deviant career models both presuppose and require deviant outcomes. In contrast, the concept of "trouble" directs attention not simply toward early phases of careers into deviance, but also toward non- and "pre-deviant" situations and settings generally. Moreover, the idea of trouble keeps open the possibility that many troubles with deviant potentiality can "come to nothing," or come to something devoid of imputations of deviance, or become one of several possible categories of deviance. In these ways, trouble comprehends and incorporates both the openness and indeterminacy of deviant outcomes, in part by abandoning the centrality of the notion of deviance itself.

Second, the micro-politics of trouble points toward a deepening of the basic imagery of deviant designation. It is axiomatic to the labeling approach that deviants are products of social definition; definition typically involving the imputation of immoral identity and defective status. Douglas, for example, views deviance as the product of a negotiation of "moral meanings" (1971), and Katz (1972:192) conceptualizes deviance as the assignment of defective moral or ontological status. But an exclusive focus on "meanings" runs the risk of being one-sided. This paper has argued that definition can both shape and be shaped by response; specifically, that deviant designation is the product of remedial efforts[7] involving both interpretative and active components which can vary independently of each other. A deviant should be understood not only as one who is morally condemned, but also as one who is sided against. And while on some occasions moral condemnation seems to precede and cause the siding against, having been sided against generates the subsequent moral opprobrium for others.

Third, our approach emphasizes a point insufficiently explicit in many studies by proponents, and totally unseen by many critics of labeling: actions directed toward another (or oneself) as a "deviant" are heavily contingent on, although not totally determined by, the frames of reference and resources of complainants, victims, and official troubleshooters, when they are

---

7. See also the specific proposal by Fletcher et. al. (1974:59) to shift the conceptual focus to "referral behavior rather than naming behavior" as the key process in the "labeling" of mental illness.

involved.[8] The "labeling approach," properly construed, does *not* hold that the activities of deviants are disregarded by complainants, victims, or officials, nor does it recommend that analysts disregard these activities. It does propose that analysts explicitly take into account *and attempt to account for* the role of complainants, victims, and officials in determining definitions and actions, and redefinitions and further actions. We both think the activities of those eventually treated as deviants (and those not so treated), and the activities of complainants, victims, and troubleshooters, are appropriately conceived as *variable* influences on both temporary and lasting outcomes. The conditions of such variation should be a major topic for inquiry and theorizing.

This consideration leads to one final implication of this approach. Although our paper has focused on the micro-political, interactional processes, we recognize and even insist that a fully developed sociology of trouble would also consider macro-politics. Such a macro-politics of trouble would inquire into the ways broader economic, political and social interests shape both the frames of reference and the institutionalized remedies available for identifying and dealing with trouble. Long-term social trends such as the formation of states and the centralization of state power, the shift from mercantilism to industrial capitalism and from laissez-faire to corporate capitalism, and the spread of bureaucratic forms of organization appear to have major implications for interpretations of and responses to troubles. It may be argued that the formation of states and the centralization of their power made some forms of punishment such as banishment and transportation impossible and helped motivate the establishment of prisons (see Langbein, 1976); that the rise of a market economy in labor helped motivate differentiation of specific categories of deviants, and that the welfare state is encouraging "decarceration" (see Scull, 1977); that legal developments are sometimes powerfully determined by economic ones, so that new forms of "crimes" are "recognized," legislated, and enforced (see Hall, 1952); or, finally, that remedial institutions in the form of bureaucracies work unceasingly to influence how certain activities, like the possession of marijuana, are treated and understood (see Dickson, 1973).

8. The difference made by the presence and preferences of complainants has been documented by the work of Donald J. Black and Albert J. Reiss, Jr. (1970), although theory about the matter remains undeveloped. Much work in "victimology" also implicitly raises some relevant questions, but so much attention has been given to the light victims can throw on "dark numbers," and the variable role of victims in "causing" deviance, that these questions have gone unanswered. A considerable amount of work in the labeling tradition has, of course, focused on the role of official troubleshooters.

This is not the place, even had we the insight, to try to spell out these matters. We strongly urge that developing a "micro"-politics of trouble should not be taken to imply that developing a "macro"-politics of trouble is unimportant; we think both need to be developed and their relations examined. Our approach suggests that in addition to exploring how larger forces may affect individual and group activities which may come to be treated as deviant, such a macropolitics of deviance should explore in detail how actions toward and understandings of such activities are affected.

REFERENCES

Allon, Natalie. 1973. "Group dieting rituals." *Society* 10 (January/February): 36−42.

Aubert, Vilhelm. 1965. *The Hidden Society.* Totowa, N.J.: Bedminster Press.

Balint, Michael. 1957. *The Doctor, His Patient, and the Illness.* New York: International Universities Press.

Becker, Howard. 1963. *Outsiders: Studies in the Sociology of Deviance.* New York: Free Press.

Bittner, Egon. 1967. "The police on skid-row: A study of peace keeping," *American Sociological Review* 32 (October): 699−715.

Black, Donald J. and Albert J. Reiss. 1970. "Police control of juveniles." *American Sociological Review* 35 (February): 733−747.

Cumming, Elaine, Ian M. Cumming and Laura Edell. 1965. "Policeman as philosopher, guide and friend." *Social Problems* 12 (Winter): 276−286.

Cumming, Elaine and Charles Harrington. 1963. "Clergyman as counselor." *American Journal of Sociology* 69 (November): 234−243.

Dickson, Donald T. 1970. "Marijuana and the law: Organizational factors in the legislative process." *Journal of Drug Issues* 3 (Spring): 115−122.

Douglas, Jack D. 1971. *American Social Order: Social Rules in a Pluralistic Society.* New York: Free Press.

Eckhoff, Torstein. 1966. "The mediator, the judge and the administrator in conflict-resolution." *Acta Sociologica* 10: 148−72.

Emerson, Joan P. 1969. "Negotiating the serious import of humor." *Sociometry* 32 (June): 169−81.

Emerson, Robert M. and Melvin Pollner. 1976. "Mental hospitalization and assessments of untenability." Presented at the Annual Meetings of the Society for the Study of Social Problems, New York.

Fletcher, C. Richard, Peter K. Manning, Larry T. Reynolds, and James O. Smith. 1974. "The labeling theory and mental illness." In Paul M. Roman and Harrison M. Trice (eds.), *Explorations in Psychiatric Sociology*. Philadelphia: F. A. Davis: 43–62.

Freidson, Eliot. 1961. *Patients' View of Medical Practice: A Study of Subscribers to a Prepaid Medical Plan in the Bronx*. New York: Russell Sage Foundation.

Garfinkel, Harold. 1967. *Studies in Ethnomethodology*. Englewood Cliffs, N.J.: Prentice-Hall.

Gibbs, Jack P. 1966. "Conceptions of deviant behavior: The old and the new." *Pacific Sociological Review* 9 (Spring): 9–14.

Goffman, Erving. 1961. *Asylums*. Garden City, New York: Doubleday.

——1963. *Behavior in Public Places*. New York: Free Press.

——1969. "The insanity of place." *Psychiatry* 32 (November): 352–388.

——1971. *Relations in Public*. New York: Basic Books.

——1974. *Frame Analysis: An Essay on the Organization of Experience*. Cambridge, Mass.: Harvard University Press.

Gulliver, P. H. 1969. "Introduction" to Case Studies of Law in Non-Western Societies. In Laura Nader (ed.), *Law in Culture and Society*. Chicago: Aldine; 11–23.

Hall, Jerome. 1952. *Theft, Law, and Society*, 2nd Ed. Indianapolis: Bobbs-Merrill.

Hewitt, John P., and Peter M. Hall. 1973. "Social problems, problematic situations, and quasi-theories." *American Sociological Review* 38 (June): 367–374.

Jackson, Joan K. 1954. "The adjustment of the family to the crisis of alcoholism." *Quarterly Journal of Studies on Alcohol* 15 (December): 562–586.

Kadushin, Charles. 1969. *Why People Go To Psychiatrists*. New York: Atherton Press.

Katz, Jack. 1972. "Deviance, charisma, and rule-defined behavior." *Social Problems* 30 (Fall): 186–202.

Kitsuse, John I. 1972. "Deviance, deviant behavior, and deviants: Some conceptual problems." In William J. Filstead (ed.), *An Introduction to Deviance*. Chicago: Markham: 233–243.

Langbein, John H. 1976. "The historical origins of the sanction of imprisonment for serious crime." *The Journal of Legal Studies* 5 (January): 35–60.

Nader, Laura. 1965. "The anthropological study of law." *American Anthropologist* 67 (December): 3–32.

Orcutt, James D. 1973. "Societal reaction and the response to deviation in small groups." *Social Forces* 52 (December): 259–267.

Parnas, Raymond I. 1967. "The police response to the domestic disturbance." *Wisconsin Law Review* 4 (Fall): 914–960.

Scull, Andrew T. 1977. *Decarceration: Community Treatment and the Deviant—A Radical View*, Englewood Cliffs. N.J.: Prentice-Hall.

Spector, Malcolm, and John I. Kitsuse. 1973. "Social problems: A reformulation." *Social Problems* 21 (Fall): 145–159.

Weiss, Robert S. 1973. "Helping relationships: Relationships of clients with physicians, social workers, priests, and others." *Social Problems* 20 (Winter): 319–328.

ERVING GOFFMAN

The Insanity of Place†

I

For more than two hundred years now the doctrine has been increasingly held that there is such a thing as mental illness, that it is a sickness like any other, and that those who suffer from it should be dealt with medically: they should be treated by doctors, if necessary in a hospital, and not blamed for what has befallen

Reprinted from *Psychiatry*, Vol. **32**, November, 1969, pages 357, 366–383, 385–388, by permission of the author and publisher.

† I am much indebted to Edwin Lemert and Sheldon Messinger and to Helen and Stewart Perry for help in writing this paper.

them. This belief has social uses. Were there no such notion, we would probably have to invent it.

However, in the last twenty years we have learned that the management of mental illness under medical auspices has been an uncertain blessing. The best treatment that money has been able to buy, prolonged individual psychotherapy, has not proven very efficacious. The treatment most patients have received—hospitalization—has proven to be questionable indeed. Patients recover more often than not, at least temporarily, but this seems in spite of the mental hospital, not because of it. Upon examination, many of these establishments have proven to be hopeless storage dumps trimmed in psychiatric paper. They have served to remove the patient from the scene of his symptomatic behavior, which in itself can be constructive, but this function has been performed by fences, not doctors. And the price that the patient has had to pay for this service has been considerable: dislocation from civil life, alienation from loved ones who arranged the commitment, mortification due to hospital regimentation and surveillance, permanent posthospital stigmatization. This has been not merely a bad deal; it has been a grotesque one.

Consequently, in the last decade some important changes have been entertained regarding treatment of the mentally ill. There has been marked improvement in living conditions in mental hospitals, albeit no more so than in other backwashes of American society recently penetrated by secular conceptions of man's inalienable right to recreational facilities. More to the point, there has been some pressure to keep the potential patient in the community as long as possible and to return the hospitalized patient to the community as quickly as possible. The legal rights of persons accused of mental illness have been sharpened—in some states, such as California, to the point where involuntary commitment is quite difficult to arrange. And the notion is abroad that the goal is not to cure the patient but to *contain* him in a niche in free society where he can be tolerated. Where a niche is not available one is sometimes built, as in the institutions of family care and halfway house. And if this new approach places a burden on the patient's home, neighborhood, or work place, there is a current understanding of mental disorder to help justify this: since the patient has been put upon, since he is merely the symptom carrier for a sick set-up, it is only fair that the whole be made to share the burden; it is only fair that the patient and those with whom he is most involved be encouraged, preferably with psychiatric counsel, to work together to work things out.

Given the life still enforced in most mental hospitals and the stigma still placed on mental illness, the philosophy of community containment seems the only desirable one. Nonetheless, it is worth looking at some implications of this approach for the patient's various "others," that is, persons he identifies as playing a significant role in his life. To do this we must examine closely the meaning of the patient's symptoms for his others. If we do this we will learn not only what containment implies, we will learn about mental disorder.

Before proceeding, I want to introduce one issue and its concepts—an issue regarding the medical world and the doctor-patient relationship.

The ideal behind medical service is much like the ideal behind other legitimate services and, as in their case, is often realized. The patient comes to the doctor on his own, places himself in the doctor's hands, follows the doctor's orders, and obtains results which amply justify the trust and the fee.

Of course there are points of tension. The patient may not know of his need for service; knowing of his need, he may apply to charlatan servers; desiring medical service, he may not be able to afford it; affording it, he may shop around too much before settling on a particular physician; settling on one, he may not follow the advice he gets from him; following the advice, he may find his situation somewhat eased but not basically altered.

More at issue, the two-party dealings and two-party relationship between the doctor and his patient can become complicated in certain ways by other parties. For example: medical group-plans of various kinds can obscure the patient's view of the agency from which he obtains treatment; communicable diseases and suspect wounds oblige the physician to act for the community as well as for the patient. I will focus on one class of these third parties, the patient's daily circles: his service community, his work place, his friendships, and particularly his family.

Traditionally in medical service the patient's family has been given certain functions. For example, very commonly the family is expected to cooperate, to help out, to mobilize the domestic resources necessary to accommodate the special temporary needs of the patient. When the illness is major, the least the family will do is to use its car to bring the patient to the hospital and fetch him therefrom; at most, the household can become a hospital away from the hospital. Whatever the extent of the family help, the physician will usually have to communicate instructions to the helpers, directly or through the patient.

Another function of the family is guardianship. Adult members of the family can be openly called on to act for the patient, typically because he is below the age of discretion or beyond it, ratifying a medical decision ordinarily requiring the free consent of the person directly affected.

Further, should the patient be a full-fledged adult and his situation desperate, the family may be brought into a secret relation with the doctor, who tells them facts about the patient's condition that they need to know for their own good or his, but that the physician feels he cannot on humanitarian or medical grounds tell the patient now. A kind of emergency guardianship is involved requiring collusion between the sick person's kin and the physician.

Here definitions might be justified. A "coalition" is a collaborative arrangement minimally between two parties who use it to control the environment of a third, the arrangement itself not being openly established and recognized in these terms. A "collusive net" or "collusive alignment" is a coalition aimed at one kind of control—the third party's definition of the situation.[1] No matter how many persons are actually involved in the various parties, only two basic roles are present: the two or more persons who collude—that is, the colluders; and the one or more persons whose definition of the situation is secretly managed, who might be called the "excolluded." Note that if collusion is to occur, the colluders must be in communication with one another, since independent response will not allow them to concert in the line they are maintaining. This collusive communication takes two forms: in one, the participants are not in the presence of the excolluded and therefore need conceal only that they are in touch; in the other, the communication occurs in the immediate presence of the excolluded, typically by means of furtive signs. The first involves open communication between concealed persons, and second, concealed communication between exposed persons.[2]

Collusion involves falseness knowingly used as a basis for action. Something of a conspiracy is therefore entailed, typically in regard to two fundamental matters. The first is reality. Collusion serves to maintain for the excolluded a definition of the situation that is unstable, one that would be disrupted and discredited were the colluders to divulge what they know, and were they to relax in their management of the evidence available to the excolluded. The second is relationships. The personal relationship that an excolluded individual feels he has in regard to each of the colluders would be undercut if he discovered that they have a collusive relationship to one another in regard to him.[3] The adulterous affair, that great training ground for off-stage acting, can be taken as a central example.

A collusive conspiracy of course may be quite benign, may be in the best interests of the person conspired against. Collusion is a normal and no doubt desirable part of social life. Children are raised by it, especially handicapped children. Everywhere egos are preserved

by it and faces saved by it. More important, it is probably impossible for interaction to continue among three persons for any length of time without collusion occurring, for the tacit betrayal of the third person is one of the main ways in which two persons express the specialness of their own relation to each other. In fact, stable triads seem always to involve at least a little round-robin collusion, with each of the three possible pairs colluding, and each of the three participants serving a turn as the excolluded.

In ordinary medical practice, collusion is of no great issue. Perhaps this is so even in the case of the dying patient (Glaser and Strauss), where it is very likely that at least for a time he will be put on regarding his future, by the hospital staff, if not by his family. As we will later see, it is in psychiatric care that collusion becomes a questionable and troublesome business.

II

We can begin to consider the insanity of place by reviewing and extending some elementary terms regarding the sociology of place.

The treatment that an individual gives others and receives from them expresses or assumes a definition of him, as does the immediate social scene in which the treatment occurs. This is a "virtual" definition; it is based upon the ways of understanding of the community and is available to any competent member, whether or not such interpretations are actually made and whether or not they are made correctly—that is, in the manner most others could be led to defend. The ultimate referent here is a tacit coding discoverable by competently reading conduct, and not conceptions or images that persons actually have in their minds. Note, a rounded definition requires a collation of relevant conduct and its interpretation, a task a lay person would be competent to do but have no reason for doing.

Virtual definitions of an individual may be "accorded"—that is, readable in the conduct of agencies seen as external to the individual himself. These definitions constitute the individual's "person." Corresponding to these accorded assumptions about him there will be virtually "enacted" ones, projected through what is seen as his own conduct. These assumptions constitute the individual's "self."[4] Person and self are

---

1. For a recent treatment of family coalitions, see Haley. A vivid treatment of collusion within the family is provided in the writings of Ronald Laing.

2. There is a parallel distinction in intelligence work between a clandestine operation and a covert operation, the first involving total concealment, the second concealment only of intent and method.

3. Once someone begins to suspect collusion and has identified the members of the net, he will no longer be in a position to have his relation to them undercut. Lemert has suggested to me that an adversary process may then emerge, the excolluded attempting to prove publicly that there is a conspiracy against him, and the conspirators attempting to deny the evidence. Of course, a person can learn (whether correctly or not) that his suspicions were unfounded, and then re-credit his relationships.

4. The distinction between accorded and enacted definitions of an individual follows Kai Erikson's distinction between role-validation and role-commitment: "For the purposes of this paper, it will be useful to consider that the acquisition of roles by a person involves two basic processes: *role-validation* and *role-commitment*. Role-validation takes place when a community 'gives' a person certain expectations to live up to, providing him with distinct notions as to the conduct it considers

portraits of the same individual, the first encoded in the actions of others, the second in the actions of the subject himself.

The individual's enacted definition of himself may be different in various ways from the definition accorded him. Further, the psychological relation he sustains to his accorded and enacted definitions is enormously complex. He will certainly be unaware of some elements of these definitions and erroneously aware of others. He can be variously attached to such definitions as he is aware of, liking or disliking what he perceives is implied about him in his dealings with others, and inwardly accepting or rejecting these assumptions in various degrees. Also, he can employ various devices to press his desires regarding these assumptions about him, or he can passively submit to definitions of him that he feels are undesirable. As Cooley argued, the self-regarding sentiments such as pride and shame will be involved. When these various relations that an individual can have to what can be read about him become patterned and habitual, they can be called his "personality" or "character," comprising what we try to assess when we consider what an individual is really like, what he is essentially like, what he is like as a human being.

It should be plain now that the implicatory aspect of the individual's conduct has a very convoluted and recursive character. Even while his overall behavior can be read for the self-assumptions which inform it, some of his minor gestures will convey what he feels about having a self that is defined in this way and what he feels about others' defining him as a given person; and these gestures in turn will be taken as part of his enacted self by himself and others, which fact can in turn be taken into consideration in the assessment he or others make of him. The individual stakes out a self, comments on his having done so, and comments on his commenting, even while the others are taking the whole process into consideration in coming to their assessment of him, which consideration he then takes into consideration in revising his view of himself.[5]

<hr>

appropriate or valid for him in his position. Role-commitment is the complementary process whereby a person adopts certain styles of behavior as his own, committing himself to role themes that best represent the kind of person he assumes himself to be, and best reflect the social position he considers himself to occupy'' (pp. 263–264).

5. I do not think there is anything like an adequate version of these complications. Little help has been provided by pencil and paper students of the self who start with a subject's verbal description of himself, often based on his selection from verbal trait-lists, instead of starting with the serious ethnographic task of assembling the various ways in which the individual is treated and treats others, and deducing what is implied about him through this treatment. The result has been a trivialization of Cooley, Mead, and social psychology. The self acquires a hopelessly shifting status: in one sentence the student refers to the tacit coding of an individual's conduct, the assumptions in effect that the

Having considered the individual's person and his self, consider now their normative regulation. A social norm or rule is any guide for action recommended because it is felt to be appropriate, suitable, proper, or morally right. Three parties are involved: the person who can legitimately "expect" and demand to be treated in a particular way because of the rule; the person who is "obliged" to act in a particular way because of the rule; the community that supports the legitimacy of these expectations and obligations.

The treatment that is accorded anyone and that he accords others is typically regulated by social norms, and so also, therefore, are the delineative implications of these dealings. When, therefore, an individual becomes involved in the maintenance of a rule, he tends to become committed to a particular set of enacted and accorded definitions of him. If the rule obliges him to do something in regard to others, he becomes to himself and them the sort of person who would naturally act in this way, correctly delineated by what is expressed in this conduct. If the rule leads him to expect others to do something in regard to him, then he becomes to himself and them someone who is properly characterized by what is implied through this way of treating him. Accepting this delineation of himself, he must then make sure that through his treatment of others and their treatment of him the rule will be followed, allowing him to be what he feels he is.

In general, then, when a rule of conduct is broken, two individuals run the risk of becoming discredited: one with an obligation, who should have governed himself by the rule; the other with an expectation, who should have been treated in a particular way because of this governance. A bit of the definition of both actor and recipient is threatened, as is to a lesser degree the community that contains them both.

Having seen that rules of conduct are fundamental to definitions of a self, we must go on to see that they are just as fundamental to corporate social life. Put simply and quickly, the activities of any organization are allocated to members, and these activities are coordinated by being subsumed under (or being allowed to fall within or be covered by) various rules. Thus, many of the obligations and expectations of the individual pertain to, and ensure the maintenance of, the activities of a social organization that incorporates him.

Let me restate this general sociological position. Through socialization into group living, the individual

<hr>

individual makes about himself, and in the next to a purely subjective mentalistic element—this itself having an inconstant referent. There is a failure to see that the term "conception" can radically shift in meaning, and that an individual's mental conception of self is merely his subjective and partial view of the effective conception he has of himself.

comes in effect to make assumptions about himself. Although these assumptions are about himself, they nonetheless are delineated in terms of his approved relationship to other members of the group and in terms of the collective enterprise—his rightful contribution to it and his rightful share in it. In brief, these assumptions about himself concern his normatively supported place in the group.

The individual tends to organize his activity as if the single key to it all were the assumptions he makes about himself. He thus anticipates that his share of group expectations and obligations will be parceled out to him on the basis of (and as a confirmation of) his particular assumptions about himself. And by and large this self-organization of the individual's activity is effective because others in the group make more or less the same assumptions about him and treat him accordingly. Self and person coincide. His treatment of them and their treatment of him can be read as making the same set of assumptions concerning him, the same except for a difference in point of reference; and this set of assumptions will not be an incidental implication of the reciprocal treatment, but its key.

Here note that the expressive idiom of the individual's society and group will ensure that evidence of his assumptions about himself will be made available not only through his performing his main substantive obligations, but also through expressive means, comprising the way in which he handles himself while in the presence of others or while having dealings with them. Through quite minor acts of deference and demeanor, through little behavioral warning lights, the individual exudes assumptions about himself. These provide others with a running portent, a stream of expression which tells them what place he expects to have in the undertakings that follow, even though at the moment little place may be at stake. In fact, all behavior of the individual, insofar as it is perceived by others, has an indicative function, made up of tacit promises and threats, confirming or disconfirming that he knows and keeps his place.

III

With these elementary concepts to serve as a frame, turn now to a specific matter: the parallel drawn between medical and mental symptoms.

Signs and symptoms of a *medical* disorder presumably refer to underlying pathologies in the individual organism, and these constitute deviations from biological norms maintained by the homeostatic functioning of the human machine. The system of reference here is plainly the individual organism, and the term "norm," ideally at least, has no moral or social connotation. (Of course,

beyond the internal pathology there is likely to be a cause in the external environment, even a social cause, as in the case of infectious or injurious situations of work; but typically the same disorder can be produced in connection with a wide variety of socially different environments.) But what about *mental* symptoms?

No doubt some psychoses are mainly organic in their relevant cause, others mainly psychogenic, still others situational. In many cases etiology will involve all of these causal elements. Further, there seems no doubt that the prepatient—that is, the individual who acts in a way that is eventually perceived as ill—may have any of the possible relations to intentionality: he may be incapable of knowing what he is doing; or he may know the effects of his acts but feel unable to stop himself, or indifferent about stopping himself; or, knowing the effects of certain acts, he may engage in them with malice aforethought, only because of their effects. All of that is not at issue here. For when an act that will later be perceived as a mental symptom is first performed by the individual who will later be seen as a mental patient, the act is not taken as a symptom of illness but rather as a deviation from social norms, that is, an infraction of social rules and social expectations. The perceptual reconstituting of an offense or infraction into a medical, value-free symptom may come quite late, will be unstable when it appears, and will be entertained differently, depending on whether it is the patient, the offended parties, or professional psychiatric personnel doing the perceiving.[6]

This argument, that mentally ill behavior is on its face a form of social deviancy, is more or less accepted in psychiatric circles. But what is not seen—and what will be argued in this paper—is that biological norms and social norms are quite different things, and that ways of analyzing deviations from one cannot be easily employed in examining deviations from the other.

The first issue is that the systems regulated by social norms are not biological individuals at all, but relationships, organizations, and communities; the individual merely follows rules or breaks them, and his relation to any set of norms that he supports or undercuts can be complex indeed—as we shall see, more of a political issue than a medical one.

The second issue has to do with the regulative process itself. The biological model can be formulated in simple terms: deviation; restorative counteractions; reequilibration (associated with the destruction or extrusion of the

---

6. Of course, some personal conditions, such as loss of memory or intense anxiety or grandiose persecutory beliefs, are very quickly shifted from offense to symptoms, but even here it is often the case that social rules regarding how a person is properly to orient himself or feel about his situation may be what are initially disturbed.

pathogenic agent); or disorganization, that is, destruction of the system. A realistic picture of social regulation is less tidy.

The traditional sociological answer to the question of regulation and conformance is found in the normative sense of the term "social control" and the corrective cycle that presumably occurs when an offense takes place.

As suggested, through socialization the individual comes to incorporate the belief that certain rules are right and just, and that a person such as himself ought to support them and feel remorse and guilt if he does not. He also learns to place immediate value on the image that others might obtain of him in this regard; he learns to be decently concerned about his reputation.

Taking the notion of personally incorporated norms as central, one can distinguish three basic forms of normative social control. First, and no doubt most important, there is "personal control": the individual refrains from improper action by virtue of acting as his own policeman. Finding that he has acted improperly, he takes it upon himself to admit his offense and volunteer such reparative work as will reestablish the norms and himself as a man respectful of them.

Second, there is "informal social control." When the individual begins to offend, the offended parties may warn him that he is getting out of line, that disapproval is imminent, and that deprivations for continuation are likely. As a result of this more-or-less subtle warning, amplified and sustained until the offense is corrected, the offender is brought to his senses and once again acts so as to affirm common approved understandings. As Parsons has remarked, this corrective feedback is constantly occurring in social life, and is in fact one of the main mechanisms of socialization and learning (p. 303).

Third, the threat that an offender introduces to the social order is managed through "formal" social sanction administered by specialized agents designated for the purpose. Criminals certainly break social rules, but there is an important sense in which they do not threaten the social order, and this by virtue of the risk they accept of apprehension, imprisonment, and harsh moral censure. They may find themselves forced, as we say, to pay their debt to society—the price presumably adjusted to the extent of the offense—which in turn affirms the reasonableness of not breaking the rules at all. In any case, they often try to conceal the act of breaking the law, claim to be innocent when accused, and affect repentance when proven guilty—all of which shows that they know the rules and are not openly rebelling against them. Note that the efficacy of informal and formal social control depends to a degree on personal control, for control that is initiated outside the offender will not be very effective unless it can in some degree awaken corrective action from within.

Personal control, informal control, and formal control are the moral means and the main ones by which deviations are inhibited or corrected and compliance to the norms is assured. But taken together, these means of control provide a very narrow picture of the relation between social norms and social deviations.

For one thing, the agencies of control that have been reviewed can be as effective as they are not because of the offender's moral concern, but because of his expediential considerations. The good opinion of others may be sought in order to render these persons vulnerable to exploitation. A fine may be viewed not as a proclamation of guilt but as a routine cost to be figured in as part of operating expenses.[7] The point here, of course, is that often what looks like automatic and dependable conformance is to be expected from the actor only over a strictly limited range of costs to him.

Further, the norms may be upheld not because of conscience or penalty, but because failure to comply leads to undesired, unintended complications which the offender was unaware of when first undertaking his offensive action.[8]

But even this expanded base for normative social control provides a partial view. The control model that is implied—a model that treats social norms somewhat like biological norms—is itself too restrictive. For when an offense occurs it is by no means the case that sanctions are applied, and when negative sanctions or penalties *are* applied, or when unanticipated penalizing consequences occur—that is, when the corrective cycle is begun—it is by no means generally true that diminution of the deviation results.

When the offense occurs, the offended parties may resolve the situation simply by withdrawing from relevant dealings with the offender, placing their social business with someone else. The threat of this sort of withdrawal is, of course, a means of informal social control, and actual withdrawal may certainly communicate a negative evaluation, sometimes unintended. But the process just as certainly constitutes something more than merely a negative sanction; it is a form of management in its own right. As we shall see, it is just such withdrawal which allows those in a social contact to convey glaringly incompatible definitions and yet get by each other without actual discord.

If the offense is such as to make legal action possible,

---

7. When the agencies of control take the same expediential view, then we might better speak of social direction rather than social control. It is thus, for example, that a subsidy policy directs crop allocation without reliance on the factor of moral sensibility.

8. This is a functionalist argument. See, for example, Nadel.

the offended person may yet desist (and withdraw) for practical reasons which sharply limit the application of formal control: the cost and time required to make a formal complaint and appear in court; the uncertainty of the legal decision; the personal exposure involved in taking official action; the reputation that can be acquired for being litigious; the danger of reprisal later by the offender.

There are still other contingencies. The individual who offends expectations can prevail, causing his others to accept him on his new terms and to accept the new definition of the situation that this implies. Children growing up in a family are constantly engaged in this process, constantly negotiating new privileges from their keepers, privileges which soon come to be seen as the young person's due. Some of the mutinies that occur in schools, prisons, and ghettos illustrate the same theme. The social changes produced by the labor movement and the suffragette movement provide further examples.

And even when withdrawal from the offender or submission to him does not occur, social control need not result. The negative moral sanctions and the material costs of deviation may further alienate the deviator, causing him to exacerbate the deviation, committing him further and further to offense. And as will be later seen, there may be no resolution to the discord that results thereby. The foreign body is neither extruded nor encysted, and the host does not die. Offended and offender can remain locked together screaming, their fury and discomfort socially impacted, a case of organized disorganization.

These limitations on the social version of the homeostatic model are themselves insufficient, for they are cast in the very assumptions that must be broadened. The issue is that the traditional social control approach assumes an unrealistically mechanistic version of the social act, a restriction that must be relaxed if the close analysis of social control is to be achieved.

As the law suggests, our response to an individual who physically performs an offensive act is radically qualified by a battery of interpretive considerations: Did he know about the rule he was breaking, and if so, was he aware of breaking it? If he did not appreciate the offensive consequences of his act, ought he to have? And if he did anticipate these offensive results, were they the main purpose of his act or incidental to it? Was it within his physical competence to desist from the offense, and if so, were there extenuating social reasons?

The answers to these questions tell us about the actor's *attitude* toward the rule that appears to have been violated, and this attitude must be determined before we can even say what it is that has happened. The issue is not merely (and often not mainly) whether he conformed

or not, but rather in what relationship he stands to the rule that ought to have governed him. Indeed, a significant feature of *any* act is what it can be taken to demonstrate about the actor's relation to such norms as legitimately govern it.

However, the actor's attitude toward a rule is a subjective thing; he alone, if anyone, is fully privy to it. Inevitably, then, an important role will be played by the readings others make of his conduct, and by the clarifying expressions that he contributes, whether to ensure that a proper purpose is not misinterpreted or an improper one is not disclosed. It follows, for example, that if a deviator is suitably tactful and circumspect in his violations, employing secrecy and cover, many of the disruptive consequences of the violation in fact will be avoided. A particular application of the rules is thwarted, but the sanctity of the rule itself is not openly questioned.

A reorientation is therefore to be suggested. An actual or suspected offender is not so much faced with an automatic corrective cycle as with the need to engage in remedial ritual work. Three chief forms of this work are available to him: accounts, apologies, and requests. With accounts he shows that he himself did not commit the offense, or did it mindlessly, or was not himself at the time, or was under special pressure, or did what any reasonable man would have done under the circumstances;[9] with apologies he shows that if indeed he had intended the offense, he now disavows the person that he was, bewails his action, repents, and wants to be given a chance to be what he now knows he should be; with requests he seeks the kind of offer or permission which will transform the act from his offense into the other's boon. With this ritual work, with explanations, propitiations, and pleas, the offender tries to show that the offense is not a valid expression of his attitude to the norms. The impiety is only apparent; he really supports the rules.

Once we see that ritual work bears on the very nature of social acts and considerably loosens what is to be meant by social equilibrium, we can readdress ourselves to the crucial difference between medical symptoms and mental symptoms.

The interesting thing about medical symptoms is how utterly nice, how utterly plucky the patient can be in managing them. There may be physical acts of an ordinary kind he cannot perform; there may be various parts of the body he must keep bandaged and hidden from view; he may have to stay home from work for a spell or even spend time in a hospital bed. But for each of these deviations from normal social appearance and

---

9. A discussion of accounts is available in Scott and Lyman.

functioning, the patient will be able to furnish a compensating mode of address. He gives accounts, belittles his discomfort, and presents an apologetic air, as if to say that in spite of appearance he is, deep in his social soul, someone to be counted on to know his place, someone who appreciates what he ought to be as a normal person and who is this person in spirit, regardless of what has happened to his flesh. He is someone who does not *will* to be demanding and useless. Tuberculosis patients, formerly isolated in sanitaria, sent home progress notes that were fumigated but cheerful. Brave little troops of colostomites and ileostomites make their brief appearances disguised as nice clean people, while stoically concealing the hours of hellish toilet work required for each appearance in public as a normal person. We even have our Beckett player buried up to his head in an iron lung, unable to blow his own nose, who yet somehow expresses by means of his eyebrows that a full-fledged person is present who knows how to behave and would certainly behave that way were he physically able.

And more than an air is involved. Howsoever demanding the sick person's illness is, almost always there will be some consideration his keepers will *not* have to give. There will be some physical cooperation that can be counted on; there will be some task he can do to help out, often one that would not fall to his lot were he well. And this helpfulness can be *absolutely* counted on, just as though he were no less a responsible participant than anyone else. In the context, these little bits of substantive helpfulness take on a large symbolic function.

Now obviously, physically sick persons do not always keep a stiff upper lip (not even to mention appreciable ethnic differences in the management of the sick role); hypochondriasis is common, and control of others through illness is not uncommon. But even in these cases I think close examination would find that the culprit tends to acknowledge proper sick-role etiquette. This may only be a front, a gloss, a way of styling behavior. But it says: "Whatever my medical condition demands, the enduring me is to be dissociated from these needs, for I am someone who would make only modest reasonable claims and take a modest and standard role in the affairs of the group were I able."

The family's treatment of the patient nicely supports this definition of the situation, as does the employer's. In effect they say that special license can temporarily be accorded the sick person because, were he able to do anything about it, he would not make such demands. Since the patient's spirit and will and intentions are those of a loyal and seemly member, his old place should be kept waiting for him, for he will fill it well, as if nothing untoward has happened, as soon as his outer behavior can again be dictated by, and be an expression of, the inner man. His increased demands are saved from expressing what they might because it is plain that he has "good" reasons for making them, that is, reasons that nullify what these claims would otherwise be taken to mean. I do not say that the members of the family will be happy about their destiny. In the case of incurable disorders that are messy or severely incapacitating, the compensatory work required by the well members may cost them the life chances their peers enjoy, blunt their personal careers, paint their lives with tragedy, and turn all their feelings to bitterness. But the fact that all of this hardship can be contained shows how clearly the way has been marked for the unfortunate family, a way that obliges them to close ranks and somehow make do as long as the illness lasts.

Of course, the foregoing argument must be qualified. In extreme situations, such as the military, when it can be all too plain that the ill person has everything to gain by being counted sick, the issue of malingering may be seriously raised and the whole medical frame of reference questioned.[10] Further, there is the special problem caused by illness directly affecting the face and the voice, the specialized organs of expression. An organic defect in this equipment may be a minor thing according to a medical or biological frame of reference, but it is likely to be of tremendous significance socially. There is no disfigurement of the body that cannot be decorously covered by a sheet and apologized for by a face; but many disfigurements of the face cannot be covered without cutting off communication, and cannot be left uncovered without disastrously interfering with communication. A person with carcinoma of the bladder can, if he wants, die with more social grace and propriety, more apparent inner social normalcy, than a man with a harelip can order a piece of apple pie.

With certain exceptions, then, persons have the capacity to expressively dissociate their medical illness from their responsible conduct (and hence their selves), and typically the will to do so. They continue to express support of the social group to which they belong and acceptance of their place therein. Their personality or character will be seen to remain constant in spite of changes in their role. This means that the illness may tax the substantive resources of the group, make tragic figures of well members, but still not directly undermine the integrity of the family. In brief, ritual work and minor assistance can compensate for current infractions because an important part of an infraction is what it can be taken to symbolize about the offender's long-range attitude toward maintaining his social place; if he can find alternate ways of conveying that he is keeping

10. Here see the useful paper by Aubert and Messinger.

himself in line, then current infractions need not be very threatening. Note that the efficacy here of excusing expressions (with the exceptions cited) is due to the fact that medical symptoms involve behavior which is either not an infraction of social norms at all—as in the case of internal tumors of various kinds—or only incidentally so. It is the incidental side effects of the physical deviation that disqualify the person for compliance. When an amputee fails to rise to greet a lady, it is perfectly evident that this failure is only an incidental and unintentional consequence of his condition; no one would claim that he cut off his legs to spite his courtesies. Almost as surely, his disqualification for jobs that require rapid movement can be seen as a side effect of his deviance and not its initial expression. He is a deviator, not a deviant. Here is incapacity, not alienation.

Now turn to symptoms of mental disorder as a form of social deviation. The most obvious point to note is that since there are many kinds of social deviation that have little to do with mental disorder, nothing much is gained by calling symptoms social deviations.[11]

The position can be taken that mental illness, pragmatically speaking, is first of all a social frame of reference, a conceptual framework, a perspective that can be applied to social offenses as a means of understanding them. The offense, in itself, is not enough; it must be perceived and defined in terms of the imagery of mental illness. By definition one must expect that there always will be some liberty and some dissensus in regard to the way this framework is applied. Many important contingencies are known to be involved, some causing the imagery to be applied to psychologically normal behavior with the consequence of reconstituting it into a mental symptom. But given this necessary caveat, we can ask: In our society, what is the nature of the social offense to which the frame of reference "mental illness" is likely to be applied?

The offense is often one to which formal means of social control do not apply. The offender appears to make little effort to conceal his offense or ritually neutralize it. The infractions often occur under conditions where, for various reasons, neither the offended nor the offender can resolve the issue by physically withdrawing from the organization and relationship in which the offense occurs, and the organization cannot be reconstituted to legitimate the new self-assumptions of the offender—or, at least, the participants strongly feel that these adaptations are not possible. The norms in question are ones which frequently apply and which are

constantly coming up for affirmation, since they often pertain to expressive behavior—the behavior which broadcasts to all within range, transmitting warnings, cues, and hints about the actor's general assumptions about himself. Finally, with the exception of paranoia of primary groups (folie à deux, trois, etc.), the offense is not committed by a set of persons acting as a team, but rather—or so it is perceived—by an individual acting on his own. In sum, mental symptoms are willful situational improprieties, and these, in turn, constitute evidence that the individual is not prepared to keep his place.[12]

One implication of the offense features I have mentioned should be stressed. Mental symptoms are not, by and large, *incidentally* a social infraction. By and large they are specifically and pointedly offensive. As far as the patient's others are concerned, the troublesome acts do not merely happen to coincide partly with what is socially offensive, as is true of medical symptoms; rather these troublesome acts are perceived, at least initially, to be intrinsically a matter of willful social deviation.

It is important now to emphasize that a social deviation can hardly be reckoned apart from the relationships and organizational memberships of the offender and offended, since there is hardly a social act that in itself is not appropriate or at least excusable in some social context. The delusions of a private can be the rights of a general; the obscene invitations of a man to a strange girl can be the spicy endearments of a husband to his wife; the wariness of a paranoid is the warranted practice of thousands of undercover agents.

Mental symptoms, then, are neither something in themselves nor whatever is so labeled; mental symptoms are acts by an individual which openly proclaim to others that he must have assumptions about himself which the relevant bit of social organization can neither allow him nor do much about.

It follows that if the patient persists in his symptomatic behavior, then he must create organizational havoc

---

11. I omit considering the popularists who have tried to establish the psychogenesis of everything that is interesting, from crime to political disloyalty.

12. Although much of mental symptomatology shares these offense features—thereby allowing us to answer to the argument that mental symptoms are not merely any kind of social deviation—it is the case that many social deviations of the situational kind do not qualify as signs of mental illness. We have been slow to learn this, perhaps because mental wards once provided the most accessible source of flagrant situational improprieties, and in such a context it was all too easy to read the behavior as unmotivated, individually generated aberrancy instead of seeing it as a form of social protest against ward life—the protest having to employ the limited expressve means at hand. In the last few years the nonpsychiatric character of considerable symptomlike behavior has become much easier to appreciate because situational improprieties of the most flagrant kind have become widely used as a tactic by hippies, the New Left, and black militants, and although these persons have been accused of immaturity, they seem too numerous, too able to sustain collective rapport and too facile at switching into conventional behavior to be accused of insanity.

and havoc in the minds of members. Although the imputation of mental illness is surely a last-ditch attempt to cope with a disrupter who must be, but cannot be, contained, this imputation in itself is not likely to resolve the situation. Havoc will occur even when all the members are convinced that the troublemaker is quite mad, for this definition does not in itself free them from living in a social system in which he plays a disruptive part.

This havoc indicates that medical symptoms and mental symptoms are radically different in their social consequences and in their character. It is this havoc that the philosophy of containment must deal with. It is this havoc that psychiatrists have dismally failed to examine and that sociologists ignore when they treat mental illness merely as a labeling process. It is this havoc that we must explore.

IV

The most glaring failure to organize conduct in accordance with assumptions about himself that others accept is to be found in those dramatic cases where the individual, perceived to be in a state of disorganization as an actor, accords himself a personal biographical identity not his own or temporarily reconstitutes himself in accordance with age, sex, and occupational categories for which he does not qualify. Often this is associated with the individual's imputing quite grandiose personal properties to himself.[13] He then makes some effort to treat others accordingly and tries to get them to affirm this identification through their treatment of him.

Note that mental hospitals can manage such diffusions and distortions of identity without too much difficulty. In these establishments much of the person's usual involvement in the undertakings of others and much of his ordinary capacity to make contact with the world are cut off. There is little he can set in motion. A patient who thinks he is a potentate does not worry attendants about their being his minions. That he is in dominion over them is never given any credence. They merely watch him and laugh, as if watching impromptu theater. Similarly, when a mental hospital patient treats his wife as if she were a suspect stranger, she can deal with this

impossible situation merely by adjusting downward the frequency and length of her visits.[14] So, too, the office therapist can withstand the splotches of love and hate that the patient brings to a session, being supported in this disinvolvement by the wonderfully convenient doctrine that direct intercession for the patient, or talk that lasts more than fifty minutes, can only undermine the therapeutic relationship. In all of these cases, distance allows a coming to terms; the patient may express impossible assumptions about himself, but the hospital, the family, or the therapist need not become involved in them.

Matters are quite different, however, when the patient is outside the walls of the hospital or office—outside, where his others commit their persons into his keeping, where his actions make authorized claims and are not symptoms or skits or something disheartening that can be walked away from. Outside the barricades, dramatically wrong self-identification is not necessary in order to produce trouble. Every form of social organization in which the patient participates has its special set of offenses perceivable as mental illness that can create organizational havoc.

One very important organizational locus for mental symptoms consists of public and semipublic places—streets, shops, neighborhoods, public transportation, and the like. In these places a fine mesh of obligations obtains which ensures the orderly traffic and commingling of participants. Modes of personal territoriality are delineated, and respect for their boundaries is employed as a key means of ordering mutual presence. Many classic symptoms of psychosis are precise and pointed violation of these territorial arrangements. There are encroachments, as when a mental patient visiting a supermarket gratuitously riffles through a shopper's cart, or walks behind the counter to examine what is contained there, or openly advances her place in the checkout line, or leans into an ongoing conversation not her own, or addresses a midpassage statement to someone who has not been brought into a state of talk. There are self-contaminations involving exposure or befoulment, as when a patient is denudative, or too easily invites conversational contact from others, or speaks aloud shameful admissions, or smears himself with half-eaten

13. Corresponding to these expressed overreachings, there will be alterations in the overreacher's subjective sense of himself. Here a very useful paper was contributed by Josiah Royce titled, "Some Observations on the Anomalies of Self-Consciousness," helpfully brought to attention in an abridged reprinting in Edgar Borgatta and Henry Meyer's *Sociological Theory*. Since Royce's statement in 1895, progress in this area has been modest.

14. A mental hospital in fact can be defined functionally as a place where persons who are still rightfully part of our daily lives can be held at bay and forced to wait for our occasional visits; and we, instead of sharing existence, can ration it. Of course, patients often can manage to hold their kinsmen at bay, too, simply by declining to meet them off the ward or by becoming upset when they visit. However, the cost of this rejection can be very high—for example, loss of an opportunity to get off the ward for a time and to obtain minor supplies. Further, what the patient can hold off is not life with his loved ones, but visits.

food, or openly toys with his mucus, or takes dirty objects into his mouth. There are "hyper-preclusions," as when a patient declines to acknowledge any conversational overture, or shies away from passing glances, or fights off a medical examination, or will not let go of small personal possessions.

From this brief look at public places and social order among the unacquainted,[15] turn to closer social organization involving sustained obligations among sets of acquainted persons. First, formal work organizations. For this I propose to review Edwin Lemert's study of mental patients with paranoid complications whose trouble appeared to be focused on the job (1962).[16]

Lemert dates the trouble-career of each member of his sample by suggesting that each had been subjected to a loss, or threat of loss, of status, on or off the job, for which apparently no compensatory alternative could be found. Apparently such an individual can respond by declining to exert control over himself, and by resisting the informal control attempted by others. His willingness to play the game while on the job declines. He begins to intrude into the decision territory of subordinates and makes improper demands upon them, by implication subordinating them to his sphere of operation. He declines to return confidences with equals, thus leaving them with unreciprocated and insecure relations to him. He becomes insulting and arrogant, failing to show expected consideration for the feelings of the others, while exhibiting an improperly elevated view of himself. He attempts to arrogate to himself informal privileges which are part of the status symbolism of the group and otherwise allocated. He attempts to use markers of place without having the place that is customarily marked by them.

The conduct so far cited violates the informal rules for the management of personal place. We see in this a simple interdependency between the actor and his others, where the disturbed boundary is the one between the actor and these others. But in addition to these direct disturbances there are some indirect ones. Given the actor's membership in a work-group which is itself a segment in the total organization, we find he is in a position to disrupt the boundary relations of his segment to other segments. For example, he overrides group cleavages, threatening the working relationship between them. And he exposes the informal power structure, jeopardizing its relationship to the overarching official structure. He uses formal and official means to force his fellows to consider his demands directly, if only because he has forced higher officials to attend to his instituted complaints.

Plainly, then, the actor's failure to keep his place has disruptive consequences for his work associates, undermining their sense that a common understanding concerning everyone's social place exists and is a viable guide for daily activity. An important part of Lemert's analysis is his consideration of the sequence of events that is set in motion by this initial disturbance.

In order to cope with the troublesome colleague, the others avoid him physically when possible and exclude him from joint decisions and joint ventures. This very exclusion begins to color these excluding events, bringing a new meaning to them. When his workmates find that face-to-face interaction with him is unavoidable, they employ a humoring, pacifying, noncommittal style of reply which serves to damp the interaction as much as possible without giving him obvious cause for complaint. In order to be better prepared for what he might do, they may spy on him, in any case coming together in his absence to share their reaction to his latest move, pool their information, consider his next move, plot out together their next move, and in general celebrate the special solidarity that antagonism to him has created. A countergroup sustained through gossip is thus formed, with him as the negative focus. He becomes the center of distraction.

In consequence of this freeze-out, the actor, recipient now of no corrective feedback, may be forced to relatively violent outbursts as a means of making some impression upon the glossily opaque shell that others have constructed around him. They in turn may find it necessary to form a collusive net so as to inveigle him into receiving psychiatric attention.

Two implications of Lemert's analysis may be suggested. First, a system of informal social control can easily go awry. Tact and secrecy can have the ultimate consequence of constructing a real paranoid community for the paranoid. Secondly, until the individual is hospitalized, or until his reputation becomes widespread so that no one takes his actions seriously (and this latter form of encapsulation is found in large-scale social organizations), his symptoms have a very disruptive effect; it is a great deal to ask that members of the organization respond with understanding and support—it's a wonder, in fact, that organizations are as tolerant as they are.

I have sketched the relation between mental symptoms and two forms of social organization—public order and formally organized work places. Turn now to the final

---

15. I have made a more extended effort along these lines in *Behavior in Public Places* and *Interaction Ritual*.

16. Lemert extensively studied 31 cases involving paranoid complications: 23 in southern California, 6 in northern California, and 2 miscellaneous cases.

unit of organization to be considered, the domestic or family establishment.

V

Approach the family—say in the American middle-class version—through conventional sociological terms. When we examine its internal functioning, its internal social economy, we find a legitimated distribution of authority, material resources, work, and free time. There is the obligation of each member to care for and protect the others, insofar as they are in need of this help and a member is able to provide it. There is a normatively established allocation of respect, affection, and moral support. Some common values and special ways of doing things will be maintained. Knowledge of the family biography will be shared, along with memory of joint experiences. A crisscross of personal relationships will be sustained. A common care will be exerted (by all but the very young), so that the damage that could easily occur to the household through fire, water, soiling, and breaking will not occur. And each member will be trusted by the others not to exploit any of the lethal instrumentalities readily available in the house for harming himself or the others. Finally, as the special feature of the family as a social organization, each member commits his own feelings and involvements to what he takes to be the personal interests and personal plight of each of the others.

If the behavior of any one member, especially that occurring in the presence of other members, is examined closely, it reveals an expressive style that affirms this allotting of obligations. The maintenance of this style by each member gives the other members constant assurance that their expectations will be lived up to and that things are as they should be. In brief, the activity of each member tends to express that he knows what his social place is in the family and that he is sticking to it. Of course, if an individual member has medical difficulties, he is likely to make extra demands, but part of the safety here is due to the ritual work he engages in which neutralizes these demands as threats to the family's normative order, ensuring constancy to the members' sense of what the ill individual is like as a personality. Nonmedical crises, such as the lengthy absence of a member for military service, can similarly be handled, provided only that appropriate ritual work is done.

Turning to the external economy of the family, we find something similar. Resources which have value in the external environment are budgeted among the members in a conserving and perceivedly equitable manner. The fund of private information about the family possessed by the members is preserved, and a united, somewhat false front is maintained before the world—as if there were a family information rule. Finally, the relationships and work/school obligations that link individual members to outside persons and organizations comply with established jurisdictional rulings whereby the family retains some rights. In any case, the family member is pulled out of the family space only by real organizations and real persons who have made a real place for him. In brief, nonfamily claims on family members are limited and regularized.

The maintenance of the internal and external functioning of the family is so central that when family members think of the essential character, the perduring personality of any one of their numbers, it is usually his habitual pattern of support for family-organized activity and family relationships, his style of acceptance of his place in the family, that they have in mind. Any marked change in his pattern of support will tend to be perceived as a marked change in his character. The deepest nature of an individual is only skin-deep, the deepness of his others' skin.

In the case of withdrawals—depressions and regressions—it is chiefly the internal functioning of the family that suffers. The burden of enthusiasm and domestic work must now be carried by fewer numbers. Note that by artfully curtailing its social life, the family can conceal these disorders from the public at large and sustain conventional external functioning. Quiet alcoholism can similarly be contained, provided that economic resources are not jeopardized.

It is the manic disorders and the active phases of a paranoid kind that produce the real trouble. It is these patterns that constitute the insanity of place.

The beginnings are unclear and varied. In some cases something causes the prepatient—whether husband, wife, or child—to feel that the life his others have been allowing him is not sufficient, not right, and no longer tenable. He makes conventional demands for relief and change which are not granted, perhaps not even attended. Then, instead of falling back to the *status quo ante,* he begins his manic activity. As suggested, there are no doubt other etiologies and other precipitating sequences. But all end at the same point—the manic activity the family comes to be concerned with. We shall begin with this, although it is a late point from some perspectives.

The manic begins by promoting himself in the family hierarchy. He finds he no longer has the time to do his accustomed share of family chores. He increasingly orders other members around, displays anger and impatience, makes promises he feels he can break, encroaches on the equipment and space allocated to other members, only fitfully displays affection and respect, and finds he cannot bother adhering to the family schedule for meals, for going to bed and rising. He also becomes hypercritical and derogatory of family members. He moves backward to grandiose statements of the high rank and quality of his forebears, and forward to an exalted view of what he proposes soon to accomplish. He begins to sprinkle his speech with unassimilated technical vocabularies. He talks loudly and constantly, arrogating to himself the place at the center of things this role assumes. The great events and personages of the day uncharacteristically evoke from him a considered and definitive opinion. He seizes on magazine articles, movies, and TV shows as containing important wisdom that everyone ought to hear about in detail right now.

In addition to these disturbances of rank, there are those related to the minor obligations which symbolize membership and relatedness. He alone ceases to exercise the easy care that keeps household equipment safe and keeps members safe from it. He alone becomes capricious in performing the little courtesy-favors that all grown members offer one another if only because of the minute cost of these services to the giver compared to their appreciable value to the recipient. And he voices groundless beliefs, sometimes in response to hallucinations, which imply to his kin that he has ceased to regulate his thought by the standards that form the common ground of all those to whom they are closely related.

I repeat that the claims and actions of the ill person are not necessarily bizarre in themselves, merely bizarre when coming from the particular patient addressing himself to his particular family. And bizarreness itself is not the issue. Even when the patient hallucinates or develops exotic beliefs, the concern of the family is not simply that a member has crazy notions, but that he is not keeping his place in relationships. Someone to whom we are closely related is someone who ought not to have beliefs which estrange him from us. The various forms of grandiosity can have the same significance.

The constant effort of the family to argue the patient out of his foolish notions, to disprove his allegations, to make him take a reasonable view—an argumentation so despaired of by some therapists—can similarly be understood as the family's needs and the family's effort to bring the patient back into appropriate relationship to them. They cannot let him have his wrong beliefs because they cannot let him go. Further, if he reverses his behavior and becomes more collected, they must try to get him to admit that he has been ill, else his present saneness will raise doubts about the family's warrant for the way they have been treating him, doubts about their motivation and *their* relationship to him. For these reasons, admission of insanity has to be sought. And

what is sought is an extraordinary thing indeed. If ritual work is a means of retaining a constancy of image in the face of deviations in behavior, then a self-admission that one is mentally ill is the biggest piece of ritual work of all, for this stance to one's conduct discounts the greatest deviations. A week of mayhem in a family can be set aside and readied to be forgotten the moment the offender admits he has been ill. Small wonder, then, that the patient will be put under great pressure to agree to the diagnosis, and that he may give in, even though this can mean that he must permanently lower the conception he has of his own character and must never again be adamant in presenting his views.

The issue here is not that the family finds that home life is made unpleasant by the sick person. Perhaps most home life is unpleasant. The issue is that meaningful existence is threatened. The definitions that the sick person tacitly accords the family members are less desirable than the ones they had before and imply that the family members are less connected to him than they had thought. If they accept this revision, then meaningful organization can be re-achieved, as happens, for example, when family cult-formation occurs or *folie à ménage*. But if they do not, there is trouble.[17]

Let me repeat: the self is the code that makes sense out of almost all the individual's activities and provides a basis for organizing them. This self is what can be read about the individual by interpreting the place he takes in an organization of social activity, as confirmed by his expressive behavior. The individual's failure to enact, through deeds and expressive cues, a *workable* definition of himself, one which closely enmeshed others can accord him through the regard they show his person, is to block and trip up and threaten them in almost every movement that they make. The selves that had been the reciprocals of his are undermined. And that which should not have been able to change—the character of a loved one lived with—appears to be changing fundamentally and for the worse before their eyes. In ceasing to know the sick person, they cease to be sure of themselves. In ceasing to be sure of him and themselves, they can even cease to be sure of their way of knowing. A deep bewilderment results. Confirmations that everything is predictable and as it should be cease to flow from his presentations. The question as to what it is that is going on is not redundantly answered at every turn but

17. Theories of *gemeinschaft* argue that intimates must agree on basic beliefs or break up their relationship, and that, by implication, the willingness of a skeptical member to come around is motivated by a desire to maintain relationships. But there are, of course, exceptions to the rule of agreement. The model here in social science literature is Mr. Keech, who quietly went about his usual business while Mrs. Keech at home was publicly organizing for the end of the world. See Festinger et al., esp. pp. 38–39.

must be constantly ferreted out anew. And life is said to become like a bad dream—for there is no place in possible realities for what is occurring.

It is here that mental symptoms deviate from other deviations. A person who suddenly becomes selfish, heartless, disloyal, unfaithful, or addicted can be dealt with. If he properly shows cause or contrition he can be forgiven; if he is unrepentant but removable he can be redefined. In either case, his others can come to terms with him, in the sense that the expressions he gives off concerning his definition of himself and them are indications that confirm the relationship they feel they now have to him. The grammaticality of activity is sustained. A patient's mental symptoms, however, are something his others cannot come to terms with. Neither he nor they withdraw from the organization or relationship sufficiently to allow his expression to confirm what his status implies. Thus his behavior strikes at the syntax of conduct, deranging the usual agreement between posture and place, between expression and position.

The domestic disorganization created by the ill person points up an important fact about social control in a unit like the family. Any grown member of the family can leave the household against the will and advice of the family, and, except for exacting financial claims against him, there is nothing that the family can do about it. The power of the leavetaker is especially strong if he departs properly, through channels as it were, with an appropriately staged announcement of intentions. On the other side, there are circumstances (varying in America from state to state) in which a family can have a member removed bodily to a place of detention. However, when, for whatever reason, neither of these forms of socially recognized departure occurs, the family and its household prove to be vulnerable in the extreme. For then the standard notion of social control effected through a corrective cycle becomes quite untenable. The simple fact is that when an offender is disapproved of and punished, and warned what will happen if he persists, it is tacitly assumed that he will be sufficiently committed to the life of the group, and to sustaining those who presume authority in it, to *voluntarily* take the sanction to heart and, whether in good grace or bad, desist from the particular offense. If the family offender elects not to heed the warning, there is then really nothing effective that can be done to him. Sheer manhandling that is not responded to by tacit cooperation requires the full effort of at least two strong adults and even then can only be managed in brief spurts—long enough to remove someone from a house, but not much longer. Even merely to stand watch and guard over a person requires more than a household can usually manage for very long. And the household itself can hardly be run if everything that

might be damageable or dangerous must be kept out of an adult's reach.

Households, then, can hardly be operated at all if the good will of the residents cannot be relied on.[18] Interestingly, it is right at the moment of punishment and threat, right when the offender presumably has additional reasons for antagonism, that the family is most clearly dependent on his self-submission to family authority. Punitive action forces the offender either to capitulate and lose face, or to disabuse his opponents of their belief that they have power over him. Just when he is most angry at them he must see that he alone can save their illusions concerning their control over him. Negative sanctions within the context of a household, then, constitute a kind of doomsday machine, forcing the last available opportunity to avoid a breakdown of order upon the stronger of the two parties, who must act as if he is the weaker. Obviously, on occasion he will not be considerate. This vulnerability of family organization is reinforced by the fact that the offender may well give less consideration to his own bodily welfare and his own interests than those who must control him.

I have considered some of the disorganizational consequences of the patient's failure to support the internal order of the family. It is, however, when the family's external functioning is considered that the full derangement is seen.

The social place of a family in the community at large is a matter of some delicacy, based as it is on personal and informal control that exposes the family to a thousand possible markets for its various resources—markets which the family itself must deal with prudently if it is to maximize its own long-range interests as these are conventionally defined. It is this circumspection, ordinarily self-imposed, that the active patient transcends.

Misplaced enterprise occurs. Family monies are squandered on little examples of venture capitalism. Grand services and equipment are bought or contracted for, nicely illustrating the democratic, accepting attitude of those who sell things and the personal control that all of us ordinarily maintain.[19] Bargains advertised in the

18. A useful recent description of the structural contingencies of disciplining an unwilling family member is provided in Louise Wilson, *This Stranger, My Son*. Mrs. Wilson describes in some detail what a child diagnosed as paranoid schizophrenic can accomplish with the domestic equipment at hand. A full picture is also available in the Bettelheim accounts of the Sonia Shankman Orthogenic School, but in this case, of course, the care that requires the staff's full-time effort *is* their official full-time job.

19. Admittedly, there are some limits due to formal social control. A thirteen-year-old cannot go down to his friendly Ford dealer and negotiate the purchase of a new Thunderbird, although a few years later he can. Similarly, although almost any adult can at will set a real estate agent to work, earnest money will eventually be needed.

newspaper are ordered in excessive quantity by phone.[20] The occupational and age-grade structure is dipped into far enough down to find commandeers and hirelings for expansive private projects. An unnecessary office or industrial layout is grafted onto the household. The patient finds that his ordinary job is cramping and gives it up or is fired.[21] A flurry of projects is initiated. A press of occupation occurs.

Contacting is accelerated. The telephone is increasingly used. Each call becomes longer and more calls are made. Favorite recipients are called more and more frequently. When the hour renders local calls a gross violation of informal rules, long-distance calls are made into acceptable time zones; when the hour prevents even these, night telegrams are dispatched.[22] A flood of letter-writing may occur.

Participation is broadened. Assistance is volunteered to persons and organizations undesirous of receiving it from this quarter—the patient appreciating that an offering is a warrantable means of making contact with the recipient. Public life is entered through its least guarded portals: participation in volunteer work; letters to politicians, editors, and big corporations; celebrity hunting; litigation. Critical national events, such as elections, war policy statements, and assassinations, are taken quite personally. Personal appearances on radio and television may be sought; press conferences and press releases may be engineered. Perceived slights in public places lead to scenes and to the patient's making official complaints to officials.

Associating is intensified. Neighbors are dropped in on at unsuitable hours. Parties are arrived at first and left last. There may be a surge of home entertainment that is unstabilizing: properly related friends attend until other commitments cause them to defect; newly formed friends are substituted, but each set wears out more quickly than the last, requiring recruitment from less and less suitable sources; ultimately the gatherings become socially bizarre. Semi-official, public-spirited purposes for home gatherings are increasingly employed, this providing some warrant for the patient's inviting persons he has merely heard about, and for aggregations of persons of widely different social rank. Invitation lists are extended right up to the last minute, as if there were a need to be in touch with all acquaintances and to pack the environment with people. Evenings of commercial recreation and weekend outings are organized repeatedly, involving much recontacting and also the mustering of unacquainted persons into one venture.

Finally, relating is expanded. Courtesy introductions and offhand referrals by others are followed up and made something of, acquaintanceship is presumed upon, and presuming requests are made across affinal lines to spouses of friends. "Middlemanning" occurs, the ill person attempting to bring into contact persons perceived as having use for each other. The functional specificity of service relations is breached. Advice is proffered to and asked of service personnel on many matters; the use of reciprocal first-naming is suggested; social invitations are extended. Corresponding to this diffusion, personal friends are loaded with service requests and enrolled in schemes and projects. Occasional workers, hired by the patient to help in projects, will be transformed into friends to fill the gap that has developed, but these will now be friends who can be ordered to come and go, there resulting a kind of minionization of the patient's social circle.[23] Minor shortcomings in services received from long-utilized professionals, tradesmen, and repairmen lead to run-ins and the immediate establishment of new service connections. Family secrets are confidentially divulged at informal gatherings to persons who are merely acquaintances. Newly formed friends are enthusiastically praised to the family, giving the impression that the patient's capacity for deep involvement is being exercised capriciously. If the patient is single, unsuitable mating may threaten to occur across age, race, or class lines; if married, then unsuitable re-mating. And some sexual promiscuity may occur of the kind that can be realized at will because it trades on marked status differences. In all of this, the patient either takes advantage of others or places others in a position to take advantage of him, in either case to the deep embarrassment of his family.

---

20. See Roueché's case study, "Ten Feet Tall." Roueché provides useful details regarding the overreaching social behavior of a man enjoying a brief manic episode due to the side effects of cortisone treatment.

21. A manic patient who can become too large for his home can similarly become too large for his job. Starting with a commendable increase in enthusiasm for his work, he begins to offer fellow workers wanted help and advice, extends this to what is seen as interference in the spheres of others, and finally takes to giving unauthorized directives and acting as a spokesman for his work-organization when he is away from it. During this process of becoming a self-appointed boss, he begins to arrogate to himself more and more equipment, space, and subordinate help. And since his private business and convivial enterprise have greatly expanded and are coming to be very ill-received at home, he shifts more and more of these activities to the work-place, spends more and more time during and after work thus engaged, and soon violates the very delicate norm governing the penetration of private interests into work. He promotes get-togethers of work personnel, and embarrasses status divisions by trying to bring together for conviviality everyone at work who is remotely within his social reach.

22. Monthly telephone bills that are twenty times normal have an interesting story to tell. Telephone companies, however, are scrupulously detached in these matters. Theirs is not to wonder why but only to collect.

23. A form of social organization sometimes bred by very high office; this is best illustrated today, perhaps, in the Hollywood entourage.

A general point can be detected here about the patient's rage for connectedness and position. Since his movement from his allotted place is to be accomplished entirely by the power of self-inclination, two spheres will be in easiest reach for him. One consists of local persons who are appreciably beneath him socially and who are willing to be approached at will because the association can mean some kind of economic gain or social enhancement. The other sphere consists of powerful and well-known personages. Of course, only the most vicarious and attenuated contact can be made with these notables, the channels here being fan letters, telegrams, attendance at personal appearances, unaccepted party invitations, and the like. Nonetheless, when actual social connections become disturbed and insufficient, these figures are there; they acquire a startling immediacy and come to serve as points of reference for self-organization.

The patient, then, is free to move in two directions: downward by means of social trade-offs; upward by means of vicarious or abortive contact. Interestingly, the more trouble at home, the greater the need to move into the lives of friends; the more this is done, the more the second circle will close itself off by virtue of being overtaxed; the more this occurs, the more fully does the patient take flight into unsuitable alliances and vicarious ones. Further, what remains of an inner circle tends to be alienated by what the patient attempts in the next concentric ring; what is there developed is undermined by his antics in a still wider circle. Tentative expansion outward thus reduces what is already possessed, and sharply increases the need to consolidate the new circle. With all of these forces working together, an explosion of dealings results. There is a flight into the community.

Without taking the time to examine in detail any of these overreachings, or to consider the clinical hypothesis that the patient may be seeking every possible external support for an internal state that is collapsing, let it only be said that so far as family organization is concerned, what happens is that the boundary between it and the community is threatened. In the extreme, the family as a unit that holds itself off from the environing world is forcibly washed away, the members literally displaced from the domestic establishment by a flood of nonmembers and by the sick person's organizational activity.

Note that the community context of family life is such that this sort of diffusion is always possible. The patient does not construct his own avenues of access; he merely uses excessively devices available to anyone in his position. To appreciate this fact, we must look at the community as a system of fences and gates, a system for regulating the formation and growth of social relationships.

A relationship cannot form unless two persons can come into personal contact of some kind (whether face-to-face or mediated), and a relationship cannot develop unless its members can interact over a period of time.

Contact itself is organizationally facilitated in certain basic ways. Contemporary social organization provides that places of residence and work can be reached by phone, telegraph, letters, and personal visits. The necessarily common use of public and semipublic facilities, especially the streets, brings a wide variety of persons within face-to-face reach of one another. The institution of acquaintanceship (established often through introduction) confers preemptive contact rights. Because of such devices, a very wide potential exists for contact, and through contact the development of relationships.

This potential, in turn, is sharply curtailed by various factors. We do not know the appearance or address of many of those we might want to be in touch with. We are bound by rules which proscribe our initiating talk with unacquainted others except on various good grounds. We are likely to be ignorant of where and when those social occasions will occur where those whose acquaintance we seek will be present, and presence itself allows for the initiation of talk. Knowing where and when, we may not be qualified by money, membership, or invitation to go. Beyond this, there are all the devices used for blocking contacts: disguise of personal appearance, avoidance of public places, nonlisting of telephone numbers, the stationing of gatekeepers to intervene at places of residence and work, segregation by cost and ecology, and so forth.[24] But note, these various blocks to association cannot be allowed to be complete. Any door that *completely* keeps out undesirables also keeps out some desirables; any means of completely shutting oneself off also shuts out contacts that would be profitable. After all, relationships that come to be close can be traced back to an overture or introduction; service dealings which prove satisfactory can be traced back to an unknown client's or customer's appearing on the telephone; successful projects, to nothing more substantial than announced intentions; valuable publicity for a celebrity, to one among the many phone calls he receives; a warning that one has dropped one's wallet, to a stranger who accosts one on the street. Who knows from whom the next phone call or letter will be and what it will be about? The most careful screening in the world must still expose someone on the staff to *anyone* who bothers to try to make contact. Presentments have to be given a moment's benefit of the doubt, lest that which will come to be desirably realized will not have been

---

24. These devices are most fully used by the famed, apparently in part because they can least rely on the probability that interested members of the public will lack detection information about them.

able to begin. We must always pause at least for a moment in our oncoming rejection of another in order to check the importuner out. There is no choice: social life must ever expose itself to unwarranted initiatings. A screening device would have no functional value if the only persons who got through it were the persons who got to it.

Mechanisms for facilitating and restricting relationship formation are reinforced by formal legal control, in the sense that persons who decline to be drawn into certain negotiations can be forced to do so by the law, as can those who decline to desist from certain importunings. Much more important, the mechanisms are reinforced by personal control and informal control, resulting in a tacit social contract: a person is obliged to make himself available for contacting and relationship formation, in return for which others are obliged to refrain from taking advantage of his availability. He incidentally can retain the illusion that he does not cut people off; they, that they would not be rejected.

This contract of association is made viable by the allowance of prognosticative expression. An open and friendly address conveys that overtures will be welcomed; a wary and stiff mien, that importunement will result in open rejection. Anyone wending his way through his daily round is guided not only by self-interest but also by these expressions. He avoids accepting subtle invitations that might lead to unsuitable associations and avoids transgressing where subtle warnings have been issued. He keeps to the straight and narrow. He handles himself ungenerously because on all sides there is something to lose.

It is understandable, then, why the patient finds himself in a disruptable world. Merely by jeopardizing a little more than persons like himself are usually willing to do—through exposing himself either to unsuitable relationships or to insulting rejection—he is in a position to penetrate all social boundaries a little. Whosoever the other, there will always be good reasons to warrant relating to him, and therefore a cover, however quickly discreditable, for the beginning of interaction with him.

A final comment. The manic activity I have described is obviously located in the life of the privileged, the middle and higher classes.[25] I think this apparent bias in

selecting illustrations is warranted. Social resources must be possessed before they can be handled in the manner that has been considered. Therefore mania would seem to be a disease of persons with social advantages—money, lineage, office, profession, education, sexual attractiveness, and a network of social and familial relationships. Perhaps impoverished expansionists, having few goods to exchange for being taken seriously, are soon forced to make ludicrous presentations, and transform everyone around them into skeptical ward attendants. Thus it could be argued that the well-stationed are prone or at least overrepresented; the insanity of place is a function of position.

I have already touched on some features of the family's response to life with the patient. Members feel they are no longer in an easefully predictable environment. They feel bewildered by the change of character and personality that has occurred. Moreover, since the dramatic change has come to a person they feel they should best be able to characterize, cognition itself becomes an issue; the very principles of judgment by which one comes to feel that one knows character and is competent to judge it can become threatened. Consider now some further aspects of the family's response.

One issue concerns the structure of attention. Put simply, the patient becomes someone who has to be watched. Each time he holds a sharp or heavy object, each time he answers the phone, each time he nears the window, each time he holds a cup of coffee above a rug,

---

25. Some empirical evidence for this argument is provided in Hollingshead and Redlich, p. 228.

For an analytical illustration, consider an extreme comparison: a black wino and a blond model, he in rough clothes and she in the style of the upper middle class. Compare their public situation—the passage of each across, alongside, or toward the paths of unacquainted others. Consider the eye practices each must face from these walkers-by.

The wino: A walker-by will take care to look at him fleetingly if at all, wary lest the wino find an angle from which to establish eye-to-eye contact and then disturb the passage with prolonged salutations, besmearing felicitations, and other importunements and threats. Should the

wino persist in not keeping his place, the discourtesy of outright head-aversion may be necessary.

The model: A walker-by will fix her with an open gaze for as many moments as the passage will allow without his having to turn his head sharply. During this structured moment of staring he may well be alert in fantasy for any sign she makes interpretable as encouraging his attentions. Note that this helter-skelter gallantry remains very well in check, no danger to the free flow of human traffic, for long ago the model will have learned her part in this ceremony, which is to conduct her eyes downward and unseeing, in silent sufferance of exposure.

Against this structural view of the public situation of the beast and the beauty (illustrating the boundaries of civil inattention), consider the consequence to each of being apparently possessed by an unsuppressed urge to enter into dealings.

Of himself the wino can make a mild nuisance, but nothing much more disarraying than that is likely to be allowed him. The more he rattles the bars of his cage, the more hurrying-by will be done by visitors to the zoo. Social arrangements are such that his screaming right into the face of an unacquainted other may only complete his treatment as someone who does not exist. The friendly model, in contrast, will find that suddenly there are a hundred takers, that strangers of both colors, three sexes, and several age groups are ready to interrupt their course for an adventure in sociability. Where'er she smiles, relationships begin to develop. A wino leaves a narrow trail of persons more fully busying themselves with their initial plans. A manic beauty may not get far enough to leave a trail. She opens up a world that then closes in on her. She clots and entangles the courses of action around her. The more delicate and ladylike, the more she is the peril the Victorian manuals should have warned the city about.

each time he is present when someone comes to the door or drops in, each time he handles the car keys, each time he begins to fill a sink or tub, each time he lights a match—on each of these occasions the family will have to be ready to jump. And when it is not known where he is or it is known that he is behind a locked door, an alert will have to be maintained for any hint of something untoward. The possibility that the patient will be malicious or careless, that he will intentionally or unintentionally damage himself, the household, or the others, demonstrates that standard household arrangements can be full of danger; obviously, it is the presumption of conventional use that makes us think that these conventional arrangements are safe.[26]

Three points are to be made concerning the family's watchfulness. First, households tend to be informally organized, in the sense that each member is allowed considerable leeway in scheduling his own tasks and diverting himself in his own directions. He will have his own matters, then, to which he feels a need to attend. The necessity, instead, of his having to stand watch over the patient blocks rightful and pleasurable calls upon time and generates a surprising amount of fatigue, impatience, and hostility. Second, the watching will have to be dissimulated and disguised lest the patient suspect he is under constant surveillance, and this covering requires extra involvement and attention. Third, in order to increase their efficiency and maintain their morale, the watchers are likely to engage in collaboration, which perforce must be collusive.

The family must respond not only to what the patient is doing to its internal life, but also to the spectacle he seems to be making of himself in the community. At first the family will be greatly concerned that one of its emissaries is letting down the side. The family therefore tries to cover up and intercede so as to keep up his front and theirs. This strengthens the collusive alignment in the family against the patient.

As the dispute within the family continues and grows concerning the selves in whose terms activity ought to be organized, the family begins to turn outward, first to the patient's kinsmen, then to friends, to professionals, to employers. The family's purpose is not merely to obtain help in the secretive management of the patient, but also to get much needed affirmation of its view of events.

26. Professionals who manage the actively suicidal are acutely alive to the unconventional lethal possibilities of domestic equipment; indeed, in published case records detail is provided. Less clearly appreciated, perhaps, is that a person with *any* type of actively expressed mental disorder can unhinge the meaning of his domestic acts for the other members of the family. What would ordinarily be an uneventful household routine can come to be seen as a deed through which the patient may intentionally or unintentionally damage the equipment at hand, the persons nearby, or himself.

There is a reversal of the family information rule. Acquaintances or other potential sources of aid who had once been personally distant from the family will now be drawn into the center of things as part of a new solidarity of those who are helping to manage the patient, just as some of those who were once close may now be dropped because apparently they do not confirm the family's definition of the situation.

Finally, the family finds that in order to prevent others from giving weight to the initiatory activity of the patient, relatively distant persons must be let in on the family secret. There may even be necessity for recourse to the courts to block extravagances by conservator proceedings, to undo unsuitable marriages by annulments, and the like. The family will frankly allow indications that it can no longer handle its own problems, for the family cat must be belled. By that time the family members will have learned to live exposed. There will be less pride and less self-respect. They will be engaged in establishing that one of their members is mentally ill, and in whatever degree they succeed in this, they will be exposing themselves to the current conception that they constitute the kind of family which produces mental illness.

While the family is breaking the informational boundary between itself and society—and an appeal to a therapist is only one nicely contained instance of this—it may begin to add some finer mesh as well as some spread to its collusive net. Some of the patient's telephone calls are tapped and some of his letters opened and read. Statements which the patient makes to different persons are secretly pooled, with consequent exposure of incongruities. Experiences with the patient are shared in a widening circle in order to extract and confirm patterns of impropriety. Discreetly planned actions are presented to the patient as unplanned spontaneous ones, or disguised to appear as if originating from a source still deemed innocent by him. This conspiracy, note, is an understandable result of the family's needing very much to know the patient's next move in order to undo it.

A review of the family's response to the patient easily suggests that members will find much cause to feel angry at him. Overlaid, however, there will be other feelings, often stronger. The damage the patient appears to be doing, especially in consequence of his overreachings outside the family, is seen to hurt his own interests even more than those of the rest of the family. Yet for the family this need not produce grim satisfaction or help to balance things out; rather, matters may be made worse. As suggested, it is the distinctive character of the family that its members not only feel responsible for any member in need, but also feel personal identification with his situation. Whenever the patient is out alone in the community, exposed and exposing himself to what can be perceived as a contamination of his self and a diminution of his character, whenever the patient must be left alone at home, exposing himself as well as the household to intended and unintended dangers, the family will know anxiety and fear.

I have suggested that a family with mania to contend with is likely to form a collusive net, the patient being excolluded.[27] Now turn and take the point of view of the patient.

The family's conspiracy is benign, but this conspiracy breeds what others do. The patient finds himself in a world that has only the appearance of innocence, in which small signs can be found—and therefore sought out and wrongly imputed—showing that things are anything but what they seem. At home, when his glance suddenly shifts in a conversation, he may find naked evidence of collusive teamwork against him—teamwork unlike the kind which evaporates when a butt is let in on a good-natured joke that is being played at his expense.[28] He rightly comes to feel that statements made to him are spoken so as to be monitored by the others present, ensuring that they will keep up with the managing of him, and that statements made to others in his presence are designed and delivered for his overhearing. He will find this communication arrangement very unsettling and come to feel that he is purposely being kept out of touch with what is happening.

In addition, the patient is likely to detect that he is being watched, especially when he approaches some domestic device which could be used to harm himself or others, or which is itself valuable and vulnerable to harm. He will sense that he is being treated as a child who can't be trusted around the house, but in this case one who cannot be trusted to be frankly shown that he is not trusted. If he lights a match or takes up a knife, he may find as he turns from these tasks that others present seem to have been watching him and now are trying to cover up their watchfulness.

In response to the response he is creating, the patient, too, will come to feel that life in the family has become deranged. He is likely to try to muster up some support for his own view of what his close ones are up to. And he is likely to have some success.

The result is two collusive factions, each enveloping the other in uncertainties, each drawing on a new and changing set of secret members. The household ceases to be a place where there is the easy fulfillment of a thousand mutually anticipated proper acts. It ceases to be a solid front organized by a stable set of persons against the world, entrenched and buffered by a stable set of friends and servers. The household becomes a no-man's land where changing factions are obliged to negotiate daily, their weapons being collusive communication and their armor selective inattention to the machinations of the other side—an inattention difficult to achieve, since each faction must devote itself to reading the other's furtive signs. The home, where wounds were meant to be licked, becomes precisely where they are inflicted. Boundaries are broken. The family is turned inside out.

We see, then, that the domestic manic breeds, and is bred in, organizational havoc, and that this havoc is all too evident. Yet here clinical reports have been very weak. I venture a Durkheimian account.

It is frequently the case that hospitalized patients who have behaved at home in the most exotic and difficult fashion are taken back into the family upon release from the hospital, and that however tentatively they are received, they are given some sort of trial acceptance. Also, it is quite generally the case that before hospitalization, the feeling of the family that the troublesome one is mentally ill will come and go: with each outburst the family will have to face anew the idea that mental illness is apparently involved, but with each moment of the patient's wonted and tranquil behavior, sharp new hope will be experienced by the family—hope that everything is coming back to normal. This readiness to oscillate, this resilience of hope on the family's part, should not be taken particularly as evidence of good will or resistance to bad-naming. In other circumstances, I'm sure, most families would be quite ready to form a rigid and stereotyped view of an offender. But the fact is that there is no stable way for the family to conceive of a life in which a member conducts himself insanely. The heated

27. If the patient is an adult, the consequences for children are especially painful. In order to protect the young from the imperious demands of the patient and from the conception of the patient that would result were his acts taken as serious ones, the young may have to be recruited into the net. This will also facilitate the collusion by reducing the number of others from whom its operation must be concealed. The children may accept this invitation, decline it, or, if careful enough, give each side the impression that its view is being supported. Whatever the response of the young, adult solidarity is clearly broken and idealization of adults undermined. Children's insubordinate treatment of the ill person can result, the other adults being unable to reinforce demands of the patient. Further, the more the ill person becomes a source of unwarranted demands upon the young, the less the other adults feel they can exert parental discipline where discipline is due.

28. For this the patient requires no special perceptiveness, sometimes attributed to the insane. It is an empirical fact that in our society the furtive signs through which a collusive alignment is maintained against someone who is present are often crude and easily available to the excolluded. Ordinarily the colluders do not discover that they have been discovered because the excolluded wants to support the surface appearance that he is not so unworthy as to warrant this kind of betrayal. Paradoxically, it is exactly such a surface definition of the situation that the colluders require in order to have something to undercut. I want to add that colluders very often decline to stage their collusion as discreetly as they could. As in many other occasions of false behaviour, the manipulators half want their dupe to be aware of what is really thought of him.

scramble occurring around the ill person is something that the family will be instantly ready to forget; the viable way things once were is something that the family will always be ready to re-anticipate. For if an intellectual place could be made for the ill behavior, it would not be ill behavior. It is as if perception can only form and follow where there is social organization; it is as if the experience of disorganization can be felt but not retained. When the havoc is at its height, participants are unlikely to find anyone who has the faintest appreciation of what living in it is like. When the trouble is finally settled, the participants will themselves be unable to appreciate why they had become so upset. Little wonder, then, that during the disorganization phase, the family will live the current reality as in a dream, and the domestic routine which can now only be dreamt of will be seen as what is real.

VI

Return now to the earlier discussion of collusive elements in the medical role. Return to the doctor's dilemma.

The traditional picture of mental hospitalization and other psychiatric services involves a responsible person, typically a next of kin, persuading, dragging, conning, or trapping the patient-to-be into visiting a psychiatrist. A diagnostic inspection occurs. It is then that the psychiatrist is likely to begin his collusion with the next of kin, on the grounds that the patient cannot be trusted to act in his own best interests, and that it will not do the patient any good to learn the name and extent of his sickness.[29] The patient, of course, is likely to feel betrayed and conspired against; and he may continue to until he is well enough to see that the collusive action was taken in his own best interests.

The great critics of the collusive management of the mental patient have been the psychoanalysts. They act on the assumption that if a real relationship is to be developed with the client, one allowing the therapist and client to work together profitably, then this relation must not be undercut by the therapist's engaging in collusive communication with the client's responsible others. If contact is necessary between therapist and patient's kin, then the kin should be warned that the patient must know what has taken place, and what in substance the therapist said to the kin. Therapists realistically appreciate that information about the patient put into the hands of his loved ones might well be used against him. This communications policy cuts the therapist off from many

sources of information about the patient, but there is an answer in the doctrine that the patient's trouble is in his style of projecting and relating, and that this can be well enough sampled by means of what is disclosed during private sessions. A parallel can be noted here to what is called hotel anthropology.

I am suggesting that therapists, especially of the psychoanalytical persuasion, appreciate the collusive implication of their contacts with the third party and go far in protecting the patient from this collusion. However, by this very maneuver they help consolidate another collusive relationship, that between themselves and the patient in regard to the responsible others. The practice of trying to get at the patient's point of view, the effort to refrain considerably from passing obvious moral judgments, and the strict obligation on the patient's part to betray all confidences if these seem relevant—all these factors in conjunction with the privacy of the therapeutic setting ensure collusive coalition formation to a degree unappreciated even by the next of kin. (Whereas ordinary relationships give rise to collusive coalitions, the therapeutic situation is a collusion that gives rise to a relationship.) This resembles a domestic handicapping system, whereby the weakest team in the family tournament is given an extra man. Let me add that collusion for hire seems a rum sort of business to be in, but perhaps more good is done than harm.

What has been considered can be reduced to a formula. Traditionally the psychotic has been treated through a collusive relation between his therapists and his family and ends up excolluded into the mental hospital, while the neurotic (who is so inclined and can afford it) has been treated to a collusive relation with his therapist against his family or boss and remains in the community.[30]

There is a collusion, then, for psychotics who end up in a mental hospital and for neurotics who stay in the community—the psychiatrist being constrained to engage in one or the other form, depending on his patient and, beyond that, his type of practice. What is to be considered here, however, is the collusion arising when psychotics of the manic kind are managed in the community.

First note that the therapeutic or patient-analyst collusion will have shortcomings. Private talks with the patient will not tell the therapist what is happening to the family or what its urgent needs are. This is indicated by

---

29. Surely this practice is not entirely a bad thing, since this information can deeply affect the patient's view of himself, and yet diagnoses seem to vary quite remarkably, depending on the prevailing diagnostic fashion and the tastes of the practitioner.

30. Admittedly in recent times some therapists have attempted to treat the same patient in and out of the hospital, in which case the usual alignments are not possible; some have engaged in "family therapy"; and some have attempted a flexible open relationship of access allowing for private and family sessions with the same patient. But even these arrangements, I think, do not prevent collusion problems.

the fact already suggested that psychotherapists have provided hardly any information about the organizational meaning of illness for the units of social organization in which the illness occurs. In any case, since the patient is likely to continue his troublesome activity unabated after beginning therapy, the family will feel that the therapist has become a member of the patient's faction. This is no small matter. The patient's domestic opponents find themselves pressed to the wall of sanity, having to betray a loved one lest his uncharacteristic assumptions about himself make their life unreal. Their social place is being undermined, and the standards they have always used in judging character and identity are in question. The failure of any other person to confirm their view of the patient, even when this failure merely means declining to take sides, adds weight to the hallucinatory possibility that they might be wrong and, being wrong, are destroying the patient. And persons distant from the family will certainly fail to confirm the family's position. A fact about the wider community must here be appreciated. Unless the patient is very ill, those who know him little—even more, those who know him not at all—may not sense that anything is wrong, and with good reason; at least for a time, all they may notice is that an individual is more friendly and outgoing, more approachable than he might be. Those in the community who *do* develop doubts about the patient are likely to be tactful enough to refrain from directly expressing them. After all, easing themselves out of contact with the troublesome one is all that is necessary. The worst that can happen to them is that they will briefly have to face how conditional their concern for another is— conditional on his being willing to withdraw in response to suggestions and hints.

The other type of psychiatric collusion may not be much better. If the family has psychiatric assurance that it is the patient who is crazy and not the family members, this mitigates somewhat their need for confirmation of their position from friends and associates, and in turn mitigates their flight into the community. But in order to contain and discipline the patient, and through this to preserve the possibility of reestablishing the old relationships later, they will feel compelled to tell him he is not himself and that so says the psychiatrist. This won't help very much. The family will almost certainly have to use this club. It won't, however, be the right one. The patient will feel that the family members are concerned not about his illness, but about their pinched status. And the patient by and large will be right. The patient then must either embrace the notion of mental illness, which is to embrace what is likely to be a destructive conception of his own character, or find further evidence that his close ones have suddenly turned against him.

In summary, the physician finds that he must join the family's faction or the patient's, and that neither recourse is particularly tenable. That is the doctor's dilemma.

VII

In this paper I have tried to sketch some of the meanings of mental symptoms for the organization in which they occur, with special reference to the family. The argument is that current doctrine and practice in psychiatry have neglected these meanings. To collapse the warfare of social place in a troubled family into such terms as "acting out" or "manic" keeps things tidy, but mostly what such terms accomplish is the splendid isolation of the person using them. A concept such as "hyperactivity," which psychiatrically denotes precisely the behavior I have been considering, seems to connote some sort of mechanical malfunctioning with little suggestion of the social overreachings that are actually involved.

A final complication. Throughout this paper I have spoken of the mentally ill patient and his mental symptoms. That was an optimistically simple thing to do. Medical symptoms and mental symptoms, so-called, are radically different things. As I have pointed out, the malfunctioning that medical symptoms represent is a malfunctioning of the human organism and only very rarely constitutes an elegant denial of social functioning. However impaired physically, the medically ill person can almost always express that he is not intentionally and openly opposing his place in the social scheme of things. So-called mental symptoms, on the other hand, are made up of the very substance of social obligation. Mental symptoms directly express the whole array of divisive social alignments: alienation, rebellion, insolence, untrustworthiness, hostility, apathy, importunement, intrusiveness, and so forth. These divisive alignments do not—in the first instance—constitute malfunctioning of the individual, but rather disturbance and trouble in a relationship or an organization. We can all largely agree that everything should be done to patch up bodies and keep them alive, but certainly not that social organizations of all kinds should be preserved. Further, as already suggested, there is a multitude of reasons why someone who is not mentally ill at all, but who finds he can neither leave an organization nor basically alter it, might introduce exactly the same trouble as is caused by patients.[31] All the terms I have used to describe the

31. An implication is that those who come to the attention of psychiatry are a very mixed bag. Given current admission procedures, and given current patient-load of nonanalytical office practitioners, I don't see how it is possible for psychiatrists to know whether or not it is mental illness that underlies the symptom with which they are dealing. Not knowing what they are dealing with, they understandably have small success in dealing with it.

offensive behavior of the patient—and the term "patient" itself—are expressions of the viewpoint of parties with special interests. Quotation marks would have been in order, but too many of them would have been necessary.

The conventional psychiatric doctrine makes a place, of course, for psychiatry. The argument goes that an individual can appear more or less normal to those in his family, his work place, or his neighborhood, and really, underneath it all, be what is called a very sick guy—one who needs some help. The prepatient and his intimates can refuse to see that anything fundamental is wrong, when to a professional eye it is plain that he is, as they say, quite sick. By the time the prepatient and his others appreciate that something is wrong, he may—the psychiatric argument goes—be very sick indeed. By that time his close others are likely to be penalizing him in all sorts of ways for his illness, and blaming him for something that they probably helped to produce. The solution is to catch things early, before symptoms become florid, the personality deteriorates, and irreparable damage has been done.

This conventional view, however, can be fatefully wrong, and wrong both for the patient and his others. For when someone not in a hospital has a manic episode, the following possibilities should be considered.

On the one hand, there may be very little wrong with the offender's psychobiological equipment. The psychological significance of the trouble for him may be relatively superficial and may, in fact, be partly understandable in terms of his changing relation to those outside the troubled organization. After all, the mess that the manic makes does not come out of his head. It comes from the vulnerabilities of domestic and community organizations to persons with social resources to expend.[32] On the other hand, those who must contain the

manic in their social organization may, because of his social behavior, find themselves fighting for their social lives. The social significance of the confusion he creates may be as profound and basic as social existence can get.

The most disruptive thing a well organism can do is to acquire a deadly contagious disease. The most disruptive thing a person can do is fail to keep a place that others feel can't be changed for him. Whatever the cause of the offender's psychological state—and clearly this may sometimes be organic—the social significance of the disease is that its carrier somehow hits upon the way that things can be made hot for us. The sociological significance of this is that social life is organized so that such a way can be found for it.

The manic is someone who does not refrain from intruding where he is not wanted or where he will be accepted but at a loss to what we see as his value and status. He does not contain himself in the spheres and territories allotted to him. He overreaches. He does not keep his place.

But more than place and the self it affords are involved. The manic does not accept tactful treatment as an exchange for not pressing too far. And he not only fails to keep the place which he and his others had allocated to him, but declines, apparently willfully, to engage in the ritual work that would allow his others to discount this failure.

In response, his others feel that his character and personality have suddenly changed, that he is no longer himself, and no longer himself in a way that disallows his close others from being what they feel they must be. Unfitting his self to his person, he unfits the persons of those around him to their selves. Wherever his dealings go, disarraying follows.

The manic declines to restrict himself to the social game that brings order and sense to our lives. Through his antics he gives up "his" self-respect, this being the regard we would allow him to have for himself as a reward for keeping a social place that may contain no other satisfaction for him.

The manic gives up everything a person can be, and gives up too the everything we make out of jointly guarded dealings. His doing so, and doing so for any of a multitude of independent reasons, reminds us what our everything is, and then reminds us that this everything is not very much. A somewhat similar lesson is taught by other categories of troublemaker who do not keep their place.

---

32. Similarly, we should appreciate that depression is not something that can be fully understood by looking inside the patient. It seems to me that depressed persons come to appreciate consciously how much social effort is in fact required in the normal course of keeping one's usual place in undertakings. Once an individual feels a little less outgoing than usual for him, a very large part of his social universe can easily become attenuated, simply because such a universe is partly sustained at the constantly exercised option of the actor. At many contact points in the individual's daily round, his others will be on the lookout for signs of disaffection and be ready to begin to withdraw from him in order to protect their own reception. A small hint that he has become less inclined toward them can begin a general letting go of him. It might be added that while the classic notion of manic-depressive cycles is no longer put forward in psychiatry—the current view being that one of the two modes predominates—it is the case that many manics experience periods of marked depression when to face any moment in the day requires a terrible effort. Again the plight of finding everything just too much of a drag is not to be attributed solely to an intrapsychic factor, but also to the fact that social place is organized so that some special effort is always required to maintain it. Given that much of social life is organized in

terms of personal control and informal control, conditions are present for multiplying in every direction a slight increase or decrease in outgoingness. Depression and mania necessarily become ready possibilities, and not surprisingly often in the same person.

REFERENCES

Aubert, Vilhelm, and Messinger, Sheldon. "The Criminal and the Sick," *Inquiry* (1958) 1:137–160.

Erikson, Kai T. "Patient Role and Social Uncertainty—A Dilemma of the Mentally Ill," *Psychiatry* (1957) 20:263–274.

Festinger, Leon, et al. *When Prophecy Fails;* Harper Torchbooks, 1964.

Glaser, Barney, and Strauss, Anselm. *Awareness of Dying;* Aldine, 1965.

Goffman, Erving. *Behavior in Public Places;* Free Press, paper edition, 1966.

Goffman, Erving. *Interaction Ritual;* Anchor Books, 1967.

Haley, Jay. "Toward a Theory of Pathological Systems," in Gerald Zuk and Ivan Boszormenyi-Nagy (Eds.), *Family Therapy and Disturbed Families;* Science and Behavior Books, 1967.

Hollingshead, August, and Redlich, Frederick. *Social Class and Mental Illness;* Wiley, 1958.

Lemert, Edwin M. "Paranoia and the Dynamics of Exclusion," first published in *Sociometry* (1962) 25:2–20, and reprinted in his *Human Deviance, Social Problems, and Social Control;* Prentice-Hall, 1967.

Nadel, S. F. "Social Control and Self-Regulation," *Social Forces* (1953) 31:265–273.

Parsons, Talcott. *The Social System;* Free Press, 1951.

Roueché, Berton. "Ten Feet Tall," *The Incurable Wound;* Berkeley Books, 1958.

Royce, Josiah. "Some Observations on the Anomalies of Self-Consciousness," in Edgar Borgatta and Henry Meyer, *Sociological Theory;* Knopf, 1961.

Scott, Marvin and Lyman, Stanford. "Accounts," *Amer. Sociol. Review* (1968) 3:46–62.

Wilson, Louise. *This Stranger, My Son;* Putnam, 1968.

DOLORES E. KREISMAN • VIRGINIA D. JOY

Family Response to the Mental Illness of a Relative: A Review of the Literature*

One of the few persistent statistics in the mental health literature is that 30 percent of patients released from mental hospitals return to the hospital during the 1st year following discharge. Over a longer period of time, the statistics are even bleaker. In New York State, for instance, more than 60 percent of all admissions to State hospitals are readmissions. For many patients rehospitalization occurs more than once and, indeed for some, becomes a way of life. It has been customary to refer to such a series of hospitalizations as the "career" of the mental patient.

The contemporary, widespread policy of short-term multiple hospitalizations has meant that the old pattern of chronic hospitalization—in which the long-

hospitalized patient each year becomes further removed from the concern of his family—is virtually a thing of the past. Increasingly, the family is becoming involved in long-term interaction with and care for the "former" patient, whether the patient returns to the family home on discharge, moves to his own quarters, or is a resident of a sheltered communal environment. Yet the mental health community's concern with the family's response to this new pattern of involvement has been meager.

In the past, the study of the family in relation to the mental illness of a relative has generally focused on its possible role as an etiological factor in the origin or outcome of the disorder. Family models of psychopathology—based on the symptomatology of the parents, the specific types of interactions between parent and child, or the idea of a disorganized family social system—have been used with varying degrees of success to explain the extent to which the family contributes to or maintains the state in which the disordered person finds himself.

Reprinted from *Schizophrenia Bulletin*, No. **10** (Fall 1974), pages 34–57, by permission of the authors.

* Studies cited in this paper often use as respondents families of hospitalized patients without regard to diagnosis. Occasionally, investigators restrict themselves to a sample of families of schizophrenics; when this occurs, it is noted in the text.

The role of the family in the etiology of schizophrenia is still uncertain (Frank 1965 and Mosher and Gunderson 1973), but we know that family members who have a psychiatric disorder can and frequently do have profound effects on other family members. The ambiguous nature of psychiatric illness (at least in its early stages) and the consequent episodic eruptions of deviant behavior require an adjustment in the family that is in itself stressful—an adjustment that includes definition and help seeking and, in all but acute cases, the responsibility for the continuing care of the patient. Additionally, family roles must shift to accommodate the behavior or deficiencies of the sick member, and the strain of this accommodation is often chronic. Considering these obvious stresses, it is surprising that the same investigators who provided ample documentation of the career of the mental patient have so sadly neglected the reciprocal career of the patient's family.

Recently, however, investigators have changed their perspective to incorporate a view of the family as *reactor* to (rather than purely causal agent in) the mental illness of a member. This change is important for its own sake. For one thing, it permits the specification of the kind of adaptation that occurs when a functioning family interacts over time with a deviant member for whom it feels and is considered responsible. For another, it permits a fuller description of the system in which the patient operates, one to which he may return and which will, in all likelihood, be a critical factor in determining prognosis.

There is still another equally beneficial consequence of research on the family as reactor (although the literature has rarely been used to this end), and that is that such research may help clarify issues of causality by isolating the part the family's reaction to deviance plays in the family's current interactional pattern. It has frequently been assumed in family research that 1) the family's behavior instigates the patient's behavior, 2) the family observed at the time of the research has remained unchanged through time, and 3) any inferences of the past that are based on observations in the present are valid if they "make sense" or if they meet the test of statistical significance for correlational analysis. Such a view has been legitimately questioned (Fontana 1966) and is clearly in need of correction. The inclusion in the description of the patient's family system of the family as responder, as well as stimulus, has immeasurably broadened its conception and has permitted an important first step to be taken toward the development of a true interactional approach.

The introduction of the family as a subject of study in the attempt to understand the response to mental illness occurred in the early 1950's when a theoretical interest in deviance and social control (Festinger et al. 1952, Parsons 1951, and Schachter 1951) and in social perception (Bruner and Tagiuri 1954) provided a conceptual framework for social scientists who had become concerned with the mentally disordered patient and his family (Parsons and Fox 1952 and Yarrow et al. 1955). Not too much later, the practical needs of hospital psychiatry to assess the effects of the then innovative programs of community care for mental patients turned the attentions of psychiatric researchers to the families of patients as agents of rehabilitation and bearers of burden (Brown, Carstairs, and Topping 1958).

The convergence of these two lines of interest, practical and theoretical, led Clausen and Yarrow (1955)[1] to undertake pioneering research that dealt specifically with the problems and attitudes of the families of mental patients. They had little relevant research to guide them, as their legitimately sparse bibliography made amply clear. Even as late as 1959, 4 years after the appearance of their report, a review of the literature by Spiegel and Bell (1959) for the *American Handbook of Psychiatry* cited Clausen and Yarrow as the major source for the section of the paper dealing with the impact of mental illness on the family.

The findings of the Clausen and Yarrow investigation reflected the natural history of the wife's reaction to her husband's deviant behavior. In ordering the literature to be reviewed in this article, we, too, employ a loosely defined natural history approach, one that derives somewhat from the Clausen and Yarrow (1955) presentation, but has the changes and extensions necessary to allow for the incorporation of new materials and different points of view. In this way we shall cover the evolution by the family of the mental illness hypothesis and the family's consequent attitudes and behavior in response to the labeling and hospitalization of the relative. In the final section, we discuss the relationship of family attitudes, particularly tolerance of deviant behavior, to outcome after discharge.

The Family's Definition of the Problem

Research on nonpsychiatrically involved samples indicates that the public labels very few behaviors as indicating mental illness. There appears also to be a

1. Throughout much of this paper, frequent reference will be made to Clausen and Yarrow (1955), Schwartz (1956 and 1957), Yarrow, Clausen, and Robbins (1955), and Yarrow et al. (1955). These articles discuss various aspects of a single retrospective study, and most were published in the *Journal of Social Issues*, vol. 11(4), 1955, under the general editorship of John Clausen and Marian R. Yarrow. The sample in this study comprised the wives and families of 20 psychotics and 13 neurotics who were hospitalized for the first time for mental disorder. Unless otherwise stated, findings reported in this article are for the total group of 33.

general consensus that the public's attitudes toward the mentally ill in affective, cognitive, and conative terms is largely negative. Given a definition of mental illness narrower than that used by professionals, and a setting in which attitudes are largely negative, how do families explain and react to the behavior of a relative who later will be labeled "mentally ill"?

The family's attempt to understand the meaning of the behaviors they observe is thought to follow a predictable course that shows both acceptance and denial, certainty and uncertainty. It is not unlike Lederer's (1952) description of the reaction of patients to physical illness. He noted three definite, established stages of response. The first of these, the transition period from health to illness, was characterized by an awareness of symptoms, anxiety over their presence, denial or minimization of symptoms, and some residual anger or passivity. If symptoms persisted and the interruption of everyday routines continued, then diagnosis and therapy resulted and the patient was encouraged to accept the "sick role." This marked the second stage. In the third stage, the patient was concerned with convalescence and the return to the functioning adult role. For part of his formulation of this sequence, Lederer drew upon Barker's (1948) discussion of the physically disabled.

Lederer's analysis of the sick role was the product of his own observations, and dealt primarily with the patient's changing perceptions. Yarrow et al. (1955) described a very similar process governing the family's coming to terms with the symptoms of mental illness. The wives of 33 mental patients were interviewed a number of times, from soon after the husband's hospitalization until 6 months after his return home or until 1 year after hospitalization. The investigators described the phases the wife went through in defining her husband's behavior: The shifting interpretations, the occasional outright denial, and the stable conclusion, once a threshold for tolerance had been reached, that the problem was psychiatric or, at least, one that could not be dealt with by the family alone. The family's naivete about psychiatric symptoms, the deviant's fluctuating behavior, and the observed presence of lesser forms of the symptoms in "normal" people all acted as factors operating against a swift recognition of mental illness. Yarrow et al. (1955) concluded:

> The findings on the perceptions of mental illness by the wives of patients are in line with the general findings in studies in perception. Behavior which is unfamiliar and incongruent and unlikely in terms of current expectations and needs will not be readily recognized, and stressful or threatening stimuli will tend to be misperceived or perceived with difficulty or delay. [p. 23]

Psychological vs. Nonpsychological View of Illness

Psychological explanations of deviant behavior were rarely invoked by the family during the early stages of mental illness (decompensation). The most frequently given explanations tended to be those attributing the behavior to character weakness, physical ailments, or situational factors. For instance, only 24 percent of the mainly middle-class wives in Yarrow et al.'s (1955) study felt something was seriously wrong when their husbands first displayed overt symptoms. When such interpretations were made, anger was occasionally used as a means of social control in an attempt to bring the husband's behavior into line. By the time successive redefinitions had taken place and hospitalization was imminent, slightly less than one-third of the total sample of the wives of neurotic and psychotic patients and 20 percent of the wives of psychotic patients still denied that their husbands were mentally ill.

Similarly, in an interview approximately 3 weeks after a family member's hospitalization, 18 percent of Lewis and Zeichner's (1960) sample of the families of 109 first admissions at three Connecticut State hospitals denied the patients' mental illness. In 40 percent of the cases, the illness was first recognized by a physician or someone outside the family. Mayo, Havelock, and Simpson (1971) reported that 19 nonpsychotic men in a mental hospital and their wives tended to accept a physical view of the husband's illness and that this general disbelief in the psychological determinants of the patients' state was at variance with the staff's view of the nature of the illness.

Some attempts to identify the correlates of a psychological versus nonpsychological view of illness were made in the works of Hollingshead and Redlich (1958), Freeman (1961), and Linn (1966). In the first two studies, social class or education was the moderating variable; in the last, family relationship. In Hollingshead and Redlich's sample of New Haven residents, the families of the three lowest class patients (classes III, IV, and V) showed a marked tendency to rely on somatic theories, heredity, or the "evil eye" to explain the patient's aberrant behavior. Classes I and II, on the other hand, had more detailed information about their relative's illness and explained the deviance on the basis of nerve strain, fatigue, or overwork. In contrast to the findings of Hollingshead and Redlich, Freeman found that education (but not other indicators of social class) and age were factors in the attitudes of relatives of discharged patients in the Boston area. He studied the relationship between relatives' attitudes regarding the etiology of mental illness and the degree to which responsibility for their condition was imputed to patients. A psychogenic view was related to the feeling that the patient could recover and was not to blame for his illness. On the whole, better educated and younger relatives had more positive attitudes toward the patient.

Linn (1966) interviewed either the wives or mothers of 34 recently hospitalized schizophrenic men and found that mothers more often than wives had a psychological explanation for their sons' illness; wives tended to believe their husbands' behavior was caused by physical and environmental factors. Linn reasoned that, since wives more than mothers were concerned with role performance, they were more likely to see the illness in terms of negligence in fulfilling role obligations, or as a result of environmental stress.

Effects of Distance or Closeness of Relationship to the Patient

The view that motivation and values could affect the perception of other people, so much a part of the zeitgeist of the 1950's, generated an interest in the psychological impediments to a mental illness explanation of deviant behavior. Generally, it was assumed that the closer the relationship to the deviant, the greater the perceived threat and anxiety resulting from a psychological definition of deviance, with the consequence that, all other things being equal, closeness would result in delay or outright denial.[2] Schwartz (1957) was the first to observe and report the occurrence of this phenomenon in her investigation of the family's response to the mental illness of a member. Shortly after, Rose's (1959) study of the families of hospitalized patients in Massachusetts and Mill's (1962) impressions of English families in a similar situation also supported the view that the closer the tie of the relative, the less ready the family to perceive mental illness.

Still further confirmation came from Sakamoto (1969), who concluded that, on the basis of his experiences as a family therapist in Japan, *distance* appears to facilitate a diagnosis of psychological disturbance. He speculated that a particular type of closeness, the symbiotic tie between parent and child, functioned to impede early parental recognition of a child's schizophrenia. Sakamoto did not believe that this relationship was culturally determined, and he found support for his

2. Another interpretation of the delaying mechanism may be derived from Goffman's (1963) work on stigma. There, it is proposed that the more intimate the relationship between two people, the more complex the picture they have of one another. If this is true, then a psychiatric symptom in a family member would not be seen as the defining characteristic of that person but would be interpreted in the context of the total person. In that case, the importance of the symptom might not be as obvious to the family as to an outsider.

conclusion in the observation of the same phenomenon in families of American patients (Wynne et al. 1958).

This line of research has not gone unchallenged, and the simple hypothesis that closeness is associated with delayed recognition has not stood the test of time. Both the type of symptom and aspects of the patient-family relationship have been shown to be related to the recognition of mental illness.

A focused interview technique was used by Clausen (1959) in interviews with the spouses of 23 schizophrenics (males and females). He concluded that when symptomatic behavior was directed against the spouse, it was more likely that a deviance framework would be used to interpret the behavior. Safilios-Rothschild (1968) replicated Clausen's study in Greece and confirmed his findings. In fact, Safilios-Rothschild disputed Schwartz's original hypothesis, because she found that spouses who were maritally satisfied, and therefore presumably close, did not arrive at a deviance explanation later than dissatisfied spouses. Both Clausen and Safilios-Rothschild observed that the definition of the behavior as deviant actually resulted in feelings of relief for the spouse, since the marriage was no longer perceived as threatened.

In another study, Sampson, Messinger, and Towne (1962) isolated two types of marital accommodations, which were so high in their tolerance of deviance that either the patient or the community was responsible for first labeling the behavior as deviance and then arranging for hospitalization. Yet neither of these accommodations could conventionally be called close, and in both cases it was the withdrawal from the deviant early in the marital relationship that permitted bizarre behavior either to go unnoticed or to be explained in normal terms. Sampson, Messinger, and Towne intensively interviewed 17 schizophrenic women and their husbands during and after the wife's first hospitalization and found that some marriages were characterized by mutual withdrawal, and others by the wife's continued intense relationship to her mother. In both situations it was not until the conventional accommodation was threatened and new role behaviors required that the deviant behavior became troublesome and consequently noticed.

Perhaps the hypothesis that emotional closeness delays labeling has attracted more attention than other problems in family labeling because it was clearly stated and could be derived from a popular theoretical position (perceptual defense theory). As a consequence, research on this hypothesis has done more than demonstrate the existence of an imperfect relationship between closeness and delay. More complex interactions invoking such variables as quality of the relationship between patient and family and whether symptoms are directed against a family member have resulted in alterations in the original formulation.

Typologies Based on Family Response

Three articles in the literature deal with typologies or classifications of the family's response to the mental illness of a member. Since these typologies have not been tested on samples other than the original and do not appear to have generated further research, neither their utility nor their heuristic power has been demonstrated. It is possible that they have not been used because it is expected that they will suffer, as do most typologies, from a lack of generalizability to new samples, an incomplete description of the data, or the inability of researchers other than the originator to use them satisfactorily. In any event, the absence of any followup study of these systems of classification makes it difficult to ascertain their value or deficiencies.

Korkes' (1959) interview study of the parents of 100 schizophrenic children yielded four basic "ideal" types:

- *Dissociative-organic type*—Parents falling into this category disavowed responsibility for the child's condition and generally offered a biological explanation for it.
- *Affiliative type*—This type of family acknowledged its own interpersonal influences as etiological factors.
- *Dissociative-social type*—The parents disavowed any responsibility and offered an extrafamilial explanation for the disorder.
- *A residual* category comprised parents who were highly and continually uncertain about etiology and the role they themselves played in their child's illness.

Korkes' data supported her expectation that parents who accepted personal responsibility were more likely to undergo profound changes in personal values, marital relationships, and child-rearing behavior. These parents perceived the patient as a human being who had comprehensible responses and who could be included in family life.

Two aspects of family response to deviance interact in an effort by Spitzer, Morgan, and Swanson (1971) to develop a typology for describing the family's role in the evolution of the psychiatric patient's career. The family's level of expected performance and its propensity to label the deviance in conjunction with the family's appraisal of deviance, its decision to seek psychiatric help, and its implementation of psychiatric care yielded eight family subtypes, which bear such engaging names

as stoics, poltroons, happenchancers, and do-nothings. Although the substantive description of each subtype does not seem to be precisely derivable from the component variables in the system, the authors were able to classify 76 of the 79 families of first-admission patients in the above typology.

A concern with the sociocultural determinants of definitions of mental illness led Schwartz (1957) to order three commonly occurring definitions of deviance (characterological, somatic, and psychological) along four variables (partial-global extent, alterability, recent-remote occurrence, and situational-somatogenic-psychogenic cause). Eighty percent of her sample of wives of recently admitted patients gave psychological explanations ("not completely crazy" or "out of his mind") of their husbands' illness. A patient who was defined as "out of his mind" was thought to have a global, unalterable, and recently occurring illness. In contrast, being "not completely crazy" was alterable, of recent origin, and only partially disabling. None of these definitions could be differentiated by cause.

Whatever the value of these particular typologies, it is clear, in reviewing the research on family labeling, that families attempting to define the problem posed by psychologically deviant behavior acted as most people do when confronted with ambiguous or stressful stimuli. They generally engaged in a process of redefinition in which they were slow, first, to view their sick member as deviant, and second, to view him as a deviant because of psychological aberrations. As expected, education and social class, which are associated with greater psychological sophistication and therefore reduce ambiguity, were related to the type of explanation used. Intimacy or psychological closeness acted as an impediment to labeling the behavior as deviant only if symptoms were not directed against a significant other. In certain cases, withdrawal, not intimacy, in an ostensibly close relationship explained the delay in defining the behavior appropriately. These findings have led to a revision of the original closeness-delay hypothesis.

It is puzzling that symptoms, the observable manifestation of mental illness, have not been more widely examined with regard to labeling. The manner of onset, the nature of symptomatic behavior, and the family's ability to tolerate those symptoms being displayed are likely to have some effect on the rapidity with which the definition of the problem occurs. For instance, when onset is gradual and symptoms are not too bizarre, as is frequently the case in the undifferentiated chronic schizophrenic, deviance may come to be expected of the individual, interpreted as "normal" for him, and perceived as neither especially different nor upsetting. Similarly, a high tolerance of deviance, resulting from the interaction of personal history and cultural expectations, may also serve to retard a psychological explanation of the deviant behavior.

The Family's Attitudes Toward Its Deviant Member

By the time hospitalization occurs, most families have come to believe that their deviant member is mentally ill. The possible consequences of such a belief can be theoretically represented by a wide range of affective and behavioral responses. On the one hand, families could show increased support and tolerance for their ill member and, because of their concern, be more aware of affectionate ties. Such positive affect would be a reaction similar to that frequently shown the physically ill. On the other hand, quite different responses may occur. When symptoms are unpredictable or bizarre, the family may become fearful. Anger may occur because of the patient's disruptiveness, or because of family resentment due to increased strain. In cases in which the appearance of mental illness arouses guilt, or when the illness is evaluated in moral terms, attitudes of shame and rejection might be expected. In reality, it is likely that a complex amalgam of all of these responses best represents the family's evaluation with variables such as length and number of hospitalizations, type of symptoms, prehospitalization family interaction, prognosis, and sociocultural status, to cite a few, determining the intensity with which such attitudes are held. A neutral affective dimension of family attitudes appears unlikely, since hospitalization cannot help but be a significant event in the family's experience.

Despite the wide range of possible responses to deviance in the family, professional interest seems to have concentrated on the negative response to the patient and particularly on the issue of stigma, with the consequence that shame and social rejection have been among the most studied aspects of family attitudes and behavior. Such a limited focus is probably the result of two factors: 1) a generalization to the family of the negative opinions the general public holds (see Rabkin 1972) and 2) the commonly held assumption shared by many mental health professionals that mental illness is indeed shameful.

In his essays on stigma, Goffman (1963) has not only summarized and elaborated on the professional consensus about the public's reaction to deviance but has provided some insights into the mitigating role that intimacy can play in that reaction. As a rule, when interaction is minimal and affective regard is low, the stigmatized person is assigned a nonhuman quality. The assignment of this quality to the deviant permits the environment to discriminate against him and encourages those who interact with him to behave as if the stigma were the essence of the person. The inevitable outcome of this process is generally believed to be rejection of the deviant.

However, the more intimate the relationship between the stigmatized and the other, the less the stigma defines the person; thus, closeness permits one to see qualities other than the flaw. But to be associated with a stigmatized person brings with it its own dilemma. Since a close relationship results in being "tainted" oneself, a relative can choose either to embrace the fate of the stigmatized person and identify with him or to reject sharing the discredit of the stigmatized person by avoiding or terminating the relationship.

Goffman presents a persuasive and tenable case for the occurrence of stigma and rejection in response to mental illness, but research on this point, as we shall see, is far from conclusive. People who have had close contact with mental patients do not appear to be as prejudiced against them as those who have not, but there is little evidence that they accept the fate of the stigmatized person for themselves. At the same time, when rejection does occur, it is not clear that its antecedents are to be found mainly in the family's sense of its own stigmatization.

Yet even within the limitations that a stigma-social rejection framework imposes, certain gaps in research interest are apparent. The literature on the family's affective response to the patient is unquestionably scant and simplistic, and research on the beliefs that families of the mentally ill have about patients generally, and their patient in particular, is virtually nonexistent. A study such as that carried out by Nunnally (1961) on the structural coherence of the affective and cognitive components of the public's attitudes toward the mentally ill has yet to be done with the family as its subject.

Social rejection studies that reflect the anticipated or actual behavioral outcome of interaction with a deviant are, as expected, more numerous. They are technically more sophisticated, but they are not especially complex in their conceptualization of the possible antecedents of rejection.

The Family's Affective Response

The family's affective response is generally assessed either through direct questioning or by the use of a semistructured interview that maximizes the probability of the occurrence of affective responses. Occasionally, affect is inferred from behavioral measures, as in the case of shame in which withdrawal from friends or the concealment of the patient's illness is considered sufficient to justify the inference.

One of the earliest studies (Yarrow, Clausen, and Robbins 1955) that examined family attitudes was done in the context of Lewin's (1948) social psychological theory of minority-group belonging. Families in that sample behaved as if they were minority-group members and characteristically showed feelings of underprivilege, marginality, extreme sensitivity, and self-hatred. Fear of the patient was reported by Waters and Northover (1965), who interviewed the wives of long-term schizophrenic patients 2 to 5 years after discharge. Wives were often found to be frightened of their husbands and experienced long periods of tension in the home. Schwartz (1956) and Clausen (1959) reported a considerable amount of anger and resentment on the part of husbands and wives toward their mentally disordered spouses prior to hospitalization.

Some studies have gone beyond the descriptive level. Hollingshead and Redlich (1958) examined social-class differences in the family response to mental illness and found that, whereas resentment and fear were prevalent reactions in lower-class families, shame and guilt were more pronounced in the upper classes. A more intensive interview of a schizophrenic subsample ($n = 25$) in that study (Myers and Roberts 1959), however, indicated that shame at having an "insane person" in the family was a common reaction in class V, the lowest social class. As a result of this shame and a general reluctance to involve themselves with authorities, class V patients were most often hospitalized by people outside the family. In contrast, class III families sought a physician's help, once decompensation occurred, and seemed to be more concerned with the patient's recovery than with feelings of shame and futility.

The general trend, however, despite the expectations of social scientists or the anticipations of common sense, is for families to report little fear, shame, anger, or guilt. For example, about 50 percent of Lewis and Zeichner's sample (1960) expressed a sympathetic understanding of the patient; only 17 percent expressed hostility or fear, and the remainder were either ambivalent or puzzled at their relatives' illness. In Rose's study (1959), relatively little stigma and shame was evident in the feelings of family members.

The most positive response to the mentally ill occurred in a sample of Cape Coloured families in South Africa. The families of a group of chronic schizophrenics who had never been hospitalized appeared to have great warmth and love for the sick person (Gillis and Keet 1965). Even those families in the comparison group who had hospitalized a relative continued to express great sympathy for him and maintained regular contact with him.

Theoretically, feelings of shame and stigma should be particularly aroused in situations in which a public display of deviance makes the label obvious to onlookers, when, as Goffman would say, the "discredit" is clearly observable. When unusual behavior is not evident, then it is less likely that shame would be a salient aspect of the attitude toward the patient. For instance, when families worry little about embarrassing behaviors or behaviors that cause trouble to the neighbors, as in Grad and Sainsbury's (1963b) study, one might deduce that symptoms are neither bizarre nor easily noticeable. In that case, little shame would be expected. This relationship was somewhat confirmed in a 2-year study of home care for schizophrenic patients by Pasamanick, Scarpetti, and Dinitz (1967). The main study group comprised potential patients who were returned to the home at the point when admission to the hospital was sought. Potential patients were given drugs or placebo, visited regularly by a nurse, and seen occasionally by a psychiatrist. The same treatment was given a second group of "ambulatory schizophrenics" (cases referred to the study by clinics or physicians in the area) who were living at home and had never sought admission to the State hospital. In both the main group and the ambulatory group, a comparison of family response at intake and 6 months later revealed that an already low level of shame and fear (approximately 15 percent) lessened even more over time for both the drug and placebo groups. At the 6-month interview, drug condition made no difference in family reports for the ambulatory group. For the main group, however, only 2 percent of the families in the drug sample reported being ashamed or afraid, whereas 7 percent of the families in the placebo sample were ashamed, and 13 percent were afraid at the 6-month interview. Since patient behavior was in part related to experimental condition, and since shame and fear decreased after contact with the hospital, it appears that when shame and fear do occur, they are as likely to be the consequences of unrestrained behavior as of the formal labeling of the patient.

Secrecy, Concealment, and Withdrawal

The relationship of secrecy, concealment, and withdrawal from friends to feelings of shame and the perception of stigma seems obvious, and Yarrow, Clausen, and Robbins (1955) and Goffman (1963) have been concerned with this problem. Goffman, whose formulations are similar to Lewin's (1948), distinguished between the discredited person who is obviously marked, and the discreditable person whose stigma is not so noticeable. For the discreditable person and his close associates, concealment is possible, and the problem for them becomes one of information management if secrecy is desired. How, then, do families deal with the question of information sharing about the sick person?

No studies have examined the issue of noticeability of symptoms, and the ease with which they can be defined as signs of psychological aberration, and related these variables to secrecy. Thus the test of the connection between secrecy and discreditability has not yet been made. There are indications, however, that at least for some families efforts at concealment do occur.

One-third of the wives in Yarrow, Clausen, and Robbins' (1955) study demonstrated a pattern of aggressive concealment. Friends were dropped or avoided, and occasionally respondents moved to a different part of town. Another third of the wives had a few favored people to whom they talked—people who would understand the problem or who had been in a similar plight. Members of the husband's family, who shared the "taint," were almost always told, particularly if they were living close by, and sometimes blamed. The remaining third of the wives could be described as communicating extensively and as expressing fewest fears of dire social consequences. While two-thirds of the sample had deliberately concealed the information about their husbands' illness to a greater or lesser degree, everyone had told at least one person outside the family, usually a personal friend.

Rose's (1959) sample did not report such seclusive behavior. He interviewed the principal or next-of-kin visitor of a sample of 100 currently hospitalized patients in a Veterans' Administration hospital in Massachusetts. The median hospital stay for the patients was 9 years. The majority of the relatives spoken with claimed that they felt no stigma and that they had discussed the illness with other people. Freeman and Simmons (1961) reported the results of a 5-item index of stigma developed for use in their long-term study of the families of recently discharged mental patients. The items dealt primarily with the respondent's behavior with regard to secrecy and social withdrawal. Only 10 percent of the sample indicated agreement with two or more of the items, and only 12 percent agreed with the most popular stigma item, "not telling fellow workers about the patient." Six percent reported avoiding friends. Agreement with at least one of the stigma items was positively related to severity of symptoms (a finding similar to that of Pasamanick, Scarpetti, and Dinitz 1967), social class, and a perception that "others" were unfriendly to them.

Unlike the subjects in Yarrow, Clausen, and Robbins' study, very few of the people in Rose's and Freeman and

Simmons' samples reported avoiding friends. This contradiction may be due to the different types of respondents sampled. Yarrow, Clausen, and Robbins' sample comprised the wives of first-admission patients. Rose's sample included the relatives of long-term patients, and Freeman and Simmons' sample was mixed in terms of number of hospitalizations. It is likely that experience with mental illness plays a role in the eventual reaction of the family to the patient. If this is so, a person faced with the first hospitalization of a relative may feel shame and anger and try to conceal the hospitalization but still not reject the patient, whereas those people whose relatives have been hospitalized a number of times, or for prolonged periods, may have accommodated themselves to the situation and no longer keenly feel and report shame. Lengthy or multiple hospitalizations may make impossible any attempts at concealment and may erode much of the willingness of the family to tolerate once again the patient's disruptive presence. So few studies have reported an analysis of data on number or length or hospitalizations that the process of accommodation to recurrent or prolonged disturbance in family life is virtually uncharted.

Social class was related to the openness with which the patient's illness was discussed by Hollingshead and Redlich (1958). There was a marked tendency for most relatives in all classes to be secretive about the mental illness. The ostensible reasons for secretiveness, however, differed in each class. Class I showed the least overt concern. Classes II and III worried about how public knowledge would affect the family's chances of getting ahead. Class IV reported the classic shame associated with stigma, and class V was secretive because of a wish to prevent snooping and interference with the family. Similar results were found by Myers and Bean (1968) in their 10-year followup of part of the Hollingshead and Redlich sample.

On the whole, the pattern of results with behavioral indicators of stigma (reports of concealment) confirms that found in attitudinal studies of affect. Shame, fear, and anger are present in some cases but do not appear to occupy as central a position as might be expected. Although it is difficult to draw any clear conclusions about the response of family members from these studies, it would be unwarranted nevertheless to underestimate the presence of negative affect, even when data to the contrary are reported. As in other areas of attitude measurement on sensitive issues, negative affect is generally underreported, and the absence of any controls for social desirability or acquiescence makes it almost impossible to judge the extent to which the respondents' statements truly reflect their evaluations. It is possible, of course, that further research, using better measurement devices and exploring interactions rather than main effects, will result in a sharper and more accurate picture of the family's feelings about a patient member. It seems equally important, however, to expand the conceptual and theoretical notions that have determined the variables chosen for research if a fuller, more complex picture is to emerge.

While contemporary usage generally regards the affective dimension as the major defining dimension for attitudes, this does not mean that nonevaluative beliefs or behavioral predispositions are unimportant. A conceptualization of attitudes, which involves affective, cognitive, and behavioral components, allows one to speak meaningfully of the psychological structure of an attitude, to investigate the relationship among these components, to assess and predict the effect of change in one on the other, and to relate these data to behavior.

Much of the research on attitudes, particularly in the mental health field, attempts to measure action tendencies and is ultimately concerned with the prediction of overt behavior. This task is certainly a most difficult one, requiring as it does knowledge of the actor's feelings, beliefs, and postulated action tendencies along with knowledge of the situational and cultural demands impinging on him. Situations of any complexity are likely to render a number of attitude systems relevant at the same time, and attempts at predicting outcome from a single variable are likely to meet with failure. To give just one example, a family may be thought to provide a proper setting for the rehabilitation of a patient because its members express affection and warmth toward the patient and want him home. Yet the family members' conviction of their inability to care for him or their fear of his bizarre behavior may become obvious in stringent attempts to monitor his activities upon his return; this situation in turn may effectively sabotage the patient's attempts at rehabilitation.

Studies of Social Rejection

Studies of the behavioral component of attitudes toward the mentally ill can most easily be grouped under the heading of social rejection, since they measure a projected tendency to accept or reject a person or class of people.

Much of the research on this subject has drawn heavily on work done in the social psychology of ethnic prejudice and, in fact, the principal measuring tool used in studies of rejection of the mentally ill (the social distance scale) was developed by Bogardus (1925) to ascertain the degree of intimacy permitted by one group of people to another. The social distance scale consists of a number of ordered statements that vary the degree of

intimacy of social interaction. The respondent is asked to indicate for each item whether he will accept a particular type of interaction with a *hypothetical* person; for example, whether he would permit a mentally ill person to work with him or to dine at his house or to marry his daughter. A person's attitude is inferred from the highest level of interaction he will accept with the target person.

The remaining studies in this section have focused on the family's attitude or actual behavior toward their hospitalized member and the willingness of the family to reaccept the patient into the home once discharge is a possibility.

Social Distance

To determine the avoidance reactions of the general public to former mental patients, Whatley (1959) administered an 8-item social distance scale to 2,001 persons in Louisiana. The items ranged from those involving "minimal ego involvement" (associating with a former mental patient) to those with "maximal ego involvement" (permitting a person who has been in psychiatric treatment to babysit with your child). The results generally indicated that the younger and more educated the respondent, the more likely he was to be willing to admit a former mental patient into a close relationship. Whatley also asked questions about whether the respondent had ever visited a mental hospital or, more crucial for our purposes, knew of any reported cases of mental illness in the family. Neither visiting a mental hospital nor having a mentally ill person in the family had any effect on attitudes toward the mentally ill—a seeming example of the relative's refusal to accept the fate of the stigmatized.

Bizon et al. (no date) studied a quota sample of Warsaw's residents and found that the closer the contact with the mentally ill, the greater was the expressed willingness to accompany former mental patients to the theater, to invite them to a birthday party, and to befriend them on a lonely trip.

The results of Chin-Shong's study (1968) of attitudes toward the mentally ill in an extremely heterogeneous, urban American sample ($n = 151$) appear less than clear-cut. Using a social distance scale similar to Whatley's, Chin-Shong examined the effects of degree of closeness to a particular mental patient on social distance from mental patients generally. Analysis of the data showed that there was a significant decrease in attitudinal distance to the hypothetical patient if the respondent had a close tie with an actual mental patient. However, the results were not linear. There was more acceptance if the patient known was a close friend than if he was a family member. It appears that having a patient in the family was sufficiently threatening to mitigate some of the effects of intimacy. While the effects of family ties in this study were not strong, they were not absent as in Whatley's original study.

Chin-Shong's data further suggest that knowing many patients casually is less effective in decreasing rejection than being closely related to a patient. People with close ties to mental patients, unlike those without them, did not reject the hypothetical patient more when they perceived him to be dangerous; they also accepted him more when they judged their patient-relatives to have improved. Chin-Shong interpreted this finding as supporting Goffman's contention that intimacy forces an awareness of the other personal characteristics of the stigmatized person. Age and education continued to be correlated with attitudes toward mental patients in the expected direction.

The question of the impact of hospitalization and its consequences for labeling was the focus of Phillips' work (1963). Phillips, like Scheff (1963), believes that the symptoms of mental illness are not easily identifiable by the lay public and that other cues are therefore necessary to define the behavior as mental illness. One such cue is the source of help that is sought to deal with the problem. Phillips studied the relationship of the type of help source to the evaluation of five people described in Star's (1955) vignettes of psychiatric syndromes in a sample of 300 married white women living in a suburb in northeastern United States. The description of a psychiatrically symptomatic person and the help source were varied in a Greco-Latin-square design. After each vignette, the respondent was asked a series of social distance questions. For each form of sickness described, the rejection score was less when no help source was mentioned and highest when the mental hospital was mentioned as the help source. This basic association was maintained within age groups, religious groups, and social-class groups. If the respondent had known either a family member or a friend who had actually sought help for emotional problems, however, the rejection scores changed. If a respondent's *relative* had sought help, then in the hypothetical cases, rejection was highest either *if no help was sought* or *if the help source was a hospital,* and rejection was lowest for those whose help source was a physician. Overall, respondents with family members who had been mentally ill were less rejecting than those who had a friend or knew no one with emotional problems.

Swanson and Spitzer (1970) wanted to test three hypotheses derived from Goffman's formulations. Specifically, they were interested in 1) how people who are mentally ill stigmatize others who are similarly afflicted, 2) how relatives of the mentally ill stigmatize the

mentally ill, and 3) how the propensity of the patient and his family to stigmatize changes as the patient moves through the prepatient, inpatient, and postpatient phases. Six hundred and seventy patients and their families were interviewed at different points in the patients' career, using Whatley's social distance scale. The results on family attitudes indicated that the significant others were less rejecting of the mentally ill than the patients themselves; they were also considerably more stable in attitude from phase to phase. This tolerance was unaffected by age, sex, social class, or diagnosis of the patient. Swanson and Spitzer see this result as evidence of a general solution of the dilemma of the tainted person. Since the attitudes of the significant others were more accepting than those of the patients, they concluded that the family had embraced the patient's fate rather than the alternative of avoiding or terminating the existing relationship.

All in all, there is a slight trend for people who have had close contact with the mentally ill to be less rejecting in terms of the degree of social interaction they say they will accept. This conclusion can only be made very warily, however, since the paucity of studies on the topic limits the generalizability of the results.

Visiting

Visiting seemed, on the whole, to be an excellent indicator of the family's attachment to the patient. While abandonment was occasionally reported, it was generally related to chronicity (Rawnsley, Loudon, and Miles 1962, Rose 1959, and Sommer 1959), class (Myers and Bean 1968 and Myers and Roberts 1959), or age (Rose 1959).

The study that most completely described visiting behavior was carried out by Rawnsley, Loudon, and Miles (1962) in Wales. The records of 230 public and private patients were searched to determine whether the patients were visited, how often they were visited, and by whom. Although 67 percent of the patients in the study had spent more than 2 continuous years in the hospital, 72 percent of the total sample were visited at least once during the year. Twenty percent of the patients had absolutely no visible contact (visits, parcels, or letters) with anyone outside the hospital. For all age groups, visiting was inversely correlated with length of hospital stay. Visiting was more frequent for married patients than for single patients, but after 10 years of hospitalization, single men and married women were the two least visited groups.

The patient's "deculturation" as a result of prolonged hospitalization was the subject of Sommer's (1958 and 1959) studies of letter writing and visiting. Approximately 12 percent of the 1,600 patients in a mental hospital in Saskatchewan had been visited at least once during the 3-week study period, and 10 percent had either sent or received a letter during a later 2-week period. When these patients were compared to a random sample of the hospital's patient population, it was found that contact was related to sex and length of stay in the hospital. Women sent and received more letters, and they were visited more often. Patients who had been hospitalized longer had fewer visitors and less letter-writing contact. Interestingly enough, distance between hospital and home residence was not related to visiting behavior.

An informal analysis of interviews with 100 patients' relatives revealed that younger patients and those with fewer years of hospitalization had more family contact (Rose 1959). This finding is similar to those of Rawnsley et al. and Sommer. The principal visitor was more likely to be the mother (a reflection of the fact that most of the sample of patients were unmarried), but when wives were the principal visitors, patients were visited less often than when parents were the principal visitors.

In contrast to Rose's study, Yarrow, Clausen, and Robbins (1955) found that wives and children of patients visited regularly, but that parents and in-laws, who would visit in the early weeks of hospitalization, were unlikely to return after one or two visits. The patient's mother was sometimes an exception to this pattern. Schwartz (1956), reporting on the same data, lists four reasons for the drop in visiting. All have an underlying anxiety dimension and deal mainly with the unpredictability of the patient's behavior and his failure to perform role functions.

It appears in one study that when the patient is visited, he is visited often, but when he is not visited, he is completely abandoned. Evans, Bullard, and Solomon (1961) found that 20 percent of their sample had not been visited at all during the previous year. However, 75 percent of those who were visited were seen at least once a month—a considerable degree of contact, especially since all of these patients had been hospitalized for at least 5 years, and 50 percent of the family sample was pessimistic about outcome for their patient-relatives.

Gillis and Keet (1965) interviewed a sample of 16 hospitalized and 16 nonhospitalized chronic schizophrenics and their relatives. Both samples consisted of South African Cape Coloureds, fairly well matched in demographic characteristics. The average duration of illness in both groups was 8 years. When the patients were hospitalized, the relatives were not uninterested in their welfare, and expressed concern by visiting and bringing gifts; they simply did not want the patient home. By placing the patient in the hospital, they had absolved themselves of all responsibility for the patient's condition and now saw the doctor as the main figure in the care of the patient.

A relationship between social class and visiting patterns was observed by Myers and Roberts (1959) and Myers and Bean (1968), whose studies indicated that less visiting, gift giving, and correspondence occurred in class V than in any other class.

The Gillis and Keet study is particularly interesting because it sets into juxtaposition two measures of social rejection, namely, visiting and reaccepting the patient. Under most circumstances, visiting is less likely than reaccepting the patient to be burdensome and/or disorganizing to the family even when the hospital is a considerable distance from the home. One person may be delegated or take on the responsibility of providing support for the patient and acting as the intermediary with the hospital, thus relieving the other members of the family of the need to concern themselves with the patient. (This may account for the dropping away of most of the family reported in Yarrow, Clausen, and Robbins 1955 and Schwartz 1956.) Not visiting can consequently be considered the strongest measure of rejection. While visiting and rejection of the patient's presence in the household seemed to be strongly related in some studies (Alivisatos and Lyketsos 1964 and Myers and Bean 1968), they were apparently independent in others (Gillis and Keet 1965 and Rose 1959). The relationship between visiting and the propensity to accept the patient on discharge would appear to yield a useful index of attachment to or rejection of the patient.

Accepting the Discharged Patient

Cumming and Cumming (1957) have recounted an instance in which a woman who had openly complained of being subjected to "sex rays" for many years was shunned by her sister only after she had been hospitalized briefly. The sister, unwilling to take the patient home, where she had been living continuously until her hospitalization, declared that now that her sister was sick there was no telling what she might do. The Cummings commented somewhat ironically, "Mental illness, it seems, is a condition which afflicts people who must go to a mental institution, but up until they go almost anything they do is fairly normal" (p. 101). While this may be something of an exaggeration, there is evidence that expectations about cure and homecoming are more pessimistic among family members than among the public at large.

In one of the rare studies comparing *beliefs* about mental patients in relatives and nonrelatives, Swingle

(1965) asked guests at an "open house" at a Veterans' Administration hospital to judge how many mental patients out of a hundred behaved in certain specified ways. He found that relatives expected approximately 50 percent of all mental patients to be incapable of returning home after treatment. Nonrelatives (guests with no relatives or acquaintances in the hospital) expected fewer patients (40 percent) to be unable to return home. Swingle also reported trends for relatives to believe that more patients would always remain patients and to perceive fewer patients as being able to conduct themselves properly in town on a 1-day pass. However, relatives and nonrelatives did not differ in their perception of the friendliness or violence of mental patients.

Pessimism about recovery has its behavioral counterparts in studies dealing expressly with family response to a patient-relative's discharge. Rose (1959) observed that whereas most families were verbally agreeable to the idea of discharge, they became resistant once the likelihood of discharge was a reality. Reluctance to take the patient home increased with the number of years the patient had spent in the hospital (see, also, Rawnsley, Loudon, and Miles 1962).

Hollingshead and Redlich (1958) noticed a similar reluctance to have the patient return in some of the families they studied and offered a social-class explanation for this behavior. Since classes IV and V (the two lowest social classes) tended least often to have a psychological explanation for the deviant behavior they were exposed to, the authors had assumed that more deviance was generally tolerated in these two classes. On closer examination, however, they discovered that many patients in class V were not discharged because nobody wanted to take them home. This last finding was confirmed and elaborated on by Myers and Bean (1968), who interviewed 387 of the 1,563 relatives of patients who were originally in Hollingshead and Redlich's sample. They found that, with each successive hospitalization, more lower-class families cut ties with the patient. The harsh reaction to the label of mental illness, as well as the alleviation of a sense of burden in the families, operated to reduce contact with the patient and interest in him. As a result, discharges in the lower classes decreased more over time than in middle and upper classes.

Perhaps the harshest judgment of patients recorded was made by the families of 300 chronic schizophrenics hospitalized in Greece. Alivisatos and Lyketsos (1964) had hypothesized that in a traditional society in which the moral obligations of the family were still strong and there were few special agencies to treat the mentally ill, patients or former patients would be readily reaccepted into the family. Instead, the investigators found that

many families ceased to consider the ill person as a family member and felt no obligation for his care at all. Families who originally had been, on the whole, quick to hospitalize (70 percent sought help within a year after they suspected a problem) were slow to accept the patient home again (88 percent of the total sample wanted the patient to remain in the hospital). In almost 50 percent of the sample, the family required total cure as a condition for the patient's return.

Another form of social rejection, the desire to separate from the patient and, more important, an actual separation or divorce from the patient, is a measure of the response to patients by people who have an acquired, terminable relationship to them. Rogler and Hollingshead (1965) did a multiple-interview study of 20 married lower-class Puerto Rican couples in which at least one of the spouses was schizophrenic; they compared the couples' responses with those of 20 neighboring couples with no known history of psychiatric disorder. When asked whether they would marry the same person, a different person, or not marry at all if they had the decision to make today, fewer of the spouses of schizophrenics said they would marry the same person than spouses of normals.

When divorce rates for patients are compared to rates in the general public, they are generally higher. Adler (1955) reported an increased divorce rate for her patient population, and former patients in an English sample had a divorce and separation rate three times the national average (Brown et al. 1966). Seven of the 11 married chronic schizophrenic patients who had been selected for special treatment by Evans, Bullard, and Solomon (1961) had been divorced or separated.

Not all studies indicated such bleak rejection on the part of the family. Some studies reported more favorable attitudes to discharge, and it appeared that the patient's return was welcome. Evans, Bullard, and Solomon interviewed the families of chronic hospitalized schizophrenics who were in a special program preparatory to discharge. Almost 50 percent of the families favored the release of patients who had been hospitalized for 5 years or more. Most of these families had a hopeful but realistic view of the patient's future behavior.

Freeman and Simmons (1963) found that 95 percent of their informants and other family members wanted the patient to live in the household. Similar figures were reported by Brown et al. (1966) in their study of 251 English families who were seen 5 years after the discharge of a schizophrenic relative. Seventy-five percent of the families welcomed the patient home, 15 percent accepted him, and only 12 percent wished him to live elsewhere. These findings are interesting in view of the fact that during the 6 months prior to the interview severe or moderate distress was reported by 30 percent of the families of first-admission patients and 59 percent of the families of multiple-admission patients. In an earlier study by some members of the same group, Wing et al. (1964) reported that of the 99 relatives of English male patients, 40 percent indicated that they would welcome the patient home, 25 percent said they would accept him, 21 percent were doubtful about how they felt, and 13 percent were actively opposed to the patients' return. No family, however, refused to take the patient back when he was discharged. The willingness of English families to care for their mentally disordered relatives and to delay sending them to the hospital is further supported by Mills (1962). Most recently, in an American study, Barrett, Kuriansky, and Gurland (1972) found that 60 percent of the 85 families interviewed 4 weeks after patients were discharged expressed pleasure at the sudden return of a patient due to an unexpected hospital strike in New York State.

The question of who is willing to receive mental patients, and why, is a complicated one. Both acceptance and rejection have been reported in the literature. Overall impressions seem to differ, depending on the values and experiences of the observer. Lidz, Hotchkiss, and Greenblatt (1957), on the basis of their collective clinical experience, have spoken of stigma and withdrawal from the patient, starting at the time of hospitalization. Lemkau (1968), on the other hand, cited the "well-known clinical experience that families often resist the hospitalization of persons and that they often remove family members from the hospital against medical advice, facts not easily made consonant with a rejecting attitude toward mental patients" (p. 353).

Certainly, the absence of systematic empirical studies that take into account such reality factors as economic and social pressures on the family, optimism about outcome, the role the patient plays in the household, and life-cycle variables permits just this sort of individual speculation based on personal experience.

While social rejection in the general population derives logically from a consideration of stigma, the relationship is not so clear-cut in the families of patients where rejection may be more closely attuned to the practical realities of life. In Grad and Sainsbury's (1963b) study, for instance, 81 percent of the rejecting and negative relatives had reality problems, whereas only 62 percent of the "accepting" group were rated as having such problems. In any case, when the family ceases to interact with the patient because it believes that the patient's condition is irreversible (Cumming and Cumming 1965)—a not untenable notion in view of current recidivism rates—or when discharge plans are met with theoretical approval but actual reluctance, then one must introduce the issue of the cost to the family of maintaining ties with the mentally disordered.

Elaine Cumming (1968) has forcefully brought our attention to the fact that we pay only lip service to the patient's own community, the family and friends who must live with him when he returns after hospitalization. In the United States, she argues, we have ignored the aggravation placed on the community by our present zeal for sending patients home. British psychiatric researchers, on the other hand, have been more concerned with the family, and indeed were the first to raise the issue of family burden in their research. The picture that has emerged from their studies is that of a family willing to receive the mentally ill member back into the home, at least after the initial hospitalizations, but nonetheless hard pressed by the strain and demands of living with a former patient. The entire family is shouldering a burden because one of its members is mentally ill. With the increasing shift in hospital policy toward early release of the patient and home care, the degree to which the family is able or desires to take on and live with this burden is an extremely important consideration.

The first study in this area was done in England in the early 1960's (Grad and Sainsbury 1963a and 1963b). The authors were interested in seeing whether the trend toward caring for the patient in the community really resulted in additional burdens for the family. Families of patients referred to two different types of hospitals were interviewed at 1 month and at 2 years after referral. One hospital had a traditional policy of removing the patient from the community; the other stressed community care. The interviewing was done by a psychiatric social worker, who estimated the burden on the family by rating the effect the patient had on the family's income, social activities, and domestic and school routines, as well as the strain the patient put on other family members, and the problems he caused with neighbors. Grad and Sainsbury's hypothesis, that the burden would be greater when the hospital had a community-care approach, was confirmed. However, the authors believed their hypothesis was borne out not because of the greater attention required by the patient in the community-care program, but because burden was significantly lightened in families in the traditional hospital condition due to the regular visits to the home by the social work staff.

Somewhat later, Hoenig and Hamilton (1969) also studied family burden in two English communities where home care was the preferred method of treatment. The sample comprised 179 families who had lived continuously with a former patient for the 4 years prior to being interviewed. The investigators differentiated between *objective* and *subjective* burden by asking the family a single question on perceived burden and comparing that to a social worker's rating of the family's objective burden. Fifty-six percent of the families were rated as operating under an objective burden, with the parental home seemingly less burdened than the conjugal home. Fourteen percent of the families reported severe subjective burden, 40 percent reported moderate burden, and 46 percent reported no burden at all. None of the families who were rated as having no objective burden reported any subjective burden. If the patient was older, was from a conjugal home, and was rated as sicker or had spent more time in the hospital during the study period, then more subjective burden was experienced. The authors concluded that there was a great deal of *subjective tolerance* in view of the high objective burden.

While 90 percent of the families in this study were rated as sympathetic to the patient, 56 percent experienced great relief when inpatient admission was resorted to. Sixty-three percent of the latter group had complained of at least "some" burden. Overall, the families reported a remarkably high degree of satisfaction with the hospital and the treatment of the patient there. It was not reported whether this was truly satisfaction, a rationalization of their decision to hospitalize, or an acquiescent or socially desirable response.

One of the British studies uncovered very little objective burden in the families of schizophrenic patients (Mandelbrote and Folkard 1961). Only 4 of 171 families were judged to be suffering any distress due to burdens imposed by the patient. Brown et al. (1966) questioned this underreporting of burden and referred to the high percentage of unemployed men (40 percent) in the sample as cause for skepticism of the findings. However, the unusually high proportion of first admissions (59 percent) in the sample may account for the low rate of observed burden.

The reduction of burden and the sense of relief that was experienced by some families as a result of hospitalization of the patient (Grad and Sainsbury 1963b, Hoenig and Hamilton 1969, and Myers and Bean 1968) may be reason enough to explain their rejecting behavior. Kelman (1964), in discussing the implications of labeling and hospitalization for the families of brain-damaged children, states that lower-class deviance, while recognized, is not assigned the same priority of familial concern and resources as other more pressing problems. In this context, hospitalization and abandonment may be viewed as the removal of one more draining problem (see Myers and Bean 1968 and Myers and Roberts 1959 on this point). As demonstrated by Barrett, Kuriansky, and Gurland (1972), when the patient contributed to the household rather than taxed its

limited resources, there was significantly greater likelihood that the patient would remain out of the hospital. In such cases, the imputation of "felt" stigma as a cause for rejection of patients in high-problem groups may hardly be relevant to the issues determining behavior in these families.

The Effects of Attitudes on Outcome

Since the results of interactions between individuals are often highly influenced by the relevant attitudes of each individual, it has been generally assumed that the impact of those attitudes would strongly affect the experiences and posthospital adjustment of the patient. Indirect support for this assumption is available from studies showing that successful outcome was associated with the family settings to which patients returned (Carstairs 1959, Davis, Freeman, and Simmons 1957, Freeman and Simmons 1963, Michaux et al. 1969, and Wing et al. 1964). It is not unlikely that differing attitudes and expectations held by parents, spouses, or siblings are at least partially responsible for such findings.

Studies in which family attitudes appear as independent variables that influence community adjustment have generally concerned themselves with 1) positive or negative attitudes toward the patient, 2) attitudes about mental illness and mental hospitals, and 3) attitudes regarding tolerance of deviance.

Usually, investigators have assessed relatives' attitudes through an intensive, generally semistructured, interview or series of interviews. Measurement techniques have varied considerably in sophistication. Both direct and indirect measures have been used; and response categories have ranged from a "yes . . . no" to a Likert format. In some cases, overall ratings were made by trained interviewers. The most commonly used indicators of outcome have been community stay versus rehospitalization, and community adjustment as shown by ratings of symptomatology and role performance.

Outcome and Family Attitudes Toward the Patient

A direct test of the hypothesis that the positive or negative attitudes of a relative were related to outcome was conducted by Kelley (1964) while working with the Psychiatric Evaluation Project of the Veterans' Administration in Massachusetts. Family acceptance, whether the patient was wanted at home, the degree of understanding of the patient, and attitudes toward the hospital and toward deviant behavior were not found to be significantly related to patient outcome as measured by exacerbation of symptoms in a group of 65 discharged schizophrenics. A replication of the study (reported by Kelley in the same article) confirmed these findings.

Significant results, however, were reported by Carstairs (1959), who found that success in remaining in the community was associated with greater welcome, the presence of a "key person" (a woman willing to involve herself with the patient), positive attitudes, and a perception that the patient was not dangerous. Similarly Barrett, Kuriansky, and Gurland (1972) reported a significant relationship of family attitude to outcome. If the caretaker family recalled that its initial reaction to the patient's return was "very pleased," the patient tended to remain out of the hospital. Fifty-seven percent of the relatives of patients who did not require rehospitalization were initially "very pleased" at the patient's release; but only 7 percent of the relatives of those who were rehospitalized responded in this way. If the attitude of the family was negative, neutral, or simply "pleased," patients tended to return to the hospital. In the same interview, when families were asked how they felt about the patient's discharge after the patient had been home awhile, this same relationship was present to an even greater degree. Standard of living was also significantly related to community stay; patients with poorer care showed a greater tendency to remain out of the hospital.

While on the surface it appears reasonable to assume that family acceptance of the patient indicates a beneficial atmosphere for the former patient and would be positively correlated to outcome, the matter is not so simple. Brown, Carstairs, and Topping (1958) found that former patients living with mothers or wives had higher readmission rates than those living with siblings, distant kin, or in lodgings. They concluded that it was not always wise to send a schizophrenic back to close parental or marital homes even if the ties were affectionate. In an attempt to explicate this finding, Brown et al. (1962) interviewed 128 recently discharged patients and their female relatives and maintained contact with them and the patient throughout the 1st year after discharge. Utilizing the notion of an optimal level of emotional arousal, the authors hypothesized that a mental patient's behavior would deteriorate if he returned to a home where there was strongly expressed emotion of any sort. They further reasoned that in those families in which emotions ran high, rehospitalization could be avoided if family contact was minimal. Emotionality was measured by rating the interaction of the patient and his key relative on content of speech, tone of voice, and gestures. Their main hypothesis was confirmed. Patients had deteriorated in 75 percent of the "emotional" homes

and only 33 percent of the "nonemotional" homes. Extent of family contact was important, however, only for those moderately or severely disturbed at discharge. When past history, home situation, and condition at discharge were taken into account, the relationship between emotionality and deterioration was weakened, although not wholly destroyed.

To extend and refine this relationship, Brown, Birley, and Wing (1972) interviewed 101 schizophrenic patients and their families both before and after discharge. As in the previous study, the interaction of patient and relative in a joint interview was rated. An emotional expression score was derived, using the number of comments denoting criticism, hostility, dissatisfaction, warmth, and emotional overinvolvement. Again a significant association between high expressed emotion and relapse was found. The most significant component of this score was number of critical comments. Warmth could not be used in the overall index because it showed a curvilinear relationship with relapse. Patients in homes showing moderate warmth had the lowest relapse rate. Low-warmth relatives tended to be critical, and high-warmth relatives were overinvolved. The data indicated that it was the emotional expression, not previous work or behavior impairment, that was associated with relapse. Symptoms were also related to relapse, but independently of emotion.

This line of research is as important for its general theoretical and methodological implications as for its substantive findings. It clearly points to the need to examine more complex relationships in an interaction framework. It is not enough to relate family attitudes to outcome. Patient attitudes, their consequences for family attitudes, and patient behavior are equally important, and have too often been ignored. In the few studies attending to both patient and family attitudes, they were rarely analyzed in conjunction with one another. Yet the interaction between these sets of attitudes, their fit with one another and with various behaviors, will have to become the focus of new research if we believe the forces that influence relapse are embedded within a social matrix context. The use of an interactionist strategy would not only be consonant with the ecological approach used by many within the field of psychology today but would inevitably lead to the much-needed use of increasingly sophisticated methodological techniques.

Outcome and Family Attitudes Toward Mental Illness and Hospitals

Among early studies relating attitudes about mental illness or mental hospitals to outcome was one by Davis, Freeman, and Simmons (1957), who found that patients with high performance levels were most likely to have relatives with an environmental view of mental illness, favorable attitudes to mental hospitals, and the belief that mental illness does not basically change a person. In a long-term study conducted by two of these authors, Freeman and Simmons (1963), similar attitudes were again measured. Relatives of successful patients tended to see them as normal, as somewhat blameless, and as having positive attitudes toward the hospital. The more educated the respondent, the less the likelihood of blaming the patient. Opinions about the etiology of mental illness were unrelated to any measure of rehabilitation, but the authors felt this to be a function of poor scale construction. They did find that the family's perception of management problems and the patient's symptomatic behavior were associated with return to the hospital (see, also, Myers and Bean 1968).

Lorei (1964) administered the Opinions About Mental Illness (OMI) scale (Cohen and Struening 1962) to the relatives of 104 released patients and correlated these scores with success or failure in remaining in the community for 9 months. Only three of the five OMI factors related significantly to outcome. Low scores on Authoritarianism and Restrictiveness and a high score on Benevolence were associated with the patient's remaining in the community. Scores on Interpersonal Etiology and Mental Hygiene Ideology were unrelated to community stay: these findings are in line with those previously noted (Davis, Freeman, and Simmons 1957). The family's perception of the patients as not unlike normals and not responsible for their condition was related to success in the community but not to recidivism.

In another study, Bentinck (1967) used the OMI to gather data from 50 male schizophrenics and their relatives and 50 male medical patients and their families 9 months after discharge from the hospital. Families of mental patients differed from families of medical patients only in that the latter endorsed items of Mental Health Ideology more than the former. Contact with a mental patient appeared to be associated with less acceptance of the medical model of mental illness. Although Bentinck simply compared the four groups and did not relate scores to outcome, her study indicated a potential source of conflict for the mental patient both in the hospital and after his return. The relatives of mental patients, who generally came from the same social background as blue-collar hospital workers, were found to have attitudes more like those of the blue-collar hospital personnel than those of mental health professionals. They were generally more pessimistic about treatment outcome, more restrictive, and more authoritarian than mental health professionals. Thus, in both the hospital and home setting patients must deal with people

who have ideologies unlike their professional therapists'.

Outcome and Family Tolerance of Deviance

Since the behavior demonstrated by a former patient is occasionally disruptive and may be considered deviant by the family, a prominent subject for investigation has been the relatives' attitudes regarding deviant behavior. For instance, Deykin (1961) interviewed either the patient or the family in a followup of 13 chronic cases and judged the patient's community adjustment by examining personal appearance, psychiatric and social functioning, and quality of interpersonal relationships. Although the families in her sample were receiving intensive casework help, which may have influenced both tolerance and outcome, she concluded that family and community tolerance for the ex-mental patient was one of the central factors relating to successful discharge, even for those patients who showed poor community adjustment. Deykin hypothesized that the family's deep love for the patient and guilt about his illness were responsible for the low recidivism rate.

Generally, however, it has been hypothesized that tolerance of deviant behavior as shown by low expectations regarding work and social participation is a key factor affecting outcome. Lower-class patients and/or those returning to parental homes (each considered to be returning to settings with lower expectations regarding performance) were expected to have fewer relapses, or at least fewer rehospitalizations. An early study by Freeman and Simmons (1958 and 1959) provided support for these derivations. Poorly performing patients who managed to remain in the community tended to be lower class, they had other males in the family to take over their roles, and they were living in parental rather than conjugal homes. Similarly, mothers were found to be more tolerant of deviant behavior in studies by Brown, Carstairs, and Topping (1958), Brown et al. (1966), and Linn (1966). On the other hand, Michaux et al. (1969) reported a greater relapse rate for those returning to parental homes, and the relationship of social class and expectations to performance did not hold up for acute female mental patients returning to conjugal homes (Lefton et al. 1962). Posthospital performance in the latter study was best predicted by illness rather than class or expectations. The authors speculated that Freeman and Simmons' results may be true only for chronic male patients.

To obtain longitudinal data and to refine and extend their ideas, Freeman and Simmons (1963) conducted their classic year-long study of the posthospital experience of 649 men and women. In this study, the culmination of earlier investigations with the Massachusetts-based Community Health Project, Freeman and Simmons interviewed a key relative twice after the patient returned home. The informant (usually spouse or mother) was seen at about 6 weeks and 1 year after discharge. The interview tapped relatives' expectations regarding work, social participation and symptomatology, and the perceived performance in these areas. With respect to tolerance of deviance, they found, somewhat surprisingly, that relatives' expectations regarding work and social participation were high. In fact, former patients were expected to perform as anyone else did. There was little change in expectations throughout the posthospital year. Tolerance of deviance was directly related to performance—the higher the expectation, the higher the performance—but unrelated to successful community tenure. Unlike the results of Freeman and Simmons' earlier study, and in partial confirmation of Lefton et al. (1962), social class was unrelated to either expectations or successful community tenure. Social class was, however, related to performance.

Tolerance of deviance, defined as the extent to which a family will keep a symptomatic former patient at home, was the subject of two reports by Angrist et al. (1961 and 1968). Drawing heavily on Freeman and Simmons' conceptual and methodological model, they focused their attention on the posthospital experience of women only. In their 1961 article they described the results of a followup study of a sample of 264 women consecutively discharged from Columbus Psychiatric Institute in Ohio. This hospital is a short-term intensive therapy facility, where 90 percent of all admissions are voluntary and 75 percent are first admissions. Thus, the patient sample was from a higher socioeconomic class and had fewer psychotics and multiple-admission patients than is usual in samples drawn from State hospital populations. A significant other, generally a husband, was interviewed 6 months after discharge by a social worker who used a structured interview. Low tolerance of deviance was significantly related to higher social class and to good posthospital performance, even when severity of illness was controlled.

The final, more extensive analyses of these same data and data from a control sample of the former patients' female neighbors and their significant others were reported in Angrist et al. (1968). A smaller sample of schizophrenics was also interviewed at 1 year after discharge, and comparisons between and within the research groups were then made. The major hypothesis that tolerance of deviance (symptom tolerance) and role expectations would predict rehospitalization was not confirmed. Similarly, social class did not have a marked relationship to rehospitalization. As in Freeman and

Simmons' study (1963), tolerance of deviance and expectations were related to performance, with high-level performers having significant others low in tolerance and high in role expectations. Social class played no part in the posthospital performance of married women, at least directly. It did influence performance indirectly via class-related role expectations. The most significant predictor of failure and rehospitalization in this study was the reappearance of symptoms.

Relatives of normals and former patients differed on tolerance of deviance on only three items. When relatives of patients having organic problems were removed (these relatives were a special group low in expectations and high in tolerance), there were no differences between relatives of normals and the relatives of former patients except, obviously, in their perception of psychological difficulties.

A recent study by Michaux et al. (1969) also examined the family's expectations of the patient and the patient's social role performance, although the investigators did not specifically focus on tolerance of deviance. Monthly interviews were conducted with patients and, in most cases, a selected family member. Among other measures, information on the level of satisfaction with the patient's free time activities, the family's satisfaction with the patient's performance, and the occurrence of symptoms was collected. The patient's poor social role performance and the families' dissatisfaction, derived from their high but unmet expectations for the patient, were significant but not powerful predictors of rehospitalization. These findings were at variance with those of Freeman and Simmons (1963) and Angrist et al. (1968). In common with the above studies, an increase in general psychopathology was noted by the family prior to hospitalization.

In summary, we find conflicting results regarding the influence of positive familial attitudes on outcome. Emotional expressiveness and differential attitudes about mental illness were significantly related to outcome. Tolerance of deviance, whether defined by low expectations for work and social participation or the extent to which families will keep a symptomatic patient at home, has been only slightly related to relapse. Returning to a family low in tolerance of deviance was likely to result in higher role performance, but it did not prevent rehospitalization. Similarly, returning to a family displaying understanding and noncritical attitudes may increase the chances for success but does not reduce rehospitalization rates when the strains become too great. Mills (1962) noted that even though families were willing to care for their symptomatic relatives, once the stress of living with the sick members became too great, the hospital was more often seen as attractive and as a place for cure. If cure did not take place, a deterioration of the relationship between patient and family ensued. This process has also been discussed by Pitt (1969), who saw the patient using up the "reservoir of good will" held by the family.

On the whole, we are confronted with a scarcity of significant results relating family attitudinal variables to successful outcome. The only finding that appears and reappears consistently in the literature is that failure in the community and subsequent return to the hospital is accompanied by the reappearance of symptoms (Angrist et al. 1968, Brown et al. 1972, Freeman 1961, Freeman and Simmons 1963, Michaux et al. 1969, and Pasamanick et al. 1967).

Conclusions

The studies of the family's early reaction to the mental illness of a relative provide a first step in understanding the initial perception of deviant behavior, attempts at explanation, and the response to the deviant. While these studies have been enlightening and heuristic, they have suffered from the shortcomings frequently found in the initial exploration of a complex phenomenon. With a few exceptions, much of this research has been impressionistic in nature, inconsistent, descriptive rather than explanatory, limited in scope and techniques, and has failed to incorporate the type of controls that would permit clear conclusions to be drawn. Further difficulties in interpretation have resulted from the use of small samples and the lack of rigorous sampling procedures.

The affective components of the attitude toward the deviant and the sense of burden that the family feels have still been inadequately treated. Also relatively untouched are the family's beliefs about their patient-relative. Some studies have inferred the family's cognitions of the patient from responses to items about a hypothetically mentally ill person, but items directly examining family members' beliefs about their own deviant family member have rarely been included as part of the research design. Finally, the interactions of the various aspects of attitude (affective, conative, and cognitive) and their relationships to behavior still remain a subject for systematic study.

Contradictory data abound on almost every subject that has been discussed in this paper. It is entirely possible that these contradictions reflect true differences in the real world. Yet scant effort has been made to explain the differences or to resolve them. Perhaps this is due to a scatter-shot approach by researchers who, with a few exceptions, have failed to follow through on promising leads in their own data. The lack of sustained interest has left us with fundamental pieces of information missing, and the promise in the early and thoughtful work reported by Clausen and Yarrow has hardly been actualized; this is unfortunate in light of the current emphasis on early detection and treatment of mental illness and the increasing trend toward shorter hospital stay and more extensive home care.

Research on the relationship of family attitudes to outcome has more often been conceptually sophisticated and programmatic. Yet here again results are inconsistent, which may be because few studies have focused on complex interrelated variables. For example, little effort has been directed at the measurement and analysis of patient and family variables in conjunction with one another. In addition, investigators have mainly studied families containing a sick member and have failed to establish any comparative baselines of attitudes for families with a member exhibiting a different type of deviance or for families without any sick member at all.

The perennial question of directionality is also a problem. Much of the research has viewed the patient in the role of reactor to the attitudes and behavior of the family. Researchers have assumed that family attitudes to deviance strongly influence the behavior of the former patient, particularly with regard to community tenure. Such a unilateral perspective has led them to neglect research aimed at distinguishing the extent to which attitudes of relatives are a function of the condition of the patients with whom they reside. Both Freeman and Simmons (1963) and Angrist et al. (1968) initiated their research with the hypothesis that family attitudes determine patient functioning. They concluded, however, that tolerance and expectations *reflect* patient functioning.

Evidence to support this conclusion is found in a dissertation that examined the effect of multiple hospitalizations on the role the patient plays within the family (Dunigan 1970). This study of the 66 husbands of patient-wives with varying numbers of hospitalizations indicated that there is a critical point at which expectations and tolerances change. Husbands seemed able to cope with one or two hospitalizations and to make temporary role adaptations to the deviant behavior of the wife-mother. With three or more hospitalizations, however, husbands withdrew from the wife, lowered their role expectations, and made other more permanent arrangements for the continued functioning of the household. These events in turn served to strain marital ties and to isolate the wife within the family setting. Dunigan concluded that families eventually exhaust their resources to expand and contract in ways that keep the wife-mother a contributing member of the family system.

This research is a promising move toward an interactional model of patient-family relationships. It would be furthered still more by the use of nonretrospective longitudinal research that would follow the family and patient through the various phases of their reciprocal role in the mental patient's career.

It is interesting to note that most investigators have concentrated on women's perceptions and expectations as they relate to male patients. While this is understandable, in terms of the supportive role that females in our society are expected to play regarding the sick, we are left with meager knowledge about the perceptions and expectations of males and the differential effect on the family of the illness of men or women. One study that did present comparative data on this point (Rogler and Hollingshead 1965) reported striking differences in the response of the family and the effects on it of having a wife or a husband as the ill member. When husbands were ill, the wife frequently added his work role to her own nurturant one and the family was maintained as a functioning unit. Illness on the part of the wife had a pervasive and destructive influence on the family organization, since the husbands were unable or unwilling to take on parts of the female role. Although this study was done in a traditional society (Puerto Rico) in which male and female roles are very clearly elaborated, it does alert us to the various modes of adaptation to a stressful situation that may occur in our society as a result of sex-role and life-cycle differences.

A final important issue pertains to the type of attitudes measured. As noted before, the appearance of symptoms preceded rehospitalization in numerous cases. At the same time, work and social participation were only weakly related to rehospitalization. It may be that family expectations regarding work, social participation, and patient behavior in these areas are not important correlates of relapse, even though they concern aspects of instrumental performance that are considered important indicators of recovery and integration within our social system. In the only study that defined tolerance of deviance in terms of symptoms, Angrist et al. (1968) asked their informants to judge symptoms for which they would return the patient to the hospital. A tolerance-of-deviance score was derived from these responses, but this score was not a strong predictor of rehospitalization. However, it is difficult to know whether family members were responding according to their perception of the severity of the symptoms or were reacting in terms of personal discomfort. An approach that emphasizes the family's personal reactions to the particular symptom the patient is exhibiting, the tolerance of the patient for his own symptoms, and the meaning the symptoms have to both the patient and the family may prove to be more fruitful.

We are dealing here with an extremely complex set of interacting variables, and it seems likely that the important information is to be found in the interactions rather than in one or another main effect. The literature we have examined tends to be inconsistent, since specified variables may have different effects, depending on their interrelationships with other variables. What appears to be required is truly multivariate research.

REFERENCES

Adler, L. Patients of a State mental hospital: The outcome of their hospitalization. In: Rose, A., ed. *Mental Health and Mental Disorder*. New York: W. W. Norton & Company, Inc., 1955. pp. 501–523.

Alivisatos, G., and Lyketsos, G. A preliminary report of a research concerning the attitude of the families of hospitalized mental patients. *International Journal of Social Psychiatry*, 10:37–44, 1964. Also in: Spitzer, S., and Denzin, N., eds. *The Mental Patient: Studies in the Sociology of Deviance*. New York: McGraw-Hill, Inc., 1968.

Angrist, S.; Lefton, M.; Dinitz, S.; and Pasamanick, B. Tolerance of deviant behavior, posthospital performance levels and rehospitalization. In: *Proceedings of the Third World Congress of Psychiatry*. Vol. 1. Toronto: University of Toronto Press, 1961. pp. 237–241.

Angrist, S.; Lefton, M.; Dinitz, S.; and Pasamanick, B. *Women After Treatment: A Study of Former Mental Patients and Their Normal Neighbors*. New York: Appleton-Century-Crofts, 1968.

Barker, R. The social psychology of physical disability. *Journal of Social Issues*, 4:28–34, 1948.

Barrett, J., Jr.; Kuriansky, J.; and Gurland, B. Community tenure following emergency discharge. *American Journal of Psychiatry*, 128:958–964, 1972.

Bentinck, C. Opinions about mental illness held by patients and relatives. *Family Process*, 6:193–207, 1967.

Bizon, Z.; Godorowski, K.; Henisz, J.; and Razniewski, A. "The Attitudes of Warsaw Inhabitants Toward Mental Illness." Unpublished manuscript, Laboratory of Social Psychiatry, Department of Psychiatry, Medical School, Warsaw, Poland, no date. (Mimeo.)

Bogardus, E. Measuring social distance. *Journal of Applied Sociology*, 9:299–308, 1925.

Brown, G.; Birley, J.; and Wing, J. Influence of family life in the course of schizophrenic disorders: A replication. *British Journal of Psychiatry*, 121:241–258, 1972.

Brown, G.; Bone, M.; Dalison, B.; and Wing, J. *Schizophrenia and Social Care*. London: Oxford University Press, 1966.

Brown, G.; Carstairs, G. M.; and Topping, G. Post-hospital adjustment of chronic mental patients. *Lancet*, 2:685–689, 1958.

Brown, G.; Monck, E.; Carstairs, G. M.; and Wing, J. Influence of family life in the course of schizophrenic illness. *British Journal of Preventive and Social Medicine*, 16:55–68, 1962.

Bruner, J., and Tagiuri, R. The perception of people. In: Lindzey, G., ed. *Handbook of Social Psychology*. Cambridge: Addison-Wesley, 1954. pp. 634–654.

Carstairs, G. M. The social limits of eccentricity: An English study. In: Opler, M. K., ed. *Culture and Mental Health: Cross-Cultural Studies*. New York: Macmillan Company, 1959. pp. 373–389.

Chin-Shong, E. "Rejection of the Mentally Ill: A Comparison with the Findings on Ethnic Prejudice." Unpublished doctoral dissertation, Columbia University, New York, N.Y., 1968.

Clausen, J. "The Marital Relationship Antecedent to Hospitalization of a Spouse for Mental Illness." Presented at the Annual Meeting of the American Sociological Association, Chicago, Ill., September 1959.

Clausen, J., and Yarrow, M. R., eds. The impact of mental illness on the family. *Journal of Social Issues*, 11(4):1955.

Cohen, J., and Struening, E. Opinions about mental illness in the personnel of two large mental hospitals. *Journal of Abnormal and Social Psychology*, 64:349–360, 1962.

Cumming, E. Community psychiatry in a divided labor. In: Zubin, J., and Freyhan, F., eds. *Social Psychiatry*. New York: Grune & Stratton, Inc., 1968. pp. 100–113.

Cumming, E., and Cumming, J. *Closed Ranks: An Experiment in Mental Health Education*. Cambridge, Mass.: Harvard University Press, 1957.

Cumming, J., and Cumming, E. On the stigma of mental illness. *Community Mental Health Journal*, 1 (Summer):135–143, 1965.

Davis, J.; Freeman, H.; and Simmons, O. Rehospitalization and performance levels of former mental patients. *Social Problems*, 5:37–44, 1957.

Deykin, E. The reintegration of the chronic schizophrenic patient discharged to his family and community as perceived by the family. *Mental Hygiene*, 45:235–246, 1961.

Dunigan, J. "Mental Hospital Career and Family Expectations." Unpublished manuscript, Laboratory of Psychosocial Research, Cleveland Psychiatric Institute, Cleveland, Ohio, 1969. (Mimeo.)

Evans, A.; Bullard, D., Jr.; and Solomon, M. The family as a potential resource in the rehabilitation of the chronic schizophrenic patient: A study of 60 patients and their families. *American Journal of Psychiatry*, 117:1075–1083, 1961.

Festinger, L.; Gerard, H. B.; Hymovitch, H.; Kelley, H.; and Rosen, B. The influence process in the presence of extreme deviates. *Human Relations*, 5:327–346, 1952.

Fontana, A. Familial etiology of schizophrenia: Is scientific method possible? *Psychological Bulletin*, 66:214–227, 1966.

Frank, G. H. The role of the family in the development of psychopathology. *Psychological Bulletin*, 64:191–205, 1965.

Freeman, H. Attitudes toward mental illness among relatives of former patients. *American Sociological Review*, 26:59–66, 1961.

Freeman, H., and Simmons, O. Mental patients in the community: Family settings and performance levels. *American Sociological Review*, 23:147–154, 1958. Also in: Spitzer, S., and Denzin, N., eds. *The Mental Patient: Studies in the Sociology of Deviance*. New York: McGraw-Hill, Inc., 1968.

Freeman, H., and Simmons, O. Social class and posthospital performance levels. *American Sociological Review*, 24:345–351, 1959. Also in: Spitzer, S., and Denzin, N., eds. *The Mental Patient: Studies in the Sociology of Deviance*. New York: McGraw-Hill, Inc., 1968.

Freeman, H., and Simmons, O. Feelings of stigma among relatives of former mental patients. *Social Problems*, 8:312–321, 1961. Also in: Spitzer, S., and Denzin, N., eds. *The Mental Patient: Studies in the Sociology of Deviance*. New York: McGraw-Hill, Inc., 1968.

Freeman, H., and Simmons, O. *The Mental Patient Comes Home*. New York: John Wiley & Sons, Inc., 1963.

Gillis, L., and Keet, M. Factors underlying the retention in the community of chronic unhospitalized schizophrenics. *British Journal of Psychiatry*, 111:1057–1067, 1965.

Goffman, E. *Stigma: Notes on the Management of a Spoiled Identity*. Englewood Cliffs, N.J.: Prentice-Hall, Inc., 1963.

Grad, J., and Sainsbury, P. Evaluating a community care service. In: Freeman, H., and Farndale, J., eds. *Trends in the Mental Health Services*. New York: Macmillan Company, 1963a. pp. 303–317.

Grad, J., and Sainsbury, P. Mental illness and the family. *Lancet*, 1:544–547, 1963b.

Hoenig, J., and Hamilton, M. *The Desegregation of the Mentally Ill*. London: Routledge and Kegan Paul, Ltd., 1969.

Hollingshead, A., and Redlich, F. *Social Class and Mental Illness*. New York: John Wiley & Sons, Inc., 1958.

Kelley, F. Relatives' attitude and outcome in schizophrenia. *Archives of General Psychiatry*, 10:389–394, 1964.

Kelman, H. The effect of a brain-damaged child on the family. In: Birch, H. G., ed. *Brain Damage in Children*. Baltimore, Md.: The Williams & Wilkins Company, 1964. pp. 77–98.

Korkes, L. The impact of mentally ill children upon their

parents. *Dissertation Abstracts,* 19 (June):3392−3393, 1959. (Abstract)

Lederer, H. How the sick view their world. *Journal of Social Issues,* 8:4−15, 1952.

Lefton, M.; Angrist, S.; Dinitz, S.; and Pasamanick, B. Social class, expectations and performance of mental patients. *American Journal of Sociology,* 68:79−87, 1962.

Lemkau, P. Evaluation of the effect of changes in environmental factors, with special attention to public attitudes toward mental health and mental illness. In: Zubin, J., and Freyhan, F., eds. *Social Psychiatry.* New York: Grune & Stratton, Inc., 1968. pp. 349−362.

Lewin, K. Self-hatred among Jews. In: Lewin, G., ed. *Resolving Social Conflicts.* New York: Harper, 1948. pp. 186−200.

Lewis, V., and Zeichner, A. Impact of admission to a mental hospital on the patient's family. *Mental Hygiene,* 44:503−509, 1960.

Lidz, T.; Hotchkiss, G.; and Greenblatt, M. Patient-family-hospital interrelationships: Some general considerations. In: Greenblatt, M.; Levinson, D.; and Williams, R., eds. *The Patient and the Mental Hospital.* Glencoe, Ill.: The Free Press, 1957. pp. 535−543.

Linn, M. Of wedding bells and apron strings: A study of relatives' attitudes. *Family Process,* 50:100−103, 1966.

Lorei, T. Prediction of length of stay out of the hospital for released psychiatric patients. *Journal of Consulting Psychology,* 28:358−363, 1964.

Mandelbrote, B., and Folkard, S. Some factors related to outcome and social adjustment in schizophrenia. *Acta Psychiatrica Scandinavica,* 37:223−235, 1961.

Mayo, C.; Havelock, R.; and Simpson, D. Attitudes towards mental illness among psychiatric patients and their wives. *Journal of Clinical Psychology,* 27:128−132, 1971.

Michaux, W.; Katz, M.; Kurland, A.; and Gansereit, K. *The First Year Out: Mental Patients after Hospitalization.* Baltimore, Md.: The Johns Hopkins Press, 1969.

Mills, E. *Living with Mental Illness: A Study in East London.* London: Routledge and Kegan Paul, Ltd., 1962.

Mosher, L. R., and Gunderson, J. G. Special report: Schizophrenia, 1972. *Schizophrenia Bulletin,* No. 7:10−52, Winter 1973.

Myers, J., and Bean, L. *A Decade Later: A Follow-up of Social Class and Mental Illness.* New York: John Wiley & Sons, Inc., 1968.

Myers, J., and Roberts, B. *Family and Class Dynamics in Mental Illness.* New York: John Wiley & Sons, Inc., 1959.

Nunnally, J. *Popular Conceptions of Mental Health: Their Development and Change.* New York: Holt, Rinehart and Winston, Inc., 1961.

Parsons, T. *The Social System.* Glencoe, Ill.: The Free Press, 1951.

Parsons, T., and Fox, R. Illness, therapy and the modern urban American family. *Journal of Social Issues,* 8:31−44, 1952.

Pasamanick, B.; Scarpetti, F.; and Dinitz, S. *Schizophrenics in the Community: An Experimental Study in the Prevention of Rehospitalization.* New York: Appleton-Century-Crofts, 1967.

Phillips, D. Rejection: A possible consequence of seeking help for mental disorders. *American Sociological Review,* 28:963−972, 1963. Also in: Spitzer, S., and Denzin, N., eds. *The Mental Patient: Studies in the Sociology of Deviance.* New York: McGraw-Hill, Inc., 1968.

Pitt, R. "The Concept of Family Burden." Presented at the Annual Meeting of the American Psychiatric Association, 1969.

Rabkin, J. Opinions about mental illness: A review of the literature. *Psychological Bulletin,* 77:153−171, 1972.

Rawnsley, K.; Loudon, J. B.; and Miles, H. L. Attitudes of relatives to patients in mental hospitals. *British Journal of Preventive and Social Medicine,* 16:1−15, 1962.

Rogler, L., and Hollingshead, A. *Trapped: Families and Schizophrenia.* New York: John Wiley & Sons, Inc., 1965.

Rose, C. Relatives' attitudes and mental hospitalization. *Mental Hygiene,* 43:194−203, 1959.

Safilios-Rothschild, C. Deviance and mental illness in the Greek family. *Family Process,* 7:100−117, 1968.

Sakamoto, Y. A study of the attitude of Japanese families of schizophrenics toward their ill members. *Psychotherapy and Psychosomatics,* 17:365−374, 1969.

Sampson, H.; Messinger, S.; and Towne, R. Family processes and becoming a mental patient. *American Journal of Sociology,* 68:88−96, 1962. Also in: Spitzer, S., and Denzin, N., eds. *The Mental Patient: Studies in the Sociology of Deviance.* New York: McGraw-Hill, Inc., 1968.

Schachter, S. Deviation, rejection, and communication. *Journal of Abnormal and Social Psychology,* 46:190−207, 1951.

Scheff, T. The role of the mentally ill and the dynamics of mental disorder: A research framework. *Sociometry,* 26:436−453, 1963. Also in: Spitzer, S., and Denzin, N., eds. *The Mental Patient: Studies in the Sociology of Deviance.* New York: McGraw-Hill, Inc., 1968.

Schwartz, C. The stigma of mental illness. *Journal of Rehabilitation,* 21:7, 1956.

Schwartz, C. Perspectives on deviance: Wives' definitions of their husbands' mental illness. *Psychiatry,* 20:275−291, 1957.

Sommer, R. Letter-writing in a mental hospital. *American Journal of Psychiatry,* 115:514−517, 1958.

Sommer, R. Visitors to mental hospitals: A fertile field for research. *Mental Hygiene,* 43:8−15, 1959.

Spiegel, J., and Bell, N. The family of the psychiatric patient. In: Arieti, S., ed. *The American Handbook of Psychiatry.* New York: Basic Books, Inc., 1959. pp. 114–149.

Spitzer, S.; Morgan, P.; and Swanson, R. Determinants of the psychiatric patient career: Family reaction patterns and social work intervention. *Social Service Review,* 45:74–85, 1971.

Star, S. "The Public's Ideas about Mental Illness." Unpublished manuscript, National Opinion Research Center, University of Chicago, 1955. (Mimeo.)

Swanson, R., and Spitzer, S. Stigma and the psychiatric patient career. *Journal of Health and Social Behavior,* 11:44–51, 1970.

Swingle, P. Relatives' concepts of mental patients. *Mental Hygiene,* 49:461–465, 1965.

Waters, M., and Northover, J. Rehabilitated long-stay schizophrenics in the community. *British Journal of Psychiatry,* 111:258–267, 1965.

Whatley, C. Social attitudes toward discharged mental patients. *Social Problems,* 6:313–320, 1959. Also in: Spitzer, S., and Denzin, N., eds. *The Mental Patient: Studies in the Sociology of Deviance.* New York: McGraw-Hill, Inc., 1968.

Wing, J.; Monck, E.; Brown, G.; and Carstairs, G. M. Morbidity in the community of schizophrenic patients discharged from London mental hospitals in 1959. *British Journal of Psychiatry,* 110:10–21, 1964.

Wynne, L.; Ryckoff, I.; Day, J.; and Hirsch, S. Pseudomutuality in the family relations of schizophrenics. *Psychiatry,* 21:205–220, 1958.

Yarrow, M.; Clausen, J.; and Robbins, P. The social meaning of mental illness. *Journal of Social Issues,* 11:33–48, 1955.

Yarrow, M.; Schwartz, C.; Murphy, H.; and Deasy, L. The psychological meaning of mental illness in the family. *Journal of Social Issues,* 11:12–24, 1955.

Acknowledgment

The preparation of this article was supported in part by National Institute of Mental Health Grant 1 RO 1 MH 21574-01. The authors would like to thank the staff of the Community Research Program for their contributions to the paper, particularly Ms. Carol Weiss, who assisted in the initial bibliographic search. They would also like to express their gratitude to Professor Richard Christie and Dr. Harold Markus for their very valuable comments about the organization and content of the paper.

ERVING GOFFMAN

The Moral Career of the Mental Patient: Prepatient Phase

Traditionally the term *career* has been reserved for those who expect to enjoy the rises laid out within a respectable profession. The term is coming to be used, however, in a broadened sense to refer to any social strand of any person's course through life. The perspective of natural history is taken: unique outcomes are neglected in favor of such changes over time as are basic and common to the members of a social category, although occurring independently to each of them. Such a career is not a thing that can be brilliant or disappointing; it can no more be a success than a failure. In this light, I want to consider the mental patient.

Reprinted from *Psychiatry,* Vol. **22,** No. 2 (May, 1959), by permission of the author and publisher.

One value of the concept of career is its two-sidedness. One side is linked to internal matters held dearly and closely, such as image of self and felt identity; the other side concerns official position, jural relations, and style of life, and is part of a publicly accessible institutional complex. The concept of career, then, allows one to move back and forth between the personal and the public, between the self and its significant society, without having to rely overly for data upon what the person says he thinks he imagines himself to be.

This paper, then, is an exercise in the institutional approach to the study of self. The main concern will be with the *moral* aspects of career—that is, the regular sequence of changes that career entails in the person's self and in his framework of imagery for judging himself and others.[1]

The category "mental patient" itself will be understood in one strictly sociological sense. In this perspective, the psychiatric view of a person becomes significant only in so far as this view itself alters his social fate—an alteration which seems to become fundamental in our society when, and only when, the person is put through the process of hospitalization.[2] I therefore exclude certain neighboring categories: the undiscovered candidates who would be judged "sick" by psychiatric standards but who never come to be viewed as such by themselves or others, although they may cause everyone a great deal of trouble;[3] the office patient whom a psychiatrist feels he can handle with drugs or shock on the outside; the mental client who engages in psychotherapeutic relationships. And I include anyone, however robust in temperament, who somehow gets caught up in the heavy machinery of mental-hospital servicing. In this way the effects of being treated as a mental patient can be kept quite distinct from the effects upon a person's life of traits a clinician would view as psychopathological.[4] Persons who become mental-hospital patients vary widely in the kind and degree of

1. Material on moral career can be found in early social anthropological work on ceremonies of status transition, and in classic social psychological descriptions of those spectacular changes in one's view of self that can accompany participation in social movements and sects. Recently new kinds of relevant data have been suggested by psychiatric interest in the problem of "identity" and sociological studies of work careers and "adult socialization."

2. This point has recently been made by Elaine and John Cumming, *Closed Ranks* (Cambridge: Commonwealth Fund, Harvard University Press, 1957), pp. 101–2: *"Clinical experience supports the impression that many people define mental illness as 'that condition for which a person is treated in a mental hospital.' . . . Mental illness, it seems, is a condition which afflicts people who must go to a mental institution, but until they go almost anything they do is normal."* Leila Deasy has pointed out to me the correspondence here with the situation in white-collar crime. Of those who are detected in this activity, only the ones who do not manage to avoid going to prison find themselves accorded the social role of the criminal.

3. Case records in mental hospitals are just now coming to be exploited to show the incredible amount of trouble a person may cause for himself and others before anyone begins to think about him psychiatrically, let alone take psychiatric action against him. See John A. Clausen and Marian Radke Yarrow, "Paths to the Mental Hospital," *Journal of Social Issues*, XI(1955), pp. 25–32; August B. Hollingshead and Frederick C. Redlich, *Social Class and Mental Illness* (New York: Wiley, 1958), pp. 173–74.

4. An illustration of how this perspective may be taken to all forms of deviancy may be found in Edwin Lemert, *Social Pathology* (New York: McGraw-Hill, 1951), see especially pp. 74–76. A specific application to mental defectives may be found in Stewart E. Perry, "Some Theoretic Problems of Mental Deficiency and Their Action Implications," *Psychiatry*, XVII (1954), pp. 45–73, see especially pp. 67–68.

illness that a psychiatrist would impute to them, and in the attributes by which laymen would describe them. But once started on the way, they are confronted by some importantly similar circumstances and respond to these in some importantly similar ways. Since these similarities do not come from mental illness, they would seem to occur in spite of it. It is thus a tribute to the power of social forces that the uniform status of mental patient cannot only assure an aggregate of persons a common fate and eventually, because of this, a common character, but that this social reworking can be done upon what is perhaps the most obstinate diversity of human materials that can be brought together by society. Here there lacks only the frequent forming of a protective group life by ex-patients to illustrate in full the classic cycle of response by which deviant subgroupings are psychodynamically formed in society.

This general sociological perspective is heavily reinforced by one key finding of sociologically oriented students in mental-hospital research. As has been repeatedly shown in the study of non-literate societies, the awesomeness, distastefulness, and barbarity of a foreign culture can decrease to the degree that the student becomes familiar with the point of view to life that is taken by his subjects. Similarly, the student of mental hospitals can discover that the craziness or "sick behavior" claimed for the mental patient is by and large a product of the claimant's social distance from the situation that the patient is in, and is not primarily a product of mental illness. Whatever the refinements of the various patients' psychiatric diagnoses, and whatever the special ways in which social life on the "inside" is unique, the researcher can find that he is participating in a community not significantly different from any other he has studied. Of course, while restricting himself to the off-ward grounds community of paroled patients, he may feel, as some patients do, that life in the locked wards is bizarre; and while on a locked admissions or convalescent ward, he may feel that chronic "back" wards are socially crazy places. But he need only move his sphere of sympathetic participation to the "worst" ward in the hospital, and this, too, can come into social focus as a place with a livable and continuously meaningful social world. This in no way denies that he will find a minority in any ward or patient group that continues to seem quite beyond the capacity to follow rules of social organization, or that the orderly fulfillment of normative expectations in patient society is partly made possible by strategic measures that have somehow come to be institutionalized in mental hospitals.

The career of the mental patient falls popularly and

naturalistically into three main phases: the period prior to entering the hospital, which I shall call the prepatient phase; the period in the hospital, the inpatient phase; the period after discharge from the hospital, should this occur, namely, the ex-patient phase.[5] This paper will deal only with the first two phases.

The Prepatient Phase

A relatively small group of prepatients come into the mental hospital willingly, because of their own idea of what will be good for them, or because of wholehearted agreement with the relevant members of their family. Presumably these recruits have found themselves acting in a way which is evidence to them that they are losing their minds or losing control of themselves. This view of oneself would seem to be one of the most pervasively threatening things that can happen to the self in our society, especially since it is likely to occur at a time when the person is in any case sufficiently troubled to exhibit the kind of symptom which he himself can see. As Sullivan described it,

> What we discover in the self-system of a person undergoing schizophrenic change or schizophrenic processes, is then, in its simplest form, an extremely fear-marked puzzlement, consisting of the use of rather generalized and anything but exquisitely refined referential processes in an attempt to cope with what is essentially a failure at being human—a failure at being anything that one could respect as worth being.[6]

Coupled with the person's disintegrative re-evaluation of himself will be the new, almost equally pervasive circumstance of attempting to conceal from others what he takes to be the new fundamental facts about himself, and attempting to discover whether others, too, have discovered them.[7] Here I want to stress that perception of losing one's mind is based on culturally derived and socially engrained stereotypes as to the significance of symptoms such as hearing voices, losing temporal and spatial orientation, and sensing that one is being followed, and that many of the most spectacular and

convincing of these symptoms in some instances psychiatrically signify merely a temporary emotional upset in a stressful situation, however terrifying to the person at the time. Similarly, the anxiety consequent upon this perception of oneself, and the strategies devised to reduce this anxiety, are not a product of abnormal psychology, but would be exhibited by any person socialized into our culture who came to conceive person socialized into our culture who came to conceive of himself as someone losing his mind. Interestingly, subcultures in American society apparently differ in the amount of ready imagery and encouragement they supply for such self-views, leading to differential rates of *self*-referral; the capacity to take this disintegrative view of oneself without psychiatric prompting seems to be one of the questionable cultural privileges of the upper classes.[8]

For the person who has come to see himself—with whatever justification—as mentally unbalanced, entrance to the mental hospital can sometimes bring relief, perhaps in part because of the sudden transformation in the structure of his basic social situation; instead of being to himself a questionable person trying to maintain a role as a full one, he can become an officially questioned person known to himself to be not so questionable as that. In other cases, hospitalization can make matters worse for the willing patient, confirming by the objective situation what has theretofore been a matter of the private experience of self.

Once the willing prepatient enters the hospital, he may go through the same routine of experiences as do those who enter unwillingly. In any case, it is the latter that I mainly want to consider, since in America at present these are by far the more numerous kind.[9] Their approach to the institution takes one of three classic forms: they come because they have been implored by their family or threatened with the abrogation of family ties unless they go "willingly"; they come by force under police escort; they come under misapprehension purposely induced by others, this last restricted mainly to youthful prepatients.

The prepatient's career may be seen in terms of an extrusory model; he starts out with relationships and rights, and ends up, at the beginning of his hospital stay, with hardly any of either. The moral aspects of this career, then, typically begin with the experience of

---

5. This simple picture is complicated by the somewhat special experience of roughly a third of ex-patients—namely, readmission to the hospital, this being the recidivist or "repatient" phase.

6. Harry Stack Sullivan, *Clinical Studies in Psychiatry,* edited by Helen Swick Perry, Mary Ladd Gawel, and Martha Gibbon (New York: Norton, 1956), pp. 184–85.

7. This moral experience can be contrasted with that of a person learning to become a marihuana addict, whose discovery that he can be "high" and still "op" effectively without being detected apparently leads to a new level of use. See Howard S. Becker, "Marihuana Use and Social Control," *Social Problems,* III (1955), pp. 35–44; see especially pp. 40–41.

8. See Hollingshead and Redlich, *op. cit.,* p. 187, Table 6, where relative frequency is given of self-referral by social class grouping.

9. The distinction employed here between willing and unwilling patients cuts across the legal one of voluntary and committed, since some persons who are glad to come to the mental hospital may be legally committed, and of those who come only because of strong familial pressure, some may sign themselves in as voluntary patients.

abandonment, disloyalty, and embitterment. This is the case even though to others it may be obvious that he was in need of treatment, and even though in the hospital he may soon come to agree.

The case histories of most mental patients document offenses against some arrangement for face-to-face living—a domestic establishment, a work place, a semi-public organization such as a church or store, a public region such as a street or park. Often there is also a record of some *complainant*, some figure who takes that action against the offender which eventually leads to his hospitalization. This may not be the person who makes the first move, but it is the person who makes what turns out to be the first effective move. Here is the *social* beginning of the patient's career, regardless of where one might locate the psychological beginning of his mental illness.

The kinds of offenses which lead to hospitalization are felt to differ in nature from those which lead to other extrusory consequences—to imprisonment, divorce, loss of job, disownment, regional exile, non-institutional psychiatric treatment, and so forth. But little seems known about these differentiating factors; and when one studies actual commitments, alternate outcomes frequently appear to have been possible. It seems true, moreover, that for every offense that leads to an effective complaint, there are many psychiatrically similar ones that never do. No action is taken; or action is taken which leads to other extrusory outcomes; or ineffective action is taken, leading to the mere pacifying or putting off of the person who complains. Thus, as Clausen and Yarrow have nicely shown, even offenders who are eventually hospitalized are likely to have had a long series of ineffective actions taken against them.[10]

Separating those offenses which could have been used as grounds for hospitalizing the offender from those that are so used, one finds a vast number of what students of occupation call career contingencies.[11] Some of these contingencies in the mental patient's career have been suggested, if not explored, such as socio-economic status, visibility of the offense, proximity to a mental hospital, amount of treatment facilities available, community regard for the type of treatment given in available hospitals, and so on.[12] For information about other contingencies one must rely on atrocity tales: a psychotic

man is tolerated by his wife until she finds herself a boy friend, or by his adult children until they move from a house to an apartment; an alcoholic is sent to a mental hospital because the jail is full, and a drug addict because he declines to avail himself of psychiatric treatment on the outside; a rebellious adolescent daughter can no longer be managed at home because she now threatens to have an open affair with an unsuitable companion; and so on. Correspondingly there is an equally important set of contingencies causing the person to by-pass this fate. And should the person enter the hospital, still another set of contingencies will help determine when he is to obtain a discharge—such as the desire of his family for his return, the availability of a "manageable" job, and so on. The society's official view is that inmates of mental hospitals are there primarily because they are suffering from mental illness. However, in the degree that the "mentally ill" outside hospitals numerically approach or surpass those inside hospitals, one could say that mental patients distinctively suffer not from mental illness, but from contingencies.

Career contingencies occur in conjunction with a second feature of the prepatient's career—the circuit of agents—and agencies—that participate fatefully in his passage from civilian to patient status.[13] Here is an instance of that increasingly important class of social system whose elements are agents and agencies which are brought into systemic connection through having to take up and send on the same persons. Some of these agent roles will be cited now, with the understanding that in any concrete circuit a role may be filled more than once, and that the same person may fill more than one of them.

First is the *next-of-relation*—the person whom the prepatient sees as the most available of those upon whom he should be able to depend most in times of trouble, in this instance the last to doubt his sanity and the first to have done everything to save him from the fate which, it transpires, he has been approaching. The patient's next-of-relation is usually his next of kin; the special term is introduced because he need not be. Second is the *complainant*, the person who retrospectively appears to have started the person on his way to the hospital. Third are the *mediators*—the sequence of agents and agencies to which the prepatient is referred and through which he is relayed and processed on his way to the hospital. Here are included police, clergy, general medical practitioners, office psychiatrists, personnel in public clinics, lawyers, social service workers, schoolteachers, and so on. One of these agents will have the legal mandate to

10. Clausen and Yarrow, *op. cit.*

11. An explicit application of this notion to the field of mental health may be found in Edwin Lemert, "Legal Commitment and Social Control," *Sociology and Social Research*, XXX (1946), pp. 370–78.

12. For example, Jerome K. Meyers and Leslie Schaffer, "Social Stratification and Psychiatric Practice: A Study of an Outpatient Clinic," *American Sociological Review*, XIX (1954), pp. 307–10; Lemert, *op. cit.*, pp. 402–3; *Patients in Mental Institutions*, 1941 (Washington, D.C.: Department of Commerce, Bureau of the Census, 1941), p. 2.

13. For one circuit of agents and its bearing on career contingencies, see Oswald Hall, "The Stages of a Medical Career," *American Journal of Sociology*, LIII (1948), pp. 327–36.

sanction commitment and will exercise it, and so those agents who precede him in the process will be involved in something whose outcome is not yet settled. When the mediators retire from the scene, the prepatient has become an inpatient, and the significant agent has become the hospital administrator.

While the complainant usually takes action in a lay capacity as a citizen, an employer, a neighbor, or a kinsman, mediators tend to be specialists and differ from those they serve in significant ways. They have experience in handling trouble, and some professional distance from what they handle. Except in the case of policemen, and perhaps some clergy, they tend to be more psychiatrically oriented than the lay public, and will see the need for treatment at times when the public does not.[14]

An interesting feature of these roles is the functional effects of their interdigitation. For example, the feelings of the patient will be influenced by whether or not the person who fills the role of complainant also has the role of next-of-relation—an embarrassing combination more prevalent, apparently, in the higher classes than in the lower.[15] Some of these emergent effects will be considered now.[16]

In the prepatient's progress from home to the hospital he may participate as a third person in what he may come to experience as a kind of alienative coalition. His next-of-relation presses him into coming to "talk things over" with a medical practitioner, an office psychiatrist, or some other counselor. Disinclination on his part may be met by threatening him with desertion, disownment, or other legal action, or by stressing the joint and exploratory nature of the interview. But typically the next-of-relation will have set the interview up, in the sense of selecting the professional, arranging for time, telling the professional something about the case, and so on. This move effectively tends to establish the next-of-relation as the responsible person to whom pertinent findings can be divulged, while effectively establishing the other as the patient. The prepatient often goes to the interview with the understanding that he is going as an equal of someone who is so bound together with him that a third person could not come between them in fundamental matters; this, after all, is one way in which close relationships are defined in our society. Upon arrival at the office the prepatient suddenly finds that he and his next-of-relation have not been accorded the same roles, and apparently that a prior understanding between the professional and the next-of-relation has been put in operation against him. In the extreme but common case, the professional first sees the prepatient alone, in the role of examiner and diagnostician, and then sees the next-of-relation alone, in the role of adviser, while carefully avoiding talking things over seriously with them both together.[17] And even in those non-consultative cases where public officials must forcibly extract a person from a family that wants to tolerate him, the next-of-relation is likely to be induced to "go along" with the official action, so that even here the prepatient may feel that an alienative coalition has been formed against him.

The moral experience of being third man in such a coalition is likely to embitter the prepatient, especially since his troubles have already probably led to some estrangement from his next-of-relation. After he enters the hospital, continued visits by his next-of-relation can give the patient the "insight" that his own best interests were being served. But the initial visits may temporarily strengthen his feeling of abandonment; he is likely to beg his visitor to get him out or at least to get him more privileges and to sympathize with the monstrousness of his plight—to which the visitor ordinarily can respond only by trying to maintain a hopeful note, by not "hearing" the requests, or by assuring the patient that the medical authorities know about these things and are doing what is medically best. The visitor then nonchalantly goes back into a world that the patient has learned is incredibly thick with freedom and privileges, causing the patient to feel that his next-of-relation is merely adding a pious gloss to a clear case of traitorous desertion.

The depth to which the patient may feel betrayed by his next-of-relation seems to be increased by the fact that another witnesses his betrayal—a factor which is apparently significant in many three-party situations. An offended person may well act forbearantly and accommodatively toward an offender when the two are alone, choosing peace ahead of justice. The presence of a witness, however, seems to add something to the implications of the offense. For then it is beyond the power of the offended and offender to forget about, erase, or suppress what has happened; the offense has become a public social fact.[18] When the witness is a mental health commission, as is sometimes the case, the witnessed

14. See Cumming and Cumming, *op. cit.*, p. 92.

15. Hollingshead and Redlich, *op. cit.*, p. 187.

16. For an analysis of some of these circuit implications for the inpatient, see Leila Deasy and Olive W. Quinn, "The Wife of the Mental Patient and the Hospital Psychiatrist," *Journal of Social Issues,* XI (1955), pp. 49–60. An interesting illustration of this kind of analysis may also be found in Alan G. Gowman, "Blindness and the Role of the Companion," *Social Problems,* IV (1956), pp. 68–75. A general statement may be found in Robert Merton, "The Role Set: Problems in Sociological Theory," *British Journal of Sociology,* VIII (1957), pp. 106–20.

17. I have one case record of a man who claims he thought *he* was taking his wife to see the psychiatrist, not realizing until too late that his wife had made the arrangements.

18. A paraphrase from Kurt Riezler, "Comment on the Social Psychology of Shame," *American Journal of Sociology,* XLVIII (1943), p. 458.

betrayal can verge on a "degradation ceremony."[19] In such circumstances, the offended patient may feel that some kind of extensive reparative action is required before witnesses, if his honor and social weight are to be restored.

Two other aspects of sensed betrayal should be mentioned. First, those who suggest the possibility of another's entering a mental hospital are not likely to provide a realistic picture of how in fact it may strike him when he arrives. Often he is told that he will get required medical treatment and a rest, and may well be out in a few months or so. In some cases they may thus be concealing what they know, but I think, in general, they will be telling what they see as the truth. For here there is quite relevant difference between patients and mediating professionals; mediators, more so than the public at large, may conceive of mental hospitals as short-term medical establishments where required rest and attention can be voluntarily obtained, and not as places of coerced exile. When the prepatient finally arrives he is likely to learn quite quickly, quite differently. He then finds that the information given him about life in the hospital has had the effect of his having put up less resistance to entering than he now sees he would have put up had he known the facts. Whatever the intentions of those who participated in his transition from person to patient, he may sense they have in effect "conned" him into his present predicament.

I am suggesting that the prepatient starts out with at least a portion of the rights, liberties, and satisfactions of the civilian and ends up on a psychiatric ward stripped of almost everything. The question here is how this stripping is managed. This is the second aspect of betrayal I want to consider.

As the prepatient may see it, the circuit of significant figures can function as a kind of betrayal funnel. Passage from person to patient may be effected through a series of linked stages, each managed by a different agent. While each stage tends to bring a sharp decrease in adult free status, each agent may try to maintain the fiction that no further decrease will occur. He may even manage to turn the prepatient over to the next agent while sustaining this note. Further, through words, cues, and gestures, the prepatient is implicitly asked by the current agent to join with him in sustaining a running line of polite small talk that tactfully avoids the administrative facts of the situation, becoming, with each stage, progressively more at odds with these facts. The spouse would rather not have to cry to get the prepatient to visit a psychiatrist; psychiatrists would rather not have a

scene when the prepatient learns that he and his spouse are being seen separately and in different ways; the police infrequently bring a prepatient to the hospital in a strait jacket, finding it much easier all around to give him a cigarette, some kindly words, and freedom to relax in the back seat of the patrol car; and finally, the admitting psychiatrist finds he can do his work better in the relative quiet and luxury of the "admission suite" where, as an incidental consequence, the notion can survive that a mental hospital is indeed a comforting place. If the prepatient heeds all of these implied requests and is reasonably decent about the whole thing, he can travel the whole circuit from home to hospital without forcing anyone to look directly at what is happening or to deal with the raw emotion that his situation might well cause him to express. His showing consideration for those who are moving him toward the hospital allows them to show consideration for him, with the joint result that these interactions can be sustained with some of the protective harmony characteristic of ordinary face-to-face dealings. But should the new patient cast his mind back over the sequence of steps leading to hospitalization, he may feel that everyone's current comfort was being busily sustained while his long-range welfare was being undermined. This realization may constitute a moral experience that further separates him for the time from the people on the outside.[20]

I would now like to look at the circuit of career agents from the point of view of the agents themselves. Mediators in the person's transition from civil to patient status—as well as his keepers, once he is in the hospital—have an interest in establishing a responsible next-of-relation as the patient's deputy or guardian; should there be no obvious candidate for the role, someone may be sought out and pressed into it. Thus while a person is gradually being transformed into a patient, a next-of-relation is gradually being transformed into a guardian. With a guardian on the scene, the whole transition process can be kept tidy. He is likely to be familiar with the prepatient's civil involvements and business, and can tie up loose ends that might otherwise

19. See Harold Garfinkel, "Conditions of Successful Degradation Ceremonies," *American Journal of Sociology*, LXI (1956), pp. 420–24.

20. Concentration-camp practices provide a good example of the function of the betrayal funnel in inducing co-operation and reducing struggle and fuss, although here the mediators could not be said to be acting in the best interests of the inmates. Police picking up persons from their homes would sometimes joke good-naturedly and offer to wait while coffee was being served. Gas chambers were fitted out like delousing rooms, and victims taking off their clothes were told to note where they were leaving them. The sick, aged, weak, or insane who were selected for extermination were sometimes driven away in Red Cross ambulances to camps referred to by terms such as "observation hospital." See David Boder, *I Did Not Interview the Dead* (Urbana: University of Illinois Press, 1949), p. 81; and Elie A. Cohen, *Human Behavior in the Concentration Camp* (London: Jonathan Cape, 1954), pp. 32, 37, 107.

be left to entangle the hospital. Some of the prepatient's abrogated civil rights can be transferred to him, thus helping to sustain the legal fiction that while the prepatient does not actually have his rights he somehow actually has not lost them.

Inpatients commonly sense, at least for a time, that hospitalization is a massive unjust deprivation, and sometimes succeed in convincing a few persons on the outside that this is the case. It often turns out to be useful, then, for those identified with inflicting these deprivations, however justifiably, to be able to point to the co-operation and agreement of someone whose relationship to the patient places him above suspicion, firmly defining him as the person most likely to have the patient's personal interest at heart. If the guardian is satisfied with what is happening to the new inpatient, the world ought to be.[21]

Now it would seem that the greater the legitimate personal stake one party has in another, the better he can take the role of guardian to the other. But the structural arrangements in society which lead to the acknowledged merging of two persons' interests lead to additional consequences. For the person to whom the patient turns for help—for protection against such threats as involuntary commitment—is just the person to whom the mediators and hospital administrators logically turn for authorization. It is understandable, then, that some patients will come to sense, at least for a time, that the closeness of a relationship tells nothing of its trustworthiness.

There are still other functional effects emerging from this complement of roles. If and when the next-of-relation appeals to mediators for help in the trouble he is having with the prepatient, hospitalization may not, in fact, be in his mind. He may not even perceive the prepatient as mentally sick, or, if he does, he may not consistently hold to this view.[22] It is the circuit of mediators, with their greater psychiatric sophistication and their belief in the medical character of mental hospitals, that will often define the situation for the next-of-relation, assuring him that hospitalization is a possible solution and a good one, that it involves no betrayal, but is rather a medical action taken in the best

interests of the prepatient. Here the next-of-relation may learn that doing his duty to the prepatient may cause the prepatient to distrust and even hate him for the time. But the fact that this course of action may have had to be pointed out and prescribed by professionals, and be defined by them as a moral duty, relieves the next-of-relation of some of the guilt he may feel.[23] It is a poignant fact that an adult son or daughter may be pressed into the role of mediator, so that the hostility that might otherwise be directed against the spouse is passed on to the child.[24]

Once the prepatient is in the hospital, the same guilt-carrying function may become a significant part of the staff's job in regard to the next-of-relation.[25] These reasons for feeling that he himself has not betrayed the patient, even though the patient may then think so, can later provide the next-of-relation with a defensible line to take when visiting the patient in the hospital and a basis for hoping that the relationship can be re-established after its hospital moratorium. And of course this position, when sensed by the patient, can provide him with excuses for the next-of-relation, when and if he comes to look for them.[26]

Thus while the next-of-relation can perform important functions for the mediators and hospital administrators, they in turn can perform important functions for him. One finds, then, an emergent unintended exchange or reciprocation of functions, these functions themselves being often unintended.

The final point I want to consider about the prepatient's moral career is its peculiarly retroactive character. Until a person actually arrives at the hospital there usually seems no way of knowing for sure that he is destined to do so, given the determinative role of career contingencies. And until the point of hospitalization is reached, he or others may not conceive of him as a

21. Interviews collected by the Clausen group at NIMH suggest that when a wife comes to be a guardian, the responsibility may disrupt previous distance from in-laws, leading either to a new supportive coalition with them or to a marked withdrawal from them.

22. For an analysis of these non-psychiatric kinds of perception, see Marian Radke Yarrow, Charlotte Green Schwartz, Harriet S. Murphy, and Leila Deasy, "The Psychological Meaning of Mental Illness in the Family," *Journal of Social Issues,* XI (1955), pp. 12–24; Charlotte Green Schwartz, "Perspectives on Deviance—Wives' Definitions of their Husbands' Mental Illness," *Psychiatry,* XX (1957), pp. 275–91.

23. This guilt-carrying function is found, of course, in other role complexes. Thus, when a middle-class couple engages in the process of legal separation or divorce, each of their lawyers usually takes the position that his job is to acquaint his client with all of the potential claims and rights, pressing his client into demanding these, in spite of any nicety of feelings about the rights and honorableness of the ex-partner. The client, in all good faith, can then say to self and to the ex-partner that the demands are being made only because the lawyer insists it is best to do so.

24. Recorded in the Clausen data.

25. This point is made by Cumming and Cumming, *op. cit.,* p. 129.

26. There is an interesting contrast here with the moral career of the tuberculosis patient. I am told by Julius Roth that tuberculous patients are likely to come to the hospital willingly, agreeing with their next-of-relation about treatment. Later in their hospital career, when they learn how long they yet have to stay and how depriving and irrational some of the hospital rulings are, they may seek to leave, be advised against this by the staff and by relatives, and only then begin to feel betrayed.

person who is becoming a mental patient. However, since he will be held against his will in the hospital, his next-of-relation and the hospital staff will be in great need of a rationale for the hardships they are sponsoring. The medical elements of the staff will also need evidence that they are still in the trade they were trained for. These problems are eased, no doubt unintentionally, by the case-history construction that is placed on the patient's past life, this having the effect of demonstrating that all along he had been becoming sick, that he finally became very sick, and that if he had not been hospitalized much worse things would have happened to him—all of which, of course, may be true. Incidentally, if the patient wants to make sense out of his stay in the hospital, and, as already suggested, keep alive the

possibility of once again conceiving of his next-of-relation as a decent, well-meaning person, then he, too, will have reason to believe some of this psychiatric work-up of his past.

Here is a very ticklish point for the sociology of careers. An important aspect of every career is the view the person constructs when he looks backward over his progress; in a sense, however, the whole of the prepatient career derives from this reconstruction. The fact of having had a prepatient career, starting with an effective complaint, becomes an important part of the mental patient's orientation, but this part can begin to be played only after hospitalization proves that what he had been having, but no longer has, is a career as a prepatient.

AUGUST B. HOLLINGSHEAD • FREDERICK C. REDLICH

Paths to the Psychiatrist[1]

Introduction

Every person who follows a path that leads him eventually to a psychiatrist must pass four milestones. The first marks the *occurrence* of *"abnormal" behavior;* the second involves the *appraisal* of his behavior as "disturbed" in a psychiatric sense; the third is when the *decision* is made that psychiatric treatment is indicated, and the fourth is reached when the *decision is implemented* and the "disturbed" person actually enters the care of a psychiatrist. Due to the limitations of the data available to us because of the nature of our research design, the paths between the first two milestones will be sketched only in outline and illustrated by typical cases. The paths between the third and fourth milestones will be traced in detail with statistical materials accumulated on all cases in the study. In our discussion of the events that link each milestone, we will focus attention upon the question: Is class status a salient factor in the determination of what path a person follows on his way to a psychiatrist?

Reprinted from August B. Hollingshead and Frederick C. Redlich, *Social Class and Mental Illness,* New York: John Wiley & Sons, 1958, pages 171–193, by permission of the authors and publisher.

"Abnormal" Behavior

"Abnormal" behavior is used here to indicate actions that are different from what is expected in a defined social situation. Thus, abnormal acts can be evaluated only in terms of their cultural and psychosocial contexts. Homicide, for example, is abnormal in a peaceful community; it is normal when inflicted on the enemy during war.

Viewed psychiatrically, the range of abnormal behavior is very great, covering in intensity mild neuroses to severe psychoses, and in duration from acute, transient "disturbances" to chronic reactions. It encompasses such well-defined phenomena as various types of schizophrenia, and many psychosocial maladjustments that never bring most persons to the attention of psychiatrists.[2] "Abnormality" depends upon appraisal.

"Appraisal"

The perception and "appraisal," by other persons, of an individual's abnormal behavior as psychiatrically disturbed is crucial to the determination of whether a given individual is to become a psychiatric patient or be handled some other way. By appraisal we mean the evaluations of family members and proximate groups of abnormal behavior of persons. The appraisal of behavior as psychiatrically abnormal precedes decisions concerning therapeutic intervention. Appraisal is carried on by individuals and groups through the interpretation of interacting responses. It may be conscious, preconscious, or unconscious; usually, it is a combination of all three. It is both interpersonal and intrapersonal. As a lay response, appraisal corresponds to the professional diagnosis. As an intrapsychic process, it designates how the prospective patient perceives his actions, particularly his disturbed actions. Appraisal, as an interpersonal process, entails how a disturbed person and his actions are perceived and evaluated by the individual and by other persons in the community. Appraisal will determine what is judged to be delinquency, bad behavior, or psychiatric troubles.

Class Status and Appraisal[3]

Inferences drawn from clinical practice, the tape-recorded interviews with persons in the 5 percent sample, and patients and members of their families in the Controlled Case Study and the Psychiatric Census indicate that class I and II persons are more aware of psychological problems than class IV and V persons. Class I and II persons are also more perceptive of personal frustration, failure, and critical intrapsychic conflicts than class IV and V persons. Perception of the psychological nature of personal problems is a rare trait in any person and in any class, but it is found more frequently in the refined atmosphere of classes I and II than in the raw setting of class V. As a consequence, we believe that far more abnormal behavior is tolerated by the two lower classes, particularly class V, without any awareness that the motivations behind the behavior are pathological, even though the behavior may be disapproved by the class norms. We will illustrate these points by drawing upon the clinical histories of several patients in our study.

The first patient is an example of a higher status person who is able and willing to utilize the help of a psychiatrist to overcome self-perceived disturbances. This patient is a 25-year-old graduate student, the son of a salaried, minor professional man in an established class II family. The patient's chief complaint is a feeling that he is not able to work to his full capacity. He first noted this difficulty as an undergraduate in a state university near his home. He discussed this problem with a college friend who was being treated by psychotherapy and, upon his friend's advice, consulted the psychiatrist in charge of the college mental hygiene clinic. However, he did not enter treatment at that time. He knew little about psychiatry when he went to the

clinic, but he began to read Freud, Horney, and others; after a period of conscious aversion, he found the materials interesting. The information gathered from them led him, after he had entered graduate school, to discuss his feelings with his friend. Upon this occasion he entered treatment. He was skeptical about psychiatric help in the first weeks of therapy, but he convinced himself that obtaining psychotherapy does not mark a person as "crazy." From this point on he was able to profit from psychiatric treatment. In the course of several months of psychotherapy, he was able to discuss with the therapist his relationships with a stern, driving father and a brother who had disgraced the family on many occasions. The discussions made him realize he was far too critical of himself and inordinately ambitious; unconsciously he was identifying with his stern father while competing with and outdoing the "bad" brother. Gradually, he realized that his unconscious motivations were related to his depression, anxiety, and inability to do graduate work the way he desired.

The patient we shall use to illustrate the lack of sensitivity to psychopathological behavior in the lower segments of the status structure is an elderly class IV man. This man's clinical history indicates that he had exhibited psychopathological behavior throughout his life, but it was not interpreted as such by his family or his associates. A few incidents will clarify the lack of appraisal by the family. In 1940, he took his thermos bottle to a chemist for examination to see if his wife was trying to poison him. Every night before his wife went to bed she secreted butcher knives and other sharp instruments to keep them away from him. He did not trust his daughter to measure medicine "prescribed" for him by a corner druggist, and he accused her of trying to poison him to get his money. He entered his daughters' bedrooms while they were dressing or undressing unless they locked their doors. He kept a razor-sharp hunting knife in the cellar. A daughter and son-in-law knew about the weapon and his constant preoccupation with sharpening it, but no action was taken. The man became violent whenever anyone told him to stop cursing or stop anything he might be doing. When this occurred, he would shout and pound on the walls; on numerous occasions he broke the plaster with the force of his blows. The family avoided bringing any liquor into the home because the father became unmanageable when drunk.

The day before Christmas, however, he requested a bottle for the holidays, and the eldest daughter and son-in-law, in order to humor him, bought a fifth of whiskey. On Christmas Eve, he drank too much, became angry, and used his full vocabulary of obscenity and profanity on the family. The daughter and son-in-law put him to bed and removed his weapons from the room. The next morning he demanded to know what had happened the previous evening, and when he was told he began to yell and curse until the entire building of flats where the family lived was aroused. His daughter in desperation called the police who took the man to the city jail. He was held until after New Year's Day before he was tried, found guilty of breach of the peace, and was sentenced to sixty days in the county jail. After transfer to the jail, he became violent, and a psychiatrist was called to the jail by the sheriff. The psychiatrist recommended commitment to the state hospital.

This man had been in the state hospital two years at the time of the Psychiatric Census. His family did not want him in the home, but they did not feel it was right for him to remain in the state hospital. His eldest daughter, who took charge of the situation, did not think he was "crazy." However, she made no active plans to care for him or to have him discharged. While the study was in progress, the man died in the state hospital.

Although the patient presents a lifelong history of hostility, suspicion, and extreme lack of consideration of others, so far as we are able to determine neither his family nor others in his environment—even when his behavior became violent—considered him a "psychiatric problem." Such an appraisal of behavior is more typical of class V than of class IV, although people in all strata have blind spots regarding psychopathological implications of unusual behavior or even deliberately avoid thinking about them. The lower status patient will attribute his troubles to unhappiness, tough luck, laziness, meanness, or physical illness rather than to factors of psychogenic origin. The worst thing that can happen to a class V person is to be labeled "bugs," "crazy," or "nuts." Such judgment is often equal to being sentenced for life to the "bughouse." Unfortunately, this sentiment is realistic.[4]

The case histories of two compulsively promiscuous adolescent females will be drawn upon to illustrate the differential impact of class status on the way in which lay persons and psychiatrists perceive and appraise similar behavior. Both girls came to the attention of the police at about the same time but under very different circumstances. One came from a core group class I family, the other from a class V family broken by the desertion of the father. The class I girl, after one of her frequent drinking and sexual escapades on a weekend away from an exclusive boarding school, became involved in an automobile accident while drunk. Her family immediately arranged for bail through the influence of a member of an outstanding law firm; a powerful friend telephoned a newspaper contact, and the report of the accident was not published. Within twenty-four

hours, the girl was returned to school. In a few weeks the school authorities realized that the girl was pregnant and notified her parents. A psychiatrist was called in for consultation by the parents with the expectation, expressed frankly, that he was to recommend a therapeutic interruption of the pregnancy. He did not see fit to do this and, instead, recommended hospitalization in a psychiatric institution to initiate psychotherapy. The parents, though disappointed that the girl would not have a "therapeutic" abortion, finally consented to hospitalization. In due course, the girl delivered a healthy baby who was placed for adoption. Throughout her stay in the hospital she received intensive psychotherapy and after being discharged continued in treatment with a highly regarded psychoanalyst.

The class V girl was arrested by the police after she was observed having intercourse with four or five sailors from a nearby naval base. At the end of a brief and perfunctory trial, the girl was sentenced to a reform school. After two years there she was paroled as an unpaid domestic. While on parole, she became involved in promiscuous activity, was caught by the police, and sent to the state reformatory for women. She accepted her sentence as deserved "punishment" but created enough disturbance in the reformatory to attract the attention of a guidance officer. This official recommended that a psychiatrist be consulted. The psychiatrist who saw her was impressed by her crudeness and inability to communicate with him on most subjects. He was alienated by the fact that she thought masturbation was "bad," whereas intercourse with many men whom she hardly knew was "O.K." The psychiatrist's recommendation was to return the girl to her regular routine because she was not "able to profit from psychotherapy."

This type of professional judgment is not atypical, because, on the one hand, many psychiatrists do not understand the cultural values of class V, and on the other, class V patients and their families rarely understand common terms in the psychiatrists' vocabulary, such as neuroses, conflict, and psychotherapy. The lack of communication between psychiatrist and patient merely adds to the hostility felt toward the psychiatrist and fear of what will happen to a member of the family if he is "taken away." A lack of understanding of the psychiatrist's goals occurs, in part, because lower class persons are not sufficiently educated, but also their appraisal of what is disturbed behavior differs greatly from that of the psychiatrist.

In class V, where the demands of everyday life are greatest, awareness of suffering is perceived less clearly than in the higher levels. The denial, or partial denial, of the existence of psychic pain appears to be a defense mechanism that is linked to low status. Also, class V persons appear to accept physical suffering to a greater extent than do persons in higher status positions. This may be realistic and in keeping with the often hopeless situations these people face in day-to-day living. In classes I and II, by way of contrast, there is less willingness to accept life as unalterable. Consequently, there is a marked tendency to utilize a psychiatrist to help ease subjective malaise or disease. Nevertheless, the individual usually tries to hide his "shame" until it is no longer concealable. Even members of the immediate family may not be told that the patient is in psychiatric treatment. For example, in an extreme case, a middle-aged class III Jewish woman takes great pains to let nobody except her favorite sister know that she is a patient. The sister, who usually brings the patient to the psychiatrist's office, insists that the patient be administered anesthesia before she receives electro-convulsive therapy. She does not think the patient should know about her "shameful" treatment.

Social Factors and Appraisal

The social factors influencing appraisal fall into two major categories: (1) access to existing technical knowledge and (2) sociocultural values. There is little doubt about the first point; without any knowledge of psychiatric therapy there can be no therapy, but prescription and application of therapy depend upon a group's access to knowledge, particularly in a popular form. The consequences of this, however, have not been understood. Only recently has health education in mental illness begun to be developed by mass communication media. We mentioned earlier that 300 years ago psychotics were considered to be witches and sorcerers. Even today, symptoms of neurosis and psychosis are thought to be caused by the "evil eye" by many class V Italians in this community. Naturally, such appraisal determined by culture is not compatible with modern psychiatric treatment.

We have begun barely to understand the appraisal process and the effects it has on who is treated by a psychiatrist and by what therapeutic techniques. A number of different things enter into it. The process of appraisal depends on individual factors of specific personality development and experience; it depends also on the values of our culture and the specific class subcultures as well as the knowledge and techniques which are available to the expert and to others who perceive and evaluate behavior in a given social situation.

Where people take their "troubles" depends on the value orientation of the individual which, in turn, depends upon group appraisal. Both interpersonal and intrapersonal appraisals are influenced by psychosocial and sociocultural factors. For example, a class I or II person who informs himself about diagnosis and treatment and who has access to the best medical opinion will appraise himself differently from the way in which a poorly informed class IV or V person will. The reasons for such differences in self-appraisal may be "deep" or "superficial." At this point, we are less concerned with individual differences than with responses to abnormality which are an integral part of a group's way of life.

Speaking broadly, a community can function adequately only by controlling members who create troubles of one kind or another for themselves and for other members of society. Through the years, special institutions have been developed to deal with particular types of chronically recurring troubles or dysfunctions, such as delinquency, poverty, and disease. Delinquency is handled by police, lawyers, judges, probation officers, and other legal functionaries. Poverty is alleviated by public and private welfare agencies. Medical institutions have been assigned the function of caring for personal crises that society defines as illness.

This neat tripartite separation of common dysfunctions works well so long as society makes clear judgments as to what agency is to care for what dysfunction. When lines of responsibility and function are unclear, as at present, problems arise. The objectives and responsibilities of psychiatric institutions often overlap with those of older welfare, legal, and medical institutions. Psychiatrists and psychiatric institutions are often asked to solve problems that involve several areas of social dysfunctions. Because of their characteristics which are as yet unclear, psychiatric institutions may be viewed as bridges between older institutions that have evolved to cope with social dysfunctions. When legal, economic, organic, and emotional factors play concomitant roles in an individual's troubles, that person may be referred to a psychiatrist mainly because traditional welfare, legal, and medical institutions have failed to handle the individual's multiple problems, possibly because no one institution is so equipped. In this sense, the psychiatrist is a community trouble shooter without a clearly defined role in relation to traditional institutions whose functions are more clearly defined and commonly accepted.

A person whose behavior is acceptable to his family, the community, and to himself is not likely to come to the attention of responsible institutional officers—parents, teachers, police, social workers, physicians, or such medical specialists as psychiatrists. However, when behavior is viewed as abnormal and a threat to the community, an individual may be brought to the attention of some official. For example, an adult male who exposes himself in public will not be tolerated by the community; at present, however, it is a moot point whether he will become a psychiatric patient or a legal case, inasmuch as our values assign the control of this kind of behavior to both penal and mental institutions. For another kind of behavior, that of a mildly hysterical class I or II female, the physician may recommend psychiatric care, but resistance to psychiatrists is so strong in our community that the chances are high she will not follow his advice. However, should she attempt suicide, she is likely to be brought forcibly into psychiatric treatment, for the class I and II subcultures attribute motivations toward self-destruction to psychopathology in the individual. In short: *Abnormal behavior that is appraised as being motivated by psychopathological disturbance in the individual is the province of the psychiatrist.*

Whether abnormal behavior is judged to be disturbed, delinquent, or merely idiosyncratic depends upon who sees it and how he appraises what he sees. To be sure, normal behavior is occasionally appraised as disturbed. Persons who perceive and appraise behavior may be classified into a number of categories: (1) the prospective patient, (2) members of the prospective patient's family, (3) friends, co-workers, neighbors, persons supplying and selling commodities, as well as leaders in community associations such as lodges and clubs, (4) professionals in the field of health (physicians, nurses, medical and psychiatric social workers, clinical psychologists), (5) professionals outside the field of health (ministers, lawyers, teachers, family case workers), and (6) officers of the community (police, attorneys, judges, and various other functionaries). Although there is some overlapping in these groups, they represent the major types of persons who perceive and evaluate behavior as normal or abnormal. Above all, these are the persons who decide whether abnormal behavior is delinquent or disturbed and who make referrals to psychiatric agencies.

Appraisals and Decisions to Act on Them

What is done about abnormal behavior that is appraised to be of psychogenic origin depends upon a number of factors. These include the assumed danger the behavior has for the disturbed individual as well as for other members of society, the attitudes, conscious and unconscious, of the individual and his family toward psychiatric treatment, and the availability of treatment. The implementation of appraisal is social, in large part, because the behavior of the persons involved, patients, therapists, or second parties, is defined in terms of cultural norms.

Among professional persons there are sharp differences in the ways behavior is perceived and appraised. Professionals—lawyers, ministers, teachers, physicians—also differ in their judgments from the perceptions and appraisals of lay persons. For example, conflicts are apt to occur when psychiatrists are asked to evaluate delinquent behavior among children and adolescents who are brought before juvenile courts. The judge may think that a child should be punished for his acts, whereas the psychiatrist may take the position that the child is disturbed and in need of treatment, not punishment. Such professional disagreements lead to fundamentally different ways of dealing with abnormal behavior which may block or delay a decision that a person is in need of psychiatric help. This is especially true when the evaluation of the expert does not coincide with "common sense" opinion.[5] Even minor professional disagreements block the implementation of a decision by a competent person that an individual ought to be treated by a psychiatrist.

These disagreements are accentuated by the ambiguous role the psychiatrist plays in our society. Law, custom, and tradition have assigned the care of the obviously psychotic person to the medical profession, but the much broader area of deviant and maladjusted behavior, although viewed as abnormal by some members of society, is not accepted fully by the public as an appropriate area for psychiatric treatment. Psychiatrists, particularly those with a dynamic orientation, consider this not only a legitimate but a most important area of professional activity.

When a psychiatrist enters the area of maladjusted behavior, he works with problems not clearly defined as being within the traditional province of medicine. As a "social" practitioner, the psychiatrist shares the appraisal of abnormal behavior with the lawyer, the clergyman, the teacher, the social worker, and the psychologist on the professional level and with parents and volunteer advisors on the lay level. The psychiatrist's role as a therapist is complicated further by the vague definitions of what facets of abnormal behavior should be handled by what agencies in the society. To be specific, delinquency as a legal problem is in the province of the courts and the penal system. Dependency is assigned to public and private welfare agencies. Yet both delinquency and dependency may be symptomatic of emotional disturbance and therefore amenable to psychiatric treatment. This is one of the areas in the society where the role and function of the psychiatrist are least clear.

Closely related to this issue is the question: Should a sex deviant be prosecuted via the courts and prison system, or should he be regarded as ill and treated in a psychiatric setting? Historically, the sexually deviant individual has been viewed as a legal case and punished by the judicial system. In more recent years some lawyers, social workers, and parole officers have held that deviant sex behavior is a psychiatric problem, but this is a minority viewpoint. What actually happens to a sexual deviant may be determined more by his class status than by what is defined by the law or by the most enlightened theory of social scientists or "progressive" dynamically oriented psychiatrists.

The differential impact of class status on what is done about disturbed behavior after psychiatrists are consulted is clear-cut when an individual's abnormal behavior has come to the attention of the police and the courts. In such cases, offenders in classes I and II are far more likely to retain a psychiatrist to protect them from the legal consequences of their acts than are offenders in classes IV and V. While this research was in progress, a class I married man, whose wife was pregnant, was arrested for exposing himself to a little girl. He was referred to a psychiatrist to avoid a possible prison sentence. This accused man retained a shrewd lawyer, well acquainted with persons in high political circles and also with the judge, a political appointee, who tried the case. The lawyer's primary expectation of the psychiatrist was to make a statement in court that would, in his words, "get his client off the hook." The accused was found guilty of breach of the peace and "sentenced" to two years of psychotherapy. From a psychiatric viewpoint, this is not a miscarriage of justice, but an enlightened sentence. The point is that such "sentences" are given rarely to the class IV and V sexual deviates, alcoholics, and drug addicts who face higher and lower courts but usually land in prison, not on a psychoanalyst's couch. Class IV and V sex delinquents, if found by psychiatric consultants to be disturbed, are committed, at best, to public mental institutions rather than sent to jail.

The generally negative attitudes toward psychiatrists and psychiatric agencies in all social strata result in persons turning in many directions for help before they go to a psychiatrist. Often this is a last resort, "a cry for help."[6] To see a psychiatrist is a rather desperate step for most persons; it is taken reluctantly after other resources, mechanisms, and compensations have failed and when the suffering person feels at "the end of his rope." Even then the patient and his associates must overcome various resistances, individual and familial; these are often linked with class status. A physician may advise a patient to see a psychiatrist, and the patient may be willing to follow the physician's advice; however, the patient's family may object strongly because they fear the social criticism that will result, or because they do not believe in it or are unfamiliar with the practice of psychiatry. On the other hand, they may want the patient

committed to a mental hospital to get him out of the family, even though they fear the resulting stigma. In most cases, the motivation to obtain psychiatric help involves ambivalent feelings and conflicting evaluations among the several persons involved.

The decision to turn to the psychiatrist is made generally only after there has been a serious breakdown in social relationships. Even when a person seeks help for a very circumscribed problem, there usually is more personality disintegration than surface manifestations may indicate. To be sure, there are differences between individuals as to the amount and kind of stress that lead to despair. There are also class-linked differences in perception of what one may do to relieve conscious and unconscious feelings of displeasure, disease, or malaise. Accordingly, in all classes there are many instances of outright refusal to cooperate to the point of physical violence among both neurotic and psychotic patients.

Awareness of disease or malaise, psychosocial sensitivity to it, and the ability to express one's feelings regarding disease are the antecedents of the action to cope with the causes of distress. In trying to understand subsequent actions, it is also important to know how psychological suffering is viewed in the several strata. It will make a difference whether suffering is considered a result of ill fate, as it tends to be in class V, or something amenable to remedial action as in the higher classes. Only when the suffering is viewed as remediable is it compatible with therapeutic intervention. Actual knowledge of the causal factors by the suffering person may be small—and need not be large—so long as the psychiatrist is accepted as a person who can help him.

A physician may form an opinion about a person with psychiatric difficulties; he may advise him to see a psychiatrist, or he may force him to enter a mental hospital by the use of an emergency certificate. The patient, though not consciously, may want the physician to do this in order to extract him from a difficult, threatening, and frustrating situation. Underlying motivations may include escape from an unbearable situation, a vague wish for love and support, and, probably less frequently, a constructive desire to work through a problem with the aid of a competent doctor.

Implementation of Decisions to Seek Psychiatric Help

A decision to obtain psychiatric help is not identical with the implementation of that decision. Implementation may not be possible because the help which is sought is not always available. Many persons who want psychiatric help or who are referred to psychiatrists are seriously frustrated when they learn that, for geographic, social, and economic reasons, psychiatry is not available to them. We want to note here, however, that the data we will present in this chapter are limited to cases where the decision to refer an individual to a psychiatrist or psychiatric agency *was* implemented by the person's entry into treatment; instances where the decision was not implemented are not included in our figures.

Sources of Referral

The decision that a person's behavior is disturbed and is amenable to psychiatric treatment may result in a recommendation for action. For our purposes, a decision made by any person that an individual, who later became a patient and was counted in the Psychiatric Census, needed psychiatric care is called a *referral*. The name of the person responsible for the referral, ascertained from the clinical record of each patient, was entered on the Psychiatric Census schedule. We pointed out in a previous paragraph that one or more of six types of responsible persons ordinarily makes the decision that a person exhibiting disturbed behavior be treated by a psychiatrist. Each type of referral will be characterized briefly before we investigate class status as a significant factor in the question of *who* makes the decision to refer disturbed persons to psychiatrists.

1. *Self-Referrals.* An individual who has enough knowledge of psychiatry and insight into himself to realize he is emotionally disturbed may decide to consult a psychiatrist about his problems. Such an individual is motivated by self-perception to seek relief through psychiatric treatment. Self-referrals are associated primarily with individuals who later are diagnosed as psychoneurotics.

2. *Family Referrals.* Family perceptions of disturbance mean that some member of the immediate family recognizes the nature of an individual's symptoms and recommends psychiatric treatment. The individual may or may not accept the family's decision. When the sick individual refuses to accept the family's view of his difficulty, a psychiatrist may be called to the home or the patient may be brought forcibly to a psychiatrist's office. On the other hand, if his behavior is not considered too severe by his family and associates, nothing may be done until the patient's behavior becomes intolerable. The realization that a person is emotionally disturbed may be made by friends and close private associates; for present purposes, such referrals will be included with the family referrals.

3. *Medical Referrals.* Medical perception of psychiatric illness usually occurs when an individual or some member of his family realizes that the person is ill but is not aware of the nature of his illness. The patient and his family may assume that the difficulty is organic and should be treated by a general practitioner or a medical specialist other than a psychiatrist. In this case, a general practitioner or a specialist concludes that the individual's difficulties are not within his domain and recommends psychiatric help. The general practitioner or specialist usually acts as an intermediary between the patient and the psychiatrist. Medical and psychiatric social workers and visiting nurses are the persons who frequently refer patients of the lower classes to psychiatric agencies.

4. *Nonmedical Professional Referrals.* Nonmedical professional personnel may observe an individual's behavior and, on the basis of their knowledge of emotional involvements, decide he needs psychiatric help. Guidance teachers in the school system and family case workers are the most common nonmedical professional persons making referrals. Ministers and lawyers may observe the behavior of disturbed persons, but lawyers make singularly few referrals.

5. *Official Referrals.* Policemen, of all community officials, are the most likely to perceive that a psychotic individual is disturbed or in need of psychiatric care. This may occur when an officer is called to a home to calm or take charge of a violent individual or where a disturbed individual is being disorderly in a public place. When police officers come in contact with a disturbed individual in classes IV and V, they usually arrest him and hold him in jail until a psychiatrist examines him; if the individual is particularly disturbed, he may be taken to the Emergency Room of the community hospital.

Usually when the police arrest a disturbed individual, they perceive the nature of his difficulty before his family does. The family may know the individual is "difficult," "quarrelsome," "ornery," "abusive," "vulgar," or "profane," but seldom realizes that the individual is mentally ill. The police officer's perception and evaluation of an individual's behavior is crucial in deciding whether the individual is to be sent to jail or to the state hospital. If the police in their investigation decide that the patient is responsible for his behavior, he will be held for trial and, in all probability, sentenced to a term in a local jail or the state penitentiary. On the other hand, if the police conclude that the individual does not understand the nature of his behavior, and therefore is not psychologically responsible for what he has done, the chances are high that he will be turned over to psychiatric authorities. Policemen are Very Important Persons in the process of "diagnosing" severely disturbed and antisocial behavior. We believe that police officers, especially in their training schools, should be given systematic training in the nature and recognition of mental illness. They should be taught also something of the reactions of frightened relatives and what is to be done with a disturbed person.

Let us examine the question of interrelationships between class status and who refers whom to psychiatric agencies. Our discussion is limited to patients in their *first course of treatment* because it is impossible in most cases to determine who made the original referral for patients who have experienced a previous course of psychiatric treatment. Also we are interested in who made the decision that first brought the disturbed person into psychiatric treatment. The data on referrals of patients in their first course of treatment are presented according to the two major groups, neurotics and psychotics. Among the psychotic patients, the schizophrenics are treated separately because of the size of the group and their referral patterns.

Sources of Referrals for Neurotics—by Class

The sources of first referrals among neurotic patients are divided, for purposes of presentation, into medical and nonmedical. Medical referrals are subdivided, in turn, into those made by private physicians and those made by clinic physicians. The nonmedical referrals are tabulated according to the typology described in the preceding section. All first referrals for neurotic patients are summarized in Table 1. Examination of the data presented in Table 1 shows a direct relationship between class status and the percentage of referrals to psychiatrists by private physicians. On the other hand, referrals from clinic physicians show an inverse relationship to class status. Although referrals from private and clinic physicians form class-linked gradients that run in opposite directions, there is no appreciable difference in the percentages of referrals to psychiatrists by clinic physicians between classes I−II and III, but there is a sharp increase in clinic physician referrals at the class IV level of the social hierarchy. Here the increase is from 9.2 percent in class III to 29.1 percent in class IV. Class V referrals from clinic physicians are essentially in the

TABLE 1

Percentage of Referrals from Specified Sources for Neurotics Entering Treatment for the First Time—by Class

	CLASS			
SOURCE OF REFERRAL	I-II	III	IV	V
Medical				
Private physicians	52.2	47.4	30.8	13.9
Clinic physicians	7.2	9.2	29.1	27.8
Nonmedical				
Police and courts*	0.0	1.3	5.1	13.9
Social agencies	1.4	5.3	4.3	36.1
Other professional persons	2.9	5.3	6.8	2.8
Family and friends	20.3	13.2	17.1	0.0
Self	15.9	18.4	6.8	5.5
$n =$	69	76	117	36

$$\chi^2 = 74.26, 9 \; df, \; p < .001$$

*χ^2 computed with *courts*, *social agencies*, and *other professional persons* combined; also with *family* and *self* combined.

same proportion as in class IV. The percentage of referrals to psychiatrists from private physicians traces a distinctly different gradient, as a glance at Table 1 will show. However, the reader should keep in mind that clinics are associated with people in the two lower classes, whereas, private practice is correlated with persons in the higher classes.

Referrals by nonmedical persons reveal an interesting series of variations from class to class. There is a definite class-linked gradient in police and court referrals; the higher the class, the lower the percentage of referrals, with a heavy concentration of referrals in class V. A few referrals are made by family and welfare agency social workers and teachers from classes I−II through IV. In class V there are more referrals from social agencies and public health nurses than from all other nonmedical persons combined. Only clinic physicians approach officials in social agencies in the frequencies of referrals of class V persons to psychiatrists. If we view the clinic physician as a "community professional" along with teachers, social workers, and nurses, then we see that almost two out of three referrals in class V are made by professional workers in the community agencies. When official referrals that are made by the police and courts are added, the proportion becomes approximately four out of five. Few referrals in any class are made by lawyers and clergymen. Referrals by family members and friends are important in the four higher classes but not in class V. Self-referrals are almost as important as referrals by family members and friends in classes I−II and III, but in class IV there are distinctly fewer self-than family referrals; there are as many self-referrals in class V as in class IV. The chi square in Table 1 reveals that *who* decides to refer disturbed persons later diagnosed as neurotic to psychiatric agencies is linked definitely to class status.

Sources of Referral for Psychotic Patients—by Class

The sources of referral for disturbed persons who are diagnosed as psychotic are more strongly associated with class status than for those who are diagnosed as neurotic. Moreover, the percentage of referrals by particular types of persons is sharply different. Both private physicians and clinic physicians make relatively fewer referrals of patients who are diagnosed later as psychotic in comparison with those who are neurotic. In classes III and IV, private physicians make the highest proportion of referrals. In class I–II, some four out of five referrals are made by the patient, his family, or his friends. There are few self-referrals in class III. The family makes about one in six, but family physicians make some three referrals out of five. Other professionals and the police make a few referrals. In class IV, clinic physicians, the police, and the courts make more referrals; social agencies play a minor role. Class V psychotics, unlike the higher classes, are referred in the same general ways as the class V neurotics, except that the percentage of referrals by clinic physicians and social agencies is lower, whereas the proportion of police and court referrals is over three times higher. A close study of Table 2 will show that in each class there is a concentration of referrals from one or two types of persons. The patient and the family are the major sources of referral in class I–II. In class III, private physicians and the family are the two principal sources of referral. In class IV, the family and clinic physicians share the decision with the police. In class V, the police and the courts, social agencies, and clinic physicians make practically all referrals.

The class-linked gradients on self-referrals and referrals by family members and friends in Tables 1 and 2 corroborate the generalization stated earlier that persons in the higher classes are more perceptive of disturbed behavior and of the potential help psychiatry offers than persons in the lower classes. For example, in class IV, only 24 percent of the neurotic patients and 11 percent of the psychotic patients entered treatment through appraisal of the patient or other persons in the primary group that the patient was disturbed. In class III, by way of comparison, the comparable figures are 32 percent for the neurotics and 23 percent for the psychotics. When

TABLE 2

Percentage of Referrals from Specified Sources for Psychotics Entering Treatment for the First Time—by Class

	CLASS			
SOURCE OF REFERRAL	I-II*	III	IV	V
Medical				
Private physicians	21.4	59.4	44.1	9.0
Clinic physicians	. . .	6.2	16.3	13.0
Nonmedical				
Social agencies	. . .	. . .	7.4	19.6
Police and courts	. . .	4.8	18.9	52.2
Family and friends	42.9	17.2	8.1	2.0
Self	35.7	6.2	2.6	. . .
Other professionals	. . .	6.2	2.6	4.2
$n =$	14	64	270	378

$$\chi^2 = 243.16, 12 \ df, p < .001$$

*Classes I–II and III were combined for the computation of χ^2 because of the small frequencies in classes I and II.

we compare class V referrals by various members of the primary group with class IV referrals, we see even a greater difference than when we compare the class III's with the class IV's. In class V there are no family referrals among neurotics, and only 2 percent of the psychotics are brought into treatment by members of their families. In class V, persons outside the family and friendship groups make practically all referrals. In this class, responsible community agents make almost all appraisals of disturbed behavior. Consequently, they are the sources of effective referrals.

Sources of Referrals for Schizophrenics—by Class

The sources of referral for schizophrenics were studied separately to determine if they are different from all psychotics. We found that schizophrenic persons in each class are referred to psychiatric agencies in almost the same ways as the total psychotic patient population. This might have been expected because the schizophrenics compose some 53 percent of all psychotics in treatment for the first time. The sources of referrals for the schizophrenic patients are recorded in Table 3. Perhaps the most striking thing about these data is that there are no self-referrals from class I–II. In these strata we might expect to find enough insight to impel a disturbed person who is diagnosed later as schizophrenic to seek out a psychiatrist; but this is not what happens. In classes I and II, most referrals are made by the family

TABLE 3

*Percentage of Sources of Referral for
Schizophrenics Entering Treatment for the
First Time—by Class*

	CLASS			
SOURCE OF REFERRAL*	*I–II*	*III‡*	*IV*	*V*
Medical				
Private physicians	45.5	66.7	35.3	10.6
Clinic physicians	. . .	3.7	23.3	12.5
Nonmedical				
Police and courts	. . .	7.4	24.8	52.3
Social agencies	. . .	. . .	3.8	17.6
Other professionals	. . .	3.7	1.5	3.7
Family and friends	54.4	11.1	9.8	3.2
Self	. . .	7.4	1.5	. . .
	$n =$ 11	27	133	216

$$\chi^2 = 129.68, 8 \; df, \; p < .001$$

*The χ^2 was computed with social agency and other professional referrals combined, and self-referrals combined with family and friend referrals.

‡In this analysis, cases in class I–II and III were combined.

after some member realizes that the patient is ill and in need of psychiatric care. When an appraisal is made that a member's behavior is disturbed the family brings the patient to the psychiatrist or calls the psychiatrist directly. Usually class I and II persons are brought to psychiatric treatment by their families after heated discussions at home. In one instance, a patient became so violent that a psychiatrist had to be called, and male members of the family held the patient while he was subdued by sedatives. The patient was then taken to a private psychiatric hospital under sedative. Ordinarily, however, the patient is aware that he is being taken to a psychiatrist or mental hospital, and violent disturbance is the exception.

Five schizophrenic patients in class I–II were referred to psychiatrists by private practitioners. Three of these referrals came from general practitioners and two from specialists. In one case, a woman went to her family physician for difficulties described as nervousness and visceral aches and pains. The physician treated her for three weeks before he came to the conclusion she was psychiatrically disturbed; then he referred her to a private psychiatrist. This woman resisted referral but after discussing the situation with her husband, her sister, and a friend in the medical profession, she went to the recommended psychiatrist. The other two persons attempted suicide. The family physicians were called by their families, and the physicians referred them to private psychiatrists. Suicidal attempts in the higher

classes provoke rather drastic, often dramatic, action. The two specialists who made referrals were internists; their referrals were made after preliminary treatment for the patient's real or imagined symptoms.

Class III schizophrenics were referred by all types of persons except social agencies. Two persons, both students, went to psychiatrists as a result of their own feelings. One, in the premedical course, came to the conclusion that his difficulties were psychiatric in nature and, as he said, "turned himself in" when he realized he was "out of contact" with reality. He was hospitalized immediately. Three patients were perceived to be ill by their families and friends. One was taken to a psychiatrist after a friend had convinced her husband that she was mentally ill. The husband and friend took this woman to a psychiatrist who previously had treated the friend. The woman accepted the situation and began ambulatory treatment. Most referrals in class III involved situations where the sick member's behavior became so disturbed that the family could no longer cope with it and called a physician. The police brought two class III persons to the attention of a psychiatrist. In one case, a young man was wandering along the street at three a.m. when he was stopped by a police car. The police realized that he did not know what he was doing and took him home. The father called a physician who examined the young man and referred him to a private psychiatrist. This case is interesting in that the man was not arrested but was taken home by the police who realized that he was ill. We infer that this action was related to the policeman's perception of the man's middle class status.

Class IV individuals are referred to psychiatrists by all types of decision-making persons, but the greatest number are seen first by private practitioners. Clinic physicians and public officers see about an equal number. Outside the family there are few referrals from any one source.

In class V, the police and courts, social agencies, and clinic physicians make over four out of five referrals. The police and courts alone make over half the referrals. The general sequence of events in these cases is as follows: The disturbed individual attracts the attention of the police, often by breach of the peace or by molesting other persons. After a complaint has been made, the police arrest the disturbed person and take him to jail where he usually remains until a psychiatrist is brought into the case. If the prisoner is obviously psychotic, the police may take him directly to the Emergency Room of the community hospital where he is seen by a psychiatrist who is on call at all times. Social workers and public health nurses make referrals when they perceive a person who is in need of psychiatric attention. This recommendation is often resisted by the patient. Schizophrenic individuals in class V often come to the attention of physicians when they come to the dispensary of the community hospital for some physical ailment. Upon examination, the physician may decide that they are in need of psychiatric care and personally take the patient to the psychiatric clinic; experience has shown that otherwise the patient may simply walk out. Systematic observance of practices in the Emergency Room of the community hospital shows that when lower status persons attempt suicide, little attention is given to the possibility that they may be disturbed. If the patient can be treated medically or surgically without being admitted to the hospital, this is done. Such a patient is discharged without a referral having been made to the psychiatric service. If the patient has to be admitted to the hospital, because of the near success of the suicidal act, a referral may be made to the psychiatric service. However, before the referral is made, the suicidal act must be appraised as the act of a disturbed individual by some responsible person in the hospital. One of our class V patients came to the attention of a clinic physician when he reported for work as an orderly. The physician realized that the man was psychotic and took him to the psychiatric dispensary. Within a matter of hours, he was in the state hospital.

Summary and Conclusions

We have discussed the milestones a person passes on his way to the psychiatrist. We illustrated the first three milestones with clinical materials drawn from the study. We stressed that the *appraisal* of abnormal behavior as disturbed, in a psychiatric sense, depends on four kinds of variables: (1) the tolerance of the individual and the society for certain kinds of behavior, (2) the general sensitivity of persons and groups to psychological components in behavior, (3) the attitudes of different responsible persons in the community toward psychiatry (this includes the type of treatment psychiatry has to offer the individual and the community to help handle abnormal behavior traceable to psychogenic or sociogenic distur-

bances), and (4) the class status of the persons whose behavior is appraised as disturbed.

The implementation of a decision that a person should be treated by a psychiatrist for his disturbed behavior is linked to class status. There is a definite tendency to induce disturbed persons in classes I and II to see a psychiatrist in more gentle and "insightful" ways than is the practice in class IV and especially in class V, where direct, authoritative, compulsory, and, at times, coercively brutal methods are used. We see this difference most frequently in forensic cases of mentally ill persons who are treated often according to their class status. The goddess of justice may be blind, but she smells differences, and particularly class differences. In sum, perception of trouble, its evaluation, and decisions about how it should be regarded are variables that are influenced in highly significant ways by an individual's class status.

NOTES

1. We are indebted to Dr. John Clausen, Chief, Socio-Environmental Laboratory, National Institute of Mental Health, for this phrase.
2. For an extensive discussion of this question, see F. C. Redlich, "The Concept of Normality," *American Journal of Psychotherapy,* Vol. 3 (July 1952), pp. 551–576.
3. Editor's note: For a description of how social class status was operationalized see the author's "Social Stratification and Psychiatric Disorders" which is reprinted in Part II-C of this volume.
4. This class V lay judgment will be supported with statistical data in Chapter Nine when we discuss duration of treatment by class status.
5. In a paper, "The Concept of Health in Psychiatry" [Leighton, Clausen, and Wilson (editors), *Explorations in Social Psychiatry,* Basic Books, Inc., 1957], Redlich cites a striking example from the court-martial scene in Herman Wouk's *The Caine Mutiny.*
6. Verbal communication by J. Rakusin.

PART FOUR

Entering the
Psychiatric Enterprise

INTRODUCTION

The preceding section focused on ways in which the community responds to individuals who produce what Goffman termed "organizational havoc." One time-honored method of accommodation to the troublesome individuals is to not accommodate them at all—the community actively excludes the troublemakers. In the medieval period expulsion assumed a particularly dramatic form. In the so-called *Narrenschiff* or "ship of fools," madmen were sometimes handed over to boatmen to be taken to distant ports (Foucault, 1967). The boatmen and their boats have since passed away, but their function has not. Individuals are still excluded and expelled from their primary groups and networks, but it is no longer the boatmen who stand at the boundary of communal membership: it is the policeman, the psychologist, the social worker, and other ancillary personnel who make decisions in the name of the mental illness enterprise. In this section we focus on gatekeeping work—on the way in which decisions to accept or reject individuals for care, treatment, or observation are made. These decisions are a function of behaviors exhibited and a variety of situational and organizational factors.

Many of the terms contained in the mental illness idiom are difficult to define with precision. Since they are ambiguous it is not surprising that they are applied in an unreliable fashion, that is, different observers apply the terms to different behavioral patterns. One person's schizophrenia is another's neurosis or yet another's normality. While studies do not quite suggest such an extreme Pirandellian world, they do indicate that psychiatric experts are frequently unable to agree on what counts as instances of madness. Many years ago, for example, Asch (1949) found that three psychiatrists were unable to agree on the major diagnostic category in more than 45.7 percent of the cases they observed and diagnosed. Subsequent studies complemented Asch's findings (Spitzer and Fleiss, 1974). As Stoller and Geertsma (1963) suggested, "Art far outweighs science when experts in the field of psychiatry try to say what they have discovered in another person, and . . . practitioners of the art disagree with each other much more than is commonly recognized.''

Although the behaviors of the patient are subject to different interpretation and the presence or absence of symptoms is loosely correlated with psychiatric decisions, the application of psychiatric labels is not a capricious process. An axiom of social psychology states that the more ambiguous or equivocal the stimulus, the more likely it is that perceptions will be influenced by extrinsic factors and forces. The axiom is an appropriate characterization of many decisions made within the mental health enterprise. Because of the nebulous character of psychiatric symptoms, psychiatric decision making is responsive to a range of situational factors other than the immediate behavioral display of the patient. An experiment by Temerlin (1968) indicates that certain psychiatric decisions are influenced by the suggestions of prestigious experts. Various groups of subjects, including psychiatrists and psychologists, were asked to diagnose a sound-recorded interview with an actor scripted to portray a normal, healthy man. Prior to hearing the interview, some of the groups were told that according to professionals of very high standing the person on tape was ''a very interesting man because he looks neurotic, but actually is quite psychotic.'' The control groups did not receive the prestige suggestion. While none of the individuals in the control groups diagnosed the individual as psychotic, and the vast majority of them felt the individual was healthy, 60 percent (fifteen of twenty-five) of psychiatrists who received the prestige suggestion diagnosed the individual as psychotic and the remainder felt that a neurosis or some other disorder was present. In a study of the actual decision making of a major psychiatric facility, Mendel and Rapaport (1969) found that while numerous factors were related to the decision to hospitalize, the severity of the patient's symptoms was not one of them. Although the decision makers felt that symptoms were a major determinant of their decision, ''the group of patients who were hospitalized could not be distinguished from those who were not hospitalized on the basis of the decision maker's estimate of the severity of symptoms.'' On the other hand, the decision to hospitalize was strongly related to whether the patient had been hospitalized previously, the profession and experience of the decision maker (social workers and the more experienced tending to commit less than others), the time of decision, and the availability of support resources. In a recent study of release decisions and the degree of dangerousness of a patient, Kress (1979) found that judgments of evaluation teams depended heavily on the orientation of the team psychiatrist. Despite the fact that all teams confronted patients fairly comparably in terms of the proportion of patients who had engaged in aggressive acts, the team containing a sociologically-oriented psychiatrist recommended continued commitment less frequently than teams containing organically-oriented or eclectic psychiatrists. In one of the more dramatic studies of recent years, Rosenhan (see Part V) demonstrated that psychiatric staff members were so affected by the perceptual set encouraged by their profession and immediate setting that they were unable to discriminate pseudopatients, who reported a few symptoms, from genuine mental patients.

One of the most interesting sources of variation in psychiatric diagnoses and decisions are organizational constraints and controls. Psychiatric decision making does not occur in a social vacuum, but in specific organizational settings that exert distinctive pressures upon the selection of decision rules. Szasz (1970) has suggested that there are deep differences between the traditional contractual psychiatrist-patient relation and the new forms of institutional psychiatry. Contractual psychiatry refers to psychiatric interventions freely sought out by a patient. The relation is based on some form of contract and may be terminated by either psychiatrist or patient. In contractual psychiatry the psychiatrist is paid by the patient, while institutional psychiatry refers to psychiatric interventions imposed on persons by agencies over whom the patients have little control. The institutional psychiatrist is a bureaucratic employee paid by public or private organizations. Institutional psychiatry includes evaluations of persons for commitment to mental hospitals, examinations of defendants to determine competence to stand trial, and examinations of employees to determine their fitness for a job. While "the contractual psychiatrist offers himself to his patients, who must pay him, must want to be his patients, and are free to reject his help," writes Szasz, "the institutional psychiatrist imposes himself on his 'patients,' who do not pay him, do not want to be his patients, and are not free to reject his 'help.' "

The institutional context determines the extent to which psychiatric personnel function as agents of the patient or of some other party. The institutional context also affects the nature of the classification system used to describe individuals and the tendency to make one or another type of classification. In situations where the psychiatrist is the agent of the patient, diagnoses are more apt to be made in accord with the patient's expressed interests. This does not necessarily preclude judgments of mental illness. Indeed, it may promote such diagnoses when they provide the client with benefits (compared to other diagnostic possibilities—such as lying or malingering). The latter labels may be invoked when the examiner is an agent not of the patient but of a bureaucratic state organization with its own goals and demands.

In "Sociology of the Therapeutic Situation" Szasz further explores the nature of the relation between physician or psychiatrist and the patient and its consequences for diagnosis. Szasz identifies three major forms of practice: private, charity, and insured, which differ in the extent to which the patient is able to exercise control over the relation. Each type of practice is further characterized by different types of rewards for the therapist. Although Szasz does not fully trace the connections of this point, it is implied that different forms of control and incentive are reflected in the types of diagnoses and decisions likely to be forthcoming. Szasz also examines the sociopolitical context of diagnosis by comparing Western therapeutic practice where it is unclear to whom the therapist is ultimately responsible and Russian state-supported medical care where the physician is clearly an agent of the state. Szasz suggests that these divergent relations affect the likelihood of mental illness being invoked as a diagnostic category. While the analysis is not as thoroughly documented as one would like, it explicates some organizational and sociopolitical factors involved in diagnostic decisions. Many studies of psychiatric diagnosis (such as the 1975 Rosenhan study found in Part V) show how psychiatric diagnosis is affected by cognitive and attitudinal factors of decision makers. Szasz's analysis suggests that these cognitive factors and decision rules are patterned by the organizational context.

Daniels (1969), in her study of psychiatry in the military, has described some of the ways in which organizational demands supersede the traditional psychiatrist-patient relationship and affect the nature of psychiatric decision making. Whereas many features of the traditional psychiatrist-patient relation are under the control of parties in that relation, the situation is different in the military. "Who may and who must see the psychiatrist, what kind of treatment may be given, and when it must be given," writes Daniels, "are all matters defined by the military organization rather than areas of negotiation open to the parties directly involved." Other contingencies also affect the nature of psychiatric decisions. During manpower shortages, pressures from high officials may promote the most strict and incautious interpretation of categories such as "unsuitable" or "inept."

In *The Taming of the Troops,* Radine examines some of the ways in which the military's manpower needs were translated into pressures on military psychologists to define as few men as possible as mentally ill. One consequence of these pressures was that individuals with complaints of a psychiatric nature were treated in comparatively cursory fashion. In the case of breakdown in combat, a man was sent back to the division psychiatrist only after a medical corpsman found he could not handle the case in a matter of hours. And even when psychiatrists saw patients, treatment was minimal. "Their direct services were limited mainly to crisis intervention and evaluation," writes Radine, "and their in-patient treatment consisted mostly of drugging the soldier to sleep for a day or so, followed by fairly brief consultation." Following the lead of societal reaction theorists, Radine suggests that it is precisely military psychiatry's reluctance to apply the label "mentally ill," and to minimize the nature of the treatment response, that accounts for the decline in neuropsychiatric casualties from an all-time high in World War II to the low level during the Vietnam War.

The military is but one organizational context of psychiatric decision making. Other contexts establish different pragmatic parameters and demands with correspondingly different effects on the nature of psychiatric reasoning and the distribution of psychiatric decisions. Emerson (1969) examined the ways in which the practices of a psychiatric clinic serving the juvenile court of a large Eastern city were shaped by organizational pressures. He noted that there were many factors that inhibited psychiatric personnel from redefining criminal events and character in psychiatric terms, thus preventing incarceration. Clinic staff were heavily dependent on the court and its probation staff for information about the referral and often looked to the probation staff for guidelines regarding a reasonable or realistic evaluation. The staff's perception was dependent upon "sources in whose eyes the delinquent may be completely discredited." Not going along with the court's initial or anticipated evaluation entailed additional time and effort from already overly scheduled personnel. As Emerson observed, "Clinic work proceeds more smoothly the more exactly one follows the expected course of events, relying on what the probation officer has worked out previously and leaving primary responsibility in his hands." These and other constraints undermined the independence of the clinic and increased compliance with prevailing court definitions of what was "reasonable" and "realistic."

The gateways to the psychiatric enterprise are not controlled exclusively by psychiatric personnel, since the decision to seek outside intervention in a trouble situation is often made by family members (Emerson & Pollner, 1978). This may involve forcing the individual to a clinic or hospital or it may entail enlisting the aid of police. The frequent involvement of police in trouble situations and their power to refer individuals for psychiatric observation and evaluation make them a most important feeder agency to the psychiatric enterprise. In "Police Discretion in Emergency Apprehension of the Mentally Ill," Bittner describes some pragmatic and organizational factors affecting police involvement in emergency situations. Bittner finds that police are reluctant to hospitalize for numerous reasons, ranging from the fact that such activity is not the sort that advances a career or gains the esteem of colleagues to the sheer tediousness of the actual procedure. Police reluctance to hospitalize does not mean that they do not hospitalize—they obviously do—nor does it mean that they refrain from engaging the trouble situation through other means. As Bittner points out, the police may use a variety of measures from "psychiatric first aid" to an informal type of "continuing care" in the interests of what police regard as their fundamental task of keeping the peace.

References

Philip Asch, "The Reliability of Psychiatric Diagnoses," *Journal of Abnormal and Social Psychology*, Vol. **44** (1949), 271–76.

Arlene K. Daniels, "The Captive Professional: Bureaucratic Limitations in the Practice of Military Psychiatry," *Journal of Health and Social Behavior*, Vol. **10,** No. 4 (December, 1969), 255–65.

Robert M. Emerson, *Judging Delinquents: Context and Process in Juvenile Court,* Chicago: Aldine Publishing Co., 1969.

Robert M. Emerson and Melvin Pollner, "The Worst First: Policies and Practices of Psychiatric Case Selection," *Sociology of Work and Occupation,* Vol. 5, No. 1 (1978), 75–96.

Francesca Kress, "Evaluations of Dangerousness," *Schizophrenia Bulletin,* Vol. **5,** No. 2 (1979), 211–217.

Michel Foucault, *Madness and Civilization,* (translated by Richard Howard), New York: The New American Library, 1967.

Werner M. Mendel and Samuel Rapaport, "Determinants of the Decision for Psychiatric Hospitalization," *The Archives of General Psychiatry,* Vol. **20** (March, 1969), 321–328.

Robert L. Spitzer and J. L. Fleiss, "Reanalysis of the Reliability of Psychiatric Diagnosis", *British Journal of Psychiatry,* Vol. **125,** (1974), 341–347.

Robert J. Stoller and R. H. Geertsma, "The Consistency of Psychiatrists Clinical Judgements," *Journal of Nervous and Mental Disease,* Vol. **137** (1963), 58–66.

Thomas S. Szasz, *Law, Liberty and Psychiatry: An Inquiry into the Social Uses of Mental Health Practices,* New York: Macmillan, 1963.

Thomas S. Szasz, *The Manufacture of Madness,* New York: Dell Publishing Co., Inc., 1970.

Maurice K. Temerlin, "Suggestion Effects in Psychiatric Diagnosis," *Journal of Nervous and Mental Disease,* Vol. **147,** No. 4 (1968), 349–53.

THOMAS S. SZASZ

Sociology of the Therapeutic Situation

Psychiatrists have traditionally regarded mental illness as a problem apart from and independent of the social context in which it occurred. The symptomatic manifestations of diseases of the body, for instance diphtheria or syphilis, are indeed independent of the sociopolitical conditions of the country in which they occur. A diphtheritic membrane looked the same whether it occurred in a patient in Czarist Russia or Victorian England.

Since mental illness was considered to be basically like bodily illness, it was logical that no attention was

Reprinted from Thomas S. Szasz, *The Myth of Mental Illness,* New York: Harper, 1961, pages 52–72, by permission of the author and publisher.

paid to the social conditions in which the alleged disease occurred. This is not to say that the effects of social conditions on the causation of illness were not appreciated. On the contrary, this sort of relationship had been recognized since antiquity. However, although it was known that poverty and malnutrition favored the development of tuberculosis, or sexual promiscuity the spread of syphilis, it was nevertheless held that once these diseases made their appearance, their *manifestations* were the same whether the patient was rich or poor, nobleman or serf. Although the phenomenal features of bodily illnesses are independent of the socioeconomic and political structure of the society in which they occur, this is not true of so-called mental illnesses. The manifestations of psychosocial disabilities vary in accordance with educational, socioeconomic, religious, and political factors.[1]

When persons belonging to different religious and socioeconomic groups become bodily ill—for example, with pneumonia or bronchogenic carcinoma—their bodies manifest the same sort of physiological derangements. Hence, in principle, for given diseases all patients should receive the same treatments, irrespective of who they are. This is the scientifically correct position with respect to physicochemical disturbances of the body. There have been attempts to apply this asocial and amoral standard of treatment to so-called mental illnesses, to which, in my opinion, it does not apply. To understand why it does not apply, it is necessary to examine and make explicit how therapeutic attitudes—or, more precisely, physician-patient relationships—vary in accordance with changes in historical and sociopolitical circumstances. In other words, our task now will be to show how the same sorts of symptoms and illnesses are differently treated in different social situations. To accomplish this, the characteristic therapeutic situations of three different sociocultural settings will be briefly described and analyzed. They are: (1) late nineteenth-century, Western European medicine; (2) medical practice in contemporary Western democracies, especially in the United States; and (3) Soviet medical practice.

The term "therapeutic situation" will be used to refer to medical and psychotherapeutic practice. Since the interrelations of social structure, value, and therapeutic situation are numerous and complex (Sigerist, 1951, 1960), two clearly identifiable aspects of the general problem will be selected for special attention. They may be stated in the form of questions: (1) Whose agent is the therapist (physician, psychotherapist, etc.)? (2) How many persons, or institutions, are directly involved in the therapeutic situation?

Nineteenth-century Liberalism, Capitalism, and Individualism

Nineteenth-century European liberalism and its concurrent economic developments had significant, but probably little understood, effects on the patterns of the physician-patient relationship. Long before this time, medical care was regarded much as other economic goods. It was a commodity that could be purchased by the rich only. To the poor, when given, it had to be given

free, as charity. This social arrangement, with its roots in Greco-Roman medicine, was firmly established by the time modern scientific advances in medicine began, during the latter half of the nineteenth century. It should be recalled, too, that this period was characterized by the rapid flowering of liberal thoughts and deeds in Europe, as manifested, for example, by the abolition of serfdom in Austria-Hungary and Russia.

As industrialization and urbanization flourished, the proletariat replaced the unorganized and sociopsychologically less well-defined peasant class. Thus, a self-conscious and class-conscious capitalism developed, and with it recognition of a new form of mass suffering and disability, namely, poverty. The phenomenon of poverty, as such, was of course nothing new. However, the existence of huge numbers of impoverished people, crowded together within the confines of a city, was new. At the same time, and undoubtedly out of the need to do something about mass poverty, there arose "therapists" for this new "disease" of the masses. Among them, Karl Marx (1890) is, of course, the best known. He was no solitary phenomenon, however, but rather exemplified a new social role and function—the revolutionary as "social therapist" (Feuer, 1959). Along with these developments, the ethics of individualism were strongly bolstered. The basic value of the individual—as opposed to the interests of the masses or the nation—was emphasized, especially by the upper social classes. The professions, medicine foremost among them, espoused the ethical value of individualism. This value gradually became pitted against its antonym, collectivism. Although the ethics of individualism and collectivism are polar opposites, their present forms were achieved through a simultaneous development, and they often exist side by side. This was already the case, to some extent, in the days of Charcot, Breuer, and Freud. This contention may be illustrated by some observations concerning the therapeutic situations characteristic of that period.

It should be recalled that the physician in Charcot's Paris (or in his counterpart's Berlin, Moscow, or Vienna) was usually engaged in two diametrically opposite types of therapeutic situations. In one, he was confronted by a private patient of means. This meant that he served, by and large, as the patient's agent, having been hired by him to make a diagnosis and, if possible, achieve a cure. The physician, in turn, demanded payment for services rendered. He thus had an economic incentive, in addition to other incentives, to help his patient. Furthermore, since some bodily illnesses were considered shameful (including not only venereal diseases but tuberculosis and certain dermatological ail-

---

1. In this connection, see Freud's discussion of the personality development of two imaginary children, one growing up in a poor, the other in a well-to-do family (1916–1917, pp. 308–312).

ments as well), a wealthy person could also avail himself of the social protection of privacy. As a rich man could buy a house large enough to provide several rooms for his sole occupancy, so also he could buy the services of a physician for his sole use. In its extreme form, this amounted to having a personal physician, much as one had a valet, maid, or cook. This custom is by no means extinct. In some parts of the world, wealthy or socially prominent people still have personal physicians whose duty is to care only for them or perhaps their families.

A similar, but less extreme, arrangement is afforded by the private, two-person medical situation. This arrangement insures for the patient the time, effort, and privacy which he considers necessary for his care and still allows the physician to care for other patients within the limits of his available time and energy. The development of privacy as an integral part of the (private) therapeutic situation seems to be closely tied to the capitalistic economic system.[2] The Hippocratic oath commands the physician to respect and safeguard the patient's confidential communications. The Greek physician of antiquity practiced, of course, in a capitalist society, selling his skills to the rich, and helping the poor without recompense.

It is implicit in this discussion that having access to a private therapeutic relationship is desirable. Why is this sort of privacy desired? The answer lies in the connections between illness (or disability) and shame, and between shame and privacy. A few brief comments concerning this subject will have to suffice here. The feeling of shame is intimately related to what other people think of one. Exposure and humiliation are feared both as punishments for shameful acts and as stimuli for increasingly intense feelings of shame (Piers and Singer, 1953). In contrast to public exposure, secrecy or privacy protects the person from being excessively ''punished'' for his shameful behavior. Irrespective of whether the shameful event is the result of physical disability, psychological conflict, or moral weakness, it is more easily acknowledged if it is communicated to a single person—as in the confessional or in private psychotherapy—than if it has to be made known to many people. Accordingly, privacy in medical or psychotherapeutic relationships is useful because it pro-

tects the patient from undue embarrassment and humiliation, and thus facilitates mastery of the problem.

In addition to protecting the patient from embarrassment, privacy and secrecy in the therapeutic situation are desirable and necessary also to protect him from ''real''—that is, social rather than intrapersonal—dangers. Social isolation and ostracism, loss of employment, and injury to family and social status are some of the dangers that may threaten a person should his condition or diagnosis become public knowledge. In this connection, such possibilities as syphilis in a schoolteacher, psoriasis in a cook, or schizophrenia in a judge may be considered. These, however, are merely illustrative examples. The possibilities both of rewards and penalties incurred for publicly established diagnoses are virtually limitless. The precise character of the rewards and penalties will vary, once again, with the intellectual-scientific development and moral climate of the society (e.g., Butler, 1872).

The second type of therapeutic situation to be considered is charity practice. The differences between it and private practice have often been overlooked as a result of concentrating on the patient's disease and the physician's alleged desire to cure it. In traditional charity practice, the physician was not principally the patient's agent. Sometimes he was not the patient's agent at all. Accordingly, a truly private—in the sense of confidential—relationship between patient and physician could not develop. The physician was technically and legally responsible to his superiors and employers. He was, therefore, bound to orient himself for his rewards, at least to some extent, to his employer, rather than to his patient (and his own conscience). This in no way negates the possibility that the physician may still remain strongly motivated to help his patient. It is often maintained nowadays that removing the financial involvement with the patient enables the physician better to concentrate on the technical task at hand (provided that he is adequately remunerated). While this might well be true in thoracic surgery, it need not be equally true in psychoanalysis. In any case, it is clear that the financial inducement which the private patient offers the physician is absent in charity practice. The main features of these two types of therapeutic situations are summarized in Table 1.

The contrast between private and public medical care is often pictured as though it were rather like the difference between a palace and a hovel. One is fine and expensive; anyone who could afford to secure it would be a fool if he did not do so, especially if he needed it. The other is inferior and second rate; at best, it makes life livable. Although physicians, politicians, and others have tried to tell the poor that medical care of the

2. I do not wish to imply that privacy (in medical or other relationships) is necessarily tied to capitalism as a socioeconomic system. Rather, it appears that the ability to command privacy (or secrecy) depends on social status or power. Money is often the means whereby such power is implemented. Significantly, however, men having high social status in communist societies may have access to privacy without this being dependent on monetary considerations, whereas highly situated persons in capitalist societies, especially if they are in the public eye, often find it virtually impossible to secure privacy in therapeutic relationships.

TABLE 1

Sociology of the Therapeutic Situation Private Versus Charity Practice

Characteristics of the Situation	Private Practice	Charity Practice
Number of participants	Two (or few) Two-person situation "Private"	Many Multiperson situation "Public"
Whose agent is the therapist?	Patient's Patient's guardian's (e.g., pediatrics) Patient's family's	Employer's (e.g., institution, state, etc.)
Sources and nature of the therapist's rewards	Patient: money, referrals, etc.	Employer: money, promotion, prestige through status
	Patient's relatives and friends: satisfaction from having helped Self: satisfaction from mastery Colleagues: satisfaction from proven competence	Patient's relatives and friends: satisfaction from having helped Self: satisfaction from mastery Colleagues: satisfaction from proven competence

indigent was as good as that of the rich, more often than not this message fell on deaf ears. The facts of life are stubborn and difficult to disguise. Thus, instead of accepting this pious message, people have tried to raise their standard of living. In this effort, the people of the United States and some European countries have been the most successful, so far. This has resulted in certain fundamental changes in the patterns of medical care— and hence in the sociology of the therapeutic situation— in these countries. I shall comment on these changes now, and shall then consider medical developments in the Soviet Union.

The Affluent Society and Its Patterns of Health Care

Several contemporary economists (e.g., Drucker, 1949) have called attention to the fact that while traditional economic thought is rooted in the sociology of poverty and want, the socioeconomic problems of modern America, and to a lesser extent those of Western Europe, must be understood in terms of the sociology of excess productivity, wealth, and leisure. In *The Affluent Society,* Galbraith (1958) has presented a masterfully executed economic portrait of the age of opulence. The medical sociology of this era has yet to be written.

Progressive technological and sociocultural sophistication has led to a number of means whereby people may guard themselves against future poverty, want, and helplessness. One of these is insurance. We shall be especially concerned with the effects of health insurance on medical and psychotherapeutic relationships.

Insured Practice

From our present point of view it matters little whether protection from illness has been guaranteed for the individual by a private insurance company or furnished by the state. Health protection by means of privately purchased insurance is in the tradition of private ownership and capitalism and is, accordingly, popular in the United States. Protection by means of taxation and socialized medicine has been the form chosen in Great Britain. To most Americans, this appears to be more socialistic and hence bad. It is essential to discard these clichés, so that we can address ourselves to the relevant variables in these situations.

Health insurance introduces a completely new phenomenon into the practice of medicine. The most significant feature of insured practice—a name which I suggest to distinguish it from both private and charity practice—is that it is neither private nor public. The physician-patient relationship is so structured that the doctor is neither the patient's nor a charitable institution's sole agent. This arrangement cannot be reduced to the old patterns of medical care, nor can it be understood in their terms. It is commonly believed that the insured situation does not differ significantly from the private practice situation. The only difference, it is thought, is that the physician is paid by the insurance company instead of by the patient. Rarely is insured medicine regarded as similar to charity practice. Yet I submit that there are probably more significant similarities between insured and charity practice than between insured and private practice. The insurance arrangement, like the charitable one, makes a two-person, confidential relationship between doctor and patient virtually impossible.

Without penetrating further into the sociological intricacies of insured medicine, I should like to offer some generalizations which may be useful for our study of hysteria and the problem of mental illness. It appears to be a general rule that the more clear-cut, "objective," or socially acceptable a patient's disease, the more closely insured practice will resemble private practice. For example, if a housewife slips on a banana peel in her kitchen and fractures her ankle, her treatment may not be significantly influenced by whether she or an insurance company or the government pays for it.

It is a corollary of this rule that the more an illness deviates from something that happens to a person, and the more it is something that the person does or makes happen, the greater shall be the differences between the insured situation and the private, two-person situation. For instance, if our patient falls in a factory rather than in her kitchen, she will then not only receive compensation but also be granted permission to stay away from work. And if she has a young child with whom she would like to spend more time at home, she will have a strong incentive to be disabled for more than a minimum length of time. Obviously, this sort of situation requires an arbiter or judge to decide whether a person is or is not disabled ("sick"). The physician is generally regarded as the proper person for this task. It may be argued that physicians in private practice also play this role. But this is fallacious argument. The physician in private practice is primarily the patient's agent. Should there be a conflict between his opinion and the presumed "real facts"—as may occur when the patient is involved with life insurance companies, draft boards, or industrial concerns—the latter groups take recourse to employing *their own physicians*. In the case of the draft board, for example, the examining physician has absolute power to overrule the private physician's opinion. And if he does not have such power, for example in the case of an industrial concern, the conflict of interests must be arbitrated by a court of law.

In the case of insured practice, the answer to the question "Whose agent is the physician?" is not clearly spelled out. As a result, it is possible for the physician to shift from one position to another. He may act entirely on behalf of the patient one minute and line up against him the next.[3] In the latter case, the patient can change physicians, if the contract permits. In any case, the entire arrangement precludes a genuine two-person therapeutic relationship.

As a third generalization, I should like to offer the following. So-called mental illnesses share only a single significant characteristic with bodily diseases: the sufferer or "sick person" is more or less disabled from

performing certain activities. The two differ in that mental illnesses can be understood only if they are viewed as occurrences that do not merely happen to a person but rather are brought on by him (perhaps unconsciously), and hence may be of some value to him. This assumption is not necessary—indeed, it is unsupportable—in the typical cases of bodily illness.

The premise that the behavior of persons said to be mentally ill is meaningful and goal-directed—provided one is able to understand the patient's behavior from *his* particular point of view—underlies all "rational" psychotherapies. Moreover, if the psychotherapist is to perform his task well, he must not be influenced by socially distracting considerations concerning his patient. This condition can be met best if the relationship is rigidly restricted to the two people involved in it.

On the one hand, therefore, the affluent society brought the widespread adoption of health insurance into being; on the other, it fostered the growth and economic rewards of private medical and psychotherapeutic practice.

The Private Practice Situation

It is necessary now to refine our conception of private practice. Thus far, this term has been used in its conventional sense, to denote the medical activities of any physician *not employed* by an institution or agency (e.g., a company or labor union). According to this definition, such a physician is engaged in private practice, irrespective of how or by whom he is paid. This common-sense definition will no longer suffice for our purposes. Instead, we shall have to adopt a more limited definition of private practice, based on strict pragmatic criteria. Let us define the Private Practice Situation as a contract between patient and physician: the patient hires the doctor to help him with his own health care, and pays the physician for it. If the physician is hired by someone other than the patient, or is paid by another party, the medical relationship will no longer fall in the category of Private Practice Situation. This definition highlights (1) the *two-person nature of the relationship,* and (2) the fundamental *autonomy and self-determination of the patient* (Szasz, 1957a, 1959d). I shall continue to use the expression "private practice" in its conventional sense, to refer to all types of noncharity, noninstitutional practice. The term Private Practice Situation (with initials capitalized) will be used to designate the two-person therapeutic situation as described above (see Table 2).

Let us remember that an opulent society fosters not only health insurance but also private practice. In the United States, a considerable proportion of the latter is psychiatric or psychotherapeutic practice. This propor-

---

3. The terms "for" or "against" the patient, and "good" or "bad" for him, are used here solely in accordance with the patient's own definition of his wants and needs. Any other definition, such as attempting to determine whether the therapist is acting on behalf of, or opposed to, the patient in accordance with the therapist's avowed intentions, can lead only to confusion and social exploitation. A good example is the notion that all psychiatrists are "therapists" acting on behalf of the patient's best interests, irrespective of what they in fact do (Szasz, 1957b, 1960b).

TABLE 2

Sociology of the Therapeutic Situation
Private Practice Versus Insured Practice

Characteristics of the Situation	Private Practice Situation	Insured Practice
Number of participants	Two Two-person situation	Three or more Multiperson situation
Whose agent is the therapist?	Patient's	Therapist's role is poorly defined and ambiguous: Patient's agent, when in agreement with his aspirations Society's agent, when in disagreement with patient's aspirations His own agent, trying to maximize his own gains (e.g., compensation cases)
Sources and nature of the therapist's rewards	Patient: money, referrals, etc. Self: satisfaction from mastery Colleagues	Patient: cure, gratitude, etc. Self: satisfaction from mastery Colleagues System or state: money, promotion, etc.

tion becomes even more significant if it is considered not in relation to the general category of private practice, but rather in relation to the narrowly defined Private Practice Situation. Indeed, it seems that psychotherapeutic practice is the most important contemporary (American) representative of a truly two-person therapeutic relationship. Deterioration in the privacy of the traditional (nineteenth-century) medical situation may have been one of the stimuli for increasing the demand for psychotherapeutic services. Inasmuch as the physician is no longer the true representative of the patient, the latter has turned to the psychiatrist and to the nonmedical psychotherapist as new representatives of his best interests.

This is not to imply that deterioration in this privacy is mainly responsible for the increasing demand for psychotherapeutic help in contemporary America. The role of affluence itself might be significant in this connection, for as soon as people have more money than is needed to provide the so-called necessities of life (whatever these may be), they will expect to be "happy." They will then use some of their money to seek "happiness." The social function of psychotherapy, from this point of view, must be compared and contrasted not only with that of religion but also with that of alcohol, tobacco, cosmetics, and various recreational activities.

These considerations touch on the relationship between social class, mental illness, and the type of treatment received for it, a subject recently explored by Hollingshead and Redlich (1958). These authors found, for example, that affluent psychiatric patients tend to receive psychotherapy, while poor patients are treated with physical interventions. Psychological help and physical therapies represent such grossly divergent types of psychiatric actions that no meaningful comparison as to which is "better" can be made between them. Hollingshead and Redlich's findings clearly demonstrate, however, that there are significant connections between economic status, education, and a self-responsible, self-determinate mode of orienting one's self to a help-seeking situation. I emphasize this because I believe that the social impact of the affluent society on psychiatry (and on medicine, generally) is such as to both foster and inhibit the growth of a two-person therapeutic situation. Better education and economic security favor the conditions necessary for a two-person therapeutic contract. At the same time, the spread of insured health protection, whether through private insurance, veterans' benefits, or government-sponsored medical care, creates a new type of therapeutic relationship that tends to preclude a truly two-person arrangement.

Finally, it is worth noting that while the Private Practice Situation is being displaced by insured patterns of care in the democracies, in the Soviet Union it was displaced when physicians became employees of the state. Medical practice in Soviet Russia will now be examined to contrast the role of the physician as agent of the individual (patient) with his role as agent of the state.

Soviet Medicine and the Problem of Malingering

The Soviet Physician as Agent of the State

The great majority of the Russian population depends on medical services furnished by the state. Private practice exists, but is available only to those occupying the top layers of the Soviet social pyramid. Another crucial feature of the Russian medical scheme is the result of the government's strong emphasis on the production of agricultural, industrial, and other types of goods (Rostow, 1952). The need to work is impressed on the people in every possible way. It follows that for those who wish to avoid working, falling sick and remaining disabled is one of the most important avenues of escape from what they experience as an intolerable demand. Since the presence of sickness is not always obvious to the layman, the physician is chosen as the expert arbiter who must decide which of the persons who claim to be ill are "really ill," and which ones only "malinger." Field (1957) described this as follows:[4]

> It stands to reason that certification of illness cannot be left, under most circumstances, to the person who claims to be sick. This would make abuses too easy. It is the physician, then, as the only person technically qualified to do so, who must "legitimize" or "certify" sickness in the eyes of society. This means, in turn, that abuses of the patient's role will consist in conveying to the physician the impression that one's sickness is independent of one's conscious motivation—whereas it actually is not. This possibility beclouds the *classical assumption* that the person who comes to the physician must *necessarily* be sick (independently of motivation): on the contrary, in certain cases, just the opposite assumption may be held. This has, of course, important implications for both physician and "genuine" patient.
>
> It is held here that a society (or social group) which, for any number of reasons, cannot offer its members sufficient incentives of motivation for the faithful and spontaneous performances of their social obligations must rely on coercion to obtain such performances. Because of the presence of coercion such a society will also generate a high incidence of deviant behavior to escape coercion. *Simulation of illness (technically known as malingering) will be one form of such behavior. Malingering can be considered as a medical, a social, and a legal problem.* It is a medical problem only insofar as it is the physician's task to certify who is a *bona fide patient* and who is a *faker*. It is a social problem insofar as the assumption that the person who comes to the physician must necessarily be sick (independently of motivation) is no longer tenable. The opposite

assumption may sometimes be just as valid. It is often a legal problem because a fraud has been perpetrated.

> Malingering may have far-reaching consequences because the "business" of society (or the group) is not done and because ordinary social sanctions are inadequate to close this escape valve. This means, in turn, that some provision must be made, some mechanism devised, to control the granting of medical dispensations. The logical point at which to apply this control is the physician ([italics added] pp. 146–148).

According to Field, Russian physicians are afraid to be lenient with patients not demonstrably ill. There is widespread anxiety that every patient is a potential spy or *agent provocateur*.

The social status of the Soviet physician is relatively low. Most of them are women. Their status is similar to that of our social workers or public school teachers. A comparison of American and Soviet medicine raises many questions concerning the merits and shortcomings of public and private systems of education and medical care. I submit that the Soviet physician, the American social worker, and the American public school teacher share a significant common feature: each functions as an agent of society. By this I mean that individuals fulfilling these social roles are hired by society or by large social bodies (e.g., a school system), to minister to the needs of groupmembers (e.g., schoolchildren, persons on relief, the sick, etc.). *They are not hired by their customers, clients, or patients and, accordingly, do not owe their primary loyalties to them.* This arrangement tends to be beneficial to the group as a whole, but is not always advantageous for the specific individuals served. The clash of interests is greatest when the needs of the group and the individual are widely divergent.

I should now like to call attention to some connections between modern Soviet medicine on the one hand and the social role of the physician in charity practice, say in Charcot's day, on the other hand. The diagnosis of malingering was frequently made in both settings. This was due mainly to two factors. First, the physician was an agent of society (or some part of it), and not of the patient. Second, the physician tacitly espoused as his own the prevalent social values concerning the patient's productive usefulness in the social structure. The Soviet physician, for example, is identified with the value of industrial productivity, just as his nineteenth-century Western counterpart was identified with certain notions concerning the woman's "proper" role as wife and mother in that society (Szasz, 1959a). Escape from both roles—whether that of downtrodden worker or downtrodden woman—was left open along a number of routes, *disability* being one. It seems to me that as the

---

4. Much of the material on the Soviet medical system is based on Mark G. Field's book, *Doctor and Patient in Soviet Russia* (1957). Field's data derive almost entirely from the Stalinist period. It seems clear now that everyday life in Russia was rather tough then, especially during the war years. Since Stalin's death, life apparently has become much easier, the pressure to work and produce less insistent. Hence, the observations cited and the hypotheses proposed, while probably accurate for Stalinist Russia, may not be entirely valid for the current sociomedical situation in that country.

investigators' interest and sympathy turned from the group exerting pressure to the individual on whom pressure was being applied, there was a metamorphosis in the very conception of the problem. The first step, taken in Western countries some time ago, was the change of diagnosis from malingering to hysteria. Perhaps chiefly because of the different patterns of social evolution in Russia, this step has not yet been taken there. One would expect, however, that this change—or one similar to it—may occur in Russia, too, in the near future.

The change in terminology from malingering to hysteria, and through it to the general notion of mental illness as a designation for all sorts of social and interpersonal happenings, is thus regarded as reflecting *social evolution.* The first step, designating the disability malingering, commits the physician squarely to the camp of the oppressor. The second, designating it hysteria, makes him the agent of a "sick" (oppressed) individual. The third step, designating it "mental illness," denotes a stage at which the physician's precise social role and function are ambiguous and officially obscure.

The following quotation from Field (1957) illustrates how strongly the Soviet physician is committed to the role of agent of society, if necessary in opposition to the individualistic needs of any one patient:

> It is perhaps significant to note that the *Hippocratic oath,* which was taken by tsarist doctors (as it is in the West), *was abolished after the revolution because it "symbolized" bourgeois medicine* and was considered incompatible with the spirit of Soviet medicine. "If," continues a Soviet commentator in the *Medical Worker,* "the prerevolutionary physician was proud of the fact that for him 'medicine' and nothing else existed, the Soviet doctor on the other hand is proud of the fact that he actively participated in the building of socialism. *He is a worker of the state,* a servant of the people . . . *the patient is not only a person, but a member of socialist society"* ([italics added] p. 174).

The Hippocratic oath was abolished, I submit, not because it symbolized "bourgeois medicine"—for charity practice is as much a part of bourgeois medicine as private practice—but rather because the oath tends to define the physician as an agent of the patient. It was suggested elsewhere (Szasz, Knoff, and Hollender, 1958) that the Hippocratic oath is, among other things, a Bill of Rights for the patient. Accordingly, the conflict with which the Russian physician struggles is an ancient one—the conflict between individualism and collectivism. (A much abbreviated summary of the contrasting

TABLE 3

Sociology of the Therapeutic Situation Western Versus Soviet Practice

Characteristics of the Situation	Western Practice	Soviet Practice
Number of participants	Two or few Private, insured, state-supported	Many State-supported
Whose agent is the therapist?	Patient's Employer's His own *Physician's role is ambiguous*	Society's Patient's (insofar as patient is positively identified with the values of the state) *Physician's role is clearly defined as agent of society*
Ethical basis of therapeutic actions	Individualistic	Collectivistic
Diagnoses encouraged or permitted	Mental illness The sick society	Malingering Psychiatric diagnoses couched in physiologic terms
Diagnoses most avoided or considered nonexistent	Malingering	Mental illness (as problem in living)
Relative social status of physician	High	Low

characteristics of Western and Soviet medical systems is presented in Table 3).[5]

The Social Significance of Privacy in the Physician-Patient Relationship

Two features of Soviet medicine—first, the Russian physician's fear lest by being sympathetic with an *agent-provocateur*-malingerer he bring ruin on himself, and second, the abolition of the Hippocratic oath—make it necessary to examine further the role of privacy in the therapeutic situation. The first-mentioned observation shows that *the privacy of the physician-patient relation-*

5. Considerations of the nature and function of private medical practice in Soviet Russia were deliberately omitted from this discussion. Accordingly, in Table 3, under the heading "Soviet Practice," the salient features of only state-supported medical care are listed.

ship is not solely for the benefit of the patient. The belief that it is solely for the patient's benefit stems, in part, from the Hippocratic oath, which explicitly asserts that the physician shall not abuse the patient's trusted communications. The contemporary legal definition of confidential communications (to physicians) lends support to this view, since it gives the patient the power to waive confidentiality. Thus, the patient is the "owner" of his confidential communications. He is in control of when and how this information will be used, or when it shall be withheld.

However, in a psychoanalytic contract—at least as I understand it (Szasz, 1957b, 1959c)—the privacy of the relationship implies that the therapist will not communicate with others, irrespective of whether the patient gives permission for the release of information. Indeed, even the patient's pleading for such action on the part of the analyst must remain frustrated, if the two-person character of the relationship is to be preserved.

The common-sense view that confidentiality serves solely the patient's interests makes it easy to overlook the fact that the privacy of the physician-patient relationship provides indispensable protection for the therapist as well. By making the patient a responsible participant in his own treatment, the therapist is protected, to some extent, against the patient's (and the patient's family's, or society's) accusations of wrongdoing. If at all times the patient is kept fully informed as to the nature of the treatment, it will be his responsibility, at least in part, constantly to assess his therapist's performance, to demand changes whenever they appear necessary, and, finally, to leave his therapist should he feel that he is not receiving the help he needs.

There appears to be an inherent conflict between the benefits which the patient may derive from a private, two-person arrangement and the guarantees of protection afforded him by a measure of therapeutic publicity (the latter providing certain official, socially administered checks on the capabilities and performances of the therapist). In a private situation, the patient himself must protect his interests. Should he feel that his therapist has failed him, his chief weapon is to sever the relationship. Likewise, severing the relationship is the only protection for the (psychoanalytic) therapist, for he cannot coerce the patient into "treatment" by enlisting the help of others, for example, family members. In sharp contrast to the privacy of the psychoanalytic situation, the publicity of the Soviet therapeutic situation—at least in cases not involving top echelon personnel—fosters the use of mutually coercive influences on the parts of both patient and doctor. Thus, physicians can force patients to do various things by certifying or not certifying their illnesses; while patients, in revenge as it were, are

provided with wide latitude for denouncing physicians and bringing charges against them (Field, 1957, pp. 176–177).

These observations also help to account for the nonexistence of psychoanalysis, or of any other type of private psychotherapy, in the Soviet Union (Lebensohn, 1958; Lesse, 1958). The incompatibility of communism and psychoanalysis has been attributed to the communist claim that problems in living are due to the inequities of the capitalist social system. It seems to me, however, that the core of the conflict between psychoanalysis and communism is the privacy of the analytic situation. The latter conflicts with too many things in contemporary and near-contemporary Russian life, such as their medical arrangements, housing conditions, etc. As long as this remains the case, the privacy of the psychoanalytic situation must appear alien and unwanted. With provisions for more ample housing, more consumer goods, and perhaps with increasing use of private medical practice, the Russian social scene may be changing. It will be interesting to observe whether private psychotherapy emerges.

Medical Care as a Form of Social Control

It is evident that anything that affects large numbers of people, and over which the state (or the government) has control, may be used as a form of *social control*. In the United States, for example, taxation may be used to encourage or inhibit the consumption of certain goods. Since Russian medical services are controlled by the state, they may readily be used for the purpose of molding society (Hayek, 1960).

The frequent use of malingering as a medical diagnosis in the Soviet Union suggests that organized medicine is used as, among other things, a form of social tranquilization (Szasz, 1960a). In this regard, the similarities between Russian medicine and American social work are especially significant. Both are systems of social care. Both fulfill certain basic human needs, while at the same time both may be used—and, I believe, at times are used—to exert a subtle but powerful control on those cared for (Davis, 1938). In Russia, it is the government (or the state) that employs the physicians, and thus may use them to control the population—for example, by means of a diagnosis of malingering. In the United States, state or local governments or private philanthropic agencies (supported by the upper classes) employ social service workers. Without wishing to deny the benefits that often accrue to social work clients, this arrangement clearly empowers the employers to exert a measure of social control—in this case, over members of the lower classes. Both systems—that is, Soviet medicine and American social work—are thus admirably suited for the purpose of keeping "in line" potentially discontented members (or groups) of society.

Employing medical care in the characteristically ambivalent manner sketched above—to care for some of the patient's needs and at the same time to oppress him—is not a new phenomenon encountered first in the Soviet Union. It existed previously in Czarist Russia as well as in Western Europe. The severity of life in Czarist prisons—and perhaps in jails everywhere—was mitigated to some extent by the ministrations of relatively benevolent medical personnel, the latter constituting an integral part of the prison-system (Dostoevsky, 1861–1862). Since this social arrangement is widespread, I believe we are justified in placing a far-reaching interpretation on it. It may be regarded as a typical manifestation of an oppressive-coercive tension in the social system, such as occurs, for example, in an autocratic-patriarchal family. In such a family, the father is a tyrant, cruelly punitive toward his children, superior and deprecatory toward his wife. The children's life is made tolerable only by the ministrations of a kind, devoted mother. The social pressures of the Soviet (Stalinist) state, demanding ever-greater productivity, are reminiscent of the role of the harsh father; the citizen is the child; the protective mother is the physician.

In such a system, the mother (physician) not only protects the child (citizen) from the father (state) but by virtue of her intervention is also responsible for the maintenance of a precarious family homeostasis (or social *status quo*). To contribute to the overt breakdown of such a balance may be a constructive—and sometimes even an indispensable—step, provided that social reconstruction is desired.

This type of medical arrangement, like the family life on which it is based, also represents a "living out," in the framework of the existing social structure, of the basic human problem of the need to handle both "good" and "bad" objects. The crudely patriarchal family structure, so well described by Erikson (1950), offers a simple yet highly effective solution for this problem. Instead of fostering the synthesis of love and hate for the same persons, with subsequent recognition of the complexities of human relationships, the arrangement permits and even encourages the child—and later the adult—to live in a world of devils and saints. Thus, the father is all-bad, the mother all-good. This leads the (grown) child to feel constantly torn between saintly righteousness and abysmal guilt. Applying this model to the Soviet medical scheme, it is apparent that this problem and its solution appear here in a new edition, so to speak. The Soviet state—or better, the principles of

the ideal Communist system—remain the perfect "good object." The state furnishes "free" medical care to everyone who needs it, and of course the care is supposed to be faultless. If it is not, the blame lies with the physicians. Thus, to some extent, the physician fills the role of the "bad object" in the Soviet social scheme.[6] The citizen (patient, child) may be viewed as being sandwiched in between the (bad) doctor and the (good) state. It is consistent with this thesis that the state gives much space to public accusations against doctors (Field, 1957, pp. 176–177). Although these complaints may be loud, one wonders how effective they are. Presumably the patient cannot avail himself of the protection provided for him in Western countries—the right to bring suit for malpractice against the physician. To do this would mean bringing suit against the Soviet government itself. The arrangement, however, serves well as a means to keep both patients and physicians in line. Each possesses enough power to make life difficult for the other, yet neither has sufficient freedom to alter his own status.

In this connection, it is significant that the Russian citizens who have fled the country because of dissatisfaction with the system have expressed a marked preference for Soviet medicine as against the medical care patterns of West Germany and the United States (Inkeles and Bauer, 1959). Here is a striking illustration of how effectively the "good" and "bad" aspects of the Soviet social system have remained isolated in the minds of these people. The Soviet government's official concern for "health" (not specifically defined) is an unquestioned, absolute value. If something in relation to it goes wrong, another part of the system—in this case, the physician—is blamed.

The roots of the physician's role as "social worker" can be traced to antiquity. The fusion of priestly and medical functions made for a strong bond which was split asunder only in recent times—then to be reunited, explicitly in Christian Science, implicitly in some aspects of charity practice, psychotherapy, and Soviet medicine. It is alleged that the great Virchow said: "The physicians are the *natural attorneys of the poor*" (Field, 1957, p. 159). This concept of the physician's role must be scrutinized and challenged. There is nothing natural

6. The famous "doctors' plot" of early 1953 lends support to this hypothesis (Rostow, 1952, pp. 222–226). It was alleged that a group of highly placed physicians murdered several key Soviet officials and were also responsible for Stalin's rapidly declining health. After Stalin's death, the plot was branded a fabrication. In other words, the plot was not "real" but "malingered." My point is that, irrespective of the specific political conflicts and motives that might have triggered this accusation, physicians—the erstwhile coarchitects of the Soviet state (Field, 1957, p. 174)—were now accused of destroying the very edifice they had been commissioned to build.

about it, nor is it at all clear that it is necessarily always desirable that doctors should act as though they were attorneys.

At this point, some connections between the foregoing considerations and the historical narrative concerning Charcot, presented earlier, may be noted. It was suggested that the change from diagnosing some persons as malingerers to diagnosing them as hysterics was not a medical act, in the scientific-technical sense of the word, but rather an act of social promotion. Charcot, too, had acted as an "attorney for the poor." Since that time, however, social developments in Western countries have resulted in the creation of social organizations and social roles whose function is to be "attorneys for the poor" (i.e., to act as representatives of their special interests). The Marxist-socialist movement itself was perhaps the first of these. There were many others, too, such as labor unions, religious organizations (which, incidentally, are the traditional guardians of the "poor"), social work agencies, private philanthropies, and so forth. In the social setting of contemporary democracies, the physician may have a multitude of duties, but being the protector of the poor and oppressed is hardly one of them. The poor and downtrodden have their own—more or less adequate, as the case may be—representatives, at least in contemporary America.[7] There is the National Association for the Advancement of Colored People, the Anti-Defamation League, the Salvation Army, and a legion of other less well-known organizations whose chief purpose is the protection of various minority groups against social injustice. From the point of view of a scientific ethic—that is, from a position that values explicit honesty as against covert misrepresentation—all this is to the good. If an individual or group wishes to act in behalf of the interests of the poor, the Negro, the Jew, the immigrant, etc., it is desirable that this be made explicit. If this is true, by what right and reason do physicians project themselves (as physicians) into the role of protectors of this or that group? Among contemporary physicians, it is the psychiatrist who, more than any other specialist, has arrogated to himself the role of protector of the downtrodden.

Concurrently with the development of appropriate social roles and institutions for the protection of the poor, the medical profession witnessed the development of many new diagnostic and therapeutic techniques. Hence, for two important reasons, it became unnecessary for the physician to function as an "attorney for the poor." First, the poor now had real attorneys of their own, and therefore no longer needed to "cheat" their

way to being humanely treated by means of faking illness. Second, as the technical task which the physician had to perform became more difficult—that is, as modern surgery, pharmacotherapy, radiology, psychotherapy, etc., came into being—the physician's role became increasingly better defined by the nature of the technical operations in which he was engaged. For example, radiologists have certain well-defined jobs, as do urologists and neurosurgeons. This being the case, they may have neither time for nor interest in the task of also acting as "attorneys for the poor."

A Summing up

The prevalence of malingering in Russia, and of mental illness in the West, may be regarded as signs of the prevailing social conditions. These diagnostic labels refer only partly to the patients to whom they ostensibly point. They refer also to the labeler as an individual and a member of society (Stevenson, 1959; Wortis, 1950). (To some extent this is true for all diagnoses.) "Malingering" is a manifestation of strain in a collectivistic society. The label also betrays the physician's basic identification with the values of the group. "Mental illness," on the other hand, may be viewed as a manifestation of strain in an individualistic society. Yet mental illness is not the antonym of malingering, for the former diagnosis does not imply that the physician functions as the patient's sole agent. Mental illness is an ambiguous label. Those who use it seem to wish to straddle and evade the conflict of interests between the patient and his social environment (relatives, society, etc.). The significance of interpersonal and social conflicts tends to be obscured by emphasis on conflicts among internal objects (or identifications, roles, etc.) within the patient. I do not wish to minimize the theoretical significance and psychotherapeutic value of the basic psychoanalytic position concerning the function of internal objects. My thesis is simply that it is as possible for a person to use intrapersonal conflicts (or past misfortunes) to avoid facing up to interpersonal and sociopolitical difficulties as it is for him to use the latter difficulties to avoid facing up to the former. It is in this connection that mental illness plays an important role as a concept that claims to explain, whereas it only explains away (Hardin, 1956; Szasz, 1959b).

The evasion of interpersonal and moral conflicts by means of the concept of mental illness is expressed, among other things, in the present "dynamic-psychiatric" view of American life (Szasz, 1960a). According to this view, virtually every human event—from personal unhappiness and marital infidelity at one end of the spectrum to political misbehavior and deviant

---

7. In this connection, see for example *Attorney for the Damned*, a selection of Clarence Darrow's addresses (A. Weinberg, 1957).

moral conviction at the other—is regarded as a facet of the problem of mental illness. Along with this *panpsychiatric bias,* and probably largely because of it, the psychiatrist has tended to assume—without, however, having made this explicit—that the psychoanalytic two-person contract somehow applies to every other so-called psychiatric situation as well. Thus, the psychiatrist has habitually approached his problem—irrespective of whether he found it in the military service, the state hospital, or the court room—as though he were the patient's personal therapist (i.e., as though he were the patient's agent). He is, therefore, bound to find "psychopathology" or "mental illness," just as the Soviet physician—functioning as an agent of the (suspicious) state—is bound to discover "malingering." Yet neither finds or discovers anything remotely resembling an illness. Rather, the first, speaking in terms of mental illness, bases his prescription on the premise that the physician is the patient's agent; the other, speaking in terms of malingering, bases his prescription on the premise that he is an agent of society.

REFERENCES

S. Butler (1872), *Erewhon,* Harmondsworth, England: Penguin Books, 1954.

K. Davis, "Mental Hygiene and the Class Structure," *Psychiatry,* Vol. **1** (1938), 55.

F. M. Dostoevsky (1861−62), *Memoirs from the House of the Dead,* translated by Jessie Coulson, New York: Oxford University Press, 1956.

P. F. Drucker, *The New Society. The Anatomy of the Industrial Order,* New York: Harper, 1949.

E. H. Erikson, *Childhood and Society,* New York: W. W. Norton, 1950.

L. S. Feuer (editor), *Basic Writings on Politics and Philosophy, by Karl Marx and Friedrich Engels,* Garden City, N.Y.: Doubleday, 1959.

M. G. Field, *Doctor and Patient in Soviet Russia,* Cambridge, Mass.: Harvard University Press, 1957.

S. Freud (1916−17), *A General Introduction to Psychoanalysis,* Garden City, N.Y.: Doubleday, 1943.

J. K. Galbraith, *The Affluent Society,* Boston: Houghton Mifflin, 1958.

G. Hardin, "The Meaninglessness of the Word Protoplasm," *Scientific Monthly,* Vol. **82** (1956), 112.

F. A. Hayek, *The Constitution of Liberty,* Chicago: The University of Chicago Press, 1960.

A. B. Hollingshead and F. C. Redlich, *Social Class and Mental Illness. A Community Study,* New York: John Wiley, 1958.

A. Inkeles and R. A. Bauer, *The Soviet Citizen,* Cambridge, Mass.: Harvard University Press, 1959.

Z. Lebensohn, "Impressions of Soviet Psychiatry," *A.M.A. Archives of Neurology & Psychiatry,* Vol. **80** (1958), 735.

K. Marx, *Capital. A Critique of Political Economy. The Process of Capitalist Production,* translated from the Third German Edition by Samuel Moore and Edward Aveling, edited by Frederick Engels, New York: Modern Library, 1890.

G. Piers and M. G. Singer, *Shame and Guilt,* Springfield, Ill.: Charles C Thomas, 1953.

W. W. Rostow (1952), *The Dynamics of Soviet Society,* New York: Mentor Books, 1954.

H. E. Sigerist, "Primitive and Archaic Medicine," in *A History of Medicine,* Vol. I, New York: Oxford University Press, 1951.

H. E. Sigerist, *Henry Sigerist on the Sociology of Medicine,* edited by M. I. Roemer, New York: MD Publications, 1960.

A. Stevenson, "Adlai Stevenson on Psychiatry in U.S.S.R., *American Journal of Psychotherapy,* Vol. **13** (1959), 530.

T. S. Szasz, "On the Theory of Psycho-Analytic Treatment, *International Journal of Psycho-Analysis,* Vol. **38** (1957a), 166.

T. S. Szasz, "Commitment of the Mentally Ill: 'Treatment' or Social Restraint?" *Journal of Nervous and Mental Disease,* Vol. **125** (1957b), 293.

T. S. Szasz, "A Critical Analysis of Some Aspects of the Libido Theory: The Concepts of Libidinal Zones, Aims, and Modes of Gratification," in L. Bellak (cons. editor), *Conceptual and Methodological Problems in Psychoanalysis, Annual New York Academy of Science,* Vol. **76** (1959a), 975.

T. S. Szasz, "The Classification of 'Mental Illness': A Situational Analysis of Psychiatric Operations," *Psychiatry Quarterly,* Vol. **33** (1959b), 77.

T. S. Szasz, "Recollections of a Psychoanalytic Psychotherapy: The Case of the 'Prisoner K,' " in A. Buron (editor), *Case Studies in Counseling and Psychotherapy,* Chapter 4, pp. 75−110, Englewood Cliffs, N.J.: Prentice-Hall, 1959c.

T. S. Szasz, "Psychiatry, Psychotherapy, and Psychology," *A.M.A. Archives of General Psychiatry,* Vol. **1** (1959d), 455.

T. S. Szasz, "Moral Conflict and Psychiatry," *Yale Review,* Vol. **49** (1960a), 555.

T. S. Szasz, "Civil Liberties and the Mentally Ill, *Cleveland-Marshall Law Review,* Vol. **9** (1960b), 399.

T. S. Szasz, W. F. Knoff, and M. H. Hollender, "The Doctor-Patient Relationship in its Historical Context," *American Journal of Psychiatry,* 115:552, 1958.

A. Weinberg (editor), *Attorney for the Damned,* New York: Simon & Schuster, 1957.

J. B. Wortis, *Soviet Psychiatry,* Baltimore, Md.: Williams & Wilkins, 1950.

LAWRENCE B. RADINE

Psychiatry in War and Peace

In my view, two general principles underlie modern methods of handling deviance within the Army. One is to preserve manpower by returning as many deviant soldiers as possible to duty. This requires some transformation of these soldiers' deviant responses as well as certain adaptations on the Army's part. But there are some soldiers whom the Army cannot reintegrate under any conditions, and this fact suggests the second principle: these soldiers must be punished or expelled from the Army in such a way as to maintain the legitimacy of the Army in other soldiers' (and civilians') eyes. The balance between expulsion (through discharges or incarcerations) and resocialization (or therapy) depends on the manpower needs of the Army. During wartime or other manpower shortages, the Army will refuse to allow recalcitrant soldiers to leave the Army and will put pressures on its deviance-control sectors to keep these soldiers in active duty. I argue that psychiatrists in garrison situations as well as those who deal with combat neuropsychiatric casualties have a strong tendency to define as ill as few soldiers as possible so the Army will not lose manpower.[1]

The psychiatrist's role in garrison situations requires him to assess GIs for the possible presence of mental illness for administrative discharge and to provide certification in court as to an accused soldier's sanity (and ability to stand trial).[2] During the Vietnam War there was considerable pressure to prevent GIs from getting out of the Army (both in combat and in garrison) for psychiatric reasons because the potential for great losses of manpower would be too great. Similarly, a commander bringing charges against a defiant GI is likely to resent a psychiatrist's giving the accused a mentally ill label because the soldier would be able to evade trial and punishment.[3] These pressures are transmitted to the psychiatrist, and the result is a minimal tendency to

Reprinted from Lawrence B. Radine, *The Taming of the Troops,* Westport, Conn.: Greenwood Press, 1977, pages 156–172, by permission of the author and publisher. Cases #1, #2, and #3 are also reprinted from H. Spencer Bloch, ''Army Clinical Psychiatry in the Combat Zone; 1967–68,'' *The American Journal of Psychiatry,* Vol. **126,** September 1969, pages 289–298, by permission of the author and publisher.

define a GI as mentally ill. Daniels cites an estimate that only two in 1,000 referrals are diagnosed as mentally ill.[4]

Why would a psychiatrist succumb to these organizational pressures? Wouldn't one expect his professionalism to be more durable and well defined than that of other ''servants of power'' (such as chaplains, psychologists, social workers, and sociologists)? There are several explanations for the accommodations that many psychiatrists make to military requirements.

To begin with, the structure of the psychiatrist's tasks makes long-term therapy impossible. The Army places so many demands on a psychiatrist's time that he cannot function in the therapy role for which he may have been trained as a civilian.[5] A visit and a diagnosis usually take less than fifteen minutes.[6] The psychiatrist may be called out on special assignments, or may be transferred, which would cause appointments to be juggled.[7] Patients similarly have demands on their time each day and are also likely to be transferred. A military psychiatrist at a state-side base reported in an interview that if the Army gave him the opportunity, he could easily cure, within a few weeks, frequent complaints among combat veterans, such as nervousness, insomnia, violent overreactions, and nightmares, all of which arose from guilt from what they had seen and done in combat. He asserted that this kind of therapy is discouraged by the Army and is rarely accomplished, or even attempted, in garrison settings. This may perhaps be as much because of organizational limitations (such as the Army's making no effort to set up treatment programs) as the view that mental symptoms are at best transient[8] and at worst evidence of malingering.[9]

Another source of difficulty is the fact that military psychiatrists do not enjoy the close relationship with their patients that most civilian psychiatrists do. Their communications are not privileged, and what a soldier tells a psychiatrist may be held against him in court.[10] For example, during the Vietnam War many symptoms that soldiers complained of were related to combat violence and atrocities or violent attitudes toward superior officers. If a soldier troubled in this way went to a psychiatrist to talk about his work problems, one of two conditions would have to prevail for psychotherapy to continue: either the psychiatrist would have to (illegally) tell the soldier he would not reveal or record anything that occurred in interviews, or the soldier would have to be able to withhold his "illegal" thoughts or acts from his conversation with the psychiatrist.[11] Ungerleider reports that few soldiers go to mental-hygiene clinics on their own initiative for relief of symptoms.[12] The great majority of referrals come through line officers or from administrative reasons.[13]

During the Vietnam War with the accompanying widespread anti-war sentiment among soldiers, how would a liberal, anti-war psychiatrist have resolved the role conflicts inherent in his position as an "internal pacification officer"?[14] There are probably as many resolutions as there are psychiatrists, but I think the response of one politically liberal psychiatrist is instructive. In 1970, I asked him if he would support resisters in the Army. Surprisingly, he said it never was a problem for him because he did not think there were any. This psychiatrist, however, held rather narrow standards of what constituted resistance; to him, a definition seemed to require a commitment to pacifism or some other "ism" and therefore had to be articulated, explained, and maybe even justified in philosophical terms. His view restricts the term *resistance* to those who can speak in middle-class terms, particularly college-educated terms.

The majority of resisters, however, are from working-class and lower-class backgrounds. If not from an urban ghetto or industrial section of a city, they are from some small town. They resist the Army as they have always resisted oppression: immediately, physically, and nonideologically. If court-martialed, they will not likely be accused of illegal distribution of a newspaper, or of uttering disloyal statements but rather be accused of going AWOL, disrespect toward an officer, refusal of a direct order, and similar disciplinary infractions. They do not have an articulate explanation for their resistance; they do not have an articulate explanation about most things, for that matter. They are not adapted to living in bureaucratic societies, and they do not comprehend bureaucratic rationality; but what they do understand of bureaucracy they immediately dislike. They have a different kind of rationality.

Thus this psychiatrist did not share this group's view of the world and rationality. Their inability to adapt to the institution seemed to this specialist to be simply stupidity. (This lack of sympathy with lower-class soldiers was shared by many college-educated enlisted men who themselves resisted the Army by organizing and writing anti-war newspapers.)

This value for manipulating bureaucracies even came

down to manipulating the psychiatrist. This psychiatrist had some contempt for soldiers he thought were too inept to know how to manipulate him properly. According to the psychiatrist, one proper way might be a forthright request to get him out of the Army.[15] Another way might be a really effective job of acting. But the middle position, that of feigning psychiatric symptoms poorly so that the psychiatrist recognizes it as a blatant "put on," causes a difficult interactive situation. If the psychiatrist went along with the act, he would look like a fool. The very attempt, therefore, is an insult to his own competence. This psychiatrist interviewee said he might respond to this ploy by using the psychiatric technique of giving the soldier "permission" to go insane—daring him to do it, knowing he could not.

This kind of resister, with his minimal experience with bureaucracies, does not understand the rationality of his psychiatrist. If he had more experience, he would know that he must allow the psychiatrist to save face. He cannot let the psychiatrist look incompetent or appear to be a "fall guy." And if he wants to be political and open about it, he must play on the psychiatrist's liberal, political conscience and let him think he is doing a legitimate or sanctified act, that is, "resisting the war machine."

This whole problem of incompatibility is a class phenomenon. The two classes do not appreciate each other's rationalities, and they do not appreciate each other's peculiar weaknesses. The Army is the overall winner in this one of many splits and antagonisms, in spite of the fact that it is probably not aware of the whole mechanism. It should be pointed out that while this class incompatibility may exist between resisters and various professionals (such as lawyers) in the Army, it was a rare psychiatrist who would have considered resisting the Army and the Vietnam War by helping GIs to escape.

If need be, such liberal (usually drafted) psychiatrists can be controlled by putting pressure on their superior medical officers (rather than on them directly). The superior medical officer, almost always a career officer in the Army, is dependent on efficiency reports for his promotions. Senior medical officers function more as administrators than as physicians. The result is that the administrator's main contact, and thus his reference group, is with senior line officers who are strongly disposed to measure competence in terms of quick recoveries and unfilled wards. Additionally, high sick-call rates reflect badly on the physician, making him appear too lenient in his definition of illness.[16]

Daniels argues that military psychiatrists' definition of what constitutes mental illness has adapted to the organizational needs of the military.[17] As a result, there is a tendency to stress adjustment rather than introspection or

self-awareness. There is also a tendency to view adapta-
bility as both a voluntary act of the soldier and a result of
psychiatrist's denial of symptoms.[18]

This approach to mental disorders is transmitted to
individual line officers. Some of my interviewees have
asserted that their commanding officers refer soldiers
whom they do not know how to handle ("troublemakers," for example) to the psychiatrist. The psychiatrist
typically will simply send them back to their unit after
minimal counseling. Some psychiatrists tell commanding officers not to refer them *any* mental cases unless
they want to (1) discharge the soldier under AR 635-212
(unfitness and unsuitability) or 635-89 (homosexuality),
or (2) court-martial him and require certification of
sanity, or (3) evaluate him for security clearance.[19] In
this manner, psychiatrists and line officers can cooperate
in denying illness (and treatment) except in those cases
where they want to get rid of the soldier.[20]

Many of these intractable—or faint-hearted—soldiers
are, of course, not mentally ill. But the question comes
to mind, how can this denial of symptoms and refusal to
engage in serious therapy be extended to combat disorders? Let us look at the kinds of prevention and
treatment that Army psychiatrists offered during the
Vietnam War.

According to Glass and others, the prevention of
psychiatric casualties can be divided into three approaches or levels.[21] "Primary prevention" consists of
attempts to influence living, working, or fighting conditions to minimize the likelihood of disabling maladjust-
ment and is a recognition of various influences upon
morale and the experience of combat.[22] "Secondary
prevention" is the early recognition and prompt management of emotional or behavioral problems that some
individuals might develop.[23] This is carried out on an
out-patient basis, so the individual remains a member of
his unit. "Tertiary prevention" is used for persistent and
severe mental disorders that require hospitalization.[24]
Here, milieu therapy is the main therapeutic tool.[25] As in
secondary prevention, this technique is oriented to rehabilitation back into military duty and the reduction of
chronic disability.[26]

The secondary prevention level is the most relevant in
a discussion of how psychiatrists prevent soldiers from
escaping combat. This approach is based on years of
experience of the many problems that arose from hospitalizing soldiers in wards far from the fighting areas.[27]
It was discovered that the "fixing" of psychiatric
symptoms (or their becoming permanent, like an image
on a photographic plate) would occur less frequently if
the soldier were treated as close as possible to his own
unit.[28] This allows other, functioning, soldiers to exert a
social control function over the soldier-patient.

A second principle is one in which the soldier is not
allowed to develop an ill role by being treated as soon as
possible after he develops the incapacitating symptoms.
The Army's use of Medevac helicopters can make this
factor one of minutes. A third principle is to deny the
seriousness of the response by the psychiatrist's communication of his expectation that the soldier will
respond favorably and return to duty within a short time.
These three principles have been termed *immediacy,
proximity,* and *expectancy.*[29]

Since the Korean War, the Army has been placing
psychiatrists at the division level, which keeps them
closer to the front.[30] In 1968 and 1969 there were seven
infantry divisions in Vietnam. To each division, comprising around 18,000 men, was assigned a psychiatrist
and his staff, which included a social work officer and
six to eight medical corpsmen who were trained in
psychiatric social work.[31] The division psychiatrist and
the social work officer usually operated from the division's base camp, while most of the corpsmen were
located at forward base camps that were closer to actual
areas of fighting.

The corpsmen themselves treated most of the less
serious cases of psychiatric (combat) breakdown.[32] If
they could not handle a case in a matter of hours, the
patient would be sent back to the division psychiatrist,
who treated the soldier but on an out-patient basis.[33] If
the division psychiatrist decided that the soldier-patient
was seriously ill or psychotic and could not be treated on
such a casual basis, he sent this individual to a hospital.[34]

As the following examples demonstrate, the enlisted
medical corpsmen were able to treat what would appear
to be debilitating psychiatric illnesses with surprising
ease and swiftness:

- Example 1. An infantry man was brought by
  dust-off (medical evacuation) helicopter to one of
  the division's clearing stations with symptoms of
  combat exhaustion. He complained of nightmares
  in which he saw eyes coming closer and closer to
  him. When the eyes were upon him a gun pointed
  at him appeared and he would awaken in a cold
  sweat. He would then force himself to think out the
  end of the dream in which he would get his weapon
  or grenade and destroy the frightening apparition.
  Specialist A talked with the soldier and learned that
  he had previously been in an ambush patrol and had
  been wounded. The infantryman related that he had
  found himself in close proximity to the enemy, "so
  close I could see the whites of their eyes," but had
  remained cool at the time and radioed for help. His
  report resulted in his being discovered and

wounded before assistance arrived. As he recovered from the injury, he became increasingly troubled by his nightmare. He began to have trouble falling asleep, lost his appetite, and was unable to concentrate.

The infantryman was extremely apprehensive about returning to the field. Specialist A consulted with a company physician who, as a result, hospitalized the soldier for 24 hours and ordered tranquilizing medication (100 mg. of chlorpromazine four times daily). The specialist told his patient he had observed that as his physical wound healed his psychological problems seemed to increase. He pointed out that the dreams were probably the soldier's way of gradually working out his anxiety about his stressful experience, which would have immobilized him had he experienced it at the time of the incident. Specialist A observed that just as the infantryman had done the right thing during the crisis and at the end of the dream, he could be assured that he would do the right thing in future times of stress. The infantryman went back to the field, and subsequent follow-up from his unit indicates he has been on patrol and is functioning effectively.

- Example 2. Another example of the ingenuity of the technicians was demonstrated by Specialist B, who evaluated and treated a new man in the field unit who had developed conversion symptoms in his first fire fight. The patient was brought to the clearing station mute and seemingly oblivious to his surroundings. Specialist B enlisted the assistance of a wounded combat veteran on the ward, who talked to the patient about his own apprehension with regard to coming to Viet Nam and going into the field. The technician then discussed the situation with the man's unit, which sent two enlisted men from its squad to express their concern about his welfare and further reassure him about their having experienced similar feelings in their first contact with the enemy. The patient asked Specialist B for permission to return with his fellow squad members to the unit. Follow-up indicates that he has functioned effectively in his unit since this time.[35]

Medical corpsmen during the Vietnam War did not undergo extensive training in the recognition and treatment of psychiatric disorders.[36] They might thus be expected to have been less sensitive to serious mental problems underlying certain symptoms. The fact that they were enlisted men themselves puts them in a position closer to that of the soldier-patient. Some of the

small-group expectations of the soldier-patient's unit would be reflected in the enlisted corpsmen's own attitudes. The corpsmen were likely to view neuropsychiatric casualties as normal reactions to combat rather than as mental aberrations.[37]

This use of medical corpsmen appears to communicate certain things to the soldier-patient and his peers. For example, the fact that he is being treated by enlisted corpsmen rather than by a psychiatrist suggests that neither the Army nor the psychiatrist takes very seriously the soldier's "psychotic" behavior. If the corpsmen do not view the soldier-patient as seriously ill, then the patient should similarly not view himself as ill.

Even when division psychiatrists saw these patients, they did not carry out lengthy therapy.[38] Their direct services were limited mainly to crisis intervention and evaluation,[39] and their in-patient treatment consisted mostly of drugging the soldier to sleep for a day or so, followed by fairly brief consultation.[40] My belief is that the brief treatment and quick reappearance in the company of a psychiatric case communicates to other soldiers that they will not be able to use psychiatric symptoms as a way out of the Army. They may learn that if the Army will not take their problems very seriously, there is no point in seeking treatment. According to this view, this phenomenon of the quick reappearance of the GI and the cursory treatment that he receives is probably the most important explanation for the low psychiatric casualty rate of the Vietnam War.

Even at the tertiary level, diagnosis and treatment seem to have been casual and brief. During the Vietnam War, tertiary treatment, or more extended clinical psychiatry, was carried out by two neuropsychiatric teams.[41] One team operated a ward in the northern half of the Republic of Vietnam and the other served the southern half. These teams consisted of three to five psychiatrists, a neurologist, a clinical psychologist, two social work officers, a psychiatric nurse, and twenty to thirty enlisted corpsmen.[42] The enlisted corpsmen worked either in ward management or in clinic work, such as taking social histories and administering psychological tests. A few other Army hospitals in Vietnam had single-staff psychiatrists who might have admitted patients to their medical wards for a week or so, but they too referred patients to the neuropsychiatric teams. The psychiatric wards carried out "intensive," though brief, treatment of psychiatric cases, maintaining the principles of immediacy, proximity, and expectancy.[43]

The approach of military psychiatrists was essentially "oriented toward intervention in the interpersonal dimension of patients' problems."[44] Like psychiatrists in garrison, they were concerned with returning the patient to duty and were thus not particularly concerned with "underlying internal emotional conflicts,"[45] which would take "much longer periods of time to resolve."[46]

Milieu therapy has the dual advantage of treating interpersonal problems as well as treating several patients at once. Group norms are mobilized in channeling behavior into ways that the Army can use. All ward patients, even the most ill, got up together and dressed and cleaned up their ward together.[47] The group decided about each patient's privilege status (such as freedom to go off the ward) and went to group therapy together five days a week.[48] Thus, the objective was to use a "highly structured program geared toward much group activity" while still trying to increase "individual patient responsibility."[49] The underlying assumption of this treatment practice seemed to be that even seriously disturbed soldiers can be effective individuals in a structured atmosphere, hence should also be able to function well after being returned to duty.[50]

The following examples, including the psychiatrist's comments, help to convey an idea of problems that were handled at this level as well as the techniques for handling them.

- Case 1. Moderately severe combat exhaustion. A 21-year-old rifleman was flown directly to the hospital from an area of fighting by a helicopter ambulance. No information accompanied him, he had no identifying tags on his uniform, and he was so completely covered with mud that a physical description of his features was not possible. His hands had been tied behind him for the flight, and he had a wild, wide-eyed look as he cowered in a corner of the emergency room, glancing furtively to all sides, cringing and startling at the least noise. He was mute, although once he forced out a whispered "VC" and tried to mouth other words without success. He seemed terrified. Although people could approach him, he appeared oblivious to their presence. No manner of reassurance or direct order achieved either a verbal response or any other interaction from him.

  His hands were untied, after which he would hold an imaginary rifle in readiness whenever he heard a helicopter overhead or an unexpected noise. The corpsmen led him to the psychiatric ward, took him to a shower, and offered him a meal; he ate very little. He began to move a little more freely but still offered no information.

  He was then given 100 mg. of chlorpromazine (Thorazine) orally; this dose was repeated hourly until he fell asleep. He was kept asleep in this manner for approximately 40 hours. After that he was allowed to waken, the medication was discon-

tinued, and he was mobilized rapidly in the ward milieu. Although dazed and subdued upon awakening, his response in the ward milieu was dramatic. This was aided by the presence of a friend from his platoon in an adjoining ward, who helped by filling in parts of the story that the patient could not recall. The patient was an infantryman whose symptoms had developed on a day when his platoon had been caught in an ambush and then was overrun by the enemy. He was one of three who survived after being pinned down by enemy fire for 12 hours. His friend told him that toward the end of that time he had developed a crazed expression and had tried to run from his hiding place. He was pulled back to safety and remained there until the helicopter arrived and flew him to the hospital.

Within 72 hours after his admission the patient was alert, oriented, responsive, and active—still a little tense but ready to return to duty. He was sent back to duty on his third hospital day and never seen again at our facility. It should be noted that he had no history of similar symptoms or emotional disorder.

[Psychiatrist's] Comment: One should note the use of chlorpromazine for sleep and the value of sleep (or perhaps chlorpromazine-induced sleep) as restitutive therapy in people who have been under great physical and emotional strain. Patients with combat exhaustion are mobilized for return to duty very rapidly, it is well known that the longer one waits, the harder it is for men to accept the idea of going back into life threatening situations.

- Case 2. Probable marijuana-induced psychotic episode. A 26-year-old Negro boat operator with three and a half months in Viet Nam was referred to the neuropsychiatry team by his dispensary physician because of violent behavior and inappropriate speech that morning. The referring note indicated that this soldier had presented behavioral problems in his unit previously. At the time of his admission no meaningful history could be obtained from him. Mental status exam revealed an agitated, unshaven man whose speech was vague and disjointed, with markedly loosened associations. His attention span, recall, and orientation were severely impaired. He was posturing, seemingly with religious connotation, frequently staring heavenward and acknowledging direct communication with God. He was extremely suspicious, with apparent ideas of reference and influence, and struck the psychiatrist when he was being sedated with intramuscular medication, he thought an experiment was being performed on him.

The patient was given a 48-hour course of sleep therapy with chlorpromazine in the manner indicated in Case 1, except that the drug was administered intramuscularly until he agreed to take it orally. Following this his agitation, unusual behavior, belligerence, posturing, and manifest paranoid ideation abated markedly. The chlorpromazine was discontinued and he was placed on trifluoperazine (Stelazine) and mobilized in the ward milieu. Over the next several days he was somewhat vague at times and always a bit tense; he claimed that this was his usual emotional state.

An anamnesis taken at that time revealed a history of behavioral problems during his growing years including difficulties with civilian authorities in his preservice life. He denied previous psychiatric hospitalization or psychotic symptomatology. When questioned about the use of drugs and specifically about the use of marijuana prior to the onset of his symptoms, he initially denied this but subsequently acknowledged it in a veiled manner. His condition remained unchanged over the next few days. He was discharged to duty on his fifth hospital day with instructions to take 10 mg. of trifluoperazine, plus trihexphenidil (Artane), four times daily for approximately two weeks.

[Psychiatrist's] Comment: Brief psychotic episodes, usually with predominantly paranoid symptoms, are a syndrome that psychiatrists and other physicians in Viet Nam have come to associate with marijuana usage there, although such syndromes are reported only infrequently with marijuana usage in the United States. The relative incidence of such reactions compared with the incidence of marijuana usage in Viet Nam is unknown, and a definite, clinically proven relationship between marijuana usage and psychosis has not been documented by a research protocol there. Nevertheless, any unusual symptom complex developing in previously healthy (though often character-disordered) men has come to make physicians in Viet Nam strongly suspect marijuana usage.

- Case 3. Anxiety reaction in a recent arrival. A 20-year-old private, an artillery observer with six months of active duty service, was referred by his division psychiatrist during his first week in Viet Nam following an overnight admission at the small division hospital for an anxiety reaction. On admission to the psychiatry ward the youthful-looking soldier was observed to be tremulous, hyperventilating, to clutch himself and rock back and forth, and to become tearful and uncommunicative. This

behavior abated with a firm approach by the interviewer. The patient communicated the following history: He had been a tense and anxious person for years, but these traits had been more prominent since he entered the service. Particularly since preparing for his tour in Viet Nam he had been aware of tremulousness, nervousness, and phobic symptoms, as well as obsessional-type thoughts and nightmares about his mother, fiancee, and brother coming to horrible violent deaths. He yearned for them, fearful of the separation. During his Army training, these symptoms had been eased by visits from his mother. However, during the week since his arrival in Viet Nam, when he was waiting to be assigned and was essentially unoccupied, the symptoms exacerbated markedly and he began to develop fearful suicidal ideas. He sought psychiatric help.

Anamnestic data revealed that he was the middle of three children raised by a nervous, histrionic mother and a much-loved stepfather. From the age of 13 he had harbored strong, unrealistic feelings of guilt and responsibility for the stepfather's accidental death and his mother's presumed near-death when she slashed her wrists after the funeral. Afterwards he became a model, compliant lad and never again experienced anger—only "nervousness" at times when anger would be appropriate. Associating to more recent events, he noted that in the setting of his impending assignment to Viet Nam, his mother's behavior had been reminiscent of the way she had shaken and trembled at the stepfather's funeral before she "went out of her mind" and cut her wrists.

This material gave rise to a working psychodynamic formulation that his concerns were like those of the phobic patient with separation anxiety who could not let persons toward whom he felt much unconscious rage out of his sight for fear that they would die because of his own hostile impulses.

During the first day of the patient's hospitalization these underlying issues were clarified with him as he experienced anxiety in the psychiatrist's office. His feelings and the issues were related both to his condition at the time of the interview and to similar experiences of anxiety in the past. Following this interview he was worked with intensively in the ward milieu. After about a day and a half of relative apathy and social isolation he began to respond rapidly to the milieu and thereafter maintained himself well. He continued to experience some anxiety but reported spontaneously that its quality as well as his ability to cope with it had changed. He still had some difficulty sleeping but no longer worried about this. He was eager to return to duty. Occasional sleeping pills were the only medications utilized during his hospitalization. He was returned to duty on the fourth hospital day after arrangements had been made with the division psychiatrist for him to be assigned to a unit without further delay.

[Psychiatrist's] Comment: Although this case might have been managed successfully by milieu therapy alone, it is one in which the intrapsychic components seemed prominent enough in the man's incapacitation to warrant the use of individual psychotherapy aimed at clarifying aspects of internal emotional conflicts in an effort to impart some insight to enhance the patient's capacity to tolerate anxiety.[51]

Apparently, even at the tertiary level, treatment is remarkably brief and appears to be singularly oriented to returning the soldier to duty. Case three is somewhat unusual in that the soldier himself sought psychiatric help. However, while this young man might have been able to benefit from some in-depth psychoanalysis, it is not clear that he received it. Simply telling a patient what the sources of his problems are is not the same as having him incorporate that explanation and truly understand it.

Treatment in cases one and two seems to rely heavily on drugs. These drugs have had a significant effect in reducing the psychiatric casualty rate and are especially effective for those psychiatric casualties resulting from shock and exhaustion. (I would expect the reliance on various mind-affecting drugs to increase in the future, perhaps to be included in training to enhance learning.)

Milieu therapy, on the other hand, is of particular value in handling problems of interpersonal adjustment, such as hating Army life.[52] Psychiatrists have been influenced by small-group cohesion-building techniques and effective leadership techniques that the Army itself has generated, and they have combined these approaches with research from their own professional fields. Military psychiatrists are trained in community psychiatry by the Army as residents.[53] Residents are given some specific knowledge of Army customs and procedures, and they are introduced to some of the operations in a military post.[54] Medical corpsmen are also trained both as military personnel and as paramedical personnel. The result, milieu and group therapy, is a collectively oriented treatment in which the GI cannot help but feel that he is important to the military psychiatrist, and thus to the Army, only as a soldier, not as an individual.

I have argued that military psychiatrists tend to refuse to define soldiers' aberrant behavior as psychiatric casualties or mental illness. In terms of the Army's overall rate of psychiatric casualties, these efforts have been very effective. Neuropsychiatric casualties dropped from an all-time high in World War II to a moderate level in the Korean War and finally to a surprisingly low level during the Vietnam War.[55]

This trend toward much lower psychiatric casualty rates is particularly interesting in light of many forces that would suggest the opposite. For example, morale among soldiers has been steadily dropping at least since World War II. The strong unit solidarity[56] that characterized that war degenerated to dyadic buddy relations during the Korean War[57] and then to a rather atomized, almost utilitarian, kind of relationship among combat soldiers in the Vietnam War.[58] The Vietnam War was, of course, the most unpopular war the United States has carried out in recent years, and there was much more anti-Army and anti-war resistance of Vietnam-era soldiers than during previous, recent wars. It can also be assumed that contemporary soldiers have a greater knowledge of mental illness that could contribute to their skill in feigning mental illness in order to get out of combat. All these lines of evidence would suggest a high psychiatric casualty rate for the Vietnam War.[59]

In part, the recent lowering of the psychiatric casualty rate is related to the shift away from policies used in World War II and earlier. The Army relied heavily on screening out potential psychiatric cases prior to induction and seemed to neglect some of the conditions of combat and the organizational situations generally.[60] Toward the end of World War II, it was discovered that unit morale, length of combat experience, leadership, and even training had an effect on the psychiatric casualty rate.[61] Since the end of World War II, these factors have been somewhat altered by the use of a shorter tour of duty, the rotation system, and more frequent rest and recreation.[62]

But the most important change is in methods of handling psychiatric disorders after they arise. In World War I and in World War II, soldiers were treated in hospital wards far removed from combat areas, and often they never returned to their unit. Clearly, significant changes have been made in these methods of treatment.

The current treatment style is a result of the discovery of the importance of labeling (or more accurately, the refusal to label) small-group normative pulls (and exploiting them by treating soldiers close to the front) and the tendency for soldiers to get attached to their symptoms (preventable by the onset of treatment immediately after symptoms appear). And finally, the

Army makes it apparent to soldiers that they will not be able to avoid combat by becoming neuropsychiatric casualties.

NOTES

1. The motto of the medical corps, "to conserve fighting strength," appears to be a guide for the Army psychiatrist and is frequently mentioned in their articles. See J. Thomas Ungerleider, "The Army, the Soldier and the Psychiatrist," *American Journal of Psychiatry* 114 (March 1963): 875; Donald B. Peterson, "Discussion" of "Army Psychiatry in the Mid-60s" by William J. Tiffany and William S. Allerton, *American Journal of Psychiatry* 123 (January 1967): 819; and H. Spencer Bloch, "Army Clinical Psychiatry in the Combat Zone—1967–1968," *American Journal of Psychiatry* 126 (September 1969): 289. Ungerleider commented on the oft-repeated medical corps phrase, "You are an [Army] officer first and a doctor second," and added, "and a psychiatrist third" (brackets in the original).
2. Arlene K. Daniels, "The Captive Professional: Bureaucratic Limitations in the Practice of Military Psychiatry," *Journal of Health and Social Behavior* 10 (December 1969): 258–60. See also Martin B. Giffen and Herbert Kritzer, "An Aid to the Psychiatrist in Military Forensic Medicine," *Military Medicine* (November 1961): 838–41; Robert L. Pettera, "Mental Health in Combat," *Military Review* (March 1971): 74–77; Arlene K. Daniels, "Military Psychiatry: The Emergence of a Subspecialty," in *Medical Men and Their Work,* ed. Eliot Friedson and Judith Lorber (Chicago: Aldine-Atherton, 1972), pp. 145–62; and Roy E. Clausen, Jr., and Arlene K. Daniels, "Role Conflicts and Their Ideological Resolution in Military Psychiatric Practice," *American Journal of Psychiatry* 123 (September 1966): 280–87.
3. See Daniels, "The Captive Professional," pp. 260–61. Daniels observed that a conscientious objector may encounter more serious disciplinary measures if a psychiatrist labels him "NPD" (no psychiatric disease).
4. Daniels cited E. L. Maillet, "A Study of the Readiness of Troop Commanders to Use the Services of the Army Mental Hygiene Consultation Service" (D.S.W. diss., Catholic University of America, 1966), p. 168. See Daniels, "Military Psychiatry," p. 161.
5. Clausen and Daniels, "Role Conflicts and Their Ideological Resolution," p. 281. Clausen and Daniels mentioned that in addition to the lack of time available to the psychiatrist, the psychiatrist must delegate a considerable amount of authority to his psychiatric team.
6. Daniels, "Military Psychiatry," p. 153.
7. Ungerleider, "The Army, the Soldier and the Psychiatrist," p. 876. Daniels argues that psychiatric therapy in the sense of a series of vis-à-vis sessions in a private office is largely confined to major military medical centers and is practiced by residents as part of their training. See Daniels, "Military Psychiatry," p. 156.
8. Arnold Rose, "Conscious Reactions Associated with Neuropsychiatric Breakdown in Combat," *Psychiatry* 19 (February 1956):87–94. See also Arnold Rose, "Neuropsychiatric Breakdown in the Garrison Army and in Combat," *American Sociological Review* 21 (August 1956): 480–88.
9. A military psychiatrist told his fellow officers that in many instances a young man "has a hard time facing decision and responsibility" because of his immaturity and "what is needed here is a firm hand from the fatherly type of person who refuses to protect him, but insists on the individual taking charge of himself and accepting responsibility for his own actions." Pettera, "Mental Health in Combat," pp. 75–76.
10. Daniels, "The Captive Professional," pp. 255–65. Ungerleider, "The Army, the Soldier and the Psychiatrist," p. 876, suggested that the lack of privileged communication explains why so few officers ever see a psychiatrist. They fear their career would be put in jeopardy.
11. Ungerleider, "The Army, the Soldier and the Psychiatrist," p. 876.
12. Ibid.
13. Daniels, "The Captive Professional," pp. 255–58. Clausen and Daniels, "Role Conflicts and Their Ideological Resolution," p. 282, stated that "referrals may regard the psychiatrist-officer with suspicion, thinking the officer's responsibility to the service makes him a 'company man' and not a man genuinely interested in their welfare."
14. I am indebted to Mark Selden for this characterization.
15. Ungerleider, "The Army, the Soldier and the Psychiatrist," p. 876, reported that some soldiers quite frankly ask the psychiatrist for discharges, compassionate transfers, or changing of overseas orders—and not for relief of symptoms. He said he frequently heard the remark, "I heard this was the place to get my orders changed (or to get out of the Army)."
16. For a discussion of the informal pressures on physicians generally, see Roger W. Little, "The 'Sick Soldier' and the Medical Ward Officer," *Human Organization* 15 (Spring 1966): 22–25. Little observed that even in a basic training company, word would get around about the leniency of various medical ward officers. If a nonsympathetic doctor were on duty, only the most seriously ill soldiers would go to him. Sometimes a soldier who was rejected on the night shift at the ward would come in again

on the day shift. Thus the rates of soldiers on sick call corresponded closely with which doctor was on duty.

17. Daniels, "The Captive Professional," p. 257, and Daniels, "Military Psychiatry," p. 160.

18. For a discussion of neuropsychiatric casualties as a failure in adaptation, often of a temporary nature, see Peter Bourne, "Military Psychiatry and the Viet Nam Experience," *American Journal of Psychiatry* 127 (October 1970): 125, 129.

19. Pettera, "Mental Health in Combat," pp. 76−77. On the difficulties involved in screening for security purposes, see Tiffany and Allerton, "Army Psychiatry in the Mid-'60s," p. 813.

20. Daniels, "The Captive Professional," pp. 255−65, argues that psychiatrists in the military shift from a counseling role to more of a controlling role whereby they become agents for eliminating deviants.

21. Albert J. Glass, Kenneth L. Artiss, James J. Gibbs, and Vincent C. Sweeney, "The Current Status of Army Psychiatry," *American Journal of Psychiatry* 117 (February 1961): 673−83.

22. Ibid. See also Chapter 4, n. 164, above.

23. Ibid.

24. Ibid.

25. Ibid.

26. Ibid.

27. For a discussion of this history, see Albert J. Glass, "Army Psychiatry Before World War II," in *Neuropsychiatry in World War II, vol. 1: Zone of Interior,* ed. Robert S. Anderson (Washington, D.C.: Department of the Army, 1966), pp. 3−23.

28. Glass et al., "The Current Status of Army Psychiatry," p. 675, and Albert J. Glass, "Advances in Military Psychiatry," *Current Psychiatric Therapies* 1 (1961): 159−67.

29. Bloch, "Army Clinical Psychiatry in the Combat Zone" p. 289.

30. The Army did occasionally assign psychiatrists to divisions in World War II (See Douglas R. Bey, "Division Psychiatry in Viet Nam," *American Journal of Psychiatry* 127 [August 1970]: 146), and in World War I (see Glass, "Advances in Military Psychiatry," p. 159). See also Glass, "Army Psychiatry Before World War II," pp. 3−26. However, the emphasis on immediacy, proximity, and expectancy clearly did not emerge until the end of World War II when it became well known that the course of psychiatric illness was highly responsive to variations in treatment methods and attitudes.

31. See Bloch, "Army Clinical Psychiatry in the Combat Zone," pp. 289−90; and Bey, "Division Psychiatry in Viet Nam," p. 147.

32. Bloch, "Army Clinical Psychiatry in the Combat Zone," p. 290, and Bey, "Division Psychiatry in Viet Nam," p.

147. Bey stated that the corpsman (social work/psychology technician) always discusses the case with the referral source and may consult with the psychiatric or social work officer.

33. Bloch, "Army Clinical Psychiatry in the Combat Zone," p. 290, and Bey, "Division Psychiatry in Viet Nam," p. 147.

34. See Bloch, "Army Clinical Psychiatry in the Combat Zone," p. 290. According to Bey, the statistics for the direct services of the division psychiatrist staff, of which he was a part, were as follows: "We average 180 new clients per month. Diagnostically the population is comprised of five percent with psychotic reactions (which include toxic psychosis secondary to drug abuse), ten percent with psychoneurotic reactions, 20 percent situational stress reactions (combat exhaustion, 'short timer's syndrome,' etc.), 25 percent with no psychiatric diagnosis, and 40 percent with character and behavior disorders. We hospitalize ten percent for two to three days in one of our clearing stations. One-half to one percent of our 180 new clients have to be sent to an evacuation hospital in order to be sent out of country; 14 percent are cleared for administrative separation from the Army; and 80 percent are returned to duty." Douglas R. Bey, "Division Psychiatry in Viet Nam," *American Journal of Psychiatry,* 1970, Vol. 127, p. 230. Copyright 1970, the American Psychiatric Association.

35. Douglas R. Bey, "Division Psychiatry in Viet Nam," *American Journal of Psychiatry,* 1970, Vol. 127, pp. 228−232. Copyright 1970, the American Psychiatric Association.

36. See Edward M. Colbach, "Morale and Mental Health," *Army Digest* 25 (May 1970): 9−11.

37. According to Bloch, "Army Clinical Psychiatry in the Combat Zone," p. 293, many cases of character and behavior disorders are not considered by the Army to represent psychiatric illness; hence, soldiers with these disorders who are not responsive to rehabilitation efforts are discharged through administrative channels rather than medical channels.

38. Ibid., p. 290.

39. Ibid.

40. Ibid.

41. Ibid., pp. 289−98.

42. Ibid., p. 290.

43. Ibid., p. 291.

44. Ibid., p. 292.

45. Ibid.

46. Ibid.

47. Ibid., p. 291.

48. Ibid.

49. Ibid.

50. Ibid., p. 292.

51. H. Spencer Bloch, "Army Clinical Psychiatry in the Combat Zone—1967–1968," *American Journal of Psychiatry,* 1969, Vol. 126, pp. 289–298. Copyright 1969, the American Psychiatric Association.

52. See Glass, "Advances in Military Psychiatry," for a brief discussion of milieu therapy in the Army.

53. Tiffany and Allerton, "Army Psychiatry in the Mid-'60s," p. 812.

54. Ibid., and Ungerleider, "The Army, the Soldier and the Psychiatrist," pp. 875–76.

55. A *psychiatric casualty* is defined as a soldier missing twenty-four hours or more of duty for psychiatric reasons.

Psychiatric Casualty Rates

WAR	Rate per 1,000 Troops per year
World War II	
Highest	101 (First U.S. Army, Europe)
Lowest	28 (Ninth U.S. Army, Europe)
Korea	
July 1950-December 1952	37
Vietnam	
Late 1965-Early 1970	13

According to Colbach, this combat psychiatric casualty rate is similar to the Army-wide rate, including garrison duty in the United States. The psychiatric evaluation rate has similarly dropped:

Evacuation Rate for Psychiatric Reasons

WAR	Percent of All Evacuees
World War II	23.0 percent
Korea	6.0 percent
Vietnam	3.4 percent

These figures are drawn from Colbach, "Morale and Mental Health," p. 11.

The low psychiatric casualty and evacuation rates continued until mid-1971, when the Army began a wide-scale urine-testing program to identify hard drug users. These addicted soldiers were usually evacuated from Vietnam for stateside involuntary detoxification. These cases were considered psychiatric casualties and as a result the psychiatric casualty and evacuation rates jumped ten or twenty times to rates comparable to those in World War II. This drug-screening program was begun after American participation in the Vietnam War had declined markedly as the "Vietnamization" policy shifted the burden of the fighting to the Army of the Republic of Vietnam. See Franklin Del Jones and Arnold W. Johnson, Jr., "Medical and Psychiatric Treatment Policy and Practice in Vietnam," *Journal of Social Issues* 31 (Fall 1975): 49–65. Jones and Johnson suggest that there was no effective policy for treating drug users in combat.

56. See Samuel A. Stouffer et al., *The American Soldier: Combat and Its Aftermath* (New York: John Wiley & Sons, 1949), pp. 96, 130–31, 135–39, 142–43, 148, 349–50, 382–83.

57. Roger W. Little, "Buddy Relations and Combat Performance," in *The New Military: Changing Patterns of Organization,* ed. Morris Janowitz (New York: W. W. Norton & Company, 1964), pp. 195–224.

58. Charles C. Moskos, Jr., *The American Enlisted Man: The Rank and File in Today's Military* (New York: Russell Sage Foundation, 1970), pp. 134–56.

59. Bourne, "Military Psychiatry and the Viet Nam Experience," p. 487.

60. Glass, "Advances in Military Psychiatry," p. 159.

61. Bourne, "Military Psychiatry and the Viet Nam Experience," pp. 123–29.

62. See Tiffany and Allerton, "Army Psychiatry in the Mid-'60s," p. 813, and Peterson, "Discussion," pp. 819–20.

EGON BITTNER

Police Discretion in Emergency
Apprehension of Mentally Ill Persons*

The official mandate of the police includes provisions for dealing with mentally ill persons. Since such dealings are defined in terms of civil law procedures, the mandate of the police is not limited to persons who for reasons of illness fail to observe the law. Rather, in suitable circumstances the signs of mental illness, or a competent allegation of mental illness, are in themselves the proper business of the police and can lead to authorized intervention. The expressed legal norms governing police involvement specify two major alternatives. On the one hand, policemen may receive court orders directing them to locate, apprehend, and convey named persons to specified hospitals for psychiatric observation and/or sanity hearings. On the other hand, policemen are authorized by statute to apprehend and convey to hospitals persons whom they perceive as ill, on an emergency basis. The first form parallels the common procedures of serving court warrants, while the second form involves the exercise of discretionary freedom that is ordinarily associated with making arrests without a warrant.[1]

The study reported in this paper concerns the rules and considerations underlying the exercise of discretion in emergency apprehensions. The findings are based on ten months of field work with the uniformed police patrol of a large West Coast city, and on psychiatric records of the hospital receiving all police referrals.[2] We shall first

consider certain attitudinal and organizational factors involved in making emergency apprehensions. Next, we shall discuss the manifest properties of cases in which emergency apprehensions are frequently made. Finally, we shall deal with procedures directed toward recognized mentally ill persons who are not referred to the hospital. In the conclusion, we shall argue that the decision to invoke the law governing emergency apprehension is not based on an appraisal of objective features of cases. Rather, the decision is a residual resource, the use of which is determined largely by the absence of other alternatives. The domain of alternatives is found in normal peace-keeping activities in which considerations of legality play a decidedly subordinate role. We shall also allude to the fact that our interpretation has important bearing on the problem of police discretion to invoke the law in general.[3]

Organizational and Attitudinal Factors Influencing Emergency Apprehensions

The statutory authorization under which apprehensions of the mentally ill are made provides that an officer may take steps to initiate confinement in a psychiatric hospital when he believes "as the result of his own observations, that the person is mentally ill and because of his illness is likely to injure himself or others if not immediately hospitalized."[4] It is fair to say that under ordinary circumstances police officers are quite reluctant

* This research was supported in part by Grant 64-1-35 from the California Department of Mental Hygiene. I gratefully acknowledge the help I have received from Sheldon L. Messinger in preparing this paper.

Reprinted from *Social Problems*, Vol. **14**, No. 3 (Winter, 1967), pages 278–292, by permission of the author and the publisher (The Society for the Study of Social Problems).

1. See, for example, *Welfare and Institutions Code*, State of California, Division 6, Part 1, Chapter 1.

2. The city has a population of approximately three-quarters of a million inhabitants and is patrolled by a uniformed police force of approximately 1,000 men. The receiving hospital is a public institution. Its psychiatric inpatient service registered a demand population of 7,500 during the period of the study, July 1, 1963—June 30, 1964. Eighty-eight percent of this population has been accepted for observation and such short-term care as is ordinarily associated with it. The average length of stay of patients is just short of five days, with a distribution that

is heavily skewed toward shorter stays. The hospital also houses a department of the court that holds sanity hearings.

3. The problem referred to is treated in Joseph Goldstein, "Police Discretion Not to Invoke the Criminal Process," *Yale Law Journal*, 69 (1960), pp. 543–594; W. R. LaFave, "The Police and Non-enforcement of the Law," *Wisconsin Law Review* (1962), pp. 104–137, 179–239; S. H. Kadish, "Legal Norms and Discretion in the Police and Sentencing Process," *Harvard Law Review*, 75 (1962), pp. 904–931; I. Piliavin and S. Scott, "Police Encounters with Juveniles," *American Journal of Sociology*, 70 (1964), pp. 206–214; Nial Osborough, "Police Discretion Not to Prosecute Students," *Journal of Criminal Law, Criminology and Police Science*, 56 (1965), pp. 241–245.

4. *Welfare and Institutions Code, op. cit.*, Section 5050.3.

to invoke this law. That is, in situations where, according to their own judgment, they are dealing with an apparently mentally ill person they will generally seek to employ other means to bring the existing problem under control. This does not mean that they attempt to deal with the problem as if it did not involve a mentally ill person, or as if this person's illness were none of their business. It merely means that they will try to avoid taking him to the hospital.

The avoidance of emergency apprehensions has a background that might be called doctrinal.[5] To take someone to the hospital means giving the facts of his illness formal recognition and using them as grounds for official action. The police, however, disavow all competence in matters pertaining to psychopathology and seek to remain within the lines of restraint that the disavowal imposes. Accordingly, the diagnosis they propose is not only emphatically provisional but also, in a sense, incidental. From their point of view it is not enough for a case to be serious in a "merely" psychiatric sense. To warrant official police action a case must also present a serious police problem. As a general rule, the elements that make a case a serious police matter are indications that if a referral is not made, external troubles will proliferate. Among these, danger to life, to physical health, to property, and to order in public places, are objects of prominent concern. Estimating the risk of internal deterioration of the psychiatric condition as such is perceived as lying outside of the scope of police competence and thus not an adequate basis for making emergency apprehensions.

While a narrow construction of the police mandate might have the consequence of eliminating certain cases from the purview of official police interest, it does not eliminate the possibility of liberal use of the authorization. Thus, it might be expected that officers would tend to refer relatively few persons who are "merely" very ill psychiatrically but many persons who are troublesome without being very ill. This expectation seems especially reasonable since the police recently have been denied the use of certain coercive means they have employed in the past to control troublesome persons.[6] On a practical level

such procedures would simply follow considerations of expediency, with the law providing a particular method and justification for taking care of matters that need be taken care of.[7] Indeed, given the heavy emphasis that mental hygiene receives in police training, it would be scarcely appropriate to attribute devious motives to the police if they were to use the "narrow construction" of the law "widely," for in many instances of untoward, but not necessarily illegal, behavior, the evidence of more or less serious psychopathology is close to the surface.[8] In fact, however, policemen do not make such use of the law. Instead, they conform in practice very closely to the views they profess. To make an emergency apprehension they require that there be indications of serious external risk accompanied by signs of a serious psychological disorder. There exist several attitudinal and organizational factors that help to explain the reluctance of the police to take official steps on the basis of the assumption or allegation of mental illness.

First, the views and knowledge of the police about mental illness are in close agreement with the views and knowledge of the public in general. Policemen, like everyone else, appear to have a correct conception of the nature of mental illness, in terms of standards of modern psychiatry, but like everyone else they avail themselves of various forms of denial when it comes to doing something about it.[9] The facts come into consciousness, as it were, without implying practical consequences; or, at least, the import of the facts is set aside in view of other considerations. Since the police almost always act on fragmentary information, their reasons for not taking any official steps are posited, among others, in the undetermined aspects of the case that must be presumed to have some undefined relevance. For example, one of the possibilities that officers must always consider is the chance that their involvement could be exploited by unknown persons for unknown reasons. Since they are not expert in symptoms of psychopathology, their desire to avoid possible future embarrassment is quite strong.

Second, policemen confront perversion, disorientation, misery, irresoluteness, and incompetence much

5. The term "doctrinal" is perhaps too strong, but only in the sense that the scheme of reasoning and justification lacks explicit formulation.

6. The literature on this topic is voluminous and heavily polemical. For a general overview, see Wayne R. LaFave, *Arrest*, Boston: Little, Brown & Co., 1965; W. T. Plumb, Jr., "Illegal Enforcement of the Law," *Cornell Law Quarterly*, 24 (1939), pp. 337–393; Jim Thompson, "Police Control Over Citizen Use of the Public Streets," *Journal of Criminal Law, Criminology and Police Science*, 49 (1959), pp. 562–568; R. C. Donnelly, "Police Authority and Practices," *Annals of the American Academy of Political and Social Science*, 339 (1962), pp. 90–110; Arthur H. Sherry, "Vagrants, Rogues and Vagabonds," *California Law Review*, 48 (1960), pp. 557–573.

7. I have dealt with the practice of invoking official rules of procedure to legitimize various "necessary" activities, as a general problem in formal organizations, in "The Concept of Organization," *Social Research*, 32 (1965), pp. 239–255.

8. The problem of the devious and exploitative use of the determination of mental illness in the administration of justice is dealt with by Thomas Szasz in a number of publications. See especially his latest book, *Psychiatric Justice*, New York: Macmillan, 1965.

9. Shirley Star, "The Public's Ideas About Mental Illness," paper presented to the National Association of Mental Health, Indianapolis, 1955, (mimeo); "The Place of Psychiatry in Popular Thinking," paper presented to the American Association of Public Opinion Research, 1957 (mimeo).

more often than any other social agent. They can readily point to a large number of persons who, to all appearances, are ready for the "booby hatch," but who nevertheless seem to lead such lives as they can without outside aid or intervention. Against this background the requirement that one should have a good brain and an even temper belong to the same category of wishes as that one should have a large and steady income. Thus, making emergency apprehensions is, among others, a matter of economy. Lower the standards somewhat and the number of apprehensions might be multiplied by a substantial factor. Similar considerations apply to making various types of arrests. Though the police could readily multiply the number of arrests for some petty offenses, they somehow manage to produce just the right number to keep the courts busy and the jails full. With the same uncanny instinct they burden the hospital just to the limit of its capacity.

Third, though policemen readily acknowledge that dealing with mentally ill persons is an integral part of their work, they hold that it is not a proper task for them. Not only do they lack training and competence in this area but such dealings are stylistically incompatible with the officially propounded conception of the policeman's principal vocation. It involves none of the skills, acumen, and prowess that characterize the ideal image of a first-rate officer. Given the value that is assigned to such traits in furthering a man's career, and as grounds for esteem among his co-workers, it is a foregone conclusion that conveying a "mental case" to the hospital will never take the place of catching Willie Sutton in the choice of worthwhile activities. The opportunities for making spectacular arrests are not so widely available to the uniformed patrolman as to compete for attention with the emergency apprehensions of mentally ill persons, but the established ways of collecting credits with one's superiors work against the development of voluntary interest with patients.

Fourth, officers complain that taking someone to the psychiatric service of the hospital is a tedious, cumbersome, and uncertain procedure. They must often wait a long time in the admitting office and are occasionally obliged to answer questions of the admitting psychiatrist that appear to place their own judgment in doubt. They must also reckon with the possibility of being turned down by the psychiatrist, in which case they are left with an aggravated problem on their hands. The complaints about the hospital must be understood in the light of a strong and widely respected rule of police procedure. The rule demands that an officer bring all cases assigned to him to some sort of closure within reasonable limits of time and effort. The ability to take care of things in a way that avoids protracted and complicated entangle-

ments and does not cause repercussions is, in fact, a sign of accomplished craftsmanship in police work that runs a close second to the ability to make important arrests. Relative to this standard, contacts with the hospital and the attitudes of psychiatrists are a source of endless frustration. Policemen are often puzzled by the hospital's refusal to lend its resources to help in keeping life outside free of violence and disorder; and, though they are relatively rarely turned down by admitting psychiatrists, many officers can cite cases in which persons who were not accepted into the hospital brought grief upon themselves and others.

Fifth, in addition to these experiences, certain other facts about the hospital exercise a restraining influence upon the making of emergency apprehensions. All officers are explicitly aware that taking someone to the hospital is a civil rather than a criminal matter. They are continually reminded of this distinction, and they employ the appropriate linguistic conventions in referring to such cases and in talking with ill persons and their relatives. The actual situation belies all this euphemizing and officers are unavoidably aware of this, too. Ill persons are, indeed, arrested on account of being ill. They are not taken to the jail, to be sure, but they are nevertheless locked up. The knowledge that the mental hospital is a place in which to lock people up is inferentially prior to the making of emergency apprehensions. It is only natural that officers would infer from witnessed hospital procedures with mentally ill patients to the conditions that presumably warrant them. To think otherwise would impugn the whole system, which operates not only under medical supervision but also under the auspices of the courts. Thus, in making an emergency apprehension the officer has to consider whether the person in question presents risks of such magnitude as warrant his confinement together with the rest of the "crazy" people who apparently require this sort of treatment.[10]

Conditions Surrounding Emergency Apprehensions

Despite the strong reluctance of the police, emergency apprehensions of mentally ill persons are quite frequent. Indeed, officers of the uniformed patrol make them about as often as they arrest persons for murder, all types of manslaughter, rape, robbery, aggravated assault, and grand theft, taken together; and more than one fifth of all

10. We propose that the degradation ceremony of the mental patient, to which Goffman refers in his work, presents itself to the policeman as a justified necessity with certain patients.

referrals to the receiving psychiatric service of the public hospital come from this source.[11]

In only a very few instances does the emergency apprehension involve the use of physical coercion. In most cases patients are passively compliant or at least manageable by means of verbal influence. At times patients go willingly, or perhaps even voluntarily.[12] In approximately half of the cases policemen encounter the patient without any warning. This happens either when officers run into the person in the course of patrolling or when they are dispatched to some address by radio, without any indication of the nature of the problem they will have to deal with. In the other half, officers are informed that they will have to deal with a possible "mental case."[13] Though the observations on which this account is based do not permit a firm inference in this matter, it appears that prior labeling does not play a role in the formation of the policeman's decision to make an apprehension.

Five types of circumstances in which emergency apprehensions are made anywhere from often to virtually always can be isolated. It is important to define the nature of this inventory. Policemen typically do not reach the conclusion that an apprehension should be made by searching for, or finding, such features as we shall enumerate. Thus, these are not, in any real sense, criterion situations. Furthermore, each of the five types encompasses cases that are linked by the rule of analogy rather than by the rule of identity.[14] By this we do not mean merely that actual instances differ over a wide range of permissible variations. Rather, we propose that the membership of any particular case in a class or in the scheme of classes in general, is based less on the presence or absence of specific characteristics than on the judgment that the case *amounts* to being of this or that class. If such a conclusion is to be reached, the case

11. During the period of the study policemen apprehended and referred to the hospital approximately 1,600 patients. The total number of arrests for the mentioned offenses, by the uniformed patrol, was exactly 1,600, according to published statistics of the police department. However, the study covered the period from July 1, 1963, to June 30, 1964, while the published statistics of the department cover the calendar year of 1964.

12. This observation is frankly judgmental; no one can estimate reliably the extent of covert coercion standing behind compliance. It is, however, not startlingly unusual for patients to ask policemen to take them to the hospital.

13. The information comes to the officer through radio code. The code contains special designations to indicate that an assignment involves a mental case, a suicide attempt, or an assignment of unknown nature.

14. Edward H. Levi has argued that reasoning by analogy prevails generally in the administration of justice; see his *Introduction to Legal Reasoning,* Chicago: University of Chicago Press, 1949. Since policemen must be attuned to the style of proof and inference that is used in courts, it would not be unreasonable to assume that they might assimilate some of this pattern of thinking.

must not be allowed to dissolve into its particulars. Instead, the conclusion is reached as much by attending to the case as such, as it is reached by attending to its contextual background.

The following three horizons of context appear to matter in cases of referrable mental illness: First, the *scenic* horizon, consisting of all the more or less stable features of the background that can be brought into play as employable resources to handle the problem, or that may assume the character of added reasons for making the emergency apprehension. Second, the *temporal* horizon, including both the changing nature of the problem as it is being attended to and what can be known or surmised about its past and future. Third, the *manipulative* horizon, which consists of considerations of practicality from the standpoint of the police officer. For example, an officer may encounter a mentally ill person in some such circumstances as we shall presently describe. He may learn that the person is a member of a stable and resourceful kinship group and that relatives can be mobilized to take care of him. In addition, there is information that the person has been in a similar state before and that he received outpatient psychiatric attention at that time. Whether this person will be moved to the hospital might then depend on whether others can take over within the limits of time the officer can allocate to waiting for them to arrive on the scene. The manipulative horizon is of particular interest and we shall discuss it more extensively in the section of the paper dealing with persons who are not referred to the hospital.

One further explanation—our description of the five categories of cases does not imply that officers themselves employ subcategories to classify mentally ill persons when they refer them to the hospital on an emergency basis. Rather, we propose the inventory as a scheme of prototypes to which policemen analogize in practice when they are confronted with a mentally ill person.

(1) When there is evidence that a person has attempted, or is attempting, suicide he is virtually always taken to the hospital. Occasionally officers have doubts about the genuineness of the attempt, but such doubts do not seem to weigh significantly against making the apprehension. In some instances the evidence in support of the presumption that an attempt has been made, or is contemplated, is ambiguous. In such cases the prevailing practice is to act on the basis of positive indications. Furthermore, the information that an attempt has been made appears to be a sufficient indication in itself for an emergency apprehension. Not only is it not necessary for the victim to exhibit other signs of a mental disorder but there is no way in which a person can demonstrate that he is not in need of psychiatric attention, once the facts

of the attempt have been adequately established. Both the most playful and the most rationally considered suicide attempts are treated as suggesting serious morbidity. The only circumstance under which officers can be dissuaded from taking a potential victim to the hospital is when a physician officially assumes responsibility for the case. Finally, when officers confront a person who shows patent signs of a mental disorder and they learn that this person has in the past attempted suicide, this information is apt to contribute significantly to the decision to make an emergency apprehension, even if the earlier attempts are not clearly connected with the present episode. In short, suicide presents the "ideal" combination of serious psychopathology and serious police business.

(2) When the signs of a serious psychological disorder, i.e., expressions of radically incongruous affect or thought, are accompanied by distortions of normal physical appearance, the person in question is usually taken to the hospital. Such things as injuries of unknown origin, seizures, urinary incontinence, odd posturing, nudity, extreme dirtiness, and so on, all tend to augment the import of psychological indications. All such features are perceived as signifying loss of control over one's appearance and as adequate grounds to expect a further proliferation of external problems. An apprehension will not be made, however, if the situation contains features indicating a mere momentary lapse of control. For example, in a case in which the police were summoned to deal with a severely retarded person living with her parents, the officers helped in restoring the normally functioning restraint and supervision. Scenically, the home environment offered a sufficient guarantee of control; historically, the situation was known to have been managed adequately in the past; and, manipulatively, the disruption could be remedied within reasonable time and with the cooperation of all parties who had a legitimate stake in the case.

(3) When the signs of serious psychological disorder are expressed in highly agitated forms, and especially when they are accompanied by incipient or actual acts of violence, the person is often taken to the hospital. Two further conditions must be met, however, before the apprehension is seriously considered. The violence or the threat of violence must be non-trivial. For example, a feeble and senile old woman assaulting her normally healthy son will not be taken to the hospital, but the son may be advised about the availability of hospitalization. Furthermore, the agitated person must be largely unresponsive to efforts to pacify him.

(4) Persons who appear to be seriously disoriented, or who by acting incongruously create a nuisance in a public place, are often taken to the hospital. Ordinarily

policemen will make an effort to induce the person to leave the scene while helping him on his way to his normal habitat. Only when it becomes clear that such a person cannot be expediently returned to a sheltered place, or remanded to some caretaker, and when he is in danger of suffering injury due to accident or exposure, will he be taken to the hospital.

(5) In the cases named so far the police act mainly on the basis of firsthand observation. Though there is always a certain amount of received information present, it plays a secondary role in the decision-making. The fifth category, however, is based primarily on received information. When requests for police aid come from complainants who stand to the allegedly mentally ill person in some sort of instrumental relationship, i.e., from physicians, lawyers, teachers, employers, landlords, and so on, the police generally, though by no means always, move the patient to the hospital.[15] It is usually assumed that the instrumentally related persons have exhausted their power and duty to help before calling the police and that there is little else left to do but to make an emergency apprehension. Interestingly, however, similar requests, in quite similar circumstances, made by family members, friends, roommates, or neighbors are usually not honored. Thus, for example, a severely depressed person may be taken to the hospital from his place of employment, on the urging of a doctor or his employer, both of whom presumably have already attempted alternative solutions, while he would be left in the care of his parent with the advice that the parent seek hospitalization for the patient.

The five types of circumstances in which emergency apprehensions are typically made are, of course, not mutually exclusive. Indeed, most actual cases are, in terms of their external circumstances, overdetermined. The general impression one gets from observing the police is that, except for cases of suicide attempts, the decision to take someone to the hospital is based on overwhelmingly conclusive evidence of illness. The very stringency of criteria would lead one to expect that the police often deal with persons who are also seriously ill but whom they do not take to the hospital. In our description of the five types we have already alluded to the fact that this is in fact so. We have also mentioned

---

15. In general, policemen insist on getting a fairly detailed story from the complainant and also on seeing the patient before they decided to make an emergency apprehension. One physician who was interviewed in the course of the study complained about this with a good deal of chagrin. From his point of view the police should take the word of a doctor without questioning him. Officers, however, maintain that the doctor's judgment would not protect them in the case of future complaints; they prefer making an "honest mistake." Policemen are generally acutely aware of the requirement of personal knowledge in finding "adequate grounds" for any action.

earlier that such persons do not fall outside the purview of police interest once it is decided that they need not be apprehended. We now turn to the description of alternative methods of handling mentally ill persons, about which no records are kept.

Non-official Ways of Dealing with Mentally Ill Persons

The following description of police dealings with mentally ill persons concerns cases in which formal emergency apprehensions are not made. We shall concentrate on encounters in which officers explicitly recognize signs of mental illness and in which they treat the illness as the primary and, in most instances, the only business at hand. That is, we will not be dealing with cases such as, for example, those involving an offender about whom policemen say, after they have arrested him, "What a nut!" Nor will we deal with cases involving various types of troublesome persons who are perceived to be, among other things, "slightly crazy." To be sure, in actual police work there exists no clear-cut dividing line segregating persons who are blatantly mentally ill from persons who are "slightly crazy." For clarity, however, we shall concentrate on extreme cases.

De Facto Emergency Apprehensions

To begin, we must consider certain types of police involvement that straddle the borderline between making and not making apprehensions. In such cases the patient usually ends up in the hospital but the police manage to avoid taking formal action. Insofar as the officers have no official part in the decision and thus no responsibilities, these cases might be considered *de facto* but not *de jure* emergency apprehensions. Occasionally policemen are summoned to aid in the move of a recalcitrant patient. The move is actually under way and the officers are merely expected, in their own words, to "do the dirty work." Though officers cannot readily avoid responding to such requests they typically do not employ coercive means. Instead, they remain in the background as a safety precaution against the possibility that the situation might get out of hand. Beyond that, they disperse curious onlookers, and at times provide help such as calling for an ambulance or a taxi. By and large they do nothing that will change the course of the ongoing development. They interpret their presence as having the value of making something that is already fully determined as peaceful and painless as possible. Insofar as they speak to the patient at all, they restrict their remarks to indicating that the move is legitimate

and in his best interest. In fact, the officers are usually the only persons on the scene who listen attentively to the patient and who use the leverage of trust to facilitate the move. Though such cases do not involve police initiative and involve no police decisions, the successful accomplishment of these referrals actually does depend on the availability of police aid. The very fact that the person who made the decision solicited help is an indication that he could probably not have prevailed by himself, or at least not on that occasion. Generally, police officers do not accompany the patient to the hospital and their involvement is not a matter of record.

Another form of *de facto* apprehension occurs when officers transport a person whom they recognize as mentally ill to a medical emergency service. In such cases it is necessary, of course, that there be present some sort of physical complaint in addition to the psychiatric complaint. It is generally expected that the admitting physician will make the further referral to the psychiatric service. By this method policemen avoid taking formal action on account of mental illness and also, incidentally, avoid having to deal with psychiatric staff which they find much more cumbersome than dealing with medical staff. Only rarely are records kept of these cases; such records as do exist identify the interventions as aiding a sick person rather than making an emergency apprehension.

Restitution of Control

By far the larger number of police encounters with mentally ill persons results neither in *de jure* nor in *de facto* emergency apprehensions. Rather, the involvements begin and end in the field. No other social agency, either legal or medical, participates in these cases and the policeman acts as the terminal, all-purpose remedial agent.

While discussing typical emergency apprehension situations we mentioned that officers often try to find competent persons to whom they may relinquish the care of the patient, or they try to return the ill person to his normal habitat in which he presumably can manage his affairs with minimal adequacy. Only in rare instances is this a simple "lost persons" problem. In these relatively rare cases, persons with stable social ties and fixed positions in the community escape the normally functioning controls or suffer a breakdown away from home. Whenever circumstances indicate that this is the case, the police will bring their technical communication and transportation facilities into play to locate caretakers for the patient. Though this is by no means always easy, it is a relatively simple problem. It may not be possible to find the caretakers within the time that can be allocated to the search, but the problem at least has a solution. In fact, when the caretakers cannot be expediently located, and the ill person is taken to the hospital, the search for the caretakers continues for the sake of informing them where the patient is. As a last resort, the identity of the lost mentally ill person is entered in the lost persons record to make it possible to respond to inquiries of caretakers. In general, however, the police are ready to devote a good deal of effort to returning persons to circumstances in which they are sheltered. As might be expected, however, persons with stable social ties and fixed positions in the community only rarely depend on the aid of the police and in many such instances the fact that the person is abroad is known before he is located because of inquiries of frantic relatives.

Much more difficult are cases in which the ill person cannot be presumed to be someone's responsibility in a structured sense, and whose living arrangements are unstable. In such cases the high proficiency of the police in tracing leads and in locating viable support are noteworthy. To solve such problems the officer invokes his detailed knowledge of people and places in the district he patrols. This knowledge, as often as not, permits him to guess who the person is and where he normally belongs. Failing this, the officer will know where to look and whom to ask for information. Bits and fragments of evidence have high informational value because the officer can fill in the missing parts out of past experiences in the same locale and with related persons.

This informational advantage is useful not only in the search for caretakers but also functions as the context for the considered transfer of responsibility. For while it is true that officers generally welcome opportunities to be rid of a mentally ill person, they are not uncritical about whom they will yield to. In one observed instance, for example, a young woman in agitated distress was taken to the hospital in part because her fiancé arrived on the scene and proposed to take over. Prior to his arrival the officers were about ready to leave the patient in the care of her mother and a neighbor who appeared to have a soothing influence on her. The entry of the fiancé seemed quite innocuous to the observer, but the officers gathered from his remarks that the arrangements he had in mind were not only not feasible but even destructive. The evaluation was possible because the officers knew many factual details about the places, persons, and arrangements the man envisioned. It is important to emphasize that the critical approach is not pursued by deliberate inquiry and scrutiny of all aspects of cases and decisions. Rather, the informational advantage of the officers automatically raises the level of demand for plausibility. That is, they can judge whether some

proposed solution is practical and acceptable with reference to empirical details of particular known places, at specified times, and in known social contexts. In the instance cited, this background information persuaded the officers that the patient could not be left safely unattended.

Among the types of persons to whom policemen most readily transfer responsibilities are family members and physicians. It is, however, not unusual to find neighbors, hotel clerks, landlords, bartenders, or shop-keepers entrusted with someone who is mentally ill. Especially in blighted parts of the city such persons are known to "keep an eye" on certain others. In such areas the policeman often stands in the midst of a referral and information system that is unstable and informally fluid, but the network of connections is so rich and ramified that an accredited member of the system is scarcely ever completely at a loss. For example, an officer might learn from a news vendor that a certain bartender might know someone who knows something about a senile old lady. If the bartender does not happen to be on duty, some patron in the bar, or the pawnbroker across the street might know. Here it is important to emphasize that news vendors and bartenders are not so much good sources of information, as that they become good sources of information, and incidentally also good resource persons, when the officer knows them personally and is personally known to them. The officer's superior competence is to a large extent dependent on the fact that he is accepted as a powerful and in certain ways uniquely authoritative member of a system of mutual aid.

Unfortunately, we know very little about the ways in which people in blighted areas of the city corroborate each others' identity and augment each others' feeble powers. But there is no doubt that the policeman is the only social agent who has some access to the functioning of this arrangement, and the only one who can employ it knowledgeably for the protection and aid of its members. The unique effectiveness of the officer as a quasi-member of this community hinges on the fact that he can invoke the powers of coercion; the effectiveness of this resource would be, however, drastically reduced if he were not also an insider who understands the dominant interests and attitudes of the denizens. It is the officer's grasp of the stable aspects of the social structure of life in slums, in rooming house sections, and in business districts—aspects that often elude the attention of outside observers—that permits him to find alternatives to the emergency hospitalization of mentally ill persons. In certain ways, dealing with persons who inhabit blighted parts of urban areas is an easier task for a seasoned foot patrolman than dealing with persons who have stable addresses and social ties, although, of course, once the latter are located a more permanent solution is guaranteed.

The relative stability of circumstances to which a mentally ill person can be returned is, of course, distributed on a continuum. At one extreme there are those patients who need only be conveyed to worried relatives, and at the other extreme there are those who can only be returned to a status of inconspicuous anonymity. With the latter, as with those who have some tenuous ties, the problem of letting the patient slip back into his normal groove is adumbrated with questions whether the normally working controls can be entrusted with "taking care of the problem." In terms of the policeman's own standards of proper procedure it is scarcely ever sufficient to remove the patient from sight. What is intended, instead, is the achievement of a solution of some degree of permanency. Although the officer's own altruism is the main acknowledged motivational impetus for this activity, the achievement of this goal is also a practical necessity. To settle for less than an adequate solution is apt to result in repeated calls and more work.

"Psychiatric First Aid"

The involvement of the police with mentally ill persons who are not taken to the hospital is not confined to finding responsible caretakers for them, or to taking them to their normally sheltered place. Nor is this always the problem at hand, for quite often the very person who is most eligible for this role is the one who solicited police intervention. In these cases officers always administer some sort of direct "psychiatric first aid," even though they repudiate this designation. It is extremely rare that officers encounter a patient who is too passive or too withdrawn for interaction of some sort. In fact, most of the patients the police encounter are in states of relatively high agitation and can be drawn into an exchange. From the officer's point of view, his task consists of monitoring the transition of a state of affairs from its dangerous phase to a phase of relative safety and normalcy.

Although police training and literature have come to include references to the handling of mentally ill persons, it is fair to say that officers are not instructed in anything that deserves to be called a technique. With no more to go on than the maxims of kindness and caution, officers tend to fall back on being formally correct policemen. To start, seasoned officers invariably remove the patient from the immediate context in which they find him. In this they merely follow good police practice in general, applicable to all types of persons who attract police attention. The object is to establish boundaries of

control and to reduce the complexity of the problem.[16] When it is not feasible to move the patient, the context is altered by removing others. The result in either case is the envelopment of the subject by police attention.

In direct dealings with the patient the policeman tries to establish and maintain the pretense of a normal conversational situation. All of the patient's remarks, allegations, or complaints are treated in a matter-of-fact manner. Policemen do not attempt to suppress or eliminate the absurd and bizarre, but rather leave them aside while concentrating verbal exchanges on the ordinary aspects of things. By this method every situation acquires a certain sense of normalcy. For example, in one observed instance a middle-aged lady complained, in highly agitated panic, that she was pursued by neighbors with an unheard-of weapon. Without questioning the lady's beliefs about what is possible in the domain of weaponry, or what might be reasonably assumed about the motives of angry neighbors, the officers went through the motions of dealing with the situation as if it involved a bona fide complaint. They searched the premises for nonexistent traces of impossible projectiles. They carefully took note of mundane particulars of events that could not have happened and advised the lady to be on the alert for suspicious occurrences in the future. The intervention, which lasted approximately one hour, terminated when the lady came to equate her predicament with the predicament of all other persons who were under some sort of threat and who apparently survive under police protection. She was visibly calmed and expressed the belief that the officers understood what she was facing and that it was within their capacity to ensure her safety. In the end, the conversation turned to such practical matters as how to summon the police quickly in situations of imminent danger and how to make doubly sure that locks on windows and doors were secure. Throughout the conversation the officers gave no hint that they doubted any part of the story. They did not challenge the statement that a projectile may travel through walls, furniture, and clothes without leaving any traces but be, nevertheless, fatal to persons. They also took pains to convince the lady that it would be tactically unwise and impractical to arrest or even interview suspected neighbors at this stage of the case.

Although the method of field work, as employed in this study, does not permit the formulation of reliable estimates of frequencies, it can be said that neither the

16. One police lieutenant explained that one of the major stresses of police work has to do with the fact that officers are often forced to reach difficult decisions under the critical eye of bystanders. Such situations contain the simple hazard of losing physical control of the case as well as the risk that the officer's decision will be governed by external influence or provocation.

observations nor the interviews with policemen suggested that the distribution of "psychiatric first aid" is anything but random, relative to social class. Furthermore, such interventions sometimes involve patients exhibiting signs of very serious psychopathology. In general, agitated patients receive much more careful and protracted attention than patients who are overtly passive, which accords with the fact that officers give high priority to risks of proliferation of external troubles. Finally, although the police occasionally encounter the same patient repeatedly, they tend to treat each confrontation as a separate emergency. Every precinct station has a fund of knowledge about persons who have been the subjects of past "psychiatric first aid," but there is no sustained concern for these persons. Whenever certain known persons come to the attention of officers, it is said that they are "acting up again." The avoidance of sustained concern and attention is part of the official posture of the police and an expression of the fact that the illness as such is of little interest and that it acquires relevance only through its unpredictable exacerbations.

The attitudes and procedures of "psychiatric first aid" are in a general sense representative of the overall involvement of the police with mental illness. The attitudes and procedures also play a role in cases in which emergency apprehensions are made. In the latter instances they provide, in part, the background for the decision, in the sense that if these measures do not succeed in reducing the potential of the external risk, the patient will be taken to the hospital. Thus, the practice of "psychiatric first aid" and the skill that it involves represent the core of what we earlier identified as the manipulative horizon of relevance in the decision-making process. The point to be emphasized about these interventions is that they involve no basic modification of police posture but rather its use for the particular purposes of dealing with patients. Though the officers are fully aware that they are dealing with mentally ill persons, they do not act in the manner of quasi-mental-health-specialists.

Continuing Care

After having placed proper emphasis on the generally prevalent pattern of the episodic, emergency, and ad hoc involvement of policemen with mentally ill persons, we turn to a significantly less frequent type of activity practiced by a limited number of patrolmen. In contrast with "psychiatric first aid," foot patrolmen, especially when they work in the slum, tenderloin, business, or rooming-house districts of the city, know some mentally ill persons with whom they have established a more or less regularized pattern of running into each other. Some of these persons are apparently chronic schizophrenics, others seem mentally defective, and others are senile. Many have a history of past hospitalization. Though the officers do not attempt to diagnose these persons, they recognize the presence of substantial psychological handicaps. Indeed, the officer's interaction with and interest in these people is basically structured by the consideration that they suffer from serious disorders.

The encounters are so highly routinized that they scarcely have an event-character of their own. It is part of the ordinary routine for a foot patrolman to meet people and to engage them in conversations. Each encounter is in its own way thematized. The themes occasionally are determined in terms of the prevailing contingencies of situations. For the most part, however, the exchanges are better understood, and often can only be understood, as episodes in long-standing relationships, with past exchanges furnishing the tacit background for presently exchanged remarks. This format of meetings holds also for the encounters with known mental patients, except that in these cases the encounters are thematized by the person's psychological handicap. Officers acknowledge that their approach and manipulation of the patient is deliberately organized around this concern.

In one observed instance a young man approached an officer in a deteriorating business district of the city. He voiced an almost textbook-type paranoid complaint. From the statements and the officer's responses it could be gathered that this was a part of a sequence of conversations. The two proceeded to walk away from an area of high traffic density to quieter parts of the neighborhood. In the ensuing stroll the officer inspected various premises, greeted passers-by, and generally showed a low level of attentiveness. After about twenty-five minutes the man bade the officer goodbye and indicated that he would be going home now. The officer stated that he runs into this man quite often and usually on the same spot. He always tried to lead the man away from the place that apparently excites his paranoid suspicions. The expressions of inattentiveness are calculated to impress the person that there is nothing to worry about, while, at the same time, the efforts the man must make to hold the officer's interest absorb his energies. This method presumably makes the thing talked about a casual matter and mere small-talk. Thus, the practices employed in sustained contacts involve, like the practices of "psychiatric first aid," the tendencies to confine, to disregard pathological material, and to reduce matters to their mundane aspects.

Conclusion

Certain structural and organizational restraints leading to an apparent reluctance on the part of the police to invoke the law governing emergency apprehensions of mentally ill persons were discussed. Next we described the external properties of situations in which the law is often invoked. This approach left a seemingly residual category of cases in which persons are judged to be mentally ill but are not taken to the hospital. The category is residual, however, only in conjunction with one particular conception of the nature of police work. According to this conception the police act with competence and authority only when their actions can be subsumed under the heading of some legal mandate. If the conditions for making an arrest or an emergency apprehension are not satisfied, then, presumably, an officer has no further legitimate business with the case. It is universally accepted that the police could not possibly conform fully to this rule. Not only is it inevitable, but it has been said to be desirable that officers use a variety of means in keeping the peace.

In real police work the provisions contained in the law represent a resource that can be invoked to handle certain problems. Beyond that, the law contains certain guidelines about the boundaries of legality. Within these boundaries, however, there is located a vast array of activities that are in no important sense determined by considerations of legality. In fact, in cases in which invoking the law is not a foregone conclusion, as for example in many minor offenses or in the apprehension of mentally ill persons, it is only speciously true to say that the law determined the act of apprehension, and much more correct to say that the law made the action possible. The effective reasons for the action are not located in the formulas of statutes but in considerations that are related to established practices of dealing informally with problems.[17]

The important point about the relevance of established practice is that it contains the means and considerations

17. We are talking about practice, of course, but the problem stands in the midst of a debate in legal theory. If it is maintained that the substance of the law is that it contains a system of rules of conduct, informing people what they must not do, and providing sanctions for violations, then neither the policeman nor the judge has any legitimate powers to exculpate a violator. If, however, it is maintained that the substance of the law is that it contains a system of rules limiting the powers of the institutions of the polity with respect to certain offenders and offensive types of conduct, then alternative means of control are not out of order, provided they are not explicitly forbidden. The former position is expressed in Jerome Hall, *General Principles of Criminal Law*, Indianapolis: Bobbs-Merrill, 1947; an exposition of the latter view is contained in Norberto Bobbio, "Law and Force," *The Monist*, 49 (1965), pp. 321–342.

in terms of which judgments are made whether there is any need to invoke the law. The practices are, of course, responsive to influences from the courts, from prosecutors, and the public. They also stand in some relationship of correspondence to the intent of the law. Some problems are routinely handled by invoking the law, in other cases it is merely one of the available alternatives. In these latter cases it is possible that an officer who merely complies with the law may nevertheless be found to be an incompetent practitioner of his craft. About him it may be said that he should have been able to handle the problem in some other way. The other ways of handling are not explicitly codified and they undoubtedly depend on personal ingenuity on the part of the officer. Their foundation, however, is in a transmittable skill.

When one defines these established practices as the focal point of reference of police function, instead of ministerial law enforcement, then the cases of mentally ill persons who are not referred to hospitals do not constitute a residual category. Instead, "psychiatric first aid" appears as the standard practice that contains within the realms of its possibilities the emergency apprehension. In certain cases, as for example in cases involving suicide attempts, the apprehension is virtually a foregone conclusion, but in general it is viewed as merely one of several ways of solving problems. It happens to be the only visible alternative, but this is an artifact resulting from existing police recording systems that note only those actions that involve ministerial law enforcement. Indeed, it can safely be said that the proper understanding of recorded interventions hinges on the knowledge of cases for which there is no official record. When, for example, we say that one of the necessary conditions for the emergency apprehension is the discernment of the risk of proliferation of external troubles, then we must add that these are such perceived risks as cannot be controlled by the ordinarily available means contained in the standard practices. Thus, to understand the perception of risk it is necessary to know the structure of what can be, and is normally done to control it.

In this paper we have tried to describe briefly certain practices of dealing with mentally ill persons and we have argued that the structure and means contained in these practices determine who will be referred to the hospital on an emergency basis. The external characteristics of cases are not irrelevant to the decisions, but their import is always mediated by practical considerations of what can and need be done alternatively. We should like to propose that such procedures as finding responsible caretakers who will "look out" for the patient, or "psychiatric first aid," or the sustained interest in some patients by foot patrolmen, are part of a larger domain of police work. We further propose that this work, which has been called "keeping the peace,"[18] in differentiation from "enforcing the law," consists of occupational routines with particular procedures, skills, standards, and information, in short, of craft, that meets certain tacit public expectations.[19] Chances are that

18. Michael Banton proposed and discussed the distinction between peace-keeping and law-enforcement functions in his book, *The Policeman in the Community,* New York: Basic Books, 1965.

19. Elaine Cumming and her co-workers define the policeman engaged in activities that do not relate to "keeping the law from being broken and apprehending those who break it" as an "amateur social worker." They do not consider, however, that their conception of the role of the policeman, that is, as being limited to law enforcement and restrictive control, may have been correct only "by definition and by law," and not in reality. Our own contention is that keeping the peace contains elements of control *and* support in a unique combination and

when police decisions are viewed from the perspective of the requirements of this craft, rather than with an interest in seeking to discover how well they correspond to the conventional formalities of the law, they may appear quite a bit less adventitious than they are generally perceived to be. To say, however, that there exists a body of methodically organized routines for keeping the peace, which in some sense influence police decisions to invoke the law, in no way settles the question whether the currently prevailing patterns of police discretion are desirable or not. It merely urges that the study of it will furnish a more realistic basis for appraisal.

that its pursuit has nothing amateurish about it. See Elaine Cumming *et al.,* "Policeman as Philosopher, Guide and Friend," *Social Problems,* 12 (1965), pp. 276–286.

PART FIVE

Structures and Ideologies of Institutional Treatment Settings

INTRODUCTION

The mental illness enterprise encompasses many lay and professional activities and organizational contexts. It includes the ephemeral moments in which friends advise and counsel one another about personal problems, office visits in which a physician prescribes a tranquilizer, and, of course, the day-to-day operations of mental hospitals and community clinics. Aspects of the enterprise have been touched upon by a number of the earlier readings. In the final two sections we focus on two prominent components of the mental illness enterprise: institutional and community-based treatment settings.

The concept of an institution devoted exclusively to the care and custody of the mad is of relatively recent origin. To be sure, for centuries there have been institutions that have housed the insane, but typically it was not insanity as such that gained individuals entry. Rather, it was their poverty. In an earlier period the organizations and institutions created to respond to problem populations did not distinguish between the mad and other "problematic groups" (Scull, 1977). From the point of view of the state there was but one undifferentiated category of persons requiring consideration—the unemployed poor.

The scope of the problem posed by the poor, according to Foucault (1954), was awesome. According to one estimate, of Paris' one hundred thousand inhabitants at the end of the sixteenth century, some thirty thousand were beggars. To the bourgeoisie, beggars were an anathema, their request for alms was an implicit tax, their idleness and seeming degeneracy morally offensive, and their aggregate presence a political threat.

In 1656, a royal edict established the Hôpital Général in Paris. Within a few months one out of every one hundred Parisians was an inmate, and by 1676, there was an Hôpital Général in every major French city. The inmates of the Hôpital were largely the poor. The insane were among them because they were among the unemployed. As Foucault noted, the Hôpital was not a medical establishment, for its primary purpose was to "prevent mendicancy and idleness."

280

> Before having the medical meaning we give it, or that at least we like to suppose it has, confinement was required by something quite different from any concern with curing the sick. What made it necessary was an imperative of labor. Our philanthropy prefers to recognize the signs of a benevolence toward sickness where there is only a condemnation of idleness.

The Hôpital Général also performed several economic functions. On one swing of the economic pendulum the Hôpital absorbed the unemployed; on the other, it provided a source of cheap labor. The connection between the Hôpital and work was further buttressed by the ethical meanings assigned to idleness. The implicit supposition of idleness was that nature would provide freely as Eden had for Adam before the Fall. Idleness represented what Foucault termed a "moral rebellion." Thus, laboring came to have an ethical significance within the houses of confinement that transcended its economic import: "Since sloth had become the absolute form of rebellion, the idle would be forced to work, in the endless leisure of a labor without utility or profit." It is in the context of the labor process within the Hôpital that the need for differentiation of the mad from their fellow poor arose, since the mad "distinguish[ed] themselves by their inability to work and to follow the rhythms of collective life." Elsewhere and at other times an institution for the mad arose for avowedly rehabilitative rather than administrative reasons.

Rothman, in *The Discovery of the Asylum*, recounts the historical circumstances that led in the pre-Civil War era to the "cult of the asylum" and to the construction of special institutions for the insane. The psychiatrists, called medical superintendents at the time, overcome by a nostalgic view of the past, believed that insanity was caused by chaotic social forces. They felt that order, discipline, and social stability, which were threatened by rapid social change, would produce a society without madness. The proper cure for insanity lay in establishing a new setting with the characteristics of quiet, serenity, order, and stability. "The charge of the asylum," writes Rothman, "was to bring discipline to the victims of a disorganized society." Psychiatrists lobbied extensively and successfully for funds to build asylums in rural, isolated areas, and by 1860 almost 85 percent of the states (there were thirty-three at the time) had built public insane asylums.

The superintendents' expectations have long since been recognized as naively optimistic. Indeed, by the end of the second half of the nineteenth century it was apparent that the asylum served a custodial and not a rehabilitative function. The superintendents anticipated asylums caring for the recently insane coming from comfortable households, while the reality was furnished by the "manic, the furiously insane and worse yet, the chronic, with no prospect of meaningful improvement."

For many observers the hospital continued to function primarily as a custodial institution. While there was considerable variation in the quality of mental hospitals and in the consequences of hospitalization, numerous scholarly studies and lay observations repeatedly noted that the large public hospitals were something less than curing and rehabilitative agencies. In "The Mental Hospital as a People-Processing Organization," Perrucci argues that many contradictory and puzzling features of hospitals become intelligible once it is understood that the primary purpose of the institution is to serve ". . . as a system of justification for a commitment process which cannot be openly admitted to be what it is; a victimization process." That hospitals are not able to rehabilitate should come as no surprise, for they were implicitly organized not to cure but to keep individuals. At the same time, hospitals maintain the collective pretense that they are rehabilitative settings.

What is life like for a patient in a large mental hospital? In "The Moral Career of the Mental Patient: In-Patient Phase," Goffman describes some of the consequences for the self of becoming an inpatient. Although the staff may view the new patients' withdrawal from social contacts as further evidence of their mental illness, this response may actually represent their response to the institution's mortification of them and simply reflect their "desire not to be known to anyone as a person who could possibly be reduced to these present circumstances."

Goffman analyzes several significant features of the mortification process: the "confessional" aspects of group psychotherapy; the sheer humiliation of failure as represented by hospitalization itself; the systematic discrediting of the patients' attempt to show themselves in a positive light; staff control over what is entered into the patients' case records and their use of this information to defame patients; and the focusing of small talk on patient behavior in such a way as to denigrate the patients.

The inmates are exposed to a ward system that places them under continual surveillance and moral review and that produces a setting where elevation of a patient's status is extraordinarily rare, if not impossible. The unfortunate inmates find that their selfhood is not viable. Their status is so low that moral norms appropriate outside may be relaxed in the hospital. For example, extramarital encounters may be permitted without censure. Patients are so low on the totem pole that they have little in the way of reputation to lose.

Goffman's powerful statement draws attention to the importance of examining stages in the morality of the self and of conceptualizing the self as that which is permitted to exist in the insane asylum's institutional arrangements.

The importance of the institution as a compelling set of constraints acting both on the patient and the staff is brought home in another fashion by Rosenhan's influential study, "On Being Sane in Insane Places." Rosenhan is interested in the issue of whether the sane can be reliably and validly differentiated from the insane. He argues they cannot and provides evidence gathered by having eight "normal" pseudopatients admit themselves to twelve different hospitals located in five states.

The pseudopatients went to the hospital admissions offices after calling for appointments and complained that they heard voices saying the words "empty," "hollow," and "thud." They falsified only their name, vocation, and employment. Other information they provided was accurate. All were admitted and diagnosed schizophrenic, except one case diagnosed as manic-depressive. Eventually each was discharged with a diagnosis of schizophrenia in remission. This study shows not only the importance of the label as a diagnostic device, but more fundamentally, it reveals how people in organizations feel compelled to fit events into existing structures of meaning. Anyone who comes to a mental hospital admissions office wishing to be admitted must be insane. Since everyone in a mental hospital is crazy, their actions can only be understood as symptomatic of their craziness. Hence, when pseudopatients took extensive notes, these activities too were interpreted in a fashion consistent with their malady. For example, when one pseudopatient began to write down the kind of medication the physician had just prescribed for him, the physician interpreted his need to do this as indicative of a poor memory.

In "The Contextual Nature of Psychiatric Diagnoses," Rosenhan reviews and discusses several questions raised by critics of the original study: How should the pseudopatients have been diagnosed and treated? Was a diagnosis of schizophrenia justified? To what extent can diagnoses be based on scientific evidence? What does "in remission" mean? How important to an understanding of the findings was experimenter bias and demand characteristics? Did the pseudopatients behave sanely while on the ward?

The sociologically trained and especially those committed to fine-grained field studies will find few surprises. Rosenhan concludes that the social system within which the patient, staff, and psychiatric diagnostician function exerts a compelling influence over psychiatric diagnosis by affecting perception, cognition, and interpersonal relationships. Since the pseudopatients occupied roles in the institution, their behaviors and the way in which they were responded to by others severely limited their choices. It is social structure that creates context and constrains behavioral opportunities.

Rosenhan's second article attacks the arbitrary character of psychiatric diagnosis, and for this reason has been highly controversial. Much of his attack has focused on the American Psychiatric Association's *Diagnostic and Statistical Manual,* which has recently been revised. The reader might wish to consult several other critiques published in the same issue of the *Journal of Abnormal Psychology*.

"Therapy and Power," by political scientist Murray Edelman, is extracted from his book *Political Language* (1977). This essay draws attention to the political character of psychiatry and related social institutions. Edelman's analysis of the helping professions, psychiatry, social work, public school education, and law enforcement, emphasizes the political impact of professional language. He argues that the helping professions define their statuses and those of their clients in their work and, in so doing, use their languages to justify a power hierarchy. The helping professions define who is worthy, in need, and dangerous, and, therefore, who should be incarcerated. Edelman demonstrates the intimate connection between the process of therapy and social conformity and social control.

Social institutions differ in the extent to which their technology is ambiguous, vague, or uncertain. Unlike the world of automobile manufacturing, for instance, whose technology is clear and well-defined, the work psychiatrists perform is permeated with uncertainty and unpredictability. The therapeutic process itself and the outcomes from this process have inherent qualities of ambiguity and vagueness. Who knows when someone is mentally ill or normal? What is mental illness? What is treatment? How can one tell if one is cured? Institutions such as psychiatry, teaching, social work, and counseling, with their intrinsically vague and uncertain technologies, must rely on consensus and conformity for information on performance effectiveness. Objective criteria simply do not exist. Therapy—which can include activities ranging from reading, bicycling, and dancing, to electric shock—becomes that which therapists do, and cures are defined as such by the very persons responsible for treatment. Psychiatry's ability to secure resources in a highly uncertain environment depends heavily on its ability to obtain the support of other powerful legitimacy-granting institutions, such as medicine, universities, law, and government. The psychiatric professional has created an ideological cocoon that is presented to the public as the valid representation of reality. The study of psychiatry as ideology draws attention to the need to explore carefully not only what psychiatrists do, but the style and the forms of language they and others use to define their actions.

The next two essays, by Szasz and Clare, consist of a debate that centers on the very meaning of "Anti-Psychiatry." They illustrate the range of commitments and values in psychiatric thought. Three positions are staked out: the antipsychiatry of two leaders of the antipsychiatry movement in England, Laing and Cooper (as depicted first by Szasz and then by Clare); Szasz's critique of contemporary psychiatry; and a defense of psychiatry by Clare, a practitioner and a moderate. Although these positions hardly exhaust the terrain, they cover quite a bit of ground.

Szasz's essay differentiates his own well-known attacks on psychiatry from those of Laing and his associates. Szasz's position has two main features: 1) ". . . that the intervention institutional psychiatrists call 'mental hospitalization' is, in fact, a form of imprisonment," and 2) ". . . that the phenomenon psychiatrists call 'schizophrenia' is not a demonstrable medical disease but the name of certain kinds of social deviance (or of behavior unacceptable to the speaker)." Both are seen as infringements on individual freedom. The essence of Szasz's opposition to traditional psychiatry lies in his fear that it strips individuals of their personal freedoms. He favors voluntary and opposes involuntary psychiatric treatment, since the latter confines people to mental institutions and "interprets disagreement as disease." Inherent in Szasz's perspective is a glorification of individual autonomy.

Szasz's criticisms of Laingian practices emphasize the similarity of Laing's image of schizophrenia to that of traditional psychiatry. Szasz points out that Laing established his own state-supported institution (Kingsley Hall) to treat schizophrenics, replete with the equivalent of patient, staff, and bureaucratic rules. He does not allege that the Laingian view of madness is the same as that of traditional psychiatry. The Laingian view, for example, uniquely emphasizes persons' impulses toward authenticity. Hence, Kingsley Hall was designed to allow patients to exhibit their "real selves" and to "work through" their problems. Szasz objects vehemently to Laing's attempt to blame madness on society, capitalism, the family, and other social institutions. Szasz feels the responsibility for madness must fall ultimately on the individual, since it is his or her weaknesses (such as lack of courage) that is fundamentally at fault: "What we call 'sanity' . . . has a great deal to do with competence earned by struggling for excellence; with compassion, hard won by confronting conflict; and with modesty and patience, acquired through silence and suffering."

Clare's view of schizophrenia, although a more gentle, understanding, and compassionate one, is no more sociological than that of Szasz (Goldstein 1980). To Clare, madness is an affliction—not, as in Laing's case, a mystical search for creativity, nor, as in Szasz's, an evasion of personal responsibility. Indeed, according to Clare, neither Laing nor Szasz take madness seriously enough. To those afflicted it is a terrifying ordeal. By intimating that the most viable remedy may be biochemical, Clare returns psychiatric thought to the very orientation from which it was jarred a number of decades ago—the medical model.

Surely the origins and sources of human misery and happiness are one of the most enduring problems in the history of social thought. In considering the ideological aspects of psychiatry we tread on perilously unfirm ground. Despite the heroic efforts of Mannheim (1936), Merton (1949), and many others, the sociological study of ideology has not solved the deep problems of objectivity. Geertz (1973) has described the evaluative problem aptly: "The familiar parodic paradigm applies: 'I have a social philosophy; you have political opinions; he has an ideology.'" Nevertheless, an adequate understanding of the place of psychiatry in modern society requires exploration not only of its social organization, but of the content and meaning of its core values and ideas as well.

References

Michel Foucault, *Madness and Civilization*, New York: New American Library, 1967.

Clifford Geertz, *The Interpretation of Cultures*, New York: Basic Books, Inc., 1973.

Michael S. Goldstein, "The Politics of Thomas Szasz: A Sociological View," *Social Problems* Vol. 27, No. 5 (June 1980), 570-583.

Robert K. Merton, *Social Theory and Social Structure*, Glencoe, Ill.: The Free Press, 1949.

Karl Mannheim, *Ideology and Utopia*, New York: Harcourt, Brace, 1936.

David Rothman, *The Discovery of the Asylum*, Boston: Little, Brown, and Co., 1971.

Andrew T. Scull, *Decarceration*, Englewood Cliffs, N.J.: Prentice-Hall, Inc., 1977.

DAVID ROTHMAN

The Discovery of the Asylum

Every general practitioner in the pre-Civil War era agreed that insanity was a disease of the brain and that the examination of tissues in an autopsy would reveal organic lesions, clear evidence of physical damage, in every insane person. Isaac Ray, one of the leading medical superintendents of the period, when presenting the consensus of his discipline to the legal profession, confidently declared: "No pathological fact is better established . . . than that deviations from the healthy structure are generally present in the brains of insane subjects. . . . The progress of pathological anatomy during the present century has established this fact beyond the reach of a reasonable doubt." Should a particular autopsy reveal no physical changes in the brain, "the only legitimate inference was that current skills were still too crude to insure accurate results.[1] Nevertheless, this view did not lead to intensive anatomical or neurological investigations to understand the etiology of the disease. Medical superintendents gave no room in their institutions to this type of research. They had no doubt that organic lesions existed, that insanity was a bodily ailment. But its first causes they assigned

not to body chemistry but to social organization. The solution to the age-old ailment would be found not in the laboratory but in the society, not by looking into the microscope but into the community.

Why were medical superintendents so convinced that dangers were omnipresent in the community? Why were their predictions so direful? For one thing, they had been taught, according to the prevailing psychological theory, that the mind operated by association and not through inherited ideas. When the mind became diseased, the fault had to rest with the associations outside it, and psychiatrists, therefore, turned attention to external influences, to the phenomena that the mind was perceiving—in other words, to the society in which the individual lived. For another, medical superintendents were eager to cure mental illness, prodded on by Enlightenment doctrines and a faith in progress, and republic patriotism. Convinced that to identify the source of the problem would be to master it, they looked avidly for faults in society. Yet, why were they, like the first penologists, so remarkably successful in their search, able to write almost endlessly about the deficiencies in American life? After all, Jacksonian society was not verging on collapse and it is doubtful, for example, whether the rates of insanity were actually increasing. (Evidence is hard to come by, but one recent study, *Psychosis and Civilization*, argues convincingly that the rate of insanity in this country has remained constant from before the Civil War to the present.[2]) Rather,

Reprinted from David Rothman, *The Discovery of the Asylum*, Boston: Little, Brown, and Co., 1971, pp. 110–111, 126–129, 130–134, 137–141, 265–268 and 285–287, by permission of the author and publisher (copyright © 1971 by David J. Rothman).

1. Isaac Ray, *A Treatise on the Medical Jurisprudence of Insanity* (Boston, 1853, 3rd ed.), 69, 129–130. The volume first appeared in 1838. For similar views see the remarks of Samuel Woodward, superintendent, Worcester State Lunatic Hospital, *Seventh Annual Report* (Boston, 1840), 65–66; see too Connecticut Retreat for the Insane, *Eighteenth Annual Report* (Hartford, 1842), 14.

2. Herbert Goldhamer and A. W. Marshall, *Psychosis and Civilization* (New York, 1953).

psychiatrists' anxieties were ultimately tied to their conception of the proper social order. Against the norms that they held, the American scene appeared chaotic.

Medical superintendents were certain that their society lacked all elements of fixity and cohesion because they judged it by a nostalgic image of the eighteenth century. Frightened by an awareness that the old order was passing and with little notion of what would replace it, they defined the realities about them as corrupting, provoking madness. The root of their difficulty was that they still adhered to the precepts of traditional social theory, to the ideas that they had inherited from the colonial period. By these standards, men were to take their rank in the hierarchy, know their place in society, and not compete to change positions. Children were to be content with their station, taking their father's position for their own. Politics and learning were to be the province of trained men, and ordinary citizens were to leave such matters to them. Family government was to instill order and discipline, and the community to support and reinforce its dictums. This was the prescription for a well-ordered society, one that would not generate epidemics of insanity.

As early as the colonial period, reality did not always fit with such a static theory. But the colonists, lacking intellectual and social incentives, had not been forced to confront the gap. Americans in the Jacksonian period, however, recognized the disparity and were frightened by it. The society was more fluid than before, and greater geographic and social mobility made it more difficult to maintain older theories. Enlightenment ideas and a faith in progress also opened up endless possibilities for achievement, and the prospect of bringing glory to the new republic made these opportunities all the more welcome. As a result, they looked closely and carefully at their society, and worried about what they saw.

Medical superintendents had little trouble comprehending the influences encouraging individualism in America. But they could not perceive what forces would prevent the separate atoms from breaking off and scattering in wild directions. Was there a nucleus able to hold these disparate elements together? This fundamental and troubling question ultimately revealed the difficulties in conceptualizing the kind of social structure that should accompany republican government. Officials and laymen alike were dubious whether a society so intent on promoting individual effort would be able to achieve cohesion. Could it withstand the strains of widespread physical and social mobility? Could it tolerate unprecedented political participation and a pervasive skepticism toward traditional ideas? Later, in the post-Civil War era, with a confidence born of survival and some

measure of success, men would emphatically answer yes. The fear of the father would become the glory of the son. The self-made man would stand as a hero, not a potential madman, a fluid society would be the pride of the country, not the chief cause of crime and insanity. But to Americans in the Jacksonian period the matter was anything but settled. The danger that under continued stress the structure might collapse seemed not at all remote.

And yet, the effect of these conceptions was to promote a vigorous and popular movement for amelioration. Rather than abandon all hope before such a depressing analysis of the nature of American society, medical superintendents and laymen issued a call for action and sparked a revolution in the practices toward the insane. For one corollary of these doctrines held that since mental illness originated in the structure of society, not in God's will or individual failings, the community incurred an inescapable responsibility. Reformers themselves felt the burden that this contention imposed, and educated the public to it. As Edward Jarvis explained, "Society establishes, encourages or permits these customs out of which mental disorder may and frequently does arise." Therefore, it had the clear obligation "to heal the wounds it inflicts." Dorothea Dix, taking her cues from this formulation, demanded of innumerable state legislatures: "Should not society, then, make the compensation which alone can be made for these disastrous fruits of its social organization?" In similar terms, Samuel Gridley Howe prodded his countrymen to make a broad commitment to the care of the insane. "This duty of society, besides being urged by every consideration of humanity," he declared, "will be seen to be more imperative if we consider that insanity is in many cases the result of imperfect or vicious social institutions and observances."[3] Having caused the pain, it was incumbent on the community to help relieve it.

An environmental conception of the causes of deviant behavior encouraged men to believe that such ailments as insanity were curable. The community not only had the moral obligation but the ability to correct the condition. Having located the etiology of the disease in social organization, medical superintendents were confident that a setting which eliminated the irritants could restore the insane to health. The diagnosis of the causes of the disease provided the clues to a cure. To be sure, the very magnitude of the problem ruled out a frontal assault. Where would one begin an effort to limit

---

3. Edward Jarvis, *Address at Northampton,* 12, and *On the Supposed Increase of Insanity,* 21; Dorothea Dix, *Memorial to the Legislature of Pennsylvania,* 5; Samuel Gridley Howe, "Insanity in Massachusetts," 5.

ambition and intellectual independence, to curb physical and social mobility, to alter the economic, political, religious, and social character of the new republic? Framed in this fashion, the question was unanswerable. But reformers devised a workable solution to this dilemma. Rather than attempt to reorganize American society directly, they would design and oversee a distinctive environment which eliminated the tensions and the chaos. They would try to create—in a way reminiscent of the founders of utopian communities—a model society of their own, not to test a novel method for organizing production or making political decisions, but to exemplify the advantages of an orderly, regular, and disciplined routine. Here was an opportunity to meet the pressing needs of the insane, by isolating them from the dangers at loose in the community, and to further a reform program, by demonstrating to the larger society the benefits of the system. Thus, medical superintendents and laymen supporters moved to create a new world for the insane, one that would not only alleviate their distress but also educate the citizens of the republic. The product of this effort was the insane asylum.

The New World of the Asylum

The sturdy walls of the insane asylum became familiar landmarks in pre-Civil War America. They jutted out from flat rural landscapes or rose above the small houses of new suburbs, visible for some distance and unmistakably different from surrounding structures. Their growth was rapid and sudden. Before 1810, only a few eastern-seaboard states had incorporated private institutions to care for the mentally ill, and Virginia alone had established a public asylum. All together they treated less than five hundred patients, most of whom came from well-to-do families. Few departures from colonial practices occurred in the first forty years after independence; the insane commonly languished in local jails and poorhouses or lived with family and friends. But in the course of the next few decades, in a dramatic transformation, state after state constructed asylums. Budding manufacturing centers like New York and Massachusetts erected institutions in the 1830's, and so did the agricultural states of Vermont and Ohio, Tennessee and Georgia. By 1850, almost every northeastern and midwestern legislature supported an asylum; by 1860, twenty-eight of the thirty-three states had public institutions for the insane. Although not all of the mentally ill found a place within a hospital, and a good number among the aged and chronic poor remained in almshouses and jails, the institutionalization of the insane became the standard

procedure of the society during these years. A cult of asylum swept the country.[4]

The movement was not born of desperation. Institutionalization was not a last resort of a frightened community. Quite the reverse. Psychiatrists and their lay supporters insisted that insanity was curable, more curable than most other ailments. Spokesmen explained that their understanding of the causes of insanity equipped them to combat it, and the asylum was a first resort, the most important and effective weapon in their arsenal.

The program's proponents confidently and aggressively asserted that properly organized institutions could cure almost every incidence of the disease. They spread their claims without restraint, allowing the sole qualification that the cases had to be recent. Practitioners competed openly with one another to formulate the most general and optimistic principle, to announce the most dramatic result. One of the first declarations came from the superintendent of the Massachusetts asylum at Worcester, Samuel Woodward. "In recent cases of insanity," he announced in 1834, "under judicious treatment, as large a proportion of recoveries will take place as from any other acute disease of equal severity." In his own institution, he calculated, 82.25 percent of the patients recovered. Still, Woodward's tone was judicious and moderate in comparison to later assertions. Dr. Luther Bell, from Boston's McLean Hospital, had no doubt that all recent cases could be remedied. "This is the general rule," he insisted in 1840; "the occasional instance to the contrary is the exception." Performance ostensibly kept pace with theoretical statements. John Galt reported from Virginia in 1842 that, excluding patients who died during treatment, he had achieved one hundred percent recoveries. The following year, Dr. William Awl of the Ohio asylum simply announced without qualification one hundred percent cures.[5]

These statistics were inaccurate and unreliable. Not only was there no attempt to devise criteria for measuring recovery other than release from an institution, but in some instances a single patient, several times admitted,

4. For asylums' dates of origin, see John M. Grimes, *Institutional Care of Mental Patients in the United States* (Chicago, 1934), 123–125. Brief histories of the nineteenth-century asylums can be found in Henry M. Hurd, *The Institutional Care of the Insane in the United States and Canada* (Baltimore, 1916, 4 vols.). A useful survey also is Albert Deutsch, *The Mentally Ill in America: A History of their Care and Treatment* (New York, 1937).

5. A convenient summary of the optimistic statements is in Pliny Earle, *The Curability of Insanity* (Philadelphia, 1887). The quotations are from pp. 23, 27–29; see too, 38–39, 209, table VI. Earle helped to puncture the myth, but he too had once been guilty of perpetuating it: *Visit to Thirteen Asylums*, 130–131. Almost every memorial of Dorothea Dix repeated these declarations.

discharged, and readmitted, entered the lists as five times cured. At Pennsylvania's Friends' asylum, for example, 87 persons contributed 274 recoveries. It was not until 1877 that the first major attack on these exaggerated claims appeared, and only at a time when the widespread faith in curability had already begun to evaporate.

Before the Civil War, these extraordinary pronouncements were widely accepted at face value, and no skeptical voices tried to puncture the balloon of inflated hopes. Psychiatrists, confident of having located the origins of the disease, were fully prepared to believe and to testify that the incredible number of cures was the just fruit of scientific investigation. Personal ambition as well as intellectual perspective made them eager to publicize these findings. The estimates were self-perpetuating; as soon as one colleague announced his grand results, others had little choice but to match or excel him. With supervisory committees of state legislatures and boards of trustees using the number of recoveries as a convenient index for deciding appointments and promotions, medical superintendents were under great competitive pressure to report very high rates. And professionals and laymen alike desperately wanted to credit calculations that would glorify American science and republican humanitarianism. A cure for insanity was the kind of discovery that would honor the new nation.[6]

The consistency of the claims quickly established their validity. With an almost complete absence of dissenting opinion, the belief in the curative powers of the asylum spread through many layers of American society. Given the hyperbolic declarations of the professionals, laymen had little need to exaggerate their own statements. The most energetic and famous figure in the movement, Dorothea Dix, took the message from Massachusetts to Mississippi. With passion and skill she reported in painful detail on the wretched condition of the insane in poorhouses and jails—"Weigh the iron chains and shackles, breathe the foul atmosphere, examine the furniture, a truss of straw, a rough plank''—and next recited the promise of the asylum. Her formula was simple and she repeated it everywhere: first assert the curability of insanity, link it directly to proper institutional care, and then quote prevailing medical opinion on rates of recoveries. Legislators learned that Dr. Bell believed that cure in an asylum was the general rule, incurability the exception, and that Drs. Ray, Chandler,

Brigham, Kirkbride, Awl, Woodward, and Earle held similar views.[7] Legislative investigatory committees also returned with identical findings. Both Massachusetts and Connecticut representatives heard from colleagues that insanity yielded as readily as ordinary ailments to proper treatment. The most tax-conscious assemblyman found it difficult to stand up against this overwhelming chorus. One after another, the states approved the necessary funds for erecting asylums.[8]

The institution itself held the secret to the cure of insanity. Incarceration in a specially designed setting, not the medicines that might be administered or the surgery that might be performed there, would restore health. This strategy for treatment flowed logically and directly from the diagnosis of the causes of the disease. Medical superintendents located its roots in the exceptionally open and fluid quality of American society. The American environment had become so particularly treacherous that insanity struck its citizens with terrifying regularity.

One had only to take this dismal analysis one step further to find an antidote. Create a different kind of environment, which methodically corrected the deficiencies of the community, and a cure for insanity was at hand. This, in essence, was the foundation of the asylum solution and the program that came to be known as moral treatment. The institution would arrange and administer a disciplined routine that would curb uncontrolled impulses without cruelty or unnecessary punishment. It would re-create fixity and stability to compensate for the irregularities of the society. Thus, it would rehabilitate the casualties of the system.[9] The hospital walls would enclose a new world for the insane, designed in the reverse image of the one they had left. The asylum would also exemplify for the public the correct

6. Pliny Earle, *Curability of Insanity,* was the most important statement; see especially pp. 9, 41–42. Some officials did admit to their techniques: Pennsylvania Hospital, *Fifth Annual Report* (Philadelphia, 1846), 25. For the defensiveness of most superintendents, see Worcester Lunatic Hospital, *First Annual Report* (Boston, 1833), 3, 22–23.

7. Dorothea Dix, *Memorial to the Legislature of Pennsylvania,* 3; quotation is condensed from the original. For other examples of her appeal, see *Memorial Soliciting an Appropriation for the State Hospital for the Insane at Lexington* [Kentucky], (Frankfort, Ky., 1846), 10–11; *Memorial Praying a Grant of Land,* 25–27; *Memorial Soliciting a State Hospital for the Insane submitted to the Legislature of New Jersey* (Trenton, N.J., 1845), 36–37.

8. *Report of Commissioners to Superintend the Erection of a Lunatic Hospital at Worcester* (Boston, 1832), 19–30; *Report of the Committee on the Insane Poor in Connecticut* (New Haven, Conn., 1838), 3–4. See too Philadelphia Citizens Committee on an Asylum for the Insane Poor, *An Appeal to the People of Pennsylvania* (Philadelphia, 1838), 9; Pliny Earle, *Insanity and Insane Asylums* (Louisville, 1841), 34–39; "Investigation of the Bloomingdale Asylum," N.Y. Assembly Docs., 1831, I, no. 263, pp. 30–31.

9. For an introduction to the literature on moral treatment, see Norman Dain, *Concepts of Insanity,* chs. 1, 5; see, also, J. Sanbourne Bockoven, "Moral Treatment in American Psychiatry," *Journal of Nervous and Mental Disease,* 124 (1956), 183–194, 299–309.

principles of organization. The new world of the insane would correct within its restricted domain the faults of the community and through the power of example spark a general reform movement.[10]

The broad program had an obvious similarity to the goals of the penitentiary, and both ventures resembled in spirit and outlook the communitarian movements of the period, such as Brook Farm and New Harmony. There was a utopian flavor to correctional institutions. Medical superintendents and penitentiary designers were almost as eager as Owenites to evolve and validate general principles of social organization from their particular experiments.

The central problem for these first psychiatrists was to translate the concept of a curative environment into reality. Rehabilitation demanded a special milieu, and they devoted almost all of their energy to its creation. The appropriate arrangement of the asylum, its physical dimensions and daily routine, monopolized their thinking. The term for psychiatrist in this period, medical superintendent, was especially apt. Every detail of institutional design was a proper and vital subject for his consideration. His skills were to be those of the architect and the administrator, not the laboratory technician.

The first postulate of the asylum program was the prompt removal of the insane from the community. As soon as the first symptom of the disease appeared, the patient had to enter a mental hospital. Medical superintendents unanimously and without qualification asserted that treatment within the family was doomed to fail. They recognized the unusual nature of their doctrine and its apparent illogic. Since families had traditionally lodged the insane, it might seem a cruel and wanton abdication of responsibility to send a sick member to a public institution filled with other deranged persons. But they carefully explained this fundamental part of their program. Isaac Ray, chief of Rhode Island's asylum, conceded that "to sever a man's domestic ties, to take him out of the circle of friends and relatives most deeply interested in his welfare . . . and place him . . . in the hands of strangers, and in the company of persons as disordered as himself—at first sight, would seem . . . little likely to exert a restorative effect." Yet he and his colleagues insisted that isolation among strangers was a prerequisite for success. Although the strategy might increase the momentary pain of the disease, it promised an ultimate cure. "While at large," Ray declared, "the patient is every moment exposed to circumstances that maintain the morbid activity of his mind . . . [and] the dearer the friend, the greater the emotion. . . . In the

hospital, on the other hand, he is beyond the reach of all these causes of excitement.''[11] How else, asked Edward Jarvis, could the insane escape "the cares and anxieties of business . . . the affairs of the town . . . the movements of religious, political and other associations. . . . Hospitals are the proper places for the insane. . . . The cure and care of the insane belong to proper public institutions."[12]

Second, the institution itself, like the patients, was to be separate from the community. According to medical superintendents' design, it was to be built at a distance from centers of population. Since it was dependent upon the city for personnel and supplies, it could not completely escape contact. But the institution was to have a country location with ample grounds, to sit on a low hillside with an unobstructed view of a surrounding landscape. The scene ought to be tranquil, natural, and rural, not tumultuous and urban. Moreover, the asylum was to enforce isolation by banning casual visitors and the patients' families. If friends and relatives "were allowed the privilege they seek,'' cautioned Ray, "the patient might as well be at large as in the hospital, for any good the latter may do him by way of seclusion." Correspondence was also to be strictly limited. Even the mails were not to intrude and disrupt the self-contained and insular life.[13]

But the most important element in the new program, the core of moral treatment, lay in the daily government of the mentally ill. Here was the institution's most difficult and critical task. It had to control the patient without irritating him, to impose order but in a humane fashion. It had to bring discipline to bear but not harshly, to introduce regularity into chaotic lives without exciting frenetic reactions. "Quiet, silence, regular routine,'' declared Ray, "would take the place of restlessness, noise and fitful activity." Superintendents had to walk a tightrope, making sure that they did not fall to the one side of brutality or the other of indulgence. "So long as the patient is allowed to follow the bent of his own will," insisted Ray, he exacerbated his illness; outside the asylum, the "only alternative was, either an unlimited indulgence of the patient in his caprices, or a degree

10. *Report of the Insane Poor in Connecticut,* 4−5.

11. Isaac Ray, *Mental Hygiene,* 316; Butler Hospital, *Annual Report for 1856* (Providence, R.I., 1857), 19.

12. Edward Jarvis, *Address at Northampton,* 21−23, 25; Pennsylvania Hospital, *Second Annual Report,* 22−23; Philadelphia Citizens Committee, *An Appeal to the People,* 10−11; Ohio Lunatic Asylum, *Thirteenth Annual Report,* 17, 21; B.P.D.S., *Thirteenth Annual Report* (Boston, 1838), 200; and *Fifteenth Annual Report* (Boston, 1840), 420−421.

13. Thomas Kirkbride, *On the Construction of Hospitals for the Insane,* 36−38; *History of the Association of Medical Superintendents,* 24. Isaac Ray, *Mental Hygiene,* 24; Butler Hospital, *Annual Report for 1856,* 24.

of coercion and confinement which irritated his spirit and injured his health.'' The charge of the asylum was to bring discipline to the victims of a disorganized society. To this end it had to isolate itself and its members from chaotic conditions. Behind the asylum walls medical superintendents would create and administer a calm, steady, and rehabilitative routine. It would be, in a phrase that they and their lay supporters repeated endlessly, ''a well-ordered institution.''[14]

The asylum's designers often labored under severe financial limitations, when legislatures and private philanthropists were not generous with appropriations. Sometimes public officials interfered with their policies, setting down admission requirements that limited administrators' prerogatives. In Massachusetts, for example, the state hospital had to admit the most troublesome and least curable cases first; legislators were more impressed with the convenience than the effectiveness of the institution. And many superintendents were discontented with one facet or another of the asylum's architecture or procedures. Nevertheless, there was usually a close correspondence between founders' ideals and the asylum reality.

The Enduring Institution

The insane asylums suffered the most dramatic decline from a reform to a custodial operation. By 1870 both the reality of institutional care and the rhetoric of psychiatrists made clear that the optimism of reformers had been unfounded, that the expectation of eradicating insanity from the new world had been illusory. The hospitals' daily procedures, as reported by medical superintendents and state investigators, revealed how inadequate treatment was; at the same time, professionals and laymen began to suggest that the disease was not as susceptible to remedy as they had once believed. Nevertheless, the insane asylum, like the penitentiary, remained central to public policy. The number of patients swelled and the size of the buildings increased. Once again an institution survived long after its original promise had dissolved.

The custodial qualities of the post-1850 asylums are easily described. The first and most common element was overcrowding and in its train came the breakdown of classification systems, the demise of work therapy, and an increase in the use of mechanical restraints and harsh

punishments to maintain order. Structures designed in the 1830's to serve two hundred patients often held twice that number in the 1850's. Visitors to state and municipal institutions told of seeing beds strewn about the hallways, because the space in the dormitories had long since been exhausted. Simple arithmetic indicated the degree of overcrowding. The Worcester state hospital, for example, had a total of 285 rooms for sleeping, feeding and employing about 250 inmates. Between 1845 and 1860 as many as 532 and never less than 301 patients filled them. Conditions were little better elsewhere. In 1871, the New Jersey asylum at Trenton squeezed 700 inmates into buildings intended to hold 500.[15]

Not surprisingly, a general disorganization of routine accompanied this change. Superintendents made little effort to keep inmates busy. When asylum officials gathered in 1862 to hear Edward Jarvis report on employment for the insane in England, almost all of them confessed an inability to put their charges to steady work. The results, in terms of the appearance and tone of the institutions, pleased no one. ''One cause of sadness felt in visiting our hospitals,'' declared a Massachusetts investigatory board in 1867, ''is the sight of so many persons of each sex, in the prime or middle of life, sitting or lying about, moping idly and listlessly in the debilitating atmosphere of the wards, and sinking gradually into a torpor, like that of living corpses.''[16] Under these conditions classification disappeared. Some institutions herded the most violent into special rooms, but without great discrimination or thoroughness. The raving and furiously insane usually mixed freely with the more peaceable and well-behaved patients.[17]

14. Butler Hospital, *Annual Report for 1850* (Providence, R.I., 1851), 23; *Annual Report for 1856*, 19; and *Annual Report for 1855*, 13–14, 18. See also Edward Jarvis, *Visit to Thirteen Asylums*, 136, and his *Address at Northampton*, 26; Philadelphia Citizens Committee, *An Appeal to the People*, 10–11; Connecticut Retreat, *Thirty-Ninth Annual Report*, 27.

15. Worcester Lunatic Hospital, *Twenty-Second Annual Report* (Boston, 1855), 8–9; *Twenty-Seventh Annual Report* (Boston, 1859), 31; James Leiby, *Charity and Correction in New Jersey*, 57–59; see, too, J. Sanbourne Bockoven, ''Moral Treatment in American Psychiatry,'' 177. By 1872, the situation was so prevalent that the Association of Medical Superintendents noted: ''The custom of admitting a greater number of patients than the buildings can properly accommodate . . . is now becoming . . . common in hospitals for the insane in nearly every section of the country.'' *History of the Association of Medical Superintendents*, 88.

16. ''Annual Meeting of the Association of Medical Superintendents,'' *American Journal of Insanity*, 19 (1862–63), 57–70. Massachusetts Board of State Charities, *Fourth Annual Report*, 1867, xl, quoted in Gerald Grob, *The State and the Mentally Ill*, 193. Professor Grob, who is writing a multivolume history of mental hospitals in the United States, kindly lent me an article summarizing some of his views, ''Mental Illness, Indigency and Welfare: The Mental Hospital in Nineteenth-Century America.'' He quotes there, p. 18, John Bucknell, *Notes on Asylums for the Insane in America* (London, 1876), with similar observations. See too Ruth Caplan, *Psychiatry and the Community in Nineteenth-Century America*, 162–163.

17. New Hampshire Asylum, *Report of 1854* (Concord, N.H., 1854), 15; J. Sanbourne Bockoven, ''Moral Treatment,'' 177–183, traces out the implications of overcrowding in detail. See too William A. Ham-

Discipline was harsh and mechanical. Superintendents frequently kept unruly patients in line by using strait-jackets, cuffs, sleeves, bed straps, and cribs. When why they did not ban such devices, as their English counterparts did, they insisted that American patients were more excitable and tougher to control, or that the British relied upon the brute force of attendants. More embarrassing were the findings of the periodic state investigations. One committee found no "gross abuses" at the New York Bloomingdale Asylum. But it had no doubt that "some instances of the improper treatment of patients by attendants have been fairly proven," and was convinced that a general laxity was to blame.[18] Many asylums of the Civil War era illustrated all too clearly the chief characteristics of a custodial operation: patients listlessly dawdled about, with every bizarre or pathetic symptom of the disease to be found in one room, while officials stood ready to adopt the most convenient tactics to keep the peace.

Medical opinion on the benefits of asylum care at this time also began to shift to a more hostile position. Superintendents admitted that earlier claims for curability were exaggerated, while a growing number of physicians insisted that the drawbacks of institutionalization far outweighed its advantages. One of the most noted retreats from an earlier optimism appeared in the writings of Pliny Earle. In the 1870's, in a widely read article, "The Curability of Insanity," he methodically demonstrated how exaggerated were the asylums' first claims to success, revealing his own disenchantment with older formulas and shocking a good many readers into agreement. Through a careful attention to the mechanics of record-keeping, Earle disclosed that the antebellum figures on the number of cures were grossly exaggerated. The annual reports had estimated percentages of recoveries not on the basis of patients admitted but on those discharged; they had counted the same patient as cured many times over, with each release after a relapse put down as another recovery. Just when Americans were learning about watered stock, they received a lesson in watered statistics.[19]

The founders of the asylum had fully expected to bring order and stability not only into the lives of the patients but, through the power of exemplification, into society as well. Retaining eighteenth-century conceptualizations of social organization, they expected to re-create, both in and out of the asylum, a well-ordered, balanced, harmonious, and ultimately homogeneous community. By the Civil War, however, these expectations appeared unrealistic and irrelevant. There seemed to be unbridgeable gaps between lower and upper classes, between Catholics and Protestants, between newcomers and natives that would not permit the reestablishment of traditional social arrangements. Reformers in the 1830's had recognized the shift away from eighteenth-century conditions; but still hoping to reverse the trend, they set about inventing new forms to restore old patterns. The passage of time, accelerating the changes that they had tried to contain, made their goals and tactics seem fanciful. This awareness in the 1850's dampened the remaining enthusiasm for the precepts of moral treatment.

But rather than lead to the dissolution of the asylum, these circumstances heightened the attractions of a custodial operation. From the perspective of the community's officials, the pauper and the immigrant insane, especially the troublesome and dangerous ones, were a convenient and practicable group to incarcerate. The program had acquired a legitimacy in the Jacksonian period which did not quickly erode. The reform ideology not only sanctioned but encouraged isolation, so that later administrators could enforce it with good conscience. And to the degree that overseers and judges used the asylum instead of a poorhouse or a jail for the insane, they could better adopt a humanitarian pose. Few countervailing influences worked to keep the pauper and the immigrant within the community. Reformers in the 1830's had already minimized the prospect of such organizations as the family or the church contributing to the deviant's welfare, and hardly anyone in the 1850's regarded immigrant associations as worth perpetuating.

Americans after 1850 were, therefore, free to follow what they considered an opportune and practical course. Convinced that the insane (especially the manic, but almost any among them) might at a moment commit some atrocious act or, less dramatically but no less seriously, spread their madness like a contagious disease, they found institutionalization a useful method for nullifying a fundamental threat. At the least, the asylum would shield society from disorder and contamination. Medical superintendents confirmed this view by devoting unprecedented attention to the dangers that the insane posed for the general public. Isaac Ray, in his widely read volume, *Mental Hygiene,* published in

mond, *A Treatise on Insanity in Its Medical Relations* (New York, 1883), 726–727; and the remarks of Edward Mann, *Second N.C.C.C.* (Boston, 1875), 62.

18. E. C. Seguin, *Lunacy Reform: Historical Considerations* (New York, 1879), Part I, 4 ff.; Franklin B. Sanborn, "Presidential Address," *Sixth N.C.C.C.* (Boston, 1879), 12–13. See too William Hammond, "A Treatise on Insanity," 725–726; Worcester Lunatic Hospital, *Twenty-Second Annual Report,* 25. On the Bloomingdale investigation, *American Journal of Insanity,* 29 (1872–73), 594–595.

19. Pliny Earle, *Curability of Insanity,* 8–9. The article of 1876 became a book in 1887. Recently, J. Sanbourne Bockoven has disputed Earle's figures for the Worcester asylum, showing that he in fact underestimated the percentage of cures: "Moral Treatment in American

1863, warned readers that "intimate associations with persons affected with nervous infirmities . . . should be avoided by all who are endowed with a peculiarly susceptible nervous organization, whether strongly predisposed to nervous diseases, or only vividly impressed by the sight of suffering and agitation." One of the great tragedies of insanity, declared Ray, was "that the poor sufferer cannot receive the ministry of near relatives, without endangering the mental integrity of those who offer them." The conclusion was inescapable: confinement of the insane was critical "not more for their own welfare than the safety of those immediately surrounding them." In a similar spirit, superintendents like Thomas Kirkbride warned that any lunatic, no matter how mild-mannered, might suddenly strike out at those around him; and such colleagues as John Gray and John

Butler recounted one horror story after another to substantiate this assertion.[20]

From this perspective, it seemed just as well that an asylum serving as a dumping ground for social undesirables should have as its common denominator a lower-class and immigrant population. These groups, many observers believed, produced many of the dangerous lunatics and the lower the social standing of the inmates, the easier for other ranks to incarcerate their most troublesome cases there. Granted, this arrangement was not without drawbacks. By giving the asylum over to the least desirable elements, the middle and upper classes restricted their own ability to utilize it. They might well hesitate to incarcerate the peaceable but still bothersome relative in such a setting. But in the end they made their choice. The returns of a custodial operation seemed worth the price.

Psychiatry," 292–298. Still, the figures that Bockoven presents are considerably lower than the claims of the 1830's and 1840's; and he makes no attempt to question just what "recovery" meant in the original records.

20. Isaac Ray, *Mental Hygiene*, 174; and his "Statistics on Insanity in Massachusetts," 92–94. See too, *History of the Association of Medical Superintendents*, 19; and Ruth Caplan, *Psychiatry and the Community in Nineteenth-Century America*, 149–151.

ROBERT PERRUCCI

The Mental Hospital As a People-Processing Organization

Whether it is referred to as the "crazyhouse," the "state hospital," or by some idyllic-sounding euphemism such as "Longview" or "Briarcliff," the mental hospital is that social organization in which society places persons who are defined as being mentally ill. Official reports which describe the philosophy and goals of mental hospitals abound with statements which emphasize the treatment and rehabilitation of patients. Milieu therapy, reality therapy, attitude therapy, and behavior modification are identified as some of the treatment techniques which are being applied to disordered minds. Also stressed is a close working relationship between the hospital, the community, and the family which is designed to facilitate planning for a speedy discharge from the time a patient is admitted to a

Reprinted from Robert Perrucci, *Circle of Madness*, Englewood Cliffs, N.J.: Prentice-Hall, Inc., 1974, pages 21–36, by permission of the author and publisher.

hospital. Such a consideration is reflected in the use of such organizational concepts as community liaisons, community reentry, family intervention, and community linkage. A final feature of official statements about philosophy and goals is the inevitable description of a new spirit of cooperation that has existed among hospital staff since the latest reorganization or since the introduction of some new administrative innovation. In this connection one is confronted with the ideas of team treatment, role blending, sensitivity groups, and management leadership.

Statements which describe the official goals of a mental hospital, or any organization for that matter, must be approached with caution, at least if one hopes to learn something about what actually goes on within that organization. Yet, despite the fact that one must be skeptical about official goals, it is very important to note the three features of a mental hospital that are being discussed in most statements about goals. First, there is the nature of the relationship that exists between the community and the hospital, and the steps that are being taken to ensure community cooperation and support. Second, there is the internal structure of the hospital in terms of the distribution of authority and responsibility. The third feature is the particular treatment technology that is being used to change patients, and hopefully, to effect their early release from the hospital.

Community-hospital relations, the internal structure of authority, and treatment technology are three central features of mental hospitals which one can use to facilitate understanding of the day-to-day life of patients and staff. These elements are in a continual state of change, reflecting shifting definitions of mental illness, the changing power of hospitals vis-à-vis the larger society, and the availability of new ideas about hospital organization and procedures. Thus, the mental hospital in its present form is an historically evolving social organization which is constantly attempting both to adapt and to control its internal and external environment. It reflects, moreover, imperfect evolution because the hospital contains elements which change at different paces, thereby producing an organization composed of "survivals" (i.e., things better suited to an earlier environment) and characterized by poor internal integration.

Here, we examine some of the organizational problems that are peculiar to the mental hospital as a special type of organization that houses persons who have been rejected by society and that tries to return those persons to society. In addition, we consider some of the characteristics that mental hospitals share with other kinds of organizations. The general focus is the influence of the external environment (i.e., society) and treatment technology upon the internal structure and processes of life inside the hospital.

Organization and Environment: The Question of Power and Autonomy

Every organization exists in a social and cultural environment that is more or less supportive of and conducive to the organization's existence. Social values, legal institutions, and the nature of the class structure create favorable or unfavorable climates for an organization, encourage or discourage people from working for or on behalf of the organization, and set limits upon the freedom with which the organization can pursue its goals.

Every organization, moreover, tries to exercise influence and control over its external environment in order to make easier the pursuit of its goals. In the most general sense, the organization-environment relationship concerns the nature of and control over the *inputs* an organization needs to carry on its work—money, raw materials, workers, physical facilities—and *outputs* of the organization. A favorable reception for an organization's output, whether it be consumer goods or "cured" ex-patients, provides an organization with a more favorable position for obtaining inputs for its continued existence.

The particular balance of power that exists between an organization and its environment is never really fixed, but is continually shifting in a manner that reflects an organization's relative success in adapting to its environment. As environment changes, so must an organization, or face the possibility of extinction. Take, for example, the Woman's Christian Temperance Union, an organization that "produced" a middle-class moral code.[1] The WCTU flourished as long as there was a natural market for its "output" or as long as it had the power to create such a market. When societal values changed, the WCTU lacked a marketable product and, hence, could not obtain sufficient resources (e.g., money, new members, support from other organizations) to stay in existence. In addition, the demise of the WCTU represents a case in which overadaptation of an organization produces success in one period but total failure in another.

Looking at the mental hospital in historical perspective, one can see periods of relative autonomy and power of the hospital in relation to the larger society with respect to both inputs and outputs of the hospital. From the work of both Foucault[2] and Rothman,[3] . . . it is apparent that mental hospitals exercised considerable control over all their activities during the period in which they first emerged. In the United States in the early nineteenth century, medical superintendents (i.e., psychiatrists) apparently had sufficient influence with state legislatures to establish extensive autonomy over the design, cost, location, and internal structure of the new asylums. They also determined who entered hospitals as patients, who was allowed to visit patients, and who should be viewed as "cured." The superintendents were quite successful, apparently, in avoiding the involvement of civil authorities in the commitment process, and in convincing patients' families that the hospital alone

1. Joseph Gusfield, "Social Structure and Moral Reform: A Study of the Woman's Christian Temperance Union," *American Journal of Sociology*, 61 (November 1955), 221–32.

2. Michel Foucault, *Madness and Civilization* (New York: Vintage Books, 1973).

3. David J. Rothman, *The Discovery of the Asylum* (Boston: Little, Brown and Co., 1971).

should determine when patients should be released.[4]

Thus, in the early stage of the establishment of mental hospitals the professional staff exercised considerable power and autonomy in relation to the larger society. This period of power and autonomy, however, started to reverse itself in the latter half of the nineteenth century. The mental hospital and the medical superintendents were faced with two problems. The first came from state legislatures which, being much concerned about rising costs for the construction and maintenance of asylums, started to reduce appropriations. The second problem was criticism about the alleged success of the new institutions in "curing" the insane which came from medical professional groups outside the asylum (e.g., neurologists, research psychiatrists, psychiatrists in private practice).

Whatever were the causes of the decline in power and autonomy of the medical superintendents, it was manifested as a loss of control in the determination of who should enter the hospital. In many states, regulations on admissions were established whereby local officials and nonhospital professions were permitted to make such determinations. Superintendents were also denied the authority to determine the type of patients that would be admitted. Whereas in the past they were inclined to admit mainly those patients who had high potential for recovery, now they were forced to take indigent, chronic cases.

The loss of control over its "input" by the mental hospital, which began over a hundred years ago, continues to find expression in current hospital-society relationships. Across the fifty states, there can be found many different ways in which people become patients. There are emergency commitments made on the evaluation of a single physician; commitments made on the evaluation of two physicians; temporary or long-term commitments made by a judge; commitments made by a formally established county commission; and commitments made with and without court-appointed lawyers. These involuntary commitments have in common the fact that the decision is made by persons and bodies outside the hospital. Even the remaining major form of becoming a mental patient, "voluntary admission," leaves the hospital with little control insofar as they cannot hold the patient against his will without obtaining from an external body a regular, involuntary commitment.

Although there was a gradual erosion of hospital psychiatrists' control over who gets into a mental hospital, they continued to have considerable autonomy over the internal life of the hospital. Let us now turn to the matter of the social structure of the mental hospital itself.

4. Ibid., p. 143.

Hospital Structure

A visitor's first experience in a mental hospital leaves him with the impression of a well-organized bureaucratic structure. The superintendent sits at the apex of a structure that divides into clinical (i.e., medical) and business hierarchies. The medical side is further subdivided into functionally organized services and wards, each reflecting some aspect of a patient's career stage or particular medical needs. The positions within this general structure follow an almost classical caste-type structure. Caste lines are marked clearly and the symbols, speech patterns, and activities which serve to locate people within the structure are noticed quickly. Combined with clear lines of demarcation between positions in the hierarchy is the fact that there is little movement up or down the caste hierarchy; that is, there is no internal mobility.

Maintenance of the formal caste-like structure depends upon spatial separation, occupational separation, prescribed and proscribed activities for each stratum, rituals of avoidance, and shared symbolic representations of rank and status. Max Weber recognized these prerequisites for a caste system when he wrote that "complete 'fraternization' of castes has been and is impossible because it is one of the constitutive principles of the castes that there should be at least ritually irremediable barriers against complete commensalism among different castes."[5]

Herein lies one of the features of the hospital structure which is difficult to reconcile with stated therapeutic objectives. Although a rigid hospital structure is maintained through the above-stated mechanisms, treatment objectives are built upon premises of "fraternization" between hierarchical levels. The "team approach" in psychiatric treatment, for example, encourages interstatus contacts, open exchange of ideas and criticism, and free and unrestrained analysis of the behavior and motives of team members as they relate to patient care. Similarly, patients are usually thought to be well enough to leave the hospital when, in a sense, they "speak the language" of the superordinate groups. They adopt, so to speak, the staff values and norms which are transmitted through interpersonal relations. Yet this seeming contradiction in structure and goals is, in reality, a paradox only if one assumes that treatment and release of patients are serious goals of the hospital.

A second feature which has profound implications for the internal structure of the mental hospital is the fact that those who care for the mentally ill share some of the stigma that society places on patients. Early in this study

5. Hans Gerth and C. Wright Mills, *Essays from Max Weber* (New York: Oxford University Press, 1958), p. 402.

the investigator had occasion to talk with people in the community nearest to a hospital about their awareness of the hospital's existence, its medical and economic role in the area, and its general influence on the attitudes of local residents. Oddly enough, rather than telling of fears of having "crazy people" so close, or expressing anticipated stereotyped views of the mentally ill, they offered views of the hospital staff which reflected a stigma that is reserved ordinarily for patients. Doctors were suspected of being "nuttier than the patients," or of being of questionable character or psychological health. For other staff, such as nurses and attendants, allegations were made that they were ex-patients themselves or had members of their family in the hospital at one time or another.

The stigma attached by the community to staff personnel exists in the hospital itself. Hospital folklore and "in" jokes reveal numerous variations on the general theme that one often is not able to distinguish patients from staff. Much more important, however, is the fact that there is a clear indication of "marginality" among the medical staff especially. There are concrete examples of personal, career, and social marginality which help to fuel the stigma that is applied to the hospital staff. There is talk about problem drinkers, or career skidders who couldn't keep a private practice. In addition, there are the hospital doctors who have come from abroad to obtain psychiatric residencies in the United States. All of this adds to the view that many of the medical staff are doctors who are marginal within their own profession and this serves to reinforce, if not to cause, the stereotypes held both by members of the community and by the hospital.

If it is true that the "keepers" share a stigma with their "charges" we know something about the source of some of the problems concerning the structure of authority in the hospital and its ability to function either bureaucratically or therapeutically. In addition, we know something about the role of the mental hospital in our society, another point to which we shall return very shortly.

A third aspect of the mental hospital of import for its internal structure is the fact that its "raw materials" are humans, who must actively participate in their own transformation and in the general support activities of the hospital.[6] If one considers the patient as a client of an organization in the most general sense, one has the relatively rare situation wherein the client is a full-time member of the organization. On occasion a particular client functions outside the client role (i.e., a patient) and becomes a member of the occupational structure of the organization, carrying out essential activities regarding laundry, food, clothing, maintenance, and housekeeping.

The situation wherein a client is a full-time member of an organization can result in a variety of control and authority problems; that is, problems which result from a patient's access to knowledge of hospital affairs to which staff members only are supposed to be privy. In addition, as a full-time working member of the hospital organization, the client plays a dual role which has considerable built-in personal as well as organizational tension. It is difficult to be a subordinate, passive person who is assumed to be experiencing problems of living, impaired reason, and irresponsibility while holding a full-time "job" in the hospital kitchen or laundry that a "normal" person would have to be hired to do otherwise.

To be a mental patient also requires one to participate actively in one's own transformation from "sick" raw material to "well" finished product. The degree of participation that is required is more than simple cooperation with the people and processes applied in order to produce a change, as would be the case for a patient in a general hospital. The mental patient must be active to the extent of negotiating with people in the environment and creating a new definition of reality for and about himself. A patient in such a situation will find incompatible demands between the needs of an orderly, bureaucratic, castelike structure and an active, potent behavior of a "normal" person.

Technology and Treatment Goals

Organizational theory provides a general hypothesis to explain why mental hospitals have little power in their relations with society, and why hospital structure, staff, and goals seem to be so unsuccessful in the treatment of mental illness. The general view is that the nature of the technology an organization uses to transform raw material has a substantial influence on the internal structure of that organization.[7] Perrow has applied this point of view most convincingly to an examination of existing technology, structure, and goals of the mental hospital.[8]

6. For a general theoretical treatment of alternative orientations of organization members or clients, see Amitai Etzioni, *A Comparative Analysis of Complex Organizations* (New York: The Free Press of Glencoe, Inc., 1961), Chapters 1–3.

7. James D. Thompson and Fred L. Bates, "Technology, Organization, and Administration," *Administrative Science Quarterly*, 2 (1957), 325–43.

8. Charles Perrow, "Hospitals: Technology, Structure, and Goals," in James G. March, ed., *Handbook of Organizations* (Chicago: Rand McNally & Co., 1965), pp. 910–71.

Perrow's basic position is that the structure and goals of a mental hospital cannot be changed successfully without a change in technology. He maintains, furthermore, that hospitals do not have a treatment technology that is suited for the large number of patients they hold. "Milieu therapy," which is often described by hospital staff as a treatment technique, is, according to Perrow, not a new technology but a humanizing influence. His position is stated clearly in an analysis of mental hospitals' greater emphasis on custodial goals rather than treatment goals.

> Hospitals are said to have "displaced" the treatment goal in favor of custody. It is more appropriate to say that the goal of "treatment" is of symbolic value only, and the real, operative goal is custody and minimal care.[9]

An extension of the logic of the technology hypothesis to several of the features of the mental hospital which were discussed earlier leads to the following interpretations. First, the limited power and autonomy of the hospital to determine its "inputs" (i.e., patients) is a result of its inability to demonstrate to society that it can "cure" mental patients. Power and autonomy flow from ability to produce a marketable product, in this case a "cured" patient whom society is once again willing to accept. When and if the hospital has a technology that produces such a product, it will have more influence than it now commands. Second, the stigma attached to hospital medical staff and their marginal status within both the hospital and their profession are also results of their inability to demonstrate competence and expertise in their work.

There is much to be said for the technology hypothesis as a way of understanding the mental hospital. I believe it is especially powerful for furthering the understanding of the internal structure of the hospital in terms of authority and power relations. Yet one must be careful not to overstate the influence of technology or to assume that the utility of technology is inherent in it, and thereby cannot help being recognized as existing. Prevailing values, interests, and power will *interpret* new technology and help to shape claims regarding its worth. Thus, it is possible that hospital psychiatrists who have societal regard *because they are doing valued work* would also have the influence to shape a belief that "milieu therapy" is effective.

This brings us to our central criticism of the technology hypothesis and the basis for an alternative view of mental hospitals which will follow. When it is argued

9. Ibid., p. 926.

that an effective treatment technology is needed to produce changes in hospital structure and goals, the basic assumption is that patients in the hospital do have something called a mental illness and do require a specific treatment in order to get "better." In short, it is assumed that the medical model of mental illness . . . contains the best explanation of why people are committed to mental hospitals. If, however, hospital commitment takes place for the reasons described in the societal reaction model, the presence or absence of an effective treatment technology will have little connection with the treatment received by patients or their chances for getting out of a hospital. In other words, if one is in the hospital because one has been rejected by society, the purpose of the mental hospital is to make sure that one doesn't return to society. This view of the mental hospital is developed next.

Patients as Victims and the Hospital as a System of Justification

One cannot begin to understand the way a mental hospital is organized and the way it operates without an understanding of why people are placed in hospitals in the first place. We, therefore, take here as our point of departure the societal reaction model of mental illness, which views patients as victims of the social networks in which they are embedded. They are victims of families and communities who can no longer tolerate rule-breaking and problematic behavior. They are victims of poverty, powerlessness, and discrimination and the resulting individual-psychological explanations for their plight as people with a mental illness. They, moreover, are often willing victims insofar as they accept and adopt the roles of madness in order to "solve" the problems of living which they are experiencing. In short, they are not in the hospital because they are mad, but because they have been rejected by society and have no suitable place in it.

The view of patients as victims is a very painful idea to accept by the individuals and families who are involved in putting someone in a mental hospital, and by the society that allows commitment to take place. In fact, the idea is so painful that individual and collective defense mechanisms develop to protect against the idea. An individual defense mechanism is the belief that mental illness is a disease, which makes it less difficult to put a family member in a mental hospital. A collective defense mechanism is the existence of a mental hospital as a social organization, which reinforces the belief in mental illness and espouses the noble goal of treatment and return of people to society, but which, in fact, functions in large part as a dumping ground for societal rejects.

The Establishment of Mental Hospitals

The question of when and why mental hospitals were established in the United States was discussed earlier. It will be remembered that Rothman[10] put forward the hypothesis that the conditions conducive to the establishment of mental hospitals could be traced to a cluster of *ideas* about how the disorganization of traditional institutions was the cause of mental illness, and how the order, regularity, and discipline of the asylum could provide a cure for mental disorders.

There is no doubt about the existence of such ideas during the time that the mental hospital was becoming an established institution. What can be disputed, however, is whether or not such ideas were causal conditions for the creation of mental hospitals rather than a set of ideological justifications for a social organization that was brought into being for quite different reasons. What, then, would be the causal factors? Let us consider the following alternate hypotheses which would be consistent with our view of patients as victims and rejects.

The period during which mental hospitals became established institutions, 1830 to 1860, was characterized by certain social conditions that could have created a segment of the population who were without social moorings and were especially vulnerable to being victimized. By 1850, a pattern of urban settlement began to be established, especially in the Northeastern states.[11] In addition, at about the same time almost one-half of the labor force was employed outside agriculture, a condition that coincided with a rural to urban area population shift and created a population of "new" people in unfamiliar surroundings who lacked supportive social ties. In fact, in 1850, 24 percent of the native-born population were residents of a state other than the one in which they were born, the highest such percentage over a 100-year period.[12]

Perhaps most significant, however, is the fact that the period of growth of asylums coincided with a period of substantial increases in immigration to the United States. The decade 1820 to 1830 brought 151,824 immigrants. From 1831 to 1840, the number increased to 599,125. For 1841 to 1850, the figure is 1,713,251, and for 1851 to 1860, the number increased to 2½ million.[13] In addition, there is some evidence that immigrants were

substantially overrepresented among patients in mental hospitals. Worcester State Hospital, for example, established in Massachusetts in 1833, had by 1851 over 40 percent foreign-born patients.[14]

Thus, it is suggested that the asylum may have emerged in America in order to deal with casualties of a changing social order in much the same way that the period of the "great confinement" in France, which marked the beginning of the institutionalization of the mentally ill there, was carried out to cope with the casualties of economic depression. In each case, it is the poor, the powerless, the socially vulnerable who are judged to be problems by families and communities, and whose problems are described as a form of illness which requires that they be expelled from normal social life.

Internal Structure: Authority of Physicians

If the societal reaction perspective has any validity as an explanation of why people enter mental hospitals, then it follows that those who are selected to care for the mentally ill are both personally oriented and professionally equipped to provide long-term care for custody rather than treatment for release. Thus, the gravitation of personally and professionally marginal physicians to positions of authority in mental hospitals serves an important dual function. First, the high social standing of the position of doctor serves to rationalize and justify otherwise painful decisions which are made by families who commit "loved ones." After all, they could say, "It's not as if we are sending him to a prison or a detention center; he is going to a medical facility where humane care and treatment are available."

Second, because the physicians are neither personally nor professionally equipped to provide treatment, and because the hospital's patient-physician ratio makes treatment impossible even if physicians were equipped to provide it, physicians serve as convenient targets for complaints of "incompetence" at such times when society's "conscience" is stirred about the plight of the mentally ill.

The combination of marginality and stigma makes the physician especially vulnerable to challenges to his authority. He faces the classic dilemma inherent in bureaucratic authority in which the holder of a position of authority does not or cannot validate positional authority with demonstrated expertise. Authority based upon position alone is unstable and will be eroded eventually in relations with subordinates.[15]

10. Rothman, *Discovery of the Asylum.*

11. Noel P. Gist and Sylvia F. Fava, *Urban Society* (New York: Thomas Y. Crowell Co., 1964), p. 50.

12. *Statistical Abstracts of the United States* (Washington, D.C.: U.S. Government Printing Office, 1952), p. 41.

13. *Statistical Abstracts of the United States,* 1961, p. 92.

14. Rothman, *Discovery of the Asylum,* p. 273.

15. Concerning this general problem in organizations, see William M. Evan and Morris Zelditch, Jr., "A Laboratory Experiment on Bureaucratic Authority," *American Sociological Review,* 26 (December 1961), pp. 883–93.

Treatment Technologies

Most large state mental hospitals have experienced similar patterns of experimentation and use of various treatment technologies. Early use of physical techniques including psychosurgery, insulin and electroshock, hydrotherapy, and drugs seems to follow a sequence of early optimism about the effectiveness of the procedure, followed by doubts and eventual cessation of use entirely. Some of the physical techniques continue to be used. During the year in which Riverview was studied by this writer, the total patient population was approximately 2,400 persons. A total of 751 patients received 4,851 treatments of electroconvulsive therapy, and 131 patients received 2,337 treatments of hydrotherapy for a total of 4,724 hours. During the same year, a total of 368 hours of individual and group psychotherapy took place, with a maximum of 45 hours in any single month. There is no record of the exact number of patients involved in such "talk therapies" but it is clear that the number is very small.

Psychopharmacological drugs are used extensively in the hospital and, like hydrotherapy, are viewed officially as parts of an overall therapeutic prescription for a patient rather than as total treatment techniques.

Following the use of physical technologies and "talk therapies," both of which were generally ineffective or impractical, came a large-scale effort to alter organizational arrangements in hospitals under the heading of "milieu therapy." Efforts to change the organizational structure concentrated upon increasing the communication between patients and staff in ways that would create consistent and reinforcing relationships among these groups. A part of milieu therapy involved the creation of "therapeutic teams" which shared total responsibility for all aspects of custody and treatment for a specific number of hospital patients. The "teams" emphasized open communication and shared authority among its members and more humane, equalitarian relations with patients.

The most recent organizational innovation that falls under the heading of milieu therapy is the transformation of the total hospital from a highly centralized, authoritarian structure to a decentralized structure with about eight to twelve treatment units which serve specific geographical areas (i.e., counties) in the state. Each unit has its own authority structure which is separate from the central administrator (i.e., superintendent) and which is based upon broadly representative committees rather than a single centralized authority. The "unit system" can be seen as an extension of therapeutic teams to the total hospital structure.

The "unit system" allows each team to develop its own programs and treatment strategies. The territorial basis for the unit encourages the development of more ties with and information about patients' families, community agencies, and community public services. All these efforts are aimed at the patient's planning discharge from the very time he is admitted.

As was pointed out earlier, Perrow's analysis of mental hospitals criticized such efforts of "milieu therapy" as being simply examples of humane treatment rather than an effective treatment technology. We feel, however, that to view the efforts of milieu therapy within the narrow framework of physical technologies which are designed to treat a disease that resides in the individual is to misunderstand their significance. The unit system, for example, has two main consequences. First, it represents an effort to wrest control from physicians within the hospital's authority structure and to give expanded power to social workers, psychologists, and those nursing-attendant staff who have a strong interest in community mental health. The community mental health perspective is less inclined to view help for a mental patient as a matter of applying an effective technology to a disease that resides in an individual, and more likely to view treatment as a matter of keeping a patient in the family and in the community by working with families and community agencies to provide support for the patient. In short, the struggle for control is seen as a struggle between those whose professional work is guided by the medical model and those whose work is guided by the societal reaction model.

The second consequence of the unit system is that it attempts to establish for the hospital the power to determine who becomes a patient through ties to community mental health facilities, and it maintains the receptivity of families to accept ex-patients through its effort to ensure that families continue to accept responsibility for any of their members who are in the hospital.

Thus, attempts at "milieu therapy" might be very effective if they are guided by an understanding of the societal reaction model, and if they do enable the hospital to exercise more control over who enters it and over families to accept former patients as family members once again. If nothing else, milieu therapy efforts such as the unit system may discourage families, community physicians, and local legal authorities from moving too quickly to label people as mentally ill and to seek their hospitalization.

What is suggested in this section, then, is that the mental hospital functions primarily as a system of justification for a commitment process which cannot openly be admitted to be what it is; namely, a victimization process. The official purposes and ideology of the hospital are consonant with the medical model of mental illness. People who have a disease called mental illness are sent to a medical facility for diagnosis, treatment, and rehabilitation. The actual goals and activities of the hospital, however, are consonant with the view that patients are victims who have been expelled from their homes and communities in much the same way that madmen were expelled from their villages in the Middle Ages. Given the way in which the hospital is funded, staffed, and organized, it cannot help preventing patient victims from returning to society unless someone wants them.

ERVING GOFFMAN

The Moral Career of the Mental Patient: Inpatient Phase

The last step in the prepatient's career can involve his realization—justified or not—that he has been deserted by society and turned out of relationships by those closest to him. Interestingly enough, the patient, especially a first admission, may manage to keep himself from coming to the end of this trail, even though in fact he is now in a locked mental-hospital ward. On entering the hospital, he may very strongly feel the desire not to be known to anyone as a person who could possibly be reduced to these present circumstances, or as a person who conducted himself in the way he did prior to commitment. Consequently, he may avoid talking to anyone, may stay by himself when possible, and may even be "out of contact" or "manic" so as to avoid ratifying any interaction that presses a politely reciprocal role upon him and opens him up to what he has become in the eyes of others. When the next-of-relation makes an effort to visit, he may be rejected by mutism, or by the patient's refusal to enter the visiting room, these strategies sometimes suggesting that the patient still clings to a remnant of relatedness to those who made up his past, and is protecting this remnant from the final destructiveness of dealing with the new people that they have become.[1]

Reprinted from Erving Goffman, "The Moral Career of the Mental Patient", *Psychiatry*, Vol. **22**, No. 2 (May, 1959), by permission of the author and publisher.

1. The inmate's initial strategy of holding himself aloof from ratifying contact may partly account for the relative lack of group formation among inmates in public mental hospitals, a connection that has been suggested to me by William R. Smith. The desire to avoid personal bonds that would give licence to the asking of biographical questions could also be a factor. In mental hospitals, of course, as in prisoner camps, the staff may consciously break up incipient group

Usually the patient comes to give up this taxing effort at anonymity, at not-hereness, and begins to present himself for conventional social interaction to the hospital community. Thereafter he withdraws only in special ways—by always using his nickname, by signing his contribution to the patient weekly with his initial only, or by using the innocuous "cover" address tactfully provided by some hospitals; or he withdraws only at special times, when, say, a flock of nursing students makes a passing tour of the ward, or when, paroled to the hospital grounds, he suddenly sees he is about to cross the path of a civilian he happens to know from home. Sometimes this making of oneself available is called "settling down" by the attendants. It marks a new stand openly taken and supported by the patient, and resembles the "coming-out" process that occurs in other groupings.[2]

Once the prepatient begins to settle down, the main outlines of his fate tend to follow those of a whole class of segregated establishments—jails, concentration

formation in order to avoid collective rebellious action and other ward disturbances.

2. A comparable coming out occurs in the homosexual world, when a person finally comes frankly to present himself to a "gay" gathering not as a tourist but as someone who is "available." See Evelyn Hooker, "A Preliminary Analysis of Group Behavior of Homosexuals," *Journal of Psychology*, XLII (1956), pp. 217–25; see especially p. 221. A good fictionalized treatment may be found in James Baldwin's *Giovanni's Room* (New York: Dial, 1956), pp. 41–57. A familiar instance of the coming-out process is no doubt to be found among prepubertal children at the moment one of these actors sidles *back* into a room that had been left in an angered huff and injured *amour propre*. The phrase itself presumably derives from a *rite-de-passage* ceremony once arranged by upper-class mothers for their daughters. Interestingly enough, in large mental hospitals the patient sometimes symbolizes a complete coming out by his first active participation in the hospital-wide patient dance.

camps, monasteries, work camps, and so on—in which the inmate spends the whole round of life on the grounds, and marches through his regimented day in the immediate company of a group of persons of his own institutional status.

Like the neophyte in many of these total institutions, the new inpatient finds himself cleanly stripped of many of his accustomed affirmations, satisfactions, and defenses, and is subjected to a rather full set of mortifying experiences: restriction of free movement, communal living, diffuse authority of a whole echelon of people, and so on. Here one begins to learn about the limited extent to which a conception of oneself can be sustained when the usual setting of supports for it are suddenly removed.

While undergoing these humbling moral experiences, the inpatient learns to orient himself in terms of the "ward system."[3] In public mental hospitals this usually consists of a series of graded living arrangements built around wards, administrative units called services, and parole statuses. The "worst" level often involves nothing but wooden benches to sit on, some quite indifferent food, and a small piece of room to sleep in. The "best" level may involve a room of one's own, ground and town privileges, contacts with staff that are relatively undamaging, and what is seen as good food and ample recreational facilities. For disobeying the pervasive house rules, the inmate will receive stringent punishments expressed in terms of loss of privileges; for obedience he will eventually be allowed to reacquire some of the minor satisfactions he took for granted on the outside.

The institutionalization of these radically different levels of living throws light on the implications for self of social settings. And this in turn affirms that the self arises not merely out of its possessor's interactions with significant others, but also out of the arrangements that are evolved in an organization for its members.

There are some settings that the person easily discounts as an expression or extension of him. When a tourist goes slumming, he may take pleasure in the situation not because it is a reflection of him but because it so assuredly is not. There are other settings, such as living rooms, which the person manages on his own and employs to influence in a favorable direction other persons' views of him. And there are still other settings, such as a work place, which express the employee's occupational status, but over which he has no final control, this being exerted, however tactfully, by his employer. Mental hospitals provide an extreme instance of this latter possibility. And this is due not merely to their uniquely degraded living levels, but also to the unique way in which significance for self is made explicit to the patient, piercingly, persistently, and thoroughly. Once lodged on a given ward, the patient is firmly instructed that the restrictions and deprivations he encounters are not due to such blind forces as tradition or economy—and hence dissociable from self—but are intentional parts of his treatment, part of his need at the time, and therefore an expression of the state that his self has fallen to. Having every reason to initiate requests for better conditions, he is told that when the staff feel he is "able to manage" or will be "comfortable with" a higher ward level, then appropriate action will be taken. In short, assignment to a given ward is presented not as a reward or punishment, but as an expression of his general level of social functioning, his status as a person. Given the fact that the worst ward levels provide a round of life that inpatients with organic brain damage can easily manage, and that these quite limited human beings are present to prove it, one can appreciate some of the mirroring effects of the hospital.[4]

The ward system, then, is an extreme instance of how the physical facts of an establishment can be explicitly employed to frame the conception a person takes of himself. In addition, the official psychiatric mandate of mental hospitals gives rise to even more direct, even more blatant, attacks upon the inmate's view of himself. The more "medical" and the more progressive a mental hospital is—the more it attempts to be therapeutic and not merely custodial—the more he may be confronted by high-ranking staff arguing that his past has been a failure, that the cause of this has been within himself, that his attitude to life is wrong, and that if he wants to be a person he will have to change his way of dealing with people and his conceptions of himself. Often the moral value of these verbal assaults will be brought home to him by requiring him to practice taking this psychiatric view of himself in arranged confessional periods, whether in private sessions or group psychotherapy.

Now a general point may be made about the moral career of inpatients which has bearing on many moral careers. Given the stage that any person has reached in a career, one typically finds that he constructs an image of his life course—past, present, and future—which selects, abstracts, and distorts in such a way as to

3. A good description of the ward system may be found in Ivan Belknap, *Human Problems of a State Mental Hospital* (New York: McGraw-Hill, 1959), ch. ix, especially p. 164.

4. Here is one way in which mental hospitals can be worse than concentration camps and prisons as places in which to "do" time; in the latter, self-insulation from the symbolic implications of the settings may be easier. In fact, self-insulation from hospital settings may be so difficult that patients have to employ devices for this which staff interpret as psychotic symptoms.

provide him with a view of himself that he can usefully expound in current situations. Quite generally, the person's line concerning self defensively brings him into appropriate alignment with the basic values of his society, and so may be called an apologia. If the person can manage to present a view of his current situation which shows the operation of favorable personal qualities in the past and a favorable destiny awaiting him, it may be called a success story. If the facts of a person's past and present are extremely dismal, then about the best he can do is to show that he is not responsible for what has become of him, and the term sad tale is appropriate. Interestingly enough, the more the person's past forces him out of apparent alignment with central moral values, the more often he seems compelled to tell his sad tale in any company in which he finds himself. Perhaps he partly responds to the need he feels in others of not having their sense of proper life courses affronted. In any case, it is among convicts, "winos," and prostitutes that one seems to obtain sad tales the most readily.[5] It is the vicissitudes of the mental patient's sad tale that I want to consider now.

In the mental hospital, the setting and the house rules press home to the patient that he is, after all, a mental case who has suffered some kind of social collapse on the outside, having failed in some over-all way, and that here he is of little social weight, being hardly capable of acting like a full-fledged person at all. These humiliations are likely to be most keenly felt by middle-class patients, since their previous condition of life little immunizes them against such affronts, but all patients feel some downgrading. Just as any normal member of his outside subculture would do, the patient often responds to this situation by attempting to assert a sad tale proving that he is not "sick," that the "little trouble" he

did get into was really somebody else's fault, that his past life course had some honor and rectitude, and that the hospital is therefore unjust in forcing the status of mental patient upon him. This self-respecting tendency is heavily institutionalized within the patient society where opening social contacts typically involve the participants' volunteering information about their current ward location and length of stay so far, but not the reasons for their stay—such interaction being conducted in the manner of small talk on the outside.[6] With greater familiarity, each patient usually volunteers relatively acceptable reasons for his hospitalization, at the same time accepting without open immediate question the lines offered by other patients. Such stories as the following are given and overtly accepted.

> I was going to night school to get a M.A. degree, and holding down a job in addition, and the load got too much for me.

> The others here are sick mentally but I'm suffering from a bad nervous system and that is what is giving me these phobias.

> I got here by mistake because of a diabetes diagnosis, and I'll leave in a couple of days. [The patient had been in seven weeks.]

> I failed as a child, and later with my wife I reached out for dependency.

> My trouble is that I can't work. That's what I'm in for. I had two jobs with a good home and all the money I wanted.[7]

The patient sometimes reinforces these stories by an optimistic definition of his occupational status. A man who managed to obtain an audition as a radio announcer styles himself a radio announcer; another who worked for some months as a copy boy and was then given a job as a reporter on a large trade journal, but fired after three weeks, defines himself as a reporter.

A whole social role in the patient community may be constructed on the basis of these reciprocally sustained fictions. For these face-to-face niceties tend to be qual-

---

5. In regard to convicts, see Anthony Heckstall-Smith, *Eighteen Months* (London: Allan Wingate, 1954), pp. 52−53. For "winos" see the discussion in Howard G. Bain, "A Sociological Analysis of the Chicago Skid-Row Lifeway" (Unpublished M.A. thesis, Department of Sociology, University or Chicago, September 1950), especially "The Rationale of the Skid-Row Drinking Group," pp. 141−46. Bain's neglected thesis is a useful source of material on moral careers.

Apparently one of the occupational hazards of prostitution is that clients and other professional contacts sometimes persist in expressing sympathy by asking for a defensible dramatic explanation for the fall from grace. In having to bother to have a sad tale ready, perhaps the prostitute is more to be pitied than damned. Good examples of prostitute sad tales may be found in Henry Mayhew, *London Labour and the London Poor*, Vol. IV, *Those That Will Not Work* (London: Charles Griffin and Co., 1862), pp. 210−72. For a contemporary source, see *Women of the Streets*, edited by C. H. Rolph (London: Secker and Warburg, 1955), especially p. 6: "*Almost always, however, after a few comments on the police, the girl would begin to explain how it was that she was in the life, usually in terms of self-justification.* . . ." Lately, of course, the psychological expert has helped out the profession in the construction of wholly remarkable sad tales. See, for example, Harold Greenwald, *The Call Girl* (New York: Ballantine Books, 1958).

6. A similar self-protecting rule has been observed in prisons. Thus, Alfred Hassler, *Diary of a Self-Made Convict* (Chicago: Regnery, 1954), p. 76, in describing a conversation with a fellow prisoner: "*He didn't say much about why he was sentenced, and I didn't ask him, that being the accepted behavior in prison.*" A novelistic version for the mental hospital may be found in J. Kerkhoff, *How Thin the Veil: A Newspaperman's Story of His Own Mental Crack-up and Recovery* (New York: Greenberg, 1952), p. 27.

7. From the writer's field notes of informal interaction with patients, transcribed as nearly verbatim as he was able.

ified by behind-the-back gossip that comes only a degree closer to the "objective" facts. Here, of course, one can see a classic social function of informal networks of equals: they serve as one another's audience for self-supporting tales—tales that are somewhat more solid than pure fantasy and somewhat thinner than the facts.

But the patient's apologia is called forth in a unique setting, for few settings could be so destructive of self-stories except, of course, those stories already constructed along psychiatric lines. And this destructiveness rests on more than the official sheet of paper which attests that the patient is of unsound mind, a danger to himself and others—an attestation, incidentally, which seems to cut deeply into the patient's pride, and into the possibility of his having any.

Certainly the degrading conditions of the hospital setting belie many of the self-stories that are presented by patients, and the very fact of being in the mental hospital is evidence against these tales. And of course there is not always sufficient patient solidarity to prevent patient discrediting patient, just as there is not always a sufficient number of "professionalized" attendants to prevent attendant discrediting patient. As one patient informant repeatedly suggested to a fellow patient:

> If you're so smart, how come you got your ass in here?

The mental-hospital setting, however, is more treacherous still. Staff have much to gain through discreditings of the patient's story—whatever the felt reason for such discreditings. If the custodial faction in the hospital is to succeed in managing his daily round without complaint or trouble from him, then it will prove useful to be able to point out to him that the claims about himself upon which he rationalizes his demands are false, that he is not what he is claiming to be, and that in fact he is a failure as a person. If the psychiatric faction is to impress upon him its views about his personal make-up, then they must be able to show in detail how their version of his past and their version of his character hold up much better than his own.[8] If both the custodial and psychiatric factions are to get him to co-operate in the various psychiatric treatments, then it will prove useful to disabuse him of his view of their purposes, and

cause him to appreciate that they know what they are doing, and are doing what is best for him. In brief, the difficulties caused by a patient are closely tied to his version of what has been happening to him, and if co-operation is to be secured, it helps if this version is discredited. The patient must "insightfully" come to take, or affect to take, the hospital's view of himself.

The staff also have ideal means—in addition to the mirroring effect of the setting—for denying the inmate's rationalizations. Current psychiatric doctrine defines mental disorder as something that can have its roots in the patient's earliest years, show its signs throughout the course of his life, and invade almost every sector of his current activity. No segment of his past or present need be defined, then, as beyond the jurisdiction and mandate of psychiatric assessment. Mental hospitals bureaucratically institutionalize this extremely wide mandate by formally basing their treatment of the patient upon his diagnosis and hence upon the psychiatric view of his past.

The case record is an important expression of this mandate. This dossier is apparently not regularly used, however, to record occasions when the patient showed capacity to cope honorably and effectively with difficult life situations. Nor is the case record typically used to provide a rough average or sampling of his past conduct. One of its purposes is to show the ways in which the patient is "sick" and the reasons why it was right to commit him and is right currently to keep him committed; and this is done by extracting from his whole life course a list of those incidents that have or might have had "symptomatic" significance.[9] The misadventures of his parents or siblings that might suggest a "taint" may be cited. Early acts in which the patient appeared to have shown bad judgment or emotional disturbance will be recorded. Occasions when he acted in a way which the layman would consider immoral, sexually perverted, weak-willed, childish, ill-considered, impulsive, and crazy may be described. Misbehaviors which someone saw as the last straw, as cause for immediate action, are likely to be reported in detail. In addition, the record will describe his state on arrival at the hospital—and this is not likely to be a time of tranquillity and ease for him.

---

8. The process of examining a person psychiatrically and then altering or reducing his status in consequence is known in hospital and prison parlance as bugging, the assumption being that once you come to the attention of the testers you either will automatically be labeled crazy or the process of testing itself will make you crazy. Thus psychiatric staff are sometimes seen not as discovering whether you are sick, but as making you sick; and "Don't bug me, man" can mean, "Don't pester me to the point where I'll get upset." Sheldon Messinger has suggested to me that this meaning of bugging is related to the other colloquial meaning, of wiring a room with a secret microphone to collect information usable for discrediting the speaker.

9. While many kinds of organization maintain records of their members, in almost all of these some socially significant attributes can only be included indirectly, being officially irrelevant. But since mental hospitals have a legitimate claim to deal with the "whole" person, they need officially recognize no limits to what they consider relevant, a sociologically interesting licence. It is an odd historical fact that persons concerned with promoting civil liberties in other areas of life tend to favor giving the psychiatrist complete discretionary power over the patient. Apparently it is felt that the more power possessed by medically qualified administrators and therapists, the better the interests of the patients will be served. Patients, to my knowledge, have not been polled on this matter.

The record may also report the false line taken by the patient in answering embarrassing questions, showing him as someone who makes claims that are obviously contrary to the facts:

> Claims she lives with oldest daughter or with sisters only when sick and in need of care; otherwise with husband, he himself says not for twelve years.

> Contrary to the reports from the personnel, he says he no longer bangs on the floor or cries in the morning.

> . . . conceals fact that she had her organs removed, claims she is still menstruating.

> At first she denied having had premarital sexual experience, but when asked about Jim she said she had forgotten about it 'cause it had been unpleasant.[10]

Where contrary facts are not known by the recorder, their presence is often left scrupulously an open question:

> The patient denied any heterosexual experiences nor could one trick her into admitting that she had ever been pregnant or into any kind of sexual indulgence, denying masturbation as well.

> Even with considerable pressure she was unwilling to engage in any projection of paranoid mechanisms.

> No psychotic content could be elicited at this time.[11]

And if in no more factual way, discrediting statements often appear in descriptions given of the patient's general social manner in the hospital:

> When interviewed, he was bland, apparently self-assured, and sprinkles high-sounding generalizations freely throughout his verbal productions.

> Armed with a rather neat appearance and natty little Hitlerian mustache this 45 year old man who has spent the last five or more years of his life in the hospital, is making a very successful hospital adjustment living within the role of a rather gay liver and jim-dandy type of fellow who is not only quite superior to his fellow patients in intellectual respects but who is also quite a man with women. His speech is sprayed with many multi-syllabled words which he generally uses in good context, but if he talks long enough on

any subject it soon becomes apparent that he is so completely lost in this verbal diarrhea as to make what he says almost completely worthless.[12]

The events recorded in the case history are, then, just the sort that a layman would consider scandalous, defamatory, and discrediting. I think it is fair to say that all levels of mental-hospital staff fail, in general, to deal with this material with the moral neutrality claimed for medical statements and psychiatric diagnosis, but instead participate, by intonation and gesture if by no other means, in the lay reaction to these acts. This will occur in staff-patient encounters as well as in staff encounters at which no patient is present.

In some mental hospitals, access to the case record is technically restricted to medical and higher nursing levels, but even here informal access or relayed information is often available to lower staff levels.[13] In addition, ward personnel are felt to have a right to know those aspects of the patient's past conduct which, embedded in the reputation he develops, purportedly make it possible to manage him with greater benefit to himself and less risk to others. Further, all staff levels typically have access to the nursing notes kept on the ward, which chart the daily course of each patient's disease, and hence his conduct, providing for the near present the sort of information the case record supplies for his past.

I think that most of the information gathered in case records is quite true, although it might seem also to be true that almost anyone's life course could yield up enough denigrating facts to provide grounds for the record's justification of commitment. In any case, I am not concerned here with questioning the desirability of maintaining case records, or the motives of staff in keeping them. The point is that, these facts about him being true, the patient is certainly not relieved from the normal cultural pressure to conceal them, and is perhaps all the more threatened by knowing that they are neatly available, and that he has no control over who gets to learn

---

10. Verbatim transcriptions of hospital case-record material.
11. Verbatim transcriptions of hospital case-record material.

12. Verbatim transcriptions of hospital case-record material.
13. However, some mental hospitals do have a "hot file" of selected records which can be taken out only by special permission. These may be records of patients who work as administration-office messengers and might otherwise snatch glances at their own files; of inmates who had elite status in the environing community; and of inmates who may take legal action against the hospital and hence have a special reason to maneuver access to their records. Some hospitals even have a "hot-hot file," kept in the superintendent's office. In addition, the patient's professional title, especially if it is a medical one, is sometimes purposely omitted from his file card. All of these exceptions to the general rule for handling information show, of course, the institution's realization of some of the implications of keeping mental-hospital records. For a further example, see Harold Taxel, "Authority Structure in a Mental Hospital Ward" (Unpublished M.A. thesis, Department of Sociology, University of Chicago, 1953), pp. 11–12.

them.[14] A manly looking youth who responds to military induction by running away from the barracks and hiding himself in a hotel-room clothes closet, to be found there, crying, by his mother; a woman who travels from Utah to Washington to warn the President of impending doom; a man who disrobes before three young girls; a boy who locks his sister out of the house, striking out two of her teeth when she tries to come back in through the window—each of these persons has done something he will have very obvious reason to conceal from others, and very good reason to tell lies about.

The formal and informal patterns of communication linking staff members tend to amplify the disclosive work done by the case record. A discreditable act that the patient performs during one part of the day's routine in one part of the hospital community is likely to be reported back to those who supervise other areas of his life where he implicitly takes the stand that he is not the sort of person who could act that way.

Of significance here, as in some other social establishments, is the increasingly common practice of all-level staff conferences, where staff air their views of patients and develop collective agreement concerning the line that the patient is trying to take and the line that should be taken to him. A patient who develops a "personal" relation with an attendant, or manages to make an attendant anxious by eloquent and persistent accusations of malpractice, can be put back into his place by means of the staff meeting, where the attendant is given warning or assurance that the patient is "sick." Since the differential image of himself that a person usually meets from those of various levels around him comes here to be unified behind the scenes into a common approach, the patient may find himself faced with a kind of collusion against him—albeit one sincerely thought to be for his own ultimate welfare.

14. This is the problem of "information control" that many groups suffer from in varying degrees. See Goffman, "Discrepant Roles," in *The Presentation of Self in Everyday Life* (New York: Anchor Books, 1959), ch. iv. pp. 141–166. A suggestion of this problem in relation to case records in prisons is given by James Peck in his story, "The Ship that Never Hit Port," in *Prison Etiquette*, edited by Holley Cantine and Dachine Rainer (Bearsville, N.Y.: Retort Press, 1950), p. 66:

"The hacks of course hold all the aces in dealing with any prisoner because they can always write him up for inevitable punishment. Every infraction of the rules is noted in the prisoner's jacket, a folder which records all the details of the man's life before and during imprisonment. There are general reports written by the work detail screw, the cell block screw, or some other screw who may have overheard a conversation. Tales pumped from stoolpigeons are also included.

"Any letter which interests the authorities goes into the jacket. The mail censor may make a photostatic copy of a prisoner's entire letter, or merely copy a passage. Or he may pass the letter on to the warden. Often an inmate called out by the warden or parole officer is confronted with something he wrote so long ago he had forgot all about it. It might be about his personal life or his political views—a fragment of thought that the prison authorities felt was dangerous and filed for later use."

In addition, the formal transfer of the patient from one ward or service to another is likely to be accompanied by an informal description of his characteristics, this being felt to facilitate the work of the employee who is newly responsible for him.

Finally, at the most informal of levels, the lunchtime and coffee-break small talk of staff often turns upon the latest doings of the patient, the gossip level of any social establishment being here intensified by the assumption that everything about him is in some way the proper business of the hospital employee. Theoretically there seems to be no reason why such gossip should not build up the subject instead of tear him down, unless one claims that talk about those not present will always tend to be critical in order to maintain the integrity and prestige of the circle in which the talking occurs. And so, even when the impulse of the speakers seems kindly and generous, the implication of their talk is typically that the patient is not a complete person. For example, a conscientious group therapist, sympathetic with patients, once admitted to his coffee companions:

> I've had about three group disrupters, one man in particular—a lawyer [*sotto voce*] James Wilson—very bright—who just made things miserable for me, but I would always tell him to get on the stage and do something. Well, I was getting desperate and then I bumped into his therapist, who said that right now behind the man's bluff and front he needed the group very much and that it probably meant more to him than anything else he was getting out of the hospital—he just needed the support. Well, that made me feel altogether different about him. He's out now.

In general, then, mental hospitals systematically provide for circulation about each patient the kind of information that the patient is likely to try to hide. And in various degrees of detail this information is used daily to puncture his claims. At the admission and diagnostic conferences, he will be asked questions to which he must give wrong answers in order to maintain his self-respect, and then the true answer may be shot back at him. An attendant whom he tells a version of his past and his reason for being in the hospital may smile disbelievingly, or say, "That's not the way I heard it," in line with the practical psychiatry of bringing the patient down to reality. When he accosts a physician or nurse on the ward and presents his claims for more privileges or for discharge, this may be countered by a question which he cannot answer truthfully without calling up a time in his past when he acted disgracefully. When he gives his view of his situation during group psychotherapy, the therapist, taking the role of interrogator, may attempt to disabuse him of his face-saving interpretations and encourage an interpretation suggesting that it is he himself who is to blame and who must change. When he claims to staff or fellow patients that he is well and has never been really sick, someone may give him graphic details of how, only one month ago, he was prancing around like a girl, or claiming that he was God, or declining to talk or eat, or putting gum in his hair.

Each time the staff deflates the patient's claims, his sense of what a person ought to be and the rules of peer-group social intercourse press him to reconstruct his stories; and each time he does this, the custodial and psychiatric interests of the staff may lead them to discredit these tales again.

Behind these verbally instigated ups and downs of the self is an institutional base that rocks just as precariously. Contrary to popular opinion, the "ward system" insures a great amount of internal social mobility in mental hospitals, especially during the inmate's first year. During that time he is likely to have altered his service once, his ward three or four times, and his parole status several times; and he is likely to have experienced moves in bad as well as good directions. Each of these moves involves a very drastic alteration in level of living and in available materials out of which to build a self-confirming round of activities, an alteration equivalent in scope, say, to a move up or down a class in the wider class system. Moreover, fellow inmates with whom he has partially identified himself will similarly be moving, but in different directions and at different rates, thus reflecting feelings of social change to the person even when he does not experience them directly.

As previously implied, the doctrines of psychiatry can reinforce the social fluctuations of the ward system. Thus there is a current psychiatric view that the ward system is a kind of social hothouse in which patients start as social infants and end up, within the year, on convalescent wards as resocialized adults. This view adds considerably to the weight and pride that staff can attach to their work, and necessitates a certain amount of blindness, especially at higher staff levels, to other ways of viewing the ward system, such as a method for disciplining unruly persons through punishment and reward. In any case, this resocialization perspective tends to overstress the extent to which those on the worst wards are incapable of socialized conduct and the extent to which those on the best wards are ready and willing to play the social game. Because the ward system is something more than a resocialization chamber, inmates find many reasons for "messing up" or getting into trouble, and many occasions, then, for demotion to less privileged ward positions. These demotions may be officially interpreted as psychiatric relapses or moral backsliding, thus protecting the resocialization view of the hospital; these interpretations, by implication, translate a mere infraction of rules and consequent demotion into a fundamental expression of the status of the culprit's self. Correspondingly, promotions, which may come about because of ward population pressure, the need for a "working patient," or for other psychiatrically irrelevant reasons, may be built up into something claimed to be profoundly expressive of the patient's whole self. The patient himself may be expected by staff to make a personal effort to "get well," in something less than a year, and hence may be constantly reminded to think in terms of the self's success and failure.[15]

In such contexts inmates can discover that deflations in moral status are not so bad as they had imagined. After all, infractions which lead to these demotions cannot be accompanied by legal sanctions or by reduction to the status of mental patient, since these conditions already prevail. Further, no past or current delict seems to be horrendous enough in itself to excommunicate a patient from the patient community, and hence failures at right living lose some of their stigmatizing meaning. And finally, in accepting the hospital's version of his fall from grace, the patient can set himself up in the business of "straightening up," and make claims of sympathy, privileges, and indulgence from the staff in order to foster this.

Learning to live under conditions of imminent exposure and wide fluctuation in regard, with little control over the granting or withholding of this regard, is an important step in the socialization of the patient, a step that tells something important about what it is like to be an inmate in a mental hospital. Having one's past mistakes and present progress under constant moral review seems to make for a special adaptation consisting of a less than moral attitude to ego ideals. One's shortcomings and successes become too central and fluctuating an issue in life to allow the usual commitment of concern for other persons' views of them. It is not very practicable to try to sustain solid claims about oneself. The inmate tends to learn that degradations and reconstructions of the self need not be given too much weight, at the same time learning that staff and inmates are ready to view an inflation or deflation of a self with some indifference. He learns that a defensible picture of self can be seen as something outside oneself that can be constructed, lost, and rebuilt, all with great speed and some equanimity. He learns about the viability of taking up a standpoint—and hence a self—that is outside the one which the hospital can give and take away from him.

The setting, then, seems to engender a kind of cos-

15. For this and other suggestions, I am indebted to Charlotte Green Schwartz.

mopolitan sophistication, a kind of civic apathy. In this unserious yet oddly exaggerated moral context, building up a self or having it destroyed becomes something of a shameless game, and learning to view this process as a game seems to make for some demoralization, the game being such a fundamental one. In the hospital, then, the inmate can learn that the self is not a fortress, but rather a small open city; he can become weary of having to show pleasure when held by troops of his own, and weary of having to show displeasure when held by the enemy. Once he learns what it is like to be defined by society as not having a viable self, this threatening definition—the threat that helps attach people to the self society accords them—is weakened. The patient seems to gain a new plateau when he learns that he can survive while acting in a way that society sees as destructive of him.

A few illustrations of this moral loosening and moral fatigue might be given. In state mental hospitals currently a kind of ''marriage moratorium'' appears to be accepted by patients and more or less condoned by staff. Some informal peer-group pressure may be brought against a patient who ''plays around'' with more than one hospital partner at a time, but little negative sanction seems to be attached to taking up, in a temporarily steady way, with a member of the opposite sex, even though both partners are known to be married, to have children, and even to be regularly visited by these outsiders. In short, there is licence in mental hospitals to begin courting all over again, with the understanding, however, that nothing very permanent or serious can come of this. Like shipboard or vacation romances, these entanglements attest to the way in which the hospital is cut off from the outside community, becoming a world of its own, operated for the benefit of its own citizens. And certainly this moratorium is an expression of the alienation and hostility that patients feel for those on the outside to whom they were closely related. But, in addition, one has evidence of the loosening effects of living in a world within a world, under conditions which make it difficult to give full seriousness to either of them.

The second illustration concerns the ward system. On the worst ward level, discreditings seem to occur the most frequently, in part because of lack of facilities, in part through the mockery and sarcasm that seem to be the occupational norm of social control for the attendants and nurses who administer these places. At the same time, the paucity of equipment and rights means that not much self can be built up. The patient finds himself constantly toppled, therefore, but with very little distance to fall. A kind of jaunty gallows humor seems to develop in some of these wards, with considerable freedom to stand up to the staff and return insult for insult. While these patients can be punished, they cannot, for example, be easily slighted, for they are accorded as a matter of course few of the niceties that people must enjoy before they can suffer subtle abuse. Like prostitutes in connection with sex, inmates on these wards have very little reputation or rights to lose and can therefore take certain liberties. As the person moves up the ward system, he can manage more and more to avoid incidents which discredit his claim to be a human being, and acquire more and more of the varied ingredients of self-respect; yet when eventually he does get toppled—and he does—there is a much farther distance to fall. For instance, the privileged patient lives in a world wider than the ward, containing recreation workers who, on request, can dole out cake, cards, table-tennis balls, tickets to the movies, and writing materials. But in the absence of the social control of payment which is typically exerted by a recipient on the outside, the patient runs the risk that even a warmhearted functionary may, on occasion, tell him to wait until she has finished an informal chat, or teasingly ask why he wants what he has asked for, or respond with a dead pause and a cold look of appraisal.

Moving up and down the ward system means, then, not only a shift in self-constructive equipment, a shift in reflected status, but also a change in the calculus of risks. Appreciation of risks to his self-conception is part of everyone's moral experience, but an appreciation that a given risk level is itself merely a social arrangement is a rarer kind of experience, and one that seems to help to disenchant the person who undergoes it.

A third instance of moral loosening has to do with the conditions that are often associated with the release of the inpatient. Often he leaves under the supervision and jurisdiction of his next-of-relation or of a specially selected and specially watchful employer. If he misbehaves while under their auspices, they can quickly obtain his readmission. He therefore finds himself under the special power of persons who ordinarily would not have this kind of power over him, and about whom, moreover, he may have had prior cause to feel quite bitter. In order to get out of the hospital, however, he may conceal his displeasure in this arrangement, and, at least until safely off the hospital rolls, act out a willingness to accept this kind of custody. These discharge procedures, then, provide a built-in lesson in overtly taking a role without the usual covert commitments, and seem further to separate the person from the worlds that others take seriously.

The moral career of a person of a given social category involves a standard sequence of changes in his way of conceiving of selves, including, importantly, his own. These half-buried lines of development can be followed by studying his moral experiences—that is, happenings which mark a turning point in the way in which the person views the world—although the particularities of this view may be difficult to establish. And note can be taken of overt tacks or strategies—that is, stands that he effectively takes before specifiable others, whatever the hidden and variable nature of his inward attachment to these presentations. By taking note of moral experiences and overt personal stands, one can obtain a relatively objective tracing of relatively subjective matters.

Each moral career, and behind this, each self, occurs within the confines of an institutional system, whether a social establishment such as a mental hospital or a complex of personal and professional relationships. The self, then, can be seen as something that resides in the arrangements prevailing in a social system for its members. The self in this sense is not a property of the person to whom it is attributed, but dwells rather in the pattern of social control that is exerted in connection with the person by himself and those around him. This special kind of institutional arrangement does not so much support the self as constitute it.

In this paper, two of these institutional arrangements have been considered, by pointing to what happens to the person when these rulings are weakened. The first concerns the felt loyalty of his next-of-relation. The pre-patient's self is described as a function of the way in which three roles are related, arising and declining in the kinds of affiliation that occur between the next-of-relation and the mediators. The second concerns the protection required by the person for the version of himself which he presents to others, and the way in which the withdrawal of this protection can form a systematic, if unintended, aspect of the working of an establishment. I want to stress that these are only two kinds of institutional rulings from which a self emerges for the participant; others, not considered in this paper, are equally important.

In the usual cycle of adult socialization one expects to find alienation and mortification followed by a new set of beliefs about the world and a new way of conceiving of selves. In the case of the mental-hospital patient, this rebirth does sometimes occur, taking the form of a strong belief in the psychiatric perspective, or, briefly at least, a devotion to the social cause of better treatment for mental patients. The moral career of the mental patient has unique interest, however; it can illustrate the possibility that in casting off the raiments of the old self—or in having this cover torn away—the person need not seek a new robe and a new audience before which to cower. Instead he can learn, at least for a time, to practise before all groups the amoral arts of shamelessness.

DAVID L. ROSENHAN

On Being Sane in Insane Places

If sanity and insanity exist, how shall we know them?

The question is neither capricious nor itself insane. However much we may be personally convinced that we can tell the normal from the abnormal, the evidence is simply not compelling. It is commonplace, for example, to read about murder trials wherein eminent psychiatrists for the defense are contradicted by equally eminent psychiatrists for the prosecution on the matter of the defendant's sanity. More generally, there are a great deal of conflicting data on the reliability, utility, and meaning of such terms as "sanity," "insanity," "mental illness," and "schizophrenia."[1] Finally, as early as 1934, Bene-

Reprinted from *Science,* Vol. **179** (1973), pages 250–258, by permission of the author and publisher.

dict suggested that normality and abnormality are not universal.[2] What is viewed as normal in one culture may be seen as quite aberrant in another. Thus, notions of normality and abnormality may not be quite as accurate as people believe they are.

To raise questions regarding normality and abnormality is in no way to question the fact that some behaviors are deviant or odd. Murder is deviant. So, too, are hallucinations. Nor does raising such questions deny the existence of the personal anguish that is often associated with "mental illness." Anxiety and depression exist. Psychological suffering exists. But normality and abnormality, sanity and insanity, and the diagnoses that flow from them may be less substantive than many believe them to be.

At its heart, the question of whether the sane can be distinguished from the insane (and whether degrees of insanity can be distinguished from each other) is a simple matter: do the salient characteristics that lead to diagnoses reside in the patients themselves or in the environments and contexts in which observers find them? From Bleuler, through Kretchmer, through the formulators of the recently revised *Diagnostic and Statistical Manual* of the American Psychiatric Association, the belief has been strong that patients present symptoms, that those symptoms can be categorized, and, implicitly, that the sane are distinguishable from the insane. More recently, however, this belief has been questioned. Based in part on theoretical and anthropological considerations, but also on philosophical, legal, and therapeutic ones, the view has grown that psychological categorization of mental illness is useless at best and downright harmful, misleading, and pejorative at worst. Psychiatric diagnoses, in this view, are in the minds of the observers and are not valid summaries of characteristics displayed by the observed.[3-5]

Gains can be made in deciding which of these is more nearly accurate by getting normal people (that is, people who do not have, and have never suffered, symptoms of serious psychiatric disorders) admitted to psychiatric hospitals and then determining whether they were discovered to be sane and, if so, how. If the sanity of such pseudopatients were always detected, there would be prima facie evidence that a sane individual can be distinguished from the insane context in which he is found. Normality (and presumably abnormality) is distinct enough that it can be recognized wherever it occurs, for it is carried within the person. If, on the other hand, the sanity of the pseudopatients were never discovered, serious difficulties would arise for those who support traditional modes of psychiatric diagnosis. Given that the hospital staff was not incompetent, that the pseudopatient had been behaving as sanely as he had been outside of the hospital, and that it had never been previously suggested that he belonged in a psychiatric hospital, such an unlikely outcome would support the view that psychiatric diagnosis betrays little about the patient but much about the environment in which an observer finds him.

This article describes such an experiment. Eight sane people gained secret admission to 12 different hospitals.[6] Their diagnostic experiences constitute the data of the first part of this article; the remainder is devoted to a description of their experiences in psychiatric institutions. Too few psychiatrists and psychologists, even those who have worked in such hospitals, know what the experience is like. They rarely talk about it with former patients, perhaps because they distrust information coming from the previously insane. Those who have worked in psychiatric hospitals are likely to have adapted so thoroughly to the settings that they are insensitive to the impact of that experience. And while there have been occcasional reports of researchers who submitted themselves to psychiatric hospitalization,[7] these researchers have commonly remained in the hospitals for short periods of time, often with the knowledge of the hospital staff. It is difficult to know the extent to which they were treated like patients or like research colleagues. Nevertheless, their reports about the inside of the psychiatric hospital have been valuable. This article extends those efforts.

Pseudopatients and Their Settings

The eight pseudopatients were a varied group. One was a psychology graduate student in his 20's. The remaining seven were older and "established." Among them were three psychologists, a pediatrician, a psychiatrist, a painter, and a housewife. Three pseudopatients were women, five were men. All of them employed pseudonyms, lest their alleged diagnoses embarrass them later. Those who were in mental health professions alleged another occupation in order to avoid the special attentions that might be accorded by staff, as a matter of courtesy or caution, to ailing colleagues.[8] With the exception of myself (I was the first pseudopatient and my presence was known to the hospital administrator and chief psychologist and, so far as I can tell, to them alone), the presence of pseudopatients and the nature of the research program was not known to the hospital staffs.[9]

The settings were similarly varied. In order to generalize the findings, admission into a variety of hospitals was sought. The 12 hospitals in the sample were located in five different states on the East and West coasts. Some were old and shabby, some were quite new. Some were research-oriented, others not. Some had good staff-patient ratios, others were quite understaffed. Only one was a strictly private hospital. All of the others were supported by state or federal funds or, in one instance, by university funds.

After calling the hospital for an appointment, the pseudopatient arrived at the admissions office complaining that he had been hearing voices. Asked what the voices said, he replied that they were often unclear, but as far as he could tell they said "empty," "hollow," and "thud." The voices were unfamiliar and were of the same sex as the pseudopatient. The choice of these symptoms was occasioned by their apparent similarity to existential symptoms. Such symptoms are alleged to arise from painful concerns about the perceived meaninglessness of one's life. It is as if the hallucinating person were saying, "My life is empty and hollow." The choice of these symptoms was also determined by the *absence* of a single report of existential psychoses in the literature.

Beyond alleging the symptoms and falsifying name, vocation, and employment, no further alterations of person, history, or circumstances were made. The significant events of the pseudopatient's life history were presented as they had actually occurred. Relationships with parents and siblings, with spouse and children, with people at work and in school, consistent with the aforementioned exceptions, were described as they were or had been. Frustrations and upsets were described along with joys and satisfactions. These facts are important to remember. If anything, they strongly biased the subsequent results in favor of detecting sanity, since none of their histories or current behaviors were seriously pathological in any way.

Immediately upon admission to the psychiatric ward, the pseudopatient ceased simulating *any* symptoms of abnormality. In some cases, there was a brief period of mild nervousness and anxiety, since none of the pseudopatients really believed that they would be admitted so easily. Indeed, their shared fear was that they would be immediately exposed as frauds and greatly embarrassed. Moreover, many of them had never visited a psychiatric ward; even those who had, nevertheless had some genuine fears about what might happen to them. Their nervousness, then, was quite appropriate to the novelty of the hospital setting, and it abated rapidly.

Apart from that short-lived nervousness, the pseudopatient behaved on the ward as he "normally" behaved. The pseudopatient spoke to patients and staff as he might ordinarily. Because there is uncommonly little to do on a psychiatric ward, he attempted to engage others in conversation. When asked by staff how he was feeling, he indicated that he was fine, that he no longer experienced symptoms. He responded to instructions from attendants, to calls for medication (which was not swallowed), and to dining-hall instructions. Beyond such activities as were available to him on the admissions ward, he spent his time writing down his observations about the ward, its patients, and the staff. Initially these notes were written "secretly," but as it soon became clear that no one much cared, they were subsequently written on standard tablets of paper in such public places as the dayroom. No secret was made of these activities.

The pseudopatient, very much as a true psychiatric patient, entered a hospital with no foreknowledge of when he would be discharged. Each was told that he would have to get out by his own devices, essentially by convincing the staff that he was sane. The psychological stresses associated with hospitalization were considerable, and all but one of the pseudopatients desired to be discharged almost immediately after being admitted. They were, therefore, motivated not only to behave sanely, but to be paragons of cooperation. That their behavior was in no way disruptive is confirmed by nursing reports, which have been obtained on most of the patients. These reports uniformly indicate that the patients were "friendly," "cooperative," and "exhibited no abnormal indications."

The Normal Are Not Detectably Sane

Despite their public "show" of sanity, the pseudopatients were never detected. Admitted, except in one case, with a diagnosis of schizophrenia,[10] each was discharged with a diagnosis of schizophrenia "in remission." The label "in remission" should in no way be dismissed as a formality, for at no time during any hospitalization had any question been raised about any pseudopatient's simulation. Nor are there any indications in the hospital records that the pseudopatient's status was suspect. Rather, the evidence is strong that, once labeled schizophrenic, the pseudopatient was stuck with that label. If the pseudopatient was to be discharged, he must naturally be "in remission"; but he was not sane, nor, in the institution's view, had he ever been sane.

The uniform failure to recognize sanity cannot be attributed to the quality of the hospitals, for, although there were considerable variations among them, several are considered excellent. Nor can it be alleged that there was simply not enough time to observe the pseudopatients. Length of hospitalization ranged from 7 to 52 days, with an average of 19 days. The pseudopatients were not, in fact, carefully observed, but this failure clearly speaks more to traditions within psychiatric hospitals than to lack of opportunity.

Finally, it cannot be said that the failure to recognize the pseudopatients' sanity was due to the fact that they were not behaving sanely. While there was clearly some tension present in all of them, their daily visitors could detect no serious behavioral consequences—nor, indeed, could other patients. It was quite common for the patients to "detect" the pseudopatients' sanity. During the first three hospitalizations, when accurate counts were kept, 35 of a total of 118 patients on the admissions ward voiced their suspicions, some vigorously. "You're not crazy. You're a journalist, or a professor [referring to the continual note-taking]. You're checking up on the hospital." While most of the patients were reassured by the pseudopatient's insistence that he had been sick before he came in but was fine now, some continued to believe that the pseudopatient was sane throughout his hospitalization.[11] The fact that the patients often recognized normality when staff did not raises important questions.

Failure to detect sanity during the course of hospitalization may be due to the fact that physicians operate with a strong bias toward what statisticians call the type 2 error.[5] This is to say that physicians are more inclined to call a healthy person sick (a false positive, type 2) than a sick person healthy (a false negative, type 1). The reasons for this are not hard to find: it is clearly more dangerous to misdiagnose illness than health. Better to err on the side of caution, to suspect illness even among the healthy.

But what holds for medicine does not hold equally well for psychiatry. Medical illnesses, while unfortunate, are not commonly pejorative. Psychiatric diagnoses, on the contrary, carry with them personal, legal, and social stigmas.[12] It was therefore important to see whether the tendency toward diagnosing the sane insane could be reversed. The following experiment was arranged at a research and teaching hospital whose staff had heard these findings but doubted that such an error could occur in their hospital. The staff was informed that at some time during the following 3 months, one or more pseudopatients would attempt to be admitted into the psychiatric hospital. Each staff member was asked to rate each patient who presented himself at admissions or on the ward according to the likelihood that the patient was a pseudopatient. A 10-point scale was used, with a 1 and 2 reflecting high confidence that the patient was a pseudopatient.

Judgments were obtained on 193 patients who were admitted for psychiatric treatment. All staff who had sustained contact with or primary responsibility for the patient—attendants, nurses, psychiatrists, physicians, and psychologists—were asked to make judgments. Forty-one patients were alleged, with high confidence, to be pseudopatients by at least one member of the staff. Twenty-three were considered suspect by at least one psychiatrist. Nineteen were suspected by one psychiatrist *and* one other staff member. Actually, no genuine pseudopatient (at least from my group) presented himself during this period.

The experiment is instructive. It indicates that the tendency to designate sane people as insane can be reversed when the stakes (in this case, prestige and diagnostic acumen) are high. But what can be said of the 19 people who were suspected of being ''sane'' by one psychiatrist and another staff member? Were these people truly ''sane,'' or was it rather the case that in the course of avoiding the type 2 error the staff tended to make more errors of the first sort—calling the crazy ''sane''? There is no way of knowing. But one thing is certain: any

diagnostic process that lends itself so readily to massive errors of this sort cannot be a very reliable one.

The Stickiness of Psychodiagnostic Labels

Beyond the tendency to call the healthy sick—a tendency that accounts better for diagnostic behavior on admission than it does for such behavior after a lengthy period of exposure—the data speak to the massive role of labeling in psychiatric assessment. Having once been labeled schizophrenic, there is nothing the pseudopatient can do to overcome the tag. The tag profoundly colors others' perceptions of him and his behavior.

From one viewpoint, these data are hardly surprising, for it has long been known that elements are given meaning by the context in which they occur. Gestalt psychology made this point vigorously, and Asch [13] demonstrated that there are ''central'' personality traits (such as ''warm'' versus ''cold'') which are so powerful that they markedly color the meaning of other information in forming an impression of a given personality.[14] ''Insane,'' ''schizophrenic,'' ''manic-depressive,'' and ''crazy'' are probably among the most powerful of such central traits. Once a person is designated abnormal, all of his other behaviors and characteristics are colored by that label. Indeed, that label is so powerful that many of the pseudopatients' normal behaviors were overlooked entirely or profoundly misinterpreted. Some examples may clarify this issue.

Earlier I indicated that there were no changes in the pseudopatient's personal history and current status beyond those of name, employment, and, where necessary, vocation. Otherwise, a veridical description of personal history and circumstances was offered. Those circumstances were not psychotic. How were they made consonant with the diagnosis of psychosis? Or were those diagnoses modified in such a way as to bring them into accord with the circumstances of the pseudopatient's life, as described by him?

As far as I can determine, diagnoses were in no way affected by the relative health of the circumstances of a pseudopatient's life. Rather, the reverse occurred: the perception of his circumstances was shaped entirely by the diagnosis. A clear example of such translation is found in the case of a pseudopatient who had had a close relationship with his mother but was rather remote from his father during his early childhood. During adolescence and beyond, however, his father became a close friend, while his relationship with his mother cooled. His present relationship with his wife was characteristically close and warm. Apart from occasional angry exchanges, friction was minimal. The children had rarely been spanked. Surely there is nothing especially pathological about such a history. Indeed, many readers may see a similar pattern in their own experiences, with no markedly deleterious consequences. Observe, however, how such a history was translated in the psychopathological context, this from the case summary prepared after the patient was discharged.

> This white 39-year-old male . . . manifests a long history of considerable ambivalence in close relationships, which begins in early childhood. A warm relationship with his mother cools during his adolescence. A distant relationship to his father is described as becoming very intense. Affective stability is absent. His attempts to control emotionality with his wife and children are punctuated by angry outbursts and, in the case of the children, spankings. And while he says that he has several good friends, one senses considerable ambivalence embedded in those relationships also. . . .

The facts of the case were unintentionally distorted by the staff to achieve consistency with a popular theory of the dynamics of a schizophrenic reaction.[15] Nothing of an ambivalent nature had been described in relations with parents, spouse, or friends. To the extent that ambivalence could be inferred, it was probably not greater than is found in all human relationships. It is true the pseudopatient's relationships with his parents changed over time, but in the ordinary context that would hardly be remarkable—indeed, it might very well be expected. Clearly, the meaning ascribed to his verbalizations (that is, ambivalence, affective instability) was determined by the diagnosis: schizophrenia. An entirely different meaning would have been ascribed if it were known that the man was "normal."

All pseudopatients took extensive notes publicly. Under ordinary circumstances, such behavior would have raised questions in the minds of observers, as, in fact, it did among patients. Indeed, it seemed so certain that the notes would elicit suspicion that elaborate precautions were taken to remove them from the ward each day. But the precautions proved needless. The closest any staff member came to questioning these notes occured when one pseudopatient asked his physician what kind of medication he was receiving and began to write down the response. "You needn't write it," he was told gently. "If you have trouble remembering, just ask me again."

If no questions were asked of the pseudopatients, how was their writing interpreted? Nursing records for three patients indicate that the writing was seen as an aspect of their pathological behavior. "Patient engages in writing behavior" was the daily nursing comment on one of the pseudopatients who was never questioned about his writing. Given that the patient is in the hospital, he must be psychologically disturbed. And given that he is disturbed, continuous writing must be a behavioral manifestation of that disturbance, perhaps a subset of the compulsive behaviors that are sometimes correlated with schizophrenia.

One tacit characteristic of psychiatric diagnosis is that it locates the sources of aberration within the individual and only rarely within the complex of stimuli that surrounds him. Consequently, behaviors that are stimulated by the environment are commonly misattributed to the patient's disorder. For example, one kindly nurse found a pseudopatient pacing the long hospital corridors. "Nervous, Mr. X?" she asked. "No, bored," he said.

The notes kept by pseudopatients are full of patient behaviors that were misinterpreted by well-intentioned staff. Often enough, a patient would go "berserk" because he had, wittingly or unwittingly, been mistreated by, say, an attendant. A nurse coming upon the scene would rarely inquire even cursorily into the environmental stimuli of the patient's behavior. Rather, she assumed that his upset derived from his pathology, not from his present interactions with other staff members. Occasionally, the staff might assume that the patient's family (especially when they had recently visited) or other patients had stimulated the outburst. But never were the staff found to assume that one of themselves or the structure of the hospital had anything to do with a patient's behavior. One psychiatrist pointed to a group of patients who were sitting outside the cafeteria entrance half an hour before lunchtime. To a group of young residents he indicated that such behavior was characteristic of the oral-acquisitive nature of the syndrome. It seemed not to occur to him that there were very few things to anticipate in a psychiatric hospital besides eating.

A psychiatric label has a life and an influence of its own. Once the impression has been formed that the patient is schizophrenic, the expectation is that he will continue to be schizophrenic. When a sufficient amount of time has passed, during which the patient has done nothing bizarre, he is considered to be in remission and available for discharge. But the label endures beyond discharge, with the unconfirmed expectation that he will behave as a schizophrenic again. Such labels, conferred by mental health professionals, are as influential on the patient as they are on his relatives and friends, and it should not surprise anyone that the diagnosis acts on all of them as a self-fulfilling prophecy. Eventually, the patient himself accepts the diagnosis, with all of its surplus meanings and expectations, and behaves accordingly.[15]

The inferences to be made from these matters are quite simple. Much as Zigler and Phillips have demonstrated that there is enormous overlap in the symptoms presented by patients who have been variously diagnosed,[16] so there is enormous overlap in the behaviors of the sane and the insane. The sane are not "sane" all of the time. We lose our tempers "for no good reason." We are occasionally depressed or anxious, again for no good reason. And we may find it difficult to get along with one or another person—again for no reason that we can specify. Similarly, the insane are not always insane. Indeed, it was the impression of the pseudopatients while living with them that they were sane for long periods of time—that the bizarre behaviors upon which their diagnoses were allegedly predicated constituted only a small fraction of their total behavior. If it makes no sense to label ourselves permanently depressed on the basis of an occasional depression, then it takes better evidence than is presently available to label all patients insane or schizophrenic on the basis of bizarre behaviors or cognitions. It seems more useful, as Mischel[17] has pointed out, to limit our discussions to *behaviors,* the stimuli that provoke them, and their correlates.

It is not known why powerful impressions of personality traits, such as "crazy" or "insane," arise. Conceivably, when the origins of and stimuli that give rise to a behavior are remote or unknown, or when the behavior strikes us as immutable, trait labels regarding the *behaver* arise. When, on the other hand, the origins and stimuli are known and available, discourse is limited to the behavior itself. Thus, I may hallucinate because I am sleeping, or I may hallucinate because I have ingested a peculiar drug. These are termed sleep-induced hallucinations, or dreams, and drug-induced hallucinations, respectively. But when the stimuli to my hallucinations are unknown, that is called craziness, or schizophrenia—as if that inference were somehow as illuminating as the others.

The Experience of Psychiatric Hospitalization

The term "mental illness" is of recent origin. It was coined by people who were humane in their inclinations and who wanted very much to raise the station of (and the public's sympathies toward) the psychologically disturbed from that of witches and "crazies" to one that was akin to the physically ill. And they were at least partially successful, for the treatment of the mentally ill *has* improved considerably over the years. But while treatment has improved, it is doubtful that people really regard the mentally ill in the same way that they view the physically ill. A broken leg is something one recovers from, but mental illness allegedly endures forever.[18] A broken leg does not threaten the observer, but a crazy schizophrenic? There is by now a host of evidence that

attitudes toward the mentally ill are characterized by fear, hostility, aloofness, suspicion, and dread.[19] The mentally ill are society's lepers.

That such attitudes infect the general population is perhaps not surprising, only upsetting. But that they affect the professionals—attendants, nurses, physicians, psychologists, and social workers—who treat and deal with the mentally ill is more disconcerting, both because such attitudes are self-evidently pernicious and because they are unwitting. Most mental health professionals would insist that they are sympathetic toward the mentally ill, that they are neither avoidant nor hostile. But it is more likely that an exquisite ambivalence characterizes their relations with psychiatric patients, such that their avowed impulses are only part of their entire attitude. Negative attitudes are there too and can easily be detected. Such attitudes should not surprise us. They are the natural offspring of the labels patients wear and the places in which they are found.

Consider the structure of the typical psychiatric hospital. Staff and patients are strictly segregated. Staff have their own living space, including their dining facilities, bathrooms, and assembly places. The glassed quarters that contain the professional staff, which the pseudopatients came to call "the cage," sit out on every dayroom. The staff emerge primarily for caretaking purposes—to give medication, to conduct a therapy or group meeting, to instruct or reprimand a patient. Otherwise, staff keep to themselves, almost as if the disorder that afflicts their charges is somehow catching.

So much is patient-staff segregation the rule that, for four public hospitals in which an attempt was made to measure the degree to which staff and patients mingle, it was necessary to use "time out of the staff cage" as the operational measure. While it was not the case that all time spent out of the cage was spent mingling with patients (attendants, for example, would occasionally emerge to watch television in the dayroom), it was the only way in which one could gather reliable data on time for measuring.

The average amount of time spent by attendants outside of the cage was 11.3 percent (range, 3 to 52 percent). This figure does not represent only time spent mingling with patients, but also includes time spent on such chores as folding laundry, supervising patients while they shave, directing ward clean-up, and sending patients to off-ward activities. It was the relatively rare attendant who spent time talking with patients or playing games with them. It proved impossible to obtain a "percent mingling time" for nurses, since the amount of time they spent out of the cage was too brief. Rather, we counted instances of emergence from the cage. On the average, daytime nurses emerged from the cage 11.5

times per shift, including instances when they left the ward entirely (range, 4 to 39 times). Late afternoon and night nurses were even less available, emerging on the average 9.4 times per shift (range, 4 to 41 times). Data on early morning nurses, who arrived usually after midnight and departed at 8 a.m., are not available because patients were asleep during most of this period.

Physicians, especially psychiatrists, were even less available. They were rarely seen on the wards. Quite commonly, they would be seen only when they arrived and departed, with the remaining time being spent in their offices or in the cage. On the average, physicians emerged on the ward 6.7 times per day (range, 1 to 17 times). It proved difficult to make an accurate estimate in this regard, since physicians often maintained hours that allowed them to come and go at different times.

The hierarchical organization of the psychiatric hospital has been commented on before,[20] but the latent meaning of that kind of organization is worth noting again. Those with the most power have least to do with patients, and those with the least power are most involved with them. Recall, however, that the acquisition of role-appropriate behaviors occurs mainly through the observation of others, with the most powerful having the most influence. Consequently, it is understandable that attendants not only spend more time with patients than do any other members of the staff—that is required by their station in the hierarchy—but also, insofar as they learn from their superiors' behavior, spend as little time with patients as they can. Attendants are seen mainly in the cage, which is where the models, the action, and the power are.

I turn now to a different set of studies, these dealing with staff response to patient-initiated contact. It has long been known that the amount of time a person spends with you can be an index of your significance to him. If he initiates and maintains eye contact, there is reason to believe that he is considering your requests and needs. If he pauses to chat or actually stops and talks, there is added reason to infer that he is individuating you. In four hospitals, the pseudopatient approached the staff member with a request which took the following form: "Pardon me, Mr. [or Dr. or Mrs.] X, could you tell me when I will be eligible for grounds privileges?" (or ". . . when I will be presented at the staff meeting?" or ". . . when I am likely to be discharged?"). While the content of the question varied according to the appropriateness of the target and the pseudopatient's (apparent) current needs the form was always a courteous and relevant request for information. Care was taken never to approach a particular member of the staff more than once a day, lest the staff member become suspicious or irritated. In examining these data, remember that the behavior of the pseudopatients was neither bizarre nor disruptive. One could indeed engage in good conversation with them.

The data for these experiments are shown in Table 1, separately for physicians (column 1) and for nurses and

TABLE 1

Self-initiated contact by pseudopatients with psychiatrists and nurses and attendants, compared to contact with other groups

| Contact | PSYCHIATRIC HOSPITALS | | UNIVERSITY CAMPUS (NONMEDICAL) | UNIVERSITY MEDICAL CENTER | | |
| | | | | PHYSICIANS | | |
	(1) *Psychiatrists*	*(2)* *Nurses and attendants*	*(3)* *Faculty*	*(4)* *"Looking for a psychiatrist"*	*(5)* *"Looking for an internist"*	*(6)* *No additional comment*
Responses						
Moves on, head averted(%)	71	88	0	0	0	0
Makes eye contact (%)	23	10	0	11	0	0
Pauses and chats (%)	2	2	0	11	0	10
Stops and talks (%)	4	0.5	100	78	100	90
Mean number of questions						
answered (out of 6)	*	*	6	3.8	4.8	4.5
Respondents (No.)	13	47	14	18	15	10
Attempts (No.)	185	1283	14	18	15	10

* *Not applicable.*

attendants (column 2). Minor differences between these four institutions were overwhelmed by the degree to which staff avoided continuing contacts that patients had initiated. By far, their most common response consisted of either a brief response to the question, offered while they were "on the move" and with head averted, or no response at all.

The encounter frequently took the following bizarre form: (pseudopatient) "Pardon me, Dr. X. Could you tell me when I am eligible for grounds privileges?" (physician) "Good morning, Dave. How are you today?" (Moves off without waiting for a response).

It is instructive to compare these data with data recently obtained at Stanford University. It has been alleged that large and eminent universities are characterized by faculty who are so busy that they have no time for students. For this comparison, a young lady approached individual faculty members who seemed to be walking purposefully to some meeting or teaching engagement and asked them the following six questions.

1) "Pardon me, could you direct me to Encina Hall?" (at the medical school: ". . . to the Clinical Research Center?").

2) "Do you know where Fish Annex is?" (there is no Fish Annex at Stanford).

3) "Do you teach here?"

4) "How does one apply for admission to the college?" (at the medical school: ". . . to the medical school?").

5) "Is it difficult to get in?"

6) "Is there financial aid?"

Without exception, as can be seen in Table 1 (column 3), all of the questions were answered. No matter how rushed they were, all respondents not only maintained eye contact, but stopped to talk. Indeed, many of the respondents went out of their way to direct or take the questioner to the office she was seeking, to try to locate "Fish Annex," or to discuss with her the possibilities of being admitted to the university.

Similar data, also shown in Table 1 (columns 4, 5, and 6), were obtained in the hospital. Here too, the young lady came prepared with six questions. After the first question, however, she remarked to 18 of her respondents (column 4), "I'm looking for a psychiatrist," and to 15 others (column 5), "I'm looking for an internist," Ten other respondents received no inserted comment (column 6). The general degree of cooperative responses is considerably higher for these university groups than it was for pseudopatients in psychiatric hospitals. Even so, differences are apparent within the medical school setting. Once having indicated that she was looking for a psychiatrist, the degree of cooperation elicited was less than when she sought an internist.

Powerlessness and Depersonalization

Eye contact and verbal contact reflect concern and individuation; their absence, avoidance and depersonalization. The data I have presented do not do justice to the rich daily encounters that grew up around matters of depersonalization and avoidance. I have records of patients who were beaten by staff for the sin of having initiated verbal contact. During my own experience, for example, one patient was beaten in the presence of other patients for having approached an attendant and told him, "I like you." Occasionally, punishment meted out to patients for misdemeanors seemed so excessive that it could not be justified by the most radical interpretations of psychiatric canons. Nevertheless, they appeared to go unquestioned. Tempers were often short. A patient who had not heard a call for medication would be roundly excoriated, and the morning attendants would often wake patients with, "Come on, you m——f——s, out of bed!"

Neither anecdotal nor "hard" data can convey the overwhelming sense of powerlessness which invades the individual as he is continually exposed to the depersonalization of the psychiatric hospital. It hardly matters *which* psychiatric hospital—the excellent public ones and the very plush private hospital were better than the rural and shabby ones in this regard, but, again, the features that psychiatric hospitals had in common overwhelmed by far their apparent differences.

Powerlessness was evident everywhere. The patient is deprived of many of his legal rights by dint of his psychiatric commitment.[21] He is shorn of credibility by virtue of his psychiatric label. His freedom of movement is restricted. He cannot initiate contact with the staff, but may only respond to such overtures as they make. Personal privacy is minimal. Patient quarters and possessions can be entered and examined by any staff member, for whatever reason. His personal history and anguish is available to any staff member (often including the "grey lady" and "candy striper" volunteer) who chooses to read his folder, regardless of their therapeutic relationship to him. His personal hygiene and waste evacuation are often monitored. The water closets may have no doors.

At times, depersonalization reached such proportions that pseudopatients had the sense that they were invisible, or at least unworthy of account. Upon being admitted, I and other pseudopatients took the initial physical examinations in a semipublic room, where staff members went about their own business as if we were not there.

On the ward, attendants delivered verbal and occasionally serious physical abuse to patients in the presence of other observing patients, some of whom (the pseudopatients) were writing it all down. Abusive behavior, on the other hand, terminated quite abruptly when other staff members were known to be coming. Staff are credible witnesses. Patients are not.

A nurse unbuttoned her uniform to adjust her brassiere in the presence of an entire ward of viewing men. One did not have the sense that she was being seductive. Rather, she didn't notice us. A group of staff persons might point to a patient in the dayroom and discuss him animatedly, as if he were not there.

One illuminating instance of depersonalization and invisibility occurred with regard to medications. All told, the pseudopatients were administered nearly 2100 pills, including Elavil, Stelazine, Compazine, and Thorazine, to name but a few. (That such a variety of medications should have been administered to patients presenting identical symptoms is itself worthy of note.) Only two were swallowed. The rest were either pocketed or deposited in the toilet. The pseudopatients were not alone in this. Although I have no precise records on how many patients rejected their medications, the pseudopatients frequently found the medications of other patients in the toilet before they deposited their own. As long as they were cooperative, their behavior and the pseudopatients' own in this matter, as in other important matters, went unnoticed throughout.

Reactions to such depersonalization among pseudopatients were intense. Although they had come to the hospital as participant observers and were fully aware that they did not "belong," they nevertheless found themselves caught up in and fighting the process of depersonalization. Some examples: a graduate student in psychology asked his wife to bring his textbooks to the hospital so he could "catch up on his homework"—this despite the elaborate precautions taken to conceal his professional association. The same student, who had trained for quite some time to get into the hospital, and who had looked forward to the experience, "remembered" some drag races that he had wanted to see on the weekend and insisted that he be discharged by that time. Another pseudopatient attempted a romance with a nurse. Subsequently, he informed the staff that he was applying for admission to graduate school in psychology and was very likely to be admitted, since a graduate professor was one of his regular hospital visitors. The same person began to engage in psychotherapy with other patients—all of this as a way of becoming a person in an impersonal environment.

The Sources of Depersonalization

What are the origins of depersonalization? I have already mentioned two. First are attitudes held by all of us toward the mentally ill—including those who treat them—attitudes characterized by fear, distrust, and horrible expectations on the one hand, and benevolent intentions on the other. Our ambivalence leads, in this instance as in others, to avoidance.

Second, and not entirely separate, the hierarchical structure of the psychiatric hospital facilitates depersonalization. Those who are at the top have least to do with patients, and their behavior inspires the rest of the staff. Average daily contact with psychiatrists, psychologists, residents, and physicians combined ranged from 3.9 to 25.1 minutes, with an overall mean of 6.8 (six pseudopatients over a total of 129 days of hospitalization). Included in this average are time spent in the admissions interview, ward meetings in the presence of a senior staff member, group and individual psychotherapy contacts, case presentation conferences, and discharge meetings. Clearly, patients do not spend much time in interpersonal contact with doctoral staff. And doctoral staff serve as models for nurses and attendants.

There are probably other sources. Psychiatric installations are presently in serious financial straits. Staff shortages are pervasive, staff time at a premium. Something has to give, and that something is patient contact. Yet, while financial stresses are realities, too much can be made of them. I have the impression that the psychological forces that result in depersonalization are much stronger than the fiscal ones and that the addition of more staff would not correspondingly improve patient care in this regard. The incidence of staff meetings and the enormous amount of record-keeping on patients, for example, have not been as substantially reduced as has patient contact. Priorities exist, even during hard times. Patient contact is not a significant priority in the traditional psychiatric hospital, and fiscal pressures do not account for this. Avoidance and depersonalization may.

Heavy reliance upon psychotropic medication tacitly contributes to depersonalization by convincing staff that treatment is indeed being conducted and that further patient contact may not be necessary. Even here, however, caution needs to be exercised in understanding the role of psychotropic drugs. If patients were powerful rather than powerless, if they were viewed as interesting individuals rather than diagnostic entities, if they were socially significant rather than social lepers, if their anguish truly and wholly compelled our sympathies and concerns, would we not *seek* contact with them, despite the availability of medications? Perhaps for the pleasure of it all?

The Consequences of Labeling and Depersonalization

Whenever the ratio of what is known to what needs to be known approaches zero, we tend to invent "knowledge'' and assume that we understand more than we actually do. We seem unable to acknowledge that we simply don't know. The needs for diagnosis and remediation of behavioral and emotional problems are enormous. But rather than acknowledge that we are just embarking on understanding, we continue to label patients ''schizophrenic,'' ''manic-depressive,'' and ''insane,'' as if in those words we had captured the essence of understanding. The facts of the matter are that we have known for a long time that diagnoses are often not useful or reliable, but we have nevertheless continued to use them. We now know that we cannot distinguish insanity from sanity. It is depressing to consider how that information will be used.

Not merely depressing, but frightening. How many people, one wonders, are sane but not recognized as such in our psychiatric institutions? How many have been needlessly stripped of their privileges of citizenship, from the right to vote and drive to that of handling their own accounts? How many have feigned insanity in order to avoid the criminal consequences of their behavior, and, conversely, how many would rather stand trial than live interminably in a psychiatric hospital—but are wrongly thought to be mentally ill? How many have been stigmatized by well-intentioned, but nevertheless erroneous, diagnoses? On the last point, recall again that a ''type 2 error'' in psychiatric diagnosis does not have the same consequences it does in medical diagnosis. A diagnosis of cancer that has been found to be in error is cause for celebration. But psychiatric diagnoses are rarely found to be in error. The label sticks, a mark of inadequacy forever.

Finally, how many patients might be ''sane'' outside the psychiatric hospital but seem insane in it—not because craziness resides in them, as it were, but because they are responding to a bizarre setting, one that may be unique to institutions which harbor nether people? Goffman[4] calls the process of socialization to such institutions ''mortification''—an apt metaphor that includes the processes of depersonalization that have been described here. And while it is impossible to know whether the pseudopatients' responses to these processes are characteristic of all inmates—they were, after all, not real patients—it is difficult to believe that these processes of socialization to a psychiatric hospital provide useful attitudes or habits of response for living in the ''real world.''

Summary and Conclusions

It is clear that we cannot distinguish the sane from the insane in psychiatric hospitals. The hospital itself imposes a special environment in which the meanings of behavior can easily be misunderstood. The conse-quences to patients hospitalized in such an environment—the powerlessness, depersonalization, segregation, mortification, and self-labeling—seem undoubtedly countertherapeutic.

I do not, even now, understand this problem well enough to perceive solutions. But two matters seem to have some promise. The first concerns the proliferation of community mental health facilities, of crisis intervention centers, of the human potential movement, and of behavior therapies that, for all of their own problems, tend to avoid psychiatric labels, to focus on specific problems and behaviors, and to retain the individual in a relatively nonpejorative environment. Clearly, to the extent that we refrain from sending the distressed to insane places, our impressions of them are less likely to be distorted. (The risk of distorted perceptions, it seems to me, is always present, since we are much more sensitive to an individual's behaviors and verbalizations than we are to the subtle contextual stimuli that often promote them. At issue here is a matter of magnitude. And, as I have shown, the magnitude of distortion is exceedingly high in the extreme context that is a psychiatric hospital.)

The second matter that might prove promising speaks to the need to increase the sensitivity of mental health workers and researchers to the *Catch 22* position of psychiatric patients. Simply reading materials in this area will be of help to some such workers and researchers. For others, directly experiencing the impact of psychiatric hospitalization will be of enormous use. Clearly, further research into the social psychology of such total institutions will both facilitate treatment and deepen understanding.

I and the other pseudopatients in the psychiatric setting had distinctly negative reactions. We do not pretend to describe the subjective experiences of true patients. Theirs may be different from ours, particularly with the passage of time and the necessary process of adaptation to one's environment. But we can and do speak to the relatively more objective indices of treatment within the hospital. It could be a mistake, and a very unfortunate one, to consider that what happened to us derived from malice or stupidity on the part of the staff. Quite the contrary, our overwhelming impression of them was of people who really cared, who were committed and who were uncommonly intelligent. Where they failed, as they sometimes did painfully, it would be more accurate to attribute those failures to the environment in which they, too, found themselves than to personal callousness. Their perceptions and behavior were controlled by the situation, rather than being motivated by a malicious disposition. In a more benign environment, one that was less attached to global diagnosis, their behaviors and judgments might have been more benign and effective.

REFERENCES AND NOTES

1. P. Ash, *J. Abnorm. Soc. Psychol.* **44**, 272 (1949); A. T. Beck, *Amer. J. Psychiat.* **119**, 210 (1962); A. T. Boisen, *Psychiatry* **2**, 233 (1938); N. Kreitman, *J. Ment. Sci.* **107**, 876 (1961); N. Kreitman, P. Sainsbury, J. Morrisey, J. Towers, J. Scrivener, *ibid.*, p. 887; H. O. Schmitt and C. P. Fonda, *J. Abnorm. Soc. Psychol.* **52**, 262 (1956); W. Seeman, *J. Nerv. Ment. Dis.* **118**, 541 (1953). For an analysis of these artifacts and summaries of the disputes, see J. Zubin, *Annu. Rev. Psychol.* **18**, 373 (1967); L. Phillips and J. G. Draguns, *ibid.* **22**, 447 (1971).

2. R. Benedict, *J. Gen. Psychol.* **10**, 59 (1934).

3. See in this regard H. Becker, *Outsiders: Studies in the Sociology of Deviance* (Free Press, New York, 1963); B. M. Braginsky, D. D. Braginsky, K. Ring, *Methods of Madness: The Mental Hospital as a Last Resort* (Holt, Rinehart & Winston, New York, 1969); G. M. Crocetti and P. V. Lemkau, *Amer. Sociol. Rev.* **30**, 577 (1965); E. Goffman, *Behavior in Public Places* (Free Press, New York, 1964); R. D. Laing, *The Divided Self: A Study of Sanity and Madness* (Quadrangle, Chicago, 1960); D. L. Phillips, *Amer. Sociol. Rev.* **28**, 963 (1963); T. R. Sarbin, *Psychol. Today* **6**, 18 (1972); E. Schur, *Amer. J. Sociol.* **75**, 309 (1969); T. Szasz, *Law, Liberty and Psychiatry* (Macmillan, New York, 1963); *The Myth of Mental Illness: Foundations of a Theory of Mental Illness* (Hoeber Harper, New York, 1963). For a critique of some of these views, see W. R. Gove, *Amer. Sociol. Rev.* **35**, 873 (1970).

4. E. Goffman, *Asylums* (Doubleday, Garden City, N.Y., 1961).

5. T. J. Scheff, *Being Mentally Ill: A Sociological Theory* (Aldine, Chicago, 1966).

6. Data from a ninth pseudopatient are not incorporated in this report because, although his sanity went undetected, he falsified aspects of his personal history, including his marital status and parental relationships. His experimental behaviors therefore were not identical to those of the other pseudopatients.

7. A. Barry, *Bellevue Is a State of Mind* (Harcourt Brace Jovanovich, New York, 1971); I. Belknap, *Human Problems of a State Mental Hospital* (McGraw-Hill, New York, 1956); W. Caudill, F. C. Redlich, H. R. Gilmore, E. B. Brody, *Amer. J. Orthopsychiat.* **22**, 314 (1952); A. R. Goldman, R. H. Bohr, T. A. Steinberg, *Prof. Psychol.* **1**, 427 (1970); unauthored, *Roche Report* **1** (No. 13), **8** (1971).

8. Beyond the personal difficulties that the pseudopatient is likely to experience in the hospital, there are legal and social ones that, combined, require considerable attention before entry. For example, once admitted to a psychiatric institution, it is difficult, if not impossible, to be discharged on short notice, state law to the contrary notwithstanding. I was not sensitive to these difficulties at the outset of the project, nor to the personal and situational emergencies that can arise, but later a writ of habeas corpus was prepared for each of the entering pseudopatients and an attorney was kept "on call" during every hospitalization. I am grateful to John Kaplan and Robert Bartels for legal advice and assistance in these matters.

9. However distasteful such concealment is, it was a necessary first step to examining these questions. Without concealment, there would have been no way to know how valid these experiences were; nor was there any way of knowing whether whatever detections occurred were a tribute to the diagnostic acumen of the staff or to the hospital's rumor network. Obviously, since my concerns are general ones that cut across individual hospitals and staffs, I have respected their anonymity and have eliminated clues that might lead to their identification.

10. Interestingly, of the 12 admissions, 11 were diagnosed as schizophrenic and one, with the identical symptomatology, as manic-depressive psychosis. This diagnosis has a more favorable prognosis, and it was given by the only private hospital in our sample. On the relations between social class and psychiatric diagnosis, see A. B. Hollingshead and F. C. Redlich, *Social Class and Mental Illness: A Community Study* (Wiley, New York, 1958).

11. It is possible, of course, that patients have quite broad latitudes in diagnosis and therefore are inclined to call many people sane, even those whose behavior is patently aberrant. However, although we have no hard data on this matter, it was our distinct impression that this was not the case. In many instances, patients not only singled us out for attention, but came to imitate our behaviors and styles.

12. J. Cumming and E. Cumming, *Community Ment. Health* **1**, 135 (1965); A. Farina and K. Ring, *J. Abnorm. Psychol.* **70**, 47 (1965); H. E. Freeman and O. G. Simmons, *The Mental Patient Comes Home* (Wiley, New York, 1963); W. J. Johannsen, *Ment. Hygiene* **53**, 218 (1969); A. S. Linsky, *Soc. Psychiat.* **5**, 166 (1970).

13. S. E. Asch, *J. Abnorm. Soc. Psychol.* **41**, 258 (1946); *Social Psychology* (Prentice-Hall, New York, 1952).

14. See also I. N. Mensh and J. Wishner, *J. Personality* **16**, 188 (1947); J. Wishner, *Psychol. Rev.* **67**, 96 (1960); J. S. Bruner and R. Tagiuri, in *Handbook of Social Psychology*, G. Lindzey, Ed. (Addison-Wesley, Cambridge, Mass., 1954), vol. 2, pp. 634–654; J. S. Bruner, D. Shapiro, R. Tagiuri, in *Person Perception and Interpersonal Behavior*, R. Tagiuri and L. Petrullo, Eds. (Stanford Univ. Press, Stanford, Calif., 1958), pp. 277–288.

15. For an example of a similar self-fulfilling prophecy, in this instance dealing with the "central" trait of intelligence, see R. Rosenthal and L. Jacobson, *Pygmalion in the Classroom* (Holt, Rinehart & Winston, New York, 1968).

16. E. Zigler and L. Phillips, *J. Abnorm. Soc. Psychol.* **63**, 69
    (1961). See also R. K. Freudenberg and J. P. Robertson,
    A.M.A. Arch. Neurol. Psychiatr. **76**, 14 (1956).
17. W. Mischel, *Personality and Assessment* (Wiley, New
    York, 1968).
18. The most recent and unfortunate instance of this tenet is that
    of Senator Thomas Eagleton.
19. T. R. Sarbin and J. C. Mancuso, *J. Clin. Consult. Psychol.*
    35, 159 (1970); T. R. Sarbin, *ibid.* **31**, 447 (1967); J. C.

Nunnally, Jr., *Popular Conceptions of Mental Health*
(Holt, Rinehart & Winston, New York, 1961).
20. A. H. Stanton and M. S. Schwartz, *The Mental Hospital: A
    Study of Institutional Participation in Psychiatric Illness
    and Treatment* (Basic, New York, 1954).
21. D. B. Wexler and S. E. Scoville, *Ariz. Law Rev.* **13**, 1
    (1971).
22. I thank W. Mischel, E. Orne, and M. S. Rosenhan for
    comments on an earlier draft of this manuscript.

DAVID L. ROSENHAN

The Contextual Nature of Psychiatric Diagnosis

One might imagine that the criticisms of "On Being Sane in Insane Places" (Rosenhan, 1973a) that have appeared here and elsewhere had quite exhausted the matter, but that is not the case. There is, in my view, yet another criticism that can be offered of that work, one that may be harsher than those printed here, and one that sets the current reaction into a comprehensible context. Stated vigorously, it is this:

"On Being Sane in Insane Places" is a negative work. It tells what is wrong with treatment and diagnosis, without telling how it might be improved. It asks us to abandon traditional psychiatric diagnosis without telling us what will replace it. It tells those who have labored to improve psychiatric care that their efforts are grossly insufficient, without offering alternatives of demonstrated value. It tells the mental health professional, on whose overworked back the burdens of mankind's anguishes fall, that even the little he can do by way of

Reprinted from the *Journal of Abnormal Psychology*, Vol. **84**, No. 5 (1975), pages 462–474, by permission of the author and publisher.

An earlier draft of this paper, entitled "The Paradigm Crisis in Psychiatric Diagnosis," was circulated to colleagues and friends, among them many who do not share my point of view. The present paper owes much to their comments and observations. Without holding them responsible for the product, I acknowledge the comments of Lee J. Cronbach, William DeJong, Peggy Thoits Doyle, Leonard Eron, Floyd M. Estess, Laurie Klein Evans, Arnold J. Friedhoff, Raquel Gur, Ruben Gur, Dillon Inouye, Seymour S. Kety, Donald F. Klein, Perry London, Theodore Millon, Loren R. Mosher, Martin T. Orne, Jerome V. Rose, Mollie S. Rosenhan, Theodore Sarbin, and Jack Zusman, as well as one reviewer who requested anonymity. This work was supported in part by a grant from K. and H. Montgomery.

diagnosis and treatment is unworthy and wrong. It even suggests that, given our current state of knowledge, symptom diagnoses may be better than syndrome diagnoses, although that suggestion is no better supported by research data than are traditional diagnoses. It suggests that the context created by the psychiatric hospital colors our perception of psychiatric patients, but it does not tell us in what way we can deal with that problem. It leaves scientists and practitioners in the lurch urging them to abandon the little they have by way of hospital treatment and diagnosis without providing them alternative tools. It would destroy a paradigm without providing an alternative. In short, it is work half done.

There is little defense against that criticism, little comfort for the anguish it expresses and the anger it conveys. That the implications of context are presently revamping large segments of personality theory, social psychology, psycholinguistics, memory, and perception is barely solace to the working clinician. The fact that my colleagues and I recognize that the work is not yet done, the fact that we have not rested, nor do we intend to rest, is again no consolation for the clinician who needs tools now. Until compelling alternatives are found, one can have little difficulty understanding those who fight mightily, even angrily, to retain current beliefs. Those beliefs were not earned without sweat in training, research, and on the clinical firing line.

Transitional eras are difficult. That seemingly endless period of time that lies between our awareness of serious shortcomings in our current views and the discovery and application of more fruitful conceptions is a breeding time for intense and conflictful emotions. But the fact is that our growing appreciation of the role that contexts play in a variety of psychological areas—a role that I will elaborate on shortly—promises improvement for the understanding, diagnosis, and treatment of psychological distress. In the final analysis, it is with that improvement that our aspirations lie. More than that, our personal appreciation of the role of context may serve to insulate us against the needless defensiveness that naturally arises during this transition period. It was with this understanding in mind that I earlier wrote:

> It would be a mistake and a very unfortunate one, to consider that what happened to us derived from malice or stupidity on the part of the staff. Quite the contrary, our overwhelming impression of them was of people who really cared, who were committed, and who were uncommonly intelligent. Where they failed, as they sometimes did painfully, it would be more accurate to attribute those failures to the environment in which they, too, found themselves than to personal callousness. Their perceptions and behavior were controlled by the situation, rather than being motivated by malicious disposition. In a more benign environment, one that was less attached to global diagnosis, their behaviors and judgments might have been more benign and effective. (Rosenhan, 1973a, p. 257)

The Contextual Nature of Psychiatric Diagnosis

The studies of diagnosis with which we are concerned are best understood in terms of the influence of contexts on perceptions. Contexts shade and color meaning; in fact, they often determine meaning. A short person among pygmies may seem to be a giant. One who is 15 pounds overweight seems stuffed on a beach but svelte at an obesity clinic. A person whose hand is missing may look tragic among factory workers but nearly unimpaired among paraplegics. Thus, contexts are powerful.

The influence of contexts of mind (sets) and contexts of natural objects and behaviors (settings) on perception and action has been a constant theme of psychological research over the decades. Gestalt psychologists were concerned with them. Kurt Lewin and his intellectual heirs were absorbed by them. And modern psychologists in such diverse fields as psycholinguistics, memory, social psychology, and personology have pursued matters of context with considerable intellectual profit. Suffice it to say that the contexts created by such matters as person, place, gender, status, and era, not to speak of relational and analytic contexts, have enormous impact on the way stimuli are perceived.

A few examples will make these matters clear to those whose interests have not been in this area. Psycholinguists observe that even the words we use create significant contexts. The question "how short are you?" carries a different presuppositional load than the question "How tall are you?", even though both have identical concrete meaning (Clark, 1969). Loftus and Palmer (1974) have shown that the very questions we use in interrogating someone may determine the kinds of answers we get, not merely regarding opinion but to the very details of fact. Researchers in memory and cognition find that the latency for detecting "0" and "1" in a string of letters is considerably shorter if those stimuli are defined as numbers (zero and one) rather than letters (Jonides & Gleitman, 1972; see also Jenkins, 1974).

All stimuli seem amenable to contextual influence, but some are more amenable than others. Contextual influence is particularly strong when stimuli are ambiguous. Stimuli that are well articulated seem much more able to defy the influence of a surrounding field than those that are ill-defined. By way of example, Figure 1, adapted from Selfridge (1955), makes the matter very clear in the area of visual perception. Most people have no difficulty in recognizing the upper part of the figure as THE CAT, even though the A and the H are identically shaped. Indeed, some readers respond so rapidly to context that they are surprised when the similarity of the shape of the middle letter is pointed out. That does not occur in the lower half of the figure. There, the A is so well articulated that perceivers see the phrase as a spelling error, and may spend some considerable amount of time figuring out what the phrase was really supposed to say.

These powerful effects occur because neither memory nor perception are passive processes. They are active,

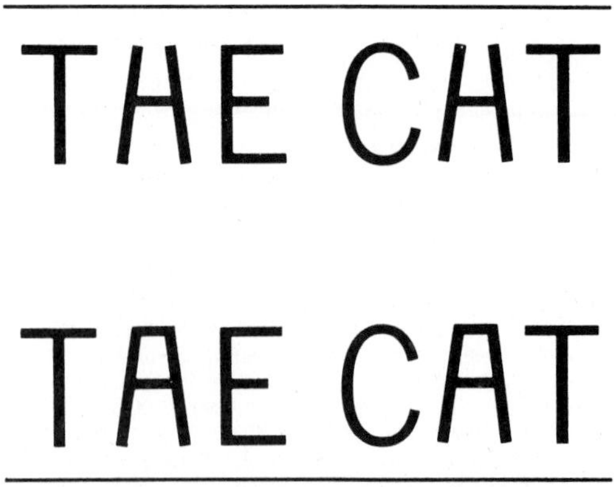

THE CAT

TAE CAT

FIGURE 1.   The influence of context on visual perception.

constructive ones in which the individual is swiftly and unwittingly processing, interpreting, construing, and reconstruing events that are observed. Seemingly small changes in context, conveyed by a word, an instruction, a setting, or even a gesture, greatly alter understanding. They affect what is retrieved from memory. They affect judgment. They affect perception. And they affect psychiatric judgment and perception no less than judgment and perception in other areas.

Psychiatric diagnoses imply that what the diagnostician sees is descriptive of the patient's condition. Much as a cancer patient has cancer, the psychiatric patient is schizophrenic or manic-depressive, no matter where he is seen. But human behavior, even distressed human behavior, is no less ambiguous than other ambiguous stimuli, and no less amenable to context-dependent interpretation. Moreover, with regard to distressed behavior, there is particular reason to believe that however deep one's belief that what is perceived is schizophrenia, that belief is by no means compelling. Another diagnostician, equally sure of his skill, may arrive at a quite different diagnosis. Indeed, if 35 years of studies on agreement among diagnosticians have taught us anything, it is that, despite subjective conviction and regardless of skill and training, coefficients of diagnostic agreement (K) between psychiatrists viewing the same behavior rarely exceed .8 (which, for purposes of individual diagnosis, is quite low[1]), are commonly in the range of .5, and can descend as low as .2. (For a recent summary of such studies, see Spitzer & Fleiss, 1974.) If anything attests to the ambiguity of such behavior and suggests the possibility that such behavior can be colored by contextual cues, these studies of agreement do.

There is yet another reason for believing that psychiatric diagnoses might be strongly influenced by contexts. Unlike most medical diagnoses, which can be validated in numerous ways, psychiatric diagnoses are maintained by consensus alone. This is not commonly known to either the consumer or the mental health profession. Spitzer and Wilson (in press) clarify the matter:

> In 1965 the American Psychiatric Association . . . assigned its Committee on Nomenclature and Statistics . . . the task of preparing for the APA a new diagnostic manual of disorders. . . . A draft of the new manual, DSM II, was

circulated in 1967 to 120 psychiatrists known to have special interests in the area of diagnosis and was revised on the basis of their criticisms and suggestions. After further study it was adopted by the APA in 1967, and published and officially accepted throughout the country in 1968.

Nothing underscores the consensual nature of psychiatric disorders more than the recent action by the American Psychiatric Association to delete homosexuality from the *Diagnostic and Statistical Manual on Mental Disorders* (DSM-II, 1968). Whatever one's opinion regarding the nature of homosexuality, the fact that a professional association could vote on whether or not homosexuality should be considered a disorder surely underscores both the differences between psychiatric/mental disorders and the context-susceptibility of psychiatric ones. Changes in informed public attitudes toward homosexuality have brought about corresponding changes in the psychiatric perception of it.

Sane in Insane Places

Turning now to the studies under review, it should be clear that if the contexts created by setting influence psychiatric perception, then sane people who enter a psychiatric hospital should be diagnosed with the common psychiatric designation for hospitalized patients (schizophrenia) even though their presenting symptoms in no way describe that disorder. Correspondingly, if the contexts created by set color psychiatric perception, then mental health professionals who expect to find pseudopatients on their ward should diagnose many true patients as pseudopatients.

Presenting Symptoms

Eight sane people[2] gained admission to 12 psychiatric hospitals by simulating a single symptom, hallucinations. These hallucinations had a special character. Their content had never been reported in the psychological literature. They were, by design, interesting auditory hallucinations that were perceived as a voice that said "empty," "dull," and "thud." It was intended that these hallucinations might lead an observer to suspect an interesting existential problem, as if these people were

---

1. "The acceptable risk depends on the type of decision being made. In individual decisions (particularly counseling), it is generally desirable to be conservative, seeking additional information rather than accepting a hazardous conclusion. When a terminal decision is under consideration, it appears reasonable to set the maximum risk as .10 or .05 meaning that 1 in 10, or 1 in 20 decisions could be wrong. An even lower level might be desired for an important decision that could not be reversed should it prove to be wrong in the light of later experience" (Cronbach & Gleser, 1959, p. 233).

2. The ambiguity of the term, mental illness, makes it difficult to find an unambiguous term that denotes its opposite. Mentally healthy, normal, and without severe psychological anguish all have difficulties of their own. I have chosen the words sane and insane to approximate the conditions I would describe. Many writers have correctly observed that these terms have legal connotations. But to my knowledge, all other terms have greater disadvantages.

looking back over their lives and characterizing them as empty and dull. They were designed primarily to get the pseudopatients into the hospital.

Hallucinations, however, were not the only symptom that was presented. Behavioral nervousness was another. Some of the pseudopatients had had only fleeting prior contact with psychiatric hospitals. Others, even though they had been employed there, were nevertheless nervous. Some of the nervousness appeared to arise from a fear of being unmasked. Some of it had its source in a fear of the familiar unknown: Although several had worked in psychiatric hospitals, they had neither been there as patients nor spent much time there at night or during the weekends. Their vantage point was commonly from behind the desk or in the nurses' station. Nothing underscored their vulnerability to forces outside their control more than their impending hospitalization as pseudopatients. Nervousness, then, was unintended but also unavoidable.

For most of the pseudopatients, then, these two symptoms—plus the fact that they showed up at the hospital in the first place—constitute the entirety of their deception. These symptoms, of course, do not in any way constitute schizophrenia. That was not the intention. They were simply intended to be sufficient to get them into the hospital. Beyond the simulation of hallucinations and some concomitant nervousness, no further alteration of history or circumstances was made. The significant events of the pseudopatients' life histories were presented as they had occurred. Relationships with parents and siblings, with spouse and children, and with people at work and in school were described as they were or had been. Despite the absence of abnormal indications beyond those described, 11 of the pseudopatients were diagnosed, initially and finally, paranoid schizophrenia, and the 12th was diagnosed manic-depressive psychosis.

Thus, set and setting, the contexts of mind and environment, heavily determine psychiatric diagnosis. But insofar as set is heavily permeated with expectation, it should prove at least partially reversible. An experiment was arranged at a hospital where the staff had heard these findings but doubted that such an error could occur in their institution. Each staff member rated every patient who appeared at admissions or on the ward according to the likelihood that the patient was a pseudopatient. Judgments were obtained on 193 patients who were admitted for psychiatric treatment. Forty-one patients were alleged, with high confidence, to be pseudopatients by at least one member of the staff, 23 patients were considered suspect by at least one psychiatrist, and 19 were suspected by one psychiatrist and one other staff member. The pseudopatient who was designated for this hospital became ill and never entered. Thus the obtained data are for real patients.

Both studies confirm the view that the contexts of mind and setting color psychiatric perceptions, and there are others that make the same point. Temerlin (1968), for example, has shown that comments about a patient from a prestigious source have remarkable effects on how he is perceived. From a tape recorded interview, a doctor described a patient as interesting "because he looks neurotic, but actually is quite psychotic." The group of psychiatrists, clinical psychologists, and graduate clinical psychology students who heard this comment rated the interviewee as emotionally ill significantly more often than the controls who had either not heard the suggestion or had heard it reversed.

A study by Langer and Abelson (1974) deals with the same issue. A videotaped interview of a young man describing his job history and difficulties was presented to clinicians who were known to have either a behavioral or a traditional psychodynamic viewpoint. Half of the clinicians were told that the young man was a job applicant, whereas the remaining half were told that he was a patient. The clinicians' evaluations of the subject were quantified on a scale that ranged from 1 (very disturbed), through a midpoint, to 10 (very well adjusted). Those words, job applicant and patient, formed entirely different contexts for these judgments among traditional diagnosticians. Enormous differences were found in their judgment of the subject's adjustment according to whether the identical tape was presented as a patient interview ($\bar{X} = 3.47$) or a job interview ($\bar{X} = 6.2$). The more traditional the orientation of the clinician, the larger the difference was.

Proper Diagnoses

What are the proper diagnoses for people (a) who manifest some nervousness, complain of hallucinations, and nothing else, (b) whose personal histories betray no sign of severe psychological distress, (c) whose relationships are basically unimpaired, (d) who have never in the past given evidence of severe psychological disorders, and (e) who apparently have nothing to gain from malingering and for whom there is no evidence of malingering?

It should be noted that no party to this debate denies that the diagnoses that were actually given to the pseudopatients were erroneous. Spitzer (1975) directly expresses the hope that, had he examined one of the pseudopatients, "I would have been struck by the lack of other signs of the disorder." Both Spitzer (1975) and Weiner (1975) go to great lengths to exonerate the diagnosticians, but all agree that the diagnoses were wrong. I agree with them and with Millon (1975) that the fault lies not with the diagnosticians but elsewhere. We shall take up this matter at greater length later. For the moment, let us note our agreement that the diagnoses were wrong.

The central issue regarding diagnosis needs to be understood (see Rosenhan, 1973b, 1973c). The issue is not that the pseudopatients lied or that the psychiatrists believed them. The pseudopatients should not have been diagnosed Munchausen disease or Ganser syndrome— diagnoses that imply that the psychiatrists understood that the patients were feigning a symptom. Such diagnoses take much more evidence than can typically be assembled in an admissions interview. The issue is not whether the pseudopatients should have been admitted to the psychiatric hospital in the first place. If there were beds, admitting the pseudopatients was the only humane thing to do.

The issue is the diagnostic leap that was made between a single presenting symptom, hallucination, and the diagnosis, schizophrenia (or, in one case, manic-depressive psychosis). That is the heart of the matter. Had the pseudopatient been diagnosed hallucinating, there would have been no further needs to examine the diagnostic issue. The diagnosis of hallucinations implies only that: no more. The presence of a hallucination does not itself define the presence of schizophrenia and schizophrenia may or may not include hallucinations.

Lest the matter reduce to one scientist's word against others', let us examine the standard for diagnosis in psychiatry, the DSM−II:

> 295. Schizophrenia. This large category includes a group of disorders manifested by characteristic disturbances of thinking, mood, and behavior. Disturbances in thinking are marked by alterations of concept formation which may lead to misinterpretation of reality and sometimes to delusions and hallucinations, which frequently appear psychologically self-protective. Corollary mood changes include ambivalence, constricted and inappropriate emotional responsiveness and loss of empathy with others. Behavior may be withdrawn, regressive and bizarre.
>
> 295.3 Schizophrenia, paranoid type . . . characterized primarily by the presence of persecutory or grandiose delusions, often associated with hallucinations. Excessive religiosity is sometimes seen. The patient's attitude is frequently hostile and aggressive, and his behavior tends to be consistent with his delusions. (pp. 33−34)

But what then is the proper diagnosis for such complaints as the pseudopatients presented? I suggest the following: Hallucinations, hallucinations of unknown origin, ?, or DD (diagnosis deferred). Millon points out that the diagnosis of hallucinations of unknown origin is fraught with contextual difficulties. There is merit in his view, and I hold no special brief for that diagnosis. Certainly it is not the ultimate diagnosis. But it may very well be the one that reflects the present state of our knowledge better than traditional nosology does. Indeed, at present, my own preference runs to omitting diagnoses entirely, for it is far better from a scientific and treatment point of view to acknowledge ignorance than to mystify it with diagnoses that are unreliable, overly broad, and pejoratively connotative.

Criticisms

Paranoid Schizophrenia: "The Most Likely Condition"?

Much of Spitzer's (1975) critique consists of the justification of the diagnosis of schizophrenia.

> Unfortunately . . . many readers, including psychiatrists, were, in my judgment, wrong in accepting Rosenhan's thesis that it was irrational for the psychiatrists to have made an initial diagnosis of schizophrenia as *the most likely condition* on the basis of a single symptom. (p. 445)

He rules out alcohol, drug abuse, organic causes, or toxic psychosis as the cause of the hallucination. He rules out affective psychosis. The evidence, he says, does not support "hysterical psychosis," and there was no reason to believe that the illness was feigned. Spitzer writes:

> Dear reader: There is only one remaining diagnosis for the presenting symptom of hallucinations under these conditions in the classification of mental disorders used in this country and that is schizophrenia. (p. 446)

This is, of course, diagnosis by exclusion. And it makes schizophrenia a wastebasket diagnosis, a designation to be applied when nothing else fits. One would not have judged as much from the quotation offered above from the DSM−II, but perhaps in practice (and with sanction) it is. If that is the case, readers will judge for themselves whether the designation is useful, whether it constitutes a diagnosis in any sense of that term, and how likely it is for misdiagnoses to occur under such conditions.

It should now be clear that it is not the psychiatrists who diagnosed the pseudopatients but "the classification of mental disorders used in this country" (Spitzer, 1975) that is being questioned by these data. That question is supported by data from others. Ward, Beck, Mendelson, Mock, and Erbaugh (1962), in a study of diagnostic disagreement, found that inadequacy of the diagnostic nosology accounted for 62.5% of the reasons for disagreement, and another 32.5% was accounted for by inconsistency on the part of the diagnostician. Despite the attempts of the DSM−II to elaborate the symptomology associated with each presumed disorder, behaviors are too variable and their meanings too dependent on contextual perception for them to be captured under the rubrics proposed by the DSM−II. The very ambiguity of behavior, the fact that its meanings are not automatically transparent, defeats such attempts at classification from the outset, at least within the psychiatric hospital.

If anything, Spitzer's comments regarding schizophrenia as "the most likely condition," support the general views that were propounded in "On Being Sane in Insane Places" (Rosenhan, 1973a). Acknowledging that the diagnosis of paranoid schizophrenia was an error in 11 out of 11 instances (recall that the 12th was diagnosed manic-depressive psychosis, a diagnosis that amounts to the same error for these purposes), Spitzer offers some illuminating insights regarding how such a patient error might nevertheless have been made. I have no disagreement with him on this score. Indeed, I concur heartily. But I emphasize, as I did in the original article, that "any diagnostic process that lends itself so readily to massive errors of this sort cannot be a very reliable one" (Rosenhan, 1973a, p. 252).

Attribution and logical analyses. The foregoing should clarify why neither attribution theory nor logical analysis (Weiner, 1975) justify the observed findings. Attribution theory is a theory of error. It is, as Heider (1958) stated, a naive psychology, one that accounts for why people might believe that the world is flat, that heavy stones fall faster than light ones, or that the sun rises in the east and sets in the west—even in the face of contrary evidence. But diagnosis should be based on scientific evidence and careful assessment of facts, not on the attributional inferences of naive observers. Indeed, Weiner's observations, like Spitzer's, support the view put forth in "On Being Sane in Insane Places" (Rosenhan, 1973a) by telling us precisely how (and how easily) psychiatric diagnosis goes astray. The present system of psychiatric diagnosis lends itself too easily to attributional errors. It needs seriously to be questioned.

In Remission Does Not Mean Sane

Spitzer (1975) points out that the designation "in remission" is exceedingly rare. It occurs in only a handful of cases in the hospitals he surveyed, and my own cursory investigations that were stimulated by his, confirm these observations. His data are intrinsically interesting as well as interesting for the meaning they have for this particular study. How shall they be understood?

Once again we return to the influence of context on psychiatric perception. Consider two people who show no evidence of psychopathology. One is called sane and the other is called paranoid schizophrenic, in remission. Are both characterizations synonymous? Of course not. Would it matter to you if on one occasion you were designated normal, and on the other you were called psychotic, in remission, with both designations arising from the identical behavior? Of course it would matter. The perception of an asymptomatic status implies little by itself; it is the context in which that perception is embedded that tells the significant story.

It is useful to observe here that the term "in remission" was used as the most conservative designation for patients' discharge diagnoses. Actually, eight of the patients were discharged in remission, three as improved, and one as asymptomatic. The latter two designations imply less of a perception of change than does the phrase in remission. But all three descriptors reify the original diagnosis. They do not imply that the diagnosis was wrong or questionable, or that over the course of the hospitalization behaviors that are inconsistent with the diagnosis of schizophrenia were observed which suggested that the diagnosis might have been an error. Nothing altered the original diagnosis. Diagnostic labels, once applied, have a stickiness of their own.

It is, in fact, a very painful commentary on the state of this healing art that, at best, only a handful of patients are discharged from psychiatric hospitals in remission, no longer ill, recovered, or asymptomatic. Because if these designations are rarely used, how much rarer must the designation "cured" be? And yet, one wonders. The literature on reactive schizophrenia conveys the impression of far greater success than is implied by Spitzer's discharge data. Could it be that we are not seeing something? Could it be that the psychiatric hospital holds many more recovered, improved, and no longer ill people who have been designated schizophrenic than our context-bound perceptions allow us to see? It is not a question that I can answer here, but it surely is one that is worthy of careful consideration.

Experimenter Bias

Is it possible that experimenter bias infected the admissions and hospitalization procedures in such a way as to guarantee one particular outcome over another? If that is the case, then both Millon and Spitzer may be correct describing the findings as trivial. Millon states it directly:

> At best, it supports the following rather trivial finding: Confederates of an experimenter who know the hypothesis being tested and who feign being psychologically disturbed, consistent with that hypothesis, will temporarily deceive unsuspecting clinicians accustomed to working in mental institutions. (p. 457)

Spitzer says that the study:

> proves that pseudopatients are not detected by psychiatrists as having simulated signs of mental illness. This rather unremarkable finding is not relevant to the real problems of reliability and validity of psychiatric diagnosis and only serves to obscure them. (p. 451)

Are they correct?

The possibility of experimenter bias cannot be dismissed. Its manifestations are legion, and many of the subtle ways by which it is communicated are as yet unknown (cf. Rosenthal, 1966). But both the history and conduct of this project, as well as an examination of the notion of experimenter bias as it might apply here, is reassuring in this regard.

This project began as, and continues to be, an investigation of the care and perception of patients in the environments in which such care occurs. Utilizing the disciplined observation technologies of social psychology and anthropology, its concern is not primarily with diagnosis but only with diagnosis as it affects perception of patients and the nature and quality of their care.

In seeking admission to psychiatric hospitals, the pseudopatients did not simulate their single symptom to trap admission officers into making an erroneous diagnosis. Their use of a single symptom, and its abandonment after they were admitted, served the central purpose of minimizing their own psychological burdens. Recall that we were not the first people to utilize pseudopatienthood to investigate the treatment milieu of psychiatric hospitals. More than two decades earlier, Caudill (1958; Caudill, Redlich, Gilmore, & Brody, 1952) had spent considerable time in a psychiatric hospital simulating a florid pattern of symptomology throughout. He was consumed with guilt over deceiving

his colleagues and his report of his experiences was an excruciating warning to subsequent scientific generations that such elaborate deceptions can have enormous personal consequences. All of the pseudopatients knew of Caudill's work and were told that the simulation of a single symptom would likely reduce these problems. Abandoning even that symptom immediately on admission would not only reduce further that potential source of stress but also allow them to move more freely on the ward and among the patients. Moreover, I was aware that the simulation of a single symptom would facilitate discharge, which was a matter of no small concern when these studies were initiated.

The history and current direction of the project then, make no presuppositions regarding the effects of any diagnosis on patient care. However, might there not have been incidental departures from protocol on the parts of the pseudopatients? Our inquiries, conducted immediately after the pseudopatients were admitted, revealed only one such incident. In that instance, a pseudopatient altered his personal history by denying that he was married and alleging that his parents were deceased. His data, however, were omitted from the study (see Rosenhan, 1973a, footnote 6), even though they were consistent with the data from another pseudopatient.

It is important, however, to ask some difficult questions of experimenter bias in this connection. Granting for the moment that experimenter bias did affect these procedures, could it possibly have accounted for these findings? I believe not, because although experimenter bias has been found to be an outcome determinant of some power, it is not overwhelmingly powerful. In the present case, 12 out of 12 sane admissions were accorded a severe psychiatric diagnosis. To insist that all of them were misdiagnosed on the basis of experimenter bias places considerably more weight on that variable than it possibly can bear. After all, not all of Rosenthal and Jacobson's (1968) late bloomers were subsequently tested in the superior intelligence range, which would have been necessary for experimenter bias to be as potent as Millon alleges.

Experimenter bias is a set, a member of the class of sets that I have subsumed under the notion of contexts. It is a context of mind, and as such it can cut two ways: It can favor or disfavor an hypothesis. Recall the challenge experiment that was arranged at a research and teaching hospital where the staff had heard these findings but doubted that such an error could occur in their hospital. There we saw an instance of bias cutting in the direction of overdiagnosing sanity, at least according to the base rate of that particular hospital. The staff were quite confident of their ability to use the DSM—II and the variants on it that they had invented, and indeed they engaged in this small study because they were certain we were wrong. However, given a set in favor of detection, they overdetected.

In this regard, I have been told that pseudopatients would have been detected in a military hospital, and quite possibly by forensic psychiatrists. And that may be the case. But observe that in the latter instances bias cuts in favor of detection. Clearly, it does not cut in that direction in the typical psychiatric institution.

Finally, discharge diagnoses are interesting because they occur after a lengthy period of observation, thus providing ample time for diagnostic errors to be corrected. Visitors' notes (including notes written by concerned members of the pseudopatients' families) provide no evidence that the pseudopatients were actively biasing their behavior in the direction of craziness. If anything, they were often attempting to impress the staff with their sanity, a complex matter to which I shall return. Moreover, true patients commonly recognized the pseudopatients as sane during their hospitalization. Nevertheless, the discharge diagnoses were consistent with the admission diagnoses. Admitted in the main with the diagnosis of schizophrenia, they were discharged with the same diagnosis, but in remission or improved. The argument for experimenter bias becomes much less convincing over the length of these hospitalizations.

Can it seriously be held with Millon (1975) that because of their biases patients prolonged their hospitalization? Anyone who has served as a pseudopatient, and most psychiatric patients, will find that view untenable. Psychiatric hospitals, even the best of them, are places as dull and difficult for people who do not belong there as they often are for true patients. It asks too much of ordinary people to remain locked into a psychiatric hospital for as long as 52 days merely to provide a diagnostic point that was made well on admission.

Demand characteristics. Millon (1975) questions whether, in addition to experimenter bias, demand characteristics might have played a role in the obtained outcome. Demand characteristics are powerful variables, as the history of hypnosis research attests (Orne, 1969). It is, however, difficult to discern from Millon's critique in what sense demand characteristics are being invoked here. Often, demand characteristics are seen to operate in the pact of ignorance that is made between an experimenter and his subjects, so that each will not reveal his secret understandings of the experiment. Surely, that could not have been the case here, at least from the admissions officer's viewpoint. Another meaning of demand characteristics refers to controlling the

setting in such a way that a particular outcome is more assured than it might ordinarily be. This is unlikely in the present instance because we did not control the setting. No other meaning of demand characteristics seems relevant to this experiment. But the fact that the demand characteristics of psychiatric hospitals lead its personnel to believe that all those who are not staff are likely to be schizophrenic or manic-depressive is certainly consistent with our view of these data.

Could the experiment have been done differently? Undoubtedly, the experiment could have been conducted another way, and because no single experiment ever fully elucidates a phenomenon, surely there will be other work in this area that tightens these findings, illuminates them further, replicates, and extends them. The use of televised stimuli, such as those employed by Langer and Abelson (1974), offers clear control advantages that may offset what is lost in ecological validity. And as far as in vivo studies are concerned, the use of new and different symptom sets might establish the limits of contextual interpretations of behavior in these settings.

Both Millon and Weiner suggest that one might simply have people come to the admissions office and request hospitalization without falsifying a symptom. This is an interesting idea, but one that I doubt would work. Diagnosticians, like anyone else, are not passive in the face of stimulus ambiguity. They inquire. They search. They attempt to obtain more data to reduce stimulus ambiguity interpretively. And what might the pseudopatient say regarding his desire to be admitted? What justification could he present?

The same problem arises with the suggestion that sane people be directly placed on the ward to see if they can be distinguished from insane ones. If such a differentiation is intended to occur without talking to patients, there would very likely be low capacity to detect. It was the common experience of pseudopatients on wards where staff dressed casually that they could not determine who was staff and who patient for some time. (One gleans similar impressions from new interns and residents who enter an informal ward—it is difficult to tell the patients from the staff by merely looking.) Talking to the real and pseudopatients is a different matter. Again, one reduces stimulus ambiguity, but one also encounters the problem of justifying the pseudopatient's presence on the ward.

Spitzer (1975) deals directly with reduction of stimulus ambiguity in my study when he asks, "What did the pseudopatients say . . . when asked, as they must have been, what effect the hallucinations were having on their lives and why they were seeking admission in a hospital?" (p. 447). They responded that the hallucinations troubled them greatly at the outset, but less so now.

They denied being greatly distracted by them, but seemed mainly puzzled and naturally concerned. They had been told by friends to come to the hospital (or mental health center). The latter response often alerted considerable surprise in the admitting psychiatrist, and several pseudopatients were carefully queried about why they had not first taken their problem to their personal physician or a psychiatrist in the community. Because the pseudopatients, with only one exception, were not hospitalized in their own communities, they indicated that they did not have a personal physician in the community. (The single exception did not, in fact, have a personal physician.) Moreover, they indicated that they had heard that "this is a good hospital" and had therefore come on their own initiative.

I have dealt with the problem of justifying the presence of the pseudopatients, either at the admissions office or on the ward, by employing a single symptom that does not qualify for a standard diagnosis. Such a symptom should, as I have earlier indicated, alert a paradox, an inquiry, or a deferral of diagnosis. Given that the admitting and attending staff are competently trained, the easy assignment of a standard diagnosis confirms the view that the diagnostic system is not working. Recall again that the central diagnostic issue is the imaginative leap that was made between a single presenting symptom and a global pejorative diagnosis.

Sanity on the ward. Did the pseudopatients' behaviors on the ward fall within an acceptable definition of sane behavior? The problem is fascinating, because it directly implicates the influence of context on meaning. Millon puts the challenge squarely. He asserts that they did not behave sanely at all.

> Quite the contrary. The behaviors they portrayed were "standard" hospital patient behaviors. Though reported in cryptic fashion, it appears that the pseudopatients sat around quietly, acted cooperatively, said they were fine in response to staff inquiries, and asked innocuous questions such as, "When will I be eligible for ground privileges?" None of these would characterize a sane person in that situation. (p. 457)

Spitzer, quoting Hunter (Letters, 1973), concurs enthusiastically in that view:

> The pseudopatients did *not* behave normally in the hospital. Had their behavior been normal, they would have walked to the nurses' station and said, "Look, I am a normal person who tried to see if I could get into the hospital by behaving in a crazy way and saying crazy things. It worked and I was admitted to the hospital, but now I would like to be discharged from the hospital." (p. 443)

These are interesting observations because they demonstrate the degree to which context colors both expectation and perception. Because patients are cooperative in a hospital, because they say "fine" in response to staff inquiries, because they are quiet and ask questions about their eligibility for ground privileges, those behaviors, ipso facto, become abnormal, without additional validation or further proof. How long might it take a true patient, behaving in this perfectly reasonable manner to convince staff that he is indeed sane? And at what point do both clinical staff and researchers take notice of the on-off behavior of true patients and begin to ask serious questions about it?

In this connection it is useful to record some of the actions of the pseudopatients and the staff responses. They occasionally intervened with staff on behalf of other patients. They were friendly toward other patients, helpful to them, active on the wards, comforting to patients in their distress, and therapeutic with patients, but because all of this occurred on the ward, it was never seen as normal behavior. Indeed, two pseudopatients who directly requested discharge from staff members were simply ignored, and treated as yet another annoying request from another annoying patient.

Given that patients are shorn of credibility and are commonly held suspect in such matters by staff, would it really have been normal to go up to the nurses' station and say, "Look, I'm a normal person?" Might that not be construed as precisely the insane thing to do? I suspect that it might, and genuine patients have the same impression. (Recall the poor soul in the film *Titticut Follies* who did insist on being discharged for these very reasons.) We commonly asked patients, "How do you get out of the hospital?" Never did a patient advise, "Just tell them you're fine now, and that you want to go home." They recognized that they would not be believed. More commonly they encouraged us to be cooperative, patient, and not make waves. Sometimes they recommended a special kind of indirection: "Don't tell them you're well. They won't believe you. Tell them you're sick, but getting better. That's called insight, and they'll discharge you!"

Much as set and setting determine what Spitzer (1975) and Millon (1975) view as abnormal behavior, so do they offer us an especially narrow view of what normal behavior in such circumstances should be. Which psychology of behavior suggests that there is one and only one normal response to a given situation? Is it abnormal to stay in a hospital because one finds it interesting (or because one has made friends, or has nowhere else to go), anymore than it is to stay at one's desk on a beautiful day because one is absorbed in one's work? How might you know whether such behavior is normal or abnormal if you didn't inquire carefully—and no one did. Is normal or abnormal behavior self-evident from outside the person? Does one not need to inquire into the reasons for staying in a hospital just as carefully as one inquires into the reasons for wanting to leave?

Finally, it was precisely on the basis of such behaviors (the normality of which Spitzer and Millon question) that the staff in the challenge experiment detected pseudopatients. Set in the direction of discovering pseudopatients, they now used those very same standard hospital behaviors to arrive at their conclusions. In isolation, such behaviors tell us little about patients' psychiatric status. They essentially serve to confirm staff biases. Identical behaviors have vastly different meanings according to staff preconceptions that are acquired through set and setting. That is precisely the meaning of context dependency in psychiatric diagnosis.

The problem of what is normal and what is abnormal behavior is a complicated one in any setting. Some would seriously question the epistemological utility of such categorizations. But regardless, Spitzer's and Millon's fairly arbitrary classification of these behaviors only further reveals their context dependency.

The Future

It is natural to infer that what I have written here argues against categorization of all kinds. But that is not the case. I have been careful to direct attention to the present system of diagnosis, the DSM−II. It may be useful to close this essay with a few words on the conditions under which diagnosis may prove useful and the requirements that we must set for those who would produce new diagnostic systems.

First, as long as differences exist between people, it is possible to classify and categorize. The thrust of any rational argument cannot be against classification, per se, but only against poor classification and misclassification as it occurs with certain systems and affects patients' welfare.

Second, scientific understanding, if not human understanding, proceeds on the basis of classification. Nothing that is said here is intended to deprive the researcher of his classificatory system. He cannot proceed without it, but as long as his diagnostic data remain in his file until they are fully validated, they can do patients and treatment no harm.

Third, with regard to new classification systems that are intended for clinical usage with patients, we can require that evidence for their utility precede its promulgation. That has not hitherto been the case. Unlike psychological tests, which need to be validated before they are distributed, the Diagnostic and Statistical Man-

uals have been promulgated by the American Psychiatric Association before being carefully validated. As I indicated earlier, they rest heavily on consensus, rather than fact.

What might we require of new diagnostic systems before they are published and officially accepted? First, we should ask that coefficients of agreements between diagnosticians in a variety of settings *commonly* reach or exceed .90. That figure, which is associated with a bit more than 80% of the variance in diagnosis, is a liberal one in terms of the possible consequences of misdiagnosis and the reversibility of the diagnoses.[1] The full reasoning behind that figure takes us away from the central thrust of this paper, but interested readers can confirm it for themselves in Cronbach, Gleser, Harinder, and Nageswari (1972) and Cronbach and Gleser (1959).

Second, we should require that the proven utility of such a system exceed its liabilities for patients. Understand the issue. Syphilis and cancer both have negative social and emotional overtones, but the treatments that exist for them presumably exceed the personal liabilities associated with the diagnosis. We ask no less of psychiatric categorization: that the diagnoses lead to useful treatments that cannot be implemented without the diagnoses.

Under such conditions, I doubt that any reasonable person would protest psychiatric classification. And until such requirements are fulfilled, protests directed against classification will seem reasonable indeed.

REFERENCES

American Psychiatric Association. *Diagnostic and Statistical Manual of Mental Disorders* (DSM−II). Washington, D.C.: American Psychiatric Association, 1968.

Caudill, W. *The psychiatric hospital as a small society.* Cambridge, Mass.: Harvard University Press, 1958.

Caudill, W., Redlich, F. C., Gilmore, H. R., & Brody, E. B. Social structure and interaction process on a psychiatric ward. *American Journal of Orthopsychiatry,* 1952, *22,* 314−334.

Cronbach, L. J., & Gleser, C. C. Interpretation of reliability and validity coefficients: Remarks on a paper by Lord. *Journal of Educational Psychology,* 1959, *50,* 230−237.

Cronbach, L. J., Gleser, G. C., Harinder, N., & Nageswari, R. *The dependability of behavioral measurements: Theory of generalizability for scores and profiles.* New York: Wiley, 1972.

Heider, F. *The psychology of interpersonal relations.* New York: Wiley, 1958.

Hunter, F. M. Letters to the editor. *Science,* 1973, *180,* 361.

Jenkins, J. J. Remember that old theory of memory? Well, forget it! *American Psychologist,* 1974, *29,* 785−795.

Jonides, J., & Gleitman, H. A conceptual category effect in visual search: O as letter or as digit. *Perception and Psychophysics,* 1972, *12,* 457−460.

Langer, E. J., & Abelson, R. P. A patient by any other name . . . ! Clinician group differences in labeling bias. *Journal of Consulting and Clinical Psychology,* 1974, *42,* 4−9.

Loftus, E. F., & Palmer, J. C. Reconstruction of an automobile destruction: An example of the interaction between language and memory. *Journal of Verbal Learning and Verbal Behavior,* 1974, *13,* 585−589.

Millon, T. Reflections on Rosenhan's "On Being Sane in Insane Places." *Journal of Abnormal Psychology,* 1975, *84,* 456−461.

Orne, M. T. Demand characteristics and the concept of quasi-controls. In R. Rosenthal & R. Rosnow (Eds.), *Artifact in behavioral research.* New York: Academic Press, 1969.

Rosenhan, D. L. On being sane in insane places. *Science,* 1973, *179,* 250−258. (a)

Rosenhan, D. L. Letters to the editor. *Science,* 1973, *180,* 365−369. (b)

Rosenhan, D. L. Letters to the editor. *Journal of the American Medical Association,* 1973, *224,* 1646−1647. (c)

Rosenthal, R. *Experimenter effects in behavioral research.* New York: Appleton-Century-Crofts, 1966.

Rosenthal, R., & Jacobson, L. *Pygmalion in the classroom:*

Teacher expectation and pupils' intellectual development. New York: Holt, Rinehart & Winston, 1968.

Selfridge, O. G. *Pattern recognition and modern computers.* Proceedings of the Western Joint Computer Conference, Los Angeles, Calif., 1955. Cited in Neisser, U., *Cognitive psychology.* New York: Appleton-Century-Crofts, 1967.

Spitzer, R. L. On pseudoscience in science, logic in remission, and psychiatric diagnoses: A critique of Rosenhan's "On Being Sane in Insane Places." *Journal of Abnormal Psychology,* 1975, *84,* 442−452.

Spitzer, R. L., & Fleiss, J. L. A reanalysis of the reliability of psychiatric diagnosis. *British Journal of Psychiatry,* 1974, *125,* 341−347.

Spitzer, R. L., & Wilson, P. T. Nosology and the official psychiatric nomenclature. In A. Freedman & H. Kaplan (Eds.), *Comprehensive textbook of psychiatry.* New York: Williams & Wilkins, in press.

Temerlin, M. K. Suggestion effects in psychiatric diagnosis. *Journal of Nervous and Mental Disease,* 1968, *147,* 349−359.

Ward, C. H., Beck, A. T., Mendelson, M., Mock, J. E., & Erbaugh, J. K. The psychiatric nomenclature: Reasons for diagnostic disagreement. *Archives of General Psychiatry,* 1962, *7,* 198−205.

Weiner, B. "On being sane in insane places": A process (attributional) analysis and critique. *Journal of Abnormal Psychology,* 1975, *84,* 433−441.

MURRAY EDELMAN

The Political Language of the Helping Professions

Hospital staff often deny or ignore the requests of angry mental patients because to grant them would "reinforce deviant behavior." Teachers sometimes use the same rationale to justify ignoring or punishing demanding students Two recent presidents of the United States declared that they would pay no attention to peace demonstrators who resort to irritating methods. We commonly regard the last as a political act and the first two as therapeutic; but whether any such action is taken

Reprinted from Murray Edelman, *Political Language,* New York: Academic Press, 1977, pages 59−68, by permission of the author and publisher (copyright 1977 by Academic Press, Inc.).

to be political or therapeutic depends on the assumptions of the observer, not on the behavior he or she is judging. Some psychologists reject the "reinforcement of deviant behavior" rationale on the ground that it pays no attention to the distinctive cognitive and symbolizing abilities of the human mind, equating people with rats. They believe such treatment too easily ignores reasonable grounds for anger and depresses the self-esteem of people who already suffer from too little of it, contributing to further "deviance," not to health. In this view the "treatment" is self-serving political repression, even if its definition as rehabilitation salves the consciences of professionals and of the public. Some psychiatrists, on the other hand, see political demonstrators or ghetto rioters as sick, calling for drugs or psychosurgery, not political negotiation, as the appropriate response; the Law Enforcement Assistance Administration has generously supported experiments based on that premise.

The language of "reinforcement" and "help" evokes a world in which the weak and the wayward need to be controlled for their own good. The language of "authority" and "repression" evokes a different reality, in which the rights of the powerless need to be protected against abuse by the powerful. Each linguistic form marshals public support for professional and governmental practices that have profound political consequences: for the status, the rights, and the freedom of professionals, of clients, and of the wider public as well; but we rarely have occasion to inhabit or examine both worlds at the same time.

Language is the distinctive characteristic of human beings. Without it we could not symbolize; we could not reason, remember, anticipate, rationalize, distort, and evoke beliefs and perceptions about matters not immediately before us. With it we not only describe reality but create our own realities, which take forms that overlap with one another and may not be mutually consistent. When it suits us to see rationalization as reason, repression as help, distortion as creation, or the converse of any of these, language and mind can smoothly structure each other to do so. When it suits us to solve complicated problems of logic and mathematics, language and mind can smoothly structure each other to do that as well. When the complicated problems involve social power and status, problematic perception and distortion are certain.

It is a commonplace of linguistic theory that language, thought, and action shape one another. Language is always an intrinsic part of some particular social situation; it is never an independent instrument or simply a tool for description. By naively perceiving it as a tool, we mask its profound part in creating social relationships and in evoking the roles and the "selves" of those involved in the relationships.

Because the helping professions define other people's statuses (and their own), the terms they employ to categorize clients and justify restrictions of their physical movements and of their moral and intellectual influence are especially revealing of the political functions language performs and of the multiple realities it helps create. Just as any single numeral evokes the whole number scheme in our minds, so a professional term, a syntactic form, or a metaphor with scientific connotations can justify a hierarchy of power for the person who uses it and for the groups that respond to it.

In analyzing such political evocations I do not mean to suggest that the helping professions cannot be rehabilitative and educational as well. Psychological distress can be as "real" as economic distress, and psychological support is often helpful for people who voluntarily seek it. There is a large literature and a complicated controversy about the links among psychological, economic, and social stress and about the effectiveness of the helping professions in achieving their goals; but this discussion focuses on the *political* consequences of professional language.

Through devices I explore here, the helping professions create and reinforce popular beliefs about which kinds of people are worthy and which are unworthy; about who should be rewarded through governmental action and who controlled or subjected to discipline. Unexamined language and actions can help us understand more profoundly than legislative histories or administrative or judicial proceedings how we decide upon status, rewards, and controls for the wealthy, the poor, women, conformists, and nonconformists.

Here I examine such political uses of language in psychiatry, social work, psychiatric nursing, public school education, and law enforcement. My observations are based on extensive (and depressing) reading in the textbooks and professional journals of these professions. I looked for covert as well as overt justifications for status differentials, power differentials, and authority.

Therapy and Power

To illustrate the subtle bearing of language on status and authority consider a common usage that staff, clients, and the general public all accept as descriptive of a purely professional process: the term "therapy." In the journals, textbooks, and talk of the helping professions, the term is repeatedly used as a suffix or qualifier. Mental patients do not hold dances; they have dance therapy. If they play volleyball, that is recreation therapy. If they engage in a group discussion, that is group therapy.

Even reading is "bibliotherapy"; and the professional literature warns that it may be advisable to restrict, supervise, or forbid reading on some subjects, especially politics and psychiatry. Such an assertion forces us to notice what we normally pass over. To label a common activity as though it were a medical one is to establish superior and subordinate roles, to make it clear who gives orders and who takes them, and to justify in advance the inhibitions placed upon the subordinate class. It ordinarily does so without arousing resentment or resistance either in the subordinates or in outsiders sympathetic to them, for it superimposes a political relationship on a medical one while still depicting it as medical.

Though the linguistic evocation of the political system is subtle, that very fact frees the participants to act out their political roles blatantly, for they see themselves as helping, not as repressing. In consequence, assaults on people's freedom and dignity can be as polar and degrading as those typically occurring in authoritarian regimes, without qualms or protest by authorities, clients, or the public that hears about them. In this way a suffix or qualifier evokes a full-blown political system. No doubt it does so for most of the professionals who draw power from the system as persuasively and unobtrusively as it does for the clientele groups whom it helps induce to submit to authority and to accept the status of a person who must let others decide how he or she should behave.

To call explicit attention to the political connotations of a term for power, on the other hand, is to rally opposition rather than support. To label an authority relationship "tyrannical" is an exhortation to oppose it, not a simple description. The chief function of any political term is to marshal public support or opposition. Some terms do so overtly; but the more potent ones, including those used by professionals, do so covertly, portraying a power relationship as a helping one. When the power of professionals over other people is at stake, the language employed implies that the professional has ways to ascertain who are dangerous, sick, or inadequate; that he or she knows how to render them harmless, rehabilitate them, or both; and that the procedures for diagnosis and for treatment are too specialized for the lay public to understand or judge them. A patient with a sore throat is anxious for his doctor to exercise a certain amount of authority; but the diagnosis is easily checked, and the problem itself circumscribes the doctor's authority. When there is an allegation of mental illness, delinquency, or intellectual incapacity, neither the diagnosis nor the scope of authority is readily checked or limited, but its legitimacy is linguistically created and reinforced.

It is, of course, the ambiguity in the relationship, and the ambivalence in the professional and in the client, that gives the linguistic usage its flexibility and potency. That is always true of symbolic evocations, and it radically distinguishes such evocations from simple deception. Many clients want help, virtually all professionals think they are providing it, and sometimes they do so. Just as the helping seems manifest until it is self-consciously questioned, and then it becomes problematic, so the political relationship seems nonexistent until it is self-consciously questioned, and then it becomes manifest.

The special language of the helping professions merges cognition and affect. The term "mental illness" and the names for specific deviant behaviors encourage the observer and the actor to condense and confound several facets of his or her perception: helping the suffering, controlling the dangerous, sympathy for the former, fear of the latter, and so on. The terms carry all these connotations, and the actor-speaker-listener patterns them so as to utilize semantic ambiguity to cope with his or her ambivalence.

We normally fail to recognize this catalytic capacity of language because we think of linguistic terms and syntactical structures as signals rather than as symbols. If a word is a name for a specific thing or action, then terms like "mental illness," "delinquency prone," or "schizophrenic" have narrowly circumscribed meanings. But if a word is a symbol that condenses and rearranges feelings, memories, perceptions, beliefs, and expectations, then it evokes a particular structuring of beliefs and emotions, a structuring that varies with people's social situations. Language as symbol catalyzes a subjective world in which uncertainties and appropriate courses of action are clarified. Yet this impressive process of symbolic creation is not self-conscious. Our naive view holds that linguistic terms stand for particular objects or behavior, and so we do not ordinarily recognize that elaborate cognitive structures are built upon them.

In the symbolic worlds evoked by the language of the helping professions, speculation and verified fact readily merge with each other. Language dispels the uncertainty in speculation, changes facts to make them serve status distinctions, and reinforces ideology. The names for forms of mental illness, forms of delinquency, and for educational capacities are the basic terms. Each of them normally involves a high degree of unreliability in diagnosis, in prognosis, and in the prescriptions of rehabilitative treatments; but each also entails unambiguous constraints upon clients, especially their confinement and subjection to the staff and the rules of a prison, school, or hospital. The confinement and constraints are converted into liberating and altruistic acts by defining them as education, therapy, or rehabilitation and by other linguistic forms to be examined shortly. The arbitrariness and speculation in the diagnosis and the prognosis, on the other hand, are converted into clear and specific perceptions of the need for control. Regardless of the clinical utility of professional terms, their political utility is manifest; they marshal popular support for professional discretion, concentrating public attention upon procedures and rationalizing in advance any failures of the procedures to achieve their formal objectives.

Categorization is necessary to science and, indeed, to all perception. It is also a political tool, establishing status and power hierarchies. We ordinarily assume that a classification scheme is either scientific or political in character, but any category can serve either or both functions, depending on the interests of those who employ it rather than on anything inherent in the term. The name for a category therefore confuses the two functions, consigning people to high or low status and power while drawing legitimacy from its scientific status.

Any categorization scheme that consigns people to niches according to their actual or potential accomplishments or behavior is bound to be political, no matter what its scientific function. IQs; psychiatric labels; typologies of talent, skills, or knowledge; employment statuses; criminal statuses; personality types—all exemplify the point. Regardless of their validity and reliability (which are notoriously low)[1] or their analytic uses, such classifications rank people and determine degrees of status and of influence. The categorizations of the helping professions are pristine examples of the function, and many of these categories carry over into the wider society. Once established, a categorization defines what is relevant about the people who are labeled. It encourages others to interpret developments so as to confirm the label and to ignore, discount, or reinterpret counterevidence. As a civil rights lawyer put it, "While psychiatrists get angry, patients get aggressive; nurses daydream, but patients withdraw."[2] The eternal human search for meaning and for status can be counted on to fuel the problematic interpretation.

The language of the helping professions reveals in an especially stark way that perception of the same act can range all the way from one pole to its opposite. Is an action punishment or is it help? The textbooks and psychiatric journals recommend actions that look like sadism to many and like therapy to many others: deprivation of food, bed, walks in the open air, visitors, mail, and telephone calls; solitary confinement; deprivation of reading and entertainment materials; immobilizing people by tying them into wet sheets and then exhibiting them to staff and other patients; other physical restraints on body movement; drugging the mind against the client's will; incarceration in locked wards; a range of public humiliations such as the prominent posting of alleged intentions to escape or commit suicide, the requirement of public confessions of misconduct or guilt, and public announcement of individual misdeeds and abnormalities.

The major psychiatric and nursing journals describe and prescribe all these practices, and more repressive ones, repeatedly. The May 1973 issue of *Psychiatry* tells of a psychiatric ward in which, as a part of her therapy, a sobbing patient was required to scrub a shower room floor repeatedly with a toothbrush while two "psychiatric technicians" stood over her shouting directions, calling her stupid, and pouring dirty water on the floor.[3] Another professional article suggests withholding meals from noncompliant patients,[4] and a third recommends that cold wet sheet pack restraints be used more often, because they gratify the patient's dependency needs.[5]

Public humiliation and pain, even when employed only occasionally and perceived as therapy, have systematic effects on people who know they may experience them and on those who use them. In the institutions run by the helping professions, the threat of their use helps keep inmates docile. Ivan Illich remarks of such "random terror" that it serves to "break the integrity of an entire population and make it plastic material for the teaching invented by technocrats,"[6] a lesson despotic governments have always been quick to learn.

The outsider acting as critic or skeptic is likely to perceive professional actions in this way, while the insider does not do so while playing the expected professional role. Yet there is ambivalence; and it is one of the functions of professional language and professional journals to help resolve it by defining constraints as help. The *Journal of Psychiatric Nursing,* for example, rarely fails to publish at least one article in each issue that encourages nurses to overcome their qualms about denying patients the rights other people enjoy; the question is presented as a search for therapy, never as a search for autonomy, dignity, or civil rights.

To describe these practices in everyday language evokes shock at the "treatments" in a person who takes the description naively, without the conditioning to the professional perspective to which everyone has in some degree been exposed. In the professionals and those who accept their perspective, on the other hand, it is the

1. See, for example, Lawrence G. Kolb, Viola Bernard, and Bruce P. Dohrenwend, "The Problem of Validity in Field Studies of Psychological Disorder," in *Challenges to Psychiatry,* ed. Bruce P. Dohrenwend and Barbara Snell Dohrenwend (New York: Wiley, 1969), pp. 429–60; Linda Burzotta Nilson and Murray Edelman, "The Symbolic Evocation of Occupational Prestige," University of Wisconsin—Madison, Institute for Research on Poverty, Discussion Paper 348–76.

2. Daniel Oran, "Judges and Psychiatrists Lock Up Too Many People," *Psychology Today* 7 (August 1973): 22.

3. D. L. Staunard, "Ideological Conflict on a Psychiatric Ward," *Psychiatry 36* (May 1973): 143–56.

4. Carl G. Carlson, Michael Hersen, and Richard M. Eisler, "Token Economy Programs in the Treatment of Hospitalized Adult Psychiatric Patients," *Mental Health Digest 4* (December 1972): 21–27.

5. Rose K. Kilgalen, "Hydrotherapy—Is It All Washed Up?" *Journal of Psychiatric Nursing 10* (November–December 1972): 3–7.

6. Ivan Illich, *Deschooling Society* (New York: Harper and Row, 1971), p. 14.

language rather than the actions that evokes horror, for they have been socialized to see these things only as procedures, as *means* to achieve rehabilitation, not as constraints upon human beings. Language is consequently perceived as a distortion if it focuses on immediate impacts on clients rather than on the ultimate ends that the professional thinks the client should read into them and that the professional himself or herself reads into them.

The professional's reaction to language of this kind exemplifies the reaction of powerful people in general to accounts of their dealings with those over whom they hold authority. Because the necessary condition of willing submission to authority is a belief that submission benefits the subordinate, it is crucial to the powerful that descriptions of their treatment of others highlight the benefit and not the physical, psychological, or economic costs of submission. The revenue service deprives people of money, almost always involuntarily; the military draft imposes involuntary servitude; thousands of other agents of the state deprive people of forms of freedom. Usually the rationale for such restraints is an ambiguous abstraction: national security, the public welfare, law and order. We do not experience or name these ambiguous and abstract objectives as any different from goals that consist of concrete benefits, such as traffic control and disease control. Linguistic ambiguity spreads the rationale of these latter types of benefits to justify far more severe constraints and deprivations (including death in war) in policy areas in which benefits are nondemonstrable and doubtless often nonexistent. We experience as radical rhetoric any factual description of authoritative actions that does not call attention to their alleged benefits to all citizens or to some, and authorities typically characterize such descriptions as subversive, radical, or treasonous. They are indeed subversive of ready submission and of political support.

The point becomes vivid if we restate the actions described above from the professional's perspective: discouraging sick behavior and encouraging healthy behavior through the selective granting of rewards; the availability of seclusion, restraints, and closed wards to grant a patient a respite from interaction with others and from making decisions, and to prevent harm to himself or others; enabling him to think about his behavior, to cope with his temptations to "elope" or succumb to depression, and to develop a sense of security; immobilizing the patient to calm him, satisfy his dependency needs, give him the extra nursing attention he values, and enable him to benefit from peer confrontation; placing limits on his acting out; and teaching him that the staff cares.

The two accounts describe the same phenomena, but they occur in phenomenologically different worlds.

Notice that the professional terms carry connotations that depict constraints as nonrestrictive. To speak of "elopement" rather than "escape," as psychiatrists and staff members do, is to evoke a picture of individual freedom to leave when one likes (as eloping couples do) rather than of locks, iron bars, and bureaucratic prohibitions against voluntary departure. To speak of "seclusion" or "quiet room" rather than solitary confinement is again to suggest voluntary and enjoyable retirement from others and to mask the fact that the patient is locked in against his or her will and typically resists and resents the incarceration. Such terms accomplish in a craftsmanlike and nonobvious way what professionals also say explicitly to justify restrictions on inmates. They assert in textbooks, journals, and assurances to visitors that some patients feel more secure in locked wards and in locked rooms, that professionals know when this is the case, and that the patients' statements to the contrary cannot be taken at face value.

To speak of "limits" is to mask the perception of punishment for misbehavior and to perceive the patient as inherently irrational, thereby diverting attention from the manifest frustrations and aggravations that come from bureaucratic restrictions and from consignment to the most powerless status in the institution.

Many clients come, in time, to use the professionals' language and to adopt their perspective. To the staff, their adoption of the approved linguistic forms is evidence of insight and improvement. All clients probably do this in some degree, but for many the degree is so slight that the professional descriptions serve as irony or as mockery. They are repeatedly quoted ironically by students, patients, and prisoners.

In the institutions run by the helping professions, established roles and their special language create a world with its own imperatives. The phenomenon helps us understand the frequency with which well-meaning men and women support governments that mortify, harass, torture, and kill large numbers of their citizens. To the outsider such behavior signals sadism and self-serving evil, and it is impossible to identify with it. To the people who avidly act out their roles inside that special world, motives, actions, and consequences of acts are radically different. Theirs is a work of purification and nurturance: of ridding the inherently or ideologically contaminated of their blight or of ridding the world of the contamination they embody. It is no accident that repressive governments are consistently puritanical. To the inhabitants of other worlds the repression is a mask for power, but to those who wield authority, power is a means to serve the public good. Social scientists cannot explain such phenomena as long as they place the cause inside people's psyches rather than in the social evocation of roles. To attribute evil or merit to the psyche is a political act rather than a medical one, for it justifies repression or exaltation, while minimizing observation and analysis. To explore phenomenological diversity in people's worlds and roles is to begin to recognize the full range of politics.

Class or status differences may also entail wide differences in the labelings of identical behaviors. The teacher's underachiever may be the epitome of the "cool" student who refuses to "brownnose." The middle class's criminal or thief may be a "political prisoner" to the black poor. Such labels with contrasting connotations occur when a deprived population sees the system as unresponsive to its needs and organized rebellion as impossible. In these circumstances, only individual nonconformity remains as a way to maintain self-respect. To the deprived the nonconformity is a political act. To the beneficiaries of the system it is individual pathology. Each labels it accordingly.

The term "juvenile delinquent" historically served the political function of forcing the assimilation of Catholic immigrants to the WASP culture of late nineteenth- and early twentieth-century America. This new category defined as "criminal" youthful behaviors handled informally among the urban Catholics and not perceived by them as crime at all: staying out late, drinking, smoking, reading comic books, truancy, disobedience. However, the definition of prevailing urban norms as "delinquency" justified the authorities in getting the Irish children away from their "bigoted"

advisers, the priests.[7] The language of individual pathology served also to raise doubts about a distinctive culture and a religion, rationalizing its political consequences in terms of its motivation of salvaging youth from crime.

Some professionals reject the professional perspective, and all, no doubt, retain some skepticism about it and some ability to see things from the perspective of the client and the lay public. The ambivalence is typically resolved in more militant, decisive, and institutionalized forms than is true of ambivalent clients; for status, self-conception, and perhaps income hinge on its resolution. In consequence, professionals adopt radical therapy, existentialist or Szaszian views, or they attack these dissidents as unprofessional and unscientific.

The lay public by and large adopts the professional perspective; for its major concern is to believe that others can be trusted to handle these problems, which are potentially threatening to them but not a part of their everyday lives. This public reaction is the politically crucial one, for it confers power upon professionals and spreads their norms to others. The public reaction, in turn, is a response to the language of the professionals and to the social milieu which gives that language its authoritative meaning.

7. Anthony M. Platt, *The Child Savers: The Invention of Delinquency* (Chicago: University of Chicago Press, 1969); American Friends Service Committee, *Struggle for Justice* (New York: Hill and Wang, 1971), p. 112.

THOMAS S. SZASZ

Anti-Psychiatry: The Paradigm of the Plundered Mind

I

With the rapid developments in syphilology, psychiatry, and psychoanalysis during the first two decades of this century, there occurred a division of the spoils, as it were, among them: paresis was claimed by syphilology, psychosis by psychiatry, and neurosis by

Reprinted from *The New Review*, Vol. **3**, No. 29 (1977), pages 2–12, by permission of the author and publisher (copyright, *The New Review*, 1977).

psychoanalysis. The result was two reciprocal series of differentiations: patients became separated into paretics, psychotics, and neurotics; doctors, into syphilologists (and neurologists), psychiatrists, and psychoanalysts (and psychotherapists). Separating the patients as, and is still, called making a 'differential diagnosis'. Separating the physicians was, and is still, called 'specialising' in the diagnosis and treatment of one or another branch of medicine.

In keeping with the general character of classifications, each of these categories of patients and doctors had a characteristic member which became its model. The paradigmatic patients displayed the supposedly typical medical diseases of their class, whereas the paradigmatic doctors displayed the supposedly typical medical intervention of theirs: paresis thus became the paradigm of neurosyphilis, schizophrenia of psychosis, and hysteria of neurosis; similarly, chemotherapy (and artificial fever) became the paradigm of syphilology, psychiatric incarceration (called 'mental hospitalisation') of psychiatry, and conversation (called 'free association' and 'interpretation') of psychoanalysis.

I emphasize these historical changes—which were partly caused by certain fresh scientific discoveries, and which generated some fresh social practices—in order to identify, as clearly as possible, the nature of 'traditional' psychiatry as it existed, say, at the end of the Second World War. As a sharpshooter must see his target clearly, so we must see psychiatry clearly—for both the so-called anti-psychiatrists and I have aimed our critical fire-power at it. As I shall now try to show, we have, however, done so in very different ways, and for very different reasons.

II

One of the developments since the first publication of my book *The Myth of Mental Illness,* in 1961, and in no small part attributable to its influence, is the so-called anti-psychiatry movement. This movement, like the movement of traditional psychiatry which it seeks to supplant, is also centered on the concept of schizophrenia and on helping so-called schizophrenics. Because both the anti-psychiatrists and I oppose certain aspects of psychiatry, our views are often combined and confused, and we are often identified as the common enemies of all of psychiatry.

It is true, of course, that in traditional, coercive psychiatry, the anti-psychiatrists and I face the same enemy. So did, in another context, Stalin and Churchill. The old Arab proverb that 'the enemy of my enemy is my friend' may make good sense indeed in politics and war. But it makes no sense at all in intellectual and moral discourse.

I reject the term 'anti-psychiatry' because it is imprecise, misleading, and cheaply self-aggrandising. Chemists do not characterise themselves as 'anti-alchemists'; nor do astronomers call themselves 'anti-astrologers'.[1] If one defines psychiatry conventionally, as the medical specialty concerned with the diagnosis

1. The term 'anti-psychiatry' is not only not good, it is also not new. It was used as early as 1912, by Bernhard Beyer to characterise an article critical of psychiatry.

and treatment of mental diseases, then one is, indeed, committed to 'opposing' psychiatry as a specialty—not of medicine but of mythology. However, since I believe that people are entitled to their mythologies, this opposition must be clearly limited to the use of force or fraud by the mythologisers in the pursuit of their ersatz religion. This is why I have always insisted that I am against involuntary psychiatry, or the psychiatric rape of the patient by the psychiatrist—but I am not against voluntary psychiatry, or psychiatric relations between consenting adults.

On the other hand, if one defines psychiatry operationally, as consisting of 'whatever psychiatrists do', then it is necessary to identify and articulate one's attitude toward each of the numerous practices psychiatrists engage in. I have tried to do this in several of my books, always indicating what I oppose, what I support, and why. As against this analytical approach, the very term 'anti-psychiatry' implicitly commits one to opposing everything that psychiatrists do—which is patently absurd. In any case, anti-psychiatrists do not clearly state whether they object only to involuntary psychiatric interventions, or also to those that are voluntary; to all involuntary psychiatric interventions, or only to those practised by their political adversaries. They do not frankly acknowledge whether they support real tolerance for contractual psychiatric interventions, or only 'repressive tolerance' for (i.e. against) them—because such practices occur in an 'exploitative-capitalist' context of free market and free enterprise.

Actually, as we shall see, the anti-psychiatrists are all self-declared socialists, communists, or at least anti-capitalists and collectivists. As the communists seek to raise the poor above the rich, so the anti-psychiatrists seek to raise the 'insane' above the 'sane'; and as certain revolutionaries justify their aims and methods by claiming that the poor are virtuous, while the rich are wicked, so the anti-psychiatrists justify theirs by claiming that the 'insane' are authentic, while the 'sane' are inauthentic.

III

Ronald Laing, who, with David Cooper, originated the so-called anti-psychiatry movement, began his work with the study of schizophrenic persons. His first book, published in 1960, is titled *The Divided Self*—an almost literal English translation of Bleuler's Greek term 'schizophrenia', and a virtual repetition of the classic psychiatric view of the schizophrenic as a 'split personality'. Four years later (with Aaron Esterson) Laing published *Sanity, Madness, and the Family*. Subtitled 'Volume I: Families of Schizophrenics', it is a report on the study of eleven hospitalised schizophrenic patients and their families. Nowhere in this book do the authors identify the legal status of any of the 'schizophrenics'—that is, whether they are voluntary or involuntary patients. There is also no mention of what, if any, roles Laing and Esterson played in depriving these persons of their liberty; or, if they were deprived of their liberty by others, what, if any, role they played in trying to help them to regain it.

Subsequently, Laing has, on some occasions, rejected the idea that schizophrenia is a disease, but he has continued to 'treat' it. The fame of Kingsley Hall—Laing's 'asylum' for managing madness—rests almost entirely on the claim that it offers a method of helping 'schizophrenic patients' superior to those offered by other psychiatric institutions or practitioners.

I have long maintained, and continue to insist, that if there is no disease, there is *nothing* to treat; and if there is no patient, there is *no one* to treat. Insofar as others make the same claim—that is, that schizophrenia (and mental illness generally) is not a disease—they are compelled, by the logic of language alone, to conclude also that there is no 'treatment' for it. However, inasmuch as many persons whom psychiatrists diagnose as schizophrenic seek help—especially if 'help' is not forced on them and if they don't have to pay for it—we are confronted with the social reality of 'psychotics', supposedly lacking 'insight' about their 'illness', clamoring for its 'treatment'.

Laing accepts such persons as 'residents' in his 'communities', and legitimises them as 'sufferers' who, because of their very 'victimisation', are more worthy than others. There is thus a moral-economic premise built into his system of asylum care which is inexplicit but is all the more important for being so. It is, moreover, the same premise that animates large numbers of men and women today throughout the civilised world. Briefly put, it is the premise that it is wicked for people to purchase, for money, medical or psychiatric (or anti-psychiatric) help, but that it is virtuous to 'purchase' it for suffering. I shall say more about this moral dimension of the therapeutic nexus presently. Here it should suffice to note that in espousing this position, Laing is hardly unconventional. On the contrary, he places himself squarely mid-stream of the main current of contemporary thought and sentiment about 'health care'. This current, in both communist and capitalist countries, is now fully Marxist, adopting, for 'suffering situations',[2] the famous formula: 'From each according to his abilities, to each according to his needs.'

Economically, Laing has thus replaced the coercion of the mental patient by the psychiatrist on behalf of the

citizen, with the coercion of the taxpayer by the government on behalf of the mental patient. Formerly, sane citizens could *detain* those whom they considered to be mad; now they must *maintain* those who undertake to 'journey' through madness.

I say this because even if a person is, in his current situation, unmolested by his family and employer, by the police and psychiatry—in other words, even if he is not actually harassed or persecuted in any way whatever—Laing still accepts him as a resident at Kingsley Hall and legitimises him as a *bona fide* sufferer. I am not contending that such persons may not, in fact, suffer—at least in the sense in which most persons often suffer from the slings and arrows of outrageous fortune. I am contending only that it does not follow logically or morally from it that such persons are entitled to services extracted by force or fraud from others—whether those 'others' be indentured torturers in old-fashioned State Hospitals or indentured taxpayers in new-fashioned Welfare States. I am trying to make explicit here something which, so far as I know, is never made explicit—either by Laing and his followers, or by their critics—namely, that the cost of the care of the 'residents' in the Laingian asylums is mainly borne by the British taxpayer; and that the British taxpayer has no more of a direct vote on whether or not he wants his hard-earned money spent that way than did the American taxpayer have on paying for the war in Vietnam. Ironically, while Laing's tongue lashes British taxpayers for funding a society that drives people mad, his hands are picking the taxpayers' pockets.

Furthermore, anti-psychiatrists resemble psychiatrists and psychoanalysts in their insistent inattention to whether the so-called mental patient assumes his role voluntarily or is assigned to it against his will. Psychoanalysts, psychiatrists, and anti-psychiatrists all talk and theorize about neurosis and psychosis, hysteria and schizophrenia, without acknowledging whether persons so identified seek or avoid psychiatric help; whether they accept or reject being diagnosed; whether they claim to be suffering or others impute suffering to them. Thus all of these seemingly different, and sometimes even antagonistic, approaches to so-called psychiatric problems display this crucial similarity: each regards the 'patient' as a 'case'—indeed, as a 'victim'. To the psychiatrist, the 'schizophrenic' is a victim of an elusive disease of the brain, like neurosyphilis; to the psychoanalyst, he is a victim of a weak ego, a powerful id, or a combination of both; and to the anti-psychiatrist, he is a victim of an intrusive family and an insane society. Each of these creeds and cults diminishes and distorts the 'patient' as the person he really is; each denies his self-explanatory act of self-definition. Thus,

2. The expression is Kenneth Minogue's.

the psychiatrist denies the 'schizophrenic's' right to reject confinement, and attributes his desire for freedom to a lack of insight into his illness and his need for treatment for it; the psychoanalyst denies his right to resist analytic interpretation, and attributes his non-cooperation with the analyst to an 'illness' that renders him 'inaccessible' to analysis; and the anti-psychiatrist denies his obligation to care for himself and to obey the law, and views his penchant for social rule-violation as proof of his superior moral virtue.

The result is a lumping together—in psychoanalysis, psychiatry, and anti-psychiatry—of the most dissimilar kinds of persons. For example, persons able but unwilling to take care of themselves are placed in the same class with those willing but unable to do so; persons who are guilty but claim to be innocent are placed in the same class with those who are innocent but claim to be guilty; and persons who are charged with and convicted of lawbreaking are placed in the same class with those who are neither charged nor convicted of any offence. In psychiatry and psychoanalysis, each of these types of persons may be categorised as 'schizophrenic'; and in anti-psychiatry, such categorisation of persons as 'schizophrenics' is, on the one hand, criticised as erroneous and, on the other hand, embraced as identifying a specific group of individuals distinctively victimised by others and especially suitable for Laingian methods of mental treatment. In all of these ways, in their approach to 'schizophrenia', the similarities between psychiatry, psychoanalysis, and anti-psychiatry seem to me to far outweigh the differences among them.

In short, insofar as anti-psychiatry is a continuation of the tradition of moral treatment in psychiatry, it is nothing new; and insofar as it is a political perspective on society and a set of practical policies about human relations, it is an inversion of certain Western values and arrangements. Some of these points have been made before by critics of anti-psychiatry (most cogently by David Martin and Lionel Trilling).

IV

The gist of David Martin's argument, with which I am in substantial agreement, is that Laing is a preacher of and for the 'soft' underbelly of the New Left. By 'soft New Leftism' Martin means, among other things, a 'syndrome of attitudes' which confront us with a 'psychological set that positively avoids careful analysis and treats the notion of fact as a treacherous bourgeois invention'. Laing's 'predominant style', adds Martin, 'is not "honourable argument"': instead it is gnomic, testamental, and confessional'. Martin calls attention to Laing's recurrent references 'to the nature of capitalist

society as being a near-universal social context in which freedom is deformed', and notes that this is a rather absurd assertion, not because it is completely false, but because it is less true of contemporary capitalist societies than of any other societies, past or present, which we know anything about. But, as Martin emphasizes, the whole point of Laing's style is to avoid and undercut the development of an exchange of reasoned assertions and denials.

Here, I might add, lies one of the most important similarities between traditional psychiatrists and Laingian anti-psychiatrists: one cannot reason or argue with any of them. Each is like a religious zealot with whom one cannot discuss or debate anything that touches on his creed. Such a person permits one only two options: total agreement and total disagreement. In the former case, one is allowed to acknowledge the psychiatrist or anti-psychiatrist as the possessor of true insight into the heart and mind of the psychotic and the defender of the psychotic's own best interests. In the latter, one is demeaned and degraded by an invidious 'diagnosis', that is, by being declared mad—the victim of insanity and brain disease in the one case, of inauthenticity and brainwashing in the other.

All of anti-psychiatry is characterised by this fateful similarity to what it opposes. In traditional psychiatry, 'We' are sane, and 'They', who defy the norms and values of our society, are insane. In anti-psychiatry, it is the other way around. 'There is in Laing's writing', remarks Martin, 'not a single word suggesting that any virtue inheres in what is his own inheritance.' That is almost putting it too mildly, for Laing is fond of tossing off remarks such as: 'The worst barbarities are still perpetrated by "ourselves", by our "allies" and "friends".' This total rejection of 'Us', and the complementary romanticisation of 'Them', is, of course, characteristic of the contemporary 'leftist' mentality in the still 'free' societies.

The image of Laing that emerges from Martin's analysis of his work is that of an angry prophet, an intolerant religious fanatic, hurling in our faces such accusations and challenges as this: 'We are all murderers and prostitutes . . .' According to Martin, Laing is

an irrationalist in that he finds rational and argued discussion of religious questions uncongenial, and insists that the essence of religion is ecstasy . . . there is in Laing's whole style a *substitution* of ecstasy for argument and a disinclination to build up a sequence of ordered points, supported by carefully collected evidence, qualified in respect to this issue or that. His method consists in random accusation and sloganised virulence, which destroys the possibility of discussion.

In short, like the mad-doctors of yore, and like the psychoanalysts of only yesterday, Laing too is a base rhetorician.

V

Lionel Trilling has also noted[3] that Laing's criticism of the existing social order is similar, in all essential respects, to that of Marxism and Communism; and that the salvation he proposes for it also resembles the solutions offered by these collectivistic creeds. Although I do not agree with Trilling's uncritical acceptance of schizophrenia as a disease (he seems to think that it is just like syphilis, only more difficult to diagnose), I regard most of his criticism of anti-psychiatry as valid and important.

Thus, Trilling is right in re-emphasising—indeed, I think his emphasis is not nearly strong enough—the economic nexus in which the anti-psychiatry movement belongs, and into which it must be explicitly re-inserted. That nexus is Marxian anti-capitalism. In it, Trilling remarks, 'money is the principle of the inauthentic in human existence'. He cites Oscar Wilde's remark, apropos of this new vision of the genuinely 'human being', that: 'The true perfection of man lies not in what man has but in what man is.' It then follows, as Trilling himself suggests, that the moral ideal is no longer that a man should *know himself,* but that he should *be himself.* This sounds nice so long as we do not ask what it means 'to be oneself'. For what is concealed in this prescription is nothing less than the whole meaning and value of life itself.

Laing's theory of schizophrenia, which serves as the moral justification and economic foundation for whatever work he does as a helper or healer, thus rests on the idea of inauthenticity and its role in this 'disorder'. It is precisely on this point that Trilling delivers his most damaging blows against Laing's work.

> . . . schizophrenia, in his (Laing's) view, is the consequence of an external circumstance, an influence exerted upon the sense of selfhood, of a person who is more disposed than others to yield to it; the schizophrenic person characteristically has what Laing calls an 'ontological insecurity', a debility of his sentiment of being. . . . It is the family which is directly responsible for the ontological break, the 'divided self' of schizophrenia; Laing is categorical in saying that every case of schizophrenia is to be understood as 'a special strategy that the patient invents in order to live an unlivable situation', which is always a family situation, specifically the demand of parents that one be what one is not. We may

3. *Sincerity and Authenticity,* Harvard University Press, 1972.

put it that Laing construes schizophrenia as the patient's response to the parental imposition of inauthenticity.

Trilling here puts a sensitive finger on the nonsensical and mischievous aspects of the cult of authenticity. This cult is, in some ways, the mirror image of the cult of modern institutional psychiatry. As in psychiatry, the core concept, the sacred symbol, is 'schizophrenia'—so in anti-psychiatry, it is 'authenticity'. In the former view, what the schizophrenic has less of than other people is the ability to 'test reality'; in the latter view, what the schizophrenic has more of than other people is 'authenticity'.

Given the problems that the 'schizophrenic' presents to himself and others, and given Laing's perspective of attributing all human problems to society, it was inevitable, according to Trilling, that the cause of schizophrenia 'be sought in social factors'. But it 'was not inevitable . . . that this line of thought should issue in the verdict that insanity is a state of human existence which is to be esteemed for its commanding authenticity'.

This is, indeed, a most unfortunate claim. By making it, Laing and Cooper, and those who support their idealisation of insanity, have, in my opinion, done a great disservice to the cause of enlarging the sphere of human decency for all people—regardless of whether they are psychotics or psychiatrists, both or neither. The proposition that the madman is sane and that society is insane is the sort of thing that Trilling calls 'cant'. In my view, it is not just cant, but rather countercant: it is the echo of the psychiatric cant which categorises disagreement as disease—which Trilling seems to think is a scientific proposition. But Trilling is right in emphasising that cant cannot be countered with logic. Many a 'schizophrenic' has discovered this, as has many a would-be critic of 'scientific' psychiatry. Trilling observes:

> To deal with this phenomenon of our intellectual culture in the way of analytical argument would, I think, be supererogatory. The position may be characterised as being in an intellectual mode to which analytical argument is not appropriate. This is the intellectual mode that once went under the name of cant. The disappearance of the word from the modern vocabulary is worth remarking.

The disappearance of this word, and also of 'rhetoric', is, of course, intimately related to the acceptance and growth of psychiatry as a 'science', a subject on which I have remarked at length elsewhere.

Trilling cites passages from Cooper and Laing to illustrate what he means by anti-psychiatric cant. For a fully balanced view of schizophrenia—from Kraepelin and Bleuler to the present—we must, indeed, be as clear and critical of the cant of anti-psychiatry as we are of that of psychiatry; and for a fully humane—by which term I here mean a candid, contractual, non-coercive—policy toward schizophrenia, we must reject the blandishments of anti-psychiatry as firmly as we do the punishments of psychiatry.

VI

We all know what psychiatric cant is: it is the material that comes packaged between the covers of textbooks of psychiatry and psychoanalysis. Anti-psychiatric cant is the same thing, turned upside down or inside out. Trilling cites this example of it from Cooper's Introduction to Michel Foucault's *Madness and Civilisation:*

> Madness . . . is a way of seizing *in extremis* the racinating groundwork of the truth that underlies our more specific realisation of what we are about. The truth of madness is what madness is, what madness is is a form of vision that destroys itself by its own choice of oblivion in the face of existing forms of social tactics and strategy. Madness, for instance, is a matter of voicing the realisation that I am (or you are) Christ.

Actually, it is easy to cite even more blatant passages of cant from Cooper's writings, as well as from Laing's. For example, in *The Death of the Family*, Cooper declares that 'all lethal diseases are suicide in the sense of refusal to love'. Cooper here confuses himself not only with Jesus Christ but also with Georg Groddeck, who came to believe that all human diseases were due to mental conflicts.

'The bourgeois state', Cooper explains, 'is a tranquiliser pill with lethal side effects.' His prescription for 'liberation' from it is equally illuminating:

> The fulfilment of liberation comes only with effective macropolitical action. So the Centres of Revolutionary Consciousness have also to become Red Bases. Macropolitical action here must be essentially negative, and takes the form of rendering bourgeois power structures impotent by any and every means. . . . Molotov cocktails certainly have their place in a significantly organised, student-worker rebellion. . . .

Cooper's comments about Red Bases and Molotov cocktails are not just asides, tossed off to impress the intellectual *lumpen proletariat;* they constitute a consistent theme, both in *The Dialectics of Liberation* and *The Death of the Family*. In the former book, he eulogises the North Vietnamese guerrillas, refers to Cuba as

'already liberated', and to the communist insurgence in Vietnam as putting that country 'inexorably on the way to liberation'. In the latter, his enmity towards capitalist leaders is as unqualified as is his endorsement of communist leaders:

> . . . false leaders are simply shadowy presences, with artificial, 'big man' images regurgitated by non-human, institutionalised social processes—for example the Hitlers, Churchills, Kennedys, etc. The true leadership principle is embodied in men like Fidel Castro and Mao Tse-tung, who lead by almost refusing to be leaders. . . .

Laing's political cant has the same ring: 'we' are wicked, and 'they' are virtuous. In an interview with Richard Evans, he offers this revealing remark about some recent atrocities:

> . . . in the sixties, the military struggle in Indochina was far more extensive than was being let on. Cambodia was being bombed. God knows what else is going on there now. Look at the German bystander's apathy about the concentration camps. Look at the British apathy when their bomber command destroyed a city like Dresden just to show the Americans and Russians what the British Air Force could do.

Neither Cooper nor Laing leaves us in any doubt what they and their anti-psychiatry are all about: they seek, by methods even more fanatical and ferocious than those they wish to replace, to impose their particular values on the world. Cooper's following proposal is typical:

> . . . for the less sophisticated middle-class and working-class men-women relationships (the upper classes being fully and finally dedicated to nonsexuality), one needs a more totally operating revolutionising activity in the whole society. This is where acutely posed strikes, bombs, and machine guns will have to come in, with a guiding compassion but also a certain reality that is wholly objective, seen and felt, by the agents of bourgeois society, towards whom we can only be compassionate at a second remove.

Kraepelin and Bleuler on the psychiatric 'Right'; Laing and Cooper on the psychiatric 'Left'. They match each other by their apparent antagonisms which conceal their actual agreements: each is convinced of the absolute righteousness of his respective position and of his right, indeed duty, to impose his will on those who resist him—by whatever force may be necessary. Kraepelin conceals imprisonment as hospitalisation and calls it psychiatry; Cooper conceals killing the 'agents of bourgeois society' and waging revolution with bombs and machine guns as liberation, guided by compassion, and calls it all anti-psychiatry. Not in their wildest moments did the ambitions of the traditional psychiatrists approximate those of the modern anti-psychiatrists. We might call this, or at least think of it, as the Romanov-Lenin effect, which I would define as follows: He who liberates you despotically from another despot will surpass in his cruelty the worst cruelties of his old antagonist.

I think we owe it to Cooper to take him seriously, and to draw from his writings the conclusions clearly implicit in them. Cooper himself cannot be faulted; he has made them explicit enough:

> All deaths in the first world are murder disguised as suicide disguised as the course of Nature. . . . Revolution, I believe, will only be a total enough social reality when white men can assume all the colours of blackness and then have babies too. In Cuba, the Guevarist doctrine of the New Man gets very close to the extended sense of revolution that I have pursued in these pages. The New Man is the pragmatic revolutionary who effectively annihilates the power structures of the feudal, bourgeois state and takes whatever power he needs to maintain an autonomous community. . . .

In short, Cooper's prescription for the conquest of insanity, alienation, poverty, and every other human misery is the old apocalyptic-millenarian dream of the collectivist brotherhood of men and women all over the world. It is an old dream that has, since the French Revolution, turned into a nightmare, and worse, for countless people all over the world.

VII

As I noted, both Martin and Trilling emphasise that Laing does not reason or argue; he blames and preaches. Accordingly, there is not the slightest effort in his works, or in those of the other anti-psychiatrists, at consistency. There is no schizophrenia, but they treat it. The sane are madder than the insane, but they operate asylums for the latter, not the former. The capitalist West is more oppressive than the communist East, but they all live in, and off, the former, and stay carefully clear of the latter.

One of the most interesting and informative documents in this connection is the *Philadelphia Association Report, 1965–1969*. This is the organisation founded by or under the guidance of Ronald Laing in 1965, for the purpose of providing asylum for—what should we call them?—schizophrenics, homeless persons, 'victims'.

Let us see how the Report handles this matter of naming the 'clients' and their 'caretakers'.

Faithfully following the style of contemporary Western collectivism, the Report has no identified or identifiable authors, and the asylums it operates have no identified staff. Indeed, individualism, self-identification as a form of self-aggrandisement, is denounced at the outset, in the dedication, which reads as follows:

> This report arises from the communal experience of many people who agreed to be together without predefined professional or social roles. To all of them, too numerous to name, this report is dedicated.

Just what, then, is the Philadelphia Association? It is 'A Registered National Charity in the United Kingdom', and an organisation which has secured for itself exemption 'from United States income tax under Section 501 (C) (3) of the Internal Revenue Code'. The purposes of the Association are set forth in its 'Articles of Association' as follows:

> To relieve mental illness of all descriptions, in particular schizophrenia.
>
> To undertake, or further, research into the causes of mental illness, the means of its detection and prevention, and its treatment.
>
> To provide, or further the provision of, residential accommodations for persons suffering or who have suffered from mental illness.
>
> To provide financial assistance for poor patients.
>
> To promote and organise training in the treatment of schizophrenia and other forms of mental illness.

This could just as well have been written by Karl Menninger as by Ronald Laing. It sounds like Laing's attempt to set up his version of the Menninger Clinic: that is, his factory called 'residential accommodations' instead of 'hospital beds' for manufacturing mental patients (called 'schizophrenics' in both cases), and for training future factory workers and managers (called 'training' persons in 'the treatment of schizophrenia and other forms of mental illness' in both cases).

The first business of the Philadelphia Association was to lease a building called Kingsley Hall for the purpose of turning it into a 'residential accommodation' or 'asylum'. Kingsley Hall, which opened its doors in June, 1965, has, we are told:

> no staff, patients, or institutional procedures. . . . Behaviour is feasible there which is intolerable in most other places. People get up or stay in bed as they wish, eat what they want

when they want, stay alone or be with others, and generally make their own rules.

There are, at least according to this Report, no obligations or duties of any kind placed upon the 'residents'. Above all, they need not pay for anything they receive. Or, if they have to pay for it, it is not mentioned. What is mentioned, indeed emphasised, is that:

> Many residents are poor, with only social security benefits. No one has been turned away for financial reasons, despite our limited resources. However, activities are restricted when funds are low.

In short, Kingsley Hall differs from the Menninger Clinic (or any other private mental hospital) in much the same way that a flophouse differs from a first-class hotel. In each case, room and board are provided by one group of persons for another, regardless of what each group calls itself or the other.

Thus, towards money, too, Laing displays the same pious posture as do institutional psychiatrists. The traditional asylum psychiatrist imposes a non-reciprocal economic relationship on the madman, ostensibly treating him as a 'solicitous' father treats his 'needy' child, while actually receiving payment for his services from others. The same economic arrangement characterises the triangular relations of guides, voyagers, and dispensers of funds in the Laingian asylums. Both settings reek of the odour of therapeutic sanctimoniousness, which the 'conceit of philanthropy'[4] inevitably exudes.

Laing imposes no explicit financial obligation on the 'patients' at Kingsley Hall. Regardless of how much money the patient may have, or of how much he may spend on liquor, tobacco, or gambling, he does not have to spend any of it on paying for 'mental health care'. How, then, does he gauge whether the patient is deserving of care? By measuring his 'need' in terms of his suffering and his willingness to submit to his helpers. This paternalistic posture has long been held to be the cornerstone of the ideal model of medical ethics. It is the role which Laing and his disciples blindly embrace, thus displaying the same contempt for their charges as the keepers of madmen at the Burghölzli, Maudsley, or Salpêtrière have always displayed.

It is clear, then, that what Laing and Cooper oppose is not so much any particular psychiatric intervention as the principle of making and keeping promises; not so much coercion as contract. In short, what they oppose is not 'therapeutic' caprice, but predictable rules binding

4. The phrase is William F. May's.

equally—morally as well as legally—on all contracting parties.

Sooner or later, it seems to me, we must all choose between the two dominant principles for regulating human relations—that is, between contracts and commands. Confronted with this choice, Laing and Cooper come down squarely in support of commands and in opposition to contracts. In this crucially important respect, too, they stand shoulder to shoulder with the traditional psychiatric authorities whom they seek to overthrow and replace. The similarities between the Laingian asylum and the lunatic asylum go, of course, even further, as I shall presently show.

There are troubling inconsistencies not only between Laing's claim that there is no schizophrenia and his claim that he possesses a superior method of treating it, but also between the Philadelphia Association's claim that it has no professional staff or hierarchy and Laing's self-identification, elsewhere, as its Director. In the journal *The Human Context,* Laing is identified as 'Director, Kingsley Hall (Clinic)'. In the Philadelphia Association's own promotional material, there is, as I noted, no director mentioned. In short, instead of demystifying the metaphors of medicine, Laing alternately denounces them, in a philosophically sweeping and politically selective way, and uses them for all they are worth, by deploying them as his own rhetorical devices.

Reflections such as these have made me conclude that in the psychiatric war with words, the metaphors of medicine do the work of hand-grenades; and that the present positions of psychiatrists and anti-psychiatrists are like those of soldiers in trenches facing each other, lobbing the same grenades back and forth, hoping they will go off in their enemies' faces rather than in their own. I am opposed to this sort of use of the medical vocabulary, regardless of the identity of the user.

Clearly, the anti-psychiatrists have accepted the central role of schizophrenia in psychiatry. What they have done, essentially, is to invert its position and significance, casting blame on the family and society instead of on the patient and his disease. They have thus argued that the schizophrenic is, at least sometimes, super-sane, in the sense that, because he is a 'victim', he is, ipso facto, more virtuous than his victimisers.

My argument against psychiatry proceeds from quite different premises and points to quite different conclusions. My primary charge against psychiatry has been aimed at the things psychiatrists actually do, and my secondary charge at their claims concerning what psychotics supposedly suffer from. Briefly put, I have maintained that the intervention institutional psychiatrists call 'mental hospitalisation' is, in fact, a form of imprisonment, and that the imposition of such loss of liberty on innocent persons is immoral (and, in the United States, unconstitutional); and that the phenomenon psychiatrists call 'schizophrenia' is not a demonstrable medical disease but the name of certain kinds of social deviance (or of behaviour unacceptable to the speaker).

VIII

While there is no need to encumber this presentation with a detailed retelling of the story of Mary Barnes, some remarks on it are essential for a rounded view of the doctrines and deceptions of anti-psychiatry.

Mary Barnes is to anti-psychiatry what the Wolfman is to psychoanalysis: each is the movement's most famous case, its most eloquent testimonial witness to the miraculous powers of its leader. The book, *Mary Barnes: Two Accounts of a Journey Through Madness,* consists of two parts, one written by Mary Barnes, the 'tourist', the other by Joseph Berke, her 'guide'. It provides 'penetrating glimpses' not so much into the 'inner world of the schizophrenic', as the publisher's blurb promises, as into the inner sanctum of Kingsley Hall, the holy mosque of anti-psychiatry.

The advertisement for the book promises one thing and implies another, both important. It promises new revelations about Laing's special method for treating schizophrenia; and it implies that there are certain similarities between this account and other testimonials of miraculous recoveries from madness, with the difference that this time, at last, psychiatry—or rather anti-psychiatry—has schizophrenia really licked.

The top line of the publisher's blurb, quoting from a review in *Publishers Weekly,* reads: 'One of the most penetrating glimpses into innovative psychotherapy techniques.' Then follows the publisher's own text, presumably approved by the authors and Laing:

> Two views of the inner world of a schizophrenic, told by the patient and the psychiatrist who helped her back to health when they lived and worked together in R. D. Laing's therapeutic community, Kingsley Hall.

Nearly every word in this blurb belies Laing's claims and the claims of those who work at Kingsley Hall:

1. Laing says that there is no schizophrenia and that there are no schizophrenics; yet here we are offered not one view but two of the 'inner world of a schizophrenic'.
2. The communards at Kingsley Hall claim that there are no patients and psychiatrists there; yet here we are told that there are.

3. The operators of this asylum claim that it is not owned or controlled by any one person, but is a communal enterprise; yet here it is explicitly identified as 'R. D. Laing's'.
4. Laing and his followers claim that the schizophrenic is not sick; yet here we are offered the account of a schizophrenic restored to 'health' in a 'therapeutic community'.

It would be difficult, even if one tried, to pack more contradictions about Laing's claims and the anti-psychiatry movement's confusions into a few sentences.

Laing's role in Mary Barnes's sojourn at Kingsley Hall, where she was cared for during her psychosis, is indicated at several points in the account, beginning in the Acknowledgments, where Berke writes:

> I would like to acknowledge my indebtedness to Ronald Laing for many of the concepts which I discuss and illustrate throughout my account. I refer, most particularly, to the awareness that psychosis may be a state of reality, cyclic in nature, by which the self renews itself; and to the awareness that a person may function at several levels of regression at the same time.

These ideas belong, of course, to Jung and Federn, and to Freud, rather than to Laing. As for Mary Barnes, she offers this revealing observation:

> Unable to cope in ways that 'grown-up' people used, I seemed at sea. Ronnie once said at dinner to the other people: 'Mary has no ego boundaries.' Just in going my own ways, being as I was seemed at times to make other people angry. Then I was surprised: 'Why Joe, I'm just getting on with myself.'

It is interesting that Laing prefers to speak about Mary Barnes in psychoanalytic jargon, rather than in ordinary language. Her remarks suggest that the 'attendants' at Kingsley Hall are not much more tolerant of psychotic coercions than are attendants in ordinary mental hospitals. Moreover, Mary Barnes's passion to control and be controlled is as plain as Laing's and Berke's passion to plagiarise psychoanalytic concepts. She writes: 'Not to be possessed and controlled can be very frightening. The hospital with its drugs and physical treatments and compulsory admission is controlling and possessing.' In a footnote she adds: 'I use the word hospital in the usual accepted way. To me the word denotes a place of healing, of therapy. Kingsley Hall is, in this sense, a real, true hospital.'

Mary Barnes, the true believer in the medical metaphorisation of human problems, here asserts herself. She is sick. Kingsley Hall is a hospital. Berke and Laing are doctors. She has made them act out the roles which she had wished to impose on them. Laing's theorising is, from this perspective, an effort to deny his actual relationship with persons such as Mary Barnes: a relationship based not on informed consent and economic contract, but on mutual coercion and celebration.

IX

Laing begins and ends *The Politics of Experience* in a way that seems to me revealing of his moral style and vision. The style is arrogant and mystical; the vision, apocalyptic and threatening. His opening sentences are:

> Few books today are forgivable. Black on the canvas, silence on the screen, an empty white sheet of paper, are perhaps feasible. There is little conjunction of truth and social 'reality'.

Does this sort of writing betoken the acceptance of psychosis and of the psychotic? Why this arbitrary and absurd condemnation of other people's writings? For it is quite clear that Laing regards his own books as 'forgivable' and 'feasible', and more. He also likes books written about him, although the trees cut down to make them possible make his ecological heart bleed. 'We shall cut down God knows how many trees to have one edition of this book', he tells Evans. 'The mind boggles at what we're doing.'

One of the characteristics of Laing's personal and literary style is his penchant for saying and writing things without asserting anything. It is what Trilling calls 'cant'; but it is a particular kind of cant—one that fairly reeks of the odour of conceit and self-importance. Here is a sample: 'I haven't met anyone with a mind quite like mine. It's somewhat original.'

Of course, Laing does make some assertions, and many of them are astonishing indeed. For example:

> The military are very interested in telepathy, hypnosis, etc. . . . There's a throb, or beat, a pulse between us that the grabby, manipulating fingers of the military-medical-scientific-industrial complex is just beginning to get hold of. The swamis are being wired up. Magic voodoo? Primitive. Hitler and his astrologists. In fact, we know that World War II was largely programmed, astrologically, by Hitler's astrological advisors. Churchill employed a state astrologer to advise him on what Hitler's astrologers were doing.

Perhaps because we all 'know' these things, Laing supplies no references identifying the sources of these 'facts'. However, he does at least tell us something

important about himself—namely, that: 'The contract I have made with my mind is that it is free to do anything it cares to do'.

Laing may be a genius at making contracts with his own mind, but there is no evidence of his even trying to make and keep real promises to real people, or of his trying to negotiate and consummate real contracts with real contracting parties. Such predictability and reliability are simply not a part of his self-image or personal style. This explains why Laing systematically avoids specifying what he himself considers to be the duties of 'therapists' or 'guides' vis-à-vis 'patients' or 'tourists' and vice versa.

Moreover, Laing also 'lets us know' that he is not satisfied with conveying his image of 'reality', but that, if he had his way, only he (and perhaps a few others) could put ink marks on 'white sheets of paper'; that, in short, he wants not to communicate but to convert. In the concluding sentence of *The Politics of Experience,* he declares: 'If I could turn you on, if I could drive you out of your wretched mind, if I could tell you I would let you know.'

There is thus a consistent symmetry between the old psychiatry and the new anti-psychiatry. In psychiatry, the dominant imagery was that of man 'losing his mind'. Curing him meant, therefore, helping him to 'find the mind he lost'; and if he refused to find it by following the psychiatrist's guidance, then it meant 'driving' him back into it. In anti-psychiatry, the dominant imagery is that of man having a 'false' or 'wrong mind'. Curing him means, therefore, helping him to 'lose' his false consciousness or inauthentic self; and if he refuses to lose it, or to give it up, by following the anti-psychiatrist's guidance, then it means 'driving' him out of his 'wretched mind'.

To be sure, occasionally Laing says almost exactly what I say about schizophrenia—namely that there is no such thing—that schizophrenia is a name and a metaphor. But then, almost as if it were enough to pay lip service to this idea, he acclaims again and again the schizophrenic's superiority over ordinary people. Here is a typical passage:

> The (future men) will see that what we call 'schizophrenia' was one of the forms in which, often through quite ordinary people, the light began to break through the cracks in our all-too-closed minds.

Laing often returns and repeats this idea. We must assume, therefore, that he means it, that it is an integral part of his vision of psychiatry and of the so-called problem of schizophrenia. But, of course, schizophrenia cannot be *both* a metaphorical illness and a psychopathological state defined by those who use the term as a literalised metaphor! Yet Laing consistently treats schizophrenia as both, without ever bothering to identify, much less to define, what it is that he refers to when, for example, he asserts that 'madness need not be all breakdown. It may also be break-through.' That sounds nice. Much nicer than Bleuler. But it is not a whit more informative, as Laing has absolutely nothing to say about which madnesses are break-downs and why, and which are break-throughs and why, and how we distinguish the one from the other when we see them. In short, Laing continues in the tradition of Bleuler and Freud in so far as he has his own categories of approved and disapproved conduct—he even calls them 'sanity' and 'madness'!—but does not tell us, clearly and unequivocally, what they are or how we can identify them.

The impression that, despite its verbal concealments, Laing's actual position on schizophrenia is quite close not only to Bleuler's but also to Freud's is also strongly supported by Laing's 'Wolf-woman'—Mary Barnes. Consider the parallels. As Freud had a famous patient psychoanalysed on the couch, so Laing has one guided through madness at Kingsley Hall. As the Wolfman had a 'neurosis', which is the sacred symbol of psychoanalysis—so Mary Barnes had a 'psychosis', which is the sacred symbol of psychiatry and anti-psychiatry. And, finally, as Freud's famous patient and the legends about him and other patients authenticated Freud as an exceptional healer of neurotics—so Laing's famous patient and the legends about her and other patients authenticate Laing as an exceptional healer of psychotics.

The general structural similarities between asylum psychiatry and anti-psychiatry are equally arresting:

The lunatic asylums were run by one set of people for the benefit of another; so are the Laingian asylums.

The people who ran the lunatic asylum insisted that their establishment was a hospital, that they were doctors, and that their clients were patients; the inmates maintained that they were confined in prison, that their keepers were jailers, and that they were prisoners. The people who run the Laingian asylum insist that their establishment is a hostel, that they are guides, and that their clients are tourists lost on their journey through madness; the inmates maintain that they are treated in a hospital, that their superiors are doctors, and that they are patients.

The struggle over definitions in much the same in the lunatic and the Laingian asylums; and there is a similar disjunction between keeper and kept in each, the former insisting on his medical or anti-medical definitions of himself and his client, the latter on his complementarily antagonistic anti-medical and medical definitions of

himself and his keepers. As against these similarities, the main differences between them are that in the lunatic asylum the guiding metaphors were medical, whereas in the Laingian they are Alpinistic; and that in the former, relations of domination-submission, coercion-countercoercion were concealed by the imagery of lost minds being restored to 'sanity', while in the latter they are concealed by lost tourists being restored to 'true sanity'. *Plus ça change, plus c'est la même chose.*

X

Mary Barnes's 'recovery' depended, it seems to me, not on her being 'guided through a journey through madness', but rather on her ability to manipulate her therapists—and their willingness to be manipulated by her; and on her eagerness to play the role of special patient, saved at Kingsley Hall—and her therapists' desire to cast, and commercialise, her in that role. In all these ways, Mary Barnes was reinflated, and inflated herself, with self-esteem. A crucial aspect of her relationship to Laing. Berke, and Kingsley Hall thus lay in her transformation from 'paranoid schizophrenic', which would have been the demotion diagnosed on her by traditional psychiatry, into 'gifted painter', which was the promotion pushed on her by anti-psychiatry. 'Harry'—she writes, referring to an artist enlisted as a 'guide' in her 'journey'—'really made me realise that I had been given the gift of God. This moved me, inside. Later, thinking of Harry and Table Mountain, I painted "Mist, Mountain, and Sea".'

This is very touching. But it is hardly a conceptual or moral breakthrough in treating children, psychotics, or others who need encouragement and are easy prey for flattery by superior persons on whom they are dependent. It is, rather, another cheap trick—not unlike, as David Martin noted, scoring debating points about making sense out of schizophrenia by making cracks about Vietnam.

And yet, the celebration of Mary Barnes as a 'resurrected' person, and her discovery as a 'gifted' painter are our final crucial clues to the ideology and interventions of anti-psychiatry. When Mary Barnes entered Kingsley Hall, she was an undistinguished, unknown, unhappy nurse. When she left, five years later, she was a woman miraculously cured of madness, a gifted painter, a celebrity well on her way towards fame as a goddess in the Church of Anti-Psychiatry. It does not surprise me that she felt better.

As the characteristic operations of institutional psychiatry diminish the mental patient's self-esteem by means of repetitive 'degradation ceremonies', so the characteristic operations of anti-psychiatry increase his or her self-esteem by means of repetitive 'promotion ceremonies'. It surely implies no endorsement of the former to be sceptical about the latter. What are these 'promotion ceremonies' about? Do they symbolise the acquisition of knowledge and skills, as do commencement exercises? Or are they ceremonial occasions of a political character, such as coronations? The distinction is important, in ways we cannot consider here. Suffice it to say that there is legitimate reason to doubt that Mary Barnes really learned to paint at Kingsley Hall. In other words, there is legitimate reason to believe that she was not discovered to be a 'gifted painter' but was declared to be one.

On the front cover of the dust jacket of her book, there is a colour reproduction of one of Mary Barnes's paintings. Inside the jacket it is identified as 'Spring the Resurrection. A finger painting on a slice of elm, done in the Spring of 1969.'

I am not an art critic. And even if I were, my judgment about Mary Barnes's talent as a painter might be mistaken or contradicted by others. But I submit that 'Spring the Resurrection' is not art; it is 'fingerpainting' defined as art.

Let us view Mary Barnes's 'Spring the Resurrection'—the name is again marvellously revealing—as a ceremonial symbol. As the name 'schizophrenia' sacralises—or satanises—the subject as a madman or madwoman, so the celebration of Mary Barnes's painting sacralises her as a 'gifted painter' or genius. Laing and Cooper should thus be regarded as priests blessing a sacramental object, transforming something ordinary and profane into something extraordinary and holy. And Mary Barnes should be viewed as having been restored to 'health' by passage through a classic ritual of purification, confirming her as 'saved', her therapists as her 'saviours', and Kingsley Hall as the St. Peter's of Anti-Psychiatry.

The anti-psychiatrists' lack of imagination in inverting not only the logic and the vocabulary, but even the trappings, of psychiatry and appropriating it all as their own 'original' theoretical principles and therapeutic methods provokes, in me at least, only contempt and pity. The Freudians discover the smearing of faeces in art; the Laingians discover art in the smearing of paint. Or, what comes to the same thing, the psychiatrists seek for the signs of madness, and find them in the paintings of genius, such as Vincent van Gogh; whereas the anti-psychiatrists seek for the signs of genius, and find them in the paintings of madwomen, such as Mary Barnes.

Lock and key fit. The psychiatrist curses and calls it diagnosis; and the patient, especially if he believes it, duly deteriorates. The anti-psychiatrist blesses and calls it discovering genius; and the patient, especially if he believes it, reverently recovers. But how many geniuses can one produce by this method? How many can the market absorb? Is every finger-painting five-year-old really the proto-Picasso his mother thinks he is? Is every Mary Barnes really the Mary Cassatt her Pygmalions claim her to be? Is every young man and woman who is bored and boring, unadmired and unadmirable—or who is just ordinary—the victim of 'plunder'? Has each of them really been robbed of his or her authenticity and sanity, like slaves of their labour and colonised people of their riches? The anti-psychiatrists answer each of these questions with a resounding Yes. But the correct answer, I submit, is No.

XI

One of the most striking things about Mary Barnes's account of her 'journey' is the frank display of her fear of, and escape from, freedom. These felicitous terms are Erich Fromm's, who introduced them to explain the popularity of totalitarian regimes in Europe after the havoc wreaked by the First World War. After the havoc that life and their 'loved ones' often wreak on individuals, they too often develop a desire to escape from freedom. They seek asylum, which is what Kingsley Hall is supposed to be. These parallels between totalitarian and psychiatric asylums, between the fear and rejection of freedom by masses of men and masses of madmen are important—and obvious. Why, then, do I emphasise them? Because although it is obvious that many adults lack freedom not so much because someone has stolen it from them as because they have thrown it away; and although it is equally obvious that persons who act this way may easily get themselves defined as psychotic (especially if that is what they want)—there is, nevertheless, no room in Laing's view of schizophrenia for any of these facts. The schizophrenic, he claims, is always deprived of freedom by others—the family, psychiatry, society. Implicitly, Laing denies that the schizophrenic ever fears freedom because it is too dangerous and demanding, or that he ever deliberately seeks escape from it in the bosom of others—the family, psychiatry, society.

Psychiatry and anti-psychiatry here again fit like lock and key. Psychiatrists deny that involuntary patients ever really want freedom; anti-psychiatrists deny that voluntary tourists ever really want unfreedom. Psychiatrists insist on seeing all schizophrenics, regardless of what they say or do, as sick and needing treatment for madness; anti-psychiatrists insist on seeing all schizophrenics, regardless of what they say or do, as tourists needing a journey through madness.

The anti-psychiatrists' view here also mirrors faithfully the envious fulminations of modern Marxists and Communists who attribute the poverty of 'underdeveloped' peoples to their being robbed, mainly by Americans, of their wealth. The Chileans would all be rich if American companies did not plunder their copper mines. In this anti-capitalist, anti-colonial perspective, riches flow from natural resources without human intervention. Such intervention only confiscates and corrupts. The Chilean sitting on top of a mountain of unmined copper is 'rich'. The child left alone with his uncorrupted self is 'sane'. Each becomes a 'victim' through plunder. Cooper articulates this imagery with unashamed naivety:

> Country A (say, the United States of America) buys tomatoes from country B (say, one impoverished South American state), and it sells them back, in tins, to country B at 300 percent profit. This is known as 'aid', and aid comes very close to help and treatment. . . .

His ideas on commerce, schizophrenia, and the whole human condition itself, are rooted in the same pattern:

> If one states the schizophrenia problem this way, namely in terms of the existence of a person being sucked out of him by others, or expressed from him by himself (in loving acknowledgment of the others' rapacious ingestion) so that finally nothing of himself is left to himself since he is altogether for the other, then we must conclude that, although being put in hospital represents a special fate, schizophrenia is nothing less than the predicament of each one of us.

Here, at last, is the fully developed image of schizophrenia as the plundered mind. Cooper, of course, overdoes it, as he overdoes everything. Plundering and being plundered are, at least, real understandable events. People do deprive others of their possessions. But how can everyone be the victim of plunder, which is Cooper's penultimate view of the world? Who, then, are the plunderers? The question is, of course, rhetorical. In the imagery that Laing and Cooper are promoting we are both victims and victimisers. Who, which, and when is not for us to ask. They will let us know when they are ready.

XII

It should be clear by now that, just as the psychiatric paradigm of paresis was not original with Kraepelin and Bleuler and their followers, so the modern anti-psychiatric paradigm of plunder is not original with Laing and Cooper and their followers. The psychiatrists have borrowed the disease model from medicine, and, on the strength of it, declared psychiatry to be a branch of medicine—a specialty based on the combination of a medical metaphor and the police power of the state. Similarly, the anti-psychiatrists have borrowed the model of exploitation—of colonialism, foreign invasion, and plunder—from the Old Left, and, on the strength of it, declared anti-psychiatry to be a branch of the New Left—a movement based on the combination of a martial metaphor and the persuasive power of apocalyptic promises and prophesies.

Actually, the proposition that the madman is sane but the society that so labels him is insane is merely an extension of Proudhon's famous proposition that 'Property is theft'. Both make use of the vocabulary of an institution to attack that institution, private property in the one instance, psychiatry in the other. In the former case, according to Searle, the moral rule or prescription that 'one ought not to steal can be taken as saying that to recognise something as someone else's property necessarily involves recognising his right to dispose of it. This is a constitutive rule of the institution of private property.' Searle then refers to Proudhon's rule-inversion about theft, and comments:

> If one tries to take this as an internal remark it makes no sense. It was intended as an external remark attacking and rejecting the institution of private property. It gets its air of paradox and force by using terms which are internal to the institution in order to attack the institution. Standing on the deck of some institutions one can tinker with constitutive rules and even throw some other institutions overboard. But could one throw all institutions overboard? . . . One could not and still engage in those forms of behaviour we consider characteristically human. Suppose Proudhon had added (and tried to live by): 'Truth is a lie, marriage is infidelity, language is uncommunicative, law is crime', and so on with every possible institution.

Interestingly, this is exactly what Laing and Cooper have done, and why, in part, they have appealed so strongly to the disaffected youth of our age who, having nothing to live for, are envious of all those who do, and want to destroy the institutions that give meaning to the lives of 'normal' people. For my part, I feel just as strongly opposed to individuals demeaning other individuals as insane as a means of gaining meaning for their lives, which is the existential cannibalism characteristic of psychiatry, as I do to individuals demeaning groups or societies as insane, which is the existential cannibalism characteristic of anti-psychiatry.

This, in short, is why I believe that psychiatry and

anti-psychiatry are two wrongs, and that two wrongs do not make a right but only a third, still graver, wrong. Psychiatry is a wrong, intellectually—because it interprets disagreement as disease; and morally—because it justifies confinement as cure. Anti-psychiatry is a wrong, intellectually—because it interprets anomie as authenticity; and morally—because by selectively condemning the behaviour of our own parents, physicians, and politicians, it justifies the behaviour of those, within our society and outside it, who would deprive us of liberty, dignity, and property because they despise us for their own personal or political reasons.

Moreover, psychiatry and anti-psychiatry resemble one another not only as opposites usually do, but also in their shared obsession with 'schizophrenia' and its management. This similarity is displayed most strikingly in the dominant images, in psychiatry and anti-psychiatry, invoked to explain this paradigmatic form of 'madness'. In psychiatry, the dominant image is that the schizophrenic had a 'sound mind' but 'lost' it. How? By destruction. Like a foreign invader burning down an occupied city and leaving it in ashes, his brain is destroyed by the invading spirochetes of syphilis.

In anti-psychiatry, the dominant image is that the schizophrenic has a 'sound mind', or could have had one, but was deprived of it or was prevented from developing it. How? By plunder. Like a foreign invader plundering a city and leaving it empty and barren, his personality is 'emptied out' by the invading 'love' of the family, (capitalist) society, the 'oppressors'.

In other words, in the psychiatric view of schizophrenia, sanity is synonymous with a biologically healthy brain, which is a nearly universal human possession, and is achieved without personal effort; and insanity results from damage to this treasured possession, to which everyone has a sort of 'biological right'. Whereas in the anti-psychiatric view, sanity is synonymous with an authentic or true self, which is conceived of, in the Rousseauesque tradition, as also a universal human possession or potentiality, and it too is achieved without personal effort; and insanity results from damage to or loss of this treasured possession to which everyone has a sort of 'political right'. The former view presupposes 'normal' brain development as a 'natural' process; the latter view 'normal' self development. This pure and healthy brain/self is then pictured as destroyed or deformed by syphilisation or civilisation. Actually, as recently as two generations ago, these two processes were said to go hand in hand. Syphilisation has since

dropped back as a major contender in the race for corrupting mankind, leaving civilisation—at least among the anti-capitalists and anti-psychiatrists—undisputedly in the lead.

Clearly, both these views contain a measure of truth; how large or small that measure is depends on time, place, and person. Syphilis does cause paresis. Parents, teachers, people in power can 'cause' extreme human anguish and misery in those who depend on them, and do, in that sense, 'drive people crazy'. But what both these models obscure are the simplest and most ancient of human truths; namely, that life is an arduous and tragic struggle; that what we call 'sanity'—what we mean by 'not being schizophrenic'—has a great deal to do with competence, earned by struggling for excellence; with compassion, hard won by confronting conflict; and with modesty and patience, acquired through silence and suffering. This image, not so much of some sort of idealistic sanity or mental health, but simply of being able to endure life with decency and dignity, cannot be fitted into the paradigms of either paresis or plunder. It requires an altogether different model or perspective—something like a sculptor carving a statue out of stone. There is no statue hidden in the stone. If a man with a piece of marble in his possession has no marble statue, it is not because his crusading enemy has smashed it—because it is the wrong idol; nor because his colonising conqueror has stolen it—because he wants it for himself; but it is because he has failed to transform the stone into a statue.

The obligation to transform oneself from infant into child, adolescent, and adult—into whatever it is we think we ought to be; and the failure to meet this obligation—for reasons too numerous to consider here but clearly including the nature of that very 'self' whose self-making is our concern—all this finds no place in the theories of either psychiatry or anti-psychiatry. Psychiatrists and anti-psychiatrists are equally simplistic in their causal imageries and remedial strategies. In the psychiatric view, medical research will make everyone sane. In the anti-psychiatric view, allowing incompetent, destructive and self-destructive persons to wallow in their self-contempt and contempt of others will suffice to guide them safely through their journey in the Alps of alienation, after which all will arrive in the neat and clean Swiss village and live happily ever after. Such are the promises of the propagandists for psychiatric research on the one hand, and for anti-psychiatric retreats on the other.

ANTHONY CLARE

Anti-Psychiatry: An Alternative View

To any intelligent and reasonably sympathetic observer, interested in acquiring a balanced and informed understanding of its theoretical basis, its clinical practice and its possibilities, the present fragmented state of psychiatry presents a formidable picture. The concept of mental illness appears to permit a bewildering number of interpretations. For some it is merely a label for socially unacceptable behaviour, behind which lurks the deviant, intent on evading the consequences of his antisocial behaviour. For others it is a purely arbitrary concept which only serves to mislead people, by virtue of its medical connotations, into believing in a 'sickness of the mind' when, more often than not, what it describes consists of disordered interpersonal relationships wherein one person is scapegoated to shoulder the responsibility for the disturbances of the entire group. Still others see it as a political device, a ruse which enables those who hold power within society to devalue and degrade the dissident and, by defining him as mentally unbalanced, to violate his freedom and destroy his dignity. Finally, there are those for whom the concept of mental illness is directly analogous to physical illness; the patient manifests not a physical pathology but 'psychopathology', exhibits disturbances in psychological rather than physical functions and, in some instances at least, suffers a significant impairment of his judgmental capabilities and personal responsibility.

Given the fractious and acrimonious debate which rages over its legitimacy, it is hardly surprising that there have even been attempts to abolish the concept of mental illness altogether and replace it by some alternative, non-medical construct such as deviance, maladaptation, social disturbance, problems of living or community disorder. Over the past fifteen years, an anti-psychiatry movement has sprung up, the central tenet of which appears to be that mental illness is a reductive smear that obscures and defiles the despairing cries of the downtrodden and exploited against an alienating and dehumanised society. Psychiatric intervention is portrayed as a violent assault perpetrated under the guise of

Reprinted from *The New Review*, Vol. 3, No. 33 (1977), pages 15–20, by permission of the publisher (copyright, *The New Review*, 1977).

treatment, and the psychiatrist is deemed to be an agent of the dominant political order, of repression and of power.

True, there are those, and they are particularly to be found within orthodox clinical psychiatry, who believe that the anti-psychiatry bubble has burst, that the heady days of the 1960s, with their psychedelia, flower power and that seductive, transparent faith in the healing properties of patience and love, have given way to a more cynical and suspicious assessment of competing creeds and claims. That grand, if improbable alliance of persecuted dissident, prosecuted criminal and incarcerated madman, fused together with such spell-binding eloquence and visceral intensity by an equally improbable intellectual clique, at whose head marched R. D. Laing and Herbert Marcuse, Timothy Leary and Stokely Carmichael, has fallen apart and dissolved and with it has evaporated much of the vitality and the urgency of the anti-psychiatry movement.

More recently, and most notably in the pages of *The New Review* by Professor Thomas Szasz, the term 'anti-psychiatry' has been criticised because it implicitly commits one to opposing everything that psychiatrists do. To those who are somewhat unfamiliar with the more subtle details of psychiatric controversies, the spectacle of Szasz attacking Laing with such uncompromising hostility must seem in the order of Lucifer turning on the Deity. They did, after all, appear such friends, united on many a banner waved below the ramparts of beleagured psychiatric orthodoxy. More than any other names in the pantheon of psychiatry's critics, these two appeared to embody the central values of radical anti-psychiatry—its anti-authoritarianism, its anti-capitalism, its anti-materialism.

It is in itself a measure of the ignorance, the relative illiteracy of so many of psychiatry's opponents that they unthinkingly bracketed Laing and Szasz together in this fashion. Laing may or may not be one of the 'self-declared socialists, communists or at least anti-capitalists and collectivists' which Szasz believes him to be (I personally feel Szasz is accurate in this respect), but there can be little doubt about Szasz's own particular position on the political continuum. Szasz refuses the tag 'anti-psychiatrist' because he insists that he is not opposed to all forms of psychiatry (which is reassuring, given that he is a professor of psychiatry and, presumably, teaches medical students the rudiments of *something*) but against what he terms 'institutional psychiatry'. The institutional psychiatrist, he defines as

> a bureaucratic employee, paid for his services by a private or public organisation . . . the actual client of institutional psychiatry is some social interest and organisation (for example, the Peace Corps, a university health service, a state mental hygiene department); its ostensible client is, more often than not, its victim, rather than its beneficiary.[1]

In what way then does the psychiatry practised by Szasz differ? The answer lies in its name, *contractual psychiatry,* itself more evocative of the world of big business and capitalist finance than of medicine and healing. The most important economic characteristic of contractual psychiatry, declares Szasz, 'is that the contractual psychiatrist is a private entrepreneur, paid for his services by his client'. In Szasz's view, this is the only economic arrangement which permits the client to retain complete control over his relations with that psychiatric expert he has called in to assist in the resolution of his personal difficulties and sufferings. Whereas the institutional psychiatrist is portrayed as someone who imposes himself on patients who do not pay him, do not want to be his patients and are not free to reject his help, the contractual psychiatrist offers himself to patients who must pay him, must want to be his patients and are free to reject his help.

Given such a formulation of the economic relationship binding patient and psychiatrist together, it is hardly surprising to find Szasz so scornful of Laing's demand that the British tax-payer finance the psychotic patient in his 'journey' through madness at Kingsley Hall. Nor is it entirely surprising to find Szasz in the van of those who are vehemently opposed to the development of a national health service in the United States to replace the entrepreneurial foundations on which American medical practice currently rests. Szasz's ideological views on such issues help to clarify and explain his idiosyncratic views on contemporary psychiatry every bit as successfully as his exposition of Laing's own political attitudes illuminates the latter's ideas on the nature of madness. Whereas Laing appears to endorse a soft, permissive and often passive attitude towards the mentally disturbed, Szasz's approach is uncompromising, harsh and often punitive. The schizophrenic, observes Szasz,

may be treated as: 1. a dangerous madman; 2. a person having highly dramatic and unusual experiences; or 3. a person disrespectful of the rights of others. The first view is that of traditional psychiatry; the second, that of the glamorizers of schizophrenia; the third is my own.[2]

Elsewhere he declares 'When Jones says he is Jesus, scientific psychiatry declares him to have a delusion. I say he is lying.' Concerning paranoid delusions, he believes that many are, in effect, 'the expression of a lack of courage':

> For example, the elderly woman who complains that her husband is poisoning her. She accuses. She complains. But she does not act. Why doesn't she kill him? Or leave him? Why doesn't she put her money where her mouth is? Because she lacks courage. She wants someone else to act on her belief and to be responsible for the consequences.[3]

In short, psychotic disturbances are games and mental illness is 'self-enhancing deception, self-promotive strategy'.

It is worth noting at this stage that throughout Szasz's voluminous writing, not a shred of worthwhile evidence is provided in support of such a view. His 'explanation' of the nature of the elderly woman's delusions ignores the fact that many patients do not restrict themselves to making verbal complaints and accusations but frequently *act* on their beliefs. Such patients are often notoriously litigious and often pursue with tenacity the innocent objects of their accusations through the courts. They are often well-known to the police and to lawyers and when they fail to persuade these representatives of the law of the truth of their assertions they not infrequently take the law into their own hands, sometimes with tragic consequences. To at least one practising psychiatrist, the conceptualisation of a paranoid patient as someone lacking in courage is a singularly unhelpful, uninformative and inappropriate declaration.

It is interesting, in view of the many books and articles that Szasz has written in which he has disputed the orthodox view of schizophrenia as a disease, to discover what he believes it to be. Schizophrenics, in his view, conduct themselves as if others had no rights. Now, few would dispute that a schizophrenic often shows scant regard for the feelings and rights of others. Careless drivers, overbearing politicians, egocentric artists, domineering prima donnas and 'stoned' pop singers likewise tend to be just a little indifferent to public sensitivity, but in each case and in the case of the

---

1. Thomas S. Szasz. *The Second Sin* p. 74. Routledge & Kegan Paul. (1974).

2. Ibid. p. 104.
3. Ibid. p. 105.

schizophrenic (and, indeed, of anyone else who manifests such regrettable self-absorption) it behoves one to ask why they behave in this way. Is the schizophrenic responsible for his behaviour when he tramples as he often, though not always, tramples on other people's rights? The orthodox psychiatrist says he may not be, in which case punishment is clearly inappropriate. Lawyers agree, it being a characteristic of sophisticated legal systems that an individual's liability to punishment, particularly for serious crimes carrying severe penalties, is made by law to depend on, among other factors, certain mental conditions, 'excusing conditions' in Bernard Hart's phrase. Szasz's response to Hart, whom otherwise he quotes with approval, is to indulge in a typical piece of debating guile:

> To the extent that a person acts involuntarily, he cannot be regarded, in the social sense of the term, as a human being. This then leads to the dilemma typical of contemporary forensic psychiatry. Either we regard offenders as sane and punish them; or we regard them as insane, and, though excusing them of crimes officially, punish them by treating them as beings who are less than human.[4]

Here Szasz sets up his premise—a person acting involuntarily cannot be regarded 'in the social sense of the word' as a human being—from which all else flows. But it is not at all clear what, if anything, such a statement means. A driver, intoxicated at the wheel of his car, is doubtless under the influence of alcohol and to that extent his mental abilities are impaired, but is he in any sense, let alone the 'social' one, any less a human being? Can a patient, confused and delirious in a toxic confusional state, be regarded as a 'human being' and if not what is he? Szasz cleverly and cunningly pairs two concepts, impairment of abilities and loss of essential humanity, in such a way that those psychiatrists and lawyers who mount a defence of diminished responsibility in a given case can be accused of denigrating their client's humanity and reducing his dignity. The choice, as Szasz ingeniously constructs it, lies between finding the offender guilty and punishing him and finding him mentally impaired and punishing him! Underpinning Szasz's entire approach to the problem of responsibility in mental disorder is his belief that all compulsory psychiatric treatment is punishment masquerading under a more acceptable name. It should be said that he has provided a sizeable body of evidence testifying to disgraceful abuse of the involuntary hospitalisation procedures in the United States and his lack of enthusiasm for such procedures is readily comprehensible. How-

ever, this is to confuse abuse of a procedure with the procedure itself.

Szasz is quite dogmatically convinced that 'the phenomenon psychiatrists call "schizophrenia" is not a demonstrable medical disease but the name of certain kinds of social deviance (or of behaviour unacceptable to the speaker)'. Szasz has been saying as much with scarcely an addendum or a modification for well over fifteen years. It must stand as one of the most impressive examples of cant, that word whose disappearance he so correctly and so mournfully laments. Szasz's ignorance of the concept of schizophrenia has already been subjected to an elegant and clinical dissection by Professor Sir Martin Roth[5] and for our purposes can for the moment be ignored. His apparent indifference to the subtleties inherent in the formulation of the disease concept itself, however, does merit some attention. For Szasz, there is no problem whatsoever:

> Disease means bodily disease. Gould's Medical Dictionary defines disease as a disturbance of the function or structure of an organ or a part of the *body*. (Italics in original.) The mind (whatever it is) is not an organ or part of the body. Hence it cannot be diseased in the same sense as the body can.[6]

Now what could be more simple? The precariousness of this position, however, is readily revealed by the simple expedient of reaching for another dictionary, in this case *The Concise Oxford Dictionary*. Here we find, among the various definitions of disease, 'Deranged or depraved state of mind or morals'. So the problem returns. Indeed were we to accept Szasz's formulation and restrict the concept of disease to those disorders in which there is an identifiable structural or functional organ change, we would be forced not merely to exclude certain psychiatric disorders but such established medical conditions as migraine, gastritis, trigeminal neuralgia and idiopathic epilepsy. The causal basis for many contemporary diseases, including cancer, arteriosclerosis, high blood pressure and peptic ulceration, remains obscure and, consequently, the main treatments employed are almost entirely palliative in their actions.

It may well be, as Kendell has pointed out in a particularly thoughtful analysis of the problem[7], that concepts such as mental illness and schizophrenia may eventually lose their usefulness and pass out of use, as earlier concepts have done. But if this should happen, it

4. Thomas S. Szasz. *Law, Liberty and Psychiatry* p. 137. Routledge & Kegan Paul. (1974).

5. Martin Roth. 'Schizophrenia and the Theories of Thomas Szasz' *British Journal of Psychiatry*. October 1976.
6. Thomas S. Szasz. *The Second Sin* p. 97 Routledge & Kegan Paul. (1974).
7. Robert E. Kendell. *The Role of Diagnosis in Psychiatry* Blackwell Scientific Publications. Oxford. (1975).

will be because they will have been replaced by other more useful concepts and not because of any sudden realisation that there is no such thing as madness. For the foreseeable future, the usefulness of the concept of mental illness is well established by the universal occurrence of the experiential and behavioural anomalies to which the term refers, which appear to remain unaffected by differences in culture or language, by the biological disadvantages associated with such anomalies, by the evidence that these abnormalities are, at least in part, genetically transmitted and by the influence on them of drugs which lack analogous effects on other people.

In arriving at his momentous conclusion that schizophrenia is not a mental illness, Szasz rejects all the theories that have been proposed for its causation, whether genetic, biochemical, social, familial or psychodynamic, and proposes one of his own which has subsequently been dubbed by Miriam Siegler and Humphrey Osmond, the 'conspiratorial' model of madness. It is this model which he shares with Ronald Laing and it is this which explains the fact that they tend, despite their obvious political differences, to be yoked together as partners in the assault on the coercive power of orthodox psychiatry. Psychiatrists are thought-police, trained to suppress and silence those who assert their individuality in the face of the prevailing power interests of society. They are today's Inquisitors, seeking in the minds and bodies of their victims the signs and the symptoms of non-existent pathology as their predecessors sought with such single-mindedness the stigmata of demonological possession. The 'mad' are our century's witches, singled out for persecution, degradation and incarceration at the hands of the official representatives of contemporary institutionalised power.

So how does such a formulation differ from Laing's? It is true that Laing's first book, *The Divided Self,* was written by someone who, while clearly preoccupied with phenomenological aspects of psychiatric abnormality, identified himself as a medically-trained clinician who accepted the existence of that category of people known as the mentally ill. The preface to the first edition of that remarkable work, in addition to acknowledging Laing's debt to phenomenologists such as Jaspers, Heidegger and Binswanger, declared the purpose of the book to be 'to give in plain English an account, in *existential* terms, of some forms of madness'. The preface thanks several medically-trained psychiatrists for their 'constructive' criticisms and expresses gratitude to two practising psychiatric clinicians 'for the facilities they provided for the clinical basis for this study and the encouragement they gave me'.[8]

Within the space of five years, all seemed to have changed. In 1964, the preface to the second edition appeared to have changed. The medical base was gone and now Laing was endorsing a conspiratorial view of the origin of the sufferings of those he had studied. All was relative. The madness of the so-called insane might well seem normal when viewed against society's accepted values and standards.

> A man who prefers to be dead rather than Red is normal. A man who says he has lost his soul is mad . . . A man who says that negroes are an inferior race may be widely respected. A man who says his whiteness is a form of cancer is certifiable. A little girl of seventeen in a mental hospital told me she was terrified because the Atom Bomb was inside her. This is a delusion. The statesmen of the world who boast and threaten that they have Doomsday weapons are far more dangerous and far more estranged from 'reality' than any of the people on whom the label 'psychotic' is affixed.[9]

This extract not merely illustrates how far Laing moved in a relatively short period of time but how closely he moved to Szasz. True, Laing quickly divided the world into 'them' and 'us' and, as Szasz points out, indulged in a total romanticisation of 'them' while savaging 'us' for our barbarities. But Szasz, too, divides the world. Ostensibly, he appears to idealise the position of those dubbed 'psychotic' (and hence he has been recruited as a guru by the many who, for a multitude of reasons, endorse the view of madness as a 'super-state', a voyage of self-exploration and self-growth) but at its heart his message is that while 'they' should be recognised as dissenters, deviants, drop-outs from the accepted behavioural and social standards of society in so far as they bother 'us' they should be punished like anyone else. His tendency to portray himself in the company of John Stuart Mill, Voltaire and Nietzsche as a redoubtable champion of the rights of the individual against the machinations of the State and to classify the mentally ill alongside witches, Jews, negroes and homosexuals, those hapless minorities hounded and persecuted for the 'crime' of being different, undoubtedly contributed to the fallacious idea that Szasz saw the psychotic as having a special role or purpose. Any lingering doubts on this matter can only have been resolved by his article in this journal. The moral righteousness, for which he roundly castigates Laing, he himself expresses when eventually he does reveal his conception of sanity and insanity:

> The obligation to transform oneself from infant into child, adolescent and adult—into whatever it is we think we ought

8. Ronald D. Laing. *The Divided Self* Preface to 1st. Edition. (1960).

9. Ibid. Preface to 2nd. edition. (1965).

to be; and the failure to meet this obligation—for reasons too numerous to consider here but clearly including the nature of the very 'self' whose self-making is our concern—all this finds no place in the theories of either psychiatry or anti-psychiatry.[10]

Such a passage reflects Szasz's American background, with its sturdy endorsement of the good capitalistic virtues of independence and self-improvement and its stern disapproval of personal failure. By the mid-1960s, however, Laing, resembling more and more a fiery evangelical Scottish puritan preacher with a penchant for socialism, was flailing society—'We are all murderers and prostitutes—no matter to what culture, society, class, nation one belongs, no matter how normal, moral or mature one takes oneself to be'—and berating witch-like parents for driving their offspring mad so that by adolescence all that remains is 'a being like ourselves. A half-crazed creature more or less adjusted to a mad world.'

The idea that the nexus of schizophrenia was to be found in the bosom of the family was a favourite Laingian theme. In a television interview with Professor Morris Carstairs, former professor of psychiatry at Edinburgh University and now Vice-Chancellor at York, Laing was asked about his pessimistic views on family life. Pressed hard by Carstairs, Laing persisted in doubting whether many people survived their early family experiences without deep scars although he did let fall a warm personal insight—'Some of the happiest and most fulfilling, rewarding, pleasant and memorable experiences have been in families in which I have lived myself.' The tribute, nonetheless, appeared grudging, an aspect of Laing which has remained somewhat puzzling but is likely to become less so with the publication of his latest book, *The Facts of Life*.[11] The book begins with an autobiographical sketch which makes up in the sickening misery of its content for the regrettable brevity of its form. The only child of parents glumly depressed with him and with each other, R. D. Laing, we learn, discovered the facts of life not from his father (though the latter did clumsily offer to reveal them), nor from his school (there appeared to be a collective confusion about which parts were for what), but from a textbook on venereal disease in a local bookstore. The family lived in a three-roomed tenement in Glasgow. Despite the ever-present threat and reality of violence, a certain genteel hypocrisy was maintained so that his mother fainted when the fifteen-year-old Ronald used the phrase 'fuckin

well' and his father was so aghast that he forgot to hit him!

These are among the few cameos that we are given of Laing's early life. The bewilderment and confusion over facts, myth, reality and meaning have remained. The rest of this book is given over to speculations and ruminations similar to those in *Knots* and *The Politics of Experience*. Whereas in *The Divided Self* he skilfully outlined the areas and borders of the fragmented mind, drawing lucidly on examples from his clinical experience to illuminate a particular point, here he drifts about aimlessly, following blind-alley trails of staggering banality. We are treated to a rambling treatise on the trauma of birth and the potential significance of intra-uterine and even pre-uterine life for our later development.

> It is at least *conceivable* to me that myths, legends, stories, dreams, fantasies and conduct may contain strong reverberations of our uterine experience.

The idea that birth produces a dramatic and possibly crucial impact on the subsequent development of the central nervous system is neither new nor, necessarily, far-fetched. However, Laing's treatment of such a theme is unforgiveably sloppy, his style and discipline utterly ravaged in comparison with his first book. He muses on the fact that he needs a daily drink around 5.15 pm. and attributes it to the fact that it was his birth hour, mourns the death of his 'intra-uterine lover' (his placenta) and attributes a whole variety of traumas and neuroses to the original anxiety following conception as the fertilised ovum waits expectantly for implantation.

Once he retreated into the mind and heart of the schizoid and, engaged on a solitary odyssey, an inward journey away from others and into the self, he howled at the arid blasphemy of the outer world. Now he has contracted still further. Compared to the rich variety of prenatal experience, the post-natal world is but a shadow. The imagination, unshackled now from the restrictions of any philosophical or phenomenological mooring, runs riot. Maybe the embryo communicates with the mother. Maybe the embryo dreams. Maybe the flu is some physical memory of living some intra-uterine crisis. Much of this and more is laid out in such a manner as to suggest either Laing believes it to be in some sense *poetic* or he anticipates that many of those likely to buy this book can hardly be expected to cope with reading a full page.

My daughter aged two and a half says to new
au pair girl

9. Ibid. Preface to 2nd. edition. (1965).

10. Thomas S. Szasz. 'Anti-Psychiatry: The Paradigm of the Plundered Mind' *The New Review*. Vol. 3, No. 29, p. 14.

Are you a Brenda?
Brenda was the first au pair girl

It is as though
we say to the breast
are you a placenta?
to a relationship one is about to get into
are you a good womb?

The book contains the usual genuflection in the direction of the value of an untreated psychosis as a journey of exploration and self-growth. One should not be surprised. Laing's intellectual sloppiness is now embarrassing and the fact that he has failed to take any account of the bankruptcy of that particular claim reflects it. His book is published hard on the heels of *Anna,*[12] the dismal and horrifying story of a girl who suffers a severe psychotic illness, and is nursed at home by her husband and a Laingian psychotherapist, supervised by Laing himself, and steadily deteriorates. Convinced that she is the centre of an elaborate persecutory system (doubtless, Szasz would insist that she was playing games), she alternated between screeching like a wounded animal, crawling around on all fours, somersaulting against the furniture and making a series of suicide attempts. Her husband, who writes the account under a pseudonym, shows a stoical devotion to the Laingian view throughout, dipping into *The Divided Self* to maintain his shaky morale. Even when he wakes one night to find his distraught crazed wife strangling their three-year-old son 'to stop him being tortured' he maintains his cool and persuades her and, even more remarkably, himself to go back to sleep. Throughout the voyage, the Laingian psychotherapist's interpretations, a mixture of banality and opacity, are treated with a totally inappropriate awe. Despairing as fleetingly lucid spells gradually give way to a steady disintegration. Reed bumps into Laing in the street and asks him why, after several months, his wife has not negotiated the voyage, has not brought her frail barque into port. Laing wearily observes, 'I feel I know less now than I did twenty years ago as a young doctor', and his latest offering only underwrites that shabby admission. This is not a voyage anywhere except down. In *The Facts of Life,* Laing regrets that there is not one psychiatric institution in the UK where a patient might be 'allowed' or even 'helped' to go 'through' what he feels impelled to go through. It is the sort of comment with which he made a striking impact a decade ago. Now, even his erstwhile companions must be beginning to doubt. 'Allowed' to go 'through', poor Anna sets fire to herself in her bath. She

dies slowly and painfully. When asked after the horrible burning whether she would have wanted to have conventional psychiatric treatment, she answered sadly: 'No. But then I wouldn't have wanted this.'

My own view, which I have argued elsewhere[13], is that the Annas of this world, in rejecting orthodox psychiatry, are rejecting its often appalling standards of practice. Its theoretical foundations, much derided by Szasz and Laing, are in fact a great deal healthier and more fertile than either of their seductive but ultimately barren philosophies. Szasz sneers at the concept of psychosis, 'the sacred symbol of psychiatry and anti-psychiatry'. His sophistical gymnastics have won him many admirers but they have nothing to offer the crazy Annas of this world; telling her that she is infringing the rights of others as she attempts to strangle her son or that she is a free, independent spirit as she burns herself may look the act of a brave realist, especially if it is dressed up with the appropriate philosophical trappings and argued with guile and force. But, in the last resort, psychosis cannot be grasped that way, a fact which more than any other explains why orthodox psychiatrists, while acknowledging Szasz's achievement in drawing attention to the abuses of contemporary psychiatric practice, regard his view on the nature of mental illness as specious.

Laing and Szasz may wrestle with each other with all the passion of the fascist and the communist waking up in the same political bed, but the differences that divide them are in the final analysis less than the sum total of that which they share. Neither takes madness *seriously;* to Szasz it is a game, to Laing a mystical experience. To those who suffer its torment, it is a misery, a terrifying ordeal which is more often than not as mysterious and odd to them as it is to those who, like David Reed, watch its remorseless progress with numbed helplessness. In *The Eden Express,* Mark Vonnegut, novelist Kurt's son, tells of the psychotic illness he underwent during a period in a hippie commune in America. Describing himself as a 'Laing-Szasz fan' who 'didn't believe there was really any such thing as schizophrenia', Vonnegut eventually was forced to conclude that the Laingian view of psychosis as a reasonable response to an insane world was bankrupt.

It's such a poetic affliction from inside and out, it's not hard to see how people have assumed that schizophrenia must have poetic causes and that any therapy would have to be poetic as well. A lot of my despair of ever getting well was

11. Ronald D. Laing. *The Facts of Life* Allen Lane. (1976).

12. David Reed. *Anna* Secker and Warburg. (1976).
13. Anthony Clare. *Psychiatry in Dissent* Tavistock Publications. (1976).

based on the improbability of finding a poet good enough to deal with all that had happened o me. It's hard to say when I accepted the notion that the problem was biochemical, it went so hard against everything I had been taught about mental illness.[14]

He had been 'taught', like so many of his generation, by Szasz and Laing. The hopelessness of dealing with schizophrenia as game or as mystical trip is known to the many psychiatrists genuinely involved in its treatment. It is becoming increasingly apparent, albeit in a tragic fashion, to some patients, a number of whom like Vonnegut can be expected to share their discovery that their theories have not been matched by reality. 'The only decent answers I've been able to come up with', concludes Vonnegut, 'are biochemical ones.' But, as he

14. Mark Vonnegut. *The Eden Express* Jonathan Cape. (1976).

points out with consummate honesty, 'biochemistry is as boring as mud next to psychology, religion and politics'. There was a time when Laing and Szasz could not have been described as boring—the very vigour and freshness of their views contrasted favourably with the aridity and prosaic flavour of orthodox psychiatric texts. Now, however, things are going full circle. *The Facts of Life* is boring, very boring indeed, I regret to say. It has nothing to offer those to whom Laing appeared to make so many promises, hold out so many hopes. As for Szasz, he meanders on, full of drive, full of energy, delivering his shafts of wisdom from his Syracuse ivory tower, unwilling to concede that the general reluctance on the part of psychiatrists, like myself, to adopt his views is not based on fear or fury, on ignorance, indifference or spleen, but on the fact that, applied to the seriously ill, the Annas and the Vonneguts seen by myself and my colleagues, they have nothing to offer at all.

PART SIX

Structures of Community-Based Treatment

Currently the most dynamic locus of change in the mental health field is the community. It is here that deinstitutionalization has created a context for action directly or indirectly involving three main components of the mental health enterprise: the *service providers* (psychiatrists, medical practitioners, clinical psychologists, social workers, marriage counselors, nurses, and many others), the *consumers* (chronic mental patients, other patients, and potential patients, and the family, friends, and relatives of patients and potential patients), and *researchers/policy makers* (physicians, psychiatrists, psychologists, sociologists, and others). Each segment has created organizations to represent their special interests (Magaro, Gripp, and McDowell, 1978). The service providers are spoken for by the American Medical Association, the American Hospital Association, the American Psychiatric Association, and many other groups. The researchers/policy makers, the least visible sector and one about which very little is known (Rogow, 1970), have national and regional professional and occupational associations and most prominently the National Institute of Mental Health to foster their interests. By far the fastest growing organizational response to decarceration has taken place among the largest and most amorphous group, the consumers. Some of their organizations, such as Network Against Psychiatric Assault, Mental Patients Liberation Front, and Mental Health Consumer Concerns, stress an advocacy process to protect mental health patient interests. Others, such as Diabasis House, Recovery, Inc., and the American Schizophrenia Association, are associated with or promote specific therapeutic technologies. For example, the latter group, which reportedly has forty-one chapters and twenty thousand members (Beels, 1978), supports the orthomolecular theory of schizophrenia. They advocate massive vitamin supplements and are backed by the enormous prestige of the Nobel Laureate, Linus Pauling. Regardless of whether or not the treatment technology they advocate is effective, this organization, which consists primarily of families of schizophrenics, merits study. It demonstrates the increasing interest of consumers and self-help groups in enlarging their participation in the mental health enterprise. The theme of this the final section of the book concerns the "working out" process in the community of the sometimes competing and sometimes shared interests of this varied and complex set of persons and organizations comprising two of the three sectors of the mental health enterprise—the service providers and the consumers. As a result of deinstitutionalization the community has become an important arena where their interests (and those of the researchers/policy makers) converge.

Historically, public policy on how and where the mentally ill should be treated has emphasized community-based care, then shifted to a focus on state institutions, and has now returned to community treatment again. The organization most symbolic of mental health practices in the 1950s and earlier was the large state mental hospital, which was typically located in rural areas so as to decrease its visibility (Belknap, 1956; Stanton & Schwartz, 1954; Goffman, 1961). The impact of the community mental health movement and the deinstitutionalization of mental illness led to the replacement of this organization with a sizeable number of specialized multipurpose organizations such as community mental health centers (CMHCs), boarding or nursing homes, methadone maintenance organizations, juvenile diversion agencies, and others (Scull, 1977; Lamb & Goertzel, 1971). These agencies were deliberately located within the urban community in order to make them more visible and more accessible to potential clients.

The very concept of community mental health is vague and amorphous. Bloom defines it broadly in the first selection as representing ". . . all activities undertaken in the name of mental health." He describes several dimensions that distinguish this field: its emphasis on practice in the community rather than within an institutional setting; its concern with a delimited geographical district (catchment area); its emphasis on prevention and indirect services such as consultation with community agencies; and its concern with "innovative clinical strategies," such as brief psychotherapy.

Sociologists, who have been using the community concept for many years, are prone to see many dilemmas in this movement. For example, the catchment area is a geographically defined population group for which a community mental health center is supposed to provide services. By federal law, the area must contain a population of between seventy-five thousand and two hundred thousand residents. One problem lies in the fact that catchment areas typically do not capture the "natural" community boundaries (Baldassare & Grusky, 1978). As a result, they fail to coincide with the residents' view of their community, and this discontinuity discourages use of their services. Another problem stems from the fact that many CMHCs were created through the efforts of professionals, such as psychiatrists, psychologists, and social workers, who were able to obtain federal funding even though they lacked a broad foundation of community support. From the beginning such centers were cast in the role of outsiders attempting to insert themselves into a community leadership that included previously established city and county mental health-related agencies. The result is strong competition between a variety of agencies, all of whom are working in the mental health field, but frequently at cross-purposes, and where none have close ties with the community they serve. Although federal agencies often argue that a solution lies in greater centralization, as Aldrich (1978) has shown, centralization favors organizations that are well-off, may decrease system reliability, and may decrease responsiveness to clients. Hence, either path, more or less centralization, has many risks.

Kirk and Therrien in their essay on "Community Mental Health Myths and the Fate of Former Hospitalized Patients" boldly criticize the community mental health system. Four major myths predominate and as a result ". . . the needs of the former hospital patient and the direction of most community mental health programs are disjointed." The myth of rehabilitation refers to the inconsistency between the *intent* of community mental health programs, which was to bring patients out of custodially oriented mental hospitals so as to facilitate their rehabilitation, and the *consequences* of their establishment, which have been the reintroduction of mental patients into new community-based institutions, such as nursing homes, which often are just as custodially oriented and depressing as their predecessors. The myth of reintegration stresses the failure of the program to effectively integrate ex-mental patients into their local community. In Hawaii, where the authors conducted their research, some patients who had Japanese, Chinese, or Hawaiian cultural backgrounds found themselves placed in unlicensed boarding homes supervised by Filipinos. They thus experienced both a neighborhood and a cultural relocation. In discussing the myth of monetary savings, the authors point out that community mental health programs were widely touted as money-savers, when in fact they were considerably *more* expensive on a per-patient basis. Their advantage for the state lay in the fact that the costs could be passed on to the federal government. Finally, the myth of continuity of care refers to problems stemming from the fragmentation of community mental health services delivery. Because they are often viewed as undesirable patients, and because of interagency conflicts, ex-mental patients fail to receive the community mental health services they desperately need.

Segal and Aviram's *The Mentally Ill in Community-Based Sheltered Care* (1978) is one of the most intensive studies ever conducted of sheltered-care facilities and their residents. These facilities are supervised living arrangements such as halfway houses, board-and-care homes, and family-care homes. (Hospitals and nursing homes were excluded from the study.) Four hundred and ninety-nine nonretarded sheltered-care residents, representing every thirty-sixth bed in a California sheltered-care facility occupied by persons between eighteen and sixty-five years of age, were interviewed. Two hundred and thirty-four facility operators were also interviewed.

The study made two important contributions. First, it provided a unique body of demographic data on released psychiatric patients. The first selection from the book answers the question "Who are the mentally ill in sheltered care?" This group has a special set of social characteristics. They are older, generally between fifty and sixty-five years of age, have less than a high school education, are white, Protestant, and have been unemployed for several years. Most live on SSI (Social Security) benefits and reside fairly close to their home town. Importantly, they are not troublesome to the community—in fact, they are *vulnerable* as a group and decidedly not dangerous. As a whole, they present mild psychiatric symptoms. However, their chances of obtaining productive jobs are slender, as is the likelihood of establishing anything resembling a close conjugal family unit.

Second, the Segal and Aviram study provided important information on the social integration of community sheltered-care residents. Social integration, the study's focal concept, referred to the extent to which residents were involved with their internal and external environments. External integration described degree of social involvement outside the facility, while internal integration meant involvement with other residents of the facility and that facility's mediation of contacts with the community. Segal and Aviram were concerned with the ability of the residents to reach out into the community and, in some cases, perhaps, to live independently from the facility. State and county mental hospitals have been roundly criticized for inducing institutional dependency to the extent that long-term residents were completely ill-equipped to ever leave (Goffman, 1961). At issue is the extent to which sheltered-care facilities are capable of assisting patients to live on their own. Segal and Aviram found that social supports such as "neighbors' positive response," "the ideal psychiatric environment," and "sufficient spending money" were effective predictors of both internal and external social integration. Social dependency items were the second most effective set of factors predicting integration. For example, it was found, not surprisingly, that a rural environment improved internal but reduced external social integration. This selection, alike the one that follows, stresses the importance of considering requirements of specific types of subgroups (depending, for example, on level of psychopathology, type of commitment, and so on) when designing community sheltered-care environments.

Although Segal and Aviram provided detailed survey data on a broad range of released patients in community care facilities, their method did not enable them to describe the role of subcultural factors in the adaptation and social integration of the mentally ill in the community at large. Vivian Garrison's "Support Systems of Schizophrenic and Nonschizophrenic Puerto Rican Women in New York City" helps fill this gap by carefully analyzing the patterns of natural support systems in a Puerto Rican community.

Garrison maintains that even chronic schizophrenics can be reintegrated into their communities if the mental health delivery system is flexible enough and sensible enough to obtain the necessary knowledge of that community and its subculture and if it utilizes non-kin alternatives to standard institutional placements. Knowledge of "natural social networks" is essential to attain this goal. Three groups of Puerto Rican neighborhood nonschizophrenics were studied in terms of their psychiatric profile, history of psychiatric treatment, and other characteristics, and compared with two samples of diagnosed schizophrenics. The latter groups differed in age and in number of hospitalizations. The support systems of all five groups were carefully mapped. Using an anthropological definition of community that defined the concept in territorial terms, seven naturally occurring types of social support systems were delineated: the rotarian, the good-friend focused, the sectarian, grouping, the cultic, the one-friend, and the null. The author first described the general features of naturally occurring social support systems. Additionally, she showed how certain patterns differentiated the schizophrenic and nonschizophrenic samples. She found greater dependence on non-kin than upon family among schizophrenic women in the Puerto Rican community. She also revealed, as others have before her, the close involvement of Puerto Rican women with folk healing cults or spiritism.

The final selection by Scull, which recapitulates his book on the subject (1977), attempts to explain in economic terms the deinstitutionalization of deviant populations, including both the mentally ill and criminals. Scull argues that decarceration has taken place not because of the advent of psychoactive drugs or because it is more humane or more effective in rehabilitating deviants, but because it saves the state and county money. The real force behind deinstitutionalization was the expansion of federal social welfare programs. Asylums were getting old and the increased number of chronic patients necessitated their expansion or alteration. Capital expenditures for these purposes would have had to be huge. Such funds could be saved by discharging patients into the community. Judicial decisions such as *Wyatt vs. Stickney,* which sought to lay down minimum treatment standards, also compelled a rise in treatment costs. By discharging patients into the community, state and county governments could save considerable sums of money that otherwise would have been allocated for new institutions. Changes in the social security laws enabled older discharged patients to collect social security benefits. This allowed states to pass on much of the cost of their care to the federal government.

An innovative feature of Scull's analysis is the linking of an economic explanation of deinstitutionalization to a functional analysis of capitalism. Scull views the expansion of social welfare programs as primarily due to class conflict. By relating the introduction of community treatment to broad changes in technology, social welfare, worker organization, and law, he demonstrates the value of a broad historical perspective.

To some extent Scull anticipated the rise of the private psychiatric hospital and nursing home industry, a business described in greater detail by Torrey

(1979). Torrey reports that seven corporations have gone into the for-profit psychiatric hospital field and that currently they are (hot financial items). One, called Hospital Affiliates, Inc., is even listed on the New York Stock Exchange and another, Community Psychiatric Centers, is listed on the American Stock Exchange. He reports that the ten largest hospital chains had gross revenues of $20 million in 1964 as compared with $2.026 *billion* in 1976 (the last data available).

The strength of Scull's analysis, its broad perspective, is also its weakness. The decarceration concept and the primarily economic approach is insufficient to comprehend the complexities of the community care process. Scull leaves no doubt about his strong opposition to deinstitutionalization: "What has the new approach meant in practice? For thousands of the old, already suffering in varying degrees from mental confusion and deterioration, it has meant premature death." Yet, Garrison's study presents a very different picture. It suggests that the new policy, if implemented with care, foresight, and respect for subcultural values, may not be as uniformly evil as Scull allows.

In the final analysis a balanced, albeit preliminary, evaluation of the consequences of the shift to a deinstitutionalization policy is sorely needed. Accepting the fact, pointed out by many observers (such as Bassuk and Gerson, 1978), that systematic follow-up studies tracing the patterns of ex-patients in and out of mental hospitals and community institutions are practically nonexistent, some tentative generalizations regarding the impact of deinstitutionalization can nevertheless be formulated. Three main propositions are proposed.

1) An unknown proportion of formerly institutionalized persons and a group who otherwise might have been institutionalized were it not for decarceration are probably better off "in the community." These are the big pluses. It is harder now in California and other states to involuntarily commit unwanted family members and others. These legislative changes have had beneficial effects.

2) Ex-mental patients with satisfactory family and subcultural support systems have a greater likelihood of coping reasonably well outside the mental hospital than those who do not have social supports (Pasamanick, Scarpitti, & Dinitz, 1967; Garrison, 1978). However, it is probable that an unexpected consequence of decarceration has been increased family distress. Bringing the mental patient back to the community may represent a transfer of strain from the mental hospital to the family context. Since the family is such a private environment we actually know very little about the extent to which family agony has been increased by the obligation to care for the ex-mental patient in the community.

3) A substantial group of ex-mental patients, namely, those without decent family connections or subcultural support systems, are probably experiencing care in community settings (board-and-care homes, sheltered-care facilities, nursing homes, welfare hotels, and so forth) that is no better and, in some cases, is much worse than that offered by state and county mental hospitals (Lamb & Goertzel, 1971; Kirk & Therrien, 1975). To make matters worse for this group, which disproportionately includes the elderly poor, federally funded community mental health centers and other mental health agencies are not adequately servicing their needs (Brandon, 1974).

It is evident that this field of endeavor is very much in flux. We do not know which sectors of the mental health enterprise (or which subgroups within each sector) have benefitted and which have suffered most from decarceration. We do not know the social characteristics or motivations of members of each sector. We are even unable to clearly identify the myriad of structures called community-based treatment agencies. In summary, we are woefully ignorant of the accomplishments, failures, and limitations of deinstitutionalization and we have only just begun to explore the characteristics and the interactions of the leading persons and organizations that constitute the mental health enterprise.

References

Howard Aldrich, "Centralization Versus Decentralization in the Design of Human Service Delivery Systems: A Response to Gouldner's Lament," in Rosemary Sarri and Yeheskel Hasenfeld (editors), *The Management of Human Services,* New York: Columbia University Press, 1978, 51−79.

Mark Baldassare and Oscar Grusky, "The Community Mental Health Center: Its Urban and Organizational Context," Mimeographed, 1978.

E. L. Bassuk and S. Gerson, "Deinstitutionalization and Mental Health Services," *Scientific American,* Vol. **238** (1978), 46−53.

C. Christian Beels, "Social Networks, the Family, and the Schizophrenic Patient," *Schizophrenia Bulletin,* Vol. **4,** No. 4 (1978), 512−521.

Ivan Belknap, *Human Problems of a State Mental Hospital,* New York: McGraw-Hill, 1956.

R. N. Brandon, "Differential Use of Mental Health Services: Social Pathology or Class Victimization?" in M. Guttentag and E. Struening (editors), *Handbook of Evaluation Research,* Beverly Hills, Calif.: Sage Publications, 1974.

E. Goffman, *Asylums,* Garden City, New York: Doubleday, 1961.

H. R. Lamb and V. Goertzel, "Discharged Mental Patients—Are They Really in the Community?" *Archives of General Psychiatry,* Vol. **24** (1971), 29−34.

Peter A. Magaro, R. Gripp, and D. J. McDowell, *The Mental Health Industry: A Cultural Phenomenon,* New York: John Wiley and Sons, Inc., 1978.

B. Pasamanick, F. R., Scarpitti, and S. Dinitz, *Schizophrenics in the Community,* New York: Appleton, Century & Crofts, Inc., 1967.

A. Rogow, *The Psychiatrists,* New York: Dell Publishing Co., Inc., 1970.

Andrew T. Scull, *Decarceration,* Englewood Cliffs, New Jersey: Prentice-Hall, Inc., 1977.

Steven P. Segal and Uri Aviram, *The Mentally Ill in Community-Based Sheltered Care,* New York: John Wiley and Sons, Inc., 1978.

Alfred H. Stanton and Morris S. Schwartz, *The Mental Hospital,* New York: Basic Books, 1954.

E. Fuller Torrey, "A Merger of Oil Filters and Ids," *Psychology Today,* (May, 1979), 120−125.

BERNARD L. BLOOM

Community Mental Health

When one reviews the events that have occurred since the inauguration of the community mental health movement in the United States, it is hard to believe that its formal beginning took place only ten years ago. While one can date its inception from the enactment of Public Law 88-164 (the Community Mental Health Centers Construction Act) in the United States Congress on October 31, 1963, its ideological roots have a considerably longer history. It is important to trace these roots not only because they are imbedded in a far broader social fabric but also because the current issues that preoccupy mental health professionals identified with the community mental health movement need to be understood in terms of this highly complex background.

The Definitions of Community Mental Health

As the term suggests, community mental health refers to all activities undertaken in the community in the name of mental health. Thus, the first dimension on which community mental health can be distinguished from more traditional clinically oriented activities is its emphasis on practice in the community as opposed to practice in institutional settings. The other aspects of community mental health are less clear from its title, but in each case they can be distinguished from clinically oriented practice. A second dimension is its emphasis on a total community or total defined population rather than on individual patients considered singly. The phrase "catchment area" has been commonly used to describe the population that can be thought of as the legitimate concern of a community mental health program. A third dimension is its emphasis on preventive services as distinguished from therapeutic services. These second and third distinguishing features of the community mental health orientation can be viewed together as the application of public health concepts to the field of psychopathology. A fourth characteristic of community mental health practice is its emphasis on indirect services rather than direct services. The clearest examples of

Reprinted from *Community Mental Health: A Historical and Critical Analysis,* Morristown, N.J.: General Learning Press, 1973, pages 1–3, by permission of the author and publisher (copyright 1973, General Learning Press).

indirect services are consultation—in which a mental health professional attempts to make a significant intervention in the lives of a group of people by working with a primary caretaking system such as teachers, clergymen, or public health nurses rather than directly with that system's clientele—and mental health education—in which mental health professionals, usually through the mass media, attempt to reach large but undefined numbers of people in order to have a positive effect on their psychological adjustment.

A fifth characteristic is its emphasis on innovative clinical strategies that have the potential for meeting the mental health needs of larger numbers of people more promptly than has ordinarily been possible. Of all the innovative approaches that have been attempted, the most common include brief psychotherapy and crisis intervention. A sixth characteristic of the community mental health orientation is its emphasis on a rational planning process in decision-making regarding mental health programs. Such planning often includes demographic analyses of the community being served, the specification of unmet mental health needs, the identification of populations within the community who are at special high risk of developing those kinds of disorders identified as mental illness, the coordination of mental health services in a community, and the establishment of priorities within a community for dealing with problems directly or indirectly related to emotional unrest. A seventh characteristic of the community mental health orientation is its innovative use of new sources of manpower. Rather than viewing appropriate sources of manpower as limited to the traditional professions of psychiatry, social work, psychiatric nursing, and clinical psychology, the community mental health professional seeks to create new sources of manpower, and such terms as the "paraprofessional" or the "indigenous mental health worker" have been coined to describe these colleagues who work with him in the community mental health center. An eighth characteristic of the community mental health movement is its commitment to what is usually called "community control." By this term is meant the belief that the mental health professional is not the sole source of data as to the mental health-related needs of the community or the best ways

363

to meet these needs. Rather, the staff of a community mental health center should join with the community or its representatives to identify needs, propose and evaluate programs to meet these needs, and plan for future program developments. The concept of community control suggests that a community mental health center operates on the behalf of the community it serves. A final characteristic of the community mental health center orientation is its interest in identifying sources of stress within the community, that is, in thinking of the community as having certain counterproductive stress-inducing properties, rather than assuming that psychopathology is exclusively within the skin of the identified individual patient.

Some Formal Definitions

Various more formal definitions of community mental health can be now scanned to see how these distinguishing features of the field are explicated. Howell [Goldston 1965, p. 197] suggests that

> Community mental health encompasses all activities which are involved in the discovery, development, and organization of every facility in a community which effects all attempts which the community makes to promote mental health and to prevent and control mental illnesses. It can be regarded as the activities in any community which take place primarily outside of a psychiatric clinic or hospital, although obviously any treatment activities are an important part of community mental health.

Lemkau [Goldston 1965, p. 197] writes

> . . . that community mental health is a *communitywide* responsibility, that the program is to be under professional and lay auspices, and that mental health is promoted and fostered not solely through medical treatment but also through a variety of institutions and agencies with numerous disciplines joining in the effort. It is through this concept that the phrase "community mental health" becomes more than a pious wish, and is a living concept whereby concern with mental health becomes truly communitywide, and hopefully, mental health becomes diffused throughout the matrix of the community itself.

The staff of the Langley Porter Neuropsychiatric Institute [Goldston 1965, pp. 197–198] have suggested that community mental health

> . . . is the broad multidisciplined field concerned with the wide variety of forces and structures in a community which affect the emotional stability (positive growth, development, and functioning) of a significant group of its members. . . . The attention is directed at social institutions including those concerned with welfare, health, legislation, minority groups, employment, education, church, and their interactions which can in their functioning either enhance or

hinder the emotional growth of a large segment of the population.

When the *Community Mental Health Journal* was founded in 1965, the editors prepared a statement entitled, "Parameters of a Community Mental Health Approach." These parameters give another view of the field [Roen 1965] and include: (1) programming of services for the prevention and control of mental disorder; (2) understanding community organization; (3) basic epidemiological studies in the field of mental illness; (4) comprehensiveness of mental health services; (5) mental health planning and decision-making as a dynamic process; (6) continuity of care; (7) optimal milieux; (8) manpower and training; (9) legislation; and (10) fresh conceptual models.

It should be mentioned at the outset that there is an implied criticism of traditional mental health activities in each of these distinctions. It has been the view of many mental health professionals that traditional mental health services have been inappropriately divorced from the communities in which patients have lived; that traditional services have been concerned too much with those individuals who find their way to the clinician, to the exclusion of developing a broader concern for a population; that the more traditional orientation has been almost exclusively focused on the treatment of psychopathology without devoting adequate resources to activities that might prevent certain forms of psychopathology from occurring; that traditional mental health professionals in their emphasis on direct patient services have neglected to develop their skills in enabling mediating caretaking agencies and persons to work more effectively with their clients; that there has been too much emphasis on long-term individual therapy to the exclusion of therapeutic strategies that might be helpful to greater numbers of patients; that too many mental health services have developed without adequate coordination with other existing services; that mental health professionals have not made adequate use of non-traditional sources of manpower; that mental health professionals have largely ignored the community in developing mental health services; and that in their failure to identify those community characteristics that appear to enhance or inhibit growth and development, mental health professionals have been engaged in an inefficient and perhaps irresponsible allocation of their limited resources.

REFERENCES

Stephen E. Goldston, ed., *Concepts of Community Psychiatry: A Framework for Training,* USDHEW P.H.S. Pub. #1319. USGPO, 1965.

Sheldon R. Roen, "Parameters of a Community Mental Health Approach," *Community Mental Health Journal,* 1965, 1:2.

STUART A. KIRK AND MARK E. THERRIEN

Community Mental Health Myths and the Fate of Former Hospitalized Patients

The State of Hawaii moved rather late into community mental health. Although catchment areas had been formed and wards of the state's only mental hospital had been allocated to each catchment area in the mid-1960s, it was not until 1971 that a concerted effort was made to reduce the hospital's resident population and that hospital personnel were assigned to staff the community mental health centers. By the end of 1973, the changes in the mental health system were apparent. The number of patients in residence, which had been declining since the late 1950s, declined sharply in the late 1960s and early 1970s. For example, prior to 1960, Hawaii State Hospital had over 1,000 resident patients, but by 1968 the number had decreased to 625. And from fiscal year 1968−69 to fiscal year 1972−73 the number of patients in the hospital further declined to 230, a 63% decrease. This occurred despite the fact that the number of annual admissions remained relatively high, growing steadily from fewer than 600 in the late 1950s to over 1,200 by the early 1970s. Patients were being kept in the hospital for shorter periods of time and long-term patients were being moved out of the hospital to community placements. At the same time, on the Island of Oahu, where approximately 80% of the state's population resides, five mental health centers were established, each with its own catchment area, staff, spectrum of services, and satellite clinics. Certainly at the level of the organization of services and the number of hospitalized patients, Hawaii has moved rapidly into community mental health programs. But what has happened to those patients who were hospitalized for long periods of time, or to similar patients who now enter and are discharged from the state hospital very rapidly? What happens to the severely disordered patient who in the past would have been a prime candidate for long-term custodial care?

Perhaps an early clue to the fate of these patients can be found in the original philosophy of community mental health programs. Although community mental health

Reprinted from *Psychiatry*, Vol. **38** (August, 1975), pages 209−217, by permission of the authors and publisher.

programs were established to supplant the traditional state mental hospital, both their ideology and their most common services are not directed at the needs of those who have traditionally resided in state psychiatric institutions. The ideology of community mental health has been primarily concerned with primary prevention, the importance of early diagnosis and treatment, consultation, social action, crisis intervention, short-term outpatient care, and time-limited, brief inpatient care. Preferred target populations for such services are clearly normal populations who are at risk, persons with mild, acute, treatable disorders, who can be handled in office practice, or severely disordered persons suffering from their first psychiatric crisis. Community mental health programs do, of course, have services for other patient populations, specifically for patients with a long history of severe psychiatric disorder, but these programs are not meant to constitute the core of community mental health practice and are usually the least prestigious of services offered, have the fewest and least trained staff, and are often viewed as undesirable but necessary services.

The transition from state hospital-based mental health services to community mental health services has not been a smooth or complete one. Nevertheless, it is becoming apparent that the needs of former hospital patients and the direction of most community mental health programs are disjointed. This disjunction, however, is not readily apparent because the ideology of community mental health serves to obscure the reality of this problem. To the extent that the belief system of the community mental health movement does not accurately reflect the fate of former patients, the beliefs may be considered as myths, collective beliefs that are built up in response to the wishes of mental health personnel rather than to the facts of the matter.

This paper will argue that there are four such myths developing in community mental health: the myth of rehabilitation, the myth of reintegration, the myth of monetary savings, and the myth of continuity of care. Each of these will be described and analyzed in terms of information obtained through various public documents, recent publications, and dozens of interviews with mental health and welfare officials in Hawaii, and also on the basis of the authors' personal observations and experiences with mental health facilities in six states.

The Myth of Rehabilitation

The community mental health movement, although resulting from changes in community attitudes and psychiatric opinion and from legal changes, was in part a response to the growing belief that hospitalization of the mentally ill was more harmful than helpful. Numerous studies of mental hospitals and, perhaps most persuasively, Goffman's description and analysis of mental institutions in his widely cited book *Asylums* (1961), suggested that mental hospitals were as much the cause of chronic mental illness as the place to cure it. There was the prevalent belief, backed by numerous studies, that admission to a mental hospital, particularly if one's residence there lasted more than several months, would eventually become a lifetime of incarceration (Zusman, 1966; Stuart, 1970). The precise validity of the observation is not as crucial as the fact that it was believed by increasing numbers of mental health professionals.

At the same time, mental health professionals and social scientists concerned with mental disorders were paying increasing attention to the importance of the social environment of the patient. Within hospitals there were moves to develop therapeutic communities on psychiatric wards and to harness group and social forces in the treatment of mental disorder. The emerging implicit belief was that the patient would be better off in the community than subject to the routines of the hospital.

As mental health policies changed, patients were discharged from hospitals in large numbers. The official ideology of the mental health enterprise encouraged this trend as an important policy reform which would facilitate the rehabilitation of mental patients. The official image of the decline of state hospitals was that patients who had been locked in back wards for decades, neglected and institutionalized, would, with the help of drugs and the new community-based mental health programs and the healthful influences of community living, be able to manage themselves better and begin to attain some minimum level of normal functioning. Both the treatment offered by community mental health programs and the avoidance of the dehumanizing forces of the state mental hospitals would together contribute to the rehabilitation of the severely disturbed patient.

This constituted the official or publicly announced objective. The implementation of such a rehabilitation program ran square into several major obstacles: (1) the lack of decent community living facilities; (2) the treatment preferences and attitudes of community mental health staff toward these ex-hospital patients and the difficulty of resocializing hospital staff assigned to community mental health programs; and (3) the lack of sufficient effective treatment methods for these patients.

The first obstacle faced by every state hospital system which wants to close down is what to do with the large number of patients currently hospitalized, some of them hospitalized for many years. Many of these patients have neither family who want them nor financial or social resources to secure adequate housing. The most immediate problem then is one of quality *placement* (Weiner et al., 1974). In Hawaii, this entailed the placement of hundreds of patients per year, but the number of licensed boarding homes available was limited and not readily accessible to the state hospital. Furthermore, the steady growth in the number of licensed boarding and care homes was not sufficient to house the increasing number of ex-hospitalized patients because these facilities also had to provide housing for the disabled, aged, and physically ill. The partial resolution of this problem was the proliferation, with the explicit encouragement of the state mental health division, of unlicensed boarding homes for the placement of ex-hospitalized patients. For example, between 1970 and 1973 the number of licensed care homes on Oahu rose from 149 to 195, a 31% increase, and by 1972 it was estimated that 68% of all the care home beds were occupied by psychiatric patients. Similarly, during those same years the number of licensed boarding homes in the state increased from 99 to 140, a 41% increase. Thus, from 1970 to 1973, approximately 87 new licensed care and boarding homes were established, although not all of them exclusively for psychiatric patients. But during that same time on Oahu the number of unlicensed boarding homes with discharged psychiatric patients is estimated to have risen from almost none to 66. For every licensed facility established for the care of the former patients, nearly one unlicensed facility was also created. Thus, initially at least, aftercare planning for the mentally ill did not consist of rehabilitation planning, but merely of ensuring that ex-patients would not have to sleep in the streets (see Lazure, 1974). Aftercare consisted, then, not in mustering new sources of help for the ex-patient, but simply in trying to *replace* the minimum life supports that were ensured in the hospital.

A second obstacle in developing a rehabilitation program for former hospital patients in community mental health centers is quite simply the fact that for the most part the staff of community mental health programs do not think very much can be done with the former hospital patients. Interviews with mental health personnel in Hawaii, for example, found that these patients are routinely referred to as "chronics," a term which connotes that the patient is hopeless, cannot be helped, and will not get better. There is a pervasive belief among staff that nothing very useful can be done for these patients, except perhaps to maintain them on high doses of antipsychotic drugs if they request help.

The belief system regarding these patients is reinforced by the fact that in Hawaii, as in other states undergoing similar reforms, many of the community mental health staff were formerly staff in the state mental hospital, many of them aides or orderlies, and they, as much as the former patients, have become deeply socialized into the values, beliefs, and attitudes fostered by that total institution environment. A repeated complaint made by the more "progressive" community-oriented mental health personnel in Hawaii is that they cannot get the former hospital staff to behave toward patients any differently than they did in the hospital environment. Nevertheless, even the more progressive and better-trained staff members of community mental health settings rarely choose to work with "chronics." They prefer the less disturbed clientele where there is a better prognosis. Consequently, chronics—if they do apply or are referred for service—are usually assigned to ex-state hospital staff who run a "day program," usually consisting of activities similar to those they would have engaged in on the hospital wards. Consequently, many ex-hospital patients involved in community mental health programs are placed in "ward-like" environments where they are supervised by ex-state hospital staff, and they participate in a state hospital routine, albeit now "in the community." But many of these former patients do not even have the limited involvement provided by a day hospital. They spend the majority of their time in a boarding home, which promotes dependency, passivity, isolation, and inactivity, qualities which formerly the state hospitals have been chided for encouraging (Lamb and Goertzel, 1971; Allen, 1974).

The third obstacle in implementing a full rehabilitation program involves the lack of knowledge about what would constitute an effective and inexpensive treatment for these patients. The only partially effective treatments available are the psychotropic drugs, but these are clearly only a first step. The patients have long-standing and severe problems, have few if any social, financial, or employment resources, and have many social and medical needs. But in the face of these massive problems the mental health system does not have an efficient or effective method of meeting these needs or of transforming backward patients into "normal" citizens. This may account for the fact that half of the schizophrenic patients discharged will be rehospitalized within two years (Gunderson et al., 1974).

The ideology of community mental health has obscured the fate of these patients and the scope of their problems by the rhetoric of rehabilitation, which has functioned to facilitate the discharge of these patients from mental hospitals, but has not provided a qualitatively different program than they had in their former institutions. The return of patients to the community has, in many ways, extended the philosophy of custodialism into the community rather than ending it at the gates of the state hospital; rehabilitation has unfortunately become more a myth than a reality.

The Myth of Reintegration

An integral component of the ex-hospital patient's rehabilitation was to be his reintegration into the community. Instead of being isolated and segregated in a state mental hospital, typically located miles from home, family, and social contacts, the patients who absolutely required hospitalization were to be hospitalized in the community and to be returned as quickly as possible to previous sources of support and previous social responsibilities. By keeping the patient *out* of the hospital, it was assumed that he would be kept *in* the community and that his tenure in the community, if it did not immediately cure him, would at least avoid the dehumanizing processes of institutionalization. This belief, which is still widely held in mental health circles and which undoubtedly has a certain plausibility, is based on a rather vague notion of what constitutes a "community" and a naive view of the patient's life "in the community."

The concept of community has been defined by the federal guidelines in terms of the artificially delineated catchment area—i.e., a circumscribed geographical area which may or may not bear any relationship to political, administrative, racial, or cultural boundaries (Connery, 1968). This has not helped mental health personnel critically appraise the important elements of a patient's relevant community (Panzetta, 1971). Furthermore, many hospitalized patients were formerly transient persons not long identified with a given location (Dunham, 1965) or have lost such identification and social ties in the course of a long hospitalization. The belief in the value of reintegration has been devoid of any systematic analysis of what constitutes a relevant community.

This lack of a critical understanding of the nature of "community" has led to a number of unfortunate developments (Kellert, 1971). First, the emphasis on the catchment area as the community has failed to distinguish separate ethnic and cultural communities. In

Hawaii, for example, many neighborhoods are strongly identified as Filipino, Hawaiian, Japanese, or Chinese and vary accordingly in language, customs, and so forth. Placement of ex-hospitalized patients, however, has not taken these cultural variations into consideration. One reason for this has been the fact that almost all boarding homes in Honolulu, both licensed and unlicensed, are run by Filipinos and are located predominantly in Filipino areas—although Filipinos constitute only 14% of the population of Hawaii. Thus, a boarding home placement for a Japanese patient is likely to mean both a neighborhood relocation and a cultural one as well. Other states have had similar experiences in the ghettoization of former patients, particularly in the poorer and more deteriorated areas of the city. This seems to have occurred in California (Aviram and Segal, 1973; Chase, 1973) and is apparently taking place in such diverse areas as Long Beach, N.Y., the Uptown section of Chicago, the Times Square and Bowery areas of Manhattan, and in the District of Columbia (Trotter and Kuttner, 1974).

But the segregation of former patients in certain areas of the community is only an indication of another, perhaps more serious, problem of reintegration—that of the social rejection of the mentally disordered, who are likely to possess multiple negative social attributes in addition to their illness: they may be poor, from a minority group, aged, etc. It has long been recognized both by mental health professionals (Joint Commission, 1961; Sarbin and Mancuso, 1970) and by sociologists who have studied deviant behavior (Scheff, 1966; Phillips, 1963) that the former patient often faces rejection by those who know of his hospitalization. There is a well-established, although slowly changing, pattern of public fear, anxiety, and revulsion in response to the mentally ill that has been evident for hundreds of years, albeit in various guises. Placing the hospitalized patient back in the community often runs the risk of subjecting the patient to these negative attitudes. Hence, former patients are not welcomed back into communities with open arms; instead they are often confronted by formal and informal attempts to exclude them from the community by using city ordinances, zoning codes, and police arrests (Aviram and Segal, 1973). They may end up residing in a relatively foreign section of the catchment area, one that is not only deteriorated, but also inhospitable to them. The belief in reintegration, then, is certainly laudable and humane, but it would be unfortunate if the belief in the benefits of community placement inhibited a recognition of the limits and dangers of the forced attempts at reintegration. Residence "in the community" can be just as disabling, frightening, de-

humanizing, and isolating as living in the back wards of more formally structured institutions.

The Myth of Monetary Savings

One of the factors that contributed to the shift from a hospital-centered mental health system to an outpatient community-based one was the realization of the tremendous financial cost involved in maintaining thousands of people inside a hospital. In addition to the expenses of treatment-related activities—e.g., salaries of clinical personnel, drugs, etc.—the hospitals were burdened with the costs of providing 24-hour supervision of the patients and all life support, such as shelter, food and clothing, as well as the costs of maintaining the physical plant. Obviously, many of these costs were required by the nature of residential facilities and not primarily because of the treatment provided. Indeed, state mental hospitals are often cited for the utter lack of treatment given to patients. The concern over the costs of hospital care for the mentally disordered, in tandem with the belief that community-based treatment programs would more effectively rehabilitate these patients, made the transition to community mental health programs seem not only humane, but fiscally sound as well.

But community mental health programs, as has been mentioned previously, neither catered to these former patients exclusively nor even gave them high service priority. Instead, because of the ideology and service biases, a new, hitherto unserviced, clientele is attracted, consisting of less disordered and more acute patients than those traditionally found in mental hospitals (Chu and Trotter, 1974). This is not to say that community mental health programs have totally ignored these patients, but simply that many former hospital patients are not given adequate care by these programs.

Perhaps more to the point of the myth of savings is the fact that total costs for mental health services have *not* declined. In Hawaii, for example, there is certainly a definite trend to increase the relative amount of money allocated to the Preventive and Clinical Services (the community mental health programs) and decrease the percent of the total mental health budget allocated for the one state hospital. Since the mid-1960s the percent of the total state mental health budget allocated to the state hospital had declined from 82% to 41% in 1973–74 and the amount allocated for the community health programs has risen from 17% to 57%. However, in terms of the total absolute amount of money allocated for mental health services, there has been a steady increase, especially since 1970. Furthermore, the amount of money allocated for the state hospital also steadily increased until the early 1970s, despite the fact that the number of resident patients had markedly decreased.

Elsewhere a similar pattern has emerged. In California, the state's appropriation for county-operated community mental health programs is four times greater than the funds currently expended for the state hospitals (Aviram and Segal, 1973). But it is not apparent that a community-based program is actually cheaper. The California Department of Finance's study of the mental health program found that in contrast to the $28 average cost per day for each patient at a state hospital, the patient cost per day at the county-level community mental health program was $98 — a 250% increase (Chase, 1973)! Thus not only is the total expenditure for mental health increasing, but the cost per patient may also be increasing under the new service delivery system. The actual costs of state hospital versus community treatment, however, must await more sophisticated cost-benefit studies.

Of greater fiscal significance in the move to community mental health programs has been the transfer of major fiscal responsibility for these patients from the mental health facilities to the public welfare enterprise—e.g., to Aid to the Totally Disabled programs. The budget figures cited above do not include the increased costs assumed by other agencies for these patients. The shelter, clothes, and meals that had been provided to former patients by the state hospital now are provided by numerous care and boarding homes and paid for not by the mental health department but by other state departments. As far as the authors are aware, no one knows the magnitude of these hidden costs of community mental health or how they compare with the costs of hospitalization.

This shift in fiscal responsibility for former patients makes these patients vulnerable to the policies of public welfare bureaucracies. One rather well-recognized objective of most state welfare bureaucracies is to reduce costs, reduce caseloads, and discourage dependency on welfare. Operationally, for former hospital patients, this means that in addition to their psychiatric disorders, they must contend with a hostile bureaucracy to meet their basic needs. In Hawaii, for example, the state payments to former patients residing in licensed board and care homes are controlled by a point system in which each recipient is evaluated in terms of disability and the payment his boarding or care home operators are given is based on this assessment. The more disabled or disturbed the patient, the more money the boarding home operator receives. The patient is caught between a welfare system that provides minimum support and attempts to exclude persons from receiving aid and the

boarding home operators, who have no incentive to help the patient get better and in fact may receive a financial reward if the patient deteriorates. Thus, this arrangement may produce increased human suffering as well as increased expenditures by welfare agencies to replace life supports which had been provided by the hospital.

In addition to these direct costs for the community care of the former patients, there are the indirect costs incurred by other community agencies that are called upon to deal with the patients. For example, the police and courts may be increasingly called upon to handle these patients, as has apparently happened in California (Aviram and Segal, 1973). Moreover, other community agencies (emergency rooms, medical clinics, family agencies, fire departments) may have increased demands for their services from this group of patients. But here, also, sound data are not available.

The myth of monetary savings has served to facilitate the transition from state hospitals to community mental health programs by allowing people to believe that community care of former patients would be much less costly. This simply may not be true, especially if total costs, direct and indirect, are considered. This possibility should not serve as an impetus to reopen or enlarge state hospitals at the expense of community mental health programs, but as an indication that care for the severely disturbed is *expensive* and that adequate care for these patients whether provided in the hospital or the community requires an enormous social and fiscal commitment.

The Myth of Continuity of Care

It has long been recognized that the delivery of human services, including mental health services, has been fragmented. This is evident in the numerous discussions of gaps in services, duplication of services, and lack of coordination, and the recurrent reports of patients who get "lost in the system." Recognizing these shortcomings, the promoters of community mental health programs place great emphasis on the idea of "continuity of care." Continuity of care refers to the idea that patients needing mental health services should be able to receive the services they need at the time they need them, regardless of the fact that the services required over the course of treatment may be offered by administratively separate agencies. A premium has been placed on the coordination of services among a variety of community service providers so that persons in need of services could move more easily among them. For example, ideally a patient being discharged from the state hospital would be followed up by the local community mental health clinic, which, if necessary, would be able to work closely with the public welfare department, the vocational rehabilitation program, or the boarding home operator.

The goal of continuity of care, however, has been more difficult to achieve than at first expected. In part, this stems from the fact that former hospitalized patients, especially those with a long history of hospitalization, are viewed as an undesirable clientele both by staff members in public agencies not directly concerned with mental health problems and by many of those in mental health agencies. These difficult patients often make little or no headway in psychotherapy, often fail to keep regular appointments, may be physically and socially unattractive, can make enormous demands on staff time and morale, and, at the end, offer the staff little sense of satisfaction or accomplishment. Patients with histories of numerous hospitalizations are simply among the most unwanted clients of health, mental health, and social agencies, and their undesirability may prevent them from receiving appropriate services (Chu and Trotter, 1974). It has been estimated that as few as 10% of discharged patients receive treatment at local community mental health centers (Weiner et al., 1974). This is by no means a problem specific to former patients of mental health agencies. A recent study revealed that among a variety of community service agencies over 50% of applicants for their services never even begin to receive help from the agencies (Kirk and Greenley, 1974).

Given that former patients may not make the most welcome clients of community agencies, the transfer of patient care from the state hospital to other community agencies becomes problematic. Agencies receiving a large number of such referrals are likely to feel that they are being burdened with a disproportionate share of the responsibility for these patients. Thus, in Hawaii, as the state hospital attempted to place its patients in the few boarding homes licensed and supervised by the state's public welfare department, it found that the public welfare officials were reluctant to accept these patients and that the lists of available boarding homes would not even be shared with the hospital. Public welfare officials felt that the limited number of boarding homes had to serve a range of diverse needs and that they were never intended to be facilities primarily for the mentally disabled. The response of the mental health organizations was to encourage the development of new boarding homes, but the public welfare agency refused to license them. These unlicensed homes, the result of inter-agency conflict, now approximately equal the licensed homes in total bed capacity.

Another source of conflict between the welfare and the psychiatric agencies in Hawaii is the "point system"

by which the welfare department assesses the needs of former patients residing in boarding homes. As mentioned, the welfare department assesses each former patient who resides in one of its licensed boarding homes; residents of unlicensed homes receive a substantially lower flat rate. The organizational conflict develops because the welfare department wants to keep expenditures as low as possible and tends to under-assess the disabilities of former psychiatric patients, while mental health personnel push for higher payments to boarding home operators, assuming that it will lead to better patient care. But, as will be recalled, boarding home operators are given no incentive by either the welfare or the mental health department to help patients become more independent. Thus, the transfer of responsibility for patients from the state hospital to other community agencies has resulted not in greater continuity of care but rather in greater inter-organizational conflict.

What appears to be lacking in the attempt to achieve continuity of care is a single agency or person acting as sole agent or advocate for the patient or having primary responsibility for seeing that the former patient's many needs are adequately met. In place of the state hospital's centralized care, the continuity of care program has produced fragmented responsibility for patient care. The state hospital was responsible for food, shelter, medical care, psychiatric therapy, vocational rehabilitation, and more. The hospital may not have adequately met these needs, of course, but at least the failure was attributable to a given institution. Continuity of care in the community for former hospital patients has partially failed, not because the idea is wrong, but because these patients are not highly valued as clientele by many community agencies.

Conclusion

In its bold new approach to the delivery of psychiatric services, the community mental health movement held out a number of promises about the likely fate of state hospital patients. The belief was that former patients would be rehabilitated by a well-integrated, coordinated system of services in the community and that the costs of this more humane and more effective program would be less than the costs of institutionalization.

These promises have been partially unfulfilled. Certainly, community mental health programs have reached their goals in relation to some patient populations and indeed have reduced the number of patients in state hospitals. The concern of this paper has been the fate of a specific group of patients: those who have been or would be likely candidates for long-term hospitalization but who, because of the decline of the state mental hospital, are now residing elsewhere. Some of the beliefs about them appear to be taking on the status of myths, reflecting more the intentions and hopes of community health than the uncomfortable realities.

REFERENCES

Allen, P. "A Consumer's View of California's Mental Health Care System," *Psychiatric Quart.* (1974) 48:1–13.

Aviram, U., and Segal, S. P. "Exclusion of the Mentally Ill," *Arch. Gen. Psychiatry* (1973) 29:126–131.

Chase, J. "Where Have All the Patients Gone?," *Human Behav.*, Oct. 1973, pp. 14–21.

Chu, F., and Trotter, S. *The Madness Establishment;* Grossman, 1974.

Connery, R. H. *The Politics of Mental Health;* Columbia Univ. Press, 1968.

Dunham, E. *Community and Schizophrenia;* Wayne State Univ. Press, 1965.

Goffman, E. *Asylums;* Doubleday Anchor, 1961.

Henderson, J. "Special Report: Schizophrenia, 1974," *Schiz. Bull.*, Summer 1974, pp. 16–54.

Joint Commission on Mental Illness and Health. *Action for Mental Health;* Wiley, 1961.

Kellert, S. R. "The Lost Community in Community Psychiatry," *Psychiatry* (1971) 34:168–179.

Kirk, S., and Greenley, J. "Denying or Delivering Services?," *Social Work* (1974) 19:439–447.

Lamb, H. R., and Goertzel, V. "Discharged Mental Patients—Are They Really in the Community?," *Arch. Gen. Psychiatry* (1971) 24:29–34.

Lazure, L. "Mental Patients' Release Is Hailed, Hit in Gardner," *Worcester Sunday Telegram*, Worcester, Mass., Oct. 13, 1974.

Panzetta, A. *Community Mental Health: Myth and Reality;* Lea & Febiger, 1971.

Phillips, D. "Rejection: A Possible Consequence of Seeking Help for Mental Disorders," *Amer. Sociol. Rev.* (1963) 28:963–972.

Sarbin, T., and Mancuso, J. "Failure of a Moral Enterprise: Attitudes of the Public Toward Mental Illness," *J. Consult. and Clin. Psychol.* (1970) 35:159–173.

Scheff, T. *Being Mentally Ill;* Aldine, 1966.

Stuart, R. *Trick or Treatment;* Champaign, Ill.: Research Press, 1970.

Trotter, S., and Kuttner, B. "The Mentally Ill: From Back Wards to Back Alleys," *Washington Post*, Feb. 24, 1974.

Weiner, S., et al. "A Report on the Closing of a State Hospital," *Admin. in Mental Health*, Summer 1974, pp. 13–20.

Zusman, J. "Some Explanations of the Changing Appearance of Psychotic Patients," *Milbank Memorial Fund Quart.* (1966) 44:363–394.

STEVEN P. SEGAL AND URI AVIRAM

Who Are the Mentally Ill in Sheltered Care?

In asking who are the mentally ill in sheltered care, we are concerned with what their experience has been with respect to social integration, what their current potential is for becoming socially integrated, and what seem to be the most formidable obstacles to integrating them into the community.

The data we present here indicate that the mentally ill population in sheltered care are a residual group, never

Reprinted from Steven P. Segal and Uri Aviram, *The Mentally Ill in Community-Based Sheltered Care*, New York: John Wiley and Sons, Inc., 1978, pages 129–144, by permission of the authors and publisher.

integrated into society's mainstream, with few prospects for complete economic and residential independence— that is, complete social integration into the mainstream of society. Our data show that the social-integration goal for this population should involve efforts to develop independent outreach and social involvements both within the facility or in the external community, on the assumption that the facility will be a base of operations.

We do not wish this rather strong statement to invoke the pessimistic attitude that assumes these residents cannot be helped. We believe their social integration can be greatly enhanced. We wish, however, to help define realistic expectations and prevent the disillusionment with helping efforts that has so often in the past led to the neglect of the population's needs.

We have defined social integration in terms of five levels of involvement—that is, presence, access, participation, production, and consumption. The social characteristics of the sheltered-care population offer some significant insights into their past involvements and future opportunities for developing these types of involvements.

Demographic Characteristics: A Unique Population

Comparison by age, sex, and marital status with the general population of California demonstrates that the mentally ill in community-based sheltered care are a unique group with unique needs. Their social characteristics place them at a disadvantage with respect to integrating themselves into society's mainstream.

Age and Sex

Almost half (46%) of the sheltered-care population between 18 and 65 years of age are 50 years old or older, compared with 25% of the general population in California and approximately 25% of the general population of mental-hospital releases (Heckel et al., 1973; Miller, 1965). This is extremely important in considering the feasibility of transition back into the community: These individuals are in need of support at a time society expects them to be most self-sufficient and is least willing to tolerate a lack of self-sufficiency.

The sex distribution of the sheltered-care population is equally balanced between male and female; yet our analysis reveals that females in the sheltered-care population are significantly older than males: 54% of them (compared with 39% of the males) are now between 50 and 65. In contrast the youth of this population are predominantly male: Almost 33% of the men are 18 to 33, compared with 19% of the women. We thus have two subgroups—older women and young men—who socially and economically have the most difficulty in finding a place in society's mainstream.

Despite the concentration of younger males in sheltered care (33%) their numbers are smaller than would be expected, given the concentration of younger males in the general population (42%). Also, mental-hospital releases, while slightly older than the general population (regardless of sex), are not as old as the sheltered-care population (Heckel et al., 1973; Miller, 1965). Thus there can be little doubt that problems will arise for this population in relation to their seniority—for example, they will need more transportation aid to make use of community resources.

Marital Status

Marital status is an index of social participation. The marital-status characteristics of the sheltered-care population indicate a lack of resources available to facilitate community transition. Table 1 vividly illustrates this by comparing this population with California's general population and with releases from state mental hospitals serving the Bay Area. While the general population figures in California show that 70% of the individuals between 18 and 65 years of age are married, this is the status of only 5% of those individuals in sheltered care. Conversely 18% of the general population compared

TABLE 1

Comparison of Marital Status in California's General Population, a General Population of Mental-Hospital Releases, and Individuals in Sheltered Care

	18-to-65-Year-Old Population Group		
Marital status	1970 Census of California Population (N = 11,652,082)	General Population[a] of California mental-Hospital Releases (N = 1039)	California Sheltered-Care Population (N = 12,430)
Married	70%	39%	5%
Never married	18%	21%	60%
Dissolved relationship (separated, widowed, divorced)	12%	34%	35%

[a] *Miller (1965) pp. 116–117 (marital status was unknown for 5%).*

with 60% of the sheltered-care population have never been married; and 12% of the general population as opposed to 35% of those in sheltered care have had marital relationships that have since been dissolved. Without speculating on the etiologic relationship between marriage and mental disorder, one thing seems sure: Individuals who lack the support of a spouse are more likely to seek social support in a sheltered living environment.

Two trends relating to marital status in addition to the very high proportion of "never marrieds" within their ranks seem to indicate that individuals in sheltered care have never been integrated into the mainstream of social life. First, follow-up studies of released mental patients show a tendency for groups of individuals returning to the hospital to be increasingly composed of "never marrieds" and people with dissolved marital relationships (Davis et al., 1974; Heckel et al., 1973; Miller, 1965; Pasamanick et al., 1967). Thus, as a group, individuals in sheltered care are a residual population of many cohorts of mental-hospital admissions. The second trend is illustrated in Table 2, which presents a breakdown of marital status in this population by age and sex. This table points to the high percentage of never-married males (73%) and the high percentage of females from dissolved marital relationships (50%). Specifically these two figures are indicative of how males and females fail socially to integrate into today's society.

These marital-status figures are not unique to California sheltered-care facilities but seem, in fact, to have much greater generality. Apte (1968), for example, in a study of transitional hostels in Great Britain, finds that 71% of his study population (both male and female) were single, but only 17% came from dissolved marital relationships. The difference between our population

and that studied by Apte seems to lie in the fact that he chose to consider only the "transitional hostel," the hostel that had at least a 50% turnover in a given year. Apte notes that this choice of a study group made a significant difference in the age of his target population. Those individuals living in the transitional facilities were significantly younger than those living in hostels he eliminated from his study. We would therefore expect him to find a smaller concentration of dissolved marital relationships than we found because at least a third of our female population who had experienced a dissolved marital relationship were over 50.

The major indication, in terms of future potential for enhanced social integration, of the marital-status characteristics of the mentally ill in sheltered care is that as a population they lack support even from the most immediate of family members—a spouse. In addition they are limited in access to two major sources of social involvement—that is, interaction with a spouse and couple-based interaction.

Socioeconomic Characteristics of the Population

In looking at the socioeconomic characteristics of the sheltered-care population, one is again struck by the extent to which individuals in this group have withdrawn from, or have never been involved in, the mainstream of social life.

Work

Work or "production" as a type of social involvement is one of the most important aspects of everyday social life in the United States. It is important, therefore, to

TABLE 2

Distribution of the Sheltered-Care Population by Sex, Age, and Marital Status

| | SEX | | | | | |
| | Males | | | Females | | |
Age	Single ($n_1 = 4870$)	Married ($n_2 = 300$)	Dissolved ($n_3 = 1540$)	Single ($n_4 = 2520$)	Married ($n_5 = 290$)	Dissolved ($n_6 = 2910$)
18-33	29%	1%	2%	16%	0%	3%
34-49	20%	1%	7%	13%	1%	13%
50-65	24%	2%	13%	15%	4%	34%
All ages	73%	4%	22%	44%	5%	50%
		n = 6710 Males (100%)			n = 5720 Females (100%)	

look into this aspect of the lives of sheltered-care residents.

Study data demonstrate that 15% of the individuals in sheltered care are in fact in the labor force. This compares with 67% of the general population in California (as found by 1970 U.S. Census figures, U.S. Bureau of the Census, 1973). Moreover, 11% of the sheltered-care population is actually employed and 4% of the population is looking for work. Whereas 4% of the general population in this age group in California were looking for work in 1970, 63% were employed. Thus the percentage of sheltered-care residents looking for work is equivalent to the general population, while the number who have found work is much lower than in the general population.

Working residents and job-seeking residents appear to be different groups in a number of aspects. Workers are equally male and female, single, white, young if female, and middle aged if male. Job seekers, on the other hand, are two-thirds male and more likely to be young, married, or formerly married. Job seekers are also more likely to be minority-group members than workers are. Residents in sheltered care tend to look for work more, and work more, if they have more education. It is also true that the less time elapsed since previous employment, the better the chance that a resident will look for work. These characteristics parallel those of workers and job seekers in the general population, yet the majority of the sheltered-care population (85%) are neither working nor looking for employment.

Workers in the sheltered-care population are different from job seekers in some other important ways. Workers come from more skilled and high-status occupational backgrounds than those people do who are looking for work and those not working. None of the sheltered-care residents who actually have a job report that this is their first working experience. These job holders are more likely to report that they have previously worked in skilled occupations such as carpentry or skilled sheet-metal work or are members of some professional group (e.g., teachers or social workers). In most cases these individuals are no longer employed in their previous vocation; often they are employed at their residence in a more menial job such as cleaning, cooking, washing, or general repair work. They have obtained their work by virtue of previously acquired and generalized work skills (such as the ability to complete an assigned task). Job seekers are more likely to report that they have had no work experience at all.

The significance of these work-related statistics for understanding the potential of the sheltered-care population to become involved in "production"-type activities as a means of enhancing their social integration lies in the observations that those with the most potential for such involvement have shown a significant drift from stable to marginal employment; those with interest in obtaining employment—the job seekers—given their backgrounds, have little chance of obtaining employment; and the majority of the population have not expressed serious interest in this type of social involvement.

Work-Related Characteristics of the Sheltered-Care Population. The lack of involvement of the sheltered-care population in production-type activities is to a large extent a function of atrophied work skills and past failures in the area in addition to their psychiatric disability. More than half of this population have been out of the labor market or away from full-time employment for 6 years or more; only a tenth were employed during the past year. In a population of which three-fourths of the individuals are over 34 years of age, only one-third have had full-time employment for 6 years or more. The employment prospects of this population are further hampered by the fact that only 66% have ever had steady employment for a year or more.

A Comparison with the General Population of Released Mental Hospital Patients. If we look at previous studies of released hospital patients, we again see that individuals in sheltered care comprise a unique population in relation to employment. Both Freeman and Simmons (1963) and Miller (1965), reporting on studies of released state-hospital patients, indicate that significantly smaller numbers of people who return to the state hospitals are employed before their return than those who manage to stay out of the hospital during the studies' follow-up period. Freeman and Simmons note that, as a total group, 33% of their study population were employed at the time of the community follow-up interview. However, 41% of those released individuals who managed to remain out of the hospital during the follow-up period were employed in some manner, compared with 20% of their hospital returnees. Miller's findings are similar. Her study found a total employment rate of 32%; she also found that 40% of those individuals who managed to stay out of the hospital during the follow-up period were employed, compared with 29% of those who returned to the hospital. Since a large portion of our study group have had several readmissions to state hospitals—a point discussed in greater detail later in this chapter—we might speculate that sheltered-care residents are, in fact, a group with a greatly diminished employment potential, at least as indicated by their employment histories. This potential is, however, indicated solely by employment history; other indicators of work potential must be considered before any final conclusions are drawn about ultimate employability.

A Perspective on Work Potential. Despite these bleak employment statistics, there is some evidence on sheltered care pointing to the possibility of improvement in California: Apte's (1968) findings show that, with a concentrated effort, as much as an additional 31% of California's sheltered-care population might be employed.

Apte (1968) reports that only 46% of the residents in the transitional hostels he studied were, in fact, totally unemployed. It is not clear what Apte means by "totally unemployed"—for example, does this mean that any type of money-making activity, even running errands, would be considered employment? If so, and this criterion is used for the California population, it could be said that 23% of the population are making some money, though the amount of work involved with 12% of the population is minimal and would not normally be considered as even part-time employment. At any rate, given Apte's criteria, we would conclude that 77% of the California sheltered-care population are totally unemployed.

Apte's population differed from the California population in two respects important in assessing employment potential: (1) Apte's subjects lived in Great Britain at a time when there was full employment (i.e., anyone who wanted a job could get one—if one could stand, one could work); (2) they lived in a subset of "transitional" sheltered-care facilities that had a turnover rate of 50% per year and emphasized employment as a program requirement for residents. Brenner (1973) has pointed out the significance of economic factors in relation to mental hospital admission, noting that in hard times there are greater numbers of admissions to mental hospitals. We thus would expect that differences in the economy and the transitional nature of the facilities that Apte studied might well account for a portion of the 31% difference in total employment between his group and the one reported on in California. In any event, even with full employment and with facilities that emphasize employment as a requirement, some residents remain unemployed in Apte's sample. In Great Britain, as in California, the types of jobs obtained by residents are menial; they tend to have little possibility for advancement and seem most vulnerable to hard times.

Education

Education speaks to potential for involvement in productive-type activities. Educationally the mentally ill in sheltered care are not very different from the general population. Though there is a tendency for them to be slightly less educated, they are also much older within the same age limits, and people get more education now than they used to; 7% of the sheltered-care population have finished college, compared with 13% in the general population. Of those completing college, slightly more are male. Both males and females in this educational group are middle aged. While this population is educated similarly to their own age group, their lack of competitive experience in the labor market would force them to compete with younger, more educated individuals for employment. Thus they in fact may be educationally handicapped in the labor market.

Socioeconomic Status

A comparison of the socioeconomic status of the resident population with that of their fathers, as demonstrated by scores on Reiss' (1961) Socioeconomic Index (SEI), reveals that this particular population is downwardly mobile. That is, of five possible index categories (professional, business/managerial, skilled worker, semiskilled worker, and unskilled worker) we find proportionately more fathers of sheltered-care residents in the professional category and proportionately more residents in the unskilled-worker category of the SEI. In general a clear downward drift is apparent from fathers of residents to the residents themselves.

Income

Income is primarily an index of ability to participate as a consumer. Only 6% of the sheltered-care population are supported solely by private funds (family, savings); the rest are supported totally or in part by welfare grants. Currently three-quarters of the residents are receiving financial support from the Supplemental Security Income (SSI); 19.5% have multiple financial sources other than SSI. To a large extent consumptive patterns in this population are determined by factors external to their control—the policies of their benefactors.

Future Prospects

Although the future prospects for social integration seem bleak, they are bleak only from the perspective of the goals of achieving totally independent living and full participation in the competitive labor market for those individuals in sheltered care. Goals emphasizing more modest achievement, such as maintaining adequate levels of social functioning and maximizing the strengths of this population for all types of social involvement, seem much more attainable and realistic. The achievement of these latter goals will, however, be most affected by current constraints on social involvements.

Constraints on Social Integration

The major constraints on social involvement for the former mental patient include geographic mobility, chronicity, psychopathology, and violence. Each of these four factors has been viewed as a characteristic of the former mental patient that detracts from his level of social integration. How do these constraints relate to the social integration of the mentally ill in sheltered care?

Geographic and Mobility Characteristics

Two geographic-mobility characteristics have been considered as important in affecting the social integration of the former mental patient. First the loss of social roles due to treatment outside of one's local area was one of the primary reasons for the initiation of the community mental-health movement (Joint Commission on Mental Illness and Health, 1961). Second, mobility itself has been viewed as in indicator of mental disorder that inhibited people from forming close relationships (Ödegaard, 1932).

Providing Care Close to Home. Fully 53% report that they are currently living in a place that they consider to be their home town. In fact 80% live within 50 miles of what they consider to be their home town. This finding must be tempered by the observation that "psychiatric immigration" may occur whereby long-term hospitalized patients come to view the area around the hospital as "home" (Satin & Gruenberg, 1975). However, since the description of the current area of residence as one's home town was in our sample, a response no more characteristic of the long-term than of the short-term hospitalized group, we would conclude that "psychiatric immigration" is not a factor in the resident's report of residing in his home town. Thus our findings indicate strongly that the community mental-health movement is meeting its goal of providing care for the mentally ill close to their actual home environments and that this constraint to social integration may be minimized.

A Relatively Stable Population. The population currently living in sheltered care is relatively stable; 60% have lived in their current facilities more than a year. Discounting rehospitalization as a move to a different living situation, only one-third of the group had moved within the last year. Yet a small portion of the population changes its residence frequently. For example, 16% of the group made several moves in the past year, and 23% lived in more than one facility in addition to their current placement.

Comparing the total sheltered-care population with 1970 U.S. Census figures for the general population in California, we note little difference between these two groups in view of their stability, though there is a slight trend for individuals in sheltered care to be more mobile. This mobility differential, however, may be a slight artifact of the overall newness of the sheltered-care system.

Young males are definitely the most mobile in the sheltered-care population; 63% of the young males have been in facilities for less than a year. In comparison we find that only 42% of young females have been in facilities for less than a year. Being female (in all age categories), as well as increasing age, is associated with residential stability. These findings regarding the mobility of young male residents are congruent with those of Segal, Baumohl, and Johnson (1977), which report a high rate of mental illness in the young, primarily male, vagrant population.

The findings that people in sheltered care are generally stable and that a small group of them tend to be more mobile are consistent with the expressed desire of residents for a stable life-style; 55% say that they wish to stay on at their facility for a long period of time.

Ambivalence about moving and its meaning is reflected in the following example:

> Judy, age 34, is one of the few board-and-care residents who is working. If she scrimps and saves, the money she makes is enough to live on. She thinks that eventually she might like to be a psychiatric nurse; her experience in the hospital prompted her interest in that field.
>
> Judy thinks that it would be wise for her to wait another year before going out to look for an apartment of her own. She has been living here since she left the hospital three years ago and is quite satisfied with her present living situation. "Like I say, it's something like taking the place of a family, although you know deep down it never could be. It's just someone to talk to, someone that knows and understands and yet keeps their nose to themselves. So that means a lot" (F.N.).*

Some mobility within the sheltered care system results from a very small number of disruptive residents who have been bounced from facility to facility within a given geographic area, usually ending up in a particular

---

* F.N. refers to field notes taken at the time of a structured or open-ended interview.

facility informally reputed to accept more difficult individuals. In addition to movement of difficult and hard-to-handle residents within this primarily stable system, there is apparently also movement of a small group of individuals out of the system. (This latter conclusion is, however, based primarily on open-ended data and is not accounted for in geographic-mobility statistics provided by the survey data.)

Those individuals moving out of the system do not necessarily move into stable life situations. They gain a modicum of independence often connected with their efforts and those of their former sheltered-living environment. For example:

Two months before the interview, Kenneth, 32, had made his move from sheltered care into an apartment. He shares his new home with a long-time school friend, a fellow with similar interests. Moving out was not an easy task for Kenneth; the longer he stayed, the more difficult it was to leave. This difficulty was attributed to the feeling of security that he derived from his former living situation, a feeling that prevailed despite the constant turnover of residents.

It was Kenneth's intention to move out with other residents as apartment mates, but these plans fell through. Fortunately for Kenneth, he grew up in this area and has a father living near the sheltered-care facility. When he first moved out of the facility he arranged to live with his father until he could move into his new apartment. Kenneth has maintained a long-term relationship with a woman who often visited him while he was living in sheltered care. Although he had little contact with the people from the facility during the first couple of weeks after he left, some new problems in his relationship with this woman have prompted him to turn to them for emotional support. The facility has hired him to work on their staff on a part-time basis; he attends staff meetings and seminars.

Given the data on geographic mobility in the sheltered-care population, we currently think that this is not a major constraint for the social integration of this group.

Chronicity: History of Mental Hospitalization

Chronicity, that is, long-term hospitalization leading to the termination of social contacts, is another constraint on social integration. In considering the history of the sheltered-care population's involvement with the state mental hospital, we should note that a quarter of the population currently in these facilities did not have their first admission to a mental hospital until after the enactment of the Lanterman-Petris-Short (LPS) legislation in 1969. Thus whereas a significant portion of the sheltered-care population is new to the state hospital system, it seems that the policy of community care for the mentally ill has the potential for producing its own residual or chronic population: The recent admissions may now represent the same residual population that in the past filled the back wards of the state mental hospitals. The possible substitution of long-term community-based sheltered care for long-term hospitalization is reinforced by the fact that a full 35% of the individuals currently living in sheltered care have cumulatively spent a year or less in a mental hospital. In fact 57% have *never* spent 2 or more continuous years in a mental hospital. Such a history is not characteristic of the former long-term mental patients who were admitted under indefinite commitment to a state hospital.

In general we found that women residents were more involved with both the sheltered-care and the hospital-care systems: Women had slightly more admissions to the mental hospitals in each age category than their male counterparts; they were more likely to be in the chronic-hospital category than men—that is, they were more likely to have spent 2 or more continuous years in a state hospital (35% of young females versus 27% of all women also spent more years in sheltered care and had been in more sheltered-care homes). In all of these figures age is an important factor. The older one is, the longer one tends to have been involved with the mental-health system. This is a traditional and expected trend. An opposite trend emerges, however, from the initiation of a revolving-door policy (i.e., a policy of easy admission and quick release, often applying to the same individual over many experiences with the mental hospital) precipitated in California by the 1969 LPS Act. For the younger and middle-aged residents we see an increase in admissions over the older group. For example, 46% of the young residents, but only 39% of the old residents, have between 3 and 25 admissions.

The effects of the 1969 LPS changes in admission and retention policies of state hospitals were studied by cross-tabulating the "years since a resident's first admission" (the assumed date of onset of his illness) with "whether or not he had spent 2 or more continuous years in a state hospital." In this analysis we are particularly interested in comparing the group of individuals whose illness began after LPS as compared with the group whose first hospitalization was before 1969. Controlling for age, we find that only 11% of the people within each age category whose first admission was since 1969 report having been hospitalized 2 or more continuous years, but within the group hospitalized before 1969 a minimum of 41% in each age category are likely to report having 2 years of continuous hospitalization. Furthermore, the earlier the first hospitalization, the higher the percentage of each age category reporting continuous hospitalization of 2 years or more. In general we find an increased number of admissions for those who have spent less than 2 years continuously in a state mental hospital in the group of more recent onsets. This is true for both sexes and all ages. We conclude that LPS has prevented the negative effects of long-term hospitalization on social integration but that, in doing so, it may be helping in the creation of a new separate system of social integration—the sheltered-care facility. Individuals may now give up their community contacts to become chronic sheltered-care residents. We consider this question in looking at those factors that facilitate and hinder the social integration of the resident.

Psychopathology

Psychopathology can be considered a major constraint on social integration in the sheltered-care population. Psychopathology has a negative influence on specific types of social involvements for a large part of the population. Our data lead us, however, to believe it is significantly handicapping—that is, an overriding factor in their daily interactions—for only a small portion of those in sheltered care. Our interviewers eliminated as too emotionally disturbed only 8% of the people we tried to interview. Indications of disturbance included a great amount of nervousness and agitation on the part of the interviewee. (In one situation the prospective interviewee hid in the closet because he was afraid of the interviewer.) In such cases no attempt was made to force the interview. The interviewers also observed that 18% of the interviewees were delusional at some time during the interview period. An additional reflection of psychological disturbance was that 10% of the population admitted that they had actually contemplated suicide during the past month.

In looking at the level of disturbance in the population, our ratings on the 16 symptom categories in the Overall and Gorham Brief Psychiatric Rating Scale (BPRS) reveal that only 16% could be considered severely disturbed, while 56% might be termed as mildly disturbed, and 28% could be regarded as lacking any overt psychological disturbance. It would appear from these data that the majority of the sheltered-care population should not find psychopathology a major constraint to attaining moderate levels of social integration. In our next chapter we discuss more specifically the relative difficulty of different types of involvements for residents and the effects of psychopathology on such involvements.

Sheltered-Care Residents as a Community Threat

We have discussed the public conception of the mentally ill as the "raving maniac"—one whose acts have no rational basis and are, therefore, unpredictable. How much of an actual threat do the mentally ill in sheltered care pose for the community? How does the perception of them as a community threat act as an impediment to their social integration?

Perhaps more directly related to age, though supported by the "revolving-door" hospitalization policy, is the finding that older residents tend to be hospitalized fewer times than younger residents with equal dates of first admission. This seems to be a function of the tendency of younger residents to pose a more active threat to the community and therefore to be more susceptible to hospitalization; 11% of the sheltered-care population reported having been arrested in the past year. The arrests were for minor offenses, primarily disturbing the peace, loitering, drunken and disorderly conduct, petty theft, and destruction of property. This may be a somewhat biased response group, however, because residents involved in the past year in serious crimes would probably no longer be living at the facility. Assuming this bias, we asked facility operators if any of their residents had been picked up by the police in the past year and what the reasons were for these police contacts; 40% responded that at least one of their residents had been picked up by the police in the past year. Only one operator (out of 92) reported that the reason for being picked up by the police was the commission of a violent act (specifically charges of armed robbery). Only 4% of the police contacts involved bizarre behavior.

The most frequent reason given for a resident's being picked up by the police—40% of the affirmative responses—involved a resident "lost and wandering around the neighborhood." It is not known whether this happened because the resident was actually lost or because a neighbor worried about the resident's standing in front of his or her house.

These statistics should lead to an appreciation of the vulnerability of this group rather than of its dangerousness. It would seem that fear of released patients' going to sheltered care is based on unfounded stereotypes rather than on actual threat to the public and that the constraint on the social integration of this population derives from these stereotypes or residents' vulnerability. With respect to the latter observation, 16% of the residents do not feel safe on the streets at any time, and another 34% feel safe only during the daytime hours. This is a significant constraint on their mobility and thus on their social-integration potential.

The Mentally Ill Resident in Sheltered Care

The typical sheltered-care resident is between 50 and 65 years of age, white, Protestant, has less than a high-school education, and has been out of the labor market for several years. The resident is generally not living far from his or her home town and is fairly settled into a stable life situation in the sheltered-care facility. The major source of financial support for the typical resident is SSI. The resident does not provoke much trouble for the community from the perspective of social disorder and manifests a mild level of psychological and emotional disturbance. Prospects for making the transition to full community life in terms of obtaining gainful employment seem small, as are prospects of establishing some sort of conjugal unit on which to base social life.

The impediments to social integration of the sheltered-care resident are those relating primarily to establishing himself more as an independent self-supporting individual. Constraints on social interaction, such as severe psychopathology, community reaction to patient stereotypes, or lack of social contacts due to mobility or long-term hospitalization, must be viewed as factors adding to the difficulties posed by a lack of previous social integration. Our efforts emphasize, therefore, the basics of social integration. The goal of our study, then, is—current constraints being taken into consideration—to assess those factors that can help improve the sheltered-care experience of these individuals and promote their efforts to reach out in a more independent manner to the external community. With this goal in mind, we now turn to a consideration of how residents use their environment.

REFERENCES

Apte, R. Z., *Halfway Houses: A New Dilemma in Institutional Care.* Occasional Papers on Social Administration, No. 27, London: G. Bell and Sons, 1968.

Brenner, M. H. *Mental Illness and the Economy.* Cambridge, Massachusetts: Harvard University Press, 1973.

Davis, A. E., S. Dinitz, and B. Pasamanick. *Schizophrenics in the New Custodial Community: Five Years After the Experiment.* Columbus, Ohio: Ohio State University Press, 1974.

Freeman, H. and O. Simmons. *The Mental Patient Comes Home.* New York: Wiley, 1963.

Heckel, R., C. Perry, and P. G. Reeves. *The Discharged Mental Patient.* Columbia, South Carolina: University of South Carolina Press, 1973.

Joint Commission on Mental Illness and Health. *Action for Mental Health.* New York: Science Editions, 1961.

Miller, D. *Worlds That Fail: Part 1. Retrospective Analysis of Mental Patients' Careers.* California Mental Health Research, Monograph #6. Sacramento, California: California State Department of Mental Hygiene, 1965.

Ödegaard, Ö. *Emigration and Insanity: A Study of Mental Disease Among the Norwegian-Born Population of Minnesota.* Copenhagen, Denmark: Evin Munksgaards Publishers, 1932.

Pasamanick, B., F. R. Scarpitti, and S. Dinitz. *Schizophrenics in the Community.* New York: Appleton-Century-Crofts, 1967.

Reiss, A. J. *Occupations and Social Status.* New York: Free Press, Macmillan, 1961.

Satin, M. S. and E. M. Gruenberg. "Immigration and Insanity: The Dutchess County Experience." Paper presented at the Fourth Tromsø Seminar in Medicine, June 5–8, 1975. Tromsø, Norway.

Segal, S., J. Baumohl, and E. Johnson. "Falling Through the Cracks: Mental Disorder and Social Margin in a Young Vagrant Population." *Social Problems,* **24**(3), 387–400 (1977).

U.S. Bureau of the Census. *Census of population: 1970,* Vol. 1, Characteristics of the Population, Part 6, California—Section 2, Part 1. Washington, D.C.: U.S. Government Printing Office, 1973.

STEVEN P. SEGAL • URI AVIRAM

Bridging the Gap: The Relation Between Internal and External Integration

Advocates of community care for the mentally ill have attempted summarily to reduce social dependency by moving individuals into the community. They hoped this tactic would stop the development of institutional neuroses, whereby individuals became so dependent upon the hospital they were unable to leave. In view of the community-care goal of involving individuals in the external environment, the importance of internal integration is the extent to which it "bridges the gap" between the facility and the community.

Bridging the Gap: A Personal Experience

It was very hard to leave the house. In fact it took me six months to move out. It was just very difficult for me— difficult for me to move in and when I got settled, it got increasingly more difficult to move out because you get the feeling of security there. The meals are there. It's a kind of psychological bind because I was afraid to move out and yet I wanted to move out. I had been there eight months. Before that there was no pressure, but after six months, there seemed to be more pressure put on the residents to move out (F.N.).*

This quote indicates the difficulty experienced by one former resident of a halfway house in attempting to bridge the gap, to move back into the outside world, the external community. This individual had relatives nearby willing and able to take him in and lived in a community where he had many friends outside the halfway house. In addition to the social supports available outside, the facility itself exerted some pressure on him to move out. Ultimately he was able to share an apartment with a friend who was not in any way involved with the facility.

Reprinted from Steven P. Segal and Uri Aviram, *The Mentally Ill in Community-Based Sheltered Care*, New York: John Wiley and Sons, Inc. 1978, pages 200–214, by permission of the authors and publisher.
* F.N. refers to field notes taken at the time of a structured or open-ended interview.

This chapter, as did our chapter on external integration, focuses on residents' efforts to reach out independently to the external community from the facility. Such efforts are a minimum prerequisite to the more difficult move to independent living reported by this individual.

Four Components of Social Integration

To understand the relationship between the environment and an individual's level of internal and external integration, we must look at four sets of facilitating or hindering factors involved in internal and external functioning, as follows: (1) social support, (2) social insulation, (3) social facilitation, and (4) social-dependency-producing variables (see Table 1). The social-support variables enhance an individual's level of both internal integration and external integration. The social-insulation variables enhance an individual's internal integration but have no effect on his external integration. On the other hand social-facilitation variables enhance an individual's external integration but have no effect on his internal integration. Finally the social-dependency-producing variables enhance an individual's internal involvement in the facility at the expense of his involvement in the external community.

In our data on the sheltered-care environment, social-support variables are found to be the strongest factors influencing both internal and external social integration.† Social-dependency-producing variables are second in importance, social-facilitation variables are third, followed by social-insulation factors.

Given the presumption in the past that social-dependency-producing variables predominate in the mental-hospital environment (Goffman, 1961), our findings indicating a predominance of social-support variables in community-based sheltered care demonstrate a major difference between these environments in the

† The relative ranking of the four sets of factors is based on the size of the average partial beta weights for each group of predictors in the external and internal integration models.

TABLE 1

Four Components of Social Integration[a]

Components of Social Integration	DIRECTION OF RELATIONSHIP	
	External	*Internal*
1. Social-support factors		
Neighbors' positive response	+	+
Ideal psychiatric environment	+	+
Sufficient spending money	+	+
Distress	−	−
Social isolation of resident group	−	−
2. Social-insulation factors		
Downtown area	n.s.	−
Operator perceives services as helpful	n.s.	+
Residence club	n.s.	−
Female operator	n.s.	+
3. Social-facilitation factors		
Involuntary resident	−	n.s.
Complaints to authorities	−	n.s.
Resident's control of money (resident pays bill)	+	n.s.
4. Social-dependency factors		
Rural area	−	+
Distance (closeness to resources produces a higher score)	+	−
Residents do not control medications	−	+

[a] *All plus and minus signs refer to the direction of the relationship indicated by the sign of the standardized partial regression weights in the external- and internal-integration models. Relationships are significant at least $p < .10$ on the assumption of a simple random sample; n.s. means not significant.*

extent to which the social-dependency-producing variables are influential in the individual's social integration. In fact, because social-support variables predominate, community-based sheltered care is a more desirable context than the mental hospital if the goal is moving someone out into the external community. This is true, of course, only to the extent that Goffman's description of the hospital as dependency producing is correct. Others have viewed the patient's role in the context of the hospital community as a more active one (Braginsky et al., 1969).

The 4 sets of factors relating to external and internal integration involve 15 independent predictors that are open to modification by policy action. Here, we see how each of these predictors relates jointly to internal and external integration, to determine how they affect one's

effort to bridge the gap between the facility and the outside world.

Social-Support Variables

In order of their relative importance for the total resident population (based on the averaged ranked importance of a factor in predicting external and internal integration) the social-support variables predictive of both external and internal integration are "neighbors' positive response," "the ideal psychiatric environment," "sufficient spending money," "psychological distress," and "social isolation of the resident group."

While "neighbors' positive response" ranked first in importance as a predictor of external integration and second for internal integration, the ideal psychiatric environment predictor ranked seventh for external and first for internal integration. Thus, in the overall perspective, the community response to individuals in the facility was most important when considered as a predictor of both social-integration variables. This result is consistent with research on the outcome of in-hospital programs (focusing on the internal environment) developed to promote external integration. Fairweather (1964), in an earlier study, developed a ward-based program that markedly changed the behavior of the residents in the hospital but had little carry-over to the outside community once the patient left the hospital. This result emphasizes again the importance of directing change efforts toward the environment in which the change is expected to occur.

Whereas positive neighborhood response and the ideal psychiatric environment enhanced the internal and external integration of the sheltered-care population when considered as a total group, they cannot be considered social-support variables for those individuals in the population who are most severely disturbed or symptomatic. For this latter group positive neighbor response is a social facilitator—promoting external and unrelated to internal integration—and the ideal psychiatric environment is a social insulator—promoting internal integration with no effect on external integration. In fact, for the severely ill, there are no social-support variables simultaneously promoting internal and external integration! This seems to be due to the fact that internal and external integration for this population subgroup are unrelated to one another. The Pearson Product Moment correlation between internal and external integration for the most severely disturbed group is .11 as compared to .42 and .31 for the mildly disturbed and asymptomatic groups respectively (both the latter correlations are statistically significant).

There are two hypotheses that offer some explanation for the lack of relationship between internal and external integration for the most severely disturbed subgroup. The first relates to the fact that the severely disturbed group has much lower levels of both internal and external integration than the rest of the population in sheltered care. Using the analogy of a developing country in economics, one can argue that, before the impact of development in one area of the economy can be experienced in another, a minimal amount of development is necessary in both areas. In other words, for internal integration to have an impact on external integration (and vice versa), a minimum amount of both assets must be possessed by the individual.

The second explanatory hypothesis involves the observation that internal and external integration have a different meaning for the severely ill population than for the mildly disturbed and asymptomatic populations. This latter argument derives from the observation made in the mental-health literature that the severely mentally ill are running away from close relationships (Ödegaard, 1932) or do better in avoiding intense emotional involvements (Brown, Birley, & Wing, 1972). Thus, for the asymptomatic and mildly ill, internal relationships may be used as a means of gaining experience and enhancing external relationships (and vice versa); for the severely ill internal relationships are avoided through the use of external involvements. For this latter group, encouraging internal involvements depends largely upon the well-designed and supportive ideal psychiatric environment.

The more externally integrated resident in the severe-pathology subgroup is more willing to move out of the sheltered-care facility than other individuals are, less likely to wish to remain at the facility for long periods of time, and more likely to spend time looking for an independent living arrangement. In considering a move out of the sheltered-care facility, this resident seems indifferent to (1) reasonable fears associated with establishing an independent household and (2) positive characteristics of the facility in which he lives. Consideration of the loneliness of living alone, the opinion that the sheltered-care facility he is currently living in is a physically and socially nicer place to live than the place the resident might find on his own, and the belief that the other residents are more of a family than the resident's natural family have no bearing on his decision to move! Indifference to such factors and a mobile orientation are characteristic of the severely ill. They are not characteristic of those individuals in the asymptomatic or mild-pathology subgroups. In fact, the more externally integrated one becomes in these latter subgroups, the more consideration he gives to characteristics of the facility in which he resides. For those with no and mild symptomatology ratings, characteristics of the facility and personal fears become important factors in considering a move.

It is possible that those residents with severe symptomatology do not consider home life to be a positive experience for them, and so they choose to focus on a life outside of the home. It therefore would not matter if an apartment of their own was not as attractive physically or socially as the sheltered-care home. A history of negative experiences with their own families may have helped to develop an external orientation, and so they may prefer to be out of the house as much as possible. It is possible that people in the "severe" group project their own unhappiness onto their immediate environment, and in their attempt to avoid this unhappiness, adopt a mobile life-style. Although Brown, Birley, and Wing (1972) speak of former hospital patients' doing better in environments with less intensive emotional involvements, we would think that the intensity and quality of such involvements need further study, since severely disturbed individuals with higher levels of internal integration wanted to stay on at the facility for longer time periods and the ideal psychiatric environment tended to promote internal integration. It would appear, however, that the severe subgroup has a more difficult time dealing with their internal environment, is in need of a more selectively designed environment, and will use external integration to avoid internal commitments.

The third most important social-support predictor facilitating both external and internal integration of the total sheltered-care population is the extent to which residents perceive they have sufficient spending money to do what they would like to do. With respect to the quality of life, having the amount of money necessary to do what one wishes to do not only bolsters the ability to reach out to the external world but also makes interaction within the facility easier. This observation is, however, true only for the largest subgroup in the population showing mild pathology. For the asymptomatic group, having sufficient spending money is a social facilitator—it promotes external integration with no impact on internal integration. The severe subgroup again differs from the other two in the impact of this predictor. For severely disturbed individuals, having sufficient spending money promotes their external integration at the expense of their internal involvements. This relationship is consistent with our observations regarding the wishes of the severely ill to avoid internal commitments and introduces a new dimension to what we might previously have conceived of as a variable, the opposite of which would have been in the social-dependency class. Given the unique character of the severely disturbed group, variables promoting their external integration at the expense of their internal involvements might be termed *social-flight*-producing factors.

Social-support predictors that reduce both internal and external integration are "psychological distress" and "social isolation of the resident group." We include these factors, most notably, level of psychological distress, as social-support variables because modifying these variables (e.g., reducing individual distress levels) will have a generalized positive impact on social behavior as measured both by internal and external integration.

The concept of "psychological distress" was initially used in the analysis of external and internal integration as an intervening variable (i.e., one that may alter the causal interpretation of the predictors to the criterion). This was done because of the underlying assumption that the disability of the mentally ill stands in the way of their social functioning. Of the 15 predictors considered as facilitators or hindrances to social integration, psychological distress was the fourth most important factor overall, as well as the fourth most important social-support variable. Its importance may be underestimated, however, because 7.6% of the sample population were not interviewed, since they were too emotionally disturbed. Higher levels of psychological distress, even within categories classified by their level of symptomatology, remained a generally negative influence on both internal and external integration.

The extent to which psychological distress can be demobilizing is vividly illustrated by the following interviewer remarks:

> The interviewer went into his bedroom to see him at 2:00 p.m. The resident had been heavily medicated and was sleeping most of the day. He was a college student who had withdrawn from contact with other residents in his facility and the social contacts in his environment after continuous unsuccessful attempts to become involved in an "intellectually challenging college career." Each attempt on his part was accompanied by a setback due to extreme psychological problems, leading to admission to a new facility, and to his progressive withdrawal (F.N.).

The negative impact of "social isolation of the resident group" on a given individual's level of internal and external integration is also quite important from a sociological perspective. This factor describes the extent to which all residents of a given facility are characterized by the operator as isolated from families and neighbors. It is a significant factor only in reducing the internal and external integration of the population subgroup having no overt symptomatology. The negative relationship to external and internal integration implies that an individual living in this context will be more isolated from social contacts outside as well as inside the facility. Whereas this could be the result of selection—that is, isolated individuals tend to be placed together in the same facility—it may also reflect an aspect of the "social-breakdown syndrome," a redefinition of one's self as chronically sick. Gruenberg (1963) has offered a tentative seven-stage formulation of the syndrome's pathogenesis:

1. Precondition or susceptibility: deficiency in self-concept (which may be characterological or precipitated by current mental turmoil).
2. Dependence on current cues.
3. Social labeling as incompetent or dangerous.
4. Induction in the sick role—that is, the suggestion that an individual adopt a passive, helpless, perhaps potentially dangerous, certainly "sick" role, with little prospect of change.
5. Learning the chronic sick role.
6. Atrophy of work and social skill.
7. Identification with the sick.

It seems reasonable for a resident to have a lower level of external integration if other residents are isolated from the community, because community rejection of the total group explains reduced acceptance of any given member. But why is there also a withdrawal from the internal community? This withdrawal indicates the existence of an additional step in the "social-breakdown syndrome," following Gruenberg's "social labeling" (step three), which we shall call "normalization." Normalization is best explained as the attempt to maintain a normal self-concept by withdrawing from the immediate community associated with illness.

Gruenberg's scheme of the social-breakdown syndrome posits too easily the change in the individual's self-concept to a negative stereotype—despite his dependency and susceptibility. Karmel (1969) found, in an empirical test of Goffman's hypothesis, that self-mortification did not occur during the first month's stay in a mental hospital. Karmel found instead that, during the first month, patients experienced "a slight gain in self-esteem and social identity" (Karmel, 1969, p. 134).

Researchers have also noted the tendency of individuals to "normalize" or interpret mental-illness behavior in a more "normal" frame of reference (Clausen & Yarrow, 1955; Starr, 1955).

Consistent with these research findings, a frequent observation by our interviewers was the tendency of residents to define everybody else in the facility, but not themselves, as "crazy." In an effort to protect their identity and combat the development of the social-breakdown syndrome, residents disassociate themselves from other residents. In an external community that disallows the participation of facility residents because it defines them as mentally ill, the residents can protect this "normal" self-image only by total withdrawal. In the following excerpt the interviewer describes a vivid example of the struggle for "normalization" of one's self-concept:

> I remember this late middle-aged gentlemen. We had a hard time finding him. He was standing in the dark in a hall closet, doing absolutely nothing, when we did locate him. Apparently this is something he always does so nobody cares or takes notice of him getting in and out of the closet.
>
> When I inquired why he was in the closet, he said he had been there all morning; he liked it in there because it was comfortable. He said he's either in the closet, in his room lying down, or eating—that's all he does.
>
> I think he enjoyed the interview because it was hard for me to get him to answer the questions. He wanted to talk to me about all kinds of things which I thought was rather strange because he didn't want to talk to anybody else. He said he was just generally tired of the people he was living with and their same old problems. It was his notion that "everybody else was crazy"; he didn't want to talk to patients; he called everybody a patient.
>
> He amazed me with his verbal ability, and though he was a little bit delusional, his affect wasn't that bland for living the type of life he was leading. . . . As soon as I explained the study to him, he just started talking right away, telling me the types of things he didn't like about the place and the improvements he would like to see (F.N.).

Social-Dependency-Producing Factors

The second most important set of predictors we found for the total resident population is social-dependency-producing factors. They comprise the most significant set of predictors from the perspective of the iatrogenic effects attributed to mental-hospital care.

Sheltered-care environments encourage a "settling-in" behavior—a predilection to become attached to one's surroundings—characteristic of the general human condition. The strongest predictor in this group of variables is the rural versus nonrural environment. The more rural environment enhances internal and reduces external integration. A good (albeit lengthy) illustration of this phenomenon emerges from one interviewer's experiences in a rural setting in contrast to a large urban area.

The area is mostly agricultural, quite a way from the city, but there are several facilities in the area. One of the homes that I went to was very pleasing; the operators were cordial, cooperative, and eager to pass along the type of program they had established so that people in other areas might establish the same types of things. The home had a massive program; the residents were much more at ease. There wasn't much tension and there wasn't much nervousness. I don't think that the degree of mental illness is any less. I just think that the atmosphere they are living in is more relaxed and more homey than the facilities I interviewed in the city.

One facility was run by a middle-aged couple. They had mostly older people there but they had a very personal relationship with their people. They have a scrapbook of all the people they've ever had. They have birthday parties for every resident. The residents, although they are elderly, are kept fairly active except for those who can't get around. They have a large garden. All the people enjoy working in the garden. They have fresh vegetables, fresh fruits, and I think the residents are very happy to do this type of work. I say this because they are all very excited and the thing they were most proud of, I could tell, was their vegetables or onions or whatever. I spent about forty-five minutes in the garden with the operators and with their guests showing me their produce. . . .

Very few facilities in this area have that peculiar or particular odor of many of the urban board-and-care homes that I interviewed in. I didn't see any places that were the least bit messy or dirty. I don't know why this is, but in many of the places in the city I was just really turned off by the smell of the homes and even the people.

There wasn't quite as much idleness with the residents in this area as in the city. Just upon walking into the house, there weren't as many bodies just sitting on the porch in front of the TV. One thing that helped is that many of these places are on farms or ranches. There is plenty of work to be done and a lot of the places have what could be considered work-therapy programs where they help out in digging ditches or planting vegetables or keeping the chickens or keeping the cows. It keeps them busy. It seems very healthy and it gives them some sense of accomplishment. I think a lot of them were glad that they were learning to do new types of things (F.N.).

This interviewer's impression of the rural area versus the urban area may sound like a nineteenth-century tract extolling the benefits of rural life. It does, however, point to the fact that very attractive and supportive environments may, by their location and their all-encompassing help and support, operate to focus all involvements within the facility at the expense of the independent involvement of residents in the outside community (a community that in rural areas is often closed to the sheltered-care resident).

Whereas this observation holds for the general population, it requires some modification for those individuals who show no overt psychological disturbance. The rural environment enhances the external involvements of this subgroup, and thus for those without psychological disturbance the farm facility takes on the character of a social-support factor enhancing both internal and external integration.

Second in order of its importance as a social-dependency-producing variable is distance. The farther the facility is from community resources, the greater the level of internal integration and the lower the level of external integration (and vice versa). While it seems logical that facilities farther away from community resources would have a lower level of external integration, the fact that they also develop higher levels of internal integration is quite interesting. To some extent our figures point out that the reason for this is that facilities removed from a concentration of community resources are more likely to be family-oriented facilities in which the operator and his family live. It is also true that facilities located away from community resources are more likely to have a therapy or rehabilitation program at the house. As a result of these two factors, plus the independent unavailability of outside community resources for residents (unless they have their own transportation, which is unusual in this population), "distance" from community resources becomes a social-dependency-producing variable.

A third social-dependency-producing factor is "resident lack of control over their medication." Facilities in which none of the residents control their own medication tend to foster an environment that increases internal and reduces external integration. The policy of selective control of medication in sheltered care leads, however, to a certain amount of risk. For example, Janet Chase (1973) writes of a patient who saved enough Miltown to commit suicide. The point of Chase's example was to expose poor medication practices in some sheltered-care facilities. However, a negative consequence of rigid supervision of medications is that residents are tied to the facility by a medication schedule that interferes with their ability to move into the external environment. We observed several facilities where, like the hospital ward, social life was organized around the dispensation of medication. This has the obvious effect of focusing an individual's life inward on the facility and increasing his internal integration.

We stress here, however, that a selective policy regarding control of medication requires responsible judgment on the part of professionals who supervise medication. Flexibility in this procedure should be given more consideration because of the impact it may have in encouraging people to move out into the community. It also appears that the type of internal integration sacrificed in the policy is one that is dysfunctional because of its emphasis on the sick role, that is, because it forces interaction around the dispensing of medication.

Social Facilitation

Social-facilitation variables tend to promote an individual's level of external integration without affecting internal integration. Three social-facilitation variables are considered here: "the involuntary resident," "complaints to authorities," and "resident control of money." Being an involuntary resident or living in a facility that has complaints made about it to the authorities leads to a reduction in residents' external integration. Having control of one's spending money increases a resident's external integration.

The involuntary resident is the strongest social-facilitation predictor even after level of psychological distress, chronicity, conservatorship, and individual ability are controlled for. This resident did not choose the facility he is currently living in. To some extent the involuntary resident has given up attempting to influence his own environment.

> One resident was transferred to his current facility by the owner of his previous facility, which had gone out of business. He expressed a sense of hopelessness and wondered if anything were worthwhile anymore. He was always bored, and had withdrawn to the point of spending most of his time in bed. Despite his dissatisfaction with his current living arrangement, he accepts what comes (F.N.).

In this case we see evidence of negative impact on external as well as internal integration: The individual is withdrawing into his bed as a result of being involuntarily moved from one living arrangement to another.

Looking within subgroups of the sheltered-care population who evidence differing levels of psychological disturbance, we found that, for those individuals showing no overt symptomatology, being unable to choose their facility is significantly and negatively related to both internal and external integration; thus, not directing or participating in the placement process takes on the character of a social-support variable for the "normals." For the mildly ill this variable takes on the character of a social-dependency-producing factor; that is, it encourages internal at the expense of external integration, and for the severely ill, it leads to social flight (discouraging internal and encouraging external integration).

Changes observed in the character of the involuntary-resident predictor for those with differing degrees of overt symptomatology appear to be related to the different stages of the social-breakdown syndrome (though we have no independent assessment of the latter other than the open-ended observations in interview reports).

We have previously observed that, after the social-breakdown-syndrome stage of being labeled "socially incompetent or dangerous," the individual may enter a stage in which his behavior can be interpreted as an attempt to retain his normal self-concept—a "normalization" stage. We have also pointed out that in this stage the individual can react by withdrawal from both the external and internal environments that have labeled him deviant. Thus the reaction of the resident in the subgroup with no overt symptomatology to the loss of his prerogative of choosing his residence is found to be withdrawal from involvements with social contacts in both the internal and external environments that have sanctioned (at least in the eyes of the individual) his involuntary placement.

Looking at the subgroup showing a "mild" or "moderate" degree of overt symptomatology, we find individuals more likely to be in the stages of (1) "induction into the sick role—that is, the suggestion that an individual adopt a passive, helpless, perhaps potentially dangerous, certainly 'sick' role, with little prospect for change" or (2) "learning the chronic sick role." At this stage the reaction to the deprivation of one's prerogative to choose one's residence leads to a withdrawal from the external community (the "normal" community)—as evidenced by the individual's reduced level of external integration—and an increase in involvement with "all the other crazy people he lives with," an increment in his internal integration. For those with mild symptomatology, then, "the involuntary resident factor" is social-dependency-producing.

Finally those individuals evidencing a high degree of symptomatology are more likely to have actually come to identify themselves with the sick role. Their identification is often, however, tinged with a learned hostility toward the system that seeks to help them. Segal, Baumohl, and Johnson (1977) report the sentiments of an eloquent "adolescent schizophrenic" regarding his unwillingness to obtain disability benefits to which he is entitled. This young man says:

> Like I don't think I'm *that* crazy. . . . But they won't give me any money until I confess my sins, man. I gotta say "yeah, man, I'm a fuckin' lunatic," and sign ten forms and

see eight doctors to prove it. And then they might really lock me up! (Segal, Baumohl, & Johnson, 1977, p. 394).

For those individuals with overt symptomatology the deprivation of the right to choose one's residence becomes a social-flight variable—a variable encouraging whatever external involvements they can muster (which we noted earlier is minimal) and discouraging their involvements with helpers and an internal environment they mistrust. These individuals have accepted the definition of themselves as sick but are avoiding the social implication of that definition in which all interactions in one's environment are made contingent upon and follow from such a definition.

In the helper's need to help lurks the temptation to take over—a temptation that may result in debilitating effects for the recipient of the help. Only 57% of the sheltered-care population respond that on a typical day most of the things they do are planned by themselves. We found that choosing one's residence is significantly related to whether or not one plans his daily activities. In the following example we note how hospital patients can be socialized into a role of being unable to plan their own activities. In commenting on her treatment at the hospital, one woman said:

> I would be out of those treatments they were giving! I have gotten tired and they was running me plum crazy, you know. Treatments, they drive me crazy. I was always shocked up. I was so nervous that I was unhappy there and I was so nervous and upset that I would just sit in one place, scared to look down the hallway because there was the room, and there were those doctors and those nurses down there. They call me at any time to take treatments (F.N.).

This woman spent almost all her time waiting to be called on. To the extent that a resident's time is organized around the needs or demands of the facility, and to the extent that he is asked to acquiesce in these needs, all his activities become contingenct upon his illness. It is such an experience that is avoided by the "well" residents through withdrawal, acquiesced in by the "mildly" symptomatic, and avoided through the flight of the most severely symptomatic.

Social Insulation

Social-insulation variables are significantly related to internal integration, enhancing or detracting from one's involvement in the facility, and have no effect on external involvements. The four variables considered, in order of their overall importance as social-insulation predictors, are "downtown area," "operator perceives services as helpful,'' ''residence club,'' and ''female operator.''

''Downtown area'' and the ''residence club'' are negatively related to internal integration. On the other hand ''perceived helpfulness of services'' and the ''female operator'' tend to increase the individual's level of internal involvement in the facility. Manipulating these factors to encourage social involvement within the facility is expedient, because they have no negative implications for external integration.

Conclusion

The positive relationship between internal and external integration and the finding that the strongest predictors of these criteria are social-support factors either facilitating or hindering both leads us to the conclusion that the appropriate focus of the design of a sheltered-care facility does not depend upon choosing between internal and external integration or using one type of integration, internal, as a means of promoting an assumedly more advanced type, external (the transitional goal); the appropriate focus is to determine how to design an environment that is dependent on factors that facilitate both internal and external integration in a manner that compromises neither—that is, does not rely primarily on social-dependency-producing characteristics.

In the designing of sheltered-care environments the needs of specific subgroups in the population must be taken into account both in terms of how characteristics affect internal and external integration in a given subgroup—that is, whether the characteristic is a social supporter, social insulator, social facilitator, or a social-dependency-producing factor—and in terms of changes in the meaning of the relationship between external and internal integration for a particular subgroup (e.g., the change we noted in distinguishing social-flight predictors in the severely symptomatic subgroup).

The danger that long-term sheltered care encourages internal at the expense of external integration will remain as long as social-dependency-producing characteristics are inadvertently allowed to operate, though a moderate level of internal integration in a long-term living arrangement may be more desirable and more realistic for much of the population.

Our goal for this population is, however, to promote both internal and external involvements to the extent possible from within the sheltered-care setting according to individual need and with a limited emphasis on transition to independent living situations.

REFERENCES

Braginsky, M., D. D. Braginsky, and K. Ring. *Methods of Madness.* New York: Holt, Rinehart and Winston, 1969.

Brown, G. W., J. L. T. Birley, and J. K. Wing. ''Influence of Family Life on the Course of Schizophrenic Disorders: A Replication.'' *Brit. J. Psychiat.* **121** (March) 241–258 (1972).

Chase, J. ''Where Have All the Patients Gone?'' *Human Behavior,* **2** (October) 14–21 (1973).

Clausen, J. and M. R. Yarrow (Eds.). ''The Impact of Mental Illness on the Family.'' *Contemporary Social Problems,* **11**(4), entire issue (1955).

Fairweather, G. W. *Social Psychology in Treating Mental Illness: An Experimental Approach.* New York: Wiley, 1964.

Goffman, E. *Asylums: Essays on the Social Situation of Mental Patients and Other Inmates.* Garden City, New York: Doubleday, 1961.

Gruenberg, E. M. ''Discussion of Critical Reviews of Pueblo, Western, and Denver Tri-County Divisions,'' in Bernard Stone (Ed.). *A Critical Review of Treatment Progress in a State Hospital Reorganized Toward the Communities Served.* Pueblo, Colorado: Pueblo Association for Mental Health May 1963 (mimeographed).

Karmel, M. ''Total Institutions and Self-Mortification,'' *J. Health and Social Behavior,* **10**(2), 134–142 (1969).

Ödegaard, Ö. *Emigration and Insanity: A Study of Mental Disease Among the Norwegian-Born Population of Minnesota.* Copenhagen, Denmark: Evin Munksgaards Publishers, 1932.

Segal, S., J. Baumohl, and E. Johnson. ''Falling Through the Cracks: Mental Disorder and Social Margin in a Young Vagrant Population.'' *Social Problems,* **24**(3), 387–400 (1977).

Starr, S. ''The Public's Ideas About Mental Illness.'' Paper presented at the Annual Meeting of the National Association for Mental Health. Indianapolis, Nov. 1955.

VIVIAN GARRISON

Support Systems of Schizophrenic and Nonschizophrenic Puerto Rican Migrant Women in New York City

Mental health professionals, under the pressures of the movement toward deinstitutionalization, have only recently developed a keen interest in the daily lives of patients with their "normal" peers in natural communities. Traditional clinical and epidemiological approaches have been focused on the individual patient, the current illness, the history of interpersonal relationships during the developmental years, and sometimes the current relationships of the adult patient to immediate family. The relationships of adult patients to non-kin have not generally been considered of great relevance to either clinical processes or etiological investigation. This leaves a gap in the clinical literature about the daily lives of patients as adults and their possible adjustments to community living—exactly the information that is now most needed in efforts to rehabilitate deinstitutionalized schizophrenics.

Sociologists and anthropologists, on the other hand, have studied routine daily life in natural communities, but their traditional focus has been on the normative and modal patterns among the presumed "healthy" population—an ideal standard of functioning that is usually unrealistic in considering the possible adjustment of a chronic schizophrenic and of little use to the clinician who would like to make a satisfactory discharge plan for an isolated and significantly psychiatrically impaired individual.

Both the clinical and the social science literature leave the same gap: How does the natural community support or not support its psychologically disabled members? Are there niches in which such persons are tolerated and perhaps even encouraged? Are there "naturally occurring support systems" (Caplan 1974) that can be tapped by mental health professionals for reintegrating the discharged patient into the support systems existing within the community? Can these systems be used as models for building new supports for patients within the

Reprinted from *Schizophrenia Bulletin*, Vol. 4, No. 4 (1978), pages 561–596, by permission of the author.

community that might be more acceptable to the community and more effective for patients than concentrating them in residence hotels and boarding homes, and more economical than day hospitals or transitional care facilities?

The thesis of this article is that many, even severely disturbed, chronic schizophrenic patients can be reintegrated into their natural communities if those communities are sufficiently well understood and if the professional care system will consider the non-kin alternatives to either family or institutional placement. The methods for doing this require nothing new—only flexible combinations of individual, family, group, and network therapies with patients in their natural setting. I will call this "natural network therapy." The information necessary to develop such strategies is available in anthropological and sociological studies of natural communities, if supplemented by adequate information on the social networks and support systems of patients with varying degrees of disability drawn from the specific community of concern. What is most needed are the conceptual and methodological tools necessary to integrate community studies of presumed "normal" or "healthy" individuals in natural communities with what is known of the needs and capacities of patients from those communities. Elsewhere, C. S. Thomas and I (1975) have argued that the concept of community from anthropology (Arensberg 1954, 1961), that of social networks from social anthropology (Barnes 1954; Bott 1957; Mitchell 1969), and that of "support system" from preventive psychiatry (Caplan 1974; Caplan and Killilea 1976) provide this integration in a way that is equally practicable for research, preventive programming, or direct patient care. Here, I hope to illustrate the practical applications of these concepts and methods to direct patient care of chronic schizophrenic Puerto Rican women.

I will draw upon my experience as cultural consultant to clinicians working with Puerto Rican patients and research done in the Tremont Crisis Center (TCC) of Bronx Psychiatric Center and Albert Einstein College of Medicine from 1972 to 1974, and upon a series of community studies conducted at Lincoln Hospital Mental Health Services (LHMHS) in the South Bronx from 1966 to 1969. This article presents a summary and reanalysis of data from these several studies, reported in greater detail elsewhere (Garrison 1972, 1974, 1977*b*; Lehmann 1970; Struening and Peck 1968), as they serve to elucidate the possibilities for fostering, rebuilding, or developing new support systems for the chronic schizophrenic patient within the Puerto Rican community.

Background—Concepts and Setting

This article is primarily concerned with what Caplan (1974) calls spontaneous or natural support systems. I, however, use a broader definition of the support system that is structurally coterminous with the anthropologists' definition of the *social network:*

> . . . the direct links radiating from a particular Ego to other individuals, and the links which connect those individuals who are directly tied to Ego, to one another. [Kapferer 1969, p. 182]

In this usage, spouse, children, parents, other kin, friends, work associates, formal or informal voluntary associations, and organized service organizations such as churches, the welfare department, physicians, and mental health services are all elements in the social network and support system of Ego. The links are interactions, which may be continuous or intermittent, frequent or infrequent, and formal or informal. Whether these interactions are supportive, indifferent, or undermining is a matter for empirical investigation.

Relationships are considered supportive when Ego reports (1) that she can count on the person (or institution, or agency) for financial help, help with household tasks, child care, or help when ill; (2) that she discusses her problems with that person (''confides'' in them hereafter); or (3) that she seeks their help in times of distress. The constellation of persons and agencies on whom the individuals depend, to whom they confide, or from whom they seek help are considered the *core support system*. This core support system, plus the surrounding constellation of relationships in the social network, which may or may not also be supportive, is called the *support system*. The social network is a structural concept that carries no implication of supportive function, while the support system concept refers to the supportive functions within that structure.

The social network is the minimal unit of study of community organization in complex societies, while communities, as anthropological constructs, are the ''basic units of organization and transmission within a society and its culture'' (Arensberg 1961, p. 248). As defined by anthropologists, community is not dependent upon ''community sentiments'' and it does not necessarily correspond to a precise geographical area. It *is* a territorial unit (delineated by patterns of movement and interaction; of dispersion and aggregation of persons), *and* it is a structured field of interindividual relationships unfolding through time—''an enduring temporal pattern of coexistences, an ordered time-progress of individuals, from their births to their deaths, through roles and relationships of each kind known to their species or their culture'' (Arensberg 1961, p. 250). Community forms in the United States, as elsewhere, vary with culture and subcultures (Arensberg 1955) defined by region, class, ethnicity, and ecological zone. They are learned in early socialization and are habitual and taken for granted as the natural way of life by culture bearers, for whom these habitual patterns of behavior and their evaluations are not fully conscious.

The community with which this paper is concerned is the Puerto Rican community of New York City. The focus within that community is upon the supports available and habitually utilized by the first generation migrant Puerto Rican woman. The sample of this community studied is a 10-census tract area of the South Bronx where LHMHS concentrated a series of innovative community mental health programs and research projects in 1965 to 1969 (Hallowitz and Riessman 1967; Peck, Kaplan, and Roman 1966; Kaplan and Roman 1973; Struening and Peck 1968). The population of this area was approximately 100,000, 60 percent of which was Puerto Rican. Over 90 percent of the Puerto Rican population was born in Puerto Rico and the majority migrated directly to the mainland from rural areas of the island in their late teens or early adulthood. Only a small proportion were born in San Juan (14 percent) or spent time there before migrating to New York.

Although the South Bronx had already been designated at that time as one of the three areas of the city with the highest rates of poverty, social disorganization, and social and psychological pathology (City of New York 1966), the neighborhood studied was, nonetheless, a workingclass, low-income, family residential neighborhood[1] and not an inner-city decayed, derelict

---

1. The housing and social characteristics of the Puerto Rican population of that area at that time are identical with those of the Puerto Rican-born population of New York City as reported in the 1970 Census (Subject Report PC(2)-1E) on the proportion of households with intact families (67 percent), educational level (mean years completed 8.6), and the proportion of individuals with incomes below the poverty level (32 percent). Indeed, all variables for which comparable data are available

TABLE 1

Criteria of subselection and classification of samples into groups reflecting degrees of emotional disturbance

Criteria	NEIGHBORHOOD SAMPLE (NONSCHIZOPHRENICS)			SCHIZOPHRENIA SAMPLE	
	Group 1 (n = 11)	*Group 2* (n = 13)	*Group 3* (n = 5)	*Outpatient* (n = 11)	*Inpatient* (n = 15)
Criteria of selection	Puerto Rican first generation migrant women, 18 and over, all groups.				
Diagnosis	—	—	—	Chronic schizophrenia, any type	
Criteria of classification					
Complaints on CMI and in interview	Insignificant	Significant in range of non-psychotic disorders	Significant, possibly psychotic	—	—
History of psychiatric treatment	None	"Nerves" treated by GP or outpatient psychiatric facility	Psychiatric hospitalization	Varied from 0 to 4 hospitalizations	Multiple hospitalizations
Age characteristics					
Mean	27	33	39	47	40
Range	18−64	20−49	20−50	32−65	20−61

area, or the disaster area it has become today. It was characterized by large family-sized apartments of three to eight rooms, occupied by intact families (67 percent), single parent families (17 percent), or extended families (12 percent). There were few single-room occupancies or isolates living either alone or in non-kin living arrangements (4 percent), and, unlike today, there were no abandoned buildings. There was an active Puerto Rican community life evidenced by many Spanish-speaking churches, *bodegas* (grocery stores), *botanicas* (religious objects stores), social clubs, *Centros Espiritis-*

tas (spiritist centers), and a variety of Puerto Rican dominated projects funded by the Office of Economic Opportunity and Model Cities. Although the neighborhood studied no longer exists as such, it can be taken as representative of the current life styles of Puerto Rican first-generation migrants living today in other areas of the city with sufficient concentrations of Puerto Ricans in the population for this active neighborhood life to develop,[2] including the areas of concentrated Puerto

2. Previous analyses of area survey data (Garrison 1972) have shown that there is very little change in the variables of social networks and support systems considered here over the lifetime of the first generation migrant. They do differ, however, between the first and second generations. Those who migrated to New York as children and entered the New York school system seem to follow the patterns of the second generation and not those of their elders. These patterns also differ by socioeconomic status and the patterns described are not those characteristic of the Puerto Rican middle or upper classes. There are also regional subcultural differences in Puerto Rico (Steward et al. 1956), which would probably be reflected in differing support system patterns if these were analyzed.

are very similar. The Puerto Rican population 18 years of age and over was 94 percent Puerto Rican-born, compared with 87 percent for the same age group in 1970—a difference that could be expected with the lapse of several years during which many of the largely young second generation reached the age of 18. Comparable data are not available in the U.S. Census for the Puerto Rican population of rural or urban birth. The largely rural origins of the population of this neighborhood, however, make it a very different population sample from that studied by Lewis (1968) selected on the basis of migration from San Juan slums.

Rican population in the Tremont area to the northeast of the original study neighborhood.

Methods of Data Collection and Reanalysis

The anthropological community study method (Arensberg 1954, 1961) involves diverse techniques of data collection and multiple levels of analysis. In the studies reported, these ranged from informal participant observations and interviews while I lived in the community for approximately 1 year, to fully standardized area surveys of two 1-percent probability samples of households conducted by the full LHMHS research team in 1966 and 1968. The combined data from these two surveys provide basic demographic, socioeconomic, and sociocultural variables for 358 Puerto Rican households. One survey provides statistical indices of social network characteristics for 117 Puerto Rican women. In between these two extremes of qualitative and quantitative data collection, there were (1) ethnographic mappings of institutions and places of congregation; (2) structured participant observations and interviews of leaders in 49 Puerto Rican churches, 14 spiritist centers, and 14 social clubs, as well as participant observations in community organizations and service agencies, and at community events, both organized and spontaneous, and (3) intensive open-ended, but structured interviews with two small samples of randomly selected community residents (*n* of Puerto Rican women = 29 and 86), Pentecostal Church members (*n* of Puerto Rican women = 54), spiritist center clients (*n* of Puerto Rican women = 35), and a consecutive sample of patients admitted to the LHMHS Outpatient clinic (*n* of Puerto Rican women = 38). In analysis of these data from multiple sources, participant observations and small samples studied intensively provide qualitative descriptions of social participation patterns and social supports, while larger survey samples provide statistical indices of the frequencies of the patterns described and measures of relationships among variables. Participant observations and small samples with greater depth of information also provide a partial test of validity and reliability of verbal reports obtained in area survey samples.

Data from all of these studies are drawn upon in this paper. The qualitative reanalysis is, however, based on intensive case studies of 55 first generation Puerto Rican migrant women drawn from several samples and reorganized into five groups reflecting increasing degrees of emotional disturbance and psychiatric impairment (see Table 1). Groups 1 through 3, hereafter called the "neighborhood sample," were drawn from a 1-percent probability sample of households in four census tracts of the LHMHS study area. The fourth group, hereafter

called the "outpatient schizophrenics," were drawn from two sources: one, a consecutive sample of admissions to the LHMHS outpatient clinic and, the other, a selected representative sample of clients in one spiritist center during a 6-month period. The last group, called the "inpatient schizophrenics," was drawn from a sample of patients studied in the TCC.

The same instruments, with minor adaptations, were used in all samples from which these cases were drawn, with exception of the TCC sample. They included an extensive "network interview,"[3] the Cornell Medical Index (CMI),[4] a medical and psychiatric treatment history,[5] and, in the case of the diagnosed schizophrenics,

3. The network interview was a semi-open-ended, semi-structured interview schedule designed to elicit, in addition to basic, demographic, and socioeconomic data, all habitual social contacts, or the total social network, of the respondent. These habitual contacts and the frequency of interaction with each person in the social network were explored in several overlapping ways. First, the respondent was asked to identify all associates and the frequency of contact with them in standard sociological categories: residents of the household, all kin outside the household by area of residence in the neighborhood, the Bronx, New York City, Puerto Rico, or elsewhere, neighbors in the building, neighbors on the block, friends and acquaintances and how they came to know them and what they did together, co-workers, if the person was employed, formal and informal group participation, and friendships developed through group participation. Once this information on the persons in the social field had been elicited, the subject was asked who he or she "counted on" for "anything" open-endedly and specific probes were made about "help with large tasks, like moving," "child care," "house-work," "help when ill," and "financial help." Thereafter a "reconstructed week" was also elicited together with habitual recreational, holiday, and seasonal activities. All linkages discovered through these habitual activities were then explored in the same manner as the relationships elicited through the use of the standard sociological categories.

4. The Cornell Medical Index is a standardized health questionnaire containing 195 "yes-no" items organized in subscales covering symptoms in eight organ systems, four areas of general medical concern, and six categories of mood and feeling state. It was designed to provide: (1) a comprehensive preexamination medical history from which a physician might derive tentative diagnoses of either physiological or psychiatric disorder by clinical interpretation, or (2) an estimate of level of emotional disturbance on a 4-point scale from none to severe by standardized scoring techniques using total number of "yes" responses and "critical scoring levels" (Brodman et al. 1949, 1952). Difficulties with the use of this and similar psychophysiological item scales for measurement of emotional disturbance in low-income populations generally and in Puerto Rican populations specifically have been discussed extensively by Dohrenwend and his colleagues (Crandell and Dohrenwend 1967; Dohrenwend 1967; Dohrenwend and Dohrenwend 1965; Dohrenwend, Egri, and Mendelsohn 1971). In this study I use it only as a measure of "perceived health status" (Suchman and Phillips 1958) and as a basis for systematically exploring the current complaints and the psychiatric and folk treatment histories.

5. The medical and psychiatric treatment history was obtained by reviewing with the respondent every positive response indicating a current symptom on the organ system subscales of the Cornell Medical Index and asking whether a doctor had been seen about each symptom and, if so, what the doctor had said. All instances of medical help-seeking over the past 2 years were explored and all instances of seeking help for nervous, emotional, family, or personal problems over a lifetime were explored. Specific probes were made of visits to general medical

either abstracts of clinical opinions in the psychiatric record or Current and Past Psychiatric Status Schedule (CAPPS) (Endicott and Spitzer 1972) protocols evaluated by a psychiatric consultant.[6] The interviews were conducted in Spanish or English, days, evenings, and weekends, and required 3 to 5 hours and one to three visits to complete. In the case of the TCC sample, a less extensive social network and support system guide was used,[7] and information was elicited in the course of routine clinical assessment and treatment interviews in which the researchers[8] participated as members of the clinical team, and sometimes assumed responsibility for continuing treatment using experimental treatment plans of the kinds to be suggested here.

For purposes of this analysis, the 29 randomly selected women in the neighborhood sample[9] are sometimes considered a sample of the general population or as a "nonschizophrenic" sample and are contrasted with either or both of the schizophrenic groups. As a group, the neighborhood sample women do not differ significantly from Puerto Rican women in area surveys on age distribution, education, socioeconomic status, or on most variables of the social network. They do differ somewhat on marital status, household composition, and religious affiliations, including a disproportionate number of separated and divorced women, single parent households, and Pentecostal women. This sample is, therefore, not considered representative of the range of variation in the general population, but it does represent the modal patterns of life (or those categories or values of variables within which the largest number of cases fall) as reflected in the larger area surveys. It also provides many examples of variant patterns that are relevant for fostering, redeveloping, or building support systems for alienated patients in this and similar communities. Variant patterns are not, however, exhaustively represented in this small sample.

For other purposes, the neighborhood sample has been divided into three groups reflecting increasing degrees of felt emotional distress as reflected in CMI responses and in the medical and psychiatric treatment history, and trends in the five groups of nonschizophrenic and schizophrenic women are examined. The criteria of subselection and of classification of these five groups are shown in Table 1. Group 1 consists of 11 women who reported no significant psychiatric complaints and no history of emotional disturbance, treated or untreated. They are assumed to be "normal," "healthy" women with no psychiatric disorder. Group 2 consists of 13 women who expressed psychiatrically significant complaints of mild or moderate severity and/or a history of treatment for "nerves" from a general medical practitioner or a psychiatric outpatient service. They are assumed to be suffering from mild to moderate emotional disturbance that would be considered significant as transient situational reaction, personality disorder, or neurotic reaction if they were to be fully evaluated psychiatrically.[10] Group 3 consists of five women who had a history of one psychiatric hospitalization. These five women had clearly significant psychiatric complaints, but only one gave any evidence of schizophrenic symptoms to lay interviewers.[11] They are classified as nonschizophrenic

---

practitioners or medical specialists other than psychiatrists for such problems; psychiatric hospitalization, psychiatric outpatient clinic treatment, private psychiatric treatment, visits to psychologists, social workers, social agencies, clergy, spiritual healers, and any help-seeking of "others" with the current or similar problems.

6. The Current and Past Psychiatric Status Schedule (Endicott and Spitzer 1972; Spitzer and Endicott 1968) is a standardized mental status and psychiatric history inventory designed for professional or lay administration in community settings, with either clinical or standardized interpretation. Gladys Egri, M.D., Clinical Associate Professor of Psychiatry, Columbia University, was the clinical consultant who provided the interpretation of these protocols.

7. The difference in data collection methods does not affect the results of this analysis as the error introduced (less exhaustive exploration of the non-kin supports) is in the opposite direction of the results (greater than expected non-kin supports), and the outpatient schizophrenics provide a partial check on the reliability of the inpatient support system data.

8. Pedro Rodriguez, M.D., then a resident in the Tremont Psychiatric Residency Training Program, Angel Mercado, M.S.W., then a Master's degree candidate, and Eugenia Pizarro, M.S.W., then research associate on this project, and I constituted the research team that conducted the study from which these patient data are drawn.

9. These 29 women were interviewed in 26 households. Eighteen males and five additional females were also interviewed in these same households, but those data are drawn upon here only insofar as they were used to elucidate the linkages in the networks of the female selected to represent the household in this analysis. Two women in each of three households were included because they were either unrelated women sharing one household or they represented different generations.

10. Subsequent analysis of the support system characteristics of 17 Puerto Rican first generation migrant women with diagnoses of nonpsychotic psychiatric disorders drawn from the LHMHS outpatient clinic sample reveals no apparent differences between them and group 2 on the social support system variables under consideration. No comparison was made of presenting complaints or mental status variables.

11. There has been a great deal of debate in the literature since the findings of Malzberg (1956) and the Midtown Study (Srole et al. 1962, pp. 290–293) about whether there is a higher incidence and prevalence of mental illness and, particularly paranoid schizophrenia, in Puerto Rican populations than among other ethnic groups (Dohrenwend 1967; Fitzpatrick and Gould 1972). The classification of women in this sample by degree of emotional disturbance is not intended to contribute to this literature. There is no representation that this classification is an accurate measure of clinical psychopathology, and it is definitely not a measure of psychiatric impairment. The proportion of "distressed" (58 percent) classified in groups 2 and 3 is greater than the 52 percent "psychiatrically impaired" found in the Midtown Study (Srole et al. 1962, p. 291), but this finding is based on the same kind of inadequate measure (psychophysiological complaints) that was used in the Midtown Study. Puerto Ricans express complaints differently than other ethnic groups (in particular, they report much larger numbers of somatic complaints) and mental illness also frequently manifests itself differently among Puerto Ricans. My own opinion is that the cultural factors that confound the

but are included as a special small group intermediate between group 2 and the outpatient schizophrenics on degree of emotional disturbance.[12] The fourth group of outpatient schizophrenics consists of 11 women, 8 drawn from the psychiatric outpatient clinic, and 3 drawn from the spiritist center sample, who have confirmed diagnoses of chronic schizophrenia but lead their lives in the community with only periodic support and treatment of either the professional or folk kind. Four have no history of psychiatric hospitalization; the rest have been hospitalized one to four times. The fifth group of inpatient schizophrenics is a more severely impaired group. They all have a history of two or more psychiatric hospitalizations and were inpatient, day hospital, or aftercare patients at the time studied.

In the qualitative reanalysis of the social network and support system data, all of the habitual social interactions (e.g., household and family members, neighbors, friends, institutions) of each subject were mapped on a field representing space (household, neighborhood, borough, city, Puerto Rico, and elsewhere). Frequency of each interaction and supportive relationships, as defined above, were also indicated. Seven patterns, including a null category, were then found in the relationships of individuals to non-kin in the networks diagrammed. These non-kin network patterns were given arbitrary descriptive labels indicating the salient features ("rotarian,"[13] "good-friend-focused," "sectarian," "grouping," "cultic," "one-friend," and a "null" category).

These patterns of non-kin network, to be described in more detail later, were then found to be associated in complex ways with variables of marital status and conjugal roles, extended kinship relationships, and the allocation of dependencies among husband, kin, and friends in the core support system. The rotarian pattern of non-kin network turned out to be associated with the ideal (verbalized values) and modal (statistically most frequent) patterns of marriage and family life in the culture, while the other non-kin network patterns were associated with the variations from the ideal or modal

patterns in either marriage or extended family relationships or both.

When these patterns of relating to non-kin were cross-tabulated with degrees of emotional disturbance, it was found that the rotarian pattern occurred only among the nonschizophrenics, and primarily among the group 1 women, while the null category occurred only among the schizophrenics, and primarily among the inpatient schizophrenics. The other patterns were found primarily among the women in the intermediate groups on degree of emotional disturbance.

The non-kin network patterns and their associated variables were then reclassified into seven patterns of *naturally occurring support systems,* arranged on a continuum from the "ideal/modal rotarian" pattern, through four variations which are considered adaptations to less than ideal family supports, to two variations which are found primarily or exclusively among the schizophrenics and are considered psychopathological variants.

Table 2 shows the classification of non-kin support networks and associated variables reclassified into support system types. Table 3 shows the cross-tabulation of these naturally occurring support system types with degrees of emotional disturbance. It will be noted that the majority of cases fall on the diagonal from group 1 and rotarian, through groups 2 and 3 in the good-friend-focused, sectarian and grouping patterns, to the outpatient and inpatient schizophrenics, falling largely in the one friend and null categories. The cultic pattern shows a distribution at the extremes of emotional disturbance off the diagonal, which will be explained later. Table 3 also shows, as a guide to the descriptions that follow, pseudonyms of typical and atypical case examples to be used to illustrate these patterns.

I will first describe the general features of the naturally occurring support systems that are common to both the nonschizophrenics and the schizophrenics. Then I will describe in some detail the ideal/modal pattern and how the schizophrenics differ and do not differ from that pattern, and, finally, I will describe and illustrate each of the variant support system types, discussing the implications of each type for patient care.

Modal and Variant Patterns of the "Natural Support Systems" of Nonschizophrenic and Schizophrenic Women

General Features

The women studied grew up and learned their basic patterns of relating to others in a very different environment, society, and culture than that in which they now

---

assessment of psychiatric disorder among Puerto Ricans have not yet been adequately understood or controlled for, and I present these data only as a description of felt emotional distress in this population sample—not as an indication of prevalence of psychiatric disorder in the population.

12. These extensive case study interviews were done by an ethnically and educationally mixed group ranging from community residents with high school education and training as community mental health workers to Ph.D. candidates in the social sciences. I did a considerable proportion of the interviews in all samples myself.

13. This use of the term "rotarian" follows its usage in neighboring studies (e.g., Caplow et al. 1964, pp. 178–179). It implies that the woman with a network of this type has many relationships of both intimate and non-intimate kinds and from many sources (all around).

TABLE 2
Naturally occurring support systems

Patterns	Non-kin network	Marital status (conjugal roles)	Kin network	Core support systems
Ideal/modal	Rotarian	Married (segregated/ independent)	Nuclear household, extended kin surrounding	Husband, kin (and friends)
Adaptation 1	Good-Friend-Focused	Single, separated, or divorced	Extended	Kin and friends
Adaptation 2	Sectarian	Varied	Weak	Church friends
Adaptation 3	Grouping	Single, separated, or divorced	Weak	Non-kin group
Adaptation 4	Cultic	Varied	Varied	Spiritist mediums
Psychopatho-logical variant 1	One Friend	Single, separated, or divorced	Missing or weak	One friend
Psychopatho-logical variant 2	Null	Single, separated, or divorced	Intergenera-tional only	Parent-child, child-parent, or institutional dependency

find themselves. There is, therefore, great discontinuity in their social fields over their lifetimes, but a remarkable continuity in their personal social networks and support systems. Despite many differences by region and class among Puerto Ricans (Steward et al. 1956) and the fact that Puerto Rico and the Puerto Rican community of New York are both changing, the women studied, whether schizophrenic or not, share many characteristics that reflect traditional rural Puerto Rican community patterns.

Very generally, in the small Puerto Rican towns and hamlets where the majority of these women grew up, the social field is relatively homogeneous by culture, class, and life experience. Independent nuclear family households dispersed in the countryside or concentrated in towns are surrounded by other households of related nuclear families and neighbors, all of whom know each other very well, and frequently these interrelated households share the domestic tasks of the nuclear family household, including child rearing. In the days when these women were growing up, private telephones were very rare, and visits to kinsmen, neighbors, or friends were generally impromptu. Time was structured by the seasons, the exigencies of the environment, and interpersonal action, more than by the calendar or clock. The only formal institutions common in rural Puerto Rico at that time were a primary school of two, four, or six grades; a church, usually with a traveling circuit priest

officiating; perhaps a clinic or a private practitioner on a part-time schedule; the *colmado* (country store), where men, but not women, congregated; perhaps some spiritists; and the municipal political organization of mayor and others, also all well-known personally to the *pueblanos* (villagers) and elected on the basis of personal qualities as much as on any particular issues.

Transplanted from their home environments, the vast majority (82 percent) of the neighborhood sample women continue to relate to others exclusively on the basis on kinship, proximity, common church affiliation, and extensions of these three bonds familiar to them from the home community, in personal, generalized role relationships. Very few have singular-interest, specialized-role relationships (18 percent) and even fewer (6 percent) participate in any formal voluntary associations other than churches and healing cults. The majority live and move about in a very limited geographical space delineated by ethnic territoriality (cf. Suttles 1968), with their social contacts limited to others of the same culture, class, and, with exception of kinsmen, the same sex. Very few (12 percent) work. Their contacts with the larger society are limited almost entirely to impersonal interactions with others of the same socioeconomic level (cf. Safa 1968) in local places of business, with representatives of agencies, and their exposure to mass media. Time is still structured by the exigencies of the environment (hours of opening and

TABLE 3

Naturally occurring support systems and degrees of emotional disturbance

| PATTERNS | NONSCHIZOPHRENICS | | | | SCHIZOPHRENICS | | |
	Group 1	Group 2	Group 3	Total	Outpatient	Inpatient	Total
Rotarian	6 Mrs. Perez	3	0	9	0	0	0
Good-friend-focused	3	2 Mrs. Serrano	1	6	1 (Juana)	0	1
Sectarian	1	4 Mrs. Velez	1	6	1	1 (Ana Maria)	2
Grouping	0	1 (Mrs. N)	2 Mrs. S Mrs. T	3	0	0	0
Cultic	1 (Mrs. Jimenez)	0	0	1	3 Mrs. Sanchez	3	6
One good friend	0	3 (Mrs. Lopez)	1 Anita	4	3	4	7
Null non-kin (parent-child or institutional dependency)	0	0	0	0	3 Mrs. Ortiz	7 Mrs. Lucas	10
Totals	11	13	5	29	11	15	26

Note.—*Married, separated, divorced, and widowed women have been given pseudonyms with the title "Mrs.," and women who have never been married are designated by a first name only. Women in the "grouping" pattern have been given one initial only merely to reduce the complexity of pseudonyms. Illustrative cases include both prototypic examples and exceptions to the general patterns. The latter are shown in parentheses.*

closing, waiting periods, lines, and block appointments) and interpersonal action (arrivals and departures of husband to and from work, children to and from school, and kin and friends who come and go from the household). The daily routine is not punctuated by family mealtimes; instead the woman of the house usually keeps food ready from about noon on, and every hungry new arrival is fed individually. The annual routine is marked by the "cold" and the "heat," and during the cold months the average Puerto Rican woman is even more restricted in her movements. Some say they do not go out at all.

Within this circumscribed geographical and social space, however, interpersonal contacts are many and frequent. Most (93 percent) know some of their neighbors and have friends (89 percent). "Friends" are usually neighbors as well, however, and friends separated by geographical distance usually lose contact. Frequency of kin interactions is also a matter of geo-

graphical propinquity, as much as genealogical closeness. Kin who live in the neighborhood are seen once a week or more; those who live outside the neighborhood are seen much less often. Women kin and friends share all aspects of their daily lives, visiting, talking, helping each other with chores, "accompanying" each other, but rarely, and only the younger unmarried ones, share any specialized interests or recreational activities outside of their respective households. Female friends, unlike male friends, do not form groups with self-consciousness as a group. They form one-to-one relationships with many linkages among them, but if they meet together at one time it is coincidental. The network of kin, neighbors, and friends, however, frequently constitutes a "quasi-group" that can become an "action set" at any time of need or common interest. The concepts of "quasi-group" and "action set" (see Mayer 1966) have most often been used in analysis of political action, but they are equally appropriate for the description of the organization of action in other spheres as well in this community. "Quasi-groups" are linkages in a network of people that may be active or dormant at any single time but can be mobilized to form an "action set" at any time of need or common interest. Such action sets are frequently mobilized at times of illness or other personal need of a member of the quasi-group, or for a social activity (such as an excursion to the country), for a big task (like moving), and other purposes, as case materials will illustrate.

Little more than half of both the nonschizophrenics and schizophrenics (57 percent) speak English adequately or fluently. The lack of English is not a great hardship in this neighborhood where one can generally count on finding someone who speaks Spanish, or, as is frequently done, take along a bilingual child or other relative to translate.

To summarize, there are many characteristics of the social networks and support systems of these women that reflect general Puerto Rican community patterns. Puerto Ricans may or may not differ from other American subcultures in these characteristics, but if the schizophrenics differ in these from their nonschizophrenic peers, it is only a matter of degree. Characteristics include: (1) a restricted use of space; (2) a structuring of time with little reference to the clock; (3) a concentration of social life in the local neighborhood; (4) a relatively homogeneous social field; (5) interpersonal relationships that are personalized, multiple-role, generalized-interest relationships, rather than the impersonal, specialized-role relationships that are said to characterize life in cities (e.g., Wirth 1938); (6) a high degree of neighboring (cf. Caplow, Stryker, and Wallace 1964, p. 156); (7) frequent church and healing cult participation; (8) a distinctive pattern of forming voluntary associations that is neither "formal voluntary association" nor "informal group"; and (9) a primary dependence upon the Spanish mother tongue.

The schizophrenic women are, expectably, relatively restricted in their movements, differentiation of time, and variety of activities and social contacts. Only one was working. These traits are considered symptomatic of schizophrenia to the extent they are related to social withdrawal, and they may well be symptomatic in the schizophrenic Puerto Rican women studied. But these are also modal patterns in this culture, which makes these particular symptoms less impairing for the Puerto Rican woman than they might be for someone from another culture.

Neighboring, friendships, and church participation, while not systematically elicited from the inpatient schizophrenics, nonetheless, show a greater than expected frequency in both the schizophrenic groups. Of the outpatient schizophrenics, all but one knew some of their neighbors and reported friendships, and 9 (82 percent) included non-kin in their core support systems. Seven went to church. Of the inpatient schizophrenics, eight, or over half, had relationships with neighbors and friends, and another eight went to church regularly. Healing cult participation, which was explored systematically, was universal among them. All had some history of involvement in Spiritism, a popular folk-healing cult that has been described by numerous investigators (e.g., Bram 1957; Garrison 1977*a* and 1977*b*; Harwood 1977; Koss 1975; Lubchansky, Egri, and Stokes 1970; Rogler and Hollingshead 1961, 1965) as a "folk psychiatry" or "folk psychotherapy," or in *Santeria*, a less frequent Afrocuban religious and healing cult (Garrison 1977*b*; Gonzalez-Wippler 1973; Sandoval 1975, 1977). Twelve were continuing to attend spiritist centers regularly or sporadically while also in psychiatric treatment.

The personal networks and support systems of all of the women studied vary in: (1) extent (numbers of persons included and frequency of interactions with all); (2) intensity (average frequency of interaction with each person in the network); and (3) the pattern of dependency on husband, kin, and non-kin. These variations are related to: (1) marital status, or the presence or absence of a husband in the traditional role of authority, guardian, and confidant; (2) the availability of extended kin in the traditional roles of providers of material, social, and psychological support; (3) residential mobility, or the time the person or the family has been in the area to permit them to either consolidate the residences of family members or to make new non-kin acquaintances; and (4) degrees and types of emotional distress.

With respect to extent and intensity of interactions in the personal network, it is generally true that the greater the degree of emotional disturbance (groups 1 through 5), the fewer the number of persons in the network and the less the total interactions, but "intensity," or the average interaction rate with those in the network, is not consistently related to degrees of emotional distress. The schizophrenic women have fewer kin and non-kin in their social networks. They are clearly different from their nonschizophrenic peers in their patterns of relating to kin, but they appear to differ less from nonschizophrenics in their relationships to non-kin. To the extent that they do differ in their relationships to non-kin, the outpatient schizophrenics, as will be shown, tend to depend more upon non-kin and less upon kin, who are most important in the support systems of the modal women and in those of the inpatient schizophrenics. Among these variations in the total social network and support systems, of greatest interest is the different patterning of dependencies upon husband, kin, and non-kin in the core support system. Before I can describe these variations, however, we must look at the typical core support system of the average woman.

The Rotarian Pattern

In this ideal/modal pattern, which includes nine of the neighborhood women with either no significant or mild emotional distress, the woman has a personal network of kin, neighbors, and friends in the immediate vicinity totaling usually 15 to 25 persons whom she names individually as important people in her life, and in addition up to 200 acquaintances. Among these kin, neighbors, and friends, there are three to five individuals (her core support system) upon whom she counts for assistance or in whom she confides. No one in this core support system, however—with the exception of the spouse and perhaps the mother—seems to be any more important to her than any other.

This social support system pattern is called "ideal/ modal" because the characteristics which define it conform to both the verbalized norms of the culture (ideals) and to the statistically modal characteristics as derived from area surveys. The women with this non-kin network pattern are, with two exceptions, married, live in a nuclear family household, and have many kin living in the immediate vicinity with whom they interact frequently. This is the ideal of the Puerto Rican family as it was described by Padilla (1958) for residents of East Harlem in the 1950s, and it is the modal pattern of family life in the South Bronx today:

> The ideal Hispano family consists of a father, mother and their unmarried children who all live together in the same household. This is the basic unit, the immediate or nuclear family. The father is supposed to impart respect to the children and to provide for the family; the mother, to care for the children and her husband and to maintain the standards of respect and good behavior set up by the father. Ideally, their home will be near those of close relatives, members of the "great family," including uncles, aunts, sisters, married children, grandchildren, and so on, and they will get along well with each other. All these relatives are supposed to help one another and to share in many common activities as members of the extended family. [Padilla 1958, p. 101]

Almost half (41 percent) of the neighborhood sample women live in such an *ideal* family arrangement. The others vary from the ideal of the nuclear family household, by either having more kin in the household (12 percent) or by having the husband missing from the family (18 percent), or both (22 percent), more than they

vary from the ideal from that of the cooperating extended kin network. It is very rare for the Puerto Rican woman to be separated from all of her own kin even after migration. Only two of the neighborhood sample had no kin living in the city and three fourths (79 percent) lived either in an extended family household or had kin living in the immediate vicinity, frequently in the same building (28 percent), with whom they interacted at least once a week. Frequently the family members of these separate household units interact as one joint family, sharing meals, domestic tasks, child rearing, and social life. The three-generation family is rarely found in single households (8 percent of 358 households surveyed), but it is nonetheless the functional family unit for one third (38 percent) of the neighborhood sample households when one considers the interrelationships among the several related households in close proximity. The ideal/modal Puerto Rican family is also characterized by a husband-wife relationship that Bott (1957), in her study of ordinary London families, described as "segregated and independent." In the modal Puerto Rican marital relationship, both partners lead relatively independent lives in separate and distinct activities with different sets of people. This "segregated and independent" pattern can be contrasted with types of marital relationships characteristic of other cultural groups. "Segregated and complementary" marital relationships, in which husband and wife do different things with different people but play roles that fit together to form a whole (as on the family farm) are most often found in preindustrial and rural societies. These marital relationships sometimes appear "disorganized" or lacking in affective intensity to middle class Americans but may be a natural concomitant of migration or the introduction of wage labor for the male. "Joint" conjugal roles, on the other hand, are the not fully realized ideal of the professional class in England and the United States. In "joint" marital relationships, the wife may work outside the home in the same or a similar occupation to that of her husband, the husband helps his wife with household tasks, and the spouses share their leisure time interests, activities, and friends, depending on one another to the exclusion of everyone else. Such a pattern is *not* the ideal of the mode of the Puerto Rican low-income family. Only 1 of the 14 married women in the neighborhood sample counted on and confided exclusively in her husband—a clearly deviant pattern in this community.

Together with this distinctive patterning of conjugal roles, there is an equally distinctive pattern of allocation of interpersonal needs among husband, kin, and friends in the core support system. The modal Puerto Rican wife counts on her own kin for the basic support functions of help when ill, help with child care, help with heavy tasks in the house, or emergency financial assistance. She discusses "everything" with her husband, seeking his advice, guidance, and approval as authority over the nuclear family.

The married woman may also confide in kin, particularly her mother, or either count on or confide in non-kin (40 percent). Supportive or confidential relationships with non-kin are, however, more frequent among the unmarried (85 percent) than the married, and among those who do not have kin on whom they can count (86 percent) than among those who do (55 percent), and among women in groups 2 and 3 (72 percent), than among the women in group 1 (25 percent). As we have seen, they are also more frequent among the outpatient schizophrenics (82 percent).

Mrs. Perez illustrates the rotarian non-kin network, the ideal and modal patterns of family life and of dependencies in the core support system, on which the schizophrenics differ qualitatively from the nonschizophrenics, and also the general features discussed above, on which the schizophrenics differ only quantitatively.

Mrs. Perez

Mrs. Perez is 30 years old, married to a 37-year-old semiskilled factory worker,[14] and has one child. She completed 7 years of schooling in Puerto Rico (mean 7.7)[15] and has been in New York for 12 years (mean 11.8). Like most women in this community (88 percent) she does not work, but also like most (83 percent) she did in the past. She worked in a factory and as a chambermaid in a hotel until she was married, but has not worked since, except to sell Avon products.

The Perez nuclear family lives in a four-room apartment of a large five-story brick walkup apartment building (the typical structure of the area). Mrs. Perez's mother and father, and a brother and one of two sisters, with their families, occupy three other apartments in the same building. She has aunts, uncles, and cousins living in six households, numbering 21 persons, in the immediate vicinity. She sees all of her kin who live in the same building daily and those in the neighborhood once a week or more. She has aunts and cousins in other parts of the city whom she sees much less often but telephones periodically. In Puerto Rico she has a sister and family to whom she writes several times a year, and three aunts and uncles to whom she writes rarely.

Mrs. Perez knows everyone in the building where she

---

14. It is the ideal in this culture that husbands should be a little older than their wives and, in fact, most are, with a mean and modal difference of 7 years.

15. Means and frequencies presented in this description are characteristics of the general population obtained in area survey samples.

---

lives and says, "Everyone in this building is like family." There are three families to whom she is particularly close. She also knows approximately 20 people on the block where she lives, but not well enough to visit with them. Other blocks are "other neighborhoods" and if the ethnic balance shifts critically from one building or block to the next, those "neighborhoods" are alien territory into which Mrs. Perez and other modal women fear to venture. She does not relate to people as neighbors who live beyond the block, and she has no friends who are not also neighbors or friends from church. If she has a choice she will select a store or clinic (or mental health facility) in her own or another "Puerto Rican neighborhood."

Mrs. Perez is a practicing Roman Catholic (76 percent) and reports that she attends mass once a week (54 percent). She also has friends in the congregation to whom she relates outside of church (16 percent). She does not go to confession, belong to a sub-society, or attend any of the social functions of the church (93 percent). She thinks she might be able to turn to the priest if she had problems (36 percent), but she has never done so (86 percent). Like many (minimum 34 percent), however, she has gone to a spiritist. She says, "I had a problem and she advised me about my marriage—I think she did me a lot of good."

Mr. Perez does not have any of his own kin living in New York, but he has a large extended family (approximately 30 adults) living in Puerto Rico. He or his wife writes one letter to his mother, grandmother, and four sisters, for sharing with the rest once every week or two. He plays dominoes with "the people upstairs" and with a group of men on the street. His best friends had recently moved away from the neighborhood and he reported, "Now, I don't have any friends." He has three chums at work, "The four of us are always together, but only at work." He previously belonged to a social club, but he thinks that they have degenerated badly, and he no longer belongs, although he is planning to organize another such club himself. He says, "I want to find a group of people who like to listen to music, rent a place, and then we can go to the club, rather than go to [night] clubs."

Mr. Perez spends his weekdays at work with his male friends, while Mrs. Perez is at home, in the homes of neighboring kin and female friends, or in the waiting rooms and lines of the clinics, post office, check-cashing place, or rental agency. She does her household tasks in no particular order. *"Hago todo a conveniencia"* ["I do everything at my convenience"], she says. The child always accompanies her and either participates in her activities or entertains himself quietly. In the evenings and on weekends, the Perezes visit relatives and friends, either together or separately, and sometimes go to a movie or dancing. Mr. Perez sets aside some specific time to play with his son. The daily routine is varied on Saturdays and Sundays when Mrs.

Perez does her major shopping at the supermarket and department stores outside the neighborhood, or, possibly, at the *Marketa* in East Harlem. Saturdays and Sundays are also days for visiting kin outside the neighborhood and for gatherings of kin, neighbors, and friends in each other's apartments. Such gatherings are frequently announced for *"la tarde,"* meaning anytime from 3 to 10 p.m., and people come and go during those hours. At other times such gatherings merely occur spontaneously as a number of unannounced drop-ins coincide at the same place at the same time. Mr. Perez spends his annual vacations looking for better jobs, and he has changed jobs four times in 4 years—"always for better pay." These job changes, which raised his weekly income from $55 to $116, made a large difference in his status in his own community, but it did not affect his position in the ranking system of the larger society (Class V in the Hollingshead [1957] system). Mrs. Perez, like most of the women studied, has no "vacation," but in the summer the family goes to the beach and parks. The Perezes do not have a car (78 percent), but some parks and beaches are accessible by subway. *Giras* (charter bus excursions) are sometimes organized by churches, *bodegas*, social clubs, spiritists, or any local entrepreneur, who rents a bus, prints up a book of tickets, and distributes them among friends to be sold to other friends.

Mrs. Perez like most Puerto Rican women (68 percent) is supported primarily by her husband's earnings and so she makes no use of health and welfare services, other than a private group medical practice two blocks from her house. Like most Puerto Rican women, Mrs. Perez does not go for periodic medical examinations but, nonetheless, she sees a physician on the average of once every 6 months.[16]

Mrs. Perez counts on her mother, father, and one sister for help with financial needs, for help with the house, child care, and in the event she is ill. She does not count on her husband for assistance in any of these circumstances. On the other hand, she does not discuss her problems with any of her family, but discusses "everything" with her husband. Mr. Perez says he cannot count on any of his family for help of any kind and he does not confide his problems to anyone but his wife. Mrs. Perez does not include any non-kin in her core support system, but more than half of the neighborhood sample (62 percent) do.

Not all of the women classified in the ideal/modal rotarian pattern have such large family and friendship

networks or illustrate so many of the ideal and modal characteristics of the Puerto Rican family as the Perezes, but Mrs. Perez is typical (excepting total extent) of the ideal and modal characteristics of family and community life. Mr. Perez also represents the typical pattern of non-kin relationships among males in this population, and the ideal male role in the nuclear family. He is, however, atypical in being separated from all of his own kin.[17]

These ideal and modal patterns of family life bear almost no relationship to the lives of the inpatient schizophrenics. Only one of the inpatient schizophrenics was married at the time of study, although all but the four whose illnesses had had a very early onset had been married (legally or consensually) at one time. None of them were currently living in a nuclear family household. With the exception of two who were heads of single-parent families, all lived in households with atypical family composition, an unusual non-kin arrangement, or alone. To live alone is considered a dreadful condition in this community. The modal woman wants to be "accompanied" at all times, if only by a child, and when she is left temporarily alone for any reason, relatives or friends frequently spend nights sleeping over "to keep her company." Isolates living alone and non-kin living arrangements were found in less than 5 percent of the 358 households studied, but nearly half (5 of 11) of the outpatient schizophrenics live alone. The schizophrenic woman living alone is sometimes surrounded by kin in nearby households, but the number of kin in her social networks is distinctively few, and the "family" of the schizophrenic woman, regardless of whether it is one household or more, usually consists exclusively of the nuclear family of orientation or procreation (depending upon the age of the woman). The schizophrenic woman, whether inpatient or outpatient, characteristically depends exclusively upon one or two family members on a different generational level (parents or grandparents in the case of young women and grown children in the case of older women). Interdependencies of parents and adult offspring are expected and normative in this culture. However, the *exclusive* dependency upon parents and, above all, the dependency of parents upon grown children are totally aberrant. Among the 40 women in the community this pattern of dependency is found only in the cases of three outpatient schizophrenics.

Also in contrast to the modal pattern, it is frequent for the schizophrenic women to have kin residing in close

---

16. Of 153 women interviewed about their visits to doctors in the past 2 years, only 5 (3 percent) had not seen a doctor in that period and 69 (45 percent) had seen doctors 8 or more times in that period. It is sometimes said that low-income people fear and avoid medical services offered. This is not the case for low-income Puerto Rican women. They do, however, fear and avoid "mental" health services. The word "mental," as has been widely reported (e.g., Rogler and Hollingshead 1965) carries a particularly strong stigma in the Puerto Rican community.

17. Previous analyses of area survey data (Garrison 1972, p. 169) revealed no statistically significant differences between Puerto Rican men and women in the number of kin in contact or the total frequency of contact with kin.

proximity with whom they have little or no contact. The "weak" extended kinship network notation in Table 3 refers either to having few living kin available or having little contact with kin. The kinship networks of all but three of the schizophrenics, inpatient and outpatient, are weak.

The modal patterns of life have less relevance for the chronic schizophrenic than the variant patterns to be described, but it is necessary to understand them, and particularly the patterning of dependencies in the core support system, in order to understand the variant patterns.

The Good-Friend-Focused Pattern

The good-friend-focused pattern is the same as the rotarian pattern except that one of the neighbors or friends in the network is counted on or confided in more than others. This pattern characterizes the non-kin networks of six of the neighborhood women and that of one unusual schizophrenic. Although these seven women have extended kin living in the neighborhood whom they see frequently, their greatest contact is with one good friend. With two exceptions, the women are single, separated, divorced, or, in one case, temporarily separated from a husband in military service. It appears that the very close friend frequently fulfills in part the role of confidant in the absence of a husband. However, only two of these women reported that they confided in their girlfriends; rather they counted on them for supports of the kind expected from kin and confided in kin or no one.

Mrs. Serrano

Mrs. Serrano is a 32-year-old high school graduate with 1 year of college. She has been married twice, and has three children. Two months before our contact with her she had separated from her second husband. Thereupon, her mother, a 64-year-old retired school teacher, moved in with her "to help."[18] Mrs. Serrano worked in the past as a clerk in a jewelry store, but she feels she no longer can because she "is always sick." She says she has had a gynecological infection for 12 years and has been told she needs an operation. Mrs. Serrano also says she gets "nervous and angry" and "shouts a lot"—"everything bothers me." She

18. The three-generation household of grandmother, mother, and grandchildren (or the "matrifocal family") is surprisingly rare in the Puerto Rican community. It was found in only 3 of the 358 households. The constellation of single-parent family with grandmother living in a nearby household also appears to be infrequent. More of the married women living in nuclear family households have parents living close by than do the single parents living alone with their children.

goes to doctors frequently, but has not seen one about her "nervousness," although she says, "I should."

Mrs. Serrano is an only child. Although she has few living kin, she sees those she has regularly. She knows five people in her building and six others on the block well enough to visit, but her particularly good friend, with whom she meets three or four times a week "to talk about each other's problems," is a neighbor from the building where she lived previously. She also knows and visits once a week with 15 other people from her "girlfriend's building." Mrs. Serrano goes to church twice a month, but does not feel she could turn to her priest or anyone in the church for help; she has no friends from the church. She went to a spiritist center once with her girlfriend but was "scared" by the experience.

None of the other nonschizophrenic women in this group have as many symptoms as Mrs. Serrano and all of them have more extensive kinship networks. But her non-kin network is typical of the "good-friend-focused" pattern, which appears to be the typical support system of the separated or divorced woman with no significant or mild emotional disturbance. Juana, on the other hand, is atypical of the schizophrenic women in having this type of non-kin social network, in having a supportive extended family, and in her level of functioning.

Juana

Juana is 32 years old, lives with a lesbian mate (her "good friend" for purposes of this analysis), and works in a factory. She has a history of mental hospitalization in childhood and a subsequent personal history that is fairly characteristic of schizophrenics (a withdrawn, "shy" adolescence, a brief period of work, and a subsequent period of living on welfare, drinking too much, and moving from place to place at brief intervals). Nevertheless, except for the fact that her mate is another woman, she has a non-kin network of the "rotarian" type, the ideal family composition, and the typically bifurcated "core support system." Juana's return to work and to relative stability coincided with her meeting and moving in with her girlfriend.

Juana has not had psychiatric treatment since her childhood hospitalization. She became part of this study when her girlfriend and her girlfriend's mother brought her to a spiritist center. This was the first, and as yet the only time, that Juana sought the help of a spiritist. She was in an acute reactive depression precipitated by a diagnosis of a possible malignancy and the necessity for an operation. At the same time, her good friend was in a family crisis that provoked her guilt about their lesbian relationship and limited her ability to be supportive of Juana. Juana had made several suicidal gestures. The spiritists provided very appropriate crisis intervention with this whole family network (to be reported in detail elsewhere) over a 6-week period. In addition, the spiritist medium, who is also a *santera*, "put necklaces on" Juana in an overnight initiation and rebirth ceremony. *Santería*, in its more traditional form and not the eclectic mixture of Spiritism and *Santería* that is now found in New York (Harwood 1977), is a secret religion with no public meeting places, organized through a system of fictive kinship in which women take on the role of *madrina* (godmother) to *ahijados* (godchildren) for life. The obligations between godmother and godchild are the same as those of biological parent and child, as well as ritual. The godchild may remain continuously dependent upon the "powers" of the godmother as one who has only "*collares*" (necklaces) or may go on for further rituals to receive a *padrino* (godfather) and later the African deities "in" his or her "own head" and become a priest in the religion and the godmother or godfather to others. Juana was projected to receive only the first initiation.

On followup 2 months after her spiritual treatment episode, Juana reported that she "felt like a new woman," she had had the operation, was still working, and had no current complaints. Although she has not felt it necessary to this date, 5 years later, she has the necklaces of this *espiritista-santera* and knows that she can return to her godmother in the event of any new crisis.

Juana's core support system consists of her girlfriend and her own kin. She is not much of a believer in Spiritism. (Like many other women, she says, "I believe and I don't believe.") Spiritism acted as the catalyst in Juana's case to mobilize an action set to deal with the multiple problems in her extended family. It helped Juana to retain her improved level of functioning, but it plays no continuing part in her life, unless the necklaces and the fictive mother they represent contribute to her sense of security. Necklaces of this kind were worn by one of the inpatient schizophrenics.

The Sectarian Pattern

This pattern characterizes the social networks of six of the nonschizophrenics (five Pentecostal, 1 Jehovah's Witness) and two of the schizophrenics (Pentecostal). It has the same overall structure as the rotarian and the good-friend-focused patterns, with the additional feature that most of the neighbors, friends, and even the professionals and business people with whom the individual interacts are connected with her directly or indirectly through their church. It is not associated with the presence or absence of a husband, but is strongly associated with weak or missing kin ties.

Pentecostalism is a fundamentalist Christian sect with the predominant feature of belief in possession by the Holy Ghost and "speaking in tongues." It involves approximately 15 percent of the Puerto Rican population (Garrison 1974). The Pentecostal church offers many social and psychological supports. Congregations are small and intimate; the average membership in 38 Puerto Rican Pentecostal churches studied is 49 people (not counting a large one that claims a membership of 600 families). Congregations are divided into sex- and age-graded societies (children's society, young people's society, men's society, and women's society, minimally) to which all members of the congregation belong. These societies are responsible for organizing services and special events that are held every night of the week except Saturday. Members call each other "sister" and "brother" and all know each other personally. During services, prayers of the total congregation are requested for anyone who is ill or suffering any other misfortune. Testimonials are also made giving thanks to Christ for any adventitious change in circumstances. Participation during services is spontaneous, and individuals are encouraged to contribute any skill they may have to the service, such as leading prayers, singing, playing an instrument, reading Biblical passages aloud, or preaching. A person does not have to be particularly good at what he does to be welcomed to perform "for the glory of the Lord."

Each of these small churches has a missionary society that answers requests of members and nonmembers, visits homes, and cares for the ill and disturbed. In addition to pastoral counseling, the ministers and the missionary societies provide emergency financial aid, go to the airport to meet new arrivals and orient them to the city, and locate housing and employment for members through the Pentecostal grapevine. All of these churches support several Pentecostal programs "to rehabilitate drug addicts, prostitutes, and other outcasts of society." Most Pentecostals go to their ministers or members of their church with any problem they might have. Services offered by the church are provided from the resources within the group and within the broader network of Pentecostal affiliations.

Jehovah's Witnesses also have small congregations that are divided into even smaller "Bible Study Groups." These groups of 5 to 10 people meet, in addition to regular Sunday services, in the members' homes at least 1 night each week. They study Biblical texts and the literature of the Watchtower Society for guidance on resolving life's every problem. Individuals and pairs from these groups then visit homes unsolicited as "Witnesses" bringing the word of God. These small groups are very supportive to their members, but they do not generally provide supporting services to nonchurch members.

The sectarian pattern is best illustrated, for our purposes, by Mrs. Velez, a group 3 woman, and by Ana Maria, an inpatient schizophrenic. It should be noted, however, that a greater than average degree of emotional disturbance is not characteristic of Pentecostals as a group. To the contrary, there is some evidence that felt emotional distress is less among them than their Catholic peers (Garrison 1974).

Mrs. Velez

Mrs. Velez is a separated 35-year-old mother of seven children, ages 6 to 19. Mrs. Velez, the oldest of 10 children, has many kin in Puerto Rico and in another borough of New York City, as well as one sister living in the neighborhood. She is not, however, in frequent contact with any of them.

At the time of the interview, Mrs. Velez had recently taken in from the street a 28-year-old separated mother and her three young children after an eviction. Mrs. Velez knows 25 people in her building, and one other on the block. She "helps out" her "tenant" and two neighbor women. She has about "50 friends," 9 or 10 of whom pass through her house every day. She knows 12 people from her church well enough that they visit together in each other's homes. Among them there is one that she considers her "best friend," and there are "a sister" and "a brother" from the church upon whom she counts and in whom she confides. She also confides in three biological sisters, although she sees them rarely. But, primarily, she handles her problems by prayer. Prayer in the Pentecostal faith, whether during church services or in private, is not a recitation of a given text, but a conversation, usually aloud, with a very personal Christ. When resolution of her problems is reached in this way, she goes to church and gives thanks in testimonials to *"El Senor."* She also goes to her minister with any problems she may have.

Although Mrs. Velez may be a moderately disturbed woman herself, and although she does not have the usual family supports found among Puerto Rican women, the church provides her the supports she needs to care for herself and seven children and leaves her strong enough to support others more disturbed than she. Ana Maria provides a good example of the sectarian pattern as it may be encountered in the clinic.

Ana Maria

Ana Maria is a 34-year-old woman who has never married. She is almost grotesque in appearance, being over-sized, cross-eyed, without eyelashes or eyebrows, and lacking many patches of hair on her head, which she keeps concealed under some kind of covering. She has a history of many physical as well as mental disease episodes. She lives with her 64-year-old chronically ill mother, her only relative in New York. Ana Maria has some college education and had worked as a teacher in her hometown until her second mental hospitalization at age 25. Between ages 25 and 34 she had been hospitalized many times.

Ana Maria was brought to the hospital by her minister and her mother after a violent episode in which she tore up the house and physically assaulted her mother. The episode was precipitated by a diagnosis of worsening of the mother's chronic heart condition. Ana Maria explained that she had been having bad thoughts, but she had subsequently been possessed by the Holy Ghost and had repented. She was delusional, hallucinating, angry, and agitated. Her behavior on the ward was considered bizarre on several occasions when she was discovered kneeling beside her bed praying aloud.

Once Ana Maria was stabilized, it was learned that she was Treasurer, Bible School Teacher, and a respected, productive member of a small society formed by the 18 members of her church. The treatment team recognized an overdependency not only of the daughter upon the mother, but of the mother upon the daughter as well. Their plan of treatment therefore involved separating the mother and daughter somewhat—if not physically, at least by encouraging them both to have other social contacts and activities.

During one visit of the minister to the hospital ward, it was learned that the church had also recognized the problem on which the treatment team was focusing. The church members had already located two small apartments for daughter and mother to occupy upon Ana Maria's discharge. Since the apartments were in a building where other members of the church lived, these neighbors would provide some of the daily care needed by the ill and infirm older woman and would see to her transportation to church, thus freeing the younger woman from some of her burden. Ana Maria was discharged to the aftercare of her minister and church.

Sectarian church membership appears to offer many of the supports ideally provided by the extended family for many women and a refuge for some who are so unfortunate or deviant that it would be difficult for them to find acceptance in a modal community life.

The Grouping Pattern

The grouping pattern is one in which social and emotional supports are found primarily or exclusively in group participation, rather than in one-to-one relationships in the fluid network of kin, neighbors, and friends as is characteristic of the majority. Only three of the women in the neighborhood sample have non-kin networks of this type. Although the women are classified nonschizophrenic, all three have significant psychiatric complaints and a psychiatric treatment history. This pattern appears to be associated with weak extended kin supports or a greater than usual degree of acculturation. Mrs. N. illustrates the relationship to acculturation.

Mrs. N.

Mrs. N. is 35 years old, married, and lives with her husband and two children, 16 and 11. She came to New York when she was 12, completed the third year of high school, and worked in the past as an educational aide and as a factory supervisor. She now considers herself *"enferma de los nervios"* (sick from nerves) and has had medical treatment for this complaint.

She has family in the neighborhood, in other boroughs, and in Puerto Rico, but she rarely sees any of them and explains "they are not very loved." Nonetheless, she says she can count on an aunt and two cousins in the neighborhood and she confides in her husband, her mother (who is in Puerto Rico and to whom she writes only once a year), and a friend. She became acquainted with this friend through group activities at her children's school where she sees her every day. Mrs. N. also has a *comadre* (ritual co-parent)[19] whom she counts on for child help but nothing else. She goes to mass every week, participates in social activities of the church, and has sought her priest's help with emotional problems. She also belongs to a political party organization, which she "counts on" for housing, legal services, employment services, and financial aid. Mrs. N. knows some of her neighbors, but none well enough to visit.

Mrs. N's social network, consisting primarily of formal voluntary association participation, specialized role relationships with fictive kin and friends, and dependence upon specialists for assistance, represents the greatest degree of acculturation found among the low-income first generation migrant women in all samples.

Mrs. S. and Mrs. T., on the other hand, are not acculturated women.

19. Close female friendships are sometimes formalized in the *compadrazco* (ritual co-parenthood), with or without the religious ceremonies that sanctify these bonds (Rogler and Hollingshead 1965, p. 348). The *compadrazco* is, however, relatively rare among the women studied, only two of whom were currently in contact with a co-parent. More may, however, have had such relationships which had merely become dormant as a result of geographical separation.

Mrs. S.

Mrs. S. is a divorced 42-year-old, with a history of one psychiatric hospitalization. She lives with four teenage children, and her oldest son lives with his wife in another apartment in the same building. Her only other living kin is a cousin in the same neighborhood whom she sees once every 3 or 4 months. She rarely goes to church and, although her family was spiritist, she does not participate in spiritists groups either. She confides in her oldest son. If that were all there were to her social network, it would be of the null category with the "parent-child dependency" pattern characteristic of the inpatient schizophrenics. But she also has a group of 14 neighbors from the building and the block who spend time in her apartment every day. She counts on these "people from the community" (her expression) when she is ill and for household tasks, but not for financial assistance; they can count on her for the same and for child care. These are reciprocal helping relationships among peers of the same generational level, and they distinguish her support system from that characteristic of the inpatient schizophrenics.

Mrs. T.

Mrs. T. is a 39-year-old married woman with nine children, and a history of one psychiatric hospitalization. She has one sister and an uncle living in the neighborhood, whom she sees daily, and another sister whom she sees much less often. She also has four neighbors she sees daily, and she participates in two groups organized by the mental health services: a Mother's Club and a Tenants' Organization. She counts on her two sisters, her father (who is in Puerto Rico), her children and "Welfare." She confides in her sister and her husband.

The three women described above represent different kinds of grouping patterns, each of which is rare among Puerto Rican women.

Mrs. N. participates in formal voluntary associations of the general American tradition derived from Western, Northern, and Central Europe. In this tradition (typified by Protestant congregationalism, and reflected in the organization of fraternal orders and self-help groups like Alcoholics Anonymous), groups are associations of like-minded people with a written creed or statement of purpose. Membership is by choice between mutually exclusive possibilities, declaration of faith, and inclusion on a formal membership list after a ritual of inclusion (e.g., baptism, initiation, or acknowledgment of an alcohol problem). Rules of inclusion usually include provisions for expulsion for either misbehavior or failure of participation. The formal voluntary associations of the Puerto Rican community all had small memberships disproportionately representing the second generation Puerto Rican and those who had been in the city for a long time. Of the 117 women surveyed, only 5 percent reported club memberships and 6 percent secular or civic group participation of any kind.

Formal voluntary associations (and informal groups) traditional in the Puerto Rican community have different and more fluid rules of organization, membership, and belonging, derived from the Roman Catholic, Southern European, and Latin American tradition. In Roman Catholicism, membership in the church is by virtue of birth, not declaration of faith, and membership list after a ritual of inclusion (e.g., baptism, initiation) and registration as a member of the parish only formalize that membership. Most churchgoing Puerto Rican Catholic women do not become "members" of the church although they may be strongly identified with the faith and perhaps even a specific parish. Memberships are not mutually exclusive—a woman does not cease to be Catholic because she attends or believes in spiritism, for example. Expulsion is never exercised for failure of participation, only for serious infringement of the society's rules of proper conduct. Similarly, all people from the hometown are nominally members of the hometown club and can participate if they want to, although these clubs also have dues-paying registered members. The spiritist centers (the typical self-help group organization of this tradition) are licensed as churches and have on paper an organization of the kind required for licensure, including provision for dues-paying members, but, in fact, only 2 of the 14 studied ever made any attempt to keep a membership list or to collect dues. People may walk in at any time, attend as long as they like, cease to attend when they choose, and return next time they feel the need, to be welcomed as a member in good standing.

The same basic differences in rules of inclusion obtain with respect to informal groups. Groups of people who meet together with a sense of belonging to a "group" with a bounded membership, or a common purpose, are only slightly more frequent than formal voluntary associations and they are limited almost entirely to adolescents, singles, and the acculturated or middle class.

Of much greater mental health importance in this community than either voluntary associations or informal groups are quasi-groups and action sets. We have seen several examples of these in the case materials presented—Mr. Perez's plan for organization of a social club, the *"giras,"* which are part of everyday life in the summer, Juana's experience with spiritism. The most common, and most relevant, example is the action set formed by the extended kin quasi-group, and probably by Mrs. S's non-kin group also, when one of the group is

ill. Kin, regardless of whether they are in contact under normal circumstances, are expected to rally to the bedside of an ailing relative. Those who do not will be sanctioned by gossip. The group of assembled kin then frequently become an action set to assist with the total array of needs of the person temporarily indisposed. This pattern of behavior is frequently seen in the families of schizophrenic patients who have periodic acute episodes. One of the inpatient schizophrenics studied, for example, is a 50-year-old woman with a history of many hospitalizations, who lives between acute episodes with her husband and his extended kin in Puerto Rico. Each time she becomes ill, her husband brings her to New York and leaves her with one of her grown daughters in a complex of related households in which the siblings share responsibility for her care for the duration of the episode.

Other common examples of quasi-group and action set formation are the Catholic or spiritist *veladas* (vigils), in which a group assembles to pray for one or more consecutive days for the recovery of the sick person, at the same time considering the practical issues of what is to be done. There are also quasi-groups of mediums and spiritist adherents who meet in their homes to address the spiritual problems of one of the group or of an acquaintance only as the need arises. Political action in this community, at least in the late 1960s, was almost entirely by mobilization of personal networks of influential community members, under the leadership of a grassroots *"caudillo"* (quasi-military/political chief), to take action, often in covert and seemingly random fashion. This mode of organization does not produce visible, identifiable political bodies, but is nevertheless effective in achieving the community's goals at times.

It is not that this community is "disorganized" or has "a minimum of organization beyond the level of the nuclear and extended family" (Lewis 1968, p. 9); rather, it is organized differently (cf. Whyte 1943). The implications for mental health care delivery to nonschizophrenics, as well as schizophrenics, are manifold.

Mrs. T. belongs to groups organized on the "helper therapy principle" (Riessman 1965) by the mental health services. This principle holds that helping others is therapeutic. People with social *and* mental health problems were, therefore, organized into groups in their local neighborhoods to first help themselves and then to help others with similar problems. This is a form of grouping which has many naturally occurring examples in the community. Although the therapeutic impact of these groups is unknown, they were a great success in the sense of attracting many people from a community that did not use traditional psychiatric services to any great extent (Lehmann 1970). The traditional group therapy model, in contrast, makes many unfamiliar demands on the patient. It requires her to leave her home and travel alone to an institution that is located outside of her neighborhood, to participate in a group with a singular common interest in the illness, to commit herself to regular consecutive attendance on a fixed schedule, to "interpret" her learned, culturally shared behavior patterns as resulting from unconscious conflicts, and to attend regularly or face "termination." Such an approach not only entails resocialization, but also reacculturation. It is appropriate only for less disturbed patients from this community—even when intended only to be supportive.

That groups in the Puerto Rican community are not "formally organized" in accordance with the patterns familiar in the Anglo tradition does not mean that they are any less supportive, or even any less therapeutic. It does mean that clinicians, administrators, or social scientists have a more difficult time in recognizing the informal groups' existence and, even more, in working comfortably with group members. While it is possible for mental health professionals to work with "quasi-groups" and "action sets" instead of, or in addition to, bounded groups and formal organizations, it would take a great deal of reorientation of clinical thinking and institutional structures. The non-kin support system of Mrs. S., for example, could be used as a model to re-create support systems for severely disturbed patients whose kinship networks are weak or nonexistent, including those whose ability to function is inadequate for them to sustain themselves in independent living. A group of neighbors on a block, including schizophrenic and nonschizophrenic patients, based in the home of the most seriously ill among them, could provide a viable living arrangement for the one most severely ill and provide resocialization for the less severely disturbed within a natural pattern. There are many possibilities.

The Cultic Pattern

In the cultic pattern the woman may or may not have kin, husband, or friends, but her primary sources of support come from spiritist cult participation. She makes relatively continuous use of spiritist consultants, and her daily life is structured at least in part around cult beliefs and practices. Included in this category are seven women: one has no significant complaints, and six are schizophrenic. The cultic category does not include the many women who, like Mrs. Perez or Juana, use Spiritism only in times of crisis. Although the pattern is associated with missing husbands, weak extended kin

ties, and severe emotional disturbance, spiritist cult participants do not as a group show these characteristics. Of 35 interviewed in depth, 51 percent were married—a proportion identical to that reported for Puerto Rican women 14 years of age and over in the 1970 Census. A greater than average proportion were working (42 percent, contrasted with 26 percent in the Census). The vast majority were also rated low on degree of impairment of function in occupational and social role performance on the CAPPS. They were, however, rated relatively higher on severity of emotional disturbance. Only three of the 35 were judged schizophrenic by the psychiatric evaluator. Most (80 percent) were rated as having a mild or moderate psychiatric disorder in the transient situational reaction, personality disorder, or neurotic reaction categories. Spiritism attracts a broad spectrum of the population of both sexes, all ages, all socioeconomic levels, and all degrees of emotional disturbance from "none significant" to "severe." The proportion of those who use spiritists as a recourse increases progressively, however, with degrees of emotional disturbance from 25 percent in group 1 to universality in group 5. More importantly, however, the patterns of beliefs and usages change.

For the group 1 and 2 women who have made use of spiritists, as with the vast majority of the spiritist clients interviewed (82 percent), Spiritism is a prevailing set of beliefs (a folk psychology, as well as a folk psychotherapy) and a recourse used episodically in times of stress. They usually go with marital, family, health, nervous, or personal problems. Smaller proportions go because they have made it their religion (2 percent) or because they like the real-life drama and spontaneous art form, are curious, or believe they can learn from it (about 16 percent). About half of the total attendance observed ($n = 180$) go "to develop spiritual faculties," as well as to seek relief of complaints. The group 1 and 2 women are about equally divided between those who are and those who are not satisfied by the ministrations of the mediums. Mrs. Jimenez and Mrs. Perez provide examples of the group 1 woman's use of Spiritism.

Mrs. Jimenez

Mrs. Jimenez is 32 years old and lives with her husband and three children. Her husband works in a restaurant and runs a spiritist center in the basement of the building where they live. Mrs. Jimenez has kin, neighbors, and friends whom she sees frequently and "counts on," but she does not confide in them. Although she considers herself Roman Catholic and attends mass regularly, she also attends her husband's and other spiritist centers regularly. Her five best friends, in whom she confides, along with her husband, are women she knows from these centers. She says "I haven't had any problems, but I like to visit them for consultation."

The group 3 women and the outpatient schizophrenics are more likely to have gone to spiritists. In their attitudes toward Spiritism, they fall into three groups: (1) those who are grateful to spiritists for the help they have received, (2) those who are afraid to go to spiritist centers because of their vulnerability to the spirits of others, and (3) those who believe their problems are spiritual but report spiritist interpretations of their problems that suggest the condition will be very difficult or impossible to cure (e.g., an "old witchcraft which has been around too long, or the condition of being in spiritual development" without having "developed"). Mrs. Sanchez is a good example of this group.

Mrs. Sanchez

Mrs. Sanchez is a 38-year-old, married, mother of four daughters. She has had two severe acute psychotic episodes since age 28 and periodically has episodes of intensified symptoms. She attributes these episodes to two works of witchcraft done against her by a woman with whom her husband had an affair just before the first episode. She believes these "works" are renewed twice annually, once on the anniversary of her first episode, and again around Christmas time, when her symptoms worsen. These "works" were purportedly done to make her and her daughters become disfigured—cause them to lose their teeth and hair, have pimples on their faces, and drive them into prostitution or an insane asylum. Mrs. Sanchez has been attending a variety of spiritist centers since the onset of her illness.

The mediums say that Mrs. Sanchez was once "in development," but "she went here and she went there, and I do not know what they did, but she lost her *facultades* (spiritual faculties)." According to them, there is nothing that can be done for her now, except to *"hacerle la caridad"* (care for her) when she comes asking for help. During the episode that was observed in the spiritist center, Mrs. Sanchez came (shortly before Christmas) complaining that her oldest daughter was "being driven into prostitution" by the spirit from this old witchcraft. Inquiry on the part of the mediums revealed that her eldest daughter had a boyfriend with whom she had been staying out late and whom she was planning to marry. The mediums helped Mrs. Sanchez to accept the inevitability of her daughter's marriage and ritually cleansed her and her home of the effects of the malevolent spirit. Mrs. Sanchez attended the center and consulted privately with the center president regularly for a period of 2 months. Once her acute symptoms were relieved, she stopped attending this center,

where she goes for crisis care, but continued to attend another center on Sunday afternoons where she is ritually cleansed (*despojada*) weekly.

Mrs. Sanchez maintains little contact with kin, does not confide in her husband, but has a number of friends and neighbors with whom she visits and one "best friend," who is a "partially made medium." The two friends confide in each other and attend centers together frequently. Her relationships with all other neighbors and friends are also based in matters of "spiritual" significance, i.e., "a woman with a *brujeria*, like me," a *"bruja"* (someone who does sorcery), etc.

Mrs. Sanchez functions as wife and mother with periodic intervention of the spiritists. Spiritism gives her an explanation of her illness that is socially acceptable in at least part of her society and culture; it also provides her with social contacts with healthy as well as other ill women. The spiritists help her cope more effectively with symptoms that they recognize cannot be relieved entirely. For Mrs. Sanchez, Spiritism is a community alternative to crisis intervention and long-term supportive psychotherapy.

Among the inpatient schizophrenics, the same three attitudes found among the outpatients were evident, but, in addition, there were several other distinctive characteristics of their use of Spiritism: (1) They believe in *brujeria* (witchcraft) as the cause of their illness, but have no interest in the more complex metaphysics of spiritism. For these women beliefs about witchcraft often express paranoid delusions, whereas for less disturbed adherents to Spiritism, witchcraft accusations are more often a socially acceptable idiom for the expression of angry feelings (not socially acceptable) provoked by actual interpersonal conflicts, particularly with other women in love triangles, with in-laws, and with neighbors. (2) They have a very concrete belief in the existence of spirits as causal agents. For most mediums and believers, spirits are concepts whose existence is verified by observations of their manifestations in thoughts, feelings, and behaviors of people. (3) They tend to describe themselves as mediums when they would not be recognized as such in the community. Laura and Dolores represent two instances of this. Like Mrs. Sanchez, they were both told at a time when they were less ill that they had been born to work *la obra* (spiritual work), but they did not "develop" their spiritual "faculties."

Laura

Laura is a very disturbed outpatient schizophrenic in her forties, who was interviewed in the community after she had made one visit to a spiritist center. Laura, the last of 10 children, remained with her mentally ill mother until the mother's death when Laura was 30. She then had three children by three casual lovers and raised them to ages 7 to 10, when they were taken from her by the courts, 1 year before my contact with her. They are the only kin Laura has, and she visits them weekly. Laura has almost no other topic of conversation than the details of how the children were taken away from her. Laura has purportedly never had psychiatric treatment, despite her involvement with the courts.

Laura has sought the help of spiritists at three times in her life, once with the problem of her mother, and twice with her problematic pregnancies. She practices Spiritism in her home to a small clientele, without which she would be totally isolated. The one client I met confided that she came, not for a consultation, as Laura assumed, but "to see how she was doing."

This independent practice of Spiritism is considered deviant by mediums in spiritist centers. One cannot become a medium without having gone through a long period of "developing" one's "faculties" through participation in center activities. Furthermore, one should not try to "work" the spirits of others, they say, unless other mediums are present in the event they should "get out of control." At least three of the inpatient schizophrenics called themselves "mediums" and worked the spirits of others in their homes without the benefit of the structured setting of the spiritist *reunion* (group meeting).

Dolores

Dolores, an outpatient schizophrenic, is a 34-year-old who has lost contact with all of her family, including an 8-year-old son. She has no friends, knows no neighbors, and has no one to "count on" or "confide in" except her *investigadora* (caseworker), the police (when she is delusional), and a spiritist medium. The medium, whom she regularly consults, advises her, among other things "to always be strong and never have to enter into a mental hospital." Dolores, unlike Laura, continues to attend spiritist centers, or at least consultations. She believes she has special spiritual faculties, which she is encouraged to use to the best of her ability. Dolores can legitimately call herself, as she does, "an almost half-made medium."

The majority of the inpatient schizophrenics considered themselves to have "spiritual faculties," usually insufficiently developed because they "have a spirit that is too strong" or they are "too weak." Others said they had an "old witchcraft" or "a spirit from another

existence" with them from before they were born. These are all culturally normal interpretations of abnormal conditions that are difficult or impossible to cure. None of the schizophrenic women would be recognized by other mediums as fully developed mediums.

In the traditional practice of mental health clinics, spiritist beliefs are taken as symptomatic of an illness, usually as delusions. Frequently this view is correct—particularly when the beliefs are self-generated attributions of symptoms to "works of witchcraft." But, in the Puerto Rican community, spiritist beliefs are a folk psychology that structures, explains, and provides behavioral prescriptions for alleviation (*despojo*) or unfolding (*desarrollo*) of the invisible forces that influence thoughts, feelings, and behaviors. In its fullest form, as represented in developed mediums, spiritism is a complex system that recognizes the full range of symptoms included in a standardized mental status examination (Garrison, in preparation; Lubchansky, Egri, and Stokes 1970). When this belief system is understood, spiritist beliefs frequently represent the patient's understanding of the symptoms and causes of the illness in a different system of conceptualization, explanation, and management of that condition. In schizophrenic patients, this recognition of the disease and self-understanding may sometimes be culturally formulated insight and the spiritist beliefs may represent coping mechanisms (Rogler and Hollingshead 1961, 1965) rather than, or as well as, symptoms.

In clinic patients, spiritist beliefs are frequently distorted by psychopathology. It is a mistake to try to understand what Spiritism is in the Puerto Rican community from psychiatric patients' reports. But if these reports are assessed objectively, they can reveal a great deal about the patient. Spiritism, as a folk psychology, as well as a folk psychotherapy, is a very important influence in the Puerto Rican community for both nonschizophrenics and schizophrenics. As such, it must be understood if the limited strengths and resources of the patient are not to be further undermined. Mental health professionals can work collaboratively with folk healers as collaterals in the treatment plan (Ruiz and Langrod 1976*a*, 1976*b*), but the complexity of the spiritist's system of thought must be fully understood before any such efforts are made.

The One Friend Pattern

Four of the nonschizophrenics and seven of the schizophrenic women have non-kin networks that consist exclusively of one very close friend. All but 1 of these 11 women are separated or divorced, and all but 2 have minimal contact with kin. All have significant psychiatric symptoms.

The prototype of this pattern is Anita, the evicted mother of three living with Mrs. Velez. Anita says she is an orphan and ''I hardly know my family.'' She has no friends, knows no neighbors, has never belonged to any groups, and does not go to church or spiritist centers. She was referred to the LHMHS Outpatient Clinic during the course of this research and the diagnosis was psychotic depression. Mrs. Velez is her one friend.

The one married woman in this group is the anomalous Mrs. Lopez, the only woman in the neighborhood sample who counts on and confides exclusively in her husband. She is 32 years old, lives with her husband and six young children, has no kin living in New York, and has only infrequent contact with kin in Puerto Rico. Her only contact outside the household is an older woman—a neighbor. Mrs. Lopez and this friend do not visit, and she does not count on or confide in her. Nevertheless, they are ''very good friends.'' The husband on whom Mrs. Lopez so heavily depends drinks to excess, and she and the children are afraid of him. Otherwise she expressed few complaints on the Cornell Medical Index and had no history of episodes of treatment for emotional problems. By the criteria of classification in this study, she was a borderline case between groups 1 and 2 on degree of emotional disturbance. Now, having viewed her social support system characteristics in the context of those of her peers, I believe a complete psychiatric examination would reveal greater psychopathology.

Two women with ''one-friend'' non-kin networks also have some kin in the neighborhood. Both women depend particularly on a family member of the younger generation (a niece and a nephew), which is reminiscent of the parent-child dependency pattern characteristic only of schizophrenics.

In 10 of the 11 cases, the one-friend role is played by a neighbor. Two of the friends are building superintendents, one is the proprietor of a *bodega* on the block, two are ''retired mediums,'' one is a *Santera,* and two were first met through children's activities at the school. The last is another patient met in the hospital. The ''one friend'' in the networks of schizophrenics in treatment can be an important source of information for workers—guiding them to the supporting others or possible ''gatekeepers'' (Caplan 1974) within any specific neighborhood.

The Null Category (Parent-Child Dependency Pattern)

This pattern, in which the person has no non-kin relationships whatsoever, is not found among nonschizophrenics and characterizes the social networks of only three of the outpatient schizophrenics. Among the inpatients, however, it is the predominant pattern. All these women are unmarried, have very small kinship networks, and depend exclusively on one or two family members. The majority rely on grown children; exceptions are two younger schizophrenics (ages 20 and 22) who depend on a mother and grandmother, and a woman without either parents or offspring, who depends on a sister. The three outpatient schizophrenics with this pattern of dependency on a grown child are all in their sixties and have been either widowed or separated for many years. Those in the inpatient group range in age from 36 to 57. Mrs. Ortiz represents the extreme of this pattern found among women in the community.

> Mrs. Ortiz is a 65-year-old mother of 10, who lives alone, has no contact with kin, no friends or neighbors, and remains in contact with only two of her children, one of whom she depends on for everything.

Dependency on the younger generation is rarely reported in this population. Under extensive probing, only three of the nonschizophrenic women, including two of those with a history of mental hospitalization, named a son or daughter as someone they ''counted on'' or ''confided in.'' It is probable, however, that some depended more on older sons and daughters than they acknowledged because such dependency is inconsistent with the culture's values. Dignity and respect are accorded to all seniors, particularly parents, and a parent who must depend on an offspring is felt to have lost face. In contrast, the dependency of an offspring on the mother is expected to be lifelong. Adults in this culture are under a strong obligation, however, not only to pay deference to parents, but also to anticipate their needs and to care for them in times of illness or other distress. Sons and daughters are expected to meet parents' needs unsolicited and, if these obligations are not fulfilled, pressure is brought and sanctions exerted indirectly through gossip and confrontations by other family members.

It is probable that the reversal of roles from the relatively authoritarian parent who demands ''respect'' and social distance to the role of childlike confidant and dependent is the most serious deterioration of adult role possible in this culture. It is also possible that clinical supportive techniques that focus on nuclear family relationships, rather than extended family or non-kin relationships, serve to reinforce this dependency of schizophrenics on adult offspring. Indeed, the clinical relationship itself may explain to some extent the disproportionate pattern of parent-child dependency in the semi-institutionalized schizophrenic population. But these questions require further research.

This group also includes one woman, but only one, who has no one at all in her social network besides the representatives of the institution. This type of support system, which I have referred to as institutional dependency in Tables 2 and 3, may be underrepresented in this patient population compared with others, particularly a long-term hospitalized population. This case, Mrs. Lucas, illustrates the extreme of social withdrawal found in the sample.

Mrs. Lucas

Mrs. Lucas was divorced after a short marriage in her late teens. Thereafter she lived alone and reared her one son of that marriage, gradually losing contact with all of her own family. When she was 43, her son married and moved away, severing all contact with his mother. At that time Mrs. Lucas had her first psychiatric hospitalization. From that time forward she became a more or less permanent patient of the partial hospitalization unit. She functioned well enough to maintain herself in an apartment alone, but she did not make friends with her neighbors or the other patients in the day hospital. Nonetheless, she came regularly to the unit and, whenever she was discharged, she would return a week or two later—angry, physically assaultive, and demanding readmission.

Mrs. Lucas, like so many other Puerto Rican schizophrenic women, believed her problems were spiritual and had a lifelong history of involvement in Spiritism. She believed she was a ''medium in development'' who had never ''developed'' and that her illness was the result of ''trials'' or ''tests'' of her ''spiritual development.'' This spiritual explanation is a culturally normal one within the logic of the diagnostic system of the folk practitioners. The spiritual prescription (*receta*) for this condition involves participating in the spiritist group, learning to help oneself, and learning to help others so that she can undergo ''spiritual development.'' The reasons she gave for not going to a spiritist center were that she did not know one near her apartment and had no one to accompany her if she went out alone at night.

The clinician in charge of this case decided to refer her to a spiritist center for socialization and asked me for an address. Not knowing one in her immediate neighborhood, I took her to the one I knew well, where I was doing participant observations, as an experimental case study. Except that she had no crisis to be resolved, she was treated like Mrs. Sanchez. The mediums were gentle and directive with her. There was no mention of witchcraft or other ''bad spirits.'' She participated appropriately, enjoyed it, took an interest in others there, and might have become a regular participant (moved back to a ''cultic'' pattern of adjust-

ment) if she had not had to travel the distance to the center alone at night.

With hindsight, after this analysis of support system data, I think that what Mrs. Lucas needs most is ''one friend,'' someone who could ''accompany'' her, not only to spiritist centers but to do other things as well. I would now suggest that Mrs. Lucas and another patient, perhaps one even more disturbed than she, be relocated to an apartment together, or located in separate but proximate apartments, or that Mrs. Lucas be moved to an apartment building where the superintendent, the superintendent's wife, or any neighbor might play the ''good friend'' role.

Teresa represents a case in which such strategies were tried with some success.

Support Systems and Natural Network Therapy—A Case Example

If the support systems I have described represent progressive stages in the withdrawal of schizophrenic patients from social contacts, as well as adaptations to the absence of modal social supports, then they also provide a guide to what can be reasonably expected of a schizophrenic patient returning to the community.

The case of Teresa, one of the inpatient schizophrenics, illustrates a dynamic movement between patterns of the support system with greater and lesser degrees of disturbance during a single episode. Teresa first appeared to be excessively dependent on one 18-year-old son (although she also had a consensual spouse who had been living with her part time and sporadically for 10 years). Later she appeared to be a fully developed medium whose whole family and social network were involved in one way or another in ''spiritual'' explanations of her condition. Still later she appeared to be a person who had only superficial relationships with everyone (consensual mate, kin, and non-kin) in her social network. At discharge she had been stabilized on medication and returned to a good-friend-focused support system reinforced by family and network therapy. Thereafter, she was followed in the community through her natural network of friends and other patients, at first with a bi-weekly appointment for medication, and later without any official contact with the mental health services.

Teresa

Teresa was an attractive 45-year-old woman brought to the hospital by the police after an argument with Carlos, the father of her two youngest children, ages 7 and 9. She had called the Police and her 18-year-old son to throw Carlos out of the house. She had then demanded that her son come to live with her and he, having recently established a consensual union of his own, had refused. The young woman with whom he was living was an ex-addict, and at the time of admission Teresa's chief complaint was of "a spirit trying to drive the whole family into drugs." She was angry, agitated, delusional, and no history was obtained. The admissions team diagnosed Teresa as being in an acute schizophrenic episode precipitated by family stresses, and admitted her for brief hospitalization, stabilization on medication, and exploration of her support system.

On the morning following her admission, Teresa refused to take medication and enclosed herself in a telephone booth where she sang, shouted, prayed, and gesticulated. She alternated between drumming the rhythm of Chango (Santeria), saying Hail Mary's (Roman Catholic), praying to *El Senor* (Pentecostal), and making *"pases"* (spiritist cleansing gestures) over herself and the phone booth. When asked what religion she was, she explained that she was now a Santera, but she had been Pentecostal. She also said that she was a "fully developed medium" (Spiritism). This made sense as Pentecostalism is the only mutually exclusive alternative among these four affiliations. When she was told that the medications she was being offered were not "drugs" of the kind addicts use, she became cooperative, took her medication, and talked coherently, but not rationally, within the logic of Spiritism, about the "spirits" that were bothering her. She also acted as if she were a medium, enacting one of the spirits that was purportedly troubling her and another one, a protecting spirit—the spirit of her deceased grandmother. While her spiritist beliefs are ones that are culturally shared, her use of spiritual explanations was not normative, her behaviors were inappropriate, and her thought processes disturbed in that system of thought as well.

Over the following few days she and her two sons (ages 18 and 20) provided some history and information about her social network. Teresa was the youngest of four sisters of a stable union. Her parents were still living in Puerto Rico and she had minimal contact with them. Two sisters and a niece were living in New York, but not in Teresa's neighborhood or borough. Her contacts with all of them were minimal. Teresa had four consensual unions, all of considerable duration, and had produced six children, none of whom she had reared beyond the age of 9. She had had two previous psychiatric hospitalizations corresponding to the points of separation from her second and third husbands at ages 27 and 34. At the time of the first episode, her two eldest children had been taken by other kin and Teresa had lost contact with them entirely. After the second episode her 18- and 20-year-old sons (then 7 and 9) had been placed in a Catholic Children's Home, where they had lived to middle

adolescence and independence almost without contact with their mother. Teresa's youngest children, a boy 9 and a girl 7, were at this time with Carlos and his mother as a temporary arrangement.

Five family meetings were held to get a better impression of Teresa's usual functioning, the stressors she was currently under, and the supports available to her upon discharge. Carlos, his mother, Teresa's two sisters, her niece, and two sons were first invited to these meetings. The first meeting was attended by all her kin, but not her mate. By the fourth meeting, only her 18-year-old son attended. The fifth meeting was attended only by Carlos and his mother who came on the insistence of clinical staff. The staff wanted him to confront Teresa directly with his intentions not to return to live with her or to let their children do so either. The picture which emerged over these five family meetings may sound bizarre to a non-Hispanic, but within the culture it is not that strange.

Teresa's two sons were convinced that her problems came from a work of witchcraft contained in a bottle of milk she had picked up the day she threw Carlos out of the house. They knew almost nothing of Teresa's psychiatric history or premorbid personality. Teresa's eldest sister was adamant that Teresa "would be all right" if she had not "gotten mixed up with the bad," and if she would "change her mind back to the way it was," and "concentrate only on the good." She and a group of friends did *veladas* in her home for 7 days to help Teresa get well. This sister reported that Teresa had always been a little unstable—she was very naive and enthusiastic. "She seems to believe anything anyone tells her," as for example, "always getting into different religions." This sister said that she and her parents had "always had to be very strong" with Teresa, even when she was a child. Teresa's other sister and niece were more flexible and accepting of her. They were also spiritist believers and reported that "Some people say that she is obsessed with the spirit of a boy she worked." All of the family said that when Teresa was well, she never wanted to have anything to do with them.

During these meetings Teresa alternately professed herself to be a "good Catholic" when she was trying to please her oldest sister or as a "spiritist" when she was opposing her. Her longing for her alienated spouse (a Cuban) she expressed by singing "Santeria, Santeria, all I want is Santeria." Her second husband was Pentecostal and during the time of that union so was she.

Carlos, Teresa's boyfriend, as it turned out had never lived with her regularly, but maintained his permanent address with his mother. He said Teresa had brought her illness upon herself by doing works of witchcraft. He did not like the company she kept—the women with whom she was involved in Spiritism and *brujeria* (sorcery, witchcraft). Teresa admitted that she had been doing works of sorcery to make Carlos more attached to her. In the fifth family meeting, when Carlos confronted Teresa with his feelings about having been thrown out of the house by the police, her response was to move over and try to sit on his lap saying "I will be a good Catholic."

Over the course of a 5-week hospitalization and these family meetings, it became clear that Teresa was a chronic schizophrenic whose usual level of functioning was considerably impaired. She lived and organized her life within a magical-religious conceptualization in which forces of evil and good (represented by "spirits" and "saints") were psychic realities, not only for her, but for all of those around her. There was little practical, pragmatic support for her among her own kin or from Carlos. The only exceptions were her 18- and 20-year-old sons, whose involvement was ambivalent and whose independent lives would be jeopardized by their commitment to emotional support of their mother. They were willing "to give her 1 month to get her life organized," during which they would share the burden of staying with her. The team, therefore, turned to the neighbors and friends in her network for practical support and to a spiritist medium for consultation on the culturally appropriate interpretation and management of the realities of Teresa's condition in that system of thinking. The whole family agreed readily to the idea of a spiritist consultation.

A sixth meeting was held to which Teresa's "best friend" and neighbor, Dona Luisa, and another friend, Mrs. Ramirez, were invited. None of the family appeared. Just before this meeting was to begin, another chronic schizophrenic patient from the outpatient clinic, who lived in Teresa's apartment building, came in agitatedly explaining that she knew what was wrong with Teresa "because the same thing happened to me." This patient's explanation was that a woman in their building had "an altar in a closet" and had done works of sorcery against both of them. Dona Luisa, a semi-retired medium who did not like to "work the spirits" anymore, but who would "*hacer la caridad*" (give caring, advice, and counseling) to those in need around her, did not accept this explanation. She explained that Teresa was not a medium but only thought she was when ill. Dona Luisa considered Teresa to be psychiatrically ill but also believed that she could be helped with appropriate "spiritual treatment." Dona Luisa was judged by the treatment team to be a mature, insightful woman, whose support and advice was practical, pragmatic, and positive. Teresa's other friend in the meeting, Mrs. Ramirez, had a history of psychiatric outpatient treatment and appeared to the team to have a hysterical personality.

A spiritist medium, well known to the treatment team and respected in the community, was invited to provide the opinion of a fully adept folk practitioner about Teresa's condition and the treatment Teresa would receive if she pursued her interests in Spiritism in the formal setting of a center. This medium participated in a clinical case conference entirely appropriately as a professional from another discipline. She asked relevant questions during the discussion of the case, explained how spiritists view some of the things discussed, but would not venture her own opinions about Teresa until she had had an opportunity to examine the patient in her own way—a spiritist *consulta* (consultation). The minimal ritual setting of a spiritist consultation (a table draped with a white sheet, a jar of water, some cigars, white flowers, and incense) was, therefore, set up in the clinic. The medium, who does not smoke in her daily life, lit a cigar to invoke her protecting and guiding spirits, concentrated and prayed to her spirit guides to assist her, gave a few rapid jerks of her upper torso and neck, and began to speak what her spirits were telling her. The medium enumerated a variety of symptoms and spiritual interpretations of each set, in part as follows:

1. "Teresa has *un espiritu obsesor*" (a low-grade ignorant spirit of darkness that fills the mind and cannot be gotten rid of). This spirit, the medium said, could be seen in her eyes, indicating what the clinical team considered her depressed mood and flat affect. There was a "work" done to separate Teresa and Carlos, to cause them to turn their backs on each other—to cause him to hate her. "Sometimes he cares for you, and other times he hates you."

2. "In addition, Teresa has a spirit that comes with her from another existence that will not let her be happy with any man."

3. "Finally, the main thing Teresa has is that she is in *desarollo espiritual* [spiritual development] and she catches everything of everyone else. Then she doesn't know how to *desenvolverse* [disengage herself] or *sacudirse* [free herself] of it."

The spiritist treatment of these conditions in the first two cases is to "mount" the molesting spirit in the body of a medium, while the client looks on, interrogate the spirit, find out what it wants and why it is there, "educate it," and "give it light" so that it can go on its way to seek its own spiritual progress. For the last condition, that of being in spiritual development, the spiritual cure for Teresa is to attend spiritist centers, participate as a medium in development, learn to communicate with her own elevated "spirit guides," and learn to "defend herself" against the low-grade molesting spirits. These were spiritual interpretations of Teresa's condition and goals for therapy that make sense to a professional psychotherapist, if the spiritist system of explanation of causality is understood and tolerated. The first diagnosis of an *espiritu obsesor* sent by sorcery explains the immediate depression. The spirit, when mounted in the body of a medium, would express the ambivalence that Carlos feels toward Teresa and the anger and longing that Teresa feels toward him. The second spirit from another existence would be a man with whom she had had a similar unresolved relationship in a previous life (the oedipal conflict projected back to previous lifetimes). The third diagnosis and treatment plan is similar to involvement of a patient in group therapy, except that it is within her own culture and community, and it is a continual resource for her.

We encouraged Teresa to pursue this course of treatment with this particular medium, at whose center I was also doing participant observations and could watch the progress. A contract was also made between Dona Luisa, Teresa, and the treatment team, in which Dona Luisa was to become a collateral in the care of Teresa upon discharge. Teresa was to be discharged to live alone until her children could be returned to live with her, with the watchful eye of Dona Luisa from upstairs. This relieved the sons of the unwanted burden of taking turns sleeping over in their mother's apartment.

Teresa was discharged and within 24 hours her children had been returned to her. Within 2 weeks Carlos began to spend 1 night per week with her. At that point, for Teresa, everything was *"lo mas bien"* (just perfect), and she felt she no longer needed therapy, medication, or *espiritismo*. She "dropped out," but the alliance between the clinic and Dona Luisa continued. Teresa was very happy to have us "keep in touch" with her through her friend and the other patients in the clinic who knew her and Dona Luisa. Our goals during this period were primary prevention in the interest of the two young children.

Through our contacts with Dona Luisa, we discovered that there were four chronic schizophrenic patients, and three patients or ex-patients with less severe disorders, living in the same building, all of whom related to Dona Luisa, to each other, and to another spiritist with a center in the next block.

It became possible, through the alliance with Dona Luisa, to keep aware of the significant events in the lives of not only one patient, but three who were the responsibility of the same treatment team, and to make inputs to those patients' lives without any greater direct intervention than was required for medication maintenance. We might theoretically have involved all seven patients and ex-patients in this supervised natural network, but one of the major problems of continuity of patient care is the lack of continuity of mental health staff. All of us primarily involved in this experimental treatment plan were nearing the end of our rotations or other tenure in that treatment setting.

What we had done in this case was to use a preexisting quasi-group for what I call "natural network therapy."

Although these women never met together in one place at one time, they all related to each other, were concerned about each other, and reported to us on each other's progress. In the event of a subsequent crisis for any one of them, we could count on hearing about it, and we could hope that one of them, particularly Dona Luisa, would organize an action set to see that serious consequences were averted.

Conclusions

The seven patterns of support systems described represent an ideal/modal pattern of relating to both kin and non-kin (the rotarian pattern); four variations that appear to be adaptive in the absence of a husband (the good-friend-focused pattern), the absence of kin (the sectarian pattern), the absence of both (the grouping pattern), or in the presence of any degree of emotional distress (the "cultic" pattern); and two patterns (the one-friend and the parent-child or institutional dependency patterns) reflecting extreme social withdrawal, which are found predominantly or exclusively among the schizophrenics.

From the ideal rotarian pattern through the one-good friend variations, a progressive decrease in reliance upon kin ties is associated with a progressive increase in reliance on non-kin ties and a corresponding increase in the incidence and severity of emotional disturbance. The last pattern, the "null" non-kin network, associated with parent-child or institutional dependency, is exclusive to the schizophrenics and characterizes, particularly, the inpatient schizophrenic group.

Social withdrawal and relative social isolation are not only characteristic of schizophrenics, but they are secondary diagnostic criteria as well. It is not surprising, therefore, to find that the schizophrenic women are relatively withdrawn and isolated. Interpersonal relationships of schizophrenics are also expected to be either shallow or overdependent and immature (parent-child rather than peer relationships). Thus, it is also not surprising to find that schizophrenic women have social networks characterized by a few overdependent relationships with family members on higher or lower generation levels and few contacts with others of the same generation level.

At this point, however, the expectations break down. Neighboring or friendship relationships and church affiliations show a higher degree of social participation than might have been expected. When relationships to non-kin in folk-healing cults were explored systematically, such non-kin affiliations were found to be almost universal even among the inpatient schizophrenics.

It is my impression from observing and participating

in clinical assessment and treatment interviews that there is an implicit assumption, in practice if not in theory, that the process of social withdrawal in schizophrenics takes place progressively: first from the most peripheral and impersonal social contacts (e.g., keeping up with world and local news, seeking new associations with strange places and persons); then from personal but non-intimate contacts with friends and acquaintances in occupational, recreational, and other social settings; and last from the immediate nuclear family of orientation or procreation, depending upon the age and marital status of the patient. The data from this study suggest that this withdrawal may occur in the reverse order: conjugal bonds appear to be severed first; relationships to nuclear and extended kin (with the exception of the parent-child bond) seem to be weakened or severed second; and finally dependence upon associations of unrelated persons (e.g., friends, neighbors, associates in church affiliations or healing cults) are retained by all but those with the greatest degree of severity of disorder, and those who have become dependent on a somewhat captive grown child or upon the institutions and their representatives (the *investigadora*, the police, and the mental health clinic).

If this is the case, it provides an empirical basis for a "natural support system" approach to rehabilitation of schizophrenic patients. Instead of looking to the family to find support for the chronic schizophrenic patient in relationships that frequently have not been supportive in the past, the clinician might seek to halt or reverse the process of withdrawal by emphasizing, reinforcing, or supplying transient non-kin supportive relationships, involvement in voluntary associations of non-kin within the natural community that are tolerant and accepting of the schizophrenic person, and development of fictive kinship relationships with age mates. Such non-kin supports might serve to dilute the overdependency of the schizophrenic on one or two family members and might ultimately make possible the restoration of real kinship relations. The approach I am suggesting would seek to reestablish successively the missing linkages of the patient to the natural community rather than to establish an artificial, protected environment for the psychiatrically handicapped. Examples from the less disturbed living within the community can be used as models upon which to pattern these linkages.

In this approach, the distinctive characteristics of the support systems of schizophrenics described, generally considered symptomatic of schizophrenia, would be viewed, instead, as the limited strengths and resources of the schizophrenic.

Some of the specific practical suggestions for rehabilitation of chronic schizophrenic patients in the Puerto Rican community that have been made here, either explicitly or by implication, are:

- Mental health services should be localized in small neighborhood units, staffed by persons who are or can become thoroughly acquainted with the concrete social systems of that specific neighborhood.
- Acquaintance with the concrete social systems of the neighborhood can be brought about through interviews with patients of all degrees of disturbance. Influential, potentially helpful members of the community can be identified through reports of patients of their daily lives.
- Severely disturbed patients might be located alone or in pairs in apartments in the community as long as there were also supportive others outside the household.
- Mapping the distribution of patients' residences within the catchment area would show clusterings of patients in close proximity to each other, which might then be organized into neighborhood-based groups or supportive networks.
- Supportive psychotherapy groups might be based in homes rather than in the clinic, and particularly in the homes of severely disturbed patients who require assistance to maintain the household.
- Neighbors, "good friends," Pentecostal people, spiritist mediums, "supers," and *bodega* proprietors are particularly likely candidates for participation in re-created support systems for chronic schizophrenics and even for foster home placements, as well as the role of "gatekeeper" (cf. Leutz 1976).
- "Living network therapy," or the maintenance of a network of natural associates in the neighborhood context, such as that illustrated in the case of Teresa, could probably be accomplished with no greater expenditure of monies or professional time than is now spent on the same group of patients in medication maintenance.
- Quasi-groups and action sets can be mobilized in the support of patients, or can be cued to mobilize themselves in times of crisis for a patient discharged into the community.
- Mental health services would probably be used more readily, and dropouts be fewer among patients from this subculture if time and attendance were structured less rigorously than is conventional in the traditional clinic. Walk-in services, without fixed appointments, and group activities, without fixed membership of groups, are two examples of patterns congenial with those found in the natural community.

• Mental health services integrated with general medical clinics would be more acceptable to this population and probably better utilized than freestanding facilities.

Some of the suggestions made are already part of standard practice in some community mental health facilities; others are not. At the TCC, all of these strategies were tried at times, but the outcome was systematically documented and evaluated only in the cases where Spiritism figured into an experimental plan of intervention.

The extent to which the findings of this research or the practical implications can be generalized to other communities or to other schizophrenic populations is a matter for continuing research. Many of the single traits found among the Puerto Ricans described have been reported for other first-generation immigrant populations, for low-income populations, for rural groups, for preindustrial peoples, and for urban proletariats. The only exactly comparable data are to be found in the data collected from Black Americans in these same studies. These suggest that Black Americans do not share the Puerto Rican characteristic of having social supports concentrated in the local neighborhood, that they do not do as much neighboring, and that their kinship networks are perhaps more extensive than those of the Puerto Ricans. Comparable data are also available in as yet unpublished analyses of the support systems of 60 deinstitutionalized patients of mixed ethnic backgrounds in a study conducted in New Jersey by the Mental Health Association of Essex County (1978). These data suggest that general mixed White Americans also do not have their support systems concentrated in the local neighborhood. Detailed analyses of non-kin relationships or of dependencies in the core support system have not yet been made with either of these comparative samples.

Pending further research, however, the support systems information needed by clinicians is readily available through patient and family interviews. If there is a mental health facility responsible for the total mental health needs of a catchment area population, such data on the support systems of nonschizophrenic and schizophrenic patients could soon be built up through the recordkeeping system of the facility. Information on the ideal and modal patterns of life is available in the literature for most American communities or subcultures varying by region, class, race, national origin, and ecological zone.

If issues of confidentiality and privacy could be overcome, patient information on supportive others could also soon build up a directory of community caretakers and gatekeepers, whose collaboration might

be sought subsequently in the management of the same and other patients.

The possibilities for a true community mental health service for deinstitutionalized schizophrenic patients are many if the professional and institutional constraints can be overcome. Third-party payment regulations, professionalism, conventions of patient confidentiality in traditional individual therapies, conventional therapist-patient roles, and boundaries in the division of labor among the several mental health specialties are all very important considerations in the institutional structure. They have little relevance to the needs of the deinstitutionalized chronic schizophrenic patient, but they prevent mental health workers from making full use of naturally occurring support systems.

Summary

Analysis of the *social networks and support systems* of patients with varying degrees of emotional disturbance reveals models of naturally occurring support systems that can be used by mental health professionals for fostering, redeveloping, or building supports for chronic schizophrenic patients in their natural communities. As a demonstration, analysis is made of the social supports of 55 Puerto Rican migrant women with five degrees of emotional disturbance. Seven patterns of social support with associated family and emotional status variables emerge. These support system patterns range on a continuum from one which reflects the ideals of the culture found primarily among women who are symptom-free, through four variations that appear to be adaptations to deficits in the *core support system* (e.g., absence of husband, extended kin, or both) found predominantly among the nonschizophrenic but disturbed women, to two culturally deviant forms found almost exclusively among the schizophrenics. The salient finding of this analysis is that there is greater reliance upon neighbors, friends, and other non-kin than upon family among the schizophrenic women who lead their lives relatively successfully within the community. It is suggested that these non-kin supports be used in *natural network therapy* to reintegrate or maintain chronic schizophrenic patients in the Puerto Rican migrant community and that similar analyses be made of the support systems of patients from other communities.

REFERENCES

Arensberg, C. M. The community-study method. *American Journal of Sociology*, 60(2):109–124, 1954.

Arensberg, C. M. American communities. *American Anthropologist,* 57(6):1143−1160, 1955.

Arensberg, C. M. The community as object and as sample. *American Anthropologist,* 63(2):241−264, 1961.

Barnes, J. A. Class and communities in a Norwegian island parish. *Human Relations,* 7:39−58, 1954.

Bott, E. *Family and Social Network.* London: Tavistock, 1957.

Bram, J. Spirits, mediums, and believers in contemporary Puerto Rico. *Transactions of the New York Academy of Sciences,* 20:340−347, 1957.

Brodman, K.; Erdmann, A.; and Wolff, H. *Manual: The Cornell Medical Index Health Questionnaire.* New York: Cornell University Medical College, 1949.

Brodman, K.; Erdmann, A.; Lorge, I.; Gershenson, C.; Wolff, H.; and Caples, B. The Cornell Medical Index-Health Questionnaire. III. The evaluation of emotional disturbances. *Journal of Clinical Psychology,* 8:119−121, 1952.

Caplan, G. *Support Systems and Community Mental Health: Lectures on Concept Development.* New York: Behavioral Publications, 1974.

Caplan, G., and Killilea, M., eds. *Support Systems and Mutual Help: Multidisciplinary Explorations.* New York: Grune & Stratton, Inc., 1976.

Caplow, T.; Stryker, S.; and Wallace, S. E. *The Urban Ambiance: A Study of San Juan, Puerto Rico.* New York: Bedminster Press, 1964.

City of New York, Institute of Public Administration. "Let There Be Commitment: A Housing, Planning and Development Program for New York City." Unpublished report of the study group of the Institute of Public Administration to Major John V. Lindsay, September 1966.

Crandell, D. I., and Dohrenwend, B. P. Some relations among psychiatric symptoms, organic illness and social class. *American Journal of Psychiatry,* 123(12):1527−1538, 1967.

Dohrenwend, B. P. Social status, stress, and psychological symptoms. *American Journal of Public Health,* 57(4):625−632, 1967.

Dohrenwend, B. P., and Dohrenwend, B. S. The problem of validity in field studies of psychological disorder. *Journal of Abnormal Psychology,* 70(1):52−69, 1965.

Dohrenwend, B. P.; Egri, G.; and Mendelsohn, F. S. Psychiatric disorder in general populations: A study of the problem of clinical judgment. *American Journal of Psychiatry,* 127(10):40−48, 1971.

Endicott, J., and Spitzer, R. L. Current and past psychopathology scales (CAPPS): Rationale, reliability, and validity. *Archives of General Psychiatry,* 27:678−687, 1972.

Fisch, S. Botanicas and spiritualism in a metropolis. *Milbank Memorial Fund Quarterly,* 46.3:337−388, 1968.

Fitzpatrick, J. P., and Gould, R. E. Mental illness among Puerto Ricans in New York: Cultural condition or intercultural misunderstanding? In: Levitt, M., and Rubenstein, B., eds. *On the Urban Scene.* Detroit, Mich.: Wayne University Press, 1972. pp. 48−64.

Garrison, V. Social networks, social change and mental health among migrants in a New York City slum. (Microfilm No. 7316203 04500) Ph.D. dissertation, Columbia University, New York, N.Y., 1972.

Garrison, V. Sectarianism and psychosocial adjustment: A controlled comparison of Puerto Rican Pentecostals and Catholics. In: Zaretsky, I., and Leone, M. P., eds. *Religious Movements in Contemporary America.* Princeton, N.J.: Princeton University Press, 1974.

Garrison, V. The "Puerto Rican Syndrome" in psychiatry and espiritismo. In: Cropanzano, V., and Garrison, V., eds. *Case Studies in Spirit Possession.* New York: John Wiley & Sons, Inc., 1977*a.*

Garrison, V. Doctor, *espiritista* or psychiatrist? Health-seeking behavior in a Puerto Rican neighborhood of New York City. *Medical Anthropology,* 1(2):65−191, 1977*b.*

Garrison, V. Espiritismo and psychotherapy: Comparative processes and relative efficacy. *Medical Anthropology,* in preparation.

Gonzalez-Wippler, M. *Santeria: African Magic in Latin America.* New York: Julian Press, 1973.

Hallowitz, E., and Riessman, F. The role of the indigenous nonprofessional in a community mental health neighborhood service center program. *American Journal of Orthopsychiatry,* 37:766−778, 1967.

Harwood, A. *Rx: Spiritist as Needed.* New York: John Wiley & Sons, Inc., 1977.

Hollingshead, A. B. *Two Factor Index of Social Position.* New Haven, Conn.: Yale University Press, Inc., 1957.

Kapferer, B. Norms and the manipulation of relations in a work situation. In: Mitchell, J. C., ed. *Social Networks in Urban Situations.* Manchester: Manchester University Press. 1969. pp. 181−244.

Kaplan, S. R., and Roman, M. *The Organization and Delivery of Mental Health Services in the Ghetto: The Lincoln Hospital Experience.* New York: Praeger, 1973.

Koss, J. Therapeutic aspects of Puerto Rican cult practices. *Psychiatry,* 38(2):160−171, 1975.

Lehmann, S. Selected self help: A study of clients of a community social psychiatry service. *American Journal of Psychiatry,* 126(10):88−98, 1970.

Leutz, W. N. The informal community caregiver: A link between the health care system and local residents. *American Journal of Orthopsychiatry,* 46(4):678−688, 1976.

Lewis, O. *A Study of Slum Culture: Backgrounds for La Vida.* New York: Random House, 1968.

Lubchansky, I.; Egri, G.; and Stokes, J. Puerto Rican spiritualists view mental illness: The faith healer as a paraprofessional. *American Journal of Psychiatry,* 127(3):312−321, 1970.

Malzberg, B. Mental disease among Puerto Ricans in New York City, 1949–51. *Journal of Nervous and Mental Disease,* 123:262–269, 1956.

Mayer, A. C. The significance of quasi-groups in the study of complex societies. In: Banton, M., ed. *The Social Anthropology of Complex Societies.* London: Tavistock Publications, 1966. pp. 97–122.

Mental Health Association of Essex County. *From Back Wards to Back Streets: A Study of People in Transition From Psychiatric Hospital to Community.* (Discharged Patient Advocacy Project) East Orange, N.J.: The Association, 1978.

Mitchell, J. C., ed. *Social Networks in Urban Situations.* New York: Humanities Press, 1969.

Padilla, E. *Up From Puerto Rico.* New York: Columbia University Press, 1958.

Peck, H. B.; Kaplan, S. R.; and Roman, M. Prevention, treatment and social action: A strategy of intervention in a disadvantaged urban area. *American Journal of Orthopsychiatry,* 36(1):57–69, 1966.

Riessman, F. The "helper" therapy principle. *Social Work,* 10(2):27–32, 1965.

Rogler, L. H., and Hollingshead, A. B. The Puerto Rican spiritualist as psychiatrist. *American Journal of Sociology,* 67:17–22, 1961.

Rogler, L. H., and Hollingshead, A. B. *Trapped: Families and Schizophrenia.* New York: John Wiley & Sons, Inc., 1965.

Ruiz, P., and Langrod, J. Folk healers as associate therapists. In: Masserman, J. H., ed. *Current Psychiatric Therapies.* Vol. 16. New York: Grune & Stratton, Inc., 1976*a.* pp. 269–275.

Ruiz, P., and Langrod, J. The role of folk healers in community mental health services. *Community Mental Health Journal,* 12(4):392–398, 1976*b.*

Safa, H. I. The social isolation of the urban poor: Life in a Puerto Rican shanty town. In: Deutscher, I., and Thompson, E., eds. *Among the People: Encounters With the Poor.* New York: Basic Books, Inc., 1968.

Sandoval, M. C. *La Religion Afrocubana.* Madrid, Spain: Playor, 1975.

Sandoval, M. C. Santeria: Afrocuban concepts of disease and its treatment in Miami. *Journal of Operational Psychiatry,* 8(2):52–63, 1977.

Spitzer, R. L., and Endicott, J. *Current and Past Psychopathology Scales (CAPPS).* New York: New York State Psychiatric Institute, 1968.

Srole, L.; Langner, T. S.; Michael, S. R.; Opler, M. K.; and Rennie, T. A. C. *Mental Health in the Metropolis: The Midtown Manhattan Study.* New York: McGraw-Hill, Inc., 1962.

Steward, J. H.; Manners, E. R. W.; Seda, E. P.; Mintz, S. W.; and Scheele, R. L. *The People of Puerto Rico.* Urbana: University of Illinois Press, 1956.

Struening, E. L., and Peck, H. B. The role of research in evaluation. In: Williams, R. H., and Ozarin, L. D., eds. *Community Mental Health: An International Perspective.* San Francisco: Jossey-Bass, Inc., 1968.

Suchman, E. A., and Phillips, B. S. An analysis of the validity of health questionnaires. *Social Forces,* 36:223–232, 1958.

Suttles, G. D. *The Social Order of the Slum.* Chicago: University of Chicago Press, 1968.

Thomas, C. S., and Garrison, V. A general systems view of community mental health. In: Bellak, L., and Barten, H., eds. *Progress in Community Mental Health.* Vol. III. New York: Brunner/Mazel, Inc., 1975.

U.S. Bureau of the Census. *Puerto Ricans in the United States. Census of Population: 1970.* Washington, D.C.: Superintendent of Documents, Government Printing Office, 1970.

Wirth, L. Urbanism as a way of life. *American Journal of Sociology,* 44:1–15, 1938.

Whyte, W. F. Social organization in the slums. *American Sociological Review,* 8:34–39, 1943.

Acknowledgment

The research conducted at Tremont Crisis Center was supported by U.S. Public Health Service Grant No. 1RO1 MH 22563, "Folk Healers and Community Mental Health Programming," to Columbia University, Department of Anthropology, New York, N.Y., Vivian Garrison, Ph.D., and Alexander Alland, Ph.D., Co-Principal Investigators. My sincerest thanks to Drs. Edward Hornick and Israel Zwerling, then Directors of the Tremont Crisis Center and Bronx State Hospital, respectively, and to all of the staff, residents, and faculty of the TCC who collaborated in this research, particularly C. Christian Beels, M.D., whose editorial assistance in preparation of this paper is also gratefully acknowledged.

The community studies conducted at Lincoln Hospital Mental Health Services were supported by U.S. Public Health Service Grant No. 5 R11 MH 02308, "Study of Neighborhood Centers and Mental Health Aides," to Albert Einstein College of Medicine, Bronx, N.Y., Elmer L. Struening, Ph.D., and Harris B. Peck, M.D., Co-Principal Investigators. The research unit at LHMHS consisted of an interdisciplinary research team under the direction of Drs. Elmer Struening and Stanley Lehmann.

ANDREW T. SCULL

The Decarceration of the Mentally Ill: A Critical View

In a colossal refuge for the insane, a patient may be said to lose his individuality and to become a member of a machine so put together, as to move with precise regularity and invariable routine; a triumph of skill adapted to show how such unpromising materials as crazy men and women may be drilled into order and guided by rule, but not an apparatus calculated to restore their pristine condition and their independent self-governing existence. In all cases admitting of recovery, or of material amelioration, a gigantic asylum is a gigantic evil, and figuratively speaking, a manufactory of chronic insanity.

John Arlidge, 1859

It is not well to sneer at political economy in its relations to the insane poor. Whether we think it right or not, the question of cost has determined and will continue to determine their fate or weal or woe.

George Cook, 1866

In recent years, a state sponsored effort to deinstitutionalize deviant populations had become a central element in the social control practices of a number of advanced capitalist societies. In varying degrees, control of such deviant groups as criminals, juvenile offenders, and the mentally ill has increasingly become "community based." Yet despite the enormous importance of this change in social policy, surprisingly little effort has been made to unravel the reasons for its appearance. Most of the time it is discussed simply in passing. Only rarely does one come across sustained discussions of the problem.

In this paper we shall consider in some detail one very important aspect of this change, the decline of the mental hospital and the shift towards community treatment as a means of handling the mentally disturbed. It is frequently suggested that this development can be attributed to the discovery in the mid-1950s of an effective antipsychotic medication, the phenothiazines, and to the demonstration by liberal social scientists that mental hospitals were fundamentally antitherapeutic institutions, having detrimental effects on their inmate populations. We shall contend here that explanation in these terms is radically implausible and unsatisfactory, that, even though the work of liberal critics of incarceration and the advent of psychoactive drugs may have been used to justify recent trends towards deinstitutionalization, the causes of the switch lie elsewhere. Briefly, and at the risk of oversimplification, we shall argue that the primary factor behind the adoption of a policy of deinstitutionalization has been a drive to control the soaring costs of incarceration, and that the need to retrench in this fashion, in turn, reflects important recent changes in the nature of advanced capitalist social formations. More specifically, it reflects the qualitative transformation that has taken place in the role of the state, and the expansion of social welfare programs that has formed an important part of that transformation. The great expansion of state activity has brought with it a growing state fiscal crisis. At the same time, the availability of welfare programs has rendered the social control functions of incarcerating the mentally ill much less salient; indeed, it has meant that other forms of social control have become equally functional. So it is that the state has maneuvered to cut back expenditures on mental hospitals and the like, even as it continues to spend money on other social services in increasing amounts.

This paper draws on a more extensive analysis of the deinstitutionalization phenomenon, which will appear as *Decarceration: A Radical View* (Englewood Cliffs, N.J. Prentice-Hall, Inc.) [Editors' Note: Published as *Decarceration: Community Treatment and the Deviant: A Radical View*, Englewood Cliffs, New Jersey: Prentice-Hall, Inc., 1977.] I am very grateful indeed to Steven Spitzer for his usual thoughtful and critical review of an earlier draft of the manuscript, and to Peter Sterling for his advice.

Reprinted from *Politics and Society*, Vol. 6, No. 2 (1976), pages 173-211, by permission of the author and publisher.

I

Most of the key features that distinguish deviance and its control in modern society from the shapes that these phenomena assume in other types of society emerged in

England and America during the early part of the nineteenth century. Of particular importance for our concerns in this paper, this period witnessed the substantial and sustained involvement of the state in this area, and the concomitant emergence of a centrally administered and directed social control apparatus committed to the treatment of many types of deviance in institutions.[1] With only relatively minor changes and additions (the most notable of which was the adoption of probation and parole as a secondary mechanism for dealing with the criminal), the dominant response to problem populations until quite recently continued to rest on a policy of segregative control, more often than not in large custodial warehouses remote from large population centers and insulated from public view.

Within the past quarter of a century, however, this policy has, for the first time since its adoption, been seriously challenged and modified, though by no means entirely abandoned. Perhaps the most striking manifestation of this change is to be found in that segment of the social control apparatus that is concerned with the management of the mad. From the establishment of the first publicly supported asylums in the early nineteenth century, a pattern of consistent year by year increases in the number of inmates confined in mental hospitals swiftly established itself, and persisted right through the nineteenth century and the first half of the twentieth century. There appeared to be a remarkably consistent tendency to underestimate the demand for asylum accommodation, no matter how careful the effort to estimate the local requirements. Moreover, as additional facilities were built to meet the apparent excess demand, they too swiftly became filled to capacity, prompting repetitions of the original cycle for as long as money was forthcoming for buildings.[2] In England, where the asylum system developed more rapidly than in America, the number of insane people grew from 21,000 (a rate of 12.66 per 10,000 people) in 1845—when provision of

TABLE 1

Resident Population in State and County Mental Hospitals in the U.S.A., 1954 – 1972

1954	554,000	1961	527,500	1967	426,000
1955	558,900	1962	515,600	1968	400,700
1956	551,400	1963	504,600	1969	no data
1957	548,600	1964	490,400	1970	no data
1958	545,200	1965	475,200	1971	309,017
1959	541,900	1966	452,100	1972	275,995
1960	535,500				

SOURCES: *NIMH Statistical Note 1; and K. A. Pollack and C. A. Taube, "Trends and projections in State Hospital Use" (paper presented at the symposium on the future role of the state hospital, SUNY, Buffalo, October 11, 1973), table 7 (for 1971 and 1972).*

TABLE 2

Resident Population of Mental Patients in England and Wales 1951 – 1970

1951	143,196	1958	142,815	1965	123,600
1952	144,583	1959	139,083	1966	121,600
1953	146,643	1960	136,162	1967	118,900
1954	148,080	1961	135,400	1968	116,400
1955	146,867	1962	133,800	1969	105,600
1956	145,593	1963	127,600	1970	103,300
1957	143,220	1964	126,500		

SOURCES: *E. M. Brooke, "Factors Affecting the Demand for Psychiatric Beds," The Lancet, December 8, 1962 (for 1951–60); and Department of Health and Social Security Figures (for 1961–70).*

asylums at public expense became compulsory—to 95,600 (a rate of 30.30 per 10,000 people) by the end of the century; by 1954, the year when the mental hospital population finally peaked, the number of patients resident in mental hospitals had grown to 148,000 (a rate of 33.45 per 10,000 people). Over the same period, the United States experienced an increase of similar magnitude, though the timing here was somewhat different. Prior to 1955, for example, "the public mental hospital population had quadrupled during the previous half century, whereas the general population had only doubled."[3]

Since the mid-1950s, however, both countries have witnessed an abrupt reversal of this trend. Dating from 1954 and 1955 respectively, the number of patients resident in mental hospitals in each country has decreased in each and every year (see Tables 1 and 2) and there has emerged in both countries an explicit commitment to a policy, which has gathered momentum over

---

1. For an account in these terms of the changing English response to insanity, and a delineation of certain other important features of this transformation of social control styles and practices, see A. T. Scull, "Museums of Madness: The Social Organization of Insanity in Nineteenth Century England," (Ph.D. diss., Princeton University, 1974); idem, "From Madness to Mental Illness: Medical Men as Moral Entrepreneurs," *European Journal of Sociology,* Vol. XVI; and idem, "Madness and Segregative Control: The Rise of the Insane Asylum" (paper read at the Annual Meeting of the American Sociological Association, San Francisco, 1975). For accounts of this transformation in America, see David J. Rothman, *The Discovery of the Asylum* (Boston: Little, Brown, 1971); Gerald N. Grob, *The State and the Mentally Ill: A History of Worcester State Hospital in Massachusetts, 1830–1920* (Chapel Hill, N.C.: University of North Carolina Press, 1966); and idem, *Mental Institutions in America: Social Policy to 1875* (New York: Free Press, 1973).

2. For a discussion and attempted explanation of this pattern, see Scull, "Museums of Madness," ch. 9.

3. *Joint Commission on Mental Illness and Health Action for Mental Health* (New York: Basic Books, 1961), p. 7.

the past two decades, of decarcerating the mentally disordered. Initially, doubts were expressed in some quarters about the significance of the decline in numbers and the likelihood of its long-term persistence,[4] but these seem to have disappeared as the fall has continued without interruption (and in some places even at an accelerated pace) for two decades now. In their place, we have seen an increasingly confident projection of existing trends to their logical limits, typified by the 1961 forecast by the British minister of health in which he expected "the acute population of mental hospitals to drop by half in the next fifteen years and the long-stay population ultimately to dwindle to zero."[5]

II

Curiously enough, while the numbers resident in mental hospitals have fallen dramatically over the past two decades, this fall has been accompanied by a steep rise in the overall admission rates. Statistically, the decline reflects a policy of greatly accelerated discharge. There is a strange historical parallel here. The establishment of the asylum system, particularly in the United States, depended heavily on the institution's presumed ability to cure. During the era of the "cult of curability,"[6] superintendents of existing institutions engaged in a bizarre competitive struggle to achieve the highest cure rates—a contest that eventually led to claims to be able to cure 100 percent of one's patients. If the asylum system thus had its roots in one sort of statistical version of cutthroat competition, its imminent demise seems to have provoked another—only this time, the hospitals, racing to discharge 100 percent of their intake within three months, seem largely unconcerned with labelling their output as cured.[7]

An explanation of the policy of early release and consequent decline in mental hospital populations that enjoys a considerable measure of popularity in some psychiatric and official circles attributes the transformation simply to the growing use and effectiveness of psychoactive drugs. In the words of the 1961 Joint Commission on Mental Illness and Health, "tranquilliz-ing . . . drugs have revolutionized the management of

psychotic patients in American mental hospitals, and probably deserve primary credit for reversal of the upward spiral of the State hospital inpatient load.'"[8] This account possesses the twin virtues of simplicity and of reinforcing the medical model of insanity by suggesting that the advent of psychoactive drugs signals a medical breakthrough in this area paralleling earlier ones allowing the successful treatment of other hitherto intractable chronic diseases.[9] Yet despite its evident appeal, as an explanation it is distinctly flawed.

Not only does such an account tend to exaggerate the therapeutic achievment that these drugs represent but, as Mechanic indicates, it is empirically inaccurate and inadequate in other ways as well. For example, studies of a number of English mental hospitals "show that new patterns of release were observable prior to drug introduction, and they suggest that the tremendous change which took place is largely due to alterations in administrative policies."[10] In the late 1940s and early 1950s, "well before the new drugs were introduced," certain hospitals had already adopted a policy of placing "an emphasis on early discharge, or the avoidance of admission altogether, in order to prevent the accumulation of long-stay institutionalized patients . . . the pioneers' use of social techniques began in certain hospitals well before the national swing was noticed in 1955, and the underlying statistical trends must have long antedated the change in overall bed occupancy."[11]

Even if this contradictory evidence had not been uncovered, to rest content with an explanation couched

4. See K. Jones and R. Sidebotham, *Mental Hospitals at Work* (London: Routledge, 1962), pp. 10ff.

5. Cited in J. Hoenig and M. W. Hamilton, *The Desegregation of the Mentally Ill* (London: Routledge, 1969), p. 2. See also A. Stewart et al., "Problems in Phasing Out a Large Psychiatric Hospital," *American Journal of Psychiatry* 125 (1968): 82–88; and A. O. Hecker, "The Demise of Large State Hospitals," *Hospital and Community Psychiatry* 21 (1970): 261–63.

6. A. Deutsch, *The Mentally Ill in America*, 2nd ed. (New York: Columbia University Press, 1949).

7. See Hecker, "The Demise of Large State Hospitals," pp. 261–62.

8. *Joint Commission on Mental Illness*, p. 39. See also H. Brill and R. E. Patton, "Analysis of 1955–56 Population Fall in New York State Mental Hospitals during the First Year of Large-Scale Use of Tranquilizing Drugs," *American Journal of Psychiatry*, vol. 114 (1957); idem, "Clinical Statistical Analysis of Population Changes in New York State Mental Hospitals since the Introduction of Psychotropic Drugs," *American Journal of Psychiatry*, vol. 119 (1962); Hecker, "The Demise of Large State Hospitals," p. 261; and Pollack and Taube, "Trends and Projections in State Hospital Use," p. 10. For England, see Chief Medical Officer's Report, *Report of the Ministry of Health for the Year 1959: Part II—On the State of the Public Health* (London: HMSO, CMND, 1207, 1959), p. 128: "The modern physical treatments and the new tranquillizing and stimulating drugs . . . explain why with a rising admission rate the number in residence now has dropped each year since 1955."

9. See J. A. Baldwin, *The Mental Hospital in the Psychiatric Service: A Case Register Study* (London: Oxford University Press, 1971), p. 18.

10. David Mechanic, *Mental Health and Social Policy* (Englewood Cliffs, N.J.: Prentice-Hall, 1969), pp. 61–62. See also George W. Brown, "Length of Stay and Schizophrenia: A Review of Statistical Studies," *Acta Scandinavia Psychiatrica et Neurologica*, 1959, pp. 414–30; George W. Brown et al., *Schizophrenia and Social Care* (London: Oxford University Press, 1966), passim, esp. p. 17; Hoenig and Hamilton, *The Desegregation of the Mentally Ill*, esp. pp. 8ff.; and J. K. Wing and G. W. Brown, *Institutionalism and Schizophrenia* (Cambridge: Cambridge University Press, 1970).

11. Wing and Brown, *Institutionalism*, pp. 174, 9.

in these terms would imply the acceptance of a naively deterministic relationship between technological advances and changes in social control styles and practices, to the neglect of the influence of the social context in determining the uses to which these advances are put. In other contexts, for example, might not the more subtle and less visible control of patient behavior that the new drugs supposedly offered have been used simply to ease internal management problems and decrease the incidence of overt, blatant physical constraint within the institution (as, indeed, has been done to some extent)[12] while having little or no effect on discharge patterns? Nor is it easy to see how a simple technological determinism of this sort can account for such things as the sudden acceleration of the decline in American mental hospital populations from the mid-1960s on when no comparable change occurred in England; or the other important aspect of the policy of decarceration, the conditions of existence endured by the mentally disabled discharged into the community.[13]

But there remains a still more damaging objection that proponents of the pharmacological explanation have been forced to finesse, namely, a growing volume of evidence that suggests that claims about the therapeutic effectiveness of so-called antipsychotic medication—mainly the phenothiazines—have been greatly exaggerated. It is becoming clear, for example, that for a substantial proportion of those labelled schizophrenic, psychoactive drugs are largely ineffective. For example, a recent double blind study of young male acute schizophrenics by Rappaport and Associates found that patients randomly assigned placebos while hospitalized and not taking phenothiazine at follow-up, "showed significantly greater clinical improvement and less pathology at follow-up, significantly fewer rehospitalizations and significantly less overall functional disturbance in the community than any other group of patients.

... Also, significantly fewer patients in the placebo group became worse from discharge to follow-up. ... In the long run, most patients *not* given phenothiazine medication do better. ..."[14] There can now be no question but that the extreme optimism that greeted the advent of psychoactive drugs, and that persisted for a number of years, reflected the weakness and poor design of many of the evaluations made at that time far more than the actual efficacy of the drugs themselves. Subsequent careful review of the relevant literature have shown that "uncontrolled studies" of a sort that remain surprisingly common in this area "gave a *systematically* more positive evaluation of drug effect than controlled studies."[15]

All of this should not be taken to imply that administration of such drugs has no behavioral effects. To the contrary, the preponderance (though by no means all) of well-designed, well-conducted studies "show that these drugs are better than placebo" if given in sufficiently high dosage.[16] There can be no question, for example, that "excessive doses of neuroleptics produce severe

12. See Brill and Patton, "Clinical Statistical Analysis."

13. A further difficulty with this approach is that it clearly cannot be extended to account for the decarceration of other types of deviants—criminals, juvenile offenders, and so on—groups that have not (at least not yet) been subject to treatment with such drugs. Yet in these areas, too, the state has pursued a policy of decarceration. See National Prisoner Statistics, *Prisoners in State and Federal Institutions for Adult Felons, 1967,* N.P.S. Bulletin no. 44, (U.S. Department of Justice, July 1969), table 1; Y. Bakal, ed., *Closing Correctional Institutions* (Boston: Lexington Books, 1973); L. T. Empey, "Juvenile Justice Reform: Diversion, Due Process, and Deinstitutionalization," in *Prisoners in America,* ed. Lloyd Ohlin (Englewood Cliffs, N.J.: Prentice-Hall, 1973); J. M. Leavey, *1973 Annual Report of the Department of Youth Services* (Boston: Department of Youth Services, 1973); and A. Liazos, "Class Oppression: The Functions of Juvenile Justice," *The Insurgent Sociologist* 5 (1974): 2–24. Instead of allowing us to see these developments as a unitary phenomenon, concentration on "the technological fix" leads us in the direction of a series of unconnected, ad hoc explanations of developments in each of these sectors.

14. M. Rappaport et al., "Schizophrenics for Whom Phenothiazines May Be Contraindicated or Unnecessary," mimeographed (Langley Porter Neuropsychiatric Institute, University of California, n.d.), p. 9, emphasis in the original. For other examples of these findings, see J. Siverman "Stimulus Intensity Modulation and Psychological Disease," *Psychopharmacologia* 24 (1972): 42–80; idem, "'Altered' States of Consciousness: Positive and Negative Outcomes" (Paper presented at the Annual Meeting of the American Academy of Psychoanalysis, 1974); J. Dabrowski and J. Aronson, *Positive Disintegration* (Boston: Little, Brown, 1964); S. Goldberg, G. Klerman, and J. Cole, "Changes in Schizophrenic Psychopathology and Ward Behavior as a Function of Phenothiazine Treatment," *British Journal of Psychiatry* 111 (1965): 120–33; the article by H. E. Lehman in *Comparative Textbook of Psychiatry,* ed. A. M. Freedman and H. I. Kaplan (Baltimore: Williams and Wilkins, 1967); L. R. Mosher, A. Menn, and S. M. Matters, "A New Treatment for Schizophrenia: One Year Follow-Up Data" (Paper presented at the 51st Annual Meeting of the American Ortho-Psychiatric Association, San Francisco, 1974); M. Goldstein, "Premorbid Adjustment, Paranoid Status and Patterns of Response to Phenothiazine in Acute Schizophrenics," *Schizophrenia Bulletin* 3 (1970): 24–37; J. W. Perry, "The Reconstitutive Process in the Psychopathology of the Self," *Annals of the New York Academy of Sciences* 96 (1962): 853–67; NIMH Pharmacological Service Center: Collaborative Study Group, "Phenothiazine Treatment in Acute Schizophrenia Effectiveness," *Archives of General Psychiatry* 10 (1964): 246–61; L. Hollister, "Adverse Reactions to Phenothiazines," *Journal of the American Medical Association* 189 (1964): 311–13; and G. Sarwer-Foner, "Recognition of Drug-Induced Extra-Pyramidal Reactions and 'Paradoxical' Behavior Reactions in Psychiatry," *Canadian Medical Association Journal* 83 (1960): 312–18.

15. John M. Davis, "Efficacy of Tranquilizing and Anti-Depressant Drugs," *Archives of General Psychiatry* 13 (1965): 552–72, esp. 552; G. A. Foulds, "Clinical Research in Psychiatry," *Journal of Mental Science* 104 (1958): 259–65; B. Fox, "The Investigation of the Effects of Psychiatric Treatment," *Journal of Mental Science* 107 (1961): 493–502; and B. Glick, "A Study of the Influence of Experimental Design on Clinical Outcome in Drug Research," *American Journal of Psychiatry* 118 (1962): 1087–96.

16. Davis, "Efficacy of Tranquilizing," p. 553.

reductions of motor activity and a general loss of spontaneity''—function, in effect, as "chemical strait-jackets.''[17] However, it has been well-established that the phenothiazines are ineffective for substantial portions of the target population and that, in any event, the types of maintenance doses generally prescribed are largely ineffective. Given this, how can anyone seriously contend that the advent of drug therapy is the primary reason for the decline in mental hospital populations (the more so since the drugs are apparently *least* effective with the groups whose release has been *most* crucial to the running down of mental hospital populations—the old, chronic cases)?

Even if most studies of the effectiveness of psychoactive drugs were far more uniformly favorable than we have seen that they are, serious difficulties would remain for proponents of the idea that the introduction of such drugs is the primary factor in the fall of mental hospital populations. For one thing, most of the studies we now possess consider short-term effects only. Where long-term follow-up studies do demonstrate the existence of a drug effect (and because of "generally faulty research designs" evidence on this point is muddled and contradictory),[18] this effect is generally quite small.[19] Moreover, "the difference between those patients treated with drugs and those not treated with drugs decreases over time. . . . As for the quality of the patient's adjustment after he leaves the hospital, the results of drug therapy are even less encouraging: the majority of those who live in the community continue to be unproductive and are often a burden to their families.''[20] At best, therefore,

one is left with the conclusion that the introduction of psychoactive drugs may have facilitated the policy of early discharge by reducing the incidence of florid symptoms among at least some of the disturbed, thus easing the problems of managing them in the community (and perhaps also by persuading doctors with an exaggerated idea of the drugs' efficacy of the feasibility of such a policy). But that their arrival can be held primarily responsible for the change is clearly highly implausible.

III

Recognizing the force of the criticism that serious account must be taken of social factors, others have sought an explanation of the decline in mental hospital populations in the growing disenchantment in this period with the adequacy of such institutions as a response to mental illness. In this view, a decisive factor underlying the transformation was the superior understanding achieved in this period of the effects of these institutions on their inmates. As Hoenig and Hamilton put it, "the policy of avoiding long-term hospitalization derives its main justification from the belief that it will protect the patient from institutionalization.''[21] A spate of social scientific research in the 1950s and 1960s (the most famous example of which was Goffman's *Asylums*)[22]

17. Crane, "Clinical Psychopharmacology, in Its 20th Year,'' *Science* 181 (July 13, 1973): 126. For further evidence that the primary effect of psychotropic drugs, given in sufficient dosage, is one of blunting the affect, see Davis, "Efficacy of Tranquilizing,'' p. 561.

18. See R. K. Gittleman, D. F. Klein, and M. Pollack, "Effects of Psychotropic Drugs on Long-Term Adjustment: A Review,'' *Psychopharmacology* 5 (1965): 317–38.

19. For example, in an eight-year follow-up study, Englehardt et al. conclude that chlorpromazine does significantly better than a placebo in preventing rehospitalization, but the difference is comparatively slight—of the order of 10 percent. See D. M. Englehardt et al., "Prevention of Psychiatric Hospitalization with the Use of Psychopharmacological Agents,'' *Journal of the American Medical Association* 173 (1960): 147–49; idem, "Prevention of Psychiatric Hospitalization: II. Duration of Treatment Exposure,'' ibid. 186 (1963): 981–83; idem, "Phenothiazines in Prevention of Psychiatric Hospitalization: III. Delay or Prevention of Hospitalization,'' *Archives of General Psychiatry* 11 (1964): 162–69; and idem, "Phenothiazines in Prevention of Psychiatric Hospitalization: IV. Delay or Prevention of Hospitalization—A Reevaluation,'' ibid. 16 (1967): 98–101.

20. Crane, "Clinical Psychopharmacology,'' p. 125. Rappaport's research suggests that the typical measures used to record improvement in a hospital context (and in terms of which the drugs are often alleged to be efficacious) may simply not tap the kinds of factors important for successful functioning in the outside world; and his finding that patients on chlorpromazine perform significantly better in a hospital setting than do those on a placebo, whereas on the outside this relationship is almost

precisely reversed, provides presumptive evidence in support of this position. See Rappaport et al., "Schizophrenics,'' esp. pp. 8, 16. More generally, the growing body of evidence on "state dependent learning" suggests that much of what is learned under the influence of drugs may not be carried over into behavior in an undrugged state. And this presents yet another serious problem for those who continue to place their faith in phenothiazines as a sort of "magic bullet''—for even if we were to grant their dubious premise, there is reliable evidence that once beyond the reaches of staff supervision, very many ex-patients simply fail to *take* their drugs on a regular basis! See L. C. Hartledge, "Effects of Chlorpromazine on Learning,'' *Psychological Bulletin* 64 (1965): 235–45; D. K. Kamano, "Selective Review of Effects of Discontinuation of Drug Treatment: Some Implications and Problems,'' *Psychological Report* 19 (1966): 743–49; L. S. Otis, "Dissociation and Recovery of a Response Learned under the Influence of Chlorpromazine or Saline,'' *Science* 57 (1964): 3–12; N. D. Vestre, "Relative Effects of Phenothiazines and Phenobarbitol on Verbal Conditioning of Schizophrenics,'' *Psychological Report* 17 (1965): 289–90; idem, "The Effects of Phenothiazine Drugs on Verbal Conditioning of Schizophrenics,'' *Journal of Psychology* 64 (1966): 257–64; L. A. Srouffre and M. A. Stewart, "Treating Problem Children with Stimulant Drugs,'' *New England Journal of Medicine* 289 (August 23, 1973): 407–12; and D. A. Overton, "Discriminative Control of Behavior by Drug States,'' in *Stimulus Properties of Drugs*, ed. G. T. Heistad, T. Thompson, and R. Pickens (New York: Appleton-Century-Crofts), pp. 87–110. See also A. Mason, I. S. Forrest, and F. M. Forrest, "Adherence to Maintenance Therapy and Rehospitalization,'' *Diseases of the Nervous System* 24 (1963): 103–4; and J. Hare and J. Wilcox, "Do Psychiatric Patients Take Their Drugs?'', *British Journal of Psychiatry* 3 (1967): 1435–39.

21. *The Desegregation of the Mentally Ill*, p. 245.

22. But see also, among others, A. Stanton and M. S. Schwartz, *The Mental Hospital* (New York: Basic Books, 1954); M. Greenblatt, R. H.

was devoted to the elucidation of the baneful effects on the patient of prolonged incarceration in a mental institution. All this research had shown, purportedly for the first time, that the defects in existing mental hospitals were not simply the consequence of administrative lapses or the lack of adequate funds, but rather reflected fundamental and irremediable flaws in the basic structure of such places, flaws so serious as to call into question their therapeutic usefulness—or rather to suggest that they were fundamentally antitherapeutic.

The consensus was clear. Presented most persuasively by Goffman, it was that the crucial factor in forming a mental hospital patient was not his "illness," but his institution; that his reactions and adjustments, pathological as they might seem to an outsider, were the product of the ill-effects of his environment rather than of intrapsychic forces; and, indeed, that they closely resembled those of inmates in other types of "total institutions," a term that came to symbolize this whole line of argument. The mental hospital, it now appeared, far from sheltering and helping to restore the disturbed to sanity, performed "a disabling custodial function."[23] The work of men like Duncan Macmillan and T. P. Rees, British pioneers of the concept of the open hospital, had demonstrated "beyond question that much of the aggressive, disturbed, suicidal, and regressive behaviour of the mentally ill is not necessarily or inherently a part of the illness as such but is very largely an artificial by-product of the way of life imposed on them [by hospitalization]."[24] Major American psychiatrists expressed fears that "the patients are infantile . . . because we infantilize them."[25] Studies of institutions as diverse as research hospitals closely associated with major medical schools, expensive, exclusive, and well-staffed private facilities, and undermanned and underfinanced state hospitals, all revealed a depressingly familiar picture. To the researchers, the very "similarity of these problems strongly suggests that many of the serious problems of the state hospital are inherent in the

nature of mental institutionalization rather than simply in the financial difficulties of the state hospitals."[26]

The conclusion was inescapable. Mental hospitals "are probably themselves obstacles in the development of an effective program of treatment for the mentally ill."[27] Policy recommendations followed naturally: "The time has come when we should ask ourselves seriously whether the interests of the mentally ill are best served by providing more psychiatric beds, building bigger and better mental hospitals. Perhaps we should concentrate our efforts on treating the patients within the community of which they form a part, and teach that community to tolerate and accept their idiosyncracies."[28] After all, considering what current research had shown, surely "the worst home is better than the best mental hospital . . . ,"[29] so that "in the long run the abandonment of the state hospitals might be one of the greatest humanitarian reforms and the greatest financial economy ever achieved. . . ."[30]

In place of the traditional stress on the need for institutionalization, there developed an increasingly elaborate attempt to convince the public, and, more importantly, the policy makers, of "the value and safety of community care."[31] In some circles, "community treatment" came to be elevated into a new therapeutic panacea, and, supported by ever larger injections of Federal funds in the United States, "community psychiatrists" became an increasingly important segment of the psychiatric profession as a whole.[32] Particularly during the sixties, "an influential group of community psychiatrists, clinical psychologists, and other professionals were being listened to increasingly at the state and federal levels."[33] In combination, it is suggested,

York, and E. L. Brown, *From Custodial to Therapeutic Patient Care in Mental Hospitals* (New York: Russell Sage Foundation, 1955); Ivan Belknap, *Human Problems of a State Mental Hospital* (New York: McGraw-Hill, 1956); T. P. Rees, "Some Observations on the Psychiatric Patient, the Mental Hospital, and the Community," in *The Patient and the Mental Hospital*, ed. M. Greenblatt, D. Levinson, and R. Williams (Glencoe, Ill.: Free Press, 1957), pp. 527–29; R. C. Hunt, "Ingredients of a Rehabilitation Program," in *Proceedings of the 34th Annual Conference of the Milbank Memorial Fund* (1957); W. Caudill, *The Psychiatric Hospital as a Small Society* (Cambridge, Mass.: Harvard University Press, 1958); and J. K. Wing, "Institutionalism in Mental Hospitals," *British Journal of Social and Clinical Psychology* 1 (1962): 38.

23. Hunt, "Ingredients of a Rehabilitation Program," p. 21.

24. Ibid., p. 13.

25. F. C. Redlich in the preface to Caudill, *The Psychiatric Hospital*, p. xi.

26. Belknap, *Human Problems*, p. 232. See also Paul S. Barrabee, "A Study of a Mental Hospital: The Effect of its Structure on its Functions" (Ph.D. diss., Harvard University, 1951); and Stanton and Schwartz, *The Mental Hospital*.

27. Belknap, *Human Problems*, p. xi.

28. Rees, "Some Observations on the Psychiatric Patient," p. 527.

29. E. Cumming and J. Cumming, *Closed Ranks* (Cambridge, Mass.: Harvard University Press, 1957), p. 55.

30. Belknap, *Human Problems*, p. 212. There is a delightful historical irony here: nineteenth-century lunacy reformers in both England and America used precisely these two potential benefits, humanitarianism and economy, as their major arguments for *building* an asylum system. See Scull, "Museums of Madness"; Grob, *The State and the Mentally Ill;* and Deutsch, *Mentally Ill in America.*

31. Hunt, "Ingredients of a Rehabilitation Program," p. 21 et passim.

32. Mechanic, *Mental Health*, pp. 96–120; G. Caplan, *Principles of Preventive Psychiatry* (New York: Basic Books, 1964); G. Caplan, "Community Psychiatry: Introduction and Overview," in *Concepts of Community Psychiatry*, ed. S. E. Goldstone (Washington, D.C.: Government Printing Office), pp. 3–18; and M. Susser, *Community Psychiatry: Epidemiological and Social Themes* (New York: Random House, 1968).

33. J. Wolpert and E. Wolpert, "The Relocation of Released Mental Hospital Patients into Residential Communities," mimeographed (1974), p. 73.

such discoveries and propaganda both logically implied and naturally produced a change in social policy.

No one familiar with the climate of contemporary liberal intellectual opinion can avoid recognizing the depths of current pessimism there concerning the value of institutional responses to all forms of deviance, or the degree to which decarceration has been elevated, in such circles, to the status of a new humanitarian myth, comparable only with the similar myth that attended the birth of the asylum. But, in general, social policy proves only mildly susceptible to the shifting intellectual fads and fashions of the day. The question remains as to why this one at least appears to have had so profound an impact. Granted that the advocates of the community approach vigorously proselytized on behalf of their cause, why were they listened to—particularly when their proposals ran counter to the deeply entrenched interests of institutional psychiatry, long a powerful interest group in the political arena?

The conventional answer to these questions has three basic elements: the emergence of a renewed concern on the part of the state for the patient's social and therapeutic rights; the therapeutic promise of community care, an appeal bolstered by the favorable outcome of early efforts in this direction; and an alleged increasing tolerance on the part of the community towards the mentally disturbed. Each of these arguments, though, is seriously defective. It is all very well to assert that "the higher level of tolerance for deviance in the post-World War II period has raised the prospect that the mentally ill and retarded could be returned to families and retained in residential neighborhoods."[34] But where this increased tolerance comes from is not explained; nor is evidence offered to demonstrate its existence—unless, of course, it is a mere tautology (such people have been returned to the community, which shows that the community must be more tolerant than it once was; therefore increased tolerance must account for the return of the insane to the community). And the issue is still more complicated than is suggested by asking why or whether a changed tolerance for deviant behavior has developed: there is also the question of whether this change is an independent (as the Wolperts would have it) or a dependent variable; whether it helped to produce the change in policy, or was itself the product of the changed policy. What evidence we do have bearing on this issue suggests the latter is the more plausible causal sequence. It quite clearly became official policy in this period to discourage the admission or readmission of patients who in an earlier era would have been taken without question, and whom relatives or neighbors actively sought to have

institutionalized.[35] Neither are the vociferous community protests that usually accompany a policy of community treatment the reaction one would expect from those becoming more tolerant of the presence of deviance.

In view of what we know of the circumstances surrounding the return of the mentally ill to the community, the claim that this change was motivated by either concern for the patients' rights, or because of the therapeutic benefits likely to ensue, seems if anything still more disingenuous. Indeed, the Wolperts' own findings reveal this to be so. In the first place, "the massive release of patients to facilities in residential neighborhoods" *preceded* "substantial data collection and analysis" on the likely effects of decarceration.[36] In fact, even now we lack "substantiation that community care is advantageous for clients." Put bluntly, "data have not been generated by the mental health sector nor by the evaluators of their programs nor by those who fund the care system . . . for determining what kinds of facilities are most beneficial or where those facilities should be sited."[37] Furthermore, "the hospital release trend is independent of community after-care facilities,"[38] and for at least one important class of ex-patients, discharge in such circumstances, far from proving therapeutic, has been positively fatal: "mortality rates for elderly patients increases [*sic*] dramatically upon release. . . ."[39]

Overall, there has been no adequate licensing, supervision, or inspection of board and care facilities for released mental patients, and no effort to avoid their "ghettoization" in the poorest, least desirable of neighborhoods.[40] And, "in the absence of adequate after-care and rehabilitation services, the term 'community care' . . . [remained] merely an inflated catch phrase

35. See Brown et al., *Schizophrenia,* chs, 3, 5, esp. pp. 51ff., for case histories of individuals exhibiting grossly disturbed behavior whose hospitalization was repeatedly resisted by the authorities even when requested by relatives experiencing severe difficulty in coping. See also *New York Times,* March 18, 1974, pp. 1, 17.

36. Wolpert and Wolpert, "Relocation of Released Mental Hospital Patients," p. 14.

37. Ibid., p. 19.

38. Ibid., p. 25. For recent criticism of New York State for announcing the restriction of hospitalization of geriatric and chronic schizophrenics without making alternative provision for such persons, see *Psychiatric News,* October 4, 1972, p. 1.

39. Wolpert and Wolpert, "Relocation of Released Mental Patients," p. 48.

40. For California, see H. R. Lamb and V. Goertzel, "Discharged Mental Patients—Are They Really in the Community?," *Archives of General Psychiatry* 24 (1971): 29–34; S. O. Silberstein, "A Survey of the Mental Health Functions of Systems of Residential Home Care for the Mentally Ill and Retarded in the Sacramento Area," mimeographed (1969). For New York and Michigan, see *New York Times,* January 21, March, 22, 24, 1974. For Canada, see Stewart et al. "Problems in Phasing Out." For England, see J. K. Wing, "How Many Psychiatric Beds?," *Psychological Medicine* 1 (1971): 188–90.

34. Ibid., p. 72.

which concealed morbidity in the patients and distress in the relatives."[41] As a natural consequence, "one form of confinement has been replaced by another, and the former patients are just as insulated from community attention and care as they were in the state hospital."[42] As far back as 1961, the Joint Commission on Mental Illness and Health, itself engaged in promoting the notion of decarceration, was forced to concede that "generally little attention is given to the psychological and social needs of these patients."[43] Over the past thirteen years the situation has not changed, and, to judge from the continuing official inaction, this does not greatly concern the authorities. Recent research has shown that it remains true that "for the long-term hospitalized patient, the move is usually into a boarding home facility . . . where little effort is directed toward social and vocational rehabilitation."[44] In practice, "it is only an illusion that patients who are placed in boarding or family care homes are 'in the community.' . . . These facilities are in most respects like small long-term state hospital wards isolated from the community. One is overcome by the depressing atmosphere, not because of the physical appearance of the boarding home, but because of the passivity, isolation and inactivity of the residents. . . ."[45] The picture is a grim one, and scarcely what one would gather from reading the liberal rhetoric on decarceration.

IV

As we have seen, a crucial element in rendering plausible the standard accounts of the move towards a noninstitutional response to mental illness has been the purported discovery by social scientists in the 1950s and 1960s of the institutional syndrome—the notion that confinement in an asylum may amplify and even produce disturbance, that in the "moral career of the mental patient" the institution may be more important than the illness. Supposedly, what had formerly been held to be the natural products of an unfolding intraindividual pathology were finally, and for the first time, seen as in large part the reflection of a natural response to a grossly deforming environment.[46] But such claims reflect the narrow and ahistorical vision of those making them. Despite the pretensions of those sociologists convinced that the understanding of society waits upon advances in

their particular discipline, recognition of the baneful effects of incarceration emerged early in the history of the asylum and took sophisticated forms. A number of nineteenth-century critics, both English and American, developed criticisms of institutionalization that in their essentials, and with respect to either their intellectual cogency or empirical support, were in no way inferior to the modern critique elaborated by Goffman and others.[47]

As this suggests, what we need to explain are the reasons why advocates of deinstitutionalization finally found a receptive audience in the 1950s and 1960s. If the shift towards community treatment was not the automatic product of advances in social scientific understanding, or of some miraculous technological breakthrough, then how else can we account for this change? To answer this question requires that we grasp the intimate relationships that exist between the nature of the social control apparatus and the social system as a whole, and the ways in which changes in the one prompt changes in the other. This is what we shall now attempt to do.

During the second half of the nineteenth century, whatever criticisms some intellectuals and professionals might make of asylums, so far as most people were concerned, such places remained a convenient way of getting rid of inconvenient people. The community was used, by now, to disposing of the derelict and troublesome in this fashion, placing them where, as one physician put it, "they are for the most part harmless because they are kept out of harm's way."[48] Asylums' earlier association with social reform gave a lingering humanitarian gloss to the huge, cheap, and avowedly custodial dumps where the refuse of the community was now gathered together. Meanwhile, medical control of these institutions, and the rhetoric about cure that went with that control, provided a further legitimation of the custodial warehousing of these, the most difficult and troublesome elements of the disreputable poor. The working people, lacking an alternative means of ridding themselves of what, in the context of nineteenth-century working-class existence, was undoubtedly an intollerable burden—caring for their sick, aged, decrepit, or otherwise incapacitated relatives—had little option but to make use of the asylum. From the upper classes'

41. Brown et al., *Schizophrenia*, p. 10.

42. Wolpert and Wolpert, "Relocation of Released Mental Hospital Patients," p. 61.

43. *Joint Commission on Mental Illness*, p. 184.

44. Lamb and Goertzel, "Discharged Mental Patients," p. 29.

45. Ibid., p. 31.

46. Brown et al., *Schizophrenia;* Wing and Brown, *Institutionalism.*

47. See, for example, S. G. Howe, "A Letter to J. H. Wilkins, H. B. Rogers and F. B. Fay, Commissioners of Massachusetts for the State Reform School for Girls" (Boston, 1854); J. Arlidge, *On the State of Lunacy.* . . . (London: Churchill, 1959); H. Maudsley, *The Physiology and Pathology of the Mind* (London, 1867); J. C. Bucknill, *The Care of the Insane and Their Legal Control* (London: MacMillan, 1880). These critics' ideas, and the reasons for their lack of impact on public policy in this period, are discussed in detail in A. T. Scull, *Decarceration*, chs. 6, 7.

48. *Hanwell Asylum Annual Report*, vol. 25 (Middlesex, England: Hanwell Asylum Annual Reports), p. 36.

perspective, the existence of asylums to treat the insane at public expense could be invoked as a practical demonstration of their own humanitarian concern for the less fortunate.

Far from asylums having been "altruistic institutions . . . detached from the social structures that perpetuate poverty,"[49] they were clearly important elements in sustaining those structures. For in this period, the influential classes in both England and America were all but unanimous in their unwillingness to insulate the population as a whole from the twin spurs of poverty and unemployment. Under the conditions characteristic of early industrial capitalism, relief threatened to undermine radically the whole notion of a labor market. It interfered with labor mobility. It encouraged the retention of "a vast inert mass of redundant labor" in rural areas,[50] where the demand for labor was subject to wide seasonal fluctuations.[51] It distorted the operations of the labor market, most especially on account of its tendency, via the vagaries of local administration, "to create cost differentials as between the various parts of the country."[52] And by its removal of the threat of individual starvation, it had a pernicious effect on labor productivity and discipline. On the ideological level, this determination to restrict relief was at once reflected and strengthened by the hegemony of classical liberalism. The latter's insistence that every man was to be free to pursue his fortune and at the same time was to be held responsible for his own success or failure, coupled with its dogmatic certainty that interference with the dictates of the free market could only be counterproductive in the long run (a proposition that could even be theoretically "proved"), rendered the whole notion of social protectionism an anathema.[53]

Hence came the stress on the principle of "less eligibility" (enforced in large part through the discipline of institutions like workhouses and asylums)[54] and the abhorrence of payments to individuals in the community (so-called outdoor relief) as the two central elements in dealing with the problems of extreme incapacity of one sort or another. For despite the ferocity of their ideological proclamations,[55] as a practical political matter, the

upper classes were aware of the impossibility of adhering rigidly to the dictates of the market. But though "the residuum of paupers could not, admittedly, be left actually to starve,"[56] the pressures of the market place must be interfered with as little as possible. Here, an institutionally based system allowed the maintenance of conditions of relief that ensured that "no one with any conceivable alternatives would seek public aid."[57] In such a context, the asylum played its part, removing from lower-class families the impossible burdens imposed by those incapable of providing for their own subsistence, and thus ensuring that a potent source of discontent could be neutralized without having to alter society's basic structural arrangements.

The rejection of anything resembling a modern system of social protection or welfare and the use of the asylum were intimately connected in yet another way, for an important implication of the highly restricted welfare policies characteristic of the United States and England until well into the twentieth century was that asylums represented one of the few costs of production that were socialized, i.e., taken over by the state rather than the private sector. Thus the fiscal pressures from this source on the state were relatively slight, and the expenses associated with a system of segregative control were more readily absorbed.

As capitalism developed further, however, so the demands on the poor-law system changed, from instilling discipline and industriousness in a period of abundant unskilled human labor, to maintaining the capacity and willingness to work of an increasingly valuable resource. By now, the "workers' physical strength and good will had become important assets. Social insurance became one of the means of investing in human capital."[58] Though slowed in varying degrees by the persisting appeal of classical liberal ideology, both societies began to construct the basic elements of the modern

49. Herbert Gans, preface to Colin Greer, *The Great School Legend* (New York: Basic Books, 1972), p. xi.

50. Redford, cited in Karl Polanyi, *The Great Transformation* (Boston: Beacon Books, 1957), p. 301.

51. Polanyi, *The Great Transformation*, chs. 7, 8; E. Hobsbawm, *Industry and Empire* (London: Penguin Books, 1969), pp. 99–100, 104–5.

52. Polanyi, *The Great Transformation*, p. 301.

53. See G. V. Rimlinger, *Welfare Policy and Industrialization in Europe, America and Russia* (New York: Wiley, 1971), esp. ch. 3.

54. See F. Piven and R. Cloward, *Regulating the Poor* (New York: Random House, 1971).

55. For example, Herbert Spencer wrote: "The well-being of existing

humanity, and the unfolding of it into this ultimate perfection, are both secured by the same beneficent, though severe discipline, to which animate nature at large is subject: a discipline which is pitiless in working out of good: a felicity pursuing law which never swerves for the avoidance of partial and temporary suffering. The poverty of the incapable, the distress which comes upon the imprudent, the starvation of the idle, and those shoulderings aside of the weak by the strong, which leaves so many 'in shallows and miseries,' are the decrees of a large, far-seeing benevolence. . . . Nevertheless, when regarded not separately, but in connection with the interests of universal humanity, these harsh fatalities are seen to be full of the highest beneficence—the same beneficence which brings to early graves the children of diseased parents, and singles out the low-spirited, the intemperate, and debilitated as the victims of an epidemic." Spencer, *Social Statics* (London: Williams and Norgate, 1868), pp. 353–54.

56. Hobsbawm, *Industry and Empire*, p. 88.

57. Piven and Cloward, *Regulating the Poor*, p. 33.

58. Rimlinger, *Welfare Policy*, p. 10.

welfare state.[59] In the remainder of this paper, I shall advance and attempt to document the contention that this development, coupled with a virtually simultaneous and massive expansion of the role of the state in other sectors of English and American society, decisively transformed the social context within which the social control apparatus was embedded; and that the ramifications of these changes account in large part for the move towards community treatment for the deviant.

To summarize my thesis briefly at the outset, I shall argue that, with the coming of the welfare state, the asylum system became, in relative terms, far more costly and difficult to justify. Formerly, there had been little or no alternative to keeping the chronically disabled cases of insanity in the asylum, for although the overwhelming majority were harmless, they could not provide for their own subsistence and no alternative sources of support were available to sustain them in the outside world. However, with the advent of a wide range of welfare programs providing just such support, the opportunity cost of neglecting community care in favor of asylum treatment—inevitably far more costly than the most generous schemes for welfare payments—rose sharply.[60] Simultaneously, the increasing socialization of production costs by the state, something that has been taking place at an increasing pace during and since the Second World War, and of which modern welfare measures are merely one very important example, produced a growing fiscal crisis, as expenditures continuously threatened to outrun available revenue.[61] In combination, a focus on the interplay of these factors enables us to resolve what at first sight is a paradox—namely, the emergence and persistence of efforts at retrenchment at a time when general expenditures on welfare items were expanding rapidly. For it is precisely the expansion of the one that made both possible and desirable the contraction of the other.

59. Ibid., chs. 5, 6.

60. Among the welfare programs adopted since World War II are: 1) in England, expansion of the state old-age and widows' pension systems, improved unemployment insurance and the provision of so-called National Assistance, compensation for industrial injuries, and state-supported health care; 2) for the U.S.A., expansion of old-age and survivors' insurance, expanded social security coverage and unemployment insurance, workmen's compensation and public assistance, and state-supported health care for the elderly and a portion of the poor.

61. In the words of James O'Connor: "Although the state has socialized more and more capital costs, the social surplus (including profits) continues to be appropriated privately. The socialization of costs and the private appropriation of profits creates a fiscal crisis, or 'structural gap,' between state expenditures and state revenues. The result is a persistent tendency for state expenditures to increase more rapidly than the means for financing them." O'Connor, *The Fiscal Crisis of the State* (New York: St. Martin's Press, 1973), p. 9. Such problems have been felt most acutely on the local, city, and (in the United States) state levels, but have also become increasingly evident at the central level. Ibid., esp. pp. 211ff.

Clearly, the advent of the welfare state reflected in some measure a lessened resistance to such legislation on the part of a capitalist class increasingly led to confront the implications of the fact that, in an advanced economy, "human faculties are as important a means of production as any other kind of capital."[62] Equally, however, the historical genesis of the welfare state is also the product of political struggles on the part of increasingly organized labor movements. To this extent, welfare measures represent social concessions made under the threat of, or in anticipation of, popular discontent and struggle.[63] More specifically, "the greater security enjoyed by many during wartime, despite the absolute fall in living standards, . . . [and] the political necessity for capitalist states to avoid a return to slumps of the interwar scale, and their ability to implement this by means of Keynesian policies . . . made demands for extended state intervention in the field of welfare irresistible. . . ."[64] The postwar growth in the relative strength of the labor movement, substantially a reflection of the largely successful pursuit of full-employment policies during this period, has produced a consolidation and extension of these earlier gains. All this has formed part of a process whereby, in all advanced capitalist societies (and particularly since 1945), there has been a prolonged expansion of government expenditures as the state moves to take on "a qualitatively expanded role in capitalist social formations."[65] Especially notable, apart from the rising outlays on social services, has been the growing expenditure on such things as aid to private industry and on items designed to improve the economic infrastructure (e.g., roads, education, and government-supported research and development).[66] The budgetary impact of all this has been startling. Even if one leaves aside the other components of state spending, in the United Kingdom, the social services have swallowed a proportion of the G.N.P. that has risen from 10.9 percent in 1937 to 24.9 percent by 1973; and an essentially similar pattern has been observable in the United States, where such outlays

62. Alfred Marshall, *Principles of Economics*, 8th ed. (New York: Macmillan, 1920), p. 229.

63. In England, for example, the Beveridge Report (which laid down the outlines of the British Welfare State), the so-called White Paper on Full Employment, and the 1944 Education Act, "were consciously seen as a necessary part of the war effort by integrating all classes and alleviating discontent." Ian Gough, "State Expenditure in Advanced Capitalism," *New Left Review* 92 (July–August 1975): 53–92.

64. Ibid., p. 69.

65. Ibid., p. 53. Gough's is the most satisfactory single analysis of this development, but see also O'Connor, *Fiscal Crisis*; D. Yaffe, "The Marxian Theory of Crisis, Capital, and the State," *Bulletin of the Conference of Socialist Economists* (1972); and idem, "The Crisis of Profitability," *New Left Review* 80 (1973).

66. Gough, "State Expenditure," p. 60; also OECD, "Public Expenditure Trends," *Occasional Studies* (July 1970), p. 48.

have risen from 9 percent of the G.N.P. in 1955 to 15 percent in 1969.[67]

A number of factors besides real improvements in the level of services have contributed to the upward pressure on state budgets in this period. The United States and England, like other developed economies in the capitalist world system, have found that the costs of state services (especially social services) rise faster than the average price level, everywhere forcing an ever higher level of expenditure merely to maintain services at the same level in real terms. Undoubtedly this reflects the fact that on the average the level of productivity rises less fast in the state than in the private sector of the economy, which, in turn, reflects the relative predominance of low-productivity-labor intensive services in the state sector. Then, too, in addition to the technical difficulties associated with any effort to raise productivity in service occupations, the situation is "undoubtedly exacerbated in the case of state services by the absence of competitive pressure to reduce costs."[68] Furthermore, it is clear that "the size of income maintenance expenditures has been heavily influenced by the growing proportion of aged in Britain and America...,"[69] and indeed, by the general "tendency of the dependent population to expand as a proportion of the total."[70]

The budgetary strains on state mental hospitals reflected the impact of these general factors making for severe cost inflation, as well as two more specific conjunctural factors. The widespread unionization of state employees and the associated "advent of the eight-hour day and forty-hour week in state institutions ... virtually doubled unit costs...."[71] On top of this, a number of class action suits on behalf of hospital inmates were brought during the 1960s and 1970s (in the United States at least). Decisions such as *Wyatt v. Stickney* (1972) attempted to lay down minimum standards of treatment, while others sought to eliminate "institutional peonage," the employment of unpaid patient labor to reduce institutional costs. To the extent that they are implemented, these decisions unquestionably "force upon the states huge expenditures...,"[72] but they will

obviously have no force if institutions can be emptied and closed instead.[73]

In such circumstances, the continuation of an increasingly costly social control policy that, in terms of effectiveness, possesses few advantages over an apparently much cheaper alternative becomes increasingly difficult to justify; and the attractiveness of that alternative to governments under ever greater budgetary pressures, whatever the political difficulties in the way of its realization, becomes steadily harder to resist. In the words of those who have served as bureaucratic managers of the system, "rising costs more than any other factor have made it obvious that support of state hospitals is politically unfeasible. . . . this is the principal factor behind the present push to get rid of state hospitals."[74] To put it bluntly, "in a sense our backs are to the wall; it's *phase out* before we go *bankrupt.*"[75]

To the extent that psychoactive drugs have played a role in the adoption of a policy of decarceration, I would suggest that it is the existence of these structural pressures that in large measure accounts for their being used in this way, rather than simply to ease the problems of internal management in asylums. Similarly, the impact of these pressures explains the differential susceptibility of the relevant audiences to the substantially identical criticisms of the asylum put forward in the 1860s and 1870s, and again in the 1950s and 1960s. The arguments had not changed, but the structural context in which they were advanced clearly had. Their contemporary reappearance allowed governments to save money while simultaneously giving their policy a humanitarian gloss. And to take the argument a step further, it is the intensity and extent of such pressures that account for the persistence of this policy despite public resistance to it, and despite the accumulation of evidence showing that, in terms of its ostensible goals, community care is substantially a failure.

As states realized that decarceration was feasible, they began to maneuver to obtain the cost savings it offered. Some of the largest savings immediately realizable came from the cancellation of planned new construction, and decisions to do this were widespread.[76] In the United

67. Gough, "State Expenditure," p. 61.

68. Ibid., p. 76.

69. Samual Mencher, *Poor Law to Poverty Program: Economic Security Policy in Britain and the United States* (Pittsburgh: University of Pittsburgh Press, 1967), p. 316.

70. Gough, "State Expenditure," p. 76. Between 1955 and 1969, for example, the proportion of elderly in the population rose in every OECD country, and it is apparent that this trend will continue for at least the next decade.

71. Paul R. Dingman, "The Case for the State Mental Hospital," in *Where is My Home?: Proceedings of a Conference on the Closing of State Mental Hospitals* (Scottsdale, Arizona, 1974), pp. 28–52, esp. p. 48.

72. M. Greenblatt, "Historical Forces Affecting the Closing of Mental Hospitals," in *Where is My Home?*, pp. 3–17.

73. David J. Rothman suggests that at least some advocates of decarceration have recognized and consciously exploited this situation. As he puts it, "they believe that the number of individuals incarcerated makes standards of the type imposed [in *Wyatt vs. Stickney*] too expensive to implement. They anticipate that a state, rather than upgrading its institutions, will recoil at the cost and abdicate its responsibility. Convinced that asylums are no more effective than prisons, they welcome this abdication; it would bring, at the very least, a drastic reduction in the number of people incarcerated for mental illness." Rothman, "Decarcerating Prisoners and Patients," *The Civil Liberties Review*, vol. 1 (1973).

74. Dingman, "The Case for the State Mental Hospital," p. 48.

75. Greenblatt, "Historical Forces," p. 8; emphasis in the original.

76. H. Brill and R. E. Patton, "Analysis of Population Reduction in

States, large cost savings for hard-pressed local governments were also available where patients could be discharged from state hospitals (where they were provided for at state expense) to private, profit-making convalescent homes—not just because provision in such places was less costly, but also because changes in the social security laws in the late 1950s made it possible for these people to collect social security (and thus be supported at Federal expense) so long as they were not in psychiatric institutions.[77] A number of states followed California's lead in providing financial inducements to counties to avoid sending patients to state hospitals for in-patient care.[78] In England, ministerial calls for ruthless cutbacks in the number of psychiatric beds were coupled with plans that included virtually no provision for increased community care. The plans promised major cost savings, and as a consequence, drew extensive support from right wing political figures.[79]

For reasons we have already discussed, the pace of expansion of state expenditures on social services in both countries increased markedly during the 1960s and 1970s. As it did so, so the incentives to accelerate the movement towards deinstitutionalization likewise intensified. And it is precisely in this period that the momentum of the drive to shut down institutions and minimize incarceration gathered its greatest force. The range of devices used to divert potential inmates away from institutions was further expanded, and those already in existence were applied with greater urgency and effect. Welfare regulations were changed to make aid to mental patients discharged into the community more readily available.[80] Screening projects were set up to encourage placement of potential admissions, particularly geriatric

cases, in nonhospital settings.[81] Involuntary commitment was made far more difficult in some jurisdictions, also helping to reduce hospital intakes.[82] Perhaps most elaborate and effective of all was the system devised by the state of California in the Lanterman-Petris-Short Act (1967). Under this approach, counties were, in effect, bribed not to use state hospitals—a scheme that led to a further acceleration in the decline of state hospital populations, allowed the closure of four state hospitals within a five-year period, and produced substantial cost savings for the state.[83]

Once the drive for control of soaring costs is seen as the primary factor underlying the move towards decarceration, both these and a number of other aspects of this change, which formerly appeared either fortuitous or inexplicable, become readily comprehensible. To begin with, this perspective allows us to see the spread of the policy of deinstitutionalization to the criminal justice sector, and the rise of efforts to decarcerate criminals and delinquents, as part of a single, unitary phenomenon. At first, movement in this direction was tentative, small-scale, and experimental. But by the late 1960s, as the pressure to alleviate the upward spiral in relief costs mounted, as the magnitude of the capital expenditure otherwise required for new prisons and reformatories became apparent, and as the size of the savings community approaches can produce on current outlays was documented, there began a rapid expansion of programs designed to divert the criminal and the delinquent away from the institution.[84]

New York State Mental Hospitals during the First Four Years of Large-Scale Therapy with Psychotropic Drugs,'' *American Journal of Psychiatry* 116 (1959): 495–508, esp. p. 495.

77. J. Myers and L. Bean, *A Decade Later: A Follow-up of Social Class and Mental Illness* (New York: John Wiley, 1968), pp. 55–56.

78. F. Chu and S. Trotter, *The Madness Establishment* (New York: Grossman, 1974), p. 42; Horizon House Institute for Research and Development, *The Future Role of State Mental Hospitals* (Philadelphia, July 1975), p. 143.

79. See National Association for Mental Health, *Report of the Annual Conference* (1961), pp. 4–10; Home Office, *Report of the Committee on Local Authority and Allied Personal Social Services* (London: HMSO, 1968), para. 339; MIND, ''Community Care Provisions for the Mentally Ill,'' MIND Report no. 4 (National Association for Mental Health, 1971); K. Jones, *A History of the Mental Health Services* (London: Routledge & Kegan Paul, 1972), ch. 13, esp. p. 326. By 1971 mental hospital populations in England and Wales had fallen by approximately 50,000; yet in the entire country there were less than 3,300 people in local-authority-provided facilities for care in the community.

80. Janet Chase, ''Where Have All the Patients Gone?,'' *Human Behavior* (October 1973), pp. 14–21; esp. p. 18; and Steven P. Segal, ''Life in Board and Care: Its Political and Social Context,'' in *Where is My Home?*, pp. 141–50.

81. L. J. Epstein and A. Simon, ''Alternatives to State Hospitalization for Geriatric Mentally Ill,'' *American Journal of Psychiatry* 124 (1968): 955–61, esp. 958.

82. Chu and Trotter, *The Madness Establishment*, p. 43; and Segal, ''Life in Board and Care,'' p. 141.

83. This involved extending the principle embodied in the earlier Short-Doyle Act along lines similar to those of the Probation Subsidy Program, which was adopted to encourage the decarceration of criminals and juvenile delinquents. See Robert Smith, *A Quiet Revolution: Probation Subsidy* (Washington, D.C.: Youth Development and Delinquency Prevention Administration, 1971), which provides compelling evidence of the degree to which decarceration on a massive basis followed on careful assessments of the relative costs of incarceration and decarceration. In essence, the scheme depended on developing an estimate of how many beds a county would need in the coming year, based on its prior usage and estimated trends of the overall decline in hospital populations. A county that used less than its allocation would then be rewarded with a payment of $15 a day per patient involved—but the following year would find its bed allotment reduced accordingly. Conversely, if a county used more than its ''share'' of mental hospital beds, it would suffer a financial penalty in the form of reduced state assistance with its budget. See Chase, ''Where Have All the Patients Gone?,'' p. 16; Chu and Trotter, *The Madness Establishment*, pp. 42–43; *Sacramento Union*, March 19, 1974; and Greenblatt, ''Historical Forces,'' p. 4.

84. For a discussion of these developments, see E. Vorenberg and J. Vorenberg, ''Early Diversion from the Criminal Justice System,'' in *Prisoners in America*, ed. L. Ohlin (Englewood Cliffs, N.J.: Prentice-

Then again, ever since segregative control became the dominant mode of managing deviance, the public has shown consistently little desire or inclination to have officially labeled serious deviants returned to their midst.[85] Studies made in the earlier phases of the decarceration movement indicated a continuing attitude of hostility, fear, and intolerance towards the mentally ill,[86] and the presence and strength of these feelings have been amply documented by subsequent reactions, as efforts have continued to return the mentally ill to the community. Residents have fought hard to ensure that if the mental patients are released, they are not released into *their* neighborhoods, a favorite tactic in this battle being the enactment of restrictive zoning ordinances.[87] Similar measures have frequently been employed to exclude such undesirable elements as criminals and addicts; and a recent study of the diversion of juvenile delinquents likewise concluded that "the actual establishment of group homes in local communities is often vehemently resisted by residents."[88]

These resistance strategies have naturally been most successfully employed by middle and upper class communities. Even those who have devoted their well-paid expertise to developing public relations techniques for the "neutralization of community resistance to group homes" have been forced to concede that these community homes have the best chance of being established in transient neighborhoods, "or where the local residents are not particularly capable of organized opposition." And they confess there are but "few strategies with potential for gaining access to a community that has the ability to organize itself in opposition, or in support of, issues."[89] In any event, on cost grounds, there has been little pressure to place ex-patients or other types of

deviants in such respectable settings. Instead decarceration has produced:

> the growing ghettoization of the returning ex-patients along with other dependent groups in the population: the growing succession of inner-city land-use to institutions providing services to the dependent and needy . . . [and] the forced immobility of the chronically disabled within deteriorated urban neighborhoods . . . , areas where land-use deterioration has proceeded to such a point that the land market is substantially unaffected by the introduction of community services and their clients. . . .[90]

In such areas there is also an absence of organized community opposition to the presence of these people.[91] As if they are industrial wastes that can without risk be left to decompose in some well-contained dump, these problem populations have increasingly been dealt with by a resort to their ecological separation and isolation in areas where they are by and large no longer visible, and where they may be safely left to prey on one another.[92]

But in many places, the sheer numbers involved have led to spillovers into residential, usually working- or lower-middle-class, communities. The opposition this has aroused has been further stimulated by complaints over the scope of after-care facilities provided (or rather not provided). If the decarceration program was to live up to rhetorical claims about its being undertaken for the ex-patients' welfare, these after-care facilities would have had to be extensively present, but this would have been extremely costly, and if the program was to realize financial savings they had to be substantially absent.

Hall, Inc., 1973), pp. 151–83; and Scull, *Decarceration*, forthcoming, ch. 3. Significantly, all this occurred in the absence of any clear-cut demonstration of the rehabilitative potential of community corrections; indeed, this still remains to be demonstrated.

85. For some nineteenth-century comments on this phenomenon, see *Massachusetts State Board of Health, Lunacy, and Charity* 3 (1881): xcix; "Non-Restraint in the Treatment of the Insane," *Edinburgh Review* 131 (1870): 215–31; esp. 221; Arlidge, *On the State of Lunacy*, p. 7; and Scull, "Museums of Madness," ch. 9.

86. J. C. Nunally, *Popular Conceptions of Mental Health* (New York: Holt, 1961); and Cumming and Cumming, *Closed Ranks*.

87. Wolpert and Wolpert, "Relocation of Released Mental Hospital Patients," p. 35; *New York Times*, February 22, March 22, 1974; and Segal, "Life in Board and Care," pp. 143ff.

88. David F. Greenberg, "Problems in Community Corrections," mimeographed (1975), pp. 28ff; and R. Coates and A. Miller, "Neutralization of Community Resistance to Group Homes," in *Closing Correctional Institutions*, ed. Y. Bakal (Boston: Lexington, 1973), p. 67.

89. Coates and Miller, "Neutralization," pp. 78-79. As this article indicates, the state has been highly manipulative in an effort to secure acquiescence in such policies.

90. Wolpert and Wolpert, "Relocation of Released Mental Hospital Patients," pp. 33, 38.

91. *New York Times*, February 1, 1974; C. Anspacher, "What Happens to Ex-Mental Patients?," San Francisco *Chronicle*, September 4, 1972; M. Schumach, "Halfway Houses for Former Mental Patients Create Serious Problems for City's Residential Communities," *New York Times*, January 21, 1974; S. Trotter, "The Mentally Ill: From Back Wards to Back Alleys," Washington *Post*, February 24, 1974; U. Aviram and S. Segal, "Exclusion of the Mentally Ill: A Reflection on an Old Problem in a New Context," *Archives of General Psychiatry* 29 (1973): 126–31, esp. 130–31; California State Employees Association, *Where Have All the Patients Gone?* (Sacramento, 1972), pp. 8–9; Chase, "Where Have All the Patients Gone?," p. 19; and Robert Reich and Lloyd Siegal, "Psychiatry under Siege: The Chronic Mentally Ill Shuffle to Oblivion," *Psychiatric Annal* 3 (November 1973): 37–55, esp. 42ff.

92. In San Jose, for example, "in a 20 square block area—an area also heavily peopled by alcoholics, drug users and prostitutes, live over 1,100 of the mentally disordered." Chase, "Where Have All the Mental Patients Gone?," p. 19. The bureaucrats in charge of the community care program offer disingenuous defenses of this: Miller, for example, the head of the California developmental disabilities program, commented: "If a patient wants to go to a lousy facility and stay there, he has as much right to do that as you and I do." Cited in ibid., p. 20.

They are absent.[93] Thus, "the actual transfer of patients has tended to favor the preferred reassignment according to economy goals. For patients who have been 'dumped' by hospitals prematurely, both therapeutic and civil rights have been violated, as well as the rights of the recipient communities."[94] Governments have consistently made the most of the opportunity to secure "a major retrenchment in the psychiatric services program, made possible by a rapidly declining hospital population. The professional administrators were unable to convince the . . . government of the necessity to greatly expand community services and to redeploy staff and resources from institutional to community services."[95] In a number of instances, the complaints provoked by this situation have grown so vociferous as to force the slowdown or halting of the release program.[96]

In the burgeoning field of community corrections, the situation is essentially no different. In 1972, for example, when Massachusetts abruptly and virtually overnight closed down all juvenile reform schools in the state, not even token efforts had been made to develop an infrastructure capable of providing community supervision or control over those released.[97] As for adult criminals, the most authoritative national survey in recent years of the corrections field pointed out that "the United States spends only 20 percent of its corrections budget and allocated only 15 percent of its total staff to service the 67 percent of offenders in the corrections workload who are under community supervision. . . ." —with the result that 67 percent of felons and 76 percent of misdemeanants were dealt with in case loads of over

one hundred per staff member.[98] Six years later, following major efforts to accelerate the diversion of criminals away from prison, the situation was essentially unchanged, perhaps worse, with the average probation officer's workload "far too great to permit adequate investigation for assessment or control purposes, let alone for appreciable assistance."[99]

It is quite clear, of course, that from the point of view of state expenditures, incarcerating problem populations of all descriptions in state institutions is extraordinarily costly, usually (though perhaps not universally) far more so than a deliberate policy of coping with them in the community. This is particularly obvious when, as has unquestionably been the case with the contemporary decarceration movement, the rhetoric of promoting rehabilitation through community treatment is taken no more seriously than similarly hyberbolic talk about treatment in the institution. Under such conditions, there emerge quite startling discrepancies in comparative costs on a per capita basis. This holds true whether one looks at the case of dependent and neglected children, criminals, juvenile delinquents, or mental patients.[100]

93. The following statement was issued by Dr. Alexander Thomas, director of the Bellevue psychiatric wards: "What is so terribly disturbing is that this policy was developed by the state without planning by the state for facilities in the community to care for these patients. The fact of the matter is that these facilities are just not available. What happens is that the individuals roam the streets, helpless victims of assault." Thomas, quoted in *New York Times,* March 18, 1974. See also Greenberg, "Problems in Community Corrections," esp. p. 7.

94. Wolpert and Wolpert, "Relocation of Released Mental Hospital Patients," p. 22.

95. Stewart et al., "Problems in Phasing Out," p. 87, in a study reporting on the progress of decarceration in Saskatchewan, Canada. See also Charles P. Hall, "The Economics of Mental Health," *Hospital and Community Psychiatry* 21 (1970): 105–10; and MIND, "Community Care Provisions." In 1968, for example, Governor Reagan of California claimed that the state faced "serious fiscal problems" and used the fall in state hospital populations to justify a cut-back of over 3,000 people in hospital staffs, and trimmed the state hospital budget by $10 million, from $122 million in fiscal 1967 to $112 million in fiscal 1968. See E. Bardach, *The Skill Factor in Politics* (Berkeley: University of California Press, 1972), p. 31, ch. 5 passim.

96. In California, the state has postponed an earlier plan to close all remaining state hospitals. See Wolpert and Wolpert, "Relocation of Released Mental Hospital Patients," pp. 54-55. Similarly, the New York program was ordered slowed recently. *New York Times,* April 26, 1974.

97. See Bakal, ed., *Closing Correctional Institutions.*

98. The President's Commission on Law Enforcement and the Administration of Justice, *Task Force Report: Corrections* (Washington, D.C.: U.S. Government Printing Office, 1967), pp. 4-5.

99. D. Glaser, "Correction of Adult Offenders in the Community," in *Prisoners in America,* ed. Lloyd Ohlin (Englewood Cliffs, N.J.: Prentice-Hall, 1973), pp. 89–116, esp. p. 99; see also Ramsay Clark, *Crime in America* (New York: Simon and Schuster, 1970), p. 237.

100. Dependent and neglected children: In California, "the ratio of institutional costs to foster family reimbursement rates is approximately 5:1." Jeffrey Koshel, *Deinstitutionalization—Dependent and Neglected Children* (Washington, D.C.: The Urban Institute, 1973), p. 39. In New York, "the cost of . . . care appears to be about five times the expense a family on a low-cost budget would incur in rearing its own child." In some cases, the costs of providing for a single family's children via institutionalization may ultimately run to over $500,000." David Fanshell and Eugene Shinn, *Dollars and Sense in the Foster Care of Children: A Look at Cost Factors* (New York: Child Welfare League of America, 1972), pp. 21–22, 30, Appendix A.

Criminals: Here, institutionalization is generally at least ten times as expensive. Recent English figures indicate that prison there costs 30–35 pounds a day versus 2 pounds for probation. *Young Adult Offenders: Report of the Advisory Council on the Penal System* (London: HMSO, 1974), p. 39. In the United States, "state institutional cost is about six times that of parole and about 14 times that of probation." *Task Force Report: Corrections,* pp. 194, 10; see also E. E. Flynn, "Jails and Criminal Justice," in *Prisoners in America,* ed. Lloyd Ohlin (Englewood Cliffs, N.J.: Prentice-Hall, 1973), pp. 49–88, esp. p. 54. In California, where a careful study was made of the comparative cost of the two approaches prior to the widespread use of decarceration, "legislators learned . . . that the total minimum cost of an inmate who served an average term in prison and on parole was $5,700 (the figure by 1971 was estimated to be 'in excess of $10,000'). The comparative cost for treating an offender on probation under the supervision of a probation officer with a maximum of 50 cases was $142." D. Ward, "Evaluative Research for Corrections," in ibid., pp. 184–206, esp. p. 200.

Juvenile delinquents: Again a number of experimental programs demonstrated the savings available before the policy was widely adopted. In California, costs per inmate per year in the probation subsidy

A more elaborate breakdown of the cost savings produced by community care, based on California data, is presented in Table 3. As these figures show (and as one would expect), the amount saved varies with the degree of disability (and hence care), but is always substantial. Moreover, the figures given tend to understate the actual savings realized, since the Community Services Division's calculations include administrative, placement, service, and Medi-Cal costs, while the Department of Mental Hygiene figures for state hospital costs fail to include all administrative costs.

One must grant, however, that reality is more complicated than these simply comparisons might suggest. Thus, in the short run at least, many of the costs of a mental hospital (or prison) system are fixed and unchangeable, regardless of the number of inmates occupying the institutions. As a consequence, a sizeable fraction of the savings potentially available from decarceration may not be immediately realizable, being postponed until the number of those incarcerated falls far enough to allow the state to close institutions and thereby eliminate fixed costs. But, on the other hand, to the extent that the adoption of diversionary policies obviates the need for massive expansion of the physical capacity of the existing institutional system (as has indubitably been the case with both asylums and prisons) decarceration provides a direct and immediate source of relief to the state's fiscal crisis whose importance is obvious, even while its dimensions are extraordinarily difficult to estimate with any precision.[101]

TABLE 3

Cost Savings in California through Transfer to Community Facilities in 1970

AGE	*Minimum to Moderate Care*	
18–64	State Hospital ($16.25/day)	$5,691.25
	Boarding Home ($7.13/day)	1,391.06
	Net Savings per patient year	$4,300.19
0–17	State Hospital ($16.25/day)	$5,691.25
	Family Care ($5.33/day)	2,151.32
	Net Savings per patient year	$3,539.93
	Intermediate Care	
0–17	State Hospital ($16.25/day)	$5,691.25
	Private Institution ($9.00/day)	3,578.00
	Net Savings per patient year	$2,113.25
	Nursing Care	
65+	State Hospital ($19.25/day)	$7,026.25
	Nursing Home ($12.04/day)	4,394.60
	Net Savings per patient year	$2,361.60

SOURCE: *California Department of Mental Hygiene Data, 1971.*

For example, on the capital budget side, by the mid-1950s much of the existing physical plant of the mental hospital systems in both England and America, largely an inheritance from the nineteenth century, was rapidly approaching a degree of decay and decrepitude that would have made replacement mandatory.[102] Moreover, annual admissions were already displaying a persistent tendency to rise markedly from one year to the next, a trend that, as Table 4 shows, grew still more prominent over the next decade and a half. If the proportion of admissions becoming chronic long-stay cases had remained at or close to its historic levels, substantial new construction would obviously have been called for. Instead, as retention rates fell sharply, mental hospitals were pictured as dying institutions on which it was naturally foolish to spend any more by way of renovation—and capital expenditure on them was reduced to a minimum.[103]

There can be no question but that the most careful efforts to derive estimates of the cost savings deinstitutionalization can produce have been with respect to the policy's impact on the handling of criminals

---

program were $142 compared with $4,500 for the institutional approach. Smith, *A Quiet Revolution,* p. 11. In the Provo experiment in Utah, cost per boy was $200 for probation, $609 for a more intensive program of supervision in the community, and $2,015 for incarceration. Empey, "Juvenile Justice Reform," p. 46. Another California program, the Silverlake experiment, indicated that community treatment produced savings of almost $2 million for every 1,000 offenders. L. T. Empey and S. G. Lubeck, *The Silverlake Experiment* (Chicago: Aldine, 1971), p. 310.

Mental patients: For example, Chien and Cole described an experimental community treatment program involving more intensive (and expensive) supervision than most ex-patients receive. The per patient-year cost of the community approach was $2,183; at the local state mental hospital, the comparable cost would have been $10,307. Chien and Cole, "Landlord Supervised Cooperative Apartments: A New Modality for Community-based Treatment," *American Journal of Psychiatry* 130 (1973): 156–59.

101. This last point is often overlooked by outside analysts. It is, for example, missed in Greenberg's otherwise useful review of the cost-benefit question. Greenberg, "Problems in Community Corrections," pp. 7–8. But to the states that would otherwise have been compelled to embark on a major expansion and renovation of the institutional sector, it is obvious.

For documentation of the consideration of cost savings (especially on capital account) in recommendations for a shift away from incarceration of the mentally defective, see California Assembly, "A Redefinition of State Responsibility for California's Mentally Retarded," *Assembly*

Interim Committee Reports, vol. 21, no. 10 (1963–65); and ENKI Research Institute, *A Study of California's New Mental Health Law* (Chatsworth, California, 1972), p. 11.

102. See Jones, *A History of the Mental Health Services,* chs. 12, 13; and Bardach, *The Skill Factor,* pp. 27–30.

103. See Powell in National Association for Mental Health, *Report of the Annual Conference;* and Brill and Patton, "Analysis of Population Reduction," p. 495.

TABLE 4

First Admissions to U.S. State and County Mental Hospitals, 1950 – 1968

1950	114,054	1957	128,124	1963	131,997
1951	112,979	1958	137,280	1964	138,932
1952	118,213	1959	137,795	1965	144,090
1953	123,854	1960	140,015	1966	162,486
1954	121,430	1961	146,393	1967	164,219
1955	122,284	1962	129,698	1968	175,637
1956	123,539				

SOURCES: *U.S. Department of Health, Education and Welfare: Public Health Service: Patients in Mental Institutions, Part II State and County Mental Hospitals 1950 – 1965*, N.I.M.H. statistical note no. 14.

NOTE: Figures for 1962 and all subsequent years were artificially deflated by changes in recording practices introduced at the end of 1961.

rather than the mentally ill. In all probability, this reflects a political demand for more precise data on cost differentials with respect to this problem population. Humanitarianism (otherwise known as being lenient or "soft" on criminals) has a distinct lack of political appeal in this context, so that in general the decarceration of criminals has been much more universally sold on cost grounds. As a result, estimates do exist of how much particular decarceration programs have saved the state. Best documented of all are those for the California Probation Subsidy Program: "Between 1966 and 1972 (using projections based on limited information for the 1971 – 72 fiscal year only) California can demonstrate that it has saved $185,978,820 through cancelled construction, closed institutions, and new institutions constructed but not opened. Total expenditure for probation subsidy . . . for the same period of time, will be $59,925,705."[104]

By contrast, for the mentally ill, adequate data on the savings thus produced unfortunately do not exist. Such data as we do possess are highly fragmentary and incomplete. One useful indicator, however, is provided by the information presented in Table 5. As these figures show, state expenditure on mental hospitals, excluding capital items, as a proportion of state expenditures had consistently fallen since the mid-1950s, paralleling the fall in patient numbers. In many states the decline has been steep and dramatic: between 1955 and 1974, from 5.26 to only 1.7 percent in Illinois, from 5.86 to 2.40 percent in Massachusetts, and from 7.04 to 3.20 percent in New York. And overall, the proportion of state

expenditures absorbed by the mental hospital sector has almost halved over the same period. These drastic reductions are all the more remarkable since they have been achieved in the face of a series of developments that appeared to threaten equally drastic increases in the proportion of state revenues absorbed by mental hospitals. We have already discussed a number of these: the general tendency of productivity to rise less fast in the state sector; the unionization of hospital workers and the advent of the forty-hour work week; the "right to treatment decisions" by the courts; and rising admissions rates. Given these circumstances, merely to have held state hospital costs down to a constant proportion of state budgets would clearly have been out of the question without vigorous attempts to divert potential patients away from the hospital, so as to at least slow the rate at which admissions were rising, and continuing efforts to shorten the stay of those who did end up as hospital inmates. Table 6 provides evidence of just how far the latter approach has gone in certain jurisdictions.

An important caveat should be added here: obviously, one needs to know whether decreases in expenditures on mental hospitals have been partially offset by associated rises in state expenditures elsewhere (for example, on welfare, or community treatment programs). Regrettably for the United States (as for England), "on a nationwide basis only speculation is possible about this question."[105] However, where data do exist, as in the case of California, they demonstrate that the financial advantages do persist even when these other factors are taken into account. Table 7 shows that incorporating expenditures on local (noninstitutional) mental health programs still leaves a substantial downward trend of state outlays in this area.[106]

The promise of such cost savings largely explains the curious political alliance that has fostered and supported

104. Smith, *A Quiet Revolution*, pp. 69ff. An early experimental version of the same program "obviated the investment of $6 to $8 million." *Task Force Report: Corrections*, p. 42.

105. Wolpert and Wolpert, "Relocation of Released Mental Hospital Patients," pp. 22 – 23.

106. Massachusetts provides a further indication of the extent to which states have used decarceration as a device to retrench expenditures on psychiatric services. "By 1973, there were [here] about ten times as many patients in various forms of extramural care as there were in intramural care." Greenblatt, "Historical Forces," p. 8. Yet despite this, the 90+ percent of patients in the community received only 20 percent of all Department of Mental Health Funds, the remaining 80 percent of the money being expended on the remnants of the institutional population. Dingman, "The Case for the State Mental Hospital," p. 35. For documentation of the similar lack of concern with aftercare elsewhere, see *New York Times*, March 18, 1974 (for New York); and ibid., March 22, 1974 (for Michigan). So far as one can tell, this policy of neglect has been a success, in the sense that "the financial savings to the State for each patient placed from a state hospital into community placement were reported as highly significant." Wolpert and Wolpert, "Relocation of Released Mental Hospital Patients," p. 51.

TABLE 5

Expenditures on Mental Hospitals as a Percentage of General State Expenditures, 1955—1974 (Selected States and Nationally)

	California	Illinois	Indiana	Massachusetts	Michigan	New York	Washington	All States
1955	2.57	5.26	3.53	5.86	2.73	7.04	1.79	3.38
1956	2.56	5.03	2.98	5.28	2.67	7.80	1.88	3.32
1957	2.60	4.48	3.29	4.93	2.63	7.41	2.00	3.25
1958	2.60	4.02	3.58	5.60	2.72	6.88	1.92	3.25
1959	2.43	4.00	3.38	5.36	2.61	6.66	1.91	3.09
1960	2.42	3.88	3.24	5.18	2.50	5.92	1.98	2.98
1961	2.36	4.01	3.06	5.67	2.34	5.73	2.15	2.99
1962	2.29	3.82	3.09	5.69	2.34	3.85	1.85	2.91
1963	2.23	3.79	3.02	5.13	2.34	5.37	1.64	2.79
1964	2.11	3.56	2.72	4.88	2.36	5.14	1.62	2.70
1965	1.97	4.08	2.65	4.65	2.37	5.45	1.61	2.68
1966	1.83	3.92	2.65	4.49	2.14	4.85	1.50	2.53
1967	1.72	4.12	2.51	4.18	2.08	4.69	1.50	2.46
1968	1.49	3.40	2.56	3.92	2.07	4.41	1.40	2.37
1969	1.34	3.10	2.51	3.49	1.99	4.12	1.49	2.29
1970	1.24	2.68	2.43	3.43	1.91	4.07	1.28	2.20
1971	1.10	2.45	2.23	3.16	1.92	3.74	1.18	2.03
1972	1.00	2.26	2.12	2.93	1.79	3.06	1.07	1.90
1973	0.93	2.07	2.08	2.51	1.69	3.04	1.04	1.90
1974	0.86	1.79	2.05	2.40	1.61	3.20	0.90	1.87
Change 1955—74	67%	66%	42%	59%	41%	55%	50%	45%

SOURCE: *U.S. Bureau of the Census: State Finances.*

NOTE: *The above figures are calculated on the basis of current expenditures. Capital expenditures are excluded.*

TABLE 6

Average Duration of Hospitalization at State Mental Hospitals in California, in Days, by Fiscal Year

Hospital	1966—67	1967—68	1968—69	1969—70
Agnews	135.9	111.0	96.5	18.0
Mendocino	108.7	88.0	72.2	8.0
Napa	150.6	135.1	108.3	61.0
Dewitt	104.1	96.9	80.3	24.0
Camarillo	145.2	123.5	128.1	18.0
Metropolitan	122.6	108.9	81.7	14.0

SOURCE: *ENKI 1972, p. 195.*

TABLE 7

California Mental Health Budget, Including Local (Short-Doyle) Programs, as a Percentage of the Total State Budget, by Fiscal Year

1959—60	2.58	1963—64	2.15	1967—68	1.80
1960—61	2.53	1964—65	2.26	1968—69	1.63
1961—62	2.46	1965—66	2.12	1969—70	1.71
1962—63	2.39	1966—67	2.00		

SOURCE: *Calculated from figures in ENKI Research Institute,* A Study of California's New Mental Health Law, *p. 6.*

decarceration.[107] Social policies that allegedly benefit the poorest and most desperate segments of the community do not ordinarily arouse particular enthusiasm among the so-called fiscal conservatives. The goal of returning mental patients to the community is clearly an exception, for from the outset, in addition to the liberal adherents one might expect, it has attracted prominent, sometimes decisive, support from conservative ranks.[108] This congruence of opinion between what are the two poles of "legitimate" political discourse has helped to render decarceration politically irresistable, since it has reduced the possibility of the movement's central premises being subjected to political scrutiny, and has lent the whole enterprise the character of being self-evident. This broad political base also helps to account for the consistency with which the policy has been pursued over time, and in places as disparate politically as New York or Massachusetts and Reagan's California.

The drive for financial savings has been evident in all phases of the program. One consequence has been ineffectual complaints from individuals who take seriously the rhetorical concern with the welfare of those who formerly ended up as "long stay," that is, lifelong, inmates of mental institutions, that the actual implementation of the policy is producing "a relatively good service for the acutely ill . . . side by side with a second class service, or no service at all, for the chronic patient."[109] But this is clearly the most desirable approach on cost effectiveness grounds—to concentrate one's efforts on those one has some prospect of restoring to the work force and to self-sufficiency, and to abandon the rest to the cheapest alternative one can find.

One group for whom restoration in those terms is by definition a hopeless goal is the aged, particularly those past the official retirement age. And despite the growing proportion of elderly people in the populations of both England and America, largely successful efforts have been made to prevent this being reflected in a parallel accumulation of the aged in mental hospitals. Restrictive admissions policies have been adopted, whose effect has been substantially to exclude the hopeless aged. For example, "in New York State a selective admission policy was introduced in 1968," aimed at diverting as many of the aged as possible to general hospitals, or to "foster homes for the aged." Within a year, this policy had effected a 42 percent reduction in the number of aged persons admitted into mental hospitals.[110] More generally, in the United States between 1955 and 1968, while the number of admissions (all ages less those over 65) rose more than 55 percent, from 89,144 to 138,474, admissions of those over 65 fell by almost 20 percent, from 33,140 to 26,594.[111]

Moving from admissions to length of stay, a similar policy has been pursued to clear elderly long-stay patients out of the mental hospitals into less expensive alternative situations. In the United States, the overall size of the resident mental hospital population fell by a relatively constant amount each year from 1955 to 1964 (1.2 percent per annum), but since 1964, there has been "an accelerated rate of discharge from year to year."[112] By 1970, for example, the rate was 9 percent a year. During this period, "discharge of the elderly patients has involved considerable transfer from the state hospital facilities to community nursing and convalescent homes."[113] A substantial proportion "of the acceleration of the population decreases in the State and county mental hospitals in the 1960's was undoubtedly due to the placement of long-term chronic patients into nursing homes " and it now "seems fairly certain that the entire range of purely *psychiatric* facilities cares for less than half of the aged mentally ill."[114]

107. See John P. Conrad, "Corrections and Simple Justice," *Journal of Criminal Law and Criminology* 64 (1973): 208–17, esp. p. 433: "In a world in which the costs of incarceration have reached annual per capita costs which far exceed average citizen incomes, the future of incarceration must be constrained by a policy of rigorous selectivity. The informed opinion that coerced rehabilitation is an impractical objective is equally welcome to humane liberals and fiscal conservatives. *The task of research is to collect the information which will support the strategy of change*" (my emphasis). The curious view of the goals of social science research implied here has obviously been one widely shared among those "objectively" engaged in studying decarceration. Usually, however, those operating on such assumptions are not so naive as to state them publicly.

108. "The fiscal conservatives have not been convinced that such institutions [state hospitals] are cost-effective given the increase in wages and other costs, and despite the apparent scale economies. Furthermore, the budgetary process was being subverted through the long-term retention of clients who no longer needed the full range of services that can be provided at such large-scale facilities," i.e., who could be "dumped" elsewhere more cheaply. Wolpert and Wolpert, "Relocation of Released Mental Hospital Patients," pp. 72–73.

109. Wing, "How Many Psychiatric Beds?," p. 190. Those in their late fifties and early sixties are also included in this group, for obsolescence on grounds of senescence comes ever earlier under advanced capitalism.

110. Pollack and Taube, "Trends and Projections," p. 14.

111. Figures calculated from NIMH Statistical Note no. 107, *Patterns in the Use of Nursing Homes by the Aged Mentally Ill* (1974). From 1968 to 1972, the fall in over-65 admissions was still more dramatic, from 26,594 to 14,490, or 46 percent, while all other admissions fell by only 9 percent. See also NIMH Statistical Note no. 14, *State Trends in First Admissions and Resident Patients State and County Mental Hospitals 1966–1968* (1970): "Only in the 65 and over age-group did first admission rates show a general decline."

112. NIMH Statistical Note no. 1, *Predictions of the Resident Population in Public Mental Hospitals Based on a Gomperz Curve* (1970), p. 1.

113. Wolpert and Wolpert, "Relocation of Released Mental Hospital Patients," p. 27.

114. Pollack and Taube, "Trends and Projections," pp. 12, 13.

Most significantly, given our present concerns, NIMH data reveal that

> the reductions in the numbers of elderly patients resident in and admitted to inpatient psychiatric services, particularly State mental hospitals, in recent years appear not to have shifted the locus of care to community-based psychiatric facilities (community mental health centers and other outpatient psychiatric services) to any great degree. Instead, they have been accompanied by substantial increases in the number of mentally ill and mentally disturbed residents in nursing and personal care homes.[115]

As Table 8 shows, between 1963 and 1969, there was a "near doubling of the number of mentally ill patients resident in these homes . . . from about 222,000 in 1963 to almost 427,000 in 1969 . . . ,"[116] and by 1972, the number had grown again, to 640,000.[117] More detailed data from the same source provide powerful support for the contention that the driving force behind this transfer has been the cost savings that result. In the first place, "the State mental hospitals which have released large numbers of elderly over the past ten or more years, have failed to play a significant role in the follow-up support of these released patients."[118] More seriously, "there appears to be a disproportionate utilization of homes offering personal (i.e., custodial-type) care only, by those elderly being transferred from mental hospitals,"[119] so that what we seem to be seeing is "the emergence of a new pattern in custodial care for the mentally ill elderly."[120] Even within the larger category of old-age homes, "as the level of provided service [and cost!] declines—from nursing-care homes to personal care homes—the admissions coming from mental hospi-

TABLE 8

Number of Patients with Mental Disorders Resident in Mental Hospitals and Nursing Homes in the U.S.A. in 1963 and 1969, Classified by Age

	1963		1969	
	State and County Mental Hospitals	*Nursing Homes*	*State and County Mental Hospitals*	*Nursing Homes*
Total	504,604	221,721	369,969	426,712
Under 65	355,762	34,046	258,549	59,126
65 and Over	148,842	187,675	111,420	367,586

SOURCE: *Adapted from NIMH Statistical Note no. 107, table 2.*

tals as a percent of total admissions to these homes increases."[121]

As this suggests, one indirect consequence of decarceration has been a much greater involvement of the private sector in coping with problem populations that were formerly the exclusive province of the state. The pattern of "the socialization of loss and the privatization of profit,"[122] already well-established in the military-industrial complex, is now imprinting itself on new areas of social existence. Particularly in America, an effort is under way to transform "social junk"[123] into a commodity from which various "professionals" and entrepreneurs can extract a profit. Medicare and the nursing home racket are merely the largest and most blatant examples of this practice. At the other end of the age spectrum, for the very young who become dependent and neglected, the system of foster care involves increasingly "heavy reliance upon the purchase by the public social welfare sector of child care services from private agencies."[124] In between, there have appeared whole chains of enterprises seeking to capitalize on this emerging market, ranging from privately run drug treatment franchises to fair sized corporations sprawled across several states dealing with derelicts and discharged mental patients.[125] Largely free of state regulation or

115. NIMH Statistical Note no. 107, *Patterns,* p. 6.
116. Ibid., pp. 2–3.
117. Paul Ahmed, "New Trusts in Unified Mental Health Care Systems, and the Status of State Mental Hospitals," mimeographed (NIMH Conference, Scottsdale, Arizona, 1974).
118. NIMH Statistical Note no. 107, *Patterns,* p. 7.
119. Ibid., p. 6. See also J. A. Collins, B. A. Skotsky, J. R. Dominick, "Is the Nursing Home the Mental Hospital's Back Ward in the Community?," *Journal of the American Geriatric Society* 15 (1967): 75–81; E. A. Hefferin and D. N. Wilner, "Opinions about Geriatric Patients in Public Mental Hospitals," *HSMHA Reports* 86, no. 5 (1971): 457–71; Epstein and Simon, "Alternatives"; E. Markson et al., "Alternatives to Hospitalization for Psychiatrically Ill Geriatric Patients," *American Journal of Psychiatry* 127 (1971): 1055–62; S. Sharfstein, "Mentally Ill Aged and Neighborhood Health Centers" (Paper presented at the 127th meeting of the American Psychiatric Association, 1974); and Roberta A. Marlowe, "When They Closed the Doors at Modesto," in *Where is My Home?*, pp. 110–24.
120. D. Frankfather, "Background and Position Paper on Mental Health Care for the Elderly" (unpublished final report for the Planning Branch, Office of Program Planning and Evaluation, NIMH, Rockville, Maryland).

121. NIMH Statistical Note no. 107, *Patterns,* p. 6.
122. N. Birnbaum, *Toward a Critical Sociology* (New York: Oxford University Press, 1971), p. 283.
123. See Steven Spitzer, "Toward a Marxian Theory of Deviance," *Social Problems* 22 (1975): 638–51.
124. Fanshell and Shinn, *Dollars and Sense,* p. 3; for the growth of this "industry" in New York City, see ibid., pp. 6–7.
125. For example, Beverly Enterprises, created in 1964, has grown from three "convalescent" facilities to more than sixty board and care facilities across the United States (including California) bringing in *net* revenues of 79.5 million dollars in 1972. Chase, "Where Have All the Mental Patients Gone?," p. 17. There are also, of course, numerous smaller, often family-run, enterprises.

even inspection, and lacking the bureaucratic encrusta-
tions of state-run enterprises, such places have found
ways to pare down on the miserable subsistence existence characteristically provided in state institutions.[126]
For our present purposes, what is important about these
places is that while, in an obvious sense, they are the
creatures of change in state policy, yet on another,
admittedly secondary, level they came to provide one of
that policy's political supports and a source of pressure
for its further extension.[127]

In this context, the reality that community care frequently involves no more than a transfer from one
institution to another institution or quasi-institutional
setting is by no means confined to the case of the aged.
Table 8 shows that in 1969 over 59,000 of those under
the age of sixty-five and officially designated mentally
ill were confined in nursing homes of various types.
Many others are in so-called halfway houses, or ex-
welfare hotels.[128] In the words of a recent report on the
situation in Michigan, many such patients have been
dumped "in facilities having fifty or more residents . . . ,
large quasi-institutional settings [that] cannot be expected to provide the anticipated [therapeutic] benefits of
community placement."[129] But, of course, they do
provide the benefit of substantial cost savings to the
state.

The discharge pattern for the elderly closely corresponds to the expanding provision of subsistence level
support for them by federal and local governments, with
the most rapid decrease coming in the late 1960s and
1970s, following the passage of Medicare.[130] Similarly,
the decarceration of other inmates has coincided with
administrative reorganizations and changes in bureaucratic regulations that have facilitated granting of the
minimal outside support that permits the return of
patients to the community. One should notice here the
effects produced by the more fragmented nature of the
United States' political structure and the differential
impact within that structure of the fiscal crisis, felt more
acutely at the state and local levels. Welfare has increasingly become a federal responsibility (or at least is
federally funded) whereas institutional programs like
mental hospitals have remained a state (occasionally a
county) responsibility. This situation has greatly mag-
nified the attractions of decarceration for states hard
pressed for money, for with some administrative jug-
gling with "conditions of eligibility," it permits the
transfer of costs to a different level of government and
thus relieves, temporarily at any rate, some of the local
fiscal crisis.[131] Almost certainly, this has had much to do
with the more rapid decline in institutional populations
in the United States, as compared with England.

Summary

Placing the decarceration movement in its structural
context, this paper has argued that this shift in social
control styles and practices must be viewed as a response
to the changing exigencies of domestic pacification and
control under welfare capitalism. In particular, it reflects
structural pressures to sharply curtail the costly system
of segregative control, once welfare payments, providing a subsistence existence for elements of the surplus
population, make available a viable alternative to management in an institution. Such structural pressures are
greatly intensified by the fiscal crisis encountered in
varying degrees at the different levels of the state
apparatus, a crisis engendered by advanced capitalism's

126. In Pennsylvania, such places were once subject to inspection.
Interestingly enough, "the same year the state stopped inspecting
boarding homes—1967—the state also began a massive deinstitutionalization program aimed at moving patients out of mental hospitals into
community programs . . . ," i.e., in many cases, boarding homes. For
an account of the resulting conditions, see the Philadelphia *Inquirer*,
September 21, 1975. Public institutions are scarcely known for their
luxury, yet in New York, the private child-care institutions used by the
city cost *at most* $26 a day; while the *least* a public shelter costs is $42 a
day, with others costing up to $52. Fanshell and Shinn, *Dollars and
Sense*, p. 10. Savings of this magnitude provide us with some clue of the
level and type of "service" these operators provide for their "clients."

127. See, for example, the activities of Bernard Bergman in New
York (as reported in the *New York Times*, January–February 1975), or
Beverly Enterprises in California (Chase, "Where Have All the Mental
Patients Gone?," p. 17). For an examination of similar links between
changes in public housing policy and the demands of landlords and the
construction industry, see Lawrence M. Friedman, *Government and
Slum Housing* (Chicago: Rand McNally, 1968).

128. *New York Times*, January 21, 1974.

129. Cited in *New York Times*, March 22, 1974. See also the
testimony of Dr. Murray C. Brown, Commissioner of Mental Health,
Chicago, before the Senate Special Committee on Aging: "Far in excess
of 50%" of the 7,000 patients discharged from Illinois State Hospitals
between January 1970 and March 1971 were "sent to nursing and
residential care homes [in Chicago]. . . . We have further learned that

such former patients were discharged not only into licensed facilities, but
into rooming houses, and converted low-class hotels, some of which the
Chicago Board of Health has been unable to locate." Brown, *Hearing on
Trends in Long-Term Care*, 92nd Congress, 1st Session, 1971, p. 1106.

130. For a summary of expanding U.S. welfare provisions in this
period, see Rimlinger, *Welfare Policy*, pp. 237–43.

131. For example, "the trend away from institutionalization gained
momentum in 1963 when the State of California, following national
guidelines, redefined disability to include severe mental illness. Mentally ill persons could now return to the community as welfare recipients,
under the Aid to the Total Dependent (AID) Program, if no purpose
would be served by further institutionalization." Wolpert and Wolpert,
"Relocation of Released Mental Hospital Patients," p. 52.

need to socialize more and more of the costs of production—the welfare system itself being one aspect of this process of socialization.

It is the pervasiveness and intensity of these pressures, and their mutually reinforcing character, that account for most of the characteristic features of the new system of community care, and that enable us to comprehend the continued adherence to this policy even where it provokes considerable opposition. The significance of the introduction of psychoactive drugs has been shown to be much less than is commonly supposed, and I have suggested that in any event their use to lessen the difficulties of managing some patients in the commu-

nity, rather than as merely an additional, less visible means of control to be used in the mental hospital, has been largely shaped by this same set of pressures. Finally, the critics of the asylum and advocates of community care on therapeutic grounds are shown to have had little influence on the actual course of policy, decarceration in practice displaying little resemblance to liberal rhetoric on the subject. Neither the arguments nor the evidence presented in their support by such people are in the least part novel, having been substantially anticipated at least a century ago. Thus their primary significance (though far from their authors' intent) would seem to be their value as ideological camouflage.

Name Index

Subject Index